Introduction to

✔ KT-440-559

Tunisia

Sun, sea and sand are what most people come to Tunisia for, and you can easily pick up a bargain holiday here from Britain, Ireland or mainland Europe, and sun it for a fortnight on the beach. But if you're a bit more adventurous, beyond the beach and hotel disco there's a land of desert oases, Roman relics, beautiful mosques and fascinating walled cities. The easiest option is to join an organized tour, but you can also rent a car or scoot around on public transport. Tunisia is friendly, safe and generally hassle-free, yet it offers an experience you can genuinely call an adventure.

 As an **Arab country**, Tunisia sometimes seems quite Middle Eastern but, sitting on the top of North Africa, it's a far cry from the oil states of the Gulf. Especially in the north, the country is recognizably Mediterranean in character and very much moulded by a century of **French colonial rule**. Tunisian culture is firmly rooted in the Islamic faith, but religion sits light, not heavy, on the lives of its citizens. They can drink alcohol if they want to – though most do not – and women have greater equality here than in most other Arab countries, largely thanks to Tunisia's liberal interpretation of Islam.

But French and Arab are only two of the many influences that have shaped this land. The country's original **Berber** inhabitants, now largely assimilated into the Arab population, are responsible for much of its culture – not least the national dish, couscous. The first cities were built by the **Phoenicians**, a maritime trading nation from Lebanon, whose Carthaginian colonists carved out an empire in their own right, and dared challenge the might of republican Rome, a challenge which ended in their destruction. And the **Romans** left behind more than just ruins: they were the people who established Tunisia's original infrastructure, and introduced the olive trees that dominate much of the countryside to this day. Even

iii

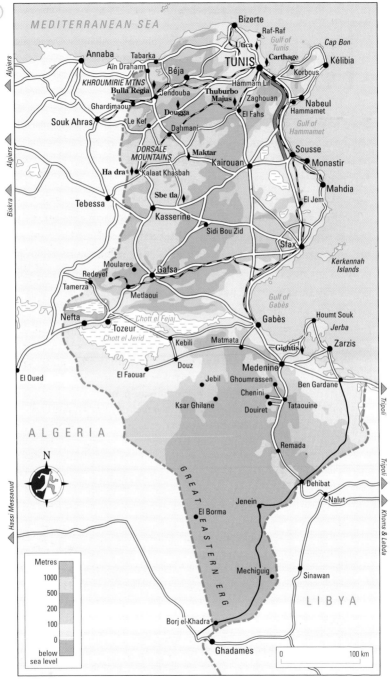

MEDITERRANEAN SEA

Bizerte
Raf-Raf
Gulf of
Tunis
Cap Bon
Annaba
Tabarka
Utica
Carthage
Kélibia
Aïn Draham
Béja
TUNIS
Korbous
KHROUMIRIE MTNS
Hammâm Lif
Nabeul
Bulla Regia
Jendouba
Thuburbo
Majus
Zaghouan
Hammamet
Ghardimaou
Dougga
El Fahs
Gulf of
Hammamet
Souk Ahras
Le Kef
Dahmani
Sousse
DORSALE
MOUNTAINS
Maktar
Kairouan
Monastir
Ha dra
Kalaat Khasbah
Mahdia
Sbe tla
El Jem
Tebessa
Kasserine
Sidi Bou Zid
Sfax
Kerkennah
Islands
Moulares
Gafsa
Redeyef
Tamerza
Metlaoui
Gulf of
Gabès
Nefta
Chott el Fejaj
Gabès
Houmt Souk
Tozeur
Chott el Jerid
Kebili
Matmata
Jerba
Gightis
Zarzis
El Oued
Douz
El Faouar
Medenine
Jebil
Ghoumrassen
Ben Gardane
Chenini
Ksar Ghilane
Douiret
Tataouine

ALGERIA

N

GREAT EASTERN ERG

Remada

Dehibat
Jenein
Nalut
El Borma

Mechiguig
Sinawan

LIBYA

Borj el Khadra
Ghadamès

Metres	
1000	
500	
200	
100	
0	
below sea level	

0   100 km

iv

Tunisia

written and researched by

Daniel Jacobs and Peter Morris

with additional research by
Sam Thorne

and contributions by
Linda Cooley, Dee Eltaïef,
Dr Carol Higham and Peter Raine

ROUGH
GUIDES

NEW YORK • LONDON • DELHI

www.roughguides.com

△ A well in the Nefzaoua

Fact file

• With an **area** of 163,610 square kilometres (63,170 square miles), Tunisia is slightly larger than England and Wales, or the state of Florida.

• Tunisia's **population** stands at around 10 million, of whom some 900,000 live in the capital, Tunis. About 99 percent are **Muslims**, with small communities of **Jews** and **Christians**.

• The official languages are **Arabic**, spoken by almost everybody, and **French**, spoken by most school-educated people. A tiny minority speaks Berber. English is not widely spoken, but more and more young people are studying it at school.

• Tunisia's main **exports** are crude oil, textiles and phosphates, and its main trading partners are France, Italy and Germany. Inflation is currently less than three percent.

• The **head of state**, President Zine el Abidine Ben Ali, took office on November 7, 1987. There is an elected **National Assembly** with a number of legal political parties, though Islamic fundamentalism is outlawed, and no serious opposition is tolerated.

the **Turks**, whose Ottoman empire was rather a loose confederation of territories, often owing only nominal allegiance to the sultan, put their stamp firmly on Tunisian culture, as seen most clearly in the country's architecture.

If the diversity of Tunisia's past cultures and their legacy of monuments comes as a surprise to most first-time visitors, the range of **scenery** can be even more unexpected. In the north there are shady **oak forests** reminiscent of the south of France, with the hill station of Aïn Draham even described as "Alpine". The south is plain **desert**, with colossal dunes, oases and rippling mirages. In fact, the landscape of the desert itself varies a great deal, from the endless dunes of the ergs in the far southwest – most people's image when they think of desert – to the rocky *hamada* to its north and east. On rugged crags in this *hamada*, Berber villages seem almost to be carved out of the rock they cling to, and indeed they partly are, since many contain homes excavated into the rock. No less precariously perched are the strange **fortified granaries** known as *ksour*, where once nomadic tribes kept their food supply, ready to defend it to the death if need be. Also here are the weird **salt flats** known as *chotts*, in particular the Chott el Jerid, which are actually seasonal lakes, dry for most of the year. In the oasis towns of

Minarets

The most outstanding feature of most mosques is the minaret, the tower (most Tunisian mosques have only one) from which the muezzin issues the call to prayer. Nowadays, he doesn't actually climb up the tower to deliver it, but uses loudspeakers installed at the top – if a recorded call to prayer isn't used, as quite often happens these days.

The earliest mosques didn't have minarets: at the dawn of Islam, Mohammed's house in Medina served as the community's mosque, and the muezzin called the faithful to prayer from its rooftop. The idea of the minaret was probably inspired by the towers of Christian churches, and the very first minaret in the world was part of the Umayyad Mosque in Damascus, though the one at the Great Mosque in Kairouan is the oldest surviving today.

Most Tunisian minarets are square in shape, a form favoured by the Malekite school of Islam, which is followed by most Tunisians. The arrival of the Ottomans in the seventeenth century saw the introduction of octagonal minarets, preferred by the rival Hanefite school. In Jerba, where many of the mosques were put up by the dissident Kharijite sect, the minarets are typically squat with a lantern-like structure at the top, and often surrounded by battlements. Even today, however, smaller mosques may well lack minarets, and it isn't unknown for the muezzin to issue the call to prayer while standing outside the front door.

the desert regions, you can stroll among date palms to escape the fierce heat of the Saharan sun. Between the extremes are lush citrus plantations, huge fields with row after row of olive trees, bare steppes with table-top mountains, and rolling hills as green and colourful (in spring) as any English county. Just offshore lie the sandy, palm-scattered **islands** of Jerba and Kerkennah.

Despite this huge variation in geography, Tunisia is a very compact country, and easy to get around. Even on a two-week holiday, you'll have no problem taking off on a tour that covers coast, mountains and desert alike. The journey from Tunis on the north coast to Tataouine in the heart of the desert can be made in a little over ten hours by bus or shared taxi. And while most trips in Tunisia are considerably shorter, the majority of journeys leave an impression of real travel, in the transformation from one type of landscape and culture to another. All this makes the country very satisfying to explore – an accessible introduction to the Arab world and to the African continent.

Where to go

Of Tunisia's cities, the capital, **Tunis**, is rather a sedate town by Mediterranean standards, and easy to explore, with a fascinating walled old city, or Medina, and a very French-influenced new town. Its museum, the Bardo, houses some of the world's finest Roman mosaics. Elsewhere on the north coast, the port of **Bizerte** has a pleasantly laid-back feel, centred around an old harbour where you can relax with a coffee and watch the fishing boats chug in and out. In the mountains of the northwest, **Le Kef** is an ideal place to rest up for a few days, built on a mountain and dominated by its fortified Kasbah. **Kairouan**, in the centre of the country, was the first Arab capital of North Africa and has a more religious feel; its Great Mosque is Islam's fourth holiest site in the world, and the Medina is chock-full of fascinating religious architecture to check out. Not far away, **Sousse** is both a major holiday resort and a vibrant town with a compact and easy-to-explore Medina. The city of **Sfax** just down the coast, though larger and more industrialized, boasts a Medina that most visitors agree is the most interesting in the country, not least because

it makes few concessions to tourism and feels far more "authentic" as a result. Beyond, **Gabès** is the gateway to the south, unique in having both an oasis and a beach together.

In terms of monuments, the **Roman sites** of the north are the best known, and, even if your interest is very casual, many are quite spectacular. In the coastal plain called the Sahel, the towering **amphitheatre** at El Jem rivals Rome's Colosseum; at Dougga you can wander around a marvellously preserved **Roman city**, complete with all the accoutrements and buildings of second- and third-century prosperity; and there are other archelogical remains, scarcely less grand, at Utica, Bulla Regia, Maktar and Sbeïtla, as well as the legendary, extensive and much-battered **Carthage**.

Roman mosaics

The Romans of course are known for their fine mosaics, which appeared in the floors of the homes of the rich as well as in public buildings, and North Africa, especially Tunisia, was where the art form reached its artistic zenith. Carthage, El Jem, Dougga, Utica, Bulla Regia and several sites in Sousse have all yielded beautiful mosaics, but few are left in situ: most – certainly the finest – have been removed to museums. The Bardo in Tunis (see p.107) holds what is undoubtedly the finest collection of Roman mosaics in the world – you'll be hard put to take in all of them on a single visit – while the museums at El Jem (see p.263) and Sousse (see p.227) house some outstanding pieces too. Serious enthusiasts may also care to check out the fine individual mosaics in the museums at Gafsa (see p.344) and Salakta (see p.262).

Favourite subjects for mosaics included gods and goddesses, the seasons, wildlife, sports and scenes from everyday life, all made up of tiny tiles, some of stone, others of coloured glass. For a selection of Tunisia's Roman mosaics on line, see Ⓦwww.tunisiaonline.com/mosaics/index.html.

△ Tunis Medina

They're all atmospheric places to visit, and at the smaller sites off the excursion routes, you'll find yourself, as often as not, enjoying them alone.

Islamic Tunisia has a varied architectural legacy, taking in early Arab mosques – most outstandingly at Kairouan – and the sophisticated **Turkish buildings** of Tunis, as well as the strange **Berber fortresses** of the south. The latter are accompanied by equally weird structures known as *ghorfas* – honeycombed storage and living quarters – and, at Matmata, by underground houses. All reward the small effort it takes to get off the more beaten tracks.

For more hedonistic pleasures, the coast is at its most beautiful – and most commercialized – around Hammamet, Sousse, Monastir and the island of Jerba, connected by causeway to the mainland. **Hammamet** is a genuinely international resort and its satellites are spreading, but by Spanish or Greek island standards, developments remain relatively small in scale and unusually well planned. Escaping them entirely is not hard either: even within sight of Hammamet, on **Cap Bon**, there is still wild coastline. **Tabarka**, on the north coast, is a quieter resort set against the

▽ Making chechias (felt hats)

ix

Films shot in Tunisia

A popular location for desert movie sets, Tunisia has starred on the silver screen as Egypt, Palestine and the planet Tatooine, and many fans make pilgrimages to see where their favourite Hollywood epics were first carved in celluloid. Films shot here include:

Jesus of Nazareth (1977) Monastir (see p.241) played the part of Jerusalem in Franco Zeffirelli's six-hour rendering of the life of Christ, originally made for TV.

Star Wars (1975) Matmata and the "Star Wars Canyon" head the list of locations in George Lucas's sci-fi blockbuster – full details in the box on p.364.

Monty Python's Life of Brian (1979) Monastir played Jerusalem once more in this controversial satire on the gospels.

Raiders of the Lost Ark (1981) Harrison Ford swashed his buckle down the Star Wars Canyon (see p.364) chasing after religious relics in Steven Spielberg's piece of Hollywood hokum.

The English Patient (1996) Tunisia took on the role of Egypt in Anthony Minghella's film version of Michael Ondaatje's haunting novel. Onk el Jemal (see p.364) was the main desert set, with the Blackmith's Souk in Sfax (p.275) doubling up as a Cairo bazaar, the former British Embassy in Tunis (see p.96) as the scene of a Christmas party, and Mahdia (p.256) in the role of Benghazi.

The Phantom Menace (1998); *Attack of the Clones* (2002) Tunisia starred again as the desert planet Tatooine in the Star Wars prequels, with locations at Onk el Jemal and Ksar Hadada – again see the box on p.364 for full details.

backdrop of the Khroumirie mountains, with its own Genoese castle. For those seeking more splendid isolation, **Raf Raf** offers Tunisia's least-developed stretches of fine sand beach. Along the east coast lies an almost unbroken succession of beaches, starting with the popular purpose-built holiday resort at **Port el Kantaoui**. Next door is the city of **Sousse**, with one of the longest beaches in the country, sharing its airport with the neighbouring resort city of **Monastir**, and in between the beaches of **Skanès**. To the south, **Mahdia**, though marketed as a beach resort, is also a charming and atmospheric old sea dog of a town. The **Kerkennah Islands**, situated just off the coast, are undoubtedly Tunisia's laziest and most laid-back holiday destination, the local people mostly engaged in fishing, using traditional methods. Finally, the island of **Jerba** offers several beautiful beaches, a fascinating interior, a unique architecture of fortified mosques, and a population more culturally diverse than any other part of the country.

To really appreciate Tunisia however, your time should

Chicha pipes

Wherever you go in Tunisia, you'll see men in cafés chugging away on hubble-bubble *chichas*, where the smoke from the tobacco is drawn through water in a glass vessel. Though the tobacco is usually pretty rough, the water is an efficient filter, as you'll see from the state of it after use. Lately *chichas* have become quite trendy, but Tunisian women don't smoke them, as smoking isn't considered ladylike in Tunisia.

The origin of the *chicha* is something of a mystery. The name is Persian for "glass", a reference to the vessel, which would appear to indicate that the pipe came to the Arab world from Iran. Another name – *nargila*, from the Persian for "coconut" – indicates what the vessel was originally made from, and suggests an origin in the tropics. The *chicha* must have predated the introduction of tobacco, as there were sophisticated water-pipes in Iran almost as soon as that pernicious weed arrived. Tobacco historian Alfred Dunhill suggested in the 1950s that the chicha started out in East Africa as a cannabis pipe (Iran had long-standing trade links with that region), and archeological finds in Ethiopia have since proved him right.

ideally include a spell in the desert and mountains, as well as on the coast. The oases at **Nefta** and **Tozeur** are classically luxuriant, while further south, the *ksour* around **Tataouine** and dunes around **Douz** give the region an almost expeditionary feel. For the really adventurous, it's possible to explore the remote desert of the far south with a four-wheel-drive vehicle.

All of this ignores one of Tunisia's best facets – its **people**. While the hassle of some tourist areas (particularly for women) shouldn't be underestimated, visitors are often startled – and exhilarated – by the hospitality which they're shown when away from the major resorts. Few independent travellers leave Tunisia without having been invited, quite spontaneously, to stay with a family. Even when Western governments do things that may be unpopular in Tunisia, the politics of the wider world rarely come between Tunisians and visitors to their country.

When to go

Tunisia has the usual Mediterranean patterns of **climate**. The best time to travel, from a scenic point of view, is **spring**, when the south has not yet reached full heat and the north looks astonishingly fertile – above all, around the orchards and vineyards of Cap Bon. Be warned, though, that March and April are the dampest months of the year in the south, and it can bucket down in the north at this time.

Summer has mixed virtues. July and August are much the hottest months of the year – if only slightly more so than in the southern parts of Italy or Greece – and the one time you really do need to lapse into the local way of life, for example resting through the midday hours at a café or taking a siesta at your hotel. Obviously this applies above all to the deep south and the *ksour*. Some of the more exposed beaches of the north coast are only warm enough for swimming from around May until October, and if you wait until **autumn**, you get the best of both worlds, with warm swimming and few crowds, even at the big resorts.

In **winter**, the north and the largely mountainous Tell region in the west can get distinctly cold; Aïn Draham, the highest mountain town, commonly has a metre of snow, and it has even been known to snow at Bizerte on the Mediterranean coast. Tunis, Cap Bon and Sousse are not so much cold in winter as dull, with sporadic rains. But this is an ideal time for covering the ancient sites at leisure and then migrating south to Jerba's beaches and the Sahara.

Average temperatures and rainfall

	J	F	M	A	M	J	J	A	S	O	N	D
Tunis												
Min night °C	6	7	8	11	13	17	20	21	19	15	11	7
Max day °C	14	16	18	21	24	29	32	33	31	25	20	16
Rainfall (mm)	64	51	41	36	18	8	3	8	33	51	48	61
Days with rain	13	12	11	9	6	5	2	3	7	9	11	14
Gabès												
Min night °C	6	7	9	12	16	19	22	22	21	17	11	7
Max day °C	16	18	21	23	26	28	32	33	31	27	22	17
Rainfall (mm)	23	18	20	10	8	0	0	3	13	31	31	15
Days with rain	4	3	4	3	2	0	0	1	3	4	4	4

△ Charms against the Evil Eye, outside a Jewish home on Jerba

things not to miss

It's not possible to see everything Tunisia has to offer in one trip – and we don't suggest you try. What follows is a selective and subjective taste of the country's highlights: distinctive architecture, a rich archeological heritage and stunning natural landscapes. They're all arranged in five colour-coded categories to help you find the very best things to do, see and experience. All entries have a page reference to take you straight into the guide, where you can find out more.

01 Bardo Museum Page **107** • The world's greatest collection of Roman mosaics, not to mention statues, frescoes and sarcophagi, all housed in a fabulous palace in Tunis.

02 Ksour Page **453** • These fortified structures built by Berber tribes to store and defend their grain, and as a meeting place for the community; now mostly disused, they're strewn over the south of the country, and well repay the time spent reaching them.

03 Couscous Page **37** • The classic North African dish, Berber in origin, consists of a meat (or occasionally fish or vegetable) stew on a bed of steamed semolina pellets. Be warned: Tunisians like it spicy.

04 Bathing in a hammam Page **57** • The luxury of a Turkish bath, at a fraction of the price you'd pay for it back home: sweat it all out and scrub it all off, or let a masseur or masseuse do the scrubbing for you.

xv

05 **El Jem's amphitheatre** Page **264** • This huge arena where gladiators once slogged it out is much better preserved than Rome's colosseum.

06 **Sidi Bou Saïd** Page **128** • A tumble of sleek whitewashed villas on a hillside overlooking the sea, this chic suburb of Tunis is a home from home to the arty, the elegant and the affluent of Tunisia and Europe alike.

07 **Carthage** Page **121** • Once the great rival to imperial Rome and home to Hannibal and his elephants, Carthage today is a scattering of ancient sites amid beautiful country by the sea.

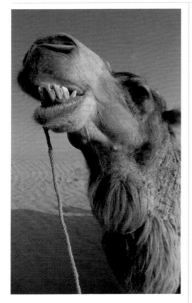

08 **Camel rides** Page **49** • An encounter with the ship of the desert can mean anything from a five-minute jaunt to a whole week or more crossing the sands on camel-back, but either way, it's an experience you won't forget.

09 **Mahdia** Page **256** • Tunisia's most charming resort, whose old city, on its own little peninsula, is protected by a sixteenth-century gateway.

10 **Festival of the Sahara, Douz** Page **382** • Tunisia's biggest celebration of desert arts and culture, featuring pageantry, poetry, and even the odd camel fight.

11 **Matmata** Page **402** • With its strange crater-like pit-dwellings dug into the soft sandstone, the landscape here has often been compared to the moon's – but Matmata has lots more atmosphere.

12 **Dougga** Page **304** • The most extensive Roman site in Tunisia, featuring a restored theatre, a town brothel and an intriguing Libyco-Punic mausoleum.

13 **The forests of Aïn Draham** Page **193** • Not the landscape you expected in Tunisia: fresh, Alpine, snowy in winter and planted with cork oak trees, whose bark is stripped periodically to make anything from bottle stoppers to floor tiles.

14 **Kairouan Great Mosque** Page **249** • One of Islam's holiest sites – four trips here, so they say, are as good as a pilgrimage to Mecca.

15 **Hammamet beach** Page **139** • Tunisia's finest beach is a sweeping curve of soft yellow sand backed by lush green vegetation, making Hammamet justifiably the country's top seaside resort.

16 **Jerban mosques** Page **437** • Built by a breakaway sect of Islam to double up as places of refuge in times of trouble, the fort-like mosques of Jerba attractively dot the island's interior.

17 **Kerkouane** Page **156** • A town whose ancient private houses, each with a characteristic red-bottomed bathtub, are almost the only surviving remnant of a Carthaginian culture systematically destroyed by Rome.

19 Troglodyte Berber villages
Page 471 • Chenini, Douiret and Guermessa, built around ancient hilltop forts, boast whitewashed mosques, antique olive-oil presses and cave dwellings.

18 Brik à l'oeuf
Page 37 • Tunisia's national snack, an egg fried in pastry, requires a certain knack to eat without the yolk spilling onto your clothes.

20 Bizerte
Page 171 • A strategic port and a pretty one, with two citadels, a Spanish fort and an Andalusian quarter.

21 **Sfax Medina** Page 272 • The most unspoiled of all Tunisia's old walled cities, and an utterly fascinating place to wander amid feverish commercial activity.

22 **Kerkennah Islands** Page 280 • Odysseus, Hannibal and former President Habib Bourguiba all enjoyed exile on these laid-back, idyllic and very friendly islands, whose shallow waters makes their beaches ideal for children.

23 **Desert dunes** Page 386 • The Sahara as you always imagined it, mile after mile of fine windblown sand; El Faouar is as good a place as any to make its acquaintance.

25 Star Wars sets Page **364**
• See where Luke Skywalker, R2-D2 and Obiwan Kenobi fought off the evil empire.

24 Nefta Page **365** • A beautiful old town of Sufi mosques and quaint alleyways, built around a palm-filled crater called the Corbeille.

26 Tabarka Page **187** • A fine beach resort dominated by its imposing Genoese castle.

ACTIVITIES | CONSUME | EVENTS | NATURE | SIGHTS |

28 **Sbeïtla** Page **327** • Capital for a year under the Byzantines, this well-preserved Roman site was once a major centre for Christianity in North Africa, as its impressive collection of ancient churches attests.

27 **Chott el Jerid** Page **372** • A shallow seasonal salt lake, dry for ten months of the year, when it's a vast flat expanse of salt crystals glittering in the sunlight and shimmering with mirages.

29 **Le Kef** Page **311** • Great views and some fascinating monuments in this strategic old town, overlooked by a solid citadel.

Contents

Using this Rough Guide

We've tried to make this Rough Guide a good read and easy to use. The book is divided into six main sections, and you should be able to find whatever you want in one of them.

Colour section

The front colour section offers a quick tour of Tunisia. The **introduction** aims to give you a feel for the place, with suggestions on where to go. We also tell you what the weather is like and include a basic country fact file. Next, our authors round up their favourite aspects of the country in the **things not to miss** section – whether it's a Roman site, a desert landscape or a special festival. Right after this comes a full **contents** list.

Basics

The Basics section covers all the **pre-departure** nitty-gritty to help you plan your trip. This is where to find out which airlines fly to your destination, what paperwork you'll need, what to do about money and insurance, about Internet access, food, security, public transport, car rental – in fact just about every piece of **general practical information** you might need.

Guide

This is the heart of the Rough Guide, divided into user-friendly chapters, each of which covers a specific region. Every chapter starts with a list of **highlights** and an **introduction** that helps you to decide where to go, depending on your time and budget. Likewise, introductions to the various towns and smaller regions within each chapter should help you plan

your itinerary. We start most town accounts with information on arrival and accommodation, followed by a tour of the sights, and finally reviews of places to eat and drink, and details of nightlife. Longer accounts also have a directory of practical listings. Each chapter concludes with **public transport** details for that region and a list of place names in Arabic.

Contexts

Read Contexts to get a deeper understanding of what makes Tunisia tick. We include articles about **history**, **wildlife** and **religion**, and a further reading section that reviews dozens of **books** relating to the country.

Language

The **language** section gives useful guidance for Arabic and French and pulls together vocabulary you might need on your trip, including a comprehensive **menu reader**. Here you'll also find a **glossary** of terms used in this book.

small print + Index

Apart from a **full index**, which includes maps as well as places, this section covers publishing information, credits and acknowledgements, and also has our contact details in case you want to send in updates and corrections to the book – or suggestions as to how we might improve it.

Map and chapter list

ALGERIA

LIBYA

N

Contents

Contexts

485–565

5

Language

Small print and Index

Basics

Basics

Getting there

Flying is the fastest and the cheapest way to get to Tunisia from most parts of the world. Scheduled flights mainly land at Tunis, though flights from Europe occasionally serve regional airports such as Tozeur and Jerba. Charter flights from Europe mostly serve Monastir, with some services to Jerba, Tozeur, Sfax and Tabarka. From the British Isles, surface options such as ferry plus train, bus or car are all feasible – if long-winded – means of getting to the country.

Airfares always depend on the season, with the highest fares in July and August. Fares drop during the "shoulder" seasons – May to June, plus September and October – and you'll get the best prices during the low season, November to April (excluding Christmas and New Year when prices are hiked up and seats are at a premium).

You can often cut costs by going through a **specialist flight agent** – either a consolidator, who buys up blocks of tickets from the airlines and sells them at a discount, or a **discount agent**, who in addition to dealing with discounted flights may also offer special student and youth fares and a range of other travel-related services such as travel insurance, rail passes, car rentals, tours and the like. Some agents specialize in **charter flights**, though these can actually be more expensive than scheduled flights, and furthermore departure dates are fixed and withdrawal penalties high.

You may well find that a **package** holiday, or flight-plus-accommodation deal, is hardly any more expensive than a flight alone. A package tour saves much time and effort in planning a trip, and for a simple beach holiday it makes much sense. For sightseeing, it does make it easier to get to all the main tourist attractions, but you'll have to go at the group's pace rather than your own, and you won't be able to pick and choose where you go.

If Tunisia is only one stop on a much longer journey, you might consider buying a **Round-the-World (RTW) ticket**, but as Tunis is not commonly included in RTW routes this is apt to be more expensive than a standard itinerary.

Booking flights online

Many airlines and discount travel websites offer you the opportunity to book your tickets online, cutting out the costs of agents and middlemen. Good deals can often be found through discount or auction sites, as well as through the airlines' own websites.

Online booking agents and general travel sites

ⓦ**www.cheapflights.co.uk** (UK and Ireland), ⓦ**www.cheapflight.com** (US), ⓦ**www.cheapflights.ca** (Canada), ⓦ**www.cheapflights.com.au** (Australia). Flight deals, travel agents, plus links to other travel sites.

Combined Trips with Libya and Algeria

At one time there were several operators covering the "North African loop" of Morocco–Algeria–Tunisia, but northern Algeria remains unsafe (see p.209), and no overland trips are passing through it at the time of writing. Libya, on the other hand, following its recent rapprochement with the West, is widely expected to open up to tourism, and trips featuring Tunisia, Libya and Egypt are already being offered by overland companies. For up-to-date information, contact an Africa specialist agent such as the Africa Travel Centre in the UK (☏020/7387 1211) or the Africa desk of STA Travel (ⓦwww.statravel.com), or an overland tour operator such as Dragoman (ⓦwww.dragoman.com) or Explore (ⓦwww.exploreworldwide.com).

ⓦ**www.cheaptickets.com** Discount flight specialists (US only). Also at ☎1-888/922-8849.

ⓦ**www.ebookers.com** Efficient, easy to use flight finder, with competitive fares.

ⓦ**www.etn.nl/discount** A hub of consolidator and discount agent Web links, maintained by the nonprofit European Travel Network.

ⓦ**www.expedia.co.uk** (UK), ⓦ**www.expedia .com** (US), ⓦ**www.expedia.ca** (Canada). Discount airfares, all-airline search engine and daily deals.

ⓦ**www.flyaow.com** Online air travel info and reservations site.

ⓦ**www.hotwire.com** Bookings from the US only. Last-minute savings of up to forty percent on regular published fares. Travellers must be at least 18 and there are no refunds, transfers or changes allowed.

ⓦ**www.lastminute.com** (UK) , ⓦ**www .lastminute.com.au** (Australia), ⓦ**www .lastminute.co.nz** (New Zealand). Good last-minute holiday package and flight-only deals.

ⓦ**www.opodo.co.uk** Popular and reliable source of low UK airfares. Owned by, and run in conjunction with, nine major European airlines.

ⓦ**www.priceline.co.uk** (UK), ⓦ**www.priceline .com** (US). Name-your-own-price website that has deals at around forty percent off standard fares.

ⓦ**www.skyauction.com** Bookings from the US only. Auctions tickets and travel packages.

ⓦ**www.travel.com.au** (Australia), ⓦ**www .travel.co.nz** (New Zealand). Comprehensive online travel company, with discounted fares.

ⓦ**www.travelocity.co.uk** (UK), ⓦ**www .travelocity.com** (US), ⓦ**www.travelocity .ca** (Canada), ⓦ**www.zuji.com.au** (Australia). Destination guides, hot fares and great deals for car rental, accommodation and lodging.

ⓦ**www.travelshop.com.au** Australian site offering discounted flights, packages, insurance, and online bookings. Also on ☎1800/108 108.

Flights from Britain and Ireland

As far as **scheduled flights** are concerned, there are direct services from London to Tunis, and indirect flights from most major British and Irish airports via London or the Continent. Flexible open tickets are expensive – London–Tunis return costs around £860 this way, for example – but you can cut costs greatly by buying a **fixed-date ticket**. There are also **charter flights**, for details of which, and bookings, see the tour-operator listings opposite. The fares below are for fixed-date tickets and include airport taxes.

From Britain

Tunisia's national airline, **Tunisair**, flies four times weekly from London Heathrow, with a return fare of around £230 for a fixed-date ticket bought at least three days in advance. The only other scheduled airline with direct flights from Britain to Tunisia is **British Airways**, who fly four times weekly from Gatwick, for around £240.

Flying from a **regional airport**, you can get a scheduled flight to Tunis with a change of plane in London or another European hub city. A typical return fare on these routes is around £280.

Charter flights are available from several British airports during the summer and from many in winter, too. Some package operators, notably Thomson, First Choice and Airtours sell flight-only deals, which vary in price with the season, from about £290 return from London in low season to about £400 at the end of July or beginning of August. The very cheapest deals of all are **last-minute** packages (see opposite).

From Ireland

For a scheduled flight to Tunis, you'll need to fly via London or another European hub. **From Dublin**, return fares to Tunis start at around €380 including tax in winter, €475 in summer. If you're departing from Belfast, BA flies via London, but their prices are relatively high. Alternatively, you could fly with BMI via Heathrow in conjunction with Tunisair, though this is also expensive.

Panorama (see p.12) runs weekly **charters** to Monastir from Dublin and Belfast, and in winter from Cork too. Airtours, Falcon/JWT and (in summer) Sunway also run charters from Dublin, and Sunnyway operate summer-only charters from Belfast. Charter flights cost around €350/£300, depending on the season.

Airlines

Air France UK ☎0845/359 1000, Republic of Ireland ☎01/605 0383, ⓦwww.airfrance.com. To Tunis via Paris from London, Dublin, Aberdeen, Birmingham (codeshare with FlyBE), Bristol, Edinburgh (codeshare with CityJet), Manchester, Newcastle and Southampton (codeshare with Britair).

Alitalia UK ☎0870/544 8259, Republic of Ireland ☎01/677 5171, ⊛www.alitalia.co.uk. London and Manchester to Tunis via Rome or Milan.

Air Malta UK ☎0845/607 3710, Republic of Ireland ☎1800/397 400, ⊛www.airmalta.com. London, Dublin, Birmingham, Cork, Glasgow and Manchester via Malta to Tunis. However, schedules are such that an extended stopover in Malta might be needed before you catch your onward flight.

British Airways UK ☎0870/850 9850, Republic of Ireland ☎1800/626 747, ⊛www.ba.com. London Gatwick direct to Tunis, operated by franchisee GB Airways, with connections from most British and Irish airports.

BMI UK ☎0870/607 0555, ⊛www.flybmi.com. Through tickets from several UK airports via Heathrow in conjunction with Tunisair, or via Frankfurt in conjunction with Lufthansa.

Lufthansa UK ☎0870/837 7747, Republic of Ireland ☎01/844 5544, ⊛www.lufthansa. com. London, Dublin, Birmingham, Edinburgh and Manchester via Frankfurt to Tunis.

Tunisair ☎020/7734 7644, ⊛www.tunisair. com. London Heathrow direct to Tunis, with onward connections to Jerba and Tozeur.

Travel agents

Bridge the World UK ☎0870/443 2399, ⊛www .bridgetheworld.com. Specialists in long-haul travel, with good-value flight deals, RTW tickets and tailor-made packages, aimed at the backpacker market.

Co-op Travel Care UK ☎0870/112 0085, ⊛www .travelcareonline.com. Tunisia flights and packages.

ebookers UK ☎0870/010 7000, ⊛www.ebookers .com; Republic of Ireland ☎01/241 5689, ⊛www .ebookers.ie. Scheduled flights and package deals.

Flightcentre UK ☎0870/890 8099, ⊛www .flightcentre.co.uk. Tunisia packages and flights.

Joe Walsh Tours Republic of Ireland ☎01/676 0991, ⊛www.joewalshtours.ie. Long-established general budget fares and holidays agent.

McCarthys Travel Republic of Ireland ☎021/427 0127, ⊛www.mccarthystravel.ie. General flight agent.

North South Travel UK ☎01245/608291, ✎ ⊛www.northsouthtravel.co.uk. Discounted fares worldwide; profits are used to support projects in the developing world, especially the promotion of sustainable tourism.

Rosetta Travel ☎028/9064 4996, ⊛www .rosettatravel.com. Flight and holiday agent, specializing in deals direct from Belfast.

STA Travel UK ☎0870/160 0599, ⊛www .statravel.co.uk. Worldwide specialist in low-cost flights, overlands and holiday deals. Good discounts for students and under-26s.

Trailfinders UK ☎020/7938 3939, ⊛www .trailfinders.com; Republic of Ireland ☎01/677 7888, ⊛www.trailfinders.ie. One of the best-informed and most efficient agents for independent travellers.

USIT Republic of Ireland ☎0818/200 020, ⊛www .usit.ie, Northern Ireland ☎028/9032 7111, ⊛www.usitnow.com. Student, youth and independent travel.

World Travel Centre Republic of Ireland ☎01/416 7007, ⊛www.worldtravel.ie. Discount air fares.

Package tours

Almost all the major British and Irish tour operators offer Tunisian holidays. Any travel agent can supply a list of relevant tour operators, and a complete list of these, in both Britain and Ireland, is available from the Tunisian National Tourist Office in London (see p.19). Packages often cost little more than a charter flight, and are mainly focused on the Nabeul–Hammamet or Sousse–Monastir coasts.

A package will include flights, accommodation and often transfers to and from your hotel, or a rental car. Some packages are straightforward travel-plus-beach-hotel affairs providing a fixed base. You can get a 14-night beach holiday with half-board in a three- or four-star hotel for around £450/ €650 off-season, or around £800/€1200 in high season, with some summer deals going for as little as £620/€900 – less if you opt for self-catering. If your trip is geared around specific interests – archeological discovery tours, trekking or desert expeditions – packages can work out much cheaper than the same arrangements made on arrival.

Tunisia is a destination to which package tours are often sold off cheap as **last-minute offers** when they approach their sell-by date. You can sometimes pick up a last-minute seven-day package holiday for as little as £100 per person, which is worth it for the flight alone.

Tunisia specialists

Aspects of Tunisia ☎020/7836 4999, ⊛www .aspectsoftunisia.co.uk. Beach holidays in Gammarth, Sidi Bou Saïd, Hammamet, Sousse, Port el Kantaoui, Jerba and Sangho (near Zarzis), breaks in Tunis, Sidi Bou Said and Tamerza, plus extensions to Ksar Ghilane, a desert tour and a Roman Tunisia tour, using scheduled fights.

Panorama UK ☏0870/759 5595, ⓦwww .panoramaholidays.co.uk; Republic of Ireland ☏0818/202020, ⓦwww.panoramaholidays. ie. Offers beach hotels in Gammarth, Hammamet, Sousse, Port el Kantaoui, Mahdia and Kerkennah, activities for kids, Sahara excursions, Tunis city breaks and golfing holidays. They operate charter flights to Monastir from Dublin, Belfast and (in winter) Cork; in the Republic of Ireland you can book these through Just Flights (☏0818/200200, wwww.justflights.ie).

Sunnyway UK ☏ 0845/130 7999, ⓦwww .sunnyway-tunisia.co.uk. Beach holidays in Gammarth, Hammamet, Sousse, Port el Kantaoui, Monastir, Mahdia, Kerkennah and Jerba, with the option of additional nights in Matmata, Douz, Kebili and Tozeur, plus golfing holidays and Tunis city breaks, using scheduled flights from Heathrow and Gatwick, or charters from several UK airports.

Other specialist tour operators

Adventures Abroad UK ☏0114/247 3400, ⓦwww.adventures-abroad.com. Seven- and thirteen-day adventure tours of Tunisia, with add-ons available to Malta, Libya, Italy and Morocco.

Andante Travels UK ☏01722/713800, ⓦwww .andantetravels.co.uk. Good value one- and two-week archeological tours with expert guide lecturers, concentrating on Punic and Roman sites.

Dragoman Overland Expeditions UK ☏08704/994475, ⓦwww.dragoman.com. Overland tours taking in Tunisia, Libya and Egypt, which extensions to neighbouring countries possible.

Erna Low UK ☏020/7594 0290, ⓦwww .bodyandsoulholidays.info. Thermal spa and "thassalotherapy" (seawater treatment) holidays in Gammarth, Hammamet and Jerba.

Explore Worldwide UK ☏01252/760000, Republic of Ireland ☏01/677 9479, ⓦwww .exploreworldwide.com. Fifteen-day overland adventure holidays in Tunisia, including a three-day camel trek.

Holt's Tours UK ☏01304/612248, ⓦwww .battletours.co.uk. Specializing in military history trips, they have occasional tours of World War II battlefields in Tunisia.

Iberian Lynx UK ☏0800/279 0345, ⓦwww .iberianlynxgolf.co.uk. Golfing holidays based in Port el Kantaoui.

Imaginative Traveller UK ☏020/8742 8612, ⓦwww.imaginative-traveller.com. A "soft" adventure operator, offering a fifteen-day tour of Tunisia using small hotels, minibuses and 4WDs.

Longmere Golf Holidays UK ☏0870/990 1420, ⓦwww.longmeregolf.co.uk. Golfing holidays in Hammamet, Port el Kantaoui and Monastir.

Mercian Travel UK ☏01562/883795, ⓦwww .merciantravel.co.uk. Bridge and bowling holidays in Port el Kantaoui.

Prospect Music and Art Tours UK ☏020/7486 5704, ⓦwww.prospecttours.com. Cultural tours, generally visiting Tunisia every year.

Remembrance Travel UK ☏01622/716 729 or 182, ⓦwww.remembrancetravel.com. Annual tour of Tunisian World War II graves and battlefields, organized by the Royal British Legion.

Select World Golf UK ☏01202/701881, ⓦwww.selectworldgolf.co.uk. Golfing holidays in Hammamet and Port el Kantaoui.

Tunisia First UK ☏01276/600100, ⓦwww .tunisiafirst.co.uk. Beach holidays in Gammarth, Sidi Bou Saïd, Hammamet, Sousse, Port el Kantaoui, Monastir, Mahdia, Bizerte, Tabarka and Jerba, plus golfing holidays, Tamerza-based desert tours and Tunis city breaks. They use scheduled flights from Heathrow and Gatwick, as well as charters from several UK airports.

Voyages Jules Verne UK ☏020/7616 1000, ⓦwww.vjv.com. Luxury cultural tours including a seven-day tour of Tunisia concentrating on Roman sites and desert oases, or a thirteen-day tour of the major Roman sites in Tunisia and Libya.

Mainstream tour operators

Airtours UK ☏0800/916 6103, ⓦwww.airtours .co.uk, Republic of Ireland ☏0818/202020. Hammamet, Sousse, Port el Kantaoui and Monastir packages; charter flights to Monastir from several British and Irish airports.

Cadogan UK ☏023/8082 8302, ⓦwww .cadoganholidays.com. Upmarket firm using scheduled flights and mostly four- and five-star hotels in Gammarth, Sidi Bou Saïd, Hammamet, Sousse, Port el Kantaoui, Monastir and Jerba. Also offers golfing holidays.

First Choice UK ☏0870/750 0001, ⓦwww .firstchoice.co.uk. Sousse, Port el Kantaoui and Monastir packages. Charter flights to Monastir from Gatwick, Luton, Birmingham, Bristol, Glasgow and Manchester.

Falcon/JWT Holidays Republic of Ireland ☏1850/946164, ⓦwww.jwtholidays.ie. Beach holidays in Port el Kantaoui; charter flights from Dublin to Monastir.

Portland Direct UK ☏0870/241 3172, ⓦwww .portland-holidays.co.uk. Holidays in Hammamet, Port el Kantaoui and Sousse. Charter flights from Gatwick, Luton, Birmingham, Bristol, Glasgow and Manchester.

Sunway Republic of Ireland ☏01/288 6828, ⓦwww.sunway.ie. Beach holidays in Hammamet and Port el Kantaoui, and summer Dublin–Monastir charter flights.

Thomson UK ☏0870/165 0079, ☏0800/000 747 for flight-only information, ⓦwww.thomson-holidays.com. Hammamet, Sousse, Port el Kantaoui and Monastir. Monastir charter flights from Gatwick, Luton, Birmingham, Bristol, Glasgow, Newcastle and Manchester.

Flights from the US and Canada

There are no direct flights to Tunisia from the US or Canada; you will have to fly via a European gateway city. In many ways Air France is the most convenient, though not necessarily the cheapest, **airline** for Tunisia, as they serve most major US and Canadian hubs and offer frequent connecting flights to Tunis. Most overnight services from North America arrive at Paris in time to connect with their morning flight to Tunis.

Flying **from the US** in low season, and particularly if you qualify for student or under-26 youth fares, you should be able to get a through ticket from New York to Tunis for around $950 in winter, $1600 in summer. Fares from Chicago, Boston or Miami will be slightly higher. From the West Coast, a ticket to Tunis out of LAX will cost from $1250 upward, rising to $1850 in high season.

From Canada, fares are typically Can$1625 in low season from Toronto, or Can$2200 from Montreal, rising in high season to around Can$2500 from either of these airports. The equivalent fares from Vancouver are Can$2700/3000.

Airlines

Air Canada ☏1-888/247-2262, ⓦwww.aircanada.com. Flights to Tunisia in conjunction with Tunisair or a European carrier.

Air France US ☏1-800/237-2747, Canada ☏1-800/667-2747, ⓦwww.airfrance.com. Flights to Tunis from plenty of major American airports, as well as from Montreal and Toronto, via Paris.

Alitalia US ☏1-800/223-5730, Canada ☏1-800/361-8336, ⓦwww.alitalia.com. Atlanta (codeshare with Delta), Chicago, Miami, New York and Toronto via Milan or Rome to Tunis.

British Airways ☏1-800/AIRWAYS, ⓦwww.ba.com. Atlanta, Dallas/Fort Worth, Detroit, Houston and Orlando to Tunis via London's Gatwick airport. Their flights from other North American airports arrive in London's Heathrow airport, from where you will have to get a bus or train to Gatwick for your Tunis flight.

Continental ☏1-800/231-0856, ⓦwww.continental.com. Flights to Tunisia in conjunction with Tunisair or a European carrier.

Delta ☏1-800/241-4141, ⓦwww.delta.com. Flights to Tunisia in conjunction with Tunisair or a European carrier.

Lufthansa US ☏1-800/645-3880, Canada ☏1-800/563-5954, ⓦwww.lufthansa.com. To Tunis from Atlanta, Boston, Chicago, Dallas, Denver, Detroit, Houston, Miami, Montreal (codeshare with Air Canada), New York, Philadelphia, Toronto and Washington, via Frankfurt.

Royal Air Maroc ☏1-800/344-6726, ⓦwww.royalairmaroc.com. New York and Montreal to Tunis via Casablanca.

United Airlines ☏1-800/538-2929, ⓦwww.united.com. Through tickets to Tunis in conjunction with Tunisair or a European carrier.

Travel agents

Air Brokers International ☏1-800/883-3273, ⓦwww.airbrokers.com. Consolidator and specialist in RTW tickets.

Airtech ☏212/219-7000, ⓦwww.airtech.com. Standby seat broker; also deals in consolidator fares.

Airtreks US ☏1-877/AIRTREKS, ⓦwww.airtreks.com. RTW specialist. The website features an interactive database that lets you build and price your own itinerary.

Educational Travel Center ☏1-800/747-5551 or 608/256-5551, ⓦwww.edtrav.com. Low-cost fares worldwide, student/youth discount offers, and Eurail passes, car rental and tours.

Flightcentre US ☏1-866/WORLD-51, ⓦwww.flightcentre.us; Canada ☏1-888/WORLD-55, ⓦwww.flightcentre.ca. Rock-bottom fares worldwide.

STA Travel US ☏1-800/329-9537, Canada ☏1-888/427-5639, ⓦwww.statravel.com. Worldwide specialist in independent travel; also student IDs, travel insurance, car rental, rail passes, and more.

Student Flights ☏1-800/255-8000 or 480/951-1177, ⓦwww.isecard.com/studentflights. Student/youth fares, plus student IDs and European rail and bus passes.

TFI Tours ☏1-800/745-8000 or 212/736-1140, ⓦwww.lowestairprice.com. Consolidator with global fares.

Travel Avenue ☏1-800/333-3335, ⓦwww.travelavenue.com. Full-service travel agent that offers discounts in the form of rebates.

Travel Cuts US ☎1-800/592-CUTS, Canada ☎1-888/246-9762, ⊛www.travelcuts.com. Popular, long-established organization, with worldwide offers for students and other travellers.

Travelosophy US ☎1-800/332-2687, ⊛www.itravelosophy.com. Good range of discounted and student fares worldwide.

Worldtek Travel ☎1-800/243-1723, ⊛www.worldtek.com. Discount travel agency for worldwide travel.

Tour operators

Abercrombie & Kent ☎1-800/323-7308 or 630/954-2944, ⊛www.abercrombiekent.com. Upmarket operator offering breaks in Gammarth.

Adventure Center ☎1-800/228-8747 or 510/654-1879, ⊛www.adventurecenter.com. Agent for Dragoman and Explore Worldwide (see p.12).

Adventures Abroad ☎1-800/665-3998, ⊛www.adventures-abroad.com. Seven- and thirteen-day adventure tours of Tunisia, with add-ons available to Malta, Libya, Italy and Morocco.

Archaeological Tours ☎1-866/740 5130, ⊛www.archaeologicaltrs.com. Annual 17-day tour of major archeological sites in Tunisia, led by specialist lecturers.

Cross Cultural Adventures ☎703/237 0100, ⊕piotrk@erols.com. Runs tours with an emphasis on culture and archeological sites. Specializes in customized trips for individual travellers and private groups.

Goway Travel Experiences ☎1-800/387-8850, ⊛www.goway.com. One- to three-week beach holidays in Hammamet, Sousse and Port el Kantaoui, or ten-day "Sahara Splendour" and "Tunisia Explorer" tours.

TunisUSA ☎1-800/474 5500 or ☎610/995 2788, ⊛www.tunisusa.com. Tunisia specialists with an emphasis on culture and history, running eight different tours for small groups with expert local guides, with customized trips possible. Offerings include a two-week culture and history tour, and one-week tours on themes such as deserts and oases, Roman Tunisia and Jewish Tunisia.

Flights from Australia and New Zealand

Reaching Tunisia from Australia or New Zealand involves travelling via Europe or the Middle East, possibly stopping over in Southeast Asia as well. A two-week return ticket from a discount agent will cost around A$2400 in high season, A$2000 in low sea-son. **From New Zealand**, two-week return tickets from Auckland to Tunis are available from discount agents for around NZ$2900 in high season, or NZ$2500 in low season.

Package tours to Tunisia from Australia and New Zealand are few and far between, and comprise mostly "adventure" tours using jeeps, minibuses and small hotels, though a couple of firms do offer beach holidays.

Airlines

Air New Zealand Australia ☎13/2476, ⊛www.airnz.com.au, NZ ☎0800/737 000, ⊛www.airnz.co.nz. From most NZ cities to Tunis in combination with Lufthansa.

British Airways Australia ☎1300/767 177, NZ ☎0800/274 847 or 09/356 8690, ⊛www.ba.com. Sydney, Auckland, Brisbane, Cairns and Perth via London to Tunis. However, fares are higher than via other routes, and furthermore the London connection involves a change of airport.

Emirates Australia ☎1300/303 777, New Zealand ☎09/377 6004, ⊛www.emirates.com. To Tunis in combination with Tunisair or a Middle Eastern carrier, via Beirut or Dubai.

Qantas Australia ☎13/1313, NZ ☎0800/808 767 or 09/357 8900, ⊛www.qantas.com. Through tickets to Tunisia from most cities in Australia and NZ in conjunction with a European carrier.

Singapore Airlines Australia ☎13 10 11, New Zealand ☎0800/808 909, ⊛www.singaporeair.com. To Tunis in combination with a Middle Eastern or European carrier.

Thai Airways Australia ☎1300/651 960, New Zealand ☎09/377 3886, ⊛www.thaiair.com. Tunis flights in conjunction with Royal Jordanian.

Travel agents

Flight Centre Australia ☎13/3133, ⊛www.flightcentre.com.au; NZ ☎0800/243 544, ⊛www.flightcentre.co.nz. Rock-bottom fares; branches nationwide in both Australia and NZ.

Holiday Shoppe NZ ☎0800/808 480, ⊛www.holidayshoppe.co.nz. Great deals on flights, hotels and holidays.

OTC Australia ☎1300/855 118, ⊛www.otctravel.com.au. Competitive deals on flights, hotels and holidays.

STA Travel Australia ☎1300/733 035, ⊛www.statravel.com.au; NZ ☎0508/782 872, ⊛www.statravel.co..nz. Specialist in low-cost flights, overlands and holiday deals. Good discounts for students and under-26s.

Trailfinders Australia ☎ 02/9247 7666, ⓦ www
.trailfinders.com.au. Well-informed, efficient agent
catering to independent travellers.

Tour operators

Abercrombie & Kent Australia ☎ 1300/851 800,
New Zealand ☎ 0800/441 638, ⓦ www
.abercrombiekent.com.au. Upmarket breaks in
Gammarth.

Adventure World Australia ☎ 02/8913 0755,
ⓦ wwww.adventureworld.com.au; New Zealand
☎ 09/524 5118, ⓦ www.adventureworld.co.nz.
Specialist in overland expeditions and trekking tours;
agent for Dragoman and Explore Worldwide (see
p.12).

Adventures Abroad Australia ☎ 1800/147 827,
New Zealand ☎ 0800/800 434, ⓦ www
.adventures-abroad.com. Seven- and thirteen-day
adventure tours of Tunisia, with add-ons available to
Malta, Libya, Italy and Morocco.

Africa Travel Centre Australia ☎ 02/9267 3048
or 1800/622 984, New Zealand ☎ 09/520 2000.
Specialist in overland expeditions and trekking tours;
agent for Dragoman and Explore Worldwide (see
p.12).

Goway Travel Experiences Australia
☎ 1800/227268 or 02/9262 4755, ⓦ www
.goway.com. One- to three-week beach holidays in
Hammamet, Sousse and Port el Kantaoui, or ten-day
"Sahara Splendour" and "Tunisia Explorer" tours.

Think! Adventure Australia ☎ 1300/135088,
ⓦ www.thinkadventure.com.au. Adventure travel
specialist; agent for Imaginative Traveller's small-
group tours (see p.12).

Overland from the UK

You won't save any money by **going overland** between the UK and Tunis but the
routes are worth considering if you want
to take in something of France and/or Italy
on the way; the route through Italy is probably the more popular. And if you're under
26, there are bargains to be had on rail tickets. Among the most used ferries to Tunis
are the sailings from **Marseille**, **Genoa** and
Trápani (Sicily); for details of these and other
ferries, see the section on pp.16–18.

By rail

By train from London, it takes around twenty
hours to reach Marseille, thirty hours to
Genoa and fifty hours to Trápani. The fastest
rail connections are the Eurostar to Paris and

the TGV on to Marseille or Milan, changing
at the latter for Genoa or Sicily. Rail **tickets**
from London to Marseille using Eurostar and
the TGV start at around £85 one-way, £165
return; to Genoa, they cost around £135
one-way, £225 return. Under-26s can get a
reduction of about 25 percent on the Paris–
Marseille or Paris–Genoa leg of the journey.
Trainseurope, European Rail and International Rail (see below) can sell through tickets
via Eurostar to Marseille, Genoa or Trápani.
Through tickets are not available from Ireland, so you'd have to travel to Britain or
France and buy an onward ticket there.

You can save more money by using ferry
services across the Channel instead of the
Eurostar, and ordinary trains instead of the
TGV. This will take you a good deal longer,
however, and you'll have to buy your train
ticket in Calais, making your own way there.

Rail passes

Worth considering if you intend to do much
travelling in Europe on the way is the **Inter-
Rail pass**, available to anyone who has lived
in a participating country (including Britain
or Ireland) for the previous six months. This
gives you half fares on trains in the country
where you buy it, and supposedly gives free
travel in all other countries covered, though
in practice you have to pay supplements
(average about £10) on all the trains you
actually want to use. A two-zone pass covering France and Italy costs around £215 for
a month if you're under 26, £300 if you're
26 or over. A three-zone pass, covering Britain and Ireland too, costs around £245 for
under-26s, £350 for over-26s. The passes
are available at main train stations throughout the UK and Ireland, or from firms like
RailEurope. For further details, price updates
and online purchasing, see ⓦ www.inter-rail
.co.uk.

Rail tickets and passes

European Rail ☎ 020/7387 0444, ⓦ www
.europeanrail.com.
Eurostar UK ☎ 0870/160 6600, ⓦ www.eurostar
.com.
Irish Rail Ireland ☎ 01/703 1885, ⓦ www.irishrail
.ie.
International Rail UK ☎ 0870/751 5000, ⓦ www
.international-rail.com.

RailEurope (SNCF French Railways) UK
℡0870/584 8848, ⊛www.raileurope.co.uk.
Trainseurope UK ℡0900/195 0101 (60p/min,
refundable against a booking), ⊛www.trainseurope
.co.uk.

By bus

Buses from London to Marseille, Genoa or
Rome take about the same time as trains
but can cost substantially less, though a
long bus ride is of course a lot less comfortable than a long train journey. Eurolines run
buses from London to Marseille (changing
at Lyon) for around £75 single/£100 return,
or London to Genoa (changing at Paris and
Milan) for £80/£135. These tickets cost
slightly more in July and August, with small
reductions for under-25s and over-65s, but
30-day advance purchase fixed-date return
tickets to either destination are available
to all comers for most of the year priced
£52. For tickets, contact **Eurolines** (UK
℡0870/514 3219, ⊛www.eurolines.co.uk;
Republic of Ireland ℡01/836 6111, ⊛www
.eurolines.ie).

Driving

Crossing the **Channel** from Britain to Europe
by car, the fastest – though not the cheapest – way is through the Channel Tunnel with
Eurotunnel; it's best to book ahead if you
can, though you shouldn't have to wait too
long if you just turn up at the port. The alternatives for most travellers are the ferry links
from Dover to Calais, Boulogne or Dunkirk,
or Newhaven to Dieppe. For any of the ferry
crossings to Tunisia, you'll need to book in
advance if you're taking a car; see below for
more on the various options.

Ferries to Tunisia

There are **ferries** to Tunisia from Trápani and
Palermo (Sicily), Genoa, Salerno, La Spezia
and Naples (mainland Italy; services from
the last two are summer-only), Marseille
(France), and even Valencia (Spain). There
are not usually any direct ferry services from
Malta, though Grandi Navi Veloci's Genoa
service and Grimaldi's Salerno service run
via Valetta on the way back, and Grandi Navi
Veloci sometimes run boats from Genoa that

call at Valetta en route. Most services arrive
at La Goulette, the port for Tunis (see p.17),
though very occasionally one or two of
CTN's services terminate at Bizerte, Sousse
or Sfax instead.

The **Trápani–Tunis** ferry crossing is the
shortest, with one service a week in summer only, run by Linee Lauro. Until recently,
a year-round weekly service was operated
by Tirrenia di Navigazione, starting in Cagliari
(Sardinia), but this was suspended at last
check. The difference in standards of service
between the Sardinia–Sicily leg, where the
passengers are mainly Italian, and the Sicily–Tunisia leg, where they are mainly Tunisian,
is quite shocking. In midsummer, especially,
you'll need to be prepared for a harassed and
frantic time buying tickets in Trápani. Booking
ahead is advisable, and essential if taking a
car across any time between mid-June and
mid-September. You would also be well
advised to get a full return ticket in advance,
especially if you're planning to return during
the last two weeks of August, when the boats
are packed with returning migrant workers.
There is also a weekly service from **Salerno**
near Naples on Grimaldi Ferries, which actually starts at Valencia in Spain, and there are
boats from **Naples** and **La Spezia** operated
by Linee Lauro, but only in summer.

Ferries from **Genoa** and **Marseille** are in
some respects more convenient and certainly pleasanter than those from Trápani. Drivers, however, will need to make reservations
three or four months in advance for summer crossings on the Marseille and Genoa
routes. Both of these are operated by **Compagnie Tunisienne de la Navigation** (**CTN**
or **Cotunav**), Tunisia's national line.

Thomas Cook's monthly *European Timetables* (the red volume), available in public libraries in Britain and Ireland, or from
any branch of Thomas Cook, carries ferry
schedules, but it's best to check with the
operators for the latest information. CTN
generally have their latest schedules and
fares on their website; other firms are less
efficient, but schedules and fares for many
services out of Italy can be found at ⊛www
.fun.informare.it/ferry/zona13uk.asp, or on
the website of Viamare Travel (who represent many of them in the UK), ⊛www
.viamare.com.

Ferry routes and prices

The prices quoted below, all for ferries to La Goulette (Tunis), are the cheapest one-way fares, and do not include port taxes. Note that fares vary with season as well as standard of accommodation. Car and motorbike prices quoted do not include the cost of passenger tickets.

From	Operator	Frequency	Time	Passenger	Car	Motorbike
Genoa	CTN	1–4 weekly	22–23hr	€108	€250	€42
Genoa	GNV	2–4 weekly	23hr	€109	€219	€46
La Spezia	Lauro	1–2 weekly June–Sept	23–31hr	€100	€175	€90
Marseille†	CTN	1–6 weekly	21–23hr	€144	€344	€65
Naples	Lauro	1–4 weekly June–Sept	19hr	€85	€165	€90
Palermo	Grimaldi	1 weekly	9hr	€45	€80	€40
Salerno	Grimaldi	2 weekly	18–21hr	€93	€129	€83
Trápani	Lauro	1 weekly June–Sept	7–12hr	€50	€175	€90
Valencia	Grimaldi	1 weekly	62hr	€222	€155	€83

† From Marseille there are very occasional sailings to Bizerte, Sousse and Sfax.

Ferry companies

Compagnie Tunisienne de la Navigation (CTN or Cotunav) ⊛ www.ctn.com.tn. UK: c/o Southern Ferries, 179 Piccadilly, London W1V 9DB ☎ 020/7491 4968. France: 21 Rue Mazenod, Marseille ☎ 04/9191 5571. Italy: Piazzale de Traghetti Iqbal Masih 5 (Nero), Genoa ☎ 010/425 8041. Tunisia: 122 rue de Yougoslavie, Tunis ☎ 71 322 775; 29 av d'Algerie, Bizerte ☎ 72 735 111; rue Abdallah Ibn Zoubeir, Sousse (by the port) ☎ 73 229 436; 75 rue Habib Maazoun, Sfax ☎ 74 228 022. Genoa and Marseille to La Goulette. The ferries operate weekly in winter, the frequency rising to as many as four a week out of Genoa and six out of Marseille in summer, supplemented by SNCM Ferryterranée boats. The Marseille service occasionally serves Bizerte or Sfax instead of La Goulette.

Grandi Navi Veloci ⊛ www.gnv.it. UK: c/o Viamare Travel, Graphic House, 2 Sumatra Rd, London NW6 1PU ☎ 0870/106040. Australia: c/o Chiariva, 530 Little Collins Street, Suite 803, Melbourne, Vic 3000 ☎ 03/9909 7266. Italy: 51 Via Milano, Genoa ☎ 010/209 4591; & c/o O.F. Gollcher, Marina Court 1, Suite No 8, 2nd Floor, Giuseppe Cali St, Valletta VLT 10 ☎ 334023. Tunisia: c/o D'Alessandro, Espace "Méditerranée", Zone commerciale Portuaire Radès (Lac Tunis) ☎ 71 448 050. Genoa to La Goulette.

Grimaldi Ferries ⊛ www.grimaldi-ferries. com. UK: c/o Viamare Travel (see under Grandi

Navi Veloci). Italy: 13 Via M. Campodisola, Naples ☎ 081/496 444; SAT Salerno Auto Terminal, Salerno Port ☎ 089/253 202. Tunisia: c/o Tamaris Voyages, 68 av Hédi Chaker, Tunis ☎ 71 790 855; c/o Agence Maritime Berrebi, La Goulette ☎ 71 737 785. Valencia, Salerno and Palermo to La Goulette.

Linee Lauro ⊛ www.lauro.it. UK: c/o Viamare Travel (see under Grandi Navi Veloci). Italy: ☎ 081/497 2222; Piazza Municipio 88, Naples; Stazione Maritima, Trápani. La Spezia, Naples and Trápani to La Goulette.

Tirrenia di Navigazione ⊛ www.tirrenia.it. UK: c/o SMS Travel, 40–42 Kenway Rd, London SW5 0RA ☎ 020/7244 8422. Italy ☎ 081/317 2999, from Italian landlines ☎ 199/123 199; Molo Sanità, Stazione Marittima, Cagliari; c/o Salvo Viaggi SRL, Stazione Marittima, Molo Sanità, Trápani; Molo Angioino, Naples; Catala Marinai d'Italia, Porto, Palermo. Tunisia, c/o CTN in Tunis. Service from Cagliari (Sardinia) and Trápani to La Goulette suspended at the time of writing but is expected to resume.

By yacht

For those with private boats, there are **marinas** at Monastir, Port el Kantaoui, Sidi Bou Said and Tabarka, a small one at Bizerte, and marinas under construction at Houmt Souk (Jerba). Although these are the only places with facilities for pleasure boats, there are a total of 26 ports along the coast where you are allowed to drop anchor, of which La Goulette, Sidi Bou Said, Hammamet, Bizerte, Tabarka, Port el Kantaoui, Sousse, Sfax, Houmt Souk and Zarzis are authorized ports of entry into the country. For further details of facilities, formalities and individual ports, see ⓦ www.noonsite.com/Countries/Tunisia.

Red tape and visas

Canadian and EU citizens need no visa for a stay in Tunisia of up to three months, US citizens for up to four months. Australians and New Zealanders need visas, however, and these are valid for stays of up to three months. New Zealanders must obtain visas in advance; Australians can get them at borders and ports on entry, though check in advance of your trip, as these things have a habit of changing. Visas cost the equivalent of 6.6TD; when applying, you'll need to provide three photos, your passport and fill in two forms. Applications usually take three weeks to process. Tunisians holding dual passports may be expected to enter and leave the country on a Tunisian passport.

Tunisian embassies and consulates abroad

Algeria 11 rue du Bois de Boulogne, El Mouradia, Algiers ☎ 021/601388; 23 av 28 Janvier, St Thèrese, Annaba ☎ 08/864568; 150 bd Col Mahmoud Cherif, BP 280, Tébessa ☎ 08/484832.
Australia Level 5, Edgecliff Centre, 203 New South Head Rd, Edgecliff, Sydney, NSW 2027 ☎ 02/9363 5588.
Canada 515 O'Connor St, Ottawa K1S 3P8 ☎ 613/237 0330; 511 pl d'Armes, Suite 501, Montreal H2Y 2W7 ☎ 514/844 6909.
Egypt 26 Sharia al-Jazira, Zamalek, Cairo ☎ 02/31 8962
Libya Sharia Bashir al-Ibrahim, PO Box 613, Tripoli ☎ 021/333 1051; Sharia al-Khadra, al-Fouihet, Benghazi ☎ 061/222 6683.
Malta 144 Tower Rd, Flat 2, Sliema SLM 08 ☎ 2134 5866.
Morocco 6 av de Fès/1 rue d'Ifrane, Rabat ☎ 037 73 06 36.
Netherlands Gentsestraat 98, 2587 HX, The Hague ☎ 070/351 2251.
Norway Håkon VII'sgt 5B, 0161 Oslo ☎ 2283-1917.
South Africa 850 Church St, Arcadia 0007, Pretoria, PO Box 56535 ☎ 012/342 5282.
Sweden Narvavägen 32, 11522 Stockholm ☎ 08/5458 5520.

UK 29 Prince's Gate, London SW7 1QG ☎ 020/7584 8117.
USA 1515 Massachusetts Ave NW, Washington, DC 20005 ☎ 202/862 1850.

Visa extensions

The practice for **extending a visa** varies, but is rarely easy. At least two weeks before your visa or permitted period of stay is due to expire, go to the police station covering the area where you are staying, with some proof that you have a reason for staying in the country, proof of accommodation (a hotel receipt for example), four passport photos, and evidence that you can support yourself (take along all your exchange slips, and either cash, or a card plus proof of funds to back it). Extensions usually take between two weeks and a month to process. Once granted, they usually give three months' residence. An alternative means of getting a renewal is to pop over to Libya, Malta or Sicily, so that you can get a new tourist stamp on re-entry. If you overstay your visa, you are committing a criminal offence, but you *may* be able to sort it out if you apply in Tunis for exceptional permission to leave the country, at the Direction des Frontières, 13 rue 18 Janvier (near the *Hôtel Africa*).

Foreign embassies and consulates can be found in the major towns. Britain, Canada and the US have embassies in Tunis (see p.118), while Britain has an honorary consul in Sfax (see p.277). Outside Tunis, Libya has a consulate in Sfax (see p.277), and Algeria has consulates in Le Kef (see p.316) and Gafsa (see p.345), though it's possible that visas will have to be applied for at the Algerian embassy in Tunis.

Customs regulations

The **duty-free allowances** for arrivals in Tunisia are 400 cigarettes, a litre of spirits or two litres of wine, 250ml of perfume and a litre of toilet water. Tunisian duty-free shops are often open at airports on arrival as well as departure, and have reasonable rates for cigarettes, tobacco for *chichas* (see p.41) and spirits. They do not take dinars, however, so don't bother to save any for a bottle on your way home.

Information, websites and maps

The state-run Organisation Nationale de Tourisme Tunisien (ONTT) have a main office in Tunis and branches throughout the country, but you can pick up most of their material in advance before you reach Tunisia if coming from the UK, USA, Canada and much of Europe. Their ⓦwww.tourismtunisia.com website has regional lists of hotels and restaurants, and glowing descriptions of Tunisia's tourist resorts, all of which would be very useful except that it is not maintained and much of the information is out of date. They have a second website, ⓦwww.tunisietourisme .com.tn, which is more up to date but has little in the way of useful information, though it does have a few ideas in the "Regional Exploration" section.

In Tunisia, you'll find a locally run tourist office, or **Syndicat d'Initiative**, in many towns, and even some villages, and they are invariably friendlier and more helpful than the ONTT. Both types of tourist office supply local information, including listings of leisure activities, bike rental outlets, laundries and countless other things; always ask for the free town plan. Many tourist offices also publish hotel and restaurant listings and give advice on the best places to go, and may even conduct free town tours.

For specialist historical and cultural information, you could try contacting the **British Tunisian Society** (c/o MBI Foundation, 78 Wigmore St, London 1U 2SJ; ☏020/7725 0986) or the **Maghreb Studies Association** (c/o The Maghreb Bookshop, 45 Burton St, London WC1H 9AL; ☏020/7388 1840). The latter publishes the most important English-language journal on North Africa, the *Maghreb Review* (ⓦwww.maghrebreview.com).

ONTT offices abroad

Algeria 1, pl Lavigerie, Hydra, Algiers ☏021/608190.
Canada 1253 McGill College, Bureau #655, Montreal PQ H3B 2Y5 ☏514/397 1182, ✉tunisinfo@qc.aira.com
France 32 av de l'Opéra, 75002 Paris ☏01/4742 7267, ✉ontt@wanadoo.fr; 12 rue de Sèze, 69006 Lyon ☏04/7852 3586.
Italy Via Calabria 25, 00187 Rome ☏06/4201 0149; Via Baracchini 10, 20123 Milan ☏02/8645 9026, ✉tunisia.turismo@libero.it; Via Cognetti 33, 77121 Bari ☏08 0522 7849.
Netherlands Muntplein 2111, 1012 WR Amsterdam ☏020/622 4971.
UK 77a Wigmore St, London W1U 1QF ☏020/7224 5598, ⓦwww.tourismtunisia.co.uk.
USA c/o Tunisian Embassy, 1515 Massachusetts Ave NW, Washington, DC 20005 ☏202/466 2546, ✉ezzeddine@ix.netcom.com.

Useful websites

There are a fair few **websites** on Tunisia, run from both inside and outside the country, mostly in French rather than Arabic, with a handful in English too. Three useful, comprehensive collections of Tunisia links are Ⓦwww.assr.org/countries/tunisia, Ⓦwww.arabinfoseek.com/tunisia.htm and Ⓦwww.sas.upenn.edu/African_Studies/Country_Specific/Tunisia.html.

General Tunisia information

Tunisia Online Ⓦwww.tunisiaonline.com Very much an official site, with features on the constitution, the president, the economy, and investment opportunities, plus latest news updates. One of the best sections is that on mosaics, with a selection of some of the best Roman mosaics from around the country.

TunisiaGlobe Ⓦwww.tunisiaglobe.com A round-up of the latest news headlines about Tunisia, with sections on business, sport and travel.

CIA World Factbook Ⓦwww.cia.gov/cia/publications/factbook/geos/ts.html A long page of statistics, facts and figures on Tunisia compiled by the American intelligence agency, with everything from the country's birth rate, sex ratio and GDP to its annual electricity consumption and railway mileage.

Weather Underground Ⓦwww.wunderground.com/global/TS.html Current weather conditions and five-day forecasts for 26 locations across the country.

Amnesty International Ⓦweb.amnesty.org/library/eng-tun/index Amnesty's reports on human rights in Tunisia.

Travel

Adventures of Tunisia Ⓦlexicorient.com/tunisia The Tunisia section of a site on North Africa, with a small write-up by Norwegian journalist Tore Kjeilen on each of over a hundred places around the country, accompanied by photos, and usually containing some interesting comments on each place covered. Absolutely plagued with annoying pop-ups, however.

The Star Wars Traveler Ⓦwww.toysrgus.com/travel/tunisia.html For serious Star Wars buffs – a site to help you track down every location used in every Star Wars movie shot in Tunisia, complete with photos showing them as they appear in the film, and as they are now.

History and culture

Global Gourmet Ⓦwww.globalgourmet.com/destinations/tunisia The Tunisia section of a site on world food – it doesn't feature a huge amount of information, but it is interesting, with recipes for harissa, vegetable couscous, Tunisian salad and lamb stew with quince.

Hannibal Barca and the Punic Wars Ⓦwww.barca.fsnet.co.uk If you're interested in Carthage and Hannibal, this is the site to check, with a vast amount of material on Carthage, its army, and in particular, Hannibal and the Punic Wars.

Web of Tunisian Jews Ⓦharissa.com/eng/objectifeng.htm A site covering all aspects of Tunisian Jewish culture, including history, arts and customs and featuring recipes, music clips and a photo gallery.

Government travel advisories

UK Foreign Office Ⓦwww.fco.gov.uk/travel
US State Department Ⓦtravel.state.gov/tunisia.html
Canadian Foreign Affairs Department Ⓦwww.dfait-maeci.gc.ca/middle_east/tunisia-en.asp
Australian Foreign Affairs Department Ⓦwww.dfat.gov.au/geo/tunisia/index.html

Maps

The maps in this book can be supplemented with free handouts from the ONTT, who print a reasonable general map of the country and a number of local town plans. ONTT offices used to give out a free 1:1,000,000 touring map of Tunisia, but you'd be hard put to find one nowadays. Tanit's 1:850,000 map is available widely and cheap (usually 1TD) in Tunisia. Both are adequate for finding your way around the country, but they are also out of date, and inaccurate in the detail. The Tunisian government's Service Topographique produce an excellent 1:750,000 map, which is usually available at their offices (listed at Ⓦwww.otc.nat.tn), but those are few and far between, and usually out of town and hard to find. In view of all this, if you want a good map of the country, it is best to buy it before you travel.

One of the best and most up-to-date and accurate Tunisia **road maps** is Michelin's (#744), which is on a scale of 1:800,000. It is particularly good on the pistes in the far south, which is handy if you plan on taking a jeep or landrover around that part of the country. Nelles' map, on a scale of 1:750,000, is a pretty good alternative. GeoCenter's, on a 1:800,000 scale, is a little bit clearer, but it is less accurate and a little bit dated, and Freytag and Berndt's 1:800,000 map is not as clear, nor as up to date. The map with the best detail of relief is the 1:850,000 map published by German guidebook firm Reise KnowHow, which has the added advantage of being printed on tear-proof paper.

Map outlets

UK and Ireland

Stanfords 12–14 Long Acre, London WC2E 9LP ☎020/7836 1321; 39 Spring Gardens, Manchester M2 2BG ☎0161/831 0250; 29 Corn St, Bristol BS1 1HT ☎0117/929 9966; ⓦ www.stanfords.co.uk.
Blackwell's Map Centre 50 Broad St, Oxford OX1 3BQ ☎01865/793 550; branches in Bristol, Cambridge, Cardiff, Leeds, Liverpool, Newcastle, Reading & Sheffield; ⓦ maps.blackwell.co.uk.
The Map Shop 30a Belvoir St, Leicester LE1 6QH ☎0116/247 1400, ⓦ www.mapshopleicester.co.uk.
National Map Centre Ireland 34 Aungier St, Dublin 2 ☎01/476 0471, ⓦ www.mapcentre.ie.
The Travel Bookshop 13–15 Blenheim Crescent, London W11 2EE ☎020/7229 5260, ⓦ www.thetravelbookshop.co.uk.
Traveller 55 Grey St, Newcastle-upon-Tyne NE1 6EF ☎0191/261 5622, ⓦ www.newtraveller.com.

US

110 North Latitude ☎336/369-4171, ⓦ www.110nlatitude.com.

Book Passage 51 Tamal Vista Blvd, Corte Madera, CA 94925 ☎1-800/999-7909; 1 Ferry Building, Embarcadero (at Market St), San Francisco, CA 94111 ☎415/835-1020, ⓦ www.bookpassage.com.
Distant Lands 56 S Raymond Ave, Pasadena, CA 91105 ☎1-800/310-3220, ⓦ www.distantlands.com.
Globe Corner Bookstore 28 Church St, Cambridge, MA 02138 ☎1-800/358-6013, ⓦ www.globecorner.com.
Longitude Books 115 W 30th St #1206, New York, NY 10001 ☎1-800/342-2164, ⓦ www.longitudebooks.com.

Canada

Map Town 400 5 Ave SW #100, Calgary, AB T2P 0L6 ☎1-877/921-6277, ⓦ www.maptown.com.
Travel Bug Bookstore 3065 W Broadway, Vancouver, BC V6K 2G9 ☎604/737-1122, ⓦ www.travelbugbooks.ca.
World of Maps 1235 Wellington St, Ottawa, ON K1Y 3A3 ☎1-800/214-8524, ⓦ www.worldofmaps.com.

Australia

Mapland 372 Little Bourke St, Melbourne ☎03/9670 4383, ⓦ www.mapland.com.au.
Map Shop 6–10 Peel St, Adelaide ☎08/8231 2033, ⓦ www.mapshop.net.au.
Map World 280 Pitt St, Sydney ☎02/9261 3601; 900 Hay St, Perth ☎08/9322 5733; Jolimont Centre, Canberra ☎02/6230 4097 and 1981 Logan Road, Brisbane, ☎07/3349 6633; ⓦ www.mapworld.net.au.

New Zealand

Map Centre ⓦ www.mapcentre.co.nz.
Map World 173 Gloucester St, Christchurch ☎0800/627 967, ⓦ www.mapworld.co.nz.

Insurance

Before travelling to Tunisia, you'd do well to take out an insurance policy to cover against theft, loss and illness or injury. Before paying for a new policy, however, it's worth checking whether you are already covered: some all-risks home insurance policies may cover your possessions when overseas, and many private medical schemes include cover when abroad. In Canada, provincial health plans usually provide partial cover for medical mishaps overseas, while holders of official student/teacher/youth cards in Canada and the US are entitled to (meagre) accident coverage and hospital in-patient benefits. Students will often find that their student health coverage extends during the vacations and for one term beyond the date of last enrolment. After exhausting the possibilities above, you might want to contact a specialist travel insurance company, or consider the travel insurance deal we offer (see box).

A typical travel insurance policy usually provides cover for the loss of baggage, tickets and – up to a certain limit – cash or cheques, as well as cancellation or curtailment of your journey. Most of them exclude so-called **dangerous sports** unless an extra premium is paid: in Tunisia this can mean scuba diving and windsurfing, though probably not jeep safaris.

Many policies can be chopped and changed to exclude coverage you don't need – for example, sickness and accident benefits can often be excluded or included at will. If you do take medical coverage, ascertain whether benefits will be paid as treatment proceeds or only after return home, and whether there is a 24-hour medical emergency number. When securing baggage cover, make sure that the per-article limit will cover your most valuable possession. If you need to make a **claim**, you should keep receipts for medicines and medical treatment, and in the event you have anything stolen, you must obtain an official statement from the police (called a *constat de vol*).

Rough Guides travel insurance

Rough Guide offers its own low-cost travel insurance, especially customized for our statistically low-risk readers by a leading British broker, provided by the American International Group (AIG) and registered with the British regulatory body, GISC (the General Insurance Standards Council). There are five main Rough Guides insurance plans: **No Frills** for the bare minimum for secure travel; **Essential**, which provides decent all-round cover; **Premier** for comprehensive cover with a wide range of benefits; **Extended Stay** for cover lasting four months to a year; and **Annual Multi-Trip**, a cost-effective way of getting Premier cover if you travel more than once a year. Premier, Annual Multi-Trip and Extended Stay policies can be supplemented by a "Hazardous Pursuits Extension" if you plan to indulge in sports considered dangerous, such as scuba-diving or trekking. For a policy quote, call the Rough Guide Insurance Line: toll-free in the UK ☎0800/015 09 06 or ☎+44 1392 314 665 from elsewhere. Alternatively, get an online quote at ⊛www.roughguides.com/insurance.

Health

Vaccinations are a small price to pay for the security they provide, though doctors differ as to which jabs they advise for travellers to Tunisia. It is wise to be up to date with polio and tetanus jabs, but not generally necessary to have inoculations against typhoid, hepatitis A or cholera.

Though most Tunisian doctors trained in France or Belgium and are as professional as their counterparts in the West, state hospitals are filthy and overcrowded, and basic services like food are not provided. On a more positive note, minor problems can be dealt with by any **infirmerie** (a surgery with a nurse), of which there's one in every town, several in bigger ones. The larger towns all have hospitals and **cliniques**, small private hospitals that are usually more pleasant than state-run ones.

Pharmacies administer most kinds of medicine – including some only available on prescription in Europe – and can often advise you about minor ailments. Pharmacists usually speak French but rarely English, so you should learn a few appropriate phrases if you have special needs. In any town of reasonable size, there will be a night pharmacy, open from evening till morning. Medicines are expensive in Tunisia, so take any basics you might need, including stomach pills and suntan lotion. Travel insurance, especially to cover medical emergencies, is an essential precaution.

The incidence of **HIV infection** and full-blown AIDS in Tunisia is almost certainly far higher than officially declared, though it is undoubtedly much lower than in most African or Western countries. From the point of view of travellers, a holiday affair with another tourist or – much more dangerously – with a Tunisian beach gigolo (see p.58) are the most likely areas of risk. Tunisian condoms are less reliable than Western ones, so be on the safe side, take some with you, and insist on using them if you have casual sex. It's also worth remembering, if you get a shave at a barber's, to make sure it's done with a new blade (they usually change it in front of you).

For updated advice on the health situation in Tunisia, check the website of the US government's Centers for Disease Control and Prevention, ⓦwww.cdc.gov/travel/nafrica .htm.

Common complaints

Most people experience some kind of **stomach problem** during a visit to Tunisia, as there are unfamiliar micro-organisms present in everything you consume. Some people drink only bottled water or use water purifying tablets and still have trouble; others drink tap water and come through unscathed. The best policy is to avoid eating places that don't look too clean, wash all fresh fruit and vegetables, and maintain good personal hygiene.

If you do go down with **diarrhoea**, it's essential to replace the fluid which is lost, since dehydration can strike very quickly. In serious cases, or if children are affected, remember that dissolving rehydration salts (*sels de rehydratation* in French, available at any pharmacy) in water helps your body absorb fluid. Failing that, half a teaspoon of table salt with four of sugar in a litre of water per day should see you through all right. Small quantities of bland starchy food such as bread, bananas and plain boiled rice or potatoes should be all right to eat, but it is best to avoid greasy food, dairy products, heavy spices, alcohol and caffeine. If symptoms persist for several days – especially if you get painful cramps, or if blood or mucus appear in your stools – seek medical advice.

Never underestimate Tunisia's **heat**, especially in the south. A hat is an essential precaution and you should take a suntan lotion with a high screen factor (particularly in summer and/or if you have a pale complexion), as the sun really is higher and therefore stronger in Tunisia than in northern latitudes. Resulting problems include **dehydration** – make sure that you're drinking enough (infrequent urination is a danger sign) – and **heatstroke**, which is potentially fatal. Signs of heatstroke are a very high body temperature without a feeling of fever, accompanied by headaches and disorientation; lowering body temperature, with a tepid shower or bath, for example, is the first step in treatment.

If you're visiting places on foot, especially in summer, take appropriate precautions – wear a sunhat, take frequent rests in the shade and carry plenty of water.

Bites and stings

Rabies exists in Tunisia, and it's wise to give certain animals a wide berth. Dogs can be very fierce, especially if you're walking or cycling; as a last resort, throwing stones (or even just threatening to) should get rid of them. A bite, scratch or even lick from an infected animal could spread the disease; wash any wound immediately but gently with soap or detergent, and apply alcohol or iodine if possible. Find out what you can about the animal and if it's known or thought to be infected, get treatment *immediately* – rabies is invariably fatal once symptoms appear. There is a vaccine, but it is expen-

Scorpions

Looking like some horrific alien creature, complete with claws and deadly sting, **scorpions** are the stuff of nightmares. At often more than 10cm from head to tail, they are the largest land invertebrates, and belong to the arachnid family, along with spiders. As well as being nocturnal, scorpions glow under ultraviolet light, so you can see them in the desert at night with the aid of a black light. The pincers are used for self-defence, digging burrows, holding prey and also courtship. Famously, when mating, the male grabs the female and the two perform what looks like a dance. In fact, the male is manoeuvering the female into a position where his genitalia can make contact with hers. Once impregnated, she may well have him for dinner unless he can make himself scarce. She does not lay eggs, but carries the young inside her until they are born, a rarity among invertebrates.

Scorpions are ideally adapted for the **desert**. They can survive the extremes of both heat and cold, and their exoskeleton protects from dehydration. Like cockroaches, they are among the species most capable of surviving a nuclear holocaust. They eat insects, spiders, and occasionally larger animals such as lizards and even mice, finding their prey with the aid of fine hairs on their pincers which detect vibrations in the air. They only sting their prey when it's necessary to immobilize it.

Only 25 out of over 1000 scorpion species in the world have a sting that can be fatal to humans, and even the sting of the most deadly species is only fatal in a small minority of cases, with children and old people the most vulnerable. It is said that Berber women in some Tunisian desert communities used to capture scorpions and boil a certain number up in milk, to give to newborn infants to build up their immunity.

The most deadly species of scorpion in Tunisia is the yellow fat-tailed scorpion (*Androctonus australis*), which is 4–10cm long. It is typically found under stones and in cracks and crevices, including cracks in the walls of houses, and is responsible for the majority of scorpion fatalities in Tunisia. Other dangerous native scorpions include the death stalker (*Leiurus quinquestriatus*), which can also reach up to 10cm and ranges from light yellow to almost orange, the blacktip scorpion (*Buthus occitanus*), up to 7cm in length and light yellow to black, the black fat-tailed scorpion (*Androctonus bicolor*), black and over 9cm long, and *Androctonus amoreuxi*, 6–9cm long and light to dark brown. Other species can give you a nasty sting, but are not dangerous.

sive, serves only to shorten the course of treatment you need and lasts no longer than three months.

Other animals to be avoided are **snakes** and **scorpions**. Both will be as keen to avoid you as you are them, and won't bite or sting unless disturbed. Don't go around barefoot in areas where there may be snakes or scorpions, wander through undergrowth in sandals, or poke about under or between rocks. If camping in desert areas, shake out your shoes before putting them on in case a scorpion has crept in. Most snakes are non-venomous, and few are life-threatening, but one or two species can be dangerous, most notably the horned viper. All scorpions sting, and a sting can be extremely painful, especially if you have an allergy to it, but again, not many are life-threatening (see box). In

fact, even in the case of potentially lethal species, death from snake bites or scorpion stings is rare, and a victim should be in no danger if treated within a reasonable time.

Nonetheless, if you or a companion are bitten by a snake or stung by a scorpion, you should seek treatment immediately. Try to remember what the animal looked like to assist in its identification when receiving treatment. Keep the victim calm and still, since moving may spread the venom. Don't bother trying to suck the venom out – that only works in movies – as attempting it may spread the poison; don't use a tourniquet either, as these are now considered dangerous. With a scorpion sting, clean the site gently with soap and water, and apply a cold compress if you have one to hand. In most cases the effects of the sting will subside within an hour, but seek treatment in any case.

The other poisonous animals you may fall foul of are **jellyfish**, now increasingly common in the Mediterranean due to the demise of sea turtles that were their main predators. Jellyfish stings are unlikely to be life-threat-ening, but are extremely painful, and again should be treated immediately.

Mosquitos can be a nuisance in Tunisia, though they don't carry malaria. It's a good idea to have mosquito repellent with you (one containing DEET is best), to be applied to all exposed skin after dark.

Costs, money and banks

The cost of travel in Tunisia is low compared with Western countries. You can get by quite easily on £150/$270 a week, with good meals, reasonable hotel rooms and a fair amount of transport, while on £250/$450 you move into relative luxury. At the bottom end, camping out or staying in the cheaper hotels, you could survive on as little as £100/$180. In general, the south of the country will be slightly cheaper than the north, and untouristed areas cheaper than resorts. Food, accommodation and souvenirs in Sousse, for example, can work out at almost double the price of equivalents in Sfax.

For students under 32, there are reductions of around 30 percent at most archeological sites and museums on production of an ISIC card.

Currency

The **Tunisian dinar (TD)** is a soft currency, whose **exchange rate** is fixed daily on a national basis (you can find it in local newspapers under "Cours des Devises"). At the time of writing, one dinar is worth about 50p sterling, US$0.90, or €0.66.

An initial source of confusion is the way in which prices are expressed. One dinar is divided into 1000 **millimes** and small, fractional prices are usually expressed in terms of millimes – 1,500, for example, instead of 1.5. "Whole" dinar prices, however, are usually written as "1TD", rather than "1,000mill". For the sake of clarity, prices in this guide are all expressed in dinars so that, for example, seven hundred millimes appears as "0.7TD".

Banknotes are issued in denominations of 5TD, 10TD, 20TD and 30TD, with silver **coins** of 5TD, 1TD and 0.5TD, and brass coins of 10, 20, 50 and 100 millimes – all identical in design, the last two confusingly similar in size. Aluminium coins of 5 millimes also exist, and are easy to confuse with 0.5TD ones. It's worth hoarding coinage,

especially the 1TD coins, as change is often in short supply.

Carrying your money

Plastic is by far the easiest and most convenient way to carry your money. Though credit and debit cards are of limited use in shops and restaurants outside tourist resorts, Visa and Mastercard can be used to draw cash from ATMs at banks and post offices in pretty much any sizeable town in the country, and some banks without ATMs will give cash advances on these cards. By using ATMs you get trade exchange rates, which are somewhat better than those charged by banks for changing cash. Your card issuer may well add a foreign transaction fee, but that is usually lower than the banks' commissions (though it's worth checking before you leave, as some banks, especially in the US, do charge quite high fees). Note also that there is a daily limit on ATM cash withdrawals, usually 500TD, and that machines tend to run out of cash quite frequently, especially at weekends. You can pay with cards (usually with Mastercard,

Visa, Diners Club or American Express, though the last two cannot be used in ATMs) in most hotels of two or more stars, and in the more upmarket restaurants. If you rent a car, a card may be essential for the deposit.

On credit cards, all cash advances and ATM withdrawals are treated as loans, with **interest** accruing daily from the date of withdrawal. Debit cards do not have this problem and are less likely to incur transaction fees, but always check with your issuer before departure. It's wise to make sure your card is in good condition, and best to use machines when banks are open, just in case they do give you any problems. Finally, before you leave home, make sure that your card and PIN will work overseas.

Cash and traveller's cheques

It's always good to have some cash to fall back on, and traveller's cheques are worth considering as a standby too. You are allowed to bring in unrestricted amounts of **foreign currency** in cash or traveller's cheques. In theory, on entering the country you should declare if you intend to leave with foreign currency whose value exceeds 1000TD, but tourists are not usually checked for currency on departure.

Euros, US dollars, pounds sterling, Canadian dollars, Japanese yen, Swiss francs and the Danish, Norwegian and Swedish currencies are exchangeable at any bank, and post offices also will often change cash. Banks and post offices don't take Australian or New Zealand dollars, nor Algerian or Libyan dinars (though they'll take Moroccan dirhams). They claim to accept Scottish and Northern Irish sterling banknotes, but in practice they rarely do so. If coming from Libya, you can change Libyan dinars with money changers at the border or in Ben Gardane, but you won't get a very good rate.

Thomas Cook, Visa and American Express are the best-known **traveller's cheques** and are accepted at most banks and many hotels, whether in sterling, US dollars or euros; Canadian dollar cheques are usually accepted as well. Tunisian banks charge a fee of 0.35TD for changing each cheque. You are supposed to keep the receipt and

a record of cheque serial numbers safe and separate from the cheques themselves. However, some banks will refuse to change traveller's cheques unless you show the receipt. In the event that cheques are lost or stolen, the issuing company will expect you to report the loss to their office in Tunisia; most companies claim to replace lost or stolen cheques within 24 hours.

A kind of compromise between plastic and traveller's cheques is **Visa travel money**, a disposable prepaid debit card with a PIN that you can use in ATMs worldwide. For more details, see the "Debit cards" section at ⓦwww.international.visa.com.

Banks and exchange

Bank **opening hours** are limited. In summer (July & Aug) they are Monday to Friday between 7.15am and noon; the rest of the year banks open Monday to Friday from 8am to 4.15pm – except during Ramadan, when it's Monday to Friday from 8.15am to 1pm. You may find, especially first thing in the morning, that banks won't change money as they haven't received the latest exchange rates. In tourist areas, banks will sometimes open outside standard hours for currency exchange, and you can often fall back on hotels; the bigger, posher ones are naturally most likely to change money.

The local STB (Tunisia's "national" bank) is generally most reliable for foreign exchange. Also worth trying are Banque de l'Habitat, Banque du Sud, BIAT and BNA. Away from tourist areas, however, exchange facilities can be few and far between. As a very last resort, if you have actual cash to change, you could try asking around the local louage (shared taxi) station, especially if it serves destinations beyond Tunisia's borders.

You are unlikely to run across **black market** currency dealers except on roads close to the Libyan border, where they wave wads of Libyan dinars at passing motorists. Moneychangers may also accost you in the street in Sfax. Black-market rates are only marginally better than official ones.

It's illegal to export Tunisian dinars from (or import it into) the country. There are strict regulations about the quantity of dinars that you can **change back when leaving** the country. You're allowed to reconvert up to thirty percent of the total amount you can prove you have changed since being in Tunisia – with an upper limit of 100TD. This means you should keep the **exchange receipts** (or ATM receipt slips) that you're given. You cannot use dinars at the airport duty-free shop, but you can use them in the departure lounge café. You will also need to show exchange or ATM receipts if buying a ticket for an international journey by air or sea.

Wiring money

Having money wired from home is not cheap, and is best treated as a last resort. Funds can be sent via **Western Union** to any major post office in the country. Fees depend on the amount being transferred, but, as an example, wiring £700 will cost around £40, while $1000 will cost around $60. The funds should be available for collection (usually in dinars) within minutes of being sent (which can be done in person or over the phone using a credit card). A simi-

lar service is available from rival firm **MoneyGram** – funds sent with them can be collected from branches of Banque Nationale Agricole (BNA) nationwide.

It's also possible to have money wired directly from a bank in your home country to a bank in Tunisia, although this is more complicated because it involves two separate institutions. If you go this route, the person wiring the funds to you will need the telex number of the bank the funds are being wired to.

Money-wiring companies

MoneyGram UK ☏ 0800/018 0104, Republic of Ireland ☏ 1850/205 800, US ☏ 1-800/955-7777, Canada ☏ 1-800/933-3278, Australia ☏ 1800/230 100, New Zealand ☏ 0800/262 263, ⓦ www .moneygram.com.
Western Union UK ☏ 0800/833 833, Republic of Ireland ☏ 1800/395 395, US & Canada ☏ 1-800/325-6000, Australia ☏ 1800/501 500, New Zealand ☏ 0800/270 000, ⓦ www.westernunion .com.

Getting around

Many visitors to Tunisia are discouraged from exploring the country by the high cost of car rental, but it's possible to reach nearly every town detailed in this guide by some form of scheduled transport or by shared taxis, known as louages. Admittedly, the rail lines are not very far-reaching, and other forms of transport may be slow, infrequent or occasionally very crowded, but transport within Tunisia is reliable enough on the whole, and distances within the country are relatively short.

Trains are generally a little faster than the SNTRI (national) buses, and cost slightly less in second class, more in first. SNTRI buses are faster and more comfortable than SRT (regional) buses, but also more expensive, and usually only ply routes to and from Tunis. Louages are faster than buses, and only slightly more expensive, but are considered more dangerous. Buses and louages have the disadvantage of stopping for an hour in the middle of any journey if it hap-

pens to be over lunchtime. A plane journey will cost about five times as much as train, bus or louage, and of course will be much quicker, airport to airport, though you still have to check in, collect bags at the other end, and travel to and from the airports, which can be time consuming.

Transport costs are moderate: Tunis–Sfax, a journey of 270km, costs around £4.20/$7.50 by second-class train, £5.50/$10 by bus, first-class train or louage, or £22.50/$40 by plane. The one general warning to bear in mind is that transport services tend to stop at around 5pm (in the far south, local transport can dry up even earlier), though there may be a night bus to Tunis via either Sfax and Sousse or Kairouan. On remote routes your only choice may be the early-morning market bus.

Buses

Tunisia's most popular form of transport, **buses** are comprehensive but complicated to master. They are run by different companies, including the **SNTRI** (pronounced "sentri", and standing for Société Nationale de Transport Rural et Interurbain) and several regional rivals known as **SRTs** (Société Régionale des Transports). Most have predictable names such as SRT Béja, or SRT du Gouvernorat de Medenine (SRTGM), but one or two have less obvious names such as SORETRAS (Sfax) and SOTREGAMES (Gabès).

SNTRI run services in and around Tunis, linking Tunis to almost every town in the country at least once a day, several times a day on important routes. A new firm, STCI, has started running buses to and from Tunis in competition with SNTRI, but is so far covering only a few major routes such as Tunis–Tozeur and Tunis–Jerba, and with only one bus a day on each. Each SRT runs local services within its own region, and some northern ones also run services to Tunis. A few long-distance services don't pass through Tunis (Sousse–Le Kef, for example), but in general it is easier to move towards or away from Tunis than across the country. SNTRI services are invariably better than SRT ones – faster, more comfortable, and much more likely to depart and arrive on time, although they also cost slightly more.

Some bigger towns have a central bus station, sometimes called the **gare routière**, but often the companies operate from their own separate locations, which are detailed throughout this guide. SNTRI generally display departure lists in both Arabic and French, but most others post them only in Arabic if at all, so unless you read Arabic finding the right bus departure can be a case of persistent questioning. The different companies often refuse to recognize one anoth-er's existence, so if you need to discover all the buses on a given route, it's important to ask at each bus company office.

SNTRI buses are air-conditioned and pretty comfortable, while SRT buses do not have air conditioning and are sometimes a little bit run-down. When travelling in the daytime, especially in summer, it's a good idea to consider which side of the bus the sun will be on, and choose a seat to avoid it.

Louages

Louages are large shared taxis, usually minibuses taking eight passengers (which have largely taken over from the old-style Peugeots taking five). Operating nonstop along fixed routes, louages are the fastest form of long-distance transport. They leave as soon as the full complement of passengers has appeared, or when the driver gets tired of waiting. In the latter case you might be persuaded to split the cost of the empty places with the other passengers; alternatively the driver may agree to let you pay the normal fare. A seat in a louage is *une place* in French, *plassa* in Arabic.

Choice of seats is on a first-come, first-served basis. The last passengers to arrive generally get palmed off with the seats immediately behind the driver on the minibuses (with little legroom) and the back seat of the Peugeots (very bouncy with little headroom), so it's best to make clear which of the remaining seats you want as soon as you find your louage.

Louages operate from informal **stations** that are liable to be elusive to the uninitiated foreigner – often a particular garage or backstreet yard. In larger towns, there are different terminals for different destinations. There is a trend now towards building a single louage station and a single bus station next to each other, out of town if need be, and these are being planned or installed in certain major towns. Once you've found the right place (they are detailed in the text, but they often change), ask for your destination – the signs on the cars only indicate where they are licensed, not necessarily where they are going. If you ask around, someone will find you a car or show you where to wait. Early morning is the best time to look for a louage – on many routes, they can get scarce at lunchtime and as the day goes on.

Usually, you will turn up to find a louage waiting. If there are a lot of passengers waiting and no louages, competition for seats can be fierce when one does eventually turn up, and you may find yourself joining a tense group of twenty people awaiting the next arrival. The time-honoured technique is to sprint for the car when you see it in the distance, grab a door handle when it slows down and hang on until the car stops. If you're carrying luggage, your only chance in this situation is to abandon it in the struggle for a seat then load it when the dust has settled. If this is too much for you, someone may get you a place for a small consideration. Louages will only stop for you on the road if they have a spare seat – the police are tough on drivers who carry more than the legal limit of passengers.

Fares are usually slightly more than the bus fare for the same route. If you think a driver is overcharging you, ask to see the official *tarif* (price list), which all louages must carry by law. Although routes are fixed, you can, of course, agree a price to charter a louage for go to a specific destination. The cost should be roughly equivalent to eight fares (five in an old Peugeot louage) to a regular destination the same distance away.

Some people regard louages as **dangerous**. Certainly, louage drivers can be frighteningly reckless, frequently overtaking on blind curves or the crest of a hill, for example, and definitely not obeying speed limits. With tariffs fixed by law and the number of possible runs in a day limited, profit margins are low and the best way for a driver to make a little extra is to squeeze in an extra run. Unsurprisingly, therefore, the accident rate for louages is even greater than the already high rate for Tunisian cars in general. Although most louage passengers do not bother with seat belts, you are strongly advised to wear them if they are available.

In addition to intercity louages, local **camionettes** (pick-up trucks) run from large towns to the surrounding villages. These don't always have a limit on passenger numbers and are very cheap, but rather uncomfortable (the benches may be very cramped, and some people may end up squatting on the floor for the duration). Occasionally, ordinary **taxis** may run a set route for a fixed fare per place like louages; this will usually be for local routes and may operate at peak times only.

Trains

Of Tunisia's rail lines, which were built by the French, only a small proportion have passenger services. Those that do are from Tunis north to Bizerte, west to Béja, Jendouba and Ghardimaou, and south to Sousse and Sfax, with fewer services on to Gabès and inland from Gafsa and Metlaoui. A branch line serves Hammamet and Nabeul. Trains on these routes are by the **SNCFT** (Société Nationale des Chemins de Fer Tunisiens) and usually operate more or less on schedule. Except at Gafsa, they have the advantage that stations are usually very near the centre of town. The disadvantage is that the network is very limited (a lot of towns with rail lines see only freight trains), as is the number of daily services. That said, some routes, like the air-conditioned service down the coast, are excellent – and a real boon in summer. Thomas Cook's *Overseas Timetable* (the blue volume), which you can find at Thomas Cook offices, in British and Irish public libraries and in many travel bookshops, gives a complete and up-to-date list of services, though if you are travelling during Ramadan, note that the timetable changes completely to fit in with fasting and eating times.

Prices are graded according to the type of service, with first and second class on all trains. First costs twenty to fifty percent more than second, and there's also a Confort class, much the same as first but less crowded and ten to fifteen percent more expensive again. A return ticket costs fifteen percent less than two one-way tickets. You can buy a one-, two- or four-week train pass called the **Carte Semaine**, which offers unlimited rail travel around Tunisia. If you plan to do a lot of travelling by train in a short time, it might be good value, at 19.5TD for a week second class, 27.3TD for first; for two- or three-week passes, multiply these figures by two or three. The pass can be bought at stations and travel agents and you need to bring a passport photo.

Students under 28 years of age can buy a 10TD **Carte Jeune**, valid for a year, which entitles them to reductions of 25–35 percent on the standard fare.

Most long-distance services, especially those that are air-conditioned (*climatisé*), can get crowded in midsummer and should be **booked** in advance if possible. Even for ordinary services, turn up early to be sure of buying a ticket – if you board without, you have to pay double.

One difficulty is that most stations only have one sign, usually at one end of the platform, so you'll have to keep a sharp eye out to know where you are. Another thing to bear in mind is that trains going in different directions often pass each other at stations, there being only single track in between, and are therefore in the station at the same time – make sure you get the right one.

Hitchhiking

Hitchhiking is generally good in Tunisia, for men at least, and can be an excellent way of getting to meet Tunisian people. Although **women** hitching alone or together can pick up lifts with car-renting tourists around Cap Bon or Jerba, it is extremely inadvisable elsewhere unless you link up with at least one male traveller.

Hitching presents no problems with officialdom and in remote areas, although there is remarkably little traffic, almost anything that passes will stop. In some of these areas, hitching is an informal kind of public transport, especially in the ubiquitous Peugeot 404 **camionnettes**. A small contribution is expected; there are no hard-and-fast rules, but the fare should be a little less than you would pay on a bus. if there are other passengers, watch how much they pay. If you're on your own, you can either try to agree on a price in advance or risk disagreement at the end should the driver try to overcharge you; in fact this is very unlikely and waiving payment is much more common. It can be hard to hitch out of Hammamet, and you have to walk a long way out of Tunis and Sfax, but other **routes** are fairly unproblematic. On main routes Tunisians usually only hitch to or from places where there is no louage service, but traffic will probably stop for you anyway.

Market days (see p.52) can be good for travel if you get up early enough. Transport usually heads out to a market first thing in the morning, returning late morning or afternoon.

Bikes

Tunisia's terrain and climate are ideally suited most of the year to **bicycles and motorbikes**, though you may get soaked in winter and spring, and strong winds can make cycling hard work. The only drawback is the lack of maintenance facilities, as there are very few motorbikes in the country (though thousands of mopeds), and though common the bicycles are also basic, so you'll have to bring specialized spare parts along. Bicycles and occasionally mopeds can be rented in big towns but, frustratingly, only for use in the town or along the beach. If you're staying some time in Tunisia and want a motorbike for transport, it's cheaper to buy abroad and import than buy locally. **Trains** will carry a bicycle for about the same fare as a passenger; **buses** usually charge about half the passenger fare.

Driving and car rental

In such a small country, driving ought to be the ideal way to get around. If you can afford to bring a car with you, this is true. Unfortunately **car rental charges** in Tunisia are phenomenal – among the highest in the Mediterranean. In general even the smallest Citroën will set you back 350TD a week, a Fiat Uno about 500TD, though it may be possible to get a better rate by shopping around and haggling, especially out of season. Officially at least, it's illegal to carry more than three passengers. Note also that rental firms don't permit their vehicles to be driven on unsurfaced roads, and can hold you liable for "any damage caused to the vehicle through driving on dirt tracks". At the time of writing, **fuel** cost roughly £0.40/$0.72 a litre for petrol (gasoline), £0.23/$0.40 for diesel; prices are fixed officially. Unleaded fuel is available at most petrol stations.

To rent a car, you'll need to be over 21 and have held a licence for at least a year. When renting a car, always check the spare wheel, jack and wrench, since suffering a flat tyre on Tunisia's ragged roads is a strong possibility. Another thing to check is the fuel tank – usually this should be full, and you will be expected to return it full, though some companies give you the car with a nearly empty tank, and you can return it the same way. You should also check the insurance and the small print very thoroughly. Hotels often have arrangements with reliable local firms. There are cheap private local companies, though note that if a car is cheap to rent it may not be very well maintained.

To bring **your own vehicle**, you will have to be over 21 and carry documents proving your ownership of the vehicle, a valid driving licence or an international one, and a green card covering Tunisia. It is often difficult to get insurance at home that will cover Tunisia.

Despite these hassles and expenses, driving has many advantages. You can visit the smaller and remoter villages seen only through dusty windows by those trapped on public transport. Picking up **hitchhikers** can be a way of making rewarding contacts with local people, but in highly touristed areas (approaching Kairouan or Matmata for example), "guides" posing as hitchhikers may want to thank you for giving them a lift by inviting you for tea at their home, except that it turns out to be a carpet shop, and you will have to worm your way out of some hard sell. Another practice, initially disconcerting, is that the police often flag down drivers to get a lift. It's best not to argue, and if you're not going their way they won't force the matter.

Rules of the road

Tunisia **drives on the right**, with priority from the right, and vehicles coming onto a roundabout or traffic circle have right of way over those already on it. **Speed limits** are (in theory, and unless otherwise indicated) 90km/h (55mph) in open country and 50km/h (31mph) in built-up areas, 110km/h (68mph) on the country's only motorway from Tunis to just south of Sousse, and 70km/h (43mph) on the island of Jerba. There are often humps in the road near schools to slow traffic down to 30km/h (18mph), and however fast you're going, it's customary to slow down when passing **highway patrols**. There are also speed

traps, and seat belts are compulsory on intercity routes for the driver and front-seat passenger. If you get stopped for speeding you have to pay on the spot. It's a good idea to have your papers available because there are frequent road checks, especially in the south and around Gafsa – usually, it's your passport rather than your driving licence that they'll want to see. If they check your vehicle, it's usually the lights and horn that they are most interested in.

Red and white stripes painted on the kerb indicate that **parking** is prohibited, and in Tunis and one or two other places, wheel clamps are used to enforce this. In Tunis, there are "blue zones" where all parking is metered and limited to two hours. Be aware also that in town, at intersections where left or right turns are banned, there may well not be a "no left turn" or "no right turn" sign at the junction, just a "no entry" sign in front of the turning.

Driving conditions

Major roads are called **grands parcours** (GP), lesser roads **moyennes corniches** (MC). Tarmac can be rather narrow and oncoming trucks tend to force cars off the edge of the road, accepted practice but a little worrying at first. Main roads are straight and surfaced and often lined with shady eucalyptus trees.

In the south, many of the routes are **unsurfaced roads**. Their condition varies: many are passable in any ordinary car, while others require a 4WD vehicle; some roads are obviously difficult, and drifting sand on others can be dangerous. In any case, you will not be able to drive on them at the same sort of speed as on tarmac; even if the going seems quite straightforward, remember that the surface can change unexpectedly, and boulders can appear as if from nowhere.

Tunisian drivers are not the safest in the world, and the roads can be quite hazardous. In fact, Tunisia has one of the highest road **accident rates** in the world. Always drive defensively, and be wary coming up to blind curves and the tops of hills, since it is quite commonplace for Tunisians to overtake approaching these. Also beware farm vehicles travelling unlit at night. Another hazard,

Desert driving

Driving in the desert is potentially hazardous and claims victims every year. You should not drive in desert regions – let alone think of leaving the main surfaced roads – without taking precautions. Don't assume everything will be fine; consider what could happen if you were to break down in the middle of nowhere with little chance of anyone passing for hours, or even days. **Mobile phone** coverage does not extend far into the desert – Ksar Ghilane is out of range for example.

First, make sure your vehicle is up to the terrain. Do all the usual fuel, oil and water checks and make sure you're carrying tools and a jack and spare tyre, preferably two. Take spare fuel if possible, and carry at least **five litres of water** per person at all times. Don't forget, either, to take high-factor suntan lotion, a sunhat and sunglasses, and appropriate clothing, including warm clothes for night-time, when the desert can get bitterly cold, especially in winter. A shovel is invaluable, as even a tarmac road can get covered in drifts, and steel sand ladders or mats will help you get unstuck too. A compass is a very good idea.

Keep to well-defined pistes as much as possible, and in open desert always travel **in convoy**, never alone. Always inform the **Garde Nationale** of your arrival and departure at every post on your journey. Tell them where you're going and when you expect to arrive (occasionally you may be refused permission). If you can't find the Garde National, tell the police instead.

Some pistes may become partially covered by sand drifts, and it is easy to get stuck if you are in a two-wheel-drive car, although you can sometimes get through by going full-throttle in third gear while waving the steering wheel sharply back and forth. If you do get stuck in sand, you will probably need help to dig yourself out, although digging the wheels out and putting stones and branches under the tyres may work. If you get stuck in a sandstorm, stop. Point your vehicle downwind and wait until the storm abates. This will avoid damage to your engine. And if you break down or get lost, there's one fundamental rule that's more likely to save your life than any other: **stay with your vehicle**. Don't go wandering off into the desert alone, as dehydration, sunstroke and heat exhaustion can strike amazingly quickly, and a car is a lot easier to find than a person wandering around.

The *Sahara Handbook*, by Simon and Jan Glen (Lascelles), contains much timeless good advice on preparing and driving a vehicle in the desert.

---

especially when passing through towns, is the lack of road sense among pedestrians, cyclists and moped riders, who all seem to meander quite happily down the middle of the road as if they'd never heard of the automobile. You will almost certainly end up using your horn more than you do at home, and you will have to reduce speed and keep your eyes peeled, especially at dusk.

In case of **breakdown**, always carry a good supply of water and, if you're planning a long journey, food and blankets. There are plenty of places that will repair a flat tyre or more serious problem cheaply – look out for workshops with tyres outside, especially on the way into and out of towns. Car rental companies should refund the cost of any necessary repairs, so long as you have kept the receipt.

International car rental agencies

Avis UK ☎0870/606 0100, ⊛www.avis.co.uk; Ireland ☎01/605 7500, ⊛www.avis.ie; US ☎1-800/331-1084, ⊛www.avis.com; Canada ☎1-800/272-5871, ⊛www.avis.com; Australia ☎13 63 33 or 02/9353 9000, ⊛www.avis.com.au; New Zealand ☎09/526 2847 or 0800/655 111, ⊛www.avis.co.nz.

Budget UK ☎0800/181 181, ⊛www.budget.co.uk; Ireland ☎0903/277 11, ⊛www.budget.ie; US & Canada ☎1-800/527-0700, ⊛www.budgetrentacar.com; Australia ☎1300/362 848, ⊛www.budget.com.au; New Zealand ☎09/976 2222, ⊛www.budget.co.nz.

Europcar UK ☎0845/722 2525, ⊛www.europcar.co.uk; Ireland ☎01/614 2888, ⊛www.europcar.ie; US & Canada ☎1-877/940 6900, ⊛www.europcar.com; Australia ☎1300/131 390, ⊛www.deltaeuropcar.com.au.

Hertz UK ☎0870/844 8844, ⊛www.hertz.co.uk;
Ireland ☎01/676 7476, ⊛www.hertz.ie; US
☎1-800/654-3001, ⊛www.hertz.com; Canada
☎1-800/263-0600, ⊛www.hertz.com; Australia
☎13 30 39 or 03/9698 2555, ⊛www.hertz.com.
au; New Zealand ☎0800/654 321, ⊛www.hertz.
co.nz.

Flights

Tunisia's size makes **internal flights** rather
a luxury, even though tickets are relatively
cheap (under £30/$50 from Tunis to Jerba,
for example). Domestic flights are run by
Tuninter (☎71 701 111, ⊛www.tunisair.com
.tn/tuninter.htm), whose tickets are available
through Tunisair or any travel agent. To be
sure of a flight, it's wise to book well ahead.

At the time of writing, domestic flights
were running on four routes, all out of Tunis:
to Gafsa, to Jerba, to Sfax and to Tozeur.
Jerba has several flights a day, but the other
airports are not served every day of the
week. Although a particular flight may call
at more than one regional airport, tickets are
only sold for transport to or from Tunis; you
cannot buy a ticket from Jerba to Sfax for
example, even if the plane stops at both.

City transport

The cheapest way to get around big towns
is by **bus**. These can be very crowded (you
often have to fight your way on and off) and
stops are not always signposted. Useful
routes are indicated in the text of the guide,
but it's often easier and more interesting to
walk. Tunis has a so-called **metro** system
that's an articulated tram rather than an

underground train, and subject to most of
the same provisos as buses.

Taxis, which you'll find in most towns of
any size, have meters and should run on
the meter, charging fifty percent extra from
9pm to 6am. In some resorts however
– notably in Hammamet and Mahdia – taxi
drivers often refuse to use the meter with
tourists so as to charge higher fares, and it's
always worth finding out in advance (from
your hotel receptionist, for example) roughly
what the fare should be. One scam worked
by taxi drivers on new arrivals coming into
town from Tunis airport is to set the meter
but take advantage of unfamiliarity with
local prices and local currency – especially
as it has three zeros at the end instead of
two – to pretend that the price shown is ten
times what it actually is, charging for example 25TD for a 2.5TD journey. Despite these
shenanigans, taxis can be very good value
for groups of up to four people to arrange
a tour of several sites by hiring a taxi for the
day. If you do this, fix the price first.

In towns with a large tourist presence,
horse-drawn carriages known as **calèches**
provide a more picturesque alternative to
taxis. Though slower and more expensive
(and given to stopping off at souvenir stalls,
where the driver gets a commission on
anything you buy), calèches are a fun ride,
especially for children. Also purely for holidaymakers are the frankly ridiculous **tourist
land trains** – known variously "le petit train",
"le train bleu", "le train rouge" or Noddy
trains – which have spread like an epidemic
to almost all of the country's resorts.

Organized tours

If time is short, you might consider an organized tour by Land Rover or even bus.
Organized excursions in Tunisia are usually termed **safaris** – though they do not
involve wildlife-spotting. These are offered by travel agents and hotels in most large
Tunisian towns and resorts, and can generally be found in our Listings sections
under "Tours". Their main advantage is that they are relatively good value (£85/$150
for three days is typical), and allow you to see far more in the way of sights than
you could on public transport. On the other hand, they rather isolate you from local
people, may move on more quickly than you would like and usually stop for meals at
places that charge quite high prices.

Accommodation

Hotels in every price range can be found in all the main tourist centres and in larger towns in the interior, but in smaller places there may only be a choice between a very basic establishment with dirty sheets or a fairly expensive hotel with air conditioning and a pool. In midsummer, any kind of room in the more popular towns can be hard to find on the spot – though if you get really stuck, someone local will probably invite you to stay rather than see the country's reputation for hospitality diminished.

High season usually means the summer (mid-June to mid-Sept, sometimes only July & Aug); **low season** is over winter (Nov–March), and **mid-season** the rest of the year. However, one or two hotels in the **desert resorts** such as Tozeur have high season in winter and low season in the summer. Not all hotels have seasonal price changes (unclassified and city hotels usually do not); some charge the same prices in mid- and high season.

Hotels and pensions

Classified hotels, officially approved for tourist use, are graded from one-star to five-star, with a wide range of prices and standards within each category. The classification of a hotel depends on factors like the size of rooms, windows and bathrooms, and the presence or absence of facilities (such as a swimming pool): it is not a reliable indication of the price nor the quality of service. Indeed, things like room service – which you might expect in Western hotels with a rating – can be slapdash or nonexistent, and even in a three- or four-star hotel in Tunisia, rooms may have a shower, not a bath. The Western practice of adding the cost of drinks bought in the bar to your room tab is rare.

There is a range of **unclassified hotels** suitable for budget travellers, even if not officially regarded as appropriate for tourists. These establishments, usually concentrated in a town's medina – just ask for an auberge (inn) or *hôtel Tunisien* – differ widely. The best of them, typically in the ❷ bracket, are often colonial relics with high ceilings and creaking fans, and are very respectable, though in winter they may be cold and draughty with no heating. Many of the cheapest ones,

though, can be rough – and they're sometimes closed to, or dangerous for, unaccompanied women. In this type of place you may be expected to share a room, or fill it, or even pay for any beds (as many as four) which remain empty. However, there are good (and perfectly safe) places even in this range and, for men at least, they're a useful standby as you can nearly always find a bed.

A few local chains, including Abou Nawas (ⓦwww.abounawas.com), Golden Yasmin (ⓦwww.goldenyasmin.com) and El Mouradi, run slightly better than average tourist hotels in the main resorts; some of these firms also run four- and five-star hotels in the cities, mainly for businesspeople. In resorts, you may occasionally also find **self-catering apartments**, often in what are styled "aparthotels". These come equipped with a kitchenette including a couple of cooking rings and a set of utensils. They're handy if you like cooking for yourself, but not especially better value than ordinary hotels.

Women looking for inexpensive accommodation will have to play it by ear much of the time. If Tunisian women are staying in a hotel, that should be a good sign; if all the clientele are male, think again. Male fellow travellers may be prepared to help out by posing as "husbands" or "brothers", but this may not excise nuisances such as the presence of Peeping Toms when you use the shared shower – and relying on male tourists can, obviously, plunge you into just the compromising situations you were trying to avoid. Another problem in sharing a room with a man who is clearly not your husband (or even if you are in fact married but retain different surnames) is that you are then assumed to

Accommodation price codes

All the hotels and pensions listed in this book have been price-graded according to the codes below, representing the **cheapest double room** in high season. Although costs will rise slightly overall with the life of this edition, the relative comparisons should remain valid. Note that many places will have pricier rooms with a higher grade of facilities or maybe a sea view, and that in the case of hostels, we quote the actual price for a **dorm bed**.

Places that are expensive in the summer may have bargain-basement prices **off season** when business is slack. Even where this isn't the case, prices may be **negotiable**, especially out of season or if you're staying for a week or more. Conversely, note that **Christmas** and **New Year** rates are likely to be even higher than the normal high-season price.

All hotels must by law display their official maximum prices in reception, usually in the form of a price per person in a double room, with a supplement for single occupancy. Places in price code ❸ or above tend to include breakfast in the rate.

❶ **Under 15TD**. Usually for bed only in a basic unclassified hotel.

❷ **15–25TD**. Bed only or bed and breakfast in a good unclassified hotel and in some one-star hotels, without en-suite facilities.

❸ **25–35TD**. One-star hotel or top-level unclassified hotels. Facilities often en suite.

❹ **35–50TD**. A good one-star or ordinary two-star hotel, typically with en suite rooms, a restaurant, perhaps a/c and a small pool.

❺ **50–80TD**. Two- or three-star hotel, with air conditioning, a restaurant and a pool.

❻ **80–110TD**. A typical three-star hotel, with comfortable a/c rooms, a pool, at least one restaurant, a bar and probably a "Moorish café".

❼ **110–150TD**. A three- or four-star hotel, with multiple pools and restaurants, and room service.

❽ **150–200TD**. In addition to most creature comforts, these hotels usually feature spacious rooms, gardens, plenty of sports facilities and punctilious service.

❾ **Over 200TD**. Hotels with everything that the slightly less expensive establishments feature, plus gourmet food, a fitness centre, shops and business facilities.

be "generally available", and Tunisian men may treat you accordingly. Very occasionally, hoteliers unused to tourists may even refuse to allow unmarried couples to share a room.

Hotels are supplemented by family-run **pensions**, found mainly in the Cap Bon area and varying widely in both price and standard. At their best they really are cheap and friendly *pensions familiales*; even at their worst they're still quite adequate, and one or two are even de luxe, with prices to match.

Youth hostels

There are more than thirty **youth hostels** in Tunisia, five of them run by Tunisia's Youth Hostel Association and the rest attached to youth centres (*Maisons des Jeunes*) run by the Ministry of Culture. Some of the *Maisons*

des Jeunes, more specifically designed for accommodation, have been designated *Centre des Stages et des Vacances*.

Youth hostels charge 4–6TD a night for a dorm bed, as much as a room in a cheap hotel, and are usually situated on the edge of town near the municipal stadium. Men and women always have separate accommodation. The hostels tend to look like barracks, feel like changing rooms, operate curfews and turf you out early in the morning. Some youth hostels seize your passport on arrival, and you'll have to track it down before you can leave or if you need to change traveller's cheques. On the positive side, youth hostels are usually clean and can be good places to meet young Tunisians. In general, YHA hostels tend to be better run than *Maisons des*

Jeunes, less heavy-handed with rules and regulations, more central and often housed in interesting old buildings.

Recommended in particular are the hostels in **Tunis Medina** and **Houmt Souk** (Jerba). Those at **Rimel** (Bizerte), **Kélibia** and **Remla** (Kerkennah) are also a cut above the norm.

Camping

There are only a handful of **campsites** in the country, but their number is growing. Some youth hostels – even a few hotels – allow camping in their grounds. Unofficially, and especially in remote areas, **camping sauvage** ("wild", meaning off-site camping) is another option. Although sleeping out on the main tourist beaches like Hammamet, Nabeul, Sousse or Monastir is either expressly forbidden or likely to be cut short by the police, there should be few problems elsewhere, and it's common at certain places around Bizerte, Raf Raf and Jerba. In the interior it's a good idea to ask the permission of the landowner. If you can't find the owner, ask the local police, who are very unlikely to say no, or will suggest an alternative site. Informing the police of your presence will also help avoid misunderstand-ings, especially if you're in a sensitive area, such as an international frontier.

Campsites vary in their **prices**, how they charge, and the facilities they provide. A typical charge would be 4–5TD per person per night, with an extra charge – maybe 5TD – for a camper van, slightly less for a car, and sometimes 3–4TD per night to pitch a tent, in addition to the per-person charge. Some campsites rent out tents, or provide huts to sleep in for those without their own canvas, and in the south they may also offer the option of sleeping in a Bedouin tent. Most campsites have hot showers, though not many have cooking facilities.

Muslims, Arabic speakers and Jewish pilgrims

Muslims or **Arabic-speaking** travellers may well receive invitations to stay from Tunisians. if you're Muslim and really stuck, you could also try the **local mosque or zaouia**. They often have hostel accommodation where pilgrims can stay – always an interesting place to meet people. **Jews** on pilgrimage, particularly in Jerba (see p.439), may find similar help from the local Jewish community.

Eating and drinking

"Chilis were essential to the full glory of Kuss Kussu; but he did not expect mere Europeans to rise to such heights. And yet he'd known one really great Englishman, a certain Captain Gordon, who could eat more chilis than any Arab."

Reginald Rankin, Tunisia (1930)

Eating out is not really an Arab tradition, but the French presence, along with the effect of tourism, have made their mark. In big cities and tourist centres you'll come across smart and essentially French restaurants offering meals of several courses; these can be excellent and are usually very good value. Every town also has less elaborate restaurants serving fare which is virtually indistinguishable from one place to the next – simple meat, chicken, fish and vegetable dishes kept warm throughout the day. You soon learn to recognize these places, known throughout Tunisia as gargotes. Cheapest are the rotisseries which, despite their name, do more frying than roasting – if you have a low tolerance for grease, you'll probably prefer the restaurants.

Rotisseries are usually open all day, their food laid out behind the counter so you can just point at what you want. Most restaurants, however, and almost all posh ones, usually open only for lunch and supper, and most display a menu; if it's in Arabic, you might want to ask to look at the dishes. Cheaper restaurants begin to close around 9pm, and the most popular dishes are often finished sometime before then. One thing that will probably throw your eating routine is the month of **Ramadan**, when Muslims fast from sunrise to sunset – see p.49 for more, including dates.

As for **prices**, a typical meal in a *gargote* is very cheap, with starters at around 1.5TD; main courses at 2–3TD; a whole meal including mineral water will come to 5TD (£2.20/$4) or so. Moderately priced places have main courses at 4–7TD, and three-course meals for 7–12TD per head. Once you're paying over 15TD (£6.50/$12) a head for three courses, or over 8TD for a main course, the restaurant ranks as expensive in Tunisia. In the big resorts, it's not unusual for restaurants aimed specifically at tourists to charge 15TD for a main course and 25TD (£11/$20) or more per person for a meal. Such prices, outrageous by local standards, are of course extremely low compared with what you'd pay for an equivalent meal in the West.

In resorts, bear in mind that anywhere worth eating in will not need to have a waiter outside hustling for business. Tourist restaurants that do not display prices invariably intend to overcharge visitors, so in such places always ask the price before ordering. Another little trick that some restaurants play is to have a huge menu outside with all sorts of great-sounding dishes to entice you in; upon sitting down, you are given a much shorter menu with the same old things served up by every other restaurant in town.

Women travellers may find that restaurants and cafés are some of the worst places for pestering. Your best bet, unfortunately, is to use the more cosmopolitan and expensive restaurants in the towns and avoid eating places in rural areas. You will also be less conspicuous drinking coffee in a patisserie than in a café. Some restaurants have separate rooms for women diners and the waiter will automatically show you in there when you arrive. There are also one or two cafés where only women can drink, but they tend to be well hidden.

Tunisian meals

If there is a **starter** at a restaurant it will probably be soup (*chorba* – oily and very spicy), Tunisian salad (basically a finely chopped green salad), or a more specifically Tunisian dish such as *brik à l'oeuf* (egg fried in a pastry envelope) or *salade mechouia* (mashed, roasted vegetables).

There are two levels of **main course**. The simplest is a starch-based dish (couscous, spaghetti or beans) with a little meat and hot peppery sauce. Unexciting but very filling, this is what most families eat at home. Paying a little more, you get more meat or fish, usually served with salad and chips. Grilled meat, lamb kebabs (*brochettes*) and fish can all be delicious, though roast chicken and chips tend to be lukewarm when served in many cheap places.

The most characteristic Tunisian dish is **couscous**, the North African staple, Berber in origin, which is based on semolina pellets. These are steamed over a meat (or occasionally fish) stew, which gives them a subtle aroma, and is poured on top of them when served. Tunisians like their **chilli**, so couscous in Tunisia is usually rather spicier than the Moroccan or Algerian variety. People in Tunisia are also fond of stews, which vary from **chakchouka**, based on vegetables and pulses, especially chick-peas (garbanzo beans), to **koucha** (lamb with potatoes in tomato sauce) and **kamounia** (meat, often liver, in a sauce heavily spiced with cumin).

Tunisia being a small country, there isn't a great deal of **regional variation** in the food, but Sfax has a reputation for good fish dishes, and one or two places have their own specialities, notably Jerba's *riz Djerbien*, rice steamed with vegetables in a couscous steamer and usually served with lamb. Larger-grained alternatives to couscous include *seffa* and *barkoukech* from Tozeur and *melthouth* from the Kerkennah

For a glossary of Tunisian food and drink, see pp.573–576.

Islands, where you'll also find an octopus soup called *tchich*. Unusual meats include camel, mainly eaten in the south (Tozeur is a good place to try it), and wild boar, which is sometimes served to tourists (Muslims don't eat it) in Aïn Draham.

Bread (*khobs*) is always included in the meal, usually with a little plate of oil and *harissa*, a concentrate of garlic and red chilli peppers which makes the average curry taste anaemic, to dip it into. The *harissa* and oil is sometimes not served to tourists, who are assumed to have an aversion to chilli, but you can always ask for it if you don't get it. There is rarely much to follow the main course except perhaps seasonal fruit or a crème caramel.

If you are invited into a **Tunisian home**, you will probably eat from a communal dish into which you dip bread to soak up the sauce. When handling pieces of food, remember to **use only your right hand** – the left is used for "unclean" functions such as wiping your bottom or washing your feet

Vegetarian and other diets

The concept of **vegetarianism** is completely alien to most Tunisians, who eat meat with every meal (or aspire to); you won't meet any Tunisian vegetarians. It is possible to tell people that you are vegetarian (*je suis vegetarien/vegetarienne* in French, *ana nabati* in Arabic) but they may still not understand what you are getting at. You may order a dish without meat, only to find that it's a meat dish with the lumps of meat (but not the gravy) removed. Don't be surprised either if you find meat or fish added to vegetable dishes to "improve" them. Canned tuna fish and – problematically for vegans – hard-boiled eggs are added liberally to all sorts of things, especially salads, so it's almost always worth specifying if you don't want them. On the positive side, in recent years a small number of restaurants in tourist areas have started to cater for vegetarians, and may offer a specifically vegetarian option (usually vegetable couscous with no added meat stock).

Vegans can get pizzas made up without cheese or live on a diet of bread and olives; otherwise about the only things vegans will be able to eat ready-cooked are chips (these may be fried in animal fat, so ask first), spaghetti in tomato sauce and *lablabi* (and even then, you'll have to watch that no eggs or tuna get into it). If you do eat eggs and dairy products, you're increasing your range considerably: besides omelettes, which are easy to order, dishes such as *chakchouka* (often topped with egg) *ojja* (a vegetable stew with egg scrambled into it), *brik* and *tajine* (a kind of baked omelette) all become possible.

The fussier you are, the harder it will be for you to eat out. You may be best advised to take a spirit stove (see p.62) or book self-catering accommodation. Staples such as rice, dried beans and pasta are available at grocers and supermarkets, and fresh vegetables are easy to find in markets.

Be aware that **hospitality** is an extremely important part of Arab culture, and if you enter a Tunisian home you're bound to be offered something to eat; your host may be insulted if you decline. One possible way round this problem is to say that it's against your religious beliefs to eat meat, an idea to which most Tunisians should be able to relate.

The Tunisian sweet tooth may be a problem for **diabetics**, especially where drinks and snacks are concerned. Artificial sweeteners are not widely used in Tunisia, diet versions of soft drinks are unavailable, and fruit juice is usually sweetened, though unsweetened juice is now available in supermarkets. Sugar will sometimes be added unrequested to coffee unless you're quick to point out that you don't want it, and may also be added to pomegranate served as a dessert. You probably won't find sugarless tea at all.

If you only eat **kosher** meat, you'll have to stick to fish and vegetables most of the time, although one kosher restaurant exists in Tunisia – a small *gargote* in Hara Kebira on Jerba (see p.439).

– and, if there is only a little meat, not to eat more than your fair share. Men and women eat separately in a Tunisian household, but visiting Western women will probably eat with the men, especially if accompanied by one. Contrary to the popular myth, you are not expected to belch loudly to show your appreciation of the food, nor are you likely to be served sheep's eyes. Should you wish to offer your host a gift, something from home unavailable locally will go down really well, or take a box of sweets from a high-class patisserie.

Pastries, snacks and breakfast

Traditional Arab and Berber **pastries** available at Tunisian patisseries are generally drenched in syrup and rather sickly. Perennial favourites include baklava (filo pastry with a nut filling), *makroudh* (semolina cake with a date filling), and *cornes de gazelle* (banana-shaped pastry "horns" filled with chopped almonds). Posher patisseries are more likely to sell French-style pastries, though these are often filled with artificial cream, and are at their best in the morning when fresh. Many patisseries also sell croissants, as do many cafés in the morning. Indeed, cafés are beginning to merge with these upmarket patisseries, many of which now serve coffee.

The perennial **snack meal** is a *casse-croûte*, a thick chunk of French bread filled with vegetables, olives, oil, and either egg, tuna or sausage. It's automatically spread with *harissa*; if you prefer to go without, specify *sans piquant* or *bilesh harissa*. Cassecroûtes can be bought at most rotisseries and many bakeries; snack bars at bus and louage stations often sell them too. Note that olives are added unstoned, so eat your *cassecroûte* with care.

Alternatively, grocers will often make up a **sandwich** for you when you buy the ingredients. Cheese is generally disappointing, though the soft white sheep's milk *maasoura*, similar to Italian ricotta, is worth a try, and sardines or tuna are other possible fillings.

The other essential for picnic meals, **fruit**, is one of Tunisia's greatest delights. Depending on the season you can gorge on fresh oranges, figs, grapes, melon, dates, pomegranates, prickly pears, strawberries and cherries. Pomegranates are often served as a dessert, broken up in a dish with the bitter yellow pith removed; if you don't want sugar on top, say so when you order. The prickly pear, or "Barbary fig", was introduced into North Africa by the Spanish in the sixteenth century, after they brought it over from the Americas. In summer they are sold by the thousand from barrows. Though they are immensely refreshing and the first remedy to try for upset stomachs, you should beware of picking them or holding them unpeeled, as they are covered in very hard-to-see spines that get into your skin and are difficult to remove.

If you want to snack while you're out and about, **nuts** and similar snacks, such as roasted sunflower or watermelon seeds, are available from shops everywhere – usually open quite late.

Most hotel **breakfasts** consist of a pot of filter coffee served with bread and jam. For a Continental breakfast – a croissant or dry cake with coffee – patisseries and cafés are the obvious place, as they have the best coffee; if a café doesn't serve croissants, it's permissible to bring them from elsewhere to have with your coffee. In less sophisticated areas some cafés still provide the traditional *ftair* (fritters) and *draw* (a porridgey concoction consisting of sweetened milk thickened with orchid root). Those who prefer a more substantial and savoury breakfast could go for a bowl of *lablabi*, bread broken up and soaked in chick-pea broth with *harissa*, cumin, egg, olive oil and often tuna, a very cheap option that's Tunisia's answer to a fry-up. This is sold at small diners, especially in big towns, which often display on their counter or in their window the soup bowls in which *lablabi* is served.

Drinking

Wine, when available in restaurants, is usually good. Alcoholic liquor is of course forbidden by Islam, and Tunisia's wine industry is a legacy of the French colonial era. The main growing regions are Cap Bon, especially Grombalia; the Tunis area, whose wines include Mornag and Tebourba denominations; the Bizerte area; and the Béja region, especially Thibar. Vieux Magon, from Tebourba, is the best red, full-bodied and comparable to an Australian shiraz. Haut Mornag and Sidi Rais, both from Cap Bon, and Koudjat from Tebourba, are all excellent table wines; Grombalia and Tardi very rough standbys. Clairet de Bizerte is the best rosé, but Gris de Tunisie is more widely available and also pretty drinkable. Cristal is a reasonable white, and Kélibia in Cap Bon produces a distinctive and unusual dry muscat. Except in the tourist hotels, wine is not served in restaurants on Fridays for religious reasons.

The local **beer** is called Celtia, and is as drinkable as any British or American bog-standard lager. French brand Löwenbrau is made here under license, but is also nothing to write home about. There are however two microbreweries, in Hammamet (see p.145) and Port el Kantaoui (see p.236), which serve excellent German-style beer. Tunisia also produces two strong **spirits**. Unless you have a throat of steel, it's best to drink *boukha* – derived from figs – in the standard combination with Coca-Cola; *thibarine*, a date liqueur, is more palatable. **Laghmi** (palm wine) is the sap of the date palm milked from the tree, and fermented for 24 hours. Both fresh and fermented versions are available around the oases in season. The unfermented version is sweet and tastes a little like barley sugar. If you're offered *laghmi* down south, be sure it's OK before drinking as it is sometimes mixed with water of dubious origin, or left too long (it goes off as quickly as it ferments). *Sirops*, non-alcoholic syrups distilled from fruit (pomegranate, orange, lemon, fig and even pistachio), are rather sickly in taste and garish in colour but make interesting mixers.

Outside Westernized restaurants, most Tunisian drinking, in big cities at least, is done in **bars** – exclusively male and still with an air of the bootleg about them, dense with smoke and invariably deafening. Still, they often serve excellent little snacks (melon, olives, even *brochettes*). In the European-style bars of the bigger hotels the drinks are more expensive but the atmosphere more relaxed, and Tunisian women can even be seen in these venues sometimes. If you're a lone drinker you can buy alcohol in liquor stores – usually hidden away in the back streets of large towns – and larger supermarkets, but you should not carry the bottles around town in public view. Prices displayed do not include the deposit on the bottle.

Other beverages include the ubiquitous **mineral waters** (Safia, Aïn Garci or Aïn Oktor), and sweet fizzy sodas (mainly international brands such as Coca-Cola) generically known as *gazouz*, which are extremely popular. Freshly squeezed orange **juice** is available from many cafés and patisseries, a real bargain, especially as Tunisian oranges are up there with the world's best. Patisseries also serve almond milk, plus *citronade* – a refreshing drink made by putting whole lemons through a blender with sugar and water and straining the result – and other fresh fruit drinks made with a blender, including *lait de poule* ("chicken's milk"), a fresh fruit milkshake with egg white. If you don't want sugar in juices or milkshakes, make it clear from the start. Note that juices are only as safe as the water that goes into them – invariably tap water.

Coffee

Coffee drinking in the ubiquitous card-playing cafés is a national pastime. The coffee (*qahwa* in Arabic, *café* in French) varies from good to horrible, and comes in several forms. *Express* is espresso; it can be good but is usually rather bitter, a fact generally disguised by the addition of large amounts of sugar. *Café au lait*, *café crème* or *qahwa bi halib* usually means filter coffee (served from an urn, bitter and not very nice), and comes with a lot of milk; with less milk it is called *shtar*. *Café filtre* is the same without milk. An espresso with milk (like a cappuccino or French *café crème*) is called a *café direct* or *crème express*. *Capucin* is not a cappuccino, but an espresso with a little milk, like a Spanish *cortado* or Italian *macchiato*. *Capucin nouveau* is the same with condensed milk added. Finally, *qahwa arbi* is Turkish coffee – finely ground coffee brought to the boil and served with the grounds still in it, often perfumed with rosewater or orange blossom water. Not all cafés serve it, but when they do, it is usually well made and very tasty – invariably the best coffee by a long chalk. Two spoons of sugar are usually assumed – to avoid them, ask for *nakas*

Chichas

Most Tunisian cafés still supply the traditional **hookah pipe** or *chicha* (pronounced *sheesha*), filled with low-grade tobacco. It is something of an acquired taste, but if you smoke you should certainly try it. Once strictly an old man's pastime, *chicha*-smoking has gone through something of a renaissance of late, and flavoured tobacco is now available in addition to the traditional *ma'asil* (which means "with honey", but is in fact flavoured with molasses – not hashish, as some tourists seem to think). The nicest is apple-flavoured (*bitufaah*), with strawberry and mint among the other popular flavours.

sukar (a little sugar) or *bilesh sukar* (without sugar).

Tea

Tea is either black (*té ahmar* in Arabic, *thé rouge* in French) or green with mint (*té akhdar* in Arabic, *thé vert* in French). Unfortunately, it is most commonly made by boiling the leaves in water, adding massive quantities of sugar and leaving it to stew for hours on a charcoal stove (*canoun*), which every household possesses for the purpose. The result is a powerful brew of almost pure tannin and sugar – said to result in cases of "tea poisoning" and even death – and too pungent for most unhabituated tastes. Green tea is not usually as stewed as black and is sometimes served with pine nuts and almonds in the brew. Tea with milk is virtually unheard of, but you may get it in expensive hotels or package tour centres; anyone used to British or Irish tea, however, will not be happy with it.

Communications

Post and telecommunications in Tunisia are up to international standards: letters arrive reasonably quickly and rarely go astray, while international calls are relatively easy, with direct dialling, immediate connection and reasonable charges. Emails can be sent from any of a growing number of public Internet offices.

Mail

Post offices (PTT) in large towns tend to follow **city opening hours** (July & Aug Mon–Fri 7.30am–1pm & 5–7pm, Sat 7.30am–1.30pm, Sun 9–11pm; Sept–June Mon–Sat 8am–6pm, Sun 9–11am; Ramadan Mon–Sat 8am–3pm, Sun 9–11am), while branch offices and those in villages and small towns follow **country opening hours** (July & Aug Mon–Thurs 7.30am–1pm, Fri & Sat 7.30am–1.30pm; Sept–June Mon–Thurs 8am–6pm, Fri & Sat 8am–12.30pm; Ramadan Mon–Thurs & Sat 8am–1.30pm, Fri 8am–12.30pm). Stamps can be bought not just at post offices but also from shops selling postcards, and occasionally from certain authorized taxiphone (public telephone) offices, which will have a sign outside to that effect.

Postal services are very reliable; **letters** to Europe rarely take more than a week, while to North America and Australasia they take around two weeks. The parcel service is slower but equally reliable. For inland post, you have the choice of ordinary mail or *lettre prioritaire*, which guarantees faster delivery. Postboxes are usually light yellow in colour, freestanding or set into walls at around shoulder height on the streets.

For **poste restante**, address letters clearly to any post office, marked "R.P." (for Recette Postale); in Tunis, use "Tunis R.P., rue Charles de Gaulle, Tunis" (the main post office). To collect poste restante mail, you'll need some form of identification, preferably your passport.

Telephones

It is almost as easy to make an **international phone call** as a local one. In most towns you can dial direct on a coin phone at the post office or a "taxiphone" or Publitel office. The last two are a sort of shop where you can phone Tunisian or international numbers; they're usually open later than the post office and have plenty of change on hand. In some post offices, you make the call yourself and pay on completion. Some shops also have a public phone; some of these phones are operated with a phonecard that can be bought at the same shop, and used nationwide. An occasional problem at taxiphone offices in larger towns is waiting for a booth: in summer, demand should be less at siesta time, from 2pm to 5pm.

Calls made from taxiphone offices cost 0.980TD a minute to the British Isles, 0.882TD cheap rate (8pm–7am and all day Sunday), 1.500TD/1.350TD to North America, and 1.750TD/1.575TD to Australasia. Calling from hotels is much more expensive than using a taxiphone office. To make a **collect call**, dial ☎17 for the international operator and ask for "*un appel en PCV*" (pronounced *pay-say-vay*).

As for **internal calls**, all Tunisian numbers are now made up of eight digits, all of which must be dialled, even locally. The old area codes have been incorporated into the number, and in the case of landline numbers, the initial 0 has been swapped for a 7. Thus a Tunis number that was ☎01/234 567 is now ☎71 234 567. Besides 71 for Tunis, 72 is for Bizerte, Nabeul and Zaghouan; 73 for Sousse, Monastir and Mahdia; 74 for Sfax; 75 for Gabès, Kebili, Medenine and Tataouine; 76 for Gafsa, Tozeur and Sidi Bou Zid; 77 for Kairouan and Kasserine; 78 for Béja, Jendouba, Le Kef and Siliana. For mobile numbers, see the following section.

Tunisian phone numbers seem to change very frequently, so don't be surprised if

To call Tunisia from abroad:
Australia ☎00 11 216 + number
New Zealand ☎00 216 + number
Republic of Ireland ☎00 216 + number
United Kingdom ☎00 216 + number
USA and Canada ☎011 216 + number

To call abroad from Tunisia:
Australia ☎00 61 + local code
(without initial zero) + number
New Zealand ☎00 64 + local code
(without initial zero) + number
Republic of Ireland ☎00 353 + local
code (without initial zero) + number
United Kingdom ☎00 44 + local code
(without initial zero) + number
USA and Canada ☎00 1 + local code
+ number

Useful numbers within Tunisia
Emergencies ☎197
Speaking clock ☎191
Directory enquiries ☎12
International operator ☎17

numbers given in this book or elsewhere are out of date. While the first two digits of a number represent the area or mobile, the next two or three digits may change for all the numbers in a town to standardize them.

Internal calls are not expensive: you will need hundred-millime coins, combined perhaps with half-dinar coins for long-distance or calls to mobiles if you intend to speak for longer than just briefly. Older payphones may not take more than one coin at a time, so you will have to continue feeding them.

Mobile phones

Mobile phones can be used in most of Tunisia, though not in remote desert areas. Coverage extends to all the towns and villages in this book with the exception of Ksar Ghilane and the area south of Remada.

There are two cellphone **networks** in Tunisia: Tunisie Telecom (formerly numbers beginning 09, now numbers beginning 97 or 98), which has the best coverage, and Tunisiana (numbers beginning 22), whose coverage is limited mostly to coastal areas and the Sahel. One or other of the Tunisian mobile service providers may well have a roaming agreement with your provider at home, but using your home mobile phone in Tunisia is expensive, and you pay to receive calls as well as to make them; US phones need to be GSM/triband to be used in Tunisia. Depending on how long you are in Tunisia therefore, it may be worth signing up with one of the local firms, using their SIM card and a Tunisian number. Alternatively you can rent a Tunisian handset from Tunisie Telecom, who have an office at Tunis airport for just that purpose. For further information about mobile phones in Tunisia, see ⓦwww.gsmworld.com/roaming/gsminfo/cou_tn.shtml; for more general advice on using a mobile abroad, see ⓦwww.telecomsadvice.org.uk/features/using_your_mobile_abroad.htm.

Email

Internet use is not as widespread in Tunisia as in the West, but it is growing; some large hotels, and even one or two small ones, now have email reservation facilities. Few people have computers at home, but most towns have **Internet offices** (we've listed locations of these throughout the guide) where you can access the Web, usually for 1.5–2TD per hour, though none serve drinks or snacks. These are often advertised under the name **Publinet**, with a purple and white sign. The downside is that connections in some places can be painfully slow (less so if you go late at night or early in the morn-

ing). Some towns have offices open 24/7, and many are open until midnight or later, depending on the number of customers. At night they often have the feel of an underground kind of club, the only thing in town that is open when all godfearing citizens are safely tucked up in bed. At such times they tend to be all-male preserves, though female tourists should have no problems.

The Internet is closely monitored and foreign websites, especially in French, may be blocked if they contain criticism of the Tunisian government. In 2002, a Tunisian journalist who ran a website that satirized the president and published statements from illegal opposition groups was jailed for eighteen months. Internet offices have also on occasion been closed down because of customers using the Web to access porn sites.

Tunisian computers are usually set up to use the **French keyboard** layout. On a PC using this layout, the "@" symbol is obtained by hitting the "0" key with Alt Gr held down. If you're a touch typist, you might want to ask staff at the Internet shop if they can change the setting to the English (QWERTY) keyboard.

It is worth noting that Hotmail sometimes goes off line in Tunisia for hours and even days at a time, for no apparent reason; most Tunisian residents therefore use alternatives such as Yahoo. If you use Hotmail and are having difficulty accessing it, you may be able to do so via ⓦwww.proxyone.com.

The media

Tunisia is almost completely bilingual, so if you're competent in either French or Arabic you should have little trouble following international news in the local newspapers or on radio or TV – though censorship is heavy and the quality of reporting and analysis is not high. Press codes determine what may and may not be published, with fines and jail sentences in force for violation, and newspapers and magazines are screened before publication. Even criticism of American foreign policy is frequently curbed, and of course no harsh examination of the Tunisian regime is allowed. Foreign newspapers and TV are easily available, but may be impounded if they contain anything critical of the regime, especially in French or Arabic.

Newspapers and magazines

The English-language weekly **newspaper**, the *Tunisian News*, has some interesting features and a small amount of international news, but what it does say about Tunisia would be better described as PR. The daily French-language newspapers *La Presse* (ⓦwww.lapresse.tn) and *Le Temps* (ⓦwww.tunisie.com/Assabah) stay close to the ruling RCD party line as, unsurprisingly, does the party's own daily paper, *Le Renouveau* (ⓦwww.tunisieinfo.com/indexrenouveau.html). *Le Temps* is the most substantial, but that isn't saying very much. Each paper lists cultural events, exchange rates, bus, train and plane departures from Tunis, and television and Tunis cinema listings.

Periodicals, less restricted than the daily press, carry interesting items from a more radical standpoint: *Jeune Afrique* (ⓦwww.jeuneafrique.com), published weekly in France but with a Tunisian editor, is excellent (its credibility is enhanced by occasional government bannings), as is the North African edition of its sister publication, *l'Intelligent* (ⓦwww.lintelligent.com).

Foreign newspapers can be bought, a day late, at newsagents and big hotels in all tourist areas (*Le Monde* almost everywhere). In the resort areas, a random selection of British national dailies is usually available, as are the *International Herald Tribune*, *Time* and *Newsweek*.

Radio and TV

There are plenty of **French-language radio stations**, including the state-run Radio Tunis (93.1FM), which is one of the more popular for music. The state broadcasting company also runs local stations in many cities. Since 2003, a privately run music and talk station, Radio Mosaïque (94.9FM), has been on the air, broadcasting in colloquial Tunisian Arabic, and mainly aimed at young adult listeners. With a combination of Arabic and Western music, phone-ins and frank chat, it has become extremely popular, and now has a massive audience share, even though at the time of writing it only covered the northern half of the country.

If you take a shortwave radio, you can pick up the BBC World Service (ⓦwww.bbc.co.uk/worldservice), which is broadcast on various frequencies through the day, from 6am to midnight local time. The most consistent reception is generally on 15,485 and 17,640 kHz (19m and 16m bands) during the daytime, or 6195, 9410 and 12,095 kHz (49m, 31m and 25m bands) after dark. You can also pick up the Voice of America (ⓦwww.voa.gov) during the day on 1197 kHz or 15,205 kHz, at night on 1593 kHz, among other frequencies. **Radio Canada** (ⓦwww.rcinet.ca) can be picked up from 7pm to 8pm local time on 11,770kHz or 13,730kHz or 15,255kHz, or from 9pm to 10pm on 13,700kHz.

There are four **local TV channels**, one in Arabic, three in French. One of the latter is a Tunisian version of the French France 2. Privately run TV stations are promised in the near future. The Italian station Rai Uno is also available, and other French and Italian channels can sometimes be picked up. Use of satellite dishes is increasing (most tourist hotels have them), giving access to many more channels in various languages, notably German, plus CNN and Eurosport in English. Most Tunisians get their news nowadays from the Qatar-based Arabic-language channel Al Jazeera (on line in English at ⓦenglish.aljazeera.net).

Opening hours, public holidays and festivals

Office hours in Tunisia are Monday to Friday from 8am to 12.30pm and 2.30pm to 6pm, except in July and August when they are Monday to Saturday 8am–1pm. Most shops open seven days a week, roughly from 8.30am to noon and 3pm to 6pm during the winter, and from 8.30am to noon and 4pm to 7pm during summer. Some shops close one day a week, usually Friday or Sunday, occasionally Monday, but this is unlikely to be true of tourist souvenir shops, which are also unlikely to close for lunch. For banking hours, see p.26.

Archeological sites and museums are typically open from 9.30am to 4.30pm. Some sites close for lunch from noon or 1pm to 2–3pm, while others open longer during the summer (July & Aug). Most are closed one day a week, usually Monday, but sometimes Sunday or Friday.

Holidays and festivals

The great national festivals of Tunisia are related to Islam and so their dates are calculated according to the **Muslim calendar**. This is a lunar system, and the corresponding dates in the Western calendar move forward by about eleven days a year.

Ramadan, the month-long sunrise-to-sunset fast required of all good Muslims every year (see p.524), would seem like a disastrous time to travel, and you certainly won't go anywhere for at least half an hour when the sun sets and everyone makes a mad dash for food as the call of the *muezzin* or the boom of a cannon marks the end of the day's fasting. Cafés and restaurants, save those that particularly cater for tourists, are likely to close during daylight, and bars will close altogether. Grocers are open so you can still buy things to eat, but, although Tunisia is not as strict about Ramadan as some Muslim countries, you may feel it inconsiderate to eat, drink or smoke in public when most people are committed to fasting.

Ramadan is also an exciting time. If those observing the fast sometimes get a little sluggish and short-tempered during the day – especially smokers deprived of their hourly

Major religious festivals

It's impossible to predict the dates of religious festivals exactly, since they are set by the Ministry of Religous Affairs and depend on the sighting of the new moon.

	2005	2006	2007	2008
Aïd el Adha	21 Jan	11 Jan & 31 Dec	20 Dec	8 Dec
Ras el Am	10 Feb	31 Jan	21 Jan	10 Jan & 29 Dec
Mouled el Nabi	21 April	11 April	31 March	20 March
1st of Ramadan (not a holiday)	5 Oct	24 Sept	13 Sept	1 Sept
Aïd el Fitr	3 Nov	24 Oct	13 Oct	1 Oct

Secular holidays

January 1	New Year	July 25	Republic Day
March 20	Independence Day	August 13	Women's Day
March 21	Youth Day	October 15	Evacuation of Bizerte
April 9	Martyrs' Day	November 7	New Era Day
May 1	Labour Day		

fix – the riotous night-time compensation more than makes up for it. Eating, drinking and smoking – with a day's consumption packed into a few hours – go on until two or three in the morning, and, for the only time in the year, **café nightlife** really takes off. Lights are strung up and you'll find performances of music, occasionally belly dancing. In Tunis, the best places to experience this are place Bab Souika and Bab Saadoun. If you're lucky enough you'll see a puppet show, enacting a tradition that arrived with Turkish rulers in the sixteenth century. Ramadan ends with a flourish in a feast called the **Aïd el Fitr**, or **Aïd es Seghir**, a public holiday on which pretty much everything closes.

The other great national festival, the feast of Abraham known as **Aïd el Adha** or **Aïd el Kebir**, is more of a family affair, the equivalent of a Western Christmas perhaps. Every family that can afford it celebrates the willingness of Abraham to sacrifice his son Ishmael by slaughtering its own sheep and roasting the meat: you can tell the *aïd* is approaching by the appearance of sheep tethered by almost every house. There's a gradual movement away from having an animal slaughtered to just buying the meat, but the festival is still the time when families are reunited and transport is packed all over the country, and it is also a universally observed public holiday, when you will find almost nothing open.

Other religious festivals are less widely observed, though the Prophet's birthday, **Mouled**, is a great event at Kairouan (see p.254), and is also a public holiday, as is **Ras el Am**, or El Hijra, the Islamic new year. Marabouts (local holy men) also have their own festival called a *moussem* or *ziara*, centred around the tomb or *zaouia* where they are buried.

National secular holidays occur on fixed dates (see box, p.45) and generally entail the closure of banks, most shops and offices. There are **local secular festivals**, some traditional, though most of them are recent creations designed to bolster tourism or agriculture. A lot of the tourist "festivals" are really just a series of rather sedate events organized by the local council or ONTT, and do not involve much in the way of celebration or festivity. The ONTT website is supposed to give current dates at ⓦ www .tourismtunisia.com/festivals, but unfortunately it was some years out of date on our last check.

Local festivals

February Olive Festival, Kalaa Kebira (near Sousse, see p.237); poetry festival, Tozeur (see p.365).

March Hammam Festival, El Hamma de l'Arad (see p.388); Festival of the Ksour, Tataouine (see p.466).

March or April Orange Blossom Festival, Menzel Bou Zelfa (see p.164).

May Matanza, Sidi Daoud (see p.160); Jewish pilgrimage, Hara Sghira, Jerba (see p.439).

June Falconry Festival, El Haouaria (see p.157); Rai festival, Tabarka (see p.193).

July Sidi Bou Makhlouf Festival, Le Kef (see p.317); International Jazz Festival, Tabarka (see p.193); Malouf Music Festival, Testour (see p.304); Plastic Arts Festival, Mahrès (see p.279); Festival du Borj, Gafsa (see p.345).

July & August Drama performances in Roman theatre, Dougga (see p.305). Also various tourist-oriented "cultural" festivals at resorts and Roman sites around the country; Carthage International Festival (see p.127); International Symphonic Music Festival, El Jem (see p.263).

August World Music Festival, Tabarka (see p.193)

Weddings

Weddings are extraordinarily public celebrations – one of the few chances people get to really let their hair down, and they make the most of it. Cavalcades of pick-up trucks loaded with people playing pipes and drums drive round the town (in Tunis, Mercedes hoot up and down avenue Bourguiba); a solemn procession carries the bride's dowry through the streets; and the celebrations, dancing and feasting can go on for several days. You can now sign up at the big hotels for an evening at a rather sad tourist version of a "typical Tunisian wedding", as tacky as you would expect. But if you do receive an invitation to a real wedding – and it is far from unusual to invite complete strangers, especially foreigners – it is well worth taking up.

September Wine Festival, Grombalia (see p.164).
October Liberation Day, Bizerte (see p.178).
November Tozeur Festival (see p.365); Date
Festival, Kebili (see p.375); Carthage Film Festival
(biennial, mainly in Tunis) (see p.117).
December International Festival of the Sahara,
Douz (see p.382).

Entertainment and spectator sport

Tunisians like going to the cinema, and the country has its own film industry which, though hardly prolific, has produced some fine movies. Most of the music you will hear in Tunisia is from Egypt or Lebanon, or raï from neighbouring Algeria, but Tunisia does have home-grown artists too, whose work is available mostly on cassette within the country, and on CD abroad. As regards spectator sport, Tunisia is as soccer-mad as every other part of the world (North America and Antarctica excepted).

Cinema

Tunisian cinemas show a mix of Hollywood, Bollywood, French, Egyptian and local movies, and the occasional Hong Kong action film. English-language films are usually dubbed into French; Indian movies are usually subtitled in French and Arabic. Longer films are not so much cut as slashed, leaving out whole reels, though actual censorship is light: controversial subjects and even soft sex scenes are usually allowed. Cinema tickets cost around 2.50TD.

Tunisia's own **film industry** has been more influenced by France than by Egypt, India or the United States. The first wholly Tunisian-produced feature was Omar Khliifi's *The Dawn* (1966), a drama about the struggle for independence. Perhaps predictably, independence and its aftermath remained the most popular theme in Tunisian cinema for some time, but other subjects included the experience of Tunisian emigrants abroad in Naceur Ktari's *The Ambassadors* (1976), social attitudes to homosexuality in Nouri Bouzid's *Man of Ashes* (1986), and rural migration to the cities in Taïeb Louhichi's *Shadow of the Land* (1982). The ill effects of tourism are well dealt with in Ridha Behi's *Sun of the Hyenas* (1977), portraying the effect of a hotel development on a small fishing village, and Nouri Bouzid's *Bez-*nez (1992), about a beach gigolo. Bouzid returned to the big screen in 1997 with *Bent Familia*, looking at three women and their relationships with men. Another Tunisian director whose films have achieved recognition outside the country is Ferid Boughedir; his best-known work, *Halfaouine* (1990), is a good-humoured coming-of-age tale set in the Tunis faubourg of the title.

The social position of women is another subject popular in Tunisian cinema. Tunisia has a growing number of fine **women directors**, starting with Selma Baccar, who broke the male mould with *Fatma 75* in 1978, and has continued to deal with gender issues in films like *Habiba Msika* (1996; see p.304). Other women film directors who have achieved international recognition include Moufida Tlatli, whose *Silences of the Palace* (1994) examines the suffering of a group of women employed as servants in a colonial palace in the 1950s, while *Season of Men* (2001) is about a Jerban woman bringing up her autistic son. Another of Tunisia's posse of women film directors is is Kalthoum Bornaz, best known for her romantic comedy *Keswa – the Lost Thread* (1997).

In even-numbered years Tunis hosts the **Carthage Festival** of African and Arab cinema, which stands alongside Burkina Faso's FESPACO (held in odd-numbered years) as Africa's most important film festival.

47

Music

The most typical Tunisian style of music is **malouf**, which is derived from the music of Islamic Andalusia. Typically it is played by a small, five- or six-piece band with a violin, an *oud* (lute), a *derbouka* (drum held under the arm) and often a vocalist. The most popular *malouf* artists today include singer **Lotfi Bouchnak** and *oud* player **Anouar Brahem**. Of Bouchnak's albums, *Lotfi Bouchnak Malouf Tunis* (1994) is easy to find on tape in Tunisia. Brahem has attained greater recognition abroad, especially in Europe, and his work for the German ECM label is easy to find. On his more recent recordings for them, *Astrakan Café* (2001) and *Le Pas du Chat Noir* (2002), his musical style tends more towards jazz. Another *oud* player whose work combines *malouf* with jazz and other outside influences is **Dhafer Youssef**, nowadays based in Vienna, whose albums include *Malak* (1999) and *Electric Sufi* (2001). Kaddour Srarfi and Khemais Tarnane have produced a good **anthology** of *malouf* music, prosaically named *Tunisie: Anthologie du Malouf* (1996), which is widely available outside the country as a set of five CDs.

Aside from *malouf*, romantic singers such as **Saber Robai** and **Latifa Arfaoui** have gone down a storm elsewhere in the Arab world, most notably in Egypt, as well as in France. Also making a name for herself abroad is actress **Ghalia Benali** (star of Moufida Tlatli's *Season of Men*) and her band Timnaa, with their eclectic combination of Arabic and European styles. You should have no trouble getting hold of their album *Wild Harissa* (2002) on CD. Another fusion artist of Tunisian origin is **Amina Annabi**, who took second place in the Eurovision song contest for France back in 1991 with "C'est Le Dernier Qui A Parlé Qui A Raison", and nowadays offers up a poppy confection of techno belly-dancing tunes.

As well as *Tunisie: Anthologie du Malouf*, referred to above, a good **sampler** for Tunisian music is the *Tunisie/Tunisia* album in the Air Mail Music series (1998), which concentrates on traditional folk dances. You can find samples of Tunisian music on line at ⓦ www.radiotunis.com/music.html and ⓦ www.focusmm.com/tunisia/tn_musmn .htm.

For live music within the country, one of the best locations is **Tabarka**, which hosts a *raï* festival in late June, followed by a jazz festival in early July, a world music festival in late August and a Latin music festival in early September. For classical music, **El Jem** hosts an International Festival of Symphonic Music in July and August every year. Music venues in and around Tunis are covered on p.116.

Football

While the best local players go to European leagues, Tunisia's top twelve domestic football **clubs** contest a league championship and cup each year. As you might expect, the clubs from Tunis and more prosperous towns are the most successful. The most important are Espérance Sportif de Tunis (EST), Club Africain (CA; who share a stadium with Ésperance), Club Athlétique Bizertin (CAB), Étoile Sportive du Sahel (ESS; from Sousse) and Club Sportif Sfaxien (CSS). Apart from Espérance, Club Africain and Stade Tunisien, they're usually referred to just by their initials. Tickets, usually costing 3–5TD, can often be bought on the gate, but are best purchased at the stadium a day or two before the match. For important games, they may even be available on line via the Tunisian Football Federation's website (ⓦ www.ftf.org.tn).

Tunisia's national team was one of the early African World Cup successes when it qualified for the 1978 finals in Argentina. They qualified again in France in 1998, when, though failing to reach the second round, they achieved respectable results against some of the world's top teams. Tunisia hosted the African Nations' Cup in 2004, when they also won it for the first time, beating Morocco 2–1 in the final.

Tunisian teams have been prominent in **African club competitions** since CAB took the African Cup Winners' Cup in 1988. Since then, CAB, Club Africain, Espérance and ESS have several times between them won the African Champions' League, the African Cup Winners' Cup, and the CAF Cup (equivalent of the UEFA Cup).

Espérance made world sports pages in sensational fashion in the African Champions' League final of 2000. Their Ghanaian opponents, Hearts of Oak, won the first leg at home in Accra 2–1, but with just fifteen minutes to go of the second leg in Tunis, Espérance were 1–0 up and looked like winning overall on the away-goals rule. At that point, Ghanaian fans started throwing missiles at one of the linesmen, and police responded by lobbing teargas canisters into the crowd. Fans of both teams poured onto the running track surrounding the pitch, and one of them passed something to Espérance goalkeeper Chokri el Ouaer, who drew it across his forehead, ran from the goal with his head streaming blood, and fell to the ground. Since pretty much everyone had seen him deliberately inflict the injury, presumably aiming to have the match abandoned with the score in Esperance's favour, the referee sent him off. When play resumed, with Esperance putting a midfielder in goal rather than their reserve keeper, Hearts of Oak scored three times to win 5–2 on aggregate. In the aftermath, Hearts were banned from playing at home in African competitions for a year, while Chokri el Ouaer was suspended for a year.

Outdoor activities

Tunisia has several golf courses, in or around Tunis (see p.118), Hammamet (see p.146), Tabarka (see p.193), Port el Kantaoui (see p.233), Monastir (see p.243), and Sidi Mahares, Jerba (see p.427). In Tozeur a new golf course is under construction which will use recycled water, Tozeur being a desert oasis town. For those contemplating a package, several British and Irish tour operators offer golfing holidays in Tunisia (see p.12).

While the Mediterranean may not have quite the diving cachet of the Red Sea or the South Pacific, Tunisia does have **diving** schools at Tabarka (see p.193), Port el Kantaoui (see p.233) and Hergla (see p.236), where you can learn the basic skills and visit reefs and wrecks. Tabarka is the only location with coral, but the seas around Tunisia are surprisingly rich in other marine life, including fish, crustaceans and sponges. Undersea fishing is subject to strict regulations, and may not normally be practised with air tanks.

Hunting has a following among some foreign visitors, from Saudi princes (whose activities threaten the protected Houbara bustard in the south) to German boar hunters based at Aïn Draham. The hunting season is winter, usually from December to February. The British tour operator Sunnyway (see p.12) offers hunting holidays in Tunisia, but if you want to arrange an expedition yourself, you'll need to sort out the necessary permits with the Fédération Tunisienne de Chasse, Club de Chasse Radès, 2040 Radès (☎71 434 910, ✉fnac@planet.tn).

Desert activities

In the desert, you'll find **sand-skiing** available at El Fouar near Douz (see p.386), made possible by the fine sand and special narrow skis. Another unusual sport available in the south of Tunisia is **land-yachting** – like windsurfing, but on dry land with wheels. The Chott el Jerid, a salt flat which is usually dry, is a perfect location for this, with a lesser site near Aghir in Jerba. The zone touristique hotels in Douz (see p.381) and Tozeur (see p.357) can often arrange for guests to go sand-yachting on the Chott, as can the Douz firm Pégase (see p.382), which also offers rides on **sand hovercrafts** and **microlights**. Pégase also have a **go-karting** track, and there's another at Ras Taguermes in Jerba (see p.429).

Douz is the main centre for **camel trek- king** (see p.383), but if you don't want to go the whole hog and spend three or four days at it, you can just take a ride on a camel. Camel drivers offer rides to tourists at Matmata (see p.405), Douz (see p.382) and Zaafrane (see p.384), or ask at the *calèche* stand in Tozeur (see p.362). **Horseback riding** is available at Hammamet (see p.143, Tabarka (see p.190), Aïn Draham (see p.195) and Tozeur (see p.365).

Crime and personal safety

You are unlikely to run into any trouble in Tunisia, where thieving is a lot less common than in most of Europe or North America. Mugging and rape are rare, though as ever it is best to avoid unlit and deserted areas of towns late at night.

Theft and scams

Tunisians are generally honest and law-abiding and **stealing** from a visitor is considered shameful. Nonetheless, foreigners are obviously targets for theft when it does occur, the main hot spots being Sousse, Hammamet and Jerba. The most common forms of theft are stealing possessions on the beach while you sleep (sometimes even from bags used as pillows); pickpocketing, especially by young kids in Hammamet, where the usual method involves an accomplice distracting your attention by asking you to change a foreign coin; and bag-snatching, especially in the Medina in Sousse. Many hotels operate a deposit service for valuables; otherwise, wearing a body belt might be good for your peace of mind.

it occasionally happens that Tunisians posing as "guides" lead tourists deep into the medina (Sousse and Kairouan being the main ones) so that they are lost and nervous, then charging them to be led out again. In such situations, you can always call on passers-by for help. Less nasty, and still relatively rare, is the practice of offering someone a gift, and then demanding an exhorbitant payment for it; food or drinks offered by people you have just met may come into this category.

The police

There are two main types of police: the blue-uniformed **ordinary police** (*sûreté* in French, *shurta* in Arabic) and the green-uniformed **Garde Nationale** (National Guard). The ordinary police have jurisdiction within town limits, and are generally the people to see to report a crime. They usually speak good French and should be able to give you directions if you're lost. The Garde Nationale have jurisdiction in rural areas and guard the country's borders. They may stop you if you're driving, especially near the Algerian border, and will ask to see your passport and question you about where you're going and why, but they won't give you any trouble. The Garde Nationale are the people you should inform before driving to remote desert areas, and in some places there is a

Drugs

Tunisia is not Morocco or Egypt: hardly any tradition of **hashish** or other drug use survives, though *takrouri* (marijuana) was smoked during the Ottoman period, and remained legal until the 1950s. With independence, however, harsh laws against cannabis were introduced, and very few people now smoke it. Those who do tend to be rich, and may feel that they have enough influence to get away with it. But use of cannabis is frowned on, both officially and popularly, and is extremely clandestine, with very stiff penalties in force. Imprisonment is the norm for possession of hashish, marijuana or any other illegal drug.

special Garde Nationale office specifically for tourists.

It is just possible, though unlikely, that you will be stopped and asked for **identification** on the street (Tunisians are issued with state identity cards, which they carry at all times). If your passport is back in your hotel, you should be okay as long as the police officer can come and inspect it there, though it's best to carry at least a photocopy of the pages containing your identification.

Reporting a crime

If you have to report a crime to the police, make sure you go to the police station covering the area where the crime was committed. You'll probably have to go during office hours and you may have to put up with a certain amount of buck-passing and time-wasting, though the police are usually kind and helpful to distressed tourists who have been the victims of crime. Whatever you do, stay calm and do not get angry or shout if

they seem to be giving you the run-around. Wearing your best clothes (and "modest" ones if you are a woman) is a good idea.

You will need a **receipt** from the police in order to get your insurance to pay up for anything lost or stolen, and for your passport in order to get a replacement. They might ask you to call back for the receipt, but should issue one for a passport immediately – if you have to insist, do so very politely. You will not get a receipt for stolen cash.

For a serious charge, such as assault, they may take you with them to try and locate your assailant, and will also expect you to come in and identify suspects face to face – this is not pleasant and they will not be happy if you back out of it, so make sure you are prepared to do this when you report the crime. Also be aware if you are a woman and sexual assault is involved that almost all police officers in Tunisia are men. However, they are usually sympathetic and the prosecution process is fast (two days on average).

Shopping

Veterans of countries like Morocco, Egypt and India will find Tunisia tame by comparison. In general, you won't be hassled endlessly by salesmen, nor will people attach themselves to you and then demand payment for having been your "guide". Shopping in most of Tunisia is relaxed, pressure-free and often conducted over a no-strings-attached cup of tea. However, some hard selling has crept into some of the more touristed areas, notably the tourist ghettos of Cap Bon and the medinas of Kairouan and Sousse.

If you're going to play the game, it pays to know the rules: A salesman invites you into his shop, maybe "for tea" because it's his birthday, or even "the birthday of the shop". You make it quite clear (and this is fundamental) that you don't want to buy anything, even if you half think you might. The salesman insists you come in just to have a look. Of course, you may not want to go in. The Arabic for "no, thank you" is *la shookran*, and if you say it with a smile,

no one can take offence. A more definitive tactic is to say you already have whatever is being offered.

A **typical scenario**, if you do enter, say, a carpet shop, begins with the trader showing you the ceiling to demonstrate what an old house he has – a "museum" of carpets; he will show you carpet makers at work, then sit you down and call for tea. A large number of carpets are brought and rolled out in front of you. He shows you examples

Weekly markets

Life in the country revolves around a cycle of weekly **markets**, often colourful affairs. The Sousse and Nabeul markets have been comprehensively "discovered"; but it's well worth timing a visit to other towns to coincide with the weekly event, which for many of them is the mainstay of the economy. Testour and El Fahs are particularly worthwhile. Market days in each region are listed in a box at the beginning of each chapter.

of the different styles, tells you how much they would be worth in your country, shows you the government seal of approval, tells you how little it will cost to send one home and demands to know why you don't want one. He brings out smaller and cheaper examples and keeps up the fluent spiel. Unless of course you do want to buy one, you will have to be insistent in declining to offer a price, and reminding the seller that it was he who insisted you "just look".

Finally, as you apologize and make to leave, he demands to know, of the carpets he has shown you, which you like. He will now probably tell you his **final price**, but any sign of interest on your part will raise it: if you're genuinely interested, you can always shop around and return any time you like. Hostility or abusiveness at this stage is still unusual, but it happens. If so, ignore it, or if you feel strongly enough report it to the local ONTT and enter it in their complaints book, naming the shop concerned.

If you're going to buy arts and crafts, it's probably worthwhile paying a visit to the local crafts shop run by the **ONA** (Organisation Nationale de l'Artisanat Tunisien, also called SOCOPA), the Tunisian crafts organization. They have a number of workshops and a showroom and shop in most big towns, listed throughout this Guide. Their goods are generally of a high quality, if a little overpriced, but it's worth visiting to get an idea of what sort of crafts are available and how much they should cost, and to help you weed out the impostors in the field – like the cheap Moroccan pottery sold as "Souvenir

of Tunisia". Indeed, quite a few things sold as souvenirs are not Tunisian at all: as well as Moroccan pottery, there are Egyptian perfume bottles and inlaid boxes, and stone eggs from around the world.

When buying something expensive like a carpet, and when buying items in ONA shops generally, you may be able to get the price down by offering **foreign currency** instead of dinars. It's sometimes possible to get a better price for souvenirs by **bartering** – the latest designer gear and trainers are always in demand.

Bargaining

When shopping, you will often be expected to **haggle** over the price. There are no hard and fast rules – it's really a question of how much something is worth to you. Don't worry too much about initial prices. Some people suggest paying a third of the opening price, but you may end up paying only a tenth or less of the opening price, or, on the other hand, not be able to get the seller much below it. If you bid too low, you may be bustled out of the shop for offering an "insulting" price, but this is all part of the game and you will no doubt be welcomed as an old friend if you return the next day.

Never start haggling for something if in fact you do not want it; if the seller asks how much you would pay for something, and you don't want it, say so. It is a good plan to have an idea of how much you want to pay, and you should never let any figure pass your lips that you are not prepared to pay – as with bidding in an auction, having mentioned a price, you are obliged to pay it. And never go shopping with a **guide**, who will get a commission on anything you buy, which means a higher price for you. If salespeople, or anyone who is trying to sell you something, asks where you are staying, they are probably trying to gauge your spending power, so naming a cheap hotel or youth hostel may give you a bit more haggling power.

What to buy

The most popular **souvenirs** are soft toy camels – useful for young relatives perhaps, though they have metal wire inside. Traditional craftwork, such as carpets and ceramics, has more lasting appeal, but you may find that items of everyday Tunisian life, domestic and otherwise, make better, cheaper and more impressive souvenirs of the country.

There are all sorts of other odds and ends you might go for, from the ornate **birdcages** sold especially in Sidi Bou Saïd to **sea sponges**. Other possibilities include **darbouka drums**, typical of Tunisia. Try the drum souk in Tunis for these (see p.98), though if you need one good enough for a serious musician you will probably want it made to order. **Desert roses**, bizarrely shaped crystals of gypsum that look a little like petrified flowers (see box, p.371), are the commonest souvenirs sold down south, and very cheap, especially around Nefta, Tozeur and Douz. They can be rather bulky but all sizes are available and you can get several very small ones for a dinar.

In the way of **antiques**, there are a lot of colonial remnants about, but nothing especially cheap. In Tunis, rue des Glacières by place de la Victoire, along with the market area around Souk des Armes and place du Marché du Blé, are likely hunting grounds for this sort of thing (see p.107). Around Roman sites, hawkers offer "Roman" and "Byzantine" coins and "old" oil lamps. Some of them are genuine (coins are sometimes found after rain and left overnight in a glass of fizzy cola to clean them), though worthless; most, however, are artificially aged fakes.

Pottery and ceramics

Of the two main pottery centres, whose wares you can find throughout Tunisia, **Nabeul** on Cap Bon specializes in pottery glazed in the Andalusian style, with stylized, plant-like patterns in bold colours, for which tourists are the main customers. Good buys include plates, vases and tiles which can be made up into a wall panel. In the other main centre, **Guellala** on the island of Jerba, ordinary Tunisians are still the main customers, and the best buys are more utilitarian. If you can cart it home, you might go for a huge "Ali Baba" jar – with room to hide at least one thief. Otherwise, you could buy a "magic camel" water jug, which is filled from the bottom and holds the water in when upright, even though the filling hole is left unplugged.

An alternative souvenir from here is a jar-like octopus trap (see p.434), but if you'd prefer a used one you should have no trouble persuading a fisherman to sell it to you. Tunisia's third ceramics centre is **Sejnane**, with its own style of "naive" ceramic sculpture available in the region or at a Tunis outlet called El Hanout (see p.92).

Carpets, rugs and blankets

There are two main regions of **carpet production** in Tunisia: Kairouan in the centre and Gafsa and the Jerid in the south. In **Kairouan**, where carpets are more finely knotted (quality being measured in knots per square metre – see p.253), they usually have geometric designs and deep colours. **Jerid** carpets are more psychedelic, with bright colours and stylized images. In **Tozeur** you may find carpets featuring the same distinctive designs used in the traditional brickwork of the houses. Other places where carpets are sold include Gabès and Jerba. **Kilims**, sold particularly in the south – Toujane near Matmata is one village with a tradition of kilim making – are woven rather than knotted. Before buying a knotted carpet, check to see that it carries the government seal of approval, which guarantees its quality, although be aware that Tunisian carpets have no special value outside the country, whatever their quality.

Jewellery

Tunisia's **jewellery** trade was traditionally run by Jews, most of whom have now emigrated. Nowadays, the jewellery shops of Houmt Souk on Jerba, often still in Jewish hands, are the best places to buy silver or gold pieces or to have them made up. The Berber regions of the south also specialize in chunky silver jewellery, often set with semi-precious stones. This, however, is less openly on sale, and you may have to ask around to find something good. One typical piece is the **khlal**, a buckle consisting of a pin attached to a silver crescent that's used to fasten clothes. In Tabarka, you'll find a lot of **coral** jewellery on sale, though perhaps you should consider the plight of its source before buying (see p.191).

Hallmarks exist for silver and gold in Tunisia, though you don't often see them. On gold, a ram's head means 18 carat (75 percent gold), a goat's head is 14 carat (58.3 percent) and a scorpion is 9 carat (37.5 percent). Silver hallmarks include grapes with a figure 1 (90 percent silver), with a figure 2 (80 percent), and an African head looking to the right (less than 80 percent).

Common **motifs** in Tunisian jewellery include the Hand of Fatima and the fish. Both are good luck symbols used to ward off the evil eye (see p.525), though some say the fish was originally a phallic fertility symbol.

Woodwork, basketwork and metalwork

There are masses of woodcarvings around, but the nicest buys are made of **olive wood**, which comes mostly from Sfax, at the centre of the main olive-growing region. Especially attractive here are salad bowls, with the bonus that they're not made at the expense of Southeast Asia's teak forests. **Basketwork** is common throughout the country, made from esparto grass, rushes or palm fronds; baskets, hats and table mats are among the items produced. Another craft worth investing in is **hammered metal**. There are some excellent plates and trays available, but also a lot of shoddy rubbish. Rather than buying from tourist shops, seek out places where Tunisians might buy and check the artistry involved.

Clothing and leather

Traditional Tunisian **clothes** can look rather silly on foreigners. **Chéchias**, red felt hats, are one possibility, or a handsome camel-hair **burnoose**, but these are expensive. If you go for a **sifsari**, a light women's shawl and head covering, get a cotton one. A cheaper way to obtain clothes is to buy the fabric and have a tailor make something to order. Alternatively, you could try the **secondhand clothes markets** in most medinas – much of the clothing is European, with some outrageous retro garments to be found. Also available are the blue jackets (called *blusa*) that are the trademark of the Maghrebi working man.

Leather can be good but it can also be awful, so check the quality before buying, especially of any stitching. Western-style gear such as jackets and handbags can be very shoddily made; more traditional items such as poufs and *babouche* slippers are usually better. Even then, any dye on them is very likely to run if they get wet. **Sheepskins** are also widely available – make sure they're well cured.

Everyday items

Often the things which will best remind you of Tunisia are everyday items sold in ordinary shops and markets. A **canoun** (charcoal stove), while not much use back home, can't fail to remind you of all those

Traditional cosmetics

Tunisians use a number of natural products as cosmetics, make-up and grooming aids, and you will see them on sale in markets nationwide, and often in use in the hammam (see p.57). Among natural cosmetics used are:

Chab Alum (aluminium potassium sulphate), a white mineral used as an antiperspirant and to stop shaving cuts bleeding.

Henna Powdered leaves made into a paste and used for conditioning hair, and for colouring hair, hands and feet. The best henna comes from Gabès.

Kohl Eyeliner made from ground antimony trisulphide (stibnite) or lead sulphide – both of which are toxic – sometimes with the addition of other materials.

Suek Walnut bark or root, used for cleaning teeth and reddening lips and gums, giving a slight, and not unpleasant, burning sensation.

Tfal Fine earth used as shampoo and traditionally kept in a container called a *tafalla*. Mixed with rose or orange blossom water, it can be used as a whole-body mudpack. The best *tfal* is said to be from Chebika cups of stewed tea you drank while waiting for louages. Alternatively, you could get a Tunisian **teapot** or a pot for making Turkish coffee, or a *chicha* (water pipe; see p.41). Failing that, esparto mats, used in pressing olives, can be used as table mats or even doormats. Olive oil and *harissa* (see p.38) are almost required purchases and cooks could try their hand at some real Tunisian

cookery with a *couscoussier* (couscous steamer). Spices are widely sold as souvenirs, but be aware that things sold as saffron are in fact safflower or turmeric – real saffron consists of fine red strands with no orange or yellow in it at all, and is rarely if ever available in Tunisia. If you own a car, you could buy some Hand of Fatima stickers to plaster it with.

 # Archeological sites and museums

Tunisian history has left a substantial legacy in the form of religious and other monuments, archeological sites and museums. The authorities are keen to promote Tunisia as more than a cheap beach, and emphasis on Tunisia's monumental heritage has resulted in sights being well maintained and accessible. Be aware, though, that the dominance of organized tourism in Tunisia means that certain mainstream sights are liable to be crowded at peak hours. For information on visiting mosques and other religious buildings, see p.56.

Many of the **lesser sites** out in the country have no entry charge, though almost all have a *gardien* (official guardian), who may be eager to show you around for a tip, and even some of the larger ones are only nominally fenced off, so outside official opening hours you can just walk in.

In the south of the country, there is now a profusion of small **museums of everyday life**, usually housing a motley collection of old pots and pans, household utensils and agricultural implements. These vary from being a waste of time to extremely interest-

ing, and the deciding factor is usually not the exhibits themselves so much as their explanation, which will usually be in French, rarely in English. Occasionally the exhibits are very well labelled, but more often it depends on the enthusiasm of the staff, a factor which can easily change.

In the large towns and tourist centres, something that calls itself a museum may well turn out to be a shop, so don't be surprised if you are sweet-talked into a "museum" (usually of carpets) where all the exhibits are on sale; see p.51 for more.

Cultural hints

As a tourist in Tunisia, you will no doubt be keen to visit mosques and religious buildings, or experience a Turkish bath (hammam). Most mosques are in fact closed to non-Muslims, but if you are allowed to visit a religious building, there are certain rules you should observe; for background on mosque architecture, see p.513. A visit to a hammam can be a little daunting for the first time, but it's an experience not to be missed and you'll soon get the hang of it.

Even though Tunisia is rather less strict than other Arab countries, **sex roles** and the division of labour are much more clearly defined in Tunisia than in the West, because of the importance of sexual segregation in Islam. Consequently male and female visitors will probably have somewhat different experiences of Tunisia. In general, it is much easier for travellers of both sexes to meet Tunisian men than Tunisian women, and Tunisian people may express surprise at seeing women travelling independently.

For some tips on table manners, see p.38.

Visiting Islamic buildings

When it comes to religious monuments still in use, the general rule in Tunisia – in contrast to Egypt or Turkey, say – is that **non-Muslims** may not enter at all. The reason for this is that a mosque is an area set aside for praying, and should not be used for any other purpose. Mosques are ritually clean and no one is supposed to enter the prayer hall without washing hands, feet, eyes, ears, nose, mouth and head in a specifically pre-

scribed manner, and removing their shoes; women are not supposed to enter a mosque during menstruation.

However there are a few major mosques and religious buildings where, during strictly regulated hours, non-Muslims can legitimately enter the complex but not the prayer hall; the same limited access may be granted to non-Muslims at one or two additional sites if accompanied by a local guide. Where non-Muslims are access to the mosque courtyard, they are expected to respect the religious nature of the building and to dress appropriately (see box, below). Mosques that are disused (one or two on the island of Jerba for example) can also be visited by non-Muslims.

It's a bad idea to try to visit mosques against the will of local people, as religion is taken very seriously here. Muslims may of course enter any mosque freely, though you may be challenged to demonstrate that you are Muslim if you do not look it.

Zaouias, also called marabouts, the tombs of holy men (see p.515), are slightly different

---

Appropriate dress

Especially for women, but also for men, Islam advocates **modest dress**, which basically means not showing too much bare flesh. Of course, you are not expected to lie on the beach fully clothed, but you should not wander round town – especially not in small towns or villages – in a swimsuit or bare-chested, nor in shorts or short skirts. Many Tunisians, especially older people, can feel seriously intimidated or affronted by scantily dressed tourists.

A woman entering a **mosque** should be covered from her neck to her ankles and wrists; she should also cover her hair and wear a skirt, not trousers. A man should be covered from over the shoulder to below the knee, so short-sleeved shirts or T-shirts are all right for men, but not singlets or shorts.

Women will find that following the above dress code will reduce sexual harassment, and make it easier to appeal for support from passers-by if it does occur.

in that they are private institutions. Unless Arabic-speaking or Muslim, you're most unlikely to be allowed into a *zaouia* still in use, but many are now either deserted or used as residences. This goes too for **medersas**, Islamic colleges. How much you impose on the occupants of secularized buildings is a personal decision; a courteous enquiry, however, can't do any harm, and many people are only too pleased to show visitors around. One or two *zaouias* are now museums or house the offices of local conservation groups (ASMs) or similar organizations, and are thus open to the public at large.

Hammams

It's difficult to understand the horror of the English woman in the 1850s who wrote that "a Moorish bath is one of the tortures with which the traveller in the East must make acquaintance". A hammam is not only civilization at its most refined, it's also a bargain at around £1/$1.80 for a steam bath, £2–3/$3.50–5.50 with a massage. You could easily pay twenty times as much for the same treatment in the West. Most Tunisians have at least one hammam a week, and for men Friday night at the hammam is the great social gathering.

Like Roman baths of old, hammams consist of a series of rooms gradually getting hotter, with hot and cold water on tap and buckets provided so that you can take and mix as much of each as you want. Not everyone uses soap or shampoo but you're welcome to do so. Older hammams follow a traditional design with a domed roof set with small panes of glass, from which shafts of light shine through the steam. Newer hammams may not be as picturesque, but are likely to be cleaner.

Hammams usually have secure **lockers** in which to leave any valuables. Always remember that total **nudity** is not acceptable in Tunisia – you have to change discreetly, and wrap a linen towel (a *fouta*, which is provided) around your waist. Women can bathe bare-breasted, but should keep knickers on. You might prefer to bring your own towel (big enough to change under) and a pair of shorts, as the authorities periodically ban *foutas* as being unhygienic. Once suitably attired, you head for the hot room to sit in or

around a very hot bath. Before long, people start scratching, using the sweat that's being induced to rub off as much dead skin as possible. If you want to be scrubbed by the masseur/masseuse (*tayyeb/harza*) – who first gives an expert massage, then uses abrasive gloves to remove every last particle of dead skin and dirt – you often have to get a *jeton* (token) at the cash desk. Alternatively, you can buy and use the gloves yourself; the best are made from loofahs. After your bath, you may care to wrap yourself up in several *foutas* and relax for a while in the cooler entrance. To find a hammam, just ask around; hammams tend to be well hidden and usually have signs in Arabic only, if at all ("hammam" is written حمّام in Arabic). Some of them have a distinctive red and green front door. Most hammams have different hours for men and women, with women usually bathing in the afternoon and men in the morning or evening. Sometimes, especially in Tunis, hammams are exclusively for the use either of males or females, and thus accessible all day. One or two beach hotels have mixed hammams that are rather pricey and for tourists only. Bear in mind that in Islam cleanliness is often quite literally next to godliness, and foreigners tend not to be welcome in hammams attached to mosques – which are used for ritual washing before prayer.

Sex and gender issues

For women visitors, the main problem will be **harassment**. Male travellers, too, can expect the occasional **sexual proposition** by Tunisian men; a polite refusal should put an end to the matter. If you find it annoying, remember that women tourists have to put up with far more, and that homosexuality is seen somewhat differently than at home (see p.59). These are symptoms of sexual repression in a society where, officially at least, any kind of sex outside marriage is frowned upon. A straight couple kissing, cuddling or holding hands in public may offend people (even if they don't say so), as may going around skimpily dressed.

Western women and Tunisian men

While some women compare Tunisia favourably with southern Europe, there's no doubt

Beach gigolos

A relatively recent phenomenon in Hammamet, Sousse, Monastir and Jerba is that of the **beach gigolo** scene, known as *beznez*, from the English word "business" and the French word *baiser*, meaning "to screw". Gigolos cruise the beaches looking for punters of either sex who will wine and dine them and give presents of money in return for sex and company. If a beach gigolo attaches himself to you and follows you into a bar or restaurant, he will expect you to pay, so make it clear if you do not intend to. If, on the other hand, you are interested in what they have to offer, be sure to use a condom, as risk of HIV infection from beach gigolos is extremely high.

The phenomenon was highlighted in Nouri Bouzid's 1992 film *Beznez*, which caused something of a stir in France, where journalists even accused Tunisia of having a sex industry akin to that of Manila or Bangkok. This was something of an exaggeration, to say the least, but it has prompted the authorities to clamp down on beach gigolos. Female prostitution is a good deal more discreet, somewhat downmarket and kept well away from tourists.

that general **harassment** is much more commonplace in Tunisia than in northern Europe. It can range from comments as you pass by in the street to persistent chatting, following you or touching; on occasions, however, friendly overtures may suddenly give way to demands for sex. You'll probably face a lot of minor hassles rather than anything seriously threatening, but it can happen with annoying frequency and be fairly persistent when it occurs. If you do feel you're in danger, don't be afraid to ask for help from passers-by or make a scene. No Tunisian man would get away with treating a Tunisian woman in this way; the Arabic word *shooma*, meaning "shame on you!" should – if shouted loudly in a public place – embarrass any man into leaving you alone.

The best solution is to be as **standoffish** as possible, even if your attitude may be misunderstood as an insult – and even if, as occasionally happens, you're accused of racist sexual preferences (this misunderstanding is often deliberately disingenuous). Other tactics to avoid harassment include wearing dark glasses to prevent eye contact (including accidental eye contact on your part), hiding your hair – especially if blonde – in a scarf, and covering arms and legs down to the wrist and the ankle (see box, p.56, for more on dress), which should not only cut down on harassment but also put passers-by more definitely on your side if you do have any trouble. Mentioning a husband waiting for you nearby may also put off someone who looks likely to start.

Also be aware of your body language, and remember that members of opposite sexes do not touch each other in Tunisia, except close family.

Do be aware, however, of the Tunisian male's point of view. It genuinely is difficult for Tunisian men to know where they stand with Western women. In particular, they are often unable to distinguish between ordinary civility and making a pass. There's a cultural difference here: Tunisian women are generally coy or aloof towards men, any other attitude being taken as a come-on (two areas where this is *not* the case are the big cities, notably Tunis and Sfax, where more relaxed sexual attitudes are emerging, and in parts of the far south).

For more in-depth coverage of these issues, three personal accounts by Western women resident in Tunisia are included in the "Women in Tunisia" section in Contexts (see pp.534–542), as is some background on issues facing Tunisian women in modern society.

Western men and Tunisian women

Foreign men should beware of talking to Tunisian women alone, especially in more traditional communities. All might seem well at the time, but the family may regard it as a breach of confidence and afterwards make life difficult for the woman. Male English teachers, for instance, are requested not to talk to female students alone behind a closed door.

Tunisia is not a country where **sexual relations** with local women are likely. You may be able to meet Tunisian women, especially in big cities; you may even be able to take them out, though you can expect dirty looks, and she can expect the occasional hissed insult (this will not be so bad if you are accompanied by other Tunisians as chaperones). But virginity at marriage is far too important for sex to be on the cards. A Tunisian woman caught sharing a hotel room with a Western man, for example, faces very serious trouble indeed, as it's a criminal offence for a Muslim to be caught in a hotel room with a member of the opposite sex other than their spouse, sibling, parent or child. Tunisia is a police state, one where people do keep an eye on each other's comings and goings, and a lot of Tunisian men are likely to be hostile to a Tunisian woman consorting with a foreign man.

Gay and lesbian Tunisia

Because of the sexual segregation endemic to Islam, **homosexual** activity is very widespread (though anal intercourse between men is illegal) but almost nobody considers themselves gay, and gay people are not identified as a group in Tunisian society. Friendships between two members of the same sex are far closer than in the West and much more physical – while it is not usually acceptable in Tunisia for a man and a woman to kiss or hold hands in public, it is perfectly normal for two men or two women to do so.

The less positive aspects are that for a man to be the passive partner during sex has connotations of femininity and weakness and is considered a disgrace, yet no such stigma attaches to the other role, and men will boast quite openly about their prowess in this position. Caution is nonetheless advised, and you should be aware that calls for money or presents in return for sexual favours are more common than sincerity and that blackmail is a possibility.

Gay women are not likely to find any hint of a community in Tunisia. **Lesbianism** is more or less invisible and its existence denied. For foreign women, therefore, the chances of making contact with local lesbians are virtually zilch.

Travellers with specific needs

Travelling in Tunisia may require some extra consideration if you are disabled or travelling with children. Senior citizens may want to travel with members of their own age group, or take tours that cater particularly for older travellers.

Travellers with disabilities

Facilities for people with disabilities are relatively undeveloped in Tunisia, and disabled Tunisians are often reduced to begging, although families are usually very supportive. Blindness is more common than in the West, and sighted Tunisians are generally used to helping blind people find their way and get on and off public transport at the right stop. Wheelchairs, though often ancient, do exist, and access ramps are gradually appearing at the entrances to post offices, museums and other public buildings, though it's a slow process and often tokenistic, as the ramps are quite frequently too steep and narrow to be of much use.

Bus and train **travel** will be difficult because of the steps that have to be negotiated, but louage travel is more feasible if you can stake a claim on the front seat, assuming there is a helper to get you in and out; people will go out of their way to be accommodating. You should also be able to get on and off planes with a lift, but check this with the airline or tour operator.

You're likely to find travelling on a **package tour** much easier than full independence. In the UK, Thomson run a client welfare service (☎020/7391 0170), which can advise people with disabilities on specific travel arrangements with them. Inform any tour operator of your exact needs before making a booking, and make sure you are fully covered by the insurance policy you take out. And use your travel agent to make your journey simpler: airline or bus companies can cope better if they are expecting you, with a wheelchair provided at airports and staff primed to help.

A number of large **hotels**, usually at beach resorts, have ramps and step-free access to some or all areas for the benefit of people in wheelchairs. Many of these are designated as "wheelchair accessible" in this book, but note that even in these hotels, ramps may be steep and narrow, and bathrooms are unlikely to be specifically designed for guests in a wheelchair; you may not be able to enter the bathroom with a wheelchair, still less manoeuvre it once inside. You should check therefore that a hotel can meet your specific needs before booking. If you use a wheelchair, you will probably not be able to stay at cheap city centre ones, which tend to have steep staircases and narrow corridors.

Accessible accommodation

Hotels in the following locations make some provision for disabled travellers, as do several hotels in Sousse (see pp.222–223) and Douz (see p.381).

Borj Cedria (Greater Tunis; see p.133) *Médisea* ☎71 293 030, ℉71 430 013, ⓦwww .mediseahotel.com.

Gabès (see pp.396–398) *Chems* ☎75 270 547, ℉75 274 485, ⓦwww.hotelchems.com.tn; *Rahma* ☎75 275 385.

Hammamet (see p.143) *Nafrawess* ☎72 288 077, ⓔnafrawess@planet.tn; *Sheraton* ☎72 280 555, ⓦwww.sheraton.com.

Jerba (see p.428) *Djerba Beach* ☎75 731 200, ℉75 730 357, ⓦiberostar.com.

Kebili (see p.377) *Oasis Dar Kebili* ☎75 491 436.

Kerkennah (see p.284) *Cercina* ☎74 489 600, ⓔhotel.cercina@planet.tn. The Sfax–Kerkennah ferry also has wheelchair access.

Matmata (see p.405) *Kouseila* ☎75 240 303.

Monastir (see p.240) *Festival* ☎73 467 555; *Kuriat Palace* ☎73 521 200, ⓔkuriat.palace@gnet.tn.

Nabeul (see p.147) *Le Prince* ☎72 285 470.

Port el Kantaoui (see p.235) *Imperial Marhaba* ☎73 246 477, ⓔimperial.marhaba@planet.tn.

Tunis (see p.81) *Sheraton* ☎71 782 800, ⓦwww. sheraton.com.

Zarzis (see p.444) *Zarzis* ☎75 684 160, ℉75 694 292; ⓔzarzis.hotel@planet.tn.

Contacts for travellers with disabilities

UK and Ireland

Holiday Care 2nd Floor, Imperial Building, Victoria Rd, Horley, Surrey RH6 7PZ ☎0845/124 9971, minicom ☎0845/124 9976, ⓦwww.holidaycare .org.uk. Provides an information sheet on North Africa, including a brief list of accessible accommodation in Tunisia. Information on financial help for holidays available.

Irish Wheelchair Association Blackheath Drive, Clontarf, Dublin 3 ☎01/818 6400, ⓦwww.iwa.ie. Useful information provided about travelling abroad with a wheelchair.

Tripscope Alexandra House, Albany Rd, Brentford, Middlesex TW8 0NE ☎0845/7585 641, ⓦwww .tripscope.org.uk. This registered charity provides a national telephone information service offering free advice on UK and international transport for people with mobility problems.

US and Canada

Directions Unlimited 123 Green Lane, Bedford Hills, NY 10507 ☎1-800/533-5343 or 914/241-1700. Travel agency specializing in bookings for people with disabilities.

Mobility International USA 451 Broadway, Eugene, OR 97401 ☎541/343-1284, ⓦwww.miusa.org. Information and referral services, access guides, tours and exchange programmes. Annual membership $35 (includes quarterly newsletter).

Australia and New Zealand

ACROD (Australian Council for Rehabilitation of the Disabled) PO Box 60, Curtin ACT 2605; Suite 103, first floor, 1–5 Commercial Rd, Kings Grove 2208; ☎02/6282 4333, TTY ☎02/6282 4333, ⓦwww.acrod.org.au. Provides lists of travel agencies and tour operators for people with disabilities.

Disabled Persons Assembly 4/173–175 Victoria St, Wellington, New Zealand ☎04/801 9100 (also TTY), ⓦwww.dpa.org.nz. Resource centre with lists of travel agencies and tour operators for people with disabilities.

In Tunisia

Association Générale des Insuffisants Moteurs (AGIM) 1 Rue des Bassatines, BP 233, Khaznadar, 2000 Bardo, Tunis ☎ 71 612 687, ⓕ 71 612 920, ⓦ www.iph.nat.tn/association .asp?AssID=3. Tunisia's main organization for people with disablities, with branches nationwide.

Senior travellers

Sedate, quiet and safe, Tunisia is a popular destination for older travellers. A number of package tours are geared especially to the needs of older travellers, offering the opportunity to travel and meet up with people of your own age group.

You'll generally be treated with respect by young Tunisians. In Tunisia, age is associated not so much with frailty and vulnerability as with wisdom and a lifetime of input into the family and the community. Older members of the family generally continue to live with their children (usually sons), care for their grandchildren and strongly influence family decisions. There are no state and few private pensions, so social security is a family responsibility.

If you are going for a sightseeing package tour, it is a good idea to check on the pace of the itinerary, and how much free time and relaxation there will be. Highly recommended are the usually twice-yearly art and archeology tours run by firms like Prospect and Andante. Mercian Travel's bridge and bowling holidays in Port el Kantaoui may also appeal to some (see p.12 for contact details).

Contacts for senior travellers

Elderhostel US & Canada ☎ 1/877-426-8056, ⓦ www.elderhostel.org. Tours for over-60s, including occasional programmes in Tunisia.
Saga Holidays UK ☎ 0800/096 0078 or ☎ 01303 771190, ⓦ www.saga.co.uk; US & Canada ☎ 1-800/343-0273, ⓦ www.sagaholidays.com. The biggest and most established specialist in holidays aimed at over-50s, they have some beach holidays in Tunisia.

Travelling with children

Tunisians, even more than other Mediterranean people, love kids. Travelling with small children in Tunisia, you may find that people will frequently come up to admire them, to compliment you on them and to caress them, which may be uncomfortable for shyer offspring. Children are very important, and numerous, in Tunisian society, and people are not really considered complete adults until they have at least one child. In Tunisian families, children stay up late until they fall asleep and are spoiled rotten by older family members. The streets are pretty safe and even quite small children walk to school unaccompanied or play in the street unsupervised.

Hotels in Tunisia usually give a reduction of thirty to forty percent for children aged under 8 or 10, though this varies with each hotel and you may have to negotiate. You won't find baby changing rooms in airports, hotels or restaurants, and will have to be discreet if breastfeeding – find a quiet corner and shield infant and breast from view with a light cloth over your shoulder. Beach hotels often have facilities such as playgrounds and children's pools; city hotels are far less likely to cater specifically for children.

Children may well enjoy a number of things that we have not particularly recommended for adults, notably calèche rides and the tourist Noddy trains found in resorts (see p.33). Short camel rides (see p.50) should also go down well. Buckets and spades are now available at some shops in big beach resorts, but **toys** in general are poor quality, expensive and in short supply, so bring along any you may need.

Disposable nappies – Peaudouce is the commonest brand – are available at most pharmacies at prices similar to what you pay at home. You may want to take along some **dried baby food**; any café can supply hot water. Bear in mind that Tunisian food can be very spicy, and you will probably want them to hold back on the harissa when serving your children. **Baby cots**, when supplied, tend to have low bars, making it easy for the more determined infant to get out. **Child car seats**, when available, are likely to be most uncomfortable unless you pad them well with something soft.

In the US, Travel With Your Children, 40 Fifth Ave, New York, NY 10011 (☎212/477 5524 or 1-888/822-4388), publish a regular newsletter, *Family Travel Times* (ⓦwww .familytraveltimes.com), as well as a series of books on travel with children including *Great Adventure Vacations With Your Kids*. You may want to try a holiday with Club Med (ⓦ www.clubmed.com), whose purpose-built holiday resorts at Nabeul, Monastir and Aghir (Jerba) feature kids' clubs, entertain- ment and sports facilities on site. Panorama (see p.12) runs kids' clubs at three hotels at Hammamet, the Kerkennah Islands and Port el Kantaoui, which are also open to children booked on Panorama holidays at other hotels in the same resort.

Directory

Cigarettes Tunisian brands are cheap but rough, with 20 Mars strong, Caravanes medium and Cristal milder. Western brands, widely available, cost about four times as much.

Clothes Two things to bear in mind are the heat, especially in the desert, and the modesty demanded by Islam (see box on p.56). You will certainly want a light sunhat, especially in summer, and light, loose-fitting cotton clothes. In winter, especially in the north, you will want at least one warm sweater.

Contraceptives Known as *préservatifs*, condoms are available from most pharmacies in large towns, but ones brought from home are more reliable. Some brands of the Pill (*la pilule*) are also available, but remember that if you get diarrhoea, oral contraceptives may not stay in your system long enough to be absorbed.

Electricity Generally 220V, 50Hz, as in continental Europe, with double round-pin sockets. British, Irish and Australasian plugs will need an adaptor; American and Canadian appliances will need a transformer too, unless multi-voltage. One or two old places, especially in Tunis, still have a 110V supply – check before plugging in.

Emergencies Police ☎197; Fire brigade (*Protection civile*) ☎198; Ambulance 190.

Laundry There are very few self-service laundries, but a few towns have places which do washing by weight. Tourist hotels usually have an (expensive) in-house service; other hotels may be able to arrange something. Dry cleaners ("pressings") are quite common, but are obviously an expensive way to get your socks and undies washed (and some may refuse to wash those in fact).

Left luggage Large train stations take left luggage (ask for the *consigne*), and many hotels have a safe room where you can leave belongings while you are away. Tourist offices may also be able to help for a short period of time, and although bus and louage stations do not have left luggage facilities, staff or local cafés may be willing to keep an eye on your baggage for you while you wander around town between buses – often just as a favour, without charge.

Photography Avoid taking photographs of government buildings, people in uniform, airports or anything even vaguely military. If in doubt, ask first or you may end up having your camera confiscated. For photography in museums, you are supposed to buy a separate ticket to your entry ticket, and tripods (and any other professional-looking equipment, including sometimes a flash) can only be used with special authorization (write to the Institut National d'Archéologie, Dar Husayn, Tunis). Most of the major brands of camera film are widely available in Tunisia, but slide film isn't easy to come by outside large towns. Videotape for cameras is expensive, where available.

Stoves Camping gas stoves are widely available, but the refills (*cartouches*) much less so. Ironmongers (*quincailleries*) and supermarkets should stock them, but supplies are sporadic. Street sellers sometimes have them when the shops have run out. In Tunis, rue al Jazira is the place to look

– especially place Cheikh el Bourzouli. Much more sensible is to take a spirit stove, since burning alcohol (*alcool à brûler*) is widely available at hardware shops. A petrol stove is also a possibility, though somewhat messier.

Time Tunisia is on GMT+1 all year round, which means that, when daylight saving time is not in effect in countries further north or south, Tunisia is an hour ahead of Britain and Ireland, six hours ahead of the US East Coast (EST), ten hours ahead of the West Coast (PST), seven hours behind Western Australia, ten hours behind east Australia and eleven hours behind New Zealand. Daylight Saving Time in those places will, however, vary the difference by an hour. Crossing from France or Italy, there is no time difference in winter, but you will have to put your watch back an hour in summer. Flying from Britain, on the other hand, there is no time difference in summer, but you will have to put your watch forward an hour in winter.

Tipping In smarter hotels and restaurants tipping follows Western practice: service is often included, and ten to fifteen percent is the standard tip for waiters (and it's worth tipping the waiter directly, or they may not see much of what you leave). Porters and chambermaids expect something, depending on the price bracket of the hotel and the length of your stay. Café waiters usually get a 0.1TD tip. Taxi drivers do not necessarily get a tip, but always appreciate one. Baksheesh is also expected for small services

such as loading your baggage onto buses or finding you a place in a louage.

Toilet paper For reasons that soon become apparent, it's a good idea to carry a stock of toilet paper around with you – it can be bought in most towns. An alternative is to use the Tunisian method – water and left hand – especially in crouching as opposed to sit-down toilets; both types are common, with sit-down toilets standard in most hotels and certainly in all tourist-oriented places.

Work and study A work permit is officially required for all foreign citizens working in Tunisia: with the economy in its present state, permits are hard to come by. English teaching is expanding rapidly, though: try contacting the British Council (Wwww .britishcouncil.org), or the Institut Bourguiba des Langues Vivantes, 47 av de la Liberté, 1002 Belvédère, Tunis (T71 832 418 or 923, Wwww.iblv.rnu.tn). Private conversation classes are sometimes possible to arrange on an informal (and illegal) basis. For almost anything else you will need at least competent French, but because the tourist industry is so highly organized there's little of the fringe market found elsewhere. As regards courses, the Institut Bourguiba offers lessons in Tunisian and standard Arabic. You can opt for a four-week intensive Arabic course (July; 380TD), with the possibility of renting accommodation in the university (80TD for the duration), or a non-intensive course (4hr per week during the academic year).

Guide

Guide

Tunis and around

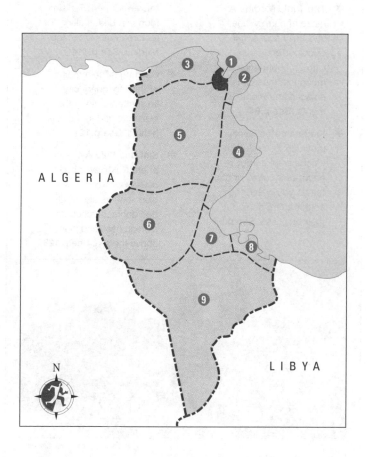

hlights

...e
...the
...t for
...and
...g up in
all sorts of ...pected
places. **See p.84**

✱ **The Tunis Medina** A
maze of narrow lanes
and busy souks, full
of colour and noise,
with an abundance of
mosques, museums,
palaces and monu-
ments. **See p.84**

✱ **Medina cafés** Gently
mouldering, thick with
chicha smoke, they're
great for a coffee or mint
tea as you watch the
souk traders go about
their business. **See p.95**

✱ **The Bardo Museum**
One of the world's finest
collections of Roman
mosaics, housed in a
grand seventeenth-cen-
tury palace. **See p.107**

✱ **The Dar el Jeld res-
taurant** Superb Tunisian
food in a beautifully
restored mansion in the
Medina. **See p.114**

✱ **Carthage** The remains
of this legendary city
lie scattered along the
seashore and in the hills
behind. **See p.121**

✱ **Sidi Bou Said** A cluster
of pretty whitewashed
houses with cornflower
blue shutters and stud-
ded doors, perched on
a steep headland high
above the sea. **See p.128**

△ The Tunis Cathedral

1

Tunis and around

TUNIS is very much a capital city: the city and its environs are home to around a sixth of Tunisia's population, the base of government and power, and the centre of virtually all that happens in the country. On first impressions it's not that attractive, as the old colonial centre becomes increasingly submerged by indistinguishable suburbs, and the streets have a rather Westernized air. But stay a few days and you'll find some allure behind this unexceptional facade. Few package tours include Tunis, and day-trippers from the beaches tend to confine themselves to one or two standard streets and monuments in the old Arab town of the **Medina**. The rest is left to the people of Tunis and anyone else who cares to explore the narrow lanes, busy markets and unrestored monuments, including huge mosques, religious schools and impressive crumbling palaces.

The Medina shelters monuments spanning one thousand years of Arab and Turkish endowment, and the French-built **New Town**, lying between the

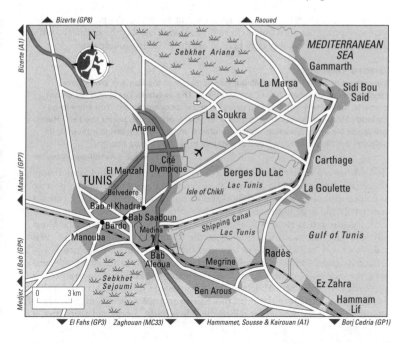

Market days

Thursday Ezzahra (by Lycée Ezzahra train station)
Friday Ariana (northern terminus of metro line #2)
Sunday Hammam Lif

small hills of Belvedere Park to the north and Jellaz cemetery to the south, has a period value of its own. These distinct phases of the city's development are intricately linked in a manner which is symbolic of Tunisia's ability to blend cultures. Moving from ninth-century mosque to eighteenth-century Turkish palace to nineteenth-century French boulevard seems almost a natural progression.

Away from the centre, but easily reached by public transport, are three more major attractions. The **Bardo Museum**, housed in a former regent's palace, has one of the finest collections of Roman mosaics anywhere in the world, best visited before seeing the Roman sites elsewhere in the country. In the other direction, overlooking the Gulf of Carthage, are the remains of **Carthage**, ancient Great Power and the enemy of Rome, and a little further in the same direction, the picturesque resort of **Sidi Bou Saïd**. Carthage can be somewhat underwhelming: the Roman invaders and then time itself were such thorough conquerors that you have to go prepared to use your imagination to a large extent. On the other hand, the views over the turquoise gulf – especially those from Sidi Bou Saïd – easily make up for any disappointment.

Any free time in Tunis can be used up on a trip to the other, less well-known, suburbs. **La Goulette**, with its Spanish fort and fish restaurants, and **Hammam Lif**, nestling below Jebel Bou Kornine – the mountain which stands guard at the bottom of the gulf – both make for worthwhile outings. The gulf shore, north from La Goulette and south from Radès, is virtually one beach, but not a very pleasant one – the proximity of Tunis and the port at La Goulette obviously has an adverse effect on the water quality. Alternatively, with Tunis as your base, almost anywhere in northern Tunisia is accessible.

Some history

We arrived at Tunis, object of all our hopes, focus of the flame of every gaze, rendezvous of travellers from East and West. This is where fleets and caravans come to meet. Here you will find everything a man could desire. You want to go by land? Here are endless companions for your journey. You prefer the sea? Here are boats for every direction. Tunis is a crown whose every jewel is a district, its suburbs are like a flower-garden constantly refreshed by the breeze.

El Abdari, thirteenth-century traveller

Tunis is rooted firmly in an Arab medieval past. For a thousand years before the establishment of Islam, it was an insignificant neighbour of the port of Carthage (although founded earlier) and its only historic role was as a base for invaders laying siege to the larger city. The Arabs, however, preferred Tunis's less exposed site, and as early as the ninth century the **Aghlabids** built the Great Mosque that still stands at the heart of the Medina. In the last years of their rule, from 894 to 909 AD, Tunis served as the Aghlabid imperial capital.

Largely ignored by the **Fatimids**, who ruled from Mahdia in the tenth century, the city really came into its own following the **Hilalian** invasion of the eleventh century, when Abdelhaq Ibn Khourassane established a principality here. Amid the chaos of the time, this **Khourassanid** state was such an island of stability that by the time it fell to the **Almohads**, a hundred years later, it had become the country's natural power centre. When the **Hafsid** complete independence in 1236, it was a capital once again.

Under the Hafsids, and especially after the fall of Baghdad to the Mongo 1258, Tunis became the western Arab world's leading metropolis, a great Medi terranean marketplace at a time of expanding trade between Christian Europe and the Muslim East. Culture flourished in the cosmopolitan atmosphere, and the university in the Great Mosque – the Zitouna Mosque – was rivalled only by those of al-Azhar in Cairo and the Kairaouine at Fez in Morocco. The Hafsids' own building programme included the first *medersas*, or Islamic colleges, many of the purpose-built souks, or markets, around the Great Mosque, the Kasbah with its mosque, and the city walls.

As Arab rule wavered before the **Ottoman Turks**, Tunis changed in appearance – becoming enclosed by fortifications – and in character, as a more foreign-dominated era emerged. Wealth from trade and piracy poured into the city, financing the building of more mosques, *medersas* and palaces. Christian traders were allowed to settle, and since many of the "Turkish" officials ruling the new **regency** were *mamelukes* (slaves of Greek or Eastern European origin taken as children), several of the buildings and even a few mosques have a strong European flavour.

Until the nineteenth century, Tunis still consisted essentially of the **Medina** and faubourgs – poor districts outside the walls – with a few elaborate palaces, such as the Bardo, set in gardens further away. But by the 1860s, several thousand European traders and advisers were living in Tunis and their presence was influential. The International Financial Commission set up by the colonial powers virtually ran the government, and newly found wealth gave merchants considerable power over the impoverished Beys, or Ottoman rulers. At this time a new European city – the **New Town**, or Ville Nouvelle – began to develop outside the city walls, and with the **French occupation** in 1881 the French set about draining the marshy land on the edge of the lake to extend this colonial domain. Today its wide avenues, jammed with traffic and beginning to crumble, still feel thoroughly *belle époque*, with their pavement cafés, iron balconies and fancy stuccowork.

Arrival, information and city transport

Tunis lies on the shore of the large, shallow **Lac Tunis**, which stretches between the town and the Gulf of Tunis. Along the gulf shore, north and south of the narrow entrance to the lake, stretches a chain of suburbs easily reached by public transport from the city centre. An independent light train line, the **TGM** (Tunis–Goulette–Marsa), crosses the lake on a causeway to the northern shore's suburbs, which include **Carthage** and **Sidi Bou Saïd**. A mainline train runs to the less attractive southern suburbs of **Radès**, **Hammam Lif** and **Borj Cedria**.

In the city itself, orientation couldn't be simpler. **Avenue Bourguiba**, the great central artery, flanked by ministries, smart hotels and shops, and divided by a tree-lined promenade, links the **Medina** in the west with the lake in the east. On either side stretches the grid plan of the French-built **New Town**, bounded by the hilltop **Belvedere Park** to the north and the sprawling **Jellaz Cemetery** to the south. Everything in this central area is within easy walking distance and, with the exception of the **Bardo Museum**, there's little to be seen in the straggling suburbs to the west.

declared

...nations and journey times, see Travel details on p.133. Note that ...show exchange or ATM receipts if you buy an international air or ...cash in Tunisia.

...rport (☏71 754 000) you can take bus #35 or #635 from Tunis Marine ...8.30pm; 30min) or the more comfortable private TUT buses from avenue Bourguiba, just east of place 7 Novembre. By taxi the journey costs 2.5–7TD depending on the time of day and traffic. The confusingly named Aeroport Station on the TGM line from Tunis Marine to La Marsa has nothing to do with the airport. Note also that the **duty-free shop** at the airport only takes hard currency, so don't save any dinars to spend in it. For airline offices, see Listings, p.117. *Le Temps* and *La Presse* list flight departure times.

By sea

If you're leaving Tunis by **sea**, get off at Goulette Vieille on the TGM line heading to La Marsa, and follow the track back for 200m to the main road, turn left and continue for some 300m, past the Kasbah (on your left) until you come to a roundabout. Turn right here and then at the mini-roundabout follow the road to the left past the CTN building and on round to the ferry terminal (☏71 735 932). Services run to Sicily, Sardinia, Malta and mainland Italy, and less frequently to mainland France. Consult the "Agenda" section of *Le Temps* for departures; for ferry company addresses, see p.17. In the summer, things can get hectic at the **ticket offices** (addresses on p.17), so it's wise to leave plenty of time for queueing, or get your ticket in Bizerte, Sousse or Sfax instead.

By train

The **train** service is pretty good along the coast, especially to the south of Tunis, but much less comprehensive once you head inland. To secure a seat, it's a good idea to turn up at the train station (☏71 334 444) an hour or so before departure to stake your claim as soon as the train arrives. Staff at its information desk hand out accurate timetables for all of Tunisia's passenger services.

By bus or louage

Buses leave Bab Saadoun (☏71 562 532) and Bab Aleoua (☏71 399 440) regularly, though during Ramadan services are greatly reduced. With few exceptions (some long-distance buses to Jerba and the Jerid), departures are during daylight hours. There are also direct services to Libya and Algeria.

  Louages (see opposite for station locations) depart from about 4am until about 6pm (the later departures are mostly local); it's better to start earlier the further your destination. One or two important destinations (such as Sfax) have louages all night, but waiting for them to fill can take a long time in the small hours.

  If you're considering crossing the Algerian border, note the warning on p.209.

The main **ONTT tourist office** is the eastern end of avenue Bourguiba, at 1 avenue MohamedV (Mon–Sat 8am–6pm, Sun 9am–noon; ☏71 341 077, ⓦwww.tourismtunisia.com), and can supply you with free maps and booklets as well a list of hotels and their prices, but that's about all.There are also tourist offices at the airport, port (☏71 738 688) and train station (☏71 241 858).

By air

Tunis Carthage Airport is a fifteen-minute drive northeast of the centre, 8km away on the shore of the lake, and has a tourist office (☏71 755 000), a

number of exchange bureaux, several travel agencies which offer
modation booking service, and **car rental** firms. The exchange bureau
baggage hall is supposedly 24-hour, and there are two **ATMs** in the air
one next to the tourist office and the other at the opposite end of the arrival
hall, past the car rental agencies.

The easiest way into the centre from the airport is by yellow **taxi**, which
should cost less than 4TD during the day or as much as 7TD at night – if you're
heading to La Marsa or Gammarth, the fares are slightly higher. Otherwise, the
#35 and #635 yellow **buses** both leave from the airport (straight ahead and to
the left as you leave the terminal) between 6.30am and 8.30pm, taking around
half an hour to reach the Tunis Marine bus station on avenue Bourguiba; other
drop-off points are the bottom of avenue Habib Thameur where it meets
avenue Bourguiba, and place Palestine, behind the République métro station.
Private TUT buses (white with blue and yellow stripes) also serve the centre
of town from the airport, finishing up opposite the ONTT office.

By sea
Ferries from around the Mediterranean dock at **La Goulette**, a port in the
city's eastern suburbs over the other side of Lake Tunis. The cheapest way into
town is by TGM train. To find the TGM, come out of the ferry terminal, go
straight ahead past the customs office and restaurants and follow the road
round to the left, until you reach the large Compagnie Tunisienne de Navigation building. Bear right at the mini-roundabout, then left at the bigger one
just afterwards and head down the straight road past the Kasbah (on your
right) and the city gate. After another 300m or so you will reach the TGM
line: turn right here and the station is 200m ahead. If your baggage is heavy,
you can always take a taxi to the TGM station – there will be a number of
them waiting at the port. With your own car, head for the TGM but instead of
turning right for the station, cross the line and take a left across the causeway
into town.

By train, bus or louage
Tunis's mainline **train station** is on place Barcelone, right at the centre of the
main hotel area, south of avenue Bourguiba, and is served by all métro lines.
Both the intercity **bus terminals** – **Bab Saadoun**, for the north of the country, and **Bab Aleoua** (also called Bab el Fellah), for the centre and south – are
well connected to the centre. Bab Saadoun (served by métro lines #3, #4 and
#5) is some 3km northwest of the train station, while Bab Aleoua (line #1)
is south of place Barcelone. City buses #72 and #78 run frequently between
the two terminals, though they stop by the Bab Saadoun city gate rather than
outside the northern bus terminal.

Louages from the north and northwest arrive outside **Bab Saadoun** bus
station; those from Hammamet and Cap Bon terminate opposite **Bab Aleoua**
bus station; while all other domestic louages use the **Moncef Bey** station, in
a vast hangar adjacent to Souk Moncef Bey, fifteen minutes' walk south of
avenue Bourguiba. International louages from Libya and Algeria have their
main stops at **Garage Ayachi** at Bab Souika (Libya) and **rue al Jazira**, just off
place de la Victoire (Algeria).

City transport

Walking isn't just the most interesting way of getting around the city centre.
In summer, when the traffic seizes up and the atmosphere in the buses is as

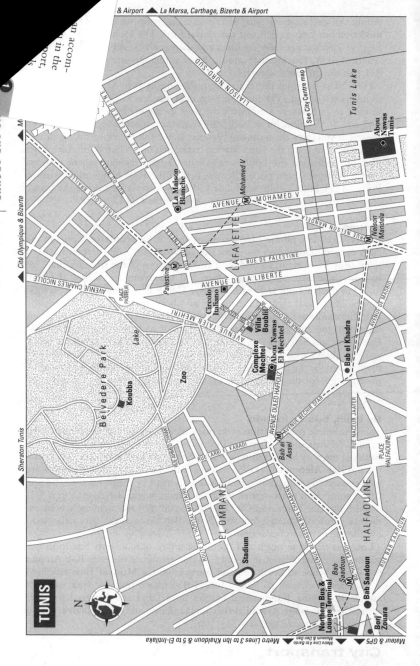

TUNIS

N

Tunis Lake

See City Centre map

Abou Nawas Tunis

La Maison Blanche

AVENUE Mohamed V Ⓜ MOHAMED V

Nelson Mandela

RUE DE PALESTINE

AVENUE DE LA LIBERTÉ

Palestine Ⓜ

Circolo Italiano

Villa Boubili

Complexe Mechtel

Abou Nawas El Mechtel

Bab el Khadra

AVENUE DE MADRID

AVENUE CHARLES NICOLLE

PLACE PASTEUR

Belvedere Park

Lake

Zoo

Koubba

AVENUE OULED HAFFOUZ

RUE NACEUR JAAFER

PLACE HALFAOUINE

Bab el Assel Ⓜ

RUE LARBI EL KABADI

RUE DE L'HOPITAL MILITAIRE

EL OMRANE

Stadium

HALFAOUINE

RUE BAB SAADOUN

Bab Saadoun Ⓜ

Northern Bus & Louage Terminal

Bab Saadoun

Borj Zouara

Bab el Khadra

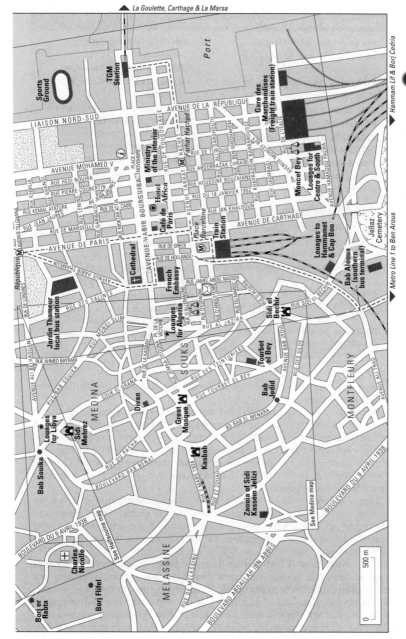

Useful bus routes and metro stations

#4a Jardin Thameur–Manouba

#5, #5c & #5d Tunis Marine–
Belvedere Park

#16b, #42 & #42a Belhouane–Tebourba

#20b Jardin Thameur–Gammarth

#20c Jardin Thameur–Carthage

#23 Jardin Thameur–Borj El Amri

#23a, #23b, #23c, #23d, #23t Jardin
Thameur–Bardo

#26a & #26b Barcelone–Mornag

#27 & #27b Rabt 10 Decembre–El
Menzah–Raoued

#31b Place Belhouane–Kalaat El
Andalous

#35 & #635 Tunis Marine–Airport

#44 Place Belhouane–Kalaat El
Andalous

#52 La Marsa (Ennassin)–Gammarth

#72 & #78 These connect the two
intercity bus terminals at Bab
Saadoun and Bab Aleoua

#116 Barcelone–Tebourba

Useful metro stations

Bab Aleoua (line #1) southern
intercity bus station and louages for
Hammamet and Cap Bon

Bab el Khadra (lines #3, #4 and #5)
Halfaouine

Bab Saadoun (lines #3, #4 and #5)
northern intercity bus and louage
station

Barcelone (all lines) Train station and
main métro interchange

Bardo (line #4) Bardo Museum

Cité Sportive (line #2) Olympic
swimming pool

Jeunesse (line #2) football ground

Palestine (line #2) Belvedere Park

République (lines #2, #3, #4 and
#5) Métro interchange, Habib
Thameur local bus station

Tunis Marine (line #1) TGM station

steamy as in any hammam, it's often the quickest and most comfortable way to get somewhere.

Bus rides in the city generally cost around 0.3TD, and tickets are purchased from a conductor as you enter the rear door of the bus. If you plan to do a lot of travelling by bus, you can buy a book of tickets from the office at the Tunis Marine bus station at the end of avenue Bourguiba, near the TGM station, but there is no discount. The other main urban **bus stations** are at Jardin Thameur (500m north of the western end of av Bourguiba) and at place Barcelone (outside the métro station).

Tunis's **métro** system is actually more of a tramway, running down the middle of the street and obeying traffic lights. Outside rush hours and lunchtime, it's not as frequent as it might be, but it is much easier to master than the bus system and costs about the same. Tickets are bought from kiosks at the stations.

The central Tunis **TGM station** is at the port end of avenue Bourguiba, next to Tunis Marine bus and métro (line #1) stations. Trains from here run every twelve minutes or so across Lake Tunis, linking the city with La Goulette, Carthage, Sidi Bou Saïd and La Marsa, at the end of the line and around 35 minutes away. Services run from about 4am to 1am. A suburban overland train line runs every ten to twenty minutes from place Barcelone station to Radès (20min), Hammam Lif (30min) and Borj Cedria (45min).

Taxis in Tunis are hailed in the street in the conventional way, and are metered. By day you'll rarely pay more than 2TD for a ride in the city centre. Between 9pm and 6am rates go up by fifty percent.

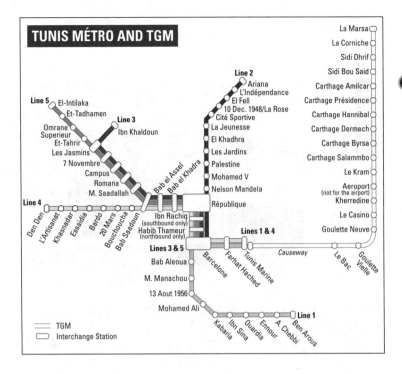

TUNIS MÉTRO AND TGM

La Marsa
La Corniche
Sidi Dhrif
Sidi Bou Saïd
Carthage Amilcar
Carthage Présidence
Carthage Hannibal
Carthage Dermech
Carthage Byrsa
Carthage Salammbo
Le Kram
Aeroport (not for the airport)
Kherredine
Le Casino
Goulette Neuve

Line 5 — El-Intilaka
Et-Tadhamen
Line 3
Omrane Superieur
Et-Tahrir
Les Jasmins
7 Novembre
Campus
Romana
M. Saadallah
Ibn Khaldoun

Line 2
Ariana
L'Indépendance
El Fell
10 Dec. 1948/La Rose
Cité Sportive
La Jeunesse
El Khadhra
Les Jardins
Palestine
Mohamed V
Nelson Mandela
République

Bab el Assel
Bab el Khadra

Line 4
Den Den
L'Artisanat
Khasnadar
Essaidia
Bardo
20 Mars
Bouchoucha
Bab Saadoun

Ibn Rachig (southbound only)
Habib Thameur (northbound only)

Lines 3 & 5
Bab Aleoua
M. Manachou
13 Aout 1956
Mohamed Ali

Lines 1 & 4

Barcelone
Farhat Hached
Tunis Marine

Causeway

Le Bac
Goulette Vielle

Line 1
Kabaria
Ibn Sina
Ouardia
Ennour
A. Chebbi
Ben Arous

TGM
Interchange Station

Accommodation

The ONTT is of limited use in finding **accommodation**; though they provide a list of hotels, they're unable to handle bookings. Many travel agencies – particularly those at the airport – offer a booking service, usually for the more expensive, classified hotels, with a few selected one-star choices at the lower end of the scale. But if you haven't booked from home, the best way to find a room is just to start walking.

Central Tunis has dozens of cheap hotels, though in midsummer the more popular ones tend to fill up disconcertingly quickly and it's wise to start looking as early as possible. Most of the **mid-range hotels** are located on or just to the south of avenue Bourguiba, while the classiest joints tend to be a bit further out of the centre. At the height of the season a few hotels let people sleep on the roof, which is cheaper than having a room and makes the humidity more bearable, though note that it's also illegal. The only real alternative to a hotel is the rather good **youth hostel** in the Medina – again, try to book ahead.

The New Town

The densest concentration of hotels – though they're also the most likely to be full – lies in the French **New Town**, between the Medina and avenue de Carthage, which cuts across avenue Bourguiba about halfway down. Most of these are mid-range to luxury, with a few cheaper dives scattered among them. All the hotels below are keyed on the City Centre map (pp.78–79), except for

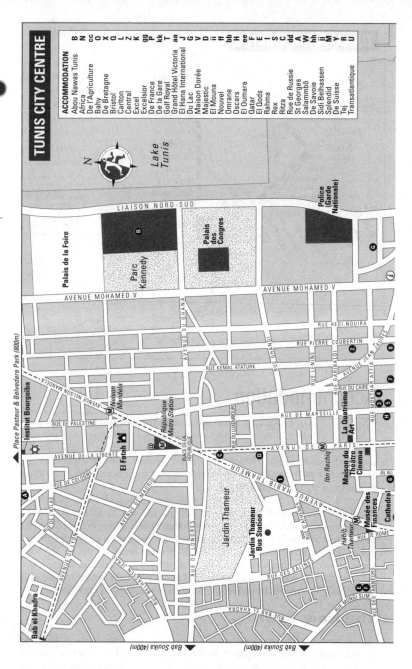

TUNIS CITY CENTRE

Lake Tunis

N

ACCOMMODATION

Abou Nawas Tunis	B
Africa	N
De l'Agriculture	cc
Bahy	O
De Bretagne	X
Bristol	Q
Carlton	L
Central	Z
Excel	K
Excelsior	gg
De France	P
De la Gare	kk
Golf Royal	T
Grand Hôtel Victoria	aa
El Hana International	J
Du Lac	G
Maison Dorée	V
Majestic	D
El Mouna	ii
Nouvel	ff
Omrane	bb
Oscars	H
El Oumara	ee
Qatar	F
El Qods	E
Rahma	I
Rex	S
Ritza	C
Rue de Russie	dd
St Georges	A
Salammbô	W
De Savoie	hh
Sidi Belhassen	jj
Splendid	M
De Suisse	Y
Tej	R
Transatlantique	U

Palais de la Foire

Parc Kennedy

Palais des Congrès

LIAISON NORD-SUD

Police (Garde Nationale)

Place Pasteur & Belvedere Park (800m)

AVENUE MOHAMED V

AVENUE MOHAMED V

RUE HEDI NOUIRA

RUE PIERRE COUBERTIN

RUE KEMAL ATATURK

AVENUE DU GHANA

RUE GHANDI

RUE LENINE

RUE GARIBALDI

AVENUE JEAN JAURES

RUE DU CAIRE

RUE DE MARSEILLE

RUE MOKHTAR ATTIA

Institut Bourguiba

Bab el Khadra

AVENUE NELSON MANDELA

RUE DE PALESTINE

Nelson Mandela

M

République Metro Station

AVENUE DE LA LIBERTÉ

RUE DE COLOGNE

El Fatah

M

PLACE DE LA RÉPUBLIQUE

RUE DU LUXEMBOURG

AVENUE DE PARIS

M

La Quatrième Art

RUE DE MADRID

RUE DE LONDRES

AVENUE HABIB THAMEUR

Jardin Thameur

Ibn Rachig

Maison du Théâtre Cinema

AVENUE DE LYON

RUE DE L'HASSEN JERAD

Jardin Thameur Bus Station

RUE D'ATHENES

RUE DES SALINES

Habib Thameur

M

Musée des Finances

AV ALI

Cathedral

RUE BAB EL KHADRA

RUE DE ROME

RUE MONGI SLIM

RUE DES TANNEURS

Bab Souika (400m)

Bab Souika (400m)

Bab Souika (400m)

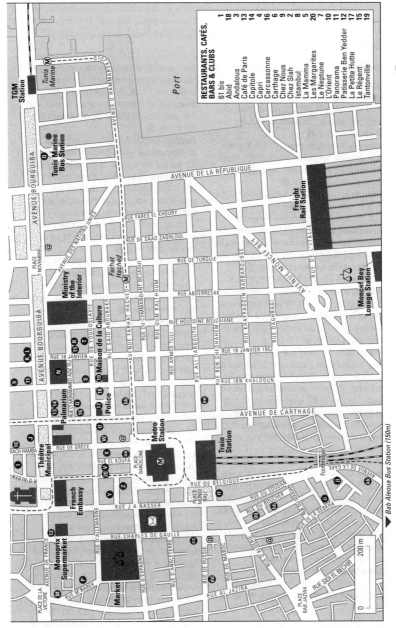

RESTAURANTS, CAFÉS, BARS & CLUBS

61 bis	1
Abid	18
Andalous	3
Café de Paris	13
Capitole	14
Capri	4
Carcassonne	16
Carthage	6
Chez Nous	9
Chez Slah	2
Istambul	8
La Mamma	5
Les Margarites	20
Le Neptune	7
L'Orient	10
Panorama	11
Patisserie Ben Yedder	12
La Petite Hutte	17
Le Régent	15
Tantonville	19

TGM Station

Tunis Marine

Tunis Marine Bus Station

Port

AVENUE BOURGUIBA

AVENUE D'HAMMARSKJOLD

AVENUE DE LA RÉPUBLIQUE

Freight Rail Station

RUE FARES EL KHOURY

RUE DE SAAD ZAGHLOUL

RUE DE TURQUIE

AVENUE DES NATIONS UNIES

PLACE 7 NOVEMBRE

Farhat Hached

Ministry of the Interior

RUE ABDERRESAK

AVENUE MONCEF BEY

RUE DE YOUGOSLAVIE

RUE SAID ABOUBAKR

Maison de la Culture

RUE DU COMMANDANT BEJAOUI

RUE OUM KALTHOUM

RUE HOUSSINE BOUZAIANE

RUE KHAYRADDIN BARBAROUSSE

RUE DAGHBAGI

Moncef Bey Louage Station

RUE 18 JANVIER

Police

RUE AHMED TLILI

RUE ALI DARGOUTH

RUE 18 JANVIER 1952

RUE IBN KHALDOUN

RUE BEN GHEDHAHEM

Palmarium

RUE T MOHAMMED AZIZIZE

AVENUE BOURGUIBA

Théâtre Municipal

BACH HAMBA

R.D'ALGER

RUE DE GRÈCE

AVENUE DE CARTHAGE

Metro Station

RUE EL KOUFA

PLACE BARCELONE

Train Station

French Embassy

RUE J A NASSER

PLACE MONGI BALI

RUE DE BELGIQUE

AVENUE DE LA GARE

Footbridge

RUE DU SOUDAN

RUE DU BOUCHER

Monoprix Supermarket

AVENUE DE FRANCE

RUE CHARLES DE GAULLE

RUE D'ALLEMAGNE

RUE DE LA SEKHA

PLACE DE LA VICTOIRE

RUE M'BAREK

Market

RUE D'ESPAGNE

RUE D'ANGLETERRE

RUE DE RUSSIE

RUE DE MAROC

RUE AL JAZIRA

PLACE BAB JAZIRA

RUE SIDI EL BECHIR

0   200 m

▼ Bab Aleoua Bus Station (150m)

the *Abou Nawas El Mechtel* and the *Sheraton Tunis* (which are on the map on pp.74–75). If you are really stuck for cheap accommodation, you can check out other inexpensive places further south around Bab Jazira, especially on rue d'Algérie and avenue Bab Jedid.

Place Barcelone and points south

Hôtel de l'Agriculture 25 rue Charles de Gaulle ☏71 326 394, ☏71 321 685. Friendly place offering clean, pleasant rooms with showers and fans. Breakfast included. ❸

Excelsior 7 rue du Boucher ☏71 342 917. No-frills budget option popular with students, though the rooms are small and dark. Not a place for women. 1.2TD per shower. ❶

Hôtel de la Gare 25 av de la Gare ☏71 256 754. Friendly, with clean but rather bare rooms, some with showers, in a fume-choked avenue. ❶

Grand Hôtel Victoria 79 rue Farhat Hached ☏71 342 863. Not that grand and can be unfriendly, but it has large rooms and is right on place Barcelone, so it's handy for bus, train and métro. ❶

El Mouna 64 rue de la Sebkha ☏71 343 375. Although not that old this hotel has already fallen on hard times, but it isn't the worst place around and the rooms without shower are the cheapest in the New Town. 1TD per shower or 5TD extra for a room with a shower. ❶

Nouvel Hôtel 3 pl Mongi Bali ☏71 345 283. Perhaps the best of the budget bunch in this area and handy for the train station, though the noise is a drawback. The rooms are small but light and well kept – the ones on the upper floors are best. ❶

El Oumara 42bis rue Ali Dargouth ☏71 333 122, ☏338 030, ☏www.hotel-eloumara.com.tn. The best of the mid-range hotels in this area, with spotless en-suite rooms, including a/c, TV and phone, and good service. ❺

Rue de Russie 18 rue de Russie ☏71 328 883, ☏321 685. Surprisingly smart hotel for the area, all rooms coming with bath, a/c, phone and TV and the better ones with balconies over the street. ❺

Hôtel de Savoie 13 rue de Boucher ☏71 253 780. Another cheapie with basic and small but reasonably clean rooms (1TD extra per shower), painted a fresh duck-egg blue. ❶

Sidi Belhassen 21 av de la Gare ☏71 343 409. Cheery sort of place with small, colourfully tiled rooms, some with showers. Rooms at the top are better. ❷

Rue de Yougoslavie/rue d'Allemagne and around

Hôtel de Bretagne 7 rue de Grèce ☏71 252 146. Some way short of spotless, unfriendly and without much security, but the rooms are a good size and reasonably priced unless you go for one with a shower, which costs about a third more. ❷

Bristol 30 rue Lt Mohammed el Aziz Tej ☏71 254 835. Basic but well located and dirt cheap. 1TD per shower. ❶

Central 6 rue de Suisse ☏71 320 422. Lives up to its name and has decent-sized rooms with showers, but you can do better for the same price. ❷

Hôtel de France 8 rue Mustapha M'barek ☏71 326 244, ☏71 323 314. Just about the best-value place in town, with pleasant staff and big, old-fashioned rooms in a 1940s building, many of which are en suite (2–3TD extra). Ask for a room overlooking the courtyard at the back to get away from the street noise. ❷

Golf Royal 51–53 rue de Yougoslavie ☏71 344 311, ☏348 155, ☏www.groupe-polycoq.com/golfroyal. Comfortable business-class place with air-conditioning, satellite TV and a bar, but not many other facilities. ❻

Maison Dorée 3 rue el Koufa ☏71 240 632, ☏71 332 401. Slightly tatty but perfectly respectable place, with a bar and restaurant, backing on to rue d'Hollande. Rooms come with balconies, some overlooking the French Embassy gardens. A/c and TV are 2–3TD extra. ❸

Omrane 65 av Farhat Hached ☏71 345 277, ☏71 354 892, ☏www.hotel-omrane.com.tn. Very well-run 1930s place, with a good bar, which still retains a touch of grandeur. Satellite TV and phones in all rooms. ❺

Rex 65 rue de Yougoslavie ☏71 257 397. Another colonial leftover that has seen better days but remains good value, with clean rooms that come with a fan, some also with a shower. ❷

Salammbô 6 rue de Grèce ☏71 334 252, ☏71 337 498, ☏hotel.salammbo@gnet.tn. Airy, spick-and-span rooms, some en suite, and a TV lounge and breakfast room. Recommended. ❸

Splendid 2 rue Mustapha M'barek ☏71 322 844. Renovation is long overdue, especially in the bathrooms, but the rooms are quite clean (if somewhat sombre) and have a certain seedy charm. An extra 2TD pays for an en-suite bath. ❶

Hôtel de Suisse 5 rue de Suisse ☏71 323 821. In an alley joining rue d'Hollande and rue Jamel Abdel Nasser, this place offers pleasant enough rooms, some with showers, but is a little overpriced. ❷

Tej 14 rue Lt Mohammed el Aziz Tej ☏71 342 629, ☏71 342 666. Decent-value mid-range place, offering comfortable en-suite rooms with a/c, satellite TV and phone, plus a café and coffee bar downstairs. ❺

Transatlantique 106 rue de Yougoslavie ☎71 240 680. Pleasant, if basic, colonial-style rooms, some with shower, and there's a beautifully tiled lobby. Rate includes breakfast. ❸

Avenue Bourguiba and points north

Abou Nawas El Mechtel av Ouled Haffouz ☎71 783 200, ℻71 784 758, ⊕www.abounawas .com. Business-class place well out of the centre towards Belvedere Park. The rooms are smart and have all you'd expect; Outdoor pool, nightclub, four restaurants and the rest. Not much cheaper than the *Abou Nawas Tunis*, and unless you have business in this area, you'd be better off there. ❾

Abou Nawas Tunis av Mohamed V ☎71 350 355, ℻71 352 882, ⊕www.abounawas.com. The city's newest luxury establishment and by far the best for tourists, offering restaurants, health clubs and pool. ❾

Africa 50 av Bourguiba ☎71 347 477, ℻71 347 432, ⊕www.elmouradi.com. Recently revamped inside and out by the El Mouradi chain, the *Africa* dominates avenue Bourguiba with its gleaming glass exterior and offers luxury rooms, extensive business facilities and superb views from the upper floors. ❾

Bahy 14 av Bourguiba ☎71 330 277, ℻71 330 425. Comfortable modern place, offering bright, airy en-suite rooms, with a/c, satellite TV, fridge and phone, plus good views over the lake in some. Also has a popular American bar and is very handy for the TGM. ❺

Carlton 31 av Bourguiba ☎71 330 644, ℻71 338 168, ℮carlton@planet.tn. Friendly and well-situated business-class hotel, in good nick after renovations a few years ago and immaculately maintained. ❻

Excel 35 av Bourguiba ☎71 355 129, ℻71 341 929, ⊕www.hotelexcel.com. Less classy than the *Carlton* but as comfortable, and including bar and satellite TV. ❺

El Hana International 49 av Bourguiba ☎71 331 144, ℻71 341 199, ⊕www.elhana.com. Not what you'd call a classy joint, in spite of its five-star rating, but popular with package tourists and businesspeople alike. ❼

Hôtel du Lac av Mohammed V ☎71 336 100, ℻71 342 759, ⊕www.hoteldulac.com.tn. Discreet and tasteful it is not, but the inverted pyramid is a landmark on the Tunis skyline and offers a bit of luxury at affordable prices. It's been suggested that this hotel inspired the sand crawler in *Star Wars*. ❼

La Maison Blanche 45 av Mohammed V ☎71 849 849, ℻71 793 842. Has more character than Tunis's other luxury choices, with individually decorated mini-suites and four-poster beds, plus a high-class restaurant. ❾

Majestic 36 av de Paris ☎71 332 666, ℻71 336 908, ⊕www.majestichotel.com.tn. Despite the elegant colonial architecture (especially the curved marble staircase leading up to the foyer), the hotel in general is getting a bit shabby; a gradual renovation is promised. ❻

Oscars 12–14 rue de Marseille ☎71 344 755, ℻71 345 558, ℮oscarshotel@planet.tn. Central, business-class hotel that has a tenuous movie theme running through its rooms and bizarrely decorated restaurant. Attached to the hotel is a small bar, café, cinema and nightclub complex. ❻

Qatar Imp. 6, rue des Tanneurs ☎71 342 522. Basic but clean rooms, some with showers. ❶

El Qods Imp. 6, rue des Tanneurs ☎71 340 404, ℻71 255 030. Next to the *Qatar*, and similarly quiet, this has recently been renovated and is in much better shape than its neighbour, especially in the bathroom department. Ask for a room with balcony. ❶

Rahma 5 rue Qadiciyah (or Kadissa) ☎71 255 566. Reasonable place with small rooms, some with sinks, in an alley behind La Parnasse cinema, though the showers are down by reception. ❶

Ritza 35 av Habib Thameur ☎71 255 428. Friendly place offering basic, clean doubles, all with showers – but overpriced. ❸

St Georges 16 rue de Cologne ☎71 781 029. If you don't mind the location (20min walk north of avenue Bourguiba), this dilapidated colonial house is a good bet, with spacious, a/c rooms, some with bathrooms (1OTD extra), and safe, off-street parking. ❹

Sheraton Tunis av de la Ligue Arabe, Notre Dame ☎71 782 100, ℻71 782 208, ⊕www.sheraton. com. Around 5km from the city centre, this luxury hotel is more convenient for businessmen than tourists, but it does have wonderful views across Belvedere Park. ❾

The Medina and Halfaouine

Hotels in the **Medina** tend to be the cheapest, but also the dirtiest, and very stuffy in the summertime and damp and cold in winter. The rooms are typically without attached bathrooms (you'll pay an additional 1TD for a hot shower), and the rate excludes breakfast. Except where otherwise stated they are not recommended for women travelling on their own. On the other hand, a stay in the Medina throws you headlong into a world that would completely pass you by in some hotels in the New Town. All the hotels reviewed here are keyed on the Medina map (pp.86–87) or the Halfaouine map (p.103).

Medina

Auberge de la Jeunesse Tunis Medina 25 rue Saida Ajoula ☏ & ℗71 567 850. Clean, friendly and well-run HI place, with central heating in winter and a/c planned for summer, but still subject to rules and curfew (midnight in summer; 10pm winter). The building is a former palace with a lovely glass-domed courtyard. Fills up quickly in summer, so book ahead. Dorm beds 6TD.

Hôtel des Amis 7 rue Monastiri ☏71 565 653. Basic but clean and friendly, with a TV room. No showers but there is a hammam close by. ❶

Hammami 12 rue el Mechnaka ☏71 560 451. Large rooms in a huge and very impressive mansion near place Bab Carthajana but it is pretty grubby and the toilets are none too pleasant. ❶

Marhaba 5 rue de la Commission ☏71 327605, ℗71 325 452. Basic but cleaner than most, and friendly and safe for women. Book ahead or arrive early in summer. ❶

El Massara 5 bd Bab Menara ☏71 563 734, ℗71 565 255. On a busy road at the western edge of the Medina; the rooms are small but clean. ❶

Medina 1 pl de la Victoire ☏71 327497, ℗71 325 452. Naturally popular: it's relatively clean and conveniently situated on the edge of the Medina. OK for women. ❶

Souk Hôtel 101 rue des Teinturiers ☏71 347 398. Small clean rooms, friendly and fine for women guests. ❶

Hôtel de la Victoire 7 bd Bab Menara ☏71 561 224. Neighbour to the *El Massara*, this is cool and airy, if rather noisy, but with friendly management and a painting in every room. Safe for women. ❶

Halfaouine

Hôtel des Amis 136 rue el Halfaouine, between Bab Souika and pl Halfaouine ☏71 566105. Relatively clean and secure, if basic, rooms around an inner courtyard. The communal showers and toilets are not so nice, however. ❶

Hôtel 20 Mars 9 rue Sidi el Aloui ☏71 566 924. Basic – and not recommended for women – but friendly, in a gorgeously dilapidated building by the Sahib et Tabaa mosque. Minimum rent is by the month (32TD).

The New Town and Belvedere Park

The area occupied by the modern colonial **New Town** consisted mainly of uncultivated land until the French took control in 1881, when they immediately set about reproducing a French provincial capital. **Avenue de France** and its continuation, **avenue Bourguiba**, run down the middle from the Medina to the port; to either side, the streets more or less follow a grid pattern. The city's main chunk of greenery is the massive **Belvedere Park**, which overlooks it from the north.

Although this isn't the most fascinating part of Tunis, it's where you're likely to spend a lot of your time eating or sleeping, since it contains the city's best hotels, most restaurants and other facilities. Incidentally, for a fantastic **aerial view** of Tunis, as well as the lake and sometimes as far as Sidi Bou Saïd to the northeast and Djebel Zaghouan 50km to the south, take the lift in *Hôtel El Hana International* to its tenth-floor rooftop bar. If you're there at dusk, you can see the flocking acrobatics of avenue Bourguiba's immense (and noisy) starling colony.

Avenue Bourguiba and around

Avenue Bourguiba is the centre of Tunis in every way. People converge here from all over the city to sit in cafés, stroll under the trees, buy a posy made of jasmine buds – above all, just to see and be seen. There's something very continental about it that's quite at odds with the Medina's cramped narrow streets.

The further you go along avenue Bourguiba from the Medina, the stronger the European influence on the architecture. Both avenue de Paris and its continuation, avenue de la Liberté, have some wonderful examples of colonial buildings, although things get more sombre towards the end of avenue de la Liberté, as you move into a zone of embassies and government buildings.

The first landmark along Avenue Bourguiba is the **Cathedral**, built in 1882 and a monstrous, bizarre mixture of Romanesque, Byzantine and Oriental styles. Just across from the cathedral, the **French Embassy** is quite modest by contrast. It was built in 1862 as the advance guard of growing French influence, and as the Résidence Générale, the centre of the Protectorate administration from 1881. Many of the important decisions of Tunisia's recent history were made within its still heavily guarded walls. A few blocks east, the old French **Théâtre Municipal**, with its bulging layers of white stucco and fantastic carved figures supporting the balcony, plays host to regular, highly recommended Arabic and classical music concerts.

North of the Cathedral, the **Musée des Finances** (foyer of the Contrôle Générale des Finances; Mon–Thurs 8.30am–1pm & 3–5.45pm, Fri 8.30am–1pm & Sat 8am–1.30pm; free) at 27 rue de Rome will appeal to numismatists. Just off avenue de Paris, the **Jardin Habib Thameur** provides a small amount of greenery but is tiny and fume laden.

South of Avenue Bourguiba is French Tunis's most lively area, with many of the city's restaurants, bars and cinemas. On rue d'Allemagne there's a huge **food market**, selling every conceivable kind of produce. Around the corner, the **Musée de la Poste** (Mon–Thurs 8.30am–1pm & 3–5.45pm, Fri 8.30am–1pm & Sat 8am–1.30pm; free), a dim and dusty room in the main post office building on rue d'Angleterre, is for ardent philatelists only.

The grid plan begins to go awry near the Medina, and the same thing happens northwest of the avenue, where the area immediately east of rue Mongi Slim and rue Bab Souika – the old **Maltese and Jewish quarters** – is agreeably chaotic. The thirteenth-century **Zeraia Mosque**, on the corner of rue Zarkoun and rue Mongi Slim, is the main sight.

Belvedere Park

Tunis is not a city greatly endowed with parks, and it is really the cemeteries – especially Jellaz (see p.107) – that provide much-needed open spaces. The exception is **Belvedere Park**, which provides an excellent reason for coming this far north. Breathing space has always been a problem in Tunis. An anonymous "English lady" of the 1850s, author of *Letters from Barbary*, reported asking to be shown a garden. Her guide led her some way through the streets, then "halted before two trees, growing against a wall, and surrounded by a plot of about four foot wide, perhaps: and this, he told us, was the biggest garden in the town". Most people today escape the summer humidity by catching the TGM to Carthage or Sidi Bou Saïd, but Belvedere Park, with its green lower area kept heavily watered, is a peaceful and accessible alternative. Vegetation grows much more sparsely as you climb the hill, but there's an excellent view from the top over Tunis to Bou Kornine (see p.133). The elaborate **koubba**, or dome, standing about halfway up, was built in 1798 for a palace in the suburbs and transplanted here in 1901.

At the bottom of the park is a **zoo** (daily: summer 9am–7pm, winter 9am–4pm; 0.4TD), where some distressingly small cages provide an eyeball-to-eyeball perspective on the fiercer species. Also here is the **Midha**, an early seventeenth-century fountain for pre-prayer ablutions, brought from its origi-

Colonial architecture

Three early examples of the French rulers trying to stamp their presence on the city are the main post office, and the Cathedral and French Residence, facing each other on avenue Bourguiba. Subsequently, architects preferred the fussiness of provincial wedding-cake elaboration, such as the theatre on avenue Bourguiba and the *Hôtel Majestic*, with occasional forays into "Moorish" kitsch.

By far the most exciting facet of the colonial heritage, however, is the wealth of **Art Deco** from the period 1925–40. Although the term Art Deco is usually associated with the decorative arts, it also relates to buildings that feature exuberantly stylized decoration and clean geometric forms. To the home-grown architects of colonial North Africa, these characteristics made Art Deco seem an appropriate and modern departure from inherited styles, as well as being up with the latest trends in France.

An architectural study has identified over four hundred Art Deco buildings in Tunis, ranging from luxurious urban villas, to apartment buildings and tenements, to functional office blocks, many of which can still be seen within the grid-plan districts of the modern city. The masterpiece of Tunis's Art Deco period is the **Villa Boublil**, near Belvedere Park at 16 rue d'Autriche. A magnificent building designed by J.G. Ellul, a member of the local Maltese community, it is, even in its semi-abandoned state, well worth a special visit for its rippling lines and elaborate metalwork. A couple of years later, Ellul also designed an office building, the Omnium Immobilier Tunisien at 12 av Habib Thameur, whose discreet elegance would not be out of place in a chic contemporary development. It remains a prestigious address.

Not all the Art Deco buildings are up to this standard, and many verge on blandness. But it's worth casting your eye above street level every now and then for the telltale semicircular balconies, crowning pylons, elaborate geometric reliefs and above all the metalwork on balconies, doors and windows. Some hallway interiors

nal site at Souk et Trouk in the Medina. The **cafés** in the middle of the zoo and on the lake just outside are two of the most relaxed in the city.

The Medina

"White, domed, studded with minarets, honeycombed with tunnel-like bazaars" – until the nineteenth century, the **Medina** *was* Tunis: an oval-shaped walled city little changed from its days as a great Mediterranean trading power. In the eighth century AD, the conquering Arabs were the first to prefer Tunis's site to Carthage, exposed out on its peninsula, and set about building the monuments that still form the heart of the Medina, most notably the ninth-century **Zitouna Mosque**, still surrounded by the central souks. Along the narrow, winding streets – typical of medieval Arab cities – subsequent generations left their own distinctive legacies: mosques, tombs, palaces and marketplaces. Most of them feature a blend of styles that mirrors the city's cosmopolitan history, although occasionally there is a more straightforward statement, such as the Mosque of Sidi Mehrez's Ottoman domes, which would not look out of place in Istanbul. Because of all this, it's no surprise to learn that the Medina is classed by UNESCO as a World Heritage Site.

In the late nineteenth century, the Medina inevitably declined when the French began to build their new capital on reclaimed land to the east, even though they made no deliberate attempt to eradicate local culture as they are also elaborately decorated. The effect is sometimes minimal, a hint of waviness in the metalwork of a balcony; other times, you find a grand statement, for example, three apartment buildings by the same designer filling one whole side of a city block (Q. Riccardini: west side of rue du 18 Janvier 1952, south of rue Ahmed Tlili; P.P. Ancona: north side of rue Ghedhahem, east of rue Ibn Khaldoun).

The densest concentration of buildings can be found north of avenue Bourguiba, and colonial archiecture can also be found in Montfleury, the suburb southwest of Bab Aleoua bus station. Particularly fine examples are listed below, with street junctions shown in brackets where appropriate.

North of rue de Londres
Villa Boublil, 16 rue d'Autriche (Ibn Tafragin)
20 rue de L'Inde (Asdrubal)
2, 43, 45 & 131 avenue de la Liberté; no. 43 is a synagogue

Central (rue de Londres to av Bourguiba)
12 avenue Habib Thameur
56 avenue de Paris

South of av Bourguiba
22 rue d'Algérie (Al Jazira)
34 avenue Farhat Hached
13 rue Oum Kalthoum

Montfleury
21 rue Allal el Fassi (Sadok)

had done in Algiers. After independence in 1956, a plan was raised to drive a continuation of avenue de France through the heart of the Medina to the government offices on the far side, which would have destroyed the quarter for ever. Fortunately, this idea was abandoned after the Association de Sauvegarde de la Medina (ASM) was set up to try to preserve the old city's heritage. But the Medina remains the most tangible evidence of Tunisia's immediate precolonial past and of the "decadence that made colonization possible", to quote a senior government official in 1961. As such, it has continued to be treated as a political football: historic buildings have been allowed to deteriorate and the authorities were slow to recognize the Medina's potential tourist value. These trends seem to have been reversed, but still few of the monuments are geared up for visitors. Many have been converted to municipal facilities of some kind, while others remain *ukalas* – large buildings subdivided for many families or businesses. The most distinctively Tunisian element are the magnificent **doorways** which, according to early traveller El Bekri, were already famous in the thirteenth century: blue or beige, set with black studs and a "hand of Fatima" knocker, and surrounded by intricately carved stone frames.

Visiting the Medina
There are many different ways to approach a visit to the Medina. Perhaps the most attractive – if not the most practical – is just to wander at random, stumbling on unexpected sights. The account below divides the Medina into three areas – **central**, **southern** and **northern**, each covered by a walking itinerary taking in the main historic sights and many lesser monuments. The walks on

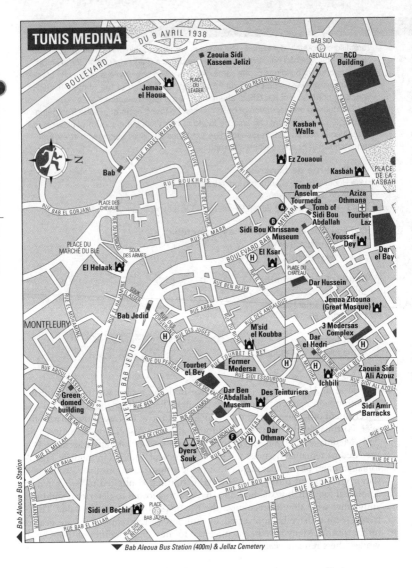

TUNIS MEDINA

BOULEVARD DU 9 AVRIL 1938

BAB SIDI ABDALLAH

RCD Building

Zaouia Sidi Kassem Jelizi

Jemaa el Haoua

PLACE DU LEADER

RUE DU RESERVOIRE

Kasbah Walls

Ez Zouaoui

Kasbah

PLACE DE LA KASBAH

Bab

RUE BAB EL GORJANI

PLACE DES CHEVAUX

RUE BOUKHRIS

Tomb of Anselm Tourmeda

Aziza Othmana

Tomb of Sidi Bou Abdallah

Tourbet Laz

Sidi Bou Khrissane Museum

Youssef Dey

Dar el Bey

PLACE DU MARCHÉ DU BLÉ

SOUK DES ARMES

El Helaak

El Ksar

PLACE DU CHATEAU

Dar Hussein

Jemaa Zitouna (Great Mosque)

MONTFLEURY

Bab Jedid

RUE DES ANDALOUS

3 Medersas Complex

M'sid el Koubba

Dar el Hedri

Tourbet el Bey

Former Medersa

Zaouia Sidi Ali Azouz

Ichbili

Green domed building

Dar Ben Abdallah Museum

Des Teinturiers

Sidi Amir Barracks

Dar Othman

Dyers Souk

Sidi el Bechir

PLACE BAB JAZIRA

RUE EL JAZIRA

Bab Aleoua Bus Station

Bab Aleoua Bus Station (400m) & Jellaz Cemetery

their own probably take a couple of hours apiece, or they can easily be combined to create a longer outing. In terms of monuments, the centre and the souks form the densest area, followed by the south and north. Halfaouine, the Kasbah district and Montfleury are suburbs outside the walls of the Medina proper and covered on pp.102–105.

The tourist authorities have created and signposted an itinerary that includes many of the major monuments and provides a quick tour (1–2hr) for visitors. A leaflet showing this route is available from the tourist office at 1 avenue Mohamed V, but don't count on the signs themselves being easily visible (most are hidden behind doors and shopfronts). Avoid wandering around the Medina

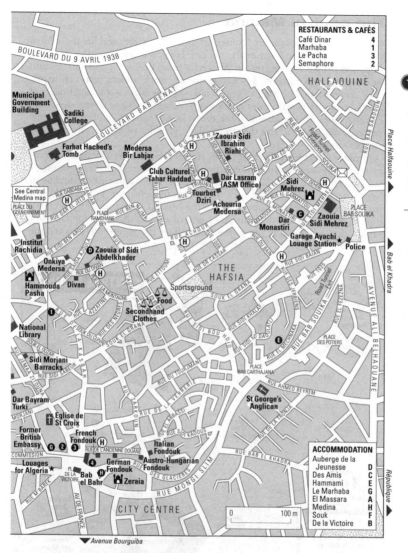

RESTAURANTS & CAFÉS

Café Dinar	4
Marhaba	1
Le Pacha	3
Semaphore	2

ACCOMMODATION

Auberge de la Jeunesse	D
Des Amis	C
Hammami	E
Le Marhaba	G
El Massara	A
Medina	H
Souk	F
De la Victoire	B

after dark, when the area is deserted, ill-lit and potentially dangerous, with incidents of mugging not unknown. Although old men are hired as watchmen, huddled around fires with baseball bats, they hardly inspire confidence for nocturnal jaunts. (Ramadan is a different story: the main streets are crammed with shoppers and families until near midnight and the cafés do a roaring trade.) Another danger in the Medina after dark is being hit by rubbish flung from windows for nighttime street cleaners to brush up, as there's not much space for garbage trucks in the narrow streets. During the day, beware of **pickpockets** in the crowded main thoroughfares, rue de la Kasbah and rue Jemaa Zitouna. Note that most of the shops and souks are **closed on Sundays**, along with the museums.

The central Medina

With the Great Mosque and souks set squarely in the middle, the central Medina was once the heart of the old city. Here, the concentration of streets, shops and people is at its greatest. At certain times of day, the main streets into the Medina from place de la Victoire are so chock-a-block you can hardly move down them. The Medina's main industry nowadays is tourism, usually of the day-trip variety, with most tour groups "doing" the same streets, sights and souvenir shops. The result is that the centre of the Medina can feel very commercial, even artificial, and the streets like a gauntlet of traders, albeit mostly amiable ones.

On **place de la Victoire** at the west end of avenue de France (the continuation of av Bourguiba), you'll notice the difference between Western symmetry and Eastern bustle. **Bab el Bahr**, the Sea Gate, stands alone in the middle of the square; before development of the European city began in the middle of the nineteenth century, it opened from the Medina onto more or less empty ground, which led down to the naval arsenal on the shores of the lake. Just outside the gate, until as late as the first half of the nineteenth century, the

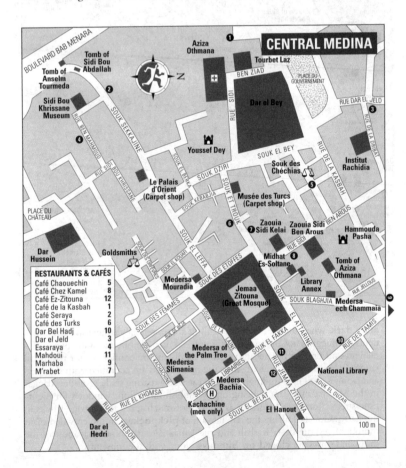

Beys used to sponsor wrestling matches between oiled Turkish wrestlers every day during the month preceding Ramadan. Once the French took over, they inevitably attached particular value to Bab el Bahr as the focal point of the meeting between Medina and European city. Ever the symbolic town planners, they knocked down the gate's surrounding houses as well as its walls so as to isolate it in a square, renaming it Porte de France. Where the houses had been, they erected an evangelical statue – now long gone – of Cardinal Lavigerie, founder of the White Fathers, a Tunisian-based order of monks who wear white burnooses.

This area of the Medina had long been a Christian ghetto, ever since the Turks allowed the first foreign embassies inside the Medina walls to be built here in the seventeenth century. By the mid-nineteenth century, growing European influence saw the positions reversed; facing the gate, the large Italianate building with shabby columns was the office of the International Financial Commission that supervised the bankrupt Beys' administration just before the French Protectorate. These French, Italian and British commissioners forced the government to grant foreigners privileges and concessions that caused much resentment at the time, and on several occasions the building was attacked by mobs.

Rue Jemaa Zitouna

Rue Jemaa Zitouna leads from place de la Victoire directly to the Great Mosque, and, as the main tourist route, it has turned into a cauldron of overflowing stalls and overeager proprietors. You can buy almost everything more cheaply elsewhere, but the shops are a useful training ground for bargaining techniques.

At no. 12 is the **Church of St Croix**, the first to be built in Tunis, in 1662. In the 1860s it became a sanctuary, protected by the French, and the source of repeated confrontation between them and the Beys. Time after time the Beys had to back down and accept that the criminals and enemies who escaped here were outside their jurisdiction.

The fine door at no. 55 belongs to the **Sidi Morjani Barracks**, built by Hammouda Bey (1777–1813) after his Ottoman troops mutinied in 1811. Hammouda was forced to recruit tribal warriors from among the Zouaoua Berbers as auxiliaries, and built them five sets of barracks, of which these are the third. At the end of rue Jemaa Zitouna, the **National Library** at no. 73 (entrance via Souk el Attarine) was originally the second barracks. The first of Hammouda Bey's barracks is now Aziza Othmana Hospital, west of the Great Mosque; the fourth is in **rue Sidi Ali Azouz**, just off rue Jemaa Zitouna (see p.96); the fifth has since been demolished.

The Great (Zitouna) Mosque

Bringing rue Jemaa Zitouna to an abrupt halt is the **Great Mosque** (daily except Fri 8am–noon; 1.6TD, camera 1TD), known as the Zitouna (olive tree) because it stands on the site of the tree under which its founder, Hassan Ibn Nooman, taught the Koran. The mosque's massive size is exaggerated by the cramped alleys around it, an effect that must have been even greater when it was completed under the Aghlabids in the ninth century. While the mosque is still the heart of the Medina, for hundreds of years it was the central point of reference for the entire city: souks were positioned deliberately around it, as well as a host of secondary buildings such as the *medersas* housing students who had come to study at the mosque.

△ The bustle of Rue Jemaa Zitouna

Successive additions over the centuries make the mosque's exterior appearance today something of a composite. In the seventeenth century Spanish architect Ibn Ghalib – who also designed the mosque complex of the second Turkish ruler, Youssef Dey – was responsible for the spacious entrance portico hanging over the **Souk el Fakka** (originally selling dried fruits, though like most of the souks it now does souvenirs) along the mosque's east side. The minaret at the northwest corner, which seems such a perfect fit, actually dates back only to the nineteenth century, when a new minaret was modelled directly on that of the 1235 Kasbah Mosque (see p.105). In the cramped surroundings of the Medina, little else is visible of the exterior except for massive blank walls.

It's worth timing a visit for the morning so that you can go inside and see the **courtyard**, which retains its original form – a vast empty space of polished marble. It is strongly reminiscent of the Great Mosque at Kairouan, built slightly earlier, and has the same wonderfully soothing effect after the bustle of the souks outside. As at Kairouan, the courtyard is surrounded on three sides by simple arcades, while the prayer hall occupies the fourth.

In its day, the **university** based in the mosque was one of the greatest in the world and its library (entry to academics only) still contains one of the world's great collections of Arabic literature. Hundreds of years before European universities had even been thought of, students were coming to Tunis from throughout the Islamic world. Tradition records that each professor had his own column, next to which he always did his teaching. Even in the 1950s there were students here, but during the 1960s the university was brought into line with the national educational system and theological students moved elsewhere.

Coming out of the mosque, turn right along **Souk des Librairies**, one side of which is lined by a series of interconnecting *medersas* built in the early eighteenth century – the **Medersa of the Palm Tree** (no. 11), the **Bachia** (no. 27) and, on the corner, the **Slimania**, which you can visit (opening times are uncertain, but at the nearby barbershop they usually know where the custodian is). These three residential Islamic colleges are part of a series founded in Tunis in the eighteenth century, and each has the classic form of a courtyard surrounded by students' cells. The story behind two of them typifies the instability of the Husaynid dynasty: the Bachia was founded in 1752 by Ali Pacha, and only two years later he dedicated the Slimania to the memory of his son Suleiman, who had been poisoned by a younger brother. There's also a long-standing **hammam** for men, Hammam Kachachine, here at no. 30 (see p.118).

The main souks

The close link between Islam and commerce could hardly be better represented than by the purpose-built **souks** around the Great Mosque. Hierarchy was symbolized by position: the closer to the mosque, the more "noble" the trade. Thus the Souk des Étoffes (cloth) and Souk el Attarine (perfume) were right next to the mosque; messier and noisier businesses such as dyeing and metalwork were relegated to the suburbs.

At the Great Mosque, turn left along Souk des Libraries and then immediately right into **Souk de la Laine** – the Wool Market, though there's not much wool here any more – which runs up the near side. At no. 21, note the doorway into the mosque, improvised out of Roman blocks. Opposite no. 9 is the **rue de Béjà**, where most of the wool and cotton weaving seems to have moved. It's interesting to watch the weaving – most of the textiles are still made

Shopping in Tunis

Tunis's **souks** still function as the backbone of the city's trading community. Souk el Kachachine is the place to come for wholesale **rugs** and **clothes**, and Souk et Trouk is where you'll find **carpet** shops. One typically Tunisian article, the characteristic red **chéchia**, or skullcap, can be bought in the Souk des Chéchias (see p.94). Souk de la Laine retains a few traditional **tailors**. **Copper and brasswork**, as well as **chicha pipes**, are best bought on Souk du Cuivre, off rue de la Kasbah (you'll also find *chichas* at the southern end of rue Sidi el-Morjani, off rue Jemaa Zitouna). Standard tourist fodder is available on **rue Jemaa Zitouna**, which has turned into a cauldron of overflowing stalls and shops that tend to be more expensive than elsewhere. Among the more interesting outlets are the stall on the corner of rue Sidi Ali Azouz, which often has old metal lamps, chandeliers and pen cases, and El Hanout, where you can find Sejnane pottery figurines and animals.

If you're interested in buying locally made crafts, a good place to start shopping is the official **ONA** showroom on the ground floor of Le Palmarium shopping centre, corner of avenue Bourguiba and avenue de Carthage. Prices here are high, but you can get a good sense of the range of goods available before entering the maelstrom of the Medina's central souks. Another hassle-free place to buy quality pieces (pottery, rugs and jewellery) is **Phenicia**, out at Carthage Salammbo (see p.123). For genuine antiques, Yousef Ayoub at 27 av Bourguiba is worth a look.

For everyday craft goods that Tunisians use, and at much lower prices, hold your fire until you get to the further reaches of the Medina – the stalls outside the Mosque of Sidi Mehrez, for example. Here there are some **pottery** shops with a good selection of low-priced plates, cups, pots and ashtrays. More unusual shopping ideas might include **olive wood crafts** from one of the shops in rue Sidi Ben Arous (see p.94) or some retro **haute couture** from the secondhand clothing stores on rue de l'Agha (see p.100).

on hand looms. At the end of Souk de la Laine, a brief detour takes in some of the further souks.

Left along **Souk des Femmes**, you cross the Souk du Coton to a junction with **Souk el Kachachine**, with its noisy wholesale bargaining for rugs and garments. Turn right at this corner, then first right onto Souk el Kouafi, then first left into **Souk des Orfèvres**. True to its name, this is still the home of gold jewellers, whose tiny, glass-fronted shops on narrow streets reflect their need for security. The souk and its surrounding streets are protected by heavy wooden doors, which are closed at night and on Sunday afternoons. Head to the junction with Souk el Leffa and a right downhill will take you to **Souk des Étoffes**, or Cloth Market, recognizable by its red and green columns. With its deep stalls, this is the most spacious souk in the Medina; elegant and refined, it comes to an end at the far west corner of the mosque. At no. 37, the **Mouradia Medersa** was built in 1673 by Mourad Bey, son of Hammouda Pacha, whose mosque is covered on p.94.

Unfortunately, the **Souk el Attarine**, which slopes down the northwestern side of the mosque, no longer specializes in perfume, although you'll find plenty of it among the ubiquitous copper ashtrays, handbags and stuffed camels; in the sixteenth century it used to stay open until midnight in order to serve women, who took their hammams in the evening. On the left of this street as it descends, steps lead up to the **Midhat es Soltane**, a fifteenth-century bathing facility attached to the Great Mosque and renowned for its beauty. It's rarely accessible, so you're unlikely to see more than the facade of the main entrance at the top of the steps, with its dramatic use of black and white marble. Reminiscent of architecture in Cairo and Syria, this technique confirms Tunis's position as a meeting place for influences from both east and west Islam. Unlike Dar Othman in the south of the Medina, though, in whose courtyard Western tilework blends with Eastern marble, the Midhat's interior limits itself to stark marble in an Eastern style.

Turning back up Souk el Attarine, continue up the hill along **Souk et Trouk**, built in the seventeenth century for Turkish tailors but now populated mainly by tourist emporiums, past the Musée des Turcs carpet shop at no. 45, with its terrace view over the Medina. Twenty metres from the top, turn left into Souk Kebabjia. The open space a little way along here is the **Souk el Berka**, once the marketplace for Tunis's slave trade (see box below).

Around place du Gouvernement

Close to the Souk el Berka, the **Mosque of Youssef Dey** dates back to 1616 and was designed by the Spanish architect who added the portico to the Great Mosque. Blending local features with influences from the East, Christian Italy and Islamic Spain, the result is an accurate reflection of the many historical and social currents to which Tunisia's geography has always made it subject. Compared with the massive simplicity of the Great Mosque, it has a more airy, complex feel.

Most obvious here is the octagonal minaret on a square base, recalling Ottoman Turkish designs and signalling the arrival of the new Turkish rulers. The shape of the lantern, with its hanging balcony from which the muezzin would originally have issued the call to prayer, is not only the first of its kind but immediately established a standard that was to appear again and again in Tunis. Next to the minaret, the **square mausoleum** also incorporates Spanish, Eastern and Italian influences, with a green-tiled pyramidal roof recalling the Alhambra in Granada; the elaborate patterns of black and white marble, Eastern in origin, had already appeared in Tunis in the Midhat es Soltane (see opposite) and the palace of Othman Dey (p.97). The form of the **prayer hall**, with eight rows of six columns, is more North African.

The Tunis slave trade

Slaves were brought to Souk el Berka in Tunis – the most unfortunate from their dungeons in the Kasbah at La Goulette – where they were displayed to prospective buyers, who would first check the strength of their teeth because unskilled slaves ended up working the corsair galleys and being fed entirely on hard biscuits. Most of the slaves were captured at sea, as far away as the English Channel – but there were also frequent raids on coastal towns in Italy, France and Spain. It was a brutal business, though Western tradition has been happy to overlook the equally ferocious Christian corsairs supplying the great slave markets at Pisa, Genoa and other European trading cities. Piracy and slavery were generally accepted (even if not officially) as a lucrative adjunct of Mediterranean trade.

By the end of the eighteenth century, European fleets had forced the corsairs from the sea. Initially the Trans-Saharan trade compensated for the declining Mediterranean supply, and in the 1790s as many as six thousand African slaves were sold in Tunis every year. Over the following decades, however, taxation, along with competition from Tripoli's markets and wars in the south, ruined the trade. Then in 1846, Ahmed Bey, building his reputation as an enlightened ruler, abolished the slave trade and the markets were closed. The Africans have remained; in the past they suffered discrimination and were often reduced to the status of domestic servants, but today they are an integral part of Tunisian society.

Continuing up past the mosque, you emerge from the Medina into **place du Gouvernement**, an open space on what was once the western edge of the Medina proper. Formerly a royal guest house, the **Dar el Bey** is now the prime minister's office, which means that government in Tunis has returned to its original site – since the Hafsids' thirteenth-century Kasbah stood just above here. Until recently you could see the excavations over the road, but they have since been covered up by a grand esplanade in front of the imposing local government headquarters; you can, however, still see the old Kasbah Mosque (where our walk to Montfleury begins; see p.105).

Also in place du Gouvernement is the **Tourbet Laz**, the tomb of a seventeenth-century Bey and his relations, now occupied by a family who may let you look inside. These *tourbets* (tombs) were very fashionable among rich Turkish families of the time and Tunis has several – the **Tourbet of Ahmed Kouja Dey** is just across the street from here.

If you head back past Youssef Dey's mosque, the street on your left behind the Dar el Bey is the **Souk el Bey**, suitably grand with its broad, pillared arcade. The third and fourth doors on the right are entrances to the **Souk des Chéchias**, another eye-catching market, selling the characteristic Tunisian skullcaps made from wool by a complicated process of carding, moulding and dyeing. During the early eighteenth century this was one of Tunisia's most important industries, but in the mid-eighteenth century European factories flooded the market with cheap imitations and the Tunisian industry was ruined. By the 1920s the remaining manufacturers faced another recession as the wealthy turned to Western dress. Until recently it was a disappearing industry, with few Tunisians under the age of 40 owning or wearing a *chéchia*, but recently it's been revived as young Tunisians discover their cultural past. In its centre is Tunis's oldest café, the *Chaouechin* (see box opposite).

Rue Sidi Ben Arous

Running along the east side of the Souk des Chéchias is **rue Sidi Ben Arous**, an attractive little street with a *chéchia* seller, a poky little café (no. 18), a bookshop (Espace Diwan) and a strange apicultural shop (no. 38) selling all manner of bee products, including jars labelled "bee venom". To the south rises the Great Mosque's minaret. In the shadow, at the end of the souk at 23 rue Sidi Ben Arous, is the **Zaouia of Sidi Ben Arous**, a fourteenth-century native of Cap Bon who brought back Sufi teaching from Morocco (see p.96). Built in 1437, this particular *zaouia*, the meeting place of a religious fraternity, quickly became too popular with women for the authorities' liking and was closed – only to be promptly reopened in the face of an ensuing uproar.

In a nearby alleyway but entered via the *zaouia*, the **Tomb of Aziza Othmana** belongs to a princess renowned for her generosity. Just before her death in 1669, she liberated her slaves and left her estate to charitable causes – funds to liberate slaves and prisoners, and a fund for poor girls who couldn't otherwise afford to marry. She's buried next to her grandfather, Othman Dey (who built the Dar Othman in the south of the Medina), and the tomb itself was built by Husayn, founder of the Husaynid dynasty and Aziza Othmana's son-in-law. The world of the Tunisian ruling classes was a small one.

On the opposite side of the street to the Zaouia of Sidi Ben Arous is the late fifteenth-century Hafsid **Zaouia of Sidi Kelai**, with inscriptions and panels of leaning keystones above its entrance. By contrast, the shocking-pink facade of the nearby **Tourbet of Hammouda Pacha** clearly belongs to a later period. With the **mosque** of the same name, it forms a complex built in 1655 and clearly modelled after the 1616 mosque of Youssef Dey, featuring the same octagonal minaret

Cafés in the Medina

Recent years have seen a surge in popularity for the Medina's gently mouldering cafés, both as daytime refuges in between sightseeing and shopping, and in the early evenings – and much later during Ramadan – when the *chicha* pipe-smoke becomes a fog. The best are reviewed below and marked on the map on p.88, apart from the *Café Dinar* on the Medina map on pp.86–87.

Café Chaouechin Souk des Chéchias. Tunis's oldest café, which occupies the main crossroad of the covered hat-makers' souk. As well as serving excellent Turkish coffee in the morning and fresh black tea in the afternoon, it puts on impromptu nocturnal music sessions during Ramadan.

Café Chez Kamel 19 rue Sidi Ben Arous. The best *chicha* in town and fine fragrant tea, with a cosy den upstairs and tables outside. Small, friendly and lacking in tourists.

Café Dinar Place de la Victoire. At the Medina's main entrance, this basic place with pleasant outdoor tables is always packed. It has all the essentials and is cheaper than the café at the nearby *Medina Hotel*.

Café Ez-Zitouna Rue Djemaa Ez-Zitouna. On the left 50m before the mosque, with Turkish decor and good *chichas*. It gets packed when football is on TV.

Café de la Kasbah Place de la Kasbah. Facing the Kasbah Mosque, this doesn't have the nicest view thanks to traffic, but it is breezy and gets plenty of afternoon sun.

Café M'rabet Souk et Trouk. From the 1930 to the 1950s this was the haunt of Tunisia's anti-colonial literary elite. The tea is sickly but the setting, in the *driba* entrance hall of this old palace-turned-restaurant, is superlative, with its simple but stately red and green pillars and mat-covered stone benches. There is also a nice terrace out back, and it is more female-friendly than most cafés.

Café Seraya Souk Sekkajine. Opposite the junction with rue Ben Mahmoud, this is another beautifully decorated café with a cosy room upstairs, serving decent coffee and cakes.

Café des Turks Souk et Trouk. Good Turkish coffee, *chichas* and a pleasant tiled upstairs hideaway.

and detached square mausoleum. In the other direction, the northern continuation of Sidi Ben Arous on the other side of rue de la Kasbah is lined by the imposing doorways of what were once senior Turkish officials' houses. These are mostly inaccessible, although the palace at no. 56 has been opened to the public.

Heading east down **rue de la Kasbah**, the other main street running across the Medina, you come to a crossroads. To the left is **rue Saida Ajoula** running past the youth hostel and into the northern Medina. To the right, however, is the **rue Djelloud**, where a further right brings you to the Impasse ech Chammaia which, surprisingly, contains two important monuments, one of which is the Tomb of Aziza Othmana (see opposite). At no. 4, the **Medersa ech Chammaia**, founded by the Hafsid Sultan Abu Zakariya in 1249, was the first *medersa* built in Tunis. For all its simplicity – a one-storey courtyard surrounded by students' cells, built in plain, undecorated limestone – it is a fine example of classic Hafsid style.

The foreign fondouks

Rue de la Kasbah continues east, downhill and out of the Medina. Just before place de la Victoire, a tiny alley on the left – rue de l'Ancienne Douane – leads to the site of the **first French Consulate** and trading post (marked by a plaque on the wall just before the Guersin baths). Along the same street are the former Italian, Austro-Hungarian and German embassy buildings, whose first-floor balconies still bear their national insignia, the only clue to their erstwhile importance. Today they're all *ukelas*, houses divided up into rented accommodation for several families, though originally the buildings were *fondouks*, trading posts where foreign merchants were obliged to live. It was Hammouda Pacha who, in 1659, gave permission for the *fondouks* to be built. These were still dangerous times for foreigners in Tunis: in 1678 Francis Baker, the English consul, reported that one Sidi Mohammed Bey "did . . . forceably and violently seize on Charles Gratiano, Consul for the French, together with ourselves . . . swearing by the Soule of his deceased he would cutt us to pieces". Fortunately Mohammed Bey fled when his brother Ali Bey returned, and the consul lived to tell the tale. The area is one of the most run down in the Medina, although the ASM is busying itself with the renovation of the *ukelas*. At the end of the rue de l'Ancienne Douane is rue Zarkoun, a kind of flea market, and just beyond you'll find yourself in a street of brothels.

Back on the corner of place de la Victoire, you'll notice the former **British Embassy**, a whitewashed mansion built in the 1860s by Sir Richard Wood. An influential British consul in the days when Britain and France were still jockeying for position here, Wood was instrumental in obtaining for a British firm the concession for the TGM, the first rail company in Tunisia, whose rail line he then succeeded in routing through the garden of his residence in La Marsa. When other nations were moving out to the suburbs the British obstinately stayed in the centre of town until 2004, when they finally bowed to the need for more space and security.

From place de la Victoire, the **rue des Glacières** leads north. Here, in the eighteenth and nineteenth centuries, huge blocks of ice shipped from the Alps were stored, to be sold at vast profit during the summer months. For a long time the street was known for its shops selling secondhand furniture and bric-a-brac, most of it left by the French in the mid-1950s (Art Deco statuettes and nineteenth-century portraits of long-forgotten soldiers), but these have now been swamped by stores selling imitation designer gear.

Southern Medina

Next to the central section of the Medina, the southern area has the greatest concentration of monumental interest, with three highlights in the Dar Ben Abdallah museum, the Dar Othman palace and the Tourbet el Bey mausoleum. As with all the non-central walks, though, it is the combination of continuing local life – children at school, vegetable markets – with hundreds of years of historical legacy that makes it so worthwhile getting off the main routes. This itinerary takes you from place de la Victoire down to the southern end of the Medina and then back up to finish on its western edge, not far from the beginning of the walk from the Kasbah district to Montfleury (see p.105).

Climbing up rue Jemaa Zitouna from place de la Victoire, you come to **rue Sidi Ali Azouz** and, turning left, at no. 7 a nineteenth-century **zaouia** of the same name. Sidi Ali Azouz was born in Fez in Morocco in the seventeenth century and settled in Zaghouan after returning from a pilgrimage to Mecca. Like Sidi Mehrez, he is one of the patron saints of the city of Tunis. Just after the *zaouia* (next left, an unnamed impasse off rue Sidi Ali Azouz) is an opportunity to see a Medina palace unaffected by the riot of decoration that covers every surface of later residences. **Dar Bayram Turki**, named after a senior official of Youssef Dey who lived here at the beginning of the seventeenth century, would originally have been approached through a typical crooked *skifa* or passage. Nowadays a simple doorway leads into a plain courtyard built of undecorated limestone, where two shallow three-arch porticoes face each other, mirrored by blind arcades on the other two sides. Compared with later courtyards, the effect is almost monastic – though far from artless: note the spaced dark stones picking out the shape of each arch, and the characteristic loop motif above. Currently the ground floor is occupied by small **workshops**, including (on either side of the entrance) a ceramics outfit which was involved in restoring Dar Othman.

A little further south, rue Sidi Ali Azouz runs past the brooding bulk of the **Sidi Amir Barracks** – one of the five built by Hammouda Bey at the beginning of the nineteenth century (see p.89). Now virtually abandoned, it feels like a massive police station – which, of course, is what it was built to be. Continuing, the street merges with a dark tunnel of the **Souk el Belat**, selling mainly food. To your right, on the corner of Souk el Belat and rue du Trésor, is the tenth-century **Ichbili Mosque** with its squat fourteenth-century minaret set well back. If you're interested in another lovely palace like Dar Bayram Turki, take a brief detour behind the Ichbili Mosque to **Dar el Hedri** at 12 rue du Trésor, easily identifiable by its Hafsid slanting arch-stones above the door and an open gallery running above the courtyard. Because it's now used as shared housing rather than workshops, this palace retains a more serene feeling. As in Dar Bayram Turki, the three-arched courtyard is in honey-coloured limestone, enlivened only by loop motifs (single and double). Instead of black arch-stones, a black design picks out the centre of the courtyard: a simple statement of the theme presented much more elaborately in the courtyard of the *zaouia* of Sidi Kassem Jelizi and on Dar Othman's facade.

Along rue Sidi Ali Azouz, the street forks just after a crossroads. Bear left and you're on **rue des Teinturiers** (Street of the Dyers). Ahead rises the minaret of the **Mosquée des Teinturiers**, also known as the New Mosque and centre of a sizable complex. The mosque was commissioned by Husayn Bin Ali, founder of the Husaynid dynasty, as his own memorial, and he lavished great expense on it, importing tiles for the prayer hall from Iznik in Turkey. The octagonal minaret recalls those of Youssef Dey and Hammouda Bey near the Great Mosque, though it was built a century later than Youssef Dey's, in 1716. In the *tourbet* attached to the mosque, Husayn buried two holy men, Sidi Kassem Sababti and Sidi Kassem el Beji, reserving the space between them for his own use. Things didn't quite work out, however, and Husayn was driven from power by his nephew Ali Pacha, who buried his own father in the position of honour. A *kouttab* and a *medersa* were added to the complex later, making it an impressive, if abortive, memorial. You can see the tombs through a window, if it's open, in rue Sidi Kassem.

Dar Othman

Almost opposite the mosque, down the passage-like rue el M'Bazaa, stands the superb doorway of **Dar Othman**, an attractive palace built by Othman Dey (ruled 1598–1610) to escape the intrigues and insecurities of life in the Kasbah – the gates closed off the street so that the palace could be defended if necessary. Its monumental facade consists of a welter of black and white marble patterns – an effect that was common further east in the Islamic world and may have been imported by the Turks. You may find it a little overdone here: in the *skifa* and the courtyard beyond, decoration continues unabated in the form of coloured tiles, offset by an attractive garden featuring three tall cypress trees in the corners and a lemon tree. If the garden feels out of place, that's because it's a twentieth-century addition. Dar Othman is not officially open to the public, as it is still in use as offices, but if you go on a weekday and ask politely, you may be allowed to look inside.

Dar Ben Abdallah

From rue des Teinturiers, turn right into rue Sidi Kassem, then left through an arch onto Impasse Ben Abdallah, where you'll find the **Dar Ben Abdallah** (Mon–Sat 9.30am–4.30pm; 1.6TD, camera 1TD), one of the finest old palaces in the Medina. The palace was originally called Dar Kahia after its builder, one Slimane Kahia el Hanafi, who achieved prominence during the reign of Hammouda Bey (1781–1813) by marrying the daughter of the next ruler, Mahmoud Bey. Slimane was a senior government official and led the ruler's vital twice-yearly *mahalla* (tax-collecting expedition) to the tribes of the interior. With up to eight thousand participants, the summer *mahalla* marched to Béja and fanned out from there across the north; in winter, its base was Tozeur. When Slimane moved to live in the Bey's entourage at the Bardo, his Tunis residence was bought by the rich landowner and silk merchant whose name it carries now.

The palace has a classic design. A *driba* (entrance hall), lined with stone benches for waiting guests, opens onto a *skifa* leading into the house proper and distancing it from the outside world. The florid decoration of the door that leads from *driba* to *skifa* is once again typical of the Italianate styles that became increasingly popular from the eighteenth century – as, too, is much of the ornamentation in the courtyard (look out for the grotesque little dolphins hanging upside down on the fountain). T-shaped reception rooms open off the courtyard; the cupboard-like rooms at the angles were sometimes used as bedrooms.

The palace has been converted into the **Museum of Popular Arts and Traditions**, with each T-shaped room devoted to an area of traditional upper-class urban life: childhood, marriage, the men's quarters. After the white stucco and light tiles of the airy courtyard, the rooms' heavily painted ceilings make for a strange contrast. Some of the rooms contain dummies dressed in traditional nineteenth-century costumes and engaged in traditional pastimes, like drinking coffee. All these displays show how even the simplest of everyday items are imbued with an elaborate sense of geometric design.

The Dyers' Souks, the Tourbet el Bey and Bab Jedid

Back on rue des Teinturiers, there's an old **hammam** on the left, which proclaims itself the "most elegant establishment of bathing baths in marble". To the south, opposite nos. 92 and 104 open the **Souks of the Dyers**, after whom the street is named. At one time, dyeing was a vital part of Tunis's economy, but now it's just one more threatened traditional craft. The first of the souks has been taken over for making drums, and you may see the odd clay body lying around, waiting for skins to be tanned before being stretched over them. The other souk is still used for a limited amount of (rather gaudy) dyeing.

Continue along rue des Teinturiers, turn right on rue Sidi el Benna, then right again on rue Sidi Zamoul, past a huge palace with lazy palm trees, to the **Tourbet el Bey** (Mon–Sat 9.30am–4.30pm; 1.6TD, camera 1TD). As its name suggests, this is a royal mausoleum, built by Ali Bey II (1759–81) and containing most of the Husaynid dynasty that followed him, right up to the last prince who was assassinated by Bourguiba partisans in 1953 (his tomb lies in the courtyard). The architecture is ornate but uninspired – one of the least successful examples of Tunisian Cosmopolitan building in the capital, perhaps because it suffers from too strong a European influence. It is fascinating to look around inside, however, at the scores of marble tombs and the flamboyant tiling and plasterwork on the walls and ceilings. The tombs of all the male members of the dynasty are topped with their headwear, carved in marble – their seniority is indicated by the number of tassels attached to their fezzes. The *gardien* is very informative and will point out much of the hidden symbolism: for example, in the princesses' tomb room, a subliminal fish scale pattern is incorporated into the tiles and a hand of Fatima motif into the plaster to ward off evil spirits. Nearby, 44 rue Sidi Essourdou was once a **medersa** founded in the eighteenth century by Husayn Bin Ali, the first Husaynid Bey.

Turning right from the Tourbet el Bey onto the street named after it, you can make a small detour by taking a left down rue des Juges and then the third right up **rue des Forgerons** (since the thirteenth century the blacksmiths' souk). This brings you out of the Medina at **Bab Jedid**, a gate built in 1276 as part of the Hafsid city wall. Up some stairs next to it is a tiny mosque, the **Khalouet Sidi Mehrez**, where the Hafsid sultans used to pay homage to the city's patron saint. You could, if you wanted, leave the Medina through Bab Jedid and join the itinerary from the Kasbah district to Montfleury (see p.105).

Returning to rue Tourbet el Bey and continuing north along it, you'll pass at no. 41 the tiny **M'sid el Koubba Mosque** where the great historian Ibn Khaldoun used to teach. Born in 1332 at no. 33 of the same street, Ibn Khaldoun anticipated a dominant theme in modern political thought by suggesting that history repeats itself in cycles (see p.563). A little further along rue Tourbet el Bey, just north of no. 20 and on the right as you emerge from underneath a **sabat** (a room located over the street), a decrepit stone archway leads into impasse du Jasmin. This was originally built in the seventeenth century as a weavers' workshop by the Spanish community, whose wealthy citizens lived on this street. Three and a half centuries later, a silk weaver is still making *sifsaris* in the workshop at no. 7.

Sidi Bou Khrissane and around

Backtracking slightly, turn right onto **rue du Riche**, then right into **rue des Andalous**, both streets having a scattering of magnificent doorways. This is where wealthier Andalusian immigrants settled while the less well-off had to petition for land in order to found towns like Testour (see p.302). At the end, a left turn onto rue du Dey then another on rue Mohsen will bring you into a small square. On your left is the **Dar Hussein**, a palace built originally in the twelfth century and enlarged in the eighteenth. Once the town hall, then the French army headquarters during colonial rule, it's now used by the National Institute of Patrimony, who will be pleased to let you have a look at the elaborate tiling and stuccowork inside for a small consideration – something well worth paying. Across the square is the **El Ksar Mosque**, founded around 1106 by the Emir Ahmed Ibn Khourassane. The minaret, an interesting blend of Ottoman and Andalusian styles, was added in 1647.

Ibn Khourassane's family, the Khourassanids, who ruled Tunis from 1059 to 1159, have their mausoleum just around the corner. Turn right out of the square into rue Sidi Bou Khrissane, then left into rue Ben Mahmoud. On your left is the **Sidi Bou Khrissane Museum** (Mon–Fri 9am–noon & 2–5pm; knock on the door – donation of around 2TD expected). Part of a cemetery dating back to the ninth century, it is really more a garden full of old tombstones than a museum. The Khourassanid emirs are interred under a cupola at the back.

Rue Ben Mahmoud finally runs out into Souk Sekkajine. Buried in a red and green box in the middle of the street on your left is **Sidi Bou Abdallah**, who died on this spot while defending Tunis against the invading Spanish. A Spaniard, however, is buried only a few metres further on, originally under an olive tree but now in a gaudy shrunken *koubba* dating from 1987, at **Bab Menara**, where Souk Sekkajine emerges from the Medina. He is Anselm Tourmeda (aka Abdallah Tourjman), a fourteenth-century Majorcan who came to Tunisia, converted to Islam and wrote religious propaganda in Arabic and Catalan.

Northern Medina

The northern Medina is largely free of sightseers and the shops here are geared for local residents. There are fewer sights as such, though the Mosque of Sidi Mehrez is as familiar to Tunisians as the Zitouna Mosque, but this is a much better part of the Medina if you just want to wander. This walk leads up to the northern end of the Medina, where you could take a detour into Halfaouine (see p.102); otherwise, it returns to place de la Victoire.

Turn off rue de la Kasbah onto rue Saida Ajoula, and the first left you see is rue Onk el Jemal, where no. 5, the **Onkiya Medersa**, was founded by a Hafsid princess in 1341. Backtracking, duck left off rue Saida Ajoula into rue du Divan. At no. 3 on the right is the **Divan** itself, home of the Divan council, which at first played a major role in the power structure of the sixteenth- and seventeenth-century Turkish Regency of Tunis. As authority gradually passed into the hands of individual beys, though, the council's function became more that of a religious court. Further on at no. 16 is the **Zaouia of Sidi Abdelkader**, built in 1851 by the Qadriya (or Kadria) Sufi brotherhood as a gathering place for their adepts.

A right at the end of rue du Divan down rue de l'Agha will bring you to an area of **secondhand clothing stalls**. Prices are ridiculously low – you can get virtually brand-new clothes for next to nothing, as well as some superb 1970s *haute couture*. Nearby, at 9 rue des Nègres, is the **Mustansiriya medersa**, founded in 1435 by the Hafsid Sultan el Mustansir and in a state of extreme disrepair. The seventeenth-century **Zaouia of Sidi Braham**, around the corner in rue el Azzafine, is famous for its collection of ceramic tiles.

Back at the junction of rue du Divan and rue de l'Agha, you can head west to little place Ramdhane Bey and have a quick look up at the elaborate set of **Ottoman windows** through the arch ahead of you in rue Bir Lahjar – a startling sight in the streets of blank exterior walls. Then head north, down **rue du Pasha**, a tidy cobbled street that was the main thoroughfare of the Turkish residential quarter, with graceful doorways befitting the homes of important officials. No. 40, on the left, is the eighteenth-century **Medersa Bir Lahjar**, which hosts frequent concerts, particularly during the month-long Medina Festival held during Ramadan (see p.116). Opposite no. 64 in the same street, follow a passageway into **rue de la Noria**, which has to be the narrowest lane in the Medina. On the left as you bear left into rue du Tribunal is **Dar Lasram**, home of the Tunis Association de Sauvegarde de la Medina and built for the Lasram family, an old Kairouan clan that claimed a direct line of descent back to the Arab conquest in the seventh century. This family palace dates originally from the mid-eighteenth century, reflected in the exuberant decoration to be seen inside. The **Club Culturel Tahar Haddad** next door is an active cultural venue for exhibitions, evening recitals and concerts. Opposite, at no. 27, is the nineteenth-century **mausoleum** of the landowning Dziri family, which is now the Maison de la Poésie and hosts mainly Arabic poetry readings.

Rue Sidi Mehrez and around

At the northern end of rue du Tribunal runs rue Sidi Ibrahim Riahi, where the **Zaouia of Sidi Ibrahim Riahi** is at no. 11, left of the junction. Originally from Testour, al Riahi was a leading member of the Tijaniya Sufi brotherhood at the beginning of the nineteenth century. Although successful as a teacher in Tunis, where religion offered greater social mobility than any other profession, he still needed a sponsor because he was not earning a decent living. Into the breach, so as to keep him in Tunisia, stepped Youssef Sahib et Tabaa, the

The Hafsia and the Jewish community

Recently redeveloped, and winning an Aga Khan award for Islamic architecture, the **Hafsia** – Tunis's erstwhile Jewish ghetto – occupies the northernmost corner of the Medina, between rue Achour and rue Bab Souika. At one time the enclave was separated from the rest of the town by a wall and its gates were closed at night. Before the status of Jews was regularized in 1861 there were many other petty restrictions: Jews had to wear black clothes of a traditional style, as European dress was forbidden; and they were not allowed to ride horses or own land outside the Hafsia. Jews had their own civil courts, but in their dealings with Muslims were subject to Islamic law, and they faced burning at the stake if found guilty of a capital offence. Although Islam regards the Jews as "people of the book" (fellow monotheists), many Muslims regarded them as heathen and treated them as such. Occasionally riots broke out and the Hafsia was wrecked by Muslim mobs, but most of the time the Jews lived in peace, however restricted.

It was the immigration of Maltese and Italian Jews, citizens of powerful European states, that allowed the Jews to escape these repressive laws. By the 1870s their wealth and connections with European governments had given them considerable power and new freedom. Then, under the Protectorate, they joined the middle class and many left the Medina for the suburbs. Nevertheless, when the Germans arrived in 1942 the Hafsia was still very crowded. Fortunately, though they imposed punitive measures, the Nazis did not pursue a policy of mass extermination against Jews in North Africa. After the war many Jews emigrated to Israel and the ghetto was finally pulled down in 1953. The remainder of the Jewish community dispersed into the suburbs.

prime minister under Hammouda Bey, and who later met a brutal end (see p.102). Follow the street the other way and around the corner in rue Achour is the seventeenth-century **Achouria Medersa**. A dogleg to the left at the end of rue Sidi Ibrahim brings you into rue el Monastiri, where at no. 9 is the entrance to Dar Monastiri, a restored early nineteenth-century palace. The street runs down into **rue Sidi Mehrez**, the last incarnation of one of the main north–south arteries of the Medina. A busy shopping street, it houses the **Zaouia of Sidi Mehrez**, fronted by a long passage. Sidi Mehrez is still revered as a patron saint of Tunis for his efforts in the tenth century: after the city's sufferings during the revolt of Abu Yazid, it was he who oversaw its revival. The original tomb has shared many of Tunis's ups and downs, and the present building is mainly eighteenth- and nineteenth-century. Traditionally, boys come to drink from its well before their circumcision ceremony.

Opposite the *zaouia*, though not visible from the street, is the **Mosque of Sidi Mehrez**, one of Tunis's most distinctive landmarks. You can climb some steps, a little beyond the *zaouia* on the right, into a shopping arcade for the best look at its heap of white domes. Dotted with pigeons, they stand out for kilometres in any rooftop view of the Medina and are the city's only example of the Imperial Ottoman building style. Presumably Mohammed Bey, who founded it in 1696, wanted to stamp a truly Turkish presence on the city, but after his early death, the assassination of his brother and the rise of the Husaynids, the mosque was left unfinished. Instead of the four circular minarets that would have conferred a fully Ottoman look, it got a small, square North African one; it's even named after the *zaouia* opposite rather than its own founder. The **pottery shops** at nos. 96 and 97 warrant a quick look. Although they don't sell the fancier souvenir products, they do have a wide range of plates, cups, pots and ashtrays, all at very low prices.

Rue Sidi Mehrez emerges from the Medina into **place Bab Souika**, once a place of public execution, and the area of the liveliest cafés during Ramadan nights. Unfortunately, controversial redevelopment, which also included the Hafsia project (see box p.101), has destroyed much of its character. Turning southeast along rue Bab Souika takes you past the Anglican **Church of St George** on the corner of rue Ahmed Beyrem (formerly rue des Protestants). Look out for the plaque commemorating John Howard Payne, a nineteenth-century US consul, better known as the author of the song "Home Sweet Home". His body had a brief sojourn in the cemetery until 1883 when a US navy frigate arrived and took him home.

The faubourgs

As well as an inner wall around the Medina, the Hafsids built an outer rampart to enclose the city's residential suburbs, or **faubourgs**, which have managed to retain a strong sense of local character and community. They are often referred to by the names of former Medina gates – thus **Halfaouine** is in the Rbat Bab Souika and **Montfleury** is in the Rbat Bab Jazira. As in the Medina, the streets of the faubourgs are often deserted and ill lit at night, and not particularly safe to wander round after hours.

Halfaouine

Halfaouine is one of Tunis's most fascinating areas, with a style completely its own. Originally a settlement outside the walls of the Medina, it was endowed with its own well and fortifications under the Hafsids. More recently, the suburb achieved a certain fame through Férid Boughedir's film of the same name, which ran away with most of the prizes at the 1990 Carthage Festival and draws the crowds in even today.

On the north side of place Bab Souika, a line of flagpoles marks the entrance to the **food markets** of rue Halfaouine. There's a fine example of Hafsid-era architecture in the **Abu Mohamed Mosque**, erected by public subscription on the east side of rue Halfouine. Associated with the mosque is a tradition of religious meetings during Ramadan to discuss the *hadiths* – the sayings of Mohammed.

Rue Halfaouine eventually gives onto **place Halfaouine**. Having begun life as one of the commodity markets common on the edges of the old city, the square had become the heart of an exclusive district by the eighteenth century, thanks largely to the efforts of Youssef Sahib et Tabaa, Hammouda Bey's last prime minister. Youssef rose from Hammouda's *mameluke* at the beginning of his reign to the post of Sahib et Tabaa, the second most powerful man in the country. He owned ships and became wealthy through piracy and international trade, using some of his fortune to commission the mosque here as well as the neighbouring Souk el Jedid, site of his personal palace. Unfortunately, Youssef's forthright personality made him vulnerable after Hammouda's death, and in January 1815, only thirteen months after his master's death, Youssef was assassinated after a rival Tunisian-born official called Larbi Zarrouk convinced Hammouda's successor, Mahmoud Bey, that Youssef was a threat.

With its trees and benches, place Halfaouine retains an air of decaying quasi-European elegance, belying the fact that this quiet backwater was once notorious for nationalist demonstrations against the French. Facing the square,

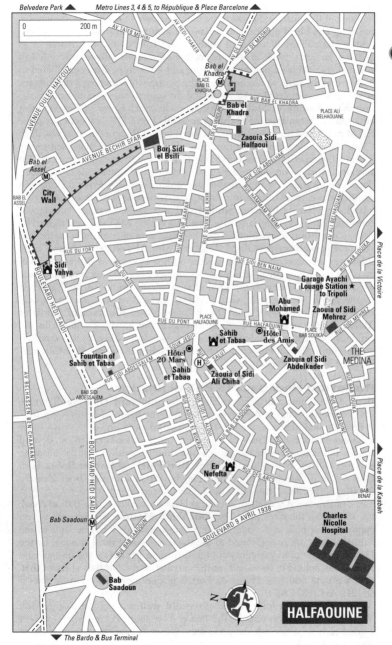

the **Youssef Sahib et Tabaa Mosque**, begun in 1812, is one of the most beautiful and unusual in Tunisia, closer to a Venetian palazzo than the Great Mosque of Kairouan, and perhaps the finest example of Tunisian Cosmopolitan building. The blend of local and Italian elements is at its most successful here, with metal railings, Neoclassical columns and flamboyant black marble – all of them foreign – made to seem perfectly in place. The minaret was only half finished when Youssef met his premature end – which perhaps contributed to a story that the same would happen to the person who completed the minaret. It was finally completed in 1970. Behind the mosque, at 9 rue du Salut, is the crumbling **Zaouia of Sidi Ali Chiha**, beside which is one of Tunisia's most atmospheric hammams, the **Hammam Sahib** (see p.118), a spectacular place full of pillars and horseshoe arches where much of Boughedir's film was shot.

Rue Sidi el Aloui leads west from place Halfouine into an elongated square full of palm trees. Cross rue Bab Saadoun here and in front of you is the **En Nefefta Mosque** on the corner of rue des Arcs and impasse de la Mosquée. The building you see is modern, but the mosque was founded in the fifteenth century and parts of the interior structure date back to that period.

Back on place Halfaouine, **Souk Jedid** is a vaulted passage leading out onto rue Zaouia el Bokria to your left and rue de Miel on your right. The souk, commissioned by Youssef Sahib et Tabaa, now specializes in clothes. As you emerge, keep straight ahead along **rue Sidi Abdessalem**, where a small *sabat* over the street about 200m further on houses a *kouttab* (Koranic school) attached to a *masjid* (small mosque). This complex of buildings is characteristic of old medina quarters – the local elementary or primary school attached to the parish church, as it were. Right at the end of rue Sidi Abdessalem on a sliver of open space stands the bulbous-domed **fountain of Sahib et Tabaa**, another of Youssef's municipal works in this quarter. The fountain was originally located just inside the Hafsid Bab Sidi Abdessalem, so that travellers arriving from the country could refresh themselves; nowadays it's usually surrounded by a small flea market.

Boulevard Hedi Saidi to Bab el Khadra

Beyond the fountain of Sahib et Tabaa runs **boulevard Hedi Saidi**, where you can pick up a bus or the métro (line #4) to the Bardo Museum (see p.107). A few hundred metres to the left, **Bab Saadoun**, once one of the city's outer gates but now a traffic island at a major road junction, looks rather lost. Beyond it is the bus station serving the north of the country. Southwest of Bab Saadoun is Rabta Hill, site of two Ottoman forts, **Borj Flifel** and **Borj er Rabta**, both built in the mid-eighteenth century. Nearby, yet another fort, **Borj Zouara** (or Borj el Andalous), dates back to the seventeenth century.

East of Bab Sidi Abdessalem, boulevard Hedi Saidi takes you to **Bab el Assel**, yet another of the city's gates. The **Sidi Yahya Mosque**, on the right as you approach, was built as a *masjid* in the fourteenth century by the saint whose name it bears, and later elevated to the status of *jemaa* (Friday mosque) by the Hafsids because of its strategic position. Turn right just before the mosque and have a look behind it, and you'll see the entrance to the old **Bab el Assel fort**, now a private house, at 25 rue du Fort. A plaque above the doorway dates it at 1216 AH (1801 AD).

Here, too, begins a huge chunk of the **old wall**, starting just past the Sidi Yahya Mosque and running by the Bab el Assel sports centre, where you get a good view of it through the perimeter railings. Follow the pavement round into avenue Bechir Sfar and take the first right into rue du Miel. The entrance to the sports centre is on your right; otherwise take a left down the little street full of carpenters' workshops. You'll be walking parallel with the wall, still there behind the workshops on your left. The street emerges at another of the old forts, **Borj Sidi el Bsili**, again dating back to the turn of the nineteenth century. The Ministry of Culture has restored it and turned it over to various craftsmen, who will be happy to show you around if you knock on the door and ask.

A left and a right turn here down avenue Bechir Sfar brings you, after 100m or so, to perhaps the city's oddest gate, **Bab el Khadra**. This double-door-wayed piece of a fairytale castle is not the fourteenth-century original, but a rebuilt version dating back to 1881. Behind the right-hand doorway is **rue de la Verdure**, whose name, like that of the gate, refers to the "greenery" of the countryside which used to start outside it. Halfway along rue de la Verdure, the impasse de Sidi el Halfaoui (on the left) leads to the **Zaouia of Sidi el Halfaoui**, containing the tomb of the seventeenth-century saint after whom Halfaouine is named. Non-Muslims can't enter, but you can glimpse the saint's tomb through a grille by the door.

Rue de la Verdure runs onto a square from where rue Hammam Remimi and a right at the end along avenue Ali Belhouane will take you straight back to Bab Souika. Much better, however, is a stroll down **rue Souiki Bel Khir**, straight ahead, which runs past various interesting cul-de-sacs and under the odd *sabat* to end up back in place Halfaouine.

From the Kasbah to Montfleury

As with Halfaouine in the north, the Medina's western and southern fringes are occupied by ancient districts dating back to Hafsid times. Directly west, the **Kasbah district** was the Hafsid seat of government, while further south **Montfleury**, also known as **Rbat Bab Jazira**, was a residential quarter.

Place de la Kasbah, on the western edge of the Medina, is always crowded with civil servants from the various government departments located hereabouts (making it a good place to catch a taxi). It gets its name from the fort that stood here above the Medina in Hafsid times, which has almost completely disappeared except for the **Kasbah Mosque** and parts of the wall to the south along rue ez-Zouaoui (heavily guarded as the Ministry of Defence occupies most of the site). More than seven hundred and fifty years after it was built, the mosque still sets a standard for Tunisian architecture. The Hafsids, arriving as part of an Almohad empire based in Marrakesh, wanted to make a clear statement of their origins, and this mosque's minaret – square, with decorated lozenge designs in relief – is immediately identifiable as part of the same family as the Koutoubia in Marrakesh, the Hassan in Rabat and the Giralda in Seville. When a new Malekite minaret was needed for the Great Mosque in 1834, this was the model that the architects used. Notice that the lozenge design is more subtle than it at first looks, with a different design on the north and south faces from the one on the east and west. Perhaps because of its elevated position, the mosque signals to the rest of the city for the call to prayer: five times a day a white flag is hung out from the scaffold protruding from the minaret.

The rest of the Hafsid kasbah stood on the other side of rue 2 Mars from the mosque, where a stark modern monument and broad **esplanade**, with great views over the city and Medina, recently replaced the last excavations. The kasbah's last occupant was a French barracks installed in 1881 and levelled in 1957, but it really lost its importance after the Turks moved the seat of government into Dar el Bey (see p.94) in the early seventeenth century. Unfortunately, the historical significance of the site made it a favourite place for architects trying to express the more grandiose aspirations of the newly independent state: the former RCD headquarters building on top of the hill was recognized as a mistake as soon as it was erected in 1974, although it has thankfully been totally obscured by the dominant new **municipal government building**, a weird mix of pink stone, concrete and blue bulletproof glass.

On the northern side of place de la Kasbah stands **Sadiki College** with its two domes, founded by Khereddine in 1875 and inevitably described as Tunisia's Eton, where Bourguiba and other future leaders were educated. Right below it, next to the street, is the **tomb of Farhat Hached**, the trade union leader murdered by reactionary French colonialists in 1952 (see p.505).

Heading up rue 2 Mars 1934 from the mosque, you pass a surviving stretch of kasbah **wall** and an old city gate, **Bab Sidi Abdallah**, before hitting boulevard du 9 Avril 1938; bear left here for a couple of hundred metres until you come to a sort of spaghetti junction, with the green pyramidal roof of the Zaouia of Sidi Kassem Jelizi at the near left-hand corner (see below). Fume-ridden city artery though it may be, boulevard du 9 Avril 1938 runs along the top of the ridge here and offers a fine view down over Sebkhet Sejoumi, round to the Jellaz Cemetery and beyond to Lake Tunis. From this viewpoint, it's easy to understand the city's appalling climate – as the eighteenth-century traveller James Bruce put it, "low, hot and damp".

The Zaouia of Sidi Kassem Jelizi and around

Fortunately, the **Zaouia of Sidi Kassem Jelizi** (Mon–Sat 8am–4pm; free) is more than adequate compensation for coming this far: the most accessible piece of late Hafsid architecture in the city, with a strong flavour of Spain and some Eastern influence as well. Abou el Fadl Kassem Ahmed as-Sadafi al-Fasi came originally from Fez, but he is thought to have learned the trade that earned him the title *jalizi* (potter) in Spain. When his mausoleum was built, in 1490, it would have enjoyed a prominent position crowning this ridge at the edge of the Hafsid city. It begins with an entrance hall leading past a small pottery workshop on the right into a courtyard. Rooms on three sides, designed originally for pilgrims and visitors but now displaying pottery exhibits, give way on the fourth to the tomb itself, whose pyramidal green-tiled roof – reminiscent of Granada and built at the time of Granada's fall to the Christians – gives the building its Andalusian feel. Looking to the other end of the Islamic world, the courtyard paving's bold geometric patterns in black marble – found elsewhere in Tunis in the Midhat es Soltane (see p.92) and in palaces of a slightly later date – are more reminiscent of Cairo. No one is sure whether the patterns here and in the Midhat are original or whether they were added later under the Turks. Inside the tomb, however, the tone is all Andalusian. In particular, don't miss the star-patterned tiles in the flat niche opposite the tomb room entrance. Outside the mausoleum proper, a small yard shelters a large collection of headstones, the Hafsid ones having plain columns and the later Turkish examples crowned with a turban. Opposite the *zaouia*, across the place du Résidence du Leader, where Bourguiba once lived, stands the strangely squat minaret of the **Jemaa el Haoua**, founded in the thirteenth century by Queen Atif, wife of the Hafsid Sultan Abu Zakariya.

Place aux Chevaux to place Bab Jezira

Make your way to the bottom right-hand corner of place du Résidence and out along rue Abd el Wahab. This shortly comes to a junction with rue Bab el Gorjani and rue Boukris. Across from here and slightly to the right, **place des Chevaux**, with its miniature football pitch, leads on to become **place du**

Marché du Blé, the start of a great junk m\
thing from old shoe buckles to metal utensils.\
the markets where city merchants would deal\
and animals from the countryside. Turn sharp left\
lowing the junk, and head downhill. At the bottom\
the broad **Souk des Armes**, formerly the weapon\
minaret of the **Mosque of El Helaak**, traditionally he\
in 1375 by a freed black slave who sold his gold jewellery\
your right, off rue el Hajamine, **Souk el Asser** is a babble\
stalls. A left here will take you to **Bab Jedid**, the Medina ga\
hill, where you could hook up with the southern Medina tou.

To continue, go straight ahead into the pillared tunnel of _____ ine
(forking right after emerging from the tunnel to stay on Hajja_ _). When
Hajjamine hits rue Abou Kassem el Chabbi, cross the road and continue past
a green-domed tomb, down into a small open space surrounded by tombs of
eighteenth- and nineteenth-century worthies. Take the lower, left-hand fork
out of here and continue on Hajjamine to where rue En Naial comes in on the
right. Immediately opposite on the left, rue Sidi Mansour heads off downhill,
passing a *masjid* with a weedy green-tiled roof at rue Er Raia, and eventually
hitting **rue Bab el Fellah** – recognizable as a main drag of the old quarter
stuffed with food stalls. Turning left on Bab el Fellah will take you back up to
Bab Jazira, the southern gate out of the Medina, which is dominated by the
minaret of the **Mosque of Sidi el Bechir**.

The Jellaz Cemetery

A right on Bab el Fellah will take you further south to Bab Aleoua bus station
and the **Jellaz Cemetery**, a huge and very pleasant hillside burial ground
founded in the thirteenth century. According to legend, the founder was a
saint whose servant bought the land from a Jew so that poor Muslims could be
buried there. In 1911 it was the scene of the first mass demonstration against
the French, when the municipal council threatened to requisition the land for
development. A shot was fired – some said by an Italian spectator, others by a
French officer – killing a young boy. In the riot that ensued, nine Frenchmen,
five Italians and over thirty Tunisians died.

The cemetery is dominated by the seventeenth-century **Borj Ali Rais**, an
Ottoman fortress visible from the whole city but, unfortunately, closed to the
public. It's also known as Borj Sidi Bel Hassen after the nearby **Zaouia of Sidi
Bel Hassen**, which was built in 1815 but dedicated to a thirteenth-century
marabout said to have introduced coffee to Tunisia.

The Bardo Museum

Housed in the former royal palace of the Bey, west of the city centre, the
Bardo Museum (Tues–Sun: April–Sept 9am–5pm; Oct–March 9.30am–
4.30pm; 4.2TD, camera 1TD) is one of those museums that is almost too well
endowed. Its encyclopedic collection of Roman mosaics is really too much to
take in on a single visit, but even a glimpse of some of the designs will flesh
out the Roman sites in the country, and a second visit afterwards will complete
the picture. The building itself is spectacular, built up over centuries and surrounded by gardens full of Roman and Punic stones; as you wander around the
collections, especially note the ornate ceilings.

...ere is on the métro: line #4 runs to the museum's ...etro. It's a thirty-minute journey from the city centre by ...nue Bourguiba, bus #3c, #4, #4c, #4d, #23, #23b, #23c or ...jardin Thameur, or several others from Bab Saadoun. A taxi from ...tre should cost around 2–3TD.

Roman and Islamic art

Africa's Roman mosaics, of which the Bardo has by far the largest collection in the world, are arguably the most colourful and vivid images left behind by a Roman Empire better known for its monumental engineering feats. Native Romans at home in Italy painted their walls so colourfully that they preferred floor mosaics to be black and white. In Africa, though, wall painting was never widespread, and mosaics developed as almost the only form of domestic decoration. Like an album of colour snapshots, these mosaics offer a direct and beautiful visual record of what was considered important by this extraordinarily powerful civilization.

Seeing the mosaics in exuberant quantity makes it easy to take them for granted. These were the Persian rugs of the ancient world, requiring enormous time and skill to lay out, and the fact that most were privately commissioned for homes reflects the status-conscious social structure of the time. The **subjects** were probably also chosen by the commissioner, so the emphasis on (broadly speaking) entertainment is significant. Hunting, fishing, the amphitheatre and, to a lesser extent, theatrical themes are all indicative of the leisure activities enjoyed by the wealthy. Even the mythological and religious scenes have a strongly hedonistic slant: **Bacchus**, the god of wine and sensual pleasure in general, features heavily, often shown triumphant over the forces of evil. **Venus**, goddess of love, usually has her vampish side strongly emphasized. Most noticeable of all, though, is the feeling of abundance. The **sea** is always shown crammed with endless varieties of fish (including the lobsters which wave in the god Ocean's hair), rural **farming scenes** are a constant, and lush vines weave their way through and around almost every scene. The mosaics evoke a life of sensual gratification and plenty, neatly summed up in an inscription found at Timgad in Algeria: "To hunt, to bathe, to gamble, to laugh, that is to live."

Towards the end of the Roman era, and into the Byzantine, the increasingly tense stylization of the mosaics reflects a less carefree society, permeated by a stricter spiritual discipline intended to preserve it in a hostile world. Although there's nothing here to match the early Byzantine mosaics of Ravenna in Italy, the tauter styles can come as a relief after the more florid imperial mosaics.

Because it had to be imported at great expense, **marble statuary** was less common in Africa than in other parts of the Roman world. Carthage, though, was richly stocked with figures of all types, primarily important men and women: generals, senators, sponsors, emperors and other worthies. The Bardo has a fine, though typically damaged selection: it's worth pointing out that the systematic **de-nosing and emasculation** of male statues was the routine work of invading Vandals, mutilating and castrating their enemies in stone as well as flesh.

There is also a stunning collection of Greek bronze and marble figures and domestic furniture, recovered from the so-called **Mahdia wreck**. In 1907 fishermen off Mahdia found this ancient shipwreck, dating from the first century BC. Its cargo gives an impression of the style in which the Romans of the time lived.

Islamic art, which shuns the human image, is at the other extreme. For the most part, Islamic artists have concentrated on decorative pattern and colour, a combination most brilliantly exemplified in a room of ceramic **tiles** taken from inside old mosques. The best are those brought by the Turks from Iznik, with their vegetal designs and bright colours still fresh after hundreds of years. There are other tiles from Tunisia itself, in characteristic blues, greens and yellows, and from Morocco, distinguishable by their tighter geometric patterns.

Confusingly, **rooms** in the Bardo are sometimes numbered and other times named after the particular sites most of the exhibits come from (and sometimes both). There is also a tendency to juggle the exhibits about, particularly the Islamic, folk-art and traditions exhibits, some of which have long been slated for a move to the Museum of Islamic Art at Reqqada, near Kairouan (see p.255), though there is little sign of this happening. In summer you might think about starting at the top of the building, so that you don't get up there just as it receives the full attention of the midday sun. English-language guidebooks (8TD) are on sale at the **gift shops** at the end of the entrance hall and at the museum exit.

While you are in the area, it is worth making a detour out to the suburb of Manouba, a couple of kilometres west of the Bardo, where you will find the **National Military Museum** (Musée Militaire Nationale; Tues–Sun 9am–4pm; ☎71 220 218; 1TD, camera 2TD), which provides an excellent account of Tunisian military history from Phoenician to modern times. Housed in the restored eighteenth-century Palais de la Rose, the museum features a fine array of weaponry and uniforms, including a particularly impressive set of sixteenth-century Ottoman muskets and gold-encrusted field guns. To reach it (it's easiest to take a taxi), head west along the Mateur road for 2km past the Bardo Museum, then turn left over the railway lines towards Manouba. The museum is on the left after 1km, signposted only in Arabic, but recognizable by its metal gates and drive lined with palm trees and tanks leading to the silver-domed palace. Bus #4a from Jardin Thameur stops about 100m down the road past the museum.

Ground floor

Prehistory (I) The gallery begins with a small collection of Capsian Neolithic flint blades, mostly from southern Tunisia (see p.341). The highlight is an apparently ordinary pile of stones, which upon closer inspection is comprised of chipped pebbles, balls of flint and bones. Found at El Guettar near Gafsa, it's considered by some to be the oldest human-made structure in the world.

Punic rooms (II–III) Clay **statues** reflect the influence of Greece on Mediterranean culture but retain an Eastern flavour. Those from the eighth century BC look like stiff Egyptian figures; by the third century BC you find a seated **Demeter** with drapery used in Greek style to allow the figure to break into three dimensions; but as late as the first century AD, a small terracotta statue of the Carthaginian god Baal Hammon (after which Room II is named) still has the two-dimensional pose of an Egyptian or early Greek figure. Grotesquely **grimacing masks** from the seventh century BC, used to frighten evil spirits away, are distinctively local.

Libyc stelae The Libyc or Numidian civilization, which followed the Punic, was one of the rare periods of Tunisian "independence", and the handful of exhibits at the end of the entrance hall – notably two **bas-reliefs** of Numidian gods and **bilingual stelae** in Libyc and Punic, and Libyc and Latin – are mere glimpses of what archeologists now realize was a far more advanced culture than had previously been thought. Excavations at the marble quarry of Chemtou (see p.206), long thought to be entirely Roman, have revealed the existence of a formidable Numidian industry there.

Sarcophagus and stele corridor In the long corridor between the Paleo-Christian room and the exit, look for an unusual and engaging **third-century AD statue** found at Borj el Amri (Inv 3047) of a hooded man with a face like a gloomy Fred Flintstone, depicted in the realistic style common at the time. Otherwise he is little more than a tailor's dummy festooned with symbols: his lionskin hood and the club he originally held in his left hand are attributes of Hercules; the drape of his tunic suggests female breasts; and in his right hand he holds a bouquet of poppies and wheat, symbols of the Greek cult of Demeter. The dog at his feet is probably the hellhound Cerberus, captured by Hercules as one of his labours.

Paleo-Christian room (V) A fifth-century **mosaic** from Tabarka on the wall (A307) shows in cartoon fashion a three-aisled basilica or church similar to many found in Tunisia's ancient cities. Similarly, the sixth-century four-way **baptistry** in the middle of the room (from as far away as El Kantara, in Jerba) was to reappear many times – including at George Sebastian's 1920s villa in Hammamet.

Bulla Regia room The prize of this collection of monumental marble statuary is a rock star-like Apollo with his lyre, who originally stood in his own temple at Bulla Regia.

Imperial Portraits room The next room contains some fine portrait heads of Roman emperors, including one ultra-realistic one (Inv 3212) of **Gordian I**, the ill-fated elderly tax collector from El Jem who ruled the Empire for a month before committing suicide.

First floor

Carthage room Set in the floor at the far end of this lavish central hall is the first of a series of documentary-like **mosaics** of rural life in Roman Tunisia (A105), dating from early third-century Oudna, alongside another of Bacchus entwined with cupids and vines. Among the colonnades are numerous statues of Roman gods, including several fine ones of Venus.

Althiburos room On the floor is an interesting mosaic of Roman boats, all labelled, while on the wall is a sixth-century depiction of Apollo and Diana in a temple, with a crane being sacrificed beneath them.

Hadrumetum (Sousse) room Three semicircular scenes from the same room in fourth-century Tabarka show the components of a large agricultural estate: the owner's house (A25); the farm building (A26); and barns and store-rooms (A27). From Carthage in the following century, the famous **Seigneur Julius mosaic** (Inv 1) shows Julius himself sitting at his leisure at bottom right, opposite his wife, who leans against a pillar (in a similar Greek fourth-century BC pose to that of the Haidra statue in the Carthage room). Above them in the middle panel stands their house – the domed roofs suggest a baths complex – surrounded by preparations for a hunt. Agricultural scenes in the top panel include olives being harvested from a tree in the top left corner. Finally, an endearingly crude mosaic from **Byzantine Gafsa** (A19) suggests that the Romans' staple leisure pursuits – like chariot racing – survived the Vandal occupation and continued into the sixth century.

Dougga room The **Cyclops Baths** in Dougga were named after A261, one of the most vivid mosaics in the museum, showing three muscular cyclopes wielding hammers as they forge thunderbolts for Jupiter. The composition is very sophisticated, with one of the group shown from behind. Originally the floor of a *frigidarium*, perhaps this mosaic's scene was designed to warm up its chilled viewers. A382, also from Dougga, shows how bathers recovered, with two servants pouring wine from amphorae on which are inscribed the message "Drink and you will live".

El Jem room A288 shows third-century hunting scenes to delight the heart of any blood-sport enthusiast.

Ulysses room Inv 2884 shows a mosaic of **Ulysses** bound to the mast of his ship and heroically resisting the calls of three sirens. Nearby, in a more flow-

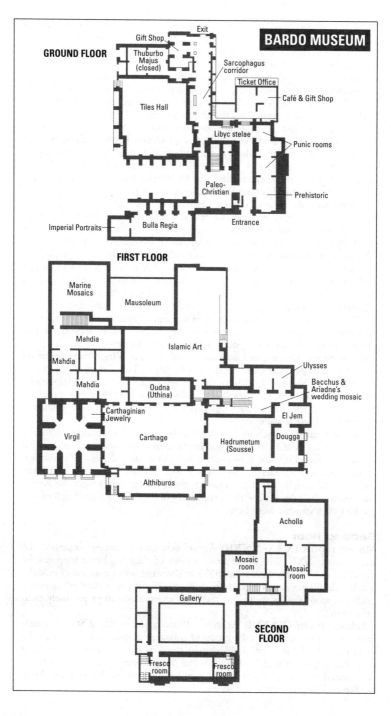

BARDO MUSEUM

GROUND FLOOR

Exit
Gift Shop
Thuburbo Majus (closed)
Sarcophagus corridor
Ticket Office
Café & Gift Shop
Tiles Hall
Libyc stelae
Punic rooms
Prehistoric
Paleo-Christian
Entrance
Imperial Portraits
Bulla Regia

FIRST FLOOR

Marine Mosaics
Mausoleum
Mahdia
Islamic Art
Mahdia
Mahdia
Ulysses
Oudna (Uthina)
Bacchus & Ariadne's wedding mosaic
Carthaginian Jewelry
El Jem
Virgil
Carthage
Hadrumetum (Sousse)
Dougga
Althiburos

SECOND FLOOR

Acholla
Mosaic room
Mosaic room
Gallery
Fresco room
Fresco room

ing style reminiscent of the Cyclopes mosaic in the Dougga room, Inv 2884A from Dougga has another nautical scene from myth. Some pirates in the Tyrrhenian Sea have attacked a ship only to find it's carrying the god **Dionysus**. Clad in a tunic and brandishing a lance, he has repelled the boarders, who hurl themselves overboard, pursued by Dionysus's panthers – unnecessarily, since the pirates are already metamorphosing into dolphins. The scene is completely stolen by the balding boozy Silenus, who clutches the steering oar for support. In the corridor outside is a fourth-century mosaic from Thuburbo Majus depicting the wedding of **Bacchus and Ariadne**.

Ship rooms This spectacular collection of **Greek bronze statuary** went down in a shipwreck off Mahdia at the end of the first century AD and lay on the seabed until discovered in 1907. Greek art was highly prized in the Roman world and travelled widely around the Mediterranean – excavations in the Roman city of Volubilis in modern Morocco unearthed a good deal of it.

Marine mosaic room Taking up most of the wall space are sections of a huge mosaic depicting dolphins, nereids and sea monsters with the buildings of third-century Carthage in the background. In the centre of the room is a half-baked recreation of a Roman garden, using fragments of statuary.

Mausoleum room Mosaic Inv 2804 once allowed wealthy citizens of Thuburbo Majus (whose floor it was) to indulge twice over in their gourmet pleasures in the *triclinium* or dining room. Munching away at their meal, they could stare at the floor and contemplate the background of a well-stocked ocean.

Oudna (Uthina) room On the left side of the door, look for A150 and A152. Remains of a feast lie on a dark background: eggshells, fish heads, lemon peel, bread. Using especially fine tesserae, the second-century artist has left an astonishingly vivid still life – you can almost smell the sauce.

Virgil room This is dominated by the eponymous **Virgil mosaic**, found in Sousse and generally dated to the third century. The author of the *Aeneid* (see p.121) sits between Clio, Muse of History (to his right), and Melpomene, Muse of Tragedy. He holds a scroll of the *Aeneid*, which Melpomene appears to be dictating to him. Just off the Virgil room is a small but spectacular collection of **Carthaginian jewellery**.

Islamic rooms Known also as the Popular Arts and Traditions rooms, the Islamic section of the Bardo is a bit overwhelmed by the wealth of Roman antiquities around it but it does contain some interesting displays of traditional female dress and jewellery, as well as perfume receptacles, ceramics, furniture and some beautifully decorated manuscripts featuring verses from the Koran. Downstairs, the Tiles Hall, with its collection of brightly patterned wall tiles, is reached via a staircase from here.

Second floor

Mosaic rooms (XXX–XXXII) An unlikely fourth-century scene from Le Kef in room XXX (Inv 2819) shows a herd of ostriches being prepared for the chase in an amphitheatre. Inv 3575 in the same room goes into unusually graphic detail: beneath the placid gaze of spectators, a lion faces off against a gladiator, who jabs his spear into the lion's chest; blood drips profusely onto the ground.

Acholla room (XXXIII) Acholla, a Roman port north of Sfax of which little remains today, produced a group of **mosaics** as spectacular as any in the country. One of these, Inv 3588, depicts the Labours of Hercules. The hero himself, equipped with lion skin, club and bow, occupies the central roundel, surrounded by others containing his opponents: triple-headed Geryon above, the River Achelous below, and so on.

Fresco rooms (XXXIV–XXXV) One of a series of rare surviving fragments of wall painting, B84 – like so many mosaics – takes for its theme the good things of life, depicting a bottle of wine wrapped in straw, a bag full of eggs and a leg of ham.

Eating and drinking

Places for **eating and drinking** in Tunis are concentrated in the New Town on **avenue Bourguiba** and the streets to either side. Since the Medina closes down fairly early in the evening, there are fewer restaurants there than you might expect, though **Bab Souika** and **Bab Jazira**, at its northern and southern tips respectively, are pretty lively in the evenings, particularly during Ramadan, with enough cafés and cheap restaurants to satisfy any appetite. For food and other supplies, the covered **market** between rue d'Allemagne and rue d'Espagne has everything you'll need, and there are also food markets along rue Bab el Fellah, rue Sidi Bou Hdid in the Hafsia and along rue Halfaouine. There's a Monoprix **supermarket** on rue Charles de Gaulle, just off avenue de France.

Restaurants and gargotes

There are plenty of inexpensive places to eat in Tunis, most of which will fill you up for 3–4TD. Cheaper still, almost every street in the city has a rotisserie, where you can either eat a plate of fried food standing up or take away a *cassecroûte*. Several rotisseries cluster around the junction of rue Ibn Khaldoun and rue de Yougoslavie. One place for good sandwiches is the trendy *61 bis*, 61 av Habib Thameur (Mon–Sat 7.30am–8.30pm), with a variety of "combos" – sandwiches, fries and a drink – for around 2TD, as well as a few other dishes.

There are better-quality mid-range restaurants south of avenue Bourguiba and, on the northern side, the early stretches of avenue de Paris and rue de Marseille. Inside the Medina there is little middle ground between the *gargotes* and a number of good, high-class establishments. With money to spare you can have a meal to remember in one of the latter places, which are housed in some spectacular restored palaces.

Fine dining is one of the legacies of French rule, and Tunis is peppered with elegant Gallic establishments. The food and ambience in these places is everything you would expect from their equivalents in France, but far cheaper: you can get a memorable meal with wine for about 15–20TD, or even cheaper with set menus. Foreign cuisines are otherwise thin on the ground – apart from the widely available, rather awful pizzas. We've included the phone numbers for restaurants where you need to book.

The New Town

South of avenue Bourguiba

Abid 98 rue de Yougoslavie. Clean, pleasant place dishing up no-nonsense Tunisian food at no-nonsense prices (*plat du jour* 3.2–4.2TD). Mon–Sat noon–10pm.

Carcassonne 8 av de Carthage. Average food, but cheap and with good service. White linen

tablecloths, white-jacketed waiters and pleasant surroundings. The 4TD menu will fill you up. Daily noon–10pm.

Les Margarites 6bis rue d'Hollande ☏71 240 632. Attached to the *Hôtel Maison Dorée*, this place has moderately priced à la carte fare but an excellent-value tourist menu at 5.5TD. Mon–Sat noon–2.30pm & 8–9.30pm.

La Petite Hutte 102 rue de Yougoslavie. Despite the overwrought African hunting lodge theme, this is a good place to go for simple, moderately priced Tunisian cooking. The fish soup is excellent. Mon–Sat noon–11pm.

Le Régent 16 rue Lt Mohammed Aziz Tej ⊕71 341 723. Tucked away at the insalubrious end of the street, this superb classy place (book ahead) is slick and discreet; 30TD will get you the works. Recommended. Closed Aug. Mon–Sat noon–3pm & 7pm–midnight.

Tantonville 96 rue de Yougoslavie. Once a busy 1940s café, now a restaurant, still popular and serving inexpensive Tunisian dishes, especially featuring seafood. A three-course set meal will cost you 7TD. Daily noon–3pm & 7–9pm.

Avenue Bourguiba and points north

Andalous 13 rue de Marseille. The decor is Moorish but the dishes typically Tunisian and good, if a little pricey. Mon–Sat noon–3pm & 7–11pm.

Capitole 60 av Bourguiba. A reasonably priced, long-established place serving filling food. A three-course set meal with extensive choices and a cup of mint tea is a bargain at 5.5TD. Unconnected with the hotel of the same name. Recommended. Daily 11am–4pm & 6–10pm.

Capri 34 rue Mokhtar Attia, one street north of av Bourguiba ⊕71 257 695. Reasonably priced Italian and Tunisian cooking – the seafood is recommended. The 8TD set meal is good value. Daily noon–11pm.

Carthage 10 rue Ali Bach Hamba ⊕71 255 614. Smart place serving French, Tunisian and a couple of Italian dishes. The food is tasty and well-presented, but the venue is a bit too brightly lit for the intimate atmosphere aspired to. The three-course set meal is good value at 12TD. Mon–Sat noon–3pm & 7–11pm.

Chez Nous 5 rue de Marseille ⊕71 254043. Fine French and Tunisian fare, rather pricey ordered à la carte, though the four-course set menu – including

a delicious chocolate mousse – is excellent value at 10TD. Muhammad Ali, Michael York and Edith Piaf are among the celebrities who've patronized it and whose photos deck the walls. Book ahead, especially Saturday nights. Mon–Sat noon–3pm & 7–10pm.

Chez Slah 14 rue Pierre Coubertin ⊕71 258 888. Discreetly tucked away in a small street of crumbling tenements and workshops, this converted private house is well worth investigating. It specializes in seafood; a three-course à la carte meal will run to around 25TD. Tues–Sun 12.15–2pm & 7.30–10pm.

Circolo Italiano 102 av de la Liberté, just after av Heidi Chaker ⊕71 781 101. A fair walk north of the centre, but easily the best Italian restaurant in the city, with prices – 40TD for two, including wine – slightly higher as a result. Reservations are essential as it's officially a private club. Daily noon–3pm & 7.30pm–midnight.

Istambul 4 rue Pierre Courbertin. Huge servings of Tunisian staples at rock-bottom prices – a three-course meal is only 4.5TD. Daily 11am–3pm & 5.30–9.30pm.

Majestic *Majestic* hotel, 36 av de la Liberté ⊕71 332 666. The 10TD set menu remains popular partly due to the slightly decaying colonial opulence of the place. For a sample of the interior you can come in just for mint tea (0.5TD). Daily noon–3pm & 7–10pm.

La Mamma 11bis rue de Marseille ⊕71 240 109. A deservedly popular place for reasonably priced pizzas, pasta and similar fare. The seafood spaghetti is particularly recommended. Puts on traditional music in the evenings. Daily noon–3pm & 7pm–midnight.

Le Neptune 3 rue du Caire ⊕71 254 820. This busy, cheap place serves decent, though not outstanding, Sfaxian-style seafood. Daily 11am–10pm.

L'Orient 7 rue Ali Bach Hamba ⊕71 252 061. Pleasantly decorated and unfailingly busy, this specializes in seafood, with a *menu touristique* at 12TD. Daily noon–3pm & 6.30–11pm.

Medina

Central Medina

Dar Bel Hadj 17 rue des Tamis ⊕71 200 894. Refined and upmarket place set in a seventeenth-century palace and catering to Tunisian elites rather than tourists. Sublime food for around 30TD. Mon–Sat noon–3pm & 8pm–midnight.

Dar el Jeld 5 rue Dar el Jeld, off pl du Gouvernement ⊕71 560 916, ⊛www.dareljeld .tourism.tn. On the western side of the Medina in a lovingly restored aristocratic residence, this is top

of the range in both price (45TD) and quality. Try the mixed hors d'oeuvres, followed perhaps by the stuffed lamb shoulder or olive beef stew. Reservations essential. Closed Aug, and open evenings only in July and early to mid-Sept; rest of the year Mon–Sat 12.30–3pm & 8pm–midnight.

Essaraya 6 rue Ben Mahmoud ⊕71 560 310. Housed in a magnificent palace tucked away in the Medina behind Bab Menara. Service and food match the stunning decor. Try the *mloukhia*. Expect to pay 30TD for a meal. Recommended. Mon–Sat noon–3pm & 8pm–midnight.

Mahdoui 79 rue Jemaa Zitouna. Right by the Great Mosque, this long-established couscous parlour has resisted the urge to go upmarket and serves good, inexpensive food. Mon–Sat 11am–4pm.

Le Marhaba 166 rue de la Kasbah. The usual Tunisian staples in a dirt-cheap spit-and-sawdust joint in the mid-Medina.

M'rabet Souk et Trouk ☎71 561 729. Situated in the heart of the Medina and built over the tombs of three holy men. Formerly the most stylish place in town to splurge seriously, but a bit touristy now. A meal and the accompanying show (belly-dancing or similar entertainment) will cost around 20TD a head. The fine café below is cheaper. Mon–Sat noon–3pm & 7–10pm.

Close to place de la Victoire

Le Pacha 1 rue Jemaa Zitouna. Good-quality but quite pricey Tunisian cuisine in an elegant, first-floor dining room overlooking pl de la Victoire. A three-course meal will set you back around 25TD, with a complimentary mint tea. Daily 7am–9pm.

Semaphore pl de la Victoire, at the corner where rue Jemaa Zitouna emerges. Workaday place with good food for 3–4TD; the soups are excellent. Mon–Sat 8am–10pm.

Cafés, patisseries and bars

Traditional **cafés**, found all over the city and usually equipped with *chichas* (hubble-bubble pipes), are crowded places where men drink coffee in various forms and women may not feel very comfortable, especially outside the main tourist areas. The **Medina cafés** (see box, p.95, for a list of the best ones) are something of an exception, where women are more likely to encounter curiosity than any unwelcome interest.

The cafés' territory has been gradually invaded by **patisseries**, which is where Tunisian women tend to go for fast food or midday breaks; there are a number of patisseries on the north side of avenue Bourguiba, where you can get sandwiches and coffee, as well as the more traditional pastries, sweets and citronade. The *Patisserie Ben Yedder*, on the corner of avenue de France and rue Charles de Gaulle, is one the best in town.

A more expensive alternative to traditional cafés, where women can feel relatively at ease, are the **café-bars** in big hotels, such as the *Africa*, 50 avenue Bourguiba, the *El Hana International*, 49 avenue Bourguiba (its rooftop bar has superlative views), or the *Majestic*, 36 avenue de Paris. The central *Café de Paris* on avenue Bourguiba is great for sitting and watching the crowds pass by – and probably the most civilized place to have a beer. The best and cheapest café-bars on avenue Bourguiba, however, are the *Capitole* at no. 60, open 24 hours and serving excellent crepes, freshly squeezed fruit juice and *lait de poule*, and over the street at the junction with rue de Marseille, the highly popular *Panorama*, which serves similar fare all day and night, as well as *shawarma*.

Tunisian **bars** – small, crowded and very male-dominated – are found mostly around the train station, though there are others scattered through the New Town on street corners (especially along avenue de la Liberté). Most close around 8pm and throughout Friday and Ramadan. The Western-style bars attached to bigger hotels or cafés tend to open later but are much more expensive. Exceptions are the American bar at the *Bahy Hotel* and the smoky little front bar at *Oscars* – though they aren't places for single women – and the more welcoming *Hotel Omrane* bar. None of these is too expensive, charging around 2.5TD for a beer.

Entertainment and nightlife

Tunis's nightlife is fairly low-key. The city closes down at about 11pm, or soon after sunset in the Medina. Crowds stroll along avenue Bourguiba, and mill around the streets to either side, but venues in the city centre are limited. During the month of **Ramadan** (see p.45 for dates), however, there's plenty of eating, drinking and merriment until the early hours of the morning, especially over the last two weeks. The uncontested centre of all this activity is the Medina, which has cafés jam-packed till well after midnight and impromptu concerts given in the Souk des Chéchias. *La Presse* covers daily listings of the numerous artistic and musical events held city-wide at this time, during the **Medina Festival** (for more on which, pick up a brochure from the Théâtre Municipal, see below, or check ⓦwww.festivalmedina.com).

Concerts

Interesting displays of live **traditional music** are provided to accompany your meal by some restaurants, including *La Mamma* (see p.114) and *Dar Bel Hadj* (see p.114). Watch out, too, for events such as concerts of Arabic and Western **classical music** at the Théâtre Municipal on avenue Bourguiba. These can be surprisingly cheap, especially if you don't mind sitting in the vertiginous upper circles. Occasional one-off performances by international bands and orchestras can be heard at government venues such as the Maison de la Culture Ibn Khaldoun, 16 rue Ibn Khaldoun.

Other venues to look out for (daily listings in *La Presse* or *Le Temps*), particularly during the Medina Festival, include: Club Culturel Tahar Haddad, 20 rue du Tribunal in the Medina; the adjacent Dar Lasram; the nearby Medersa Bir Lahjar, 40 rue du Pacha; and the excellent occasional concerts of traditional music held in Sidi Bou Saïd at Dar Ennejma Ezzahra, Baron d'Erlanger's Orientalist palace (see p.128; tickets and information from Maison de la Culture Ibn Khaldoun). The Rachidia Institute's palatial headquarters on rue de la Dribat (just northeast of the Great Mosque) has monthly concerts of classical *malouf* music. The old Cathedral of St Louis in Carthage (see p.125) is a classy setting for the international singing stars of the Arab world.

Theatre

Tunis's thespian pride and joy is the ludicrous Art Nouveau **Théâtre Municipal** on avenue Bourguiba (☎71 259 499), which regularly puts on plays as well as some opera and rock concerts. Another venue to look out for is Espace el Teatro, Complexe el Mechtel, avenue Ouled Haffouz (☎71 791 795, ⓦwww.elteatro.net), which stages works of a more modern flavour. La Quatrième Art, 27 avenue de Paris, is a converted cinema but is now home to the Tunisian National Theatre (TNT), directed by the energetic Mohamed Driss. Listings for these and other theatres are found in the daily *Le Temps* and *La Presse*.

Films

Cinema-going is a popular pastime in Tunis, with well over a dozen **cinemas** dotted around town. Matinées commence at around 3pm (tickets 1TD) and evening shows usually screen at 6pm and 9pm (2.5–3TD); the listings are published every day in *La Presse* and *Le Temps*.

The only art-house cinema in the city is Maison de Théâtre et du Cinema Ibn Rachiq, at the corner of avenue de Paris and rue Mokhtar Attia, which occasionally screens films with French subtitles. More mainstream cinemas include ABC, 8 rue Ibn Khaldoun, and Le Mondial, 10 rue Ibn Khaldoun. Along avenue Bourguiba, you'll find Colisée at no. 45 (in the arcade), Le Palace at no. 54, Capitole at no. 60 and Parnasse at no. 63 (in the arcade). The Maison de la Culture at 16 rue Ibn Khaldoun mounts seasons of classic movies.

The **Carthage International Film Festival**, a celebration of Arab cinema, takes over the capital's cinemas every second November (even years) – probably your best chance to see some Tunisian films. Events are listed in *La Presse* and *Le Temps*.

Nightclubs

Discos don't offer a very exciting alternative to just sitting at a café and watching the world go by, but if you feel the urge to get hot and sweaty under the disco lights, try *Club 2001* at the *Abou Nawas El Mechtel* on avenue Ouled Haffouz, or the *JFK* club at *Oscars Hotel*, 12–14 rue de Marseille. There are more sophisticated places out in the suburbs of La Marsa and Gammarth.

Listings

Airlines Air France, 1 rue d'Athènes ☏71 355 422; Alitalia, Imm. Maghrebia, bd 7 Novembre ☏71 708 312; British Airways, Residence LAKEO, rue du Lac Michigan, Les Berges du Lac ☏71 963 120; Egyptair, 49 av Bourguiba, in the back of the *Hôtel El Hana International* ☏71 341 182; Libyan Arab Airlines, 49 av de Paris ☏71 341 646; Lufthansa, Imm. Maghrebia, bd 7 Novembre ☏71 940 551; Syrian Air, 2 av Carthage (southeast of the train station) ☏71 341 127; Tuninter, at the airport ☏71 701 717; Tunisair, 48 av Bourguiba ☏71 336 500; Turkish Airlines, Complexe El Mechtel, av Ouled Haffouz ☏71 787 033.

American Express c/o Decouvertes de Sotuvit, 14 rue Ibn Tafargine, off av Hedi Chaker (☏71 783 513), who take care of hotels and flight bookings but do not offer a mail service. The UBCI bank on the corner of avenue Bourguiba and rue d'Hollande takes AMEX cards.

Art galleries Tunis has a wealth of exhibition space, including state-owned, commercial, religious and private galleries. All are worth a look, especially during one of Tunis's many thematic city-wide festivals, such as Photography Month (Dec) or the Medina Festival (Ramadan). You'll find listings of what's on in *Le Temps* and *La Presse*. Palais Kheireddine, rue du Tribunal (near Dar Lasram in the Medina) has a superlative setting, but some exhibits disappoint. Galerie Yahia/ Palmarium, 3 av de Carthage, is a commercial gallery, strong on photography and modern plastic arts. One of the most energetic venues is Club Culturel Tahar Haddad, 20 rue du Tribunal in the Medina, which is highly regarded for both Tunisian and international art. For a strictly Tunisian feel

there's the Dar Hussein, place du Château (near Bab Menara), a wonderful old mansion with month-long exhibitions. El Teatro in the Complexe el Mechtel, av Ouled Haffouz, puts on avant-garde works by Algerians in exile. Finally, the Medina Gallery, in an old Medina town house at 11 rue dar el Jeld, displays occasional retrospectives and generally modern paintings. Also worth checking out is the Maison de la Culture Ibn Khaldoun, 16 rue Ibn Khaldoun, which stages a variety of exhibitions.

Banks and exchange Visa and MasterCard ATMs are scattered along av Bourguiba, in pl Barcelone and also in the Medina near the mosque. The banks on av Bourguiba tend to get crowded in summer. Less packed locations include the Franco-Tunisian Bank, 13 rue d'Alger; Banque du Sud, 45 av de la Liberté, next to the Bourguiba School; and BIAT, 21 rue d'Algérie, by Bab Jazira. Outside banking hours, you can change cash and traveller's cheques at most big hotels. You can change foreign notes at BIAT near the Théâtre Municipal, the UBCI on the same block, the Amen Bank at 13 av de France, and Banque de Tunisie at 3 av de France.

Bookshops There's a limited selection of English-language novels at Librairie El Alamia, 17 av de France, opposite Magasin Général; Claire Fontaine, 4 rue d'Alger; and Mille Feuilles in La Marsa. For books in French about Tunisia and the Maghreb, try Claire Fontaine, Mille Feuilles or Espace Diwan at 9 rue Sidi Ben Arous, just up from the Great Mosque in the heart of the Medina. Secondhand books in English can be found at Abdessattar M'zoughi, 10 rue d'Angleterre; secondhand French books are sold on the street stalls on rue des Tanneurs.

Bicycle rental There's no official bike rental shop but there are many bicycle shops on av de Madrid (between Bab el Khadra and av de la Liberté), that may consent to an informal deal; 10–12TD for a full day is reasonable.

Car rental There are several agencies on av Bourguiba and in the big hotels. The main ones also have a desk at the airport. Reputable city centre offices include: Ben Jemaa, 55 av de Paris ☏71 258 871; Budget, 17 av Kheireddine Pacha ☏71 289 225; Europcar, 1 rue Hedi Nouira ☏71 340 303; and Hertz, 29 av Bourguiba ☏71 256 451. Avis is in the *Sheraton* (☏71 787 167) and also further out in the Zone Industrielle Charguia (☏71 807 252).

Car repair Any French make, and Land Rovers, can be handled at most garages, and mechanics' workshops can be found on av de Carthage south of the train station. Dealers in British and American vehicles are in very short supply. If you need towing, call SOS Car Haul (☏71 801 211).

Churches St George's Anglican church, at pl Bab Carthajana on the edge of the Medina, has Sunday services at 10am and 12.30pm. Catholics can go to Mass at the Cathedral at 6.30pm or at St Jeanne d'Arc church on pl Palestine, where there's an English service at 10am every Sunday. The Greek Orthodox church is on rue de Rome (round the corner from the Cathedral) and worth a visit just to see the icons. Tunis's main synagogue is the heavily guarded 1930s Art Deco building at 43 av de la Liberté.

Doctors For minor complaints or injuries, an *infirmerie* should be able to sort you out. A wound dressing and tetanus jab, for example, will cost around 3TD. There are *infirmeries* at 20 av de la Liberté and 51 rue al Jazira. There are two recommended *cliniques*, the Ettaoufik (☏71 800 211) and the El Manar (☏71 885 000). For specialized treatment, ask your consulate or embassy for a list of doctors.

Embassies Algeria, 18 rue de Niger ☏71 783 166 or 71 789 038; Australia, c/o Canadian Embassy; Canada, 3 rue de Sénégal ☏71 104 000; Egypt, rue 8007, Montplaisir ☏71 792 233; France, 79 rue de Yougoslavie ☏71 358 000; Ireland, c/o UK embassy; Libya, visa section 74 av Mohammed V ☏71 842 202; New Zealand, c/o UK embassy; UK, rue du Lac Windermere, behind the *Acropole Hotel* in Berges du Lac ☏71 108 700 (see p.132); US, rte du Lac, 3.5km east of pl Tahar Haddad in Berges du Lac ☏71 107 000 (see p.132).

Emergencies The tourist police are at the Ministry of the Interior, 32 av Bourguiba (☏71 830 802). For other emergency numbers, see p.62.

Football Tunis has two main clubs, Espérance Sportif and Club Africain, who have monopolized the Tunisian league over the years and, during the 1990s, had some success in pan-African cup competitions as well. They share the El Menzah ground in the Cité Olympique north of the centre, where they play at home alternate weeks, usually Sunday at 2pm or 4pm, depending on the time of year. The best way to get up to El Menzah is by métro to Jeunesse or Cité Sportive (line #2). To avoid the mad scramble for tickets, you're advised to arrive well before the match. Other metropolitan teams are Avenir Sportif de la Marsa (ASM) and Club Sportif de Hammam Lif (CSHL).

Golf The Carthage Golf Club in La Soukra has an eighteen-hole course (☏t71 765 919).

Hammams Ubiquitous but mostly well hidden, hammams in Tunis are usually single-sex, which means that you can use them throughout the day. The most atmospheric, if not always the cleanest, are in the Medina and in Halfaouine, of which the most spectacular is undoubtedly Hammam Sahib et Tabaa, close to pl Halfaouine (men 5am–1pm & 7pm–1am, women 1–7pm). The men-only Hammam Kachachine at 30 Souk des Librairies (Mon–Sat 7am–4pm, Sun 7am–2pm), near the Great Mosque, is almost as atmospheric. There's a women's hammam at 1 rue de la Noria (daily 6am–9pm), by the Club Culturel Tahar Haddad.

Hospitals The best hospital is the Hôpital Charles Nicolle, bd 9 Avril 1938, northwest of the Medina by Bab Benat (☏71 578 000).

Internet access There are a number of Publinets dotted around the city centre, including: Cyber Barcelone, 1st floor, 14 rue de Grèce (daily 8am–midnight); Publinet Le Passage, 7 av de la Liberté (Mon–Sat 8.30am–11pm, Sun noon–11pm); and other Publinets at 28 av Bourguiba (Mon–Sat 11am–10pm), 158 rue Bab Souika (daily 8am–3am) and 10 rue de Russie (daily 9am–midnight), with another signposted off rue d'Algérie, just west of the intersection with rue Charles de Gaulle (daily 9am–midnight). All charge 1.5–2TD/hr.

Laundry Laverie, 15 rue d'Allemagne, charges by the kilo (closed Sun).

Newspapers A wide range of foreign papers can be bought at the stands under the trees in the middle of av Bourguiba and at Librairie El Alamia (see p.82).

Passport photos A lot of places do these fast and cheaply. Try 23 rue Jemal Abdel Nasser (near the post office), 32 rue al Jazira (on the corner of rue Écosse), av de France (next to the Cathedral, on the corner of rue de Rome), or several places up av de la Liberté on your way to the embassy zone.

Pharmacies All-night pharmacies in the centre include Jenane, 44 av Bab Jedid ☎71 240 994; Karray, 20 av de la Liberté ☎71 243 520; and Khabthani, 43 av Bourguiba ☎71 252 507.

Post office The main post office, for stamps and poste restante, is on rue Charles de Gaulle (Mon–Sat 8am–6pm). Mail is kept in poste restante for fifteen days and there is a 0.39TD charge for each item. The parcels office (Colis Postaux) is on av de la République, just off av Bourguiba. There is a branch at 1 av Habib Thameur and a very helpful one at the Bab Aleoua bus station.

Swimming There's a public pool at the Cité Olympique in El Menza (métro line #2 to Cité Sportive), for which you have to buy a monthly ticket (12TD). The *Abou Nawas Tunis* (see p.81) has a first-rate pool that non-residents can use for 10TD per day.

Telephones There are Publitel and Taxiphone offices dotted all over the city. Some of these also send and receive faxes and have photocopiers.

Travel agents The many travel agents that line av Bourguiba are all very similar, offering combinations of car rental, organized tours, flights, ferry tickets, hotel bookings and so on. As for student travel agents, there is STAV, 2 rue de Sparte ☎71 348 011, but its special deals are not spectacularly cheap. Many ordinary agencies will give a 25 percent discount for a student card, as will Tunisair and some other airlines if you're under 31.

Visa extensions If your ninety days are coming up, you either need to leave Tunisia briefly to get a fresh entry stamp (the cheapest and easiest way is to go by ferry to Trápani in Sicily) or else apply for a visa extension at a police station; see p.18 for more.

Lac Tunis and the Gulf shore

On a hot summer evening, there's no better way of enjoying Tunis than to get out of the city centre by catching the TGM train across the lake to one of the suburbs on the northern shore of the gulf, where the sea breezes clear away the city's oppressive humidity. Modern-day **Carthage** is the suburb built over and among the remains of the ancient capital of the Carthaginian Empire, second city of the Roman world. The physical extent of the ruins can be disappointing but not the sense of history nor the scenery. Moving up the coast from Carthage, you move towards upmarket resorts that tend to cater for French tourists seeking a more refined alternative to staying in Tunis – **Sidi Bou Saïd**, a cliff-top village of considerable charm; **La Marsa**, **Gammarth** and **Raoued** for swimming and nightlife. Just south of Carthage, **La Goulette** is known for its Kasbah fortress and fish restaurants. Remember, however, that half of Tunis converges on these places in summer, especially at weekends. Beyond La Marsa, the terminus of the TGM, there are #247 buses and green TCV buses along the coastal road through Gammarth, the latter service continuing to Raoued.

The suburbs of the southern gulf shore, reached by mainline train, are distinctly downmarket, while *bidonville* (literally, "oil-drum town") shanties spread out to the west and southwest of town beyond the boulevard du 9 Avril 1938. But **Hammam Lif**, dating from the turn of the last century and dominated by Jebel Bou Kornine, retains some character of its own.

Lac Tunis

The **causeway** on which the TGM crosses **Lac Tunis** was built in the 1870s, when the suburbs that now run from La Goulette to Sidi Bou Saïd barely existed. The train was originally routed directly to La Marsa (through the British Consul's garden, see p.118) along the mainland north of the lake.

On the **Isle of Chikli**, north of the causeway, **Fort St Jacques** sits mysteriously, built by the Spanish in the sixteenth century. Once used as a prison, it is now a stopover for migrating **birds**, and indeed Lake Tunis offers the chance to see some of Tunisia's more exciting birdlife. Head for the southern half of the lake (the northern shores are being reclaimed for hotel and other developments), which attracts flamingos, waders, gulls and terns. Numbers are particularly high in spring and autumn, when they're swollen by migrants. The best vantage point is the lake's southeastern corner; take the TGM to Le Bac and the ferry across to **Radès** port, from where you can stroll 3km down into Radès along the lakeshore.

Some of the fields just northeast of the lake between Carthage and Sidi Bou Saïd have wonderful **wildflower** displays in spring; look for yellow chrysanthemums, scarlet poppies, blue borage and pink campions. Brilliant goldfinches are common in the area, while butterflies including swooping swallowtails and orange tips and, in spring, hundreds of migrating painted ladies feed on the sea stocks at the back of the beach.

La Goulette

LA GOULETTE (meaning "the gullet", or "throat") is the port of Tunis and increasingly a dormitory suburb for the capital, easily reached by the regular TGM services (10min). However, it still has a lively atmosphere of its own, as well as some excellent fish restaurants – the main reason for coming here, along with the ferries.

The road from the causeway and TGM towards the port (from Goulette Vieille TGM station, head back towards Tunis for 200m then turn left at the Esso garage) passes, on the left, a rather run-down area reminiscent of a poor district in southern Europe, complete with church – the area is unsubtlely shielded from the main road by a series of enormous, rusting billboards. In the middle of the same road is La Goulette's **city gate**, part of the Spanish king Charles V's walls but now standing alone, shored up with concrete.

The **Kasbah**, a massive fortress built in 1535 by Charles V to defend his bridgehead in Tunisia, is a little further on the left and really the only monumental sight here. As a key strategic point in the sixteenth-century struggle for control of the western Mediterranean, it saw some torrid times, finally falling in 1574 to "four hundred and seventy-five thousand" Turks, Moors and Arabs – the figure quoted by Miguel de Cervantes, author of *Don Quixote*, who fought in its defence. Despite being captured, he and many others were glad to see the Kasbah lost – it was a "breeding-place and cloak of iniquities, a glutton, sponge and sink" of all the money spent on it in a futile policy of prestige. Over the next centuries the Kasbah was used as a dungeon for prisoners, who would be taken from here to the Souk el Berka in the Medina to be sold into slavery.

Continuing past the Kasbah and bearing right takes you to the **port** (see p.72). To go into La Goulette **town**, take a left up avenue Farhat Hached immediately before the Kasbah to place 7 Novembre. This is the main area for **fish restaurants**, and there's a great variety, from very cheap to upmarket. From place 7 Novembre, where *La Victoire* has a good-value tourist menu for 9TD, avenue Bourguiba splits to the left and avenue Franklin D. Roosevelt to the right. Franklin D. Roosevelt is better for food, with cheap places like the *Stambali* offering meals for around 5TD, alongside smarter establishments such as *Le Chalet* at no. 42, *La Spigola* at no. 52 and *Le Café Vert* at no. 68 (☎71 736 156; closed Mon), where a meal will set you back around 30TD with wine. If you feel the need to stay in La Goulette, there are two comfortable beach **hotels** on the seafront one block east of place 7 Novembre – the *Lido* (☎71 738 045, ℻71 735 117; **❻**) and *La Jetée* (☎71 736000, ℻738396; **❼**), which has a pool.

Carthage

Aeneas looked wonderingly at the solid structures springing up where there had once been only African huts, and the gates, the turmoil, and the paved streets. The Tyrians were hurrying about busily, some tracing a line for the walls and manhandling stones up the slopes as they strained to build their citadel, others siting some building and marking its outline by ploughing a furrow . . . At one spot they were excavating the harbour, and at another a party was laying out an area for the deep foundations of a theatre; they were also hewing from quarries mighty pillars to stand tall and handsome beside the stage which was still to be built . . . Aeneas looked up at the buildings. "Ah, fortunate people," he exclaimed . . .

Ever since Virgil wrote the *Aeneid* in the first century BC, the ancient port of **CARTHAGE** has been suffused in a legendary aura of romance, power, cruelty and decline. "Any man who could survey the ruins of Carthage with indifference," wrote one Edward Blaquière, a typical nineteenth-century traveller, "or not call to mind the scenes of its past glories and misfortunes must, indeed, be devoid of sensibility." The image is made that much more potent by the yawning gap between the myth and today's reality. The remains consist of a series of widely spaced sites, with only a little standing above ground level, lurking among the plush villas of Tunis's wealthier commuters. Still, if you approach Carthage with some imagination and a willingness to be impressed, it has a good deal to offer – not least the wide views over the Gulf of Tunis and back to the city.

The Roman sites lie between Carthage Salammbo and Carthage Amilcar stations on the **TGM** line, taking around twenty minutes from Tunis. Visiting all the sites on foot makes a good day's ramble, though this can be quite forbidding in midsummer. An alternative would be to pick and choose, using the TGM wherever possible, and perhaps combining Sidi Bou Saïd and La Marsa with a couple of sessions at Carthage. For a worthwhile abbreviated visit, you could take the TGM to Carthage Dermech for the **Carthage Museum**, which also offers a wonderful view over the Gulf; wander north to the **Villas Romaines** or **Antonine Baths**; then catch the TGM again at Carthage Hannibal to move on to Sidi Bou Saïd or back to Tunis. If you get tired, just go on to Sidi Bou Saïd for the evening, where the mood of dusk falling over the Gulf often revives the romance.

There are not many places to **stay** in Carthage, and nowhere cheap at all. The most spectacular is the *Villa Didon*, rue Mendès France, on Byrsa Hill (T71 733 433, F71 733 488, Wwww.villadidon.com; **9**). A chic, ultra-modern hotel, it's fitted out with cutting-edge designer furniture and has a swanky restaurant belonging to Alain Ducasse's *Spoon* chain. The ten rooms (or minisuites, as the hotel prefers to call them) feature open-plan marble jacuzzis and showers, and wonderful views over the gulf, but at 350TD they are expensive considering the hotel's lack of a pool and other five-star facilities. If you decide not to stay, do at least drop in for a drink at the bar or splash out on a **meal**

Entry to all of Carthage's major Roman sites, as well as the Carthage and Paleo-Christian museums, is by the 5.2TD **global ticket** (camera 1TD). Tickets are most reliably bought at the Tophet, Carthage Museum, Antonine Baths or Villas Romaines. The sites and museums are all open daily from 8am to 7pm from April to mid-September and from 8.30am to 5pm from mid-September to March. Tickets are only valid for one day, so unless you're happy rushing about, you'll have to buy another to complete the tour of the sites.

TUNIS AND AROUND | Carthage

121

(daily noon–3.30pm & 8–11pm), which will cost around 70–80TD a head à la carte or 42TD for the lunchtime menu. A bit more affordable and just as inviting is the *Résidence Carthage* at 16 rue Hannibal, near the Tophet (☎71 730786, ℉71 720135; ❼), which has another good restaurant, making half-board (10TD extra) an attractive option. The *Hôtel Amilcar* (☎71 740788, ℉71 743139, ⓦwww.hotel-amilcar.com; ❼), on the beach up towards Sidi Bou Saïd, enjoys a good location and is mainly used for package tours.

Some history

Carthage (Qart Hadasht, or "New City") was founded, according to legend, in 814 BC by **Phoenicians** from the eastern Mediterranean. One of a number of such settlements on the North African coast, it gradually became the most important, especially after a 507 BC treaty with Rome banned foreign shipping from the others.

Remarkably little is known about the appearance of Carthage, except that it grew up around the ports on the shore and the acropolis on the Byrsa Hill, where today's museum and cathedral now stand. The first detailed accounts come from the Romans, who gleefully describe how thoroughly they destroyed the city in 146 BC. Having left Carthage in ruins, the Romans made Utica capital of their African province, but in 46 BC **Julius Caesar** refounded Carthage as a symbol of the planned resurrection of Africa, and it grew to a huge size – the second city of the Empire after Rome. Estimates of its population range from 200,000 to 700,000, and it was as cultured as it was cosmopolitan, with a large university.

As the Empire's moral and military foundations began to tremble, Christianity became the voice of the establishment, but it was too late to halt the decline. Regarded as a typically decadent Roman city, Carthage was a natural target for Christian abuse. St Augustine lambasted a group of its citizens: "Up to very recently these effeminates were walking the streets and alleys of Carthage, their hair reeking with ointment, their faces powdered white, with enervated bodies moving along like women, and even soliciting the man on the street for sustenance of their dissolute lives".

Although the Vandals and Byzantines tried to keep up the imperial lifestyle, time was running out. The Arab invaders made almost as thorough a job of destroying Carthage as the Romans had done, and what was left was carted away over the next centuries for buildings in Tunis, Kairouan and elsewhere.

Dido and Aeneas

According to a myth that plays on the Phoenicians' celebrated commercial astuteness, their queen, **Dido**, landed on the North African coast and requested as much territory as could be enclosed by an ox hide. The request willingly granted, she proceeded to cut the hide into a long strip that gave her room for a city, Carthage. According to Books 1 and 4 of Virgil's epic poem the *Aeneid*, **Aeneas** – sole survivor of the Greek destruction of Troy and charged by the gods with a mission to found a new Troy in Italy – turned up while she was building the city. Taken in and sheltered by Dido, Aeneas became increasingly torn between his divine mission and his love for the Carthaginian queen. All this was probably intended as high-class propaganda to explain the rivalry between Rome and Carthage, and Rome's superiority. But Virgil found himself unable to depict Aeneas as the sort of brainless Roman hero required by the official line, and the episode became the first classic tragic love story in European literature. Historically there's no chance of it being true, as Troy was destroyed five centuries before Carthage was built.

"In the beginning of the sixteenth century," according to Edward Gibbon, "the second Capital of the West was represented by a mosque, a college without students, twenty-five or thirty shops, and the huts of five hundred peasants, who, in their abject poverty, displayed the arrogance of the Punic senators."

The two main obstacles to **excavating Carthage** have been that the original city was thoroughly destroyed by the Romans – and what was left of the Roman city after the Vandal and Arab invasions was used either for building material or, more recently, buried under suburban housing. Nonetheless, a UNESCO-inspired project involving Tunisian, French, German, British, Canadian and American archeologists has excavated areas of the Carthaginian and Roman cities for over 5km along the shore on either side of the TGM train line.

Southern sites

From Carthage Salammbo TGM station, head down towards the sea on avenue Farhat Hached. About 200m down, rue Hannibal leads off to the left; 50m down it, on the right, are the remains of the **Tophet** (global ticket), or sanctuary, of the Carthaginian divinities Tanit and Baal. A rare patch of undeveloped suburban land, dug down into deep pits and scattered with Punic stelae (headstones), this conceals a lurid past. According to legend, the Carthaginians eagerly and frequently brought their children here to be ritually slaughtered. Urns containing the ashes of children have been found on the site, but the practice was almost certainly not as common as Roman propagandists would have had people believe.

The **Punic Ports** lie just 500m away, at the end of rue Hannibal (or straight down av 2 Mars from Byrsa TGM station). Once the foundation of Carthaginian prosperity and power, these harbours were a source of fascination, second only to Hannibal's elephants for the envious Romans. What you see today looks like two suburban ponds: the northern, circular one was the naval harbour, linked by a narrow channel (the sea opening is modern) to the rectangular merchant harbour. The best way to get a sense of what it all meant is to cross the bridge over the channel joining the two ports and bear left to a small building on the edge of the naval harbour, where the British excavating team has left behind a detailed scale **model** (times variable; free). This shows the island as one big shipyard, surrounded by slipways. One of these, left uncovered on the far side of the island, seems surprisingly small considering the awe in which Carthage's fleet was held, suggesting that a Carthaginian naval vessel was only around 34.5m long by 5m wide. There's little to see at the merchant harbour, although excavations there unearthed a wealth of the kind of trade-related material that is now displayed at the Carthage Museum.

Back by the bridge is the recently modernized **Oceanographic Museum** (Tues–Sat 10am–1pm & 3–6pm, Sun 10am–6pm; 1TD), which first opened in 1924. The US$2.25 million refit has been a sea change, with nifty interactive computer consoles as well as the usual tanks of perennially grumpy groupers and melancholic turtles.

Inland on avenue Bourguiba, between Byrsa and Dermech TGM stations, is the **Paleo-Christian museum**, so called after some early Christian remains were unearthed here. It includes excavations and a building housing some fragments of mosaic and a statuette of Ganymede, with Jupiter in the form of an eagle, taking him heavenward to be cupbearer for the gods. There are explanations in English.

Also on avenue Bourguiba, a couple of minutes' walk south of Salammbo TGM station at no. 229, is **Phenicia** (Mon–Sat 9.30am–7.30pm; ☏ 97 512846,

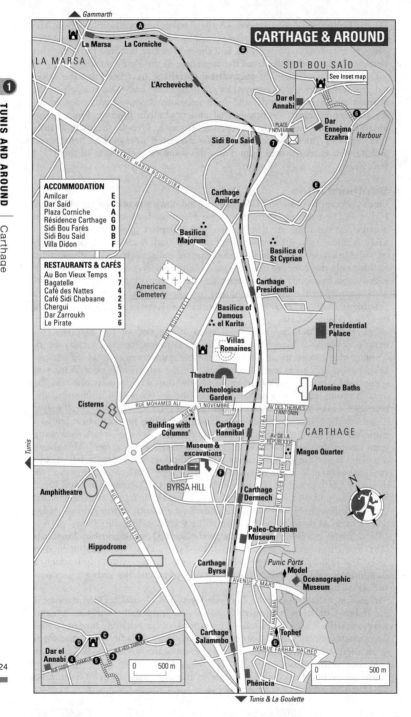

CARTHAGE & AROUND

Gammarth

La Marsa   La Corniche

LA MARSA

L'Archevêche

SIDI BOU SAÏD

See inset map

Dar el Annabi

Dar Ennejma Ezzahra

Harbour

PLACE 7 NOVEMBRE

Sidi Bou Said

AVENUE HABIB BOURGUIBA

Carthage Amilcar

ACCOMMODATION
Amilcar	E
Dar Said	C
Plaza Corniche	A
Résidence Carthage	G
Sidi Bou Farès	D
Sidi Bou Said	B
Villa Didon	F

Basilica Majorum

Basilica of St Cyprian

RESTAURANTS & CAFÉS
Au Bon Vieux Temps	1
Bagatelle	7
Café des Nattes	4
Café Sidi Chabaane	2
Chergui	5
Dar Zarroukh	3
Le Pirate	6

American Cemetery

Carthage Presidential

Basilica of Damous el Karita

Villas Romaines

Presidential Palace

Theatre

Archeological Garden

Antonine Baths

RUE MOHAMED ALI

Cisterns

AVENUE 1 NOVEMBRE

AV DES THERMES D'ANTONIN

'Building with Columns'

Carthage Hannibal

CARTHAGE

AVENUE BOURGUIBA

AV DE LA RÉPUBLIQUE

Museum & excavations

Magon Quarter

RUE TAIEB MEHRI

Cathedral

BYRSA HILL

Amphitheatre

RUE TAHA HOUSSINE

Carthage Dermech

N

Paleo-Christian Museum

Hippodrome

Punic Ports Model

Carthage Byrsa

Oceanographic Museum

AVENUE 2 MARS

RUE HANNIBAL

Tunis

Dar el Annabi

RUE HEDI ZARROUK

RUE HABIB THAMEUR

Carthage Salammbo

Tophet

AVENUE FARHAT HACHED

0   500 m

Phénicia

0   500 m

Tunis & La Goulette

Ⓔ katedaoud@yahoo.fr), a shop run by an expat British woman who has lived in Tunisia for over thirty years and tries to preserve Tunisian handicrafts by travelling to remote communities where traditional arts are losing out to modern materials. The shop stocks fabulous pottery, rugs and re-invented traditional jewellery, and has some great photographs for sale.

Byrsa Hill

Byrsa Hill, where the Cathedral of St Louis and the Carthage Museum now stand, was the heart of Carthage under Punic rule and the focus of Roman fury when they sacked the city so thoroughly in 146 BC. The meagre remains outside the museum building itself, on the southern edge of the hilltop, are the most extensive remnant of pre-Roman Carthage. Ironically, it was the Romans' decision to refound the city a hundred years later that helped preserve at least this much. To provide a platform for their civic centre they levelled the top of the hill, and the Punic quarters clustered around the top were buried under the rubble tipped over the sides, and thus saved for the meticulous French **excavations** that you can see on the southeast side. The French have uncovered a domestic quarter similar to that at Kerkouane (see p.156), though here the buildings had as many as five storeys and the streets were narrow, as in the Medina. Each house had its own cistern and a rudimentary drainage system. The scorched material found above these foundations has proved that vindictive Rome did indeed burn Carthage to the ground after the siege.

You can get up the hill quite easily from Dermech or Hannibal TGM stations. From Dermech, you can stop for a breather on the terrace of the *Villa Didon* hotel, from where you can survey the whole area. Dominating the hill is the pseudo-Oriental heap of the **Cathedral of St Louis** (daily 9am–6pm; 2.5TD), built in 1890 and dedicated to the thirteenth-century French king who died at Carthage while laying unsuccessful siege to Tunis in the hope of converting the Hafsid ruler El Mustansir. "Instead of a proselyte, he found a siege," wrote Gibbon, "the French panted and died on the burning sands; Saint Louis expired in his tent." In 1930 the French Catholic Church held a grandiose conference here to proclaim a revival of Africa's great Christian tradition, which is said to have played an important part in arousing Bourguiba's nationalist feelings. The cathedral is now leased by a private entertainments company, and is known officially as the **Acropolium** (☎71 733866, Ⓦwww .acropolium.com.tn), which hosts fascinating traditional music concerts and a music festival in October.

Carthage Museum

Beyond the cathedral and housed in the former headquarters of the White Fathers missionaries of wine and "Thibarine" fame (see p.201), the **Carthage Museum** owns a substantial collection of Carthaginian, Roman and Christian artefacts excavated from the area. At the time of writing, however, much of it was in storage pending a large-scale, World Bank-financed renovation programme that will probably take several years to complete. In the meantime, the museum is restricted to two halls in the main building containing a few interesting exhibits, though nothing to match the Bardo. On the **ground floor**, look out for a striking third-century marble statue of a charioteer and his wife among the Roman sculptures and a beautifully detailed, Christian-era ivory plaque of Daniel in the lion's den among the display cases of Punic, Roman and Christian ceramics. On the **first floor** are a few fragments of frieze and some damaged marble heads, along with some forgettable displays of Carthaginian ceramics, jewellery and domestic implements with explanations in French only. A **garden** outside the museum is crammed with architectural bric-a-brac, including – incongruously – the tombstone of Mathieu Maximilian Prosper de Lesseps, French consul general in Tunis in the early nineteenth century and brother of the builder of the Suez Canal.

If the museum's full collection is on show again, there are several highlights to look out for, including an unusual display that illustrates the complexity of current conservation techniques. Among the museum's Carthaginian and Roman **sculptures**, the prize exhibits are a life-size man and woman, carved around the fourth century BC, each lying on top of a stone sarcophagus. The man's naturalistic head would not be out of place on the statue of a fourth-century Greek philosopher, and the fall of the woman's robe over her upper body is similarly Greek. But the way both lie on top of the sarcophagus suggests an Etruscan influence, while the woman's coiffure and the bird's wings protectively wrapped around her lower body are both reminiscent of old Egypt. This striking blend of different Mediterranean influences is a theme that recurs throughout Tunisian culture. The museum's Punic collection contains many similarly pan-Mediterranean items, as well as a *tophet* in which child sacrifice was carried out, a solely Carthaginian custom. There's also a case devoted to the Punic Ports, which makes an adequate substitute for a visit to the actual site by the shore if it's too hot or you have limited time. Look out also for a pair of rare early **mosaics**, which demonstrate the transition from plain pink Carthaginian floors towards the Romans' later, more elaborate work. In the example from the fourth century BC, found in a house near the theatre, the band of simple square tesserae is the earliest known instance of true mosaic technique in the Mediterranean. The attractive first-century AD mosaic incorporates a black panel decorated with sections of coloured marble. Finally, an excellent exhibit succeeds in bringing to life the apparently dull subject of amphorae across the centuries.

Behind the hill

The **amphitheatre** (covered by the global ticket) behind Byrsa Hill, in sketchy but recognizable condition, was the site of numerous early Christian martyrdoms. Perhaps most notorious were those of SS Perpetua and Felicitas, who were brought into the arena in 203 AD, stripped naked and placed in nets. Even Romans were horrified when they saw that "one was a delicate young girl, and the other a woman fresh from childbirth with the milk still dripping from her breasts", so they were taken out to be brought back in again, dressed in unbelted tunics; Perpetua was killed by a heifer, Felicitas by a gladiator's sword.

Just over the road is a collection of huge **cisterns**, some inhabited and others decaying, which once received part of Carthage's water supply from the Zaghouan aqueduct.

The Magon Quarter and Antonine Baths

Continuing up the shore from the Punic Ports or heading directly seawards from Hannibal TGM station across avenue Bourguiba, you'll come to the **Magon Quarter** (global ticket). Located next to the water's edge, this residential quarter is named after Mago, an early king of Carthage. The German excavations here are neat, tidy and well laid-out, but not really very interesting.

A couple of blocks north, and signposted from Hannibal TGM, the **Antonine Baths** (global ticket) are the most extensive example of their kind in North Africa and were once the largest in the Roman world. The entrance to the site takes you through a park full of flowers and date palms, with paths following the streets of the Roman city; you enter along Kardo 16 (a *cardo* is a north–south Roman street). Nos. 17, 15 and 14 run parallel, and all are crossed after two blocks by Decumanus (east–west street) 4. Left from the entrance is the bunker-like doorway to a little seventh-century Christian **chapel**, complete with mosaics, which has been moved here from elsewhere. The contrast between this secret cave – built about the time that the Arabs swept in from the east – and the expansive self-confidence of the Roman baths down on the beach needs no further comment. Further on, a *schola*, or young men's club, is identifiable by an unusual mosaic showing children at some sort of ritual exercise; and further still up the hill is the Byzantine **basilica of Douimes**, in which was found a poignant inscription from the Epistle to the Romans: "If the Lord is with us, who can be against us?"

The **baths** themselves are down on the beach. Once again it's a case of using your imagination, since what remains is only the basement level of a massive complex – it's almost impossible to convey the original size. The central pool alone was as big as an Olympic swimming pool, and when the curved public latrines were first discovered they were taken for a theatre. None of the original mosaics or statuary decorating the public areas have survived, but the complex remains a potent symbol of Roman imperial presence. Next to the site is a modern **presidential palace**, whose soldiers do not like cameras to be pointed at it.

The Villas Romaines and northern sites

Heading inland from the baths, cross avenue Bourguiba onto avenue 7 Novembre, carry on under the train line and the **Villas Romaines** site (global ticket) is 150m up on the right. It's really little more than a series of foundations of Roman villas and an "Antiquarium" where a few stunted columns and statues have been collected to make a foreground for photographs of the gulf. The sight of modern villas below is hardly new – over 1500 years ago wealthy Tunisians and expatriates were already making this idyllic stretch of coast their own. Right on top of the hill are the bare foundations of the Roman **Odeon**, a type of theatre, which is overshadowed now by the massive new **mosque**, built in honour of the President Ben Ali. Big enough to house 12,000 people, the mosque dwarfs the similarly shaped cathedral on adjacent Byrsa Hill.

The small **archeological garden** across the street, containing a few Roman odds and ends, might be a good place for a breather. Further up, a **"building with columns"**, or what's left of it, may be the Baths of Gargilius where St Augustine called a conference of bishops in 411 to trick the dissident Donatist church into being a party to its own prohibition.

Back on avenue 7 Novembre, a little further up the hill, is the entrance to the Roman **theatre** (global ticket), extensively restored for the modern Carthage International Festival (see box below) and bearing scant resemblance to the original. Carthage's theatres became infamous for the immorality they portrayed and encouraged; several hundred years later a Christian critic wrote of the last days of the African Empire: "The arms of Barbarian people were

---

Carthage festivals

The **Carthage International Festival** (@www.festival-carthage.com.tn) is Tunisia's biggest cultural celebration, running from July to August every year. Events of all sorts – dance, cinema, music, theatre – are staged at the restored Roman theatre. The events are largely in French and are well advertised on hoardings and in the press – tickets can be bought at the theatre. For details of the biennial **Carthage Film Festival**, see p.117.

resounding against the walls of Carthage; and yet the Christian population was going wild in the theatres and enjoying itself in the circuses. Some were having their throats cut outside the walls; others were fornicating inside the walls."

Climbing over a fence on the far side of the Odeon and cutting across the fields brings you past the new mosque to the **Damous el Karita Basilica**. At 64.5m long and nine aisles wide, this is the largest ancient church known in North Africa. Though little more remains than a ground plan and rows of broken grey columns, there is at least a superficial similarity between this forest of columns and the one built only a few hundred years later in the prayer hall of the Great Mosque at Kairouan – perhaps even incorporating material from here. Another example of continuity is the site's name, an Arabic transliteration of the Latin Domus Caritatis (House of Grace).

The **American cemetery** (daily 8am–5pm) beyond – cross the road and take a short cut between the fields on the other side – presents an interesting contrast in style to the British, French and German cemeteries elsewhere in the country. Most Americans killed in action in Tunisia during World War II are buried here and, in contrast to the Commonwealth cemeteries, it goes all out for size and grandeur. The caretaker is something of an authority on the war in Tunisia. Close by, to the northeast, are the scant ruins of an old Byzantine church, the **Basilica Majorum**, and, east of here across the train line, another old Byzantine basilica, alleged to be the **Basilica of St Cyprian**.

Sidi Bou Saïd

Somehow, **SIDI BOU SAÏD**, a few kilometres north of Carthage (see the map on p.124), shrugs off its two and a half centuries as a tourist trap and remains a place of extraordinary charm. Today, it's a favourite retreat for the wealthy, but even on summer evenings you can have Sidi Bou to yourself by wandering through the silent backstreets past white, cubical houses and their studded blue doors.

You certainly won't see such a concentration of wealthy residents and visitors anywhere else in Tunisia, as Sidi Bou Saïd is as chic as they come. It seems that every artist and every writer who has visited Tunisia spent some time here, including Cervantes, Paul Klee, Simone de Beauvoir, André Gide and Jean Foucault. In 1939 Sacheverell Sitwell was told that Sidi Bou Saïd was the finest town in all Tunisia in which to see harem ladies in their silken dresses, but gold jewellery and tanned flesh are more the style now, especially around the expensive and rather snooty *Café des Nattes* in the main square.

The first building on this strategic cliff-top was a *ribat* or monastic fortress built in the early years of Arab rule, part of the chain stretching through Sousse and Monastir to Tripoli in Libya and over whose foundations a modern lighthouse is built. The village grew up around the tomb and *zaouia* of the thirteenth-century holy man Sidi Bou Saïd, still celebrated in the central **mosque** and during the August festival in his honour. According to one inventive but unlikely story, the saint was none other than St Louis, fresh from defeat at Carthage (see p.125), who retired here incognito to marry a local girl.

Around the beginning of the twentieth century the village was discovered by wealthy French and other expatriates, who bought houses and went to great lengths to "preserve" the town's character. As a result, there's very little here that is not Tunisian in origin – and there's nowhere else in Tunisia quite like it. One of the grandest of these houses is **Dar Ennejma Ezzahra** on rue 2 Mars (Tues–Sun: summer 8.30am–1pm & 3–6pm; winter 9am–1pm & 2–5pm; 3TD), the French Baron Rodolphe d'Erlanger's monumental and exquisitely beautiful folly. Built between 1912 and 19? **Arab and Mediterranean Music**. Beside mixture of "pure" Tunisian and Romantic Orie its collection of musical instruments, though you (20TD) to put them into context. A dedicated m. one of the moving spirits behind the important ina Music, held in Cairo in 1932, the first time that Arab as a whole and as a cultural heritage worthy of both s. There are sometimes performances of "endangered" mus about which can be obtained from the Maison de la Cultu. Tunis (see p.116).

Another opulent Tunisian house that can be visited is **L   ...abi** (Tues–Sun 9am–6.30pm; 3TD), on the left three-quarters of th.   .y up rue Dr H. Thameur. Originally owned by a local *mufti* (religious leader), the house passed to his son who served as a minister under Bourguiba. Some of its 55 rooms are still lived in by the present owner, the *mufti*'s grandson, a cardiologist. The house has a wonderful terrace from which you can enjoy panoramic views over the town and gulf, a pleasant courtyard garden in which to sip mint tea and several beautiful rooms complete with eerily realistic mannequins in everyday poses.

From Dar el Annabi, rue Dr H. Thameur continues up to the town's main square, from where rue Hedi Zarrouk continues on to end at **Cap Carthage**; on a clear day, you can see right across the bay to Korbous on Cap Bon. Below, the rain has exposed several fragments of **Punic flooring**, indicating the presence of villas here even in the third century BC.

Practicalities

The **TGM** from Tunis (30min) leaves you a five-minute walk from the town centre uphill towards the sea. Turn right from the station and walk until you reach the roundabout at place 7 Novembre; just off this square are a couple of **banks**, the **post office** and a **supermarket**. From place 7 Novembre, rue Dr H. Thameur heads up the hill to the small square dominated by the steps of the *Café des Nattes* and the central mosque's minaret rising picturesquely behind it.

There are some excellent little retreats where you can **stay** in Sidi Bou Saïd, though be aware that they're booked up months in advance in season. The most economical option is the *Hôtel Sidi Bou Farés* (℡71 740091, ℻71 728868, ⓔhotel.boufares@gnet.tn; ❺), in the stairway of the same name off the main square. It's set around a fragrant fig tree branching over a peaceful patio and its owner is something of a musician. Also off the main square, on rue el Hedi Zarrouk, is the recently renovated and excellent *Dar Said* (℡71 729666, ℻71 729599, ⓦwww.darsaid.com.tn; ❽), in a former palace with charming rooms, wonderful views and a small pool. Another high-class option is the *Hôtel Sidi Bou Saïd* (℡71 740411, ℻71 745129; ❽), about 1km out of town around the cape past the lighthouse and also enjoying good views.

Eating

Eating in Sidi Bou Saïd isn't cheap. For budget meals you'll have to trek to place 7 Novembre and its *gargotes* and sandwich bars, especially the *Bagatelle*, 9 av Bourguiba, which has good local specialities. The cheapest choice in the old town is the reasonable *Restaurant Chergui*, rue el Hedi Zarrouk (daily: summer noon–midnight; winter noon–8pm), with a pleasant rear terrace, where you can enjoy a meal for around 12TD. Otherwise, *Au Bon Vieux Temps*

.pm), further along at no. 56, is swish and expensive,
⎯nd 25TD and superb views from its dining room. *Dar*
⎯ging to the *Dar Said* hotel opposite (Tues–Sun noon–2.30pm
⎯m), is another high-quality establishment, with a lovely terrace and
or around 30TD. *Le Pirate*, near the bottom of a stepped path down to
⎯ie harbour at the foot of the cliffs (daily noon–2.30pm & 7pm–midnight),
is set among pleasant gardens and specializes in seafood (meals 20–25TD);
if you're staying in town the walk back up will easily burn off any calories
acquired during the meal.

For hanging out with the beau monde, the *Café des Nattes* in the main square
may be at the heart of the scene, though the café at the bottom of its crowded
steps is cheaper. But the place to really chill out is the *Café Sidi Chabaane*,
further along rue el Hadi Zarrouk. A steep series of narrow terraces set spectacularly in the cliff overlooking the gulf, it's the perfect place in town to relax
in romantic company with a glass of pine-nut tea. Doughnut fans should try a
bonbalouni from the stall just past the *Café des Nattes*.

La Marsa

LA MARSA, next in the long chain of suburbs along the northern shore, is
a place of some antiquity. In past centuries, when transport was less easy, the
entire court moved out here for the summer. "It is adorned with a royal palace,
and pleasant places," wrote John Ogilby in 1670, "whither the rulers of Tunis
in the summer go to take their pleasure, and keep their court." A restored
Hafsid-era **palace** can be seen in the centre of La Marsa, a few minutes' walk
inland from the TGM station behind the Tunisie Telecom building on place 7
Novembre. In the nineteenth century, when the last of Tunisia's independent
beys favoured La Marsa, many more beylical palaces and those of their ministers were built inland – two of the best are the residences of the British and
French ambassadors, both sadly inaccessible.

Today La Marsa is easy to get to on the TGM and, in summer, has become a
weekend resort for all of Tunis – or so it seems. The long **beach**, backed by an
attractive palm-lined corniche road, is what draws the crowds, and though it is
slightly less crowded than those further down, you still feel like a lemming.

Practicalities

La Marsa is quite a large town compared with Sidi Bou Saïd. From the **TGM
station** (35min from Tunis), at the southern end of the corniche, follow the
road straight ahead for about 300m until you come to a roundabout, from
where tree-lined avenue Bourguiba cuts back left to place 7 Novembre, where
you'll find **banks**, Tunisair, pharmacies and **buses** for Tunis (#20, #20d and
#20g) and Gammarth (#247). If you turn left from the TGM station, you
will find the **post office** on rue 9 Avril 1938, behind the mosque. Continue
to the end of rue 9 Avril, skirting an **amusement park** on your left (daily
8am–6.30pm; 1TD), and you will come out just south of place 7 Novembre. If
you want to access the **Internet** while you're in La Marsa, Le Net Club on rue
Cheikh Zarroukh (Mon–Sat 9am–midnight, Sun 10am–midnight; 2TD/hr),
left off avenue Bourguiba 200m from place 7 Novembre, down towards the
sea, will serve the purpose.

Options to **stay** here are limited. The unsigned *Pension Predl*, 7 rue Mohamed
Salah Melki (☎71 749 529; ❹), is left off avenue Bourguiba about 250m from
place 7 Novembre, one block beyond Le Net Club and immediately on the left
as you turn into rue Melki. It has the cosiest family atmosphere of any pension

in Tunisia. Alternatively, there's the pleasant *Hôtel Plaza Corniche* at 22 rue du Maroc (℡71 743 577, ⓦwww.plaza-corniche.com; ❼), five minutes' walk from the TGM station back towards Sidi Bou Saïd. With a pool, bar and nightclub, in season it gets booked solid. There's also a *Maison des Jeunes* at the northern end of the beach (℡71 774 074).

La Marsa's cheap **restaurants**, among them *El Hana* and *du Peuple* (daily 8am–9.30pm), are off the corniche around the avenue 20 Mars arcade, opposite the modern Zephyr shopping centre. A little further towards the beach, on rue Mongi Slim, where it crosses beneath the corniche, the *Restaurant Mexicane* serves up moderately priced pizzas and the like (Tues–Sun noon–3pm & 6.30–9pm) amid bits and pieces of Americana and a mounted wild boar's head, though nothing particularly Mexican. Where rue Mongi Slim meets the sea is the *Koubet El Haoua* (℡71 729 777; Mon–Sat 12.30–3pm & 7.30pm–midnight), an amazing piece of Art Deco that has been converted into a posh French/Italian restaurant and piano bar, with panoramic sea views. Another good upmarket option is the restaurant at the *Plaza Corniche* (daily 10am–3pm & 8pm–midnight). For a quick bite, try *Baguette & Baguette* to the left of the TGM (daily 8am–8pm), part of a sandwich chain where you can get a combo (sandwich, fries and a drink) for around 3TD, or one of the sandwich shops and ice cream parlours in the Zephyr centre, which also has a Monoprix **supermarket**. The most interesting place in town for a **mint tea** or Turkish coffee is the *Café Saf Saf*, opposite the mosque, whose terraces surround a public well dating back to the Hafsid period. If you're lucky you might see a camel working the wheel, but the *Saf Saf* has clearly declined since the memorable performances of the tragic chanteuse Habiba Msika in the 1920s (see p.304).

Gammarth and Raoued Beach

GAMMARTH (bus #20b from Jardin Thameur in Tunis or #247 from La Marsa; 6TD by taxi from Tunis) is the next suburb along the northern coastline. It grew up around the series of beaches dubbed **Baies des Singes** (Bays of the Monkeys) by local fishermen – reputedly after the Europeans who sunbathed in the nude there in the 1950s. Up on the hill is the **cemetery** of the Free French killed during World War II.

Beyond Gammarth, signs of civilization start to thin out as the road runs between a salt flat and **Raoued Beach** (#247 bus from La Marsa or Gammarth), a broad expanse of sand where families used to camp en masse in summer but which is gradually being taken over by a string of new resort hotels. With so many people and relatively few facilities, the water becomes almost visibly unhygienic in the peak season.

The **hotels** in and around Gammarth are fairly expensive; if you want to spend several days by the beach, Hammamet, Sousse and Jerba are better destinations. Accommodation here is a strange mixture of average package-tour places, hideous five-star carbuncles and a handful of smarter new hotels along Raoued Beach. Least offensive of the established hotels is the small *Abou Nawas Gammarth* on the coast road between La Marsa and Gammarth (℡71 741444, ℻71 740 400, ✉gammarth@abounawas.com.tn; ❻), with all the creature comforts. By the shore, the *Megara* (℡71 740366, ℻71 740 916; ❻) is in a nice location but slightly dilapidated and rather overpriced. In Gammarth itself is *La Tour Blanche* (℡71 774 788, ℻71 747247; ❺), which has also seen better days and doesn't offer great service. One kilometre further on, rounding the cape, is *Le Palace* (℡71 912 000, ℻71 911 442, ⓦwww.lepalace.com.tn; ❾), rigged with all the state-of-the-art fittings and five restaurants. On the far side of the cape, the main road turns inland while the old route Touristique veers off back to the coast. Here are cheaper package-type options, including the *Cap Carthage Méditerranée* (℡71 740 320, ℻71 911 980; ❺), which has tennis courts and a host of activities. Among the hotels that have opened further along the beach are the package-style *Acqua Viva*, about 1500m to the west (℡71 741 374, ℻71 911 503; ❻), featuring a pool with water slides, and the plush business-class *Renaissance* (℡71 910 900, ℻71 910 295; ❾), another 1500m towards Raoued village.

Among the **restaurants** in Gammarth, there's *Les Dunes*, a lovely villa with seaviews up towards Cape Carthage, and the fractionally cheaper but equally good *Les Ombrelles*, just before *Les Dunes* on the beach; *Sindbad*, next door to *Les Ombrelles*, is popular with young chic folk. All three are open daily between noon and 3pm and from 6pm until at least 10pm, and will cost upwards of 20TD for a meal. Along with *Sindbad*, the *Grand Bleu* up on the headland just before *Le Palace* is a popular place for a **drink**, while *Le Cotton Club*, by *La Résidence*, and *Cyclone*, belonging to *La Tour Blanche*, are two of the best **clubs**.

La Soukra and Berges du Lac

A few kilometres inland of La Marsa is the burgeoning suburb of **LA SOUKRA**, once covered in orchards but now being transformed into a leafy residential district for wealthy Tunisians and expats. As well as being home to Tunisia's oldest golf course, La Soukra shows more recent signs of affluence, notably a vast Carrefour **hypermarket** next to the Tunis–La Marsa highway. At the same time antique shops and galleries have opened up on the main drag, avenue Fatouma Bourguiba, along with a handful of trendy **bar-restaurants**, including the popular *Le Boeuf sur le Toit*, which has a dance floor and is really more about letting your hair down in cosmopolitan company than having a meal.

Part of the reason La Soukra has become such a desirable address is its proximity to the airport and the new **BERGES DU LAC** development (buses #20d and #28d from Jardin Thameur in Tunis) on the south side of the Tunis–La Marsa highway. Overlooking the northern shore of Lac Tunis, Berges du Lac has proved a magnet for business, with its gleaming new office blocks, and is home to the new British and American embassies. The district centres on a roundabout, place Tahar Haddad, with a wide boulevard, the route du Lac, stretching to either side and providing easy access to the modern grid of streets, all named after famous lakes of the world. Most of Berges du Lac's leisure facilities lie to the west of the main roundabout, including the **Tunisia Happy Land Park** (Mon & Wed–Fri 2–9pm, Sat & Sun 11am–9pm), which is more substantial than the average Tunisian fairground, with a rollercoaster and a Ferris wheel that is something of a landmark here. There are a few restaurants and a nightclub on the lake-shore promenade near the fairground and further west, 2km from place Tahar Haddad, a **bowling** complex, Bowling du Lac (daily 9am–midnight).

As you approach place Tahar Haddad from the highway turn-off, you pass a large **shopping centre**, the Lac Palace, on the left. On the far side of place Tahar Haddad is the smart, business-orientated *Acropole* **hotel** (℡71 963 000, ℻71 962 044, ✉acropole@planet.tn; ❽), with the **British Embassy** behind it on rue du Lac Windermere on the lake shore. In the other direction from place Tahar Haddad, 3.5km along the route du Lac towards La Marsa, is the new **American Embassy**, fortress-like with its huge walled compound and turret poking out of the main building.

The southern Gulf shore

Easily reached by **train** (every 10–20min; 5am–midnight) from Tunis's main station, the suburbs along the **southern shore** of the gulf are for the most part shapeless areas of commuter housing, with warehouses and light industry filling the gaps between what were once smart resorts. Once the last stage on the caravan route from the south, where merchants paid tax before entering the capital, **HAMMAM LIF** was a popular spa in Carthaginian and Roman days, and emerged again as a resort under the Protectorate. By far the busiest and most established of the Gulf of Tunis resorts, it's a pleasant place to pass a few days. Palm-lined avenues and an old seafront casino give the town an air of faded grandeur in its dramatic setting under Bou Kornine, but it rarely throws off its rather listless feel – except on Sunday, the market day, which is the busiest time of the week. The *Casino* is now a **bar-restaurant** – an excellent place to pop in for a beer and where women need have no worries. As for the decor, as one writer remarked, it's like "Elvis on acid". If you want time to inspect this display, you can **stay** at the basic *Bon Repos*, 14 rue Ibn Rochd (☎71 291 458; ❶).

The imposing two-pronged mountain of **Bou Kornine**, heavily forested lower down but with a more open maquis vegetation at the top, is theoretically a national park. In practice, it has become a military zone and you are liable – though unlikely – to be arrested if you try to go further than the *Chalet Vert* restaurant, about 1km up the hill and with a fine view north over the Gulf of Tunis. A road leads up to the restaurant from the main Tunis road, a few hundred metres towards Tunis from Hammam Lif. Beyond the restaurant, it's another hour or so on foot along good paths to near the top before the paths begin to disappear.

BORJ CEDRIA is the last desultory resort before Soliman Plage (see p.142). Just beyond, off the main road, there's a discreet sign pointing a few hundred metres inland to the **Deutscher Soldaten Friedhof**, a German military cemetery from World War II. Built in 1975 on a slight rise near the site of the final German surrender, this grim collection of rectangular lockers represents yet another approach to the issue of the World War II dead, a stark contrast to British pastoral, American razzmatazz and French militarism. If you want to stay in the area, there are a few rather tired and downmarket package **hotels** on the beach, including the wheelchair-accessible *Medisea* (☎71 430 261, ☎71 430 013, ⓦwww.mediseahotel.com; ❻), with bikes for rent and watersports on offer. There is also a basic **campsite**, *La Pinède* (☎71 430 621).

Travel details

Trains

Tunis to: Béja (7 daily; 1hr 50min); Bir Bou Regba (10–12 daily; 50min); Bizerte (4 daily; 1 hr 25min–1hr 40min); Borj Cedria (every 10–20min; 45min); Bou Kornine (every 10–20min; 20min); Dahmani (3 daily; 3hr 50min); El Fahs (4 daily; 1hr 30min); El Jem (5 daily; 2hr 50min); Enfida (5–6 daily; 1hr 15min); Ez Zahra (every 10–20min; 25min); Friguia Safari Park (4 daily; 1hr 10min); Gaafour (3 daily; 2hr 15min); Gabès (4 daily; 6hr 20min–6hr 40min); Gafsa (2 daily; 7hr 45min); Ghardimaou (5 daily; 3hr); Hammam Lif (every 10–20min; 25min); Hammamet (2 direct daily & 4–6 daily connecting at Bir Bou Regba; 1hr 15min–1hr 45min); Jendouba (5 daily; 2hr 30min–2hr 45min); Kalaa Khasbah (2 daily; 5hr); Kalaa Sghira (near Sousse; 6–7 daily; 1hr 35min–2hr); Mahdia (1 daily; 4hr); Mateur (4 daily; 1hr–1hr 25min); Medjez el Bab (5 daily; 1hr); Metlaoui (1 daily; 8hr–8hr 30min); Monastir (1 daily; 3hr); Nabeul (1 direct daily & 4–6 daily connecting at Bir Bou Regba; 1hr 20min–1hr 50min); Radès (every 10–20min; 20min); Sfax (7 daily; 3hr 25min–3hr 40min); Sousse (8–9 daily; 1hr 50min–2hr 05min); Tinja (4 daily; 1hr 20min).

Tunis Marine TGM (every 12min) to: Carthage

(20min); La Goulette (10min); La Marsa (35min); Sidi Bou Saïd (30min).

Buses

Tunis Bab Aleoua (Bab el Fellah) to: Douz (3 daily; 8hr); El Haouaria (7 daily; 3hr); El Jem (8 daily; 3hr 45min); Enfida (hourly; 1hr 30min); Gabès (18 daily; 6hr 30min); Gafsa (10 daily; 5hr 30min); Grombalia (every 20min; 1hr); Hammamet (hourly; 1hr 30min); Jerba (Houmt Souk; 3 daily; 8hr 30min); Kairouan (10 daily; 2hr 30min); Kasserine (7 daily; 5hr); Kebili (3 daily; 7hr); Kélibia (hourly; 2hr 30min); Korba (every 30min; 2hr); Korbous (4 daily; 3hr); Maktar (7 daily; 3hr); Medenine (11 daily; 8hr); Nabeul (every 30min; 1hr 30min); Nefta (2 daily; 7hr 30min); Ras Ajdir (1 daily; 10hr); Sbeïtla (7 daily; 4hr); Sfax (11 daily; 5hr); Sidi Bou Zid (4 daily; 5hr); Sousse (7 daily; 2hr 30min); Tatouine (3 daily; 9hr); Tozeur (5 daily; 7hr); Tripoli (Libya; 1 daily Mon–Sat; 15hr); Zaghouan (7 daily; 1hr).
Tunis Bab Saadoun to: Aïn Draham (4 daily; 4hr); Béja (14 daily; 2hr); Bizerte (every 30min; 1hr 30min); Ghar el Melh (2 daily; 2hr); Jendouba (6 daily; 3hr); Le Kef (12 daily; 3hr); Mateur (hourly; 1hr 30min); Medjez el Bab (every 30min; 1hr); Menzel Bourguiba (hourly; 1hr 30min); Raf Raf (2 daily; 2hr); Ras Jebel (5 daily; 2hr); Tabarka (6 daily; 4hr); Téboursouk (6 daily; 2hr 20min); Testour (hourly; 1hr).

Louages

Tunis Bab Aleoua (Bab el Fellah) to: El Haouaria (1hr 45min); Enfida (1hr 30min); Grombalia (1hr);

Hammamet (1hr 30min); Kélibia (2hr 30min); Korba (2hr); Korbous (1hr); Nabeul (1hr 30min).
Tunis Bab Saadoun to: Aïn Draham (4hr); Béja (1hr 45min); Bizerte (1hr 30min); Ghar el Melh (2hr); Jendouba (3hr); Mateur (1hr 30min); Medjez el Bab (1hr); Menzel Bourguiba (1hr 30min); Raf Raf (2hr); Ras Jebel (2hr); Tabarka (4hr); Téboursouk (2hr); Testour (1hr).
Tunis Moncef Bey to: El Jem (occasional; 2hr 45min); Gabès (6hr 30min); Gafsa (5hr); Jerba (Houmt Souk; 8hr 30min); Kairouan (2hr); Kasserine (5hr); Kebili (7hr); Le Kef (3hr); Maktar (3hr); Matmata (7hr); Medenine (7hr 30min); Monastir (2hr 20min); Ras Ajdir (10hr); Sbeïtla (4hr); Sfax (4hr 30min); Sidi Bou Zid (4hr); Sousse (2hr); Tataouine (8hr); Tozeur (6hr); Zaghouan (45min); Zarzis (9hr).
Tunis rue al Jazira to: Annaba (Algeria; 5hr 30min).
Tunis Garage Ayachi to: Tripoli (Libya; 13hr).

Ferries

Tunis La Goulette to: Genoa (3–8 weekly; 27hr); La Spezia (June–Sept 1 or 2 weekly, 24hr); Malta (2 weekly; 10hr); Marseille (1–6 weekly; 24hr); Naples (June–Sept 1–4 weekly; 19hr); Palermo (1 weekly; Salerno (2 weekly; 18–21hr); 9hr); Trápani (2 weekly; 8–12hr); Valencia (1 weekly; 62hr); Valetta (2 weekly; 10hr).

Domestic flights

Tunis to: Gafsa (2 weekly; 1hr); Jerba (6–7 daily; 1hr); Sfax (4 weekly; 45min); Tozeur (1 daily; 1hr).

Arabic place names	
Tunis	تونس
Bardo Museum	متهف البارد
Tunis environs	
Borj Cedria	برج السدرية
Carthage	قرطاج
Gammarth	قمّرت
Hammam Lif	حمّام اللانف
Jebel Bou Kornine	جبل بو قرنين
La Goulette	حلق الوادي
La Marsa	المرسى
Raouad	روّاد
Sidi Bou Saïd	سيدي بو سعيد

Hammamet and Cap Bon

ALGERIA

LIBYA

N

CHAPTER 2 # Highlights

✱ **Hammamet beach** For all the crowds and parasols, the beach here, with its luxuriant green backdrop, manages to look even lovelier than the brochure pictures. See p.144

✱ **Nabeul** The beach might not be as nice as Hammamet's, but the pottery and other crafts are well worth coming to see. See p.147

✱ **Kélibia** A busy fishing port dominated by a massive hilltop fort, with some pretty sandy coves to the north. See p.153

✱ **Kerkouane** The largest Carthaginian site in Tunisia, notable for the curious private baths in virtually all the houses. See p.156

✱ **El Haouaria** Pleasant little town below the last hump of Cap Bon, known for its falconry festival and some amazing Roman quarries. See p.157

✱ **Korbous** An ancient spa on the craggy slopes of Jebel Korbous, with a hot spring nearby that gushes into the sea. See p.160

△ Hammamet

Hammamet and Cap Bon

Protruding like a crooked finger into the Mediterranean, the **Cap Bon peninsula** is Tunisia's traditional resort area. Indeed, glancing at the brochures – with their staggering hotel capacities – it looks a little ominous, particularly along the coast around **Hammamet**. But although Hammamet, the best-known resort in the country, has been heavily developed, images of a Spanish-like *costa*, with tourists crowded in like cattle, don't apply. The beaches, for a start, are too big and too luxuriant, and the hotels are kept discreetly down to a few storeys, strung out along the tree-lined shore. Twenty minutes away, **Nabeul** has less perfect beaches and a less glamorous image, but does have cheaper places to stay and good transport links to other areas of the peninsula.

Among these areas, one of the most worthwhile targets is **El Haouaria**, a village at the end of the peninsula with the twin attractions of a remote white strand and an ancient quarry complex. **Kerkouane**, south along the coast from here, is the largest Carthaginian site yet uncovered, while **Kélibia**, a few kilometres on and dominated by a massive Spanish castle, is the busiest fishing port and quietest beach resort on the east coast. Over on the west coast of the peninsula, the venerable spa of **Korbous** is the best-known lure, while if you're after seclusion and have transport, the coast beyond is literally one long and as yet undiscovered beach.

The peninsula is at its best in spring, when it becomes a mass of colour with its fruit orchards and vineyards. If you can make it in March or April, try to coincide with the orange blossom festival at **Menzel Bou Zelfa**. By Septem-

Market days

Monday Kélibia
Tuesday Menzel Temime
Thursday Hammamet, El Haouaria, Maamoura (near Nabeul), Menzel Bou Zelfa
Friday Nabeul
Saturday Soliman
Sunday Béni Khiar (near Nabeul), Dar Chaâbane (also near Nabeul), Korba

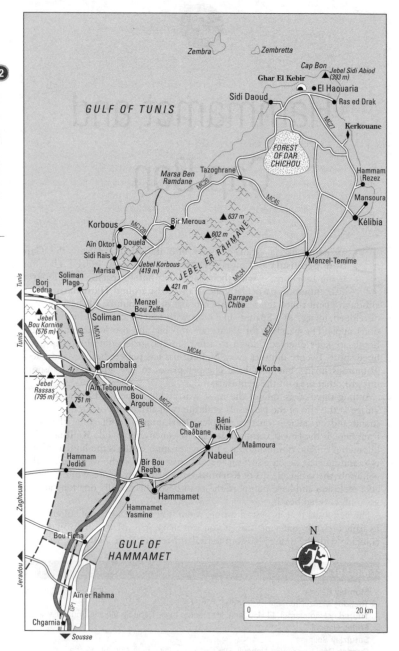

Zembra ○ Zembretta

GULF OF TUNIS

Cap Bon
Jebel Sidi Abiod
(393 m)
Ghar El Kebir
Sidi Daoud ● El Haouaria
● Ras ed Drak

Kerkouane

FOREST
OF DAR
CHICHOU

*Marsa Ben
Ramdane*
MC26 Tazoghrane
Hammam
Rezez

MC45
Mansoura

Korbous
MC128
Bir Meroua
▲ 637 m
Kélibia

Aïn Oktor
Douela
Sidi Rais
▲ 602 m
JEBEL ER RAHMANE

Marisa
▲ *Jebel Korbous
(419 m)*
MC34
Menzel-Temime

Soliman
Plage
▲ 421 m
*Barrage
Chiba*

Borj
Cedria
Menzel
Bou Zelfa
MC27

*Jebel
Bou Kornine
(576 m)*
MC41
Soliman

GP1
MC44
Korba

Grombalia

*Jebel
Rassas
(795 m)*
A1
Aïn Tebournok
▲ 751 m
Bou
Argoub
MC27

Dar
Chaâbane
Béni
Khiar

Hammam
Jedidi
Bir Bou
Regba
Nabeul
Maâmoura

Hammamet

Hammamet
Yasmine

Bou Ficha
*GULF OF
HAMMAMET*

N

Aïn er Rahma

Chgarnia
▼ *Sousse*

0 ———————— 20 km

Tunis ◄
Tunis ◄
Zaghouan ◄
Jeradou ◄

ber the ground is parched – although liquid compensation is afforded by the wine festival at **Grombalia**, held around this time of year.

Nabeul is the main centre for **road transport** in Cap Bon, and anyone visiting the peninsula will probably pass through here. Both Grombalia and Bir Bou Regba are on the main Tunis–Gabès **rail** line, the latter town having a branch-line connection to Nabeul and Hammamet.

Hammamet

At the beginning of the last century, **HAMMAMET**, some 60km southeast of Tunis, was a small fishing village making some extra money by selling lemons from its dense citrus groves to Sicily for export to America. It was not until the 1920s, with the arrival of Romanian millionaire Georges Sebastian, that the town found its true vocation. Sebastian built a fabulous villa just above the beach, described by Frank Lloyd Wright as the most beautiful house he knew. Others followed, and soon Hammamet was part of the Orientalist legend of a sensual Tunisia – somewhere between an intellectual resort and a luxurious bohemia for Europe's prewar moneyed classes. Today, with more than a hundred hotels and around forty thousand beds, Hammamet is considerably less exclusive. If you don't mind being surrounded by burger bars, pizza joints and carpet shops, then there's a lot to be said for Hammamet as a beach resort. Otherwise, give it a wide berth and head further south – to Mahdia, for example (see p.256) – or else into the Cap Bon peninsula, for less crowded beaches.

Arrival, information and transport

Hammamet's two main streets begin at the Medina, with **avenue de la République** heading towards Nabeul and becoming **avenue de la Libération** further along, and **avenue Bourguiba** going inland towards the **train station**. If you arrive by **bus** from Tunis or Nabeul, you'll be set down in the middle of town on avenue de la République near the tourist office; other buses stop on avenue Hedi Ouali, ten minutes' walk north of the centre. The main **louage station** is at Baraket Essahel, near the *Hôtel Samaris* on the GP1 Tunis–Sousse road, though Tunis louages terminate in a triangular square 50m west of *Hôtel Khella* and avenue de la République. From the louage station,

---

Moving on from Hammamet

For a list of destinations and journey times, see Travel details on p.164.

Buses to Tunis and Nabeul (where you can change for other Cap Bon destinations) leave from avenue de la République near the ONTT tourist office. Buses en route from Nabeul to Sousse, Monastir and Kairouan stop on avenue Hedi Ouali, near its junction with avenue Bourguiba. **Louages** to Tunis gather in a small triangular piazza off avenue de la République near *Hôtel Khella*, while those to Sousse, Kairouan and Zaghouan leave from the main louage station. There are no louages to Nabeul, so if you don't want to get there by bus or train, take a shared taxi (around 1TD per place) or one of the metered **taxis** (about 7TD) that wait near the tourist office on avenue de la République.

There are frequent **trains** to Nabeul and Bir Bou Regba, from where you can connect for Tunis or for points south. There's only one direct train to Tunis (Mon–Sat 6am). The station is on ☏72 280174.

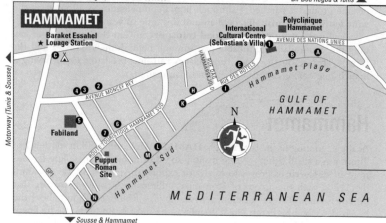

it's a six-kilometre taxi ride into town, much shorter to the resort hotels in Hammamet Sud and Hammamet Yasmine. The **train station** is on avenue Bourguiba, north of the junction with avenue Hedi Ouali.

If you want a very slow ride along the coast, via all the big hotels, there's a tacky toy-town **tourist road train** from outside the Medina. The trains, which leave fairly often, are operated by four different companies, and tickets (5TD) are not interchangeable.

The main **ONTT** (Mon–Sat: July & Aug 7.30am–1.30pm & 3–8pm; Sept–June 8am–6pm; ☎72 280 423) is in the centre of town on avenue de la République. Staff here are pretty helpful and can provide a map and accommodation price list. There is a **Syndicat d'Initiative** around the corner on avenue Bourguiba in a small building facing the beach (Tues–Sun: July & Aug 7.30am–10pm; Sept–June 9am–noon & 3–6.30pm; ☎72 262 891).

Accommodation

Most of Hammamet's hotels are spread out along the beach in both directions from town in the *zones touristiques* of Hammamet Nord, Hammamet Plage, Hammamet Sud and its new extension, Hammamet Yasmine. About two kilometres west of the town centre, the most attractive patch of beach begins to curve away southwest towards Hammamet Sud, with views of the Medina all the way along. In the opposite direction, it's about 17km northeast to Nabeul; we've listed fewer on this stretch of coast as the beach here is more exposed and less attractive.

There's a central **youth hostel**, the *Maison des Jeunes* at avenue Assad Ibn el Fourat (☎72 280 440; dorm beds 5TD), offering the usual concrete bliss. Six kilometres southwest of town, the one-star *Samaris* hotel (see p.143) has a **campsite** (☎72 226 353) and a pool that campers can use.

Petty thieving is common in Hammamet, stuffed as it is with tourists. Take care of your valuables, both on the beach (never leave things unattended) and on the street, where small children might try to distract you with posies of flowers or other objects while someone else runs off with whatever is accessible.

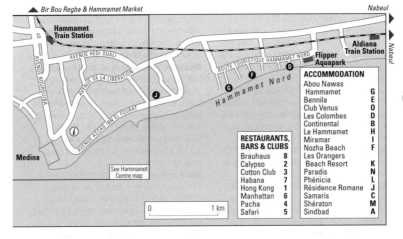

Hotels

Three-star (and better) beach hotels generally offer good, en-suite rooms equipped with satellite television, telephones and air conditioning, as well as swimming pools and rather insipid restaurants serving international rather than Tunisian cuisine. Unless otherwise mentioned below, rates include breakfast. Prices everywhere in the area plunge spectacularly in winter, sometimes as low as a third of high-season rates.

Most hotels will organize **excursions**, many of which are rather antiseptic, but still the easiest way to see the sights of the town if time is limited. Outside Cap Bon, trips can range from a half-day to several days to the usual destinations of Kairouan, Sousse, Tozeur and Matmata. If you want to organize trips yourself, the hotels in town are not only more convenient for transport but also cheaper than beachfront places.

The town centre

Except for the *Résidence Romane,* the hotels listed here are shown on the map on p.145.

Baie du Soleil av Assad Ibn el Fourat ☎72 280 298, ℗72 280 407. Quiet, leafy and right on the beach just east of the centre, though the rooms are a bit spartan and there's no pool. Half board doesn't cost much more than paying for accommodation only. ❺

Bel Azur av Assad Ibn el Fourat ☎72 280544, ℗72 280 275. Part of the *Sol Azur* complex, this is more expensive than most three-stars, but is high-quality, with landscaped gardens and its own beach, and offering boat trips and water sports. ❼

Belle Vue av Assad Ibn el Fourat ☎72 281121, ℗72 283 156, ✉kaismohdi@yahoo.com. Excellent seafront location close to the Medina, with most rooms overlooking the sea and its own private section of beach. Rooms are pleasant, though they were a bit tired at the time of writing – something

that should be rectified by a promised facelift. Fills up in season, so book ahead. ❺

Dar Hayet 33 rue Farhat Hached ☎72 283 399, ℗72 280 424, ✉dar.hayet@planet.tn. The closest five-star to the centre, and right on the beach with its "feet in the water", as the French say. The marble lobby is very classy but the rooms – for two to six people – and the hotel's other facilities fail to live up to its billing (or price). ❾

Kacem av Bourguiba ☎72 279 580, ℗72 279 588. The closest hotel to the train station. The rooms, sleeping two to four people, have a small kitchenette and fridge. Facilities also include two pools, a gym and a rooftop barbecue area. ❻

Khella av de la République ☎72 283 900, ℗72 283 704. Prettily furnished place, similar to the *Sahbi* and just north of it on the same street. Fair value. ❺

141

Milano rue des Fontaines ☎72 280 768. Small place which, at the time of writing, was being converted from a pension into a three-star hotel, with a private area on the beach. More personable than the larger package places; after the renovations, likely to be ➏

Le Mirage 173 av de la République ☎72 280 601, ☎281 568. Friendly new hotel with spacious, comfortable rooms – though the bathrooms are a bit cramped – and a nice roof terrace with views over the town. ➎

Olympia av du Koweit ☎72 280 622, ☎280 969. On a busy road, but perfectly adequate and quite inexpensive by Hammamet standards. ➎

Résidence Amine av de la Libération ☎72 765 500. A comparatively new, good-value hotel run by the affable Ramdane Kochkache, and featuring enormous, tastefully decorated rooms that sleep two to five people. ➎

Résidence Hammamet 60 av Bourguiba ☎72 280 406, ☎72 280 396. Pleasant, comfortable place only 300m from the Medina and even nearer to the beach, with rooms for two to four people and equipped with kitchenettes. Smarter and better value than the nearby *Kacem*. ➎

Résidence Romane av Assad Ibn el Fourat ☎72 263 103, ☎72 261 681, ☺rommene.sami@gnet .tn. Very nice family-run place with quite classy rooms, as well as self-catering apartments for two to four people, and villas for up to six, at eminently reasonable prices. As well as a pool, there is a small complex attached to the hotel containing a pizzeria, grocery store, hairdresser and games room. ➎

Sahbi av de la République ☎72 280 807, ☎280 134. Described in their brochure as "Moorish style" (no doubt referring to the colossal carpet shop on the ground floor), this place has big, clean rooms at a reasonable price. Fills up with package tourists, mainly Czech, in summer. No breakfast served in winter. ➎

Hammamet Plage

Beginning 2km from the Medina, Hammamet Plage is the nearest southern "resort" from town. The hotels are generally more downmarket than at Hammamet Sud, but are more discreetly tucked away in verdant grounds. The streets behind the hotels feature plenty of restaurants, grocery stores, newsagents, travel agents and car rental outfits.

Bennila rue des Hôtels ☎ & ☎72 261 894. Set back from the beach, with tidy rooms and a pool. Closed Oct–May. ➍

Continental av des Nations-Unies ☎72 280 220, ☎72 281 667. Right on the beach and within walking distance of the town centre, this early 1970s package hotel is now showing its age, though it does have an indoor and outdoor pool, and a restaurant serving reasonable international fare. Good rates in winter but overpriced in summer. ➐

Le Hammamet rue des Hôtels ☎72 280366, ☎72 282105. Between the *Oranger Beach Resort* and the *Miramar*, this hotel has no beach frontage, but is very good value for a four-star – exceptional value in winter. Facilities include two pools (indoor and outdoor), fitness centre, jacuzzi and sauna. Also has apartments for four people. ➏

Miramar rue des Hôtels ☎72 280 344, ☎72 280 586, ☺miramar.hammamet@planet.tn. Three hotels in one: the oldest, dating from 1959, has been renovated up to the standards of the two modern wings, which comprise bungalows and apartments with cooking facilities. The garden leads to the beach, where you'll find a full range of aquatic activities and boat trips. ➑

Les Orangers Beach Resort rue des Hôtels ☎72 280144, ☎72 281077, ☺www.tunisia-orangers.com. Very pleasant family-oriented place with facilities for water sports, including windsurfing and jet skis. ➑

Sindbad av des Nations-Unies, before the International Cultural Centre ☎72 280122, ☎280004, ☺www.hotel-sindbad.com. Five-star comfort, with a beauty centre, hammam and tennis courts in addition to all mod cons in the rooms. ➒

Hammamet Sud

Until Hammamet Yasmine came along, this run of hotels, 5–7km from the centre, was the most extensive in the area. Most of Hammamet's nightlife takes place here, with a plethora of "British pubs" (the Spanish *costa* version), bars and discos lining the two main roads behind the hotels. Most hotels here are blessed with maturing, shaded gardens, and the more exclusive establishments have courtesy buses into town – otherwise, you can catch a taxi or the tourist road train (see p.140).

Club Venus rte Touristique Hammamet Sud ☎72 227 211, ℗72 226 304. Very well endowed for its three-star rating, with recently done-up rooms, three pools, a sauna, mini golf, a grass football pitch – plenty to keep you occupied. Good value. ❽

Paradis rte Touristique Hammamet Sud ☎72 226300, ℗226860, ℮paradis.hotel@planet.tn. Tackiest and cheapest of Hammamet Sud's establishments, stuffed with package-holiday guests in summer – it's a good laugh with no pretensions. Large range of activities, and the outdoor pool has a waterslide (there's a heated indoor pool too). ❼

Phénicia rte Touristique Hammamet Sud ☎72 226533, ℗226337, ℮hotel.phenicia@planet .tn. With its own beach, this place lives up to its four-star rating, with the usual facilities, plus three

swimming pools and activities in[...] and horse-riding. ❾

Samaris 6km west of Hammamet, on the Tunis–Sousse road ☎72 226353. Strictly speak ing not part of Hammamet Sud, but a reasonably priced and friendly place, with a pool, a nice lounge and good food. The only disadvantage is that it's a couple of kilometres down to the beach. Self-catering apartments, sleeping up to three, are available too. ❺

Shératon av Moncef Bey ☎72 226555, ℗227301, ℮reservations_hammamet_tunisia@sheraton.com. A cut above its business-class namesakes elsewhere in the world, with accommodation in tasteful chalets and a good range of water sports offered. Some rooms are suitable for disabled guests. ❽

Hammamet Yasmine

Some 9–12km from town, the new purpose-built resort of Hammamet Yasmine contains over forty massive hotels, a 740-berth marina and even an imitation Medina that would not look out of place in Disneyland. The resort is well connected to the centre of town by half-hourly buses and by the tourist road train. Almost all the hotels here are four- and five-stars with all the trimmings, but they lack charm, and as yet there is hardly any greenery to soften the concrete feel of the place or shelter the beach from the wind and sun.

Hasdrubal Southern end of Hammamet Yasmine ☎72 248800, ℗248923, ☜www.lhw.com. A member of the Leading Hotels of the World group, this is Hammamet's premier hotel and it offers a level of opulence and service to match. Unfortunately it's miles out of town and costs a packet. ❾

Le Royal Northern end of Hammamet Yasmine ☎72 226 935, ℗226 965, ☜www.leroyal-hammamet .com. One of the first hotels to be built on the strip,

the *Royal* (formerly the *Occidental*) has the usual five-star luxuries plus a landscaped garden, which sets it apart from most of the other hotels here. ❾

Safa Centre of Hammamet Yasmine on the seafront boulevard ☎72 248790, ℗72 248700. One of the few three-stars in Hammamet Yasmine and consequently among the least expensive options, with modern rooms, indoor and outdoor pools and various water sports on offer. ❼

Hammamet Nord

Although this area contains many pricey five-stars, it is slightly cheaper than Hammamet Sud in general, and the beach isn't as nice. The more easterly hotels can be reached by train – all Hammamet–Nabeul services call at Aldiana station.

Abou Nawas Hammamet rte Touristique Hammamet ☎72 281 344, ℗72 281 089, ☜www .abounawas.com. Up to the chain's usual high standard and right on the beach. Mod cons include a gym, tennis court, pools and shops, and ample gardens to lose the kids in. ❽

Les Colombes rte Touristique Hammamet ☎72 280049, ℗280899. Built in 1970 and slightly tacky, this is very much package-tour heaven (or

hell): right on the beach, with water sports, an embarrassing disco and plenty of cheerful holiday-makers from all over Europe. Full board only. ❽

Nozha Beach rte Touristique Hammamet ☎72 280 311, ℗280 157, ☜www.nozhabeachhotel .com. Large 1980s hotel, with the usual facilities. Well equipped for sports such as tennis as well as a range of aquatic activities. Camel and horse rides available. ❼

The Town

Hammamet's centre is a little cape sticking out into the sea with the **Medina** standing neatly on its point, the newer quarters spreading out behind, and most of the hotels spaced to either side along the beach. The tiny walled Medina but been swamped by tourist emporia, although Boutique ...n & 3–6.30pm) at 9 bis place Pasteur, opposite the Kasbah ... quality locally made traditional clothes at fixed prices. The ...**Great Mosque** boasts an attractive minaret, while the over-...ntury **Kasbah** (daily 8am–7pm; 1.6TD, camera 1TD) in the ...stern corner is of little interest apart from its views.

...na, avenue de la République heads towards Nabeul, passing ...the municipal museum at no. 21. The building is sometimes stu.. ... llery: entry is free, and one or two relics remain inside. On the street corner next to it is an old olive oil press. The town hall on avenue Bourguiba, in the very centre facing the beach, was formerly the *Hôtel de France*, once popular with Europe's rich and famous.

The main business of Hammamet, of course, is the **beach**. Even with the fast-food stalls, the forests of sunshades and the herds of bored-looking camels, the sheltered curve of the bay – backed by luxuriant greenery which conceals the low-built hotels – still manages to look even more beautiful than the brochure pictures.

There's little more to the seashore than the beach and the hotels, but at some point it's well worth heading out on the road west of town to **Sebastian's Villa** (daily 8am–6pm; 1.5TD), built by George Sebastian in the 1920s and now a state-owned **International Cultural Centre**. You can look around the house and assess Frank Lloyd Wright's impression of its beauty – it really is fantasy material, with an arcaded swimming pool, a baptistry-like bath in solid marble built for four and a black marble poolside table. During the war, the villa was used by General Rommel as his headquarters in the North African campaign. If you can't make the visiting hours, wander into the grounds and look around the garden and the mock-Greek **theatre** built for the **Festival de Hammamet** during July and August. Although geared primarily for tourists, many of the events are interesting (note that most are in French or Arabic) and it's worth looking at a programme from the ONTT here or in Nabeul to check out what's on.

Further along the beach, 6km south from town, is the Roman site of **Pupput** (daily: summer 8am–7pm; winter 9am–5pm; 1.1TD). The limited remains of baths and houses aren't terribly impressive; much better are some of the Christian tomb mosaics displayed on a wall.

For kids, there's **Fabiland**, a small funfair with a few rides, it's near the Pupput site at the western end of avenue Moncef Bey, while over in Hammamet Nord near the *Hôtel Les Colombes*, there's the summer-only **Flipper Aquapark**, with pools and waterslides. Out beyond the train station, a short way off the road to Bir Bou Regba, a **market** is held every Thursday.

Eating and drinking

As you'd expect, **restaurants** in Hammamet are plentiful, both in the town and in most of the hotels – and if you're on a budget it's still surprisingly easy to find a cheap Tunisian meal around the town centre. Most of the places on avenue Bourguiba between the Medina and the tourist office are solely geared for tourism, and overpriced.

There are comparatively few **cafés** in the centre of town. A pleasant place to sip tea or coffee and watch the world go is *Café Sidi Bou Hdid*, on the beach outside the Kasbah walls (daily 7am–10pm). Not far away on rue Ali Belhouane, *Gelateria Artigianale Italiana* does delicious ice creams to take away (daily 9.30am–11pm).

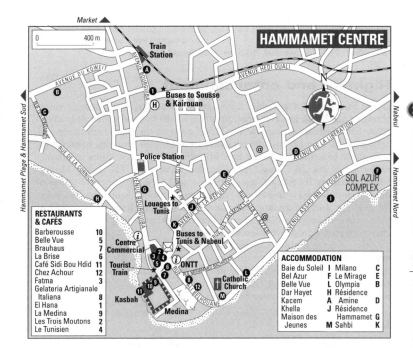

Market ▲

0   400 m

Train Station

Buses to Sousse & Kairouan

Police Station

Louages to Tunis

Buses to Tunis & Nabeul

SOL AZUR COMPLEX

ONTT

Catholic Church

Centre Commercial

Tourist Train

Kasbah

Medina

RESTAURANTS & CAFÉS

Barberousse	10
Belle Vue	5
Brauhaus	7
La Brise	6
Café Sidi Bou Hdid	11
Chez Achour	12
Fatma	3
Gelateria Artigianale Italiana	8
El Hana	1
La Medina	9
Les Trois Moutons	2
Le Tunisien	4

ACCOMMODATION

Baie du Soleil	I	Milano	C
Bel Azur	F	Le Mirage	E
Belle Vue	L	Olympia	B
Dar Hayet	H	Résidence	
Kacem	A	Amine	D
Khella	J	Résidence	
Maison des		Hammamet	G
Jeunes	M	Sahbi	K

Hammamet Plage & Hammamet Sud

Nabeul

Hammamet Nord

HAMMAMET AND CAP BON | Hammamet; eating and drinking

Most **drinking** establishments can be found in Hammamet Sud, where there is an array of British-themed bars serving pints and advertising live football. If you want to drink in slightly more exotic surroundings (but still with pints and big-screen sports), try the African-themed, 24-hour *Safari*, next to Fabiland at the western end of avenue Moncef Bey.

Restaurants

Barberousse On the Medina wall next to *La Medina*. Should have re-opened by the time you read this, and serving typical fare and seafood for around 10TD, with good views.

Belle Vue At the southern end of av Bourguiba. Usually dependable, with seafood dishes priced at 4–12TD. Daily 8am–1am.

Brauhaus Opposite the Medina, with a branch in Hammamet Sud. Used to be fantastically Teutonic, complete with *bockwurst*, litre steins of beer brewed on the premises, and filled with Germans. The beer and Germans are still there but the owners have decided that German food does not cut the mustard, so they've switched to Tunisian staples and pizza. A basic meal with a beer will set you back 10–15TD. Daily 8am–midnight.

La Brise 2 av de la République. Serves tasty and decent-sized traditional dishes for 6–13TD in a clean, congenial dining room. Recommended. Daily 10.30am–8pm.

Chez Achour rue Ali Belhouane ☎72 280 140, ⊛www.chezachour.com. The best seafood in town – the fish couscous is renowned – at 25–30TD for a full meal. Daily noon–midnight.

Fatma At the southern end of av Bourguiba. Marginally more expensive than its neighbour the *Belle Vue*, with similar fare. Daily 11am–midnight.

El Hana Corner of av Bourguiba and av Hedi Ouali. Big portions for the lowest of prices, up towards the train station. Daily 7am–10pm, or later.

Hong Kong av des Nations Unies, near the Hammamet Plage turn-off ☎72 242 825. For that unexpected craving for Chinese cuisine, this place does tasty, predominantly Cantonese fare, quite expensive à la carte but with a 12TD tourist menu. Daily noon–3pm & 7pm–midnight.

La Medina Next door to the *Barberousse*, on the Medina wall. Good views and the usual offerings, with a 10TD tourist menu. Daily noon–10pm.

Les Trois Moutons In the Centre Commercial, just off av de la République ☎72 280 981. Refined and quite pricey (20–25TD for two courses and wine),

145

with excellent lobster and shellfish dishes. Daily noon–3pm & 7pm–midnight.
Le Tunisien In the Centre Commercial. Family-run place with a good-value 5.5TD menu. The salads are not great but briks, couscous and fish stew all hit the spot. Daily noon–9pm.

Nightlife and entertainment

Outside the more "respectable" hotels, who put on the usual anodyne entertainment, **nightlife** involves large quantities of alcohol and sexual advances in a number of sweaty nightclubs. You'll find most of these in Hammamet Sud, on avenue Moncef Bey and the parallel route Touristique, running immediately behind the beach hotels. At the time of writing, the hottest **clubs** in summer were the *Calypso* and *Cotton Club* on avenue Moncef Bey. The cheesy *Manhattan*, on the route Touristique, operates year round. One of the best venues in or out of season is the *Habana Club* on the route Touristique, which serves tapas in the evenings and has dancing, live music, shows or salsa lessons later on. Next to the *Cotton Club* on avenue Moncef Bey, *Le Pacha* puts on spectacles of snake charmers, *gargoulette* dancers and belly dancers.

There are three **casinos** in which to tempt Lady Luck. Of the two in Hammamet Yasmine, the swisher is the Grand Casino towards the south end (daily 5pm–5am), which reserves the right not to admit persons who have a "neglected aspect". There's another Grand Casino in the *Hôtel Sol Azur* complex, just to the east of town on avenue Assad Ibn el Fourat.

Listings

Banks and exchange There are several banks on av de la République and av Bourguiba, many of which have ATMs. The BIAT next to the *Belle Vue* restaurant has a note exchange machine, and many shops and hotels will change money outside banking hours. The larger hotels have their own exchange services, and there are also exchange shops near concentrations of hotels in Hammamet Plage and Sud.

Car rental Avis, rue Dag Hammarskjold ☏72 280 164; Hertz, rue des Hôtels ☏72 280 187. Operators down av des Nations-Unies on the hotel strip include Budget (☏72 280 606), a little beyond the rue des Hôtels turning, and Europcar (☏72 280 146), a couple of hundred metres further west on the corner of rue Dag Hammarskjold. There are several other local rental agencies around rue des Hôtels and rue Dag Hammarskjold.

Car repairs A number of garages and spare parts shops can be found on av du Koweit near the *Olympia Hotel*.

Church Catholic church on rue Abou Kacem Chabbi, with services on Saturday at 5pm and Sunday at 11am.

Cinema The cinema in the Centre Commercial, av Bourguiba, screens mainstream releases from the West, dubbed into French.

Diving Trips can be arranged through many of the hotels – the Venus Diving Centre (☏72 227 211 or 98 345 960) at *Club Venus* charges 40TD for an introductory or exploratory dive and 45TD for a night dive. Courses are available.

Golf Hammamet has three eighteen-hole courses: two at Golf Citrus (☏72 226 500, ⊛www.golfcitrus .com) and one at Golf Yasmine (☏72 227 001).

Hammams There's a hammam in the Medina, opposite the mosque, and another at the junction of av Bourguiba and av Hedi Ouali. Both are open for women in the afternoon and for men in the morning and evening.

Hospitals The regional hospital (☏72 285 022) is around 10km out of town on the road to Nabeul. More convenient is the new 24hr Polyclinique Hammamet (☏72 266 000) on av des Nations Unies. There are *infirmeries* next to the police station on av Bourguiba (☏72 282 333) and at 27 av de la République (☏72 280 223), plus an emergency doctor's surgery (☏72 282 333) opposite the *Hôtel Sol Azur*.

Internet access The Publinet on rue Taieb el Azzabi (daily 8am–midnight) and the Public Internet Centre, 117 av de la Libération (daily 8.30am–11pm), both charge 2TD/hr.

Newspapers English-language newspapers are available on av de la République, as well as in the Centre Commercial near the Medina, and on rue des Hôtels in Hammamet Plage.

ONA No matter what the touts tell you, there's no official craft shop in Hammamet; Nabeul is the nearest place to find one.

Pharmacy There's an all-night pharmacy at 138 av de la République.

Police av Bourguiba ☎72 280 079.

Post office At the time of writing, the main post office (city hours) had "provisionally" moved from its usual site near the tourist office to 125 av de la République.

Supermarket In Central Hammamet, try the Magasin Général, on av de la République opposite the Medina (daily 8am–7pm); there are plenty of grocery stores in Hammamet Plage and Hammamet Nord.

Telephones You'll find coin-operated taxiphones in the Centre Commercial on av Bourguiba and opposite the Medina next to the *Brauhaus*. There are also numerous taxiphone and Publitel offices at intervals along the strip.

Tours If your hotel doesn't offer excursions around Cap Bon and elsewhere, try any of the travel agents along av de la République and in Hammamet Plage: the Tunisian Welcome Service in the Centre Commercal (☎72 280 924) is as good as any. Other tour operators include Carthage Tours, rue Dag Hammarskjöld (☎72 281 926), and CT Tours, 7 av Assad Ibn el Fourat (☎72 281 322). Boat trips are available in summer from Hammamet Travel Service on rue Dag Hammarskjold (☎72 280193).

Nabeul and around

NABEUL, 17km northeast along the coast from Hammamet, is the seat of the Governorate of Cap Bon, a market centre and the pottery and stonework capital of Tunisia, with a busy working atmosphere quite different from its near neighbour. With its easy access to the fertile hinterland of Cap Bon, Nabeul has always been an industrious place. The inhabitants of Roman Neapolis supported themselves by manufacturing *garum*, a sort of fish sauce used as basic seasoning in almost every savoury dish. "Take the entrails of tunny fish," a second-century recipe instructs, "and the gills, juice and blood, and add sufficient salt. Leave it in a vessel for two months, then pierce the vessel and the *garum* will flow out." Potteries, too, are long established in this area and remain the principal industry – along with tourism.

Hotels dot the beach between Hammamet and Nabeul, but not much development has gone on here in the last decade compared to the coast southwest of Hammamet. Though the sand is just as extensive, the beach lacks Hammamet Sud's gentle curve and lush green backdrop, and on a windy day can feel distinctly exposed.

Arrival and information

The centre of town is where the main east–west road, avenue Habib Thameur, crosses the Tunis road, **avenue Bourguiba**; the latter runs straight through the town almost to the beach – around a fifteen-minute walk. A few blocks seawards of this central junction is place 7 Novembre and the **train station**.

There are two combined **bus and louage stations**. Buses and louages arriving from Hammamet or outside Cap Bon use the station 400m west of avenue Bourguiba on avenue Habib Thameur. Arriving from places within Cap Bon other than Hammamet, you'll be dropped at the station 600m east of avenue Bourguiba on rue el Arbi Zarrouk, opposite the Friday market site.

The helpful **ONTT** is on avenue Taïeb Mehiri, not far from the beach (July & Aug Mon–Sat 7.30am–1.30pm & 5–9pm, Sun 9am–noon & 5–9pm; Sept–June Mon–Thurs 8.30am–1pm & 3–5.45pm, Fri & Sat 8.30am–1.30pm; ☎72 286800). There is an excellent **website** with news and cultural information on Nabeul and Cap Bon: ⓦwww.nabeul.net.

Moving on from Nabeul

For a list of destinations and journey times, see Travel details on p.164.

Nabeul is the main transport centre of Cap Bon. From the station on rue el Arbi Zarrouk, it's easy to reach most parts of the peninsula, other than Hammamet, via regular bus services run by SRTG Nabeul, or by louage. The main bus station on avenue Habib Thameur (☏72 285 873) has a list of bus destinations elsewhere in the country and times; buses leave every half hour during the day to Tunis and to Hammamet, with much less frequent departures to destinations further south. Louages mostly travel the same routes as the buses but do not go to Hammamet; for that you will have to take a shared taxi (around 1TD per place) or a metered **taxi** (about 7TD) – there is a taxi rank outside the hospital.

There are up to ten daily **trains** (the station is on ☏72 285 054) through Hammamet to Bir Bou Regba on the main line between Tunis and the south, with daily connections to Sousse, Monastir, Mahdia, Sfax and Gabès. For Tunis, there's a direct train daily at 5.45am, excluding Sundays and holidays.

Accommodation

Although it has been somewhat left behind by Hammamet as a tourist resort, Nabeul is not short of **hotels**, most of which are closer to standard European package places than Tunisian in feel. The big hotels are on the beach, but the town also has an unusual and welcome sprinkling of *pensions familiales*, along with a good youth hostel and campsite. As with Hammamet, rates for the bigger places take a plunge off season, to as little as a third of the summer rate.

There's a pleasant, shady **campsite** attached to the *Les Jasmins* hotel on rue Abou el Kacem Chabbi (same phone; see below). There are also camping facilities in the compound of the *Auberge de la Jeunesse Nabeul* on avenue Mongi Slim (☏72 285547; dorm beds 5TD), which has a great location right by the beach. Its dorms fill up in summer but are empty the rest of the year.

Hotels

Hôtel Byzance bd de la Corniche ☏72 271 000, ☎72 287 164, ✉www.hotelbyzance.com. One of the newest hotels in town (albeit opened in 1995), in a prime location 100m from the beach, with pool, jacuzzi, disco and karaoke evenings. ❻

Club Med Nabeul rte Touristique, on the beach ☏72 285 777, ☎72 285 682, ✉www.clubmed .com. Large establishment with full facilities, fortified against any possible intrusion by anyone or anything remotely Tunisian. Closed Nov–March. ❾

Hôtel Fakir rte Touristique ☏72 285477, ☎287616. A small place, just outside the Roman remains of Neapolis and within easy reach of the beach. ❺

Pension el Habib av Habib Thameur ☏72 224785. On the road to Hammamet by the *oued*, this is clean and friendly, with a small library of left-behind paperbacks. ❷

Hôtel Imène 28 av Bourguiba ☏72 222 310, ☎72 272 380. Very comfortable, with big rooms, but rather impersonal and fraying slightly at the edges. ❻

Hôtel les Jasmins av Habib Thameur ☏72 285343, ☎72 285073. Attractive place with a

leafy garden. It's liable to be booked up in season. Camel rides available. ❻

Hôtel Kheops av Mohamed V, just off av Habib Bourguiba ☏72 286 555, ☎72 286 024. Nabeul's top choice, swapping the usual package-tour atmosphere for more of a business look. It features all facilities and an Olympic-sized pool. ❼

Hôtel Lido 3km east of town on the beachfront; turn right off av Ali Belhouane after Oued Sidi Mousa ☏72 362 988, ☎72 361 487, ✉h.lido@planet.tn. Nabeul's biggest complex after *Les Pyramides* and better value, with two- and four-bed bungalows with kitchenettes available, as well as normal rooms. All the amenities you would expect are on offer, plus water sports and a spa centre. ❻

Pension Monia Club rte Touristique, opposite the Neapolis site ☏72 285 713. Officially a pension, this is really more a restaurant and bar with staying guests. Okay for the price. ❸

Pension Mustapha av Habib el Karma ☏72 222262. A nice little place, clean and welcoming. ❸

Pension les Oliviers rue Abou el Kacem Chabbi ☏72 286865. Deservedly, this family-run pension

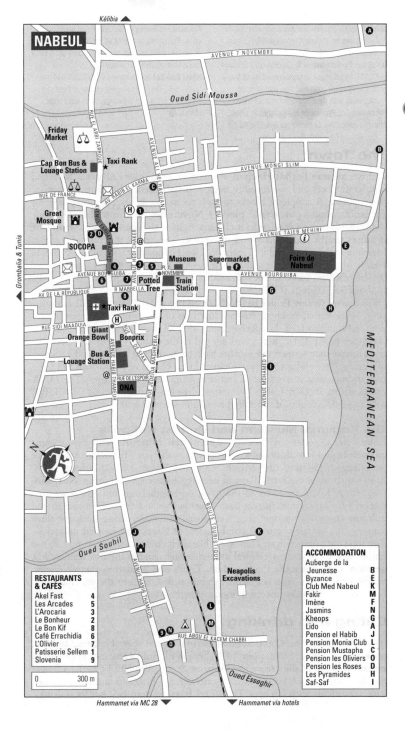

NABEUL

Kélibia ▲

Oued Sidi Moussa

Friday Market

Cap Bon Bus & Louage Station

Taxi Rank ★

Great Mosque

SOCOPA

Museum

Supermarket

Foire de Nabeul

Potted Tree

Train Station

Taxi Rank ★

Giant Orange Bowl

Bonprix

Bus & Louage Station

ONA

AVENUE 7 NOVEMBRE

AVENUE MONGI SLIM

AVENUE TAIEB MEHIRI

AVENUE BOURGUIBA

RUE DE FRANCE

RUE EL ARBI ZARROUK

AV. HABIB EL KARMA

AVENUE ALI BELHAOUANE

RUE DU 18 JANVIER

RUE HEDI CHAKER

AVENUE FARHAT HACHED

AVENUE BOURGUIBA

AV DE LA RÉPUBLIQUE

PL 7 NOVEMBRE

R MARBELLA

RUE SIDI MAAOUIA

RUE DE SFAX

RUE FARHAT HACHED

AVENUE HABIB THAMEUR

RUE DE L'ESPOIR

RUE TEBÉDA MAGHRÉBIA

AVENUE MOHAMED V

◄ Grombalia & Tunis

MEDITERRANEAN SEA

N

Oued Souhil

AVENUE HABIB THAMEUR

ROUTE TOURISTIQUE

Neapolis Excavations

RUE ABOU EL KACEM CHABBI

Oued Esseghir

0   300 m

RESTAURANTS & CAFÉS

Akel Fast	4
Les Arcades	5
L'Arocaria	3
Le Bonheur	2
Le Bon Kif	8
Café Errachidia	6
L'Olivier	7
Patisserie Sellem	1
Slovenia	9

ACCOMMODATION

Auberge de la Jeunesse	B
Byzance	E
Club Med Nabeul	K
Fakir	M
Imène	F
Jasmins	N
Kheops	G
Lido	A
Pension el Habib	J
Pension Monia Club	L
Pension Mustapha	C
Pension les Oliviers	O
Pension les Roses	D
Les Pyramides	H
Saf-Saf	I

opposite *Hôtel les Jasmins* has a glowing reputation, with simple, pleasant rooms and balconies overlooking olive trees. **❹**

Hôtel les Pyramides av Bourguiba ☎72 285444, ℱ72 287 461. Large complex consisting of the main (overpriced) hotel and two sets of apartments, each with their own kitchens. Of these, *Résidence Les Pyramides* is much better value than the expensive *Les Jasmins* apartments. **❻**

Pension les Roses 3 rue Sidi Abd el Kader, just off av Farhat Hached ☎72 285 570. The cheapest of the pensions and not at all bad; room no. 5 even has a little marble colonnade. **❷**

Hôtel Saf-Saf av Mohamed V ☎72 286 044, ℱ286 198. One of the newer places in the hotel district; smaller and less impersonal than most others. **❻**

The Town

Touristy **avenue Farhat Hached**, also known as Souk de l'Artisanat, is packed with craft stores and has recently been pedestrianized, with plans for further development. A couple of blocks towards the sea from here, an unsubtle giant pot built around a pine tree at **place 7 Novembre** proclaims Nabeul's major industry. If you're a die-hard kitsch fanatic, then the giant ceramic **bowl of oranges** nearby should have you in raptures – it's at the junction of rue Sidi Maaouia and avenue Habib Thameur. Like Hammamet's shoreline, Nabeul's **beach** is hotel-strewn but still attractive, with nothing except a sprinkling of tourist-oriented cafés and restaurants, as well as the ubiquitous water-sport facilities (see Listings, p.152).

The town's weekly Friday **market** out on rue el Arbi Zarrouk (the continuation of av Farhat Hached) has become one of the country's biggest attractions, with busloads of shoppers arriving from all over Tunisia to pick up local crafts (see box, p.151). There's nothing out of the ordinary about it except size and convenience – since the tourists have been coming it's sprouted a section specializing in holiday souvenirs. Despite its nickname of "Camel Market", the only dromedaries you're likely to see are of the cuddly-toy variety. The **ONA crafts shops** at 93 av Habib Thameur and 144 av Farhat Hached (SOCOPA) have a good selection of officially priced and selected items.

The Regional Museum and Roman Neapolis

Nabeul has a modern, well-designed **Regional Museum**, with explanations in English, at 44 av Bourguiba, by the tree in the pot (Tues–Sun: April–Sept 9am–1pm & 3–7pm; Oct–March 9.30am–4.30pm; 1.1TD, camera 1TD). Along with some colourful Roman mosaics discovered at Roman **Neapolis**, a couple of kilometres west of the town centre, the museum also has a collection of Carthaginian pieces from Kerkouane and from Thinissut in the hills just above Hammamet. The Kerkouane statuettes, dating from the third century BC, display the usual combination of Greek and Eastern influences. The terracotta figures from Thinissut – like their companion pieces now in the Bardo – show these cross-cultural influences surviving in the first century AD, into the Roman era: the Punic goddess Tanit's lion head, for example. A new addition to the museum is a small exhibition dedicated to the excavations at Neapolis and the fish-processing industry here.

Eating and drinking

It's a shame that, given Cap Bon's richness in fruit and vegetables, meat and fish, cooking is hardly the high point of Nabeul. With only a few exceptions, most **restaurants** are of the greasy-spoon variety, and you might be better off getting half-board in a hotel, or else self-catering: *Les Pyramides* and the *Lido* both have apartments with kitchens. The **hotel bars** are your best bet for a drink.

Nabeul crafts

Many of the souvenirs on display in Nabeul, in s[...]
Palace and Aladdin's Cave, are standard wares ava[...]
there's a special emphasis on **pottery** in Nabeul beca[...]
the national centre of the craft. In fact, the potters of [...]
Jerba, attracted perhaps by the quality of the local clay. [...]
was the arrival in the seventeenth century of Andalusian[...]
them the artistic traditions of Muslim Spain. The same tradi[...]
in Morocco, and Nabeul's ceramics often resemble those of [...]

Pottery has a long history in Tunisia – the Roman provin[...]
standard red tableware all over the Empire – and thanks to the [...]
traditional craft that appears to have a healthy future, even if so[...]ucts
are in highly dubious taste. Most shops will be happy to show yo[...] workshop
of one of their suppliers if you ask about an *atelier* (craftsman). Two particularly good
workshops that welcome visitors are Kedidi, 1500m down the Tunis road (⊕72 287
576), and Poterie Gastle, a little further on (⊕72 222 247). The industrial potters, who
actually make bricks, are not as glamorous or well known, but are no less interesting. The small humps dotted around the eastern edge of the town, especially near
the market, are the ovens in which the bricks are fired, and when they're in operation
(usually in the evening) they produce a thick black pall of smoke. You'll probably be
invited to clamber down into the inferno-like subterranean chamber where the oven
flames are kept fired through the night.

Other crafts are worked in and around Nabeul. **Beni Khiar**, a village 2km east
(walk up av Ali Belhouane), specializes in **wool products**, possibly a legacy of Hilalian nomads who first settled here in the eleventh century. The village centres around
its little daily fish market. Before this, on the left-hand side of the road, you'll find a
weaving co-operative, with jackets and carpets a third cheaper than the same stuff
in Nabeul's emporia. The workers are happy to show you their craft. Another nearby
village, **Es Somaa**, just inland, specializes in **straw mats**.

But the big craft, after pottery, is **stonecarving**. This is less amenable to souvenir
production, but flourishes thanks to the policy of incorporating traditional elements
in modern buildings, including hotels and houses. Doorways, columns and benches
in Tunisia have long been carved with intricate geometric patterns – witness the
Tunis Medina – and it's fascinating to watch the process. Most of the stonework is
done in **Dar Chaâbane**, a small village to the east that is now virtually a suburb of
Nabeul. The main street is lined with workshops clinking to the sound of chisels,
while a pile of raw stone on the pavement outside announces the trade. Its weekly
market, where you'll find the results on sale, is held on Sunday mornings.

Likewise, **cafés** are for the most part uninspiring. Two places worth trying are
the *Patisserie Sellem* on avenue Hedi Chaker (daily 7am–7.30pm), serving good
cakes and citronade, plus savouries; and the *Café Errachidia* on the corner of avenue
Bourguiba and avenue Habib Thameur (daily: summer 8am–1am; winter until
8pm), also serving delicious cakes and the fanciest place in town for mint tea.

Restaurants

Akel Fast Corner av Bourguiba and av Farhat
Hached. Serves up decent sandwiches, burgers
and vast salads (1–3TD) in a fastidiously clean
environment. Daily 8am–9pm.

Les Arcades av Bourguiba, diagonally opposite
the train station. Good, simple, fresh Tunisian food
in pleasant surroundings for under 10TD. Daily
9am–10pm.

L'Arocaria (aka *Chez Haddad*) Just off av Bourguiba, just along from *Les Arcades*. Cosy little
place cluttered with rustic junk and serving home-
made pizzas for 2.5–3TD. Daily 10am–11pm.

Le Bonheur At the bend in av Farhat Hached by
the *Pension les Roses*. The best of the cheapies,
with Tunisian staples for 5–8TD. Daily 8am–5pm.

Le Bon Kif Corner rue Marbella and av Habib
Thameur ⊕72 222 783. In the same league as

...u is especially
...se meal will set you
...on–3pm & 7pm–midnight.
...l Chaker ☎72 286 613. Still the
...ul's restaurants, a classy French-style
...ith matching prices (full meals 20–25TD).
...aily noon–3pm & 6–11pm.

Slovenia av Habib Thameur, next to *Hôtel les Jasmins* ☎72 285 343. Serving up a range of international dishes prepared by Rafik Tlatli, who is rated as one of Tunisia's best chefs. A full meal should set you back no more than 25–30TD. Daily noon–2.30pm & 6pm–midnight.

Listings

Banks There are lots of banks on and around avenues Bourguiba and Habib Thameur, and at least one should be open in the morning at weekends. A few have ATMs, including BIAT on av Bourguiba.

Car rental Hertz, av Habib Thameur ☎72 285 327; Nova Rent-a-Car, 54 av Bourguiba ☎72 285 967.

Cinema Films dubbed into French are screened and some plays staged on Sundays by the Maison de la Culture, 75 av Hedi Chaker.

Festivals The summer festival, a programme of cultural events for tourists, takes place over July and August in the open-air theatre at the beach end of av Bourguiba, the only time it's ever used; details can be obtained from the tourist office. The Foire de la Fleur d'Orange, held in late April and early May in the Foire de Nabeul site between avenue Bourguiba and avenue Taieb Mehiri, is basically a glorified souk.

Hammams There's one at 42 av Hedi Chaker (men mornings, women afternoons), another at 37 rue Sidi Bel Aissa and a women-only one, Bain Sidi Maaouria, at 19 av Habib Thameur.

Hospital The large hospital in the centre of town (☎72 285 633) only deals with casualties; for other complaints you'll need to visit the regional hospital (☎72 285 022), 5km out of town on the road to Hammamet. There is an *infirmerie* at 10 rue Ibn Badis and *cliniques* on av Mongi Slim (☎72 285 199) and on the Hammamet road (☎72 286 183).

Internet access Both Publinet, on the corner of av Hedi Chaker and Taieb Mehiri (daily 8am–midnight) and Internet, av Habib Thameur opposite the bus station (daily 8.30am–8pm), charge 2TD/hr.

ONA craft shops 144 av Farhat Hached and 93 av Habib Thameur.

Pharmacy The night pharmacy is at 37 av Habib Thameur.

Police av Taïeb Mehiri, just off av Ali Belhouane ☎72 285 474.

Post office av Bourguiba, north of the junction with av Habib Thameur (city hours). You can make international phone calls here. There's also a branch on av Habib el Karma.

Supermarkets There's a Bonprix on av Habib Thameur, just east of the bus station, and another supermarket down an alley opposite *Café Errachidia*.

Taxis Express Taxi ☎72 222444.

Telephones At the post office, or the taxiphone offices at 168 av Habib Thameur and av Habib el Karma, up from *Pension Mustapha*.

Tours For tours around Cap Bon and further afield to Tozeur and Matmata, contact Delta Travel, 113 av Bourguiba (☎72 271077); your hotel will most likely also arrange tours.

Water sports Windsurfers and other aquatic gear can be rented at *Hôtel Lido*, *Hôtel le Prince* (on the beach near *Hôtel Saf-Saf*) and *Hôtel Les Pyramides*.

The coast from Nabeul to Kélibia

The coast north of Nabeul is one endless stretch of white beach backed, as far as Menzel Temime, by unsightly salt flats, and after that by rich farmland. There are few towns, fewer places to stay, and little reason to stop off except for a minimal change of beach scenery.

KORBA, the next town north from Nabeul, is a large agricultural centre with a Sunday **souk** and minor Roman remains. **Birdwatchers** should find it worth a stop, as there are lagoons and a salt marsh just to the north, which hold flamingos, spoonbills and avocets in the spring, a good range of migrants in spring and autumn, and ducks over the winter. Another kind of song can be heard around the third week of Ramadan at Korba's **Amor Yedess Festival**, where Sufi liturgical chants, specifically of the Soulamia brotherhood and otherwise almost impossible for an infidel to hear, are performed. Generally more sober than the often hypnotic and bizarre Aissawiya chants, the Soulamia are a good introduction to the form. The tourist office in Nabeul may have dates nearer the time.

If you want to **stay**, there is a very good four-star signposted off the main road 1km south of town: the *Africa Jade* (☎72 384 633, ℉385 353; ❼), with pleasant rooms, an attractively designed pool and a swath of unpopulated white sand beach out front. Otherwise there is a *Maison des Jeunes* **youth hostel** in town (☎72 289 296), which closes erratically; to reach it, turn right off the main Nabeul–Kélibia road through town by the BNA bank, then left onto a wide boulevard and carry on for 300m until you come to the hostel on your right. Korba has a **post office** (country hours), a number of fast-food places and several **banks** clustered near the **bus station** on the main road in the centre of town. The smart new El Ambra shopping centre by the *Africa Jade* turn-off south of town has an Amen bank with a Visa and MasterCard ATM, and a good Bonprix **supermarket**.

Menzel Temime

Another 25km further along the coast, **MENZEL TEMIME** has no special attractions except for its **beach** (rather windy and some way from town) and its Tuesday **souk**, which takes up most of the town centre. The **bus and louage station** is a roundabout on the Kélibia road, here called avenue de la République. Buses and louages head to Nabeul, Kélibia, Menzel Bou Zelfa and Tunis, while early-morning services from Kélibia to destinations further afield such as Kairouan, Monastir and Sousse also stop here. Running inland from the roundabout is **avenue Bourguiba**, along which the residents at nos. 41 and 45 have put a lot of work into the design of their front doors. The **post office** (country hours) is 50m further on at no. 39, and beyond that are two **banks**, with another on the main square at the end.

Also on the square, next to a cavernous café, the two-star *Hôtel Temim* offers pleasant, clean **rooms** with a choice of bath or shower (☎72 344 947; ❹), but closes sporadically. The only other accommodation is the *Maison des Jeunes* **youth hostel** behind (☎72 344 116), signposted in Arabic and also prone to occasional closure. There are a number of cheap **restaurants** on the main square and on the market square behind the *Temim*. On Tuesdays, the streets round here are crammed with market stalls. A Bravo **supermarket** is located by the roundabout on the main road.

Kélibia, Mansoura and Kerkouane

With all the ingredients for tourism, **Kélibia**, 50km along the coast from Nabeul, has mostly resisted development as a resort and remains an agricultural centre, with a major fishing port nestling under a huge sixteenth-century fortress. The port is pleasantly unspoilt, although the backdrop to neighbouring **Mansoura**, with its stunning white-sand coves, has been marred by the construction of a package hotel. Thankfully, plans to develop the coast further – a project known as Kélibia la Blanche – appear to have stalled at the time of writing, and the beaches here still feel very removed from Hammamet. You can combine the beaches with a visit to the Carthaginian site of **Kerkouane** by taking some food and strolling along the shore, though be warned that it's about four-and-a-half hours' walk.

Kélibia

Part of the charm of **KELIBIA** is the feeling that it's something of a backwater, but this hasn't always been the case. Some fine remains including mosaics, which can be seen in the various patchy **excavations** around the town (free entry; you may be asked for a photo fee but this is a scam), bear witness to a sizeable Roman presence, while for the Byzantines, who built the first fortress here, Clupea (Kélibia) was reputedly the last place of refuge after the Arab invasion. Later, the town and fortress were sacked three times by the Spanish between 1535 and 1547.

Some 2km east of the centre, the towering **fortress** has recently been restored (daily: summer 8am–7pm; winter 9am–5pm; 1.1TD), and though there's little to see in itself, the views from the ramparts are superb. At the foot of the hill on which the fortress stands lies the **port**, crammed with colourful fishing boats, trawlers and, on the dockside, fishermen mending their nets, a daily **fish market** and the State Fishing School. Kélibia is the best natural harbour on this stretch of coast north of Sousse, which explains both the fortress and all the boats – Cap Bon's largest fishing fleet. The main **beach** lies south of the fishing port at the end of avenue Erriadh, but unfortunately it's covered in seaweed and gunk from the port.

Practicalities

You'll most probably arrive at the **bus and louage station** on avenue Ali Belhaouane (☏72 296208). Early-morning bus departures for Monastir, Sousse and Kairouan pass through Hammamet; to reach Hammamet at any other time of day, you'll have to change at Nabeul. For El Haouaria, standard yellow taxis perform the same function as louages on a price-per-place basis.

The **post office**, which has Western Union money transfer, is on avenue Bourguiba (country hours) and there are Publitel and taxiphone offices on avenue des Martyrs near the centre, as well as a couple out beyond the *Hôtel Palmarina*. There's a **Publinet** on avenue des Martyrs not far along from place de la République (daily 8.30am–11.30pm; 1.5TD/hr). There is no tourist office here.

Both the BNA **bank** on place de la République and the Amen bank on rue

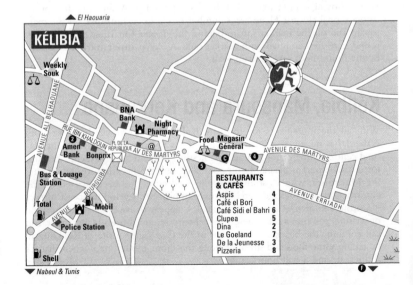

Ibn Khaldoun have ATMs accepting Visa and MasterCard. The **night pharmacy** is at the beginning of avenue des Martyrs, around the corner from the post office. The **police** are on avenue Bourguiba (☎72 296 343) on the way out towards Nabeul.

There's a small food **market** where avenue Erriadh meets avenue des Martyrs. The Monday **souk** takes place just north of avenue Ali Belhaouane but also has stalls set up all the way to the food market. Daily necessities can be bought at the Bonprix **supermarket** on rue Ibn Khaldoun, or at the Magasin Général, on avenue des Martyrs by the food market.

Accommodation

There's a reasonable selection of medium-priced **accommodation**. The *Pension Anis* (☎72 295 777, ℻72 273 128; ❹), off avenue Erriadh between the town centre and the beach, is the best option, with spotless, airy rooms and squeaky-clean shared bathrooms. Down the beach, the old favourite, the 1940s *Hôtel Florida* (☎ & ℻72 296 248; ❹), has en-suite rooms, though it's now rather shabby. Next door is the modern *Hôtel Palmarina* (☎72 274 065, ℻72 274055; ❺) and, a couple of hundred metres towards the centre, the newish *Belle Étoile* (☎72 274374, ℻72 275302; ❺); both offer a pool and other three-star comforts. The package-type *Mamounia* (☎72 296 088, ℻72 296 858; ❻), some way along the beach, has similar facilities.

The drab *Maison des Jeunes* (☎72 296105), on the Mansoura road by the port, is unusually friendly. You can sometimes **camp** in the grounds, which have a small, unearthed Roman site in front.

Eating and drinking

There are plenty of **restaurants** in Kélibia, though a couple of the more obviously touristy ones have an unwelcome tendency to overcharge – check the price before ordering. In the town itself, the *Pension Anis* (daily noon–3pm & 7–11pm) is the classiest choice, with service to match. Budget options include the very good *Dina* on rue Ibn Khaldoun (daily 8am–11pm), with tasty pizzas and excellent fish *chorba*, and another pizza joint, *Restaurant Aspis* (daily

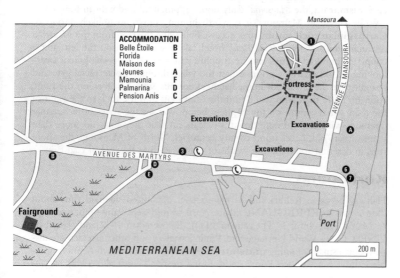

9am–midnight), a pleasant place on avenue des Martyrs, just round the corner from *Pension Anis*, which serves cheap pizzas and big, tasty sandwiches.

Out by the port, the *Restaurant de la Jeunesse* (daily 11am–3pm & 7pm–midnight), on avenue des Martyrs just after the *Hôtel Palmarina*, has reasonable seafood dishes for 6–15TD. The *Palmarina* itself has an expensive restaurant, *Les Arcades* (daily noon–3pm & 7–10pm), which is strong on shellfish; a meal here will set you back around 20TD. Further on, the *Café Sidi el Bahri* (daily 6am–2am) has good views but is better for drinks than the rather ordinary and overpriced food. Much better is *Le Goeland* next door (daily: summer 8am–midnight; winter 11am–10pm), serving good fresh seafood with most mains at 6–8TD. If you're travelling with kids, you might consider the pizzeria at the southern end of avenue Erriadh, which doubles as a patisserie and is open the same times as the small **fairground** next door (weekends only in winter).

For **cafés**, the aforementioned *Sidi el Bahri* and *Le Goeland* have seafront terraces and chairs on the beach, while *Café el Borj*, up by the fort, has bird's-eye views over Mansoura to the northeast. **Drinkers** can take refuge in the *Restaurant Clupea*, on avenue Erriadh opposite the food market, in the *Hôtel Florida* bar and at the bar attached to the *Restaurant de la Jeunesse*.

Mansoura

Far more alluring than the beach in Kélibia is the series of beautiful coves 2km north at **MANSOURA**, backed by a small community nicknamed "Little Paris", with its fancy holiday houses. In recent years, Mansoura's exclusivity has been eroded by modern villa developments and by the unsightly new *Kélibia Beach* **hotel** (☎72 277 777, ☏72 275 274, ✉recp.kelibia@planet.tn; ➒), which looms over the northern horizon a bit like a giant hunk of cheese. It has all the facilities you'd expect of an all-inclusive four-star package hotel, but be warned that they are snooty about accepting reservations from within Tunisia. There's only one alternative to the *Kélibia Beach* – the nearby *Résidence Mansoura*, a cluster of white-domed bungalows, just behind the beach (☎98 901 549; 450TD per week for a five-person bungalow). On a rocky promontory nearby is the excellent **café-restaurant**, the *Mansoura* (daily noon–10pm, until midnight in summer).

While you're in Mansoura, it is worth hunting down an unlikely group of **Carthaginian rock tombs** (free access). Following the road from the *Mansoura* restaurant towards the *Kélibia Beach* hotel, take the first road on the left after a couple of hundred metres and head uphill past a new villa development overlooking an old quarry. Continue past the villas, through a blue metal gate and straight over the crossroads immediately afterwards, with a factory on the right. After no more than 50m you'll find the tombs cut into the rock to the right of the road; you're almost on top of them before you see the series of rectangular openings with steps leading down, so clean cut that they look no more than twenty years old, never mind twenty centuries. North of Mansoura, the shore runs in deserted and tempting swaths of white beach to the end of Cap Bon.

Kerkouane

Halfway between Kélibia and El Haouaria, a signposted sideroad runs about 2km down to **KERKOUANE** (daily: April to mid-Sept 9am–6pm; mid-Sept to March 9am–4pm; 2.1TD, camera 1TD), discovered in 1952 and classed by UNESCO as a World Heritage Site. Punic jewellery and other artefacts are displayed in a small adjoining **museum** (Tues–Sun same hours), whose most notable exhibit is a wooden Punic statue found nearby. There's also a clay *tabouna* oven, very similar to bread ovens still in use today in some Cap Bon villages.

There was much excitement at first about the character of the streets and housing, and the curious absence of public buildings, giving rise to an eccentric theory that this was a fifth-century BC holiday resort – a sort of Carthaginian *Club Med*. It's now understood that the town's main industry was manufacturing a purple dye for which Carthaginians and Phoenicians were famous, named after a species of shellfish called *murex*. Hundreds of these creatures were collected and left in large pits in the ground to rot; the smell must have been overpowering, but the decomposed mess was somehow made up into the dye known by the Romans as "Tyrian purple" (after the Phoenician capital, Tyre), much beloved as the imperial colour.

Almost all the **houses**, whose foundations line the easy-to-follow streets, follow the same plan: a narrow corridor leading into a small courtyard, with a water well and sometimes an altar to the household gods. Kerkouane's houses are most famous, however, for their private **baths**, neatly lined with reddish cement, some of them covered with plain pink and white mosaic. Virtually every house has its own, which says something about Carthaginian society – while the Romans spent vast sums on public baths, the Carthaginians kept a private, low-key profile. The town was abandoned sometime in the second century BC, after the destruction of Carthage, and never reoccupied by the Romans – which explains its remarkable state of preservation.

If Kerkouane, the largest Carthaginian site yet discovered, seems like a meagre remnant of a major civilization, it's worth remembering that outsiders were as impressed by the Carthaginians' agricultural prowess as they were by their navy. A description of the interior of Cap Bon by Diodorus Siculus, a historian writing in Rome in the first century BC, but drawing on earlier accounts, still holds true today:

It was divided into market gardens and orchards of all sorts of fruit trees, with many streams of water flowing in channels irrigating every part. There were country houses everywhere, lavishly built and covered with stucco, which testified to the wealth of their owners . . . Part of the land was planted with vines, part with olives and other protective trees. Beyond these, cattle and sheep were pastured on the plains, and there were meadows filled with grazing horses.

A bus or louage from Kélibia to the Kerkouane turn-off will cost 1.3TD, a taxi around 5TD (settle the price before you start). Leaving the site, you'll probably have to take potluck and hitch, or hail a passing bus or louage on the main road. It is possible to **stay** at Kerkouane, at the new *Pension Dar Zenaidi* (☎98 300 822 or 22 774 705, ✉darzenaidi@planet.tn; ➏), signposted down a track to the right just before you reach the site; the location is idyllic, the rooms (in two separate buildings) modern and comfortable, and it also has a pool. Prices are negotiable and meals can be ordered in advance. There is also a private house, *Villa Tanit* (☎72 295752, ⓦwww.dartanit.com), by the turn-off for *Dar Zenaidi*, which has a homely apartment annexe with kitchen (around 80TD per night).

El Haouaria and around

Just below **Jebel Sidi Abiod**, the defiant last hump of Cap Bon, the pretty little town of **EL HAOUARIA** is best known as the centre of falconry in Tunisia. In an annual **festival** held around the end of May, young birds are caught on the mountain, trained for a month, then used for hunting game birds on the mountain and the heaths below. Two species of birds of prey are involved – sparrowhawks, which are trapped in nets on the mountain as they migrate, and female peregrine falcons, which are taken as young from the nests on the rocky cliffs. The males, it is said, soon die of a "broken heart". The number of birds each falconer can catch is supposed to be strictly limited; they may not be sold, and the sparrowhawks are later returned to the wild, but what happens to the peregrines is uncertain. About 1km from the centre of town, just uphill from *Pension les Grottes* (see opposite), there's an informative **falconry centre** (variable hours; ☏72 269 117), run by the Association des Fauconniers du Cap Bon, which occasionally puts on demonstrations of the art for tourists. The building – white with blue shutters – is called the Aquilaria, after the Latin for "eagle", and the name of the town is thought to have derived from the same word. The town itself is a sleepy agricultural centre that turns its back on the Mediterranean to focus on Cap Bon's rich hinterland.

El Haouaria is pleasantly out of the way, and its inhabitants will assume you've come to see the **Ghar el Kebir** (daily: summer 8am–7pm; winter 9am–5pm; 1.1TD), a remarkable complex of ancient quarries right on the seashore a couple of kilometres to the north, reached by following the road straight through the town past the cemetery and beyond the *Pension les Grottes*. To the left you'll see electricity-generating windmills as you descend towards the complex's car park, from where a short stroll brings you to a group of pyramid-shaped chambers poised above crashing breakers. Quarrying operations started here by the Carthaginians were continued by the Romans and Byzantines – the latter installing a military garrison – and the stone was used for buildings all around the Gulf of Carthage. The locals here recount vivid stories of slaves who spent their whole lives working inside the caverns. You can still see the marks made by their tools on the walls in the dim illumination afforded by small skylights cut out of the chambers' rock ceilings.

A second complex of caves – the **Grotte des Chauves-Souris** up on the mountain – is full of bats but is now closed to visitors to preserve their delicate habitat. This situation is unlikely to change, but you may wish to check with the Association des Amis des Oiseaux (see box opposite); if you are permitted access to the caves, you will need a guide and a torch to make close acquaintance with the creatures. Whether or not bats appeal, the mountain is a wonderful place for long windy walks, where you can reflect on the strategic position that played such a large part in Tunisia's history, with Sicily just 150km away. A road leads from the town past the bat caves, a couple of kilometres out, and on up to a telecommunications mast on the summit.

Southeast of El Haouaria, at the very beginning of Cap Bon's east coast, hides the area's most beautiful and least-known beach, **Ras ed Drak** – known as El Haouaria Plage these days. The white sands are sheltered here and given an extra dimension by the mountain's craggy shoulder. A four-kilometre road (signposted "Le Port") leads from El Haouaria over heathland to the assortment of villas and farms on the slopes behind the beach where, in season, there's a restaurant. Many of the villas are advertised for rent, should you want to stay for any length of time, and there is a small shop 100m before the beach. In the lee of the mountain to the north, a small fishing **port** was built in 1998 to access the rich waters this side of the cape. The futuristic complex on the shore to the south is a station on a gas pipeline running between Algeria and Italy.

The *Daurade* restaurant in El Houaria (see opposite) can arrange **boat trips** around the cape, although a minimum of ten people is required (35TD per person). If you are on your own or in a smaller group, you could organize a trip instead through the *Pension les Grottes* (see opposite) for a negotiable price.

Birdlife around El Haouaria and the Cape

The rocky hillsides around the mountain of Jebel Sidi Abiod and the walk to Ras ed Drak beach are rich not only in flowers but also in **birdlife**. The fields have abundant finches, buntings and warblers, along with stonechats – the black-headed males perching prominently on bushes and telegraph wires. Down on Ras ed Drak, the scrub behind the beach is often full of migrating birds, with the unusual blue rock thrush and Moussier's redstart both relatively common residents. The sea is worth watching too, and vast numbers of breeding pairs of the stiff-winged Cory's shearwater, as well as gulls and gull-billed and sandwich terns, can often be seen flying past, the last two species occurring as winter visitors and passage migrants.

The actual headland of Cap Bon is special because it is the last jumping-off point for migrating birds of prey before they cross the Mediterranean. April and May are the peak spring passage months, with lesser numbers coming back each autumn. Honey buzzards are the dominant species, although black kites, marsh harriers and common buzzards also occur in good numbers, together with a variety of migrating eagles, sparrowhawks and hobbies (the small, rather dashing falcons, midway in size between kestrel and peregrine, that prey mostly on swallows and the like – they follow the migrating swallow flocks up from Africa).

The best place for viewing the migration is the top of Jebel Sidi Abiod. The local **Association des Amis des Oiseaux** (☎72 269 200, ✉aao.capbon@gnet.tn) organizes excursions up to an observation post on the mountain every weekend in migration season. Their office (variable hours) is located behind the police station on avenue Bourguiba, 500m from the town centre on the way to the Ghar el Kebir, and has plenty of information about local wildlife.

Both will take you into some otherwise inaccessible coves and provide you with a barbecue lunch.

Practicalities

There's a frequent **buses** and **louages** from El Haouaria's main square to Kélibia and less frequent departures to Tunis via Soliman. For Kerkouane (see p.156), buses and louages to Kélibia can drop you at the turn-off, while a couple of louages go to and from Sidi Daoud to the west; alternatively, a **taxi** to either will cost no more than a few dinars. The main square has a couple of **banks**.

There is no tourist office in El Houaria, but very good budget **accommodation** in the form of the *Pension Dar Toubib* (☎72 297 163; ❷), tucked away down the side streets but well signposted (follow the blue signs). If you'd prefer more comfort, the alternatives are the friendly two-star *Hôtel l'Épervier* (☎72 297017, Ⓕ297258; ❹), on the main street, and the *Pension les Grottes* (☎72 297078, Ⓕ269070; ❹), at the top of the hill leading down to Ghar el Kebir, with en-suite a/c rooms and a pool to go with its views. **Camping** on Ras ed Drak is feasible, as is renting a villa.

Across the street from the *Épervier* in El Haouaria, the *Restaurant de la Jeunesse* (Mon–Sat 5.30am–2pm) serves basic **meals**. The *Épervier's* restaurant (daily 8am–midnight) is reasonably priced, with a set meals for 8TD, though you can order à la carte instead. *Pension les Grottes* also has a restaurant (daily 9am–3am), but it fails to take advantage of its beautiful location. By far the best place is *Restaurant la Daurade* (☎72 269 080; daily noon–midnight), right on the seashore next to the caves, with its cosy indoor section and series of outdoor terraces. Their speciality is, unsurprisingly, daurade fish; a three-course meal can be enjoyed for around 20TD.

Sidi Daoud and around

Seven kilometres on past El Haouaria, down the west coast of the peninsula, a turning leads 2km west to **SIDI DAOUD**, the sleepiest of sleepy fishing villages. Almost totally dormant for ten months of the year, it bursts into life around May for the **Matanza**, a spectacular if gory tuna harvest with a technique going back to Roman times. A huge net is laid about 4km out to sea, stretching from surface to seabed to catch the fish as they migrate around the coast to spawn. The net forms a series of chambers of decreasing size, and when the final one – the *corpo*, or death chamber – is full, it is closed. Then the boats converge around the net and raise it from all sides until the fish are virtually out of the water, at which point the fishermen jump into the net and set about the fish (some of which weigh as much as 250kg) with clubs and knives.

It used to be possible to get a **permit** from the National Fisheries Office to watch the Matanza from one of the boats but, after disagreements with the tourist authorities, this scheme has lapsed. If you're interested, it might be worth checking the permit situation with the Arondissement de Pêche at the fishing port in Kélibia (☎72 296021) before you come up here. To avoid a paper chase, however, you could simply try to sort something out with the local office at the dockside. If you do get permission and decide to try it, be warned that the smell of fish lingers for some days afterwards.

Off the coast north of Sidi Daoud, the islands of **Zembra** and **Zembretta** are now off limits, having been declared a nature reserve under army protection. Zembra, with sea birds, beautiful scenery and excellent snorkelling, used to host a scuba-diving centre run by the Centre Nautique de Tunisie. If you want to try for a permit to visit, you could write to the Ministry of Defence (Ministère de la Defense Nationale, bd Bab Menara, 1008 Tunis; ☎71/560244) well in advance of your trip, stating reasons (don't expect success). Access to the island is by fishing boat from Sidi Daoud, and you'll have to do a day-trip as there's nowhere to stay on Zembra.

The only other diversion around Sidi Daoud is the **Forest of Dar Chichou** to the southeast. A road runs inland from Sidi Daoud, through the forest to emerge on the south coast between Kerkouane and Kélibia. On the way, you pass a fenced-off **nature reserve** devoted, strangely enough, to **gazelles**; you should be able to glimpse some from the road, especially if you stop and wait quietly for a while.

From Sidi Daoud down Cap Bon's western coast to Bir Meroua, the road stays several kilometres inland, skirting country that is surprisingly mountainous – even reminiscent of Scottish heathland. For most of the way, the coastline is one deserted beach, backed by farmland with any number of possible tracks down to the shore.

A couple of **louages** shuttle between Sidi Daoud and El Haouaria, and you may also be able to flag down a bus or louage on the main road. Buses between El Haouaria and Tunis run along here (local people will know current times), but louages heading south are likely to be full.

Korbous and around

Protruding like the knuckle of Cap Bon's finger, the massif of **Jebel Korbous** looms over the ancient thermal resort named after it. Apparently the waters are good for curing arthritis, rheumatism, hypertension, obesity and cellulite.

Famous since Roman times as Aquae Calidau Carpitanae, and heavily developed by the French, **KORBOUS**, 30km along the coast from Sidi Daoud, has seen better days and now exudes a seedy, turn-of-the-twentieth-century air reminiscent of Hammam Lif (see p.133). It remains a popular weekend excursion, though, and the scenery is dramatic, with waves crashing onto rocks below the Jebel Korbous's craggy green slopes – ideally you'd want your own transport to take you all the way round the mountain. There are a few **buses** daily to Korbous from Tunis's Bab Aleoua station and from Soliman, as well as **louages** from Tunis, Soliman and, less frequently, Nabeul and El Haouaria.

Korbous is set in a steep ravine where the Romans first came to take the waters. At the end of the nineteenth century the spa was redesigned by a French civil engineer, who then retired to the villa – now a presidential retreat – perched on an outcrop overlooking the main street. Below the villa, the **Zarziha Rock** has been polished smooth by generations of women sliding down it to cure infertility. The focal point of the village is still very much the **spa**, at the bottom of the main street, which offers various reasonably priced thermal cures (daily 8am–8pm) – "the largest dose will be taken first thing in the morning while fasting in several successive swallows", according to ONTT literature. Next door is an ancient and suitably grotty **hammam**, the Arraka (24hr: women Tues, Thurs & Sat 7.30am–9pm, men at all other times), which is thought to have origins in Roman times.

There isn't a great deal to Korbous apart from the spa and the main street, which is lined with souvenir stalls for daytrippers on Sundays and two **hotels**: the deteriorating and overpriced *Hôtel les Sources* (☎72 284540; ❺) and the preferable *Hôtel des Thermes* (☎72 284520, ℱ284755; ❸), at the top of the main street, with basic en-suite rooms in its original block and pricier, more modern a/c rooms in the new block opposite. There is a reasonable **restaurant** in the old block (daily 1–2.30pm & 7.30–10.30pm) and a pizzeria in the new part. The best place to eat, however, is the pleasant and moderately priced *Restaurant Dhib* (daily 10am–8pm), a short way down the main street, which does good seafood.

Once you've seen Korbous, follow the road north for a kilometre and you'll come to a spring called **Aïn el Atrous** (Goat Spring), which shoots out of the mountain through a pipe below the road. At the point where the hot sulphurous spring water meets the salty Mediterranean, a small pool containing both waters has formed, which is wonderfully relaxing and good for skin complaints and rheumatism. You can also dangle your feet in the hot water where the stream has been channelled through a small esplanade, down some steps off the road. If you continue down another flight of steps, you'll come to a narrow strip of beach, beyond which people camp (though it looks very exposed). Several cafés and souvenir stalls operate around the spring.

Beyond Aïn el Atrous the road climbs hundreds of metres up the mountain's north shoulder and down onto a high plain and the village of **Douela**, where you can turn right towards the main road south to Soliman or carry straight on to the small settlement of **Bir Meroua**, also on the main road. Not far beyond Douela, and a couple of kilometres short of Bir Meroua, a road (signposted "El Bekakcha") leads off left towards the long, pristine white beach of **Marsa Ben Ramdane**, one of the most spectacular in the country. About 4km from the turn-off, the road turns into a track (negotiable by car in normal conditions), which continues downhill for another 4km to the beach dominated by a fort that's been converted into a private house. The only permanent inhabitants down here are a few fishermen who operate from a wooden pier; camping should not be a problem.

△ The spring at Korbous

South of Korbous, the coastal road skirts the foot of the mountain for 3km before hitting the diminutive spa town of **AÏN OKTOR**. Buses to Tunis used to pass this way but the road beyond Aïn Oktor has been closed because of falling rocks. A new road is being built to replace it, climbing from Aïn Oktor over a southern spur of the Jebel Korbous to join up with the old road at the tiny, rickety settlement of **Sidi Rais**, 3km further south. Dubbed the Route des Crêtes, the new road should be spectacular (it should have opened by the time you read this). There are plans to renovate the long-closed *Hôtel Oktor* (☎72 284 874) in Aïn Oktor to take advantage of the increased traffic that will pass this way. Beyond Sidi Rais – once a fashionable seaside resort but now comprising little more than a few fishing boats hauled up on the beach – the road passes through the more substantial settlement of **MARISA**, where the *Hôtel Chiraz* (☎72 398 143; phone to check that they are open) has eight basic rooms, a restaurant and a pool overlooking a lush orchard. One kilometre past the *Chiraz* you rejoin the MC26 south to Soliman.

Soliman and Soliman Plage

Eighteen kilometres south of Korbous is **SOLIMAN**, a seventeenth-century Andalusian settlement whose **mosque** is almost the only remnant of that time. Today the town is a prosperous agricultural centre with an attractive tree-filled square next to the mosque, whose semicircular Spanish roof tiles can just be made out. Look out, too, for a **fountain** surrounded by colourful ceramic work.

Rue Habib Thameur runs from the town centre around the mosque to end up near the **bus station**. As well as several bus services, there are also **louages** to Tunis and Grombalia, which leave from near the bus station. There are no buses or louages for Soliman Plage; taxis leave from place 7 Novembre, the other side of the town centre, or you could walk. The **post office** (country hours) is at 35 rue Habib Thameur.

There are no hotels in Soliman itself, only at **SOLIMAN PLAGE** (also known as Plage Ejjehmi), 3km away. The sand is white enough and there are good views of the mountains – Jebel Bou Kornine to the west and Jebel Korbous to the east – but the desolate stretch of beach, isolated on the edge of a marshy plain, makes for one of the least attractive resorts in Tunisia. At the end of the road from Soliman is a **café** and two hotels, both catering for European package tourists, a few hundred metres up the beach to your left (to get straight to them, turn off the Soliman road 500m before hitting the beach). The *Hôtel el Andalous* (☎72 290 199; ❹) has waterskiing and riding; a bit smarter and rather Teutonic is the large *Hôtel Solymar* (☎72 290 105, ☎72 290155, Ⓔsolymar@planet.tn; ❻). Between the café and the hotels, straw beach cabins are used by Tunisian holidaymakers during July and August, when the beach is packed solid. Beyond the *Solymar*, the beach continues round to Borj Cedria (see p.133), where there are a few more package options.

Grombalia and around

South of Tunis, the A1 motorway and the old GP1 cut through the fertile bottom end of Cap Bon. Originally settled by Spanish Muslim immigrants in the seventeenth century, the region was later popular with European farmers under the French regime, who left behind the many red-tiled farms and crumbling gateposts scattered among its vast vineyards and orchards.

There's little reason to stop here, unless you happen to coincide with one of the seasonal festivals. **GROMBALIA**, straddling both GP1 and the main north–south rail line, is the largest market town in the area and celebrates a **wine festival** every August or September to coincide with the harvest. Grombalia's **train station** serves Mahdia, Monastir, Sousse, Bir Bou Regba (for connections to Hammamet and Nabeul) and Tunis. There are also hourly **buses** and frequent **louages** to Menzel Bou Zelfa, Nabeul, Soliman and Tunis. **MENZEL BOU ZELFA**, 8km east of Grombalia, has an **orange festival** to celebrate the appearance of orange blossom in March or April, as well as an important seventeenth-century **zaouia**, a multi-domed structure in the centre of town.

If you have your own transport, and fancy an excursion into the hills west of Grombalia, take the road opposite the Société Tunisienne de Banque on the main road, which leads 8km over the motorway up to the village of **AÏN TEBOURNOK**. Just before Aïn Tebournok, look out north of the road for a grotesque **colonial mansion**, a fantasy Moorish pile with a quasi-minaret for a central tower, staring out over the plain. Aïn Tebournok itself sits in a bowl of hills, built around an ancient spring where Roman remains lie forlorn and deserted.

Some 10km south of Grombalia on the road to Hammamet is **BOU ARGOUB**. There's little enough to this tiny village apart from a **villa** built for Mussolini by the Fascists of Tunisia's Italian community. Relations between Mussolini and the French were never good: the Italians always felt they had been cheated out of Tunisia in 1881 and had to settle for second best with Libya. Mussolini was continually preparing to invade Tunisia and, with more Italian colonists in the country than French, this appeared no empty threat. Ultimately, however, the Abyssinian campaign distracted "Il Duce" and the villa, now a girls' school, was never occupied by him.

Travel details

Trains

Bir Bou Regba to: Gabès (3 daily; 4hr 45min–5hr 10min); Grombalia (6–8 daily; 15–20min); Hammamet (8–10 daily; 5min); Mahdia (1 daily; 3hr 5min); Monastir (1 daily; 2hr 10min); Nabeul (8–10 daily; 25min); Sfax (5 daily; 2hr 30min–3hr); Sousse (8–9 daily; 1hr–1hr 15min); Tunis (10–12 daily; 50min).

Grombalia to: Bir Bou Regba (6–8 daily; 15–20min); Gabès (1 daily; 5hr 25min); Mahdia (1 daily; 3hr 20min); Monastir (1 daily; 2hr 25min); Nabeul (1–2 direct daily; 50min); Sfax (1 daily; 3hr 10min); Sousse (5–6 daily; 1hr 15min–1hr 30min); Tunis (6–8 daily; 35–50min).

Hammamet to: Bir Bou Regba (8–10 daily; 5min); Nabeul (8–10 daily; 20min); Tunis (1 direct daily; 1hr 20min).

Nabeul to: Bir Bou Regba (8–10 daily; 25min); Hammamet (8–10 daily; 20min); Tunis (1 direct daily; 1hr 35min).

Buses

El Haouaria to: Kélibia (3 daily; 30min); Nabeul (3 daily; 1hr 30min); Soliman (7 daily; 1hr 15min); Tunis (7 daily; 2hr).

Grombalia to: Menzel Bou Zelfa (hourly; 15min); Nabeul (hourly; 45min); Soliman (hourly; 15min); Tunis (hourly; 45min).

Hammamet to: Hammamet Yasmine (every 30min; 15min); Kairouan (3 daily; 2hr 15min); Monastir (1 daily; 2hr); Nabeul (every 30min; 15min); Sousse (2 daily; 1hr 45min); Tunis (every 30min; 1hr 30min).

Kélibia to: El Haouaria (8 daily; 30min); Hammamet (2 daily; 1hr); Kairouan (1 daily; 3hr 30min); Korba (hourly; 45min); Menzel Bou Zelfa (hourly; 1hr); Menzel Temime (hourly; 15min); Monastir (1 daily; 3hr); Nabeul (hourly; 1hr); Soliman (hourly; 1hr 15min); Sousse (1 daily; 2hr 45min); Tunis (hourly; 2hr 30min).

Menzel Bou Zelfa to: Grombalia (hourly; 15min);

Kélibia (hourly; 1hr); Menzel Temime (hourly; 45min); Soliman (hourly; 15min); Tunis (hourly; 1hr).

Nabeul to: Borj Cedria (every 30min; 1hr); El Fahs (4 daily; 1hr 45min); Grombalia (every 30min; 45min); Hammamet (every 30min; 15min); Hammamet Yasmine (every 30min; 30min); Kairouan (3 daily; 2hr 30min); Kélibia (hourly; 1hr); Korba (hourly; 15min); Menzel Temime (hourly; 45min); Monastir (1 daily; 2hr 30min); Sousse (2 daily; 2hr 15min); Tunis (every 30min; 1hr 30min); Zaghouan (7–9 daily; 1hr 30min).

Soliman to: El Haouaria (7 daily; 1hr 15min); Grombalia (frequent; 15min); Kélibia (frequent; 1hr 15min); Korbous (5 daily; 15min); Menzel Bou Zelfa (frequent; 15min); Tunis (every 15min; 45min).

Louages

El Haouaria to: Grombalia (1hr 15min); Kélibia (yellow taxis serve as louages for this route; 20min); Sidi Daoud (15min); Soliman (1hr); Tunis (1hr 45min).

Hammamet to: Nabeul (yellow taxis serve as louages for this route; 15min); Sousse (1hr 15min); Tunis (1hr).

Kélibia to: El Haouaria (yellow taxis serve as louages for this route; 20min); Korba (30min); Menzel Temime (10min); Nabeul (45min); Tunis (2hr).

Nabeul to: Enfida (1hr 30min); Hammamet (yellow taxis serve as louages for this route; 15min); Kélibia (45min); Sousse (1hr 30min); Tunis (1hr); Zaghouan (1hr 15min).

Soliman to: Grombalia (15min); Menzel Bou Zelfa (15min); Menzel Temime (45min); Tunis (45min).

Arabic place names

Aïn Tebournok	عين تبرنق
Bir Bou Regba	بئر بو رقبة
Bou Argoub	بئر عرقوب
El Haouaria	الهوّارية
Grombalia	قرمبالية
Hammamet	الحمّامات
Kélibia	قليبية
Kerkouane	كركوان
Korba	قربة
Korbous	قربص
Mansoura	منصورة
Menzel Bou Zelfa	منزل بو زلفة
Menzel Temime	منزل تميم
Nabeul	نابل
Sidi Daoud	سيدي داود
Soliman	سليمان

Bizerte and the north

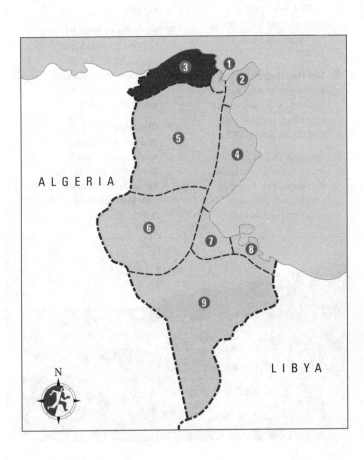

ALGERIA

LIBYA

N

CHAPTER 3 # Highlights

* **Bizerte** This underrated city has a magical old fishing port, surrounded by forts, markets and mosques. See p.171

* **Lac Ichkeul National Park** An ornithologist's delight, particularly in winter, when it is a haven for migrating birds. See p.180

* **Raf Raf Beach** A fabulous curve of white sand backed by dunes, forest and steep fields of figs and vines. See p.182

* **Tabarka** This is just about the prettiest resort in the country, in a sheltered sandy bay, with great diving and music festivals all summer. See p.187

* **Khroumirie Mountains** Leafy forests, fabulous views and cool temperatures make for superb hiking country. See p.195

* **Bulla Regia** With its opulent underground villas, this is one of the most extraordinary Roman sites in the world. See p.202

* **Chemtou** The marble quarries here were renowned throughout the Roman Empire, but the excellent museum is now the main draw. See p.206

△ Sidi Mechrig

Bizerte and the north

S parsely populated and with few roads, Tunisia's **northern coast** has played little part in the country's touristic development until recently. **Bizerte**, the one town of any size, is far more of a port than a resort, despite the excellence of the beaches in the area. Even if you get no further, Bizerte is worth a few days of your time – easily reached from Tunis, and with a monumental heritage covering centuries of strategic importance. Closer to the capital, and very much the preserve of Tunisians, are the superlative long white strands of **Raf Raf** and **Ras Sidi el Mekki**. Beaches with few equals in Tunisia, they are cut in two by the steep green flanks of **Cap Farina**, with its crumbling old pirate base of **Ghar el Melh**. **Utica**, a Roman city famous for its part in the civil war between Julius Caesar and Pompey, lies not far from Ghar el Melh on the road from Tunis. Inland, **Lac Ichkeul** and its national park form an ornithological highlight.

West of Bizerte along the coast, buses are infrequent and often erratic, but it's possible to reach some beautiful and remote beaches poised between deep forested headlands: **Cap Serrat** and **Sidi Mechrig** are both feasible targets. **Tabarka**, long popular as a resort for independent travellers and a recent target for major tourist development, has perhaps the best beach of all, overlooked by a spectacular island castle. Just inland from here, **Aïn Draham** is reckoned the coolest place in the country in midsummer; and around, in the **Khroumirie Mountains**, there are some impressive hikes.

In contrast to the coast, the **Medjerda Valley**, formed around the country's one permanently flowing river, has always had a considerable urban population. **Béja** is the most attractive of the modern centres, though more intriguing are the Roman settlements of **Bulla Regia** with its underground villas, unique in the ancient world, and **Chemtou**, with its marble quarries and fine museum.

Market days

Monday Aïn Draham
Tuesday Béja, Bizerte, Ghardimaou, Souk es Sebt
Wednesday Jendouba, Menzel Bourguiba, Nefza
Thursday Bou Salem, Sejnane
Friday Tabarka, Ras Jebel
Saturday Bizerte, El Alia, Hammam Bourguiba, Mateur
Sunday Bezina, Fernana, Menzel Bourguiba, Thibar

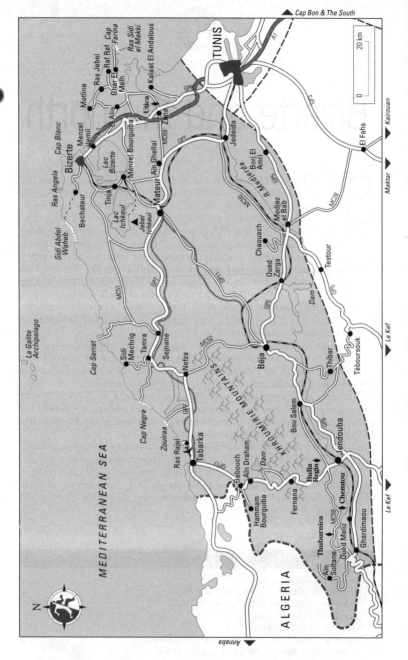

The coast

To visit anywhere other than the major centres along the **north coast** without a car means either hitching or fighting for a place in the occasional louage. Trains run only as far as Bizerte, and there is only one bus a day between Bizerte and Tabarka; otherwise the whole coastal region is somewhat inaccessible. The payoff lies in the rugged, unspoiled shoreline. Soaking up the sun on the best beaches and stopping off to explore the historic sights could fill a couple of weeks; it's best not to hurry, taking leisurely trips and avoiding the searing summer heat.

Between **Raf Raf beach** and Tunis, the northern shoreline consists of barely inhabited alluvial farmland. Beyond, the coast becomes thickly populated and culminates in the port of **Bizerte**, where the population thins out again until **Tabarka**, which has been developed substantially for tourism but is not yet despoiled beyond recognition.

Bizerte and Lac Bizerte

BIZERTE, also called Benzert or Bizerta, is the most underrated of Tunisia's resorts – perhaps because it's not so much a resort as a historic port that happens to have beaches. These aren't as opulent as those on the east coast, but if you're looking for a town with both swimming and character you won't find much better. The town stands at the mouth of **Lac Bizerte**, a saltwater lake connected to the sea by a canal, along which the modern port is located. An older outlet connects the fishing port to the sea. Guarded by two forts and overlooked by a dignified mosque, the fishing port is the place to get a sense of Bizerte's pre-colonial identity.

Some history
One of the great natural ports of the Mediterranean, Bizerte was exploited early by the **Phoenicians**, who improbably called their town Hippo Diarrhytus and dug the first channel linking the lake to the sea. When the Romans arrived they improved the existing facilities, and imperial prosperity gave the town its first taste of popularity – the Younger Pliny described it as "a town where people of all ages spend their time enjoying the pleasures of fishing, boating and swimming".

The **Arabs** changed the name to **Benzert**, and under the Hafsids its prosperity continued, when it had a great hunting park. Bizerte inevitably found itself in the front line during the Turco-Spanish struggles of the sixteenth century, and **Charles V** punished the town for supporting the corsair Barbarossa with a brutal raid in 1535. It continued to absorb large numbers of Andalusian immigrants, however, and was rewarded with considerable attention from the **Turkish** rulers, who developed its amenities during the seventeenth and eighteenth centuries. **Piracy** was rife at this time but, with the demise of the slave trade and increasing European domination of the Mediterranean, Bizerte went into decline until the opening of the Suez Canal brought renewed strategic importance. The **French** then set about building up the port's facilities – strictly for commercial purposes, they claimed. Even after World War II, Bizerte inspired lust in the hearts of Western strategic planners, and following independence the French simply stayed on. When they still refused to evacuate after the bombing of Sakiet Sidi Youssef (see p.318), Tunisian forces blockaded the military base in 1961. The French responded by trying to break the blockade, and Tunisia's army undertook its first **military action**. More than a thousand Tunisian lives were lost before the French finally withdrew on **October 15, 1963** – no longer a national holiday, but still a day of celebration in Bizerte.

Thanks to the French legacy (and departure), the main thrust of Bizerte's development has been **industrial**, and its naval arsenal has been converted into a vast complex, including what was once North Africa's first blast furnace. **Tourism**, which has dropped off sharply here over the past few years as Tabarka and the east-coast resorts continue to expand, comes a distant second.

Arrival, information and accommodation

The **train station** is by the docks at the western end of rue de Russie and rue de Belgique, a ten-minute walk to the centre. Outside is a **louage station**, where regional services (from Mateur, Sejnane, Menzel Bourguiba and Béja) will drop you. If you're coming from Tunis, the louages drop you outside the main SRT Bizerte **bus station**, at the bottom of avenue d'Algérie and rue Ibn Khaldoun. Other buses, from Kairouan, Sousse, Sfax and Jerba, stop at the SNTRI depot in rue d'Alger, while SRT Jendouba buses terminate near the train station.

You'll find the **tourist office** on quai Khemais Ternane in the Old Port (July & Aug Mon–Sat 7.30am–1.30pm; Sept–June Mon–Thurs 8.30am–1pm & 3–5.45pm, Fri & Sat 8.30am–1.30pm; ☏72 432897). Note that **street names** in Bizerte are mainly posted in Arabic and locals tend not to number buildings and houses, so locating specific places can be a problem.

Accommodation

Most of the cheap (and generally tawdry) **hotels** are in town, with a couple of more expensive and modern hotels just north of town in the half-hearted *zone touristique* of Sidi Salem, and older package-type places strung out beyond along the Corniche for 4km towards Cap Bizerte. The *zone touristique* hotels are within walking distance of the city centre; for the Corniche, take a bus

---

Moving on from Bizerte

For a list of destinations and journey times, see Travel details on p.211.

Buses to Tunis leave more or less half-hourly from the SRT Bizerte bus station (☏72 431 371); there are also frequent services to Ras Jebel, where you can change for Raf Raf. Outside the bus station building is the stop for services to Menzel Bourguiba, close to Lac Ichkeul, via Rimel. There are other buses from SNTRI's unpromising-looking depot in rue d'Alger (☏72 431 222): twice a day to Houmt Souk on Jerba, via Sousse and Sfax, and daily to Kairouan. SRT Jendouba buses leave from near the train station. For Tabarka, note that there's only one bus a day; if you miss it, you can get a louage 40km south to Mateur, on the route of several buses daily to Tabarka from Tunis.

    Louages to Tunis (red stripes), Ras Jebel, Raf Raf and Ghar el Melh (blue stripes) leave from outside the SRT Bizerte bus station. For other departures to locations within this chapter, including Sejnane and (very occasionally) Tabarka, the stop is outside the train station. There are very occasional louages to Tabarka. The **train station** (☏72 431071) has services to Tunis via Tinja and Mateur. For the address of the **ferry** company CTN, see p.17.

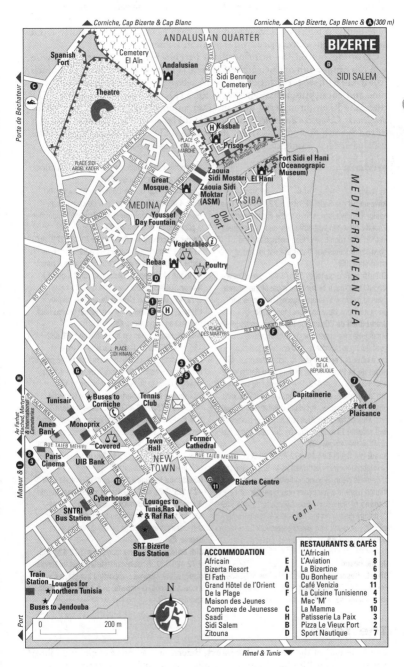

BIZERTE

ANDALUSIAN QUARTER

SIDI SALEM

Corniche, Cap Bizerte & Cap Blanc — Corniche, ▲ Cap Bizerte, Cap Blanc & Ⓐ(300 m)

Porte de Bechateur ▲

Spanish Fort

Cemetery El Aïn

Andalusian

Sidi Bennour Cemetery

Theatre

Ⓒ

Kasbah

PLACE SIDI ABDEL KADER

Prison

Zaouia Sidi Mostari

Fort Sidi el Hani (Oceanograpic Museum)

El Hani

Great Mosque

Zaouia Sidi Moktar (ASM)

MEDINA

KSIBA

Youssef Day Fountain

Old Port

Vegetables Ⓘ

Rebaa

Poultry

MEDITERRANEAN SEA

Ⓖ

Ⓗ

PLACE SIDI HINAN

PLACE DES MARTYRS

Ⓕ

PLACE DE LA RÉPUBLIQUE

Ⓗ

Tunisair

Buses to Corniche

Tennis Club

Capitainerie

Ⓖ

Ⓗ

Port de Plaisance

Amen Bank

Monoprix

Av Farhat Hached, Martyrs & International Cemeteries

Mateur & Ⓘ ▲

Ⓗ

Ⓘ

Ⓑ Ⓘ

Paris Cinema

UIB Bank

Covered

Town Hall

Former Cathedral

NEW TOWN

Cyberhouse

Bizerte Centre

SNTRI Bus Station

Louages to Tunis, Ras Jebel & Raf Raf

Canal

SRT Bizerte Bus Station

Train Station

Louages for northern Tunisia

Buses to Jendouba

Port ▲

0   200 m

N

Rimel & Tunis ▼

ACCOMMODATION
Africain	E
Bizerta Resort	A
El Fath	I
Grand Hôtel de l'Orient	G
De la Plage	F
Maison des Jeunes Complexe de Jeunesse	C
Saadi	H
Sidi Salem	B
Zitouna	D

RESTAURANTS & CAFÉS
L'Africain	1
L'Aviation	8
La Bizertine	6
Du Bonheur	9
Café Venizia	11
La Cuisine Tunisienne	4
Mac 'M'	5
La Mamma	10
Patisserie La Paix	3
Pizza Le Vieux Port	2
Sport Nautique	7

from the "Cheikh Idriss" bus stop at the corner of boulevard Hassan en Nouri and avenue Bourguiba. Because business is slow, there tends to be less variation here between high- and low-season prices than in more popular resorts; about a third off high-season prices is the norm in winter.

Camping out on the main northern beaches may be tolerated; otherwise you can camp south of town at the *Centre de la Jeunesse de Rimel* in Rimel beach (☎72 440 819; see p.177 for directions). A sylvan and peaceful place smelling of pine and eucalyptus, it has dorm beds for 5TD and camping spaces for 2TD; the sea is 300m through the trees and over a dune. North of town, the *Maison des Jeunes Complexe de Jeunesse*, on boulevard Hassan en Nouri just to the west of the Spanish Fort (☎72 431608; dorm beds 4TD; check in after 6pm), is the usual charmless monolith; there's a sports hall and a covered pool.

Hotels

In Town

Africain 59 rue Sassi el Bahri ☎72 434 412. This basic, friendly place is favourable to the nearby *Zitouna*, although both are noisy due to the street market. The rooms are clean enough but the downstairs toilets and baths are not in such a good state. ❶

El Fath av Bourguiba ☎ & ☎72 430 596. A new-ish addition that's better than most of the alternatives in town, with simple rooms, balconies and en-suite baths but communal toilets. ❸

Grand Hôtel de l'Orient 38 bd Hassan en Nouri (no phone). Has air-conditioning – which makes it worth considering in summer – and en-suite toilets with the rooms, but nothing else to justify the price. ❹

Hôtel de la Plage 23 av Mohammed Rejiba ☎72 436 510, ☎72 434 412. The newest and best of the town hotels, only 50m from the seafront, with basic, clean doubles, triples and family rooms, with and without facilities. Also has a rooftop terrace and satellite TV lounge. Run by the same management as the *Africain*. ❸

Saadi rue Salah Ben Ali ☎72 422 528. A couple of hundred metres northwest of av Bourguiba, this cheapie is clean, if basic and without hot showers, though there is a hammam next door. ❶

Zitouna pl Slahedinne Bouchoucha ☎72 438 769. Definitely dingy and the hot water is temperamental, but you won't find any cheaper. Ask for a room with a window. ❶

On the beach

Bizerta Resort In the *zone touristique* ☎72 436 966, ☎72 422 955, ⊕www.bizerta-resort.com. Easily the smartest place hereabouts, with comfortable, well-equipped rooms, a pool, jacuzzi, sauna and other luxuries. ❼

Club Jalta 1km up the Corniche ☎72 443 100, ☎72 436 888. Friendly but run-down package place offering horse-riding, windsurfing in summer, a pool and other facilities. ❹

Corniche 2km up the Corniche ☎72 421 222, ☎72 422 515. Bigger and grander than the other Corniche hotels, but the uninspired rooms don't match up to the gleaming marble and chrome lobby. ❻

Nador 1500m up the Corniche ☎72 431 848, ☎72 433 817. Like *Club Jalta*, another slightly decrepit place undergoing renovation to woo back the package operators. ❺

Petit Mousse 3.5km up the Corniche ☎72 432 185, ☎72 438 871. Dating back to 1946, with friendly staff and a touch of class, this is the pick of the Corniche hotels. There are only twelve rooms, so you'll need to book ahead in summer. ❻

Résidence Aïn Meriem 1km up the Corniche ☎72 422 615, ☎72 422 459. Large modern *aparthotel* offering a range of upmarket self-catering studios sleeping three, five or seven, as well as apartments and chalet-villas, which are a bargain only if you're in a big group (five or seven people) or if you stay off season. ❽

Résidence Essaada 2km up the Corniche ☎72 423 433, ☎72 423 790. Better value than the *Aïn Meriem*, with big, comfortable bedrooms, spotless bathrooms and a decent-sized TV room in self-catering apartments sleeping two to eight people. ❼

Sidi Salem In the *zone touristique* ☎72 420 365, ☎72 420 380, ⊕hsalem.bizerte@planet.tn. Newish place, with clean, well-appointed bungalows, with a choice of bath or shower, plus a bar, restaurant and disco. ❻

The Town

Until the end of the nineteenth century, Bizerte was a compact city straddling a natural channel leading from the Mediterranean into Lac Bizerte, its centre standing on an island in the middle and with heavy fortifications punctuating its surrounding walls. The French colonial planners filled in most of the channel, built their new town on reclaimed land south of avenue Bourguiba and, in the 1890s, dug the modern shipping canal to provide superior access to the lake. The lift-bridge over the canal looks pretty impressive when raised, its middle section towering straight up and visible right across town.

Bizerte still consists of a grid-pattern **French new town** – a wholly unscenic place that has a curious gritty charm, with a green and spacious central square and grandiose buildings along the seafront. The new town sits alongside the remains of the old walled town with its harbour, the **Old Port**, built to serve as a major Mediterranean naval and military base and guarded at the entrance by the twin forts of the **Kasbah** and **Fort Sidi el Hani**. Next to the harbour are the narrow streets and monuments of the **Medina**, overlooked from the top of the hill behind the town by the so-called **Spanish fort**, begun by the Spanish but finished by their enemies, the Turks.

The Old Port

Surrounded by cafés, narrow streets and forts, the **Old Port** is the heart of Bizerte. Originally it split into two arms, one running along what is now place Lahedine Bouchoucha and one continuing around today's tourist office building. Reuniting on avenue Bourguiba, the channel went behind an island and continued into the body of Lac Bizerte. The island in the channel – nowadays the area around the tourist office, the covered market and the **Rebaa Mosque** – lay within the city walls, and in pre-colonial times, this was where the European population lived in detached splendour. Most of old Bizerte lay west of the channel, making up what is now known as the Medina. Its western wall followed the path of boulevard Hassan En Nouri up to the Spanish fort on the hill behind town, before returning back down the hill to the Kasbah. You can still get a sense of the historic town by heading for **place Lahedine Bouchoucha**, on the edge of the Old Port, with its busy shops and markets (the covered vegetable market is particularly colourful).

It's a long time since any fishing boats or corsair privateers sailed all the way through town, along the channels and below the minarets, on their way to and from Lac Bizerte. But the Old Port retains a magical feeling, especially in the evening. Café tables are set out along the **quay** and, as darkness falls, illuminated **boats** chug off for the night's fishing, accompanied by the call to prayer from the minaret of the Great Mosque that stands just next to the harbour. In the daytime, the quaysides are a peaceful retreat where you can have a coffee or wander up to the prosaic modern **bridge** between the twin fortifications of the Kasbah on the left and Fort Sidi el Hani on the right.

The Kasbah and Fort Sidi el Hani

At the mouth of the port, the **Kasbah**, with its massive walls, is hard to miss. Although its general form suggests a Byzantine foundation, like many of Bizerte's monuments, it dates mainly from the seventeenth century. Virtually untouched by the modern city outside, it's a wonderful place to wander around, as beyond its single, heavily defensive gate lies a miniature old town of passages, arches and walls painted in pastel shades. Outside, through an entrance in the southeast bastion facing the port, you can also reach a promenade running around the top of the Kasbah **walls** (July & Aug daily 9am–12.30pm & 4pm–midnight; Sept–June Mon 3–7pm, Tues–Sun 9am–12.30pm & 3–7pm; 0.5TD). It's the best place to get a view of the historic town's layout, and there's the bonus of a café.

Facing the Kasbah on the other side of the harbour channel, the smaller **Fort Sidi el Hani** is the other half of what must have made a formidable defensive ensemble, though the effect is now somewhat muffled by the modern bridge over the channel. Parts of the fort – the round tower and the wall facing the channel – date back to Byzantine times. It is now a small **Oceanographic Museum** (Tues–Sun 9am–12.30pm & 3–7pm; 0.5TD), though aside from a few glum turtles and forgetful fish it's not up to much. The area immediately behind the fort is called the **Ksiba** (the diminutive of Kasbah, meaning "little fort"), and still houses local fishermen, who moor boats outside their doorsteps.

The Medina

Overwhelmed by the colonial town and bombed during World War II, the **Medina** is nonetheless a good place for a wander – despite a sparsity of monuments and souks, in parts the overused adjective "labyrinthine" really does apply. The most impressive monuments lie conveniently next to the Old Port in what was once the heart of the town. If you walk up place Lahedine Bouchoucha towards the port, you'll come upon a great horseshoe to your left, in alternating black and white marble; this once belonged to a **fountain** erected in the seventeenth century by Youssef Dey, second of Tunis's Turkish rulers and founder of a mosque in Tunis's Medina (see p.84). Like the mosque in Tunis, the fountain was designed by an architect of Spanish origin – he is identified in its inscription as El Andaloussi. The fountain's inscription advises passers-by in both Arabic and Turkish to use its water until such time as the waters of Paradise become available to them. Originally the water would have been fed by a *nouria* waterwheel powered by a camel, like the one in Kairouan (see p.248), but sadly both camel and water are long gone.

Bizerte's **Great Mosque**, built in 1652, lies a little way beyond the fountain. Its minaret is visible either from the cramped rue des Armuriers or – even better – from the other side of the port, where you can watch its reflection jostling in the water with brightly coloured fishing boats, while the walls of the Spanish fort loom on the hillside behind. Dating, like the fountain and Youssef Dey's mosque in Tunis, from the first years of Turkish rule, the minaret belongs recognizably to the same school, its octagonal shape (signifying Hanefite sympathies) and hanging balcony reminiscent of contemporary Tunis monuments.

Just north of the Great Mosque, on the corner of rue des Armuriers and an alley leading down to the quay, the **Zaouia of Sidi Moktar** is now the headquarters of the local ASM (Association de Sauvegarde de la Medina), who have a fascinating map of Bizerte, drawn to show the city as it was in 1881, before the new town and canal were built. They sometimes use the *zaouia* to put on exhibitions about the Medina and the ASM's work in restoring and maintaining it. A little further still towards the Kasbah on rue des Armuriers is the seventeenth-century **Zaouia of Sidi Mostari**. To explore the old streets of the Medina, you can head back down rue des Armuriers, which twists the length of the old town as rue Bab Jedid, and take any number of side alleys to your right.

The Andalusian Quarter and the Spanish fort

Just below the walls of the Kasbah, a small open square makes a pleasant place to sit at a café table. Beyond it, outside the old city wall, lies the former **Andalusian Quarter**, populated by Spanish Arab and Jewish immigrants who arrived following the Christian reconquest of Spain. There are some old streets and a whitewashed mosque, flanked by two **cemeteries** – Sidi Bennour, on empty ground outside the Kasbah walls, and El Aïn, whose gravestones sprinkle the hillside below the Spanish fort.

③

Like its contemporary at La Goulette outside Tunis, the massive **Spanish fort** dates back to the sixteenth century, when Tunisia was the front line in the war between Christian Spain and Ottoman Turkey. On taking control of Tunisia in 1535, the Spanish dismantled Bizerte's existing fortifications. Later, as their struggle with the Turks continued, they realized that they would need defences in this key port and began building the fort in 1570, probably not even completing it before the Turks ejected them in 1573. Since then it has undergone significant alterations and additions; in its original form, it was a star-shaped polygon with a central courtyard and one huge entrance gateway from the town. All it really offers now is the view from its battlements, a couple of World War II Italian guns and some rusty old cannons that were mentioned by Alexandre Dumas on his visit in 1848. A large Roman-style **theatre** just below the fort is used for concerts during the Bizerte festival (see p.178).

The Martyrs and International cemeteries

Echoes of past battles can be found in two other cemeteries which are poignant memorials to those who died while liberating or defending Bizerte. The **Martyrs Cemetery**, dedicated to Tunisians who fell during the 1963 liberation from the French, can be found by taking avenue Farhat Hached northwest out of town for a kilometre, then bearing left and uphill at the fork in the road; you'll see the ten-metre-high monument ahead, and the pristine cemetery lies across the main road. In contrast, the **International Cemetery** at the end of rue Pasteur is ramshackle, but contains some grand tombs (especially those of the Italians). To get there, follow avenue Bourguiba west out of town to where it meets rue Hedi Chaker, with a post office on the corner. Turning right up rue Pasteur, with a large military installation on your right, you'll find the cemetery at the end.

The beaches

Bizerte's main beach runs alongside the **Corniche** – a strip of sand varying in width and crowdedness as it stretches the five kilometres from **Sidi Salem**, by the Old Port bridge, north towards **Cap Bizerte**. Beyond lies the pretty and secluded small beach of **Les Grottes**, reached by walking the last 2km from where the bus stops or by taxi from town (around 3TD). Buses up the Corniche (#2) leave town from "Cheikh Idriss", a bus stop on boulevard Hassan en Nouri by the corner of avenue Bourguiba. You can also catch the bus from just north of the Old Port.

Three kilometres southeast of town, the beach of **Rimel** (meaning "sand") is definitely lusher, if a little exposed. It's reached by bus #8 from the main bus station to the "Menzel Jemil" stop, a fifteen-minute ride, from where it's a further fifteen-minute walk, or directly by taxi for around 3TD. There's a youth hostel and campsite just behind the beach (see p.174). The **shipwrecks** on Rimel beach can be seen from the bridge over the canal, and are about a fifty-minute walk down the beach from the hostel and campsite, away from town. Both hulls are from Italian vessels wrecked in 1940. For beaches further afield, see p.186.

Eating and drinking

Because Bizerte is so undeveloped for tourism, its **restaurants** are rather thin on the ground, especially the mid-range ones, and most close during Ramadan. On the other hand, there are enough *gargotes* to keep you satisfied, and Bizerte is one of the best places in Tunisia for a real splurge too, with several places to treat yourself along the Corniche. There are also a couple of excellent **patisseries** in town on rue 2 Mars 1934: *La Bizertine*, on the corner of rue du 1 Mai, serves delicious cakes, canapés and citronade, while the nearby *La Paix* is not quite as good for pastries but is well known for its ice creams in summer.

The hotels *Corniche, Jalta* and *Sidi Salem* have **bars** serving alcohol, as well as **discos**. The *Café Venizia*, on the first floor of the Bizerte Shopping Centre on quai Tarik Ibn Ziad, has a rather seedy atmosphere but provides a good view over the canal and the lift-bridge.

Restaurants

In town

L'Africain rue Sassi el Bahri, next to *Hôtel Africain*. Limited menu but the food is good and cheap (around 3TD). Daily 7am–9pm, later in summer.

L'Aviation (aka *Le Roi de Mechoui*) Corner av Thaalbi and av Bourguiba. Tasty couscous and grilled meats for under 5TD. Daily 11am–3pm & 6–9pm.

Du Bonheur av Thaalbi, near the corner of av Bourguiba ☎72 431 047. Smartish restaurant with good set menus at 14 and 15TD and à la carte for a little more. The owner was preparing to open a floating restaurant down at the Old Port at the time of writing. Daily 7am–3am.

La Cuisine Tunisienne rue 2 Mars 1934, near the corner of rue d'Istamboul. You can silence a grumbling stomach for 2–4TD in this pleasant *gargote*. Mon–Sat noon–11pm, Sun noon–3pm.

Mac 'M' rue 2 Mars 1934. A cheap and modern *gargote*, also serving – you guessed it – pizza. Mon–Sat 5am–9pm.

La Mamma rue Ibn Khaldoun. Good, affordable (3–5TD) Italian (and Tunisian) food in pleasant surroundings. Daily noon–10pm, later in summer.

Pizza Le Vieux Port (aka *Chez Bellahouel*) Apex of rue de Tunis and rue Ali Belhouane. Cheap pizzas and sandwiches. Daily 9am–2am.

Sport Nautique bd H Bougatfa, at the harbour mouth in the Port de Plaisance ☎72 432 262. A posh restaurant which offers a nice terrace to enjoy a plate of oysters over a bottle of wine. Expect to pay 25–30TD per person for a meal, with alcohol. Daily noon–3pm & 7.30–11.30pm.

On the Corniche

Belle Plage Beyond the *Petit Mousse* ☎72 431 817. Good selection of fish and other seafood, with full meals for 20–25TD, though the service is a bit laboured. Daily noon–3.30pm & 6.30–11.30pm.

Eden 2km up the Corniche ☎72 439 023. A fairly classy joint specializing in seafood and charging 20–25TD for a full meal. Daily noon–3pm & 7–11pm.

Petit Mousse 3.5km up the Corniche ☎72 432 185. An excellent seafood meal in this hotel will set you back 25–30TD including wine. Daily noon–3pm & 7–10pm.

Listings

Airlines Tunisair, 76 av Bourguiba ☎72 432 201.

Banks The main concentration of banks is in the new town between the bus station and av Bourguiba. UIB on av Taïeb Mehiri at rue Moncef Bey has an ATM accepting Visa, while Amen Bank on av Bourguiba near rue d'Alger has a Visa and MasterCard ATM.

Bike rental Bizerta Quads, opposite *Résidence Aïn Meriem* on the Corniche (☎72 443 563), rents out bikes for 15TD per day and also runs quad bike excursions (24TD/hr) into the Nador forest behind town as far as the beach at Aïn Damous (see p.186). *Club Jalta* also rents out bicycles in summer, while you may be able to strike a deal at one of the bike shops on av Bourguiba, between rue Ibn Khaldoun and rue du 1 Mai. Bikes are ideal for exploring the otherwise hard to get to (and around) Lac Ichkeul National Park (see p.180).

Car rental Ada, 27 rue d'Alger ☎72 431 508; Avis, 7 rue d'Alger at rue Habib Thameur ☎72 433 076; Hertz, Bizerte Centre ☎72 438 388.

Car repairs bd Hassan en Nouri, just down from the *Maison des Jeunes*, has a string of garages, mechanics and spare parts shops.

Cinemas Casino, pl des Martyrs; Majestic, rue de Tunis; Paris, 43 av Taïeb Mehiri at av Bourguiba.

Festivals Street celebrations and a carnival of sorts celebrate the city's 1963 liberation from the French on October 15. The Festival de Bizerte, held annually from mid-July to mid-August, sees international music hosted at the Spanish Fort. The Saints Day of Sidi Selim was formerly tied to the Islamic calendar, but is now incorporated into the Festival de Bizerte.

Football The local club is CAB Bizerte, winners of the 1988 African Cup Winners Cup, but currently only bobbing around the first division. Their ground is up by Porte de Bechateur northwest of town. Matches usually kick off at 2pm on Sundays.

Hammams The best hammam in town is the Hammam Sidi Abde el Kader (formerly Hammam de la Régence) off pl Lahedine Bouchoucha on rue Sassi el Bahri, diagonally opposite the *Hôtel Africain*. Another is in the Kasbah, and there's one in rue Salah Ben Ali, near the *Hôtel Saadi*. Hours at all of these are 6am–noon and 6–9pm for men, noon–6pm for women.

Hospital The regional hospital (☎72 431 422) is up rue Ibn Khaldoun; at the roundabout, bear up into rue Saussier.

Internet access Cyberhouse on av Habib Thameur (daily 9am–midnight; 2TD/hr) has a good connection and plenty of posts. Otherwise, try Futur Net in the Bizerte Centre (daily 7am–10pm; 1.3TD/hr) or the Publinet at 76 bd Hédi Chaker, round the corner from the *Hôtel Saadi* (daily 8am–10pm; 1.2TD/hr).

Newspapers English-language newspapers are available at the *Bizerta Resort* hotel.

Pharmacy There's a night pharmacy at 28 rue Ali Belhouane (☎72 432 461).

Police rue du 20 Mars 1956 ☎72 431 200.

Post office av d'Algérie at rue du 1 Mai (city hours); it changes cash, has Western Union money transfer and phones in the side entrance.

Supermarkets Monoprix, rue 2 Mars 1934 at rue Ibn Khaldoun.

Swimming There's a municipal pool on bd Hassan en Nouri by the *Maison des Jeunes*. Otherwise, try the Corniche hotels.

Taxis Allo Rapide Taxi ☎72 531 531.

Telephones There is a taxiphone with glass booths on rue 2 Mars 1934 near rue du 1 Mai, as well as other taxiphone and Publitel offices throughout the city.

Tours Some of the big hotels, notably the *Club Jalta*, run trips – for example, half a day in Raf Raf and Utica, a day in Kairouan or a three-day "safari" in the south (not a wildlife trip, but a whirlwind tour of the key sites), or you could try Aphrodite Tours, 12 rue Ahmed Tlili (☎72 436 195), or Via Bizerte, 1 rue du 1 Mai (☎72 432 901).

Lac Bizerte

South of Bizerte, the villages of **MENZEL ABDERRAHMAN** and **MEN-ZEL JEMIL** (short journeys from Bizerte's main bus station along the Tunis road) were both founded by the Aghlabids in the ninth century and make attractive places from which to view Lac Bizerte. Menzel Abderrahman is right on the shore, while Menzel Jemil – now virtually a suburb of Bizerte – perches on a hillside, its dapper old central **square** dominated by a fortress-like whitewashed mosque.

On the south side of the lake, **MENZEL BOURGUIBA** (formerly the French garrison town of Ferryville) is pretty dreary but is the closest jump-off point for the Lac Ichkeul National Park (see p.180), whose main gate is 7km away. The centre of Menzel Bourguiba is a leafy square with a bandstand, just off which is the lively *Moderne* **bar** in rue d'Alger. During World War II, soldiers on both sides had occasion to drink here, and the venerable *patron* who served them still runs the place. The **train station**, a couple of hundred metres further down rue d'Alger, no longer has any passenger services – the nearest passenger train station is at **Tinja**, 6km west on the Tunis–Bizerte line. Turn left just before the station and continue for 100m to find the Tunis **louage** station, or cross the tracks and turn right to the site of Menzel's Wednesday and Sunday **market**, where you can pick up louages to Mateur (an important transport hub with a busy Saturday market) and, less frequently, to Ichkeul, by the park gate. To find the **bus station**, and louages for Bizerte, go back up rue d'Alger, turn left at the bandstand and go straight on past a six-way roundabout and standard-issue monument to the November 7, 1987 "chargement". There are regular buses to Tunis and Bizerte, and half-hourly buses to Tinja.

The only **hotel** in the area is the *Ichkeul*, some way out of Menzel Bourguiba in **GUENGLA** (☎72 461 606; ❸), right on Lac Bizerte, though it was being renovated at the time of writing and was due to reopen in summer 2005. Buses to Tinja pass by the hotel, while a taxi from the centre of town will cost you a couple of dinars. If you have your own transport, follow signs for the hospital from place 7 Novembre, then turn left with the tarmac at the barracks entrance and carry straight on for another 2km until you come to the hotel on your right. The hotel is in a pleasant spot, and ideally placed for exploring Oued Tinja, the river that connects Lac Ichkeul with Lac Bizerte. The proprietor also runs the Tardi wine company, which bottles many of the region's **wines**, and visits can be arranged to the cellars at **Aïn Ghellal**, 10km to the south.

Lac Ichkeul National Park

The sixty-square-kilometre **LAC ICHKEUL**, linked to Lac Bizerte by a narrow channel near Tinja, is non-tidal, slightly saline and too shallow to be navigable, making it an ideal habitat for fish and bird life. The lake's unique ecosystem is protected as a **national park** (daily: summer 6am–8pm; winter 8am–6pm; free), although this hasn't prevented it coming under threat from dams constructed on its feed rivers. These dams, along with several years of low rainfall, lowered the water level in the lake and caused salt water from Lac Bizerte to flow back into it, killing off some of the water plants on which Lac Ichkeul's delicate ecosystem depends. More recently, conditions have improved thanks to a couple of years of better rainfall and a water pipeline to Bizerte from the mountains behind Tabarka, which has reduced the heavy demand on the lake's water. The park authorities are optimistic about the lake's future, believing that they can control its water level and salinity using a system of locks.

In winter, Lac Ichkeul is an ornithologist's delight as a haven for birds migrating from northern Europe (see box on p.181). Non-tidal and slightly saline, the lake also abounds in **frogs** and **toads**, including a very handsome, vocal species with green stripes down the back; there are **terrapins** too. The **Sejnane marsh** on the lake's north side is a good place to look for these. Rising directly from the southern edge of the lake is a superb limestone mountain, **Jebel Ichkeul**, which was a royal hunting park in the thirteenth century. **Wild boar** and **jackals** still live on its flanks, as do **porcupines**, **mongooses**, **otters**, **tortoises** and a small herd of **water buffalo** – descended, it's said, from a pair given to the Bey of Tunis by the king of Sicily in 1729. During the war, US troops stationed nearby developed a taste for the meat and the herd was virtually wiped out.

The **flowers** up on Jebel Ichkeul are utterly dependent on the winter rains and you can walk through a carpet of colour or over barren straw, depending on recent weather. Interesting flowers also grow around the rivers feeding the lake – around the River Douimis on the north shore, for instance, you'll find a white Star of Bethlehem and a delightful, tiny narcissus. The **agricultural weeds** are spectacular even in a dry year, since many of the fields to the north of the lake are irrigated. Look out for fields ablaze with poppies and wild chrysanthemums, and for various colourful convolvulus species around the edges. Honeywort, with its strange pendulous yellow and brown flowers, is also common by the roadside, and there's a shocking-pink soapwort in the fields.

Practicalities

Getting to the park is not easy by public transport, and it's a good idea first to visit Bizerte's tourist office (see p.172) for advice and information. You can

Birdwatching on the lake

Waterfowl are Lac Ichkeul's high spot. Ducks feed on the extensive beds of pond-weed and greylag geese on the club rush. These plants, together with the sheer size of the lake, make it North Africa's principal wildfowl wintering ground, with up to 150,000 birds at its peak.

Although huge flocks are present only between October and February, ducks remain in good numbers until the spring, with a few staying on and occasionally breeding over the summer. The birds move around the lake depending on the distribution of the plants they feed on, but in general the best viewpoints are from the shore below the mountain (there's a good track along it starting from the museum), or from the Douimis and Sejnane marshes on the north side. The latter marsh requires a walk along the river from the road.

As well as ducks and geese, the lake supports a variety of **wading birds** around its fringes. If the water level is high enough, both the Douimis and Sejnane marshes are good all year round for waders, with sizeable populations of avocets, black-winged stilts and Kentish plovers. These are augmented in winter by black-tailed godwits, redshanks and the smaller sandpipers. If it's wet, the edge of the Joumine marsh closest to the level crossing outside Tinja is a great spot to watch waders, but beware of the dogs around here. Herons and egrets breed among the reeds, the grey heron is a resident and purple heron is a summer visitor, and there's sometimes a colony of night herons in the reeds at the bottom of the mountain. The unmistakable white storks don't breed in the park but they nest close by and often feed around the lake's edges. The lake's **speciality birds** include the purple gallinule, a rarity rather like a huge red-billed coot; the marbled teal, a small, shy duck with a mottled brown plumage; and the white-headed duck, a universally rare bird which winters in small numbers.

With all these water birds about, as well as small mammals, reptiles and amphibians, the lake also attracts **birds of prey**. Marsh harriers are the most dominant species, identifiable by their upturned wings as they drift over the reed beds and surrounding fields in search of small prey. Of the falcons, peregrine, lanner and kestrel all breed on the mountain, Bonelli's and short-toed eagles wheel high in the sky, and long-legged buzzards breed here too.

Don't ignore the **smaller birds**, either. Reed warblers and great reed warblers breed here in summer, nightingales are common, and bee-eaters breed in the river banks. Quail, the smallest game bird, breed in the park too; listen for their "whic whic" call from the surrounding fields in spring – they're notoriously hard to spot. Moussier's redstarts are common among the scrub on the mountain, and Sardinian warblers are everywhere. Woodchat shrikes perch on telegraph wires and lone trees in summer, and a related and very rare species, the black-headed bush shrike, breeds here in very small numbers. Nightingales, known in Arabic as **bulbuls** – like drab blackbirds but with a loud and mellifluous song – reach the most northerly part of their range in Tunisia (they're primarily Asian and African birds). Incidentally, if you've come with weighty telephoto lenses and other photographic equipment, be discreet, as officially **photography** is not permitted in the park due to a number of military and air bases around it.

---

enter the park from the southeast or the north. The turning for the **southeastern section** of the park is on the Bizerte–Mateur road 7km south of **Tinja**, just after the road crosses the rail line; you can be dropped here by buses and louages travelling between Bizerte and Mateur. The **park gate** can be reached from the main road along 4.5km of good piste across a marsh. Alternatively, you can catch a bus or louage to **Menzel Bourguiba** (see p.179), then try to find a louage or taxi to **Ichkeul**, the settlement by the park gate. A *gardien* should be there to greet you at the gate, but if he's not, you're perfectly all right to continue. The track beyond the gate skirts around the bottom of Jebel Ichkeul, past some domed bathhouses, to a sign for the **ecomuseum** (same hours as park; free) about 3.5km from the gate. The museum, which sits on a ridge above the track (be prepared for a steep climb), is really of interest only to keen ornithologists and geologists, with a good collection of stuffed birds and explanatory maps and diagrams of the lake's ecosystem. For the **northern shore** of the lake, the bus from Bizerte to Sejnane (see p.172) skirts the water's edge, passing both the Douimis and Sejnane marshes.

If you're staying at the *Ichkeul Hôtel* (see p.179) outside Menzel Bourguiba, you can take the local bus to Tinja and hitch from there either along the north shore or, with more promise, the south side of the lake to the gate mentioned above. Finally, note that a **bicycle** would really come into its own here; see p.178 for details on renting one in Bizerte.

The Raf Raf coastline

A beach of legendary beauty, **Raf Raf**, 30km east of Bizerte, is the best-known attraction on a stretch of coast that remains surprisingly undeveloped. Conventional tourist facilities are sparse in this area of conservative farmers, but the rewards are there if you make the effort to explore, with some beautiful clifftop scenery towards **Cap Farina** and another wonderful beach at **Ras Sidi el Mekki**.

Transport to the area can be confusing until you master the local geography. Frequent buses from Bizerte and several from Tunis go to **Ras Jebel**, from where local services continue to Raf Raf town and down to the beach (specify "Raf Raf Plage"). Plenty of louages ply the same route, and some travel directly between Bizerte and Raf Raf Plage. During summer you can usually get a louage direct to the beach from Tunis as well, though you'll have to fight for a seat at weekends. For **Ghar el Melh**, there are a few buses from Bizerte and more frequent transport from Ras Jebel.

Ras Jebel

At the centre of the region is **RAS JEBEL**, a farming town which makes few concessions to visitors and is really only useful as a transport connection. The road into town from the east divides before reaching the centre, with the main square and its towering minaret straight ahead and the **bus** and **louage station** a short way along the left-hand fork and down another street to the left. Just after the point where the road forks, a street drops to the right, passing a large **café** and the **market** on the left before reaching a basic **hotel**, the *Okba* (☎72 449 840; ❷), further round to the right. The town's single other notable feature is a Lee Cooper jeans factory.

Although Ras Jebel has its own **beach**, 2.5km down a signposted road, it's small and gets crowded in July and August, when families camp there on a long-term basis and conditions become less than hygienic. You can avoid this just by walking along to the west until you find a deserted cove.

Raf Raf beach

The real attraction on this part of the coast is **Raf Raf Beach**, an almost endless curve of white sand backed by dunes, forest and steeply sloping fields of figs, vines and rustling cane. At its eastern edge is the long claw of **Cap Farina**, the cliffs of its ridge hidden in shadow or gleaming in the sun, to the west a small, knobbly hill, and out in the bay, the rocky islet of **Pilau**. If you feel an urge to do other than swim, sunbathe and eat grapes and figs (some of the best in the country), Cap Farina makes a spectacular walk. The easiest way up is from Raf Raf town, along a track to an old watchtower. More daring is to climb the gash of sand visible on the mountain from the beach, from the top of which the whole coast opens out, west to Raf Raf's curve, east down to the lagoon of Ghar el Melh and Ras Sidi el Mekki beach.

The beach is popular, formidably so at weekends, but even then it's easy to escape the crowds. The friendly *Hôtel Dalia* (☎72 441668; ❺) has good, if overpriced, en-suite **rooms**, some with sea views. If you ask around, you might also be able to find some villas for rent. Otherwise, you could rent one of the straw shacks (in season) or sleep out if you're discreet.

Ghar el Melh

GHAR EL MELH, 4km along the coast from Raf Raf beach, means "Cave of Salt", perhaps a reference to the lagoon which the River Medjerda has created around the town, ruining the harbour facilities that once made Porto Farina (as it was then called) a notorious haunt of **pirates**. In 1654 the English Admiral Blake attacked and destroyed the port, in an action described by Lieutenant Colonel Sir Lambert Playfair, the British consul in Algiers, as "one of the most brilliant victories in the history of the British Navy". By the next century, however, the port had been rebuilt with three forts and an arsenal. Piracy and smuggling continued to be the town's main source of revenue well into the nineteenth century – carried out, for the most part, by the British and the Maltese. The government only clamped down in 1834, when a huge arsenal – kept by one of the Maltese smugglers in his basement – exploded, taking many of the surrounding houses with it. Ahmed Bey tried to turn the port to more legitimate trade, building new jetties and forts. But by this time the estuary had started to silt up, and today Ghar el Melh is a small farming town, half asleep under the green flank of the mountain, where the **forts** and the crumbling walls of the **old port** are steeped in a sense of nostalgic melancholy.

Ras Sidi el Mekki

Ghar el Melh should really be left to slumber gently, but its peace would be forever destroyed if long-standing plans to develop the beach at **RAS SIDI EL MEKKI**, 5km beyond, at the tip of Cap Farina, are ever fulfilled. The authorities like to call this beach "Polynesian", which does at least convey the stillness of the water and the isolation. It's little known for the moment, though, and the facilities consist of just a few straw huts in season, a **café-restaurant** with good fresh fish (mid-May to Sept daily noon–6pm; Oct to mid-May Sat & Sun only), and a few holiday **villas** for rent (ask around), so camping is the ideal solution.

The turn-off to Ras Sidi El Mekki is on the left just over 2km beyond Ghar el Melh, from where the beach is another 3km. The right-hand fork in the road veers off to a modern fishing **port**. If you don't have your own transport, you'll have to hitch to the beach or walk from Ghar el Melh, where the bus stops.

Utica and around

The ancient site of **UTICA** (Tues–Sun: April to mid-Sept 8am–7pm; mid-Sept to March 8.30am–5.30pm; 2.1TD, camera 1TD) lies in the broad alluvial plain of the **River Medjerda**, whose banks, so British traveller Sir Grenville Temple (see p.561) reported in the nineteenth century, "were witnesses to the well-known combat between the forces of Attilius Regulus and an enormous serpent, in 225 BC". The river – the only permanently flowing one in the country – plays a vital part in irrigating the north, but for centuries it has also been silting up this section of the coast, locking in what were once great ports. Utica lies just off the main Tunis–Bizerte road, a two-kilometre walk from the village of **Zana**, and just over 30km southeast of Bizerte.

Now a smallish site marooned 10km from the sea, Utica predated Carthage as the first **Phoenician** trading post on this coastline. It never really reconciled itself to Carthage's supremacy, backing the losing mercenary army in its revolt against Carthage in 240 BC and then supporting Rome in the 146 BC campaign which ended in Carthage's destruction; a century later it supported **Pompey** against Julius Caesar in the Roman Civil War. One of Pompey's backers, **Cato the Younger**, was in control of the city when he heard of Caesar's decisive victory at Thapsus, near Mahdia. Having decided to kill himself rather than surrender, he fell on his sword in time-honoured fashion, and when doctors tried to repair the damage, he thrust them aside and rent his innards asunder with his bare hands. This was the sort of gesture which went down well with the Romans: they immediately erected a statue of Cato, facing heroically out to sea, and enshrined him in national myth. With the resurrection of Carthage as the new Roman capital, though, Utica began a decline that was then accelerated as silt from the river gradually put an end to the city's port and *raison d'être*.

The site and museum

Despite the size and wealth of the Roman city, its remains are not extensive. The central feature is the **House of the Cascade**, whose doorway still stands. The private residence of some very well-off citizen, it gives an impression of staggering affluence even without walls or decoration. The ground floor was almost entirely devoted to entertaining, with the main complex of rooms to the right of the pool in the centre of the house. In the middle of this side, the *triclinium* (dining room) is identifiable by the U-shape of its floor decoration. Couches, on which Romans lay to eat their meals (Cato was a source of amazement because, Stoic that he was, he actually ate sitting up), occupied the three sides around the walls. Of the orange and green paving in the middle of the floor, the orange "Numidian" marble came from Chemtou (see p.206), while the green was imported from Euboea, today's Evvia, in Greece. On either side of the *triclinium* is a garden well and another reception room: one well contains the running fountain arrangement (all in mosaics) which gives the house its name. The other rooms around the central pool are smaller reception chambers, except for a stable to the left of the entrance; note the feeding troughs. The stable for the horse-drawn carriage is on the other side of the entrance, with a wide doorway.

The residences surrounding the House of the Cascade are less affluent, but still part of an exclusive district. The **Forum** was only a block away to the north, beyond the **Punic necropolis** excavated at a lower level, and the sea was not much further. A little way west along the ancient shoreline – remi-

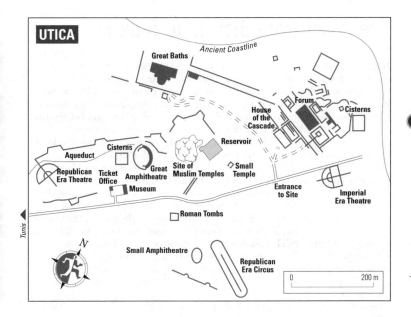

niscent of Carthage's Antonine Baths (see p.126) – stood Utica's own massive **baths complex**, whose remains are still visible. It is not certain where the shore was when the Medjerda started silting it up, but it would have been close to the bottom of the slope – from the House of the Cascade's roof you could watch ships sailing in from Spain, Carthage and Alexandria.

A few hundred metres west of the site entrance is a **museum** containing mainly domestic and funerary objects, illustrating the life led by Uticans for more than a thousand years. The Punic pottery and grave reliefs (note the angular Punic script) in the right-hand room date from its first six hundred years. The Phoenicians were traders and merchants, and when they weren't fighting the Greeks they were doing business with them; look out for a fine Greek *skyphos* (wine goblet) painted with a Maenad chasing a Satyr. The Roman relics, as so often, are prosaically domestic, and the quantity of marble statuary is a clear indication of the city's wealth. None of it is of a particularly high standard – the Reclining Ariadne and Satyr (recognizable by his tail) are poor versions of stock garden figures – and because North Africa has no white marble of its own, all this had to be imported at great expense from elsewhere in the Mediterranean.

Kalaat el Andalous

KALAAT EL ANDALOUS, 5km from Utica as the crow flies, is the village just visible to the northeast of Utica, on what was once another headland in the sea. Not much is left now of the original village founded by Spanish immigrants during the seventeenth century, but the walk from Utica across the rich river plain is pleasant, and there's a magnificent view from the steep cliff on the far side – from Bou Kornine and Sidi Bou Saïd in the south to Cap Farina in the north. **Buses** #31b and #44 from place Belhouane in Tunis pass through here regularly.

The coast from Bizerte to Tabarka

North of Bizerte, the beaches run in shallow curves until the hump of **Cap Blanc**, 8km along the coast, often said to be the northernmost point in Africa, although that is actually a few kilometres west at **Ras Angela** (aka Ras Ben Sekka). As with all the beaches on the north coast, when the wind blows here it can feel pretty exposed, but in summer it's never unpleasant. The Roman writer Pliny the Younger tells how a boy out swimming here was befriended one day by a dolphin so tame that it carried him out to sea for rides. The dolphin soon acquired a cult following, but this was too much for the local bureaucrats of the Roman Empire, who had the dolphin killed.

For a distant view of Cap Blanc, catch a #6 bus from boulevard Hassan en Nouri in Bizerte to the village of **BECHATEUR**, a side trip which reveals some of the unexpectedly bleak scenery behind the coast at this point. Bechateur itself is a tiny hamlet on a windswept hilltop that was once inhabited by the Romans, and blocks of their masonry can be seen in the walls of the village here and there. The bus stops at Bechateur, but a track continues for 15km to the beach of **Sidi Abdel Waheb** – worth exploring, if you have the means of getting down there. The area still yields unexpected discoveries: between Cap Blanc and Ras Angela, at **Aïn Damous**, a recently discovered underwater cave is said, rather implausibly, to be an entrance to Roman catacombs leading all the way to Utica.

From Ras Angela, the coastline consists of a series of isolated coves, backed by increasingly thick forests, whose inaccessibility pays dividends to those in search of wilder shores. Most of the coves are uninhabited, putting them beyond the reach of all but the most dedicated. Unless you have your own transport, you'll need plenty of time and you'll probably have to negotiate a taxi or charter a louage from **SEJNANE**, 40km west of Mateur on the GP7. The best base for accessing the beaches, it's a peaceful country town, living off agriculture and mining, and with its own unique style of **pottery**. Pots and beaches aside, there's little reason to stop here (unless for the Thursday **market**) except to enquire about transport out again – which is mainly back to Mateur.

Due north of Sejnane are the remote beaches of the promontory of **Cap Serrat**, down a well-signposted thirteen-kilometre road that turns off the C51 and runs steadily down through heavily forested land. At the end of the road the mountains subside into a broad valley with a scattered settlement and a spectacular empty **beach**. If you have a 4WD, you might want to head west along a sandy track to the next named beach, **Sidi Mechrig**, which boasts a small settlement and a **hotel**, *Auberge Sidi Mechrig* (no phone; ❷), as well as some scanty but picturesque **Roman ruins** of a bathhouse. For an easier approach to Sidi Mechrig, continue from Sejnane along the GP7 to just before **Tamra**, where a potholed eighteen-kilometre road leads off to the right.

Next in the line of named beaches along the coast is **Cap Negre**, reached by a road signposted about 6km west of the Sidi Mechrig turning. It's barely inhabited except for a National Guard post occupying the remains of a French coral-fishing establishment, sacked in 1741 by the same expedition that ejected the Genoese from their fort at Tabarka. West of **Nefza**, 15km beyond the Cap Negre turning, a road leads down past a large reservoir to yet another beach, **Zouiraa**.

Just after **RAS RAJEL**, 12km east of Tabarka, the road passes a **Commonwealth War Cemetery**, whose green pastures face a petrol station on the other side of the road. From the middle of Ras Rajel, a new road runs 2km north to the long-promised international **airport** (see p.188), whose arrival is a sign of changing times in the Tabarka area.

Tabarka

The setting of **TABARKA** is all that anyone could ask for – a natural harbour first used by the Carthaginians, situated where the Khroumirie Mountains subside suddenly into a fertile plain and dominated by an offshore rock crowned by a **Genoese Castle**. The surrounding region is one of the richest natural habitats in Tunisia, with cork oak forests around Aïn Draham (see p.193) dropping down to the "coral coast" around Tabarka.

Roman **Thabraca** was the main port of exit for Chemtou marble from south of the mountains (see p.206), and thanks to this and grain exports it became a substantial town, wealthy enough to produce the fine early Christian mosaics on display in the Bardo Museum in Tunis. Decline set in after the fall of the Empire, but the eleventh-century geographer El Edrisi was still impressed by "ancient monuments of fine construction", and by the twelfth century trade was sufficiently brisk as to convince the commander of a shipwrecked Genoese boat in the service of the Knights of St John to stay. His descendants kindly bought the island in 1542 and built the castle on it (see p.191). The **French** colonials used Tabarka as a hunting resort (wild boar and game birds) in a small way; in 1952, it was still considered remote enough to be a suitable place of exile for Bourguiba. **Coral** diving and **cork** growing in the mountain forests behind the town, as well as fishing, farming and tourism, provide the area with its industry and income today.

Tabarka's success as a **resort** has taken what was basically a sleepy country town by surprise. Independent travellers used to arrive in July and early August, making the atmosphere like a big easy-going campsite. When they left, the town would settle back to being a market centre (the Friday souk is just out of town on the Aïn Draham road) and small fishing port. Alas, the tourist authorities and developers are trying to recreate in Tabarka the perceived success of resort developments like Sousse. Along with the new airport, several massive hotels and a golf course have been conjured out of the previously pristine beach running east of town, and more hotels are under construction; downtown, the fishing port has been endowed with an oversized development called **Porto Corallo**, complete with a fifty-berth marina reminiscent of a downmarket Port el Kantaoui, while old buildings continue to be torn down and replaced with unattractive apartment blocks. Clearly, Tabarka is undergoing significant change and you're going to find yourself sharing it with more and more fellow visitors, but for now it remains a place of considerable charm, far prettier and more laid-back than Tunisia's east-coast resorts.

Arrival and information

Ignoring the sprawling modern "Medina" – something of a slum – the town itself is tiny: essentially just a main street, **avenue Bourguiba**, and a few blocks on either side. In the middle of avenue Bourguiba is Tabarka's main square, where you'll find a covered market and the town hall. From the main square, avenue Bourguiba runs northwest towards the Needles on the coast (see p.191) and in the other direction towards the roundabout for Bizerte and Aïn Draham. Running parallel to avenue Bourguiba are avenue 7 Novembre and, next to the beach, the Route Touristique, which leads from the Porto Corallo development past the regional **tourist office** (July & Aug Mon–Thurs 8am–8pm, Fri & Sat 8am–2pm; Sept–June Mon–Thurs 8.30am–1pm & 3–5.45pm, Fri & Sat 8.30am–1.30pm; ☎78 673 555) and continues east to the *zone touristique*, known as **Tabarka Montazah**, where you'll find the big hotels and a golf course.

Moving on from Tabarka

For a list of destinations and journey times, see Travel details on p.211.
Flights out of Tabarka's airport (☏78 680 005) are infrequent charters to continental Europe. From the SNTRI **bus** station (☏78 670 404) there are services to Tunis via Nefza (where you can change for a louage to Béja), Sejnane and Mateur, and one via Béja; for Aïn Draham, Jendouba, Le Kef, Bou Salem or Bizerte, use the SRT Jendouba station (☏78 670 087). SRT Béja runs buses to Béja, which stop in Tabarka's main square; check also with SNTRI to see who has the next bus out. **Louages** – most of them for Jendouba via Aïn Draham – leave from avenue Bourguiba by the roundabout southeast of town. Otherwise, **hitching** to Aïn Draham is pretty standard practice.

The **airport** is 14km east of town near Ras Rajel (see p.186); if you arrive here you'll have to get a **taxi** into town (around 7TD), hitch a lift with a hotel bus or walk 2km straight ahead to the main road and flag down a louage or bus. In town there are two **bus stations**: SNTRI at 12 rue du Peuple and SRT Jendouba at 72 av Bourguiba. SRT Béja buses stop in Tabarka's main square. **Louages** arrive at the southern end of avenue Bourguiba, opposite the *Hôtel Mimosas* turn-off near the main roundabout. Incidentally, the Mateur–Tabarka rail line shown on many road maps is well and truly defunct.

Accommodation

The old town, on and around avenue Bourguiba, is the best place for budget **accommodation**, while the *zone touristique* east of town offers more upscale alternatives. The latter hotels are within forty minutes' walking distance, and the inevitable **tourist train** links the *zone* with the town (Porto Corallo) in summer. There are also **taxis** (2TD) and hourly **buses** at a quarter to the hour (more frequently in summer) to the hotels, leaving from outside the BNA bank on the corner of avenue Bourguiba and rue Ali Chaawani. Most hotels are half price or even cheaper in the low season.

The town centre

Les Aiguilles av Bourguiba ☏78 673 789, ☏78 673 604. One of the new developments, comfortable and pleasant if a little overpriced. **❻**

Andalous Corner of av Bourguiba and av Hédi Chaker ☏78 670 600, ☏78 671 132. The smartest of the hotels in the old town, with comfortable, well-equipped rooms and balconies. Negotiable rates. **❻**

Corail Corner of av Bourguiba and rue Tazerka ☏ & ☏78 643 082. Large, clean rooms with sink, plus communal toilets and showers, but it charges far too much for such basic facilities. A new block of en-suite rooms is promised for 2005. **❹**

Mamia 3 rue de Tunis ☏78 671058, ☏78 670 638. The best budget option, with basic but cosy rooms (with toilets) set around a courtyard. **❸**

Les Mimosas Up the hill above town ☏78 673 028, ☏78 673 276, ☏www.darhotels.com. The elegant old-fashioned alternative to the newer hotels. The rooms in the old wing have been updated and offer stupendous sea views; those in the modern wing don't have quite such good views

and lack balconies. There is a small pool and terrace café. Recommended. **❻**

Novelty 68 av Bourguiba, just east of the central square ☏78 670 176, ☏78 673 008. Reasonably smart and comfortable family-run place, though overpriced. **❻**

De la Plage 11 av 7 Novembre ☏78 670 039, ☏78 670332. Bright and clean, offering basic rooms without showers and smart en-suite a/c rooms with satellite TV in a modern extension. Both types of room are good value, particularly off season. **❹**

Résidence Tabarka Porto Corallo ☏78 670 840. Recently built time-share block, which has studio apartments with kitchenettes and larger apartments for rent by the day; book ahead in summer. Residents get to use the pool and gym. **❺**

The zone touristique

Abou Nawas Montazah ☏78 673 532, ☏78 673 530, ☏www.abounawas.com. One of the more tastefully designed *zone* hotels, with facilities including an Olympic-sized pool and five tennis courts. **❼**

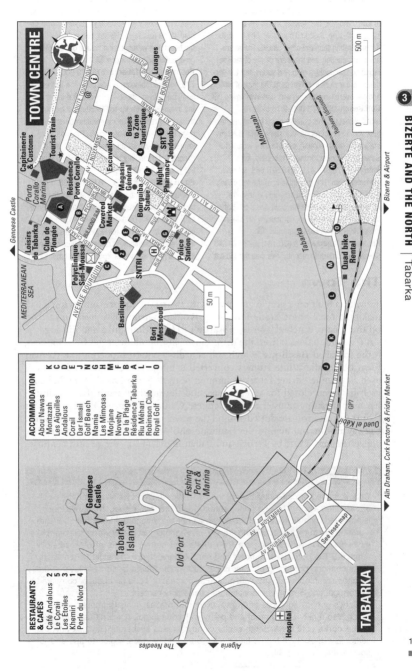

RESTAURANTS & CAFÉS

Café Andalous	2
Le Corail	5
Les Étoiles	3
Khemiri	1
Perle du Nord	4

ACCOMMODATION

Abou Nawas	K
Montazah	C
Les Aiguilles	D
Andalous	E
Corail	J
Dar Ismail	N
Golf Beach	G
Mamia	H
Les Mimosas	M
Morjane	F
Novelty	B
De la Plage	A
Résidence Tabarka	L
Riu Méhari	I
Robinson Club	O
Royal Golf	

TOWN CENTRE

MEDITERRANEAN SEA

Genoese Castle ▲

Porto Corallo Marina

Capitainerie & Customs

Tourist Train

Loisirs de Tabarka

Club de Plongée

Résidence Porto Corallo

Excavations

Covered Market

Magasin Général

Buses to Zone Touristique

Bourguiba Statue

SRT

Night Club

Pharmacie

SNTRI Jendouba

Police Station

Polyclinique Sidi-Moussa

Louages

Basilique

Borj Messaoud

0 — 50 m

TABARKA

Genoese Castle

Tabarka Island

Old Port

Fishing Port & Marina

Hospital

See Inset map

AV 7 NOVEMBRE

AV BOURGUIBA

◀ The Needles   ◀ Algeria

▲ Ain Draham, Cork Factory & Friday Market

▶ Bizerte & Airport

Montazah

Tabarka

Oued el Kebil

ROUTE TOURISTIQUE

GP7

Quad bike Rental

Banlieue (disused)

0 — 500 m

Dar Ismail ☎78 670 188, ℻78 670 343, ℮hoteldarismail@shti.com.tn. The closest hotel to town, and also the newest, this is the only five-star on the strip, though it's unclear why it merits a higher rating than the other places. The rooms are smart enough and there are plenty of facilities, including two pools, a gym and sauna, but the gardens were a work in progress at the time of writing and the overall impression was underwhelming. **❽**

Golf Beach ☎78 673 002, ℻78 673918, ℮tit@planet.tn. This opulent place has all the facilities you'd expect for its four stars, but the rooms are a little disappointing, despite their wonderful views of the ocean or the hills behind. **❼**

Morjane ☎78 673 411, ℻78 673 888, ℮www .darhotels.com. The granddaddy of the lot, dating from 1968 and, like most veterans of that era, its ideals and standards have slipped a bit. But it's still reasonable value, particularly off season. Horse-riding available in summer. **❻**

Riu Méhari Tabarka ☎78 670 184, ℻78 673 943, ℮www.riu.com. Until recently, this was the top cat here, part of a Spanish group, with all the facilities you'd expect, plus a small thalassotherapy centre. It also has roomy self-catering bungalows over the road at the *Résidence Méhari*, set well back from the beach but within a sand wedge of the golfing greens. Bungalows for two **❼**, hotel **❽**

Robinson Club Tabarka ☎78 670 000, ℻78 671 770, ℮www.robinson-tunisie.com. The furthest hotel from town, about 4km away, and easily the swankiest, with tip-top facilities including a thalassotherapy centre, clay tennis courts and a huge theatre for evening shows. The rooms are immaculate, with all the mod cons you would expect. Caters mainly to German package tourists. Full board only; **❾**

Royal Golf ☎78 673 899, ℻78 673 838, ℮royal .golf@gnet.tn. Set back a little way from the beach, this place was built in 1994 and is already starting to look a bit dated (as well as overpriced compared to its neighbours). On the plus side, it has plenty of facilities, is close to the golf course and has great sea views from some rooms. **❼**

The Town

Tabarka is built on a simple grid plan, with the **main square** and its town hall making a focal point. Some interesting Roman remains have been unearthed on the square, watched over by a **statue** of Habib Bourguiba and his dog.

A few minutes' walk from the main square, just uphill from the *Café Andalous*, is the so-called **Basilique**, which was actually a cistern supplying the Roman town before the White Fathers converted it into a church. The garden is still used as a venue during Tabarka's summer festivals (see p.193), but the building itself has been closed for several years, and the small museum that was inside has been awaiting transfer to the Genoese Castle ever since. Other patches of Roman excavation are dotted around the town, including the **Borj Messaoud** halfway up the hill behind the Basilique, also originally a Roman cistern but converted into a fort by French and Italian merchants in the twelfth century.

Cork

Cork is made from the outer bark of the cork oak, which grows all around the western Mediterranean. The first cork **harvest**, when the tree is about 15–20 years old, is achieved by making a careful cut – so as not to damage the inner bark beneath – around the trunk just above the ground, and another just below where the branches begin. Four vertical cuts are then made and oblong panels of cork carefully removed. The outer bark regrows and can be harvested every eight to ten years. Trees continue producing cork for about 150 years. Tunisia is a small player in the Mediterranean cork industry, with only three percent of world production, compared to Portugal and Spain, who account for over eighty percent.

Cork's springy lightness is due to millions of tiny air pockets trapped within it, which also make it waterproof and pretty well soundproof. It wasn't used to make **bottle corks** until the fifteenth century, and that was almost its only use until the veritable explosion of recent times – life buoys, table mats, cigarette tips and, of course, floor and wall tiles.

Coral

Mediterranean **coral**, Tabarka's favourite souvenir, has been collected for jewellery use for centuries, and was one of the luxury items exported from North Africa to Europe. Avenue Bourguiba in Tabarka is lined with shops selling jewellery made by local artisans out of the coral brought up by divers, at prices considerably lower than in Tunis. The coral is now fast declining and has been listed as an endangered species – think twice, therefore, before buying a coral souvenir in one of the many shops throughout northern Tunisia.

Along with coral (and the ubiquitous stuffed camels), **cork** is one of the most prominent handicrafts on sale in Tabarka, thanks largely to a factory a couple of kilometres outside town on the Aïn Draham road. The best place to look for cork products is the shop belonging to Hmissi Abdelmagid Ben Brahim on the roundabout at the southern end of avenue Bourguiba, although it is due be closed for several months in 2005 for renovation or possibly relocation to the town centre; ask at the tourist office for details.

The Genoese Castle

Compared with the **Genoese Castle**, a twenty-minute walk from the centre over a causeway, the town centre's minor monuments seem rather feeble. The castle's origins were as dramatic as its appearance is now: in 1541 the Turkish corsair Khair ed Din Barbarossa surrendered it to Charles V of Spain in return for his colleague Dragut, who had been languishing in a Christian jail, and the next year Charles sold the coral fishing rights and the island to a Genoese family called Lomellini. Having built the castle and enough of a town to support twelve hundred inhabitants, they managed to stay, despite Turkish control of the mainland, for two centuries. One of their main sources of income came from acting as agents for ransoming slaves in Tunis, a service for which they charged a three-percent commission. Then in 1741 they found themselves in need of ransoming when an Ottoman expedition sacked the outposts here and at Cap Negre, selling the Christian inhabitants into slavery in Tunis, where the name Tabarchini still survives.

The romance of the place was dealt a blow when the French built a causeway to the castle's island after World War II, but the silhouette on its rocky pinnacle has lost none of its allure – it's a fabulous place, especially at sunset when the sun sinks gingerly over the Needles and glints in the other direction off the cliffs of La Galite (see p.192). The castle has long been occupied by the military, although in theory part of it has been set aside to house a **museum**, formerly in the Basilique, of mosaic reproductions, objects from local excavations and a few old anchors.

The coast

The **beach** east of town stretches 4km round the bay, where the presence of the coral makes for some of the best **snorkelling** in the Mediterranean. You should be able to find some space on this beach, even at its most crowded. A kilometre or so down towards the *zone touristique* hotels, a few remnants of World War II wrecks just protrude from the water.

The coast west of town is a series of rocky coves whose beginning is marked by the grotesquely shaped **Needles**, jagged blades of rock standing in a row that juts out towards the castle. For a pleasant **walk** on this side of town, go up rue Farhat Hached from avenue Habib Bourguiba, and then take a path off to the right, which scrambles up to the road by the army camp. Turn left

La Galite

La Galite is a small volcanic archipelago 40km off the coast, 60km from Tabarka. The largest of the islands is only 5km long, with a tiny seasonal population that at one time included Bourguiba (on yet another bout of exile). The sea here is rich in fish, with great snorkelling in summer if you get the chance, and this is one of the only places in the Mediterranean where it's possible to see the exceedingly rare **Mediterranean monk seal**, numbered in the low hundreds. La Galite is a strictly protected area – until recently closed to all except genuine scientific expeditions – but a project is now underway to repopulate the islands with a view to expanding tourism. At the moment, the only way of visiting La Galite is on a day-trip organized by Loisirs de Tabarka, at the fishing port (☎78 670 664); the fee of 70TD per person includes snorkelling, a walk around the main island and a barbecue lunch.

along this road, and follow it as it winds up through shrub-covered hillside. The sandy rock doesn't support a great variety of flowers, but there are some unusual species – the Mediterranean **medlar tree** and heavily grazed **mastic trees** and **Kermes oaks**. Turn right off the road and head towards the coast. Look closely under the **white-flowered rockroses** on the hill and you'll find the extraordinary parasitic plant **cytinus**: with red and yellow waxy flowers and no green leaves, it gets its energy from its host plant, and is particularly common around here. In between the shrubs is **romulea**, an abundant and very beautiful tiny purple relative of the crocus. You can return to Tabarka along the cliffs – where blue rock thrushes are common – and pass above the Needles on your way.

Eating and drinking

Fish is the main source of sustenance in these parts, and excellent it is too, with large, succulent whole specimens being the rule in cheap places as well as the more expensive **restaurants**. Of the *gargotes*, *Les Étoiles* (daily 7am–9pm), at 11 rue du Peuple, is one of the best, with meals for under 5TD and a good-value *plat du jour* for 1.8TD. The friendly *Restaurant Le Corail* (daily 11am–9pm) on avenue Bourguiba offers a more congenial setting with a small but tasty menu and a filling three-course set meal for 7TD.

For something a bit classier, try the mid-priced *Khemiri* at 11 av Bourguiba (daily noon–4pm & 7–10pm), which serves delicious seafood for around 15TD for two courses (unless you go for a 70TD lobster) but no desserts. The food at the *Hôtel Mimosas* (daily 12.30–2.30pm & 7.30–9.30pm) is similarly priced, with a set menu for 15TD, while the views are unsurpassed and the atmosphere more refined; it's also good for a quiet drink or a game of pool. Also in this range is the excellent *Perle du Nord* (daily 10am–midnight), at the corner of avenue Bourguiba and rue Ali Zouaoui, serving seafood specialities à la carte for around 15TD, unless you snap up the lobster (70TD apiece); note, however, that the bar takes over as the main business off season, making it pretty rowdy and smoky. The restaurants attached to the hotels *Novelty* (daily noon–3pm & 6–10pm) and *Aiguilles* (daily 11.30am–3pm & 5.30–10pm) both have set meals for 10TD, but are pretty charmless.

For tea or coffee and a *chicha*, don't miss Tabarka's trendiest rendezvous, the *Café Andalous*, on the corner of rue du Peuple and rue Hedi Chaker, with its bizarre, and rather atmospheric, collection of bric-a-brac. As for **nightclubs**, hotels *Abou Nawas Montazah* and *Royal Golf*, both in the *zone touristique*, have discos where local boys try out their latest chat-up lines on holidaymakers.

Listings

Banks The STB bank at 30 av Bourguiba and Habitat on av Bourguiba next to the *Aiguilles* hotel both have ATMs which accept Visa, MasterCard and Cirrus.

Boat trips Trips in a glass-bottomed boat are run in summer by Aquavision, in the marina next to the Porto Corallo development. You can even head all the way out to the La Galite archipelago on a day-trip organized by Loisirs de Tabarka (see box opposite).

Car rental Hertz (℡78 670 670) and Europcar (℡78 670 834) have offices in the Porto Corallo development. The Centre d'Animation Touristique Ben Ali (℡98 213 074), near the *Hôtel Morjane* in the *zone touristique*, rents out mopeds and runs quad-bike excursions.

Diving The Club de Plongée at the fishing port (℡78 671 478), where the local coral divers are trained, offers a *baptême* (first dive) to outsiders for 20TD and training to the first grade for 310TD, including membership of the club, equipment and a diploma. The course lasts seven days and includes up to ten dives; you must be over 14 and have a medical certificate, which both the club and the Polyclinique Sidi-Moussa on av Bourguiba can provide. Loisirs de Tabarka (see box opposite) offers similar diving packages. The *Hôtel Riu Mehari* also has a dive centre (℡78 671 444), which offers introductory dives for 15TD and a range of courses from first grade (230TD) up to instructor level (600TD).

Festivals Tabarka is developing a reputation for the quality of its summer music festivals, the main one being the week-long jazz festival at the beginning of July, along with a *raï* festival at the end of June, a world-music festival at the end of August and a Latin music festival at the beginning of September. There are also concerts of local traditional music through most of July and August. Most events take place in the garden of the Basilique or at the *Café Andalous*.

Golf The entrance to the scenic eighteen-hole golf course (℡78 670 028, ℡78 674 026, @www.tabarkagolf.com) is 4km east of town after the *Hôtel Morjane* in the *zone touristique*.

Hammams rue Farhat Hached, on the corner of rue de Tunis (daily: men 5am–noon & 5–10pm; women noon–5pm).

Hospital Western end of rue Farhat Hached ℡78 673 661. The 24hr Polyclinique Sidi-Moussa is at the northern end of av Bourguiba (℡78 671 200).

Internet access Publinet, near the tourist office on the Route Touristique (daily 8am–8pm; 2TD/hr).

Pharmacy There's a night pharmacy, Noureddine, at 17 rue Ali Zouaoui (℡78 673 314).

Police rue de Tunis ℡78 671 021.

Post office rue Hedi Chaker (country hours).

Supermarket Magasin Général on the main square (Mon–Sat 8am–7pm, Sun 8am–1pm).

Taxis AlloTaxi ℡78 673 636.

Tours The *Mimosas* and the big hotels in the *zone touristique* all organize day excursions to places such as Bulla Regia and the Khroumirie Mountains.

Aïn Draham and the Khroumirie Mountains

The small eruption of forested mountains in the northwest corner of Tunisia is called the **Khroumirie**, but in practice you're more likely to hear the area referred to as **Aïn Draham**, after its one sizeable town and effective capital. The region stretches from Tabarka on the coast to **Fernana** 50km south, and its mountains rise steeply from the sea to a height of over 1000m, covered with leafy forests of **cork oak** (see box on p.190) and ferns – and reputedly bristling with wild boar – before dipping down to the Medjerda Valley at Jendouba. This sudden mountainous barrier gives rise to enormous amounts of rain which never reach other parts of the country, and in winter it's not unusual to find a metre of snow at Aïn Draham. In summer the mountain air is refreshing, and Aïn Draham has become an unassuming resort, though there is little here in the way of sights.

Aïn Draham

In **AÏN DRAHAM**, 25km south of Tabarka and 800m above sea level, the French tried to recreate a small Alpine village in what was the equivalent of the British Shimla in India, and many of the older buildings appear to have been spirited out of Switzerland and the Jura mountains in France and plumped down on this remote mountain in North Africa. Today Aïn Draham (the name means "Springs of Silver") is popular with Tunisians who can afford to escape the heat of the capital – which means that prices have been pushed a little higher than usual. Most holidaymakers here rent out villas on the outskirts of the town for a longish stay, leaving the centre largely unspoiled. The steep main street, **avenue Bourguiba**, lined with a few cafés, general stores and the town's prettiest building, the **police station**, runs down the flank of Jebel Bir, the highest point in the area at 1014m. It doesn't quite have the full Swiss Alpine atmosphere sometimes claimed, but the combination of forested slopes, fresh air and red-tiled roofs is European enough for a minaret to look incongruous.

Coming here in summer, it's almost a shock to find exercise suddenly a pleasure instead of a penance. There are two standard **walks** around town. One is to the **Col des Ruines**, the ridge opposite Jebel Bir, which you can either scramble up directly, or gain access to from a side road 1500m north of Aïn Draham off the main Tabarka road. The other is the hike to the summit of **Jebel Bir**, which offers great views – east over mountains shaved with firebreaks like a reverse Mohican hairdo, north to Tabarka on its plain, and west over more mountains into Algeria (you can make out the coastal town of El Kalaa as a white smudge on the horizon). A side road to the summit runs from the main Jendouba road near the *Hôtel Rihana*: the pylon at the top is easy to spot and home in on. Both walks are about a three- or four-hour round-trip from the town and are occasionally steep, but not particularly strenuous.

Practicalities

All buses leave from the **bus station** on avenue 7 Novembre, which forks away from avenue Bourguiba at the bottom of the hill. **Louages** on their way to Tabarka stop opposite the bus station, though they are usually full at this point, while louages for Jendouba and Tunis can be found a couple of hundred metres past the bus station, just below avenue 7 Novembre to the right. Local louages run to Babouch on the Algerian border from next to the Esso station a little way up the Tabarka road. There are also yellow shared **taxis** to Hammam Bourguiba on avenue 7 Novembre just uphill from the bus station.

Most of the necessities of life are to be found along avenue Bourguiba, including the **Syndicat d'Initiative** at no. 57 (variable hours; ☎78 655 052 or 78 655 115), a couple of **banks** and the **post office** (country hours) at no. 114, where you can make international phone calls. On avenue Habib Thameur, which leads off to the right by the Esso station as you come into town from the north, you'll find the municipal **swimming pool**, the regional **hospital** (☎78 655 047) and the Clinique Sidi Abdallah (☎78 655 101).

Accommodation and eating

The town itself has only a couple of **places to stay**. The *Hôtel les Pins* on avenue Bourguiba (☎78 656 200, ⓕ656 182; ❹), just round the corner from the bus station, has clean, pleasant doubles with bathrooms and balconies enjoying pleasant views. Near the top of avenue Bourguiba, the *Hôtel Beau Séjour* (☎78 655363, ⓕ655527; ❹) is a remnant of the French hunting parties, with stuffed boars' heads on its walls, but is to close for extensive renovations until spring 2006. A bit further still, the *Maison des Jeunes* (☎78 655 027) offers the usual Colditz-like accommodation. More attractive and remote are three alternatives in the surrounding forests, easily reached by taxi from the bus station. The *Hôtel Nour el Aïn* (☎78 655 000, ⓕ78 655 185; ❺), in the trees just above the

Col des Ruines turn-off 1500m north of town, is reasonably priced and quite plush, with well-equipped rooms, an open fire in the lobby, an indoor pool, hammam and gym. A kilometre beyond the *Maison des Jeunes*, on the road to Jendouba, the *Royal Rihana* (☎78 655 391, ℱ78 655 578; ❺) is older and not quite as swanky as the *Nour el Aïn* but has comfortable rooms, an indoor pool, a super bar and offers **horse-riding** expeditions into the mountains. The third, and newest, option is the *Hôtel La Forêt* (☎78 655 302, ℱ78 655 355, ⓦ www.hotellaforet.com.tn; ❽), with all mod cons and Chemtou marble staircases in a pleasant setting 5km south of town, but overpriced compared to the other two.

Aïn Draham is one of the few places in the country where you can eat **pork**, with wild boar available in the *Hôtel Beau Séjour* and other hunting-oriented hotels during the season; the *Beau Séjour* does a set menu for 15TD (daily noon–3pm & 7–10.30pm). Other town eating places, mostly in avenue Bourguiba, are cheaper, including *El Qods* (daily 7am–8.30pm), more or less opposite the *Beau Séjour*, and, further down the hill, *Khemir* at no. 77 (daily 7am–10pm).

The Khroumirie Mountains

Looking over the **Khroumirie Mountains**, it's easy to see why the **Khroumir Berber** tribespeople who lived here were virtually independent of the country's rulers. They had a reputation for ferocity, regularly raiding the surrounding tribes and even crossing into Algeria to steal herds. But, despite their strength, they kept clear of the dynastic quarrels that embroiled – and destroyed – other tribes. When Mohammed Bey's disgruntled nephew fled here after an abortive coup in 1867, he was sent packing. Fourteen years later, however, the bey's inability to stop cross-border raiding provided the French with the excuse they needed to invade Tunisia from Algeria in 1881.

East below the mountaintop of Jebel Bir lies the lake of the **Beni M'tir dam**, surrounded by forests. A detour south of Aïn Draham leads down here before rejoining the main road just before **Fernana**. The town took its name from the only tree for miles around (now vanished), which stood near this bleak settlement. The tree's singularity gave rise to a legend about its special powers. On their annual tax-collecting rounds the bey's officials never dared penetrate further into the Khroumirie than here. The story goes that the Khroumiris would consult the tree about how little they could get away with declaring, and it would rustle its answer. According to one tale, it was the tree's error of judgement that caused the French invasion.

North of Aïn Draham, the road winds along the edge of the great natural bowl which surrounds the Tabarka plain, the only settlement it passes through being **BABOUCH**, just before the Algerian border. Like Aïn Draham, Babouch was a great hunting centre in colonial times, and the last lion and leopard were shot here around eighty and sixty years ago respectively. Babouch and Aïn Draham are surrounded by **cork oak woodland**, and almost any walk from either will take you through the forests; the valley leading from Babouch towards Hammam Bourguiba is one especially beautiful and rewarding area, although be aware that the troubles in Algeria have made the border area particularly sensitive in the past. This is the only large deciduous forest in Tunisia, and the wildlife is distinctive. You may notice how individual **woodland birds**, familiar from northern Europe, are developing differences that will, in tens of thousands of years, lead them to be classed as separate species. The blue tit here has a black head; the chaffinch is pale, without a red breast; the green woodpecker is greyish and lacks the red "moustache"; and the jay is quite different, with a red, black and white head.

Louages run from Babouch to **HAMMAM BOURGUIBA**, 12km southwest, a resort used by the ex-president. Here you can take a thermal cure – or perhaps an anti-stress massage or ominous-sounding *cure d'enveloppement* – in the four-star *Hammam Bourguiba* (☎78 610 555, ℻78 610 557, ✉info.hb@elmouradi.com; ❻), which has recently been taken over and tarted up by the El Mouradi chain. If you want to pamper yourself for a night, this is the place to do it, with a beautiful alpine setting, spacious rooms and gleaming new facilities for much less than you would pay on the coast. As yet unexcavated **Roman ruins** indicate, as ever, that the Romans were the first to discover the beneficial effects of the waters here, believed to be especially good for respiratory conditions.

The Medjerda Valley

The **Medjerda Valley** is the most fertile and best-watered region of Tunisia. In Roman times it supplied much of the grain that fed Rome, its perennial river, unique in Tunisia, allowing the fields to be irrigated and the grain transported. During the 1930s and 1950s the French improved irrigation by building numerous dams, so harnessing the winter floods for the summer. More recently, their feats were surpassed by Chinese engineers who built a canal and pipeline that takes water to Cap Bon without a single pumping station en route. Most of the valley's towns are prosperous market centres, but the region's main attractions are its Roman ruins, most spectacularly those of **Bulla Regia**. Inevitably and enticingly, the valley forms a stark contrast to the coastal route, and it's straightforward enough to combine both in a looping, wandering journey starting and ending in Tunis.

Medjez el Bab and around

MEDJEZ EL BAB was a seventeenth-century Andalusian foundation on the Roman site of Membressa, but little remains of either except for the mosque just back from the main square and a few miscellaneous fragments in the garden of the town hall. Today it's a main crossing point over the Medjerda, one of a number of small farming centres dotted along the main roads of northern Tunisia.

Built in the seventeenth century (a plaque in the middle dates it at 1088 AH, or 1677 AD), the river **bridge** is the only real reminder of that period, but only by chance did it survive the bitter battles for Medjez in the winter of 1942–43. A **Commonwealth War Cemetery**, 4km west along the Kef road, bears eloquent and emotional witness to the 2904 Commonwealth soldiers killed here; a taxi to it from town will cost around 2TD.

Buses and louages stop in a square just across the bridge, where there are also two **banks**. There are frequent **buses** to Béja and Tunis, and **louages** to Béja,

War graves

The Imperial War Grave Commission, subsequently renamed the Commonwealth Commission, was set up after World War I to arrange for the burial of Britain's **war dead** in specially designed **cemeteries**. Its general principle was to bury the dead near where they died, and wherever possible in the countryside. Timeless English Pastoral was the desired atmosphere, and it's something of a shock to find these little pieces of England, with lawns and trees in the middle of Tunisia. As you move along the seemingly endless rows of names, it's important to recognize the nightmare they represent, yet impossible to fully comprehend it. An unnamed grave means that a body could not be identified from the remains, and headstones are grouped together when several were indistinguishable. The cemeteries are moving, and their spirit is summed up in the words of English war poet Keith Douglas, who fought in Tunisia in 1943 before being killed just after D-Day aged 24: "Remember me when I am dead/And simplify me when I'm dead."

There are **Commonwealth cemeteries** at Medjez el Bab, Messicault (see below), Ras Rajel (see p.192), Oued Zarga (see p.198), Béja (see p.200), Thibar (see p.201), Enfida (see p.217) and Sfax (see p.277). Indian servicemen are buried at Sfax, Jews at Borgel Jewish cemetery in Tunis, and victims of World War I in Bizerte International Cemetery.

American servicemen killed in action in Tunisia (and a number of Commonwealth soldiers) are buried at Carthage American Military Cemetery (see p.128). There are **French** military cemeteries at Enfida (see p.217), Gammarth (see p.131) and Haffouz (see p.327), and a **German** one at Borj Cedria (see p.133).

Tunis and Testour. The **train station** is 2km out of town on the left bank of the river. You could **stay** at the *Hôtel Membressa* (☎78 460 121; ❷), on the west bank of the river overlooking the bridge, though it's something of a dive, frequented mainly by inebriated male clients in the rather raucous bar. They should have food if you ask them early enough.

Around Medjez el Bab

After the war graves experience, you might want to clear your head by taking a taxi-truck or bus up the road to Toukabeur and Chaouach, two villages high on the mountain wall to the north, for a magnificent view over the surrounding countryside and a reminder that Medjez was once a strategic point. **CHAOUACH**, at the end of the road, is built on the site of a Byzantine **fort** on a rocky outcrop, the fort itself assembled from the remains of Roman Sua just below. **TOUKABEUR**, 3km below Chaouach on the same road, has more scant remains – the garage on the main square is a converted Roman cistern. On April 12, 1943, a unit of the British 1st Army captured a hill just north of Chaouach. One member of the unit was Sidney Keyes, among the most promising English poets of World War II. "Algeria is a pleasant enough country," he wrote home, "but Tunisia is like what Scotland must have been in the eighteenth century, a mass of bald mountains, terribly cold at night." Two weeks later, at the age of 20, he was killed just outside Medjez, and he lies buried in plot number 2.K.15 in the **Commonwealth War Cemetery** at **MESSICAULT**, 1km east of Borj el Amri on the GP5 Medjez–Tunis road, some 30km from Tunis.

West from Medjez, the road hugs the north side of the Medjerda Valley. When the huge **Sidi Salem dam** was completed in 1982, the river had to be diverted, and the people of **OUED ZARGA**, nearly due west of Medjez, were entirely rehoused in smart new homes. The old village was the site of a notorious massacre in September 1881, when the French stationmaster and ten other European staff were burnt alive in a sudden uprising by the local people. A conflagration from another era is commemorated at Oued Zarga's **Commonwealth War Cemetery**, left behind in the old village. A signposted track starting a couple of kilometres beyond the modern village leads over a hill to the cemetery.

Béja and around

Head west of Oued Zarga on the GP6, and **BÉJA** comes into view after 25km, after you've climbed over a high ridge. Spread over the slopes of a mountain rather like Le Kef to the south, Béja is an important grain town and, although there's little of outstanding interest, it's well worth stopping off here if you're passing through, especially on a Tuesday, when the weekly **souk** is held.

Since Roman times, Béja has held the biggest **grain market** in the north, and has paid the price of prosperity with a torrid history of destruction and recovery. The first of these cycles began in 109 BC, when a Roman garrison was massacred by a population keen to show its support for the Numidian **King Jugurtha**. The only survivor of the disaster, one Turpilius, turned out to have made a grave error of judgement, because, when his supreme commander Metellus arrived and punished the town by razing it to the ground, he had Turpilius flogged and executed. "A man who in such a calamity could prefer dishonourable survival to an untarnished name must have been a detestable wretch," the historian Sallust explained helpfully.

The town recovered, only to be levelled again by the Vandals in the fifth century, Abu Yazid in the tenth, and the Banu Hilal in the eleventh. By 1154, however, according to El Edrisi, it was a "beautiful city, built on a plain extremely fertile in corn and barley, so that there is not in all the Maghreb a city so important or richer in cereals". It has remained an important agricultural centre ever since, attracting large numbers of Europeans under the French, who left their mark in the form of striking buildings and a well-populated cemetery.

The Town

Béja's backbone is **avenue Bourguiba**, which climbs from an overpass across the rail line at the bottom of the hill up to the town's main square, place du 7 Novembre, and beyond. Bisecting avenue Bourguiba, avenue de France runs east towards the train station – with the **modern town** beginning from place de l'Indépendance – and rue Kheredine runs northwest up towards the Great Mosque, with the Medina behind.

Climbing avenue Bourguiba, you'll come across the huge and extraordinary **church** (now a cultural centre), built by Béja's large colonial population in a bizarre confusion of dimly remembered European styles, with a few local additions – the tower, for example, looks like a minaret. You can study more of Béja's outrageous colonial architecture at the building immediately behind the former church and opposite the top of rue Habib el Meddeb. Reminiscent of Tunis's Christmas-cake colonial style, the building is dated 1912, suggesting how important an agricultural centre such as Béja was in the colonial scheme of things; it's now a row of shops.

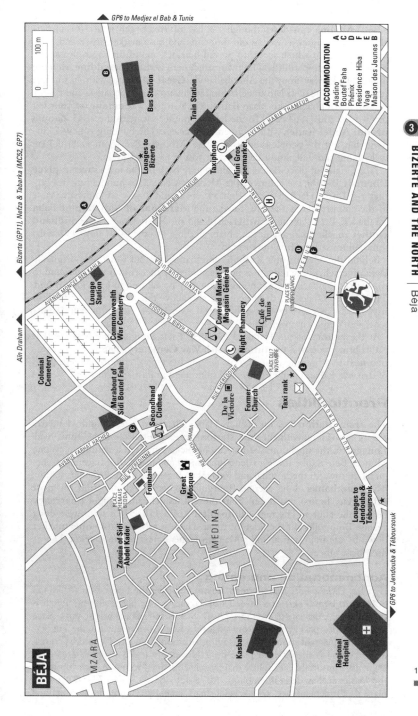

BÉJA

MZARA

MEDINA

Kasbah

Regional Hospital

Zaouia of Sidi Abdel Kader

Fountain

Great Mosque

PLACE HEMAIS BEDDA
RUE CHEFEDDINE

De la Victoire

Former Church

RUE KHEREDDINE

RUE EL HEDI HAMBA

Secondhand Clothes

Marabout of Sidi Boutef Faha

AVENUE FARHAT HACHED

Taxi rank

Colonial Cemetery

Commonwealth War Cemetery

Louage Station

AVENUE MONCEF BEN KAMLA

RUE HABIB EL MEDEB

AVENUE BOURGUIBA

Covered Market & Magasin Général

Night Pharmacy

Café de Tunis

PLACE DU 7 NOVEMBRE

PLACE DE L'INDÉPENDANCE

AVENUE BOURGUIBA

AVENUE DE LA RÉPUBLIQUE

AVENUE DE FRANCE

Mini Gros Supermarket

Taxiphone

Train Station

Bus Station

Louages to Bizerte

AVENUE HABIB THAMEUR

AVENUE HABIB THAMEUR

Louages to Jendouba & Téboursouk

0   100 m

N

GP6 to Medjez el Bab & Tunis

Bizerte (GP11), Nefza & Tabarka (MC52, GP7)

Ain Draham

GP6 to Jendouba & Téboursouk

ACCOMMODATION
Aladino A
Boutef Faha C
Phénix D
Residence Hiba F
Vaga E
Maison des Jeunes B

Béja's **Medina**, run-down though it is, has survived largely intact. It is unusually full of mosques, as well as old fountains and busy market streets and, with the cool climate which seems to prevail here, it's one of the most pleasant to wander through in Tunisia. The main street here is **rue Khereddine**, running only a block away from the Almohad-style **Great Mosque**, with an unusual red minaret. Rue de la Mosquée, behind it, emerges into a square as rue Blagui. Ahead, bearing right into place Bab el Aïn, you pass a **fountain** on your left dated 1219 AH (1804 AD). To the left, in another square, is the 1843 **Zaouia of Sidi Abdel Kader** with its green-tiled *koubba*. The building is now a kindergarten, but the people who work there (Mon–Sat 8am–5pm as a rule) are welcoming and will almost certainly let you in to have a look.

Take a right off place Bab el Aïn and you're back on the main street at **place Khemais Bedda**, the centre of the Medina. A couple of hundred metres further, rue Farhat Hached on the right sweeps round to give an impressive view of the countryside to the east, passing the **Marabout of Sidi Boutef Faha** on the left. Between rue Farhat Hached and rue Khereddine is a **secondhand clothes market** where you can obtain all those ghastly 1970s and 1980s fashions you missed the first time round.

Behind the Medina, the **Kasbah**, dominating the old town, was originally Byzantine; what little remains is now occupied by the army. If you go round to the gate at the back and ask politely, you may be allowed in for a look round. The **Mzara** district, north of here and also above the old town, is said still to have one or two cave dwellings, but this is a very poor part of town and sightseers aren't especially welcome.

At the bottom of rue Habib el Meddeb, a left along avenue Moncef Ben Kahla brings you to a **Commonwealth War Cemetery**, unusual for its position next to a housing estate. On its far side is a typical colonial cemetery, full of dynastic Italian family tombs now smothered in dust and cobwebs.

Practicalities

The **train station** lies on avenue Habib Thameur, a few hundred metres east of the centre, with the **bus station** across the tracks on the Tunis road. **Louages** in the direction of Tunis can be picked up from a station on avenue Moncef Ben Kahla, those to Jendouba and Téboursouk from avenue Bourguiba up towards the hospital and louages to Bizerte from near the bus station. There are **banks** along avenue Bourguiba, where you'll also find the **post office** (city hours) just uphill from the old church, and a night **pharmacy** behind the church. The regional **hospital** (℡78 451 431) is southwest along avenue Bourguiba on the edge of town. There is a Mini Gros **supermarket** down by the train station and a Magasin Général next to the **market**. There's no tourist office.

Accommodation and eating

Béja has a *Maison des Jeunes* **youth hostel**, opposite the bus station (℡78 453 621; dorm beds 4TD), and several **hotels**, the newest player among which is the two-star *Aladino* (℡78 455 077, ℱ78 458 661; ❺), a bright pink place across the overpass at the bottom edge of town. Convenient for the bus station, it has pleasant modern rooms with bathrooms, satellite TV and balconies. More central is the *Vaga* on place du 7 Novembre (℡78 450818, ℱ456902; ❹), with comfortable, if slightly shabby, self-contained rooms. A nicer option is the *Phénix* at 8 av de la République (℡78 450 188, ℱ78 456 344; ❸), just off place de l'Indépendance, with several smart, recently renovated self-contained rooms – and more to follow. Opposite, the friendly *Résidence Hiba* (☎78 457 244, ⓕ456 299; ❷) has a range of characterful, high-ceilinged rooms with sinks, bidets and sometimes balconies. Far cheaper than any of these is the *Boutef Faha* (no phone; ❶), opposite the marabout of the same name in rue Farhat Hached, next to a large café; rooms are adequate, some with a terrace, and you're at the edge of the Medina, but it's a bit grotty.

As far as sustenance goes, you're not exactly spoiled for choice in Béja, and in Ramadan even the few places below close for the month, making picnics the only option. Mind you, this is a pleasure in Béja, with its lovely fresh vegetables (in the Medina and market), a profusion of sweets and cakes available everywhere, and good selections of olives, cheeses and pickles. There are a few cheap **restaurants** in the Medina, such as the *Restaurant de la Victoire* at 25 rue Khereddine (daily noon–3pm). Otherwise you're limited to hotel restaurants; the one at the *Vaga* (daily 10am–11.30pm) has a set menu for 10TD, while the cheaper, but even duller, *Hiba* (daily noon–3pm & 7–10pm) does a 7TD set meal. The top recommendation, especially for its seafood, is the *Hôtel Phénix*'s restaurant (daily noon–3pm & 7–11pm), where you'll get an excellent meal for around 15TD. A good place to watch the world go by is the *Café de Tunis* just off place du 7 Novembre.

Thibar

Eleven kilometres south of Béja on the GP6, a road branches off towards Téboursouk (see p.310), passing a farmstead that looks like a fort with an egg on top, and runs through the pleasant little village of **THIBAR**, which has a farm and monastery set up by the White Fathers in 1895 that's still in use today. Thibarine date liqueur and Thibar wine are made here and, if you're lucky, you may be able to visit the wine cellars. Behind the farm buildings, yet another **Commonwealth War Cemetery**, a small one this time, broods among trees full of birds.

There are some scant **Roman remains** south of the village, not really worth seeing but an excuse for an hour-long stroll. Head past the site of Thibar's Sunday **souk**, taking the right-hand fork in the road, signposted "Bou Salem". At the crossroads 1500m further on, turn right as signposted; you're now on an avenue of eucalyptus trees with vineyards on the left, then a peach orchard. After a kilometre or so, you pass a water-pumping station on your left and, 100m beyond, a path to the left takes you around a field and across an *oued*. The remains, such as they are, lie on the other side.

Jendouba and around

JENDOUBA is not a particularly interesting town but it does have a couple of reasonable accommodation options, plus banking and transport facilities, making it a good base for visiting the impressive Roman site of **Bulla Regia** in the hills above the Medjerda Valley, as well as the ancient marble quarry of **Chemtou**, once renowned throughout the Roman Empire, and the lesser remains of **Thuburnica** to the west. There are a few Roman remains in Jendouba, lifted from Bulla Regia and now sitting in a small garden – along with a monument to Jendoubans who died fighting the French for control of Bizerte in 1961 (see p.172) – down rue Hedi Chaker on place des Martyrs.

Arriving in Jendouba by bus or louage, you're likely to find yourself at the main transport focus of place 7 Novembre, a large roundabout on the western

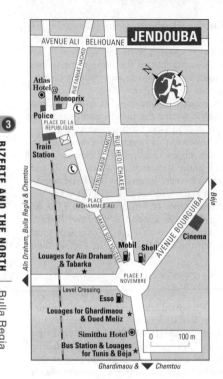

AVENUE ALI BELHOUANE · JENDOUBA

Aïn Draham, Bulla Regia & Chemtou

Atlas Hotel
Monoprix
Police
PLACE DE LA REPUBLIQUE
Train Station
RUE FARHAT HACHED
AVENUE HABIB THAMEUR
RUE HEDI CHAKER
PLACE MOHAMMED ALI
Béja
AVENUE BOURGUIBA
Cinema
Mobil Shell
Louages for Aïn Draham & Tabarka
SAYET SIDI YOUSSEF
PLACE 7 NOVEMBRE
Level Crossing
Esso
Louages for Ghardimaou & Oued Meliz
Simitthu Hotel
Bus Station & Louages for Tunis & Béja
0   100 m
Ghardimaou & ▼ Chemtou

edge of town with a weird tripod structure in the middle. On one side, by a level crossing, is the station for **louages** to Aïn Draham and Tabarka (passing the Bulla Regia crossroads). On the other side are the louage stations for Ghardimaou and Oued Meliz, and beyond them the **bus station** and louages for Le Kef, Béja, Bizerte and Tunis. The **train station** is tucked away in a corner of the main square, place de la République, by the police station.

You'll find pretty much everything you need on or around the main square, including the **post office** (city hours), a Monoprix **supermarket** and several **banks**, which are concentrated on rue Farhat Hached and rue Ali Belhouane – day and night **pharmacies** can be found on the latter. You can access the **Internet** at a Publinet opposite the *Hôtel Atlas* on rue 1 Juin (Mon–Sat 8am–midnight; 1.5TD/hr). Of the two **hotels** in town – both of which are ageing but adequate two-stars – the *Atlas* (☎78 603 217, ℻78 603 518; ❸), just behind the police station on rue 1 Juin, is better value and in a nicer location than the *Simitthu* (☎78 604 043, ℻78 602 595; ❹), out by the bus station.

There are plenty of cheap **restaurants** in the town centre, and the *Atlas* and *Simitthu* hotels (both daily noon–3pm & 6.30–10pm) do moderate set menus for 8TD and 10TD respectively. If your stay in town becomes prolonged, there's a **flea market** of sorts off place 7 Novembre, and a **cinema** 100m down avenue Bourguiba from place 7 Novembre. There's no tourist office in Jendouba.

Bulla Regia

BULLA REGIA (daily: April to mid-Sept 8am–7pm; mid-Sept to March 8.30am–5.30pm; 2.1TD, camera 1TD) is one of the most extraordinary Roman sites anywhere in the world. Its **underground villas** – the distinctive feature here – were built by wealthy inhabitants and, though they have their modern parallel at Matmata (see p.402), were unique in the Roman Empire. Equally striking are the intact and beautiful **mosaics** left *in situ*, all too rare now that the museums have taken the best mosaics at other sites.

As with the troglodytes at Matmata, no one knows for certain why Bulla Regians went underground, given that the rock in other hot settlements was also soft and hence easy to excavate. This has always been an important region, though, and Bulla Regia played much the same market-centre role as Jendouba does today. The "Regia" in its name refers to royal connections before the arrival of the Romans, when it was associated with one of the native Numidian kingdoms. Subsequently, it became yet another prosperous Roman town and was still occupied in the Byzantine era, but was abandoned after the Arab conquest in the seventh century.

The **site** itself lies just north of Jendouba, 6km along the GP17 Aïn Draham road, then signposted 3km to the right along the minor C59. A **taxi** from Jendouba to the site shouldn't cost more than 4TD from the flea market off place 7 Novembre, or there are shared taxis for 0.7TD. Louages and buses between Jendouba and Aïn Draham can drop you at the turn-off. Make it clear that it's just the turn-off (*croisement*) that you want; if the driver thinks you want the site itself, he may direct you to a taxi.

The Memmian baths and Treasure House

Bulla Regia's most prominent remains – the **Memmian Baths** – stand just by the site entrance and were named after the wife of Septimius Severus, the first African emperor of Rome; the large central hall was a *frigidarium*. From here, take the track leading north to the Quartier des Maisons; you'll shortly come to the first of the buried villas, the **Treasure House**, so called after a cache of seventh-century Byzantine coins discovered inside. The standard pattern for villas built in this curious way was to have a normal ground floor, with a dining room and perhaps bedrooms sunk underground. The relatively small Treasure House conforms to this pattern, with a large dining room downstairs (identifiable by the pattern of the floor mosaic, showing where couches were positioned around three walls), flanked by two smaller rooms. At least one of these was a bedroom, so presumably eating and sleeping were the two daily functions for which the wealthy Roman citizen most wanted to remain cool.

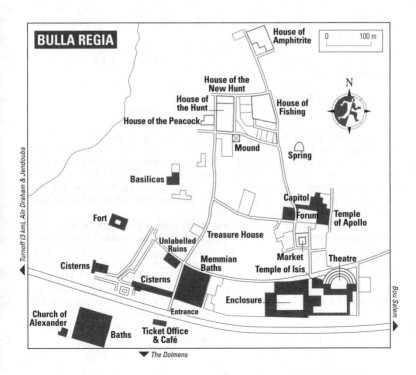

The Peacock, Hunt, Fishing and Amphitrite houses

Back at ground level, some columns standing over to the northwest of the Treasure House belong to a pair of basilica **churches**, one of which has a baptismal font at its western end. From here an artificial **mound** in the middle of the site is visible: this gives a good view over the whole area, and especially the residential quarter directly below it.

Just left of the crossroads next to the mound is the **House of the Peacock**, whose eponymous mosaic has been removed to the Bardo Museum in Tunis, but it's the fully excavated block on the other side of the street that's most fascinating. Almost the whole block is occupied by the huge **House of the Hunt**, whose basement even includes its own colonnaded courtyard, off which opens a magnificent dining room with its mosaics still in place. Bedrooms also open off the courtyard. Note, too, the hexagonal holes in the superstructure of the courtyard, designed to lighten the load, and the clusters of what are apparently broken clay pipes in the walls – these were piled together, then plastered over, forming a light but strong construction unit which helped make these basements possible. A private baths complex and some latrines on the ground floor suggest that the owner of this house was something of a plutocrat.

Leaving the House of the Hunt, head north along the street running alongside, then take a right at the top of the **House of Fishing**. This has a huge basement built like a bunker, with a semicircular fountain that would have produced refreshing jets of water, which faces a small room containing part of a mosaic depicting fishermen and their prey. Take the street leading north from here to the **House of Amphitrite**, a sea goddess, justly famous for the magnificent mosaics on the basement level. The star of the main scene in the *triclinium* is actually Venus, not Amphitrite. You have to delight in the attendant Cupid who manages to ride a dolphin and admire his chubby features in a mirror at the same time. When Bulla Regia was first excavated, one disturbing discovery was made in this house, a skeleton tied to a chair with an iron ring around its neck, inscribed: "Adulterous prostitute: hold me, because I ran away from Bulla Regia." The later building over the street was a **baths** complex.

Around the Forum

Head back down the street, then off left to the **spring** – as at Sbeïtla (see p.327), the ancient source is still in use today. Beyond lies the administrative quarter of the town, the first grassy open space being the **Forum**, flanked to the west by the **Capitol**, a true-blue Roman temple on a podium, and to the north by the **Temple of Apollo**, in the African pattern of a courtyard with a small sanctuary opening off it. The best statues in Tunis's Bardo Museum were found here. A broad street leads south from the Forum, past the **market** on the right – an important facility in a town like this, its small shops around the sides could be locked up when not in use.

Continuing down the street, you pass another set of **baths** on the left, with an octagonal *frigidarium*, before reaching the back of the **theatre**. It's still possible to enter this by the original galleries, known graphically as *vomitoria*. The first three rows of seats, wider than the rest, were reserved for local dignitaries – who were separated from the proles behind by a solid railing. Bulla Regia's loose and immoral ways, focusing as ever on the theatre, were notorious. St Augustine preached a famous sermon here at the end of the fourth century, berating the citizens for their impropriety and imagining them welcoming strangers to the town with "What have you come for? Theatrical folk? Women of easy virtue? You can find them all in Bulla."

△ The Amphitrite House, Bulla Regia

Immediately south of the theatre, blocked originally by the stage building, is a rectangular plaza. Making your way west from here, you pass the small podium of the **Temple of Isis**. Its remains are unremarkable, but the cult it served was a cosmopolitan one characteristic of the Roman Empire. Starting life as an Egyptian goddess, Isis was taken up as early as the first century BC by Romans searching for new deities to brighten up their spiritual lives. Isis worship became institutionalized but always kept an air of mystery; in *The Golden Ass* it is Isis to whom Apuleius turns in his plea to be transformed back from a donkey to a man: "She is the shining deity by whose divine influence not only all beasts, wild and tame, but all inanimate things are invigorated; whose ebbs and flows control the rhythm of all bodies whatsoever, whether in the air, on earth, or below the sea." Beyond the temple you pass a sizeable **enclosure** on the way back to the site entrance, with a central area, presumably once a garden, surrounded by deep water channels.

South of the main road

For enthusiasts only, a jumble of ruins south of the modern road belongs to a set of **baths**, next to what is now misleadingly called the **Church of Alexander**. An inscription from the Psalms was found over the door here ("May the Lord guard your coming in and your going out, now and for ever more, Amen"). The trough-like stones (as at Le Kef, Haïdra and Maktar) were probably connected with the distribution of food and commodities. Half a kilometre or so south of here is an area of pre-Roman **dolmens**.

Chemtou

The other Roman site in this part of the country is **CHEMTOU** (daily: April to mid-Sept 8am–7pm; mid-Sept to March 8.30am–5.30pm; 2.1TD, camera 1TD), an apparently unremarkable place that was once famous throughout the Roman world as Simithas, the source of **Numidian marble**, a lurid red-yellow-pink variety much in vogue with imperial builders. Plainly recognizable on an isolated hill on the plain, the site lies just off the C59 road, 10km east of Thuburnica and 16km west of the GP17 Jendouba–Aïn Draham road. To get there, take a local **louage** from Jendouba or Ghardimaou, preferably along the Thuburnica road or, failing that, to **Oued Meliz**, on the main GP6 road 3km southwest of the site (and on the rail line). From Oued Meliz, you can either catch a louage to the site or walk: the signposted turn-off 1km to the east of the village leads after 2km to a low concrete bridge over the River Medjerda, which is overshadowed by the remains of a much larger Roman bridge nearby (see p.208). The site is just beyond on the right. Easiest of all is to arrange for a **taxi** to take you directly to the site from Jendouba and wait to drive you back; this should cost around 20TD for a return trip.

The museum

Newly victorious in 146 BC, the Romans used the Chemtou marble widely and closely identified it with extravagance and luxury. "No beams of Athenian stone rest in *my* house," wrote the poet Horace, "on columns quarried in furthest Africa." As a result, the industry supported a sizeable town which has been excavated by a team from Tunis and the German Archeological School in Rome. The fruits of their findings are displayed in an excellent US$1.5 million **museum**, which is really the chief draw. There are three main rooms, each illustrating aspects of Chemtou's past. The first room contains rock samples, and explains the **geology** and morphology of the region, and so the creation of

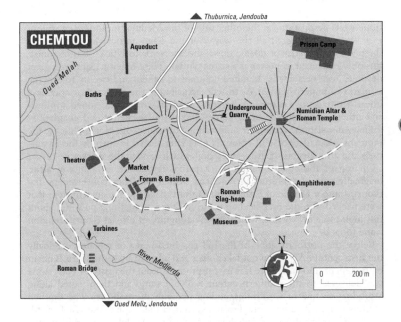

Thuburnica, Jendouba

Aqueduct

Prison Camp

Oued Melah

Baths

Underground Quarry

Numidian Altar & Roman Temple

Theatre

Market

Forum & Basilica

Roman Slag-heap

Amphitheatre

Turbines

Museum

Roman Bridge

River Medjerda

N

0   200 m

Oued Meliz, Jendouba

marble. There are also some **Numidian** artefacts, including a lovely carving of a **mounted god**, as well as reliefs dedicated to Baal and other funerary pieces, some from the region of the Berber King Micipsa dating from 148–118BC. The relics are remarkable in that pre-Roman, Numidian excavation of marble was for a long time unknown to archeologists and suggests that Numidian culture, of which very little remains, was more sophisticated than previously thought.

A doorway leads out of the first room into a courtyard featuring a recon-struction of the **temple** found on the eastern summit of the hill above (see p.208), with a striking series of mosaics and massive reliefs showing shields and other accoutrements that decorated the Roman successor to the original Numidian hilltop altar. On the other side of the courtyard, the second main room has a fascinating display explaining the **excavation** of the marble, while the third room contains various bits of Roman statuary and tombstones. One of the most exciting discoveries at Chemtou was made during the building of the museum, when a hoard of 1647 solid **gold coins** and one silver coin was uncovered, visibly testifying to the riches of what was an immensely wealthy town. Unfortunately the coins are stored in a bank vault, although a couple can be seen at the Musée des Finances in Tunis (see p.83).

The site

Saddling the middle of the hill are the marble **quarries** themselves – just gap-ing holes in the rock now, but their emptiness seems to preserve an indefinable memory of the skill and sheer hard work of so many men over so many years. The Romans declared the quarries imperial property under Emperor Octavius Augustus, a decision which led to the building of an entire city. They had the industry highly organized, with every single block stamped with the names of the emperor, the consul in office and the local official, along with a production number so that it wouldn't go missing. The effort involved in transporting the stone to its destination on the other side of the Mediterranean was enormous – it was either dragged all the way over the Khroumirie Mountains to be shipped from Tabarka, or floated down the Medjerda to Utica – but of course, this only enhanced its power as a status symbol. The Emperor Hadrian, a great devotee, once presented a hundred columns to Athens and twenty to Smyrna as marks of imperial favour. As to who actually did the work, excavators have unearthed traces of a mammoth **prison camp**, in which condemned criminals and others were kept, covering some 20,000 square metres and guarded by military installations. A number of remaining miscellaneous blocks illustrate the Romans' particular sense of colour, a taste later shared in turn by the Byzantines and a nineteenth-century operation which revived the workings.

On top of the eastern summit is a partial restoration of a hilltop **altar**, originally part of a Numidian sanctuary which was later converted by the Romans into a Temple of Saturn. You can just make out the ancient steps that were hacked into the rock leading up to it. There's something powerful about this high place of worship, which the civic dignity of official Roman religion came to lack.

Below the northern slope of the hill is a broad area of remains, originally the first-century AD camp but taken over and adapted by some sharp Roman entrepreneur into an on-site factory for products from the quarries. Raw stone was delivered to the southern entrance of the camp and then passed along a production line of workshops, ending up with the polishers. The finished utensils and small statues were dispatched all over the empire. Also visible north of the hill are stretches of aqueduct heading into the hills, from where they brought the water that fed the town.

South and west of the hill were the residential and official quarters of the town, far away from the prison camp, below which, towards the tumbledown Roman bridge, you can make out the remains of a basilica and a half-buried theatre. The bridge, whose massive remains bear elegant testimony to the Romans' civil engineering, carried the main Sicca–Thabraca (Le Kef–Tabarka) road, along which much of the stone was hauled for export. Among the tangled ruins on the northern bank, you can see the unusual industrial feature of three parallel grooves – unique in North Africa – which forced the flowing water to drive turbines to grind grain.

Ghardimaou

GHARDIMAOU, 30km west of Jendouba on the GP6, is a small border town and unglamorous in the extreme. Its only virtue is its setting, a misty river plain overshadowed on three sides by mountains that pile up steeply towards Algeria. The only real reason for coming here is to visit the minor Roman site of **Thuburnica**, featuring a miraculously preserved bridge, or the mountainous **Forest of Feija**, a national park 20km northwest of Ghardimaou, right on the Algerian frontier.

Ghardimaou's **train station** is centrally placed, with services to Jendouba, Béja, Oued Zarga, Medjez el Bab and Tunis. There's a single basic **hotel** in town, the *Thuburnic*, overlooking the station (☎78 660 043; ❷). There is some activity in its bar and restaurant but, as a depressed resident admitted, "there's no ambience in Ghardimaou". A good alternative to staying here is the *Centre des Stages et des Vacances* (no phone) in the village of **AÏN SOLTANE**, some 20km northwest, but ask around in Ghardimaou before making the trip to check that it's open. **Louages** to Aïn Soltane and Thuburnica depart from the main road, just after it curves round to the right across the rail line towards

Travelling to Algeria: a warning

Since early 1992, when the government cancelled elections expected to be won by the **FIS** Islamic party (Front Islamique de la Salvation), Algeria's internal security situation has been virtually a **civil war** between the forces of the establishment (in essence, the army) and the Islamic fundamentalist movement. By 2004, over 150,000 people had died in the vicious struggle between hardliners on both sides. Victims of the security forces have included ordinary citizens suspected of allegiance to their Islamist opponents and whole villages thought to have voted for the FIS in 1992, while the Islamists have targeted not just security and government officials, but anyone involved in what they perceive as a West-tainted activity: this has included journalists, a *raï* (a form of Algerian pop music) star, feminists and sporting officials. Compared to the total number of victims, only a small proportion have been foreigners, but Islamist paramilitaries have explicitly targeted foreigners in the past and anyone who visits the country is at high risk.

Compared to the 1990s, the security situation in Algeria had improved a great deal at the time of writing, culminating in the largely peaceful re-election of President Abdelaziz Bouteflika in April 2004. But while order had more or less returned to city centres, terrorist attacks continued sporadically in rural areas, particularly in the north of the country, where large-scale massacres of Algerian villagers have occurred regularly over the years. The south of Algeria was also unsafe, as shown in February 2003 when 32 foreign tourists travelling overland across the desert were abducted by bandits and held in captivity for several months. Unless the situation improves drastically, any journey to Algeria, particularly the north, is extremely dangerous.

Algeria. Louages for Jendouba or Tunis can be found louages near where the street down to the train station leaves the main road.

The region around Ghardimaou is true border country – never more viciously or tragically so than during the Algerian War of 1954–62. In 1957, the French built the infamous **Morice Line** to prevent the Algerian ALN (Armé de la Libération Nationale), based in "neutral" Tunisia, from reinforcing their FLN (Front de la Libération Nationale) counterparts inside the country. Three hundred kilometres long, the Morice Line was brutally effective, a 2.5-metre-high electric fence, charged to 5000 volts, flanked by minefields and defended by eighty thousand French troops using the latest in electronic surveillance technology. It ran from the Mediterranean in the north to the Sahara in the south, where no one could hope to cross the border unnoticed. One three-day assault in April 1958 saw the ALN push eight hundred men at the line just north of Souk Ahras. In a subsequent week-long running battle, six hundred of them were killed or captured. After the line was built, the ALN never did succeed in providing significant support across the border.

The **border crossings** here and further north at Babouch are the most heavily used in the country. Travelling close to the Algerian border was not a problem at the time of writing, but during times of unrest in Algeria, it would be advisable to stick to the road and have a hotel and destination in mind if questioned by security forces.

Thuburnica

A visit to the Roman site of **THUBURNICA** (free access) on the north side of the river plain gives ample chance to see the region's scenery. With your own transport, take a right turn on the edge of Ghardimaou, after crossing the bridge towards Algeria, onto the minor MC59 road signposted "El Kalaa–Chemtou". The road passes through the village of **El Kalaa** after 9km and then reaches Thuburnica's memorable little **bridge** 2km further on; **louages** and taxi-trucks pass regularly along the MC59 from near the bridge in Ghardimaou. The bridge's Roman builders are nearly two thousand years gone, but the structure looks as if it might have been put up twenty years ago and still carries the road over one of the deep stream beds that hurry out of the foothills. The rest of the ancient town is scattered in smallish fragments over the hill to the west – a ruined Byzantine castle stands on top and a fine two-storey **mausoleum** about halfway up – but much of the hill is fenced off inside a military base.

Arabic place names

Aïn Draham	عين دراهم
Aïn Ghellal	عين غلال
Babouch	ببّوش
Bechateur	بشاطر
Béja	باجة
Bizerte	بنزرت
Bulla Regia	بولا ريجية
Chaouach	شوّاش
Chemtou	شمتو
Fernana	فرنانة
Ghar el Melh	غار الملح
Ghardimaou	غار الدماء
Hammam Bourguiba	حمام بورقيبة
Jebel Ichkeul	جبل إشكل
Jendouba	جندوبة
Kalaat el Andalous	قلعة الاندلس
Lac Ichkeul	بحيرة إشكل
Mateur	ماطر
Medjez el Bab	مجاز الباب
Menzel Bourguiba	منزل بورقيبة
Oued Zarga	وادي زرقة
Raf Raf	رفراف
Ras Jebel	رأس الجبل
Ras Sidi el Mekki	رأس سيدي المكي
Sejnane	سجنان
Tabarka	طبرقة
Thibar	تيبار
Toukabeur	توكابر
Utica	أوتيقا

Travel details

Trains

Bizerte to: Mateur (4 daily; 40min); Tinja (4 daily; 20min); Tunis (4 daily; 1hr 40min).
Ghardimaou to: Béja (5 daily; 1hr 15min); Jendouba (5 daily; 30min); Medjez el Bab (5 daily; 2hr); Oued Meliz (5 daily; 15min); Oued Zarga (5 daily; 1hr 45min); Tunis (5 daily; 3hr).

Buses

Aïn Draham to: Béja (4 daily; 2hr); Bizerte (2 daily; 4hr); Hammam Bourguiba (2 daily; 30min); Jendouba (8 daily; 1hr); Le Kef (2 daily; 2hr); Tabarka (hourly; 1hr); Tunis (4 daily; 4hr).
Béja to: Aïn Draham (6 daily; 3hr); Bizerte (7 daily; 3hr); Jendouba (6 daily; 1hr 30min); Medjez el Bab (every 30min; 1hr); Siliana (1 daily; 5hr); Sousse (2 daily; 3hr 30min); Tabarka (5 daily; 1hr 30min–2hr 30min); Tunis (every 30min; 2hr).
Bizerte to: Aïn Draham (1 daily; 5hr); Béja (2 daily; 2hr); Gabès (2 daily; 8hr); Ghar el Melh (4 daily; 1hr); Jendouba (2 daily; 3hr); Jerba (Houmt Souk; 2 daily; 10hr); Kairouan (1 daily; 5hr); Menzel Bourguiba (every 30min; 45min); Ras Jebel (hourly; 1hr); Sfax (2 daily; 6hr); Sousse (2 daily; 4hr); Tabarka (1 daily; 4hr); Tunis (every 30min; 2hr).
Jendouba to: Aïn Draham (5 daily; 1hr); Béja (8 daily; 1hr 30min); Bizerte (3 daily; 3hr); Ghardimaou (6 daily; 1hr); Le Kef (7 daily; 1hr 10min); Medjez el Bab (8 daily; 3hr); Tabarka (4 daily; 2hr); Tunis (8 daily; 4hr).

Medjez el Bab to: Béja (every 30min; 1hr); Jendouba (8 daily; 3hr); Le Kef (hourly; 1hr 30min); Téboursouk (hourly; 1hr); Testour (hourly; 30min); Tunis (every 30min; 1hr).
Ras Jebel to: Bizerte (hourly; 1hr); Ghar el Melh (8 daily; 45min); Raf Raf (every 30min; 30min); Tunis (5 daily; 2hr).
Tabarka to: Aïn Draham (hourly; 1hr); Béja (4 daily; 2hr 15min); Bizerte (1 daily; 4hr); Jendouba (5 daily; 2hr); Le Kef (2 daily; 3hr); Mateur (4 daily; 3hr); Sejnane (4 daily; 2hr 30min); Tunis (5 daily; 3hr 45min).

Louages

Béja to: Bizerte (1hr 30min); Jendouba (1hr); Medjez el Bab (45min); Nefza (for Tabarka and Sejnane; 45min); Téboursouk (1hr); Thibar (40min); Tunis (1hr 45min).
Bizerte to: Béja (1hr 30min); Jendouba (2hr); Mateur (45min); Menzel Bourguiba (30min); Raf Raf (30min); Sejnane (2hr); Tunis (1hr 30min).
Jendouba to: Aïn Draham (45min); Béja (1hr); Bizerte (2hr); Ghardimaou (30min); Le Kef (50min); Oued Meliz (20min); Tabarka (1hr 30min); Tunis (3hr).
Medjez el Bab to: Béja (45min); Testour (20min); Tunis (45min).
Tabarka to: Aïn Draham (40min); Jendouba (1hr 30min).

Kairouan and
the Sahel

ALGERIA

LIBYA

N

CHAPTER 4

Highlights

* **Sousse** Tunisia's liveliest resort, with a historic Medina and an excellent archeological museum to add to its beaches and nightlife. **See p.218**

* **Monastir** More good beaches and a magnificent fortress with a Monty Python connection. **See p.238**

* **Great Mosque at Kairouan** The most important religious site in the country, powerful in its simplicity. **See p.249**

* **Mahdia** The prettiest town on the east coast, its Medina poking out to sea along a narrow, rocky peninsula. **See p.256**

* **El Jem** The amphitheatre here is the single most impressive Roman monument in Africa – a match even for the Colosseum in Rome. **See p.263**

* **The Medina in Sfax** With a thriving community within its massive walls, this unspoilt (and untouristy) Medina is refreshingly different to any other in the country. **See p.272**

* **Kerkennah Islands** For a few days of peace and tranquillity, these flat, sleepy islands are hard to beat. **See p.280**

△ city walls, Sfax

Kairouan and the Sahel

airouan – the Holy City – is only the most obvious attraction in the **Sahel**, an area that is central in every way to Tunisia. (The Arabic name "Sahel" means "coast" or "margin" and, in the case of the sub-Saharan Sahel, the edge of the desert.) Ranging back from the east coast, the Sahel's fertile plains have long been the heartland of the country's agriculture, and a focus during each shift of power. The Romans planted millions of olive trees throughout the region, and under Arab rule it was the base of the great Aghlabid dynasty, which launched a successful invasion of Sicily from the port of Sousse in the ninth century.

Monuments from this and ensuing dynasties grace most of the Sahel's larger towns. **Kairouan**, the first Arab capital in North Africa, is pre-eminent – above all for its Great Mosque, justly Tunisia's most famous building as well as its spiritual centre. But **Sousse**, **Sfax**, **Monastir** and **Mahdia** are each highly rewarding for their architecture, while **El Jem** shelters what is arguably the Roman world's finest surviving amphitheatre. Add to this an impressive series of beaches and it's easy to understand the region's popularity – and why the **coast** around Sousse and Monastir has become the country's most highly developed for tourism. Yet there are still places – in particular, parts of the **Kerkennah Islands** off Sfax – where you can find virtual isolation. For naturalists, too, the area is interesting, with marshland, mud flats and saltpans all the way down the Sahel coast and around the bay of Gabès, attracting large numbers of wading **birds** and associated species.

Market days

Monday La Chebba, El Alia, El Jem, Kairouan, Ksour Essaf, Mahrès, Msaken
Tuesday Ksar Hellal, Remla (Kerkennah)
Wednesday Moknine
Thursday Bou Thadi, Kalaa Sghira, Sbih, Sidi el Hani
Friday Kalaa Kebira, Mahdia, Sahline, Sfax, La Skhirra
Saturday El Hencha, Hammam Sousse, Monastir, Sidi Bou Ali
Sunday Enfida, Graïba, Ksar Hellal, Sousse

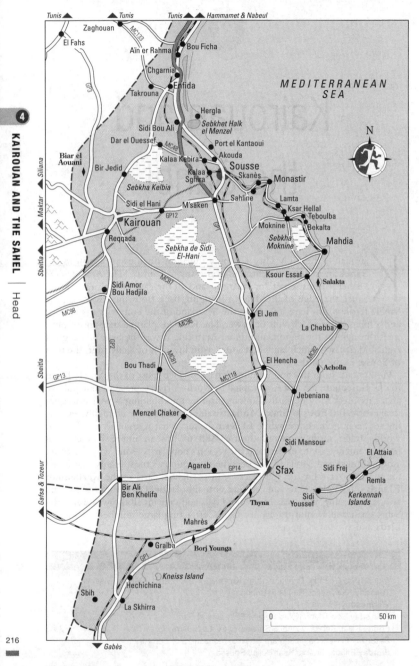

Enfida and Takrouna

ENFIDA, formerly Enfidaville, is the administrative centre for a vast and fertile agricultural estate that was an indirect cause of French colonial intervention in 1881. The estate's original owner, the reforming Turkish official Khaireddin, put it up for sale when he was recalled to Constantinople, and the Franco-African Company immediately submitted the highest bid. The Tunisian government tried to keep the estate out of French hands, but the attempt backfired and helped to convince the French that the time had come to take full control of the country.

The estate is still heavily cultivated, but the town has been bypassed by the coastal road to Sousse, and its dusty streets would hardly be worth a visit were it not for the breathtaking village of Takrouna nearby and the small town **museum**, in the old French church on the main street (Tues–Sun: April to mid-Sept 9am–1pm & 3–7pm; mid-Sept to March 9.30am–4.30pm; 1.1TD, camera 1TD). The collection of mosaic epitaphs and tombstones vividly illustrates the mix of cultures and values prevalent here in ancient times – Berber, Carthaginian, Roman and Christian. Many of the tombstones are dedicated to priests of Saturn, a Roman transplant of the Carthaginian god Baal – hence the un-Roman symbols such as crescent moons. When Christianity came, the Berbers adapted once again, and names in the epitaphs like Filocalus, Gududa, Jades and Vernacla show that local people as well as overlords took to the new religion. The mosaics from the nearby site of Uppena reveal persecution of Catholic Christians by the Vandals, who followed the Arian heresy. One depicts the deaths of sixteen Catholic martyrs, while two more are epitaphs to bishops summoned to a church convention in 484 AD by the Vandal king Huneric, who kept them here until their deaths.

During World War II, heavy fighting took place around Enfida in the final weeks of the North African campaign, as the retreating Germans attempted to hold a line here against the Eighth Army. A melancholy reminder of this are the two **military cemeteries** – a Commonwealth one on the western edge of town (follow signs for Zaghouan) and, 3km further on, below the looming presence of Takrouna's rocky outcrop, one for the French forces. They make an interesting comparison – the French one is austere and militaristic, with a helmet placed on each grave, while the Commonwealth cemetery is green and rustic.

Between Enfida and Bou Ficha on the GP1, just north of Chgarnia, the **Friguia Safari Park** (daily: mid-June to mid-Sept 9am–6pm; mid-Sept to mid-June 9am–4pm; ⓦwww.friguia-park.com; 5TD; tour available from the *Hôtel Kanta* in Port el Kantaoui, see p.235) is operated in collaboration with the Tunisian forestry commission and the Paris zoo. It runs a breeding and reintroduction programme for threatened species, and also features lions, giraffes, elephants and other African wildlife. The park has its own **train station**, with services to Tunis and Sousse.

Practicalities

Most of Enfida is spread out along one main street. At the western end is the turn-off for Zaghouan and, less than 100m east of it, the turn-off for Sousse. Buses and louages heading to or from Tunis can be picked up at the main **bus station**, 100m east of the museum across the main road. One or two services between Sousse and the north have to be picked up at the relevant turn-off – the people in the bus station should be able to advise. The **louage station** for Sousse is a little way down the Sousse road. From the **train station**, head north for a couple of hundred metres and you will emerge on the main street about 20m east of the museum..

On the northern side of the main street are the **post office**, **police** and museum, with a couple of **banks** and cheap *gargotes* opposite them. A street opposite the post office leads to a square, off which is the main **market**. There's no tourist office or accommodation in town.

Takrouna

The victims lying in the military cemeteries died fighting for **TAKROUNA**, a Berber village 7km northwest of Enfida and perched high on a rock, whose inaccessibility long made it a natural defensive position. The final Allied assault on it in 1943 was made by thirteen New Zealanders, most of them Maoris, scrambling up the sheer rock under fire from besieged Nazi troops. Today the village can be reached from Enfida by local **louage**, picked up at the Zaghouan turn-off.

The Berbers have always cherished their independence, and Takrouna is typical in its isolation and impregnability. It's crowned by a green-domed **marabout**, and the view from the top is mind-blowing – from the sinister gleaming blade of Jebel Zaghouan behind to the broad sweep of the coastline. All this has placed Takrouna firmly on the tourist map, and busloads are rushed in and out along a specially built road. Unfortunately, Takrouna's touristic exploitation has changed the attitudes of villagers to visitors, and today the hassle can be quite off-putting. The road that goes past Takrouna continues to Zaghouan through some lovely remote heathland, passing two more Berber villages – **Jeradou** and **Zriba** – which are similar to Takrouna, but less visited (see p.295).

Sousse and around

As a tourist destination, **SOUSSE** seems to have everything going for it: a historic **Medina** containing two of Tunisia's most distinctive monuments, an excellent **museum** second only to the Bardo, and endless stretches of white **beach**. Little wonder it has become Tunisia's most popular resort. But if the town has become rather a tourist trap, the benefits are that it has plenty of facilities, a number of cultural events and a wide choice of restaurants and places to stay.

Sousse is surrounded by the very old and the very new – the latter in the form of a massive tourist development at **Port el Kantaoui**, and the former by the clifftop village of **Hergla** and a group of timeless hamlets in the hills a few kilometres inland. The best areas around Sousse to see the coast's birdlife are the **Oued Sed** and **Sebkha Kelbia**.

The Sahel métro

The coast between Sousse and Mahdia is served by a regular and fairly reliable **métro** service, which runs in both directions from about 5am to 10pm, stopping at all the resorts and small towns on the way, as well as Monastir airport. Trains run every 45 minutes or so between Sousse and Monastir, and slightly less frequently to and from Mahdia. Journey times from Sousse are about 20 minutes to the airport, 40 minutes to Monastir and 1 hour 40 minutes to Mahdia. A single ticket from Sousse to Monastir costs around 1TD, to Mahdia about 2.5TD.

Moving on from Sousse

For a list of destinations and journey times, see Travel details on p.285.

Sousse is well connected, with bus, train, louage and air services all close at hand, plus the métro train. **Monastir airport** (☎73 520 000) has scheduled flights to various European destinations. For the local address of the **ferry** company CTN, see p.17. In addition to regular modes of land transport, there are tuk-tuks – expanded six-seater versions of Thai auto-rickshaws – and Noddy trains shuttling along the hotel strip between Sousse and Port el Kantaoui.

By bus

All non-local bus services leave from the **gare routière** (☎73 237 978). Local bus services depart from **place Sidi Yahia** in the northeast corner of the Medina, serving Hergla (#18) via Port el Kantaoui (also served by #12) and Chott Mariam; Kalaa Sghira (#20); Kalaa Kebira (#15) via Akouda (also served by #14); Monastir via the airport (#52); and Mahdia (#30).

By louage

All **louages** leave from the new station on rue du 1 Juin 1955 (☎73 339 525). Located in a vast hangar, it is surprisingly modern and well-organized for a louage station, and there is even a ticket office for the major routes with a TV screen informing you of seat availability. Yellow **shared taxis** to Hergla and Kalaa Sghira (identifiable by the blue stripes running down the sides, though the destinations on the roof signs are in Arabic) can be picked up from place Sidi Yahia and function as louages, taking four passengers for a set fare; make clear you are paying for places in the vehicle unless you actually want to charter a taxi privately.

By train

Train services leave from the **main station** on boulevard Hassouna Ayachi (☎73 225 321), although express trains and most southbound services now bypass Sousse and stop instead at Kalaa Sghira, 6km to the west (bus #20 or 3TD in a taxi). Nevertheless, there remain ten daily departures for Tunis from the main station, including four that stop at Kalaa Kebira and Enfida, and five that connect at Bir Bou Regba for Hammamet and Nabeul. In the other direction, one morning train and a couple of night trains serve El Jem and Sfax, continuing to Gabès, and one night train goes to Gafsa and Metlaoui. From Kalaa Sghira, there are two trains to El Jem, four to Sfax and two to Gabès.

The Sahel **métro** to Monastir via the airport runs from 5am to 8.10pm (from 6.40am Sun) from **Bab Jedid station**, 200m south of place Farhat Hached on boulevard Mohammed V. Most of the trains continue to Mahdia.

Some history

Founded as the Phoenician colony of **Hadrumete**, probably in the ninth century BC, Sousse was Hannibal's naval base in his struggle against the Romans. Since then, thanks to its natural harbour and central position on the fertile eastern seaboard, it has been a vital port for every civilization occupying this stretch of North African coast, each remodelling it in their own image – Roman Hadrumetum, Vandal Hunericopolis and Byzantine Justinianopolis. Hadrumete avoided Carthage's fate by wisely backing Rome in the third and final Punic War (see p.490), and even when the all-conquering Oqba Ibn Nafi, leader of the **Arab** invaders (see p.493), destroyed the town in the seventh century, it wasn't long before Soussa – the Arabic name still most commonly used – revived. Sousse was the main outlet to the Mediterranean for the **Aghlabids** ruling in Kairouan, and they launched their invasion of Sicily from here in 827. It was later occupied by the **Normans** (then masters of Sicily) in the twelfth

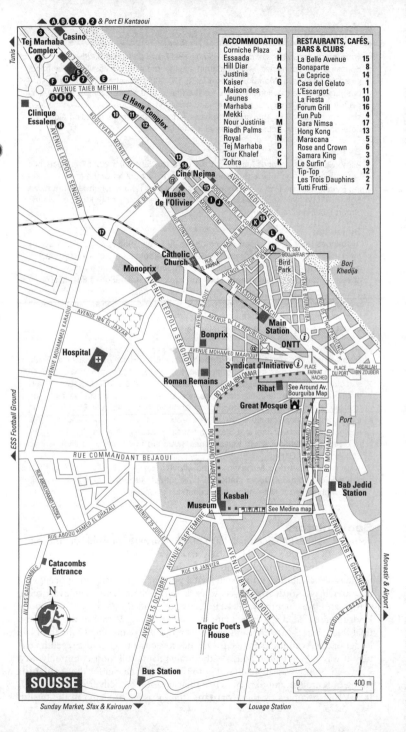

▲ ⒶⒷⒸ❶❷ & Port El Kantaoui

Tunis ▲

Tej Marhaba
Complex

Casino

Clinique
Essalem

El Hana Complex

ACCOMMODATION	
Corniche Plaza	J
Essaada	H
Hill Diar	A
Justinia	L
Kaiser	G
Maison des Jeunes	F
Marhaba	B
Mekki	I
Nour Justinia	M
Riadh Palms	E
Royal	N
Tej Marhaba	C
Tour Khalef	D
Zohra	K

RESTAURANTS, CAFÉS, BARS & CLUBS	
La Belle Avenue	15
Bonaparte	8
Le Caprice	14
Casa del Gelato	1
L'Escargot	11
La Fiesta	10
Forum Grill	16
Fun Pub	4
Gara Nimsa	17
Hong Kong	13
Maracana	5
Rose and Crown	6
Samara King	3
Le Surfin'	9
Tip-Top	12
Les Trois Dauphins	2
Tutti Frutti	7

AVENUE TAIEB MEHIRI

BD 7 NOVEMBRE

BOULEVARD MONGI BALI

AVENUE LEOPOLD SENGHOR

Ciné Nejma

Musée
de l'Olivier

RUE DE RABAT

BOULEVARD DE LA CORNICHE

AVENUE HEDI CHAKER

RUE CONSTANTINE

RUE MONGI SLIM

Catholic
Church

Monoprix

RUE EL KAHNA

RUE NACEUR BEY

AVENUE VICTOR HUGO

Bird
Park

Borj
Khedija

AVENUE LEOPOLD SENGHOR

AVENUE IBN EL JAZZAR

AVENUE MOHAMED KARAOUI

Hospital

AVENUE 3 AOUT

AVENUE DE LA REPUBLIQUE

Bonprix

AVENUE MOHAMED MAAROUF

Syndicat d'Initiative

BD HASSOUNA AYACHI

Main
Station

ONTT

AVENUE BOURGUIBA

RUE DE L'INDEPENDENCE

PL. SIDI
BOUJAAFAR

PLACE
FARHAT
HACHED

PLACE
DU PORT

ABDALLAH
IBN ZOUBEIR

Roman Remains

BD YAHIA IBN OMAR

Ribat

See Around Av.
Bourguiba Map

Great Mosque

Port

RUE COMMANDANT BEJAOUI

BOULEVARD MARECHAL TITO

Kasbah

Museum

See Medina map

Bab Jedid
Station

AV HABIB THAMEUR

BD MOHAMED V

ESS Football Ground ▲

RUE NOUREDDINE YASSINE

RUE ABOU HAMED EL GHAZALI

Catacombs
Entrance

AV. DES CATACOMBES

AVENUE 25 JUILLET

AVENUE 3 SEPTEMBRE

RUE 18 JANVIER

AVENUE 15 OCTOBRE

AVENUE IBN KHALDOUN

RUE DU 1 JUIN 1955

AVENUE TAIEB EL GHACHEM

RUE FERHAT ESSAFA

Monastir & Airport ▶

N

Tragic Poet's
House

SOUSSE

Bus Station

0   400 m

Sunday Market, Sfax & Kairouan ▼

▼ Louage Station

century, the **Spaniards** in the sixteenth, and was bombarded in turn by the **French** and Venetians in the eighteenth century. By the end of the nineteenth century the resilient town was becoming increasingly important to the French colonists. Since then Sousse's growth was impeded only in World War II when, as an important German supply port, it suffered heavy Allied bombing. It is now Tunisia's third largest city, with a population of over 300,000, and textile production to some degree balances tourism, the biggest industry by far, which at times seems to completely swamp the place.

Arrival and information

Monastir airport (see p.239) is 15km southeast of Sousse and connected to the town by tourist hotel buses, taxis (8TD), city bus #52 and a métro train, which continues down the coast to Monastir and Mahdia. The main **train station** is in the centre of town on boulevard Hassouna Ayachi, while regular **métro** services from Mahdia, Monastir and Monastir airport leave you at **Bab Jedid station** on boulevard Mohamed V, just south of the centre.

Arriving by **bus** from Monastir or Mahdia, you will be dropped at place Sidi Yahia in the Medina's northeast corner. Buses from elsewhere use the *gare routière* some 2km out of town on the Sfax road, by the Sunday market, from where avenue 15 Octobre runs 1km to the southwest corner of the Medina; a taxi into town will cost around 1.5TD. The **louage station** is located a couple of kilometres south of the centre on rue du 1 Juin in the suburb of Ettoufala; the taxi fare into town from here should be about 1.5TD.

There's a well-organized ONTT **tourist office** at 1 avenue Bourguiba (July & Aug Mon–Sat 7.30am–7pm, Sun 9am–noon; Sept–June Mon–Thurs 8.30am–1pm & 3–5.45pm, Fri & Sat 8.30am–1.30pm; ☎73 225 157), with train and bus schedules, fares and a hotel price list. The Syndicat d'Initiative nearby on place Farhat Hached (June–Aug Mon–Sat 8am–noon & 3–7pm, Sun 9am–noon; Sept–May Mon–Sat 8am–noon & 3–6pm) is also helpful and offers much the same.

Accommodation

Most of the cheaper **hotels** are situated within the Medina, with classier options in the new town. The gleaming white monster beach hotels begin at the northern end of avenue Bourguiba and go on for miles. Almost all of them offer full board and an in-house disco; in low season many have bargain rates and can be warmer at night than the draughty Medina hotels.

Camping is strictly forbidden on most of the beaches, though it is possible at the *Maison des Jeunes* on avenue Taïeb Mehiri (☎73 227548). The hostel is the cheapest place to stay in Sousse if you're on your own, but has rather barrack-like dorms (5TD) and a midnight curfew.

Hotels

Hotels in the new town are shown on the map on p.222, except for the *Corniche Plaza*, which is on the map opposite, as are the beach hotels closest to the centre. For hotels in the Medina, see the map on p.225.

New town

Abou Nawas Boujaafar av Bourguiba, corner of pl Boujafaar ☎73 226 030, ℗73 226 595, ✉www .abounawas.com. A grandiose business hotel, especially known for its seawater thalassotherapy centre. ❼

Claridge 10 av Bourguiba ☎73 224759, ℗73 227 227. An old favourite and city landmark, with a/c, central heating and shower or bath (but no toilet) in every room. Room service is available, as well as discounts on low-season stays of three days or longer. ❹

Corniche Plaza bd de la Corniche ⊕73 226 763, ⊕73 226 433, ⊛www
.corniche-plaza.com. A small place with pleasant, efficient staff. The rooms are plain but large and airy; all are en suite and have a balcony. **❹**

Fares bd Hassouna Ayachi, corner of rue de l'Algérie ⊕73 277 800, ⊕73 227380. An alternative to the *Hadrumète*, with a choice of bath or shower and balconies in all rooms. Some rooms have good views over the Medina. **❹**

Hadrumète pl Assad Ibn Fourat, off pl Farhat Hached ⊕73 226 291, ⊕73 226 863. The Roman torso in the lobby hints at a more auspicious past, as do the slightly tatty rooms. On the fourth floor rooms come with balconies, and many have views over the port. Off-season rates are good value. **❺**

Monia rue de Remada ⊕ & ⊕73 210469. An immaculate little place tucked away behind av Bourguiba, with comfortable en-suite rooms (5TD extra for a/c and TV). **❹**

Hôtel du Parc rue de Carthage ⊕73 220 434, ⊕73 229 211. Comfortable enough, with friendly staff, but it has seen better days and is popular for illicit liaisons (so it sometimes has a dubious clientele). All rooms are en suite. **❷**

Sousse Azur 5 rue Amilcar, near the bird park ⊕73 227760, ⊕73 228145. Spotless place with welcoming smiles. Some rooms have balconies; all are en suite and equipped with a/c and TV. **❺**

Sousse Palace 30 av Bourguiba ⊕73 219220, ⊕73 219 221, ⊛www.soussepalace.com. A 1960s package hotel reborn as a swanky, plush establishment in the heart of town, boasting a magnificent lobby bar, large pool, fitness centre and gym, plus a children's club in summer to amuse the littl'uns while you hit town. Rooms are tastefully done out in turquoise. Exceptionally good value off-season. **❼**

Medina

El Aghlaba 2 rue Laroussi Zarrouk ⊕73 211 024. Simple, pleasant family-run place with shared, single-sex showers. Not all rooms have outside windows. Dorm beds (3TD) available for men only. **❷**

Ahla pl du Grande Mosquée opposite the Great Mosque ⊕73 220 570. Rooms are a bit spartan, but clean enough and good value considering the location. Shared bathrooms open 8am–8.30pm only. **❶**

Emira 52 rue de France ⊕73 226 325, ⊕73 225 723. Clean and friendly; each room comes with its own bath or shower and some rooms have a balcony. In summer there are evening barbecues on the roof terrace. Breakfast included. **❸**

Gabès 12 rue de Paris ⊕73 226 977. Friendly, basic hotel with decent doubles (plus 7TD singles on the top floor), and communal showers with hot water round the clock. For 5TD, in summer you can sleep on the roof terrace, which offers great views. **❶**

Medina 15 rue Othman Osman, by the Great Mosque ⊕73 221 722, ⊕73 221 794. Much posher than the other establishments in the Medina and the only hotel here used by tour groups. The rooms are spick and span and en suite; the rate includes breakfast. **❹**

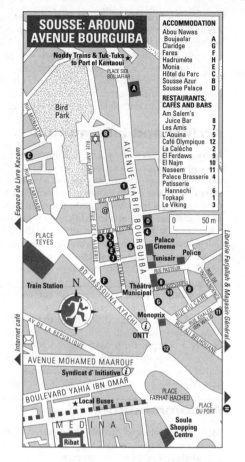

SOUSSE: AROUND
AVENUE BOURGUIBA

Noddy Trains & Tuk-Tuks to Port el Kantaoui

PLACE SIDI BOUJAFFAR

Bird Park

Espace de Livre Kacem

RUE DE MONASTIR

RUE AMILCAR

RUE DE CARTHAGE

AVENUE HABIB BOURGUIBA

RUE D'ITALIE

RUE DE PALESTINE

RUE DE L'ALGÉRIE

PLACE TEYES

Palace Cinema

Police

Tunisair

BD HASSOUNA AYACHI

Train Station

N

Internet café

AV DE LA REPUBLIQUE

Théâtre Municipal

RUE PASTEUR

RUE DU CAIRE

RUE KHALED IBN WALID

RUE AL BELHOUANE

Monoprix

ONTT

AVENUE MOHAMED MAAROUF

Syndicat d' Initiative

BOULEVARD YAHIA IBN OMAR

Local Buses

MEDINA

Ribat

PLACE FARHAT HACHED

PLACE DU PORT

Soula Shopping Centre

Librairie Farjallah & Magasin Général

0   50 m

ACCOMMODATION

Abou Nawas Boujaafar	A
Claridge	G
Fares	F
Hadrumète	H
Monia	E
Hôtel du Parc	C
Sousse Azur	B
Sousse Palace	D

RESTAURANTS, CAFÉS AND BARS

Am Salem's Juice Bar	8
Les Amis	7
L'Aouina	5
Café Olympique	12
La Calèche	2
El Ferdaws	
El Najm	10
Naseem	11
Palace Brasserie	4
Patisserie Hannechi	6
Topkapi	
Le Viking	3

Mestiri 19 rue el Aroua ☎73 222 120. Just about the cheapest place in town, nothing fancy and the rooms are poky. Dorm beds 4TD. ❶

Hôtel de Paris 15 rue du Rempart Nord ☎73 220 564, ℗73 219 038. Boasts pristine if small rooms, a large sunny terrace and friendly management; the shared showers have hot water round the clock. ❷

Beach area

Essaada av Leopold Senghor ☎73 219 515, ℗73 227 277. Friendly and reasonably priced, but the location isn't great, on a busy road 700m from the beach. All rooms en suite, with bath or shower. ❹

Hill Diar bd 7 Novembre ☎73 241811, ℗73 242 836, ℮hilldiar@planet.tn. A very pleasant, laid-back hotel 3km from the centre, set in lovely gardens with a little collection of aviaries plus sheep, goats and guinea pigs. The rooms are sunny and airy (with bungalows available in summer), and there are flowers all over the place indoors and out. Prices are negotiable if you reserve in advance. ❻

Justinia & Nour Justinia av Hedi Chaker ☎73 211 845, ℗73 211 844, ℗www.justinia.com. Sharing a pool, these are the nearest beach hotels to the centre but are not as smart as those further up the beach. Both offer reasonable deals off season, especially for full- and half-board, and the *Justinia* has self-catering rooms. ❺

Kaiser av Taïeb Mehiri ☎73 228 030, ℗73 224 683, ℮hkaiser@planet.tn. A small, mainly package-tour place near the *Tej Marhaba*, about 400m off the beach, though it does have a swimming pool. Also has external glass-windowed elevators. ❺

Marhaba, Marhaba Club & Marhaba Beach bd 7 Novembre ☎73 242 170, ℗73 243 867, ℮marhaba@planet.tn (for *Marhaba* & *Marhaba Club*); ☎73 240 112, ℗73 240 688, ℮marhaba .beach@planet.tn (for *Marhaba Beach*). Also see ℗www.marhababeach.com. A group of three hotels that share facilities. Good value – especially for single rooms off season – and deservedly popular with British holidaymakers. The *Marhaba Beach* is a bit smarter and more expensive. ❼

Mekki rue 2 Mars ☎73 227 127. A quiet pension with spacious en-suite rooms and balconies in a cul-de-sac one block behind bd de la Corniche, but pretty basic and shabby for the price. ❹

Riadh Palms bd 7 Novembre ☎73 225700, ℗73 228 347, ℮palms.reservations@planet.tn. A large package-tour hotel well situated on the best bit of beach in Sousse, but otherwise nothing special. Wheelchair accessible. ❼

Royal 4 rue Teboulba la Corniche, near the bird park ☎73 220 536, ℗73 260 115. A friendly pension not far from either the beach or the town centre, with simple, cosy en-suite rooms. ❷

Tej Marhaba av Taïeb Mehiri ☎73 229 800, ℗73 229 815, ℗www.marhababeach.com. Large and classy, with a well laid-out outdoor pool area, and an indoor pool too; wheelchair accessible. The hotel's beach is 200m away across a main road. ❼

Tour Khalef bd 7 Novembre ☎73 241 844, ℗73 243 868, ℮tourkhalef@planet.tn. Another well-regarded package hotel with plenty of facilities, and wheelchair accessible. It's popular off season (when the rates are very reasonable) with older travellers on longer-stay holidays. ❼

Zohra rue Naceur Bey ☎73 227 423. Tucked away 50m off the beach a block past the *Justinia*, this small hotel offers spotless rooms (en suite with balcony) and a sun terrace. Popular with Scandinavians, as a Swedish woman used to run it. ❹

The City

The hub of the city is **place Farhat Hached**, a huge "square" – if it can be called that – which becomes, on its outer fringes, variously place des Martyrs, place Sidi Yahia and place du Port. Here all traffic and activity seem to converge, and even the main rail line used to cross it – the tracks are still there. To the north is the **new town**, which has been almost entirely rebuilt since the war, and to the south is the **Medina**. The **port** is so close that it's unsettling at night to see a large ship, all lit up, apparently being towed across the square – a surreal image that used to be heightened when the train to Sfax edged its way through in front. The inevitable **avenue Bourguiba** leads from here up to place Sidi Boujaffar, where the **beach** begins, backed for a kilometre by **avenue Hedi Chaker**. Further along, **boulevard 7 Novembre** follows the coast, separated from the beach by a line of hotels, all the way to Port el Kantaoui.

There isn't a great deal to see in the new town, and little in the way of excit-ing colonial architecture, but Sousse does have a few **Art Deco** buildings that enthusiasts may like to check out. One is the ABC Cinema on avenue Habib Thameur, backing onto avenue Mohamed Ali just to the east of the Medina;

Given the large numbers of tourists who come here, it was inevitable that the Sunday **market** in Sousse, a couple of kilometres out towards Sfax, would be "discovered", and images of huge camel sales are used to entice people. Unfortunately, camels are no longer sold here, so if you were hoping to buy one you're out of luck. A taxi from the middle of town should cost around 1.5TD; ask for the Souk Dimanche.

Less touristy is the weekly market at **Hammam Sousse**, 6km northwest of town on the way to Port el Kantaoui. Housed in a walled compound, the market is full of local colour without the tacky souvenirs and takes place on Friday evenings and Saturday mornings. A taxi there – ask for the Souk Samedi Hammam Sousse – will cost about 4TD from the town centre.

another is an office building on the corner of rue de l'Algerie and rue de Palestine, just across the street from *Restaurant le Viking* and west of avenue Bourguiba. There are two more Art Deco structures near the Catholic church on rue Constantine, northwest of the train station – a crumbling house on the corner of boulevard Hassouna Ayachi and avenue Victor Hugo and a building on the corner of rue Constantine and rue el Kahna. Three Art Deco-style private houses can be found on boulevard de la Corniche, one on the west side about 100m northwest of place Boujaffar, opposite the *Hôtel Justinia*, with two others at no. 31 (near the Ciné Nejma) and no. 85 (opposite the El Hana complex).

A couple of blocks behind boulevard de la Corniche, also near the El Hana complex, the interesting new **Musée de l'Olivier** (Mon–Thurs, Sat & Sun 9am–7pm, Fri 9–11.30am & 2.30–7pm; 2TD) is devoted to the olive industry that the Sahel region is famous for (see also box, p.279). Set in the house of a former olive merchant, the museum uses traditional tools to demonstrate how olives are crushed, pressed and filtered to produce olive oil, as well as showing the many other uses that olives are put to in the region. You can sample the museum's own olive oil (included in the entry price) in the pleasant rooftop café or buy a range of home-made produce in the gift shop.

The Medina

The monuments in the walled **Medina** testify to the city's long-lasting importance; in particular the Ribat and the Khalef Tower indicate Sousse's strategic significance, especially to the Aghlabids. You might expect the old city in such a resort to have lost all charm and character in a deluge of tacky souvenir shops. But while there are plenty of these, with a ready spiel for eager punters – and often abuse for less eager ones – the Medina has clung to its individuality. If you fancy a spot of **shopping**, one good place to check out is the Soula Shopping Centre in the northeastern corner of the Medina, where you can browse at leisure without pressure, and where prices are fixed and displayed. Note that there have been one or two cases of bag-snatching in the shopping areas of the Medina, so keep your eyes open and don't dangle valuables temptingly about the place.

The ramparts

Although the Ribat was primarily defensive, only six years after it was begun the Aghlabids were strong enough to launch a successful invasion of Sicily. The city's defences remained important, however, against both Christians at sea and the Berbers inland – hence the thickness of the Medina **ramparts** on the western, inland side. The ramparts were put up under the Aghlabids in 859 AD, following foundations laid by the Byzantines; the gap in the northeast corner

SOUSSE MEDINA

N

AVENUE MOHAMED MAAROUF

PLACE
FARHAT
HACHED

ACCOMMODATION
El Aghlaba   C
Ahla   B
Emira   G
Gabès   E
Medina   D
Mestiri   F
De Paris   A

Syndicat
d'Initiative

BOULEVARD YAHIA IBN OMAR

RUE DU REMPART NORD

Local
Buses

PLACE SIDI YAHIA

Av. Leopold Senghor

RED LIGHT AREA

Dar Essid

RUE SAIDA NEJMA

Zaouia
Zakkak

RUE DE SMYRNE

Ribat

Ticket Booth

Soula
Shopping
Centre

PL DES
MARTYRS

RUE DAR SULTAN

RUE DE MALTE

PLACE DE LA
GRANDE MOSQUEE

Abdel
Kader
Mosque

Tower of
Sidi Ameur

RUE EL AGHLABA

Hammam
Sidi
Bouraoui

Great
Mosque
Police

RUE OTHMAN OSMAN

RUE LARGUESS ZARROUK

RUE D'ANGLETERRE

RUE DE PARIS

Bab el
Finga

RUE SIDI SAID

SABAT DALMA

S O U K S

RUE TIBILIS

RUE DE FRANCE

AVENUE MOHAMED ALI

Police

RUE SOUK EL CAID

Old
Town Hall

EL RBA
SOUK

Kalaout
el Koubba

Old Fondouk

Bab
Jedid

Bab el
Gharbi

Sofra

RUE DE LA KASBAH

Sidi Ali el
Ammar Mosque

Market
Lookout
Tower

RUE SALEM BEN HAMIDA

BOULEVARD MARECHAL TITO

RUE IBN RACHID

RUE SIDI BAZAIZ

RUE EL MAR

Kasbah
Museum

Khalef
Tower

Bou Fatata
Mosque

PLACE
JEBENET
EL GHORBA

Bab El Khabli

RESTAURANTS
Dodo   4
National   2
Du Peuple   1
El Soffra   3

0   100 m

by place Farhat Hached was caused by Allied bombing in 1943. Unfortunately, you're not allowed to climb onto the walls except for a very small section within the Kasbah museum (see p.227).

The Ribat and the Great Mosque

At the northern end of the Medina, the **Ribat** (daily: mid-April to mid-Sept 8am–7pm; mid-Sept to mid-April 8am–5.30pm; 2.1TD, camera 1TD) was begun by the Aghlabids in 821. It's a well-preserved example of a style peculiar to this period of North African history, when the Muslim inhabitants were under constant threat from marauding Christians based in Sicily. The word "ribat" is related to "marabout", and the buildings served a religious as well as a military purpose, housing devout warrior troops broadly comparable to crusading Christian orders such as the Knights Templar. When necessary, the men would fight; in times of peace they lived and studied in the bare cells around the Ribat's inner courtyard. The simplicity of the fort reflects the men's dedication to their second role. The entrance was built with columns and capitals taken from Roman and Byzantine buildings; the only large communal room is the **prayer hall** over the entrance. Until superseded by the Khalef Tower at the opposite corner of the Medina, the Ribat's **tower** served as a lookout point and would pass on beacon messages – messages could be relayed from Alexandria in Egypt through to Ceuta in Morocco in a single night.

Opposite the Ribat stands the **Great Mosque**, Sousse's other great early Islamic monument (Mon–Thurs, Sat & Sun 8am–2pm; Fri 8am–1pm; 1.1TD; tickets from kiosk opposite the main entrance; free loan of cover-all *jellabas* available). Although founded in the ninth century, like the great mosques of Kairouan, Tunis and Sfax, it has a sparer quality than its contemporaries, perhaps because it has received fewer subsequent additions. The original concept of uncomplicated forms remains evident, giving added emphasis to the minimal decoration of the inscription around the wall of the courtyard. The little domed **kiosk** atop the eastern corner was added in the eleventh century to act as a minaret; its wide staircase is a feature more commonly seen in Arab countries further east.

On and north of Rue el Aghlaba

Down a side street near the Ribat you should be able to see a curious open minaret, like stone crochet-work, which belongs to the **Zaouia Zakkak** – Turkish-built, as the octagonal shape reveals. Nearby, rue el Aghlaba climbs to leave the Medina at **Bab el Finga**, passing en route the 1852 **Abdel Kader Mosque** opposite no. 29 and, a little further at no. 52, the square stone **Tower of Sidi Ameur**, like a minaret without a mosque.

The area just north of Bab el Finga is a red-light district, which can only be entered here since all other exits have been walled off. On rue du Rempart Nord, just before you get to the wall of the red-light district, **Dar Essid** is a beautifully restored traditional home, complete with its own tower, now open to the public as a **museum** (daily: May–Sept 10am–7pm; Oct–April 10am–6pm; 2TD, camera 1TD). A stone above the doorway of one room off the inner courtyard appears to date the building at 928 AD, although a closer inspection reveals that the initial digits of "1346 AH/1928 AD" have been erased. Whatever the date, the man of the house had two wives, each with her own bedroom, containing one bed to sleep in and another for marital relations. Next to the first wife's marital bed is a Roman oil lamp: apparently, her husband had to keep up his lovemaking while the lamp was burning and could only climax when it went out; the lamp's design reflects this function. An allegedly Roman urinal has been plumbed into the bathroom for good measure. After looking round the rooms, it's well worth climbing the spiral staircase up the **tower**: at the top is a terrace café with commanding views over Sousse and the surrounding coastline, as well as the Medina ramparts and red-light district immediately below.

The souk area

Back at the other end of rue el Aghlaba, rue d'Angleterre leads south past the tourist stalls to an area of covered souks, which is closed up at night. Turn right here onto rue Souk el Rba, and almost immediately on the right is the **Kalaout el Koubba**, an eleventh- or early twelfth-century Fatimid building whose original function remains unknown. In the fourteenth century it became a *fondouk*, later a café; now it's a fascinating **museum** (Mon–Thurs & Sat 9.30am–1pm & 3–5.30pm, Sun 10am–2pm; 2TD, camera 1TD). Tableaux with life-size plaster models illustrate Tunisian marriage customs and household activities, and there's an English-speaking guide to show you around and explain the details. The building itself is also worth more than a passing glance, with a *koubba* whose design, with external zigzag fluting, is unique in Africa. Parallel with rue d'Angleterre, running south from the Great Mosque, **rue de Paris** is the main street of tourist souvenir shops, selling the usual goods at not exactly bargain prices. One place worth a quick look is no. 54, an old *fondouk*.

Rue el Maar and the southeast of the Medina

At its southern end, rue de Paris joins rue d'Angleterre to become rue el Maar. Just beyond, on the left at no. 3, you can make out the delicately carved facade of the **Sidi Ali el Ammar Mosque**, which dates from the Fatimid period, next door to the white dome of a hammam. A turning to the right, opposite the hammam entrance, leads past a spice, grain and coffee-grinding shop at no. 16, exuding all kinds of wonderful smells, to a blank and impenetrable wall which surrounds the **Sofra**, an early Islamic cistern complex. Near the end of rue el Maar you pass a small, austere mosque on the left, named after one **Bou Fatata** and built, around 840, in a style that's in marked contrast to the elaboration of the Fatimid buildings.

Rue el Maar comes to an end at **Bab el Khabli**, the gate of the southern wall of the Medina. From here, a left within the wall takes you to place Jebenet el Ghorba, where there's a dusty football pitch, then north up rue Salem Ben Hamida and alongside the eastern rampart up to **Bab Jedid**. The woman at no. 3, a house with a lookout tower built into the wall, sometimes lets tourists climb it for a small fee.

The Kasbah and Museum

Leaving the Medina at Bab el Khabli and climbing the windswept street to the right alongside the southern wall, you'll come out eventually onto boulevard Marechal Tito, giving access to the former **Kasbah** in the Medina's southwestern corner. The Kasbah grew up around the **Khalef Tower**, built here in 859 at the highest point in the city to improve on the view given by the Ribat tower, put up thirty years earlier.

Today the Kasbah houses an excellent **museum** (mid-April to mid-Sept Tues–Thurs 9am–noon & 3–7pm, Fri–Sun 9am–6pm; mid-Sept to mid-April Tues–Thurs 9am–noon & 2–6pm, Fri–Sun 9am–6pm; 2.1TD, camera 1TD), whose exhibits – predominantly mosaics – are of a consistently high quality and, unlike those of the Bardo (see p.107), don't threaten to overwhelm by sheer quantity. Many mosaics and tombstones were found in the region's Christian catacombs and, with their familial and domestic epitaphs, are distinguishable by the XP symbol (the "X" is actually a Greek "CH", and the "P" a Greek "R", together standing for "Christ").

Entering the museum, you come first into a cloister; ahead, on the wall to your left, are a number of epitaphs. One long message reads:

This was Eusebia, brothers, a rare and most chaste wife who spent with me a life of marriage, as time tells: sixty years, eight months and twenty days. God himself was pleased with her life, as I say. Truly a gentle wife of the rarest sort: I, Sextus Successus, lawyer, her husband, beg that you always remember her in your prayers, brothers.

The room diagonally across the cloister from the entrance has a number of striking **mosaics** from the second and third centuries AD. Facing you as you come in is Neptune triumphant in a chariot pulled by mer-horses. To the left on the wall behind you, a large early third century AD mosaic shows Bacchus in Triumph in a chariot pulled by tigers, with a lion and a leopard in the foreground. In the late third-century mosaic next to it, four fishing boats sail a sea full of beautifully detailed (and zoologically accurate) fish and other sea creatures. A similar subject is on the same wall at the other end of the room. Facing it, there is a beautiful but sadly incomplete mosaic of different birds and animals, while a little to its left is a yin-yang sign, a Chinese symbol that came to the Romans with the silk trade. As you leave the room, check the mosaic above the door of Venus bathing, surrounded by a group of rather stern-looking portraits.

The next room round the cloister contains some old **tombstones**, and the next door after that leads into the courtyard, with other rooms off to the right as you go through. A series of mosaics are displayed in a trio of rooms straight across the courtyard. The first room features theatre scenes and a first-century work containing swastikas, an Indian sun symbol with no sinister connotation in those days. Like the yin-yang and the tigers in the other mosaic room, it shows that the Romans were not cut off from India and China, as medieval Europe was following the rise of Islam. The third room has some amazing amphitheatre mosaics of gladiators facing, and preparing to face, all manner of wild animals. From the courtyard a small piece of the **rampart** is accessible, but most of the Kasbah is closed to the public.

The House of the Tragic Poet and catacombs

If you head south from the Kasbah along rue Ibn Khaldoun and bear right at the fork after 200m onto rue du 1 Juin, you'll come to the **House of the Tragic Poet**, a tiny Roman site with mosaics of dramatic themes along the lines of its namesake in the ruins of Pompeii in Italy. Another area of Roman remains can be glimpsed from avenue 3 Août, just northwest of the Medina, but is currently closed to the public.

Another suburban attraction is the **Catacombs of the Good Shepherd**, about 1km southwest of the Medina (Tues–Sun: mid-April to mid-Sept 8am–noon & 3–7pm; mid-Sept to mid-April 9am–noon & 2–6pm; 1.1TD). You can reach it by taking rue Commandant Béjaoui from Bab el Gharbi (the Medina's western gate), turning left after 500m, then right onto rue Abou Hamed el Ghazali and left after 100m. One of four sets of Roman catacombs in Sousse, this was the burial place of early Christians from the third and fourth centuries. A small part of it has been restored – perhaps a little too tastefully. It is illuminated with flickering lights and, though most of the tombs are bricked up, one or two are fronted with glass to reveal the skeletons inside. The part open to the public only extends for a couple of hundred metres, but the whole complex has over 5km of catacombs in total, and contains over fifteen thousand tombs.

The beach

What brings most tourists to Sousse is its **beach**. Though inferior to Hammamet's – the shore is more exposed, urban and often windy – it has a more eminent literary history. Somewhere on the sands beneath where the hotels now stand, French novelist André Gide had his first sexual experience, at the age of 23, in 1893. His partner was his porter, Athman, who appears in Gide's semi-autobiographical novel, *L'Immoraliste*, though the author leaves out any mention of the sexual encounter.

The beach stretches from the centre of town to Port el Kantaoui, 7.5km up the coast. The southernmost part, south of Borj Khedija, is dirty and litter-strewn. North of it is the city beach, also called **Boujaffar Beach**, with avenue Hedi Chaker running alongside to form a promenade. This part of the beach is relatively narrow and usually pretty crowded. The choicest bit, with the widest sand, is 500m further along, between the *Hôtel Riadh Palms* and Oued Blibane, beyond which the hotels become sparser. As you round the cape by the *Hôtel Alyssa*, 4km out of town, the beach narrows again, but is almost free of hotels and their guests until Port el Kantaoui.

Large slices of beach are privately owned by the hotels, with small **public areas** in between which, especially where there's direct access to the road, can get very busy in summer as Tunisian families pile in with everything but the kitchen sink in tow. The **private sections** are usually marked by umbrellas and sunbeds, and generally charge a moderate fee (around 3TD) for their use. It may be worth paying for a chair and umbrella, if only for the security of having someone watch over your things while you swim or visit the hotel's snack bar, though of course you should never leave valuables unattended. If you're female, the security in a private section will protect you from the advances of young Tunisian men. The level of vigilance varies from lax to hawk-like, depending on who's in charge of your particular slice of sand; the *Marhaba* hotel complex is one of the best security-wise. Apart from petty thieving gangs of kids, look out for beach sellers of cigarettes, candied almonds and such sundries. Most vendors are honest, but some will overcharge new arrivals unfamiliar with Tunisian money, and may lift unattended or unwatched valuables.

You can take part in various **water sports** at four posts on public areas of the beach, allocated as franchises by the city council. These are: between the *Jawhara Club* and the *Marhaba* hotels; by the *Hôtel Tour Khalef*; "Tina's", in front of the *Hôtel el Ksar*, just south of the *Hôtel Hill Diar*; and to the north of here by the *Hôtel Orient Palace*. Franchisees at all four posts have agreed prices and charge standard rates. Activities include parasailing (20TD), waterskiing (15TD) and windsurfing (20TD/hr), as well as jet-skiing (20TD/10min) and inflatable bananas and doughnuts (7TD). **Pedalos** are available at various sites along the beach.

There is a small **bird park** (daily 8am–5pm; 0.2TD) just across place Boujaffar at the southern end of the promenade. Really just a small patch of greenery with a few aviaries, it does offer at least a change of scene. From this end of the promenade it's also possible to rent **calèches** (horse-drawn carriages) or catch the tuk-tuk or noddy train to Port el Kantaoui (see p.235).

Eating and drinking

Sousse has plenty of quality **restaurants** and **cafés**. Tourists are catered for with European cooking but Soussis favour haunts that have much less in the way of finesse but serve equally palatable food at a cheaper price. A lot of the beach hotels have buffets and set menus at moderate prices, too. The tourist-driven places in Sousse tend to be tacky and poor value, and generally speaking anywhere that displays its menu outside in several languages, with a waiter trying to hustle you in as soon as you stop to look, is worth avoiding.

Sousse does not really have any licensed **bars** like Sfax or Tunis, but some places attached to hotels or restaurants serve alcohol. Of these, the terrace bar of the *Claridge Hôtel*, 10 av Bourguiba (daily 6am–11pm), is a good place to relax with a beer during the afternoon. Some 100m up the road, the *Palace Brasserie* (daily 5am–8pm) by the Palace cinema is more like an ordinary Tunisian bar. An alternative up in the hotel zone, and more comfortable for women, is the *Rose and Crown* (daily 11am–midnight or later), an English-style pub, as you may guess from the name; it's on boulevard 7 Novembre in the Tej Marhaba shopping centre, belonging to the *Hôtel Tej Marhaba*. As well as beer – Tunisian, not English – the *Rose and Crown* serves food, including a full English breakfast. For a decent pint, however, your best bet is about 100m north of the Hammam Sousse turn-off at the far northern end of the hotel zone; here *Golf Bräu* brews and serves the best beer in Tunisia.

Restaurants

Around avenue Bourguiba

Les Amis rue de Remada. Good, cheap place serving a tasty *kamounia* and *salade mechouia*. Daily 11am–midnight.

L'Aouina rue de Remada. The couscous is spicy and very good at this low-priced restaurant. Daily noon–10.30pm.

La Calèche 6 rue de Remada ☎73 226 489. One of the better posh gaffs in town, and not at all expensive, with particularly good-value set meals. Daily noon–3pm & 6pm–midnight.

El Ferdaws rue Braunschweig. Decent food at a reasonably priced cheapie whose staples include pasta, chicken and chips, and sometimes couscous. Near the *Claridge Hôtel*. Daily 6am–9pm.

El Najm (Hamza) rue Braunschweig. It's signed in Arabic only, opposite *Am Salem's Juice Bar*. A small, cheap Tunisian diner, known for having the best *lablabi* in town, and also serving excellent *chakchouka*, *merguez* and other traditional specialities. The owner speaks English. Daily except Tues 6am–10pm.

Naseem Corner of rue Khaled Ibn el Walid and rue de l'Indépendance. Signed in Arabic only, this busy and popular little place serves couscous, grilled chicken, *chakchouka*, *kamounia* and other typical Tunisian dishes. Daily 8am–9pm.

Le Viking rue de l'Algérie ☎73 228 377. Another good, central, upmarket option, named for the owner's long sojourn in Nordic climes, and very popular with Scandinavian tourists. Daily noon–midnight.

Medina

Dodo rue el Hajra ☎73 212 326. A moderately priced establishment at the southern end of the Medina with a fine stone-walled upstairs dining space, serving pizzas as well as other European and Tunisian dishes. Daily noon–9pm.

National rue el Aghlaba, near the Great Mosque. A *gargote* serving grilled meat, chicken *shawarma* and staples such as pasta, beans and chips. Daily 9am–9pm.

Du Peuple rue du Rempart Nord, next to the *Hôtel de Paris*. A very pleasant and well-priced little place, good for couscous and tajines. Mint tea and dessert are free. Daily: June to mid-Sept 7am–1am; mid-Sept to May noon–10pm.

El Soffra 6 rue el Soffra. Highly regarded, spotless place offering a choice of seven or eight excellent-value Tunisian dishes that change from day to day. Daily noon–4pm.

Beach area

La Belle Avenue bd de la Corniche. One of the first – and best – of a host of Western-style fast-food takeaways, with cheap burgers, pizzas, chips and the like. Daily noon–midnight.

Le Caprice bd de la Corniche. A friendly, moderately priced place with pizzas and a selection of salads. Daily noon–midnight.

L'Escargot 87 bd de la Corniche ☎73 224 779.

Pleasant, upmarket restaurant with great seafood and grilled meats, plus of course snails for starters (with garlic or bacon). Mon–Sat 10am–2pm & 5.30pm–1am, Sun eve only.

La Fiesta rue Mongi Slim ☎73 225 112. Offering a decent choice of tasty fish or meat dishes, a bit pricey à la carte, though there's a good-value 9TD set menu. Also has live music Mon, Fri & Sat eve. Daily noon–midnight.

Forum Grill av Hedi Chaker ☎73 228 399. A friendly, moderately priced place on the beachfront with good food – particularly *brik* and fish soup – and service.Daily noon–3pm & 6–11pm.

Hong Kong rue de Rabat, opposite the *El Hana Beach Hôtel* ☎73 221 366. Sousse's only Chinese, with a 9TD set menu or expensive à la carte dishes, including pork and duck. Daily noon–3pm & 6pm–midnight.

Le Surfin' av Taïeb Mehiri. Fixed-price fish dinners, pricey at 20TD (half-price for children) but worth every penny, including an eight-plate hors d'oeuvre, fish soup and whatever fish is fresh in, plus sorbet for dessert. Choice is limited but it's always fresh and competently prepared. Daily noon–4pm & 6pm–midnight.

Tip-Top 73 bd de la Corniche ☎73 226 158. Consistently good, moderately priced establishment with great fish dishes – including fish couscous – and pizzas. Set menus 7–10TD. Daily 11.30am–1am.

Les Trois Dauphins bd 7 Novembre, 2km north of town near *Hôtel Tour Khalef* ☎73 270 397. Excellent eating out in the hotel zone, with a choice of indoor or terrace dining or, in summer, a barbecue in the beer garden. All sorts of food is on the menu, mostly French and Italian, plus English or Continental breakfasts. You can pop in just for a beer or a coffee. Daily 9am–1am.

Snack bars and patisseries

Am Salem's Juice Bar rue Braunschweig. The best place in town for real fruit juice – they only have what's in season – and keenly priced compared to all the tourist places. They also do scrumptious cakes. Daily except Tues 5am–10pm.

Casa del Gelato bd 7 Novembre, by the *Hôtel Hill Diar*. Delicious ice cream out in the hotel zone, in a snazzy cubical glass building, with a pizzeria upstairs. Daily 7am–midnight.

Gara Nimsa av Leopold Senghor, near corner of rue de Rabat. Locally renowned bakery and patisserie, with ice creams and pizzas too (the neon sign outside just says "Jus – Glaces – Pizza – Gateaux"). Daily 6am–midnight.

Café Olympique 1 av Bourguiba, corner of pl Farhat Hached. Pleasant, conservatory-style café in which to watch the world go by, serving decent breakfasts, *shawarma* sandwiches, pastries and ice cream. Daily 6am–10pm.

Patisserie Hannechi av Bourguiba, opposite Palace cinema. A good place to drop in for cakes or ice cream. Daily 3am–11pm.

Tutti Frutti bd 7 Novembre, next to Tej Marhaba complex. Glitzy new place serving super ice creams, cakes and a range of coffees. Daily 7.30am–11.30pm.

Nightlife

Avenue Bourguiba and avenue Hedi Chaker are where people eat, drink, meet or simply stroll the promenade in the evenings. The only **nightclub** down here is *Topkapi* at 65 av Bourguiba, mainly gay and rather seedy – and closed for renovations at the time of writing. About 2km north of the town centre, the *Samara King Disco* on boulevard 7 Novembre (entry 6TD), is very lively, especially on Friday and Saturday nights in summer. The club usually gets going around 11pm, continuing until 4am or later if people are still on the dance floor. The *Maracana Club*, in the Tej Marhaba complex just south of the *Samara King*, is similar but newer; in winter it sometimes closes during the week. There is also a reasonably popular disco in the *Hôtel Tour Khalef* called *La Grotte*, which some wags unkindly say lives up to its name.

Opposite the *Samara King* used to be a glitzy casino doubling as a cabaret theatre, but it was closed at the time of writing and its future was unclear. Also in this part of town are a couple of trendy **dance bars**: at the *Restaurant Bonaparte* on avenue Taïeb Mehiri and the *Fun Pub* at *Hôtel Rym*, north of the junction of avenue Taïeb Mehiri and avenue Leopold Senghor; both open around 10pm and carry on into the small hours. A newer venue, and closer to the centre of town, is the *Latino Bar* at the *Justinia Hotel*, open till dawn.

Listings

Airlines Tunisair, 15 av Bourguiba ☎73 227 955.

Banks and exchange There are plenty of banks on av Bourguiba, one or two of which open Sat & Sun morning. A solution to the summertime queues is to try banks further afield (such as the STB on av Leopold Senghor opposite the junction with av de la République). After hours, try the big hotels for money-changing. There are plenty of ATMs dotted around.

Bookshops Librairie Farjallah at the corner of rue Ali Belhouane and rue Avicenne has a small selection of English classics, while Espace du Livre Kacem, near the train station at 17 bd Hassouna Ayachi, has some more contemporary choices. The secondhand bookstalls by Sidi Yahia bus station have the occasional English title.

Car and moped rental Avis, bd de la Corniche ☎73 225 901; Budget, bd de la Corniche ☎73 227 614; Europcar, 49 bd de la Corniche ☎73 226 252; Hertz, 77 av Bourguiba ☎73 225 428. For details of Monastir airport offices, see p.239. There are lots of local agencies clustered about halfway up bd de la Corniche near the Ciné Nejma. Motorbikes, scooters and mopeds can be rented from Ali's Motos Rent on bd 7 Novembre (☎73 226 519), just beyond the Tej Marhaba complex.

Car repairs Garages and spare parts stores are concentrated on av 15 Octobre, down towards the *gare routière*, and on bd Mohamed V, south of Bab Jedid station.

Churches St Felix Catholic church, 1 rue Constantine (☎73 224 596), has Mass at 6.15pm weekdays and 9.30am Sun. Protestant services in English are held at 16 rue de Malte in the Medina (Sun at 10am; ☎73 224 073). There's a synagogue hidden away in an alley next to the *Sousse Azur Hotel*, with a service on Saturday morning.

Cinemas The Théâtre Municipal on av Bourguiba, a block north of the *Hôtel Claridge*, screens arty films (and stages plays and classical concerts). Otherwise, there's the Palace a few doors up and the Ciné Nejma on bd de la Corniche.

Dentists Recommended English-speaking dentists include Kamel Bouslama on av Habib Thameur by the old ABC cinema (☎73 224 699) and Hosni Sriha on av Mohamed Maarouf opposite the Lycée des Garçons (☎73 211 833).

Doctors Big hotels have their own doctors on call, but otherwise, recommended doctors include Dr Mounira Kadhraoui Zahra at 1 rue Essarouel, 2km north of town in Khezzama (☎73 242 251), whose husband (☎98 400 838), also a doctor, speaks English and makes house calls for around 20TD.

Ferry companies CTN has an office in town (see p.17), but tickets are best obtained from travel agents in town, such as Chams Tour at 8 rue Ali Belhouane (☎73 225 357) and Sahel Voyages at 6 rue de Palestine (☎73 220 531).

Festivals Both Sousse and Port el Kantaoui have high-season programmes of cultural events for tourists, known respectively as the International Festival of Sousse and the El Kantaoui Festival. Every 24 or 25 July, there's a carnival in aid of a mythical marabout named Baba Aoussou, featuring a procession of floats with music and dancing, making its way down from Port el Kantaoui into town. There's also a spring festival in mid-March and an olive festival in Kalaa Kebira (see p.237) at the beginning of December.

Football The main local team is Étoile Sportive du Sahel (ESS), whose ground is west of the Medina (out of Bab Gharbi and straight ahead up rue Commandant Béjaoui for 2km); matches are usually played on Sunday afternoons.

Hammams Hammam Sidi Bouraoui in rue Sidi Bouraoui (off rue Aghlaba by no. 23) is one of the oldest in the Medina (daily except Tues: men 6am–1pm, women 1.30–7.30pm). Hammam Sidi Ali al Ammar at 3 rue el Maar, next to the mosque of the same name, is also recommended but was closed for renovations at the time of writing. A more sanitized (and expensive) version of a hammam is available at the *Hôtel Chams el Hana* on bd de la Corniche, where couples can also go along together in the morning (Tues–Sun: mixed 10am–1pm, women 1–7pm, men 7–9pm).

Hospitals Farhat Hached University Hospital is on av Ibn el Jazzar (☎73 221 411), off av Leopold Senghor, behind the Medina. The Clinique des Oliviers on bd 7 Novembre (☎73 242 711), just past the *Hill Diar Hotel* on the left, is generally preferable. The modern Clinique Essalem, by the junction of av Leopold Senghor and av Taïeb Mehiri (☎73 210 375), is also rated highly, with 24hr casualty admissions.

Internet access The biggest place is Publinet Sousse Centre in Immeuble Gloulou on av Mohamed Maarouf, 100m west of the post office, though you have to pay by the hour rather than the quarter-hour (Mon–Sat 8am–1am, Sun 3pm–1am; 2TD/hr). Other places include: Cybernet, first floor, Immeuble Kassaa, at the north end of rue Remada (daily 8am–midnight; 2TD/hr); Publinet Century 21 on rue de Rabat, just west of rue Mongi Slim (Mon–Sat 9am–2am, Sun noon–2am; 2TD/hr); and Club Génération Informatique behind *Cala Pi Nou* pizzeria on rue des Jardins in El Khezama, 100m west off bd 7 Novembre just south of *Casa del Gelato* (daily 9am–10pm; 3TD/hr).

Massages As well as the version on offer at the hammams, aromatherapy and reflexology are offered for women only by Dee Eltaïef at 93 bd 7 Novembre, just north of the Tej Marhaba complex (☎73 227 109, ✉dee@topnet.tn), currently for 25TD and 22TD a session respectively.

Newspapers English-language papers can be found at the Espace du Livre Kacem bookshop (see p.232), as well as some of the beach hotels.

Pharmacy There's a night pharmacy at 38 av de la République.

Police The central station is on rue Pasteur off av Habib Bourguiba (☎73 225 566), with smaller ones by the Great Mosque's southwest corner, and inside Bab el Gharbi.

Post office At the corner of av de la République and bd M Naarouf (city hours), with a bureau de change for cash and Western Union.

Supermarkets The best supermarket in town is Bonprix on av Victor Hugo, just north of av Moham-

ed Maarouf. Otherwise, there's a Monoprix at the beginning of av Bourguiba by pl Farhat Hached and a large new one on av Leopold Senghor, 100m north of the av de la République junction, and two branches of Magasin Général, one on bd de la Corniche and one on the corner of rue de l'Indépendance and rue Avicenne. There is another good supermarket by the *Riadh Palms* hotel, slightly pricier but with a better choice of groceries.

Swimming pools Non-residents should be able to use hotel pools for a small fee.

Telephones There are taxiphone offices on almost every street corner, most staying open from about 7am to 10pm.

Tours Try the big hotels, or agencies like Cartours on bd de la Corniche (☎73 224 092), who do trips such as a three-day "safari" (not a wildlife expedition) around the south, a day in Gabès and Matmata and excursions to Kairouan, El Jem and Mahdia. You should book a couple of days in advance.

Port el Kantaoui

Nine kilometres north of Sousse, **PORT EL KANTAOUI** offers Tunisia without tears for the delectation of the international tourist. With the help of Kuwaiti investment, a vast pleasure complex has been conjured out of a stretch of empty coast, including a "genuine" Tunisian yacht harbour in "authentic" Andalusian style. Call it artificial, soulless, even anaemic, it has nonetheless become one of Tunisia's most popular resorts and, if you don't mind being in a tourist ghetto cut off from the rest of the country, it does have a lot going for it. Tunisians find the place fascinating and come down by the busload in season to see how the other half lives and to join foreigners in dancing the night away.

The **marina** is a popular winter refuge among Mediterranean yachting folk, who come here for its mild climate and very reasonable mooring fees – you'd have to go through the Suez Canal into the Red Sea to beat either – while package tourists flock to the marina for its well-designed hotels and range of facilities. The **SDANEK Diving Centre** (☎73 246 374, ✉sdanek@planet.tn) at the end of the quay offers lessons for beginners and advanced divers, with daytime and nighttime dives. **Sailing excursions** are available along the quayside too, on glass-bottomed boats, yachts, fishing boats and imitation galleons.

Other attractions in Port el Kantaoui include the **Zoo Kantaoui**, a garden of birds and of aromatic and medicinal plants (daily 8am–7pm; 3TD), near where the road into the centre of Port el Kantaoui leaves the main road. Just across the way, **Hannibal Park** (daily 10am–10pm) is a collection of fairground-type rides for children, including a train, a merry-go-round and trampolines; entry is free – you pay by the ride. On the other side of the main road is the **Acqua Palace** (daily: April–June & Sept–Nov 9.30am–6pm; July & Aug 9am–10pm; 10TD), a water amusement park featuring slides, water toboggans, wave machines, spa pools and all sorts of splashy fun for adults and children alike. There are two eighteen-hole **golf courses** (☎73 348 756, ⓦwww.kantaouigolfcourse.com .tn) a few hundred metres north along the main road; a round will set you back 60TD. A popular day-trip from Port el Kantaoui is the **Friguia Safari Park** (see p.217) by bus from the *Hôtel Kanta*, which can be booked through the Panorama tour agency at the hotel and costs 28TD per person.

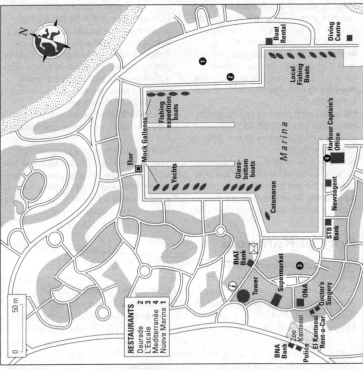

RESTAURANTS

Daurade **2**
L'Escale **3**
Mediterranée **4**
Nuova Marina **1**

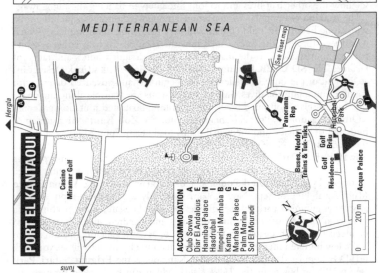

PORT EL KANTAOUI

MEDITERRANEAN SEA

ACCOMMODATION

Club Soviva **A**
Diar El Andalous **E**
Hannibal Palace **H**
Hasdrubal **I**
Imperial Marhaba **B**
Kanta **K**
Marhaba Palace **F**
Palm Marina **C**
Sol El Mouradi **D**

Practicalities

It's easy to reach Port el Kantaoui by bus from place Sidi Yahia in Sousse (#12 or #18, running half-hourly). In Port el Kantaoui, buses to Sousse or Hergla, and louages to the same destinations, can be picked up on the main road, as can the regular **noddy trains** that most tourists bound for Sousse seem to prefer (3.5TD return – note that you have to return on the same colour train that you leave on, or else buy a new ticket). Another alternative is the **tuk-tuks** (auto-rickshaws), which leave every ten minutes or so from the same place as the Noddy trains, heading for place Boujaffar in Sousse's centre. For **car rental**, try Kantaoui Rent-a-Car by the zoo (℡73 241 318).

Most of the hotels here have everything you could possibly want for a fortnight in the sun, and around the marina you'll find shops, a bar, car and boat rental offices, banks, a post office, a doctor and an **ONTT** (July & Aug Mon–Sat 7.30am–1.30pm, Sun 9am–noon; Sept–June Mon–Thurs 8.30am–1pm & 3–5.45pm, Fri & Sat 8.30am–1.30pm; ℡73 348 799). Panorama's tour rep, in an office at the back of the *Hôtel Kanta* (daily 9am–noon & 4–6pm), is also a good source of information.

Accommodation

The original **hotels** in the centre of the resort are generally better than the newer ones to the north and south, some of which are more slapdash affairs built to cash in on the resort's name.

Hôtel Club Soviva 1700m north of the marina ℡73 246 145, ℗73 246 258, ⍟www.soviva.com. Reasonable for the price, but most notable for its aquapark swimming pool complete with amazing giant slide and water chute, sadly out of bounds for under-10s, but otherwise open for a fee to non-residents who can't face the trek down to the Acqua Palace. **❼**

Diar El Andalous 1km north of the marina ℡73 246 200, ℗73 246 348, ⍟www.abounawas .com. Very stylish with comfy rooms, bars and restaurants in massive grounds with thirteen tennis courts. **❽**

El Hana Hannibal Palace 300m east of the main junction ℡73 348 577, ℗73 348 321, ℮hannibal .elhana@planet.tn. The largely green decor of this impressive-looking hotel greets you as you enter the marina area. This was one of Port el Kantaoui's original hotels, and is still one of the nicest, but the lack of an indoor pool belies its five-star rating. **❽**

Hasdrubal 200m southeast of the main junction ℡73 348 944, ℗73 348 969, ⍟www.hasdrubal -hotels.com. Quiet and restful, with a large pool and seawater thalassotherapy spa. **❽**

Imperial Marhaba 1700m north of the marina ℡73 246 477, ℗73 246 377, ⍟www .marhababeach.com. The most stylish of the hotels, with a full range of facilities and a very swish atrium-style lobby done out in marble, with glass lifts. **❽**

Kanta 400m north of the main junction ℡73 348 666, ℗73 348 656, ⍟www.kantahotel.com. Friendly rather than grandiose, with an emphasis on service rather than palatial-style decor. It also has a self-catering annexe, the *Hôtel Résidence Kanta*. **❼**

Marhaba Palace 300m north of the marina ℡73 243 633, ℗73 243 639, ⍟www.marhababeach .com. Scores highly across the board, with a palatial lobby, pleasant rooms and cheerful service. **❽**

Palm Marina 1700m north of the main junction ℡73 246 900, ℗73 246 921, ℮palm .marina@planet.tn. It's worth popping in just for a look at the beautifully designed lobby with its reception desk backed by a sea view. The rooms are cool and tasteful. **❽**

Sol El Mouradi 1500m north of the main junction ℡73 246 355, ℗73 246 070, ℮elmouradi .resa@planet.tn. A decent three-star with its own hammam and a selection of pinball machines and video games. **❼**

Eating and drinking

For a change from hotel food, there are some excellent **restaurants** by the quayside, with prices that will make you blench if you are used to typical Tunisian places, but which still represent extremely good value compared to what you'd pay for the same food in the West. Notable among them are the

Daurade (☎73 348 893; Tues–Sun noon–11.30pm), a tip-top fish restaurant offering seafood bisque with champagne, fish hotpot and paella, and baked Alaska among the desserts; and across the quay, by the harbourmaster's office, the *Méditerranée* (☎73 348 788; daily except Tues noon–11pm), which offers a selection of fish or steak cooked to your specifications, as well as vegetarian dishes and a 18.5TD tourist menu. Also recommended is *L'Escale*, near the tower and port entrance (☎73 347220; daily 11am–midnight), which has some excellent meat and poultry dishes, including turkey à l'orange, and a good-value tourist menu at 14TD. Of the cheaper places, try *Nuova Marina*, set back from the quay near the *Daurade* (daily 11am–midnight), which does starters for 5TD, pasta and pizza for 6TD, meat and fish dishes for 8TD and a limited selection of desserts for 3.5TD.

For a **beer**, the best place in Port el Kantaoui, and indeed the whole of Tunisia, is *Golf Bräu* (daily 10am–1am), a German-run microbrewery on the main road junction between Hannibal Park and the Acqua Palace. It produces its own pilsner, white beer and black ale, all absolutely delicious, with free bar snacks thrown in (food is also available). The beer costs about double what you'd pay for a Celtia in Sousse, but is well worth the difference.

Hergla

Fifteen kilometres north of Port el Kantaoui, and 24km north of Sousse, **HERGLA** is a pretty village perched on a cliff, which can be reached by bus (#18, running roughly hourly via the hotel zone and Port el Kantaoui) or by yellow shared taxi from place Sidi Yahia in Sousse. Hergla has a long history, including a time when it marked the boundary between two Roman provincial subdivisions. Its romantic setting should have belonged to a pirate's lair, but the inhabitants have always made their living from weaving **esparto grass** – brought from as far inland as Kasserine – into filters used in pressing olives for oil. A fishing harbour has since been built, rather marring the sea views, but it remains a spectacular place, dense with whitewashed houses and topped, as in the hill villages, by a **mosque**. Built in the eighteenth century and named after a local man called Sidi Bou Mendel (who, the story goes, flew back from Mecca in the tenth century on his handkerchief), the mosque overlooks a cemetery and a drop to the harbour and the deep blue sea beyond.

The paltry remains of Roman **Horrea Coelia** (a few mosaics and minor excavations) are 800m down the cliff road from the mosque to the south: look for a blue metal fence by a tarmac road leading down towards the sea (Mon–Sat 9am–4pm; free, token payment to the *gardien* at your discretion). To the north of the village is a **beach**, narrow and flotsam-strewn, but deserted. There are also snorkelling possibilities and a **scuba diving** centre down by the harbour (☎73 231 386). Two kilometres west of the village, towards the Tunis–Sousse highway, is **Hergla Park** (July–Sept daily 9am–2am; Oct–June daily except Tues 9am–7pm; pay by the ride), a collection of fairground rides and two go-karting tracks – a full-sized one (950m) for adults, and a junior version (450m) for kids.

There is nowhere to stay in Hergla, but there are a couple of **restaurants** – the cheap and cheerful *L'Étoile* on the main square (daily 7am–9pm), which offers Tunisian staples such as couscous, and the smarter but still not especially pricey *Boumendil* on avenue de Bizerte, the narrow road up to the clifftop (☎73 251 299; daily 8.30am–10pm), serving your choice of the day's catch freshly grilled. Around the mosque, where the bus stops, there are a handful of cafés and **souvenir shops**, where you can check out the local woven goods.

The Oued Sed and Sebkha Kelbia

Some 4km south of Hergla, the road crosses the **Oued Sed**, a freshwater and reed-bed area, whose river flows under the main road and eventually ends up in **Sebkhet Halk el Menzel**, a salt lake close to the sea. Any passing bus can drop you off here.

As always, freshwater is a magnet for **birds**, and if there's enough water in the river and the lake, the area is well worth a trip, with all the usual wading and waterside birds, including spoonbills, plus occasional sightings of purple gallinule and marbled teal. Peregrine falcons and marsh harriers hunt over the area – the latter feeding on the abundant frog population. **Flamingos** are present whenever there's enough water, and you can sometimes see large flocks of migrating cranes, too.

In the past, **Sebkha Kelbia**, a huge salt lake 30km inland from Sousse, was a major site for wintering wildfowl and waders, but dams have been built on its feed rivers, cutting off the water supply. After a very wet winter, though, it would certainly be an outstanding site. The lake can be best explored from the village of **Dar el Ouessef** at the northern tip where the Oued Sed flows out, or (with a bit of a walk) from the village of **Bir Jedid** at the southwestern corner.

The fields around Kelbia are rich in **gypsum** and, in spring, hold a very colourful and characteristic **flora**. Vast areas of the *sebkha* itself, in common with all salty mud flats, are dominated by species of salt-resistant glasswort. Tamarisk bushes form a shrubby fringe, and birdwatchers will find them worth scouring for small warblers.

Hill villages

Once picturesque and still quite traditional, if rather nondescript, are three hill villages just a few kilometres inland from Sousse – **KALAA SGHIRA**, **KALAA KEBIRA** and **AKOUDA** – all of which date back to Aghlabid times, and preserve a sort of bustling venerability, with ancient winding streets and doorways. Before they became so sprawling, each village stood perched on a green hill topped by a mosque, and this still forms the heart of each one. In 1864 their tranquillity was shattered when the villagers joined forces with the tribes from the interior in a **revolt** against the bey's demands for increased taxation. They came near to overthrowing the government but soon fell out with each other, giving General Zarrouk a chance to gather his troops and defeat them piecemeal. The retribution he exacted was terrible, with heavy fines imposed on the villagers. Those who could not pay were seized, tortured and executed; landowners with no cash were forced to sell their acres to merchants from Sfax, who had wisely remained loyal to the bey, and thus the villagers became labourers rather than landowners. Many were totally impoverished. Even today, Zarrouk's name is considered synonymous with cruelty, and historians identify the year 1864 as the turning point in the region's economy. Thereafter a steady decline set in.

You can reach the villages by bus from place Sidi Yahia in Sousse (#20 to Kalaa Sghira leaving half-hourly; #15 to Kalaa Kebira, #14 or #15 to Akouda, leaving every 10min). Kalaa Kebira holds a **festival** every December to celebrate the olive harvest, with music, dancing and general merrymaking.

Monastir and around

Coming from almost any other part of the country, it's a shock to discover just how densely populated this small triangle south of Sousse is, with a thriving town every few kilometres. This was the case even in the time of the Romans, and the coastline is littered with vestigial remains of many of their settlements. But it was under the Aghlabids, when Kairouan was the capital, that this area moved ahead of the rest of the country.

Most of the towns are virtually indistinguishable, with crowded streets and a purposeful atmosphere that's very different from elsewhere in Tunisia. **MONASTIR**, however, has a special appeal. A former fishing port on the Sahel coast just 20km southeast of Sousse, it has never been allowed to forget that **Habib Bourguiba** (born here August 3, 1903) emerged from its industrious middle class, which later provided his power base. With a festival every year on the late president's birthday, along with the Bourguiba family mausoleum, the Bourguiba Mosque and a presidential palace, Monastir has uneasily adjusted to a role in the national limelight. As well as this attention, the town has had to cope with the international film industry and a level of tourist development that has all but swamped it. Needless to say, all this detracts somewhat from its older heritage.

Moving on from Monastir

For a list of destinations and journey times, see Travel details on p.285.
For most destinations, you are better off looking for public transport in Sousse
than Monastir, although there is one daily departure for Enfida, Bir Bou Regba and
Tunis from the **train station** (☎73 460 725). From here, there are also regular **métro**
services to Sousse and Mahdia (via Ksar Hellal and Moknine). The **bus station** (☎73
461 059) has services to Le Kef, Kairouan, Kélibia and Nabeul, among others. For all
other long-distance destinations you must go to Sousse (bus #52; every 20min). To
get to the **airport** (☎73 520 000), the métro is the obvious means (10min), although
there's also bus #52.

Arrival, transport and information

Monastir airport, right in the middle of the country's tourist haven, is connected
to the town by the Sahel **métro train** (see p.218), whose platform is 100m from
the air terminal, and by **bus** (#52).You can catch a **taxi** into Monastir for around
5TD, though you'll have to haggle – taxi drivers are quick to take advantage of
tourists. A number of **car rental** firms operate from the airport (see p.221); you
should be able to pick up a car immediately on arrival. There is also a **tourist
office** (variable hours), which stays open for inbound flights.The **train station** is
on avenue des Martyrs in the centre of town, as are the **bus** and **louage stations**,
side by side a couple of hundred metres up the street.The *zone touristique* is served
by three métro stations – L'Aéroport, Les Hôtels and Sahline Sabkha – with plenty
of trains daily to Monastir (10–15min) and Sousse (15–20min).

The **ONTT** (July & Aug Mon–Sat 8.30am–1.30pm & 3–6pm; Sept–June
Mon–Thurs 8.30am–1pm & 3–5.45pm, Fri & Sat 8.30am–1.30pm; ☎73 461
960), on place de l'Indépendance opposite the Bourguiba Mosque, has a pam-
phlet containing a hotel price list and a fairly basic map of the town and *zone
touristique*. There's another regional tourist office (same times; ☎73 520 205),
fronted by the helpful and knowledgeable Ayara Moncef; it's just up the coast
in the **Zone Touristique de Skanès**, near Les Hôtels métro station off the
road to the *Skanès Palace Hôtel*.

Accommodation

All the *zone touristique* hotels are perfectly decent for a beach break, and you're
not missing much by staying out of Monastir. Hotels in Monastir itself are almost
all reserved for package tours, with the exception of the *Monastir Beach*, plus a
trio of rather gloomy places out on the Ksar Hellal road, and the *Maison des Jeunes*
on rue de Libye (☎73 461 216; dorm beds 5TD), which is in reasonable nick.
For real budget accommodation, you're much better off staying in Sousse or at *Al
Jazira* in Mahdia and visiting Monastir as a day-trip. Because the package hotels
are mainly prebooked, you'll pay full whack if you just drop in, but prices take a
nose dive out of season, with fifty to seventy percent lopped off high-season rates,
making them much better value than the low-end places in town.

Hotels

In town

Le Cristal av Habib Bourguiba ☎73 460 129,
☎73 460 126. New hotel with bright, comfortable
a/c rooms and some self-catering apartments. ❻
Esplanade rte de la Corniche ☎73 461 146, ☎73

460 050. The most central of the hotels,with sea
views and a couple of pools among other facilities. It has seen better days but is very reasonably
priced. ❺
El Faouz pl du 7 Novembre ☎73 448 280, ☎73
448 221. The best-equipped of three slightly forlorn
hotels on a busy roundabout about 800m up the

239

Ksar Hellal road from the junction of av Bourguiba and av des Martyrs. Rooms have a/c and private bathrooms – and TV for 5TD extra. The management is open to bargaining – and you should take them up on it because the rooms are overpriced. ❺

Kahla av Taïeb Mehiri ☎73 464 586, ℗73 467 881. Next door to *El Faouz*, this place has basic en-suite rooms and some apartments. ❸

Marina Cap Monastir Port de Plaisance ☎73 462 305, ℗73 464 999, ⊛www.caesium.fr/capmonastir. Ranged along the northern edge of the marina, with two-, four-, six- and eight-bed apartments with TV, a/c, kitchen and balcony. Past its best and lacking beach or pool, it's still a good deal for a group staying a week or more, especially outside summer. ❼

Monastir Beach rte de la Corniche ☎73 464 766, ℗73 463 594. Located literally underneath the corniche road halfway down some steps onto the beach, this is the only one of the cheaper hotels in Monastir with much going for it – primarily its proximity to the town centre and beach. Rooms are basic but have a/c and are en suite, and there is a café-bar with pool table. ❹

Monastir Centre av Habib Bourguiba ☎73 467 800, ℗73 467 809. Fairly new, well run and very well equipped hotel in the centre. Within a few minutes of the beach, it has all the usual activities, a large pool and a good restaurant. Recommended. Half board only. ❻

Regency Port de Plaisance ☎73 460 033, ℗73 460 727. Monastir's poshest hotel, with all mod cons and right by the marina – park your yacht while you pop in for dinner. ❽

Yasmine rte de la Falaise ☎73 501 546. Small family-run pension with pleasant rooms and good breakfasts, but 2km out of town, and quite pricey in summer. Half or full board only. ❺

The Zone Touristique de Skanès

Abou Nawas Sunrise 12km away at La Dkhila ☎73 521 644, ℗73 521 282, ⊛www.abounawas .com. Downmarket by usual Abou Nawas standards and very 1970s Ibiza, but with nice two-floor chalet accommodation, and good value for full board, which is all they offer anyway. Closed winter. ❽

Emir Palace 1km west of Les Hôtels métro ☎73 520 900, ℗73 521 823. The *zone*'s fluffiest kennel. Everything you could want, and totally Tunisia-proof. ❾

Kuriat Palace 5km from the centre, near Aéroport métro station ☎73 521 200, ℗73 520 049, ✉kuriat.palace@gnet.tn. Among the most expensive four-stars in the *zone*, but well equipped with loads of restaurants, bars, health centre and good water sports activities. Wheelchair accessible. ❼

Sahara Beach 2km west of Les Hôtels métro ☎73 521 088, ℗520 466, ⊛www.iberostar.com. Over a thousand rooms, three pools, various restaurants and bars, water sports and horse-riding. ❼

Skanès el Hana 2km west of Les Hôtels métro ☎73 521 055, ℗520 709, ✉skanes .elhana@planet.tn. More stylish and cheaper than adjacent *Sahara Beach*, and complete with the usual water sports and horse-riding. ❻

The Town

The heart of the town is the **Medina**, skirted to the north and east by rue d'Alger, to the south by avenue Bourguiba and to the west by avenue des Martyrs. Some parts of its walls are eighteenth century, others more recent, and there are gratuitous additions in the 1980s Andalusian style used at Port el Kantaoui. The **Bourguiba Mosque** on rue de l'Indépendance follows classic Hafsid design, but the rest of the Medina has been so blatantly gentrified that it hardly even merits a stroll. In fact, the real Medina was originally the area around the Ribat; what is called the Medina today was a walled suburb, like the faubourgs of Tunis. One little curiosity is the **tower**, which protrudes, for no apparent reason, from the wall opposite the post office. Just up from here, it's difficult to miss the **golden statue of Bourguiba** in the square by the Gouvernorat office, which beats even Nabeul's potted tree and giant orange bowl for sheer tackiness. The statue commemorates Bourguiba's schooldays – ironically, the school itself was demolished to make way for the monument. Close by, beside the tourist office on rue de l'Indépendance, is the small, dusty **Museum of Traditional Costume** (Tues–Sun: April to mid-Sept 9am–1pm & 4–7pm; mid-Sept to March 9am–4pm; 1.1TD), with a diverting display of local clothes.

To go with its national prominence, the town centre east of the Medina has had its houses razed and replaced by a bleak esplanade designed to show

△ Monastir's ribat

off Monastir's monuments to the best advantage. Overlooking the sea, the old **Ribat of Harthema** (daily: April to mid-Sept 8am–7pm; mid-Sept to March 8.30am–5.30pm; 2.1TD, camera 1TD) was the first *ribat* in Tunisia to admit female professors and students. Begun in 796, it has undergone so many reworkings that even experts have difficulty in dating its various parts. The core structure follows the same plan as at Sousse, however, with a courtyard surrounded by cells for the fighters, and on one side a prayer hall now used as a rather good **museum** (closed Mon) to display ancient Islamic writings, fabrics and pottery – look out here for eleventh-century Coptic fabric from Egypt and an ornate 1774 Turkish marriage certificate. A map of the original Medina shows how comprehensively the old town was levelled in the pursuit of modernity, creating the sterile esplanade outside the Ribat. Traditionally the Ribat has been a favourite backdrop for filmmakers wanting to evoke the biblical world – this is where Jesus trod the battlements in Zeffirelli's *Jesus of Nazareth*, as did Brian in Monty Python's alternative scenario. Next door stands the ninth-century **Great Mosque**, while the smaller **Ribat of Sidi Dhou-wayeb** lies between the mosque and the Medina.

The **Bourguiba Mausoleum**, just to the north of the centre (Mon–Thurs 2–4.30pm, Fri–Sun 9am–4.30pm, until 6pm in summer; no shorts; free), is undoubtedly the most eye-catching of the monuments, unmistakable with its gilt cupola and twin minarets. Housed within are the tombs of Bourguiba's close family in the two rooms off to the left, and the man himself in a marble sarcophagus in the central chamber, complete with 365-piece crystal chandelier. The mausoleum stands in a cemetery named after the **Koubba of Sidi el Mezeri**, the tomb of a twelfth-century saint. The inscription on the gateway, apparently written by the saint himself, mentions one Princess Mona, after whom the town is said to have been named.

Monastir's busy **marina** (ⓦ www.marinamonastir.com) is to the north of the Ribat. From here the corniche road leads west along the coast past more resort development and Bourguiba's favourite **palace**, where the ex-honcho lived out his dotage. In contrast to the modern marina is the old **fishing port**, just over 1km to the southeast in a rocky inlet. It must have been a pretty place once, but the corniche is now so loaded with hotels that it looks distinctly out of place. The **house** where Bourguiba was born is located in place 3 Août (his birthday), just before the port. From here, the promenade turns due south and into a more workaday district, the shore lined with larger modern fishing vessels. A weekly **souk** is held here on Saturdays.

Eating, drinking and nightlife

Good, inexpensive **eating** is hard to come by in Monastir, and if you're on a beach holiday you might consider opting for full or half board in your hotel. You'll find most restaurants and fast-food places on the streets enclosing the Medina, many with reasonable if unexciting tourist menus for 5–7TD. Of these, *Restaurant les Remparts,* on avenue Bourguiba near the tower (daily noon–4pm & 6.30pm–midnight), is the most popular with decent pizza and a range of set menus starting at 7TD; nearby, against the Medina wall, *Restaurant du Bonheur* is also good and cheap (daily 8am–midnight). Inside the Medina itself, a third budget place to try is *El Medina* on place de l'Indépendance (daily 11am–10pm), serving reasonable pizzas and a few Tunisian dishes.

The marina is full of fancy restaurants for a splurge. Alternatively, you'll find one of Monastir's oldest establishments, *Restaurant la Plage* (daily except Fri noon–3pm & 6–11pm; closed Ramadan), above the old fishing port at place 3 Août, serving a fine line in fish; try the *shirkau*, a local speciality of tiny fish made into a kind of patty. Expect to pay 20–25TD for a full meal à la carte or 19.5TD for the tourist menu, a veritable seafood feast.

In July and August each year, the **Monastir International Festival** (ⓦ www.monastir.org) receives a number of international Arab singing stars and orchestras. For the rest of the year nightlife is typically low-key, except for a couple of rather dreadful **nightclubs** at *Hôtel Sahara Beach* and *Hôtel Kuriat Palace*, both in the *zone touristique*. In summer, most package hotels also put on various dubious entertainments in the evenings.

Listings

Airlines Nouvelair, Zone Touristique Dkhila, near the *Hôtel Sahara Beach* ☎73 520 600; Tunisair, in the Ribat complex on av Bourguiba ☎73 462 550.
Banks Near the post office on av Bourguiba, with more on pl de l'Indépendance in the centre of the Medina. Several have ATMs accepting Visa and MasterCard.
Boat trips It's possible to visit the Kuriat Islands, a deserted archipelago 15km off the coast, where Phoenician ruins have been found. Fishing trips or days out on a boat can be arranged from the marina – the yacht *Sidi Bou* will take a group

of four out for half a day for 130TD and kids go along free.
Car rental Avis (☎73 521 031), Budget (☎73 520 000), Europcar (☎73 520 799) and Hertz (☎73 521 300) each have counters at the airport. There's a cluster of local agencies around the Ribat complex on av Bourguiba, including Nova Rent (☎73 467 826).
Diving Monastir Plongée et Loisirs, at the marina (☎73 462 509 or 98 457 393), organizes trips; the minimum charge for a day-trip is 200TD for boat and skipper. They may be closed out of season.

Golf courses The Flamingo Monastir (☎73 500 283, ◉www.golfflamingo.com) is next to the Ouardanine road, which leads from the town centre towards Kairouan. Another eighteen-hole course, Golf Palm Links (☎73 521910), is way out along the *zone touristique* hotel strip near the *Sunrise Hôtel*. In season, daily shuttle buses operate between it and the major *zone touristique* hotels; ask at your hotel for details.

Hammam rue de Tunis, in the Medina (daily: men 6am–1pm, women 1–5.30pm).

Hospital The regional hospital is on av Farhat Hached (☎73 461 144).

Internet There is a Publinet (24hr; 2TD/hr) at the train station and another on rue Mohammed M'hallah (daily 8am–midnight; 2TD/hr).

ONA crafts shop rue Abdessalem Trimêche, corner of rue de l'Indépendance.

Pharmacy There's a night pharmacy 200m off av Bourguiba down rue Chedli Kallala, past the market.

Police rue d'Alger ☎73 461 431; the tourist police can be found in the *zone touristique* near the *Hôtel Sahara Beach* (☎73 521 771).

Post office av Bourguiba, opposite the Medina wall (city hours).

Supermarkets There's a Magasin Général on rue de l'Indépendance and a Monoprix on av Bourguiba, which has longer opening hours (daily 9am–9pm).

Swimming pools Most of the beach hotels will let you use their pools for a small fee and also Turkish baths for around 5TD.

Telephones International calls can be made from the taxiphone office next to the train station and others dotted around town.

Tours and travel agents Most of the *zone touristique* hotels offer reasonably cheap bus or 4WD excursions to Matmata and other attractions in the south. Otherwise, there are plenty of agencies at the airport, or try C.T. Tour at the Ribat complex on av Bourguiba (☎73 449 606).

South of Monastir

The settlements south of Monastir are constantly expanding and merging with each other, and travelling through them – to the buzz of a thousand mopeds – you get a vivid sense of why this region is such an economic powerhouse. The easiest way to get around here is on the Sahel **métro** (see p.218), which runs frequently between Monastir and Mahdia via Lamta, Ksar Hellal, Moknine and Bekalta. If you want to reach Mahdia by louage, change at Moknine or Ksar Hellal.

Two thousand years ago, this area was already industrious and heavily settled. **LAMTA**, 15km southeast of Monastir, was once Leptis Minor, cousin of the much larger Leptis Magna, whose ruins on the modern Libyan coast are among the most spectacular Roman sites in the world. The **museum** on the northern edge of town (Tues–Sun: April to mid-Sept 9am–1pm & 4–7pm; mid-Sept to March 9.30am–1pm & 2–5pm; 1.1TD, camera 1TD), next to the Monastir road though quite a walk from the train station, is worth a visit if you're passing or interested in industrial-type archeology, which seems to be a speciality of this region. Like the British team at Salakta (see p.262), an American-funded excavation here focused on pottery, as Leptis exported so-called red slipware all over the Mediterranean for five hundred years. The museum explains techniques and processes – with English labels – and also has one unique piece of fine art in a carved Christian sarcophagus found in 1975 and probably imported from France or Rome.

A few kilometres south of Lamta, bustling **KSAR HELLAL** is an old textile centre where silk is still made. The thread is dyed in large vats, and handlooms are used to weave the cloth. Sadly, the resulting article is disappointing – usually plain, with none of the geometric designs that you find on coarser textiles, and very expensive. The town's other claim to fame is as the venue for the 1934 Neo-Destour Party Congress in which Habib Bourguiba emerged as leader. From here disciples went throughout the country encouraging strikes and civil disobedience that came close to overthrowing the Protectorate. Ksar Hellal fades into **MOKNINE**, another sprawling town known for its pottery.

Moknine has a small regional **museum** (closed for renovation at the time of writing; ask at the Skanès tourist office), 100m to the left on the main road entering town and housed in a disused mosque, with exhibits of coins, manuscripts, pottery and weapons from different periods. If you want to see some modern **pottery**, drop by the Poterie Abdel Ali on the road to Teboulba. Here you can watch the craftsmen at work, or go along to the town's busy Wednesday **market**. To the southeast of Moknine, on the coast 6km east of **Bekalta**, Roman **Tapsus** was the site of a battle in 46 BC that ended the Roman civil war between Julius Caesar and Pompey.

Kairouan and around

"What a Hell of a place to put a Holy City," wrote *The Times'* military correspondent of **KAIROUAN** in 1939. In midsummer, when the town bakes like a brick on its barren plain, it's hard to disagree. But Tunisia's oldest Arab city and Islam's fourth most holy centre – after Mecca, Medina and Jerusalem – is an exceptionally rewarding place. The whole city is a UNESCO World Heritage Site; its architectural interest is unrivalled, and the strong Eastern flavour it retains comes as a surprise if you visit after passing through Sousse. Kairouan has a special place in international Islamic consciousness, and representatives from all over the world converge on the city for the annual Mouled celebration.

Some history

Not surprisingly, perhaps, it was divine inspiration that led to the choice of this infernal site. In 670 **Oqba Ibn Nafi**, advancing west, called a routine halt here with his army. A golden cup was found on the ground, which he recognized as one he had lost at Mecca; then a spring was discovered, and declared to be connected to the holy well of Zem Zem at Mecca. Having first banished for eternity the "noxious beasts and reptiles" which had been present in some abundance, Oqba founded his capital on the spot. There was sound strategic sense behind the inspiration, as the new city was a reasonably secure and central base for the new rulers, halfway between the seaborne threats of the Mediterranean and the mountainous homes of the rebellious Berbers. Despite this security, extremist **Kharijite** Berbers took the city in 757, and their behaviour (such as massacring their opponents and stabling horses in the Great Mosque) shocked more moderate Kharijites, who drove them out and installed one Abderrahman Ibn Rustam as their ruler. In 761, Egyptian forces loyal to the Caliph retook the city, and Ibn Rustam set up shop in Tahirt (Algeria), from where his family (the Rustamids) ruled the south of Tunisia.

As the **Aghlabid** capital, Kairouan quickly developed into one of the world's great cities, its monuments surpassed only by the level of its scholarship and its

Moving on from Kairouan

As Kairouan is pretty central, it has bus services to most parts of the country; the bus station is on ☏77 300 011. There are **louages** to Maktar, Sbeïtla, Sfax, Sousse and Tunis, but none to El Jem or Mahdia – you have to go via Sousse or, for El Jem, pay the full fare to Sfax and ask to be dropped along the way. Note that Sfax louages do not leave from the louage station but from a side street just off the post office roundabout.

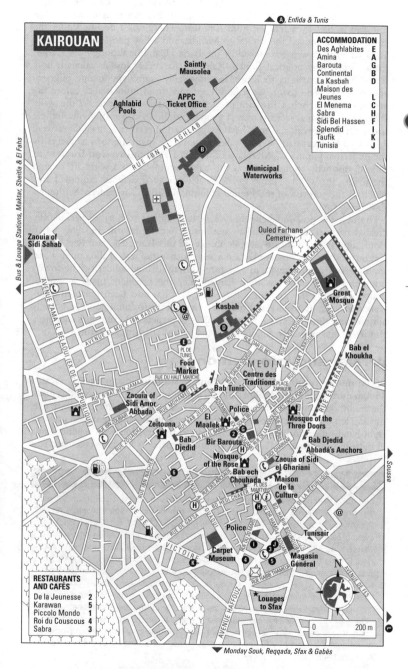

KAIROUAN

▲ Ⓐ, Enfida & Tunis

Saintly
Mausolea

APPC
Ticket Office

Aghlabid
Pools

ⒷⒸ

Rue Ibn al Aghlab

❶

Municipal
Waterworks

Zaouia of
Sidi Sahab

Ouled Farhane
Cemetery

Great
Mosque

◄ Bus & Louage Stations, Maktar, Sbeitla & El Fahs

Avenue Zama el Belaoui Ex de la République

Avenue el Moez Ibn Badiss

Avenue Ibn el Jazzar

Kasbah

Ⓒ@

Ⓔ

PL DE
TUNIS

Food
Market

Rue du Haut Marche

MEDINA

Bab el
Khoukha

Ⓕ

Centre des
Traditions

Bab Tunis

PLACE
ZARROUK

Zaouia of
Sidi Amor
Abbada

Police

Zeitouna

El
Maalek

Ⓖ

Bab
Djedid

Bir Barouta

Ⓗ

Mosque of the
Three Doors

Rue R'bai Ben Jamaa

Rue Zouaghi

Rue Ibn Nahhes

Mosque
of the Rose

Bab ech
Chouhada

Zaouia of Sidi
el Ghariani

Bab Djedid

Abbada's Anchors

❻

Maison
de la
Culture

Ⓗ

Rue de la Victoire

Rue de Gafsa

Ⓗ ⓘ

Bd Hedi Chaker

Police

Rue 20 Mars

Rue Habib Thameur

Tunisair

@

Avenue de Fes

Carpet
Museum

Ⓚ

❹

Louages
to Sfax

Rue Habib Thameur

❷

❶

❸❺

Magasin
Général

N

Sousse ►

0   200 m

ACCOMMODATION

Des Aghlabites	E
Amina	A
Barouta	G
Continental	B
La Kasbah	D
Maison des Jeunes	L
El Menema	C
Sabra	H
Sidi Bel Hassen	F
Splendid	I
Taufik	K
Tunisia	J

RESTAURANTS
AND CAFÉS

De la Jeunesse	2
Karawan	5
Piccolo Mondo	1
Roi du Couscous	4
Sabra	3

▼ Monday Souk, Reqqada, Sfax & Gabès

influence, which reached far across the Islamic world. The Kairaouine Mosque in Fez – still the centre of Morocco's religious life – is so named as it was founded in 857 by a refugee from Kairouan. There was a decline under the Fatimids, who moved the capital to Mahdia, and a low point was reached in 1057 when the town was sacked by the Banu Hilal. But although the Hafsids made Tunis their political capital, Kairouan has never lost its ancient, holy status, with seven visits to Kairouan supposedly equivalent to one pilgrimage to Mecca. The town was jealously guarded from infidels and, before the arrival of the French, Christians needed a beylical permit to enter the walls. Even then, personal security wasn't guaranteed. In 1835, Sir Grenville Temple had a permit to visit, and may have exaggerated in reporting that "if we were known to be Christians, whilst walking about, we might be torn to pieces by the infuriated populace". Members of the 1881 **French invasion force** were, indeed, distinctly apprehensive as the tribes assembled in a wide arc around the town. But when it came to the final battle their defence crumbled and, much to the surprise of the French column, the town surrendered without a shot being fired.

Through the post-independence years, its religious authorities periodically created friction over Bourguiba's attempts at secular reform. In 1960, when Bourguiba urged national abandonment of the Ramadan fast (see p.506), Kairouan pointedly observed it a day longer than the rest of the country and simultaneously with Egypt, in a gesture of Arab–Islamic solidarity. The town's boulevard Bourguiba was only named after the president made a visit of conciliation in 1969, and the greater part of it has now been renamed again. Kairouan today is a successful market centre for agricultural goods, especially apricots and almonds, and a major producer of carpets and Caravanes cigarettes. But it remains intensely religious, a living centre of Islamic doctrine.

Arrival and information

A taxi into town from the **bus** and **louage stations**, inconveniently located 1500m northwest of the Medina, should cost around 1TD. If you want to reach the centre on foot from the bus station, head straight out of the main entrance, turning left on to a wide boulevard after 100m with the louage station on your right hand side. Another 200m brings you to the junction with avenue Zama el Belaoui (avenue de la République on most maps). A left here takes you past

---

Street names in Kairouan

Streets in Kairouan seem to **change their names** even more indiscriminately than elsewhere in Tunisia, and many streets have two or more names. Avenue de la République, southeast of the Medina, was formerly called rue Farhat Hached; avenue Zama el Belaoui used to be avenue de la République; avenue 7 Novembre was avenue Ali Belhouane, which itself replaced avenue Bourguiba; and boulevard Hedi Chaker (alongside the city wall between place des Martyrs and rue de Gafsa) was also avenue Ali Belhouane. Rue Mohamed Fez is still frequently called boulevard Sadikia, while avenue Ali Zouaoui is also called boulevard Driss 1, boulevard Idris Snoussi, or avenue Belaghjie. To add to the confusion, most maps of Kairouan (including ones in the tourist office) are extremely inaccurate and name streets differently or wrongly. However, the main sights are prominently signposted, and attempts are being made to complement the old Arabic-only street-name plaques with signage in French. Where an old street name is still often used, both new and old have been marked on our map.

the Zaouia of Sidi Sahab to the Aghlabid pools; a right leads down eventually to the big roundabout by the post office. **Louages from Sfax** terminate in a side street just off this roundabout.

The newer **French quarter** to the south of the Medina contains the banks and administration, but most of the life of the town remains centred on the main street through the Medina, avenue 7 Novembre. At its southern end, in place des Martyrs opposite Bab ech Chouhada, is the reasonably efficient **ONTT** (July & Aug Mon–Sat 7am–7pm, Sun 7am–noon; Sept–June Mon–Thurs 8.30am–1pm & 3–5.45pm, Fri 8.30am–1pm, Sat 8.30am–1.30pm), with brochures and a list of hotels. From Bab Tunis at the northern end of avenue 7 Novembre, avenue Ibn el Jazzar (aka rue des Aghlabites) leads north to the Aghlabid pools, which is a good place to buy a **global ticket** for Kairouan's monuments (see box, p.248).

Accommodation

Hotels in Kairouan run the gamut from cheap and basic to five-star luxury, though if you're used to accommodation standards on the coast you may be a little disappointed. There is a *Maison des Jeunes* on avenue de Fes, 1500m southeast of Bab ech Chouhada (℡77 230 309; dorm beds 5TD), open all day with a midnight curfew.

Des Aghlabites pl de Tunis ℡77 230 880. Large and reasonably clean budget place, popular with Tunisians, with showers in some rooms and set around an enormous courtyard. Women should feel safe here. **❷**

Amina 2km up the Tunis road from the Aghlabid pools ℡77 226 555, ℻77 235 411. This hotel suffers from its location miles out in a garbage-strewn wasteland, though it does have a pool and mod cons. **❻**

Barouta Opposite *Restaurant de la Jeunesse*, just off av 7 Novembre (no phone). Not suitable for women on their own and only really worthwhile if you're after the cheapest deal. Cold water only; passably clean. **❶**

Continental rue Ibn al Aghleb, opposite the Aghlabid Pools ℡77 232 006, ℻229 900. Large, well-appointed rooms with a/c and satellite TV, plus a pool. Recommended. **❺**

La Kasbah av Ibn el Jazzar ℡77 237 301, ℻77 237 302. Kairouan's only top-notch hotel, in the converted Kasbah, is basically a brand new building with the Kasbah's facade. While there are some excellent features such as the fabulous pool in the central courtyard and a café in the former prison, the maze of bland corridors leading to the rooms are unimaginative given the potential of the location. Nevertheless, it has all you would expect for its five stars and isn't overly expensive. **❼**

El Menema rue el Moez Ibn Badiss ℡77 226 182, ℻77 235 033. Clean and pleasant, with large

cool rooms, some with private bathrooms (and heaters in winter). Their card promises "you would find your pleasure, your good freedom and much courtesy". **❷**

Sabra pl des Martyrs ℡77 230 263. Deservedly popular place, shabby around the edges, though some rooms, bathrooms and toilets have recently been renovated. Rooms have sinks and are usually clean; there are hot shared showers (and a hammam next door). You can sleep on the roof (which has excellent views) in summer. Breakfast included. Bargainable. **❷**

Sidi Bel Hassen rue Mohamed Fez (formerly bd Sadikia) ℡77 230 676. Turn left just out of Bab Tunis. A mixed bag of rooms, some without windows; the better rooms face the street and Medina wall (which conceals an alley of brothels). Not particularly friendly. **❶**

Splendid rue 9 Avril, off av de la République ℡77 227 522, ℻77 230 829. Pleasant hotel with an air of subdued grandeur. Rooms are spacious and all have bathrooms, and there's a bar. Recommended. **❹**

Taufik rue de la Victoire ℡77 234 634. One of the cheapest in town but not at all bad, and little visited by tourists. Shared facilities. **❶**

Tunisia av de la République ℡77 231 855, ℻77 231 597. Decent-sized clean rooms with a choice of bath or shower. Not quite as nice as the nearby *Splendid*, and slightly more expensive, but a good fall-back option. **❹**

The Medina

Kairouan's **Medina** stretches east to west, the **Great Mosque** at its far north-eastern corner and its main street, **avenue 7 Novembre**, seeing most of the city's life. The ancient suburbs lie to the north and west, with the newer **French quarter** to the south. When planning your route, especially on a hot day, bear in mind that two of the city's main attractions lie some way from the Medina – the Aghlabid pools to the north and the Zaouia of Sidi Sahab to the northwest, not far from the bus station.

Although the Medina is smaller than the one in Tunis, it has a mystique that has always affected Western travellers. In 1914, the artist Paul Klee remarked that the Medina was "the essence of *A Thousand and One Nights*, with a 99 per-cent reality content". Shortly after, he declared euphorically, "I am a painter!" and cut short his trip to plunge himself into a frenzy of artistic productivity that lasted to the end of his life.

The Medina **walls** were originally built by the Zirids on foundations dating from 761, but it was only a few years before they were wrecked by the Hilalian invasion, and they have undergone repeated destruction and restoration ever since. The most recent damage was during World War II, when the Germans needed to build an airfield in a hurry. The most impressive remaining walls are those around Bab ech Chouhada at the south end of avenue 7 Novembre, and those around Bab Tunis at the north end, which still protect local sensibility from a cul-de-sac of brothels, nestled just within the walls.

Bir Barouta

Lurking just east of avenue 7 Novembre, the tunnel-like **souks** are surprisingly easy to miss, as is the **Bir Barouta** (daily 8am–5.30pm; global ticket), which looks more like a mosque than a well. Up some steps is an unlikely camel, clad in a natty set of green fluffy harnesses, tramping endless circles to draw water that you can, supposedly, drink – though you may be pressed to cough up a small sum for the privilege. Some say that this is the well connected to Mecca which Oqba found in 670, but its name refers to a holy man of the thirteenth century whose prayers for water were answered when his dog, Routa, scratched the ground until water gushed forth. A taste of the water, it's said, will bring you back one day to Kairouan.

Just behind Bir Barouta, on the right of rue Barouta heading to Souk Belaghjia, is the ONTT's **Centre des Traditions et des Métiers d'Art**

The global ticket

You can enter all of Kairouan's most important monuments using one **global ticket** (4.2TD), which can be bought from the headquarters of the **APPC** (Agence de Mise en Valeur du Patrimoine et de Promotion Culturelle; July & Aug daily 7am–1.30pm; Sept–June Mon–Thurs, Sat & Sun 8am–5.30pm, Fri 8am–noon) out by the Aghlabid pools, and also at the Great Mosque and at the Zaouia of Sidi Sahab. The ticket is valid, in theory, only on the day of issue, though you may be allowed to use it for an extra day. It covers the **Great Mosque** (Mosque of Oqba), the **Zaouia of Sidi Sahab** (Mosque of the Barber, or Mausoleum of Abou Zammaa el Balaoui), the **Aghlabid pools**, the **Zaouia of Sidi el Ghariani**, the **Museum of Islamic Art** at Reqqada, the **Zaouia of Sidi Amor Abbada** and **Bir Barouta**. For **photography**, note that an additional 1TD ticket is required, covering all sites, and that the Museum of Islamic Art has an extra entry fee of 1.1TD. You can gain free entrance to the Aghlabid pools by its western entrance (or view them from the roof of the APPC office). The APPC office also offers **guided tours** at 10TD for a couple of hours.

(Mon–Thurs 8.30am–4pm, Fri & Sat 8am–1.30pm; July & Aug closes early), housing apprentice workshops at which the finer of Kairouan's crafts are taught: silversmithing and woodwork, weaving and filigree embroidery. The pupils are usually happy to explain and show you their work – an ideal way of getting a feel for the goods before entering the hard sell of the bazaars.

The Great Mosque

In its grand simplicity, the **Great Mosque** (or Mosque of Oqba; Mon–Thurs, Sat & Sun 8.30am–2.30pm, Fri 8.30am–noon; global ticket; prayer hall closed to non-Muslims), at the Medina's eastern end, is one of the oldest, largest and most important mosques in the country. Compared with the delicate elaboration of later periods, its massive buttressed walls feel more like a fortress, and it's hard not to be impressed by such a powerful and beautiful expression of faith.

Only one of the several monumental entrances is now used, but the **Lalla Rihana Gate** on the east side, dating from 1294, deserves a quick detour. Typically Hafsid, with the characteristic arches and cupola, the gate was built more than four hundred years later than most of the present mosque, which was

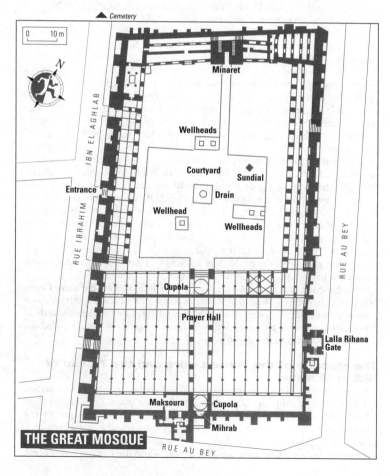

THE GREAT MOSQUE

erected by the Aghlabid Ziyadatallah in 836 and greatly influenced mosques built at the same time in Sfax, Sousse and Tunis.

Framed by Hafsid and Turkish colonnades, the vast **courtyard** was never just an aesthetic addition. In a town so short of natural water sources, the courtyard was used as a catchment area, with rainwater channelled to the curiously shaped drain in the centre and into huge cisterns below. The curious notches in the **drain** were designed to remove dust from the water before it went down into the cistern. The **wellheads** used to draw from the cisterns are made out of antique column bases; the grooves in the rims come from centuries of rope friction. The oversized **sundial** in the courtyard is one of two: the other, a smaller one for afternoon use, is on the superstructure of the eastern colonnade.

Although the age of the **minaret** is disputed, its lowest storey is thought to date from 730, a century before most of the present mosque. This fact might explain why it stands off-centre, and would certainly make it the oldest surviving minaret in the world. The minaret's blunt form is more imaginative than it first appears, particularly in the way the windows increase in size as ascending storeys grow smaller. Two blocks bearing Roman inscriptions are built into the minaret, one of them upside down.

Neither the minaret nor the courtyard is symmetrical, which emphasizes by contrast the layout of the **prayer hall**, which has six aisles to either side in the colonnade and eight in the hall itself, with the entrance set off by the cupola above. The elaborate wooden doors into the prayer hall date from the nineteenth century. With its roof supported by columns (mainly from Roman sites), the hall has been likened to a forest by centuries of pilgrims and travellers. The central aisle, higher than those on either side, is further marked out by stone reliefs below the ceiling. A transverse aisle, connecting the Gate of Lalla Rihana to another on the far side, is also distinguishable. Wooden pillows separate the capitals from the higher elements of the columns, designed to soak up any shifts caused by earth tremors. There are endless stories about these columns. According to one, anyone who counts them all will become blind; in another, the pairs operate as a sort of Muslim eye of the needle – those who cannot squeeze between them, it is said, will never reach Paradise. Dimly visible at the far end of the central aisle are 130 faïence tiles around the mihrab, imported from Baghdad in the ninth century. The wooden *minbar* just next to the *mihrab* is another important example of early Islamic decorative art, also carved in the ninth century by order of Ibn Aghlab himself. The wooden enclosure, or *maqsoura*, to the side of the *minbar*, was installed by a Zirid ruler in 1022 so that he did not have to pray among the hoi polloi.

Just outside the wall by the Great Mosque, the little **Ouled Farhane Cemetery** with its whitewashed gravestones makes a pretty backdrop for souvenir snapshots, while at the other end of boulevard Ibrahim Ibn Aghlab, **Bab el Khoukha** is the oldest of the Medina's remaining gates, originally called the "Sousse Gate" when built in 1705.

The Mosque of the Three Doors and the Zaouia of Sidi el Ghariani

Two remarkably photogenic streets – rue Khadraouine and rue Tahal Zarrouk – lead southwest from the Great Mosque down to place Zarrouk, south of which you pass though a street of woodcarvers to reach the **Mosque of the Three Doors**. Closed to non-Muslims, the mosque is a rare nineteenth-century survivor. Above the three doors, the top two bands of inscriptions date from the mosque's foundation, the lowest band – and the minaret – from later additions. Between the top two bands is a row of stones with floral decorations, of which no two are decorated the same.

A few minutes' walk away is the **Bab ech Chouhada**, the gate at the southern end of avenue 7 Novembre, and the **Zaouia of Sidi el Ghariani** (daily 8am–5pm; global ticket), with its formidable entrance. Although the building dates from the beginning of the fourteenth century, it is now named after a native of Gharian in Libya, who died a hundred years later. In 1891, according to Sir Lambert Playfair, it was still the case that the hereditary governor of Kairouan was one of Abd el Ghariani's descendants. Since then the *zaouia* has seen hard times, but it has been restored and is now the home of the ASM (Association de Sauvegarde de la Medina). Notice especially the green and black columns of the *mihrab*, and the typically dark wooden ceiling of the tomb. The *zaouia* is not where it's marked on most maps; that spot, about 100m further along the street, is an old beylical palace, now a carpet shop, Tapis–Sabra. The salesman here may try to entice you inside by asking for your ticket and claiming the shop is a museum.

Outside the Medina

After the bustle of the Medina the tranquillity on the outside comes as some relief. The **Aghlabid pools** are a keen reminder of the ingenuity of Arab engineering, while the **Zaouia of Sidi Sahab** and **Zaouia of Sidi Amor Abbada** are rich in architecture. If you are interested in buying a carpet (see box, p.253), it's worth having a look first at the **Carpet Museum**, which provides a good introduction to this knotty subject.

The Aghlabid pools

About 800m from the Medina at the north end of avenue Ibn el Jazzar, the **Aghlabid pools** (July & Aug daily 7am–1.30pm; Sept–June Mon–Thurs, Sat & Sun 8am–5.30pm, Fri 8am–noon; global ticket, or free entry via western gate) were incorrectly ascribed to Roman engineers by blinkered nineteenth-century French historians who imagined that Arabs of the time could not have conceived such a technically complex project. After extensive restoration, the pools (four of a presumed fourteen have been excavated) have the bland feel of a municipal waterworks – which is not surprising, since that's what they were. The vital importance of water would have been foremost in the minds of the newly arrived Arab builders as they conjured this city from the desert more than a thousand years ago, and such utilities were an essential feature of urban life in the area.

Water arrived here by aqueduct from Jebel Cherichera, 36km to the west, to be settled in the smaller basins before being stored in the largest pool, 128m across. The buttresses around the sides of this pool have something of the Great Mosque's monumental purity, while the small stand in the middle of the pool held a pavilion in which the Aghlabid rulers could recline. It was hoped that the pools, as well as holding water, would help relieve the town of its summer heat – instead, they were a terrific mosquito breeding ground and consequent source of malaria. Incidentally, the city's modern waterworks – not entirely dissimilar – are only a stone's throw away, next to *Hôtel Continental*.

The Zaouia of Sidi Sahab

Following the main avenue west from the Aghlabid pools (most maps label the road avenue de la République, though officially it's known as rue Ibn al Aghlab), you arrive at the **Zaouia of Sidi Sahab**, or more correctly the Mausoleum of Abou Zammaa el Belaoui or Mosque of the Barber (daily 8am–6pm; global ticket). Its occupant was a companion, or *sahab*, of the Prophet, and his distinguishing characteristic was that he always kept with him three hairs of the Prophet's beard – one under his tongue, one on his right arm and one next to his heart, hence the tendency to call him the Prophet's barber. The mosque and its surrounding complex remain a much-venerated place of pilgrimage, where families – both Berber villagers and prosperous town-dwellers – come to pay their respects. Most of the existing buildings date from the seventeenth and nineteenth centuries, and their elaborateness contrasts with the less fanciful form of the Great Mosque.

The entrance to the main complex ducks under an Andalusian-style minaret, where an ornate passage of marble columns and Italianate windows leads to an equally rich courtyard, its walls and ceilings lined with green-blue tilework and white plaster stucco. In a small room to the left of the courtyard is the **tomb of Sidi Sherif Ben Hindu**, the architect of the Great Mosque. Sidi Sahab himself lies buried in the room on the far side (closed to non-Muslims). This central court is a wonderfully peaceful place to sit on a hot afternoon, the trees outside waving overhead. The mosque is also a popular place to have boys circumcised, and the climax of the ceremony happens in this courtyard. Over the preceding weeks the boy's family will have filled a large jar with sweets and nuts before sealing it. At the moment of the big snip, the jar is smashed in the centre of the courtyard, and the waiting children scramble for its contents.

The Zaouia of Sidi Amor Abbada

Continuing south from Sidi Sahab along avenue Zammaa el Belaoui for half a kilometre or so, you can take a left down rue Ibn Zoubair, followed by a second left after 100m, to reach the **Zaouia of Sidi Amor Abbada** (Tues–Sun 9am–4pm; global ticket). Sidi Amor Abbada was a nineteenth-century blacksmith who, though somewhat loopy by all accounts, must have operated successfully enough to build this seven-domed tomb which is now a museum of some of his artefacts – mostly giant and rather useless iron objects. Until recently the collection included two enormous, blunt and unwieldy swords, which were supposed to protect Kairouan against the infidel. Alas, they were stolen in 1996. Still, it would seem that Kairouan remains safe, on account of two enormous anchors (another two have disappeared), which Amor Abbada claimed had come from Noah's Ark on Mount Ararat, and which currently fasten Kairouan to the soil in the roundabout outside the city's southern Bab Djedid, just east of Bab ech Chouhada. A rival theory suggests that they came from the silted-up port of Porto Farina, now known as Ghar el Melh (see p.183).

From here you can head into the Medina, making for the western Bab Djedid, next to the over-restored **Zeitouna Mosque**. En route you pass through one of the town's ancient suburbs, particularly well endowed with **doorways** painted in disturbing colour combinations, featuring the brown and blue that seem to be a Kairouan speciality.

The Carpet Museum

The former ONTT crafts shop on avenue Ali Zouaoui, just up from the post office, no longer sells carpets but functions as a **Carpet Museum** (Mon–Thurs 8.30am–1pm & 3–7pm, Fri 8.30am–1pm, Sat 8.30am–1.30pm; free), with mostly modern replicas of the many traditional types hung on its walls. It is heavily involved in quality control, and every carpet for sale is inspected and awarded a **rating** – *Deuxième Choix*, *Première Choix* and *Qualité Supérieure* – which is stamped on it. Any carpet without this rating has not been passed.

Carpet magic

Carpet making in Kairouan belongs to a tradition going back many hundreds of years. The authorities will tell you that every Kairouan woman – doctor, lawyer or shop assistant – knows how to make them, and that five thousand families in the town are engaged in the industry. However, you can safely discount the vendors' claims to either a carpet's antiquity (which usually means "secondhand") or the claim that the marriage shawls on sale were made by the bride for her own wedding. The ones on sale are mostly made by professional (male) weavers. After all, would you sell your wedding dress to a tourist? Furthermore, many shops offer tempting credit facilities as part of their hard sell; sceptical caution is advisable.

Knotted carpets

All knotted carpets are handmade, but there are two basic types. The more expensive ones, recognizable by the pile, are made to 40,000, 90,000 or 160,000 knots per square metre. These carpets are luxury items produced by a sophisticated urban culture and their designs are based on a central diamond-shaped lozenge derived originally from the lamp in the Great Mosque, though infinite variation is possible. Traditionally, each design is passed on and evolves from generation to generation within the family. An important subdivision is between Alloucha and Zarbia: Alloucha carpets use a range of colours which can be naturally derived from the wool – beiges, browns, whites and blacks (a recent innovation, perhaps in deference to Western "ethnic" tastes); the traditional Zarbia carpets use rich polychrome shades of deep blue and red.

Woven carpets

Woven carpets, or Mergoum, come from a very different culture, that of the nomadic Berbers. Instead of being urban luxuries, these carpets were literally the roof over a family's flocks. Mergoum use brighter colours, the sort of intense reds and purples which Berber women still wear, and more strictly linear geometric patterns. Because Mergoum are cheaper, they're more open to abuse – the designs of roofline mosque silhouettes have very little to do with traditional forms. For a look at some traditional designs, call in at the carpet museum, which has a small collection of old Mergoum.

The carpet market

If you're really committed to bargaining, it's possible to buy direct from the women who make the carpets; head to the carpet market in **Souk Belaghjia** (Mon, Wed, Thurs & Sat noon–2pm). Be aware, however, that the retailers don't like foreigners cutting into their business, and if you don't speak Arabic you'll need a translator. The scene is fairly frenetic, with a row of women sitting on one side of the alley displaying their carpets and a row of merchants standing on the other; in between them runs an independent auctioneer who takes bids for the carpet on offer. The whole thing is done at feverish pitch and the atmosphere is electric. It's well worth a look, even if you don't intend to buy. If you do, then prices can be less than half those in the shops, though watch out: the nicest old lady can be a shark and you could easily pay good money for junk. Around 1pm or 2pm on Monday or Saturday is the best time to go.

Eating, drinking and nightlife

Buses between Tunis and the south often have to wait, even in the middle of the night, while all the passengers get off at Kairouan to buy the **sweets** for which the city is famous – the best known of which is *makroudh*, a honey-soaked cake with a date filling. The city's foremost patisseries are in the Medina along avenue 7 Novembre.

4

For something more substantial, the budget-priced *Restaurant de la Jeunesse* on avenue 7 Novembre (daily 7am–10pm), almost opposite Bir Barouta, will feed you for under 5TD; their couscous in particular is recommended. Other options include the spotlessly clean and family-run *Karawan* on rue Soukeina Bent el-Haussein near the post office (daily 8am–11pm), which serves up traditional meals for 7–8TD; and the *Sabra* opposite (daily noon–9pm, later in summer), fronting onto avenue de la République, which dishes up fairly tasty food and has a set meal at 7.5TD. You can also fill up on chicken and chips for 2TD at any of the dirt-cheap rotisseries at the post office roundabout, although, as with everything in Kairouan, ask the price before you tuck in or you'll get stung. For something a bit classier, try the restaurant at *Hôtel Splendid* (daily noon–3pm & 7–9pm), with a 9TD set meal, or the upmarket *Sofra* (daily noon–2.30pm & 7–9pm), which serves a wide range of expensive dishes in an original and atmospheric part of the *Kasbah Hôtel*.

As a conservative town, Kairouan has little local **nightlife**, except for some raucous restaurants-cum-bars around the roundabout by the post office, such as the *Roi du Couscous* (closed Fri) at rue 20 Mars. Otherwise, the Aghlabid pools are a popular summer venue for evening stroll, and if you're peckish you can take with you a cheap pizza from *Piccolo Mondo*, 200m south of the site (daily 8am–10pm, later on Sat), as many locals do. The most popular **cafés** are those on place des Martyrs, along with an unnamed cavern on the left side of avenue 7 Novembre just before rue Bab Jedid, and another nameless café on rue Dr Hamda Laouani, which offers good *chicha* pipes. More expensively, you could smoke a *chicha* and slurp on a coffee at the *Café Chicha*, in the former prison of the kasbah in the *Kasbah Hôtel*. For a calm **beer**, try the *Hôtel Splendid*.

Listings

Airlines Tunis Air, rue Khawarezmi, off bd Bourguiba ☎77 230 422. Hend Voyage, nearby on av Dr Hamda Laouani (☎77 227336), serves as an agent for most other airlines.

Banks There are several in the centre between Bab ech Chouhada and av de la République, one of which should be open weekend mornings. The STB on the corner of av Dr Hamda Laouani and av de la République has an ATM accepting Visa and MasterCard.

Car rental Hertz, av Ibn el Jazzar ☎77 234 529, near the *Kasbah Hotel*.

Cinema Maison de la Culture, bd Bourguiba.

Festivals The Mouled Festival, a celebration of the Prophet's birthday, is a big event in Kairouan. A seasonal pudding called *assida* is a speciality of the celebration, whose date varies according to the Islamic calendar (see p.45).

Hammams Men can use the hammam attached to the *Hôtel Sabra* (daily 5am–10pm), as well as one in the Medina near Bir Barouta. There is a women's hammam on av Ali Zouaoui, 20m from the junction with bd Hedi Chaker on the left, through a whitewashed archway next to a dry cleaner.

Hospital Ibn el Jazzar University Hospital, av Ibn el Jazzar ☎77 230 036.

Internet access Publinet Horizon, next to *Hôtel El Menema* (daily 8am–midnight; 1.5TD/hr). Slightly more difficult to find is Publinet L'Univers (daily 8am–8pm; 1.5TD/hr), in a back street: from the Tunis Air office, take the next left by the sign for the *Maison des Jeunes*, follow the road round to the left, then turn right and the Publinet is on your right.

Markets A busy daily food market is held in the streets between Bab Tunis and pl de Tunis. There's another food market, which combines with a flea market, just south of the bus and louage stations, best on Sundays. Also well worth heading for is the distinctly untouristy Monday souk, attracting Berbers and others from all around; it's held about 500m down av Haffouz (aka av Beit el Hikma) from the post office.

Pharmacy There's a night pharmacy at 44 av Ali Zouaoui (☎77 230 069), less than 100m north from the junction with bd Hedi Chaker on the right.

Police On av 7 Novembre by Souk Belaghjia (daytime only), and on rue du 20 Mars (24hr), opposite *Hôtel Splendid*.

Post office On the large roundabout where av de la République meets rue de la Victoire and av Haffouz (city hours; bureau de change).
Supermarket Magasin Général on bd Bourguiba, just south of Bab ech Chouhada.

Swimming pools Non-residents can use the pool at the *Continental* for 5TD and at the *Kasbah* for 5.5TD.
Telephones There are numerous taxiphone offices in both the Medina and new town.

Around Kairouan

On the flat plain surrounding Kairouan are the remains of some palace complexes built by the ninth-century Aghlabid rulers, testimony to their feelings of insecurity even in such a prosperous period. The minimal remains are hardly worth a visit for their own sake, but those at **Reqqada** could be combined with a visit to the National Museum of Islamic Art.

Reqqada

The main reason for visiting **REQQADA** (or Rakkada), 11km south of Kairouan, is the **National Museum of Islamic Art** (Tues–Sun: July & Aug 8.15am–2.15pm; Sept–June 9am–4pm; closes 1pm on Fri; ☎77 223 337; global ticket plus 1.1TD), which opened in 1994 to great fanfare in a former presidential palace. Sadly, it is a bit of a letdown. The collection features some jumbled ancient Koranic manuscripts, old gold and silver coins from the earliest period of Arab rule and some desultory ceramics, glassware and stoneware, with little in the way of background explanation. For years, the museum has been gearing up to receive a wealth of material formerly exhibited in other museums – such as the exquisite ninth-century Cordoban astrolabe formerly at Monastir and a part of the Bardo's Islamic collection – but at the time of writing there was still no sign of this happening.

There has been talk of the museum setting up a minibus link to Kairouan; ask at the tourist office, but don't hold your breath. Until then, you can get there by taking the **bus** for students of Reqqada's Faculté des Lettres, which leaves every half hour to an hour from Kairouan's Cité Mohammed Ali station (about 300m down av Haffouz from the post office roundabout) between 7.30am and 8pm except on Sundays and during the summer vacation. When you arrive at the Faculté des Lettres stop, the museum is a kilometre further on and signposted to the right. Alternatively, you can find yellow-striped louages to Reqqada about 200m further down avenue Haffouz from the Cité Mohammed Ali station, on the left, either side of a *oued*; they will drop you at the museum turn-off. Simplest of all is a taxi from Kairouan (around 5TD).

As you walk towards the museum from the bus stop, you'll find the minimal remains of a **palace**, built in 876 by the Aghlabid sovereign Ibrahim II, in a field on the right. The Aghlabids' reasons for wanting a palace out of town included avoiding troop rebellions and being able to have a reasonably pleasurable lifestyle beyond the withering gaze of Kairouan's religious lobby. Another reason for choosing Reqqada was its agreeable climate, believed to have dynamic powers: "Every time the doctor Zian Ibn Khalfoun left Kairouan for Reqqada," wrote El Bekri, the early traveller, "he took off his turban in order to receive directly on his head the beneficial effects of this atmosphere."

Raqqada's predecessor was **El Abbasiya**, built 5km southeast of Kairouan after a troop rebellion of 809, in which the Kairouanis had joined. Even less remains of this than of the palace in Reqqada, but it has given rise to an intriguing theory. El Bekri's description of a minaret which once stood there fits that of the Leaning Tower of Pisa, itself built in 1174. The theory begs the question of whether this is more than coincidental, given that Pisan ships took part in the Norman campaign in Tunisia between 1141 and 1160.

Scanty remains of another old palace, **Sabra**, are to the left off the Reqqada road a couple of kilometres out of Kairouan, and not easy to find. The palace was built for the Fatimid ruler El Mansour on the site of his final victory over the Kharijite rebel Abu Yazid in 947 (see p.495). Abu Yazid is said to have died of his wounds exactly a year later.

Biar el Aouani

North of Kairouan, after an easy run across flat empty country, the GP3 road to El Fahs and on to Tunis skirts the southern edge of the Zaghouan massif, last remnant of the Dorsale range. The only diversion on this route, 20km from Kairouan, is **BIAR EL AOUANI**, with its perfect turreted Byzantine **fort** on the bare hillside, and a little local museum (variable hours) whose curator rushes up to greet any car that stops. The isolation makes the site all the more attractive.

Mahdia and around

Georges Sebastian, whose fabulous villa helped launch Hammamet as an internationally famous resort, regarded **MAHDIA**, 50km south along the coast from Sousse, as the only other place in Tunisia that could compare. It's easy to see why. Despite the installation of a large *zone touristique* on the beaches to the north, the historic old town remains remarkably unspoilt. This, as well as the light and colour of the place, makes Mahdia well worth a few days' stay.

The Mahdi

Just as Jews look forward to the coming of the Messiah, and Christians to the second coming of Jesus, so Muslims look forward to the coming of the **Mahdi** or "divinely guided one", whose arrival will herald the final victory of Islam. Muslim belief in the Mahdi is based on the *hadith* (sayings of the Prophet), but some *hadith* are more reliably authentic than others, and those that refer to the Mahdi are not in the category considered most reliable. In one of them, Mohammed says that the Mahdi "will fill the earth with fairness and justice as it was filled with oppression and tyranny", while in another he tells that "the Mahdi will be from my family, a descendant of Fatima". Fatima is the Prophet's daughter, from whom the Fatimids claimed descent.

The Mahdi is not a prophet or Messiah, but a rightful caliph or imam, the divinely appointed leader of Islam. The question of who is the rightful caliph has been disputed by Sunni and Shi'ite Muslims since the time of Ali, the fourth caliph, who was Fatima's husband and Mohammed's son-in-law. When he died in 661, Shi'ite Muslims refused to accept the legitimacy of the Umayyad caliphs who succeeded him. Instead, they regarded as legitimate leaders of Islam only Ali's direct male heirs, to whom they gave the title "imam". Most Shi'ites ("Twelvers") recognize twelve imams, of whom the last, Mohammed al-Muntazar ("the Expected One") disappeared in 873. According to legend, however, al-Muntazar did not die; he is simply "hidden", and it is he who will return one day as the Mahdi, the hidden imam revealed.

Belief in the coming of Mahdi originated among Shi'ites, but soon spread to Muslims of all schools, although Sunnis and non-Twelver Shi'ites do not accept that it will be al-Muntazar. Throughout history, and especially at times of crisis, leaders and would-be leaders have claimed to be the Mahdi, especially in North Africa. Like most, Obaidallah Said, the "Mahdi" from whom Mahdia takes its name, conveniently ignored certain aspects of the Mahdi legend: the Mahdi, for example, will reign for only seven years, after which comes Judgement Day and the end of the world.

Mahdia's position on a narrow peninsula in the belly-like bulge of the Sahel coast has defined its history. After defeating the last of the Aghlabids in 909, the new Fatimid ruler of Tunisia – the self-styled **Mahdi** (see box opposite) – needed a capital to provide security from the hostility of the Sunni majority. The heretical Fatimids overthrew the complacent Aghlabids with the aid of Berber dissidents, but were neither popular nor concerned to be so. They wanted Tunisia as a base to conquer Egypt and Iraq, the heart of the Arab world. It was with this in mind that the historian Ibn Khaldoun later called Mahdia a "dagger held in the fist".

Mahdia made the ideal capital, its narrow entrance easily closed off by the massive wall begun in 916. Behind the wall the Mahdi built a Great Mosque, a harbour, a palace and other installations, with everything else relegated outside the wall. A few merchants were allowed to trade inside, but had to live outside, and the Mahdi claimed that his aim was to separate them from their wives during the day and from their goods at night.

For the next six hundred years, Mahdia was to be one of the most formidable fortresses in the Mediterranean. Its first test came with a siege in 944–45 by **Abu Yazid**, "the man on a donkey" (see p.495), and his Kharijite revolt from Tozeur, but this was soon beaten off. After the Fatimids left for Cairo in 970, Mahdia shared the chequered fortunes of other coastal towns. In 1057 the **Zirids**, supposedly the country's rulers, were forced to take refuge here by the invading Banu Hilal, and thirty years later a joint Genoese–Pisan force seized the city, and the Zirids had to buy it back. Taken again by the Norman king Roger II of Sicily in 1148, Mahdia was returned to Islamic control in 1160, which brought prosperity through trade and piracy and, in 1390, another unsuccessful siege by the French, English and Genoese.

The wars of the sixteenth century, however, brought Mahdia's period of greatness to an end. In 1547 the corsair **Dragut** made the town his centre of operations, causing the Spanish to storm it in 1550. Rather than have to return, when they left in 1554 they brought the walls down. Since then – apart from routine pillagings by the Spanish in 1597 and the Knights of Malta in the seventeenth century – Mahdia has been a peaceful fishing port.

Arrival and information

The main square, place de l'Indépendance, is next to the port; on or just off the square you'll find the town hall, police station, a couple of banks and entrance to the Skifa el Kahla gate-tunnel, which joins the **new town** to the west with the peninsular **Medina**. Stretching off into the new town is avenue Bourguiba, running parallel to the **beach** until the coastline curves away to the north. The *zone touristique* doesn't start until about 4km from the Skifa.

The **train station** is centrally located on avenue Farhat Hached by the port. **Buses** drop you outside the **louage station**, inconveniently located 3km west of the Medina on avenue Belhouane, which arcs round from avenue 7 Novembre in the north to avenue Farhat Hached in the south. You can walk to the Medina by turning left out of the station with the railway to your right, then left at the level crossing, right at the end of the street, and left again onto avenue Farhat Hached, with the port to your right. Alternatively, a taxi should cost around 1.5TD to the Medina, a bit more to the *zone touristique* hotels.

Just through the Skifa in the Medina is the **ONTT** (Mon–Sat: July & Aug 8.30am–noon & 2–7pm; Sept–June 8.30am–noon & 2–5.45pm; ☎73 681 098), which is helpful and has a hotel price list but no maps (these can be purchased in the gift shops on the west side of pl de l'Indépendance).

Moving on from Mahdia

For a list of destinations and journey times, see Travel details on p.285.

Buses stop outside the **louage station** (☏73 680 372). You can walk there by turning right onto avenue Taïeb Mehiri about 1km down avenue Farhat Hached, then left after 200m and right again at the end (before the level crossing) onto avenue Belhouane, from where the station is 500m on the right. Note that if you want to go to Monastir by louage, you'll have to change at Moknine or Ksar Hellal. For Kairouan, you're best heading to Sousse for a connection. The **train station** (☏73 680 177) has one daily service to Tunis, along with regular **métro** services (see p.218) to Monastir, Monastir airport and Sousse, via Moknine, Ksar Hellal and Lamta.

Accommodation

There are only two **hotels** in the Medina (book ahead in summer, especially for the *Al Jazira*) and a smart new four-star nearby on avenue Bourguiba, with the rest along the beach to the northwest in the **zone touristique**, which has around twenty hotels and more planned. Most are expensive, though out of season prices plunge, with half- or full board not much more than bed and breakfast. As a rule of thumb, the further out the hotel, the better and more modern the facilities. **Taxis** to the *zone touristique* hotels should cost no more than 2TD. Alternatively, the Sahel **métro trains** from Mahdia to Monastir and Sousse call at two handy stations: Sidi Messaoud, near *Hôtel El Mehdi*, and Mahdia Zone Touristique, near *Hôtel Mahdia Palace* towards the end of the *zone*.

If you prefer a beach location without the luxuries, there's an unofficial **campsite** between the closed-down *Sables d'Or* and the *El Mehdi* hotel. The *Maison des Jeunes* on rue Ibn Rached (☏73 681 559; ❶, dorm beds 5TD; closed daytime) is centrally placed and unusually pleasant, with double rooms available; from the train station, turn left opposite the Esso garage and you'll find the hostel in the second (narrow) street on your left.

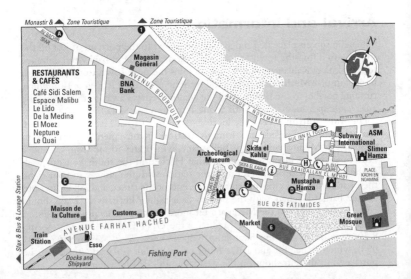

Hotels

Town

Al Jazira 36 rue Ibn el Fourat ☎73 681 629, ℻73 680 274. With cosy rooms, clean shared bathrooms and heating. Some rooms have jaw-dropping views over the sea just 10m away (no. 9 especially), and the management is friendly and ever helpful. Highly recommended. ❷

El Medina rue el Kaem, in the Medina ☎73 694 664, ℻73 696 384.Though lacking the sea views of the *Al Jazira* and a touch more expensive, it's still a good place, offering pleasant, airy rooms set around a courtyard and a roof terrace. ❷

Le Phénix de Mahdia Corner of av Bourguiba and av Bachir Sfar ☎73 690 101, ℻73 690 108, ⊛www.phenixmahdia.com. Recently opened luxury hotel with comfortable, well-equipped rooms and a rooftop pool offering fabulous views over the Medina and surrounding coast. ❻

The zone touristique

Abou Nawas Cap Mahdia 4km from the Skifa ☎73 680 300, ℻73 696 332, ⊛www.abounawas .com. Relatively established member of the *zone*, offering horse-riding and water sports as well as archery and some marvellously tacky evening entertainment. Full board only in high season. ❽

Cap Sérail 5km from the Skifa ☎73 695 011. Much smaller and more intimate than most *zone* hotels, and offers water-sports facilities. ❼

Corniche av 7 Novembre, just before the *zone touristique* ☎73 694 201, ℻73 691 422. Unremarkable place, with some en-suite rooms, and next to the beach. Reasonable value but not as good as the Medina cheapies. ❸

Mahdia Palace 5.5km from the Skifa ☎73 696 777, ℻73 696 810. Mahdia's swankiest, easily justifying its prices. All mod cons, fantastic outdoor (and indoor) pools, tennis courts, health club and several bars and a nightclub. ❽

Thapsus 6km from Skifa ☎73 695 530, ℻73 695 374, ⊛www.thapsus-hotel.com. One of the newest, and most distant, in the *zone*, which means that the beach to the north is virtually deserted. Water sports and horse-riding available. ❼

The Town

Mahdia's **Medina** is only a tiny quarter now of what's otherwise a typical, thriving Sahel town, but its maritime atmosphere sets it apart from Tunisia's other old cities, and even the stones of the houses look more seaworn than weather-beaten. The dominant sound, on the other hand, is not the breaking of waves but the working of looms, since weaving is the main cottage industry here.

ACCOMMODATION
Al Jazira	B
Maison des Jeunes	C
El Medina	D
Le Phénix	A

MAHDIA

Cap d'Afrique

AVENUE 7 NOVEMBRE

RUE SIDI JABEUR

RUE SIDI JABEUR

RUE HAJ MOHAMED ARESSALEM

Lighthouse

Borj el Kebir

Excavations

RUE DU BORJ

Rocks

Fatimid Port

0   100 m

MEDITERRANEAN SEA

Dominating the main square and forming the dividing line between the old and new towns, the **Skifa el Kahla** is a sixteenth-century reconstruction of a gateway the departing Spaniards blew up in 1554. The gate – once the only entrance to the city – stood in the middle of a wall as much as 10m thick, stretching right across the neck of the peninsula. It's staggering to think that the defences destroyed by the Spaniards 450 years ago were already 600 years old. The Skifa in particular quickly became legendary: each section of its vaulted passage could be closed off by lowering an iron grill weighing as much as eight tons. But it was the narrow passage itself, immortalized in the name *skifa el kahla*, "The Dark Passage", which became most notorious: "So dark," according to John Ogilby, translating Olfert Dapper's *Africa* compendium of 1670, "that it is terrible to strangers, seeming rather a murdering den than an entrance into a city". Nowadays the murdering den is an informal souk, which comes into its own on Fridays with a number of perfume, magico-mineral and jewellery sellers.

On place de l'Indépendance beside the Skifa, the regional **Archeological Museum** (Tues–Sun: April to mid-Sept 9am–1pm & 3–7pm; mid-Sept to March 9am–4pm; 1.1TD, camera 1TD) is a light and airy place whose ground floor houses Punic, Roman and Christian ceramics, mainly oil lamps (the Roman models are particularly intricate) and *amphorae*, as well as statues and mosaics from Thysydrus (El Jem). The Islamic Art section upstairs includes ceramics, calligraphy, mosaics, wooden chests and examples of traditional local dress together with the looms used to weave them. Labelling is in French and Arabic.

The street on the far side of the Skifa cuts through Mahdia's main tourist drag, with souvenir shops and persistent hard sell. Beyond it, you come to **place du Caire**, one of the most perfect little squares in all Tunisia. Sit at the café here under the small minaret of the **Mustapha Hamza Mosque**, and the only reminder of time passing is the tortoise-like movement of old men who shift their seats slowly round the square in pursuit of shade. The two **cafés** here form Mahdia's main nocturnal attraction.

Also worth a visit if you want to learn more about the Medina is the local branch of the **ASM** (Mon–Thurs 9am–1pm & 3–5.30pm, Fri & Sat 9am–1pm), in an old palatial residence on avenue 7 Novembre, which organizes projects to renovate the houses within the Medina. If you're interested in **weaving**, the Medina is full of workshops whose loom workers are friendly and usually willing to chat about their craft to passing tourists. Prices range from 4–6TD for a synthetic bedspread, to 35–40TD for a pure silk sash, and up to 600TD for a silk, gold and silver thread bridal wedding shawl made to order. This is some of the most beautiful craftwork you'll find anywhere in Tunisia; a good place to sample it is the loom and workshop around the corner from the *Al Jazira* on rue du Caire.

The daily fish **market** by the modern fishing port and the weekly Friday market are both lively; look out especially for octopuses, which are sold by the bunch. They're caught by boys who can be seen any morning picking their way round the shallow rocky pools on the peninsula's shore, armed with spiked canes.

The Great Mosque

Straight on from place du Caire, beyond another Turkish mosque (the Slimen Hanza) on the left, the fortress-like **Great Mosque** dominates the expanse of place Kadhi en Noamine. By the 1960s the whole building was so decrepit that it was entirely reconstructed; the original was built by Obaidallah Said in the tenth century, incorporating some characteristic Fatimid elements. Most prominent of these is the monumental entrance, a Fatimid innovation which owes its form to Roman triumphal arches and its function to the elitism of Fatimid doctrine. Only the Mahdi and his entourage were allowed to use the main entrance, and the same distinction carried over to the prayer hall, where the central aisle was reserved for those in the ruler's favour. Deep niches, used in the entrance gate and in the prayer-hall facade, represent another Fatimid innovation, and the two bastions at either corner of the north wall were cisterns for collecting water from the roof. The courtyard was used as a cemetery by the Spaniards in 1551, but when they left in 1554 they exhumed the bodies and took them to Palermo. Suitably dressed non-Muslims may be allowed in outside prayer times, though this can't be assumed.

Most of the peninsula itself is rocky, but some steps going down from the *Café Sidi Salem* at rue du Borj on the south side of the peninsular, 200m beyond the Great Mosque, provide good **swimming** off the rocks below the excavation site. The café itself (see p.262) has wonderful views.

Borj el Kebir and Cap d'Afrique

Passing the fenced-off Fatimid excavations to your left, the hilltop **Borj el Kebir** (Tues–Sun: April to mid-Sept 9am–1pm & 3–7pm; mid-Sept to March 9am–4pm; 1.1TD, camera 1TD) looms large over a cemetery beyond. Dating from 1595, it was first just a simple rectangle; the corner bastions were added in the eighteenth century. As forts go, this one is bleak and uninteresting, but it does offer a great view over the town (mornings are best for photography from this angle, although Mahdia's evening light often takes your breath away).

The *gardien* may talk of a subterranean tunnel leading off the narrow entrance to El Jem and describe how elephants were used to transport building blocks for an amphitheatre from the port at Mahdia to the middle of the Sahel. But it is unlikely that there was any Roman settlement here, as the crumbling **port** below the fortress was built by the Fatimids. The port once had a tower on either side of the entrance with a chain suspended between (which Christian attackers broke through in 1088). Once home to a Mediterranean strike-force, the port is now used only by a few small, brightly painted fishing boats, themselves left behind by the modern vessels and the new port in town.

The old port and the few confused remains of the Mahdi's **palace** almost breathe melancholy, an impression not helped by the fact that the end of the peninsula is a large **cemetery**. The red **lighthouse** at the tip is operated by the military, though there are no problems with photography, or clambering around the very sea-worn ruins right at the end – **Cap d'Afrique**.

Eating, drinking and nightlife

You don't have to stray far from the main square by the port to get some great **food** at prices you won't believe if you've just come from Sousse or Monastir. At the *Restaurant el Moez* (daily 9am–9pm), down an alley by the Skifa, you can fill up on the dishes of the day, which might include their excellent fish soup, a deliciously spicy *kamounia* or stuffed calamari for 2.5–3.5TD. For not much more, the friendly *Restaurant de la Medina* (daily 8am–10pm), in the same building as the market, does succulent fish and excellent soups served by a handlebar-moustached waiter in a canary-yellow waistcoat. More upmarket restaurants can be found along the quayside avenue Farhat Hached, best of which are *Le Lido* (daily 11.30am–midnight) and *Le Quai* (daily 8am–midnight), both offering three courses for around 15TD, though the difference in price and attitude isn't reflected in the quality of the food. On the north shore, another pricey alternative is the *Neptune* (daily 8am–midnight), avenue 7 Novembre, 300m from the Skifa, which has a good tourist menu for 15.5TD.

There are a couple of **cafés** on rue des Fatimides, just off the main square, including *Espace Malibu* (daily 6am–10pm), which is female-friendly and has a shady pergola to sit under if you can stand the traffic noise. Much the best place for a drink, however, is the *Café Sidi Salem* (daily 9am–11pm, later in summer), on rue du Borj on the south side of the peninsula, which offers superlative sea views and reasonable food as well, with sandwiches for up to 1.5TD and seafood dishes for around 8TD. You'll find the usual unremarkable **nightclubs** at many of the *zone touristique* hotels, with the pick of the bunch probably *Samba* at *Hôtel el Mehdi*.

Listings

Banks There are several at the northern end of av Farhat Hached and the eastern end of av Bourguiba. BNA and Amen banks, about 200m up av Bourguiba from pl de l'Indépendance, have ATMs accepting Visa and MasterCard.

Car rental Avis, av Bourguiba ☎73 696 342. There are a few local agencies on av Bourguiba towards the junction with av Belhouane, a couple of kilometres from pl de l'Indépendance.

Diving The Club de Plongée le Mahdois (☎73 680 300) is based at the *Abou Nawas Cap Mahdia* and offers diving equipment and lessons, as does Subway International (☎98 556 542, ✉subway@topnet.tn), on av 7 Novembre next to *Al Jazira*.

Festivals A fishing festival and the Nights of Mahdi Festival take place in July. Information on both is available at the tourist office nearer the dates. Most events are held in the Borj el Kebir.

Hammam rue Obaidallah el Mehdi in the Medina (men 6am–noon & 6–11pm, women noon–6pm).

Hospital The regional hospital is on rue Mendès France (☎73 681 005).

Internet access Cybernet, av Belhouane, near the CNSS College (Mon–Sat 9am–midnight, Sun 10am–midnight; 2TD/hr). To get there from the Skifa follow av Bourguiba for a couple of kilometres, turn left onto av Belhouane and it's on the left after 100m.

Pharmacy There are several pharmacies on av Bourguiba; the night pharmacy is in the market building off rue des Fatimides (☎73 681 490).

Police pl de l'Indépendance ☎73 681 419.

Post office The main office (city hours) is on av Bourguiba, about 2.5km from the Skifa in the new town. There is a small branch on place du Caire.

Supermarket Magasin Général, 63 av Bourguiba (Mon–Sat 8am–noon & 3–7pm, Sun 8am–12.45pm).

Taxis There's a taxi rank on the corner of pl de l'Indépendance and rue des Fatimides (☎73 695 900).

Telephones International calls can be made from taxiphone offices opposite the market, on rue Obaidallah el Mehdi between the Skifa and place du Caire, and on the west side of the main square.

The coast south of Mahdia

The ruins at **SALAKTA**, a small coastal village on the site of Roman Sullecthum, are really only for the enthusiast, though it's a pleasant enough place with a modern fishing harbour. The village is a little way south of Mahdia; the nearby village of **Ksour Essaf** is the jumping-off point, with shared taxis running to and fro between Ksour Essaf and the shore. Right on the beach is a Roman cemetery, next to a **museum** (Tues–Sun: April to mid-Sept 9am–1pm & 4–7pm; mid-Sept to March 9.30am–4.30pm; 1.1TD, camera 1TD), much of which is devoted to the work of a British-funded team on Roman pottery from the region. Among the other exhibits is the mosaic of a lion 4.5m long from nose to tail, and the funerary breastplate of a general from Hannibal's army. Also in the museum is an enlarged photograph of a mosaic found in Ostia, Rome's port town, showing ships in front of the office of a group of traders who specialized in trade with Sullecthum – a vivid reminder of how close trade links across the Mediterranean were.

South along the shore are other vestigial **remains** of baths, houses and walls, some of them actually in the sea. A little further on are the **Catacombs of Arch Zara**, or Ghar Dhaba, quite an extensive series of niche-lined tunnels, which you'll need a light of some kind to explore. To look for them, follow the coast road south from the museum for just over a kilometre until you come to a junction. Turn right inland, and continue for about 300m until the tarmac turns right again, but instead of following it, turn left with the main power lines. After nearly 1500m of piste, a track to your left heads towards a building with a blue-tiled onion dome on the roof. The path takes you after 100m to three pits, one of which has steps leading down into the catacombs. Just before the path, also on your left, an old Roman **cistern** is used by a local family to keep their rabbits in. The piste continues 500m to emerge on the Ksour Essaf–Sfax road by the "Sfax 87/Mahdia 18" marker.

The coast between here and Sfax is largely bare, but the town of **LA CHEBBA**, 20km south, has beaches of a sort, and a couple of places to **stay**. In town, the *Hôtel Lahmar* is reasonable enough (☏73 641 805; ❷), and there's a *Maison des Jeunes* 5km north of town (☏73 643 815), 1500m off the main road; call them to check they're open before traipsing out there. A couple of hundred metres away is a sand and rock beach, full of black seaweed and washed-up garbage, but free of people. You can **camp** at the hostel, though note that meals are only available in the summer. The peninsula protruding into the sea for 4km east of town ends at the most easterly point in the belly of the Sahel, **Ras Kaboudia**, a corruption of Caput Vada, its ancient name. A **lighthouse** here incorporates the remains of a Byzantine fort.

Another Roman site, **Acholla**, lies on the coast between here and Sfax. Originally founded by Maltese Phoenicians, the site boasted some mosaics, which were plundered and hauled off to the Bardo in Tunis, but ruins of a **bathhouse** and two **villas** – one the home of a second-century AD Roman senator – remain.

El Jem

The extraordinary **amphitheatre** at **EL JEM**, midway between Sousse and Sfax, is the single most impressive Roman monument in Africa, its effect magnified by the sheer incongruity of its sudden appearance, surrounded by a huddle of small houses in the middle of the flat Sahel plain. There is a reasonable hotel here, but transport is good and there's no reason to stay longer than it takes to see the amphitheatre and the excellent **archeological museum**. A good time to visit is in the early morning before the tour groups arrive, or else late afternoon when they've gone. Every year, from mid-July to mid-August, the amphitheatre becomes the setting for performances of both classical Arab music (including *malouf*) and classical European orchestral pieces, as part of the **International Festival of Symphonic Music** (☏73 630 224, ⊛www.festivaleljem.com).

Ancient El Jem was probably larger than the modern town, full of luxurious villas owned by men who had grown rich trading olive oil with Rome. As the Romans expanded from grain into oil, the Sahel began to grow rich, and it was during the second century AD that **Thysdrus**, set here at a crossroads of the area, first started to expand so spectacularly. Prosperity brought the villas, mosaics and the amphitheatre – but eventually also the town's downfall. The citizens rose in revolt against the level of Roman taxation around 230 AD, killing the collector of taxes and proclaiming the 80-year-old Imperial official **Gordian** as

Emperor of Rome. This action introduced an unsettled period for the empire and did Thysdrus little good. The one memorial to Gordian's short rule (soon defeated – he committed suicide) is the amphitheatre, begun in his time and left unfinished at his death. According to one legend, the amphitheatre saw the last heroic stand of **Kahina**, Jewish prophetess and leader of **Berber resistance** to the Arab invasion in the seventh century. Certainly it would be even better preserved today if, in 1695, Mohammed Bey had not blown up most of one side in order to evict the followers of Ali Bey.

4 The Town

The remains of the **amphitheatre** (daily: April to mid-Sept 7am–7pm; mid-Sept to March 8am–6pm; 4.2TD, camera 1TD) are among the best preserved of their kind – finer than the Colosseum in Rome, and not much smaller. The amphitheatre's original capacity is estimated at around thirty thousand, more than the population of Thysdrus itself; people would have come from all around to watch the games here, boosting the town's civic prestige.

Chambers underneath the middle of the arena held **gladiators**, animals and theatrical scenery, and an elaborate system of lifts delivered them directly to the arena. Animals would be hoisted up in cages, which could then be opened in safety using pulleys from below. Following extensive restorations, you can wander around the underbelly of the complex. To recreate the scene, picture an amphitheatre mosaic you've seen, and imagine the roars and stench of animals and the fear of those about to face them in this claustrophobic space, which was lined with marble so neither combatant nor animal could escape.

Roman entertainment

Circus shows were the opiate of the Roman masses, used unashamedly by rulers to keep their huge urban populations happy, and the whole ritual played an important part in cementing the paternalistic relationship between rulers and ruled. A royal box was situated at each end of the arena, from where the charitable sponsor of the show would watch the proceedings and intervene when necessary. The defeated gladiator in a duel had the option of throwing himself on the mercy of the ruling official in his box. The official would give a signal by lying on his back and raising his left arm. If the crowd thought his courage had earned him his life, they would give the thumbs-up sign – but the final decision was the official's alone: if his thumb was pointed down, the victim was killed on the spot. Doubtless, prudent officials tended not to offend the crowd too often.

The only disadvantage of the shows for the rulers was their in-built inflationary spiral. The more spectacular the show, the higher the expectations next time. **Wild animals** played a large part in the proceedings and were plentiful here in Africa. Animals would be pitted against each other or against gladiators, or else unarmed victims would be thrown into their midst. On the day that Rome's Colosseum opened, five thousand animals are said to have perished. But the appetite for blood grew ever stronger, and human life was sufficiently cheap for **armed gladiators** to be in plentiful supply. They were mostly prisoners or criminals, or even bankrupts on a contract to pay off their debts – if they survived. Gladiators were surrounded by a macabre sort of glamour: they had their own fan clubs, and sometimes banquets were put on at which the public could meet the next day's combatants.

Perhaps the most disturbing aspect of all this is that people enjoyed it so much. When a gladiator was on the point of dispatching his victim, the crowd would scream "Bene lava!" ("Wash yourself well [in blood]"), a homely little tag usually found on the doorsteps of houses and public baths.

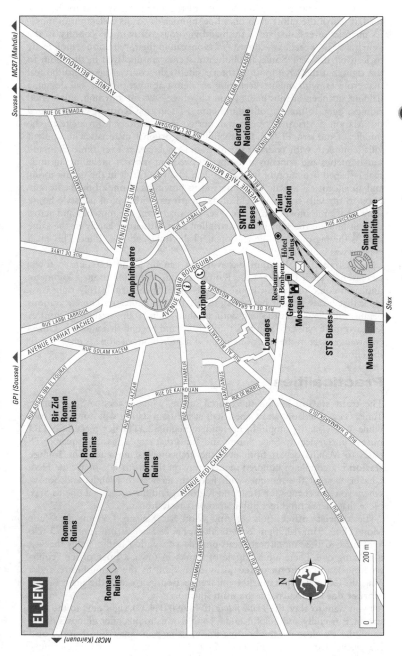

EL JEM

MC87 (Mahdia) ▲

Sousse ▲

GP1 (Sousse) ▲

MC87 (Kairouan) ▲

Stax ▶

AVENUE A BELHAOUANE

RUE DE REMADA

RUE EMIR ABDELKADER

RUE DE L'ADJUDANT

RUE M'HAMED ALI

RUE DE LIBYE

AVENUE MONGI SLIM

RUE O. TNEZAK

RUE I KHALDOUN

RUE H JABALLAH

AVENUE TAIEB MEHIRI

S BEL HAJ

AVENUE MOHAMED V

Garde
Nationale

Train
Station

RUE AVICENNE

SNTRI
Buses ★

Hôtel
Julius ⊙

Smaller
Amphitheatre

Amphitheatre

AVENUE HABIB BOURGUIBA

ℹ

Taxiphone 📞

Restaurant
du Bonheur ⊡

⊠

Great
Mosque 🕌

STS Buses ★

RUE DE LA GRANDE MOSQUÉE

RUE LARBI ZARROUK

AVENUE FARHAT HACHED

RUE GOLAM KACEM

RUE AIT BELHASSEN

Louages ★

Museum ▪

RUE ASSAD IBN EL FOURAT

RUE IBN EL JAZZAR

THAMEUR

RUE HABIB

RUE GARDIANUS

RUE DE BUZRITE

RUE D'HAMMARSKJOLD

Bir Zid
Roman
Ruins

Roman
Ruins

Roman
Ruins

RUE DE KAIROUAN

AVENUE HEDI CHAKER

RUE DU NID D'UN

Roman
Ruins

Roman
Ruins

RUE JAMMAL ABDENASSER

RUE DU 20 MARS 1956

N

0   200 m

265

The **Archeological Museum** (same times and ticket as amphitheatre, except closes 5.30pm in winter), south of the amphitheatre next to the Sfax road, is worth the effort even on a hot summer day, as its collection of mosaics includes several that are as fresh and vigorous as any in the country. In the courtyard, two peacocks – almost Art Nouveau in their stylization – look ready to leap off the wall. Some amphitheatre scenes are displayed in the room to the right, but the large room at the far side of the courtyard contains the real masterpieces, with mosaics featuring an almost abstract peacock-tail design, a balding, drunken Silenus being bound by three boys for a nymph, and a child riding a tiger. To the rear of the museum, a fascinating **Roman villa** (dubbed the Maison d'Africa) has been transported in its entirety from a site in the middle of modern El Jem and rebuilt using original materials. The opulent villa, complete with courtyard garden and pool, covers over three thousand square metres and contains a number of excellent mosaics, including an unusual T-shaped depiction of fish, seafood and bowls of fruit in the dining room, and an allegorical mosaic of Rome and its provinces in one of the bedrooms. Next to the villa is a small field of **excavations**, with typical peristyle house plans and some mosaics in place. Over the road from the museum and across the rail line are the remains of a **smaller amphitheatre**, hardly in the same state as the big one but free and open all the time, and less visited. This small version was built first.

Another patch of **Roman excavations** can be found just outside town; take avenue Hedi Chaker – the Kairouan road – west for about a kilometre until you come to the last house on the right. Then turn sharply right up a track that heads straight back towards the big amphitheatre. The excavations begin immediately on the left, with another group 100m straight in front. A left turn there will take you to a third group, and beyond that a fourth. Unless you want a walk in the sun, none of these scattered bits of stone is really worth the effort.

Practicalities

The **train station** lies on the central square, with services to Sfax, Sousse, Tunis, Gafsa, Metlaoui and Gabès. Staff at the train station will store your bags while you visit the amphitheatre and museum (2.3TD per piece). SNTRI **buses** run services to Sfax, Sousse and Tunis that stop across the square; STS buses to Mahdia depart from near the archeological museum. The **louage station** is a couple of hundred metres away on the north side of avenue Hedi Chaker, west of the mosque, with frequent services to Mahdia and Sousse, where you can change for Tunis and Kairouan, and the occasional one to Sfax. Note that there's no direct public transport to Kairouan.

The **tourist office** (July & Aug Mon–Sat 8.30am–1.30pm; Sept–June Mon–Thurs 9am–12.30pm & 3–6.30pm, Fri & Sat 8.30am–1pm; ☎73 630 438) next to the amphitheatre can provide you with a leaflet about the site, if nothing else. There are a couple of **banks** in town, a **post office** (country hours), a **taxiphone office** (daily 8am–9pm) by the amphitheatre, and a Magasin Général **supermarket** on avenue Bourguiba near the main square. **Market day** is Monday (in the main square).

If you want to **stay**, the *Hôtel Julius* (☎73 690 044; ❹), right next to the train station, is friendly and helpful, and a couple of its rooms offer glimpses of the amphitheatre, although the hooting from passing trains may disturb you. **Food** is available at the hotel (daily noon–3pm & 6–10pm) and at the simple, inexpensive *Restaurant du Bonheur* nearby (daily 11am–midnight). For something even cheaper, there are a couple of *gargotes* around the marketplace by the main square. There are a few **cafés** around the entrance to the amphitheatre, but the *Hôtel Julius* is about the only place in town where alcohol is served.

Sfax and around

The writer Ronald Firbank once took it into his head to call **SFAX** "the most beautiful city in the world", for which he has been ridiculed ever since by travel writers, their readers and at least one mayor of the town. Granted some exaggeration, Sfax *is* a much more attractive place than is usually supposed. Somehow everything seems a little easier here, from bureaucratic operations to a certain no-nonsense attitude that other Tunisians often dislike. Indeed, with its two excellent museums and consistently underrated Medina, Sfax can claim to be the most sophisticated town in the country. Ferries also run regularly from here to the **Kerkennah Islands** (see p.280), another good reason for passing through.

Some history

Sfax's lack of interest in tourism is significant: as the wealthiest, most successful city in the country, it has no need to rely on tourists either for revenue or for self-esteem. Founded in 849 near the site of a small Roman town, Taparura, Sfax took its name from a species of cucumber (*faqous* in Arabic) and made its money from a trading fleet and the products of the Sahel's olive trees. By the tenth century it was already wealthy.

During the **Hilalian invasion**, a member of the Zirid family, one Ibn Melil, set up a principality in Sfax, with hopes of reuniting Tunisia around it, but the Normans already had their eyes on it, and the town fell to them in 1148. The Sfaxians plotted their resistance and began manufacturing arms in secret. Posing as beggars, they went from door to door recruiting fighters. As a signal they would be given a number of beans corresponding to the number of combat-worthy men in the house. Then, on New Year's Eve 1156, which the Christians celebrated with fireworks and a procession of bejewelled cows, the Sfaxians mingled with the Normans and surprised them mid-carnival, recapturing the town. With money from the cows' gold, they built the "Cisternes des Vaches" a few hundred metres northwest of the Medina – the site is now a school, but the district still bears the name – and even today New Year's Eve is celebrated in Sfax with beans and fireworks.

In 1546, under the crumbling rule of the Hafsids, Sfax again became a principality under the cruel adventurer **El Mokkani**. It was rescued fifteen years later by the pirate **Dragut**, who reunited it with the rest of Tunisia. Then began the period of Sfax's greatest prosperity, which reached its height in the eighteenth century. When the French came in 1881 they met fiercer resistance here than anywhere else, and the city was bombarded by nine warships and four gunboats. Having taken Sfax, the French proceeded to sack the city, profane its mosques and kill hundreds of its inhabitants. Later it was here that **Farhat Hached**, the UGTT leader, found fertile ground for trade unionist resistance to French rule.

Today Sfax occupies a unique position in Tunisia. Politically, the Sfaxian lobby is very powerful, its clout deriving from Sfax's role as a major centre for manufacturing (mainly of olive oil, almonds, phosphates and textiles), a port and a financial and commercial hub. Feelings about Sfax in the rest of

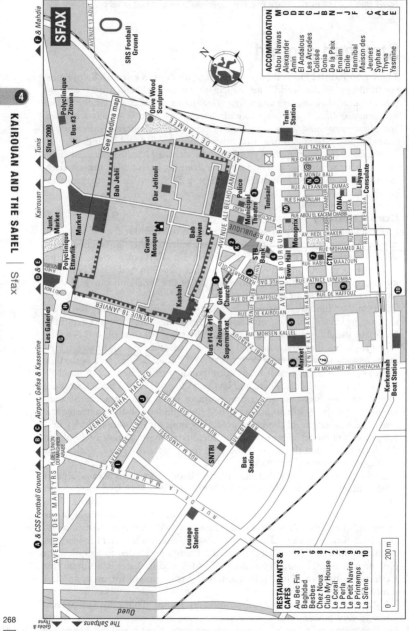

▲ Sidi Mansour

SFAX

AVENUE 13 AOÛT

◀ F & Mahdia

SRS Football Ground

N

Polyclinique Zitouna
Bus #3

Sfax 2000

◀ Tunis

◀ Kairouan

Olive Wood Sculpture

AVENUE DE L'ARMÉE

See Medina map

Train Station

RUE TAZERKA

RUE CHEIKH MEGDICH

RUE MONGI BALI

RUE ALEXANDRE DUMAS

RUE S HARZALLAH

Libyan Consulate

Bab Jebli

Dar Jellouli

Junk Market

Polyclinique Ettaawfik

Market

Great Mosque

Bab Diwan

Kasbah

Police

Municipal Theatre

Tunisair

AVENUE ALI BELHOUANE

AVENUE DE LA RÉPUBLIQUE

Monoprix

AV. ABOU EL KACEM CHABBI

AV. HEDI CHAKER

ONA

RUE TAHAR SFAR

RUE DE REMADA

RUE ABOU EL KACEM CHABBI

STB Bank

CTN

RUE MOHAMED ALI

RUE HABIB MAAZOUN

RUE PATRICE LUMUMBA

RUE DE HAFFOUZ

RUE DE HAFFOUZ

AVENUE BOURGUIBA

AVENUE HAMMADI TAIEB

AVENUE DAG HAMMARSKJOLD

Town Hall

Greek Church

RUE DE HAFFOUZ

RUE DE KAIROUAN

RUE MOHSEN KALLEL

Zeitouna Supermarket

Bus #14 & #16

AVENUE 18 JANVIER

Les Galeries

RUE 7 NOV

◀ D & E

◀ B, C, Airport, Gafsa & Kasserine

◀ A & CSS Football Ground

AVENUE DES MARTYRS

PLE DE L'UNION DU MAGHREB ARABE

AVENUE FARHAT HACHED

AVENUE DE L'ALGÉRIE

RUE M. JAMOUSSI

RUE DE LA MAURITANIE

Market

AV MOHAMED HEDI KHEFACHA

RUE ARBI ZARROUK

AVENUE ALI BACH HAMBA

RUE SAKIET SIDI YOUSSEF

AVENUE DE RABAT

SNTRI

Bus Station

Kerkennah Boat Station

Louage Station

RUE DE LA MAURITANIE

Oued

◀ Gabès & Thyna

◀ The Saltpans

0   200 m

RESTAURANTS & CAFÉS
Au Bec Fin   3
Baghdad   1
Besbes   6
Chez Nous   8
Club My House   7
Le Corail   2
La Perla   4
Le Petit Navire   9
Le Printemps   5
La Sirène   10

ACCOMMODATION
Abou Nawas   M
Alexander   O
Amin   D
El Andalous   H
Les Arcades   G
Colisée   L
Donia   B
De la Paix   N
Ennaim   I
Étoile   J
Hannibal   F
Maison des Jeunes C
Syphax   A
Thyna   K
Yasmine   E

Moving on from Sfax

For a list of destinations and journey times, see Travel details on p.285.

The **train station** is central and easy to find, right at the eastern end of avenue Bourguiba (℡74 221 999), and has several services daily to Tunis, Sousse and Gabès. As for **buses**, city bus #16 to the war cemetery and out towards the Thyna turn-off can be picked up on avenue de l'Algerie by the small gardens opposite the Kasbah, and #3 to Sidi Mansour from just off avenue des Martyrs. Both run every twenty minutes during the day. From the bus station, **SORETRAS buses** serve Gabès, Gafsa, Kasserine, Le Kef, Mahdia, Medenine, Ben Gardane, Jerba, Kairouan, and Nefta (via Tozeur, Moulares and Redeyef). Buses also run to Mahrès, La Chebba, Sidi Bou Zid and Agareb. **SNTRI buses** leave from outside the SNTRI office opposite (℡74 222 355), with regular departures to Tunis and Sousse – via El Jem or Mahdia – and one continuing to Bizerte. The **louage station** is on ℡74 220 071.

Ferries for the hour-long journey to the Kerkennah Islands are operated by Sonotrak, down at the port on rue M Hedi Khefacha (℡74 222 216; see box on p.282 for details). For contact details for CTN, see p.17.

Sfax's **airport** (℡74 278 000) is not very well connected, but it offers flights to Tunis, as well as charters. Bus #14 from avenue de l'Algerie drops you at the airport turn-off on the Gafsa road (still nearly a kilometre from the airport itself), so your best bet is to take a cab.

the country are a mixture of admiration, envy and resentment, while Sfaxians are known as "the Jews of Tunisia" (an indication of residual anti-Semitism), and the stories and proverbs about their competitive nature are endless. The Sfaxians just go about their business knowing – as does everyone else – that the town is successful.

Arrival and information

Sfax's main thoroughfare, avenue Bourguiba, runs roughly east–west across town. The modern town centre is spread astride it, with the Medina to its north. Arriving by **train**, you'll find yourself at its eastern end, still pretty well in the town centre. The **louage station** is 200m west of the **bus station** along rue Commandant Bejaoui at the western end of town. A taxi from the bus or louage stations should cost no more than 1TD to most parts of town). Sfax's **airport** is 7km west of town off the Gafsa road (also called route de l'Aéroport), from where taxis to the city centre cost around 3TD; the #14 bus travels into town from the main road outside the airport.

The **ONTT** is on avenue Mohamed Hedi Khefacha, near the Kerkennah boat station (July & Aug Mon–Sat 7am–7pm, Sun 9am–noon; Sept–June Mon–Thurs 8.30am–1pm & 3–5.45pm, Fri & Sat 8.30am–1.30pm; ℡74 497 041). Staff are friendly and have a number of maps, information leaflets and hand-outs.

Accommodation

The Medina has a variety of cheap **hotels**, shown on the map on p.273. These are mostly very basic and unsuitable for women travelling alone (the *Ennacer* is an exception, and *El Medina* and *Hôtel du Sud* also claim to be suitable for women); there is a better-value budget option, the *Hôtel de la Paix*, in town. Mid-range, you get a slightly wider choice, and if the town-centre hotels are full, there are others further afield, notably to the west of town. A number of upmarket establishments cater mainly for visiting business people. Hotel **prices** in Sfax do not vary with the season, reflecting the city's untouristy nature. For the very cheapest Medina hotels, you usually pay per bed rather than per room.

The *Maison des Jeunes* is at the beginning of route de l'Aéroport (☎74 243 207, ℱ74 246 745; dorm beds 6TD, camping possible). It has clean three- and four-bed dorms, with shared toilets and segregated showers, and operates a midnight curfew.

Hotels

New Town centre

Abou Nawas av Bourguiba ☎74 225 700, ℱ74 225 521, ⊛www.abounawas.com. Well-placed, business-oriented hotel with all mod cons including a rooftop pool, but the service is not all that great. ❼

Alexander 21 rue Alexandre Dumas ☎ & ℱ74 221 613. Next door to the central *La Paix* and rather more sedate, with good value en-suite rooms and friendly, efficient staff. ❸

Colisée 32 av Taïeb Mehiri ☎74 227800, ℱ74 299 350. Friendly, comfortable and central. All rooms are en suite and offer a choice of shower or bathtub, plus TV and a/c for a moderate supplement. ❹

Hôtel de la Paix 17 rue Alexandre Dumas ☎74 296 437, ℱ74 298 463. An old favourite, and cheapest of the city-centre bunch. It's safe and friendly if rather sombre, with some en-suite rooms. The cheapest single rooms on the roof (7TD) cost not much more than a bed in the small Medina hotels, and are far better value. ❷

Thyna 35 rue Habib Maazoun ☎74 225 317, ℱ74 225 773. Comfortable rooms with a/c and TV, and recently refitted bathrooms. ❺

Medina

Besbes 23 rue Borj el Nar ☎74 210 962. Pretty spartan, but clean and reasonable for the price. ❶

Ennacer 100 rue des Notaires ☎74 211 037. The best hotel in the Medina: bright and clean, with spotless communal showers (though hot water can be sporadic) and a roof terrace. ❶

El Habib 25 rue Borj el Nar ☎74 221 373. A cut above most of the other Medina cheapies. Some rooms have their own toilet, though showers are communal. ❶

El Jemia 89 rue Mongi Slim ☎74 221 342. Reasonably clean, with communal showers and hot water at least some of the time. ❶

El Jerid 61 rue Mongi Slim; no phone. Small, clean rooms around a sunny landing above a clothing shop – you enter through the shop. ❶

El Magreb 18 rue Borj el Nar ☎74 220 057. Basic but clean and friendly, with shared showers and hot water at least some of the time. ❶

El Medina 53 rue Mongi Slim ☎74 220 354. Cleanest, friendliest and the most respectable of the rue Mongi Slim hotels. Should be fine for women (indeed the sexes have separate toilets). ❶

Moktar 19 rue Borj el Nar ☎74 220 892. Friendly though pretty basic – no washbasin in the rooms for example, though there are shared showers with hot water at least some of the time. ❶

Hôtel du Sud 42 rue Dar Essebai ☎74 297 208. Family-run with very basic rooms but spotless toilet and shower facilities, and a nice patio with tiled seats. ❶

Out of the centre

Amin av Mejida Boulila ☎74 245 600, ℱ74 245 603. On a busy road 800m north of the Medina and near the hospital, this is one of the best-value mid-range options. All rooms are en suite with a/c and satellite TV, though the perfumed air-freshener they spray them out with every day is a definite minus point. ❺

El Andalous av des Martyrs ☎74 405406, ℱ74 406 425. Not to be confused with the hotel of the same name in the Medina, this place is large and efficient, catering for tourists and businesspeople alike, with small but comfortable rooms, all with a/c and satellite TV. ❺

Les Arcades av des Martyrs ☎74 400700, ℱ74 405 522. A rather pricey competitor to the *El Andalous*, with quite spacious rooms, bigger at the front though quieter at the back, all with a/c and satellite TV. There's a big garden out back, and underground parking facilities. ❻

Donia rte de l'Aéroport ☎74 247714, ℱ74 248552, ⊛www.doniahotel.com. Comfortable enough place near the stadium, it's used as an overnight stop by Land Rover tour groups and by visiting sports teams (with conference rooms for pre-match briefings and team meals). ❺

Ennaim 46 rue de la Mauritanie ☎74 227 564, ℱ74 220 363. Large, pleasant rooms, some en suite (second-floor rooms are better than those on the first floor), and all with a phone. There's a café downstairs. ❷

Étoile 9 rue Mohamed Janoussi ☎74 296 091. Off av Farhat Hached west of town, the *Étoile* is quiet, amiable and good value. Some rooms are en suite. ❷

Hannibal rue Mohamed Rachid Ridha, off rte de Mahdia ☎74 234 329. Two kilometres from the centre, Sfax's only pension is a bit tatty but eccentric and characterful, as well as quiet and good value, with spacious rooms, massive bathrooms and the possibility of full board. ❷

Syphax rte de Soukra ☎74 243333, ℻74 245 226, ✉sangho.syphax@planet.tn. Inconveniently

located 1500m west of the Medina, beyond the football ground, though the pool and gardens are very pleasant, the staff are efficient and the food is good. ❻

Yasmine av 7 Novembre ☎74 401 000, ℻74 402 004. Relatively new hotel 400m north of the Medina, with nice-sized, immaculate, cosy rooms, a/c and satellite TV, plus tasteful red and white tiled bathrooms. ❻

The New Town

At first the city seems to vindicate all criticism with its sprawling suburbs of housing and industry, but Sfax's centre is as compact as that of Sousse. The Medina is separated from the port by a French grid-plan **New Town** that is pretty light on things to see but contains almost everything you need in the way of facilities. The pedestrianized **boulevard de l' Republique** connects the Medina's main entrance at **Bab Diwan** to the thoroughfare that runs through the New Town, **avenue Bourguiba**.

The New Town was largely rebuilt after heavy bombardment during World War II, and today it's less crowded and more open than the Medina, with paved esplanades, green spaces and tree-lined streets, as well as a large port with a busy daily **fish market**. Besides fish, sponges and seashells are landed: there's a warehouse for these at 1 avenue M.H. Khefacha, next to the *Besbes Restaurant*, where you can pop in and buy a genuine **sponge** for your bathroom.

Admirers of **Art Nouveau architecture** will find interest in nos. 39–41 avenue Bourguiba, a stucco confection on the corner of rue Patrice Lumumba, while the colonial mock-Moorish style of the castle-like building on the corner of avenue Bourguiba and avenue Hedi Chaker (opposite the Town Hall) is worth a second glance, as are the cherub-surmounted windows of 10 rue d'Athènes, behind the Greek Orthodox church.

The Archeological Museum

Very stylish, if a touch incongruous, is the French-looking clock tower on the Town Hall in place Hedi Chaker, which houses the musty and rather neglected **Archeological Museum** (Mon–Sat 8.30am–1pm & 3–6pm; 1.1TD). In the entrance hall are a few nondescript Roman remains, including a headless statue, plus some Islamic antiquities, notably a couple of Korans with beautiful calligraphy. Room 2, to the left of the entrance, has early Christian relics from La Skhirra (see p.280), including mosaics from the sixth-century Basilica and a nicely executed fifth- or sixth-century mosaic of Daniel in the lions' den. Room 3, opposite, contains Roman relics, including a third-century funerary urn painted with scenes of people hunting and fishing, some rare fragments of second-century frescoes, a third-century mosaic featuring two pairs of naked wrestlers, and a collection of oil lamps illustrating their development from Punic through Roman and Byzantine to early Islamic styles. Next door, a long, thin and ill-lit room houses fragments of mosaics from Thyna (see p.277) that are difficult to see well because there is no room to stand back and look at them. The room opposite, with a similar viewing problem, has an interesting mosaic of an amphitheatrical bear hunt. Finally, a glass kiosk to the left of the stairs contains prehistoric stone tools and decorated pieces of ostrich egg-shell from near Gafsa, relics of the Capsian culture.

The Medina

Sfax's **Medina** differs from many in Tunisia in that it is still a thriving community. This is no tourist spectacle, but a real city where people live and work, and you won't find souvenir stalls or tour groups trailing after a guide. Not that you'll be made to feel in any way unwelcome; on the contrary, the pleasant reaction you get in the shops where Sfaxians make routine purchases comes as a refreshing contrast to the tedious *"kommen sie hier, mein freund"* of Tunis and Kairouan's souvenir emporiums. The Medina is changing, however, becoming more commercial in fact, as residents move out and businesses move in, but it only serves to make the place even more animated (except on Mondays, when businesses within the walls close).

The Medina's near-complete **ramparts** make for a dramatic first impression. In view of the many bombardments the city has endured, they're in remarkable shape, with some parts dating back to the ninth century. If you want to walk around the walls on the inside, you can follow them almost all of the way in the Medina's western corner from Bab Jedid to Bab Gharbi. One curious feature of the Medina is the multitude of first-floor **workshops**: narrow staircases lead up to these cramped rooms, where small businesses – tailors, shoemakers, engravers – beaver away using traditional techniques and equipment. Few of them mind being interrupted, and their terraces offer wonderful rooftop views.

The **Kasbah** in the Medina's southern corner was originally constructed in 1849 as a *ribat*, and was later the governor's residence and the headquarters of the town's militia. It is now restored as the **Museum of Traditional Architecture** (Tues–Sun 9.30am–4.30pm; 1.1TD, camera 1TD), featuring exhibits on private, public and religious buildings, plus an interesting model showing the different stages involved in building the Medina walls – but the best thing about it is that you can climb up the bastions and walk along the battlements. On leaving, check out the attractive tiled doorway of the school across the square. Just north is the whitewashed **Sidi Karray Mosque**, dating back to 1654 and surrounded by some classic Sfaxian doorways decorated in pink Gabès stone, notably that of 31 rue Ben Kaddour. The mosque is the focus of Sfax's Mouled festivities to celebrate the Prophet's birthday.

Rue de la Kasbah runs alongside the southern wall from the Kasbah, past the *Café Diwan* and into a small square. On the corner as you come into the square is the **Zaouia of Sidi Bahri**; note the double inscription above the door, again in pink Gabès stone. If you cross the square from here, the multiple arches of **Bab Diwan**, the Medina's main entrance, are to your right. As at Tunis, Bizerte and Sousse, this main gate into the Medina was once much closer to the sea. Only its westernmost, horseshoe entrance is ancient, going back to the fourteenth century. Along with Bab Jebli, it was one of just two original city gates, both still retaining their iron-clad doors, which were once closed nightly. Opposite the inward side of Bab Diwan, is the **Ajouzin Mosque**, restored in the nineteenth century. Rue de la Grande Mosquée runs next to it, up towards the Great Mosque.

Rue Borj el Nar and the Dar Jellouli Museum

Straight on down rue Borj el Nar to the east of Bab Diwan, the **Amar Kamoun Mosque** – to the right (south), after about 150m – is between nos. 50 and 52; look out for its small stone minaret. The mosque was rebuilt, like so many of Sfax's monuments, in the eighteenth century, when the city became a major commercial centre, though the style of the minaret gives away its earlier origins.

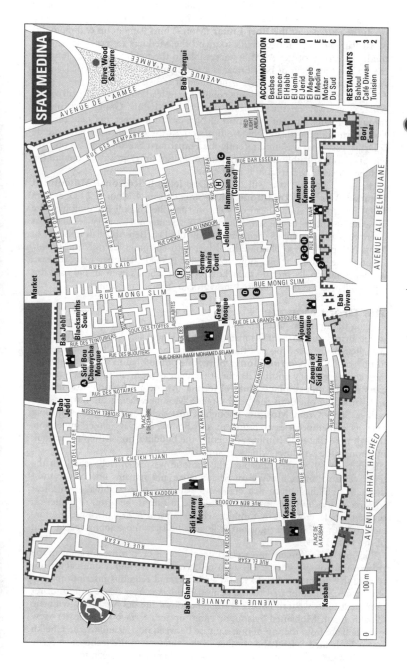

SFAX MEDINA

ACCOMMODATION
Besbes   G
Ennacer   A
El Habib   H
El Jemia   B
El Jerid   D
El Magreb   I
El Medina   E
Moktar   F
Du Sud   C

RESTAURANTS
Bahloul   1
Café Diwan   3
Tunisien   2

Olive Wood
Sculpture

AVENUE DE L'ARMÉE

AVENUE DE L'ARMÉE

Bab Chergui

Bab Jebli

Market

Bab Jedid

Bab Gharbi

RUE DES REMPARTS

RUE DES FORGERONS

RUE SIDI KHELIL

RUE KHAIREDDINE

RUE CHEIKH

RUE DU CAÏD

RUE MONGI SLIM

RUE DES TEINTURIERS

Blacksmiths
Souk

Sidi Bou
Choueycha
Mosque

SOUK DES ÉTOFFES

RUE DES BIJOUTIERS

RUE CHEIKH IMAM MOHAMED SELAMI

RUE DES NOTAIRES

RUE ABDELKADER

RUE SIDI BEL HASSEN

PLACE
5 DÉCEMBRE

RUE CHEIKH TIJANI

RUE BEN KADDOUR

Sidi Karray
Mosque

RUE DE LA MECQUE

RUE EL KSAR

RUE SIDI ALI KARRAY

RUE HANNON

RUE BEN KADDOUR

RUE CHEIKH TIJANI

RUE BAB EJEDIDE

Kasbah
Mosque

PLACE DE
LA KASBAH

RUE EL KSAR

Kasbah

AVENUE 18 JANVIER

RUE DE LA KASBAH

AVENUE FARHAT HACHED

Zaouia of
Sidi Bahri

Ajouzin
Mosque

RUE DE LA GRANDE MOSQUÉE

Great
Mosque

RUE DES

AGHLABITES

Former
Sharia
Court

Dar
Jellouli

Hammam Sultan
(Closed)

SIDI ALI ENNOURI

RUE DE LA DRIBA

RUE DAR ESSEBAI

RUE DU KHALIFA

RUE DU CADHI

RUE BORJ EL NAR

Amar
Kamoun
Mosque

Borj
Ennar

Bab
Diwan

RED
LIGHT
AREA

RUE MONGI SLIM

AVENUE ALI BELHOUANE

N

0   100 m

4

KAIROUAN AND THE SAHEL | Sfax: the Medina

273

Another 100m along the same street, follow a sign to the right through a small archway between nos. 76 and 78 and then turn left and right again to reach the entrance of the **Borj Ennar** (Mon–Thurs 9am–noon & 3–5pm, Fri & Sat 9am–noon), a fortress built to guard the Medina's eastern corner. Now the headquarters of the **ASM**, it's accessible to the public. The area alongside the wall to the north of Borj Ennar is a red light district, best avoided, and in any case walled off so that there is no through access.

West of the Borj's entrance, some cobbled steps lead down into a small square where a gateway on the left leads out of the Medina. Going back instead through the archway onto rue Borj el Nar, cross the street and take rue Dar Essebai, running north straight ahead of you. At the end, turn left into rue de la Driba, past what was until recently the **Hammam Sultan** at no. 78 on your left, Sfax's oldest bathhouse. Dating back to Hafsid times, it was restored in the eighteenth century, but sadly is now closed.

After the hammam you will see the **Dar Jellouli Regional Museum of Popular Arts and Traditions** (Tues–Sun 9.30am–4.30pm; 1.1TD, camera 1TD) just to the right ahead of you, on rue Cheikh Sidi Ali Ennouri. The museum is not to be missed, housed in a seventeenth-century residence as interesting as the exhibits themselves. As in the Dar Ben Abdallah museum in Tunis (see p.98), these illustrate local life, with costumes, utensils and manuscripts. One exhibit shows how rose water is made, another how Tunisian women traditionally prepare their kohl eyeliner. There's even an old cannabis pipe similar to the ones still used in Morocco (though not Tunisia).

The Great Mosque

Leaving the museum, turn left and continue up rue Cheikh Sidi Ali Ennouri, which brings you to a small square. Rue Sidi Khelil, left off the square under a small archway, takes you past the former courthouse on the left (nos. 36–40). Just beyond, you cross **rue Mongi Slim**, one of the Medina's main thoroughfares and perpetually bustling. Rather than get caught up in the flow, however, carry straight on past **place Souk el Jemaa**, the site of a hectic Friday market, and you come out onto rue de la Grande Mosquée, facing the northeastern wall of Sfax's **Great Mosque**. Though at first sight lower and less imposing than its contemporaries at Kairouan and Sousse, it repays closer inspection, though note that only Muslims can enter the building; non-Muslims can look in through the windows, which are normally open.

Begun in 849 by the Aghlabids, the mosque was extensively rebuilt in the tenth century under heavy Fatimid influence and remains one of the most distinctive buildings from that era – more so even than Mahdia's own Great Mosque (see p.260). The most characteristic feature is the series of niches on the east facade, crowned by toothlike rims – a form of articulation quite foreign to both the simple Aghlabid style and the later, more sophisticated calm of the Hafsid styles.

This love of movement in external decoration is even more apparent in the **minaret**, whose wedding-cake layers of decoration are highly unusual for this region; the geometric bands, round windows and religious inscription seem almost frenzied compared to the Kairouan minaret. You can see the minaret from next to its western corner at the junction of rue des Aghlabites with rue Cheikh Imam Mohamed Selami, or climb up to a terrace for a clearer view – the best are from the top of one staircase between nos. 59 and 61 rue Cheikh Imam Mohamed Selami and another in the entrance to the teahouse at 5 rue des Aghlabites, where you can also get an excellent cup of green tea.

A curiosity worth looking out for is the stone embedded above the fourth window from the left in the mosque's northeastern facade. Originally Byzantine, it depicted two peacocks (the ancient Greek symbol of eternity or immortality) surrounded by grapevines and small birds, with a Greek inscription above and probably a cup or fountain between them. Such obvious pictures of animals and plants are very rare in Islamic architecture, but the spirit of the inscription ("Good deeds and happiness accompanying them enrich Your holy abode") was considered sufficiently Muslim for its inclusion in the mosque.

The souks

Heading north from the Great Mosque, you pass under an arch into rue des Aghlabites, on the other side of which is the area of the main souks. More or less straight ahead is the **Souk des Étoffes**, specializing in fabrics, with rich garments all around, gradually giving way to carpets as you move up the souk. Parallel, one street to the left, is rue des Bijoutiers, the **jewellers' souk**. Cross rue Okba at the end of Souk des Étoffes, and follow rue des Teinturiers (once the dyers' souk) until you come to **Bab Jebli**, currently closed, but one of the city's original gates and worth a glance.

Just to the left is the **Sidi Bou Choueycha Mosque**, recently restored. The older of its two prayer halls is Zirid or Hafsid, but the later one, added in 1683, marked a new phase in Sfaxian architecture, establishing a style which was to dominate eighteenth-century construction in the city. If you're Muslim, you should definitely pop in for a look at the stonework and tiled *mihrab*. In the other direction, opposite no. 19 in rue des Forgerons, an archway leads through to the **blacksmiths' souk**, where the smiths are hard at work amid the noise and grime. However, a glance at the upper storey, reached via a staircase to your left as you go through the archway, reveals that this was once a *fondouk*. In fact it dates back to the tenth century and was associated with Bab Jebli, outside which there was a marshalling point for trans-Saharan caravans, whose passengers would stay overnight at the *fondouk*. More recently, it featured as a Cairo bazaar in the film of *The English Patient*.

Coming out of the blacksmiths' souk, you can take a right turn to reach the northern end of rue Mongi Slim, opposite which crowds squeeze through a narrow Medina entrance in a crush worthy of Cairo. The large food **market** complex on the other side is one of the most successful modern uses of the old vaulted forms to be seen in Tunisia, and, unlike so many other new market buildings, is a delight to wander through.

Eating and drinking

As with accommodation, the Medina is the obvious place to go for **budget eating**. On the other hand, if you feel like treating yourself, you'll find the expense well worth it, as Sfax has some first-class **restaurants** at prices that are very cheap by Western standards, though often quite pricey by Tunisian ones. Sfax is noted in Tunisia for its fish and seafood, but there are those who avoid the local fish because of sea pollution from the phosphate plant just south of town. For those with a sweet tooth, a number of places in rue de la Grande Mosquée in the Medina do **waffles** with chocolate sauce: try nos. 73 or 77.

For a cup of **tea or coffee**, head for the *Café Diwan* off rue de la Kasbah by no. 37 (daily 7am–11pm) – an amazing place in the Medina, actually inside the city wall (go upstairs for a better view). With pine-nut tea, rose-water Turkish coffee, a relaxed atmosphere and arguably the smoothest *chicha* in the country, it's recommended for women as well as men. Other cafés – and bars – are located around boulevard de la République and in the grid zone south of avenue Bourguiba; *Club My House* (see below) has a pleasant lounge in which to refuel but does not serve alcohol.

Bars serving alcohol tend to be rather raucous and very male-dominated. A quieter, and more female-friendly, beer can be had at the bars of hotels like the *Alexander*, the *Colisée*, the *Andalous*, the *Arcades* and the *Donia*.

Restaurants

New Town

Alexander *Hôtel Alexander*, 21 rue Alexandre Dumas ☎74 221 613. The restaurant here serves excellent meat and fish dishes (prawn bisque, prawn brochette, stuffed sole), with good-value starters but slightly pricey mains, and a 10TD set menu. Daily 10am–2.30pm & 6–11pm.

Au Bec Fin pl 2 Mars, near the post office. Pleasantly situated and with decent, if not very exciting, reasonably priced fare. Mon–Sat noon–3pm & 6–9.30pm, Sun noon–3pm.

Baghdad 63 av Farhat Hached ☎74 223 856. Excellent Tunisian cooking – some would say the best in town. Moderately priced à la carte and with a good-value 7TD set menu. Daily except Fri noon–3pm & 7–11.30pm.

Besbes 79 av Bourguiba, on the corner of av Mohamed H. Khefacha. Very inexpensive couscous, meat and fish dishes. Daily 8am–10pm.

Chez Nous 28 rue Patrice Lumumba ☎74 227 128. Good food and meticulous service, at moderate prices. Daily noon–3pm & 6.30–10.30pm.

Club My House rue Mohamed Ali. Trendy new place spread over three floors, serving good cheap burgers, pizza and pasta, with a 3.5TD set menu. Upstairs is a nice lounge with comfy leather sofas, where you can enjoy paninis, crepes and other snacks, along with tasty milkshakes, fruit juices and flavoured coffees. Mon–Sat 8am–10.30pm.

Le Corail 39 rue Habib Maazoun ☎74 227 301.

Fairly chic, with fine Tunisian cooking, angling for the moneyed tourist market. The set menu costs 16.5TD. Mon–Sat 11.45am–3pm & 6.30–11.30pm.

La Perla 18 av Bourguiba ☎74 229 456. Good Tunisian food at moderate prices, with entertainment in the form of a singer from about 8.30pm nightly. Daily noon–midnight or later.

Le Petit Navire 125 rue de Haffouz ☎74 212 890. Fine seafood – try the fish soup – and some Italian dishes in an elegant, first-floor vaulted dining room overlooking the old fishing port. Offers a lunchtime set menu for 15TD. Daily 11.30am–3pm & 6pm–midnight.

Le Printemps 55 av Bourguiba ☎74 226 973. Very smart, with excellent and not too pricey French cooking. Mon–Sat noon–2.30pm & 6–10pm.

La Sirène Across the rail line from the bottom of rue Haffouz, or across the bridge from the Kerkennah ferry port ☎74 224 691. Excellent, though expensive, fish restaurant – choose your fish and have it barbecued while you wait. Great octopus salad among other seafood entrées. Daily except Fri noon–3pm & 6–11pm.

Medina

Bahloul 25 rue Hannon. Hidden away inside the Medina, this is a clean, good-value place to have lunch. Daily 8am–4pm.

Tunisien 16 rue Borj el Nar. Best of a number of cheap places just inside Bab Diwan, serving spit-roast chicken, couscous and basic Tunisian dishes at very low prices. Daily 9am–10pm.

Listings

Airlines Air France, c/o Yassine Travel Agency, 15 rue Taïeb Mehiri ☎74 224 847; Tunisair, 4 av de l'Armée ☎74 228 028.

Banks Banks are mainly concentrated on av Bourguiba and bd de la République; STB in bd de la République is probably the best. One bank will be open at weekends. BNA at 1 av Taïeb Mehiri has an ATM that accepts Visa and Mastercard. The post office will change cash.

Bookshops Librairie la Caravelle, 22 av Bourguiba (on the corner of rue Habib Maazoun) has some English titles – mainly classics, but also some recent bestsellers.

Car rental Avis, rue Tahar Sfar, at rue Habib Maazoun ☎74 224 605; Europcar, 40 rue Tahar Sfar ☎74 226 680; Hertz, 47 av Bourguiba ☎74 228 626. A number of small firms have their offices around the junction of rue Habib Maazoun and rue Tahar Sfar.

Car repairs and spares Mechanics and car spares stores are concentrated in the area to the east of place de l'Union du Maghreb Arabe, along and between av des Martyrs and av Farhat Hached.

Churches As well as the Greek Orthodox church at 1 rue d'Athènes, there's a Catholic church behind at 4 rue Dag Hammarskjold (Mass Sat 6.30pm & Sun 9.30am), and a synagogue at 71 rue Habib Maazoun.

Cinemas Atlas, 103 av Hedi Chaker; Le Colisée, 27 rue Tahar Sfar at av Hedi Chaker; Étoile, 50 bd de la République.

Consulates The Libyan consulate at 35 rue Alexandre Dumas (☏74 223 332) has been known to issue visas, but at the last check was sending people to Tunis to apply. UK honorary consul: Moncef Sellami, first floor, 55 rue Habib Maazoun (☏74 223 971).

Festivals The International Festival of Sfax in (July & Aug) features cultural events including music, dance and theatre, many held at the municipal theatre on bd de la République. Also in July, there's a "fantasia" of traditional Arab equestrianism in Agareb, 22km west of Sfax.

Football Sfax's main club, the Club Sportif de Sfax (CSS), has its ground behind the youth hostel near the beginning of the airport road. Sfax Railway Sport (SRS) play in among the railway sidings just south of av 13 Août.

Hammam Hammam El Jemni, 25 rue Sidi Khelil in the Medina (daily: men morning and evening, women afternoons).

Hospitals The main hospital is on route de l'Aïn, west of the town centre (☏74 244 511), with the Polyclinique Ettawfik on av des Martyrs at the corner of rue Hedi Nouira (☏74 404 306), and the Polyclinique Zitouna further east on av des Martyrs

opposite the Sfax 2000 building (☏74 211 611).

Internet access Publinet offices are at 7 rue Ali Bach Hamba (daily 8.30am–11pm; 2TD/hr) and on rue Ahmed Sikelli, 50m north of av des Martyrs near the *Hôtel Les Arcades* (daily 8am–9pm; 2TD/hr).

Newspapers English-language papers are available at two kiosks in a little square off the southern end of bd de la République, diagonally opposite the town hall, and at a larger kiosk on the square in front of the *Hôtel Thyna*.

ONA crafts shop 10 rue Lt Hamadi Taj, beween rue Alexandre Dumas and rue Abou el Kacem Chabbi (Mon–Sat 10am–noon & 3–6pm).

Pharmacy There's a night pharmacy at 23 Les Galeries, 50m up bd 7 Novembre from av des Martyrs.

Police rue Victor Hugo ☏74 229 700.

Post office av Bourguiba, by the train station (city hours).

Pool halls There are several in the town centre, including two on rue de Haffouz at nos. 51 and 125.

Supermarkets Monoprix has a branch at 12 rue Abou el Kacem Chabbi and another in the Sfax 2000 building on av des Martyrs (the latter has more convenient hours: daily 8.30am–7pm). There's also Zeitouna, at the corner of rue Kairouan and av de l'Algérie.

Swimming There's a 25m municipal pool on rte de l'Aérodrome, near the youth hostel (Tues–Sat 7am–8pm, Sun 9am–1pm; 2.5TD/hr).

Around Sfax

The nearest **beach** to Sfax is 12km to the north at **SIDI MANSOUR** (reached by city bus #3 from avenue de l'Armée and avenue des Martyrs). Sidi Mansour is also home to an annual **festival** in honour of its marabout, usually held in July or August, with horse-racing, boat-racing and music. On the way is the source of all the olive-wood salad bowls, chess sets and other souvenirs that are sold in Sfax's few souvenir shops: the **Maison du Bois d'Olivier** (☏74 272 094), signposted off the road 9km out of Sfax. They usually have only a few things in stock, but you can call in advance to have things made to order, or pop in and see what's in their showroom.

To the south of Sfax, 2km down the Gabès road, the **Commonwealth War Cemetery** is as well kept as ever, next to an ordinary Christian cemetery that isn't. Indian soldiers are segregated off in a little enclosure at the back: Muslims to the right, Sikhs and Hindus to the left, together with a few graves from World War I. The cemetery can be reached from town on city bus #16.

Thyna and the saltpans

Ten kilometres south of Sfax, **THYNA** (free access) is the site of Roman Thaenae, and the source of some of the mosaics in the Sfax museum. The turn-off from the Gabès road is signposted, but not too conspicuously, so keep your eyes peeled. Any bus bound for Gabès or Mahrès should drop you there (ask for the Thyna *croisement*), while city bus #16 leaves you 300m short. From the

The wildlife of the saltpans of Sfax

The saltpans south of Sfax support large winter populations of **flamingos**, rare **spoonbills** and a variety of **herons**, **egrets**, **gulls** and **terns**. The whole area offers exceptional birdwatching, partly because of the sheer numbers and range of species, but mostly because the birds have become used to saltpan workers and shell fishers, making them very approachable. If you're remotely interested in wildlife, it's not a site to pass up.

The little inlet closest to Sfax is magical in the early morning sunlight, with hundreds of **wading birds** among the shell fishers. Although the largest numbers of birds are recorded from November to the end of February, many are still present through to April, and some species (such as avocet, blackwinged stilt and redshank) stay on to breed in the coastal salt marshes surrounding the mud flats. As well as the waders, Sfax is a good place to watch for **sea birds**, including the region's largest tern, the Caspian, with its long red beak. In winter, you can also see hundreds of **black-necked grebes**, bobbing on the water like miniature round ducks.

The feeding grounds in the mud flats beyond the saltpans are the actual reason why the birds congregate at Sfax, and a few hours watching the area gives a fascinating insight into their **feeding habits**. You'll see everything from flamingos doing their inverted side-to-side sieving of the shallow water with their huge bills, to spoonbills with their own usefully shaped mouthparts; from herons and egrets standing poised, ready to pounce, to the true waders (stints and dunlins, curlews and godwits) probing the mud, each species to a different depth and for different prey.

turn-off, follow the Thyna road left towards the sea until you see a lighthouse; go straight on past it and take a track off to the right, following the arrow, just after it. The main relic here is the **Baths of the Months**, whose mosaics are still in place but covered with sand. The desultory remains to the south are of a smaller **bathhouse**. Another track runs a little inland alongside the ramparts of the Roman town; on the other side are the main buildings so far excavated, including a **temple** – whose mosaics have been carted off to the museum – and a **Roman street** with remains of houses. Chances are that the *gardien* of the site will find you and give you a guided tour.

The **saltpans of Sfax** stretch almost continuously from Sfax to Thyna, and produce some 300,000 tonnes of top-grade sea salt a year. More significantly, they're the Mediterranean's single most important site for wintering **wading birds**, making them a focus of international scientific interest. At low tide, the combination of a shallow coast and a tidal range of 1–2m – a highly unusual feature in the largely tideless Mediterranean – exposes huge areas of mud flats rich in the small creatures that form the bulk of a wading bird's winter diet.

You can access the southern end of the saltpans from the site at Thyna, and the whole shebang is theoretically under development as a national park. In the meantime, you can access the northern end by taking avenue de l'Algérie westward out of town, turning onto the Gabès road (boulevard de l'Environnement) and then taking the third left, just over the *oued*. Walk up that, and the mud flats start on your right; the birdlife are found on the mud flats at low tide, and on just a few of the saltpans, depending on their salinity. Though the mud flats are public land, they're unsafe to walk across as well as being foully polluted with Sfax's effluent. The best way to see the birdlife is to wander along the banks on the seaward side of the saltpans – private land, whose **entrance** has a gate and a high wire fence and is marked "Cotusal"; you'll need to ask permission at the gate. There are fifteen square kilometres of saltpans, so it may take some time to find the birds' location.

Mahrès and La Skhirra

Continuing south from Sfax for 30km or so, you pass through **MAHRÈS**, an unexciting beach resort with a Monday market and three hotels. The **beach** is not really suitable for swimming, being covered with slimy green seaweed, but there's a very pleasant sandy one at **Chafaar**, 5km north along the shore or 8km up the main road; turn seaward just after a level crossing and continue down a track for 4km. You should be able to **camp** here.

Simple **accommodation** in the centre of Mahrès is available at the *Hôtel Younga* (T74 290 334; ❷), with the hotel entrance at the back and the very reasonable *Restaurant de la Corniche* at the front (daily 9am–10pm), where you may need to ask for the receptionist. Just north of town is the two-star *Marzouk* (T74 290261, F74 290866; ❺), with clean rooms, all en suite and with a/c, and a pool; next door is the three-star *Hôtel Tamaris* (T74 290 950, F74 290494; ❺), better value with a larger pool, bougainvillea-wreathed gardens and paintings in each room by the owner's wife, based on traditional carpet designs. The hotel also has rather a posh and expensive **restaurant** (daily noon–3pm & 5–10pm), with musical entertainment in the evenings.

Mahrès's three **banks**, a taxiphone office and, bizarrely, the skeleton of a whale, are to be found along the main street. The town hosts an annual **International Festival of the Plastic Arts** at the end of July, and it has a permanent, if rather neglected, **park of modern sculptures**, including a doughnut man, and a giant metal jasmine seller, with stairs inside his legs up to benches in his belly, which are only open during the festival. The *Cafétéria du Festival* opposite is a good place to sit and watch the world go by. **Buses** and **louages** for Sfax can be picked up by the *Hôtel Younga*, and there's a bus station 100m south on the other side of the road and a **train station** inland, with daily services to Sfax, Sousse and Tunis, as well as to Gabès, Gafsa and Metlaoui.

Olive trees

Whether you find the roads out of Sfax scenically appealing depends on your reaction to row upon row of **olive trees** – the age-old industry of the Sahel ever since the Romans introduced them to replace grain. It was in the early nineteenth century, however, that the olive plantations really came into their own. Most of the olive oil was shipped to Europe, where, too coarse and strong-tasting for dainty European palates, it was made into soap. The markets seemed bottomless and the price high, encouraging many Sfaxians to occupy lands belonging to the surrounding Methelith tribes in order to plant trees. By the 1830s, the German traveller Prince Puckler-Muskau claimed that the trees already stretched further than the eye could see.

Most of the trees are planted a standard 20m apart, the optimum distance, and the **harvest** begins in November. As it has to be done by hand, the process is highly labour-intensive, with teams of seven combing the branches, protecting their fingers with hollowed-out goat horns (more recently with plastic substitutes). An average tree around Sfax produces 50kg of olives a year, almost all of them sent to factories on the outskirts of the city. Unfortunately, recent increases in productivity and production – not only in Tunisia but throughout the Mediterranean – have led to **overproduction**. In the last couple of decades prices have tumbled, and after a good harvest Tunisia can't sell the bulk of its oil, whatever the price. Now the government encourages farmers to uproot the older plantations and plant cereals, and so history has turned full circle.

South to La Skhirra

If you're a sucker for ruined castles, you might make the effort to get to **Borj Younga**, a Byzantine fortress rebuilt by the Aghlabids, 11km south of Mahrès. The turn-off is marked only by a stop sign, just before a couple of shops in the middle of nowhere. From there, it's a three-kilometre walk down a track to the fort, the shell of which remains, adorned by graffiti, next to a marabout, a couple of houses and a well. It looks rather more impressive from a distance than when you actually reach it. Gabès-bound buses (except SNTRI services) will drop you off at the turn-off.

Forty-five kilometres south of Borj Younga and 50km north of Gabès, **LA SKHIRRA** has a big oil terminal for pipelines coming from Algeria and Tunisia. Until the second half of the nineteenth century it was simply a summer camp for the Mehadhaba tribes. Then, in 1871, the Perry Bury Company of Lancashire began exporting esparto grass for paper manufacture from here. It quickly became one of the region's most important commodities and the town grew up on this British link.

In case you should need to stay here, there is a two-star **hotel** 2km south of town, the *Bab Essahara* (☎74 295 175, ☎74 295 223; ❸). The oil terminal is in fact 14km north of town at **Hechichina**, where there is also an archeological **site**, many of whose finds are now in the museum in Sfax, leaving little to see. Three kilometres offshore here is **Kneiss Island**; if you're lucky, you might be able to get someone to take you over to it for some isolated birdwatching, but check with the port police first.

The Kerkennah Islands

Throughout history the **Kerkennah Islands**, 20km off the coast of Sfax, have been a place of exile – the Carthaginian general Hannibal, Roman outcasts, adulterous Muslim wives and Habib Bourguiba have all been sent here at one time or another. Now this isolation is an attraction for tourists. Conventionally promoted as the poor folks' Jerba, the islands are distinctively quieter than Jerba and make an ideal spot for doing nothing for a few days or weeks – even energetic swimming is out of the question as the sea is so shallow, though this does make it highly suitable for young children to play in.

Strictly speaking there are two inhabited islands – **Chergui** (Eastern) and **Gharbi** (Western), also called **Mellita** after the village at its centre, which was founded by migrants from Mellita in Jerba (see p.434) – but the channel between them was bridged by a causeway in Roman times, so for all practical purposes there's only one. It's now a hypnotic expanse of windblown date palms on sandy ground that never rises more than 13m above sea level. The trees are rather tatty and their dates generally inedible (although figs grow well here), but many people think this the most beautiful spot they know and return year after year. Apart from the dominant palms, there are some interesting **flowers** – in particular, a small type of asphodel (see p.548), and a low plant with sprawling thin leaves and a beautiful flat purple flower that goes by the inelegant name of *fagonia*. Other common seaside plants include dandelions and cottonweed, covered with fine silvery hairs and with yellow "everlasting" flowerheads. Both of these species combine with pale-blue sea lavender to form a fine carpet of colour at the edges of the beaches and rocks. **Birdwatching** in Kerkennah is also generally good, with a number of waders

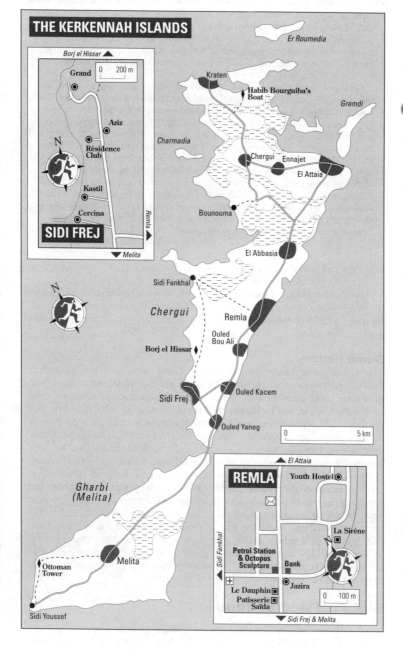

THE KERKENNAH ISLANDS

Er Roumedia

Kraten

Habib Bourguiba's Boat

Gremdi

SIDI FREJ

Borj el Hissar

Grand

0   200 m

Aziz

N

Résidence Club

Kastil

Cercina

Remla

Melita

Charmadia

Chergui   Ennajet

El Attaia

Bounouma

El Abbasia

Sidi Fankhal

N

Chergui

Remla

Ouled Bou Ali

Borj el Hissar

Sidi Frej

Ouled Kacem

Ouled Yaneg

0   5 km

Gharbi (Melita)

Melita

Ottoman Tower

Sidi Youssef

REMLA

El Attaia

Youth Hostel

La Sirène

Sidi Fankhal

Petrol Station & Octopus Sculpture

Bank

Jazira

Le Dauphin

Patisserie Saïda

0   100 m

Sidi Frej & Melita

Getting to and from the Islands

There are eight daily **ferries** to and from Sfax (1hr) from mid-November to mid-April, with as many as sixteen crossings a day at the height of summer; the timetable is published in the back of *La Presse*. The ferries are operated by Sonotrak, down at Sfax's port on avenue Mohamed Hedi Khefacha (☎74 222 216; passengers 0.65TD, car 4.4TD). There is access if you are in a wheelchair, but you will have to spend the journey on the car deck.

On Kerkennah the ferry docks at **Sidi Youssef**, the westernmost tip of the first island, not far from the crumbling **Ottoman tower**, 3km along the north shore. The island's sole **bus** line rumbles north along a single road over the causeway to Chergui; buses connect with the ferries and run to Sidi Frej, Remla and El Attaia. Quicker and more flexible about where they drop you are **shared taxis**, which also meet the ferries and function in the same way as louages, costing about 1.5TD to Sidi Frej and 2TD to Remla. The other way, buses leave Remla an hour before the boat's scheduled departure (although the journey only takes 25min); all except the first bus of the day are supposed to call at Sidi Frej but, especially outside the main tourist season, they may not do so, so you would be better off walking to Ouled Yaneg and picking up the bus there. A surer, and not much costlier, option is again to take a shared taxi, which your hotel can order for you. The *Grand Hôtel* also sometimes runs a minibus to Remla, and to meet the ferries.

easily spotted in the shallow waters around the islands; Bounouma, El Attaya, Gremdi and the causeway are favoured locations.

There's an excellent **website** on the islands, Ⓦ www.kerkennah.com, run by two Kerkennian residents in the US, with features on history, the various villages and traditional fishing techniques, plus photos and samples of Kerkennian music to download.

Some history

The islands' name came from the nymph **Circe** who, according to legend, imprisoned Odysseus here because she could not bear to let such a handsome man leave. Since then, the only historical events interrupting the islands' calm were their 1286 seizure by **Roger de Lluria**, the Catalan ruler of nearby Sicily, their 1335 repossession by the **Hafsids**, and an attempt to occupy them in 1510 by the Spanish. At the time, the Spaniards held Tripoli and felt they needed a backup base. They tried to take Jerba without success, and left four hundred men on Kerkennah to occupy it. All were massacred by the Kerkennians within the next year, and they didn't hold Tripoli for long, either.

Today, many of the islands' people find the desert island atmosphere less appealing than do the tourists, and depopulation has been a problem for some years. In the early 1960s a company called Somvik was set up to exploit the tourist potential and revive the islands' fortunes, but this has done little more than bring a small strip of low-key hotels, so isolated that unless you're staying in one it would be easy not to notice them at all. Happily, there are signs that the economy is picking up, and the island people remain some of the most hospitable in the country.

Sidi Frej and around

A left turning just after the causeway to Chergui leads to Kerkennah's main resort, **SIDI FREJ**, on the west coast. If heading this way by bus, make sure you take the right one when you get off the ferry, otherwise you could get dropped off at Ouled Yaneg and be left with a two-kilometre walk. That said, if you arrive on a ferry in the early morning, there probably won't be a bus to Sidi Frej, so you'll have to take a shared taxi.

Sidi Frej is a very pleasant and low-key place compared to the resorts at Hammamet, Sousse and Jerba, although it is rather isolated, with just a few hotels and very little else. Consequently, much revolves around the swimming pools and organized activities in the hotels. The **beach** at Sidi Frej is certainly not the best on Kerkennah, and the *Grand Hôtel* really has the only bit worthy of the name, but you can always lounge around the hotel **swimming pools** instead: non-residents can use the pool at the *Grand Hôtel* for 4TD, as well as the *Appart-Hôtel Aziz*'s and the *Résidence Club*'s, which is the biggest, for 3TD (free of charge if you're dining at the hotels' restaurants). The *Grand Hôtel* has the best facilities, including **windsurfing** (8TD/hr), **pedalos** (10TD/hr) and a **kids' club** organized by the Panorama tour rep. Note that the pools and most of the other facilities are out of action off season.

To see more of the islands, you could rent **bicycles** from the *Cercina* (1.5TD/hr or 10TD/day) or the *Grand* (3TD/hr or 12TD/day). One short trip is to **Borj el Hissar**, a ruined fort 2km or so up the coast along a track from the hotel zone, put up by the Aghlabids on a Roman site, later rebuilt by the Spanish, and supposedly destined to become a museum. In front of it on the shore, some **Roman mosaics** have been excavated. If you don't fancy biking, Samir's Horse and Camel Hire (you should find Samir outside the entrance to the *Grand Hôtel*) offers rides to Borj el Hissar in summer. Five kilometres further, **Sidi Fankhal** is Kerkennah's finest beach, also accessible by piste across a salt flat from Remla on the other side of the island.

Practicalities

You can **eat** at all the Sidi Frej hotels and, if you're lucky, try local Kerkennah specialities such as *tchich* (octopus soup) and *melthouth* (something between pasta and couscous). The best food is to be found at the *Cercina*, whose restaurant serves excellent fresh fish (daily noon–midnight). Otherwise, the *Grand Hôtel* does a buffet for 15TD and the *Aziz* a tourist menu for 7TD. The *Kastil* is slightly more expensive but has a nice terrace, while the *Résidence Club* does a beach barbecue in summer, in addition to its usual restaurant food. For a **drink**, the *Cercina*, *Aziz*, *Résidence Club* and *Grand Hôtel* all have bars worthy of a visit: the *Cercina* for a cool lunchtime beer on the terrace, the *Aziz* perhaps for a

---

Fishing excursions

Doing anything energetic on Kerkennah really defeats the object of coming here, but one popular **excursion** is to go out with one of the fishermen, who take people aboard for a small fee, usually cooking a meal of fresh fish into the bargain. The islanders use a curious fishing technique involving screens made of palm fronds set in V-shapes in the waters all around the shore. A trip in one of their small sailing boats, as the sun falls behind the palms and floods the sea a deep blood red, is one of Tunisia's most idyllic experiences. The going rate is about 15TD per person for a day; contacts are easily made at the *Jazira* in Remla (fee by arrangement with fishermen), the *Cercina* (15TD) and *Aziz* (20TD) in Sidi Frej, or by just asking around the fishing boats. Longer trips of up to a week for up to ten people going round the islands in a *felucca* (the larger boats that took people to the mainland before the ferry service started in the 1970s) can also be arranged through the *Café Archipel* in El Attaia. One boatman offering such trips is Samir Bouzida ("Captain Sam"), who can be contacted on ☎74 484 330.

relaxed evening. In the way of nightlife, the *Résidence Club* and the *Aziz* have what look to be the best **nightclubs**.

Hotels

Appart-Hôtel Aziz 700m from the main road junction, on the right (east side of the road) ☎ & ☏74 489 932. Offers large, cool rooms or family apartments with satellite TV, a/c and the possibility of self-catering, although supplies are limited to the shop within the hotel. It also has a pool, a jacuzzi, a pleasant bar and a nightclub, with a DJ box resembling King Kong's head. ❺

Cercina Just off and west of the junction of the Ouled Kacem and Ouled Yaneg roads ☎74 489 600, ☏74 489 878, ✉hotel.cercina@planet.tn. The first hotel you come to, with a choice of simple but pleasant en-suite a/c rooms in the old block, mostly with sea views, or spacious, airy rooms without the view but smarter, more expensive and with satellite TV in the new block, and designed to accommodate wheelchair use. The reception has displays of local seashells and ancient artefacts dredged up from the seabed by local fishermen. ❹

Grand Hôtel At the end of the road, 1500m from the main junction ☎74 489 861, ☏74 489 866, ⊕www.grand-hotel-kerkennah.com.tn. Has the best facilities of the Sidi Frej hotels, and the best bit of beach, catering for mainly British package tourists. ❻

Kastil 200m north of the junction of the Ouled Yaneg and Ouled Kacem roads, on the west side of the road ☎74 489 884. A group of small cubical huts with shared washing facilities. Was closed for renovation at the time of writing (though the restaurant was open); the huts will need to improve if they are not to remain a fall-back option. ❸

Résidence Club 600m from the main road junction, on the left ☎74 489 999, ☏74 489 777, ⊕www.residence-club-kerkennah.com.tn. Good-value en-suite a/c bungalows, a large pool and an impressive array of evening venues, including a poolside bar, another bar indoors (complete with spherical seating nests to relax in around the dancefloor), a beachside mini-theatre and a huge nightclub opening onto the poolside terrace. Activities on offer include horse-riding and windsurfing. ❹

Remla

REMLA, the "capital", lies on the east coast 8km from Sidi Frej and contains about three-quarters of all the shops on the islands. As a beach, it has nothing to recommend it, but as a village it is quiet and amiable, making no attempt whatsoever to jolly along the islands' sleepy way of life. It boasts the islands' only other **hotel** – the friendly *Jazira*, on the main street (☎74 481 058,☏74 482 001; ❷), with clean if rather plain rooms and shared washing facilities, which have recently been renovated. The hotel also has the only **bar** in town. The *Centre des Stages et des Vacances* **youth hostel** (☎74 481 148), a couple of hundred metres further up the main road and then right down towards the beach, is clean and welcoming, open 24 hours, with a mix of Tunisian and foreign guests and the option of **camping**. Remla also has a **bank** (on the main crossroads), with a Visa and MasterCard ATM, a **hospital** (100m towards Sidi Fankhal; ☎74 481 052), a petrol station, pharmacy, **police station** (☎74 481 053), a couple of taxiphone offices and a **post office** (country hours).

For **food**, the *Dauphin*, opposite the *Jazira* (daily 7.30am–7.30pm), serves good basic Tunisian dishes, while the *Patisserie Saïda*, a few doors further away from the crossroads, sells excellent cheap sandwiches. Alternatively, you can eat at the *Jazira* (daily 9am–midnight), whose meals are cheap to moderate, depending on the current price of fish, or at the slightly more expensive but excellent *Sirène* by the beach (☎74 481 118; daily 10am–3pm & 6–11pm), with delicious fish and seafood.

Remla is the main centre for the Kerkennah Islands' two annual **festivals**: the week-long Sirène Festival in August, with a series of mainly musical events, and the three-day Octopus Festival held at the beginning of the octopus fishing season around March 20, with exhibitions, competitions and much eating of eight-tentacled sea beasts. A **sculpture** of an octopus and octopus trap in the centre of town, in front of the petrol station, celebrates the industry.

El Attaia and Gremdi

From Remla, the road keeps straight on for 12km to the fishing village of **EL ATTAIA**, reached by the ferry buses, which stop in Remla and then carry on up the island, or by shared taxi (1.5TD). The village is home to a **restaurant**, the very reasonably priced *Resto le Regal* (℡74 484 100; daily noon–9pm, but hours vary), offering *fruits de mer* such as seafood risotto and couscous with fish, octopus or cuttlefish. Beyond the village, on the way to the fishing port, the *Café Archipel* is a nice spot for a snack and drink by the sea. A turning to the left (north) on reaching El Attaia leads through some small settlements to the shore near **Kraten**, another fishing village. En route, at **Ennajet**, there used to be a **museum** devoted to Habib Bourguiba's dramatic escape from French custody in 1945, when he passed through the village. The museum is now closed, but the boat he used and the house he sheltered in can still be seen by the shore at a turn-off some 5km out of El Attaia.

Across a narrow stretch of water from El Attaia lies the uninhabited island of **Gremdi**, to which local fishermen will row you for a small consideration and come and collect you by arrangement. Together with the beach at **Bounouma**, 6km west of El Attaia, Gremdi is a favourite spot for **camping**. Finally, en route to El Attaia, you might try to find the meagre **Roman remains** near the village of **El Abbasia**, 4km north of Remla; the same village was also the birthplace of Farhat Hached, the UGTT leader gunned down by die-hard French settlers in 1952.

Travel details

Trains

Enfida to: Gabès (1 daily; 5hr 30min); Grombalia (4 daily; 40–50min); Mahdia (1 daily; 2hr 40min); Monastir (1 daily; 1hr 50min); Sfax (2 daily; 2hr 20min); Sousse (5 daily; 45min); Tunis (3–4 daily; 1hr 15min–1hr 30min).

El Jem to: Gabès (2 daily; 3hr 25min–3hr 40min); Gafsa (1 daily; 4hr 45min); Metlaoui (1 daily; 5hr 20min); Sfax (4 daily; 45min); Sousse (4 daily; 1hr); Tunis (5 daily; 2hr 45min).

Kalaa Sghira (near Sousse) to: Gabès (2 daily; 3hr 20min–3hr 50min); Sfax (4 daily; 1hr 20min); Tunis (4 daily; 1hr 40min–2hr).

Mahdia to: Ksar Hellal (14–16 daily; 35min); Moknine (14–17 daily; 30min); Monastir (14–17 daily; 1hr); Sousse (14–17 daily; 1hr 30min); Tunis (1 daily; 3hr 45min).

Mahrès to: Gabès (2 daily; 1hr 25min); Gafsa (2 daily; 2hr 45min); Metlaoui (2 daily; 3hr 20min); Sfax (3 daily; 30min); Sousse (2 daily; 2hr 30min); Tunis (3 daily; 4hr–4hr 30min).

Monastir to: Enfida (1 daily; 1hr 35min); Ksar Hellal (15–17 daily; 25min); Mahdia (15–17 daily; 1hr 15min); Moknine (15–17 daily; 30min); Sousse (19–21 daily; 30min); Tunis (1 daily; 2hr 50min).

Sfax to: Bir Bou Regba (4 daily, 2 connect for Hammamet & Nabeul; 2hr 50min); Gabès (2 daily; 2hr 40min); Gafsa (2 daily; 3hr 30min); El Jem (5 daily; 45min); Kalaa Sghira (3 daily; 1hr 20min); Mahrès (4 daily; 35min); Metlaoui (2 daily; 4hr 10min); Sousse (4 daily; 1hr 45min); Tunis (5 daily; 3hr 45min).

Sousse to: Bir Bou Regba (10 daily, 5 connect for Hammamet & Nabeul; 1hr); Enfida (4 daily; 40min); El Jem (3 daily; 1hr); Friguia Safari Park (3 daily; 45min); Gabès (2 daily; 4hr 30min); Gafsa (1 daily; 6hr 30min); Kalaa Kebira (4 daily; 15min); Kalaa Sghira (1 daily; 10min); Mahdia (14–17 daily; 1hr 30min); Metlaoui (1 daily; 7hr 15min); Monastir (19–21 daily; 30min); Sfax (3 daily; 1hr 50min); Tunis (10 daily; 1hr 50min).

Buses

Enfida to: Bizerte (2 daily; 3hr); Hammamet (1 daily; 1hr 15min); Kairouan (4 daily; 1hr); Kélibia

(1 daily; 2hr 30min); Nabeul (3 daily; 1hr 30min); Sousse (hourly; 1hr); Tunis (hourly; 1hr 30min). **El Jem** to: Mahdia (5 daily; 40min); Sfax (5 daily; 1hr 15min); Sousse (3 daily; 1hr); Tunis (5 daily; 3hr 45min).

Kairouan to: Douz (1 daily; 6hr 30min); Enfida (4 daily; 1hr); Gabès (7 daily; 4hr); Gafsa (7 daily; 4hr); Hammamet (6 daily; 2hr 15min); Jerba (Houmt Souk; 3 daily; 4hr 30min); Kasserine (6 daily; 2hr); Le Kef (3 daily; 3hr 30min); Maktar (3 daily; 2hr); Medenine (5 daily; 5hr); Nabeul (6 daily; 2hr 30min); Nefta (3 daily; 5hr); Sfax (3 daily; 2hr); Sousse (16 daily; 1hr–1hr 30min); Tataouine (1 daily; 5hr 30min); Tozeur (6 daily; 5hr 30min); Tunis (10 daily; 2hr 30min).

Mahdia to: Ksar Hellal (hourly; 30min); Moknine (hourly; 20min); Nabeul (2 daily; 3hr 30min); Sfax (2 daily; 2hr 30min); Sousse (hourly; 1hr 30min); Tunis (2 daily; 4hr).

Monastir to: Kélibia (1 daily; 3hr 30min); Kairouan (1 daily; 1hr 30min); Ksar Hellal (hourly; 35min); Le Kef (1 daily; 4hr); Moknine (hourly; 40min); Nabeul (3 daily; 3hr 30min); Sousse (every 20min; 45min).

Sfax to: Agareb (9 daily; 30min); Bizerte (1 daily; 6hr 30min); Ben Gardane (2 daily; 4hr 30min); Douz (1 daily; 4hr); El Jem (5 daily; 1hr 15min); Gabès (19 daily; 2hr); Gafsa (5 daily; 3hr); Jerba (Houmt Souk; 4 daily; 4hr 30min); Kairouan (1 daily; 1hr 30min); Kasserine (4 daily; 3hr); Kebili (2 daily; 3hr 30min); La Chebba (10 daily; 1hr 30min); Le Kef (3 daily; 4hr 30min); Mahdia (10 daily; 2hr 30min); Mahrès (20 daily; 40min); Medenine (5 daily; 3hr); Nefta (1 daily; 5hr 30min); Sbeïtla (4 daily; 2hr 30min); Sidi Bou Zid (3 daily; 2hr); Sidi Mansour (every 20min; 30min); Sousse (10 daily; 2hr 30min); Tataouine (2 daily; 4hr); Tozeur (1 daily; 5hr); Tripoli (3 weekly; 12hr); Tunis (10 daily; 5hr); Zarzis (1 daily; 4hr).

Sousse to: Akouda (every 10min; 15min); Béja (2 daily; 4hr); Ben Gardane (2 daily; 7hr); Bizerte (1 daily; 3hr 30min); Chott Mariam (14 daily; 30min); Douz (2 daily; 6hr 30min); Enfida (17 daily; 45min); El Fahs (2 daily; 1hr 30min); Gabès (18 daily; 4hr 30min); Gafsa (3 daily; 5hr); Hammamet (5 daily; 1hr 45min); Hergla (hourly; 45min); El Jem (3 daily; 1hr); Jerba (Houmt Souk; 2 daily; 6hr 45min); Kairouan (16 daily; 1hr); Kalaa Kebira

(every 10min; 20min); Kalaa Sghira (every 30min; 20min); Kebili (1 daily; 6hr); Le Kef (2 daily; 4hr); Mahdia (hourly; 1hr 30min); Matmata (1 daily; 5hr 30min); Medenine (3 daily; 5hr 30min); Nabeul (5 daily; 2hr); Port el Kantaoui (every 30min; 30min); Sfax (11 daily; 2hr); Monastir (every 20min; 45min); Tataouine (1 daily; 6hr 30min); Tozeur (1 daily; 5hr 30min); Tripoli (Libya; 3 weekly; 14hr); Tunis (11 daily; 2hr 30min); Zaghouan (1 daily; 1hr 15min); Zarzis (1 daily; 6hr 30min).

Louages

Enfida to: Sousse (50min); Tunis (1hr 30min).
El Jem to: Mahdia (40min); Sousse (50min).
Kairouan to: Maktar (2hr); Monastir (1hr 15min); Sbeïtla (1hr 40min); Sfax (2hr 30min); Sousse (1hr); Tunis (2hr).
Mahdia to: El Jem (40min); Ksar Hellal (30min); Ksour Essaf (15min); La Chebba (30min); Moknine (30min); Sfax (1hr 30min); Sousse (1hr 30min).
Monastir to: Kairouan (1hr 15min); Ksar Hellal (40min); Lamta (35min); Moknine (45min); Ouardanine (10min); Sousse (20min); Tunis (2hr 20min).
Sfax to: Agareb (30min); Bir Ali (1hr); El Hencha (40min); El Jem (1hr); Gabès (2hr); Gafsa (2hr 30min); Jerba (Houmt Souk; 4hr 30min); Kairouan (2hr 30min); Kasserine (3hr 30min); La Chebba (1hr); Le Kef (4hr 30min); Mahrès (30min); Mahdia (1hr 30min); Maktar (3hr); Medenine (3hr); Sidi Bou Zid (2hr); Sousse (2hr); Tozeur (4hr); Tripoli (9hr); Tunis (4hr 30min).
Sousse to: El Jem (50min); Enfida (50min); Hammamet (1hr 15min); Kairouan (1hr); Kasserine (3hr 30min); Ksar Hellal (30min); Ksour Esaf (1hr 30min); La Chebba (1hr 20min); Mahdia (1hr 30min); Moknine (50min); Monastir (20min); Nabeul (1hr 30min); Port el Kantaoui (15min); Sbeïtla (3hr); Sfax (2hr); Sidi Bou Ali (30min); Sidi Bou Zid (3hr); Siliana (2hr 30min); Tunis (2hr).

Ferries

Sfax to: Kerkennah (Sidi Youssef; 8–16 daily; 1hr).

Domestic flights

Sfax to: Tunis (5 weekly; 45min).

Arabic place names

Akouda	اكودة
Biar el Aouani	بيار العواني
El Jem	الجم
Enfida	النفيضة
Hergla	هرڤلة
Kairouan	القيروان
Kalaa Kebira	القلعة الكبرى
Kalaa Sghira	القلعة الصغرى
Kerkennah Islands	جزر قرقنة
Ksar Hellal	قصر هلال
La Skhirra	الصخيرة
Lamta	لمطة
Mahdia	المهدية
Mahrès	المحرس
Moknine	المكنين
Monastir	المنستير
Port el Kantaoui	القنطاوي
Remla	رملة
Reqqada	رقّادة
Sebkha Kelbia	سبخة الكلبية
Sfax	صفاقس
Sidi Frej	سيدي فرج
Skanès	صقانص
Sousse	سوسة
Takrouna	تكرونة
Thyna	طينة

5

The Tell

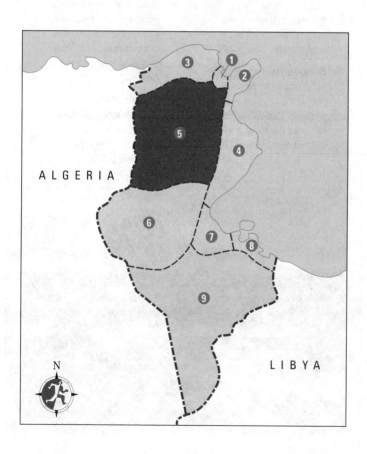

CHAPTER 5 **Highlights**

✳ **Zaghouan** Pretty market town with an alpine feel, clinging to the slopes of Tunisia's most spectacular mountain. **See p.294**

✳ **Thuburbo Majus** Perhaps the most idyllic of the major Roman sites, surrounded by rolling wheat fields. **See p.297**

✳ **Dougga** The largest and most dramatic Roman site in the country, with a majestic Capitol looking out over the town and valley below. **See p.304**

✳ **Le Kef** Little-visited town in a breathtaking location, sprawling down the side of a mountain beneath its historic Medina and Kasbah. **See p.311**

✳ **Haïdra** An old Roman border town, minimally excavated but stunning in its remoteness close to the Algerian frontier. **See p.320**

✳ **Sbeïtla** The remarkably well-preserved Roman Forum here offers the ultimate photo opportunity. **See p.327**

△ Jugurtha's Table

5

The Tell

M
uch of central Tunisia lies within the **Tell**, a region which begins
to the southwest of Tunis with fertile plains – good, well-watered
farming land – but rises quickly into the **Dorsale mountains**, the
highest in the country, forming a barrier from Zaghouan to Kasserine. Beyond, to the south, lie empty and infertile steppes which fade towards
the east into the Sahel. The plains have been heavily populated since Roman
times, though over the centuries the southern parts were steadily taken over
by esparto grass and left to sheep and camel herds. The tribes that lived here
in the nineteenth century were notorious for their banditry; the **Hammama**,
centred on Sidi Bou Zid, used to raid as far as the very gates of Sfax, over
100km to the east. During the protectorate large areas of public grazing land
were taken over by colonists, and the tribes were left to fight over the scraps.
Most of the population lived by working on colonial estates and gathering
esparto grass.

Despite a number of mines and modern industrial plants in the south, the
economy remains largely agrarian, and vulnerable to external economic crises.
The bloodiest of these was in 1984, when the IMF-backed removal of bread
subsidies led to nationwide riots, which started here in Kasserine and led to the
deaths of eighty people (p.508). Nowadays the economy has revived, but the
region still lags behind the rest of Tunisia's "economic miracle", and workers
still leave for larger towns. Nonetheless the Tell remains a deeply rewarding,
if divided, region to travel through, both in terms of its obvious attractions
– landscape and its numerous ancient sites – as well as the striking and unaffected pride of the people.

Tour groups make their way from the coast to the main Roman sites of
Thurburbo Majus, **Maktar**, **Sbeïtla** and, above all, **Dougga**, but they largely
neglect the region's less obvious attractions. To be fair, however, there are very
few **hotels** in the region. Wild camping is a good as well as rewarding way
around this problem, though most sizeable places tend to have at least one
"**hôtel populaire**": dirty, hidden away and not suitable for women. **Zagh-**

Market days

Monday Kasserine, Maktar, Sidi Bou Zid, Tajerouine
Tuesday Dahmani, Haffouz, Kasserine, El Krib, Sidi Jedidi
Wednesday Menzel Chaker, Sbeïtla
Thursday Le Kef, Siliana, Téboursouk
Friday Testour, Thala, Zaghouan
Saturday El Fahs, Sidi Bou Zid

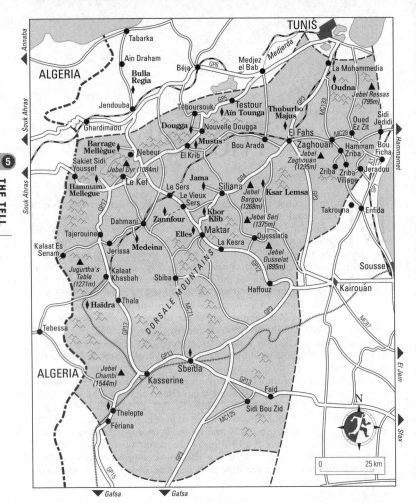

ouan, an unspoilt market town just an hour from Tunis, sits below the country's most spectacular mountain, **Jebel Zaghouan**, whose foothills harbour a group of isolated Berber villages. **Testour** was built up by Andalusian settlers and retains a very Spanish flavour, with a glorious seventeenth-century minaret more like a Toledo church tower. Over by the Algerian border is **Le Kef**, a historic mountainside town that looks out over landscapes reminiscent of the American West. Hidden here, and virtually unvisited, are **Haïdra**, one of the most majestic Roman sites in the country, and **Jugurtha's Table**, a flat-topped mountain that served as a bandit's lair for many centuries.

Le Kef and Kasserine are the main **transport** centres, reasonably well connected to other parts of the Tell and beyond. Places on the edge of the region often have better connections to other parts of the country than to the interior of the Tell. The only passenger **rail service** in this area is from Tunis to Kalaat Khasbah via El Fahs, Gaafour, Le Sers and Dahmani; at the time of writing there were three trains a day between Tunis and Dahmani, with one service daily continuing on to Kalaat Khasbah.

La Mohammedia and Oudna

The most direct route from Tunis into the Tell, the **GP3**, holds little of interest before Thuburbo Majus (see p.297), save for a ruined beylical palace not far out of the capital's sprawling southern suburbs and an impressive stretch of Roman aqueduct beside the road a little further on. With a little time and your own transport, however, you could make a worthwhile detour to the underrated Roman site of **Oudna**, set amid olive and cypress trees in the rolling hills to the east of the main road.

Tunisia has a large number of redundant and ruined beylical palaces – perhaps because of the superstition that it was unpropitious for a bey to rule from the palace of his predecessor – and little but a shell now remains of the summer palace called **La Mohammedia**, 16km from Tunis on the road to El Fahs. Senior state officials had long kept country residences in the area, including Youssef Sahib et Tabaa, who built the mosque in Tunis (see p.104), and Shakir Sahib et Tabaa, both of whom met early deaths. In the 1840s Ahmed Bey (1837–56) began to build a palace complex here, hoping the result would surpass even Versailles in its grandeur. Following his state visit to France in 1846, Ahmed Bey aimed to incorporate some of what he had seen in Europe. This included a French optical telegraph system – then the latest in telecommunications – which the French, rulers of Algeria since 1830 and already jockeying for position in Tunisia, were only too glad to provide. Lines were set up linking La Mohammedia to the Bardo Palace and to La Goulette, but the system was barely used before being abandoned after Ahmed Bey's death. The site still has the bare outlines of the palace buildings and associated barracks, but all the roofs have collapsed and most of the tiles have been pillaged.

Oudna

A few kilometres beyond La Mohammedia, the road runs parallel to the Roman **aqueduct** which carried water from Zaghouan to Carthage. First built in the second century AD, it was reconstructed by the Byzantines after the Vandal invasion, and later by the Fatimids and Hafsids. At the point where the aqueduct turns sharply away from the main road to the east, a six-kilometre minor road leads to the hillside remains of Roman Uthina, now called **OUDNA** (daily: April to mid-Sept 8am–7pm; mid-Sept to March 8.30am–5.30pm; 1.6TD). From Tunis, just 30km away, **bus** #24 from place Barcelone runs to the nearby village of Ferch el Annabi (roughly half-hourly); alternatively you could haggle a taxi driver down to a realistic 20TD for a trip to Oudna and back.

Unfortunately some excellent mosaics have gone to the Bardo from the site, but a number of surprisingly opulent buildings have been uncovered during excavations (still ongoing), including a Capitol temple, a spectacular amphitheatre, public baths, cisterns and a theatre. There is a World Bank-financed project to expand the site over the next few years and add a museum, but at the moment it is quite undeveloped and receives few visitors, making a pleasant change from the busier Roman sites.

The **amphitheatre**, partly hollowed out of a hill, is now thought to have been the third largest in Africa, holding around sixteen thousand people. Half of what remains of it has been fully restored using original materials, giving an idea of its former dimensions; further tiers would have risen out of the hillside. The **Capitol**, which sadly has been built over by a nineteenth-century farmhouse, occupies a commanding hilltop position. However, its main interest lies in its huge underground vaults, miraculously intact after so many centuries. Air vents down to the vaults indicate that they may have been used as grain silos.

Zaghouan

Almost alpine in feel, with its green slopes and the grey crags above, **ZAGH-OUAN**, 60km south of Tunis, is perhaps the most refreshing town in Tunisia. Although a fair number of tourists stop by to see its Roman ruins, few stay long, leaving the town surprisingly unspoilt; if you have the choice, come on a Friday for the **market**.

The old town's steep, narrow streets crisscross a low ridge of Jebel Zaghouan – not quite the highest mountain in the country, but easily the most spectacular. Cold water gushing from the mountain springs used to supply Carthage via a 132-kilometre Roman aqueduct, part of which can be seen next to the GP3 road southwest of Tunis (see p.293). One end of the ridge on which the town sits is punctuated by the old church spire and the new mosque's minaret; nearer the middle are the nineteenth-century **Great Mosque** and the **Mosque of Sidi Ali Azouz**, named after the patron saint of Tunis (where he is commemorated with his own *zaouia* and mosque; see p.96). Below the new mosque, just above the main road running through town, is a second-century Roman **triumphal arch**, with a bull's head on its keystone.

The principal Roman remains, dubbed the **Temple des Eaux**, lie about 3km above the town centre. On foot, you can head up past the triumphal arch and Sidi Ali Azouz Mosque; in a car, turn uphill at the roundabout on the main road with the fountain in the middle, overlooked by the Magasin Général. Follow signs for the Temple des Eaux and turn right when you eventually come to the *Club de Chasse* after a couple of kilometres. The Roman "temple" is little more than a backdrop – it's not a temple at all, in fact, but a grand fountain of the type found in all Roman towns. The twelve niches above the basin once held a statue for each month of the year. There is a **café** just below the remains, where you can sit and enjoy the view, extending over the bare plain below and up into the mountain behind.

Visible within a seventy-kilometre radius and, at 1300m, rising high above the surrounding plains, **Jebel Zaghouan** is typical of the Dorsale mountains that form Tunisia's backbone. From a naturalist's point of view, its highlight is an abundance of **birds of prey**, of which up to a dozen species can be sighted in a few hours, including eagles, vultures, kites and falcons, wheeling around their nest sites, or soaring hundreds of metres before gliding out over the plains in search of food. They're active most of the day, but early morning and evening are the best times to watch.

If you feel inspired to climb the craggy, limestone ridge of Jebel Zaghouan, either take the sixteen-kilometre track leading to the relay station on the summit (from where there are superb views over the countryside), or scramble up directly from the temple in a couple of hours to the lower peak nearer the town. It's very hard going, rough on exposed legs and a good place to twist an ankle, and the mountain is not a place to get caught out on after dark.

While you're in Zaghouan, look out for the roses for which the town is famous. The nurseries were introduced by Andalusian refugees in the seventeenth century and are used to make rose-water and perfume. There's a **rose festival** held here in May.

Practicalities

Transport around Zaghouan is not that extensive, but interesting excursions can be made west to El Fahs and Thuburbo Majus (see p.296), or southeast to the Berber villages of Zriba and Jeradou (see below). **Buses and louages** operate from the bottom of the old town, 200m down a side street opposite the Roman arch. There is no tourist office in town, thought there are a couple of **banks** with Visa and MasterCard ATMs on the main street and a **post office** (country hours).

You can **camp** wild on the slopes around the Temple des Eaux. Unfortunately, the only **hotel** – the pleasantly located *Nymphes* (℡72 675 708), high up among the trees near the Temple des Eaux (turn left at the *Club de Chasse* instead of right to the temple) – has been closed for several years, and there was no sign of it reopening at the time of writing. The *Maison des Jeunes* (℡72 676 630), a barrack-like affair on top of the next ridge over from the town centre, has also been closed intermittently over the past few years, so call ahead if you hope to stay there.

The **café** at the temple (daily 7am–8pm, until midnight in summer) serves food, as does a newish **restaurant**, the *Aigle Royal*, a couple of hundred metres down the road (daily 7am–10pm). In the centre of town, on the main street below the Roman arch, *Restaurant La Source* (daily noon–11pm) is blessed with great views; a meal here will set you back 12–15TD.

East of Zaghouan

The roads southeast towards Enfida and the Sahel lead past a couple of dramatic **Berber villages** perched in the dying fall of the Dorsale mountains, and similar to Takrouna outside Enfida (see p.217). The most remote is the now abandoned **ZRIBA** (also called Zriba Tunisien), 12km southeast of Zaghouan and confusingly located amid Hammam Zriba and the French-built Zriba village. You'll need to find your way first to **HAMMAM ZRIBA** – turn right 7km out of Zaghouan on the MC133 road to Enfida and continue for a couple of kilometres through the modern settlement to the shops and cafés around the **hammam** itself, which occupies the opening of a narrow gorge leading into the hills. You should be able to find a bus or a lift from Zaghouan this far – especially at weekends, when the hammam is a popular excursion. There are communal baths (0.7TD) and a small jacuzzi-like one that holds four people (10TD/hr) at the end of the entrance to the old hammam. The gorge is apparently where Gustave Flaubert drew inspiration for the massacre of the mercenaries in *Salammbô*. The *Complex Touristique 7 Novembre* next door (℡72 677 533; ➎) has enormous rooms with bathrooms, and is packed with Tunisian hammam-goers, so you will need to book ahead.

To continue to Zriba, you'll need to find a rough eight-kilometre track that heads southeast past the entrance to an ugly open-cast mine. As you walk or bump over the hills, you'll catch glimpses of the village in the distance, clinging to the edges of an outlying jag of the mountain behind. The village itself is less striking than its setting, with narrow lanes crawling up and down the steep ridge.

Similar to Zriba, **JERADOU** is more accessible if you have transport. A minor road (10km) leads east to it from the Zaghouan–Enfida road some 7km south of Zriba village. Like Zriba, Jeradou occupies an outlying pinnacle of a mountain and consists of narrow streets leading up to a saint's shrine on top of the ridge. Look out for Roman remains in the field of olives below the village.

From Jeradou, a minor road heads south through **SIDI KHALIFA**, a small settlement with a multi-domed shrine. A track leads a short way south from here towards a low forested hill, at the foot of which lie the unexpected remains of Roman **Pheradi Maius** – baths, a triumphal arch and, on the hill-top above to the east, a temple to Baal. The road through Sidi Khalifa goes on to join the coast road halfway between Bou Ficha and Enfida.

Sidi Jedidi and Oued ez Zit

The direct Zaghouan–Hammamet road (MC28) leads east off the Bou Ficha road through open countryside, cultivated with wheat, olives and almonds and populated with Berbers and their flocks of sheep and goats. Twelve kilometres on, the village of **SIDI JEDIDI** has become the target of tourist excursions from Hammamet, especially to coincide with the Tuesday **market**. The setting, in the shoulder of the hills, ridged with strange, needle-like rock outcrops, is spectacular. From the top of the ridge here you can look down towards the coast, where your first sight of the resort complex may be of parasails floating above the beach. There are a few **cafés** and cheap **restaurants** here, but not much else.

The main road between Zaghouan and Tunis, the MC133, runs northwest to join the GP3 between El Fahs and Tunis. If you have transport or happen to find a lift, you might want to think about taking the back way to Tunis, first taking the MC28 east across the fertile plain below Zaghouan to **OUED EZ ZIT** ("River of Oil"), a small village with some Roman remains. From here the MC35 heads north and enters a lonely pass between Jebel Zit and Jebel Marchana, either of which makes attractive walking country. Towards the end of the pass, the road offers a dramatic view of the back of **Jebel Ressas**, the lonely trapezoid mountain more usually seen lurking behind Jebel Bou Kornine from Sidi Bou Saïd. Beyond the mountain, the road runs through vineyards towards the straggling southern end of Tunis.

El Fahs and Thuburbo Majus

The only reason to come to **EL FAHS**, a sizeable but nondescript market town 60km southwest of Tunis, is to see the Roman site of **Thuburbo Majus** 3km to the north. El Fahs has good transport connections, making a day-trip to Thuburbo Majus straightforward.

El Fahs has few attractions of its own, with the exception of the Saturday **market**, one of the largest in the area and totally devoid of tourist buses. The marketplace is next to the rail line near the **train station**. **Buses** stop on the main road outside the train station, as do **louages**. East and west of El Fahs, good minor roads lead through empty country to Zaghouan and (with limited public transport) Medjez el Bab. More heavily travelled are the main roads south to Kairouan via the fort at Biar el Aouani (see p.256) and southwest to Siliana and Maktar (see p.323). There's no tourist office in town, nor are there any hotels.

△ view of Zaghouan from Thuburbo Majus

Thuburbo Majus

The ruins of **THUBURBO MAJUS** (daily: April to mid-Sept 8am–7pm;
mid-Sept to March 8.30am–5.30pm; 2.1TD, camera 1TD) lie behind a low
rise 3km north of El Fahs on the Tunis road, beyond a bridge over the Oued
Miliane. Under French rule, El Fahs was known as Pont du Fahs, and as you
cross the river you can see the remains of a bridge left behind by the Romans
in the riverbed to the east. If you're on foot, ignore the signpost for the site
– which seems to take you halfway around northern Tunisia – and walk instead
straight up to the dip between two small hills, the eastern edge of the Roman
city. Minibuses here from El Fahs cost 0.5TD, though you might have to wait
for one to fill up. There's a small **café** and toilets at the main entrance.

   Thurburbo Majus was a Berber–Carthaginian settlement long before the
Romans arrived. The name was actually based on a common root in the
indigenous local language, used in place names like Thuburbo Minus (modern
Tebourba), Thuburnica near Ghardimaou (see p.209) and Téboursouk near
Dougga (see p.304). For the Romans (and later the French) it was an important
market centre and grew rich on the proceeds. Like so many other provincial
towns, it acquired the trappings of Rome – a Forum, a Capitol, and the
semblance of an orderly grid plan at the heart of an older, meandering town.
The site was abandoned after the seventh-century Arab invasion and was only
rediscovered in 1875. As Roman sites in Tunisia go, it lags slightly behind the
likes of Maktar and Sbeïtla but is easier to reach from Tunis and the coastal
resorts.

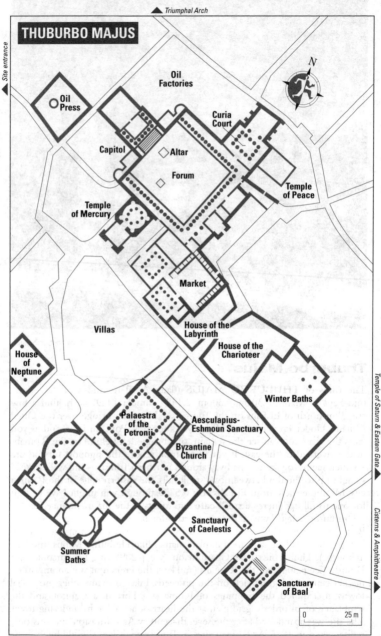

THUBURBO MAJUS

Triumphal Arch

Site entrance

N

Oil Press

Oil Factories

Curia Court

Capitol

Altar

Forum

Temple of Peace

Temple of Mercury

Market

Villas

House of the Labyrinth

House of the Charioteer

House of Neptune

Winter Baths

Palaestra of the Petronii

Aesculapius-Eshmoun Sanctuary

Byzantine Church

Sanctuary of Caelestis

Summer Baths

Sanctuary of Baal

Temple of Saturn & Eastern Gate

Cisterns & Amphitheatre

0   25 m

The Forum and around

The town's public buildings date mainly from the great imperial era of the second to third century AD. The **Forum** – the paved open space at the centre of the site, laid out between the years 161 and 192 AD – was its most characteristically Roman feature, something that any self-respecting imperial town had to have. A colonnade ran around three sides, the fourth left open for the **Capitol temple**, which catered for the imperial cult of Jupiter, Juno and Minerva. The podium and the vertical emphasis of the columns are very much the norm, and if you walk round behind it's easy to see just how much effort had to go into giving the temple a massive base so that it would dominate the Forum in the prescribed manner. In fact, the whole of one side of the Forum had to be raised on an artificial platform to create the required level space – a graphic illustration of the influence of the Roman role model over status-conscious provincial citizens.

The area of housing behind the Capitol was later converted into **oil factories**. You can see clearly where one massive circular press was installed so that the oil would drip into a pool originally designed for human bathing – a sad illustration of the change in Thuburbo's circumstances, with industry supplanting leisure. To the north, one of three surviving **triumphal arches** marks the outskirts of town.

Behind the colonnade on the other three sides of the Forum stood temples and municipal buildings. On the right-hand side if you peer out from the Capitol is a curious **Temple of Mercury**, built in 211 AD to the local and not the Roman pattern, and featuring an outer courtyard – circular, with niches making corners – leading into the sanctuary. Mercury was the god of trade (as well as thieving), and the three split-level courtyards below the temple formed the town's **market**, where stalls can still be made out.

The residential areas

The Mercury temple looks out over an area of jumbled streets and houses, predating the Forum, in a layout that was anathema to the Romans. Several hundred metres beyond, towards another triumphal arch in the distance, is a second residential quarter with regular streets, a Roman addition as the town expanded. In many ways, the contrast between the two areas is similar to the difference in modern Tunisia between traditional medinas and French grid plans – like the Romans before them, the nineteenth-century colonial powers imported their own ideas when it came to town planning.

However rambling the streets in the quarter below the Forum, though, the houses in this central district were as Roman as their wealthy inhabitants could make them. Some fine colourful **mosaics** are visible in the so-called **House of Neptune**, where columns have been re-erected around the central courtyard.

The Palaestra of the Petronii and around

Just east of the House of Neptune stands a well-preserved row of blue-grey columns which still support an entablature. These made up one side of the 225 AD **Palaestra of the Petronii**, where young men took part in boxing, wrestling and running before heading to the **Summer Baths** behind. Carved in the paving of the Palaestra's southern corner, you'll find some letters that make up a Roman game used to learn the alphabet. The most striking part of the baths beyond, confused in plan after being remodelled in 361 AD, is an impressive semicircular portico which housed not statuary but latrines – whose users sat over a still-visible channel of running water.

Nothing could be more Roman than the Palaestra, but three hybrid centres of worship are reminders of the cultural blend in Roman North Africa. In the far corner of the Palaestra is the first of these, a small **shrine** to the healing god Aesculapius, here worshipped under the joint name of Aesculapius-Eshmoun. An inscription reveals that those wishing to enter the sanctuary had to observe a three-day ritual when they were forbidden bathing, shaving, beans and pork, and sexual relations.

From the Palaestra, a street leads off to the left past the impressive façade of the **Winter Baths**. The small temple podium a little further up the slope on the right is the **Sanctuary of Baal**, the top deity in the Phoenician pantheon, which was erected in the second century under Roman rule. The courtyard just over the street (with its entrance re-erected) was a **Sanctuary of Caelestis**, the Roman version of Carthaginian Tanit. Later it was fashioned into part of a Byzantine church. Standing among the columns of its nave and two aisles, in the former courtyard between the Palaestra and Sanctuary of Caelestis, you can easily make out how a rectangular church plan was imposed on the existing square courtyard. An apse is recognizable at one end, a baptistry at the other.

The southern edge of the site

Ruins discernible on the hillside south of the Baal temple comprise perhaps the most monumental **cistern** to be seen in Tunisia, even boasting an inner gallery around the top of the deep storage tank. An **amphitheatre** above is just recognizable. There's a fine view from here of Jebel Zaghouan (see p.294) dominating the whole region, and across to the eastern gate of the town on the next hill. Above this gate are the remains of a **Temple of Saturn**, who was the Roman equivalent of Baal; temples to him tend to stand near the city boundaries, as at Dougga.

El Fahs to Maktar via the GP4

The **GP4** road southwest of El Fahs makes up one side of the scenically rewarding El Fahs–Maktar–Kairouan triangle. This is some of the most remote country in the Tell, difficult to reach without your own transport, though **Siliana** has reasonable transport connections and one of the few hotels in the area, making it one of the few feasible bases for exploring the triangle.

The most obvious single sight here is the massive Byzantine fortress of **Ksar Lemsa**, 20km down a southward turn off the GP4 towards Ouesslatia. Sitting below the massive presence of Jebel Bargou, Ksar Lemsa guarded one of the routes north into the more fertile but vulnerable areas of the Tell. Continuing south along the Ksar Lemsa road will bring you to a fork where you can go east to Kairouan or west to Ouesslatia (see p.327).

Staying on the GP4, you could take a southward turn 20km east of Siliana at **Bargou** (also known as Rabaa or Robaa) for a scenic one-way route into the heart of the **Jebel Bargou** massif. Twenty kilometres further on along the GP4, **SILIANA** itself is, like Ouesslatia, a lowland equivalent of Maktar: a dull modern farming centre where you wouldn't want to stay for its own sake. It is, however, the site of a **hotel** – the *Zama* (℡78 871121, ℻78 870 751; ❺) – as well as a **youth hostel** (℡78 872 871; call ahead to check that it's open). There are a couple of daily **buses** from here to Béja (2hr), though they may well stop at every stone along the way.

Roman remains within reach of Siliana, accessible down a nine-kilometre minor road and recommended for enthusiasts only, are the vestigial ruins at

△ Triumphal arch, Maktar

Jama of what is thought to be Zama Minor, site in 202 BC of the climactic battle of the Second Punic War, in which Scipio (soon to become Scipio Africanus) defeated Hannibal.

It's uphill most of the way from Siliana to **Maktar** (see p.323). About 10km outside Siliana, a lonely minor road signposted "Le Sers" turns west to cut across for 20km to the Maktar–Le Kef road (GP12), covered on p.323. About halfway down this lonely road, which bumps up and down over steeply rolling country, you pass two solitary Roman-era monuments, both easy to miss. The first, known as **Ksour Toual Zouamel**, is a two-storey square mausoleum, which sits below and to the north of the road, halfway up a hill. About 1km further, the second, known as **Kbor Klib**, is a couple of hundred metres south of the road on the ridge of the same massif. A huge block of masonry, originally 45m long by 15m wide and 6m high, it remains uncertainly identified, and is said to be either a Numidian sanctuary, similar to the one which stood on top of the hill at Chemtou, or a victory altar erected by Julius Caesar to celebrate his Civil War triumph.

Testour and around

From Tunis, the main westward route into the Tell, the **GP5**, runs along the Medjerda Valley as far as Medjez el Bab (see p.196), at which point the GP6 forks off it to the north and climbs over the Téboursouk range. The GP5 continues southwest along the Medjerda River before reaching **TESTOUR**, 75km from the capital and – its modern concrete outskirts aside – the clearest remaining evidence in the country of the Spanish immigration of the early seventeenth century. A cluster of tiled roofs on a mound above the River Medjerda, the heart of Testour looks so Spanish that it's no surprise to find that it was built by Andalusian refugees in the 1600s. Its appearance and the local way of life have changed very little since, and this, along with the almost pristine rural feel of the place, gives it a particular fascination, the more so if your visit coincides with the Friday regional **market**, although the daily souks are bustling nonetheless. It's worth a stop en route from Tunis to Dougga and Le Kef, an easy enough road to travel by bus or louage.

Some history

Some of the **Andalusian Muslims** evicted from Spain (see p.499 for more) in the wake of the Christian reconquest were wealthy enough to settle in Tunis itself, where the rue des Andalous is a reminder of their presence. Others had to petition the authorities for land, and in 1609 they were granted the old Roman site of **Tichilla**, today's Testour. The new Andalusian communities were renowned throughout North Africa for their commercial abilities and hard work, but were conscious of their outsider status. Both feelings are neatly expressed in a myth about Testour's foundation. According to this story, the first group of settlers originally stopped about 12km north of the current town, where some of them planted vineyards. The Turkish authorities were so impressed when they saw the result that they slapped on taxes at a punitive level – whereupon the disgusted settlers uprooted their vines and themselves and moved on to Testour's current site.

From its foundation, Testour's economy centred on the agricultural activities of the region – for which it still provides an important market – but there were also skilled artisans among the immigrants. The town was long famed for its

chéchias, made from the wool of local flocks. These have almost disappeared, but the other main trade – traditional **roof tile production** – has survived. The factory down by the river below Testour's Great Mosque is one of only two left in all Tunisia (the other is at Tozeur); it produces up to two thousand tiles every week.

The Town and around

In Testour, the bourgeois pride and culture of the Andalusian settlers found permanent expression in mosques and public buildings that are redolent of rural Spain. Local legend tells that there were once fourteen mosques here, built on virtually every side street off the main avenue and serving the specific needs of local communities, playing host to business and municipal meetings as well as everyday prayer. Only a handful remain, but almost without exception they consist of a bell-tower-like round crown on a square base.

The **Great Mosque**, with its distinctive tiled octagonal minaret – unmissable if you are approaching the town from the east – is the largest and most beautiful of an extraordinary number of mosques built here in the early seventeenth century. It stands just off the main square, its walls the texture of crumbled biscuit, surmounted by a ribbed tile roof. Inside, the delicate arcades of the two courtyards, one hung with white jasmine, are in marked contrast to the generally heavier local styles. Yet even here you can see that Roman bits and pieces – door frames, capitals, columns and oil presses – have been reused in the paving. One corner column in the main courtyard sports a milestone proclaiming "Carthage 66 miles", which, as it happens, is just about right.

The **minaret** dominates the mosque, just as it dominates the old town and the surrounding river valley, with its nostalgia for Spain. Most obviously Spanish is the superimposition of an octagonal crowning section, lavishly decorated with tiles, on a square base, which recalls church bell towers in Aragon and Castile. In the base, the builders used a Toledan technique in which rectangular patches of rubble somehow become decorative when surrounded by brick. Least obvious, but perhaps the biggest giveaway, is the clock on the south face, which doesn't appear on a minaret anywhere else in the world. Note that the numbers go backwards, allegedly because the Andalusians wanted time to go back so that they could be returned to their homeland.

Testour's Spanish immigrant citizens could hardly have provided a clearer demonstration of their identity than the Great Mosque and its minaret, although it is actually the second great mosque that they built. (The remains of the first – a floor plan, a bricked-in mihrab and the bottom half of a smaller minaret – lie not far to the northeast.)

Just downhill from the main street, on rue Kortouba, is another seventeenth-century survivors, the **Abdellatif Mosque**, whose minaret has some rows of faïence tiles. "Kortouba" is Cordoba in Spain; just before it, on the same side of the main street, notice also rue Ichbilia (Seville).

Uphill from the main street, at the end of rue 26 Fevrier 1953 on the GP5 through road, stands another graceful reminder of Andalusian culture – the **Zaouia of Sidi Naseur el Baraouachi**, built around his tomb in 1733. It begins in a lengthy passage and passes through a green door whose studded nails have been painted a hallucinatory red. Inside, however, all is calm, with a tiny paved courtyard surrounded by small chambers under a tiled arcade and almost swamped by an orange tree. The tomb itself, under its green-tiled dome and decorated with stucco and faïence tiles, is still an object of veneration; the stains on its far wall were made by hands coated in henna to ward off the evil eye.

Most of the Andalusian immigrant communities in Tunisia included **Jews** as well as Muslims, though many of the Jews have left for Israel over the past few decades. Testour was formerly the site of a Jewish pilgrimage from all over Tunisia to the tomb of Rabbi Fraji Chawat, said to be a native of Fez who died here. More recently, the town became tangled in the torrid story of a Jewish woman called Habiba Msika, born in 1895, who became one of the country's best-known singers and actresses during the musical revival in the early twentieth century. She is largely remembered today for her gruesome death in 1930, when her jealous lover Elyaou Mimouni – a wealthy native of Testour – doused her in petrol while she slept, burning her alive. Her story is told in the 1996 film *Habiba Msika*, directed by Selma Baccar.

Mimouni's house now serves as Testour's **Maison de Culture** on rue Kortouba, beyond the Abdellatif minaret, with an Arabic plaque on the wall in which the fateful year of 1930 is recognizable. If you can find someone to show you round this incongruously lavish 1920s mansion, you can see Mimouni's massive safe, some splendidly vampish photos and even an auditorium that was purpose-built for Msika. The Maison de Culture is also the place to ask about Testour's annual **Festival of Malouf Music**, which takes place in the second half of July in the large café opposite the Great Mosque.

At **AÏN TOUNGA**, 9km west of Testour on the Le Kef road, there is an ancient site (free access), which includes one of the most impressive **Byzantine fortresses** in Tunisia. Remains of its walls and towers, some half-buried but still enormous, loom over the modern road, which sees plenty of bus and louage traffic. Above the fortress are the remains of Roman **Thignica**: a residential quarter crowned by a temple, with the outline of a theatre, baths and an arch hidden away in a garden below to the right.

Practicalities

There have been few incursions into the fabric of the old town; most of the straggle of new development flanks the main road heading west to Le Kef. The **main street** through the old town leads straight ahead as the GP5 loops off to the left at the eastern edge of town; a few hundred metres further on the main street rejoins the GP5 by a Shell petrol station. **Buses** stop a couple of hundred metres west of the Shell station, outside the new Municipalité building. There are no hotels in town, and there's no tourist office.

Dougga and around

"Dougga very big city" is what the hopeful guides hanging around the entrances will tell you, and they're right. The Roman site of **DOUGGA** (daily: April to mid-Sept 8am–7pm; mid-Sept to March 8.30am–5.30pm; 2.1TD, camera 1TD) is both the largest and most dramatic in Tunisia, and contains what some consider the most beautiful single Roman monument in North Africa. If you see only one Roman site in the country, it should undoubtedly be "these magnificent remains of taste and greatness, so easily reached in perfect safety by a ride along the Medjerda", as the English traveller James Bruce noted in 1765. The city was accorded World Heritage Site status by UNESCO in 1997.

Dougga's name suggests non-Roman origins, as does its site high on the side of the valley – the Romans preferred flatter sites more suited to their standardized urban forms. Here they seem to have adapted well to a town that had already been described in the fourth century BC as being "of an impressive size". By the second century BC it had become the seat of Numidian king **Massinissa**, whose support for Rome in the last war against Carthage gained much credit for the town. From the second century AD, under Roman administration, it began to enjoy a period of great prosperity. At its peak the Roman town had a population of ten thousand and, although the surrounding countryside now looks empty, aerial photography has revealed no fewer than ten other settlements within a ring of just six square kilometres.

The Byzantines built huge fortifications and, after their departure, the local inhabitants remained among the ruins until excavating archeologists at the end of the nineteenth century forced them to move 3km down the hill into the purpose-built village of **Nouvelle Dougga**, a drab modern place on the Tunis–Le Kef road. **Access** is pretty easy from Nouvelle Dougga: hourly buses between Tunis and Le Kef pass through the village (the stop is called Borj Brahim; last bus to Tunis at 6pm), though you may want to find a taxi to continue to the site itself. The other approach, better for finding a taxi, is from Téboursouk (see p.310), about 7km northeast of the site, from where a side road follows the wall of a valley up and around to Dougga. The taxis hereabouts are white minibuses with yellow stripes, functioning like louages though you can pay around 3TD to hire a taxi privately for the trip to Dougga from Nouvelle Dougga, 4TD from Téboursouk (you can arrange for the driver to pick you up later for the return trip for the same price). The nearest place to stay is Téboursouk, but Dougga can be visited as a day-trip from Le Kef or even Tunis.

The **main entrance** to the site is on the Téboursouk side, where there is a **café** and toilets; there's also a ticket office on the Nouvelle Dougga side. There are two official **guides** who request around 10TD an hour, but you should be able to bargain them down to 6–7TD, especially if it's quiet. As for **food**, the *Restaurant Mercure*, near the ticket office on the Nouvelle Dougga side, caters mainly for package tours, with a reasonable, if uninteresting, menu at 10TD (daily 9am–midnight; closed Mon in winter).

The theatre and Temple of Saturn

The road to Dougga from Téboursouk ends at a car park next to Dougga's heavily restored **theatre**, almost at the top of the steep slope over which the grey remains are spread. Originally built in 168 AD, the theatre was one of a string of monumental projects from the second and third centuries financed by Dougga's wealthy land-owning families. An inscription proclaims that one Publius Marcius Quadratus erected the theatre, the halls flanking the stage, the porticos, the statue platform and the scene building. Today the theatre is used for performances of the French classics during the **Dougga Festival** in July and August.

Up on the hilltop behind the theatre are some early and peripheral odds and ends, beginning with the **Temple of Saturn**, whose columns overlook the road. These columns formed the facade of a courtyard which in turn led into three inner chambers, the typical African pattern for a temple. This is not surprising, since underneath the second-century Roman remains were found traces of a pre-Roman sanctuary of Baal, the Carthaginian god. In the paving opposite the central sanctuary chamber, look out for a pair of mysterious footprints in the floor, remnants of some unknown ritual.

From the top of the cliff by the Temple of Saturn, you can cut across west to some occupied houses that huddle under the remains of the pre-Roman Numidian defensive wall. Otherwise, return to the theatre and make your way

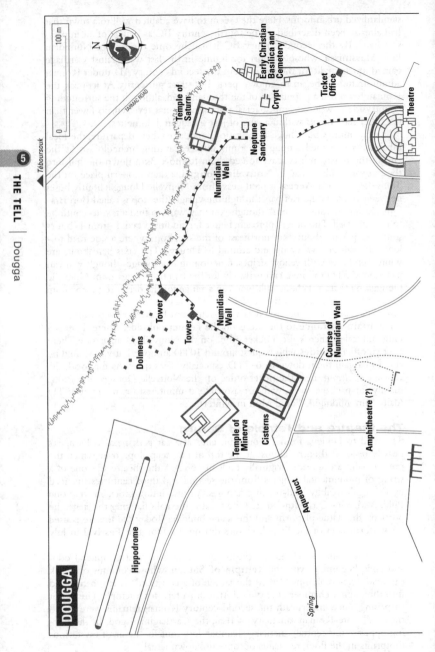

DOUGGA

◀ Téboursouk

N

0   100 m

Hippodrome

Spring

Aqueduct

Temple of Minerva

Cisterns

Amphitheatre (?)

Course of Numidian Wall

Dolmens

Tower

Tower

Numidian Wall

Numidian Wall

Neptune Sanctuary

Temple of Saturn

TARMAC ROAD

Crypt

Early Christian Basilica and Cemetery

Ticket Office

Theatre

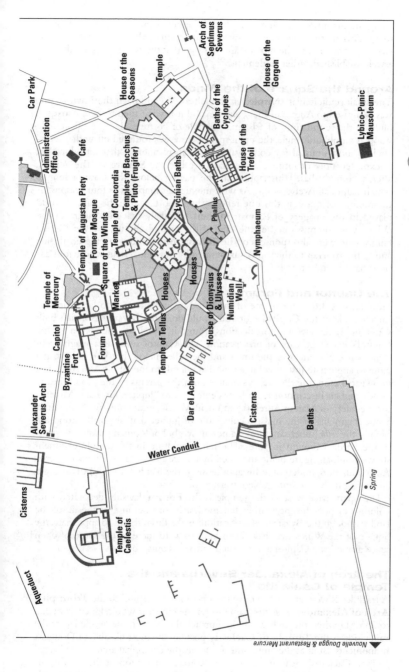

Nouvelle Dougga & Restaurant Mercure

Car Park

House of the Seasons

Temple

Arch of Septimus Severus

Administration Office

Café

House of the Gorgon

Temple of Augustan Piety

Former Mosque

Temples of Bacchus & Pluto (Frugifer)

Temple of Concordia

Baths of the Cyclopes

Lybico-Punic Mausoleum

Temple of Mercury

Square of the Winds

Lycinian Baths

House of the Trefoil

Capitol

Market

Houses

Forum

Houses

Phallus

Byzantine Fort

Temple of Tellus

House of Dionysius & Ulysses

Nymphaeum

Alexander Severus Arch

Dar el Acheb

Numidian Wall

Cisterns

Water Conduit

Cisterns

Baths

Temple of Caelestis

Spring

Aqueduct

along the main track leading towards the Capitol at the centre of the Roman town. This in turn becomes a paved Roman street that seems narrow and twisting compared to the norm – another sign that the Romans here inherited a well-established earlier settlement.

Around the Square of the Winds

The small semicircular **temple**, on the left as you approach the town centre, was dedicated to Augustan Piety, and beyond it is what used to be a **mosque**, built on the foundations of a Roman Temple of Fortune. Because this temple stood at an oblique angle, the open space below was rounded off with a semi-circle – most unusual for conservative Roman planners – that introduces an unexpected note of intimacy. The plaza is called the **Square of the Winds**, after a compass-based inscription in the paving below the Capitol temple which names all twelve winds. As with mosaics illustrating the four seasons, or the months of the year, this one reflects the important role the natural world played in the imagery of Roman Africans. It's likely that the Square of the Winds was commissioned at the end of the second century by the Pacuvii family, who were also sponsors of the **Temple of Mercury** on the north side and of the **market** to the south, surrounded by individual stalls whose foundations have been restored.

The Capitol and Forum

Heading west from the Square of the Winds, you come face to face with the huge temple of the **Capitol** – or you would do, if the Byzantines hadn't built some highly disorienting fortifications around it, which are the reason for the Capitol's excellent state of preservation. The Capitol really is a magnificent sight as it looks out over the town and the valley below, but you have to get close to appreciate just how huge it is. It was a gift to the city in 166 AD – just two years before the theatre was built – from the parents of the proud theatre donor, and an inscription records its dedication to "Jupiter, Juno and Minerva for the safety of Marcus Aurelius and Lucius Verus", joint emperors at the time. Some fragments of the massive cult statue of Jupiter that originally stood 6m high in the *cella* (inner sanctum) – a potent symbol of Roman power – are now in the Bardo Museum in Tunis. The relief sculpture in the temple pediment shows a human figure being molested by a large bird – the previous emperor, Antoninus Pius, undergoing his apotheosis at the hands (or claws) of an eagle, and a singularly uncomfortable reward it looks, too.

The open space west of the temple is the **Forum**, lavishly decorated with columns of polychrome marble, but modest in size because of the lie of the land. Although the Byzantine fortifications make this difficult to appreciate, the Square of the Winds may have been built so as to increase the sense of open space around the Capitol and give it an urban Roman quality.

The Arch of Alexander Severus and the Temple of Caelestis

A track leads west among the olive trees behind the Capitol to the **Triumphal Arch of Alexander Severus**, named after the emperor who reigned from 222 to 235 AD, when the arch was built. Further along, set in the gentle lap of the valley side, is the **Temple of Caelestis**, possibly the most likeable of Dougga's monuments. Built at the same time as the nearby triumphal arch, it's dedicated to Juno Caelestis (Heavenly Juno), the Romanized version of the Carthaginian god Tanit, and thus makes a pair with the Temple of Saturn on the far side of the city (but it's the truly Roman cult which is given central position in the Capitol). The temple itself, featuring podium and columns with attractive Corinthian capitals, is nothing out of the ordinary, but the semicircular colonnaded portico behind it is, like the Square of the Winds, unusual in the conservative architectural atmosphere of Roman Africa, where innovation seems to have gone against the grain of the designers; far away at the other end of the Roman Empire (Turkey and Palestine, for instance), this sort of touch was commonplace. The portico was inscribed with the names of distant provinces of the empire – Dalmatia, Judaea, Mesopotamia, Syria and Laodicea – as well as Carthage and Thugga. They may all have been centres of the Caelestis cult.

The residential quarter below the Forum

Head back towards the city centre along the track which turns into a Roman street just below the Forum and runs past an imposing doorway to the right. This is now known by the Arab name of **Dar el Acheb**, and the original function of its courtyard is not known. Beyond Dar el Acheb, the main street cuts through the centre of the town's most exclusive residential quarter. Large houses are crammed into all available spaces on the narrow side streets, and it's hard to imagine how it once looked when the walls stood to their full height. As the street follows the contour of the hill around, one sharp left and a left again leads between houses to the **Temple of Tellus** (Earth), dated to 261 AD and identifiable by a small peristyle (columned courtyard) leading to a sanctuary room with niches in the far wall, a recognizably African temple pattern. Further round the hill, the **House of Dionysus and Ulysses** is named after the famous mosaic of Ulysses tied to the mast of his ship while the Sirens sing; it's now in the Bardo (see p.110).

By now you are below the fortress-like remains of the **Licinian Baths**. Look for a barrel-vaulted passage – originally a tradesmen's entrance – which takes you into the baths from here. The official entrance was down some steep steps into a room on the northwest side of the complex, where mosaics and columns still stand. A headless statue here probably represents one of the Licinii family who donated the baths to the city in the third century AD. The large central room was the *frigidarium*, which opened through a smaller *tepidarium* to the southwest on to the *caldarium*, situated above the tradesmen's entrance and facing south to catch the sun. In the other direction, the large peristyle room in the northeast corner was the *palaestra*, a sort of training room for athletes.

A right turn at the end of the main street brings you to the large **House of the Trefoil**, which has had its history censored. A stone with a relief of a phallus stood outside the door, identifying the town brothel, until it was removed some 1800 years later by authorities concerned for tourist sensibilities. If you'd like to see it, look twenty metres away on a terrace above the road, west of the house and behind the Licinian Baths. A staircase leads down between two standing columns to a wide courtyard surrounded by rooms, one (its roof heavily restored) in the clover-leaf shape that provides the building's name – a name that carefully avoids any suggestion of the house's original function.

Beside the brothel stood a small private **baths complex**, now named after the magnificent mosaic in the Bardo of three bodybuilder Cyclopes swinging their hammers to forge Jupiter's thunderbolts. The baths were presumably connected with the brothel and still contain a well-preserved row of toilet seats.

The Arch of Septimius Severus and the Libyco-Punic Mausoleum

Heading down the hill past the baths leads eventually to the **Triumphal Arch of Septimius Severus**, built in 205 AD, a few years before the one near the

Caelestis Temple. A track originally left the city through this arch to join the main road below from Carthage. Septimius Severus, who came from Libya, was the founder of the dynasty of Roman emperors which ended with Alexander Severus (dedicatee of the Triumphal Arch near the Caelestis temple). The accent of Septimius's wife was notorious in Rome, but not that of the emperor himself, according to one tactful poet: "Your speech is not Carthaginian, nor your dress, nor is your spirit foreign: you are Italian, Italian . . ."

A track to the right, just before the arch, winds down to the **Libyco–Punic Mausoleum**, built in the second century BC for "Ateban, son of Ieptamath, son of Palu", which is important as one of the few surviving examples of pre-Roman monumental building in Tunisia. Although the mausoleum managed to survive the Roman Empire more or less intact, in 1842 it fell victim to the British Empire when the British consul, Sir Thomas Reade, dismantled it to get at the bilingual inscription which provides the names mentioned above. The inscription remains in the British Museum in London, where Libyco–Punic script was deciphered for the first time. Ironically, it was with the help of a sketch by the English traveller James Bruce that the French authorities reconstructed the mausoleum at the turn of the last century. Like other remnants of immediately pre-Roman North Africa – the sarcophagi in the Carthage Museum (see p.126), for example, and the recently reconstructed temple at Chemtou (see p.207) – the mausoleum is a mélange of different influences. Greek culture contributed the Ionic order in the second storey, but most of the elements are more recognizably Eastern, influenced by Carthage's Phoenician links; the overall form is similar to Anatolian and Syrian monuments, and the lotus-flower pilaster capitals on the corners of the first and third storeys speak with an Egyptian accent.

The Temple of Minerva and around

North of the Capitol, on the summit of the hill behind, are a few traces of the pre-Roman town, as well as some peripheral Roman structures. A track which veers right, uphill, from the Roman road between the theatre and Capitol leads past a group of seven massive **cisterns** on the right, each 35m long and 5m wide, with newly restored pink roofs. An aqueduct fed water into these from the spring located a little way west. Above the cisterns, a **Temple of Minerva**, built in the second century AD, follows the African pattern, with a colonnaded courtyard leading into a sanctuary room. Beyond the temple, the track runs along what looks like a long, flat field that was once the municipal **Hippodrome**. Two small heaps of rubble facing each other 190m apart were the ends of the *spina*, the central barrier around which the chariot races were run. If this seems like a bleak kind of place to watch a chariot race, sitting on the bare rocks opposite, the man who donated the land to the city in 214 AD knew better – he provided it "ad voluptates populi" (for the pleasure of the people), and numerous mosaics in museums around the country support his judgement.

Back to the east, beyond the end of the *spina*, is an area of **dolmen tombs** dating from the third century BC to the first century AD, sited just below the walls of the Numidian city, of which some remains and even a tower can be seen behind.

Téboursouk

For most tourists, **TÉBOURSOUK**, 30km south of Béja, is simply a point of transit on the way to nearby Dougga. While it's probably not worth visiting for its own sake, there is enough to repay a brief wander – it is a venerable and attractive market town in its own right, with a Thursday **souk** just off the main road to Le Kef and a Byzantine **fortress** dominated by a **marabout** clinging to the hill above. Like Dougga, just along the valley side, it affords balcony views south over the broad agricultural lands of the Tell.

The only places to **stay** in town are the *Maison des Jeunes* (℡78 465 095) and the rather staid but comfortable *Hôtel Thugga* (℡78 466 647, ℻78 466 721; ❹), below the town on the main road to Testour, with various Roman artefacts tastefully arranged outside. **Buses** stop by the fort in the centre of town, **louages** opposite.

Mustis

Twenty kilometres southwest of Téboursouk, the road to Le Kef runs past a well-preserved triumphal arch standing casually by the side of the road. This was the outskirts of Roman **Mustis** (free access), today a site of middling-to-limited interest whose central ruins sit right by the edge of the road, with an attractive **zaouia** a little further along.

Mustis was originally an unremarkable farming town much like modern **El Krib**, a kilometre further down the road. On the left of the entrance are remains of the **temples** of Ceres and Apollo. Then a paved Roman street leads uphill through an arch, with two massive pieces from an olive press leaning against a wall at the top of the street; the remains of the structure they came from are recognizable over to the left, beyond the **Temple of Pluto**. Just north of here are traces of a three-aisled Christian **church** ending in an apse.

From here you can already see the walls of the Byzantine **fort** that dominate the site – a sign that Mustis, like so many similar towns, ended its life as a frontier outpost. From inside, the fort offers a vivid sense of the precariousness of life at the turn of an era. Perhaps this is because it is smaller than the likes of Aïn Tounga (near Testour) or Haïdra (south of Le Kef), and there is barely room for it to contain everything the inhabitants would have needed, such as cisterns, living quarters and defensive walls.

Le Kef

The first sign of **LE KEF** (or El Kef), just 45km east of the Algerian border, is a gleaming ribbon of rock that twists round Jebel Dyr under the mountain's flat summit. Clinging just below the cliff at the southern end of the table top is the old town, while the newer quarters spill ever wider down the hillside below. It's a breathtaking setting – the more so in its isolation close to the Algerian border – and the kind of place where you feel involved just wandering round, contemplating the vistas below. But there's more than just views here: the town's long history has left a legacy of monuments, and it also has an interesting museum of popular arts and traditions.

Some history

Le Kef is still regarded as the unofficial capital of western Tunisia, but its predecessors enjoyed more prominence. The area was inhabited very early: Neolithic tools have been found nearby and the Numidians built megalithic tombs here. After the Second Punic War the area became the Carthaginan urban centre of **Sicca**. Unable to pay its defeated mercenary army, Carthage packed them off here, a move which rebounded when the mercenaries rose in revolt and waged a four-year struggle in which they were only suppressed with the aid of yet more mercenaries. This war – of a legendary brutality – inspired Gustave Flaubert's blood-and-guts novel *Salammbô*. The town was annexed in 46 BC by the Romans, who attached the title "Veneria", reflecting its special appeal. The Arabs, who took it in 688, called it Chakbanaria, but renamed it El Kef (The Rock) in the seventeenth century.

Since the Islamic conquest, Le Kef's strategic position between the Tunisian hinterland and the Algerian interior put it at the centre of so many inter-factional struggles that it never quite regained its former eminence, although Le Kef was made provisional capital of Tunisia during World War II. The town was bypassed when the rail line to Algeria was built in the last century, the line passing through Jendouba and Ghardimaou to the north. Algerians have, however, had occasion to be thankful for Le Kef, which was the main base and command centre of the FLN, the Algerian armed resistance, until 1962.

In the years since independence the town has felt itself a victim of the national bias towards the Sahel region (both Bourguiba and Ben Ali come from there) – feelings which erupted particularly strongly in the 1984 troubles. For a town of its size it is desperately short of work and recreational outlets and, even though the townspeople are proud to have one of the largest schools in Africa, the pupils it educates find little employment here.

Arrival, information and accommodation

The **bus** and **louage** station is in the new town, south of the old town, on the road to Dahmani. From the station, it's a twenty-minute walk uphill to the centre (1TD taxi), past the modern administrative buildings; turn right off the road at the top of the hill to reach **place de l'Indépendance** at the heart of town. **Avenue Bourguiba** follows the curve of the hill round to the east from here, a tremendous belvedere for the plains below. On the uphill side of the avenue is the **Medina**, with narrow cobbled streets winding up to the **Kasbah** at the cliff's edge.

There is no ONTT in town, but the Association de Sauvegarde de la Médina (ASM) runs a **Syndicat d'Initiative** on place de l'Indépendance (Mon–Sat 10am–noon & 3–6pm; ☎78 201 148). If it's closed, try the ASM headquarters nearby on rue de la Source, which holds temporary exhibitions, or the excellent Museum of Popular Arts and Traditions (see p.315), also a good source of information.

Le Kef has several **hotels**, mostly inexpensive or mid-range. The *Maison des Jeunes* (☎78 204 424), near the post office on rue Mohamed Gammoudi, doesn't have rooms at the time of writing but has vague plans to build some around 2006.

Hotels

Leklil 3km out of town on the Tunis road ☎78 204 747, ⒻS78 204 746, ⓌSwww.hotel-leklil. planet.tn. New hotel on a wooded hillside a little way out of town, with pleasant, comfortable rooms and good views but little atmosphere as yet. ❺

Medina 18 rue Farhat Hached ☎78 204 183. The rooms here aren't as promising as the lobby suggests but are usually clean, and there should be hot water. A decent bet. ❶

Les Pins av de l'Environnement, 2km out of town on the Tunis road ☎78 204 300, ⒻS78 202 411.

A very well priced modern place owned by the same folk as the *Venus*, with superlative views from most rooms, good facilities and a nice swimming pool. Recommended if you don't mind staying out of town. ❹

Ramzi rue Hedi Chaker ☎78 203 079. Relatively new hotel and pretty good, with spotlessly clean tiled rooms, some of which are en suite. ❹

Les Remparts rue des Remparts ☎78 202 100. Centrally located opposite the post office, this place is less personable than the *Venus* but has good en-suite rooms and is quite a bit cheaper. ❷

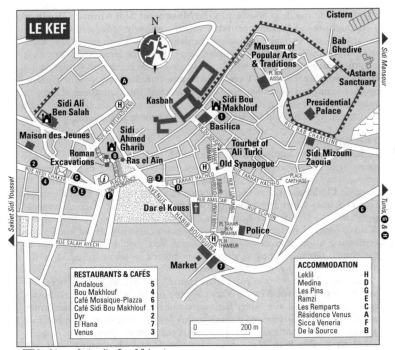

LE KEF

RESTAURANTS & CAFÉS
Andalous	5
Bou Makhlouf	4
Café Mosaique-Plazza	6
Café Sidi Bou Makhlouf	1
Dyr	2
El Hana	7
Venus	3

ACCOMMODATION
Leklil	H
Medina	D
Les Pins	G
Ramzi	E
Les Remparts	C
Résidence Venus	A
Sicca Veneria	F
De la Source	B

0   200 m

▼ Bus & Lougue Stations, New Town & Dahmani

Sicca Veneria pl de l'Indépendance ☏ 78 202 389. Central and in good condition, with a choice of bath or shower. ④

Hôtel de la Source rue de la Source ☏ & ⒻⓉ78 204 397. Something of a grotty travellers' hotel, popular with Algerians, too. All rooms except one are the usual budget affair, the better ones facing the street. The exception is the legendary four-bed *chambre de famille*, where a huge double bed reposes under an ornate vaulted stucco ceiling.

This may be the nearest you'll come to sleeping like an eighteenth-century Tunisian bey, give or take the odd grubby sheet. ②

Résidence Venus rue Mouldi Khamessi, off rue Ali Belhouane ☏ & Ⓕ 78 204 695. A friendly, laid-back pension five minutes' walk north of pl de l'Indépendance. The best bet in town, with neat, comfortable rooms, mostly en suite, and a satellite TV lounge downstairs. ④

The Town

Le Kef – or plain Kef as it's usually known – is a great place just to wander at random, catching glimpses, between houses or over the trees in the park, of the chequered plains below. **Place de l'Indépendance** forms the heart of the town, but is little more than a crowded traffic junction bordered on the south side by a park. Just north of here, the **spring** of Ras el Aïn rises in the open space just below the *Hôtel de la Source* on the square; Roman blocks which channelled the water can be made out. The spring has supplied all the cities on this site, receiving cult reverence through the centuries. Just next to the locked door of the spring proper is a small niche, a **shrine** to the Islamic saint Lalla Mna who was originally a Roman nymph, but was later renamed and Islamicized. She remains a living cult, and there are often recent offerings in the niche.

313

Uphill along rue de la Source, past the **Mosque of Sidi Ahmed Gharib**, is a confused area of **Roman remains** which are slowly being restored. Above the street is the entrance to a huge Roman **cistern** which stored the water that fed the more interesting complex across the street. Here at the far end is a **nympheum**, or fountain, which would have been lined with statues, and a **baths complex**. The baths were subsequently converted into a church whose geometric mosaics are visible; one wall is lined with the tombstones of Roman worthies. Before emerging onto rue Ali Belhouane, rue de la Source runs through an attractive old **vaulted passage** containing food shops.

The Medina

Le Kef's main attraction is its **Medina**, which has managed to retain not just monuments from successive periods in its history, but also a neighbourhood feeling, away from the bustle of the new town. Closest of the monuments to place de l'Indépendance is the well-preserved (if rather dull) fourth-century **Dar el Kouss Church** – take the first right off rue Farhat Hached immediately after it leaves avenue Bourguiba, and the church is on the first corner. A small room in its far right-hand corner has a curiously carved lintel stone combining a Greek cross and a palm frond. You should find the *gardien* in the church during normal working hours; otherwise ask at the ASM or the Museum of Popular Arts and Traditions.

From here you can rejoin rue Farhat Hached, the Medina's main street, and turn right to meet rue Marakit Karama going uphill and rue Bahri Barbouch coming down it. At rue Bahri Barbouch you leap forward to Turkish times, when the street was reserved for the town's Jewish community. The building on the northeast corner of this junction is the former **synagogue**, recently – and remarkably, here in the distant interior of an Arab country – restored. The synagogue's walls are now lined with items evoking the not-so-distant world of Tunisia's Jewish community, such as Hebrew tablets, photos of local life in the 1950s and a wedding invitation from 1960. A rota of *gardiens* should keep the synagogue open at all times – if not, ask at the ASM office. Incidentally Le Kef's last Jewish citizen died peacefully in 1995.

Le Kef was one of three *ghribas* in the eastern Maghreb – the other two being in Annaba, Algeria (presumably disappeared) and Jerba (see p.440). The town had a sizeable Jewish community, though virtually all left for Tunis, France or Israel in the years following World War II and especially during independence. Their traditional specialization in **jewellery** lives on in the shops which line rue Bahri Barbouch, where you will also find spectacular wedding costumes and one small jewellery shop with a fine old painted wooden shade.

Le Kef has also played its part in recent Tunisian history. The father of Husayn Bin Ali, the Husaynid dynasty's founder, is entombed just up the hill; you pass his somewhat derelict **Tourbet of Ali Turki** at the top of rue Marakit Karama and rue du Soudan. Ali Turki was born in Crete but came to Tunisia and enrolled in the army during the reign of Mourad Bey. While serving in Le Kef he married two local Tunisian women, each of whom gave birth to a son: one of them was Husayn Bin Ali (ruled 1705–35; see p.500); the other was the father of Ali Pacha, Husayn's successor (ruled 1735–56).

Place Bou Makhlouf

If you continue up rue du Soudan you'll come to **place Bou Makhlouf**, an open space below the Kasbah that lay at the heart of the souks of the old town. Here was the town's Great Mosque, the monumental building now known as the **Basilica**, whose origins are uncertain but which was used for hundreds of years for Muslim worship. The building now serves as a **museum** of local antiquities (daily 8–11am & 3–6pm; free), although it is more interesting for its own sake. Built either in late Roman or Byzantine times, it takes the form of a spacious courtyard (look for columns of unusual green stone) leading into a cruciform room ending in an apse. Both the apse and the arms of the cross are lined with niches (23 in all), with a carved lintel running above them.

The diminutive **Mosque of Sidi Bou Makhlouf** at the end of place Bou Makhlouf, along with the complex of streets around it, is one of the most captivating spots in Tunisia. The mosque – named after the patron saint of Le Kef, who originally came from Fez – is a small masterpiece, the bare whitewashed courtyard leading into a domed prayer hall resting on antique columns and lined with white stucco work. On the outside, its dome has an unusual ribbed appearance, similar to the domes of Tunis's Sidi Mehrez (see p.101). At the beginning of the nineteenth century this complex became home to Le Kef's branch of the Aissaouia Sufi brotherhood, renowned for some of the more outlandish Sufi rituals. On one side of the cobbled street leading up to the mosque is a blue door into a former *fondouk*, which has a Roman tombstone for a tap in its central water trough. Opposite it is the pleasant *Café Sidi Bou Makhlouf* (daily 7.30am–10pm, open late in summer), with some chairs in the square. For a magical experience, take your drink up to the Kasbah ramparts above. It's the perfect place to sit and watch the changing patterns of light over the plains and is especially enchanting under a full moon.

The Kasbah and around

The views from the **Kasbah** (daily: summer 7am–7pm; winter 8am–5pm; free, though the *gardien* will expect a tip) attest to the prime military importance of Le Kef. The smaller and lower of the **forts** here is a legacy of the border struggles under the beys: Hammouda Bey added it in 1813 to house a guard of ultra-faithful troops, because of Algerian designs on the town. Excavations here during the current refurbishment uncovered the remains of a number of Turkish clay pipes made in Smyrna (now Izmir) on Turkey's Aegean coast. The older, larger fort dates back to 1601 and was converted during the French occupation into a prison for Tunisian nationalists. Now abandoned by the military, the Kasbah has been renovated to house a cultural centre in the large fort, where the region's cultural archives – currently in the ASM headquarters – may one day be kept. Currently the only cultural activities inside the fort are during the annual two-week **Festival de Sidi Bou Makhlouf** held from mid-July, when there are theatrical and musical performances.

Following rue el Kasbah round above the Basilica and rue Sidi Bou Makhlouf to place Ben Aissa, you'll find the worthy **Museum of Popular Arts and Traditions** (Tues–Sun: April to mid-Sept 9am–1pm & 4–7pm; mid-Sept to March 9.30am–4.30pm; 1.1TD, camera 1TD), housed in the restored Zaouia of Sidi Ali Ben Aissa. Its exhibits beautifully evoke the way of life of the nomads in particular, whose tents can still be seen on the surrounding plain. Put up in 1784, the building that houses the museum was originally the headquarters of a Sufi brotherhood called the **Rahmania**.

The old town walls run almost continuously from the Kasbah around to the east, finally encircling a **presidential palace**. This is something of a sore point in the town, as it occupies a prime site but is hardly ever used; a swimming pool beckons invitingly in its grounds, while the municipal pool in the park has never been opened. Just below the palace walls is the nineteenth-century **Zaouia of Sidi Mizouni**, which is the local headquarters of the Qadriya, probably the oldest of the Sufi brotherhoods.

Bab Ghedive and beyond

Just above the palace, **Bab Ghedive** (Gate of Treachery) gives entrance to the town and earned its name in 1881 when the governor and town notables, having received no orders to fight, opened the gate to the French army on its "temporary mission" – even though the townspeople were prepared for a long siege. They surrendered the most important frontier defences without a shot being fired. Through the gate, the transition from town to country is startlingly abrupt. Just ahead, an iron ladder leads down into a vast **Roman cistern** that's twelve gloomy chambers in length and one of the coolest places in Kef – but an alcoholics' den at night.

Over to the right from here, across the road, are more fragmentary remains, the first set of which may be the ancient **Sanctuary of Astarte** – so notorious for its erotic mysteries. Roman moralists professed shock that young Carthaginian girls of noble birth were forced to sacrifice their virginity here to the goddess, ensuring the fertility of the land on which Sicca depended, but it was the Romans who gave the town the suffix "Veneria". Sex still enjoyed a high profile here in Christian times; the second area of remains, below the disused **Christian cemetery**, may have been the **Ksar el Ghoula Basilica**, which reputedly possessed a magic mirror – men who suspected their wives of infidelity could look at the glass and find the face of their rival. Beyond it, a **Jewish cemetery** stretches all the way back to the wall, the part nearest to it being much older than the rest of the Jewish and Christian cemeteries.

Eating and drinking

Food is generally good and cheap in Le Kef with numerous perfectly decent *gargotes* on and around avenue Bourguiba. Best of the cheap **restaurants** are the *Andalous* (daily 9am–2am), diagonally opposite the post office on rue Hedi Chaker, which does great couscous; the *Bou Makhlouf* (daily 5am–10pm), a little further down the street; and the *El Hana* (Mon–Sat 7am–8pm, Sun 7am–1pm) in avenue Bourguiba above the market. All of these places will fill you up with standard tasty fare including soups, couscous, chicken and steaks for 3–5TD. For a cheap pizza with a view but lots of cigarette smoke, try the *Café Mosaique-Plazza* (daily 6am–9.30pm, later in summer), a few hundred metres east of the *El Hana* on the road to Tunis.

For a smarter, more expensive meal, try the *Hôtel Sicca Veneria*'s restaurant (daily noon–3pm & 6pm–2am). Alternatively, if you've never had supper at a petrol station, the *Restaurant Dyr* (daily noon–10pm), above Esso's pumps in rue Hedi Chaker, 50m past the post office, serves a surprisingly good meal for 10–15TD. A final, more upmarket alternative is the *Restaurant Venus*, just off avenue Bourguiba on rue Farhat Hached (daily noon–3pm & 6–10pm; closed Fri eve), which belongs to the *Résidence Venus*.

If you want to **drink** in the evening, try the cheap, unnamed bar-restaurant up behind the post office at 4 rue Salya. The *Sicca*'s bar is only slightly more refined.

Listings

Banks There are several banks around town, especially at the top of rue Salah Ayech and rue Ali Belhouane; others can be found in av Bourguiba above the market, and opposite the bus station on the hill down into the new town. They run a weekend rota, so there should be at least one open in the mornings. The post office changes money and has a Visa ATM outside.

Cinemas Ciné Pathe, av Bourguiba (no sign).

Consulates The Algerian consulate is at 3 rue Hedi Chaker. For visas, they will probably say to apply in Tunis.

Festivals The annual two-week Festival de Sidi Bou Makhlouf is held from mid-July, during which time theatre and other performances are held in the Kasbah. The first day sees a procession by the Aissouia Sufi brotherhood through the streets. Another good date to be in town is Ramadan 27, which also sees religious parades and music.
Hammams The best is on rue Ali Belhouane – follow rue de la Source to its end, through the tunnel and turn right. Others are at pl Habib Thameur, at the bottom of rue Habib Karma, and at 33 rue Farhat Hached.
Hospital On the Sakiet Sidi Youssef road (☎ 78 420 900).

Internet There is a Publinet on place de l'Indépendence (daily 8.30am–2am; 1.5TD/hr).
Police Just off pl Tahar Ben Brahim.
Post office rue Hedi Chaker (city hours).
Supermarket Monoprix is 100m left off the Dahmani road down into the new town, just above the bus station.
Swimming There is a good pool at *Hôtel les Pins*, free to guests at the *Résidence Venus* and open to other non-residents for a small fee.
Telephones Numerous taxiphone offices are dotted around the centre of town.

North and west of Le Kef

If the view across the plains around Le Kef tempts you, there are several good hiking possibilities and particularly rewarding excursions north and west of town. One of the best short walks from Le Kef is to **SIDI MANSOUR**, a small village around 4km from town. Leave Le Kef by Bab Ghedive and scramble up the rocks below the TV mast; from here a rough path leads north through a small eucalyptus plantation and onto the top of the plateau, opening out on an immense view over the broken forests along the Algerian border and the glint of the lake behind the Mellegue Dam. The village, a small farming community, is soon reached. Just to the west, beyond a deep river canyon, are wide caves gouged in the rock – a popular picnic spot inhabited in prehistoric times. Not far north of the village is the other end of the plateau; or you can climb up to the east, then bend down and around and come back into Le Kef by the palace.

The artificial **Lake Mellegue** that gleams in the distance from Sidi Mansour was created by damming the River Mellegue. From Le Kef, buses head in this direction to the attractive village of **Nebeur**, 17km northeast below the northern tip of the mountain of **Jebel Dyr**, and then 5km on to **Barrage Mellegue**, a small cluster of houses on the dam itself. The water crashing out at the bottom has the colour and consistency of liquid chocolate. The reason for coming to the dam, though, is to **hike** back to Le Kef through open country – a five-hour walk, but a rewarding one. There's no danger of getting lost as Jebel Dyr is always in sight and, once you get to the mountain, Le Kef is only 5km further on. If you aim for the top of Jebel Dyr, then head round its western face below the cliff edge, you should hit a winding track that runs all the way to Sidi Mansour. It climbs through clumps of pines, foothills of the mountain proper, to emerge onto broader slopes which sweep up like waves against the rock. The scenery is tremendous, and the hike gives an insight into the pace of life in this part of Tunisia, and an appreciation for the value of **water**. When you set out on the walk, take as much water as you can carry; if you need a refill, you'll be dependent on the infrequent springs that the isolated local farmhouses rely on for their daily needs. On reaching these, you'll be surrounded by a group of children who have walked several kilometres with donkeys and cans to fetch the day's supply.

West of Le Kef

At the western end of Lake Mellegue, the restored Roman spa of **HAMMAM MELLEGUE** is at the end of a twelve-kilometre piste off the road to Sakiet Sidi Youssef. The closest you'll get to the spa on a Sakiet bus is the piste junction, about 10km west of Le Kef; alternatively, ask around for a lift at the market in Le Kef. The hot spring water provides a communal bath (women in the morning, men in the afternoon), which is very popular with people from the surrounding villages.

Thirty-five kilometres west of Le Kef, **SAKIET SIDI YOUSSEF** is the last village before the Algerian frontier. The border post here is sometimes open, and accessible from Le Kef by louage, but you should check this before setting out – the main crossing is 30km north at Ghardimaou (see p.209). Otherwise there's little reason to visit Sakiet, although it does have a historical notoriety. It was here, in the midst of the Algerian War in 1958, that the French bombed the civilian population. The incident was denounced as a "new Guernica" and caused a rapid decline in relations between France and newly independent Tunisia. One outcome was the Tunisian attempt to eject the French navy from their base at Bizerte (see p.172).

Between Le Kef and Kasserine

The area south of Le Kef – before the fertile plains climb up onto bleaker steppes around Kasserine – is right off the tourist routes, yet is a quietly rewarding region to explore. The scenery, always impressive, becomes eerily compelling around the craggy mountain of **Jugurtha's Table**, and there are two virtually untouched Roman sites at **Medeina** and, a little further afield, at **Haïdra** (see p.320). Each of these – particularly Haïdra – has an aloof grandeur in its remoteness, inspiring an excitement quite absent from the more domesticated major sites.

Tajerouine and Jugurtha's Table

TAJEROUINE, 25km from Le Kef, is the first town of any size on the main road south, and is quite a transport centre. The **bus station** is in the middle of town on the main road, with plenty of buses to Le Kef. **Louages** stop nearby, down a side road next to the mosque. Tajerouine has a Monday **souk**, and there are **banks** and a Magasin Général **supermarket** opposite the bus station, but the town has no hotel and little character: it's hardly more than an outgrown roadstead. Beyond the town, however, you emerge onto the plains – vast open spaces with isolated **mountains** that jut out like islands in a calm sea. There is a good deal of mining on the plain, with major producers of iron and phosphates dotted about.

To reap the best rewards of the scenery around here, head west to **Kalaat Es Senam**, just 6km from the Algerian border. This small village sits at the foot of the mountain known as **Jugurtha's Table**, a flat-topped peak like Jebel Dyr to the north but more sharply defined, with its tilting plateau standing out for kilometres around. Louages go to Kalaat es Senam either direct from Le Kef or with a change at Tajerouine. Stock up with water while you can, because it's a good two hours' walk from the village to some steps in the middle of the mountain's north side, though the steps themselves make for an easy ascent.

The name "Jugurtha's Table" refers to the tradition that it was the stronghold of the Numidian king **Jugurtha** in his struggles against the Romans during the second-century BC. This role is echoed in more recent times by the name Kalaat es Senam – "Fort of Senam", after a local bandit who made similar use of the mountain against the armies of the beys. This dramatic past seems very close as you climb the steps to the summit, which are hacked into the rock and lead to a Byzantine gateway. The lunar-like surface is littered with remains, which include troglodyte **caves** and a spooky **marabout**. Romance apart, the mountain also provides a magnificent view and, if you have camping gear, it's an extraordinarily remote place to spend the night.

Medeina

MEDEINA, Roman Althiburos (free access), isn't the easiest site in Tunisia to reach. You have to get the bus from Le Kef to **Dahmani** (also known as Ebba Ksour), a small tree-shaded farming town, and then walk or hitch 6km down the Jerissa road; the turning to Medeina is on the left, and the site is about a four-kilometre walk away.

Despite its present remoteness, Medeina once stood on the main Roman road from Carthage to Tebessa. Today its ruins are attractive enough, rambling above a green riverbed, though hardly extensive. The first glimpse is of a third-century AD **Triumphal Arch**, almost hidden in a field to the left. Beyond, towards the centre of the site, the most distinctive building is the **Capitol**, just above the riverbed, to one side of the paved **Forum**, opposite the remains of a **temple**. A street runs southeast through the Forum; following it you'll find a well-preserved **fountain** on a street corner. Further in this direction are the remains of a **theatre**.

Back in the Forum, alongside the temple opposite the Capitol is the **House of Sixteen Bases**, whose name refers to the unusual reliefs on the bases of its inner portico. Some way north of here, across a stream bed, is the **Building of Aesclepia**. No one knows its precise function, but having begun life as a private house it seems to have become the home of some sort of cult connected with the healing god Aesculapius. This explains the extraordinary number of baths found here, and the quality of the mosaics (now removed to the Bardo Museum in Tunis), most of them third- or fourth-century AD.

Kalaat Khasbah and Haïdra Town

Midway between El Kef and Kasserine, **KALAAT KHASBAH** (also known as Kalaat Jerda) is an old Italian mining town retaining echoes of its colonial influence, with tiled houses, profuse greenery and abandoned mining machinery, including an enormous chimney stack. But the real reason for coming here is to catch a lift to the Roman site of **Haïdra**, 18km away.

Kalaat Khasbah is the terminus for passenger **rail** services, with one train a day from Tunis via Le Sers, Gaafour and El Fahs. There are onward **buses** and **louages**

Travelling to Algeria

At the time of writing, it was still extremely dangerous to travel to Algeria; you should also think carefully before going off the beaten track anywhere near the border. Be aware that Tunisian sensitivities about people travelling near the Algerian border have been quite high in the past – with increased passport checks and the like – although this was not the case at the time of writing. See p.209 for more details.

to Thala, Kasserine and Le Kef, but just about no public transport to Haïdra. **Hitching** to Haïdra from Kalaat Khasbah is quite easy, however – there's only one road, so virtually everything that passes will stop. On your way down this road, look out to the north for glimpses of Jugurtha's Table (see p.318), ducking above and below the skyline – a bit like the prow of a ship. The modern settlement of **HAÏDRA TOWN** has even more of a dead-end border feel than Ghardimaou, enlivened only by a grotesque train station. With its extraordinary combination of Classical order and 1930s Art Deco, this would look weird in the middle of a big European city, let alone miles from anywhere on a North African frontier. The **border post** here is usually open, but little used.

Haïdra

The Roman site of **HAÏDRA** (free entry), 18km southwest of Kalaat Khasbah, is remotely positioned by the Algerian frontier and only minimally excavated, meaning that the surviving monuments are exceptionally well preserved. Coming upon them, you feel something of the awe early travellers must have experienced when confronted with remains of a mysterious and magnificent past.

Ancient Haïdra, Roman **Ammaedara**, was in its way a border post like the modern village of the same name, founded as a base for the Third Augustan Legion, whose job was to protect Rome's new province from hostile incursions. When the legion was moved further west, the camp became an important town, but after the Islamic conquest, it reverted to its border role.

The ruins sprawl beside the road just to the east of the modern settlement. If you've managed to get a ride in from Kalaat Khasbah, ask to be dropped off outside the Byzantine fort at the centre of the ancient remains, opposite the former **French customs post**, where you will find Haïdra's friendly *gardien* Saadi Adel. The customs post, identifiable by a hemispherical arch and dated 1886, is being converted into a museum, which should open sometime in 2005.

The site

East of the customs post are the remains of Haïdra's "**building with troughs**" (see also p.322). A **Vandal Chapel** behind it is so called because of the crude inscriptions on its paving stones dating it to the reigns of the kings Thrasamund (510 AD) and Ildirix (526 AD), who sound as though they come from an Asterix and Obelix storyline.

Man bites lion

The area around Haïdra was notorious among early European travellers for the lawlessness of its inhabitants. Although James Bruce (see p.561), passing this way in 1765, managed to avoid mortal danger, he did have a curious gastronomic experience. A recent predecessor, one Dr Shaw, had claimed that the inhabitants of Haïdra ate lions, but was promptly accused of "traveller's licence" by the learned doctors of Oxford University, who took it as "a subversion of the natural order of things, that a man should eat a lion, when it has long passed as almost the peculiar province of the lion to eat man". Ever the vigorous empiricist, Bruce was not much impressed by expert opinion, and was glad to be able to report that he had "eaten the flesh of three lions – that is part of three lions – in the tents of the Welled Sidi Boogannim". He found the texture like old horseflesh, palatable except for a strong smell of musk. As for the locals, he sniffed, "a brutish and ignorant folk, they will, I fear, notwithstanding the disbelief of the University of Oxford, continue to eat lions as long as they exist".

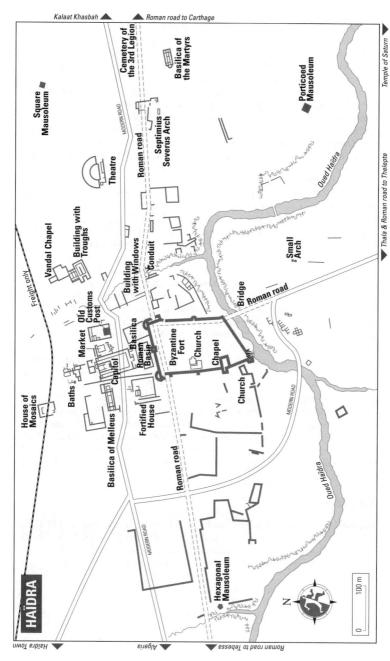

HAÏDRA

Kalaat Khasbah ▲   ▲ Roman road to Carthage

Temple of Saturn ►

Cemetery of the 3rd Legion

Basilica of the Martyrs

Square Mausoleum

Porticoed Mausoleum

Theatre

Septimius Severus Arch

Roman road

Vandal Chapel

Building with Troughs

Building with Windows

Conduit

MODERN ROAD

Oued Haïdra

Freight only

Old Customs Post

Small Arch

Market

Basilica

Thala & Roman road to Thelepte ►

House of Mosaics

Baths

Capitol

Roman Basin

Byzantine Fort

Church

Chapel

Bridge

Roman road

Basilica of Melleus

Fortified House

Church

MODERN ROAD

Roman road

MODERN ROAD

Oued Haïdra

Hexagonal Mausoleum

N

0   100 m

◄ Haïdra Town

◄ Algeria

◄ Tébessa   Roman road to Tébessa

321

5

On the west side of the customs post, a **market** can just about be made out as a square depression, followed by the **Capitol** temple with only its podium recognizable, and then the more interesting **Basilica of Melleus**, featuring two rows of columns, some in Chemtou marble, clearly defining the nave. Entrance to the church was through three doors at the eastern end, which connected with a courtyard. An apsidal structure at the western end was the *presbyterium*, reserved for clergy. Spidery inscriptions from the sixth and seventh centuries, still visible on the paving stones, suggest something of Haïdra's turbulent history. They include the gravestones of two bishops buried here – Victorinus, a Vandal Arian Christian, and Melleus, a Byzantine Catholic.

Across the road from the basilica lies a **fortified house**, another structure containing some troughs. A little to the east of this are the five empty windows of the "**building with windows**", whose function is not known. Behind that looms the mother of all Byzantine **fortresses** in Tunisia, 200m long by 100m wide, with stretches of wall and towers still standing 10m high. Stretching down to the river valley at the bottom of the hill, the fortress was built to guard an important frontier crossroads when the Byzantines retook Tunisia from the Vandals in 533 AD; the north wall was rebuilt much later under the Turks. Roads from Carthage and Tebessa entered through fortified towers at the top of the fortress, while the road from Thelepte (see p.333) crossed a Roman **bridge** – whose remains can still be seen in the riverbed – then entered through the southeastern tower. The interior presents a jumble of unexcavated remains except for the evocative **chapel**, built against the southwest wall, with its apse and green columns, and a newly excavated **church** and temple just up the slope. If smaller Byzantine fortresses such as Mustis (see p.311) reek of panic on the frontier, this one conveys instead the determination, however doomed, of a Byzantine empire based thousands of kilometres away to defend what it saw as its rightful inheritance.

The site's eastern outskirts contain two well-preserved square **mausoleums**, the golden-coloured southern one with its four-columned second storey standing in splendid isolation above the river. Between them, next to the modern road, stands the **triumphal arch** of Septimius Severus (195 AD). Like the arch at Maktar and the Capitol at Dougga, this owes its crisp preservation to fortifications that the Byzantines built around it; here, the Byzantine work has been only partially dismantled, and the arch emerging from its casing looks for all the world like a piece of sculpture coming out of a plaster cast. West of the site, again just above the river, stands another well-preserved **mausoleum** – this time hexagonal.

Thala

The only village of any size between Kalaat Khasbah and Kasserine is **THALA**, 10km south of Kalaat, on the steep slope dividing the plains of Le Kef from the more forbidding steppes around Kasserine. At an altitude of 1017m, it is a refreshing place in summer but a cold one in midwinter. The village's only claim to fame is a notorious incident in 1906, when a marabout, **Amor Ben Othman**, inspired the local Fraichich tribes to take up arms against the colonists who had stolen their lands. In the ensuing riot sixteen men, women and children died, causing an outcry across North Africa. Amor Ben Othman was brought to trial and the press clamoured for his execution. Only Myriam Harry, a reporter on *Le Temps*, cared to look behind the scenes and describe the poverty and deprivation suffered by the Fraichich tribe under colonial rule. "Oh little Joan of Arc of this desert," she wrote, "what pity you inspire in me." Her sympathy could not help the marabout and his accomplices: all were hanged with great ceremony as a warning to others.

There are a few minor **excavations** on the main street in Thala, and a **marble factory** in the lower outskirts of the village, but unless you arrive on a Friday (**market** day) there is little reason to linger. The **bus station** is 200m uphill from the excavations; **louages** leave from next to the excavations. Should you want to **stay**, there is the cheap and popular *Hôtel Bouthelja* (☎77 480 047; ❷), a little way uphill from the excavations off the main street to the right, but it is basic and for males only. The main street has a few cheap **restaurants**, a **bank** and a couple of **petrol stations**.

Maktar and the GP12

At nearly 1000m in altitude, **MAKTAR** (or Makthar) dominates the surrounding country and would be worth passing through for the scenery and fresh mountain air alone. As it is, the town is also blessed with extensive remains of a much earlier, mainly Roman settlement, and it has a relaxed feel that can come as a welcome relief. The only pretence to bustle is **market** day on Monday.

The three main approaches to Maktar all take in some beautiful countryside. The **GP4** route from El Fahs is described on p.296, while the journey southeast on the **GP12** from Maktar towards Kairouan is covered on p.244. In the other direction, the GP12 winds 60km from Le Kef to Maktar, passing through some preliminary foothills to **Le Sers**, a French railway town sitting in the middle of a vast natural bowl that contains some of the most fertile land in the country. Passing through **Le Vieux Sers**, a few kilometres further south, you come to a track leading to the unexcavated but quite substantial remains of Roman Assuras at **Zannfour** (6km) and a minor road leading to **Elles** (9km), with megalithic tombs and a meagre Roman settlement that produced the Bardo's bizarre fourth-century mosaic of a stressed Venus being crowned by two female centaurs. The GP12 goes on to climb up the southern side of the bowl, and on neighbouring hilltops beyond the rim are the ancient and modern towns of Maktar, separated by a modern road junction at a Roman triumphal arch.

Ancient Maktar

The **site** of ancient Maktar (daily: April to mid-Sept 8am–7pm; mid-Sept to March 8.30am–5.30pm; 2.1TD, camera 1TD) was only rediscovered in the nineteenth century by the French officer, Captain Bordier, who founded the modern town. Dominating the surrounding country, ancient Maktar was founded in the second century BC by a Numidian king trying to protect his domain from Berber incursions. Even after it was Romanized in the second century AD, Maktar kept a strong local tone, and the city wasn't abandoned until the Hilalian invasion of the eleventh century. Today the ruins are of a similar extent to those at Sbeïtla (see p.327), though Maktar's mountaintop setting is much more spectacular.

The entrance to the site is next to the **museum**, full of objects (tombstones in particular) that illustrate the hybrid nature of North Africa's rural Roman culture. Displays of neo-Punic stelae, many dedicated to Baal Hammon, show the enduring local influence over the early colonizers. Although Roman ele-

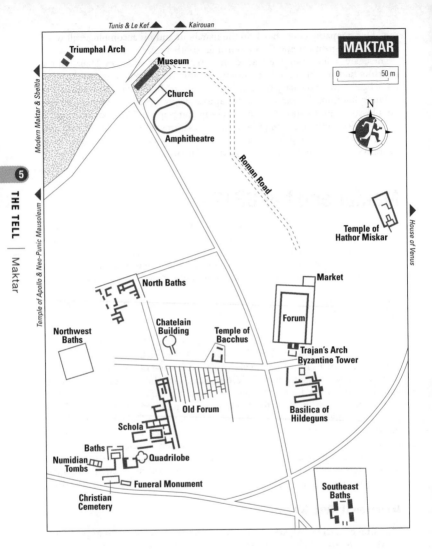

MAKTAR

Tunis & Le Kef ▲   ▲ Kairouan

Triumphal Arch

Museum

Church

Amphitheatre

Roman Road

0   50 m

N

Temple of Hathor Miskar

North Baths

Market

Chatelain Building

Temple of Bacchus

Forum

Northwest Baths

Trajan's Arch
Byzantine Tower

Old Forum

Basilica of Hildeguns

Schola

Baths

Numidian Tombs

Quadrilobe

Funeral Monument

Christian Cemetery

Southeast Baths

ments gradually appear on the stones (note the family emphasis, increasing depth and architectural frames), the basic sculptural style is a primitive naivety that makes the figures look like rag dolls.

Outside the museum garden, beyond a church built on top of an earlier temple, is a small **amphitheatre** which has been substantially restored. From the middle of the arena, surrounded by gates where you can still see the slots for doors, it has the feel of a Spanish bullring.

The Forum and around

Following the track up the slope to the level hilltop brings you to a scant **Forum**, built at the same time as the **Triumphal Arch** on its south side, dedicated in 116 AD to the Emperor Trajan, whose accomplishments as "Conqueror of the Germans, Armenians and Parthians" sound very impressive. As at Dougga and Haïdra, this arch was fortified by the Byzantines and used again at the turn of the last century by Captain Bordier, who installed himself in the Southeast Baths.

At the northeast corner of the Forum, a **marketplace** can be distinguished, surrounded by stalls and with an altar dedicated to Mercury. A short walk further in this direction takes you to the remains of the **Temple of Hathor Miskar**, a local divinity, and the large **House of Venus**. The Hathor Miskar temple is more interesting for the material it contained, revealing that local cults survived well into the Roman era.

Back at the Forum, a solitary tree just south of Trajan's Arch stands over two rows of double columns belonging to the fifth-century Vandal **Basilica of Hildeguns**. Its baptistry, hidden behind the apse at its eastern end, is reminiscent of the one in Sbeïtla's Basilica of St Vitalis, though less lavishly decorated. After the Byzantines ejected the Vandals, they buried some of their dead in the church. From here it's a short walk south to the unmissable **Southeast Baths**. Thanks again to Byzantine fortifications, whose remnants can be made out, these are some of the most impressively preserved Roman baths in Tunisia, with massive walls and pillars and some lovely geometric mosaic floors still in place.

The west edge of the site

A smooth paved road leads west from the Forum past a **Temple of Bacchus** on the right (look for the cave uncovered in its cellar) and an irregular paved open space on the left. This is another **Forum**, an older African one that predates the rigid Roman lines of the model next to the Triumphal Arch. The original wasn't any less functional than the new Forum; it's just that custom demanded one in the Roman style.

The **Châtelain Building** at the road junction is named after its excavator but is little understood, while the **North Baths** date from Byzantine times. The **Northwest Baths**, dating from the second century AD, were converted into a church in the fifth or sixth century. Roman blocks were cut down (look for an interrupted inscription) to obtain the square posts that define the nave and two aisles.

A path leads southeast from here to the prettily ruined **Schola**, its columns and trees reminiscent of Olympia in Greece. This was basically a clubhouse for a young men's association, where well-born youths of the town would meet both socially and as a sort of police force. Their complex here consisted of the main building, later confused by being turned into a well-defined church with apse and columns and, just to the south, the so-called **quadrilobe**, whose windows with troughs make it one of the mysterious "buildings with troughs" (see also p.322). Here the troughs were perhaps used for the collection of contributions by the association's members.

It was this sort of voluntary association, with its implicit faith in the Roman order, that formed the backbone of the empire. If it had been able to offer the rural Berbers what it offered the urban citizens, it might have lasted longer. A remarkable gravestone found at Maktar, belonging to the so-called "Maktar Reaper", records a rare case of upward mobility. The inscription, thought to date from the second half of the third century AD, tells the "local boy made good" story with relish – how the deceased had worked his way up the social scale by the sweat of his honest brow. You too, it concludes encouragingly, can be a success: "Learn, mortals, to lead a blameless life. Those who have lived honourable lives have earned an honourable death". Behind the Schola, some jumbled remains belong to a **cemetery** that was in use for six hundred years. Its earliest tombs were megalithic chambers active before the arrival of the Romans, and still used in the first century AD.

Monuments outside the site

Five hundred metres west of this cemetery, outside the site wall, beyond a **Muslim cemetery** that surrounds a white-domed **koubba**, stands an Oriental-looking neo-Punic **mausoleum** similar to the one at Dougga. Getting over the site wall is a bit of a scramble – you may prefer to go back to the site entrance and walk up the road. If you use the latter route, don't miss the **herm** (entry stone with phallus) which stands outside the excavation headquarters. The mausoleum's pyramidal roof and angular design are distinctly un-Roman, though the monument may in fact have been built during the imperial epoch. Another 500m northwest of here is an African-style **Temple of Apollo**. A second **triumphal arch**, on the modern road junction below the museum, is impossible to miss, unlike the square **Mausoleum of the Julii**, across the road from the museum, and, even easier to miss, a tumbledown **dolmen tomb** in the middle of the modern town.

Modern Maktar

Modern Maktar, across a ravine from the ancient town, is quite a tempting place to stay. At nearly 1000m in altitude, the air is fresh, the scenery tremendous, and the relaxed feel to the town can come as a welcome relief. The only pretence to bustle is **market** day on Monday. **Buses** to and from Le Kef and Kairouan leave from the road at the bottom of the town overlooking the ravine, round the corner from the triumphal arch, as do **louages** for Kairouan and Sousse. Buses for El Fahs, Kasserine and Tunis, and louages for El Fahs, Siliana and Tunis, all leave from the main street, which runs parallel one block up the hill – turn left out of the *Hôtel Mactaris*, then left again and at the top you'll see the departure point.

Accommodation is available at the basic but adequate *Hôtel Mactaris* (☎78 826 465; ❶), near the bus and louage stop at the bottom end of town. The town's main **bar** and **restaurant** share the ground floor of the hotel.

Southeast of Maktar

The most exciting route south from Maktar is the GP12 road to Kairouan, which runs through some of the most rugged scenery in the country. After about 10km you enter the vast **Forest of Kesra**, a blanket of bright-green Aleppo pine named after **LA KESRA**, a Berber village clinging almost invisibly to a mountain face at an altitude of 1078m.

Side roads connect the village to the main route from both east and west, the western one slightly shorter at about 3km – the western junction, in modern Kesra, is also where you're more likely to find a lift. If you catch it open, the *Hôtel des Chasseurs*, 1km west of the junction on the main road, offers spectacular **views** up to the village and down onto the plain; the hotel part has been closed for several years but the ground-floor bar is still up and running. Although steep, the climb up to La Kesra offers a foretaste of the *ksour* in the south, as well as a reminder of similar villages further north, such as Chaouach (p.197) and Jeradou (p.296). The houses merge with the slope, leaving no doubts about the defensive necessity – the warding off of threats from open plains to the south – which saw settlements like these built; Maktar shared the same vulnerability. Nowadays the only defence is a pair of **cemeteries** at either end of the village, each surrounding a white-domed tomb of a saint.

Back below, at a village called **El Garia**, the main road soon punches through the last ridge of hills, a final reminder of the Tell before you descend onto the plain of the Sahel. If you're going through to Kairouan, you face another 90km of barren emptiness, broken by only the barest of diversions. Just east of the roadside town of **HAFFOUZ**, 35km east of La Kesra, is an old and neglected French **war cemetery** for Muslim soldiers. Twenty kilometres further, as the road crosses Oued Chnihira, look out to the north of the road for remains of the **aqueduct** which carried water from the mountains to Kairouan's Aghlabid pools (see p.251).

Ouesslatia

About 15km beyond the tunnel at El Garia, a turning goes left to **OUESS-LATIA**, another 10km away. This road offers an alternative route into the exciting El Fahs–Maktar–Kairouan triangle (the other being off the GP4; see p.301). Another drab modern farming settlement of little interest for its own sake, Ouesslatia is the principal settlement inside the triangle, lying in the broad valley between Jebel Ousselat to the southeast and Jebel Serj to the northwest, and just off the GP12 Maktar–Kairouan road. Another route to it is the road southeast from Siliana, which curls round the flank of **Jebel Serj**, at 1357m not much lower than Tunisia's highest mountain, Jebel Chambi outside Kasserine. About 10km before Ouesslatia, as the road descends to leave the mountain massif behind, the remains of Roman **Aggar** tumble down the slopes to the north of the road; just prior to this, look out for the massive pillars of a Roman **bridge** across a riverbed, next to a rickety-looking modern equivalent.

In the eighteenth century, and for hundreds of years before, these mountains were the home of the eponymous Ousselatia, a tribe that, like the Khroumir Berbers of the Khroumirie Mountains (see p.195), remained outside the control of central government in Tunis. In the dynastic quarrel of the 1730s the Ousselatia made the mistake of backing Husayn Bin Ali, and on his death in 1740 Jebel Ousselat was taken by his rival, Ali Pacha. According to the chronicler Mohammed Seghir Ben Youssef, Ali Pacha had all the olive trees cut down and exiled the survivors to the corners of the regency, from where they were never allowed to return. Despite its fertility, the mountain is still deserted, its empty villages having remained untouched for two hundred years. Like much of the terrain around here, it's good **walking** country, with limited public transport.

Sbeïtla and Sidi Bou Zid

The dusty modern market town of **SBEÏTLA**, 30km east of Kasserine, is unexciting in the extreme, enlivened only on Wednesdays by the weekly **souk** held mainly on avenue Ali Belhouane and from mid-July by a month-long **festival** of folk culture. What makes a detour here advisable is its proximity to the site of Roman **Sufetula**. Approaching Sbeïtla from the east, the GP3 from Kairouan skirts the southeastern edge of the Dorsale range, while the GP13 from Sfax fails to provide even this limited interest, though you could take a short detour to the pilgrimage town of **Sidi Bou Zid,** about 40km from Sbeïtla.

Very little is recorded about Sufutela, apart from one moment of abortive glory in 646 AD, when the Byzantine Prefect Gregory declared the African province independent in anticipation of the coming Arab invasion. Much good it did him or the province: the Arabs won a famous victory here in 647, making Sbeïtla the shortest-lived of all Tunisia's capitals. What remains of Roman Sufetula sits on a level plain with little scenic interest, but it does boast the best-preserved complex of Forum temples in the country. These have long been famous, inspiring one of the prints of Sir Grenville Temple (see p.561) in 1835, an enlargement of which is on display in the museum here.

The site

The **site** (daily: April to mid-Sept 7am–7pm; mid-Sept to March 8am–5.30pm; 2.1TD, camera 1TD) lies along the Kasserine road, northwest of the new town. From the bus station, walk straight ahead and about half a kilometre up rue Taïeb Mehiri to where it joins the Kasserine road, then continue another few hundred metres past a **triumphal arch** on the right, which straddled the main Roman highway east to Hadrumetum (Sousse). The **ticket office** is in a modern complex of shops and cafés just before the site entrance on the opposite side of the road. A small **museum** (Tues–Sun 8.30am–1pm & 2.30–5pm) is next door, featuring archeological finds and explanatory displays. Apart from the Temple print mentioned above, look out for a round fifth-century altar table that looks at first like an olive press and an attractive mosaic featuring a cross in red and yellow. The museum also has some fine Christian remains and the most unadulterated Roman city plan in Tunisia. Touts hanging around outside sell "Roman" coins and plaster moulds of sculptures; some of the coins may actually be genuine although almost worthless.

Opposite the museum, you enter the site past a small Byzantine **fort**, and an immediate left turn takes you past another on the right. Both were little more than fortified houses, with no door on the ground floor (entrance would have been via a wooden staircase). Climbing up to look down into the second fort, you can see how crammed the rooms are: you wouldn't have wanted to withstand a long siege in here.

Beyond the fort, opposite a plan of the site on the left, are the best-preserved remains of an **olive press** in Roman Tunisia, with massive standing stones that remind you what a serious industry this was in the region. After the olive press, turn right towards the centre of the site. It's immediately apparent that you're already walking along a regular grid plan, suggesting that, unlike most of the other major Tunisian sites, Roman Sbeïtla did not grow out of an earlier African foundation.

After two long blocks, you reach the well-preserved **baths** on the right, with paved pools and hypocaust heating systems visible everywhere. Entrance was down some steps from the street on the north side; the double pillars of a *palaestra* exercise yard are straight ahead through two rooms, flanked immediately to the left by the *frigidarium* and, beyond, the *caldarium*. The sad remains of a **theatre** overlook the river below the baths. It's not hard to imagine what a pleasant spot it must once have been.

Back on the main road that runs towards the Forum at the centre of the complex, the **Church of St Servus**, carved out of an existing temple in the African style, is recognizable by the four standing corners of its baptistry. The baptistry was originally the temple sanctuary, reached through a square-porticoed courtyard to the south; the body of the church was laid east–west across the courtyard, with a *presbyterium* apse just recognizable at the west end.

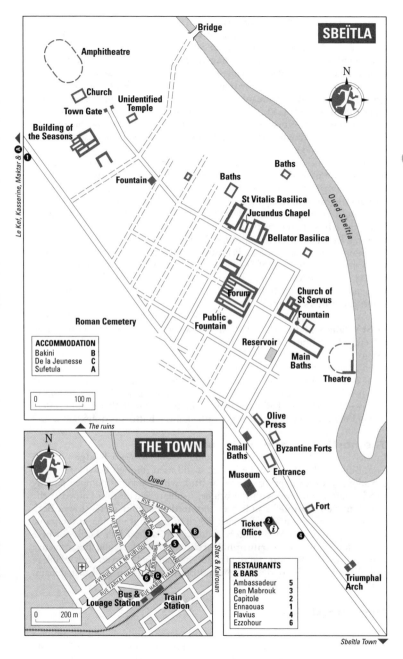

SBEÏTLA

Bridge

Amphitheatre

Church

Unidentified Temple

Town Gate

Building of the Seasons

Fountain

Baths

Baths

St Vitalis Basilica

Jucundus Chapel

Bellator Basilica

Oued Sbeïtla

Forum

Church of St Servus

Fountain

Roman Cemetery

Public Fountain

Reservoir

Main Baths

Theatre

ACCOMMODATION
Bakini	B
De la Jeunesse	C
Sufetula	A

0   100 m

Le Kef, Kasserine, Maktar & ⓐ ①

Olive Press

Small Baths

Byzantine Forts

Museum

Entrance

Fort

Ticket Office ②ⓘ

④

Triumphal Arch

The ruins ▲

THE TOWN

N

Oued

RUE 2 MARS

AVENUE AL

RUE TAÏEB MEHIRI

RUE FARHAT HACHED

AVENUE DE LA RÉPUBLIQUE

RUE BOURGUIBA

RUE HABIB THAMEUR

③

ⓗ

ⓑ

⑤

⑥

ⓒ

Bus & Louage Station

Train Station

Sfax & Kairouan ▶

0   200 m

RESTAURANTS & BARS
Ambassadeur	5
Ben Mabrouk	3
Capitole	2
Ennaouas	1
Flavius	4
Ezzohour	6

Sbeïtla Town ▼

The Forum and basilicas

Highly photogenic due to its uniquely well-preserved condition, the **Forum** ensemble – dated to 139 AD by an inscription on the entrance archway – is Sbeïtla's big draw. The two side **temples** of Juno and Minerva were approached by flights of steps, while Jupiter's in the middle stood on a podium and was accessible only from the side. For perhaps the only time in Tunisia, you get a real sense of the dominant impact of a Roman civic centre. Although the Byzantines may have made use of the enclosure wall as a defence, it is probably too thin to have been built as a fortification and, in any case, the original Forum was undoubtedly surrounded by a wall, as well as a colonnaded portico inside on three sides.

Passing out of the Forum between the temples, you can turn northeast towards a complex of Christian buildings, which after being installed on top of existing Roman structures underwent constant shifts in configuration to reflect changes in Christian doctrine. Furthest to the right, with an apse at each end (and tombs visible in the apse nearest the street) is the **Basilica of Bellator**. In its first Christian incarnation, this was flanked to the west by a freestanding baptistry, later converted into a chapel. You can see where a reliquary column was inserted in the middle of a baptistry basin that was in the curiously elongated shape characteristic of Sbeïtla. The relics in question, which would have resided in the hollow on top of the column, are thought to have been those of Jucundus, a Catholic bishop martyred by the Vandals – hence the building's name, **Jucundus's Chapel**.

Next door to the chapel lies the largest building in the complex, the **Basilica of St Vitalis**, with five aisles divided by rows of double columns. Dating from the end of the fifth century, it would have had only fifty years of use before Gregory's defeat by the Arabs in 647. Even so, like Bellator's Basilica, it went through adjustments which produced an apse at both ends of the central nave. In its original form it would have had only the one nearest the street, behind which is hidden a magnificently decorated baptistry basin. The inscription in its mosaic says that the basin was built at the instigation of Vitalis and Cardela. Beyond the northwest corner of the cathedral is a **baths complex**.

The northern edge of the site

In the distance, looking north, you should be able to see a **bridge** over the *oued*. Built by the Romans, the bridge is still used (though heavily restored), providing access to a spring on the far bank whose water is pumped directly to Sfax. Just about level with the bridge, a solitary square ruin known as the "**unidentified temple**" stands over the northwest limit of the town. Both feature in the foreground of Temple's sketch of the ruins in 1835, as the frame for some picturesque Arab hunters standing over a dead lion. Look out here for the foundations of a **triumphal arch** over the street, and the attractive **Building of the Seasons** on the far side, its colonnade carved with a vine in typical local style. Beyond a low mound outside the town is all that remains of the **amphitheatre**.

Practicalities

The train station, on rue Habib Thameur at the southern end of modern Sbeïtla, has no passenger services, but the **bus station** next door has daily services to Kasserine, Sidi Bou Zid, Tunis, Sfax, Kairouan and Sousse; there are also **louages** from here to Sidi Bou Zid and Kasserine. There is a **tourist office** in the modern complex opposite the Roman remains (July & Aug daily 7.30am–5pm; Sept–June Mon–Thurs 8am–1pm & 3–5.30pm, Fri & Sat 8am–1pm), which has information and leaflets about the region – as well as a **taxiphone** office and a **Publinet** (daily 8.30am–10pm; 1.5TD/hr). There's a **bank** on avenue Ali Belhouane near the central roundabout at the end of avenue Bourguiba. The **post office** (country hours) is on avenue Farhat Hached, towards the bus station.

Should you want to **stay**, the best-value place in town is the friendly *Hôtel de la Jeunesse* (℡77 466 528; ➋), on avenue Bourguiba near the bus station, with clean and pleasant rooms, some en suite. The two-star *Bakini*, near the mosque on rue 2 Mars (℡77 465 244; ➍), is perfectly acceptable but does not offer much more than the *Jeunesse* for double the price. Out on the Kasserine road beyond the site, the tour parties' favourite, the two-star *Sufetula* (℡77 465 074, ℻77 465 582; ➎), is due to undergo extensive renovations until September 2005, when, all being well, it should offer smart, spacious rooms with views over the ruins; the swimming pool (closed in winter) should also be open to non-residents for 5TD. A fourth option, the *Flavius* (℡97 357 767), next to the tourist office complex, should be open by the time you read this, and will compete price-wise with the new improved *Sufetula*.

For **food**, a good cheap option is the recently opened *Ambassadeur* (daily 7am–9pm), off avenue Ali Belhouane just south of the central roundabout, with traditional Tunisian food in a pleasant dining room for under 5TD. A bit more rough and ready is the *Ben Mabrouk* (daily 8am–10pm), overlooking the roundabout – it's marked in Arabic on a yellow sign with "Restaurant" written underneath – while the inexpensive *Ennaouas* (daily 9am–9pm) is opposite the amphitheatre a few hundred metres out towards the *Sufetula*. A classier option in the tourist office complex is the *Capitole* (closed for renovation at the time of writing), which serves three-course meals for around 15TD, is used by package groups during the day and locals for drinking in the evening. Next door, the restaurant at the *Flavius* (daily noon–midnight) is up and running and offers a tourist menu for 11TD. Finally, the *Bakini* has a restaurant with a 10TD menu and a sedate **bar**. Rather raucous by comparison is the *Ezzohour* bar, opposite the bus station at the start of avenue Bourguiba.

Sidi Bou Zid

About 40km east of Sbeïtla, then 8km south of the Sfax road on the MC125, is **SIDI BOU ZID**, a notoriously drab town, most of whose population works in Sfax. The focus of interest here is the **Zaouia of Sidi Bou Zid** and the nearby *zaouia* of his son, which though unexciting from the outside (entry reserved for Muslims), are a centre of pilgrimage and the historical base of the Hammama tribal confederation. The weekly **souk** takes place on Saturday near the *zaouias*.

The **bus and louage station** is about 1km north of the town centre, along the MC125 – here called avenue Bourguiba – towards the Sfax road. There are two one-star **hotels** in Sidi Bou Zid, both north of the main square. The *Hôtel Chems* (℡76 634 465; ➋), about 300m up avenue Bourguiba, is small and welcoming, if charging over the odds, though its budget-priced restaurant (daily 8am–11pm) does a good *steak au poivre*. Also clean and friendly is the *Hôtel Horchani* (℡76 634 635, ℻76 633 775; ➌), 500m down the Meknassy road (turn right off avenue Bourguiba just north of the *Chems*). The *Maison des Jeunes* (no phone), next to the *Horchani*, is the usual affair. Most of the action, such as it is, takes place around the main square, where there are a few cheap **restaurants** and other facilities. The town's **post office** (country hours) is 300m south of the main square.

Kasserine and around

From the edge of the high steppes at Thala, the Gafsa road passes through empty and unrelenting country populated mainly by lonely shepherds and their flocks. Fifty kilometres south of Thala – and just 30km west of Sbeïtla – **KASSERINE** proves a sprawling and unattractive town under the equally uninspiring **Jebel Chambi**, Tunisia's highest peak, at 1554m. The town centre is focused on a huge barracks and a conspicuously ugly American-aided cellulose factory, which accounts for the periodic stench of chlorine in the vicinity. It's a depressed as well as a depressing place, and it's no surprise that the bread riots of January 1984 (see p.508) began here. Although Kasserine is the site of the remains of Roman Cillium and a large mausoleum, both are some way from the town centre and barely worth the effort except for enthusiasts.

The main square that marks the town centre boasts trees and flowers, three **banks** and a couple of cheap **restaurants**. **Buses** and **louages** leave from a large dusty expanse surrounded by apartment blocks 1500m out, just off the road to Sbeïtla. There's a **hospital** (☎77 474 022) out towards the ruins, with buses running from the main square every fifteen minutes. You can access the **Internet** at a Publinet (daily: summer 24hr; winter 8.30am–2am; 1.5TD/hr) on the first floor of a peach-coloured complex with a sprinkling of shops and cafés; it's 200m west of the main square on the road out to the ruins. Kasserine has no tourist office.

There are quite a few **hotels** in town, with budget places like the *Hôtel Ben Abdallah*, 40 rue Habib Thameur (☎77 470 568; ❶), near the Magasin Général; and the Colditz-style barracks of the *Maison des Jeunes* (☎77 474 053), 1km from the town centre on avenue Bourguiba, on the left going towards Cillium. Slightly more comfortable are the *Hôtel de la Paix* on avenue Bourguiba, 50m from the main square on the Sbeïtla road (☎77 471 465; ❷), and the rather officious *Pinus* (☎77 470 164; ❷), 600m from the main square towards Sbeïtla. Top of the list is the friendliest hotel in town, the circular *Cillium* (☎77 473 682; ❹), near the junction with the Thala road, with huge rooms and nice views over the ruins of the same name, although it feels a bit old and tired. **Food** is available on the main square and behind it in avenue Taïeb Mehiri, where there are several patisseries, rotisseries and cafés. A number of **bars** are located on avenue Bourguiba near the main square: the *Hôtel de la Paix* has one, and there's another next door.

Cillium and the Mausoleum of the Flavii

The remains of Roman **Cillium** (free access) are just off the Thala road near the *Hôtel Cillium*. To walk there from the town centre (some 3km), head west along avenue Bourguiba from the main square (the opposite direction to Sbeïtla). After a kilometre you'll come to the cellulose factory on your left before you cross a small *oued*. After another 500m you cross a bridge over a wider river. Fork right at the junction on the other side and after 100m you come to the remains of a Roman mausoleum on your right. A couple of hundred metres past the mausoleum, at another junction by the hospital, a left fork takes you up a small hill to Cillium, the hotel and ruins. If you don't fancy walking all the way or taking a taxi, get a bus to the hospital and walk from there. The ruins are fenced off about 100m beyond the hotel on the left and are spread out over quite an area. The most impressive feature of a not very outstanding site is the third-century **arch**. Nearby is a group of rather pretty whitewashed **marabouts**.

The **Mausoleum of the Flavii**, which you pass on the way, is rather more engaging than Cillium's rather limited remains. The best-preserved example of its kind in the country, it stands three storeys high next to the main road and is decorated with a 110-line falteringly poetic inscription to the dead Flavius. Four lines sum up the Roman dedication to conspicuous consumption:

Who could fail to be mind-blown as he stands here, who would not marvel at this construction and be staggered at the wealth which has caused this monument to rise to the heavenly skies . . . ?

Onward to Gafsa and Tébessa

There's nothing to stop off for on the road between Kasserine and Gafsa, one of the bleakest in the country. The only town of any size is **FÉRIANA**, 5km after the minimal remains of Roman **Thelepte**, which look as if someone has just scattered a handful of hefty blocks across the road: the basilicas, baths and a theatre in the home town of St Fulgentius (467–532) are barely visible. If through some mishap you do get stuck in Fériana, it offers the *Mabrouk* **hotel** (☎77 441 202; ❷) on the main road, along with a couple of **banks**.

Travel details

Trains

Dahmani to: El Fahs (3 daily; 2hr 30min); Gaafour (3 daily; 1hr 35min); Kalaat Khasbah (1 daily; 1hr 10min); Le Sers (3 daily; 35min); Tunis (3 daily; 3hr 50min).

Kalaat Khasbah to: Dahmani (1 daily; 1hr 10min); El Fahs (1 daily; 3hr 40min); Gaafour (1 daily; 2hr 45min); Le Sers (1 daily; 1hr 45min); Tunis (1 daily; 5hr).

Buses

El Fahs to: Kasserine (hourly; 3hr); Le Kef (2 daily; 2hr); Maktar (hourly; 1hr 30min); Nabeul (2 daily; 2hr); Siliana (hourly; 1hr); Sousse (2 daily; 2hr); Tunis (hourly; 1hr); Zaghouan (7 daily; 30min).

Kalaat Khasbah to: Kasserine (5 daily; 2hr 30min); Le Kef (4 daily; 1hr 30min); Thala (6 daily; 2hr).

Kasserine to: El Fahs (6 daily; 4hr); Gabès (2 daily; 4hr); Gafsa (2 daily; 2hr); Kalaat Kasbah (3 daily; 2hr 30min); Le Kef (3 daily; 4hr); Maktar (7 daily; 2hr); Sbeïtla (8 daily; 30min); Tunis (9 daily; 5hr).

Le Kef to: Béja (3 daily; 2hr); Bizerte (1 daily; 4hr); El Fahs (3 daily; 2hr); Gafsa (1 daily; 4hr 45min); Jendouba (10 daily; 1hr 10min); Kairouan (2 daily; 3hr 30min); Kalaat Khasbah (8 daily; 1hr 30min); Kasserine (4 daily; 4hr); Maktar (3 daily; 1hr 30min); Medjez el Bab (hourly; 1hr 30min);

Nabeul (1 daily; 4hr); Sakiet Sidi Youssef (2 daily; 1hr 10min); Sfax (3 daily; 4hr 30min); Sidi Bou Zid (4 daily; 3hr); Sousse (3 daily; 3hr 45min); Tajer-ouine (hourly; 30min); Téboursouk (hourly; 40min); Testour (hourly; 1hr); Thala (5 daily; 1hr 45min); Tunis (hourly; 3hr).

Maktar to: El Fahs (4 daily; 2hr); Kairouan (4 daily; 2hr); Kasserine (4 daily; 3hr); Le Kef (4 daily; 1hr 30min); Siliana (4 daily; 30min); Tunis (7 daily; 3hr).

Sbeïtla to: Kairouan (5 daily; 2hr); Kasserine (8 daily; 30min); Sfax (7 daily; 3hr); Sidi Bou Zid (4 daily; 1hr); Sousse (3 daily; 3hr); Tunis (7 daily; 4hr).

Sidi Bou Zid to: Gabès (2 daily; 4hr 30min); Gafsa (5 daily; 2hr); Kairouan (5 daily; 1hr 30min–2hr); Le Kef (1 daily; 3hr); Sbeïtla (4 daily; 1hr); Sfax (6 daily; 2hr); Tozeur (5 daily; 4hr 30min); Tunis (3 daily; 5hr).

Siliana to: Béja (2 daily; 3–4hr); El Fahs (4 daily; 1hr 30min); Maktar (hourly; 30min).

Téboursouk to: Béja (1 daily; 1hr); Le Kef (hourly; 40min); Medjez el Bab (hourly; 1hr); Testour (hourly; 30min); Thibar (2 daily; 30min); Tunis (hourly; 2hr 20min).

Testour to: Le Kef (hourly; 2hr); Mejdez el Bab (hourly; 30min); Téboursouk (hourly; 30min); Tunis (hourly; 1hr 50min).

Thala to: Kalaat Kasbah (every 30min; 20min); Kasserine (10 daily; 45min); Le Kef (7 daily; 1hr 45min); Tajerouine (7 daily; 30min); Tunis (4 daily; 5hr).

Zaghouan to: Enfida (2 daily; 45min); El Fahs (7 daily; 30min); Hammamet (7 daily; 1hr); Nabeul (7 daily; 1hr 30min); Sousse (2 daily; 2hr); Tunis (6 daily; 1hr).

Louages

El Fahs to: Kasserine (2hr 45min); Le Kef (1hr 45min); Maktar (1hr 30min); Nabeul (1hr 45min); Sousse (1hr 45min); Tunis (50min); Zaghouan (20min).

Kalaat Khasbah to: Kasserine (2hr); Le Kef (1hr); Thala (1hr 30min).

Kasserine to: Fériana (45min); Kalaat Khasbah (2hr); Sbeïtla (20min); Thala (1hr 30min); Tunis (4hr).

Le Kef to: El Ksour (50min); Jendouba (50min); Kalaat Khasbah (1hr 15min); Kalaat es Senam (1hr 15min); Tajerouine (20min); Tunis (3hr).

Maktar to: El Fahs (1hr 30min); Kairouan (1hr 30min); Siliana (30min); Sousse (2hr 30min); Tunis (2hr).

Sbeïtla to: Kasserine (20min); Sidi Bou Zid (45min).

Sidi Bou Zid to: Gabès (2hr); Gafsa (1hr 30min); Meknassy (1hr); Sbeïtla (45min); Sfax (1hr 30min); Tunis (3hr 15min).

Téboursouk to: Béja (45min); Medjez el Bab (45min); Nouvelle Dougga (15min); Thibar (20min); Tunis (2hr).

Thala to: Haïdra (50min), Kalaat Khasbah (15min); Kasserine (30min).

Zaghouan to: Enfida (30min); El Fahs (20min); Hammamet (1hr); Nabeul (1hr 20min); Sousse (1hr 20min); Tunis (1hr).

Arabic place names

Barrage Mellegue	سد ملاق
Dougga	دقّة
El Fahs	الفحص
Elles	اللاس
Fériana	فريانة
Haffouz	حفّوز
Haïdra	حيدرة
Jama	جامة
Jeradou	جرادو
Jugurtha's Table	مائدة يوغرطة
Kalaat es Senam	قلعة سنام
Kalaat Khasbah	القلعة الخصبة
Kasserine	القصرين
Ksar Lemsa	قصر اللمسة
La Mohammedia	المحمّدية
Le Kef	الكاف
Maktar	مكثر
Medeina	مدينة
Mustis	موستي
Nebeur	نبّر
Oudna	أوذنة
Oued ez Zit	واد الزيت
Ouesslatia	الوسالتيّة
Sakiet Sidi Youssef	ساقية سيدي يوسف
Sbeïtla	سبيطلة
Sidi Bou Zid	سيدى بوزيد
Sidi Jedidi	سيدي الجديدي
Sidi Khalifa	سيدي خليفة
Tajerouine	تاجروين
Tébersouk	تبرسق
Testour	تستور
Thala	تالة
Thuburbo Majus	طوبوربو مايوس
Zaghouan	زغوان
Zannfour	زنفور
Zriba	الزريبة

6

The Jerid

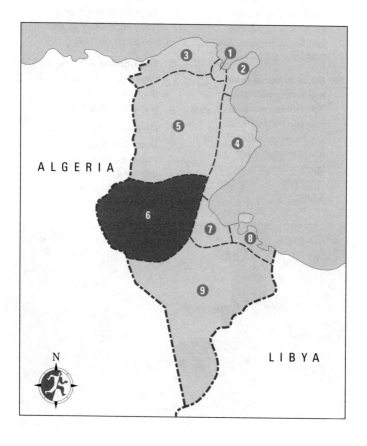

ALGERIA

LIBYA

N

CHAPTER 6 # Highlights

* **The Lézard Rouge** Make like a nineteenth-century bey and view the rugged Seldja gorge from this antique train. See p.348

* **Tamerza** A picturesque abandoned village with three marabouts, adjoining an oasis, a gorge and two waterfalls. See p.351

* **Ouled el Hadef quarter, Tozeur** Navigate palm-roofed tunnels and admire traditional brickwork in a district that seems to have barely changed since the fourteenth century. See p.358

* **Dar Cheraït Museum, Tozeur** Three exhibitions, all completely tacky and strictly for tourists, but fun none-theless. See p.360

* **Nefta** This sleepy town is full of Sufi shrines and labyrinthine alleys, and has a huge oasis gouged into its centre. See p.365

* **The Chott el Jerid** A huge salt lake, usually dry and encrusted in crystals. See p.372

* **Festival of the Sahara, Douz** Camel fights and poetry jousts are part of this celebration of desert culture, held every December. See p.382

△ The mausoleums at Sidi Aïch

6

The Jerid

Rich in the phosphates which play a major role in Tunisia's economy, the **Jerid** – the parched terrain spreading west from Gabès all the way to the Algerian frontier – is an arid land of bare pink hills punctuated only by mining towns and sporadic oasis-villages built around springs and deep gorges. These take time to explore, but are memorable places to experience the precariousness of oasis life. In contrast, the oasis at **Tozeur**, a popular tourist resort, and the quieter neighbouring oasis of **Nefta** – both reached quite easily – are vast folds of luxuriance, set right at the edge of the **Chott**, a bizarre salt flat shimmering with shifting colours and mirages. Nefta has long been a centre of Sufism, whose monuments add an intriguing dimension to its character. Across the Chott lie further oases – the scattered centres of the **Nefzaoua**, under constant threat from the dunes of the Great Eastern Erg. **Kebili** and **Douz** are the two main towns, but what supplies the interest is the access they offer to the vastness of the desert. Good roads and regular bus and louage services link all the main towns covered in this chapter, though rail connections (which reach Gafsa, Metlaoui and Redeyef) are a lot less convenient.

Jerid wildlife

The steppes cover a vast area of the centre of the country – from the southern foothills of the Dorsale ridge down to the Chott el Jerid. Most are degraded forests; it's a sobering thought that Hannibal probably got his elephants from this region a few thousand years ago. Over the centuries, the wood has been felled and the land grazed by sheep, goats and camels, resulting in a landscape only barely productive for agriculture.

The steppes, and particularly the low hills and wadies rising up from them, are rich in unusual **small birds**. Worth special mention are crested larks, hoopoe larks (so called because of their long decurved bill and black and white wings), and the even more peculiar Temminck's horned lark, a striking bird with a black and white head pattern and, in breeding plumage, two distinct black "horns". In the rockier parts, look out for the trumpeter finch, a thick-billed pink bird with a weird nasal call. **House buntings** are common in villages and, as they're treated with some reverence by local people, are extremely tame.

Out in the wilder areas, you may see – with some patience and luck – some of the true **desert mammals**. Jerboas and gerbils are reasonably common, as are susliks, a sort of short-tailed ground squirrel with an upright "begging" posture. Most of the larger desert **antelopes** have been hunted out of existence here, but an ambitious reintroduction programme is under way at the Hadaj and Bou Hedma national parks (see p.347).

Market days

Tuesday Kebili, El Guettar
Wednesday Gafsa, El Gola'a
Thursday Douz, Nefta
Friday El Faouar, El Hamma de l'Arad, Tamerza
Saturday Jemna
Sunday Metlaoui, Moulares, Redeyef, Souk Lahad, Tozeur

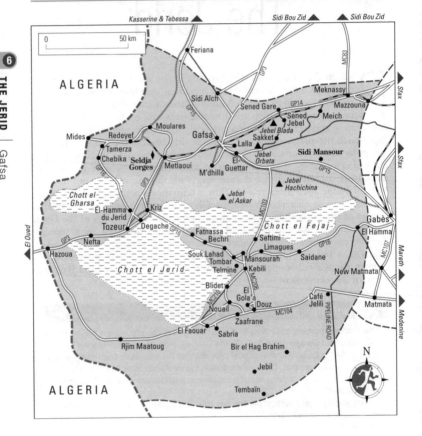

Gafsa and around

For hundreds of years **GAFSA**, 130km northwest of Gabès, has inspired the sort of impression that the Edwardian traveller Norman Douglas (see p.561) quoted from an old Arab song: "Gafsa is miserable; its water blood; its air poison; you may live there a hundred years without making a friend." Douglas agreed – "one dines early in Gafsa and afterwards there's nothing, absolutely nothing, to do". After a brief flirtation with tourist development, the town now seems resigned to its fate as a stopover for tour parties heading south. But it isn't really as bad as people like to make out, and it's worth passing through to check out the mosaics in its museum and enjoy the scenery. Indeed Gafsa's scenery is its most striking feature, with one long tongue of bleak hills passing behind the town to the west, another parallel in the southern distance. On the edge of this pocket is the **Gafsa oasis**, west of the Kasbah, large but more diffuse than those of Tozeur or Nefta.

Some history

Gafsa's history is one of the longest in the Maghreb, let alone Tunisia. The prehistoric Capsian culture which spread all over Africa is named after implements found near the site of Roman **Capsa**. In 107 BC, the Roman town's Numidian predecessor was famously captured by the Roman general **Marius** from the troublesome Jugurtha. "Except the immediate neighbourhood of the town," wrote the historian Sallust, "the whole district is desolate, uncultivated, waterless, and infested by deadly serpents, which like all wild animals are made fiercer by scarcity of food, and especially by thirst, which exasperates their natural malignity." Not short on malignity himself, Marius sacked the town and slaughtered the population – giving the excuse that the inhabitants were a "fickle and untrustworthy lot". An important Roman colony, Capsa was heavily fortified by the Byzantines and renamed **Justiniana** after the emperor – neither of which moves proved any deterrent to Arab **Oqba Ibn Nafi**, who captured the city and took 80,000 prisoners in 668. Despite the conquest, and large-scale conversion to Islam, El Edrisi reported Latin still being spoken here in the twelfth century.

Gafsa's most recent world headlines were in January 1980. On January 27 a mysterious group of unidentified soldiers took over the town in a night-time operation. It took several days for the army to evict them, after 48 deaths; of the 60 captured, 13 were hanged on April 17. To this day the incident remains shrouded in mystery. Rumour has it that the leader was a native of Gafsa who had fled to Libya in the wake of the Ahmed Ben Salah purges of 1969, and the common thread in suggested explanations seems to be that the men came from Libya. As to their purpose, however, nothing is clear; if the Tunisian south was expected to rise spontaneously and declare allegiance with Libya, its mood had been severely misjudged. But it is significant that Gafsa was chosen as the target. As the economic and administrative capital of the Jerid, whose phosphates play such a large part in the national economy, there is some resentment among the citizens that they don't benefit more from the industry. True or not, the common view in the town, that the profits all go to rich businessmen in Sfax, suggests considerable disenchantment.

Putting the devil back in hell

Gafsa has a literary claim to fame in Boccaccio's 1353 classic, the *Decameron*, being the home of Alibech, the innocent virginal heroine of the book's thirtieth and most infamous tale. Setting off into the desert to learn how to serve God, Alibech encounters the pious young hermit Rustico, who agrees to teach her. Rustico, however, soon gets other ideas and persuades her to join him in a rather unorthodox enactment of putting the devil into hell, thus coining a sexual euphemism current in the Italian of the time. When the women of Gafsa find out how Alibech and Rustico have been serving God out in the desert "they laughed so hard that they are laughing still". English translators, though, found it no laughing matter. Even into the twentieth century, they refused to translate the crucial passages into English, leaving readers to fathom the finer points of Rustico's method from the original Italian text.

Moving on from Gafsa

For a list of destinations and journey times, see Travel details on p.390.

From the **bus station** (⊕76 220 335 for SRT services, ⊕76 221 587 for SNTRI) and Iouage station, there are regular departures to Tozeur, Kasserine, Gabes, Sfax, Sousse and Tunis. Most Tunis-bound SNTRI buses pass through Kairouan. Gafsa Ksar **airport** (⊕76 273 700) is best reached by taxi, although there are hourly local buses from in front of the bus station on place 7 Novembre, the same stop where you'll find local buses to Sidi Aïch and the **train station** (⊕76 270482). The best train to Tunis is the overnight service via Sfax and Sousse, though there's a day train to Sfax which connects for Tunis but not Sousse. For Hammamet and Nabeul, the day train is best, although you'll need to change at both Sfax and Bir Bou Regba. There are two daily trains to Metlaoui, but neither arrives at a convenient time for either the Redeyef train or the Lezard Rouge; you're better off going to Metlaoui by bus or Iouage.

Arrival, information and accommodation

Arriving by **train**, you are left way out in the suburb of Gafsa Gare on the Gabès road, 3km to the southeast. Your best bet is to take a taxi into town (1.5TD or so), or walk (bear right opposite the station and straight on) up to the main road, where there are more taxis – and some buses, but not early enough for the arrival of the morning train. The **bus station** is off avenue 2 Mars, right in the centre of town behind several cheap hotels, and the **louage station** is also more or less in the centre of town (for place 7 Novembre, turn left out of the exit and right at the next road junction). If you arrive at **Gafsa Ksar** airport, 5km from town on the Tunis road, the best way into Gafsa is by taxi, which should cost around 1.5TD, though if you walk 100m to the main road there are hourly buses from 7.30am to 6.30pm.

The town centre is marked by the triangular garden officially known as **place 7 Novembre**, tucked in between avenue Taïeb Mehiri, avenue 2 Mars and avenue 13 Février. The Medina lies west of here, across avenue 13 Février, which continues as **rue Ali Belhouane**, where most of the budget hotels are located. On the west side of the Medina is **avenue Bourguiba**, running from the Roman Pools up to the post office, where it meets the Tozeur road, officially renamed boulevard de l'Environnement. The helpful **ONTT** (July & Aug Mon–Sat 7.30am–1.30pm; Sept–June Mon–Thurs 8.30am–1pm & 3–5.45pm, Fri & Sat 8.30am–1.30pm; ⊕76 221 664) is next to the museum by the Roman Pools. On the east side of place 7 Novembre, **avenue Taïeb Mehiri** is Gafsa's main thoroughfare, and where you'll find the central **market**.

Accommodation

The choice of accommodation is Gafsa is not great. Most of the budget **hotels** are on rue Ali Belhouane, and rather squalid. Upmarket hotels – such as there are – can be found close to the centre of town, but a brand new five-star hotel, the *Gafsa Palace*, is currently under construction and due to open soon by Orbata Park (see p.346) and the airport. Mid-range accommodation is thin on the ground, but is at least decent and good value.

There is a *Maison des Jeunes* on rue du Caire (⊕76 224 468, ⊕76 225 599; dorm beds 3TD), with three- to five-person **dorms** and a 10pm curfew in winter, 11pm or later in summer. It's often fully booked by sports groups. To get there, take the Tozeur road past the *Hôtel Moussa*, then the next right and the second left; the hostel is 200m down on the left. **Camping** may be pos-

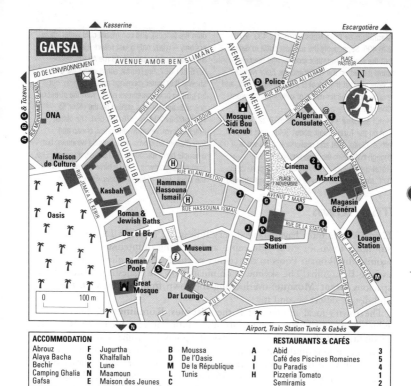

GAFSA

Kasserine

Escargotière

Place Pasteur

N

Avenue Amor Ben Slimane

Avenue Taïeb Mehiri

BD de l'Environnement

ONA

Avenue Habib Bourguiba

Rue F. Hached

Rue Bou Yacoub

Mosque Sidi Bou Yacoub

D Police

Rue Mohamed Ali Alhami

Algerian Consulate

Maison de Culture

Kasbah

Rue Jema'a el Kebir

Hammam Hassouna Ismail

Rue Kilani Metoui

F

Oasis

Roman & Jewish Baths

Dar el Bey

Rue Hassouna Ismail

Avenue 2 Mars

Cinema

Market

Magasin Général

Museum

Roman Pools

Rue de la Station

Bus Station

Louage Station

Great Mosque

Dar Loungo

0   100 m

N

Airport, Train Station Tunis & Gabès

THE JERID | Gafsa: Accommodation

6

sible at the hostel, though there is a good campsite, *Camping Ghalia*, in the oasis (☎76 229 135; 4TD per person, 4TD per tent, 3.5TD per car or 4TD per campervan). This has plots for tents and campervans, electricity, a pool, hot showers (2TD) and a café that serves pizzas. To get there, follow rue Jema'a el Kebir from behind the Kasbah, cross rue Ali Belhouane and head into the oasis, taking a right after 700m or so by a marabout (the campsite is signposted most of the way).

Hotels

Abrouz 29 rue Kilani Metoui ☎76 227 357. Cheap and friendly but basic, none too clean, and not recommended for women travelling alone. Cold showers only, but there's a hammam nearby. ❶

Alaya Bacha 10 rue Ali Belhouane ☎76 202 029. Small but decent rooms, some with showers, and hot water at least some of the time. ❶

Bechir 40 rue Ali Belhouane ☎76 223 239. Very much a fall-back option, with small rooms and cold showers. ❶

Gafsa 10 rue Ahmed Snoussi ☎76 224 000, ⓕ76 224 747. Catering mainly for tour groups, but not a bad choice, with reasonable rooms, clean bathrooms, a/c and satellite TV. ❹

Jugurtha Sidi Ahmed Zarroug ☎76 211 201. Luxury hotel 4km west of town in a small oasis (see p.346), with pool and a great view over the desert. Currently closed for renovation and upgrading. Owned by the same firm as the *Maamoun*. ❾

Khalfallah av Taïeb Mehiri ☎76 225 624, ⓕ76 290 228. A touch classier than the other budget hotels, but also pricier. All rooms have their own showers, but toilets are on the landing. Breakfast isn't included in the rate, but costs very little extra. ❸

Lune rue J Abennaceur ☎76 220 218, ⓕ76 220 980. Much better value than the *Gafsa* or the *Maamoun*, with pleasant rooms and friendly staff, though the bathrooms could do with a lick of paint. ❹

343

Maamoun av Taïeb Mehiri ☎76 222 433, ☎76 226 490. Supposedly the poshest outfit in Gafsa, but the rooms are rather gloomy, and the only thing it's got on the *Gafsa* and the *Lune* (where rooms are half the price) is its swimming pool and a reception counter made of yellow marble from Chemtou. ❻

Hôtel Moussa av de la Liberté ☎76 221 333. Out on the Tozeur road, about 300m past the post office. Clean, neat and reasonably good value, though bathroom facilities are shared. ❷

Hôtel de l'Oasis 7 rue Ali Belhouane ☎76 222 371. Not very clean rooms with windows opening onto the landing, and communal cold water showers only – really only a last resort. ❶

Hôtel de la République 28 rue Ali Belhouane ☎76 221 807. Big rooms, some with their own shower (hot water mornings and evenings), but a bit grubby and sometimes noisy, with the street on one side and the bus station on the other. ❶

Tunis 62 av 2 Mars ☎76 221 660. The oldest hotel in town, recently renovated, cheap and friendly. Not all rooms have outside windows, but a couple have balconies, and there's a terrace. The communal showers (1.5TD) have hot water round the clock. Best of the cheapies. ❶

The Town

Gafsa's centre must have changed very little since Norman Douglas's day. It's still not a town for great sightseeing, and anything of interest is concentrated around the Roman Pools in the corner of the Medina at the bottom end of avenue Bourguiba. The skyline is dominated by the majestic minaret of the spacious **Great Mosque**, overlooking the town from nearby, with the oasis and distant desert beyond it.

The town's focal monument is the **Piscines Romaines** (Roman Pools), which every small boy will automatically assume you've come to see. Recently reconditioned, the two open-air, rectangular pools, in familiar Roman masonry with inscriptions on the side of the larger (upper) pool, have a hot spring coming up through the bottom of them; you can bathe here if you don't mind sharing the pools with a large contingent of local schoolboys. The arcaded building overlooking the lower pool is called the **Dar el Bey**, after the ruler who built it. Behind an iron door on the far side, steps lead down to what was a hammam using the pools' overflow.

On the square by the pools, a small **museum** (Tues–Sun: April to mid-Sept 7.30am–noon & 3–7pm; mid-Sept to March 9.30am–4.30pm; 1.1TD) exhibits stone tools, arrowheads and shards of decorated ostrich eggshells from the Capsian culture, and some mosaics from Roman Capsa. The two most impressive mosaics, both from the early fourth century, show the goddess Venus on a fishing trip, and athletes engaged in a series of different pugilistic sports. Some of the Stone Age tools in the museum come from a mound known as **l'Escargotière**, whose name ("the snailery") comes from the fossils of snails that are found there. Should you want to find it (there is little to see), head up rue Houcine Bouzayen, bear left at place Pasteur, and then head off to the right after 500m or so; a map in the ONTT shows its exact location.

The path behind the large pool and the *Café des Piscines Romaines* leads back to rue Ali Belhouane. Where the path widens to accommodate cars, you can check out the large whitewashed mansion known as **Dar Loungo**. Recently restored, it is worth a look around if you can get somebody to let you in. The roof offers excellent views over the town – although the best vistas over both the town and oasis are to be had from **Jebel el Meda**, the rocky hillock opposite the *Hôtel Moussa* on the Tozeur road.

A little way up avenue Bourguiba from the Roman Pools stand the pinkly picturesque crenellated walls of the **Kasbah**. It has had a chequered career since it was built by the Hafsids on a Byzantine foundation – it resisted a Turkish corsair's siege in 1551, only to surrender to the same opponent five years later. Its worst moment came in 1943, when an explosion in an Allied ammunition dump blew out most of one wall. This was subsequently replaced, to universal dismay, with new law courts, and the Kasbah remains a rather soulless place until sunset, when the walls glow in harlequin shades of limpid colour. The best view of it is from the back, where the walls remain intact.

On the southern side of the Kasbah, a small egg-domed **marabout** conceals another **hammam**, Roman in origin and using water from the Roman Pools, with an entrance for women one side and men on the other. Next to the men's hammam, right up by the walls of the Kasbah, is an ancient **Jewish ritual bath**. These baths are in a disgusting state, being used as an unofficial public toilet, but there are plans to clean them up and use them again as a hammam.

The road south from here skirts the oasis and passes the Great Mosque before crossing rue Ali Belhouane and continuing into the oasis. If you're here at the right time of year, you can see some vintage technology in action 100m past the junction, in the form of an electric-powered **olive press**, used during the November to January harvest.

Eating and drinking

Most of the **restaurants** around the bus station and cheap hotel area are little more than overpriced *gargotes*. The *Abid* near place 7 Novembre (daily 10am–11pm) has good food though small portions, and gets quite packed at times (though the crowds do not spill over into the second-rate imitator next door that has brazenly taken the same name). Otherwise, you could try the *Restaurant du Paradis*, opposite the *Hôtel Maamoun* on avenue Taïeb Mehiri (daily 7am–9pm), which also offers low-priced dishes, sometimes including couscous, though on a bad day the choice is limited to spit-roast chicken. For a pizza, try *Pizzaria Tomato*, close to the Algerian consulate on avenue Abou el Kacem Chabbi (daily 8am–10pm).

More sophisticated eating places, with moderate to high prices, include the *Restaurant Semiramis* on rue Ahmed Snoussi (daily noon–2.30pm & 6–10.30pm), the *Hôtel Gafsa* restaurant opposite (daily 11am–3pm & 6–11pm), and the *Hôtel Maamoun* (daily noon–2.30pm, & 7.30–10pm), which is rather expensive à la carte, but has a reasonable 10TD set menu.

A good place for members of both sexes to relax with a coffee during the day is the outdoor **café** at the Maison de Culture, behind the Kasbah on the edge of the oasis. Alternatively, try the *Café des Piscines Romaines* overlooking the Roman pools.

Listings

Banks There are several banks on av Taïeb Mehiri, including a couple by the cinema. There is a weekend rota, so one bank will be open Saturday and Sunday mornings. Banque de l'Habitat on av Taïeb Mehiri at the corner of rue Houcine Bouziane, and UBCI on av J Abennaceur near the *Hôtel Lune* are among those with ATMs.

Car repairs and spares There are mechanics and spare parts suppliers in and around rue de la Station, on bd de l'Environnement (the Tozeur road) and rue Mohammed Glanza, and on av Taïeb Mehiri south of town near the *oued*.

Cinema On av Taïeb Mehiri, opposite the *Tunis*

Hôtel, next to the central market. The Maison de Culture behind the Kasbah has a cinema that also screens mainstream films.

Consulates Algeria, behind 37 rue Houcine Bouzayen (entrance in rue Abou el Kacem Chabbi; ☎76 221 366).

Festival The Festival du Borj is a series of theatrical and musical presentations in the Kasbah throughout July.

Hammams Hammam Hassouna Ismail, on rue Hassouna Ismail, one corner from its western end, is new and clean (women 10am–4pm, men 7–10am & 4–8pm). There's an older one, Hammam Khalil, at 101 rue Kilani Metoui, with two doors – the right-hand one for men, the left-hand one for women (men 4–10am & 4–8pm, women 10am–4pm).

Hospital The regional hospital is on rue Ibn Sina (☏76 225 177); head up rue Houcine Bouzayen to pl Pasteur, then head right.

Internet access Univers de l'Internet, av Abou el Kacem Chabbi, opposite the Algerian consulate (daily 8.30am–midnight; 1.2TD/hr).

ONA craft shop Rue Mohammed Glanza, inside the ONA administrative building (same hours).

Pharmacy There are several on av Taïeb Mehiri, including one in the market. There's a night pharmacy at 16 av Amor Ben Slimane.

Police av Taïeb Mehiri next to the *Hôtel Khalfallah* (☏76 225 012).

Post office On the corner of av Bourguiba and bd de l'Environnement, the Tozeur road (city hours). Stamps are also sold at a small office on av 13 Février at the northern end of pl 7 Novembre.

Supermarket There is a Magasin Général on av Abou el Kacem Chabbi, behind the market.

Swimming Non-residents can use the pool at *Camping Ghalia* for 3TD.

Around Gafsa

Gafsa's position at a transitional point, between the last remnants of the central steppes and mountains to the north and the desert to the south, has always made it an important place. Its significance as a desert "port" can best be appreciated by visiting two of its satellite oases, which can be seen as small islands in the desert, with Gafsa the big port on the shore. Local buses leave regularly from in front of the bus station for the **Lalla** oasis, 7km east of town. Stay on the bus until it turns around at the end of its route, then walk on a bit further to a small café and two prolific springs. The stark contrast here between shady green and glaring pink hills really brings home the fragility of oasis existence. **Sidi Ahmed Zarroug**, the other oasis, lies 4km west of town and is now occupied by the luxurious *Hôtel Jugurtha* (see p.343). The view out over the desert from the bald ridge which towers over the hotel is little short of magnificent, especially if you climb it in time for sunrise. You can also take a walk into the *hamada*.

There is a **zoo** at **ORBATA** (daily 7am–6.30pm, later in summer; 0.2TD), 5km out on the GP3 Tunis road just past the airport. On Wednesdays, there's also a livestock **market** next door. Attached to the zoo is a two-square-kilometre animal park where ostriches and gazelles roam freely, but to visit this permission must be obtained from the Direction des Forêts on the route de Gabès (Mon–Thurs 8.30am–1pm & 3–5.45pm, Fri & Sat 8.30am–1.30pm; ☏76 221 485), which is just past the rail line on the left if you're heading out of Gafsa. Orbata can be reached by local bus from in front of the bus station in Gafsa (hourly 7.15am–6.15pm), or by taxi (about 1.5TD).

Two Roman **mausoleums** can be visited just outside the village of **SIDI AÏCH**, 48km north of Gafsa on a turning off the Sidi Bou Zid road. They stand in splendid isolation at the beginning of a piste to Fériana with a lovely backdrop of jagged mountains striped with layers of rock. The original Roman inscriptions are joined by more recent carvings, some as modern as the nineteenth century. Regular louages and three buses a day head to Sidi Aïch from Gafsa.

El Guettar

Some 20km east of Gafsa on the Gabès road is another oasis, **EL GUETTAR**, known for its pistachio nuts. Reached by bus or louage from Gafsa, the town is nothing much in itself, a ribbon of modern concrete houses along the road, but the huge palmery is rarely visited and farmers here still use old techniques and equipment such as the *noria*, a water wheel with buckets attached, which is used to draw water from wells by animal power. In ancient times, water was carried down from aquifers on high ground by irrigation tunnels called *foggara* or *khriga*, some of which can still be seen in the region (and also near Douz – see p.377). Teams of workers would dig holes along the course of the *foggara* to excavate the earth and rock, and the holes were used to maintain the system. From the road, these circular pits, some of them 30–40m deep, are all you can see of the *foggara*. Close up, the amount of work that has gone into the kilometres of tunnels below becomes evident. But those here are considered small; in Iran, where the practice originated, the *qanat*, as they term them, can extend for hundreds of kilometres.

Sakket, Sened Jebel and Meich

East of El Guettar, the main GP15 highway continues across the steppe to **SIDI MANSOUR**, a small village with an important marabout, and thence to Gabès; buses run regularly along here both ways. At the eastern end of El Guettar itself, a turning to the left leads to the remote Berber mountain villages of **SAKKET** (14km), **SENED JEBEL** (27km) and **MEICH** (42km). These are highly worthwhile targets if you're prepared for a moderate adventure and want to meet the locals, though the presence of an outsider still causes a stir, the women hiding in their houses and the men gathering into groups to discuss the *hawaja*, or foreigner.

Little has changed here in the past two centuries. As in Berber villages in the far south of the country, the villagers retain their distinct ethnic identity (though none has spoken Berber since the nineteenth century), and traditional dress and customs persist. Women wear the *bakhnug*, a shawl embroidered with geometrical patterns to shelter them from the eyes of strangers. Many of the men wear the knee-length trousers that used to be common before World War II. At the centre of each of the villages are marabouts' tombs, with rags and flags hanging from poles; this is the last place in Tunisia where you can see votive offerings to these village saints. The village oil presses are still animal-powered (in Sened Jebel, some old oil presses lie within a number of disused cave dwellings), and women grind their own flour by hand. In winter many people migrate into the pastures with their herds, and the villages are virtually deserted. Today, however, a different type of migration is slowly eroding the community, as many families abandon their villages for an easier life in the city.

Getting to these villages is difficult. If you catch a louage to El Guettar or **Sened Gare** (on the Gafsa–Sfax road), you could negotiate with the driver to take you the rest of the way, or from the latter you could walk or hitch the 10km to Sened Jebel. It's possible to catch a bus to El Guettar and walk from there or, if you're lucky, to get a lift to Sakket.

Meknassy and Bou Hedma National Park

The road from Gafsa to Sfax takes you across the barren steppes between the Dorsale mountains to the north and the Chotts to the south. The only town of any size on this route is **MEKNASSY**, just under 80km east of Gafsa, where you might conceivably need to change louages (they go from here to Sfax, Sened Gare, Sidi Bou Zid and direct to Tunis). Meknassy hosts a **Cavalry Festival** of horsemanship every November.

With your own vehicle, you could visit **Bou Hedma National Park** and the adjoining **Hadaj National Park**, just south of Meknassy, where an ambitious programme is in progress to reintroduce gazelle, oryx and addax, as well as ostriches, which only disappeared from the south of the country in the twentieth century. To visit Bou Hedma, you'll first need permission from the Direction Général des Forêts in Tunis, at 30 rue Alain Savary, 1002 Tunis Belvédère (☎71 891 497). You may be able to phone them and arrange to pick up your permit at the forestry office (Direction des Forêts/Triq el Ghaba) opposite the train station in **Mazzouna**, 25km east of Meknassy. From there, you take the Skhirra road, turning right (no signposting) after 7km and arriving at the park after 10km of tarmac and 10km of piste which is due to be surfaced. Even then, much of the park is inaccessible without a 4WD. For Hadaj, you should be able to obtain a permit from the Direction des Forêts in Gafsa, route de Gabès, just past the train station (☎76 221 485).

The mining towns: Metlaoui to Redayef

The region west of Gafsa is rather bleak and industrial, and not one frequented much by tourists, who mainly pass through here on their way to Tamerza and Chebika, though many stop off to ride the **Lézard Rouge** train. The phosphate industry that dominates the local economy dates back to 1896, when a French army vet and amateur geologist, Philippe Thomas, found phosphate deposits around **Metlaoui**. Previously known only for his work on goat diseases, Thomas became a national hero in France, and his discovery turned an insignificant village into an important mining centre.

The transformation took little over a decade. Thousands of miners were recruited from Algeria and Libya as local people were at first reluctant to work in the mining towns and were later excluded because the mine owners feared they would campaign for better conditions. Conditions were certainly bad; companies provided no accommodation and huge *bidonvilles* (shanty-towns) grew up without any planning or services. At work there were few safety measures, and one third of employees had to retire – without compensation – because of injury. Unions were discouraged by the companies' policies of maintaining a high turnover of personnel and by pitting ethnic groups against each other, paying Algerians more than Libyans, and Libyans more than Sudanese. So tense were relations that fights used to break out between them, and on one occasion the Algerians burnt down a Libyan *bidonville*, killing over a hundred people. It was only in the 1930s that the unions managed to unite the work force and direct their anger against their bosses rather than each other – and conditions then improved radically.

By 1899, phosphate from Metlaoui was being exported to France via the new railway to Sfax, and other mines were being dug in the surrounding hills. The Compagnie des Phosphates de Gafsa was established after independence, and Tunisia is now the fourth largest phosphate producer in the world. Now however, reserves are running low, and the spectre of mass redundancy looms large over a region in which phosphate production is virtually the only industry, and unemployment is already high. The quantity of phosphates mined in Metlaoui and its sister towns of **Moulares** and **Redeyef** has already fallen to a fraction of the amount once extracted here, and reserves seem unlikely to last much into the 2010s. Metlaoui is in a slightly better position than its sister towns, since the phosphates are actually processed here. One consequence of the industry's decline is the large-scale migration to the richer towns of the Sahel, in particular Sousse, where there is a suburb called Moulares on account of its domination by immigrants from there.

Metlaoui

METLAOUI is an odd jumble of French houses dwarfed by overhead phosphate conveyors and heavy mining equipment. The **Musée National des Mines** (Mon–Sat 8am–noon; free) was built to house Philippe Thomas's natural history collection about 800m up the Tamerza road, just before the louage station. It's rather a dry and dusty old place and sadly many of the original exhibits, and their labels, were lost in the ten years the museum was closed. The main highlights are two fossilized Eocine turtles in among the old photos and piles of rock, but the museum is worth a look if you're passing through.

The Gafsa road runs through the centre of town until it meets the Tamerza–Tozeur road at a T-junction by a petrol station, bank and cinema. The **bus station**, about 800m up the Gafsa road from the main junction, just past the level crossing, is served by both SNTRI and SRT Gafsa, with departures to east to Gafsa, Tozeur and Sfax, west to Nefta, Moulares and Redeyef, as well as services further afield. **Louages** operate a yard 50m west of the bus station, with a kind of auxiliary station about a kilometre up the Tamerza road by the museum, sometimes cruising from one to the other in search of passengers, though the one near the bus station is a safer bet. Louages can be a bit sparse; mornings are the best time to find one. The **train station** is 1500m from the main junction on the Gafsa road, with an overnight service to Tunis via Gafsa, Sfax and Sousse, and a morning service to Sfax where it connects for Tunis. In the other direction, there is a daily afternoon service to Redeyef via the Seldja gorge, which doesn't particularly connect in either direction with the Sfax or Tunis trains.

The **post office** (country hours) is off the Gafsa road, about 200m from the main junction, and there's also a Magasin Général **supermarket** about 700m up the Tamerza road, just before the museum. The municipal **swimming pool**, which is off the Gafsa road just 50m from the main junction, is open mid-June to mid-September only.

Metlaoui's only **hotel** is the two-star *Hôtel Selja* (also spelt *Thelja*), a kilometre towards Gafsa from the main junction (☎76 241 570, ℗76 241 486; ❺), which is decent enough, with air conditioning and satellite TV in all rooms, plus a bar, and a restaurant with a 7TD set menu (daily noon–3pm & 7pm–midnight). Cheaper eating can be found at the *Restaurant Ellafi* (daily except Sun 7am–9pm), 100m towards Gafsa from the main junction, serving the usual staples such as couscous and lamb chops.

The Lézard Rouge

From Metlaoui, a special **tourist train**, the Lézard Rouge, runs to Seldja and back (5 weekly; 20TD return). Originally used by the bey, the train consists of original nineteenth-century carriages, including the bey's private car, which is restored in red velvet and leather. The other seating is pretty bog-standard, apart from a couple of compartments, so get there early to grab the best seats. The train leaves Metlaoui at 10am on Tuesday and Thursday, 10.30am on Monday, Friday and Sunday, taking an hour and 45 minutes for the round trip. Further information is available from the Galilée Travel/Lézard Rouge office at Metlaoui's train station (☎76 241 469, ℗76 241 604), through whom reservations can be made, although off season you should be able to turn up at the station just before the train's departure and buy a ticket there and then. The train itself isn't as exciting as it might sound, but the scenery the ride offers is dramatic, as the train passes through a succession of narrow **gorges** between sheer rock on either side.

△ The Lézard Rouge

Seldja

SELDJA, 16km west of Metlaoui, comprises only a neat white signal box stuck in the middle of nowhere, built by the French along with a remarkable series of bridges and tunnels through rugged ravines. Previously, the Romans had diverted water from these ravines by aqueduct to supply nearby agricultural land. Their caravans from Sbeïtla took a short cut through here en route to Ghadames in present-day Libya. From the signal box you can walk back down the tracks to some of the more impressive parts of the gorge, its sheer sides worn completely smooth by the river. Phosphate trains do still pass at regular intervals, so watch your step. As well as the Lézard Rouge (see above), you can reach Seldja from Metlaoui on the afternoon Redeyef train, returning on the same train an hour and a half later. An alternative route to the gorge is by road from Metlaoui, where a track leads out over the flat plain for 5km – too hot to walk for most of the year – to a rock passage known as the **Coup de Sabre**, or "sword thrust". Legend says that the warrior Al Mansour cut into the rock with one stroke to prepare a bed for Leila, a princess escaping from her husband. There's a four-kilometre path along the foot of the gorge to the signal box. If you walk it, you'll see the wheeling silhouettes of birds of prey overhead – be sure to carry enough water with you, or they'll be looking a whole lot more sinister.

Moulares and Redeyef

On the road between Metlaoui and Redeyef, the nondescript mining town of **Moulares** does not warrant a stop; the only thing of note as you pass through is the little mining train on display by the Metlaoui road on the edge of town. **REDEYEF**, the last of the mining towns, is 17km further on from Moulares and, like Metlaoui, has grown up around an old French community, with its bungalows and church. There's nothing much to see here, but it's a pleasant enough little town. The Gafsa road meets the Tamerza road in front of the **post office** (country hours), and another road off the main junction leads to the square, with a **mosque** and, in front of it, rather resembling a toy train, a mining locomotive and bogeys built by Schötter GmbH of Bremen, Germany. Beyond the main square is the **market**, at its busiest on Sunday, and a **bank**. There is no accommodation in Redeyef.

The **bus station**, at the beginning of the Gafsa road, has services to Metlaoui, Gafsa and Tozeur, among others. Buses to Tamerza can also be picked up at the other end of the market, where you'll also find pick-ups for the same destination. SNTRI buses to Tunis leave from the main square. The train station, with its single late-afternoon departure for Metlaoui, is 100m up the Tamerza road and off on the left. For the intrepid, it is possible to find scenic pistes that can be driven, with care, in an ordinary car; one, leading to **Chebika**, was built by Rommel's forces during World War Two, but even with your own transport, you'd need a guide to find them, best organized at *Restaurant Gelain* or the Syndicat d'Initiative in Tamerza.

Tamerza and the Chott el Gharsa

West of Redeyef, the towns lose their industrial ugliness and become a series of lovely oases that some consider the most beautiful in the country. Certainly, their remoteness and inaccessibility leaves them unspoilt compared to places like Tozeur and Nefta; but it also means that facilities are few and public transport rare. The first settlement you come to if travelling from Redeyef is **Tamerza**, where scenic views are to be had over the abandoned old town and out across the desert. South of here, the recently surfaced road to Tozeur crosses the **Chott el Gharsa**, a salt plain giving a taste of the larger Chott el Jerid (see p.372). Although it is possible to reach Tamerza by bus or louage from Tozeur, sparseness of transport makes a day trip very difficult if you want to take in two nearby towns: **Chebika**, where a pleasant walk through a gorge follows a small stream to its sources, and **Mides**, another oasis with a gorge, where the scenery is more dramatic. You would need to start off very early in the morning, and be prepared to hitch between Chebika and Tamerza, and to hitch or even walk between Tamerza and Mides. An alternative to take a tour with a company such as The Green Travel (see p.365) who organize day-trips from Tozeur.

Tamerza

TAMERZA (also spelt "Tamaghza"), 85km west of Gafsa, is one of the least spoiled of all the Jerid oases, densely cultivated and featuring two picturesque waterfalls. The oldest mud-and-stone houses here, to the south of the road from Redeyef, were abandoned after torrential floods in 1969. The new village, a kilometre further on, is built in traditional style, with high blank brick walls facing the main street, which is called avenue 7 Novembre. Three **marabouts** are still maintained in the old village, the most striking being that of Sidi Dar Ben Dhahara with its pointed green dome. Tamerza hosts an annual **festival** at the end of March, featuring music, dance and equestrian events.

There are buses between Tamerza and Redeyef, Tozeur and Tunis, among other destinations; in Tamerza, the buses drop you on the main road in the centre of town. The **Syndicat d'Initiative** at 22 avenue 7 Novembre (daily 8am–noon & 3pm–6pm; ☎76 485 288) keeps a list of local guides and can arrange excursions on foot or by donkey, for example over the hill and along the gorge to Mides (see below).

The very classy four-star *Hôtel Tamerza Palace* (☎76 485 344/5, ℗76 485 322, ⓦwww.tamerza-palace.com; ❾), perched above a *oued* at the northern end of town, has excellent views over the oasis and old village from its poolside terrace and each of its rooms. A mid-range hotel, *Résidence des Oasis Montagneuses*, is due to open shortly on avenue 7 Novembre, 100m towards Chebika from the Syndicat d'Initiative, but in the meantime the only other accommodation is in the rather grotty and overpriced palm-frond bungalows of the *Hôtel des Cascades* (☎ & ℗76 485 332; ❸), down avenue de l'Environnement, a street off avenue 7 Novembre. As the name suggests, the *Cascades* is just above one of Tamerza's two **waterfalls** – the other is beyond the edge of town, a couple of kilometres towards Chebika. There are panoramic views over the second one from the Chebika road. It is possible to park up in a campervan or pitch a tent overnight near the second waterfall at a place called Marah Azazia, though it isn't an official campsite.

Avenue de l'Environnement has a few places to **eat**. Here you'll find the reasonably priced *Restaurant Chedli* at no. 54 (daily 7am–9pm), which has a set menu at 7.5TD, excellent couscous, and home-made *harissa* to dip your bread into on request. At no. 56, the *Restaurant Gelain* (daily 8am–9pm or later) has a 6.5TD set menu and good brochettes.

Mides

The mountain oasis of **MIDES**, a few kilometres west of Tamerza, can be reached by a surfaced road from a junction 4km north of Tamerza towards Redeyef (a piste from the same junction passes a customs post before crossing the border into Algeria). Alternatively you can get there on foot or by donkey from Tamerza, taking a scenic 4.5-kilometre route over a hill and through a dramatic narrow **gorge** – the Syndicat d'Initiative in Tamerza can arrange donkeys and guides. The walk should take about two and a half hours at a steady pace (guides and donkeys are about 15TD apiece for this route). Take water with you, and in summer take precautions against heatstroke – it can get roasting hot.

An abandoned Berber village and the new Mides settlement stand at opposite ends of the oasis, where palms provide shade for pomegranates, which in turn shelter lemon and orange trees. Only from the top of the hill, above the ruins and the network of narrow paved streets, can you make out the spectacular position of the old houses, clinging to the sheer rock face of a deep and extremely impressive **gorge**. This stretches for 3km around the village, providing a natural defensive position. The four campsites by the Berber village are currently closed by official order; following an incident at Chebika (see opposite), it appears that the government has cause for concern about fundamentalist incursions across the border. As it is, Mides is full of plain-clothes police keeping a close watch on things. Also by the Berber village is a **café** where you can buy fossils and rock crystals, and where you can find local guide Brahim Eidini. He can take you on a walk to see some of the herbs and medicinal plants that grow wild in the area, though it's best to call him in advance to arrange things (☎76 460 384; preferably after sunset).

Tamerza to Tozeur

The road south from Tamerza leads across the Chott el Gharsa to El Hamma du Jerid and Tozeur, the route plied by louages and two daily buses. The road is surfaced all the way, though the first section is rather rough, characterized by sharp bends, sheer drops and breathtaking scenery (there's a great spot for panoramic views 4km out of Tamerza) before it comes down onto the plain for the last 5km before the small oasis of **CHEBIKA**. Behind the new settlement by the road, the old village (abandoned after floods in 1969) perches on a rock platform, bordered by palms and, on the far side, a steep gorge. This was the site of the Roman outpost of **Ad Speculum**, from where signals were sent by mirror (*speculum*) to track caravans en route to Tozeur. Because of its exposed position, the village was later named Qasr el Shems (Castle of the Sun). Tourist transport parks up by a small group of cafés and souvenir stalls, from which steps and a path lead through the gorge to a small **waterfall**, and on to the mouth of the spring which waters the oasis. The springs are said to have risen up at a point where a wandering camel carrying the body of a holy man, Sidi Sultan, finally came to a halt; the **marabout**, attributed with the usual powers, is buried in a tomb near the ravine. Next to the spring, steps and a steep climb lead up to the summit, where you are rewarded for your effort with great views. Along the path to the spring, local residents sell fossils and minerals, though what looks like amethyst is on closer inspection a creation made with rock crystals and purple ink.

Chebika is the village described by Jean Duvignaud in his book *Change at Shebika* (see p.565), in which he tells of the open rivalry between Chebika and nearby Redeyef since mining began. Wealthy miners bought land here in the oasis, when an annual cathartic ritual stood in for open warfare right up until independence. The people of Redeyef used to go to a selected spot between the villages, lay out some bread and then hide behind a rock. When the people of Chebika arrived on the scene and pretended to steal the bread, the owners would run out and perform a mock fight before both sides settled down to eat together. Duvignaud describes how other traditions led to the destruction of the very community they were supposed to sustain. The men from here, for example, often married women from El Hamma du Jerid, and ceded land from the oasis to the bride's father, depriving the village of its property and increasing the power of the absentee landlord. Agricultural production seldom increased, since the new owners (like the miners) were unskilled, and local families had to borrow to survive.

Chebika was also the scene of an alarming incident in early 1995, when fundamentalist insurgents from Algeria crossed the border and murdered six members of the National Guard as they sat down at sunset to break their Ramadan fast. The BBC's Arabic service reported the attack but there was no mention of it in the Tunisian media until a week later, when newspapers carried the story that the National Guard officers had been killed in a car crash.

The Chott el Gharsa and El Hamma du Jerid

Beyond Chebika, the road cuts across the corner of the **Chott el Gharsa**, a salt flat lying in a depression below sea level. Like the Chott el Jerid, it's not a lake – though mirages suggest it might be, and maps invariably show it as one; it's only covered in water after (rare) heavy rainfall. On the other side of the Chott, **EL HAMMA DU JERID**, with its six springs and 110,000 palms, signals the beginning of the large oases around Tozeur. El Hamma has a hot spring whose waters, rising at a temperature of 38°C, were much favoured by the Romans, though a later traveller compared the bath to a mustard plaster, and emerged feeling like a boiled lobster. The baths today are in a building just off the road from Chebika, with pools and showers, and separate facilities for men and women, who can both use the baths daily from 6am to 9pm (0.5TD). There are also open-air hot spring pools for both sexes 100m into the oasis (same hours).

Tozeur

TOZEUR has always been the commercial and political centre of the Jerid, and for many years had greater regional power than the central government. This it owed to the date harvest, which made the town an important market and attracted caravans and merchants from the far south. Parts of the old four-teenth-century quarter still survive, but the **oasis** is the main feature.

In recent years, like so many other parts of the country, Tozeur has been gearing itself up as a major tourist centre. First came the jeep-loads of day-trippers on "safari" from the coast, then the airport with a few charter flights, and finally the route Touristique, lined with package hotels to make this a fully fledged desert resort. Tozeur still retains much charm, but it is now very much a tourist town.

Some history

After the first **Arab invasions**, the Berbers of Tozeur joined the Arab army, which swept west through the Maghreb. By 900, however, Tozeur's radical **Kharijite sect** had begun to resist the rule of the Shiite Fatimids, and in 944 the legendary figure of **Abu Yazid** (or Abu Himara, "the man on the donkey") moved north from Tozeur to lay siege to the Fatimid capital at Mahdia. The rebellion failed and Abu Yazid was killed in 947, but the legend of the unruly southerner became part of Tunisian mythology. Over the next centuries, Tozeur continued to be a centre of revolt; the **Almoravids** found strong support here when they tried to overthrow the **Almohads**, and the town's rebelliousness was only finally suppressed by the **Hafsids** in the four-teenth century.

Thereafter Tozeur lost its military might but developed as the major trading post for southern Tunisia. When Scottish traveller Dr Thomas Shaw arrived in 1757, he noticed the "great traffick" in slaves, brought from as far away as the River Niger; the exchange rate was one slave for two or three quintals of dates (100kg to the quintal). James Bruce, heading for the Nile in 1765, reported that Tozeur was used by merchants from Timbuktu and other Saharan oases, dealing in sufficient wool and dates to load twenty thousand camels each year. But by the middle of the nineteenth century, the Saharan trade had dwindled to one or two small caravans each year, and the oasis was thrown back on its own, still plentiful resources.

Until the French occupation the town had a strangely ambivalent relation-ship with the beys. Although there was a governor, or *caid*, who usually lived in Tunis, the town was actually administered by its own council of elders. Every winter the bey had to send a *mahalla*, a military expedition to force the town and surrounding tribes to pay their taxes and allow the *caid* to carry out his administrative duties. After a couple of weeks the *mahalla* would leave and the town once again became autonomous – until the following winter.

Arrival and information

Tozeur's backbone is its main street, **avenue Bourguiba**, lined with tourist souvenir shops selling carpets and desert roses. About halfway down is the cen-tral **place Ibn Chabbat**, flanked by the market and post office. Avenue Bour-guiba is flanked by **avenue Farhat Hached** to the northwest and **avenue Abou el Kacem Chabbi** to the southeast; at the western end of the latter, the road turns a corner by the Dar Cheraït Museum to become the **Route Touristique**, meeting up with avenue Farhat Hached at the airport turn-off.

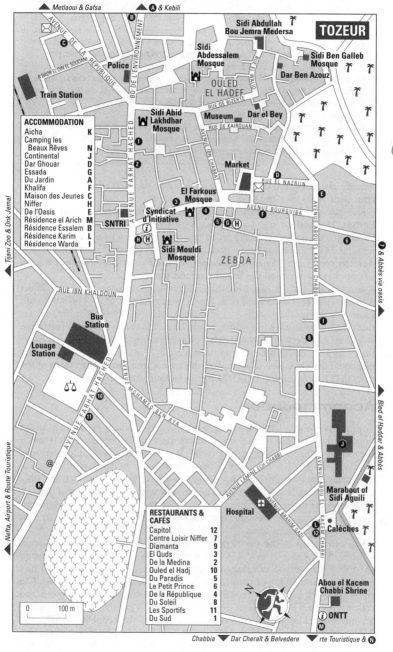

▲ Metlaoui & Gafsa   ▲ Ⓐ & Kebili

TOZEUR

Sidi Abdullah
Bou Jemra Medersa

AVENUE DE LA REPUBLIQUE

Ⓒ

R BADR EL DIN EL SOUDANI

Police

Sidi
Abdessalem
Mosque

Sidi Ben Galleb
Mosque

Dar Ben Azouz

Train Station

OULED
EL HADEF

RUE DE BIZERTE

ACCOMMODATION

Aicha	K
Camping les	
Beaux Rêves	N
Continental	J
Dar Ghouar	D
Essada	G
Du Jardin	A
Khalifa	F
Maison des Jeunes	C
Niffer	H
De l'Oasis	E
Résidence el Arich	M
Résidence Essalem	B
Résidence Karim	L
Résidence Warda	I

Sidi Abid
Lakhdhar
Mosque

Museum

Dar el Bey

RUE DE KAIROUAN

Market

Ⓓ

RUE EL NAZRIIN

Ⓔ

El Farkous
Mosque

Syndicat
d'Initiative

AVENUE BOURGUIBA

Ⓕ

SNTRI

ⓗ Ⓗ

Ⓗ Ⓗ

Sidi Mouldi
Mosque

ZEBDA

Ⓖ

 Tijani Zoo & Onk Jemal

Ⓘ

RUE IBN KHALDOUN

Ⓘ

Bus
Station

Ⓑ

Louage
Station

⚖

Ⓘ

Ⓘ

⑩

⑪

Nefta, Airport & Route Touristique

@

Ⓚ

Ⓙ

Marabout of
Sidi Aguili

Calèches

Ⓛ

⑫

**RESTAURANTS &
CAFÉS**

Capitol	12
Centre Loisir Niffer	7
Diamanta	9
El Quds	3
De la Medina	2
Ouled el Hadj	10
Du Paradis	5
Le Petit Prince	6
De la République	4
Du Soleil	8
Les Sportifs	11
Du Sud	1

Hospital

Abou el Kacem
Chabbi Shrine

Ⓜ

ⓘ ONTT

0   100 m

N

Chabbia ▼   Dar Cheraït & Belvedere ▼   rte Touristique & Ⓝ

▲ Ⓐ & Kebili

Ⓑ

▶ & Abbès via oasis

▶ Bled el Haddar & Abbès

Bled el Haddar & Abbès

355

Moving on from Tozeur

There are regular **buses** to Metlaoui and Gafsa, with SNTRI services continuing to Kairouan and Tunis. There are also buses to Kebili, two continuing to Gabès, two to Douz, though you may in fact have to change buses at Kebili. In the other direction, there are regular services to Nefta, and two that continue to the Algerian border at Hazoua.

    Louages leave from a yard opposite the bus station. You should have no trouble getting a vehicle from here to Tunis, Nefta, Tamerza, Metlaoui, Gafsa, Kebili, Degache or El Hamma du Jerid; direct louages for Sfax and Gabès are less frequent but do run, especially early mornings and Sundays.

    Tozeur's **airport** (⊕76 453 388), best reached by taxi, has flights to Tunis. There are no longer any passenger **train** services to or from Tozeur, though the line (partly washed away by flooding) has been repaired, and the station renovated, a sign of possible reinstatement of passenger services in the future, *insha'allah*.

Straight ahead, off the tarmac, is the road out to the **Belvedere**, a rocky outcrop with views over the oasis.

The **bus** and **louage stations** are on the main Nefta–Kebili road, **avenue Farhat Hached**, at the northern end of avenue Bourguiba. If you arrive by **air**, there's no public transport to take you the 3km to town except taxis (around 3TD); Europcar have a desk at the airport (⊕76 453 388) in case you want to rent a car. There are **calèches** on hand on avenue Abou el Kacem Chabbi to take you into the oasis or around town.

The **ONTT** (July & Aug Mon–Sat 7.30am–1.30pm; Sept–June Mon–Thurs 8.30am–1pm & 3–5.45pm, Fri & Sat 8.30am–1.30pm; ⊕76 454 503), with some English-speaking staff, is at 89 avenue Abou el Kacem Chabbi, not far from the *calèche* stand. More conveniently located is the **Syndicat d'Initiative** at 143 avenue Bourguiba (Mon–Thurs 8am–noon & 3–6pm, Fri & Sat 8am–noon, sometimes open beyond these hours), by the corner of avenue Farhat Hached. They have lists of bus and air departures, and can arrange tours of the oasis (5TD/hr by camel, 10TD/hr for up to four people by *calèche*).

Accommodation

Tozeur has plenty of **hotels**, and some very good choices particularly at the upper end of the low-budget range, where most places even have a/c, though they usually charge a supplement to use it. The route Touristique overlooking the Belvedere has a number of three- to five-star tourist hotels, each with swimming pools, nightclubs and money-changing facilities; in fact, the only thing missing is a beach. Prices tend not to vary with the season, but, if they do, high season is often winter not summer. Note that unless you make arrangements in advance, you are unlikely to find any hotels open if you arrive at 4am on the night bus from Tunis.

You can **camp** at the *Camping les Beaux Rêves* on avenue Abou el Kacem Chabbi (⊕76 453 331, ⓕ76 454 208, ⓦbeauxreves.koi29.com), 500m beyond the ONTT. Here you can sleep in your own tent, in a Bedouin version in a palm-frond hut (7TD), or on a hammock hung between two date palms. The site is very well kept, with trees, a stream behind it, running water, showers and toilets. Camping excursions in jeep and tent are also possible if enough people are interested. The *Maison des Jeunes* at 29 avenue de la République (⊕76 452 335), a couple of hundred metres up the Gafsa road from its junction with avenue Farhat Hached, was closed for repairs at last check, but used to charge 4TD for a dorm bed, with a 10pm curfew.

THE JERID | Tozeur: Accommodation

6

Hotels

Town centre

Aicha 156 av Farhat Hached ☎76 452 788, ℗76 452 873. Good value, with all rooms en suite, many with a bath, and also a/c (3TD), but the decor is a bit hit-and-miss, and some rooms can be smelly at the wrong time of year. ❷

Continental 79 av Abou el Kacem Chabbi ☎76 461 411, ℗76 452 109. Comfortable if rather impersonal, with big rooms and a pool. It's used mostly by tour groups whisked in from Hammamet and Monastir on whirlwind jeep "safaris" of the south. ❺

Dar Ghouar rue el Nazriin ☎76 452 666, ℗76 461 923. Adequate if a little neglected; all rooms are en suite with a/c and TV, but they're rather gloomy. The mattresses can be a bit ropey, so check yours before taking the room. Some rooms have a small balcony, and there's a pool. ❺

Essada 65 av Bourguiba ☎76 460 097. Off the street itself, opposite the market, this is the cheapest place in town, simple but clean and good value, with hot shared showers, and rooms around a central patio full of jasmine and bougainvillea. ❶

Hôtel du Jardin bd de l'Environnement ☎76 454 196, ℗76 454 199. A lovely little place, though a little way out of town; it's set in a large, pretty garden full of trees and singing birds, 100m east of *Résidence Essalem*. The rooms are pleasant and tasteful, in a choice of yellow, pink or blue decor. ❹

Khalifa 35 av Bourguiba ☎76 454 858. Basic but clean rooms, those upstairs en suite, though some have windows onto the corridor rather than outside. In summer you can sleep on the roof (5TD). Rate includes breakfast. ❷

Niffer 4 rue Général Hussein, at the junction of av Bourguiba with av Farhat Hached ☎76 460 555, ℗76 461 900. Bang in the centre, offers airy, en-suite a/c rooms, reasonably spacious, and breakfast is included. ❷

Hôtel de l'Oasis 1 av Abou el Kacem Chabbi ☎76 452 300, ℗76 461 522, ℮oasisdartozeur@gnet .tn. Rather a classy joint but friendly with it, and definitely preferable to the three-stars out in the Route Touristique, with comfortable rooms, pleasant gardens, a pool and smart service. ❻

Résidence el Arich 93 av Abou el Kacem Chabbi ☎76 462 644, ℗76 461 544, ℮www.elarichtozeur.8m.com. A pleasant little hotel with cool, clean rooms, all en suite with a/c (3TD), and some self-catering family apartments. Breakfast, included in the rate, is on the roof terrace. ❸

Résidence Essalem 21 bd de l'Environnement ☎76 462 881, ℗76 454 199. A quiet, family-run place on the Kebili and Degache road, east of town, clean and friendly, with hot water round the clock, no a/c but ceiling fans, and some rooms en suite (these cost no extra). Rate includes breakfast. ❷

Résidence Karim 150 av Abou el Kacem Chabbi ☎76 454 574. Opposite the calèche stand, a bright clean place, and very friendly, with pretty tiles, en-suite rooms, a/c (4–7TD), and a roof terrace with a vista over the oasis. The rate includes breakfast. Plans for the future include central heating for the winter months, when Tozeur can get surprisingly cold at night. ❷

Résidence Warda 29 av Abou el Kacem Chabbi ☎76 452 597, ℗76 452 744. An old favourite, with very helpful staff, hot water round the clock, breakfast (included in the rate) and all bar four rooms en suite (some feature a shower, some a bath) with ceiling fans and, if those aren't sufficient, a/c (3.5TD). There's a pleasant garden, and a covered roof terrace with views over town. ❷

The route Touristique

Abou Nawas Tozeur ☎76 453 500, ℗76 452 686, ℮www.abounawas.com. Pleasantly peaceful with tastefully decorated rooms, all with TV, a/c, terrace or balcony, and bathroom. Facilities include a pool and fitness centre. ❼

Basma ☎76 452 488, ℗76 452 294, ℮hotel. basma@gnet.tn. Friendly and relaxed, with a lot of young French guests, and the usual three-star facilities, including a pool, though the rooms are smallish. Activities include *pétanque*, and there's also a massage service. ❻

Dar Cheraït ☎76 454 888, ℗76 454 472, ℮www.darcherait.com. A very pricey deluxe establishment (rooms start at around 270TD), adjoining the museum complex, with junior, senior and presidential suites available. ❾

Ksar el Jerid 186 av Farhat Hached, just off the rte Touristique ☎76 454 323, ℗76 454 515. Cool and comfortable with spacious, well-furnished a/c rooms, friendly, efficient staff, and all mod cons, including a pool. ❼

Palm Beach Palace ☎76 453 111, ℗76 453 911, ℮www.accorhotels.com. Tozeur's classiest establishment, purring with understated luxury; facilities include fitness centre, hammam, Jacuzzi, pool and three restaurants. Note that rates almost double over Christmas and New Year. ❾

Phedra ☎76 452 185, ℗76 452 799, ℮www .phedra-tozeur.com.tn. A friendly place with great views of the sunset over the Belvedere, even when actually in the pool. Ask for a room with a view. ❼

THE JERID | Tozeur: Accommodation

357

The Town

The most interesting part of Tozeur is the ancient **Ouled el Hadef** quarter, between avenue Farhat Hached and avenue Bourguiba, where the architecture, like the lives of its people, is largely traditional. Avenue Abou el Kacem Chabbi runs west alongside the quarters of **Zebda** and **Chabbia**, which have been less zealous about preserving their traditions than Ouled el Hadef.

You may notice that the traditionally dressed women in Tozeur and the oasis wear a distinctive **black gown** decorated with a single stripe. Originally, a white stripe was worn by women from Tozeur, and a blue one by women from Nefta, but the blue seems to have largely taken over in Tozeur too. An unmarried girl will have a narrow stripe on her gown, changing it for a broader band when wed.

Ouled el Hadef

The oldest part of town is the fourteenth-century **Ouled el Hadef**, its entrances marked by plans of the quarter. As at Tamerza, the high walls are faced with small rectangular bricks, presenting a blank exterior to the narrow streets. The windowless walls ensure the privacy that is prescribed in the Koran – in fact, the Arabic word for a house, *maskin*, is related to *sakina*, which means "peaceful and holy". A fifteenth-century legal ruling of one Sidi Khalil, brief and to the point, states that "anyone may climb up his date palm but only if he previously informs the neighbour into whose house he might obtain a view". Only traditionally made bricks are used and the brickwork in the quarter is almost unique in Tunisia (see box below); the only other place it can be found is in neighbouring Nefta. The bricks themselves are made near the Belvedere.

This is an excellent place to wander around and get lost, despite groups of young boys who sometimes like to bait tourists. Things to look out for, apart from the brickwork, are the palm-trunk ceilings overhead as you pass under archways, and large doors equipped with three knockers that some houses are still fitted with. Men, women and children each have a different one with its own tone (men left, women right, children underneath the other two), so

---

Brickwork in Tozeur and Nefta

The **houses** in the old quarters of Nefta and Tozeur are unique in Tunisia. They are constructed of yellowish handmade bricks, some of which protrude in ornate geometrical designs in relief on the walls of the houses, and their shapes and motifs are repeated on local carpets and shawls. The decorative technique was first used in Syria and Iraq during the eighth century and was carried west by the Arab invaders in the tenth century. The only other place it is practised today is in Iran.

The old quarters have been extensively restored, the work largely carried out in the traditional manner. To make the bricks, local clay and sand are mixed, soaked in water and left to mulch for a day. The mixture is then shaped in a wooden frame and left to dry in the sun. Finally, the bricks are baked in a kiln for three days at temperatures of up to 1000°C. The industry is on something of an upturn at the moment as people are returning to locally made bricks – which provide better insulation against extremes of temperature than breeze blocks. The pattern-making protruding bricks also create small patches of shade on the wall, generating convection currents that cool the surface.

For everything you could possibly want to know about the bricks, their manufacture and use in local buildings, a book called *Brick of Tozeur* by Haddan Abdelhamid is available locally (for example at Cheraiet Atef, 31 av Farhat Hached, and sometimes at *Résidence Warda*).

that any visitor can be greeted by the appropriate member of the household. A door with only two knockers indicates a family without children. Poorer families have doors made of palm-trunks, while richer ones have doors made of true wood. Designs in nails on the doors include horseshoes, for good luck of course, fish to ward off the evil eye, crosses with arrows, and tridents. A green door indicates a religious building rather than a residence.

The main street of the quarter, **rue de Kairouan**, leading from the *Hôtel Splendi* and the *Hôtel de l'Oasis*, runs from one side to the other. Mohammed Said, who runs a shop on rue de Kairouan, 50m southeast of the museum, is a mine of information on the quarter, and is usually happy to explain its quirks to those who are interested. On the east side of the street is the fourteenth-century **tomb of Sidi Bou Aissa**, now converted into a **Museum of Popular Arts and Traditions** (Tues–Sun 8am–noon & 3–6.30pm; 1TD), with some friendly young ladies from the Syndicat d'Initiative to show you around. Among the exhibits are objects from the traditional marriage ceremony – the wooden chests for the bride's clothes, an Egyptian silk dress, and ornamental green and yellow pottery. A collection of manuscripts includes a timetable for the distribution of water through an oasis, devised by Ibn Chabbat in the thirteenth century as a way of ensuring equal supplies for every landowner and only printed by the French. In the courtyard, among miscellaneous statuary, is a traditional three-knocker door, in case you didn't spot any while wandering around the old quarter.

If you leave rue de Kairouan at its northern end, two right turns will take you down rue de Bizerte. The rue el Walid, left at the end, leads to the **Medersa of Sidi Abdullah Bou Jemra**. A right, on the other hand, takes you to the main square of the quarter, where a room in the former bey's mansion, **Dar el Bey** (no. 9) was used for the cave in the film *The English Patient*. The family are usually happy to let visitors in at any reasonable hour, but will expect a gratuity for it. Not far away to the north is the mosque whose minaret dominates the quarter, that of **Sidi Abdessalem**.

Avenue Bourguiba, the markets and Tijani zoo

The mosques on avenue Bourguiba are of limited interest. The **El Farkous Mosque**, with its tall, slender minaret, is attractive and distinctive, but not very ancient. The **Mosque of Sidi Mouldi**, down the road by the Syndicat d'Initiative, has a minaret in a similar style, restored in 1944, but you probably won't be allowed up it to admire the view.

The main section of the **Sunday market**, which actually starts on Saturday afternoon and finishes shortly after lunch on Sunday, takes place in an enclosure by the bus station; there's also a **livestock market**, mostly for sheep, goats and horses, on avenue de la République (the El Hamma road), 150m past the post office, where the railway crosses the street.

North of town, animal lovers will want to avoid the cruel little cages of the **Tijani Zoo** – left from avenue Bourguiba into avenue Farhat Hached, then signposted (right) after some 150m and off to the right a few hundred metres up (daily 8am–nightfall; 2TD). This was once a snake farm, but the reptiles are nowadays a very minor attraction, not even easy to spot beneath their wire gauze. The biggest attraction is a Coca-Cola-drinking camel.

South of town

Avenue Abou el Kacem Chabbi is named after the great Tozeuri poet (see p.555), who is buried in a shrine tucked away by the ONTT. With the northern edge of the oasis on one side, it also skirts the quarters of Zebda and

Chebbia. **Zebda** borders avenue Bourguiba, across which it glared angrily at Ouled el Hadef, the two in a state of mortal feud until the nineteenth century. **Chabbia**, a little further west along the road, was one of the last places in Tunisia where the bride rode in a camel-borne litter at her marriage ceremony. The camel still joins the procession, but nowadays the bride walks alongside it. If you want to see the real thing, you'll have to go to Jerba. Behind the *Hôtel Continental*, near where the camels and calèches hang out, is the photogenic little **Marabout of Sidi Aguili**, a favourite on postcards of the region.

Dar Cheraït

At the end of avenue Abou el Kacem Chabbi is the **Dar Cheraït complex** featuring a museum, an Arabian Nights grotto, a restaurant, café and deluxe apartments, with all sorts of additions and extensions in the pipeline. The **museum** (daily 8am–midnight; 3.4TD) gives an upmarket, sanitized view of Tunisian life based on waxwork-style tableaux, but it's well laid out, with treasures formerly belonging to the bey, among other fascinating antiques, all with English explanations. If you so desire, attendants dressed up like the bey's servants will escort you round. The **Arabian Nights Grotto** (same hours as museum; 5TD) is a kind of overblown fairground funhouse complete with mirrors, scary effects and fluorescent decor, based loosely on ideas from the *Thousand and One Nights* (which are mainly set in Egypt and Iraq, and don't actually mention Tunisia). There is a leaflet (0.5TD) offering some explanation, and a cassette outlining the story as you enter, and you may recognize images such as Ali Baba's cave, Aladdin's genie and Sinbad and the Roc. Best visited after dark, when the tableaux are spotlit, the grotto definitely has its moments and is fun in a tacky sort of way, but you should try to avoid getting tangled up with a tour group. There is also now a third exhibition in the complex, **Dar Zamen** (same hours as museum; 5TD), illustrating the history of Tunisia from the days of the dinosaurs, with tableaux and an explanatory booklet (1.8TD). The escorts on all these tours are generally used to showing round groups, and can get impatient with individual tourists, but you've paid your money, so don't let them rush you. After a tour, the complex's café is a handy place to stop for a drink, so long as you don't mind paying well over the odds for it.

The Belvedere and beyond

The paved track west of Dar Cheraït follows the main watercourse out to **Parc Ras el Aïn**, a landscaped garden with no entry times or charges as yet, that encloses an open-air bathing pool fed by hot and cold springs (hence the park's name, which means "head of the spring" or "fountainhead"), some children's playground attractions (slides, roundabouts and see-saws), and also a series of large rocks that used to be called the **Belvedere**. These have now been decorated – some would say defaced – with some rather ugly sculptures, but they have also had steps built into them, and can be climbed for a view over the oasis. At night the Belvedere is lit up for the sake of tourists in the *zone touristique* hotels, who have a view onto it. Beyond the Belvedere, a **golf course** is being constructed, which will use recycled waste water.

Beyond the golf course, south and west, the shards glinting on the ground like broken glass in the sun are in fact **rock crystals**. A little further, for the time being, are the open-air traditional **brick factories**, whose workers are usually happy to show tourists how they make the bricks used in Tozeur's distinctive architecture. Two brothers at the first brick factory double up as Tozeur's only potters, and will make pieces to order. The scrub area around the factories is an excellent and easily accessible place for spotting desert bird life.

The oasis

Tozeur's vast **oasis** covers around ten square kilometres planted with some 200,000 palms and fed by 200 springs, the water channelled along dykes, or *seguias*, and controlled by a series of sluices. At the time of Ibn Chabbat, in the eleventh century, these streams were blocked with sections of palm trunks, which were opened and closed by orders of the warden. Most tourists visit the

Dates and date farmers

Of all the 120 varieties of date palm (for more on the trees themselves, see p.400), the finest is the **deglat en nour**, or "finger of light", so called because of the translucent quality of the ripened fruit. Tozeur and Nefta produce 1000 tonnes of these dates every year, most of which is exported to Europe for Christmas. According to legend, a poor village woman died before she could make the pilgrimage to Mecca and was buried with her humble string of beads, made from date stones. The tears the Prophet shed in sympathy germinated the stones and created not only an oasis but also the new variety of date. The palms are artificially pollinated in April and June each year, and the fruit harvested by hand at the beginning of winter. Each tree is yields some fifteen or twenty clusters of dates, each weighing about 10kg. The date is extremely **nutritious** – not only high in energy but also rich in niacin, iron, potassium, phosphorus and pantothenic acid. It can be preserved, and when properly stored, will keep for a year or more. On long journeys, when food is scarce, it's possible to survive on dates alone. The stones are also used to feed camels, which happily munch away on them.

Palm wine, known as *laghmi*, is simply the sap of the palm, collected from the top of the trunk by cutting off one of the fronds and letting it drip into an earthenware pot tied to the trunk. Tapping the tree for palm wine will weaken and eventually kill it, so palms producing eating-quality dates are not used. *Laghmi* takes 24 hours to ferment, and is available in sweet (fresh) and fermented versions. The latter needs to be treated with caution as it's unpredictably potent and goes off quickly. The wine is generally available between April and October – ask around in the oasis in Tozeur or Nefta, but be discreet, since sale of fermented *laghmi* is strictly speaking illegal. You'll find the unfermented version on sale in front of the municipal market in Tozeur during the season (look for the earthenware jugs plugged with palm fibre from which it is sold). As for buying the dates themselves, in season the market in Tozeur is as good a place as any, and you can also get them easily in Gafsa and Douz, but beware that they sometimes have maggots inside (especially if slightly old), and may need opening and checking individually before eating.

The sharecroppers' tale

Most of the palms are owned by wealthy (often absentee) landlords, who employ labourers as **sharecroppers**. Instead of a salary, they each receive a share of the harvest. Out on the plains where the main crop is barley, this share is about one-fifth – a share that gives them their name, the *khammes*. In the oases, however, the figure falls to one-tenth, sometimes less, because the date harvest is so valuable.

Without capital of their own, and since they are paid only at the end of the agricultural year, the *khammes* have to borrow from their employers to tide them over. Paying high rates of interest on these loans forces them into heavy debt, which, after a poor harvest, they are often unable to repay. And so they fall into a sort of debt bondage, bound to the employer in perpetuity because they cannot pay off the ever-increasing loans. Since Independence the government has tried to improve their status by introducing a union to combat the employers. Strangely enough the *khammes* have been far from enthusiastic. They see the weather, the cause of poor harvests, as the source of their condition rather than the employers' exploitation of their poverty.

oasis on a calèche from the stand opposite the *Résidence Karim* on avenue Abou el Kacem Chabbi, but for those who don't mind a long walk, shanks' pony is an equally pleasant way to wander through the oasis, and one that allows you more flexibility to stop where you fancy.

The main road into the oasis branches off avenue Abou el Kacem Chabbi by the *Hôtel Continental*. Just over 500m along it is the village of **Bled el Haddar**, site of Roman **Tusuros**, where a partially restored brickwork **minaret** stands on a course of Roman stonework in an enclosure to the right of the main road. Also in the enclosure is the **Great Mosque**, built around 1190 by the Almoravid Ibn Ghaniya who, like so many others, came to Tozeur to start a rebellion. Its beautiful stone **mihrab**, all the more striking in this plain interior, was the work of craftsmen from the Balearic islands. Like many Islamic buildings, the mosque exploits sunlight, which, during the afternoon, streams through the narrow windows down the central nave to the mihrab. The classic minaret above begins as a circle, develops into an octagon and ends up square; the "crow's nest" is a later addition. On the other side of the tower, a path leads to the reconstructed **tomb of Ibn Chabbat** (first built in 1282), who devised the complex irrigation and cultivation system used in the oasis.

The road continues through some of the oasis's best cultivated land, reaching, after a couple more kilometres, the little village of **Abbès**. Just beyond it is the **Marabout of Sidi Bou Lifa**, overshadowed by a venerable old **jujube tree** apparently planted by the saint himself; both are reputed to be over 700 years old. Jujube trees, which originated in China, bear fruit which taste a little like dates and can be eaten fresh or dried; in the USA the fruit is used to make large sucking sweets. From here the road meanders lazily a few pleasant kilometres through the oasis, before bringing you back to Tozeur near the southern end of avenue Bourguiba.

Two hundred metres past the tree and marabout is a garden and zoo, unassumingly called **Paradis** (daily 8am–nightfall; 2TD). The menagerie includes gazelles, several tormented baboons, snakes, and a family of lions, all kept in overcrowded captivity. If you arrive at the same time as a tour group, you can also see such spectacles as performing scorpions and a Coke-drinking camel. More interesting perhaps, though overpriced, are the pistachio, rose, violet and pomegranate syrups made from plants in the garden and sold at the entrance.

A kilometre further, Tozeur's mayor, Abderrazak Cheraït, the man behind the Dar Cheraït complex, is busy setting up his latest project, the much larger and more ambitious **Chak-Wak**, named after one of the lands visited by Sinbad in the *Thousand and One Nights*. It starts with a history of evolution from the dinosaurs to prehistoric humans, illustrated by a large number of models, and a reconstructed volcano that you can stroll through. This is followed by a history of the Jewish, Christian and Muslim religions from Adam and Eve and Noah's ark through to Moses, Jesus and Mohammed, including a walk through the parted waves of the Red Sea, though the biblical personages themselves are not represented, such depictions being against koranic law. The exhibitions should be up and running by the time you read this.

Eating and drinking

There are a number of budget and mid-range **restaurants** along avenues Bourguiba, Abou el Kacem Chabbi and Farhat Hached. For something a little classier, apart from the *Petit Prince*, your best bets are the restaurants of the various tourist-class hotels, most of which do set menus and/or buffet lunch and supper: try the *Continental*, *L'Oasis* and *Dar Ghouar*. The restaurants on avenue

Abou el Kacem Chabbi are not allowed to serve alcohol, so if you want beer or wine with your meal, eat elsewhere.

Several of the moderately priced places offer local specialities, which usually need to be ordered in advance for at least four people, though some places are flexible. One Tozeur speciality is *metabka*, sometimes referred to as "Berber pizza". Strictly for onion lovers, it consists of a *harissa* and onion sauce between two chapatti-like griddle-baked unleavened breads. Other local dishes include *seffa* and *barkoukech*, both based on something like couscous, though with larger grains; *seffa* is made with vegetables and contains no meat, while *barkoukech* is served with a sauce that contains two or three meats such as rabbit, chicken and lamb. There is even a special regional version of couscous: *couscous helba*, made with saltfish.

Restaurants

Capitol Restaurant 158 av Abou el Kacem Chabbi ☏76 462 531. Pleasant and moderately priced, offering *metabka*, *seffa* and *barkoukech* (these usually need to be ordered in advance for a minimum of four people, but ask), and camel steak. They also serve the usual staples, and veg couscous. Daily 11am–3pm & 6.30–10pm.

Restaurant Diamanta 94 av Abou el Kacem Chabbi, opposite the road to Bled el Haddar. Moderately priced traditional fare, including a good lamb couscous. Daily noon–3pm & 7–10pm.

Restaurant de la Medina 19 av Farhat Hached. A reasonably cheap place serving couscous, tajine and *metabka*. Daily 11.30am–3pm & 6.30–9.30pm.

Restaurant Ouled el Hadj av Farhat Hached. A popular low-priced Tunisian restaurant, serving standards like roast chicken, lamb and *riz Djerbien*. Open outside the little lunchtime and supper-time "windows": daily 7am–midnight.

Restaurant du Paradis 75 av Bourguiba, but in fact in a small street off av Bourguiba opposite the market. Serves a small selection of very low-priced Tunisian dishes including either spaghetti or couscous or rice with lamb. Daily noon–3pm & 6–10pm.

Restaurant le Petit Prince Off av Abou el Kacem Chabbi near the top of av Bourguiba ☏76 452

518. Pricier restaurant and bar offering fine French and Tunisian cooking, including roast rabbit and six different types of coucous, with a band playing most evenings except Monday. Daily 12.30–3pm & 7.30pm–midnight.

Restaurant de la République Through the arches between 99 and 101 av Bourguiba. An excellent establishment, popular with tourists and Tunisians alike, with good service, good food and moderate prices. They do one vegetarian main course, *chak-chouka*. Daily noon–3pm & 7–10pm.

Restaurant du Soleil 58 av Abou Kacem el Chabbi, opposite the *Résidence Warda* ☏76 454 220. Good food and pleasant dining at moderate prices, with veggie couscous for non-carnivores and, if ordered in advance, *seffa*, *barkoukech* or camel-meat couscous. Daily except Fri noon–3pm & 6.30–10pm.

Restaurant les Sportifs 163 av Farhat Hached. Cheap and cheerful Tunisian diner, serving chicken, chips, lamb chops and the like. Daily noon–3pm & 7–9pm.

Restaurant du Sud 11 av Farhat Hached, opposite the Agil station. Sfaxian specialities at moderate prices, including spaghetti *aux fruits de mer*, plus *metabka* and four kinds of couscous. Daily 9am–3pm & 6–10pm.

Cafés and bars

The best **patisserie** in town is the *El Quds* at 60 avenue Bourguiba (daily 6am–10am), which does fresh fruit milkshakes and a choice of almond, pistachio or hazelnut baklava. The former *Hôtel Splendid*, opposite the Dar Ghouar, is now a **bar**, a bit raucous; the bars of the upmarket hotels such as the *Ksar el Jerid* are your best bet for a quiet drink, especially for women. For a **coffee or tea** in beautiful surroundings, try the *Centre Loisir Niffer* in the oasis (daily 9am–midnight), an outdoor café among banana trees and bougainvillea-swathed date palms, with a swimming pool and sometimes entertainment in the evenings. To find it, continue for 200m past the *Restaurant le Petit Prince* to the statue of Ibn Chabbat, where you bear left (the right fork leads after 4km to Abbès), then take a right after 100m and it's 150m further on your right.

Few films have such a devoted cult following as *Star Wars*, and Tunisia provided locations for the original 1977 movie, and the first and second prequels, *The Phantom Menace* (1998) and *Attack of the Clones* (2002). In each film, Tunisia plays the role of the desert planet Tatooine (named after the town of Tataouine), home of Luke Skywalker. As a result, the country has begun to attract quite a number of *Star Wars* fans eager to find themselves a long time ago in a galaxy far, far away. Some locations can be visited with Tunisian travel agencies such as The Green Travel in Tozeur (see opposite), but it's also possible to visit others under your own steam, especially if you have transport.

Onk Jemal 30km north of Tozeur (no public transport). The site where Quinion and Darth Maul slogged it out in *The Phantom Menace*, and the background for the pod race in the same film, is a popular stop for jeep-borne tour groups. The set is still in place, and open to visitors. The same site was also used in *The English Patient* – indeed, the piste to get here was made specifically for its film crew. The name Onk Jemal, meaning "Camel's Head", comes from a rock formation resembling the head and hump of a camel.

Shubiel Gorge By the marabout of Sidi Bou Helal near Kriz (see p.373; no public transport). The location for two ambush scenes in *Star Wars*, of R2-D2 by robotnapping space nomads, and of Luke Skywalker and his robot chums by Sand People. It was christened "Star Wars Canyon" by the film crew, and also used as a location in *Raiders of the Lost Ark* and *The English Patient*, as well as *The Phantom Menace*.

Chott and dunes near Nefta 10km west of Nefta (no public transport). A piste crossing the main road leads south down onto the *chott* to a site used for exterior shots of Luke Skywalker's home, although little remains of the set now. To the north, the same road leads to the dunes where R2-D2 and C-3PO landed in an escape pod at the beginning of *Star Wars*. Neither site is easy to find, and you'd really have to be an enthusiast to go out looking for either of them.

Ajim Jerba (see p.434; easy access by public transport, though specific sights want searching out). In town, on avenue Abou el Kacem Chabbi (first right off avenue Salah Ben Youssef, the Guellala road, 100m east of place 7 Novembre, the roundabout in the centre of town; if you're approaching from avenue Salah Ben Youssef, it's the domed building, now abandoned, 50m down on the right), though barely recognizable nowadays, is the entrance to the bar at the space port of Mos Eisley where Luke and Obiwan meet Han Solo in the original *Star Wars*. Obiwan's house in the film is an old mosque 3km up the west coast road towards Borj Jillij, on the seaward side; the entrance to Mos Eisley is another old mosque and domed marabout, 11km further north, again on the seaward side of the road.

Matmata (see p.402; easy access by public transport). The *Hôtel Sidi Driss* was the set for the interior shots of Luke Skywalker's home at the beginning of *Star Wars*. You can sit down to a meal in the exact spot Luke had dinner with his aunt and uncle. The main courtyard also served as a location in the second prequel, and most of the set is still in place.

Ksar Haddada Near Ghoumrassen (see p.460; accessible by public transport). Used for the filming of the Mos Espa slave quarters in *The Phantom Menace*.

Ksar Ouled Soltane 30km south of Tataouine (see p.470; accessible by public transport). Used for pick-up shots of the Mos Espa slave quarters in *The Phantom Menace*.

Further details on these locations and their film roles, with photographs and movie stills, can be found at ®www.toysrgus.com/travel/tunisia.html.

Listings

Airlines Tunisair, opposite Hertz on the Nefta road (℡76 452 127), also representing Tuninter.

Banks Banque de Tunisie at 113 av Bourguiba and STB at no. 36 both have ATMs taking Visa and Mastercard. There are two more banks just round the corner in av Farhat Hached (without ATMs). Tozeur's banks maintain a weekend rota, which means that one bank in town will always be open Saturday and Sunday mornings 9am–noon.

Bike rental At the Ameur kiosk, 75 av Abou el Kacem Chabbi, nearly opposite *Restaurant Diamanta*, you can rent out bicycles (3TD/hr) or mopeds (5TD/hr). Agence Slim at 138 av Abou el Kacem Chabbi ℡76 461 555 rents bicycles (43TD/hr), scooters (25TD/hr), and quads or beach buggies (30TD/hr).

Car rental Avis, 96 av Farhat Hached ℡76 454 356; Europcar, 279 av Farhat Hached ℡76 471 119; Hertz, 223 av Farhat Hached ℡76 460 214.

Festivals Every year around November, a series of camel races and Bedouin spectacles, including camel wrestling (camel versus camel), takes place on a site 500m off av Abou el Kacem Chabbi. This being Abou el Kacem Chabbi's birthplace (see p.555), there is also a modern poetry festival in February.

Hammams Hammam el Nakhla is at 8 rue Omar Ibn Abdelaziz, behind the Syndicat d'Initiative (daily: women 10am–1pm & 6–10pm; men 4–10am, 1.30–6pm & 10pm–1am).

Horse-riding You can ride a horse, accompanied by a guide, at Ranch Equi-Balade, rte du Belvedere (℡76 452 613; 15TD/hr, 45TD for half a day), just past the *Hôtel Dar Cheraït*.

Hospital The regional hospital is on av Brahim Gadi (℡76 453 400), off av Abou el Kacem Chabbi, opposite the *Hôtel el Jerid*.

Internet access Palmnet, 140 av Farhat Hached (daily 8am–midnight; 2TD/hr); Tozeur Publinet, 8 rue 4 Août, near *Résidence el Arich* (daily, supposedly 8am–midnight, but often closed earlier; 2TD/hr).

Newspapers Some English-language papers and magazines are available at 9 av Bourguiba, between the *Hôtel Khalifa* and av Abou el Kacem Chabbi.

Pharmacies Several around town, for example at 27 & 118 av Abou el Kacem Chabbi, 74 av Farhat Hached, 76 av Bourguiba. There is a night pharmacy at 157 av Farhat Hached, 100m west of the junction with av Mohamed Ben Aya.

Police The regular police are at the junction of bd de l'Environnement with av de la République (℡76 452 129); the National Guard are at 180 av Farhat Hached ℡76 454 295.

Post office In place Ibn Chabbat, just off av Bourguiba (city hours); changes cash. There's another post office by the *Maison des Jeunes*.

Supermarket Magasin Général, 245 av Farhat Hached, out towards the airport turn-off (Tues–Sat 8am–12.30pm & 2.50–7pm, Sun 8am–1pm).

Swimming The hotels *Continental* and *Oasis* have pools you can use for a few dinars, as do the hotels on the rte Touristique (the *Phedra*'s has a view). Use of the pool at the *Centre Loisir Niffer* oasis café is free for customers.

Tours The Green Travel, rte Touristique (℡76 454 520), opposite Dar Cheraït complex, offer trips which can be booked at most of the budget hotels, in particular *Résidence Warda*, who keep thorough details of itineraries. The most popular outings are half-day excursions to Chebika, Tamerza and Mides (see p.351; 30TD), and to the *Star Wars* set at Onk Jemal (30TD). Another option is a two-day excursion to Ksar Ghilane (see p.475; 120TD).

Nefta

After you've travelled west from Tozeur through almost totally barren and dusty land, the oasis 25km away at **NEFTA** is quite a shock. You don't notice it immediately as you approach – the drab buildings on the edge of the town shield its beginnings – but suddenly its extent becomes clear, as does that of the **Corbeille**, a crater-like central depression densely planted with palm trees. The site of Roman Nepte, Nefta, according to the legends, was settled by Kostel, "son of Shem, son of Noah", at the place where water boiled for the first time after the Flood. It is now one of the most important religious centres in Tunisia, traditionally linked with the mystical brotherhoods of **Sufism**; the ridge above the Corbeille is cluttered with simple whitewashed domes and the old quarters somehow manage to pack in 24 mosques and over a hundred shrines.

All **bus** services stop at the bus station, although the two SNTRI buses to Tunis actually start at the *Hôtel Neptus*, and the morning service parks up there overnight. Regular daily local services run to Tozeur and to the Algerian frontier at Hazoua; there are some through services to major towns such as Gabès and Sfax, as well as to the capital, but for most destinations you'll need to pick up onward transport at Tozeur. **Louages** leave from avenue Bourguiba about 100m west of the Syndicat d'Initiative, serving Hazoua (yellow-striped vehicles), Tozeur (red- or blue-striped vehicles) and occasionally (usually early morning) direct to other places such as Gafsa and Sfax.

West to the Algerian border

The road west from Nefta continues to the Algerian border, 36km away at **Hazoua**, passing the open-air traditional brick factory, 5km out of town, and a market for desert roses (see box p.371), which takes place daily 10km west of town on the south side of the road. The 5km between the Tunisian and Algerian border posts is plied unreliably by occasional Algerian louages. On the other side, there are buses to El Oued, and from there onward to Toggourt and then Hassi Messaoud, Ouargla and Ghardaia. Algerian dinars should be available for cash at the border post.

In the past, the border crossing at Hazoua was on one of the main trans-African overland routes to Mali or Niger. Travellers still continued using this route, even after northern Algeria became pretty much a no-go area, but in early 2003, fundamentalist insurgents kidnapped 32 foreign tourists in southern Algeria, one of whom died in captivity though the others were eventually freed. At time of writing it remains **dangerous** to travel to many parts of Algeria (see p.209 for more information).

Arrival and information

Avenue Bourguiba, the main road from Tozeur to the Algerian border, splits the town neatly in two. Coming in from Tozeur, it descends into the **Corbeille**, which it bridges at the narrowest point – the area south of here is **Ouled ech Chrif**, one of Nefta's old quarters, and over the bridge is **place de la République**, the centre of town. The main road, boulevard de l'Environnement, swings south from here, skirting the quarter of **Beni Ali** on one side and the main hotel zone on the other, before continuing on its way towards Algeria. South of the hotels is the **oasis**, and beyond that the silvery gleam of the Chott el Jerid, which really does look like sea from here. Should you wish to drive around the town, the whole ensemble is neatly encircled by a belt of tarmac, the northern part of which goes right round the top of the Corbeille.

Nefta's **bus station** is on avenue Bourguiba next to the Mobil petrol station, opposite the **Syndicat d'Initiative** (daily 8.30am–noon & 3–6pm); the office is very helpful and can fix you up with a guide at 15TD for a one-and-a-half-hour tour of the town and the oasis. If you have a vehicle, you can hire a guide for a 25TD half-day tour of Nefta and the oasis including a trip out to the dunes, or 50TD plus lunch on you for a full day visiting Chebika, Tamerza and Mides (see p.351). **Louages** arrive at avenue Bourguiba, halfway between the bridge and the Syndicat d'Initiative. **Calèches** hang out off boulevard de l'Environnement near *Hôtel Marhala*, or cruise around town hustling for custom. Expect to pay 6TD per hour for up to four people, but you'll have to haggle, and keep track of the actual time spent.

NEFTA

ACCOMMODATION
Bel Horizon A
Caravanserail H
Habib G
Marhala D
Mirage C
Neptus F
Rose E
Sahara Palace B

RESTAURANTS, CAFÉS & BARS
El Ferdaous 3
Jawhara 2
Les Sources 1

N

▲ *Tozeur*

Bus Station

RUE ALI ALISAWI

i

Sidi Abdallah Laamoud Mosque

Bank

Police

AVENUE BOURGUIBA

ROUTE DE LA CORBEILLE

EZ ZAOUIA

Bank

Louages

2

Sidi Boucetta Mosque

OULED ECH CHERIF

PLACE DE LA LIBÉRATION

Sidi Mohamed Bel Hai Mosque

Sidi Ameur Mosque

Sidi M'Khareg Mosque

Dar Djerid ▼

Dar Houidi ▼

Sidi Zmourtine Mosque

AVENUE DES SOURCES

H

PLACE DE LA RÉPUBLIQUE

Hospital

Sidi Ben Abbes Mosque

CORBEILLE

Pool

EL BAYADHA

Café de la Corbeille

G

Zaouia of Sidi Brahim

Sidi el Hachani Mosque

Sidi Dhaifallah Mosque

Sidi Ahmed Miaad Mosque

Sidi el Tabai Mosque

Sidi Salem Mosque

AVENUE ABOU ESSENNI

Marabout of Sidi Bou Ali ▼

PLACE DE L'INDÉPENDANCE

Sidi Lahmadi Mosque

Sidi Houssine Mosque

Sidi Ahmed Ben Rabah Mosque

BENI ALI

Sidi Mustapha Ben Azouz Mosque

Calèches

★

BOULEVARD DE L'ENVIRONNEMENT

ROUTE TOURISTIQUE

D

H

F

E

▲ *Onk Jemal*

ROUTE DE LA CORBEILLE

A

B

0   200 m

THE JERID | Nefta

6

Hazoua & Algeria ▼

367

Accommodation

Nefta doesn't have the widest choice of **accommodation** in Tunisia. Though there are some reasonable mid-range choices, accommodation at the very top and bottom ends of the spectrum leaves much to be desired. The town was formerly home to Tunisia's last old-school travellers' hotel, the *Hôtel de la Liberté*, a leftover from the days when Nefta was a stop on the overland route from Europe to West and Central Africa; unfortunately, this closed following the death of its owner. As a result, the only budget accommodation is the rather grotty *Habib*, though camping is possible at the *Hôtel Marhala*.

Hotels

Bel Horizon rte de la Corbeille ☎76 430 088, ℻76 430 500, ✉hotelbelhorizon@yahoo.fr. Quiet and comfortable, with a nice pool and a/c rooms that boast balconies and a view over the Corbeille. A definite cut above the other three-stars in town. ❻

Caravanserail rte Touristique ☎76 430 355, ℻76 430 344, ✉hotelcaravanserailnefta@planet.tn. Opposite the *Marhala*, and with a choice of three-star or four-star wings – the latter newer, with TV and mini-bar in all rooms, plus a bathtub as opposed to just a shower. The price in both wings is the same, so ask for the better one. ❼

Habib pl de la Libération ☎76 430 497, ℻76 430 036. The cheapest hotel in town, nicely located but none too clean. The rooms have their own shower; toilets are shared. ❶

Marhala rte Touristique ☎76 430 027, ℻76 430 511, ✉marhala@yahoo.fr. A better deal than its three-star neighbours, though it pretty well equals them in facilities, with a/c rooms and a pool. You can camp here and use the hotel's facilities. Staff can be a bit scarce if you arrive in the middle of the day. ❸

Mirage rte de la Corbeille ☎76 430 622, ℻76 431 182. This hotel was closed for seven years and in

places it looks like it was rebuilt in a hurry, but it's not bad value, with a/c and en-suite bathrooms throughout, plus a small pool. ❹

Neptus rte Touristique ☎76 430 221, ℻76 430 186. Good value, with a large pool and nice airy a/c rooms – ask for an upstairs one with a view of the oasis. They usually give discounts on the official rate. The hotel is also handy for the morning bus to Tunis, as the bus parks up outside and the driver spends the night here. ❺

Rose rte Touristique ☎76 430 696–7, ℻76 430 385. A comfortable tourist hotel with a/c rooms and a big pool, but not worth the premium over the cost of staying at the *Bel Horizon* or the *Neptus*, which have much the same facilities. ❷

Sahara Palace rte de la Corbeille ☎76 432 048, ℻76 431 444, ✉www.saharapalace.com.tn. Nefta's poshest establishment, and supposedly a five-star hotel, this was at one time quite a classy joint, patronized by the likes of Catherine Deneuve, Habib Bouguirba, Jacques Chirac and Brigitte Bardot. It still has the best view and the biggest pool in town, but the service leaves much to be desired, and it's really just another process-the-punters tour group hotel nowadays. ❾

The Town

The most rewarding pastime in Nefta is wandering round the **old quarters** – Ouled ech Cherif, El Bayadha, Ez Zaouia and Beni Ali – where you can admire the distinctive local architecture and, through the ancient doorways, see the looms and rugs which provide a living for most of the people.

Sadly, torrential rain and flooding in 1990 caused considerable damage to Nefta's ancient buildings – especially in El Bayadha, when a chunk of the old quarter fell into the Corbeille. Although the mosques and many homes have been rebuilt, there are still quite a few gaps in between. Ouled ech Cherif, south of avenue Bourguiba, remains the least affected quarter if you fancy a walk to check out the traditional brickwork (see p.358); in the other quarters, much of it has been replaced with cheaper, less attractive materials.

Ouled ech Cherif

At the heart of **Ouled ech Cherif** is place de la Libération, the main square of the quarter. The streets north of place de la Libération are a maze of brick

The Sufi tradition

Sufism, *tasawwuf* in Arabic, is the Divine Wisdom contained within the *tariqah*, the spiritual way or path laid down in the Koran. Participants are called faqirs or dervishes, meaning "poor", and strictly speaking the Sufi is one who has reached the end of the path, which is a direct personal experience of the Unity of God. A Sufi teacher, variously called a faqir, sheikh or *murshid*, prescribes the chants, recitations and body exercises which have made this sect so famous. Besides the Koran and the Hadith (sayings of the Prophet), the Sufi looks to the Hadith Qudsi, in which God speaks in the first person through the Prophet. "My slave", reads one typical verse, "comes ever nearer to me through devotion of his free will, until I love him, and when I love him, I am the hearing with which he sees and the hand with which he fights and the foot with which he walks."

Threatening to usurp religious law and to substitute **mysticism** for the knowledge of the truth contained in the Koran, Sufism has often had an awkward relationship with orthodox **Sunni Islam**. This was partially resolved as early as the eleventh century by saying that Sufism was a way of "apprehending reality", not of finding out new facts about God.

In Tunisia Sufis have long held considerable power. With the breakdown in the control of central government, from the Almohads in the thirteenth century onwards, the sheikhs had great influence in rural areas, setting up *zaouias* which provided shelter and teaching, and administered justice. In the twentieth century, Tunisian liberals as well as the French attacked the *zaouia*'s autonomy and what they considered an obsolete code of conduct. Many devout Muslims, however, continued to practise the hypnosis, trance-like meditation and saint worship, or maraboutism, with which Sufism had always been linked.

alleyways and tunnels roofed with palm beams, while the quarter's most outstanding mosque, that of **Sidi M'Khareg**, stands on the edge of the oasis, its four-domed minaret restored after severe damage in the floods. On the southern edge of the quarter, a couple of hundred metres southeast of the *Restaurant Bar el Ferdaous*, the **Dar Djerid Museum** (daily 9am–8pm; 2.5TD) illustrates the traditional lifestyle of local people, the collection including kitchenware, tools for handicrafts, and bedrooms of the late nineteenth and early twentieth centuries. The visit includes a tour and explanation in French by the friendly and enthusiastic staff. Nearby, the newly opened **Dar Houidi** (daily 8.30am–midnight; 3TD) houses a collection of furniture, clothing and utensils in the seventeenth-century home of its proprietor, who is on hand to show visitors around. The exhibits don't amount to much, but it's a chance to see the interior of a traditional Neftawi house, and there's a café where you can relax with a nice cup of mint tea after your tour.

Ez Zaouia and El Bayadha

Heading west along avenue Bourguiba, you come to place de la République, where a left turn takes you into the heart of the oasis, while a right turn up **avenue des Sources** takes you along the edge of the Corbeille and then crosses it into the **Ez Zaouia** quarter. The edge of the Corbeille offers good views but in general Ez Zaouia is less interesting than the other old quarters and still sustains considerable flood damage. Of its two mosques, **Sidi Mohamed Bel Haj** got away reasonably unscathed, while **Sidi Ameur** was left virtually a ruin, but has since been restored.

Some of the most important monuments in Nefta are along the edge of the Corbeille in the **El Bayadha** area. In the northwest corner of the Corbeille, by the *Hôtel Mirage*, the former *Café de la Corbeille* is now closed, but its terrace is still accessible and offers great views over the Corbeille. Just down the road is the **Zaouia of Sidi Brahim**, a complex of tombs, courtyards and teaching rooms belonging to the Qadria, the most important of the Sufi orders represented here. Members of the order are often buried here near the saint, who also belonged to it. Heading east from here along the southern edge of the Corbeille, you pass five **mosques**, all small, simple in design and packed closely together. The first is the **Sidi el Hachani Mosque**, then the mosques of **Sidi et Tabaï** and **Sidi Ahmed Miaad**. The oldest is the **Mosque of Sidi Salem**, sometimes called the Great Mosque, approached through an unobtrusive doorway off the narrow street; apart from one strip of carving around the walls, its fifteenth-century courtyard is completely unornamented. Finally comes the **Mosque of Sidi Ben Abbes**, the smallest. The road continues from here across an open space that was until recently the town brickworks. The brickworks have moved 5km out of town along the Hazoua road and the site now hosts Nefta's Thursday **market**. Beyond it, the road leads out onto avenue des Sources near place de la République.

Don't take it personally if the *gardiens* of the *zaouia* and mosques turn you away. Nefta is considered a religious city, and local people generally don't like tourists wandering around their monuments. If you are Muslim, you should have no trouble gaining entrance, but if not, you may be luckier with a Syndicat d'Initiative guide.

The Corbeille

The **Corbeille** is a vast sunken extension of the oasis, like a massive crater full of palm trees gouged out of the middle of Nefta, with steep sides to protect it from the harsh desert wind. North of the bridge, it bends around to the west, spreading into a wedge that takes out a large chunk of town; at its northern extremity, the Corbeille measures almost a kilometre across. The springs which irrigated it were beneath the defile, but with the receding water table, these have disappeared and water now has to be pumped from a large pool in the northwestern corner to irrigate the crops in the Corbeille and indeed the whole oasis. The best way through the Corbeille from avenue des Sources is to follow the stream from the west to the east end of the valley, which saves trampling on cultivated land.

Norman Douglas (see p.561) liked the Corbeille so much that he wanted it replicated in Tozeur – "all the elements are present," he explained; "it only requires a few thousand years of labour, and what are they in a land like this?" Good views over the Corbeille can be had from the former *Café de la Corbeille* in the northwestern corner, as well as from the *Hôtel Sahara Palace*, and the neighbouring *Hôtel Bel Horizon*.

The oasis

The **oasis** proper, on the south side of avenue Bourguiba and boulevard de l'Environnement, extends for some ten square kilometres. Wells drilled here in the 1960s reduced the flow from the springs in both the oasis and the Corbeille, and in fact, the springs in the oasis have completely dried up; the date palms were beginning to die from lack of water before the pool in the Corbeille was built to irrigate the oasis artificially.

Numerous tracks lead through the palm groves, all best explored on foot. Set right in the heart of the oasis is the **Marabout of Sidi Bou Ali** – take the road south from place de la République past the hospital and continue for

Desert roses

Desert roses, known in French as "sand roses" (*roses de sable*), are ubiquitous throughout the south of Tunisia – some big, some small, some absolutely enormous, piled high on souvenir stalls, strewn about hotels as part of the decoration, and occasionally mounted at road junctions as part of the street furniture. There is even a daily market dedicated to them 10km west of Nefta. These brown crystalline rock formations that so resemble a petrified flower are in fact formed from rising ground water rich in **gypsum** (calcium sulphate), which crystallizes when the water evaporates. Pure gypsum is white and transparent, but desert roses, found in the valleys between dunes, are brown and opaque due to particles of sand trapped in the crystal. The large ones are rarer and can be pretty impressive, but the small ones make more practical souvenirs – you should be able to pick up several for a dinar in places like Tozeur, Nefta, Douz and Kebili.

It is possible to find your own desert roses, but you'd need transport and a guide. One place to find the formations is off the road from Kebili to El Fouar – Arafat at *Les Amis du Camping* in Kebili (see p.377) may be able to guide you there if he is free. The other place known for desert roses is near Bir Pastor in the very far south (see p.481), but getting there would be a major expedition.

500m. This is a major place of pilgrimage, particularly on the third day after the Aid el Kebir. The marabout is closed to non-Muslims, but it's worth the short walk just to get among the surrounding gardens and to see the other, smaller marabouts (also closed to non-Muslims) along the way. Sidi Bou Ali was born in Morocco and came to Tunisia in the thirteenth century, hoping to resolve the religious disagreement which had divided the area. The legend that he planted the first palm trees in the Jerid (bringing the plants from Touggourt in Algeria) doesn't seem very likely, since Ibn Chabbat had already reorganized the oasis at Tozeur.

Eating and drinking

There's a dearth of **restaurants** outside the hotels. Of the cheap hole-in-the-wall restaurants on avenue Bourguiba, around the louage station, the *Jawhara* (aka *Chez Laroussi*; daily 5am–3pm & 4–11pm) is by far the best. The *Restaurant Bar el Ferdaous* (aka *Bar de la Palmerie*), just inside the oasis south of the Sidi M'Khareg mosque (daily noon–midnight), is good for cheap meals as well as for drinking, inside and outside among the date palms. In the party atmosphere in the evenings, everybody makes a great fuss of unexpected guests – women may find it a little intimidating then, but should be fine having a drink outside in the daytime if they are with a male companion. For something more refined, and female-friendly, the moderately priced *Restaurant les Sources* by the Syndicat de l'Initiative, where avenue Bourguiba meets the route de la Corbeille (daily 12.30–3pm & 6.30–9.30pm). Though the menu is limited, the food here is good, with a couple of vegetarian options such as *chakchouka* in addition to the usual couscous, chicken or grilled lamb, and the choice of indoor or outdoor terrace eating.

Of the **hotel restaurants**, the *Marhala* is the cheapest (daily noon–2pm & 7–9.30pm), with a 10TD set menu and à la carte. The *Neptus* (daily 12.30–2pm & 8–9.30pm) also offers a set menu (14TD), as does the *Bel Horizon* (daily 12.30–2pm & 7.30–9.30pm; 10TD), which also has a small à la carte restaurant. Both the *Bel Horizon* and the *Caravanserail* (daily 12.30–2pm & 7.30–9.30pm) offer an eat-as-much-as-you-like buffet for a few dinars more. The poshest nosh is to be found at the *Sahara Palace* (daily noon–2pm & 8–9.30pm), where dining is à la carte, though at midday the restaurant often seems to be full of tour groups eating a set menu or buffet lunch.

The most congenial place for a **drink** is the *Bar de la Palmerie*, although the *Caravanserail* and the *Neptus* also have bars, where women may feel more comfortable, especially if they are without male travelling companions.

Listings

Banks There are two banks on av Bourguiba, one opposite the Syndicat d'Initiative, the other not far from the post office (where you can change cash too). At the time of writing, there were no ATMs in Nefta.

Festivals The Dakhla pilgrimage on the third day after Aid el Adha (see p.45) is an important *ziara*, featuring Sufi chanting and dancing centred around the Marabout of Sidi Bou Ali.

Hammams Hammam el Baraka, pl de la République (men daily 5am–noon & daily except Mon & Fri 5pm–midnight; women daily 1–5pm, and later on Mon & Fri); Hamman Lahmar, on rue Ali Aisawi just south of the mosque, is open similar hours.

Hospital The regional hospital is on rue des Martyrs (☎76 430 193), south of pl de la République.

Pharmacy There's one on av Bourguiba between the post office and Syndicat d'Initiative, and another in pl de l'Indépendance.

Police On av Bourguiba (☎76 430 134), about 100m west of the Syndicat d'Initiative.

Post office On av Bourguiba just by the bridge (city hours). International phone calls and currency exchange available.

Swimming pools Most hotels will let non-residents use their pools for a few dinars, while anyone dining at them can normally use the pool without charge.

The Chott el Jerid and Kebili

The **Chott el Jerid**, the largest of Tunisia's desert salt pans, was once called the "Lake of Marks" – after the palm trunks planted across its normally parched surface to guide trading caravans. On maps it is usually shown as a lake, and strictly speaking, that's what it is, a huge salt lake, except that it is completely dry for nine or ten months of the year, though it does flood after rain and is covered in water (never very deep, due to evaporation) for at least some of the time between December and March. In 1885, Sir Lambert Playfair, the British consul in Algiers, was shown a circular platform in the middle of it, called the "Middle Stone", where camels could pass the night. Although the *chott* can be crossed on foot at virtually any point for most of the year, tradition has it that leaving the recommended path can be fatal. Tijini, the fourteenth-century Arab historian, recounts the apocryphal story of the death of a thousand camels and their attendants in black mud beneath the thin salt crust. Now the army has built a causeway and road between Tozeur and Kebili, making this once lengthy journey quick and easy.

Villages north of the chott

DEGACHE, 10km northeast of Tozeur, claims to have the very best dates in the region. The town has basic facilities such as **banks**, a **post office** (country hours) and a municipal **swimming pool** (mid-June to mid-Sept), but nowhere to stay and nowhere very appetizing to eat.

A couple of kilometres beyond Degache at **OULED MAJD**, a newly rebuilt but originally ninth-century brick **mosque** stands in the oasis by the remains of the old town – take a track off the main road to the right (south), just east of the date-packing plant. A glance at the base of the minaret reveals that, like

Roudaire and Ploughshare: the West's plans for the Chott el Jerid

In 1876, one Captain Roudaire, working for the French Ministry of War, put forward a plan to dig a **canal** from the coast at Gabès to the Chott el Fejaj, a finger-like extension of the Chott el Jerid pointing eastwards towards the coast. The sea water, he supposed, would flood the entire area of the salt flats, creating a huge inland sea. In part this scheme was prompted by legends from the past: Roudaire thought the *chott* was the site of the ancient Bay of Triton, birthplace of Poseidon, crossed by Jason with the Argonauts, and a Roman galley had been found on the northern shores. The bey would not agree to "so dangerous an experiment", but, once the French had occupied Tunisia, engineers no longer had to worry about his opinion. The project looked set to go ahead and Ferdinand de Lesseps, architect of the Suez Canal, became involved. At that point, to general embarrassment, preliminary surveys revealed that the *chott* was, in fact, above sea level.

If Roudaire's project sounds daft, then still worse was to follow. In 1962 the American **Atomic Energy Commission** set up the benignly named Ploughshare Program to enquire into "the peaceful use of nuclear explosions". In an associated paper, a leading scientist explained how the radiation would be just an "operational nuisance, quickly localized and easily controlled". For some reason, he couldn't put his finger on anywhere in the USA worthy of the detonation, but the *chott* seemed like an ideal place. With the mighty atom, the whole of the south and parts of the Sahara could be turned into a lake, open to mineral exploration and tourism. Like the programme itself, the idea was quietly cast aside.

the one at Bled el Haddar, it rests on Roman foundations. The minaret with four cupolas is typical of the region, unlike that of the Salaam Mosque on the main road, which bears a striking resemblance to a church tower. From the old mosque, a small road leads east into the oasis, ending after a kilometre at a T-junction, where the **remains** of Roman Gibba can be found just 50m down the right-hand road, mostly lying to the left of it. The ruins, unexcavated and largely overgrown, are all that is left of what was once a palatial mansion.

Continuing east, you cross into the next village, **ZAOUIET EL ARAB** where, north of the main road at its far end, the pretty white **Marabout of Sidi Mohammed Krisanni** sits behind a more recent, and less picturesque, wall of grey breeze blocks. At one time there were seven wells here, in whose memory the village has been rechristened **Saba Abar**, meaning "seven wells", with all the road signs changed accordingly. Local residents, however, continue to use the original name.

The next village, **KRIZ**, begins just east of the marabout, and has also been renamed, as **El Mahassen**. At the other end of the village, 800m up the Gafsa road, just past the railway tracks, the hot spring **baths** (daily: men 5am–8pm front entrance; women 5am–5pm side entrance), are clean first thing in the morning, but a bit soupy by lunchtime – those at El Hamma de l'Arad (see p.38) are cleaner.

Two kilometres south from Kriz on the Kebili road is a turn-off to the east, signposted "Dghoumes"; two kilometres along this on the left, a road leads up to two **marabouts** perched on the mountainside. The larger, left-hand one is the tomb of Sidi Bou Helal, a thirteenth-century hermit and holy man, the disciple of Sidi Bel Abbes, who lies buried in the other marabout. These marabouts are the site of a large joint *moussem*, held on the first Wednesday of the spring school holiday in March. This otherwise desolate spot was used in the filming of *Star Wars* (see box, p.364), and the gorge by the marabouts was christened "Star Wars Canyon" by the film crew.

Beyond the Dghoumes turn-off, the main road begins to drop down towards sea level as you cross the **chott**, giving a perfect view of the pale expanse of salt and sand, marked only by a single black tarmac strip. To the east, the mountains gradually march into the distance and the crystal surface is concealed by mirages on every side. The mirage, or *fata morgana*, is caused by the refraction of light from the sky and from objects such as trees as it hits the thin heated air rising from the sun-baked ground. The light is bent upward so that it appears to come from the surface, and is perceived as a reflection, making the sand or tarmac look like water, which always seems to begin a few hundred metres ahead of you. However, it's a shore that constantly recedes, so that in the shimmering heat, the *chott* becomes a surreal land of dreamlike optical effects reminiscent of a Tanguy painting.

The Nefzaoua

The southern side of the Chott, the region called **Nefzaoua**, is an area full of oases, smaller but more frequent than those further north, with lonely clumps of palms standing among the dunes or on the salt flats.

Most of the **oasis villages** are stretched out along the road from Tozeur. They are largely ugly, but if you want to see traditional oasis agriculture it's interesting to roam around the palmeries, where villagers will proudly show you their plots and present you with fruit straight from the trees. Just get off the bus or ask the louage to stop at any point; the road is busy, so you should be able to pick up a passing bus or louage to Kebili later.

Just after the road rises out of the Chott proper, a turn-off to the south leads to **FATNASSA** and **DEBEBCHA**, the latter a beautiful site with a marabout, palms, a couple of dunes and some fabulous yardangs (wind-sculpted rocks). It's a great place to watch the sun go down, though not unknown to the jeep "safari" mob. A café here provides refreshments. A few kilometres further up the Debebcha road, there's a break in the water channel on your left where, if you wander up to the dunes, you'll be greeted by a brilliant vista over the *chott*.

SOUK LAHAD, as its name suggests, hosts a lively Sunday market, as well as a couple of cafés and a bank. There's also a three-star **hotel**, the *Les Dunes* (☎75 480 711, ℗75 480 563; ●), 7km north, complete with swimming pool, restaurant (daily noon–2.30pm & 7.30–9.30pm; 15TD buffet) and the usual amenities. It might not be a bad place to stop for lunch if you're passing, since the tour groups who are its main customers tend to arrive in the evening and depart the next morning, leaving it pretty quiet around midday. If you're staying overnight, it's worth asking for one of the larger rooms, which cost no extra. The hotel's outstanding feature is a tower which you can climb to survey the surrounding landscape.

Six kilometres south of Souk Lahad, a road off to the east, just after the village of Tombar (signposted "Rabta"), leads in 4km to **MANSOURA**, where you can bathe in pools originally built by the Romans (daily: men 5–9am & 5–9pm; women 9am–5pm). The village itself is famous for its melons. About a kilometre further on the main road, you reach **TELMINE**, now a compact place whose oasis was reputedly planted by conquering Egyptians. It was one of a series of outposts used by the Romans to guard against insurrection, and later became a thriving city – which the Almohads destroyed in 1205. The houses, crowded around narrow streets, still give it a medieval look, and a couple of Roman **reservoir pools** still survive. The **Mosque of Oqba** in the centre, formerly the site of a church, was rededicated by Oqba Ibn Nafi in the seventh century.

The Nefzaoua and the bey

Ibn Khaldoun, writing in the fourteenth century, describes the Nefzaoua people as an independent group of Berbers mixed with nomadic Arabs, and in the twelfth and thirteenth centuries they played an important part in the Almoravid rebellion. During the Turkish administration, the Nefzaoua was ruled first from Tripoli and then, in the sixteenth century, from Tunis. Sir Grenville Temple (see p.561) visited in 1835 and found the people quiet after another bout of insurrection. To punish their "rude conduct" the bey had imposed a fine of 15,000 piastres – much more effective, Temple saw, than the "cutting off of heads: for, as they remark, 'what signify a few heads more or less? We have plenty of them but very few piastres.'" When Kebili became the centre of another revolt twenty years later, the bey had clearly had enough – he gave orders that the village was to be evacuated and its residents exiled to Cap Bon. Four years later he relented, but only after the villagers had bought back their lands at an extortionate price.

Kebili

KEBILI, an important market town for slaves until the nineteenth century, is now the administrative centre of the Nefzaoua, 85km southeast of Tozeur. It is not a major centre for tourism, but there are a couple of points of interest, and it is an important interchange, especially for Douz.

The town's main square, **place de l'Indépendance**, is south of the bus and louage stops and just off avenue Bourguiba, which joins the roads to Gabès and Douz. Downhill is the main road to Tozeur. Off the Gabès road just out of town is the MC103 road to Gafsa, via Seftimi, the Chott el Fejaj and the Hachichina mountains.

South of the centre, Avenue Bourguiba continues round an S-curve to become boulevard de l'Environnement and the main road to Douz. Four hundred metres after the S-curve is a fountain that was used as a bathing pool as long ago as Roman times, and after that a hammam with natural hot water from a three-kilometre-deep borehole. The hammam should be open round the clock, with separate entrances for each sex.

Just before you get to the fountain, a road on the right leads west down a hill and then 4km through the oasis to **Old Kebili**, the town's original site, complete with four marabouts and a mosque. The old town has been deserted since 1980, though the mosque still blares out the "Allah-o-akbar"'s five times daily and an annual date harvest **festival** is held here at the end of November. Also here is a small square called **El Bortal** (the gateway), site of the former slave market where people from West and Central Africa were traded as chattel, after being kidnapped and marched across the desert. Though on nothing like the scale of the trans-Atlantic slave trade, the trans-Saharan trade was just as brutal and murderous; on the cross-desert journey, the many who fell by the wayside were simply left to die. In 1848, Tunisia became the first Arab country to abolish slavery, but the forced migration of Africans from south of the desert is still reflected today in the high proportion of Nefzaoua people who are black.

A turning on the left just before you reach Old Kebili from the modern town leads, after 500m, to the ruins of **Dar el Kehia**, the "chief's house". The chief in question was Ahmed Ben Hamadi, Kebili's first local administrator, appointed by the French in 1882. A cruel opportunist, Ahmed had raced across the *chott* to surrender to the French while the elected village sheikh vacillated. His reward was command over his fellow villagers, whom he ruled tyrannically for three terrible years. His palace, as he liked to call it, was built from the stones of

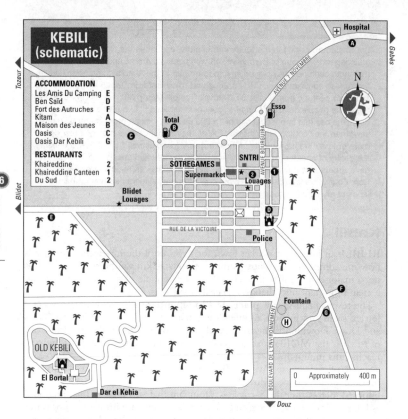

his neighbours' homes, which he had destroyed. Eventually however, even the colonialists realized that Ben Hamadi's excesses were causing discontent and making it harder to extract taxes efficiently, and so, to the relief of the villagers, they gave him the boot and installed a more capable administrator.

Practicalities

SOTREGAMES and other SRT **buses** stop in front of, or across the street from, the supermarket (the office and waiting room is across the street and 50m down, but isn't usually staffed). The SNTRI office is just behind the supermarket, with louages for local destinations such as Mansoura and Souk Lahad in the lot next door. The main **louage** stand is across the street, with vehicles to Tozeur, Gabès, Gafsa and (usually in the morning) Sfax and Tunis. Louages for Douz are in the next street over to the south, but for Blidet they leave from the Blidet road (down the hill from place de l'Indépendance, or 300m south of the Total station and then right).

Two **banks** – Banque du Sud, about 100m north along avenue Bourguiba, and Banque de l'Habitat, just west near the bus stand – have ATMs that take Visa and Mastercard, and the **post office** (city hours) will change cash. There's a good **Internet** café in the *Maison des Jeunes* (daily except Mon 9am–1pm & 2–10pm). The **regional hospital** is on the edge of town out on the Gabès road (Ⓣ 75 490 027).

For a low-priced bite to **eat** in clean surroundings, try the *Khaireddine Restaurant* by the louage stand (daily 8am–11pm), or *Restaurant du Sud* behind it (same hours). The *Khaireddine* also has a self-service canteen two blocks east (daily 10am–4pm). For something with a bit more class, your best bet is the *Hôtel Oasis Dar Kebili*, which has a large restaurant with a 14TD set menu and a smaller, more intimate à la carte restaurant (both daily 12.30–2pm & 7.30–9pm).

Accommodation

Kebili has a very good budget **hotel**, the *Hôtel Ben Saïd* on avenue Bourguiba (T75 491 573; ❶), opposite the street leading to place de l'Indépendance, which is friendly and pleasant, with shared showers and hot water round the clock; the proprietor is young and speaks good English. It is certainly a much better proposition than the ramshackle and run-down *Hôtel Oasis* down the Tozeur road (T75 492 430; ❶), which costs the same but is rather dirty, with no hot water and few outside windows, though some rooms have their own bathroom. The friendly, two-star *Hôtel Fort des Autruches* (T75 492 104, F75 204 290; ❺), signposted east off avenue Bourguiba, past the *Ben Saïd* towards Douz, has small en-suite rooms, a small pool fed by a hot spring, and a sometimes rather raucous bar. For a bit more comfort, featuring a larger pool and a quieter lobby bar with a more intimate upstairs section, try the nearby four-star *Hôtel Oasis Dar Kebili* (T75 491 436, F75 491 295; ❼). The rooms here are pleasant, with a/c, TV and mini-bar, and there are ramps for wheelchair users. At the edge of town on avenue 7 Novembre (the Gabès road), the two-star *Hôtel Kitam* (T75 491 465, F75 491 076; ❹) has reasonable en-suite rooms.

The **Maison des Jeunes** behind the Total station is not too bad (T75 490 635; dorm beds 5TD), with small, clean dorms, refurbished bathrooms and friendly staff; you can come and go as you please during the day, but there's a 10pm curfew. Near Old Kebili there is a low-priced and friendly **campsite**, *Les Amis du Camping* (T75 492 710; 2.5TD per person), on the Blidet road in the oasis, 1500m out of town. It has space for tents and camper vans, plus small Bedouin tents with bedding for those who don't have their own, and hot showers. An on-site café provides drinks and meals.

Douz and around

The road south from Kebili takes you along the edge of the **Great Eastern Erg**, a sea of sand where the dunes reach hundreds of metres in height. Here, at its northerly extent, they are a touch less impressive, but you can at least get the feel of the desert. And to add a little local colour, scattered around are date palms fed by small springs and several nondescript hamlets. **Jemna**, the largest of the villages on the road, once had a roadside fountain gushing out gallons of sweet water per second, and people from all over the region came to fill up their jerry cans from it, as most of the region's other water sources were brackish. With the retreat of the water table, however, the water now has to be pumped up; the fountain is now housed in a small building on the west side of the main road by the clock tower in the centre of town. Just south of here, and west of the main road, is a hammam using water from a natural hot spring (women 6am–6pm, men 6pm–6am).

Twenty-seven kilometres south of Kebili, **DOUZ** calls itself "the gateway to the Sahara" and with some justification. Even though it has become the tourist

Douz is the centre for the **Mrazig**, originally the family of seventeenth-century patriarch Sidi Merzoug, now a people numbering about 45,000, whose lifestyle is traditionally nomadic. With the development of schools, medical facilities and housing, however, the Mrazig have largely abandoned the life which led them to three different areas every year. Even today though, most Douz residents still keep a few sheep and goats, a patch of desert to pasture them and a tent to sleep in when they pop over to tend it, usually during school holidays. For the rest of the year, they leave their animals in the care of a *gardien* belonging to the small contingent of Mrazig who remain completely nomadic. Following the traditional lifestyle, these Mrazig move south in spring, when the rains provide good pasture for the sheep and goats. After the shearing of the sheep during April, the women make rugs from the wool to sell in the large towns. The Mrazig nomads return to the comparative cool of the oasis for the summer, where the men look after the land and dates and the women prepare food for the coming winter. Two months later, the animals are taken north to fresh lands near Gabès or Gafsa, and the people set up their tents nearby. At the beginning of winter, they return to pick dates or press olives and spend the cooler months around their home base.

The Mrazig are one of four traditionally nomadic tribes in the Nefzaoua, all descended from the Banu Suleim, a tribe from the Arabian peninsula who migrated to Egypt in the eighth century, moved into Libya in the tenth, and settled in southern Tunisia at the end of the thirteenth century (see pp.495 & 498). The land used by the Mrazig to pasture their livestock lies to the southeast of Douz. The **Adhara**, based at Zaafrane, use the land to its south, while the **Ghrib**, based at El Fouar and Sabria, take their flocks southwest. The area to the north, as far as the Chott el Fejaj, belongs to a fourth tribe, the **Beni Yaqoub**, who base themselves in Kebili.

centre of the region, it's remarkably unspoilt: the people are an amiable lot and their town is a pleasure to stay in, though the sights, apart from the market, are not particularly spectacular. It is also a good base from which to explore the isolated oases to the south.

Arrival and information

Arriving by public transport, you'll be dropped at the **bus and louage station** just north of the town centre. The **ONTT** in place des Martyrs (daily 8am–6pm; ☏75 470 351) is friendly, helpful and enthusiastic, if a little officious, loves answering questions, and can provide services such as camel rental (10TD/hr) and calèches (5TD/hr for up to four people). Douz's *zone touristique* is on the far side of the oasis by a large dune known prosaically as the Great Dune, about 2km south of the town centre.

Accommodation

Most of the budget **hotels** are near the market square, with pricier options out in the *zone touristique*. More than anywhere else in the country, however, the difference between the warm welcome you get in some of the cheaper places, and the impersonal processing of tourists through the *zone touristique* hotels, means that less is definitely more here. On the other hand, the tourist hotels are usually empty in the daytime, as the tour groups that use them arrive around 4pm and leave in the morning, so you'll have the run of them in between times. Most of them, the *Mouradi* in particular, claim to be wheelchair-accessible, though check that they cater for your particular needs. Note too, that

Kebili ▲

Matmata & Ksar Ghilane ▲

Bus & Louage Station

0   100 m

RUE EL ADAALA

Police

Bank

AVENUE BOURGUIBA

AVENUE MOHAMED EL MARZOUGUI

Cemetery

Bank

AVENUE MOHAMED EL MARZOUGUI

Pharmacy

RUE ALI BEN LATIF

N

Douz Voyages

RUE OMAR EL MAJOUN

❸ ❷

Horizons Déserts

RUE DE LA LIBERTÉ

RUE HAMED ABDEL MALEK

Zaafrane & El Faouar ◄

RESTAURANTS
Ali Baba	1
De l'Arc	5
Errimel	4
Les Palmiers	2
Rendez-Vous	3

Ⓐ

Ⓑ

Ⓒ

RUE GHARA JAWAI

AVENUE 7 NOVEMBRE

AV DE LA RÉPUBLIQUE

AVENUE TAIEB MEHIRI

RUE 20 MARS

@

MARKET SQUARE

ACCOMMODATION
20 Mars	C
Camping Desert Club	H
Centre des Stages et des Vacances	G
El Houdou	F
El Medina	E
Méhari	N
Mouradi	L
Résidence Bel Habib	D
Résidence Essaada	A
Sahara Douz	M
Saharien Paradise	I
Sun Palm	K
De la Tente	B
Touareg	J

Ⓓ

AVENUE DES MARTYRS

AVENUE MONGI SLIM

RUE DES AFFECTIONS

Ⓔ

Animal Market

AVENUE FARHAT HACHED

Ⓕ

Supermarket

❺

Oasis

Oasis

▼ **Place des Martyrs**   **El Gola'a & Kebili** ▲   ▼ **Camping Desert Club**

0   500 m

RUE EL AFRAH

Ⓖ

AVENUE MOHAMED EL MARZOUGI

See Inset map

Museum of the Sahara

ⓘ

AV 7 NOVEMBRE

Zaafrane & El Faouar ◄

Matmata & Ksar Ghilane ▶

PL DES MARTYRS

AVENUE DES MARTYRS

Hospital

Ⓗ

Maison de la Culture

Oasis

Oasis

Zoo

Ⓘ

N

Ⓙ

Ⓚ Ⓛ

Ⓜ

Camels ●

Ⓝ **Café des Dunes**

PLACE DU FESTIVAL

Great Dune

DOUZ

▼ *Bir el Hag Brahim, Jebil & Tembaïn*

Buses and louages all leave from the station north of the cemetery. Minibus louages have now almost entirely superceded bus services to destinations west of Douz such as Zaafrane, El Fouar, Sabria and Nouail. Although there are infrequent direct buses to many destinations, and three a day to Tunis, for most southern destinations you'rxe best off taking a louage to Kebili and continuing from there. There is no direct public transport from Douz to Matmata.

Douz to Ksar Ghilane

The round trip to Ksar Ghilane (see p.475) from Douz takes approximately ten days by camel (see p.383 for operators); by jeep, you can do it in two days. It is sometimes possible to get there from Douz on a supply truck (around 50TD return), but if you do travel with one, you're dependent on it for your return, which would probably entail leaving Douz on a Saturday afternoon and coming back on a Sunday morning.

Most jeep tours, the supply truck, and almost everybody with their own transport takes the **pipeline road**, a piste which branches south from the Matmata road (MC104) at the *Café Jelili*, 68km east of Douz (see p.476). It is just about possible to cover this road – with care, and preferably with a local guide – in an ordinary car, but it can be tricky because there are frequent sand drifts and it's easy to get stuck (see p.32 for advice about driving in the desert).

Camel treks and a few 4WD tours make a beeline for Ksar Ghilane across open desert. One feature of the journey is that the sand gradually reddens in colour, from light beige around Douz to a deep orange by the time you reach Ksar Ghilane. The route passes **Bir el Hag Brahim**, 40km out of Douz and supposedly the gateway to the desert, where the *Café Restaurant du Porte du Désert* is open September to June for travellers passing through. A slight deviation south from the main route passes **Jebil**, an area of high ground 80km from Douz and 50km west of Ksar Ghilane, where Douz-based travel firms (see p.383) run campsites for their clients. It's a good area to spot wildlife, with animals such as gazelles attracted by the slightly cooler temperatures, as is **Tembaïn**, another piece of high ground, 20km to the south, where some excursions stop on their way to Ksar Ghilane.

---

during the Douz Festival at the end of December (see p.47), the small hotels fill up very quickly and it's wise to reserve ahead.

Douz has two **campsites**. On the northern edge of the oasis, *Camping Desert Club* on rue des Affections (℡ & ℻75 470 575, ⓦ www.desertclub.it) is a European-style campsite with a pitch for every tent or vehicle, complete with electric socket. Passports must be surrendered on arrival. Fees are cheap (4TD per person including tent, 4TD to park a camper van) but meals are expensive by local standards. Three kilometres out on the edge of town, the *Centre des Stages et des Vacances* on route de Matmata (no phone) has space for tents or vehicles (2TD per person), clean bungalow accommodation (❶), a kitchen and hot running water, and bedding and even tents provided if you need them.

Finally, if you yearn for the vastness of the open desert, you could opt instead to stay in the nearby oases of Zaafrane (see p.384) or El Faouar (see p.386).

Hotels

The town and oasis

Hôtel 20 Mars 23 rue 20 Mars ℡75 470 269, ℻75 472 922, ⓔhotel20mars@planet.tn. A great little place, excellent value with sparkling rooms, most en suite, with solar-heated water and friendly staff. [16TD b&b without bathroom, 20TD en suite] ❷

Hôtel el Houdou 3 av des Martyrs ℡ & ℻75 470 430. Basic and not tremendously clean, though it's the cheapest hotel in town. Rate includes breakfast. ❶

Hôtel el Medina rue des Affections ℡75 470 010. A nice new hotel, some of whose rooms are en suite with a/c. There's a café downstairs and a big, bare roof terrace giving views over the oasis and out to the desert, though the mosque across the street may not be too appealing when it blares out the early morning call to prayer. Rate includes breakfast. ❷

Résidence Bel Habib 10 rue Palestine ☎ & ⓕ75 471 115. A bit grubby and really a fallback option, though it does have a Bedouin tent for tea and *chichas* on the roof. Some rooms are en suite and have a/c. Breakast included in the rate. ❷

Résidence Essaada 18 rue Ghara Jawai (aka rue 1 Juin; no phone). Rather run down, but clean enough, with a roof terrace; handy as a fall-back if the *20 Mars*, *de la Tente* and *el Medina* are full. ❶

Hôtel Saharien Paradise In the oasis ☎75 471 337, ⓕ75 470 339, ⓦwww.sdts.tourism.tn. Approaching from the east, turn left off av des Martyrs before the tourist office and it's 500m down on the left, in the oasis. Somewhat better value than its three-star equivalents in the *zone touristique*, with nicely furnished rooms, all with a/c and bathtub, and no less than four pools, including one indoor with hot spring water. Wheelchair accessible. ❻

Hôtel de la Tente 8 rue des Affections ☎ & ⓕ75 470 468, ⓔhoteldelatente@yahoo.fr. Clean, friendly and good value, with English-speaking staff. Some rooms have their own shower, though not all have outside windows, and there's also a garage to keep bicycles and motorbikes. ❶

The zone touristique

Méhari ☎75 470 088, ⓕ75 471 589, ⓦwww.goldenyasmin.com/douzmehari/en/. The oldest of the *zone touristique* hotels, with cool, pleasant rooms, and a hot-spring pool in addition to the swimming pool. ❻

Mouradi ☎75 470 303, ⓕ75 470 905. The newest and plushest of the *zone touristique* hotels, with spacious rooms, some with views of the Great Dune, plus indoor and outdoor pools, and a hammam, sauna and fitness room. ❻

Sahara Douz ☎75 470 864–5, ⓕ75 470 566. There's an indoor hot-spring pool and a hammam, all rooms have a terrace or balcony (some have a bath en suite, others a shower), the food's good, and the staff even smile. ❻

Sun Palm ☎75 410 123, ⓕ75 470 525, ⓦwww.goldenyasmin.com/douzsunpalm/en/. Reasonably spacious a/c rooms, plus a pool and a hammam, and four suites, but nothing really to raise it above the level of a bog-standard tour-group three-star. ❻

Touareg ☎75 470 057, f 470 313, ⓦwww.hotel-touareg.com. Cheapest of the *zone touristique* hotels, with cosy a/c en-suite rooms, most with balconies. You can specify if you want a bathroom with a bath rather than just a shower. ❺

The Town

On Thursdays, Douz is transformed by the weekly **market**. Townspeople, nomads, people from nearby villages and tourists pour in to participate in one of Tunisia's most engaging souks, and it says something for Douz that the presence of tourists seems to add to rather than detract from the whole affair. The centre of activity is, of course, the market square itself. Here you can find many of the traditional goods (jackets, leather shoes and slippers) which end up in the cities. You can also buy souvenirs like petrified wood or the inevitable desert roses, or get desert shoes made to measure overnight. In season, you'll find the region's famous *deglat en nour* dates for sale behind the southern side of the square. Don't expect to find many camels nowadays in the livestock section southwest of the square, where most of the animals sold are sheep and goats – if there are any camels, they'll be just to your right as you come down the stairs into the compound, along with horses and donkeys.

Top of the list of sights, such as they are, is the **Museum of the Sahara** on place des Martyrs (Tues–Sun: June–Aug 7–11am & 4–7pm; Sept–May 9.30am–4.30pm; 1.1TD), with a small but interesting collection of exhibits illustrating the traditions of the region's nomadic peoples, with features on camels, the construction and furnishing of bedouin tents, weaving and textiles, and clothing, jewellery and tattoos, all well explained in Arabic and French. The road to the right of the museum (as you face it) leads past a natural **hot-spring bath** into the oasis. The bath is open 6am to noon and 3pm to 7pm for both sexes (separate entrances) and you have the choice of individual bath or communal pool, but you have to bring your own towel and, for the pool,

The wintertime Festival of the Sahara, held at the end of December, celebrates everything from popular pottery and a traditional marriage to camel fighting (camel versus camel, that is), sand hockey and greyhound racing. It all takes place at a special festival site out beyond the *Hôtel Saharien Paradise*. Associated cultural activities such as music, singing and poetry contests take place in the Maison de la Culture in place des Martyrs. Local poet Abdellatif Belgacem Merzoughi, who runs the Museum of the Sahara, is likely to read samples of his immensely popular verse. Hotels tend to fill up quickly at this time of year, so it's a good idea to arrive early or book ahead. The tourist office will have the latest details, or check the festival website ⊛www.douz.org.

bathing costume. Further into the oasis on the way to the *zone touristique* is the **Borj Shara Zoo** (daily 7am–sunset; 2TD), a sad spectacle of wild desert animals pacing their undersized cages and cowering in fear as visitors approach.

A little further along the same road, you emerge out of the oasis into the *zone touristique*, by the village of Gleissia. Beyond is another popular attraction for tour groups on day-trips, the **Great Dune**. The rumour that it was built with the aid of bulldozers is not true, but even if it were it probably wouldn't make much difference to most of the people who come here. The dune is a chance to play in the sand for those without the time to get further into the desert – or to go to the beach. If you want a quick ride on a camel in the desert without spending a day or a week on one, it might fit the bill. About a kilometre beyond the *zone touristique* hotels, at the *Café des Dunes*, a firm called Pégase (℡75 470 793) runs a track for desert **go-karts** (10TD a lap, 20TD for three), with the option of guided desert excursions on them, and also offers rides on microlight planes (60TD for a 10–12min flight), with rides on sand hovercraft also possible if you book in advance.

A word of **warning** for women travelling alone in Douz: it is not a good idea to go wandering in the oasis alone, as there have been instances of sexual harassment and even rape.

Eating and drinking

For **eating**, Douz's greatest culinary experience has got to be the *Restaurant Ali Baba* on the Kebili road (daily 8am–11pm), with low prices, legendary couscous, fine Mrazig welcome and relaxed atmosphere. You can eat in a Bedouin tent out the back, or go out there for a tea, a chat, and even a hookah after your meal, all for a good price. There is no upmarket eating in town as such, but for something posher and a little pricier, try the Italian restaurant at *Camping Desert Club* (in theory daily: summer 7–11pm, winter 5–9.30pm, but in practice open only for lunch and supper when there are enough people staying at the campsite), or the restaurant at the *Hôtel Saharien Paradise* (daily 12.30–2.30pm & 7.30–9pm), which has a 14TD buffet.

Otherwise, most of the cheap hotels double up as eating places, offering the likes of couscous, stew and chicken for a few dinars. The *Résidence Bel Habib*'s restaurant (daily 7am–11pm) serves breakfast and has a limited menu but does offer meat-free couscous for vegetarians. There are also a few *gargotes* in town including the *Errimel* on avenue Taïeb Mehiri (daily noon–9pm), which offers mostly stews; the *Restaurant de l'Arc* by the arch on avenue des Martyrs, which has chops, liver, chicken or couscous; and the *Restaurant des Palmiers* at 13 avenue Taïeb Mehiri (daily 10am–10pm). Next door to the *Palmiers*, the *Rendez-Vous* is slightly more refined, but the long menu outside belies the limited choice of dishes, mostly grills, which they give you when you actually sit down.

If you fancy a beer or two, *Camping Desert Club* has a reasonable **bar** (daily noon–midnight when there are enough people staying at the campsite), as does the *Saharien Paradise*.

Listings

Banks Banque du Sud is on av Bourguiba, just north of the junction with av Taïeb Mehiri; STB (with an ATM) is on av Taïeb Mehiri 100m to the west. The post office, plus some of the cheap hotels and some shops, also change money.

Bike rental Available from Grand Sud, 22 av Taïeb Mehiri by *Café el Amel* (☎75 471 777, ✉saharaking@voila.fr, or c/o *Hôtel 20 Mars* if the office is closed; 2TD/hr).

Car repairs Sahara Assistance (☎75 471 152), off av des Martyrs just west of the arch, opposite no. 6 have a good reputation as mechanics for 4WD and two-wheel-drive vehicles. Smaller workshops can be found on av Taïeb Mehiri and streets off it near the junction with rue de la Liberté, and there's another garage specializing in 4WDs at 12–14 av Taïeb Mehiri.

Hammams As well as the natural hot-spring baths (see p.381), there's Hammam el Hana, 100m north of the louage station past the cemetery (daily women 8am–5.30pm, men 6–10pm).

Hospital Just off av des Martyrs, 100m east of the tourist office ☎75 470 323.

Internet access There is a Publinet office at 24 rue des Affections (daily 8am–midnight; 1.6TD/hr).

Pharmacy The town pharmacies run a rota for night duty, posted in the window. The largest is at the corner of av Taïeb Mehiri and av 7 Novembre.

Police The main police station is on av Bourguiba, just north of the junction with av Taïeb Mehiri (☎75 470 333). The Garde Nationale are at pl des Martyrs (☎75 470 554).

Post office Av Taïeb Mehiri, opposite the end of rue 20 Mars (country hours); it changes cash and has a coin phone.

Supermarkets Magasin B Abdennour on av Taïeb Mehiri, opposite the *Hôtel el Houdou* (daily 8am–8pm).

Swimming pools The municipal pool is behind the water tower off pl des Martyrs (July & Aug daily 9am–6pm; 0.2TD). Otherwise, for a few dinars you can use the pools at the *Hôtel Saharien Paradise* (including the indoor thermal pool) or the *zone touristique* hotels (whose pools are little used during the day); the best belong to the *Méhari* and the *Sahara Douz*, both of which have a natural hot-spring pool as well as a conventional swimming pool.

Tours There are many reputable operators in Douz offering excursions to Ksar Ghilane, Jebil or Tembaïn (see box, p.380), but there are also a lot of sharks and cowboys offering deals that are cheap in every sense, neither officially sanctioned nor covered by insurance. Among legitimate operators, the biggest and oldest is Douz Voyages at 7 av Taïeb Mehiri, on the corner of rue Ghara Jawai (☎75 470 178–9, ✆www.chez.com/douzvoyages). Nefzaoua Voyages at the *Hôtel 20 Mars* (☎75 472 920, ✆www.nefzaoua-voyages.com) offer excursions to various destinations by camel, jeep or bicycle. Horizons Déserts at 9 rue des Affections (☎75 471 688, ✆www.horizons-deserts.com) specialize in tailor-made excursions. Camel treks cost about 35TD a day, and a three-day excursion to Tembaïn and Ksar Ghilane might cost around 350TD per person all-in, including accommodation, food, guide and sleeping bag. Always check exactly what's included in the cost – not all agencies supply sleeping bags for example, and you'll need them, as well as warm clothing, especially in winter.

Around Douz

A good road leads west out of Douz to the oases of **Zaafrane**, **El Faouar** and **Sabria**. As well as buses from Douz, pick-ups do the run cheaply enough, but transport back to Douz dries up around 4pm. If driving in this region, take the usual precautions for desert driving (see p.32). There are other, smaller oases, unmarked on any of the available maps, between El Faouar and Zaafrane. If you're hitching, you might be dropped off on the way, and there will always be shade and an occasional car later in the afternoon.

On the way out of Douz, a piste turns south off the Zaafrane road, 100m past a school and a sign marking the end of the town limits. After about 4km it passes under a power line which, if you follow it to the right, leads to a *khriga* (see p.346) that once took water from a spring – now dried up due to the falling water table – to the grove of palm trees that lie to your right. The maintenance shafts for the *khriga* are unmarked and unfenced, so if you come here to check out the *khriga*, be careful not to fall down them.

Zaafrane

Ten kilometres west of Douz, **ZAAFRANE** is the real gateway to the Grand Eastern Erg. The village lies close to the main road and is surrounded by endless dunes on one side and by a cool **oasis** on the other. Zaafrane is the centre for the traditionally nomadic **Adhara** people, whose large black tents, often pitched near their brick and concrete houses, are made from long strips of wool and goat hair, supported by two wooden poles. Paths lead from the main road to the sand dunes at the far edge of the village. From here the desert stretches into the distance, beyond the remains of old stone houses, washed over by the sand. The strictly unofficial **Syndicat d'Initiative** at the western end of town (daily sunrise–sunset; ☎98 232 148) is less a tourist office than a shop, café and agency for the local camel drivers, and can organize camel rides and treks. Prices here are much the same as in Douz (about 10TD/hr, 45TD/day, plus the same again for a guide for every two or three people); as in Douz, avoid ultra-cheap deals from unauthorized operators.

Almost opposite the Syndicat d'Initiative there is a **hotel**, the one-star *Zaafrane* (☎75 450 020, ℉75 450 033; ❸), which is not a bad old place, with nice en-suite rooms, all with heating and air conditioning. They usually allow

The ship of the desert

The one-humped **Arabian camel**, or dromedary, is native to North Africa, southwest Asia and the Arabian peninsula, where it was first domesticated some 3000–4000 years ago. Camels can cover 160 to 200 kilometres in a day and have been used since the Middle Ages for long-haul **desert travel**, in particular for the pilgrimage to Mecca. They also played a vital role for the Saharan economy in the caravans that traded across the desert.

Arabic has many different words for camels, depending on their age, sex and breed, just as English does for horses. There are four basic varieties, distinguished by the colour of their coat. The **white camel** (*mehari*) is the fastest, used for hunting and warfare. The **red camel** is used to transport goods, as it can carry the heaviest loads. The **yellow camel** is used, if male, as a stud, and can be bred with females of other varieties to produce both its own breed and its mate's. The **black camel** (*azraq*, meaning "blue") is used for smuggling, since its dark coat makes it hard to spot at night. Camels of mixed breed are considered the best for eating and, if female, milking.

The camel is well adapted to the desert, with long double eyelashes to keep sand out of its eyes, nostrils that it can close, and broad, soft, padded feet that are ideal for walking on sand, though not slippery mud or sharp stones. Because the camel moves its left and then right legs together, rather than front and then back legs like a horse, it has a rolling gait that makes for a smoother ride. Camels have callused pads on their knees and chest to kneel and set down in the hot sand, which they will do on command if trained, but they will usually bellow in protest when being loaded up with goods or passengers to carry. In fact camels are usually docile, good-tempered animals, though the male goes into rut in spring, when it becomes rather grumpy and can kick and bite, and spit its regurgitated stomach contents in anger.

Camels space themselves out over a wide area to **forage**, and eat only a small amount from each plant they find, which allows the plants to continue growing and also lets other animals such as sheep and goats graze in the same area. If really

camping in the grounds (10TD per camper van, 5TD per tent) and have a set menu for a few dinars (daily noon–3pm & 6pm–midnight) and a bar if you're in need of a cold beer. You can use their pool for 5TD (for free if you're eating there). The hotel runs another campsite, 10km into the desert towards El Fouar. There is a campsite next to the hotel and directly opposite the Syndicat d'Initiative, *Campement de Désert* (☎75 450 172, ⓦwww.campingdudesert .com), where you can stay in your own tent (5TD per person) or in a Bedouin tent (8TD per person). The campsite is rather rustic and has no showers as yet, but there are plans to install them in the near future.

Whether or not you use public transport to Zaafrane, you'll probably end up hitching back to Douz or on to El Faouar; most passing vehicles will pick up hitchhikers, and there are louages stopping here to drop off and pick up.

Sabria

Beyond Zaafrane, it's no problem getting a louage on to Sabria and El Faouar. The main attraction is simply the drive through the desert. The road divides after 34km, branching left to **SABRIA**, a village which is the centre for the people of the same name, Arabized Berbers who are part of the larger Ghrib confederation. Spectacular views over the desert greet you when you climb up some of the high dunes around Sabria, with a vast expanse of sand stretching in every direction, dotted with little green oases.

Sabria is one of the few places where the "**Danse de la Chevelure**" is still authentically performed during marriage celebrations. On the first night of the marriage ceremony, the women remove all their jewellery and woollen head

hungry, camels will eat almost anything – coarse, thorny vegetation, twigs and dried grass, date stones, even prickly pear cactuses – and they thrive on plants with a high salt content that other animals cannot eat.

Most famously, the camel can go for days – a week in summer, two in winter – without **water**. This is partly because, already well insulated by its thick coat, it is protected from the heat of the day, and does not need to keep its body temperature down by sweating. The camel's hump stores reserves of fat that can convert into energy, and the hydrogen in the fat can also be oxidized into water when necessary. In fact, a camel can shed up to 40 percent of its body weight through dehydration, and then put it all back by drinking as much as a hundred litres in ten minutes flat; furthermore, camels can drink salty or brackish water. The hump is firm and straight when "full", but becomes soft and leans over as its reserves are depleted.

For many of the nomads in the south of Tunisia, camels represent their worldly wealth, but a camel also has a lot of practical uses. As well as a pack animal and a means of transport, it is a source of meat and also of milk. Its hide can be used for leather, and its hair, which it sheds in huge clumps every spring, is extremely light and durable, providing excellent insulation against extremes of heat and cold. The best examples of the traditional North African coat, the **burnous**, are made of camel hair – though the fur of the two-humped Bactrian camel is considered superior to that of its Arabian cousin.

Camels are often left to roam the desert freely, but can be matched to their owner by means of a **brand**. In the Nefzaoua, the brand is always made on the right back leg, and is based on a shape not unlike the letter H on its side. Additional markings indicate the tribe, clan and family who own the camel. In fact, many nomads can identify a camel – especially a male camel – simply from its footprints, which are distinctive in the way fingerprints are to humans, except that a male camel's footprint will follow the pattern of its father's.

coverings and parade before the assembled men and musicians. To the beat of the *tambour*, and encouragement of the crowd, each dancer whirls her long hair round her head faster and faster. Over several hours the women gradually drop out, and the dance ends when just one is left on the floor.

The old French army fort, **Borj Sabria**, 1km beyond the village, is now a **bar**, **restaurant** and **campsite** (☎75 754 077; 12TD per person in your own tent, or 18TD per person with half board in a Bedouin tent). Here you can stop for a tea or a beer, eat an inexpensive meal featuring either couscous or *mechoui*, and stay the night in your own tent or vehicle, or in a Bedouin tent complete with beds and palm-frond fencing to keep out the wind. The roof of the fort offers fabulous views across the desert, and a stroll into the dunes will soon leave you feeling fantastically remote. To get here, bear left at the fork in the road at the entrance to the village, follow the tarmac till the end, and then continue along the sandy track until it ends at the fort.

El Faouar

Back on the main road, most traffic goes straight on past the Sabria turn-off to **EL FAOUAR** (also called Sabria el Faouar), 41km west of Douz, which has a Friday souk. This is the home of the Ghrib who, until recently, were a wholly nomadic community, breeding camels, goats and sheep. Like the Mrazig and the Adhara, the Ghrib have partly abandoned their nomadic lifestyle, but many of them continue to live in the traditional way, and the majority still keep livestock, often leaving their animals in the care of a *gardien* and visiting the desert during the school holidays to tend them in person.

El Faouar is connected with Douz by louages, and by local buses; there are also buses to Kebili, Gabès and Tunis. The one **hotel** – the three-star *El Faouar* (☎75 460 531, ☎75 460 576; ❻) – is a reasonable place, especially when not too swamped. Off on the left as you come into the village from Zaafrane, it has a bar and restaurant with a menu costing 10TD or so (daily noon–2pm & 7.30–9pm). The hotel also has a pool, which non-residents can use for a small fee, and rents out sand skis (10TD/hr). As well as the rooms, each decorated with its own mural, there is the cheaper option of sleeping in tents (30TD per person including breakfast). While the **dunes** behind the hotel aren't as huge as those deeper into the erg, they do stretch immensely to the horizon and satisfy most visitors' desires to be, at last, really in the desert.

Nouail and Blidet

Paved roads branching off on your right (if coming from Douz) 5km before Zaafrane and 10km after El Fouar (signposted "Dergine") lead to Kebili via **NOUAIL**, where a *campement* offers **accommodation** in two-person "bungalows" or in Bedouin tents (☎75 455 118, ☎75 455 014), and allows you to pitch your own tent (10TD in own tent or campervan, with bed-and-breakfast bedouin-tent or bungalow accommodation available for a few dinars more). There are hot showers, but the bungalows have no electric power. Meals are available at the restaurant. Between Nouail and Kebili is the picturesque village of **BLIDET**, with a ruined **medina** on a hill topped by a **marabout** and flanked by minor **oases**.

There is no direct transport from Zaafrane, Sabria or El Fouar to Blidet or Nouail, though there are louages between Blidet and Kebili, and between Nouail and Douz. As for buses, there are a couple of services each day between Douz and Nouail, plus five daily buses from Kebili to Blidet, two of which continue to Nouail.

El Gola'a

A pleasant day-trip from Douz is the pretty little village of **EL GOLA'A**, reached by heading west off the Kebili road or using the direct road from Douz. At the village's highest point, adjoining the Great Mosque, a small park gives views over the whole of El Gola'a, and to the five oases surrounding it. In the past, any force approaching the village could be spied and sized up before they arrived. Nowadays, it's a good spot for watching sunrises and sunsets. As for the mosque itself, the small square minaret is original; the tall octagonal one was added in the 1990s. Down the hill towards the Kebili road, the modern Salaam mosque has an unusual round minaret, which looks particularly funky when lit up at night.

El Hamma de l'Arad

For Thomas Shaw in the 1750s, the area **east of Kebili** towards the coast was a "lonesome and uncomfortable desert, the resort of cut-throats and robbers". He recalled, "We saw the recent blood of a Turkish gentleman, who, with three of his servants, had been murdered two days before by these assassins". Nowadays there's no blood and little of interest until **EL HAMMA DE L'ARAD**, 70km east of Kebili and 31km west of Gabès, whose main point of interest is its natural **hot baths**. At **Saidane**, 40km east of Kebili, the old French fort, once a hotel, is now a Garde Nationale post, so resist the temptation to photograph it as you pass. Looking out for the desert birds and mammals that can be spotted along the road between Kebili and El Hamma may help pass the time.

Some history

In the sixteenth century, unlikely as it may seem, El Hamma was a substantial town and a major **staging post** on the trans-Saharan routes. Then, in the 1630s, the **Matmata** people who lived here refused to pay their taxes to the bey. He had the town razed to the ground and its citizens expelled, and Arab nomads of the Beni Zid tribe then settled here in place of the recalcitrant Berbers.

El Hamma has quite a history of militancy in modern times too. Its centre is a square called place Daghbaji, with a statue of the man it is named after, **Mohammed Daghbaji**, one of the very first Tunisian fighters for independence from colonial rule. The story goes that in his youth Daghbaji was beaten for no good reason by a French soldier. He later absconded with his weapon after being conscripted to serve in the French army and, taking to the hills with a band of fighters in 1915, began an armed campaign to rid his land of infidel rule. Daghbaji's campaign coincided with the Ouderna rebellion in the south (see p.460), and the Berber rebellion against Italian rule in Libya (see p.477), and years before Bourguiba and the Neo-Destour Party came on the scene, his men proved a major thorn in the side of the colonialists, and killed numerous French soldiers before their leader was finally captured and shot in 1924.

Nor was Daghbaji the only son of El Hamma whose radicalism was ahead of his time. Just 200m further south, near the turn-off for the piste to Matmata, is the bust of local theologian and writer **Tahar Haddad**. A staunch supporter of women's rights, Haddad argued in his 1930 work, *Our Women between Sharia and Society*, that the oppression of women was contrary to the law of Islam, and called on religious grounds for the abolition of polygamy and the veil, and for equal access to education for both sexes. Haddad pointed out that nothing in the Koran or the Hadith (sayings of the Prophet) supports the imposition of purdah or sexual segregation, arguments echoed nowadays by Muslim women worldwide. A third native of El Hamma whose miltancy predated that of his better-known successors was Haddad's friend **Mohammed Ali el Hammi**, a pioneer of Tunisian trade unionism, who in 1924 founded the Confédération Générale Tunisienne des Travailleurs. Even today, El Hamma retains a tradition of militancy, and support for Islamic fundamentalism is strong here, though largely unvoiced in the current political climate.

The Town

The town's **hot baths** have long attracted visitors from far and wide, and gave it the Roman name Aquae Tacapitanae. Sixteenth-century traveller Leo Africanus was not a fan, noting somewhat irrelevantly, "the hot water tastes like brimstone so that it will in no way quench a man's thirst". Today the baths are housed in a modern building called Hammam Sidi Abdel Kader (24hr), which is 100m west of the central place Daghbaji, and based on Roman foundations. The entrance on the left is for women; men go round the corner to the right. The spring water rises at 47°C, and you can sit in it on submerged seats in a shallow pool, as well as using it for ordinary hammam washing. On Fridays, an additional attraction is the **market**, centred on the market building just east of place Daghbaji and around the hot baths. There is a **hammam festival** in March, which is in fact nothing to do with baths but features the usual cultural pageantry.

El Hamma's other sight is the **Morabi**, the tomb of a local Jewish holy man, Rabbi Sidi Youssef, and scene of an annual Jewish pilgrimage around December. At one time El Hamma had quite a thriving Jewish community, but all of them left for Israel, Tunis or Jerba in the 1950s. To find the tomb, take the street leading east from the main road just south of place Daghbaji, and follow it for some 500m, past a palm grove and a mosque to a little square, where you turn right, and the tomb – a white building with a blue Hebrew inscription – appears on your right after 500m. Apart from the December pilgrimage, the Morabi is also visited by Jewish pilgrims who have come to Jerba for Lag beOmer, in late April or early May (see p.439).

Practicalities

El Hamma is strung out along a single main road that runs through it roughly from north (toward Gabès) to south (toward Kebili), parts of which have been variously named avenue Bourguiba, avenue 7 Novembre and avenue de l'Environnement, according to the political whim of the day, though of course none of the official names are actually used by local residents. The **bus and louage station** is some 500m north of place Daghbaji, with SRT bus services to Gabès, Kebili and beyond, and SNTRI departures to Tunis and Kebili. A couple of **banks** are situated opposite the *Hôtel Thermes*, and there is a **post office** (country hours) 50m north of place Daghbaji.

The town has two **hotels**, both simple but clean: the *Hôtel Thermes* on the east side of the main road, 50m north of place Daghbaji (☎75 331 120; ❶), and, 30m further north, the slightly better *Hôtel el Hana*, also called *Hôtel de la Quiétude*, at 15 rue Abdel Karim el Khatabi, 30m down a side street off the east side of the main road (☎75 334 497; ❶). Neither hotel has showers, but the hot baths are close at hand. In the way of **eating**, there are a few small restaurants in town, including the *Restaurant el Adouani*, a cheap diner just 200m north of place Daghbaji on the east side of the main road (daily 7am–6pm), and the slightly less basic *Restaurant Tunisien* on the west side of the main road, just to the north of place Daghbaji (daily 7am–9pm).

Arabic place names

Abbès	عبّاس
Bled el Haddar	بلد الحضر
Blidet	بليدات
Bou Hedma	بو هدمة
Chebika	الشبيكة
Debebcha	الدبابشة
Degache	دقاش
Douz	دوز
El Faouar	الفوّار
El Gola'a	القلعة
El Guettar	القطار
El Hamma de l'Arad	الحامّة عراد
El Hamma du Jerid	الحامّة الجريد
Fatnassa	فطناسة
Gafsa	قفصة
Kebili	قبلي
Kriz (El Mahassen)	قريز (المحاسن)
Mansoura	المنصورة
Mazzouna	المزّونة
Meknassy	المكناسي
Metlaoui	المتلوّي
Mides	ميداس
Moulares	ام العرائس
Nefta	نفطة
Nouail	نويل
Orbata	عرباطة
Ouled Majd	أولاد ماجد
Redeyef	الرديّف
Sabria	الصابرية
Saidane	سعيدان
Sakket	السكّات
Seldja	ثالجة
Sened Jebel	السند الجبل
Sidi Mansour	سيدي منصور
Souk Lahad	سوق الأحد
Tamerza	تمغزة
Telmine	تلمين
Tozeur	توزر
Zaafrane	زعفران
Zaouiet el Arab	زاوية العرب

Travel details

Trains

Gafsa to: Bir Bou Regba (for Hammamet and Nabeul; 1 direct, 1 connecting daily; 6hr 25min); El Jem (1 direct, 1 connecting daily; 4hr 15min); Mahrès (2 daily; 2hr 45min); Meknassy (2 daily; 1hr 25min); Sened Gare (2 daily; 50min); Sfax (2 daily; 3hr 15min); Sousse (1 daily; 5hr 15min); Tunis (1 direct, 1 connecting daily; 7hr 15min).

Metlaoui to: Bir Bou Regba (for Hammamet and Nabeul; 1 direct, 1 connecting daily; 7hr 10min); El Jem (1 direct, 1 connecting daily; 5hr); Gafsa (2 daily; 45min); Mahrès (2 daily; 3hr 30min); Meknassy (2 daily; 2hr 10min); Redeyef (1 daily; 1hr 30min); Sened Gare (2 daily; 1hr 35min); Sfax (2 daily; 4hr); Seldja (Lézard Rouge; 5 weekly; 1hr 30min round trip); Sousse (1 daily; 6hr); Tunis (1 direct, 1 connecting daily; 8hr).

Buses

Douz to: El Faouar (3 daily; 1hr); El Hamma de l'Arad (3 daily; 2hr); Gabès (3 daily; 2hr 30min); Gafsa (1 daily; 3hr 30min); Kairouan (1 daily; 6hr 30min); Kebili (10 daily; 30min); Nouail (2 daily; 40min); Sabria (3 daily; 40min); Sfax (1 daily; 4hr); Sousse (2 daily; 6hr 30min); Tozeur (2 daily; 2hr); Tunis (2 daily; 9hr); Zaafrane (3 daily; 15min).

El Faouar to: Douz (3 daily; 1hr); Gabès (1 daily; 3hr); Kebili (2 daily; 50min); Tunis (1 daily; 7hr).

El Hamma de l'Arad to: Douz (3 daily; 2hr); El Faouar (1 daily; 2hr 30min); Gabès (22 daily; 40min); Jerba (Houmt Souk; 1 daily; 3hr); Kebili (7 daily; 1hr 30min); Sfax (4 daily; 2hr 30min); Sousse (4 daily; 5hr); Tozeur (1 daily; 3hr); Tunis (4 daily; 7hr–8hr 10min).

Gafsa to: Douz (1 daily; 3hr 30min); El Guettar (14 daily; 30min); Gabès (3 daily; 2hr 30min); Kairouan (7 daily; 4hr); Kasserine (2 daily; 2hr); Kebili (1 daily; 3hr); Le Kef (1 daily; 4hr); Metlaoui (21 daily; 1hr); Nefta (7 daily; 3hr); Redeyef (6 daily; 2hr); Sened Gare (13 daily; 1hr); Sfax (5 daily; 3hr); Sidi Aïch (3 daily; 1hr); Sidi Bou Zid (5 daily; 2hr); Sousse (3 daily; 5hr); Tozeur (12 daily; 2hr 30min); Tunis (10 daily; 5hr 30min).

Kebili to: Blidet (5 daily; 30min); Douz (10 daily; 30min); El Faouar (2 daily; 50min); Gabès (7 daily; 2hr); Gafsa (1 daily; 3hr); Kairouan (1 daily; 6hr); Nouail (2 daily; 45min); Sfax (2 daily; 3hr 30min); Sousse (2 daily; 6hr); Tozeur (4 daily; 1hr 30min); Tunis (4 daily; 8hr 30min).

Metlaoui to: Gabès (1 daily; 3hr 30min); Gafsa (21 daily; 1hr); Kairouan (6 daily; 4hr 30min); Moulares

(11 daily; 40min); Nefta (9 daily; 2hr); Redeyef (11 daily; 1hr); Sfax (4 daily; 4hr); Sousse (2 daily; 5hr 15min); Tozeur (15 daily; 1hr 30min); Tunis (7 daily; 6hr 30min).

Nefta to: Gabès (1 daily; 4hr); Gafsa (7 daily; 3hr); Hazoua (3 daily; 25min); Kairouan (2 daily; 6hr); Metlaoui (9 daily; 2hr); Redeyef (2 daily; 3hr); Sfax (1 daily; 5hr 30min); Sousse (1 daily; 6hr); Tozeur (13 daily; 30min); Tunis (2 daily; 7hr 30min).

Redeyef to: Gafsa (6 daily; 2hr); Moulares (11 daily; 20min); Metlaoui (11 daily; 1hr 30min); Nefta (2 daily; 3hr); Tamerza (6 daily; 40min); Tozeur (4 daily; 2hr 30min); Tunis (2 daily; 8hr).

Tozeur to: Chebika (2 daily; 1hr); Douz (2 daily; 2hr); Gabès (2 daily; 3hr 30min); Gafsa (12 daily; 2hr 30min); Hazoua (2 daily; 1hr); Kairouan (6 daily; 5hr 30min); Kebili (4 daily; 1hr 30min); Metlaoui (15 daily; 1hr 30min); Nefta (13 daily; 30min); Redeyef (4 daily; 2hr 30min); Sfax (1 daily; 5hr); Sousse (1 daily; 5hr 30min); Tamerza (2 weekly; 1hr 15min); Tunis (5 daily; 7hr).

Louages

Douz to: El Faouar (30min); Gabès (2hr); El Gola'a (10min); Kebili (30min); Nouail (30min); Sabria (30min); Zaafrane (15min).

Gafsa to: El Guettar (20min); Fériana (1hr); Gabès (2hr); Kasserine (1hr 40min); Metlaoui (40min); Nefta (occasional; 2hr); Redeyef (1hr 20min); Sened Gare (45min); Sfax (2hr 40min); Sousse (4hr); Tozeur (1hr 30min); Tunis (5hr).

Kebili to: Blidet (20min); Gabès (1hr 30min); Gafsa (3hr); Sfax (mornings only; 3hr); Tozeur (1hr 30min); Tunis (7hr).

Meknassy to: Sened Gare (40min); Sfax (1hr 45min); Sidi Bou Zid (1hr); Tunis (4hr 30min).

Metlaoui to: Gafsa (40min); Redeyef (40min); Tamerza (1hr); Tozeur (50min).

Nefta to: Gafsa (occasional; 1hr 30min); Hazoua (25min); Sfax (occasional; 4hr 30min); Tozeur (30min).

Redeyef to: Gafsa (1hr 20min); Metlaoui (40min).

Tozeur to: Degache (10min); Gabès (mornings and souk days only; 3hr) Gafsa (1hr 10min); El Hamma du Jerid (10min); Kebili (1hr 30min); Metlaoui (40min); Nefta (25min); Sfax (mornings only; 4hr); Tamerza (1hr); Tunis (6hr).

Domestic flights

Gafsa to: Tunis (2 weekly; 1hr).

Tozeur to: Tunis (4 weekly; 1hr 15min).

Gabès and Matmata

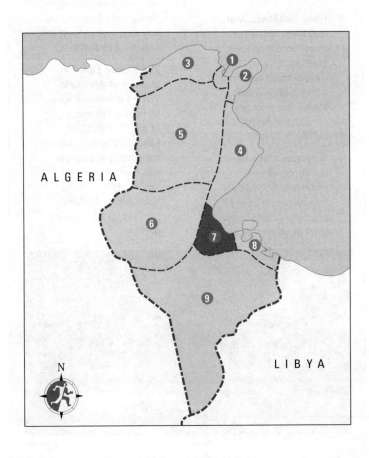

CHAPTER 7 # Highlights

* **Boulbaba Museum** This pink stone *medersa*, in Gabès, belongs to a mosque dedicated to Mohammed's barber, with ancient artefacts and a lovely little garden. **See p.399**

* **Hôtel Sidi Driss, Matmata** Not only is this a real troglodyte cave dwelling, it's also part of the set from *Star Wars*, where Luke Skywalker ate his last meal with his adopted family. **See p.406**

* **Tamezret** A little Berber village clinging to a mountain, topped by a mosque and a café with great views, and boasting a museum featur-ing traditional Berber domestic interiors. **See p.408**

* **Toujane** A stunningly scenic village built on two sides of a gorge in the shadow of a mountain, with breathtaking views, herb-flavoured tea and a cottage industry in carpets. **See p.409**

* **The Mareth Line** The museum at this World War II site features well-laid-out explanations of the 1943 Battle of Mareth. With your own transport, you can also visit the nearby mountain stronghold where Nazi Germany's "Desert Fox" set up his HQ. **See p.411**

△ Matmata

![7](circle with number 7)

Gabès and Matmata

T he towns of **Gabès** and **Matmata** lie in a tract of land that swoops below the belly of the Sahel, the fertile terrain stretching south of Sousse. For the most part nondescript, it is punctuated by fecund emerald oases and hemmed by mile upon mile of coast along the gulf. Almost every traveller heading south passes through Gabès, but few take the time to explore its historic quarters and adjacent oasis – both remnants of a

GABÈS AND MATMATA

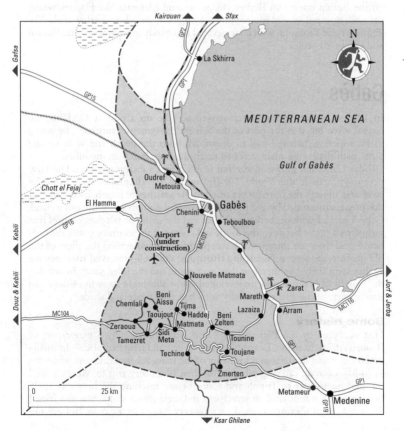

393

Market days

Tuesday Nouvelle Matmata
Wednesday Mareth
Thursday Tounine
Friday Tamezret
Saturday Techine
Sunday Gabès, Zeraoua

turbulent era in Tunisia's past, when the extensive oases were important staging posts for caravans from the other side of the Sahara. Better known – and decidedly more spectacular – are the weird lunar landscapes and **troglodyte villages** around Matmata, a town blown to fame by the filming there of scenes in the *Star Wars* movies.

Sometimes the demands of tourism seem disturbingly overbearing in this region, and unless you are with a tour group, it's difficult to make your way around without a car. Gabès is a major **transport** hub, and Matmata and Mareth are no trouble to get to by bus or grand taxi, but smaller places in this chapter are less well served by public transport. If you've got your own vehicle or are willing to hitch, the most genuine experiences are to be found some way off the beaten track – in Berber villages around Matmata like Haddej, where the underground way of life continues unaffected, or others further afield like Tamezret and Taoujout, which are isolated and barely visited, deeply traditional and extremely scenic.

Gabès

In 1886, a French administrator arrived to take up a post at **GABÈS**, the coastal town billed as the port of the Sahara. "Imagine my surprise", he wrote to his superior, "when I had to disembark onto the beach and walk up the dusty path that is the main street to reach the only building, my office."

Today Gabès has grown in size but is still rather a disappointment. The busy new town, rebuilt after World War II, stretches for kilometres away from the coast and, though the palm groves reach to the sea, they're largely inaccessible at this point, surrounded by the port and industrial complex. On the other hand, Gabès's pivotal position between the sea and the *chotts*, or salt flats, ensures that virtually all traffic between the south and centre of the country passes through here – and there are things worth stopping for. Tucked among the alleys of the old quarters are several fascinating **mosques**; the well-preserved **markets** are as alive with daily commerce as they ever were; and the long, sandy **beach** has the benefit of being almost undeveloped. Most alluringly, away from the main streets, parts of the vast **oasis** really are a haven of peace and shade.

Some history

First occupied by the Phoenicians, Gabès was subsequently a major port of Roman Africa, its name, Tacape, meaning "a wet and irrigated place". In medieval times it was the terminus for many of the trans-Saharan caravans, while the main hajj caravan, carrying pilgrims on their obligatory trip to Mecca, passed through on its way to Tripoli and Cairo before reaching the holy city itself, bringing with it thousands of merchants and their goods. Gabès was also famed for its silk, from silkworms raised on mulberry bushes in the oasis. But even in those times the oasis had its darker side. The tenth-century traveller Ali Mahalli complained that the oases were "the home of plague and death" and advised others to avoid the place or stay as short a time as possible.

Like Jerba, Gabès fell easy prey to seafaring European states, with the **Aragonese** the first to invade in 1279. However, when central government was weak and there were no Europeans about, the town was quick to reassert its independence. It did this during the Hilalian invasions and, later, whenever the Hafsids were too busy fighting among themselves to do much about it.

By the time of the Ottomans in the late sixteenth century, the city was divided into three separate quarters: **Jara**, with a large Jewish community, in the north, **Menzel** in the west and **Boulbaba** a couple of kilometres south. According to Leo Africanus, the entire region was surrounded by a dyke which could be flooded in times of war – though for much of the time the city quarters expended their energies fighting one another. Their quarrels came to a head in 1881, when Jara sided with the French, inciting its neighbours to attack. Without the help of a large French landing party and gunboats offshore, the Jews would inevitably have been massacred. As it was, Menzel and Boulbaba were fined heavily and denied permission to hold a market, so forcing local trade into the hands of the Jews. The communities' rivalry and mutual loathing simmered throughout the Protectorate period, exploding again in 1942 when anti-Semitic riots, encouraged by the Germans, persuaded most of the Jews to leave for Jerba.

Under the French, Gabès became the key garrison point of the south, and a massive **fort** was built on the outskirts of the town in readiness for a tribal revolt or Italian invasion. Today the region remains strategically sensitive, and the town is full of Tunisian conscripts. Their presence is also explained by the fact that the Gulf of Gabès has considerable reserves of **oil**, claimed by both Tunisia and Libya, though the dispute was settled in 1981.

Moving on from Gabès

For a list of destinations and journey times, see Travel details on p.411.

Gabès is the main transport link between the south and the centre of Tunisia, so it's a very good place to pick up connections to anywhere in the country. There are four daily **trains** to Tunis via Sfax, of which the fastest is the night train, which leaves just after midnight and will get you into Tunis at a bleary 6am. The afternoon train connects at Ghraïba (not far north of La Skhirra) for Gafsa and Metlaoui, though this is strictly for train buffs, as it's a long way round.

From the **bus station** there are services operated by SNTRI, Gabès's own SRT (called SOTREGAMES), and three other SRTs. There are regular buses to Tunis – some via Kairouan, some via Sfax and Sousse, with a couple continuing to Bizerte, as well as services to major towns all over south and central Tunisia. As for local destinations, there are buses to El Hamma, Matmata, Tamezret, Techine, Toujane, Mareth and Zarat; the Zarat buses, travelling via Mareth, leave from rue de Bizerte by the Great Mosque, though Mareth itself is served by most soundbound buses.

If you're getting a **louage** from the louage station, you'll need to pay at the ticket office before boarding (unless you're on a louage to Libya). Note that louages for Mareth leave from rue de Bizerte by the Great Mosque, while those for Nouvelle Matmata (where you can change for Matmata) depart from avenue Farhat Hached, just west of the junction with rue Haj Jelani Lahbib and rue Ali Jemel. Buses for Matmata stop here too. If you want a louage to a less well-served destination such as Tozeur or Douz, start out early; otherwise, change at Kebili.

Gabès has an **airstrip**, but this isn't used for passenger flights, and the new airport under construction on the Nouvelle Matmata–El Hamma road isn't going to be up and running until 2010.

Arrival and information

Arriving by **train**, you find yourself bang in the middle of town on rue Mongi Slim and not far from the beach. Road transport from Matmata may leave you on avenue Farhat Hached, just west of the junction with rue Haj Jelani Lahbib and rue Ali Jemel; local services from Mareth terminate on rue de Bizerte by the Great Mosque. The main **bus and louage stations** are opposite the calèche stand at the far western end of town, where avenue Farhat Hached meets avenue de la République and the road to Sfax. From here, two main roads head east through the city centre, with most of the services and shops concentrated along them. Rue Lahbib Chagra branches northeast to become **avenue Bourguiba**, which curves past the main **market** before turning a sharp bend seawards past several of the town's best hotels and restaurants. The other main artery, **avenue Farhat Hached**, follows a more or less straight line towards the sea, meeting avenue Bourguiba again at the other end of town. Just beyond the junction where they meet up again is the **ONTT** (July & Aug Mon–Sat 7.30am–1.30pm & 5–7pm; Sept–June Mon–Thurs 8.30am–1pm & 3–5.45pm, Fri & Sat 8.30am–1.30pm; ☎75 270 254), with a list of bus and train departures posted outside. Beyond it, the main road continues seaward towards the **port** and **beach**. Gabès is small enough to be able to get around on foot, though **taxis** and **calèches** can be handy for visiting the oasis.

Accommodation

Gabès has plenty of budget **accommodation**, though you may well find much of it full if you arrive late in the day. There is less choice among the more expensive hotels, with nothing over two stars except a couple of package-type places by the beach. Apart from these, most hotels are in the centre of town around avenues Bourguiba and Farhat Hached. There is a **youth hostel** in the well-kept *Centre des Stages et des Vacances*, rue de l'Oasis, Petite Jara (☎75 270 271; dorm beds 5TD, breakfast 1.5TD), where you can come and go as you please. **Camping** is possible here for 3TD per person.

Hotels

Atlantic 4 av Bourguiba, at the junction of av Farhat Hached ☎75 220 034, ☎75 221 358. This enormous white French colonial building dating from 1912 is the oldest hotel in town and creaks with character, but has seen better days, though it remains excellent value. All rooms – some pretty large, others quite small – are en suite, with either a bath or shower; some rooms have a/c, and there's a family suite. Often full in summer, so book ahead. This is slightly better value for an en-suite room than the *Mourad*. The rate includes breakfast. ❷

Ben Nejima 68 rue Ali Jemel, on the corner of av Farhat Hached ☎75 271 591. Although the rooms are clean and the management friendly, the place is a bit noisy. Bathroom facilities are shared. ❶

Chems On the beach ☎75 270 547, ☎75 274 485, ✆www.hotelchems.com.tn. The most modern hotel in town, with a nice pool and big spotless rooms, some with a sea view, and all en suite. Wheelchair accessible, though you'd need help up the ramp. Reservation by fax preferred. ❻

Houda av de la République ☎75 220 022, ☎75 271 145. Cool and comfortable, with good views from the top floor and the roof terrace. Most rooms have bathroom and balcony, but some have just a shower. ❷

Medina rue Haj Jilani Lahbib ☎75 274 271. A good-value little hotel in the Menzel quarter, with decent rooms and shared bathrooms. ❶

Mourad 300 av Bourguiba, above the UIB bank ☎75 273 926. Clean, quiet and very good value. Most of the upstairs rooms are both large and en suite. Best of the cheapies. ❶

M'Rabet rue Ali Zouaoui, near the train station ☎75 270 602. Open 24hr, so handy for train arrivals at any time of the day or night. The lobby is rather pleasantly kitsch, and most of the nice, clean rooms have showers; the others either have a toilet and/or balcony. Rate includes breakfast. ❷

L'Oasis On the beach ☎75 270 381, ☎75 271 749, ✆www.sdts.tourism.tn. A reasonably posh tourist hotel with the usual facilities, including a/c and TV in all rooms, a sea view from some of them

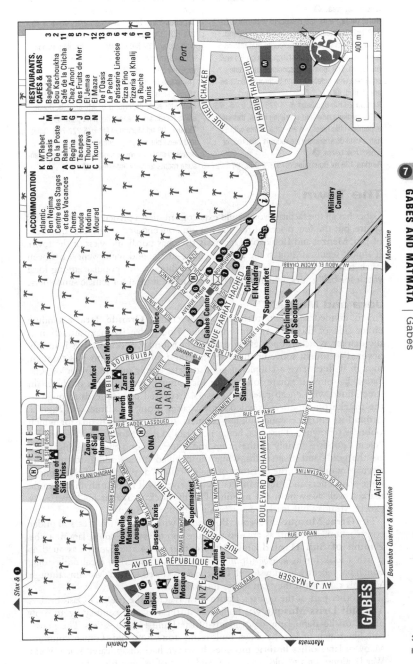

ACCOMMODATION			
Atlantic	H	M'Rabet	K
Ben Nejma	B	L'Oasis	M
Centre des Stages		De la Poste	I
et des Vacances	A	Rahma	H
Chems	O	Regina	O
Houda	F	Tacapes	J
Medina	E	Thouraya	D
Mourad	C	Tkouri	N

RESTAURANTS, CAFÉS & BARS	
Baghdad	3
Bou Kachoukha	2
Café de la Chicha	11
Chez Amori	8
Des Fruits de Mer	5
El Jemaa	7
El Mazar	12
De l'Oasis	13
La Pacha	9
Pâtisserie Lineoise	6
Pizza Pino	4
Pizzeria el Khalij	1
La Ruche	6
Tunis	10

GABÈS

and a pool fed by a natural hot spring, though the food is not great. ❻

Hôtel de la Poste rue Belgacem el Bazmi ☏75 222 182. The second-oldest hotel in town, and a long-time backpackers' favourite that retains a small amount of 1920s charm, though it's well run-down. The rooms are spacious and come equipped with bidets, though bathroom facilities are shared. ❶

Rahma 26 rue Boulbaba ☏75 275 385, ℻75 275 710. Spanking new and sparkling clean, this well-appointed little hotel has en-suite rooms with TV and a café downstairs. One room is adapted for wheelchair users. ❹

Regina 138 av Bourguiba ☏75 272 095, ℻75 221 710. The rooms are around an interior patio, all en suite, clean and fresh. Good value. ❶

Tacapes 55 av Bourguiba ☏75 270 700–1, ℻75 271 601. The rooms are clean and comfortable with a/c and TV, but the place is showing its age somewhat, and could do with a lick of paint. Rate includes breakfast. ❸

Thouraya By the bus station ☏75 274 160. A slightly scruffy but friendly hotel by the bus station, handy for early departures or late arrivals. Downstairs rooms are cheaper but a bit poky. ❶

Tkouri 399 bd Mohamed Ali ☏75 277 706. Quiet and clean but not very central. There's a choice between small rooms without bathroom, or big en-suite rooms for very little more. ❷

The Town

Gabès has all the facilities you would expect from such a pivotal communications centre, but the few places of real interest are concentrated in the **old quarters** of Jara, Menzel and Boulbaba. The **oasis** stretches north and west of the town. It almost seems as though the **beach** – litter-strewn and windswept – has been stuck on the eastern end of town as an afterthought. It's popular among local youth for ball games, which doesn't exactly make it ideal for female sunbathers.

Jara and Menzel

Jara is divided into two parts, the larger chunk, **Grande Jara**, extending either side of the western end of avenue Bourguiba. Its main attraction is the market, which is open every day except Monday, and nowadays is mostly devoted to tourist souvenir shops serving the tour groups who pass through, though it does have a couple of good cassette shops on the corner of Rue Sadok Lassoued if you're looking for local music. To the north of the main street, lined with cheap cafés and *gargotes*, a covered passage leads through to the **marketplace**, once crowded with caravans from Ghadames and Algeria. Around its entrance stand bulging panniers, filled with the henna for which Gabès is renowned. This area, being near Jara's Great Mosque, is reserved for "clean" goods – mainly clothes, rugs and spices. Among the adjoining shops are the gold- and silversmiths, while the cobbled street leading down to the river were originally the territory of the so-called "dirty" crafts of blacksmiths, knife-sharpeners and metalworkers. By the river itself is the unhygienic cattle market, well away from the mosque. The livestock market is held every day except Monday, but market day, when it is busiest, is Sunday.

The **Great Mosque** on avenue Bourguiba, with its huge minaret, still under construction, is recent, as are most of the mosques in Grande Jara, but the **Zaouia of Sidi Hamed**, around the corner at 44 rue Sadok Lassoued, is worth a look for its *koubba* (dome) and doorways carved in local pink stone, which has recently been restored. The *zaouia* is closed to non-Muslims, though Muslims can visit if they can locate the *guardien*.

The other part of the quarter, **Petite Jara**, is across the rue de l'Oasis bridge. The **Sidi Driss Mosque** was built here in the eleventh century by an Arab prince of the Banu Jami, descendants of the Banu Hilal invaders. The prayer hall, like much of Jara, has been built using stone from old Roman columns. Many of Jara's other historic mosques, however, have disappeared since World War II, along with its old synagogues and most of its Jewish heritage.

The monuments of **Menzel** – the area around avenue de la République – seem to have survived rather better, such as they are. Menzel's Great Mosque, in a square just west of avenue de la République, and the **Zaouia of Sidi Bnei Isa**, down a side street on the other side of the avenue, are both old and attractive buildings, and a stroll down rue Bechir el Jaziri will take you past the **Zem Zmia Mosque**. Even if you don't track all these down, Menzel is the only quarter of Gabès that really retains its ancient feel, and is definitely the best part of town for an aimless wander. It also has its own **market**, on rue Omar el Mokhtar.

Boulbaba

The third historic quarter, **Boulbaba**, is somewhat removed from the town centre, down at the end of avenue de la République and along avenue J.A. Nasser, then along rue 6 Octobre, some twenty minutes' walk away – look out for the tall minaret. Bus #2 runs to Boulbaba half-hourly from rue Jilani Lahbib; ask the driver for Sidi Boulbaba. A taxi will cost about 1.5TD.

It's worth making the effort to get out here to see Gabès's most important and oldest religious monument, the **Mosque of Sidi Boulbaba**, containing the tomb of the saint who was Mohammed's barber. The mosque is located in the quarter's main square, on the opposite side from the mosque with the tall minaret. Boulbaba arrived here in the seventh century and, like many holy men and marabouts in the south, united warring factions to bring prosperity to the town – of which he is now the patron saint. The surrounding village, which took his name, stood on the site of Roman Tacape and was closed to local Jews and Christians. Non-Muslims may enter the mosque's courtyard – which is particularly beautiful, surrounded by colonnades and decorated with tiles – but not the prayer hall.

Next to the mosque is an imposing old *medersa*, built in 1692 and now the **Museum of Popular Arts and Traditions** (Tues–Sun: mid-April to mid-Sept 8am–1pm & 4–7pm; mid-Sept to mid-April 9.30am–4.30pm; 1.1TD). The people who run it are welcoming and happy to show you around. The pink stone building itself holds more interest than the exhibits, which include everyday objects, textiles, a Punic ossuary, and a little garden planted with henna, pomegranates, bananas and grapes. Some locally excavated Roman artefacts decorate the grounds.

The oasis

Part of the **Gabès oasis** starts just behind Petite Jara, leading along to the Sfax road and, in the other direction, to the sea. There are 300,000 palms here, but many are in poor health, spoilt by the damp sea air. The land has changed little since the days when the Roman writer Pliny observed: "Here in the midst of the sand, the soil is well cultivated and fruitful. Here grows a high palm and beneath that palm are olives and under that a fig tree. Under the fig tree grows a pomegranate and beneath that again a vine. Moreover, beneath these there are sown corn, then vegetables or grass." This tiered intercropping continues today, allowing farmers to cultivate an astonishing range of crops, some four hundred varieties in total, including henna and spices.

The main oasis villages are on the other side of the Gabès–Sfax road; most worthwhile – although also most touristed – is **CHENINI**. The small direct road there (head past the louage and calèche stands, then talke a right turn over the river) winds around the irrigation ditches in a swirl of right-angle bends to reach **EL AOUADID**, some 3km away. If you turn left here, the road meanders past the *Café des Cascades*, a pleasant spot for an open-air tea or coffee

The amazing date palm

Dates are a big export industry, and bring much needed foreign currency into the Tunisian economy. But to the people of the desert, the cultivation of dates is more than just business: it supplies them with a vital source of food, fuel and building materials, to the extent that life would be unimaginable without it.

Although the fibrous **trunk** of the palm is not a true wood, it is sturdy enough to saw into planks to make doors, window shutters and floorboards. In the old quarters of Tozeur (see p.358) and Nefta (see p.368), where the alleys pass under buildings, the boards overhead are of palm wood, just as they are in the entrances to many of the southern *ksour*. The doors of *ghorfas* in the *ksour* are also made from palm wood, along with many doors of homes in the old quarters of the desert towns, and the conduits which carry water from spring to cistern. For more on *ksour* and *ghorfas*, see p.453.

Palm wood is too valuable to burn, but the **fronds** of the tree make excellent fuel. Alternatively, they can be used for fencing, to protect crops and gardens from wind and sand – you will often see such fencing installed along the top of roadside dunes to prevent their advance across the road. The fronds are also used to make the huts that nomadic families live in, and to thatch the roofs of houses built with other materials. The spines of the frond can be turned into chairs, beds and other furniture, while the tough green leaves are woven to make anything from baskets to floor matting and fans for keeping the charcoal alight on a *chicha*. Even the stalk on which the dates grow can be used as a broom once the dates have been taken from it.

Dates aren't the only food that can be derived from the palm: **palm hearts** are a very tasty luxury, and the tree can be tapped for *laghmi* (palm wine). For more on dates themselves and palm wine, see the box on p.361.

in the palm trees, eventually arriving at a **crocodile farm** (daily 8am–sunset; 0.5TD). At present this contains a rather unimpressive zoo, but it is due to metamorphose into a **Nature Museum**, with exhibits on wildlife in the oasis, the mountains, the desert and the Gulf of Gabès, including an aquarium as well as a zoo. Beside it is an open-air café restaurant with a family section, complete with swings and slides for the kids, and in front of the zoo is a rather underwhelming **Roman dam**, made up of several layers of stone holding back a small reservoir. A path behind the dam goes on to some impressive **gorges** at the southwest tip of the oasis. The road along the top leads past the **Marabout of Sidi Ali Bahoul** and on to Chenini itself.

The walk to Chenini is a nice stroll in spring or autumn but a hot four-kilometre trudge in summer, and most people actually take a **calèche tour** of the oasis (15TD for up to four people). The tours all follow much the same route, with obligatory stops to buy souvenirs. Alternatively, you can get there on the hourly bus #7 from Gabès, which leaves from opposite rue Jilani Lahbib near the junction of avenue de la République (even though #7 isn't listed at the bus stop), or you can take a place (*plassa*) in a shared taxi from the same spot (0.4TD).

Eating and drinking

Food isn't one of Gabès's high points, but reasonable meals can be found in every price range if you know where to look. If your budget is really tight, there are some *gargotes* on avenue de la République and around the market, and around the Nouvelle Matmata louage station on avenue Farhat Hached.

Among **cafés**, the *Café la Chicha* on rue Ibn Jazar at the junction of avenue Bourguiba and avenue Farhat Hached (daily except Fri 6am–9pm) is a refined if slightly pricey place, where women as well as men can relax with a coffee and *chicha*. The same is true of the open-air café just east of the tourist office. Women will not, however, feel at home in the town's **bars**, which include the *Tunis* at 8 avenue Farhat Hached, and the one attached to the *Hôtel Atlantic*. The best **patisserie** in town is *Patisserie Lineoise* at 134 avenue Farhat Hached, with several varieties of croissants as well as pastries, savouries and cold drinks.

Restaurants

Baghdad 175 av Bourguiba. Low-priced, reliable Tunisian food – salads, merguez, brochettes, roast chicken and so on. Mon–Sat noon–3pm & 6–10pm, Sun noon–3pm.

Bou Kachoukha 60 rue Ali Jemel. The usual staples (chicken and chips, spaghetti and such like). Daily noon–3pm.

Restaurant Chez Amori 84 av Bourguiba. Watch French TV while you eat cheap, substantial meals such as couscous royale (couscous with all the trimmings), lamb chops or brochettes. Daily 11am–9pm. Also has a sandwich bar two doors down.

Restaurant des Fruits de Mer rue Hedi Chaker by the fishing port. Excellent food including treats like spicy stuffed cuttlefish (*sêche farci*), barbecued freshly landed fish, even roast rabbit, all at low prices. Daily 7am–10pm or later.

Restaurant el Jemaa av Bourguiba, by Banque du Sud and two doors from the post office. Cheap, clean diner, handy for for sandwiches, spit-roast chicken and shawarma. Daily 5am–10pm.

Restaurant el Mazar 39 av Farhat Hached ☎75 272 065. Highly regarded and rather refined, serving French-style food as well as well-prepared Tunisian dishes. Steaks and grills share the menu with fish and prawns. Daily noon–3pm & 6–11pm.

Restaurant de l'Oasis 17 av Farhat Hached ☎75 270 098. This established place is Gabès's top

restaurant, with a 9TD set menu, and specials like paella if you order in advance, though the more exotic dishes advertised on the menu, such as young rabbit in mustard sauce, are not actually available. Daily noon–3pm & 7–10pm.

Restaurant la Pacha 38 av Farhat Hached ☎75 272 418. Formerly a posh French restaurant, this place is now rather more popular, partly because it serves alcohol, and partly because it serves good French-style fare in generous portions and at moderate prices. Daily except Fri noon–3pm & 6–11pm.

Pizza Pino 114 av Bourguiba. A pleasant and moderately priced little place, doing very passable pizzas, including a "pizza gabèsienne" with *harissa*, egg and canned tuna fish. Daily except Sun noon–3pm & 6–10pm.

Restaurant Pizzeria el Khalij 142 av Farhat Hached. A passable Tunisian restaurant, serving the usual grills and couscous (though not pizzas at last check, despite its name), plus beer and wine. Daily except Sun noon–3pm & 6.30–11pm.

Restaurant la Ruche rte de Sfax, 1km out of town. A popular bar-restaurant with a small selection of inexpensive, competently prepared meat dishes such as steak or lamb chops to wash down with beer or wine, though women may not find it a comfortable place to eat in the evening due to the prevailing tavern atmosphere. Daily 11am–10pm.

Listings

Airlines Tunisair, 172 av Farhat Hached ☎75 271 250.

Banks Several on av Bourguiba, including four near the Gabès Center with ATMs that take Visa and Mastercard. There are three more on av Farhat Hached. In Menzel, there's the Banque du Sud at the corner of av de la République and rue Omar el Mokhtar.

Bookshop Librairie Béchraoui at 75 av Bourguiba has the odd English title among its dusty piles of used books.

Car rental Avis, 4 rue 9 Avril ☎75 270 210; Europcar, 6 av Farhat Hached ☎75 274 720; Hertz,

6 av Farhat Hached ☎75 270 525; Olympique, 337 av Mohammed Ali ☎75 273 780.

Car spares and repairs You'll find a few mechanics' workshops on av J.A. Nasser southwest of town, on the right just before it crosses the *oued*, with spares shops dotted around town, for example at 44 av Mohammed Ali (Peugeot), and at the start of the Sfax road (Renault, Opel, Isuzu).

Cinema El Khadra, rue Abou el Kacem Chabbi, near the corner of av Farhat Hached.

Hammams The most central is on rue de Palestine, just off rue Sadok Lassoued – look for the blue and white door (daily: men 5am–12.30pm

& 6–9pm, women 12.30–6pm). Others in town include Hammam el Hana, rue Général de Gaulle, just off av Bourguiba (daily: men 7am–noon & 6–9pm, women 1–6pm); and Hammam Sidi Driss, rue Sidi Driss, Petite Jara (daily: men 5am–1pm & 6–10pm, women 1–5pm).

Hospitals and clinics The regional hospital is in rue Romdhane Ali Dhari, 3km down the Medenine road (℡75 282 700). More central is the Clinique Bon Secours at 12 rue Mongi Slim (℡75 271 400 or 75 277 700), which has an emergency department. There's an all-night pharmacy at 55 rue Mongi Slim, at the corner of rue Ali Ben Khalifa.

Internet access The most central Publinet office is at unit 146 upstairs in the Gabès Centre (daily 8am–10pm; 2TD/hr), but there's a cheaper one that stays open later in Gallerie Ben Jaber at 145 rue Bechir Jaziri, opposite the Zem Zmia Mosque (daily 8am–midnight; 1.5TD/hr).

Laundry Nettoyage Daim, 144 av Bourguiba, has self-service machines at 3TD for up to 5kg of washing.

Newspapers Maktaba el Jemaa, at the corner where av Bourguiba does a bend, just south of *Hôtel Mourad*, stocks British tabloids.

ONA crafts shop av Farhat Hached, opposite the post office (Mon–Thurs 8.30am–1pm & 3–5.45pm, Fri & Sat 8.30am–1pm).

Police The main police station is 1km out of town on the Medenine road (℡75 270 844). There's a more central station on av Bourguiba, near the junction with rue 18 Janvier.

Post offices At the corner of av Farhat Hached and rue Bechir el Jaziri (country hours), and on av Bourguiba at the corner of rue General de Gaulle (city hours). Both have money-changing facilities (for cash) and international phones. There are also a few smaller offices around town, open country hours.

Supermarkets Magasin Général has two branches, one in Menzel at the corner of rue Omar el Mokhtar and rue Bechir el Jaziri, the other at the junction of bd Mohammed Ali and rue Mongi Slim. Both are open Mon–Sat 8am–7pm, Sun 8am–1pm.

Swimming pools The *Hôtel Chems* will let you use their pool for a few dinars.

Tours To cover some of the more inaccessible parts of the south, you might consider a tour, mostly by Land Rover, run by operators such as Sahara Tours at 11 av Farhat Hached (℡75 270 930). A two-day excursion into the desert, including a night at Ksar Ghilane (see p.375) will set you back around 110TD.

Matmata and around

As the Romans of Bulla Regia once did (see p.202), the Berbers of **MAT-MATA**, some 40km due south of Gabès, live underground in **pit dwellings** consisting of a courtyard dug straight down into the soft, crumbly sandstone with rooms excavated into the surrounding walls, and it is these troglodyte dwellings that provide the town's main attraction. In 1959, however, the government began construction of a modern settlement at Nouvelle Matmata, 15km up the road to Gabès, and people started moving in three years later. By the 1970s, when **Star Wars** (see box on p.364) was filmed here and Matmata was discovered by the tourist industry, many Matmatis were already living in more conventional housing, either in Nouvelle Matmata or in the original village. This was not because the new houses were preferred, but rather because they were easier to construct, and there was a need for housing for young people. Those who had traditional homes preferred to keep them, except where their location made them prone to flooding.

Tourism proved a mixed blessing for the town, and completely changed the local way of life, with tour groups on "safari" pouring in and tramping around the village, peering into the pits to take photographs of people in their homes. This is tourism at its most voyeuristic, and barbed wire and dogs around many of the pits demonstrate that not everyone in town is happy about it. Others take a more resigned attitude to what is now by far the biggest local industry, and a source of income after all. You'll get repeated invitations into people's houses but these are not gratis: be prepared to either pay a fee, especially for photographs, or to buy the local handicrafts in exchange for a quick peep. In the evenings, when the tour groups have all gone home, Matmata becomes

The Matmata Berbers

The Matmata tribe of Berbers once lived near the hot springs of **El Hamma de l'Arad** (see p.387), but were expelled from their original home following a failed rebellion in 1630. While some Berbers did join the Hilalian armies that swept west into Morocco, the Matmata tribe preserved its autonomy until the end of the seventeenth century. The Ottomans always had trouble collecting taxes in this area, and Mohammed Bey was forced to build forts at El Hamma to the north and Bir Soltane in the desert to the west in order to keep the Matmata under control. By the eighteenth century, however, these forts had been abandoned and military expeditions remained the only means of asserting government authority, sometimes with success, sometimes ending in humiliating failure. In 1869, for instance, General Osman led his army into the foothills only to be surprised at night and forced to flee, leaving behind his artillery and richly adorned tent.

Under the French, the Berbers maintained their own **tribal court**, called the *miad*, which settled questions according to Berber law. In common with all the villages in the south, Matmata was still ruled by a sheikh, or administrator of the community, answerable to a *khalifa* (deputy governor) and the *caid* (governor) at Gabès. The system continued until independence, and the French officers of the Service des Affaires Indigènes, who supervised tax collection and public works, usually kept out of village affairs. Although the Berbers enjoyed some autonomy under colonial rule, the government presence was still strong, as the fort on the outskirts of town – now an army base – testifies.

a much more pleasant, laid-back kind of place, and it's also a useful base for exploring the other villages of this remarkable region.

If you're on the way to Matmata from Gabès, look out for two concrete bunkers, one on each side of the road, half a kilometre past the "Matmata 37km/Gabès 5km" milestone. Dated "le 28.1.36", they were command posts for the wartime **Mareth Line** (see p.411). Matmata buses from Gabès stop briefly on the way at **Nouvelle Matmata** (change here if you're travelling by louage), before climbing to the top of the Demer mountains and then descending to Matmata in the valley on the other side. With the virtual absence of any buildings above ground, Matmata looks deserted as you approach, though in fact, five thousand people still live in the "craters" which come into view as you head further down the road, and the town centre is now marked by some ordinary above-ground buildings.

The Town

Matmata is spread out across the saddle of the mountain, around three main roads – to Gabès, Toujane and Douz respectively, the roads meeting in the centre of town. Despite its obvious centre, Matmata seems almost too diffuse to be a town; the structures which have sprung up above the ground in the centre now give the lie to its much-heralded "lunar" landscape, while the busloads of snap-happy day-trippers and camel-riding tourists manage at times to completely swamp the place.

Before the bulk of the Matmata tribe moved here in the sixteenth or seventeenth century, a much smaller community lived in ancient Matmata, around the *kala'a*, or **fortress**, just discernible on the heights above today's town. Their homes, built into the mountainside, have been abandoned in favour of the pit dwellings. Trying to climb up there is inadvisable since the *kala'a* overlooks an army camp on the road to Toujane, and your appearance on its ramparts may lead to trouble.

The pit dwellings

The pit dwellings in Matmata follow a regular design some 400 years old. Most are based around a **circular pit** with vertical walls, 7m deep and 10m in diameter. Their construction takes advantage of the relative softness of the local sandstone which is easy to dig into. First the pit is excavated, making a central sunken courtyard, equivalent to the patio of a normal Tunisian home; then caves are dug into its sides at the level of the courtyard to serve as rooms. Smaller chambers may be dug out at higher levels, with steps leading up to them. These are usually cisterns or store-rooms, and may have holes in the ceiling to allow grain to be poured into them. A small, covered passageway, sometimes lined with recesses for animals and their fodder, leads from ground level down to the sunken courtyard. In fact, the pit may be dug into a small hillock, so that the tunnel runs horizontally out of the side of it. A simple dwelling takes six to eight months to build, while the largest houses, consisting of two or three pits linked together, take even longer.

The rooms in these troglodyte dwellings have the advantage of **natural temperature control**. In Iraq and Iran people escaped from the intense heat by building wind towers, a primitive kind of air conditioning which forced any breeze down into the rooms. At Matmata this was unnecessary since, as at Bulla Regia (see p.202) and at Gharian in Libya, the insulation of the earth was even more effective in providing cool temperatures during summer and warmth in the winter, making the rooms comfortable at any time of year.

There are a number of ways to see a pit dwelling while respecting the privacy of local residents. You can visit or stay in one of three **hotels** originally built as troglodyte homes, or you can visit the **museum** (daily except Sun 8am–5pm; 2TD), behind the *Hôtel Sidi Driss*, where a group of local women have set up a display of furniture, utensils and wedding costumes in a former dwelling, with one room now given over to carpet making. The tour is a little bit cursory (most of the women do not speak much French, let alone English) and the exhibits are not really explained, but it's the architecture you've really come to see. Finally, you may be **invited** to visit someone's home; kids generally wander round the village accosting tourists with invitations. These will either be for money (it's best to agree a price beforehand – the going rate is around 5TD), or for the opportunity to sell you souvenirs. If no one approaches you, note that there are houses 2–3km along the Douz road and 3–4km along the Gabès road with signs outside inviting tourists to view them.

Moving on from Matmata

For a list of destinations and journey times, see Travel details on p.411.

Daily buses run from Matmata to **Gabès**, one continuing to Jerba, and there's a summer-only (plus school holidays) SNTRI bus serves Tunis via Sousse and Sfax. The school bus to **Tamezret** at 6am and 1pm takes other passengers too, but returns immediately, and there's a school bus at the same times to Techine. On Mondays and Tuesdays – souk days in Matmata and Nouvelle Matmata – there are also louages to Tamezret. Otherwise, louages serve only **Nouvelle Matmata**, from where there are connections to Gabès. The road to **Douz**, 100km west, is surfaced and easily motorable, but isn't served by any public transport.

The pipeline route to **Ksar Ghilane** (see p.476), which branches off 32km west of Matmata, is usually passable with care by car, though it is easy to get stuck in sand drifts, and always wise to take along somebody who knows the road. If you do attempt it, do check conditions locally before setting off, inform the National Guard of your plans and heed the advice on desert driving on p.32.

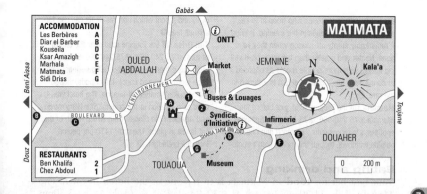

ACCOMMODATION
Les Berbères   A
Diar el Barbar   B
Kouseila   D
Ksar Amazigh   C
Marhala   E
Matmata   F
Sidi Driss   G

RESTAURANTS
Ben Khalifa   2
Chez Abdoul   1

Practicalities

Buses and **louages** will drop you in or by the market place, which is just off the junction where the Gabès, Douz and Toujane roads meet up. There's a helpful **ONTT** 200m up the Gabès road from here (July & Aug Mon–Sat 7.30am–1.30pm & 5–7pm, Sun 10am–noon & 5–7pm; Sept–June Mon–Thurs 8.30am–1pm & 3–5.45pm, Fri & Sat 8.30am–1.30pm; Ramadan Mon–Thurs & Sat 8am–2pm, Fri 8am–1pm; ☎75 240 075), and an equally helpful **Syndicat d'Initiative** 400m along the Toujane road (Mon–Thurs & Sun 8am–noon & 3–5.30pm, Fri & Sat 8am–noon, and often staffed outside those hours; ☎75 240 114). The Syndicat can organize camels (5TD per person per hour), *calèches* (5TD per person per hour) and guides (10TD for a standard 1hr 30min tour), and provide information on Matmata's annual tourist festival, held in March and featuring the usual "folkloric" performances.

There are no banks in Matmata (the nearest is at Nouvelle Matmata), but the **post office** (country hours) in the centre of town at the beginning of the Gabès road will change cash, as will the *Kouseila* hotel.

Three of Matmata's **hotels** (the *Sidi Driss*, *Marhala* and *Berbères*) are converted pit dwellings, consisting of several courtyards joined together by underground passages with excavated rooms. A fourth, the *Diar el Barbar*, is a massive – and utterly audacious – modern deluxe version of the same design. Most Matmata hotels do good deals for half board.

Hotels

Les Berbères Off the Douz road, near the centre of town ☎75 240 024, ☎75 240 097. A friendly hotel in a converted pit dwelling, smaller and quieter than the other pit-dwelling hotels in town. Individual travellers can take a bed in a large, shared room for 12TD. Both this price and the usual room rate include breakfast. **❷**

Diar el Barbar 1500m up the Douz road ☎75 240 074, ☎75 240 144. An amazing new hotel modelled on a pit dwelling but on a massive scale, incorporating traditional and modern features, with two underground levels of deluxe troglodyte rooms built around several huge courtyards, plus another storey of ordinary rooms on top. All the four-star trappings are here, with all rooms en suite, and

with a/c and heating in case you are not satisfied with the natural variety. There's also a pool and a large terrace with a panoramic view of the mountains. **❺**

Kouseila On the Toujane road ☎75 240 303, ☎75 240 265. A conventional modern hotel with cool, comfortable a/c rooms. Wheelchair accessible. **❺**

Ksar Amazigh 1km up the Douz road ☎75 240 088, ☎75 240 173. This is where most upmarket tour groups stay. Its pool, bar, restaurant and "Moorish" café are very peaceful during the day as the groups are all out touring, and the bungalow-style rooms are nice and cool, with a/c in case you need them cooler. **❺**

Marhala Off the Toujane road ☎75 240 015, ☎75 240 109. The most popular place in town, especially with tour groups who troop in to eat, mostly returning to Gabès in the evening, leaving it remarkably empty off-season when they've gone. Neater and quieter than the other pit-dwelling hotels, with more double rooms as opposed to dorms. Also has a bar. Breakfast is included in the rate. ❷

Matmata Off the Toujane road, just before the *Marhala* ☏75 240 066, ℻75 240 177. Spacious, spotless, a/c rooms (some of which don't have outside windows, though the rooms aren't troglo-

dyte) and a pool which non-residents can use for a small fee. ❹

Sidi Driss Off the Toujane road near the centre of town ☏75 240 005, ℻75 240 265. Slightly more basic than the other two pit dwellings, with each room crammed chock-full of beds, though that shouldn't matter off-season. The hotel was used as a location in the original *Star Wars* movie and *Attack of the Clones*, from which much of the set is still in place. The rate, 14TD per person, includes breakfast. ❸

Eating and drinking

Your best bet for **food** in Matmata is to try one of the hotels in town. The *Marhala* (daily 11.30am–2.30pm & 6.30–9pm), *Berbères* (daily 11am–3.30pm & 6–10pm) and *Sidi Driss* (daily 11am–3pm & 7–9pm) all do set menus of salad and couscous. The *Marhala* is the cheapest at 5TD, but at the *Sidi Driss*, for a few extra dinars you get to eat in the courtyard where Luke Skywalker had dinner with his aunt and uncle in *Star Wars*. Alternatively, you can try *Chez Abdoul (Restaurant Ouled Azaiza)* in the very centre of town (daily 8am–midnight), also with a reasonably priced set menu, including the option of vegetarian couscous for non-carnivores. *Restaurant Ben Khalifa*, 50m down the Toujane road (daily 8am–10pm) has low-priced Tunisian standards such as *mechoui*, couscous or chicken and chips. The *Hôtel Diar el Barbar* offers an all-you-can-eat buffet (12.15–4pm & 7.30–9pm) for 12TD including beer or wine, and with lots of salads and vegetarian options. For **drinking**, the obvious place is the *Hôtel Sidi Driss*, the most convivial bar in town.

Tijma and Haddej

To get some idea of what Matmata must once have been like, it's worth taking in the less touristy village of **Haddej**. The Syndicat d'Initiative in Matmata may be able to arrange transport, failing which it's a question of walking or hitching 4km north along the main road to **Tijma**, where you turn right for Haddej (signposted), about 3km up into the hills. There's a direct footpath between Matmata and Haddej, which you may enjoy if you like hiking (don't forget precautions against heatstroke and dehydration): follow the Gabès road to the edge of town then take a path to the right just after a café-souvenir shop, following the most trodden route at every junction thereafter. One problem on this path is fierce dogs, especially likely to take umbrage if you stray into someone's garden.

In the valleys between Tijma and Haddej, the luxuriance of the olive, almond and fig trees contrasts with the barrenness of the slopes. The trees flourish on hidden reservoirs of water stored in the thick soil of terraces called **jessour**. Every last drop from the winter downpours on the mountains is channelled into these terraces by shallow ditches and walls and is contained for the long dry summer, and the *jessour* also protect the plain below from flooding. To create the *jessour*, huge quantities of earth need to be piled up behind dry stone walls built across the valley floors. The work involved in building and maintaining them is formidable, and it's hardly surprising that they're no longer built. Most of the local men work in the cities and agriculture has been neglected, with the result that the region's terraces, its agricultural capital, are literally being washed away. Recently however, work has been done to conserve and renew the *jessour* (as at Douiret near Tataouine – see p.474), and many of them have been repaired and restored to their former condition.

Tijma

The **House of Fatima** in the tiny settlement of **TIJMA**, not signposted but on the west side of the main road 100m south of the Haddej turn-off, has long been owned by a woman of that name, and presents itself as a typical pit dwelling. Due not least to its unusually sanitized condition, this house is now on the tourist route and the current Fatima, plus daughter, receive the hordes with much aplomb. A bedroom, with its *dukkana* (a sort of bench used as a bed), and a kitchen, with pots and postcards for sale, are both open to view.

Haddej

Three kilometres northeast of Tijma, **HADDEJ** was formerly the region's most important village and home of the *khalifa*. A primary school among the palm trees marks the centre of town, and the **pit dwellings** lie up ahead. As soon as you arrive, the village children will surround you, asking for pens and offering to show you around (for a little baksheesh, naturally). It's a good idea to take up their offer as the buildings are even better concealed than those at Matmata, and the kids will probably follow you in any case. Many of the pits were abandoned after floods in 1969, when the water covered the courtyards for a week, but an underground **grain store** at the top of the slope is in remarkably good condition. Two tiers of interlocking, arched storerooms have been built into a rock, like the *ghorfas* which dominate the landscape further south.

On the left-hand side of the path leading to the pit dwellings is an **olive press**, one of several in the village, and also subterranean. At the centre of a small domed chamber is a circular stone, connected by a wooden shaft to the ceiling; a stone roller fixed to an axle is pulled around this shaft, crushing the olives spread out on the slab. The skins are taken from the stone and pressed again by a heavy palm trunk fastened at one end to the wall. Oil runs through a series of esparto grass mats into a jar, and the underground location provides the warmth in winter that's needed to separate the waste, which is fed to camels. In a final room, the olives are fermented to give the oil the musty flavour the people of the south appreciate.

Nearby is an underground **marabout** occupied only by its custodian. Another pit house, to the left of the olive press, was used for the village's **marriage ceremonies**. Seven days before the wedding, the bride's family would go into the large underground room to prepare the feast. On the wedding day the bride was brought here on a camel and taken into a small room, reached by the steps leading up from the basement (take a light if you visit). The husband, who was staying in a cell further inside the rock, went through to see the bride and to sign the marriage contract. Taking a back staircase up to ground level, he was led round to the front door to be formally received. When the feast was over, bride and groom would be taken into a cave room at the far end of the house, to remain in conjugal seclusion for several days. Meanwhile, the celebrations went on outside with a company of African comics, jesters and dancers.

Beni Aissa

Neither easy to find nor to get to (there's just one daily minibus from Nouvelle Matmata), **BENI AISSA** is a lovely little village where the people live in the same underground dwellings as in Matmata. About 1.5km west of Matmata, an unpaved road leads off to the right; some 4.5km along here is another turn-off (left) that takes you after a couple of kilometres to the village. A car will cover the route with no difficulty.

Beni Aissa is a far cry from tourist-driven Matmata, and people here are not used to sightseers coming to look at their homes, and may not take kindly to it. On the other hand, you won't have hordes of kids following you about, or encounter any tour groups, so a visit here will be quite a different kind of experience, and a rewarding one, so long as you respect the privacy of local residents. Look out for the group of **marabouts** 100m or so beyond the school, bus stop, shop and postbox that mark Beni Aissa's centre.

West of Matmata

The main road west from Matmata to Douz skirts the edge of a valley cultivated using the *jessour* system (see p.406). About halfway between Matmata and Tamezret, set 1km back from the road to the right, is the village of **SIDI META**. The first you see of it is a white *koubba* high up on the hillside, all that remains of the old village. At some time in the last two centuries the villagers moved down into the valley below, where, as at Matmata, they dug houses into the soft soil. Like Beni Aissa, Sidi Meta is rarely visited by tourists, and the people, as a result, are very accommodating. There's an **oil press** and an **underground mosque** that are worth seeing, and the village has a shop where you can buy bottled drinks.

TAMEZRET, built above ground, is packed around several steep slopes, topped by a **mosque**. One path between the tumbledown houses will take you to the **café** at the summit (open irregularly), where you can get a cup of green tea with almonds and climb onto the roof to see the village of Zeraoua in the distance. There are also some interesting oil presses (*massera*), both ancient and twentieth-century, if you can get somebody to show them to you. Tamezret and the villages around are known for their **woollen shawls**, the ceremonial *bakhnoughs*, with striking geometric designs identical to the facial tattoos sometimes seen on older women. The shawls, along with traditional tools, cooking utensils, carpets and costumes, can be seen at the **Berber Museum** (irregular hours; free, but donations appreciated), run by the enthusiastic and knowledgeable Mongi Barras. The museum is a little below the mosque, and also has a recreation of a traditional marriage room, an ancient cave dwelling and a seventh-century Berber home. When wandering around town, be sensitive to the privacy of local residents, especially if you have a camera.

West of Tamezret, the road continues across the desert to Douz (see p.377). Tracks lead north from Tamezret to the villages of **TAOUJOUT** and **ZERAOUA**. Both are walkable – 4km and 7km respectively, though the paths are not always easy to follow – but, like Tamezret, neither has accommodation (although someone may take pity on you and put you up). The views across the plateau and into the desert are stupendous, as are the villages – tightly knit communities living in compacted houses that look like a continuous wall from a distance.

The only one of the above villages with regular transport from Matmata is Tamezret, with school buses serving the route; you could catch the afternoon bus (see box on p.404) out to Tamezret if you don't mind walking 10km back to Matmata afterwards. On Mondays and Tuesdays, souk days in Matmata and Nouvelle Matmata respectively, you may also find louages to Tamezret.

Southeast of Matmata

The route east from Matmata past the *kala'a* leads on to Metameur (55km) and Medenine (60km) by way of **Toujane**, 23km from Gabès. The old town – not to be confused with Nouvelle Toujane (or Dekhila) down below – is one of the most dramatic of the Matmata region villages. The road from Matmata is now surfaced, and there may in the future be a bus service along it, though this was not certain at the time of writing. Most traffic to Toujane still uses from Mareth on the Gabès–Medenine road (there is a daily bus to Toujane from Gabès and Mareth, and there are louages from Mareth), and there's a surfaced road from Nouvelle Matmata too. Great views are to be had from all the roads into Toujane, particularly the one from Mareth, which commands a spectacular panorama of the coastal plain as far as the sea, and a lovely tableau of Toujane itself just before the descent into the village.

The road from Matmata begins to flatten out about 3km out of town, revealing the **Marabout of Sidi Moussa** on a peak to the left. In the early summer this is the scene of an ancient *ziara*, a tribal pilgrimage attended by thousands of villagers from Matmata; on the rocks around the tomb you can see the blood-stains from animal sacrifices. Some 8km further along, just off the road, is the village of **TECHINE** (served by two daily buses from Gabès and Matmata), known for its furniture, made from branches covered with clay, plaster and whitewash. It also has a traditional olive press, worked by a donkey.

A further 4km down the Toujane road – 15km from Matmata – a turn-off on the north side of the road winds for 8km down an incredibly steep gorge and out onto the plains to reach **BENI ZELTEN**, perched – like Tamezret – on the top of a small hill. Here though, the hilltop village has been deserted in favour of underground dwellings and houses on the valley floor. Nevertheless, it remains a remarkable site, and one that's unknown to most visitors. The road beyond the village continues to Nouvelle Matmata.

Toujane

Ignoring these detours and continuing along the Matmata–Medenine road, you cross a series of deep gorges and then pass along the escarpment with spectacular views of the plains below. Suddenly the road drops again, this time

△ Toujane

giving a bird's-eye view of **TOUJANE**, the old town spreading across two sides of a deep gorge and built around the foot of a mountain, from whose heights rear two brooding *kala'a* (fortresses). The local green tea, made with mountain herbs rather than just mint, is quite refreshing and worth a try.

Once isolated and untouched, Toujane is now sufficiently on the beaten track for a couple of **auberges**, offering half board, to have sprung up. The first *auberge* you come to if arriving from Matmata or Mareth is *Auberge Shambhala* (T98 663 482; half board ❸), very welcoming, with small but decent rooms in a former troglodyte home at street level, or more spacious and comfortable rooms up on the hillside, plus hot showers, free tea, dinner with the family, and the chance to see local crafts such as carpet weaving. At the Medenine end of town, *Auberge Hasnaoui* at the Medenine end of town (T98 913 919; ❷), is cheaper but less well run, with a traditional oil press, a café, and guided walks into the mountains. The auberges sells such items as locally made carpets (Toujane's main cottage industry) somewhat more cheaply than in the tourist emporiums of Houmt Souk, where many of them end up. They also sell olive oil and thyme and rosemary honey (if you're tempted by this, note that many countries, including the UK, prohibit the import of unsterilized honey). Shops along the main road may claim to be *auberges* and offer to put you up in rooms in the proprietors' homes, but will not have facilities such as showers, and are actually illegal.

Mareth and around

Midway between Gabès and Medenine, **MARETH** has long suffered from its important strategic position, commanding the narrow coastal plain between the Gulf of Gabès and the mountains. In 1936, the French army built a **defensive line** here to withstand a possible attack by the Italians in Libya. After the Italians and then the Germans occupied Tunisia however, the latter used the Mareth Line against the Allies, to block the Allied advance from the east in 1943; in the ensuing battle and Allied capture, the line and Mareth itself were virtually destroyed.

Apart from the busy Wednesday **market**, the new town is not wildly interesting, but if you're **staying** the options are the *Hôtel el Iman* (T & F75 321 035; ❶), on the east side of the main road, 200m south of the Gabès bus and louage stop, or the *Hôtel du Golfe* (T75 321 135; ❶), 100m south on the other side of the main road, which is basic but very friendly. Both hotels have cafés. For changing money, there are three **banks** in town but no ATMs.

Leaving Mareth, there are **buses** north to Gabès via Zarat, and south to Toujane, Medenine and Houmt Souk as well as further afield (see p.412 for details). Other services reach Tataouine, Zarzis, Ben Gardane and Ras Ajdir. **Louages** go to Gabès and (from across the street) Medenine, and occasionally to Tunis, but not usually to Houmt Souk. However, it is not difficult to hitch to Jorf, from where you can pick up the ferry to Jerba (see p.418). Louages (with a yellow stripe) to Toujane leave from opposite *Hôtel el Iman*. **Shared yellow taxis** for Zarat and Lazaiza leave from the junction between *Hôtel el Iman* and the Gabès bus and louage stop.

Zarat

A kilometre north of Mareth, a road branches off east to the town of **ZARAT**, a windblown, dead-end place, 2km beyond which is a **beach**, marked by a line of roofless white beach huts. It's not the nicest in Tunisia – the sand is hard and the shoreline covered in black seaweed – but you won't see another tourist here.

The Mareth Line

Three kilometres south of Mareth, just before the Jorf turn-off, the main road crosses **Oued Zigazou** on a zigzag bend. It's a seasonal river, dry most of the year, with the main emplacements of the Mareth Line spread out along it. On the *oued*'s north bank is the **Military Museum of the Mareth Line** (Tues–Sun 9am–4pm; 1TD including English tour, camera 2TD), run by the Ministry of Defence. Exhibits include maps and reconstructions illustrating Tunisia's role in World War II and the Battle of Mareth, as well as various small arms, and a French gun emplacement that looks remarkably like a dalek from *Dr Who*. Outside the museum are **concrete bunkers** that were actually part of the Mareth Line. These have been dug out – they were previously half-buried – and you can go inside them.

Rommel's command post, as illustrated in the museum, has also been tidied up by the army and is open to the public (same hours as the museum, and it may be left open at other times), though you are supposed to call at the museum first and take a guide. To get to it, take the Toujane road from Mareth – west off the main road between the two hotels – for 5km to the village of **LAZAIZA**, just beyond which there's a track to the right that seems to head for an upright rectangle on top of a hill, which is in fact a seismograph. Follow the track for 2km, round the back of the hill with the seismograph, and you will see the command post. Of the two entrances, the one on the left leads into the sleeping quarters, but you'll need a light of some kind in order to see anything. At the top of the hill by the seismograph are the remains of **trenches**, and there's a stunning view over the whole plain, which illustrates very clearly indeed how strategic the position was. Rommel set up his HQ here following orders from the Axis high command to strengthen the Mareth Line after their October 1942 defeat at the battle of El Alamein. Fortifications were built up along Oued Zigazou, which was in full flood at the time of the battle, and the post was chosen for its commanding view over the plain and the whole of the Mareth Line. It was the road to Toujane, then just a path, that allowed Montgomery's eighth army to outflank the German lines by advancing during a single night.

Travel details

Trains

Gabès to: Bir Bou Regba (2 daily; 5hr – connecting for Hammamet & Nabeul); El Jem (3 daily; 3hr); Ghraïba (2 daily; 1hr 10min – 1 connecting for Gafsa and Metlaoui); Mahrès (2 daily; 1hr 30min); Sfax (4 daily; 2hr); Sousse (2 daily; 3hr 45min); Tunis (4 daily; 5hr 50min).

Buses

Gabès to: Ben Gardane (6 daily; 2hr 15min); Bizerte (2 daily; 8hr); Douz (3 daily; 2hr 30min); Gafsa (3 daily; 2hr 30min); Ghoumrassen (3 daily; 2hr 15min); El Hamma (22 daily; 40min); Jerba (Houmt Souk; 11 daily; 2hr 30min); Kairouan (7 daily; 4hr); Kasserine (2 daily; 4hr); Kebili (7 daily; 2hr); Nefta (1 daily; 4hr); Mareth (roughly hourly; 40min); Matmata (8 daily; 1hr); Medenine (16 daily; 1hr 15min); Ras Ajdir (4 daily; 3hr); Sfax (19 daily; 2hr–2hr 30min); Sidi Bou Zid (2 daily; 4hr 30min); Sousse (18 daily; 4hr 30min); Tamezret (2 daily; 1hr 20min); Tataouine (6 daily; 2hr 15min); Techine (2 daily; 1hr 40min); Toujane (1 daily; 1hr 20min); Tozeur (2 daily; 3hr 30min); Tripoli (3 weekly; 9hr 30min); Tunis (18 daily; 6hr 30min); Zarat (6 daily; 1hr); Zarzis (7 daily; 2hr 30min).

Matmata to: Gabès (8 daily; 1hr); Jerba (Houmt Souk; 1 daily; 4hr); Sfax (1 daily summer and school holidays only; 3hr); Sousse (1 daily summer and school holidays only; 5hr 30min); Tamezret (2 daily; 20min); Techine (2 daily; 30min); Tunis (1 daily summer and school holidays only; 7hr 30min).

Mareth to: Ben Gardane (6 daily; 1hr 40min); Bizerte (2 daily; 8hr 30min); Gabès (roughly hourly; 40min); Jerba (Houmt Souk; 11 daily; 2hr); Medenine (16 daily; 40min); Kairouan (8 daily; 4hr 30min); Ras Ajdir (4 daily; 2hr 30min); Sfax (9 daily; 3hr), Sousse (7 daily; 4hr); Tataouine (6 daily; 1hr 40min); Toujane (1 daily; 40min); Tunis (15 daily; 7hr); Zarat (6 daily; 20min); Zarzis (7 daily; 2hr).

Louages and shared taxis

* indicates a route served by shared taxis.

Gabès to: Ben Gardane (2hr 30min); Chenini (Gabès oasis)* (10min); El Hamma (30min); Gafsa (2hr); Jerba (Houmt Souk; 2hr); Kairouan (3hr 30min); Kebili (1hr 30min); Mareth (30min); Medenine (1hr); Nouvelle Matmata (25min); Sfax (2hr); Sousse (4hr); Tataouine (1hr 45min); Tozeur (3hr); Tripoli (7hr); Tunis (6hr 30min); Zarat (30min); Zarzis (2hr 30min).

Mareth to: Gabès (30min); Lazaiza* (10min); Medenine (30min); Toujane (30min); Zarat* (10min).

Nouvelle Matmata to: Gabès (25min); Matmata (10min).

Arabic place names

Beni Aissa	بني عيسى
Beni Zelten	بني زلتن
Gabès	قابس
Haddej	الهدّاج
Lazaiza	العزيزة
Mareth	مارث
Matmata	مطماطة
Tamezret	طمزرت
Techine	تشين
Tijma	تجمة
Toujane	توجان
Zarat	زراط
Zeraoua	زراوة

8

Jerba and the southeast coast

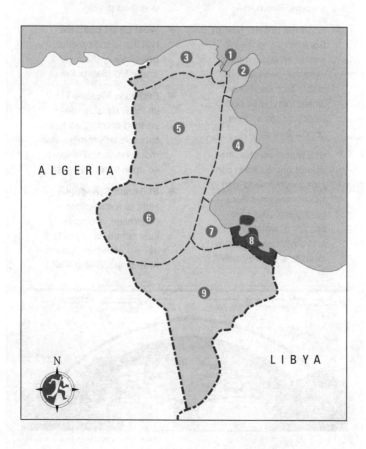

CHAPTER 8

Highlights

* **Cycling around Jerba**
Touring this compact, flat island by bicycle is a great way to discover its hidden treasures, from Jerban mosques and ruined mansions to Punic tombs and Roman remains. **See p.418**

* **Fondouk hotels, Houmt Souk** Your chance to stay in an ancient cara- vanserai, once an inn, stable and warehouse where merchants both slept and stored their goods. **See p.421**

* **Sidi Mahares** Mile after mile of golden sand car- peted with wall-to-wall lobster-coloured Euro- pean flesh, plus para- scending, water-skiing and other beach holiday amusements. **See p.427**

* **Djerba Explore** An excellent museum of Islamic art, an educa- tional exposition of Jer- ban crafts and agricul- ture, and the most croc- odiles you've ever seen in your life, all rolled into one. **See p.429**

* **West coast beaches** Not the island's nicest, but certainly the most unspoiled. **See p.434**

* **Fadloune Mosque** This strange, squat, white- washed building, so typi- cal of Jerba's fort-like little mosques, is now disused, so open to all. **See p.437**

* **El Ghriba Synagogue** Host to a springtime pilgrimage, and spir- itual centre for the oldest Jewish community in the Arab world. **See p.439**

△ Qasr Hamida Ben Ayed, near Sedghiane

8

Jerba and the southeast coast

The island of **Jerba**, joined to the mainland by a causeway since before Roman times, perches at the southern end of the Gulf of Gabès, enclosing the smaller **Gulf of Bou Grara** between island and mainland. To the southeast, the coast dips past the modern town of **Zarzis** and the Bahiret el Biban lagoon before disappearing over the border into Libya.

This sun-soaked corner of Tunisia boasts some of the finest **beaches** in the Mediterranean, arguably *the* finest. Unfortunately, the best of these, in Jerba's northeastern corner – from **Sidi Mahares** round to **Aghir** – have largely been swamped in recent years by large-scale package tourist developments, and beach hotels are beginning to spread, too, along the mainland coast around Zarzis. In midsummer it's probably a good idea to seek nirvana elsewhere.

Jerban society is quite distinct in many ways from that of mainland Tunisia. Its population forms a patchwork of different **ethnic and religious groups** – Arabs, Berbers and black Africans, Muslims (both Ibadite and Sunni) and Jews – who all differ slightly in their traditions, style of dress, the names they bear and the way they speak. However, all of them share a common Jerban identity: their traditions differ from those of the mainland as much as from each other. One overriding Jerban trait is the business acumen of its people – especially the Ibadites (see box on p.432) and Jews (see box on p.440) – and over the centuries this has been of lasting importance to Jerba.

Today, however, with the present **tourist influx**, it seems no exaggeration to talk of a **crisis** in Jerba's identity. Nowhere in Tunisia is there such an obvious and direct clash between a still very traditional society and the demands of foreign culture. Services have become strained, prices inflated, and local culture and

Market days

Monday Houmt Souk, Zarzis
Tuesday Sedghiane, Sedouikech
Wednesday Guellala, Mouansa
Thursday Houmt Souk
Friday Midoun, Zarzis
Saturday Ben Gardane, El May, Souihel
Sunday Ajim, Guelalla, Hara Sghira, Mellita, Sidi Chammakh

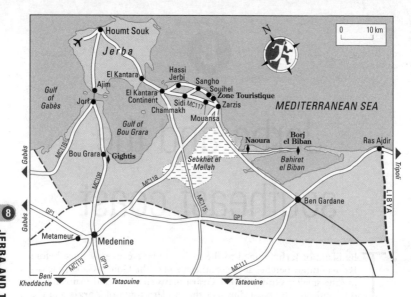

agriculture increasingly ignored. People whose parents worked the land are no longer interested in breaking their backs when easier work and more money are to be had in the tourist industry and its related services. Meanwhile, the demand on water is beginning to threaten the island's drinking water supplies as salinity creeps into the water table, which will also make agriculture more difficult.

Even more serious a threat to the Jerban way of life is **emigration**, with traditional communities disrupted by the departure of Jews to Israel and of young men off to seek their fortunes elsewhere, usually by opening shops (known in Tunisia simply as "jerbans"). People from the island now work as grocers all over Tunisia, and there are Jerban communities throughout Europe and as far away as Brazil.

Jerba

On the tenth [day] we made the country of the Lotus-Eaters, a race that live on vegetable foods . . . I sent some of my followers inland to find out what sort of human beings might be there, detailing two men for the duty with a third as messenger. Off they went, and it was not long before they were in touch with the Lotus-Eaters. Now it never entered the heads of these natives to kill my friends: what they did was to give them some lotus to taste, and as soon as each had eaten the honeyed fruit of the plant, all thoughts of reporting to us or escaping were banished from his mind. All they now wished for was to stay where they were with the Lotus-Eaters, to browse on the lotus and to forget that they had a home to return to. I had to use force to bring them back to the ships, and they wept on the way, but once on board I dragged them under the benches and left them in irons. I then commanded the rest of my loyal band to embark with all speed on their fast ships, for fear that others of them might eat the lotus and think no more of home. They came on board at once, went to the benches, sat down in their proper places, and struck the white surf with their oars.

So we left that country and sailed on sick at heart.

Homer, The Odyssey (Book IX)

Jerba, like Gozo and Menorca, claims to be the legendary land of the **Lotus-Eaters** and – low-lying, semi-desert island that it is – it makes good territory for such myth and fantasy. The coast consists largely of beautiful sandy beaches while, inland, unique mosques and houses are scattered among palm groves. Its history and culture are to some extent different from those of the mainland; its architecture is quite distinctive, its ethnic background more diverse. Jerba is not really an island of towns and villages, but of individual homes. The only apparent villages are the two Jewish "ghettos" of Hara Sghira and Hara Kebira. The island's capital **Houmt Souk**, once just a marketplace, only became a town in the twentieth century.

Unfortunately, Jerba's seductive packageable charms and easy access through an international airport have brought **tourism** on a big scale. Dozens of hotels line the northern coast, which the government has declared a *zone touristique*, and many of the people who come to stay here see the island as nothing more than a beach in the sun. And indeed Jerba is an excellent **beach resort**: the palm-rustled strands themselves are wonderful, the sea warm and limpid, the mood relaxed and the general scene idyllic. Moreover, the hotels here are some of the country's best and more than adequate by any standard.

If all you want is sun and sand, Jerba is just the place to come; on the other hand, if that is all you want, you're missing out. The intimate, farm-divided **interior** exudes a certain magic you won't find anywhere else, a district of country lanes through date and olive groves, the sea never far away. The beautiful white-washed, fortified mosques are unique in Tunisia and the island also boasts three historic forts and scattered Roman remains, so far unexcavated. It's a big enough area (around 25km by 22km) to explore, but small enough to do so by bicycle.

Getting to Jerba

Jerba is linked by reasonably inexpensive Tuninter **flights** with Tunis, as well as with western Europe by international scheduled and charter flights. The **airport** is at Mellita (☎75 650 233), 6km from Houmt Souk and 12km from the heart of the hotel strip at Sidi Mahares. There are only three daily buses into Houmt Souk, so if you don't have transport laid on by a hotel, and if the bus fails to connect with your arrival, you'll have to take a metered taxi to Houmt Souk (3–5TD) or to the *zone touristique* (6–15TD). Avis, Budget, Hertz and Europcar all have **car rental** desks at the airport (all on ☎75 650 233), and there are banks, an ATM and a change machine that takes bank notes – US and Canadian dollars, pounds sterling (not Scottish notes) and euros.

Jerba can be reached easily enough by road. Most **buses** from the south of the country take you straight through to Houmt Souk via the El Kantara causeway, sometimes taking a detour to call at Zarzis. Coming from Gabès and

The **tap water** in Zarzis, which is also piped to Jerba (in the large pipe by the causeway) is slightly saline and, due to the region's high water table, not as safe to drink as in the rest of the country. The people who live here don't drink it, and visitors with delicate digestive systems should definitely stick to bottled water.

#10 Houmt Souk–El May–Mahboubine–Midoun–Aghir, with some services continuing to Sidi Mahares and then back to Houmt Souk
#11 Houmt Souk–Sidi Mahares, with some services continuing to Midoun, Mahboubine, El May and returning to Houmt Souk
#12 Houmt Souk–Ajim (for the ferry)
#13 Houmt Souk–Sedghiane–Midoun–Mahboubine
#14 Houmt Souk–Hara Sghira–Guellala, with some services continuing to Sedouikech, El May and returning to Houmt Souk
#16 Houmt Souk–El May–Sedouikech–Guellala–Hara Sghira–Houmt Souk

the north, it's faster to use the Jorf–Ajim **ferry** (passengers free, 0.8TD for cars, 0.2TD for motorbikes), with half-hourly services between 6.30am and 9.30pm, then hourly till 11.30pm, and a few sailings through the night. Try to avoid crossing on weekend evenings when there can be long queues (going to Jerba on Saturdays, coming back on Sundays). There are also one or two buses going the long way round to Jerba via Medenine and Zarzis.

For **travelling around** the island, the metered **taxis** are probably your best bet, though there is also a network of **bus routes** (see box above). **Bicycles and scooters** are an inexpensive way to get to out-of-the-way places, including most of the mosques and antiquities, and are especially useful for exploring the inland areas. They can be rented easily in both Houmt Souk and the *zone touristique*, where you can also rent **motorbikes**. Failing that, **hitching** is very

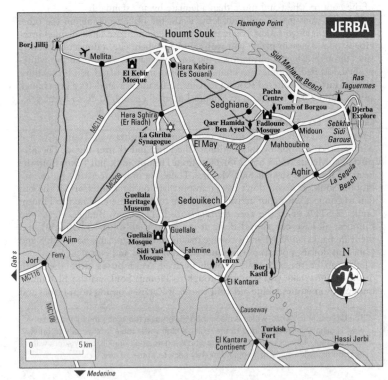

easy in Jerba, and, depending on the heat, even **walking** is not out of the question for getting around parts of the northwest of the island. If you are **driving**, note that Jerba has a speed limit of 70km/hr, rarely obeyed but sometimes enforced. Jerbans seem to know where the police are waiting to pounce, but tourists are better off keeping within the limit.

Some history

The **Carthaginians** who first settled on Jerba called it Meninx – "land of the receding waters", a reference to the highest tides anywhere in the Mediterranean. With its virtually landlocked gulf, it was an ideal haven for any sheltering fleet, and quickly gained a reputation for trade and commerce. The **Romans** built an extensive city on the southern shores, exporting cloth (coloured imperial purple using dye from the murex shellfish) throughout the Empire.

Under the **Arabs**, Jerba was a centre of almost permanent revolt as it constantly struggled to assert its independence from its overlords. The island strongly supported the **Kharijite rebellion** (see p.494) in 740 and, when the Aghlabids retook the north of Tunisia, Jerba became part of the Rustamids' Kharijite state (based at Tahirt in Algeria). Later, Jerba supported **Abu Yazid**'s 944 Kharijite rebellion against the **Fatimids**, and also rose unsuccessfully against their successors, the **Zirids** in 1047. The island is still one of Kharijism's last strongholds. In the centuries prior to French domination, it remained a hotbed of defiance, never at peace for long, as the architecture of its mosques (see p.432) and homes (see box below) testifies.

From the twelfth century, Jerba came under serious threat from the Christian kingdoms, especially whichever one had control of Sicily, just across the water. Like Sicily, Jerba was the object of Muslim–Christian rivalry due to its strategic position. In 1135, Sicily's Norman king **Roger II** invaded Jerba, massacring or enslaving much of the population. The island resisted with little success, and remained in Christian hands until retaken by the Almohads in 1159. In 1284, Jerba again suffered a bout of brutal Christian rule under **Roger de Lluria** of Aragon. When the island rose up in 1310, Aragonese troops under **Ramon de Muntaner** murdered or enslaved three-quarters of the island's population and strangled its economy with punitive taxes. In 1333, rebellion by Muslims throughout Aragon's territories in Sicily and North Africa freed Jerba once more, but when the Hafsids attempted to impose their authority on the island, its residents made repeated attempts to regain their autonomy,

---

Jerban homes

Jerban homes, spread around the countryside, take the form of a **houch** (traditional house) inside a **menzel** (parcel of land), each one belonging to a different family. Like the mosques, these houses were designed in response to numerous invasions from the twelfth century onwards (see above), and it's been suggested that the basic plan was taken from the Roman forts, or *limes*, on the mainland.

From the outside, a *houch* looks like a small square fortress, with blank white walls and, at each corner, a tower called a *ghorfa* or *kouchk*, often crowned with a dome. Three large rooms surround the central courtyard, each used by one section of an extended family. The parents in each section sleep in the tower. This is the only part of the house with external windows, traditionally placed higher than a man on horseback. The breeze is fed down below through holes in the floor, cooling the entire house. Near the house is a simple guest room (usually facing east) and a threshing floor. The distinctive Jerban **well** is flanked by two upright supports for a system of pulleys operated by camel or mule, a system you can see all over the island.

and for much of the fifteenth century, under the **El Samumni** family, it was virtually independent. The Christians tried to retake it several times, but local resistance rebutted them. During this period, there was also an internal struggle for political and religious domination of the island by two parties representing different strains of Kharijism, the Wahabites and the Nakkarites, the former eventually predominating.

Piratical **merchant-sailors** wrought havoc in Jerba in the sixteenth century. The corsair Aruj **Barbarossa** made his base here in 1510, as did his protégé **Dragut** in 1535. Trapped with his fleet by the flotilla of Charles V of Spain in 1551, Dragut made a famous **naval getaway** (see p.430) from the island. Later putting himself at the disposal of the Turks, he returned with an **Ottoman** fleet to set up shop in 1560, and completely trounced the coalition of European forces under Philip II of Spain that attempted to drive him out.

Under the Ottomans, Jerba became a centre of silk and wool production and its economy thrived. It was also a major terminal for trans-Saharan goods until the trade in its main commodity, African **slaves**, was banned in 1846. European merchants preferred to trade here rather than with the unpredictable mainland – if there was an uprising on the mainland, business could go on as usual on the island. This is just what happened in 1881: the islanders, fearing that Jerba would be occupied and sacked by the rebellious tribes on the mainland, welcomed the **French** invaders, gaining for themselves the lasting gratitude of the conquerors.

Houmt Souk

The island's capital and its one real town, **HOUMT SOUK** (meaning "marketplace" – it was originally the site of the island's market, with everything built outwards from the souk) is a lively and interesting place and, at only 1500m from end to end, a very easy one to find your way around. Although Houmt Souk is becoming increasingly commercialized, the Association de Sauvegarde de l'Île de Djerba has made great efforts to preserve its distinctive architecture over the last decade.

Moving on from Houmt Souk

For a list of destinations and journey times, see Travel details on p.447.

Local buses serve the *zone touristique* of Sidi Mahares (#11; 14 daily), Midoun (#10; 12 daily) and Aghir (#10 & #11; 24 daily). There are also services to Hara Sghira (#14; 9 daily), El May (#10 and #16; 18 daily), Guellala (#14; 9 daily), Ajim (#12; 8 daily), Sedouikech (#16; 6 daily) and the airport (#15; 3 daily). A map on the bus-station wall shows routes on the island, though note that some buses terminate midway along their designated route. Intercity buses run by regional SRT companies serve Ben Gardane, Medenine, Tataouine and Zarzis, with SNTRI and STCI services to Sousse, Kairouan, Tunis and Bizerte. Gabès and Sfax are served by a combination of regional and national buses. There's also a bus to Gabès to connect with the overnight **train** to Tunis. For destinations north of Gabès, and especially for Tunis, buses are often full and need booking in advance. For bus information, call ☏ 75 650 076 for local and SRT services, ☏ 75 652 239 for SNTRI services.

  Louages leave Houmt Souk's louage station bound for Ben Gardane, Gabès, Medenine, Tunis, Zarzis, and (usually only mornings) Sfax and Tataouine. The only Jerban destination served by Houmt Souk louages is Ajim, the vehicles leaving from avenue Bourguiba by Tunisair.

Arrival and information

Houmt Souk's **bus station**, run by SRTG Medenine, is off avenue Bourguiba just south of the town centre, with the **louage station** opposite. For details of the airport, see p.417. The **ONTT** is on boulevard de l'Environnement (July & Aug Mon–Sat 7.30am–1.30pm & 5–7pm; Sept–June Mon–Thurs 8.30am–1pm & 3–5.45pm, Fri & Sat 8.30am–1pm; ⊤75 650 016), the coast road to Sidi Mahares, and there's a **Syndicat d'Initiative** (Mon–Thurs 8am–noon & 3–6pm, Fri & Sat 8am–noon; ⊤75 650 915), on avenue Bourguiba, opposite place Mongi Bali. Most services and shops are on the two main north–south roads, **avenue Bourguiba** to the west and **avenue Abdel Hamid el Kadhi** to the east.

Accommodation

Unless you want to stay by the beach at Sidi Mahares or Aghir, you'll probably end up in one of Houmt Souk's **hotels**. Five of these (including the town's youth hostel) are old converted **fondouks** or *caravanserais*, once offering food and shelter to itinerant merchants and pilgrims. They share a common plan, with a large open courtyard surrounded by arches or colonnades. At the centre, camel trains would once have been tethered by the well, their goods securely stored on the ground floor.

Houmt Souk has an HI **youth hostel** at 11 rue Moncef Bey (⊤ & ⑦75 650 619; ❶, dorm beds 6TD), which has double rooms, though it is perhaps a little too basic for some. It is reasonably friendly, however, and there's a distinct lack of rules and regulations, though in principle there's a midnight curfew. There are two **campsites** are at Aghir, and it's possible to camp *sauvage* at Flamingo Point, Ras Taguermes or on the west coast.

Fondouk hotels

Arischa 36 rue Ghazi Mustapha, near the Catholic church ⑦75 650 384. Getting a bit run-down, this once rather pleasant hotel now seems to do more business as a bar, which makes it a bit noisy. It has a plunge pool and a nice roof terrace. Some rooms have private bathrooms. Rate includes breakfast. ❷

Erriadh 10 rue Mohamed Ferjani, off pl Hedi Chaker ⑦75 650 756, ⑦75 650 487. Nice, clean rooms with bathroom, some with a/c, others with a ceiling fan, but some windows open onto the central patio rather than the exterior. Breakfast included in the rate. ❸

Marhala 13 rue Moncef Bey ⑦75 650 416, ⑦75 653 317. Next door to the youth hostel, and sharing management with its namesakes in Nefta and Matmata. Clean if basic rooms, some en suite, and the best bar in town. ❷

Sindbad pl Mongi Bali ⑦75 650 047, ⑦75 652 602. Pleasant, en-suite rooms around a larger, more open courtyard than the other *fondouk* hotels have, decorated with pretty ceramic tiles. Best value of the *fondouk* hotels, though the rate doesn't include breakfast. ❷

Other hotels

Ben Abbes 158 av Bourguiba ⑦75 650 128. Out towards the hospital. Clean, modern and quite pleasant self-catering apartments, each with their own kitchen. ❷

Dar Faiza av de la République ⑦75 650 083, ⑦75 651 763, ⓦwww.darfaizadarsalem.com. Up near the Borj is this charming and well-run place with en-suite rooms, some a/c, a small pool, a family atmosphere and customers who come back year after year. Advance reservation is a good idea, especially in season. ❺

Essada 6 av Habib Thameur ⑦75 651 422, ⑦75 652 520. Cool and quiet, with quite large en-suite rooms, all a/c, some with balcony, and a games room with pool tables. ❸

Essalem rue de Remeda, off pl 7 Novembre ⊤ & ⑦75 651 029. Good-value cheapie, tucked away in the backstreets of the town centre. Rooms have ceiling fans but bathrooms are shared. It's worth checking the sheets before taking a room. ❷

Hadji 44 av Mohamed Badra ⑦75 650 630, ⑦75 652 219. Large a/c rooms, some with shower, some with bath. Could do with a lick of paint. Breakfast included in the rate. ❸

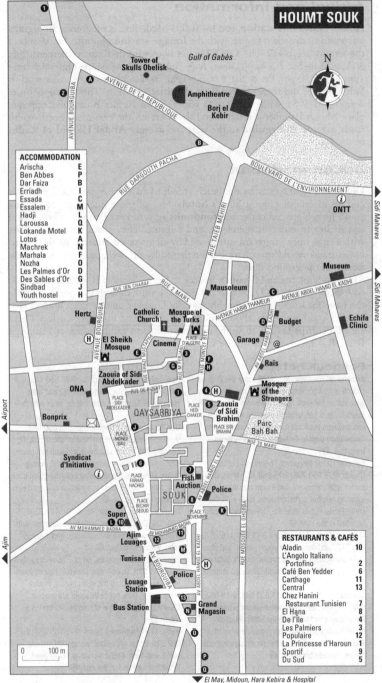

HOUMT SOUK

Gulf of Gabès

The Port

Tower of
Skulls Obelisk

Amphitheatre

Borj el
Kebir

AVENUE BOURGUIBA

AVENUE DE LA RÉPUBLIQUE

RUE DARGOUTH PACHA

BOULEVARD DE L'ENVIRONNEMENT

Sidi Mahares

RUE TALEB MEHIRI

ONTT

ACCOMMODATION
Arischa   E
Ben Abbes   P
Dar Faiza   B
Erriadh   I
Essada   C
Essalem   M
Hadji   L
Laroussa   Q
Lokanda Motel   K
Lotos   A
Machrek   N
Marhala   F
Nozha   O
Les Palmes d'Or   D
Des Sables d'Or   G
Sindbad   J
Youth hostel   H

RUE IBN CHARAF

RUE 2 MARS

Mausoleum

AVENUE HABIB THAMEUR

AVENUE ABDEL HAMID EL KADHI

Sidi Mahares

Museum

Hertz

Catholic
Church

Mosque of
the Turks

El Sheikh
Mosque

Cinema

PLACE
D'ALGERIE

Budget

Garage

Echifa
Clinic

RUE MONCEF BEY

RUE GHAZI MUSTAPHA

RUE M'FERDJI

Raïs

@

Zaouia of Sidi
Abdelkader

ONA

RUE DE BIZERTE

PLACE SIDI
ABDELKADER

Bonprix

PLACE
MONGI BALI

QAYSARRIYA

PLACE
HEDI CHAKER

Zaouia of Sidi
Brahim

PLACE SIDI
BRAHIM

Mosque
of the
Strangers

Parc
Bah Bah

RUE 20 MARS

Syndicat
d'Initiative

PLACE
FARHAT HACHED

PLACE
BECHIR SEOUD

SOUK

Fish
Auction

Police

AV ABDEL HAMID EL KADHI

RUE MOSQUÉE EL GHORBA

Super

PLACE 7
NOVEMBRE

AV MOHAMMED BADRA

AV MOHAMMED BADRA

Ajim
Louages

Tunisair

AV BOURGUIBA

Police

AV ABDEL HAMID EL KADHI

Louage
Station

Bus Station

Grand
Magasin

El May, Midoun, Hara Kebira & Hospital

RESTAURANTS & CAFÉS
Aladin   10
L'Angolo Italiano
  Portofino   2
Café Ben Yedder   6
Carthage   11
Central   13
Chez Hanini
  Restaurant Tunisien   7
El Hana   8
De l'Île   4
Les Palmiers   3
Populaire   12
La Princesse d'Haroun   1
Sportif   9
Du Sud   5

Airport

Ajim

0   100 m

422

8

JERBA AND THE SOUTHEAST COAST | Houmt Souk

Laroussa (aka El Aroussa) av Bourguiba ☎75 650 788. A quiet place with a car park, down towards the hospital; a lot of the clientele are holidaymakers from other Arab countries. All rooms have ceiling fans; some have balconies. Rate includes breakfast. ❷

Lokanda Motel passage de la Municipalité ☎75 651 513. Not the best hotel in town, but the cheapest, and clean, though there's no hot water. ❶

Lotos 18 av de la République ☎75 650 026, ℗75 651 127. A friendly pension with large, clean, en-suite rooms, and a quiet bar and restaurant. It's associated with the nearby *Hôtel Dar Faiza*, whose pool and tennis courts are open to *Lotos* guests. ❹

Machrek av Bourguiba ☎75 653 155 or 6, ℗75 653 157, ✉hotelelmachrek@planet.tn. The best hotel in town, with smallish but comfortable

rooms, a/c (summer only) and attached bathrooms throughout. There are balconies in some rooms. ❹

Nozha 150 av Bourguiba ☎75 650 381, ℗75 620 758. Friendly, if a little shabby, but all the rooms have en-suite bathroom, a/c and satellite TV. You can have a room with a balcony and/or a bathtub if you want, at no extra cost. ❹

Les Palmes d'Or 84 av Abdel Hamid el Kadhi ☎75 653 369 or 370, ℗75 653 368, ⌨www .djerba.biz/hotellespalmesdor. A cool, quiet place with small but pleasant en-suite rooms, most with balcony and all with a/c and satellite TV. It's a bit pricey, though they offer a discount if you stay more than three nights. ❺

Hôtel des Sables d'Or 30 rue Mohamed Ferjani ☎75 650 423. Not a *fondouk* but an old palatial house built around a central patio, with small, immaculate rooms, private showers and shared toilets. ❸

The Town

With a history as stormy and an identity as strong as Jerba's, it is hardly surprising that its capital is full of interest. Though Houmt Souk's nooks and crannies are gradually being pedestrianized, and its cottage industries are giving way to shops and restaurants that aren't patronized by Jerbans, the town still has loads of charm and remains one of the country's most pleasant. While non-Muslims can't enter any of the mosques or *zaouias*, the **fort and museum** are open to everyone, and both are worth investigation. Just south of town, the Jewish village of **Hara Kebira** is an interesting target for an afternoon's stroll (see p.439).

The souk and around

At the very centre of the town is the **souk**, with its *qaysarriya*, a warren of arched and covered passageways to the north of place Mongi Bali. Traditionally the *qaysarriya* were where the most expensive goods were sold, such as prized Egyptian cloth and filigree silver. Coral and jewellery are now the market's pricey mainstays; the leather goods are often pretty shoddy. In the less-tourist-oriented part of the souk, the daily **fish auction** is interesting to visit. Mondays and Thursdays are the souk's busiest days, with traders coming in from around the island. The market is then full of people selling straw baskets and mats, along with musicians from Midoun (see p.435) playing and selling their instruments.

To the east of the *qaysarriya*, in the northwest corner of place Sidi Abdelkader, is the **Zaouia of Sidi Abdelkader**, home of the Association de Sauvegarde de l'Île de Djerba (ASSIDJE), who have restored its pretty, tiled courtyard. Mornings are the best time to pop in for a look, when the sun shines right into it. East of the *qaysarriya*, the **Zaouia of Sidi Brahim**, with its heavily buttressed walls, is typical of the ascetic Ibadite style of architecture (see box on p.432) and looks more military than religious. Building was begun in 1674 but only completed thirty years later under the bey Mourad Ben Ali, and it was subsequently used for worship, teaching and as a rest house for travellers. Today it contains the tomb of the saint and his followers and it is still used for prayer, so non-Muslims are not allowed to enter. Across the road is the extravagant **Mosque of the Strangers**, whose contrast with the *zaouia* could hardly be greater – this mosque is covered with domes and topped by an extravagantly carved minaret. Again, it is closed to non-Muslim visitors. Nearby on rue 20 Mars, kids young and old will appreciate **Parc des Loisirs Bah Bah**, a small fairground with rides at 0.6TD a go or 5TD for ten (summer daily 5pm–1am; winter Mon–Fri 3–7pm, Sat, Sun & school hols 10am–9pm).

Rue Moncef Bey, just to the west of the *zaouia*, leads to the smaller **Mosque of the Turks**, the most interesting of all Houmt Souk's mosques. The unusually shaped minaret was first dubbed "phallic" by the Victorian polymath Sir Harry Johnston – a contentious description that has rather stuck. Johnston was convinced of "an unrecognized system of phallic worship throughout the south, and on Jerba all but the most recently built mosques have a phallic emblem on the summit of the minaret".

Just around the corner in a quiet cul-de-sac, the **Catholic church** offers no such mysterious symbols for interpretation: this strange Baroque building was once the centre of a thriving Christian community on Jerba. From the 1840s Greeks, Italians and Maltese came to the island for the sponge-fishing. Some stayed on, and by the 1890s several thousand Europeans were living here. With independence, however, most left and the church fell into disrepair.

Opposite the *Hôtel Marhala* is another reminder of the island's European links, the **Maltese fondouk** at 30 rue Moncef Bey, where merchants and sponge-collectors once stored their goods. In one of the upstairs rooms, a silk weaver (listen for the tell-tale "clack clack" of his loom) makes traditional Jerban wedding dresses – very beautiful, and a snip at around 180TD.

The Borj el Kebir and Libyan market

From the Mosque of the Turks, rue Taïeb Mehiri leads to the fort, variously called the **Borj el Kebir** or **Borj Ghazi Mustapha** (daily except Fri: April to mid-Sept 8am–7pm; mid-Sept to March 9.30am–4.30pm; 1.1TD). The fort has been substantially restored, and contains a miscellaneous collection of pieces of mosaic, columns and statues, plus a large number of large stone balls used as ammunition by medieval catapult machines. There are even a couple of Punic stelae with the symbol of Tanit carved on them.

The site was originally occupied by the Romans, but it was the Aghlabids who converted it into a square *ribat*, like those of Sousse (p.226) and Monastir (p.241), which now forms the inner core of the fort. The fort was captured by the Aragonese king of Sicily, Roger de Lluria, in 1284, and the outer wall was added under the Hafsid sultan Abou Fars in 1432. It's easy to make out the remains of the *ribat's* round corner turrets – there's one straight in front as you enter. There's little in the way of explanation in the fort, but if you turn left on entry, the first room on your left has some photos, engravings and a ground plan. The engravings include two pictures of the tower of skulls (see below) before it was dismantled, and the photos show the fort before and during restoration. At the far end of the courtyard, the tomb of Ghazi Mustapha (who had the fort rebuilt under Ottoman rule) stands on the site of a thirteenth-century mosque, and you can climb up onto the battlements and walk round them on the landward side.

The fort's most famous moment came in 1560 when, after Philip II of Spain's armada was wiped out by Dragut's Ottoman fleet, his men retreated inside the fort, only to be massacred by the Turks. The skulls of the Spaniards (by various accounts numbering 500 or 5000) were piled up in a great tower – which stood until European powers prevailed on the bey, despite strong local opposition, to bury them in 1848. All that remains of this tower of skulls is a discreet **obelisk** marking the site, 100m over towards the port, behind the amphitheatre (under construction, and which may in the future become the viewing stand for a sound and light show). Those of Dragut's forces who died in the fighting are commemorated by a little **mausoleum** on rue Taïeb Mehiri near the corner of rue 2 Mars.

A couple of hundred metres south of the fort, spread out along rue Taïeb Mehiri (though it has a habit of changing locations), a **"Libyan market"** takes place on Monday and Thursday mornings, with bargains and goods brought across the border. At one time, most of the traders were Libyan and all sorts of rarities unavailable elsewhere in Tunisia could be found here. Nowadays, the market has become much like any other in Tunisia, though still worth a browse. If you want something approaching the real thing, you'll have to go to Ben Gardane (see p.445).

The Museum of Arts and Popular Traditions

Not far from the fort is the **Museum of Arts and Popular Traditions**, at the eastern edge of town on avenue Abdel Hamid el Kadhi (daily except Fri: April to mid-Sept 8am–noon & 3–7pm; mid-Sept to March 9.30am–4.30pm; 2.1TD), housed in two former *zaouias* – religious centres set up by holy men, who in this case are not buried here. Its exhibits, labelled in French and Arabic, are not massively exciting, but are worth half an hour of your time, and an attendant will happily show you round and rattle off a spiel in English if you want.

The museum's first section is housed in the eighteenth-century **Zaouia of Sidi Ameur**. Its first room contains **costumes** worn on special occasions and in different parts of the island. To the left are wedding clothes worn by a bridegroom, and musical instruments used to celebrate the marriage, as well as traditional costumes worn by women in Midoun and women of Bedouin origin. To the right are the traditional wedding costumes of a Jewish bride and groom from the island. Off to the right as you enter, a small room with stucco, tiles and a pottery roof was formerly the *zaouia's* library. Wedding dresses worn by women of Guellala and Houmt Souk flank the door at the far end of the first room, which leads through to the museum's second room, the late eighteenth-century **Zaouia of Sidi Zitouni**. This still has its original roof of glazed tiles overlaid fish-scale style, with pottery pipes on the inside, though the stuccowork on the walls has been restored. Display cases contain ornamental **jewellery** made by the island's Jewish community. The long ornamental brooches are worn to indicate tribal allegiance: a Malekite (Sunni, that is, as opposed to Ibadite) would wear such a brooch on the left, a Berber in the middle and a Bedouin on the right. Downstairs is a reconstruction of an old pottery workshop of the sort still used at Guellala (see p.431). A room across the next courtyard was once used as a **kitchen** by pilgrims staying at the sanctuary and contains a number of painted wooden chests. As you leave the museum, have a look at the **weaver's hut**, the *harout*, with its triangular front and sunken external buttressing; like the *houch* (see p.419), these are unique to Jerba.

Eating and drinking

Houmt Souk has a reasonable range of **restaurants**, with plenty of tourist ones (such as the *El Hana* and *de l'Île*) around place Hedi Chaker and place Sidi Brahim, and cheaper places tucked away around town. Inexpensive and plentiful, Houmt Souk's **cafés** and **patisseries** are popular places to start the day, with croissants, pastries and sandwiches on sale from early morning onwards. *Café Ben Yedder* in the northeastern corner of place Farhat Hached is a cut above the rest, with a large selection of excellent pastries, as well as sandwiches and of course coffee. The best cakes and ice cream in town however come from *L'Angolo Italiano Portofino*, 25 avenue Bourguiba (daily 8am–midnight).

As for **drinking**, most places are closed by 8pm. The *Hôtel Marhala* stays open late, with its courtyard serving as a lively saloon bar, but it's sometimes restricted to hotel guests. The *Arischa* is quieter and sometimes stays open late in summer. After closing time, your best bet is to find a restaurant where you can get away with ordering just beer, and perhaps a snack to go with it. Otherwise, you'll have to get a taxi out of town to a hotel such as the *Dar Salem* or the *Strand* in Sidi Mahares, where you can drink till midnight or so. Make sure you arrange transport back if you do this.

Restaurants

Aladin 40 av Mohamed Badra. Next door to the *Hôtel Hadji*, this is one step up from a simple *gargote*, offering couscous, spaghetti, fish or grills. Daily 11am–9pm.

Restaurant Carthage 11 av Mohamed Badra. A reasonably priced but very presentable restaurant, with good-sized portions of pizza, chicken and grills. Specialities include an excellent *riz Djerbien*. Daily 10am–10.30pm.

Central 128 av Bourguiba, near the bus station. A calm atmosphere with good and reasonably cheap couscous, though the other dishes are variable. Daily 8.30am–10.30pm.

Chez Hanini Restaurant Tunisien In the central souk. This market canteen is a bargain place for a good feed; grilled fish is a particular speciality. Daily except Sunday 11.30am–3pm.

Hôtel Dar Faiza rue de la République ☎75 650 083. The best of the hotel restaurants, with good fish and a 9TD set menu. It seems to cater mostly for elderly European tourists who can't handle spices, so the food can be a bit bland. Daily 12.30–2pm & 7–9.30pm.

El Hana pl 7 Novembre ☎75 650 568. Expensive tourist restaurant tucked away by the souk entrance, with specialities like "Sole Lord Nelson" or a "Captain's Fish Plate", or even a cheese fondue if you order it a day in advance. Daily 10am–2pm & 6–10pm.

Restaurant de l'Île pl Hedi Chaker ☎75 650 575. Better than most of the tourist traps, not too pricey and with quite a good 9TD set menu. For vegetarians, they do a meat-free veg couscous. Daily noon–3pm & 6–10.30pm.

Les Palmiers rue Mohamed Ferjani, off pl d'Algérie. Excellent Tunisian food at pretty low prices, complemented by a pleasant ambience and good service. The *spaghetti aux fruits de mer* is particularly recommended, and there's a meat-free veg stew for non-carnivores. Daily noon–3.30pm & 6.30–10pm.

Populaire 21 av Mohammed Badra. Low-priced *gargote* serving couscous, *kamounia*, *kefteji* and other Tunisian fare. Daily 10am–9pm.

La Princesse d'Haroun At the harbour ☎75 650 488. A posh, pricey but excellent fish restaurant, with a 15TD set menu as well as à la carte. Specialities include *langouste* and *gargoulette* of grouper, and there are a couple of vegetarian options too. Daily noon–3pm & 6–10pm.

Sportif 147 av Bourguiba. Moderately priced, moderately good downtown restaurant, serving mostly meat dishes. Daily 11am–9pm.

Restaurant du Sud pl Sidi Brahim. One of the better tourist restaurants, with a 6TD basic set menu, a 9TD menu based on brochette, fish or couscous, a 30TD special seafood menu including wine, or à la carte dining at around 25–30TD a head. Daily noon–9.30pm.

Listings

Airlines Tuninter, at the airport ☎75 650 233; Tunisair, av Bourguiba ☎75 650 159.

Banks Mostly in the centre of town on av Bourguiba, with at least one open weekday lunchtime and weekend mornings. There's no shortage of ATMs.

Bike rental Bicycles (10TD/day) and scooters (45TD/day) can be rented from Raïs, 155 av Abdel Hamid el Kadhi (☎75 650 303).

Boat trips Excursions by boat to Flamingo Point (see opposite) leave from the port most days

around 8–9am, returning mid-afternoon, and cost around 20TD per person including a barbecued fish lunch. Ask around the evening before to find out which boats are going. You get a better deal on the smaller boats at the southern end of the quay than on the large, shallow-bottomed and rather stupid-looking mock galleons. If you prefer to call in advance, one operator to try is Tour Mar (☎75 673 818).

Car rental Avis, bd de l'Environnement ☎75 650 151; Budget, 197 av Abdel Hamid el Kadhi ☎75

653 444; Europcar, 161 av Abdel Hamid el Kadhi ⊕75 650 357; Hertz, 91 av Bourguiba ⊕75 650 196. Avis, Hertz, and Europcar all have desks at the airport (⊕75 650 233). There are also a large number of local firms on av Habib Thameur and av Abdel Hamid el Kadhi near the museum.

Churches Catholic mass is held Sun at 10am at 2 rue Ghazi Mustapha (⊕75 650 215), behind the old cathedral.

Cinema pl d'Algérie, opposite the Mosque of the Turks.

Festivals A Ulysses festival is held in July or August, with performances of traditional dance and music. At the beginning of September, there's a windsurfing regatta round the island from Houmt Souk to Ajim.

Hammams The oldest, friendliest and most central hammam is by the *zaouia* at 17 pl Sidi Brahim (daily: men 5am–noon, women 1–6pm). The Hammam Ziadi at 93 av Bourguiba is cleaner but less friendly (daily except Tues: men 6am–noon, women 1–6pm). There is another one with similar hours at 117 av Abdel Hamid el Kadhi.

Hospitals and clinics The regional hospital is at the southern end of av Bourguiba (⊕75 650 018). There's also a private clinic, the Echifa, near the museum (⊕75 652 441). One GP used to treating foreigners is Dr Ben Sabah at 164 av Bourguiba (⊕75 650 238). The doctor at 188 av Bourguiba

(⊕75 620 550) is on duty 8pm–8am nightly and all day Sun.

Internet access The most central place to get online is just off av Abdel Hamid el Kadhi north of the Mosque of the Strangers (daily 8am–10pm or later, 1.5TD/hr). There's also a place just south of *Hôtel Laroussa* on av Bourguiba (daily 8am–midnight; 1.5TD/hr).

Newspapers A random selection of British dailies, plus *Time* and *Newsweek*, are usually available from the bookshop at 127 av Bourguiba, near the post office.

ONA crafts shop 97 av Bourguiba, 100m north of the post office.

Pharmacy There's a night pharmacy at 166 av Bourguiba.

Police av Abdel Hamid el Kadhi, just north of pl 7 Novembre ⊕75 650 015.

Post office av Bourguiba, opposite pl Mongi Bali, with a special desk just for tourists (July & Aug Mon–Fri 7.30am–1pm & 5–7pm, Sat 7.30am–1.30pm, Sun 9–11am; Sept–June Mon–Fri 8am–6pm, Sat 8am–12.30pm; Ramadan Mon–Thurs & Sat 7.30am–1.30pm, Fri 7.30am–12.30pm).

Supermarkets The best is Bonprix on the airport road 200m west of the post office, but there's also Super at the corner of av Bourguiba with av Mohamed Badra, and Grand Magasin at 24 av Abdel Hamid el Kadhi.

Sidi Mahares beach

East of Houmt Souk, before the package tourists' haven of Sidi Mahares, the low sandy peninsula of Ras Rmel – known as **Flamingo Point** – stretches lazily out into the sea. Between November and March, you'll see pink waders here, and often **dolphins** too, just a few metres offshore. Tunisians and Libyans like to **camp** out here in summer, as they do at the other end of the *zone touristique*, and there is no reason why you shouldn't join them.

Bus #11 from Houmt Souk will take you past Flamingo Point and out along **Sidi Mahares beach**, past the tourist complex and the string of hotels along 8km of wide, sandy beach and surf until you reach the lighthouse at Ras Taguermes. Unfortunately, pollution is a problem on the beach, and most of the hotels provide diesel to wash tar off feet. **Beach sports** are available all the way along, and include parascending (20TD), water-skiing (20TD), jetskiing (40TD per 15min for up to three people) and windsurfing (20–30TD per hour). You can also rent a pedalo (10TD/hr), or be towed behind a speedboat on an inflatable "banana" (7TD per person). Most of the hotels run stables for horse-riding and rent out bicycles.

There is a **golf course** (⊕75 745 054/5) with its entrance 1km west of the *Dar Jerba* hotel complex, 500m east of the *Djerba Palace*. A rather snazzy **bowling alley**, Grand Bowling Djerba, can be found just west of *Dar Jerba* (daily 10am–4am; ⊕75 745 101–3; 5TD per person till 8pm, 7TD thereafter), with a bar and restaurant attached.

ACCOMMODATION

Le Beau Rivage	**A**	La Pacha	**J**
Dar Salem	**E**	Résidence Dar Ali	
Djerba Beach	**G**	Royal Garden	**H**
Djerba Palace	**I**	Strand	**C**
Al Jazira	**F**	Ulysse Palace	**B**

Practicalities

Unless you're booked on a package, rates at the **hotels** on Sidi Mahares beach are very inflated, especially in summer, though most of these establishments are good and easily bear comparison with their equivalents in, say, Greece or Spain. Only a few operators – among them Panorama (see p.12) – offer package holidays here from Britain and Ireland. Bus #11 stops at most of the hotels; specify which one you want as you buy your ticket.

On Sidi Mahares's main road, which runs about 200m inland from the beach road, you can rent a **bicycle** (15TD a day), **scooter** (40–45TD a day) or **quad** (35TD a day) from Djerba Quad Découverte (☎98 212 397), 100m west of the Midoun road (bd de l'Environnement) that starts just by the *Hôtel Djerba Beach*. Daly Cyclos (☎75 757 726), 50m east of the two turn-offs for the *Hôtel al Jazira*, rent out bicycles (12TD a day) and scooters (45TD a day). English-language **newspapers** are available at hotels used by UK tour operators such as the *Djerba Palace* and the *Djerba Beach*.

Traditional Tunisian **food** at a fair price is available on the Midoun road near Djerba Quad Découverte at *Restaurant Luna*, an oasis of good honest grub in a desert of tourist traps (daily 10am–10pm). Very near Djerba Quad Découverte, there are two grocers calling themselves supermarkets (one just to the west, the other in the Pacha Centre at the junction with bd de l'Environnement). An ordinary Tunisian grocer, selling yoghurt and *leben* among other things, can be found just across boulevard de l'Environnement, from the Pacha centre, and 50m up.

Most of the beach hotels feature **discos** and **bars**, though the choice of booze is rather limited. A hard-currency foreigners-only **casino**, the Pasino (daily 10am–4am; ☎75 757 534), lies on the main road 1km west of bd de l'Environnement.

Hotels and pensions

Le Beau Rivage 100m from the beach, at the western end ☎75 758 230, ☎75 758 123, ⓦwww.djerba.biz/beaurivage. A friendly, intimate little *pension* between the *Ulysse Palace* and the *Al Jazira*, with a pool and a small restaurant. **❹**

Dar Salem Western end of the beach, 300m east of the *Al Jazira* ☎75 757 667–8, ☎75 757 677, ⓦwww.darfaizadarsalem.com. A new hotel opened by the owners of Houmt Souk's *Dar Faiza*. The rooms are not huge but are tasteful and comfort-

able, with a/c. There's also a pool and private beach, but what makes this a cut above similar *zone touristique* hotels is the personal touch and the friendly efficiency of the staff. **❻**

Djerba Beach Near the centre of the beach ☎75 731 200, ☎75 730 357, ⓦwww.iberostar.com. Smaller, quieter and friendlier than a lot of the package hotels, wheelchair accessible and right on a very nice bit of beach. **❼**

Djerba Palace Eastern end of the beach ☎75 732 600, ☎75 732 635. A complex used by British tour operator Panorama, containing three hotels which share facilities. These include four pools (one of them indoor), a fitness centre and a children's club, all with friendly staff used to English-speaking tourists. *Cesar Palace* & *Djerba Palace* ❾; *Miramar Park* ❼

Al Jazira Western end of the beach ☎75 758 860, ℻75 758 870, @bravoclub@planet.tn. The first of Jerba's beach hotels, originally put up in 1962, then pulled down and rebuilt from scratch, to emerge as an all-inclusive and very well-run beach club popular with Italian sunworshippers. Though most guests are here on packages, you can book privately and discounts on the official rates are usually available. Reserve at least two weeks ahead in summer. Full board ❾

La Pacha Pacha Centre, junction of the main road and bd de l'Environnement, 500m from the beach ☎75 731 827, ℻75 731 171, @hedi.sassi@tunet .tn. Officially a *pension*, this is a small but very comfortable place with biggish rooms, a/c, en-suite bathrooms and satellite TV. Just about within walking distance of Midoun (3km) and some of the sights of inland Jerba mentioned on p.435. ❺

Résidence Dar Ali Western end of the beach ☎75 758 671, ℻75 758 045. A good *pension* with spotless, comfortable rooms and a small pool; English is spoken. ❻

Royal Garden Eastern end of the beach ☎75 745 777, ℻75 745 570, @riu.royalgarden@planet.tn. The smartest, most expensive and most luxurious hotel on the island, done out on a grand scale, with doubles starting at 330TD in high season. ❾

Strand Western end of the beach, 600m east of the *Al Jazira* ☎75 757 406, ℻75 757 014, @www .will-liz.freeserve.co.uk. Not as chic as the other beach hotels, without any of their facilities, but comfortable and has its own small pool and private beach. Its main interest lies in the fact that its bar is reasonably priced and open till midnight. ❹

Ulysse Palace Western end of the beach, 400m west of the *Al Jazira* ☎75 758 777, ℻75 757 850, @www.movenpick-djerba.com. At one time the best of the beach hotels, and still relatively stylish, all done out in cream, with lobby areas in a smooth hard plaster called *tadelakt*, tradionally used for hammams. ❽

Ras Taguermes to Aghir

The cape at the end of Sidi Mahares beach, called **Ras Taguermes**, is marked by a red- and-white-striped **lighthouse**. The main local attraction here is the **go-kart track** (daily 9am–6.30pm; 6TD for ten laps). Two hundred metres east, at the beginning of the El Kantara road, is a refined and rather pricey **restaurant**, *Le Phare* (daily noon–3pm & 6pm–midnight; ☎75 745 382), specializing in seafood, and also serving *gargoulette* if ordered in advance, with a pleasant terrace for outdoor eating and a bar.

Opposite the *Le Phare* restaurant, 200m down the El Kantara road from the junction by the lighthouse, is the island's newest attraction, **Djerba Explore**, a complex of three sections (daily mid-June to mid-Sept 9am–8pm; mid-Sept to mid-June 9am–6pm), completely wheelchair accessible. For the culturally inclined there's the **Lalla Hadria Museum** (5TD), a very impressive collection of Islamic art from the seventh to the twentieth century, laid out thematically, with exhibits to be labelled in French and Arabic; English-speaking guides are available, and English-language catalogues explaining each exhibit are promised for the future. The first five rooms hold art from around the Muslim world, in particular Iran, while rooms 6 and 7 focus on the Maghreb, and the remaining rooms on Tunisia. There are excellent sections on calligraphy, textiles, carpets and ceramics, including coverage of Tunisian ceramics and costumes. **Djerba Heritage** (4TD) is a garden of traditional-style buildings housing a weaving loom, a pottery and an oil press, with explanations on how they work, and the chance for visitors to try some of them out; there's also a functioning well and typical Jerban irrigation system, not to mention a very friendly camel. But if the first two sections of the complex are largely educational, the third is purely for entertainment, and named with a terrible pun: **Croco d'Île** (6TD) is a crocodile farm consisting of a series of interconnected pools and the most snappers you've ever seen in your life. Feeding time is Wednesday, Friday and Sunday late afternoons (times vary depending on the season), sometimes other days too. The complex also contains the *Djerba Explore Museum Hôtel*, consisting of four- and six-person self-catering apartments and a smallish pool, 300m from the beach (T75 745 277, F75 745 255, ⓔdjerbaexplore.commercial@planet.tn; ❻).

Across from the Ras Taguermes lighthouse begins a **sand spit** enclosing the **Sebkha Sidi Garous** lagoon. In summer, *camping sauvage* is the order of the day, as Tunisian and Libyan families pitch tents or sleep out on the beach. Some 5km down the spit, the two-star *Hôtel Tanit* (T75 757 034, F75 757 033) offers an alternative for those who don't want to camp out, but was closed on our last check, though there are other package-tour beach hotels at the spit's northern end. The spit continues for another 2km beyond the hotel. In winter, look out for **flamingos** and other birds in the lagoon.

❽ La Seguia and Aghir

Around the point of Ras Taguermes, on **La Seguia beach**, is a carefully restricted Club Med with three branches – *Jerba la Fidèle*, *Jerba la Douce* and *Calypso*; *Jerba la Fidèle* has the nicest beach on the island fenced off and monopolized. While the beach at **AGHIR**, a few kilometres further on, is not quite up to Sidi Mahares's standards in terms of sandiness, it is a lot less crowded. After storms, however, the water tends to be infested with jellyfish. The pricey but rather jolly and well-managed *Palma Djerba Hôtel* (T75 750 830, F75 750 832, Ⓦwww.palma.djerba.com; half board ❽) has the best bit of Aghir's beach. Next door, near the beach road's junction with the road to Midoun and El Kantara, the *Centre des Stages et Vacances* **youth hostel** and **campsite** (T75 750 266) is friendly and comfortable, with the choice of refurbished four-bed dorms (5TD per person) or camping (2.5TD per person plus 2.5TD per tent or vehicle), but only does food if there is a group or a substantial number of people staying. Otherwise, you have the choice of eating at neighbouring hotels, going into Midoun or getting in supplies at the grocery store a couple of kilometres up the road by the junction between Aghir and La Seguia. There are regular **buses** from Aghir to Houmt Souk via Sidi Mahares or Midoun. Doing the journey by taxi will cost 6–8TD.

El Kantara and around

A single twelve-kilometre road leads southwest from Aghir to **EL KANTARA**, passing some deserted beaches on the way. Without your own transport, the nearest you can get to El Kantara is Guellala or Sedouikech, both a few kilometres away and served by bus #16. Halfway along the Aghir–El Kantara road, on the left if you're heading southwest, a track heads 8km over the sand and out along a strip of land to the fort of **Borj Kastil**, built by Alfonso V of Aragon during his brief mid-fifteenth-century tenure of the island. The surrounding rocks are said to be good for underwater fishing.

It was the Carthaginians who created the **causeway** which stretches 7km from El Kantara to the opposite shore. In 1551, Dragut the pirate, trapped with his fleet by the flotilla of Charles V of Spain between the causeway and the fort, made his famously daring naval getaway here. To gain time, he barricaded himself in the fort and held off the Spaniards while his men, under cover of darkness, dug through the causeway, enabling his fleet to escape into the Gulf of Bou Grara.

Although it could still be forded at low tide in the intervening period, the causeway was not repaired for over four hundred years, finally re-opening in 1953.

The site of ancient **Meninx** is spread around the road junction by El Kantara. Very little now remains of the city established by the Phoenicians and rebuilt by the Romans, but there are two patches of **unexcavated remains** (freely accessible). One area is spread up the Aghir road for 2km or so on both sides, the main area of blocks and fallen columns being about 1km from the causeway on the seaward side of the road, where the forum once stood. A little to the north, on the inland side of the road, a mound marks the site of the former Roman bathhouse, and a kilometre or so further are some Punic catacombs, associated with the Punic port that once stood at the north end of the bay between here and the peninsula where Borj Kastil stands. None of these sites are obvious to the untrained eye however, nor are they easy to find. The other patch of remains is about 100m north of the road to Guellala, less than a kilometre from the causeway (just before the date palms begin), and includes the remains of a basilica whose font is now in the Bardo Museum in Tunis. Again, there is nothing spectacular to be seen, but it is worth a stroll, and a number of nooks and crannies repay closer inspection.

For the intrepid, a small piste leads inland 400m north of the remains just mentioned, opposite what's left of a Roman cistern (there are also third- and fourth-century catacombs to the north of the road here). About 1500m up this piste is the ancient and very interdenominational **Jema'a Haratt Ouirsighen**, originally a Roman temple, then a synagogue for Meninx's Jewish community, which became a church in the fourth century, a Byzantine basilica, and finally a mosque.

Guellala

GUELLALA, on the island's south coast, is the stronghold of Ibadism and the Berber language in Jerba. It also rivals Nabeul in Cap Bon as a centre for handmade **pottery**. The clay is dug out of the hillside on the road to Sedouikech, then bleached and cleaned in the sea. All the products were once exported from a port down the road, and people used to travel around the markets near Tataouine selling their goods. The staple of the industry, the large terracotta vessels used for storing and cooling water and oil, went to markets as far afield as Benghazi in Libya and Constantine in Algeria. Pottery workshops line the main street though, of the ones operating, only one is still in the original style, partly underground and insulated with stone and soil to protect the drying clay from the heat and wind. The three hundred kilns in the village are constructed with special bricks, made from earth, which has been washed with alluvial deposits. Most of the glazed ware is garish and geared to the market in cheap souvenirs, though the Berber bowls, baked at the lowest temperatures, are more authentic and interesting. A Guellala speciality nowadays is the "magic camel", a water jug in the shape of a camel, with a hole in the base through which it's filled. When placed the right way up, the water miraculously fails to escape from this hole and pours only from the mouth.

The town has an underground oil press (the yard with the big blue door, 50m up the road for Hara Sghira and Ajim, from the police station and bank). It's accessible through any of the neighbouring shops, though of course you'll be expected to stop for some shopping. A more interesting visit can be had half a kilometre up the El Kantara road where, opposite a taxiphone office, you'll find "**Ali Berber's Cave**". Ali Berber, the indefatigable proprietor, gives a highly entertaining tour of his allegedly Roman and undoubtedly ancient

Ibadites and Berbers

From the earliest Arab invasions, Jerba became a centre for the **Kharijites**, an ascetic Islamic sect hostile to the caliphs who ruled the Arab empire, and whose origins go back to the very beginning of the schism between Sunni (orthodox) and Shiite Muslims. The Sunnis supported the Omayyad caliphs and their Abbasid successors, while Shiites believed that only the prophet's son-in-law Ali and his descendants had the right to the caliphate. But in the early days of the dispute, when Ali agreed to arbitration over the question, a group of his followers withdrew their support, declaring that God was the only arbitrator. Taking their name from the Arabic for "to leave" (*kharaja*), they became an ascetic and highly puritan sect, hostile to Sunnis and Shi'ites alike (it was a Kharijite who eventually assassinated Ali), but they had a considerable following among the Berbers, especially since the Kharijites saw piety rather than (Arab) pedigree as the main criterion for leadership of the Islamic community. With the fall to the Fatimids in 909 of their North African states based at Sijilmasa in Morocco and Tahirt in Algeria, Jerba became one of the Kharijites' last refuges, along with the Mzab in Algeria, the Jebel Nafusa in Libya, and the island of Zanzibar in Tanzania.

For many years, the Kharijite population in Jerba was divided between two factions, the Wahabites (followers of Tahirt's Rustamid ruler Abdallah Ibn Wahab, whose territory included Jerba) and the Nakkarites (the faction followed by Tozeuri rebel Abu Yazid – see p.495). From the eighth to the fourteenth century, between uniting to fight the common Christian foe, these two factions struggled for political and religious dominance of the island. Eventually, the Wahabites prevailed, and in fact many of the Nakkarite party eventually converted to Sunni Islam. (The Wahabite faction of Kharijism has nothing to do with the eighteenth-century Wahabite movement from the Arabian peninsula.)

Today, Jerba's Kharijites, usually referred to as Wahabites or **Ibadites**, form nearly half the island's Muslim community and are concentrated in the south and west. They are extremely strict in their religious practice, and follow the dictates of the Koran even more scrupulously than other Muslims. They also differ from Sunni Muslims in certain details of their religious rituals. The austerity of their religion is best expressed in their architecture: they built the most simple and severe of the three hundred mosques and marabouts around the island. In times of war these semi-fortified buildings would serve as a place of refuge for those outside the *houch*, the country houses in the interior (see p.419).

Most of Jerba's dwindling minority of **Berber speakers** are Ibadites. They live in the south of the island, especially around Ajim, Guellala and Sedouikech. Because they speak a different first language, they tend to be at a social disadvantage (getting a job is always a problem, for example), and the low social status of Berber is the main factor behind the decline of the language.

underground pottery and oil press, with a full explanation in French. The only **oil press** in use here today is on the edge of town (continue 200m past Ali Berber's towards El Kantara and it's on the right, before the 7km milestone), is actually much more interesting – a wonderful piece of vintage science-museum technology – but is only open in November and December.

The Guellala Heritage Museum

About 2km up the Sedouikech road, on a hill overlooking the town, the **Guellala Heritage Museum** (daily: summer 8am–11pm; winter 8am–6pm; 5TD, camera 1TD, video camera 3TD) is housed in a whitewashed ensemble of traditional-style buildings. It's a tacky but quite amusing collection of tableaux illustrating Jerba life using showroom dummies, with labelling in English and several other languages. Jerba has its own **marriage rituals** (depicted in scenes 1–5), now threatened by increasing costs and the demand for high dowries from the bride's father. Six weeks before the wedding day, red or yellow eggs are sent as invitations to the guests, and during the week before the wedding the bride will receive presents from her husband and his family, including jewellery and ceremonial dress. She must apply henna (on two different occasions) to the whole of her palms, fingers and feet; a Berber might also use a black paint called *ouchi*. At some stage, both the man and woman will be led in procession around a fertile olive tree, striking their companions with a branch to hasten other marriages in the village. On the Friday before the wedding the bride is formally presented and unveiled to her family, who traditionally throw money at her feet. Finally she is carried to the groom in the privacy of a palanquin placed on the back of a camel.

Scenes 8 and 19 in the museum depict circumcision, thankfully without the gory details, while scenes 9–14 show traditional wedding dresses from different regions of the country, definitely worthwhile for those with an interest in costumes and textiles. Some of the labels in the museum are a little bit cryptic (scene 5: "third day of the marriage – the bride steps over the fish"; scene 24 "egg ceremony – the wedding night"). The last few "galleries" are actually shops.

The coast near Guellala

South of Guellala, along the shore, are a couple of interesting mosques and a few bits of Roman masonry. The **Guellala Mosque**, by the beach (1km out of town; take the first surfaced left turn opposite the "Robbana" sign after 200m heading from the police station towards Hara Sghira, and continue straight ahead when the tarmac veers off to the right), dates back to the fifteenth century and is a favourite on the ubiquitous "Mosquée de Djerba" postcards. It's a lovely place to watch the sun set over the sea between the mosque and the neighbouring palm tree, bathing the seaward-facing walls in a rosy light as it goes down. Half a kilometre west up the beach, you'll find the odd piece of Roman wall; there's more underwater just offshore, and local farmers often turn up pieces of marble and mosaic in their fields. In the other direction, 1500m southeast along the coast, the tenth-century **Mosque of Sidi Yati** (another postcard favourite) stands disused and crumbling by the shore.

Practicalities

There are nine **buses** a day (#14) here from Houmt Souk, while a **taxi** costs about 6TD, and it's not hard to **hitch** via either Sedouikech or Hara Sghira (Er Riadh). Guellala has a **bank** (but no ATM), should you need to change any money to invest in a bit of pottery.

Sedouikech

SEDOUIKECH, 6km from Guellala and El Kantara, stands on a small plateau, which is the one prominence on the island. The main mosque here is Sunni, but somewhat more interesting is the twelfth- or thirteenth-century Ibadite **Louta Mosque**, which is subterranean. Only its two cupolas are above ground, a design that takes the squat windowless form of the typical Jerban mosque to its fullest extreme. Since this is the highest point on the island, the mosque was not only a house of prayer, but also a vantage point from which any approach could be seen. It was restored in the 1990s by the Institut National du Patrimoine. Three kilometres east of Sedouikech lies the mausoleum of sixteenth-century hermit **Sidi Satouri**, visited by childless women who pray here in the hope that the saint's *beraka* (blessing) may help them to conceive. According to legend, Sidi Satouri once turned to stone members of a wedding party who interrupted him at prayer. Perhaps the legend derives from the **megalithic dolmens** that stand 200m to the northwest, of unknown antiquity, but quite probably the oldest artefacts on Jerba.

The west coast

Long and wild, virtually uninhabited and empty of tourists, the **west coast of Jerba** is not as postcard-pretty as the other coasts, nor as good for swimming, with a rocky shore and shallow water for quite a way out. It is, however, *the* place to really get away from it all – if you can get there, that is. At its northern end is the island's airport; to the south, Ajim, Jerba's main port; and in between no public transport at all. If you stay anywhere along this twenty-kilometre shore, you'll be camping or just sleeping out – no hardship so long as you have adequate supplies of food and water. Two old mosques along this coast appeared in *Star Wars* – see the box on p.364 for details.

Two roads run out to Jerba's west coast from Houmt Souk. The airport road, which is surfaced, passes **MELLITA** and some of the oldest *menzels* (parcels of land) on the island. Four kilometres out of Houmt Souk to the south of the road is the **El Kebir Mosque** which, despite the name ("Great Mosque"), is no bigger than any other inland Jerban mosque, and very typical in appearance, with its whitewashed windowless walls and battlement-like mini-minaret resembling a lookout on a mini-fort. It is in fact Jerba's oldest mosque, dating back to the ninth century, when it was considered one of the most important Kharijite mosques in North Africa. If you are Muslim, you can pop in to admire the tenth-century *mihrab* and *minbar*. After Mellita, the road passes Jerba's airport and continues to **Borj Jillij**, where a lighthouse was first constructed in the sixteenth century on the site of an earlier fort. A new fort was built here in the eighteenth century under Hammouda Bey, but it is now used as a lighthouse once again, running on electricity rather than olive oil lamps. From Borj Jillij you can drive or cycle back along a track by the sea to Houmt Souk, a distance of about 11km.

The main Houmt Souk–Gabès road leads through dull countryside to the fairly dreary port of **AJIM**, the most important centre for sponges, which are still taken from the sea floor by divers – now mainly Tunisians, but originally Greeks and Maltese. Ajim is also a centre for the local date harvest, though compared with the *deglat en nour* variety of Tozeur the crop here is poor – three varieties of palm provide nothing edible at all, and are kept only for *laghmi*, palm wine (see p.361). Be careful if you go swimming here, as the channel swarms with large jellyfish, constantly chewed up in ferry propellers. The channel is also full of octopuses; all along the quay you'll see stacked piles of **octopus traps** in the form of ceramic pots, which are laid on the seabed in the evening. The creatures, looking for hiding places at the end of a night's foraging, crawl into them only to be hauled out in the morning. The raucous and exotic bar in *Star Wars*, or at least the outside of it, was in fact a house in Ajim (barely recognizable these days), while Obiwan Kenobi's house was an old mosque 3km up the coast – see the box on p.364 for details.

There are frequent **louages** between Ajim and Houmt Souk, and regular **ferries** between Ajim and Jorf on the mainland (see p.448). Ajim has a **bank** on the main road, but no hotels.

Sponges

The Mediterranean Sea is very rich in **sponges**, particularly soft and flexible ones, and people living around the Mediterranean have used them for centuries: the Romans, for example, used them as toilet paper. There are over five thousand species in the world; some gather on rocks like moss, while others are free-standing, and only attached at the bottom. Sponges go back a long way in time; indeed, some fossilized examples from Tunisia date back to the Jurassic period, when the country was underwater.

Once thought to be a plant, a sponge is in fact one of the simplest forms of animal life; if part of a sponge is broken off it will become an independent animal. The sponge has no organs – no heart or brain for example – but consists of cells with different functions. A sponge is covered with small holes, or pores, which continually suck in water. Inside the sponge, special cells called choanocytes extract oxygen, and also food in the form of planktonic plants. Waste is expelled through a larger hole in the top called the osculum, or through medium-sized holes called ostia. Sponges are hermaphrodite, but when mating, each sponge takes the role of one sex. The tiny larvae released by the sponge playing the female role drift in the plankton for just a few days before attaching themselves to rocks to start growing.

Most bathroom "sponges" used nowadays are artificial, made of plastic foam or other chemical products. Tunisia is a good place to find the real thing.

Inland Jerba

Inland Jerba is a quiet expanse of sleepy homesteads and fortified mosques, their architecture attesting to the island's stormy history. People live in homes dotted around the countryside, and places that appear on the map to be villages – **El May**, **Midoun**, **Mahboubine**, **Guellala** – are really little more than markets: people shop and work in them, but few people live there. The only settlements that really qualify for the title of village are the two Jewish "ghettos" of **Hara Sghira** and **Hara Kebira**, whose residents, unlike most of their fellow Jerbans, actually do live in houses grouped closely together.

Midoun

MIDOUN, the island's second town, is really little more than a bunch of souvenir shops, a trio of banks and a few restaurants, but it's quite a lively place during the Friday souk, when there's also a livestock **market** just out to the southeast. The other event of the week is a "**fantasia**" of music and dance every Tuesday in the open-air theatre (Jan–June & Sept–Dec 3pm, July & Aug 5pm; 2TD), including a mock Berber wedding and a performance by a band of *ouled jema'a* musicians, black descendants of slaves who brought their musical traditions with them across the desert.

Midoun's underground **olive press** (*massera*) is worth a look. You'll find it between the mosque on avenue Farhat Hached (the Sidi Mahares road) and the taxiphone office on avenue Salah Ben Youssef – look for the ground-level dome (you can see in through the windows in the dome if the press is closed). As at Haddej and Matmata (see p.402), underground air ensures humidity throughout the winter, necessary to separate the oil. A mule or camel used to turn the stone roller around its base, crushing the olives, but the press is now motor-driven. After pressing, the skins are transferred to a sieve (*chamia*) which

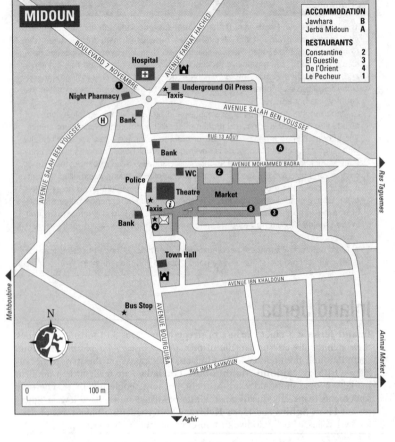

is squashed by the weight of a palm trunk, hinged at the wall; the oil and vegetable water drip through into a jar and separate. Around the main room are storage chambers, used by each family for their olives.

Practicalities

Frequent **buses** run here from Houmt Souk (#13 direct, #10 via El May and Mahboubine, #11 via Sidi Mahares), and there are also buses from the hotel zone (#11). Buses departing Midoun serve Houmt Souk (#10, #11 and #13), the hotel zone (#10), Mahboubine (#10, #11 and #13) and Aghir (#10), and there are long-distance departures to Zarzis and Medenine. **Taxis** wait by the main roundabout (around 3TD to Aghir or Ras Taguermes, 6TD to Houmt Souk). There's a **Syndicat d'Initiative** (Mon–Thurs 9am–noon & 3–5pm, Fri & Sat 9am–1pm; ☎75 658 116) in the street leading to the market, and a **hammam** on avenue Salah Ben Youssef (Thurs–Sat: men 6am–12.30pm & 6–10pm; women 12.30–5.30pm). For medical needs, apart from various **pharmacies** (including a night pharmacy), Midoun has a **hospital** (☎75 730 280) and a very reputable **doctor**, Dr El Messabi, Midoun's former mayor, at 20 avenue Bourguiba (☎75 730 305).

For **accommodation**, the budget option is the pleasant *Hôtel Jawhara* off the market square (☎75 600 467; ❷). It has en-suite rooms, though some have no outside window. A more luxurious choice is the spotless *Jerba Midoun* on rue 13 Août (☎75 730 006, ☎75 730 093; ❺), with such modern conveniences as air conditioning and a breakfast terrace. The *Restaurant de l'Orient* on the main roundabout does cheap and filling Tunisian **food** (daily 8am–5pm), as does the *Restaurant Constantine* at 11 avenue Mohamed Badra (daily 7am–5pm). For more refined eating, there's the reasonably priced *Restaurant le Pêcheur* (daily 10am–10pm) on boulevard 7 Novembre (the Houmt Souk road) and, just off the market square, the pricier and more tourist-oriented *Restaurant el Guestile* (daily noon–midnight), both of which which specialize in seafood.

Around Midoun

If you take the direct road from Midoun to Houmt Souk, there are a couple of things en route worth breaking the journey for. Two kilometres out of Midoun, a pyramid-shaped pile of weather-worn sandstone blocks north of the road marks the Punic **Tomb of Borgou** (free access). The sarcophagus was in an underground chamber which is accessible but not very pleasant, since its entrance has been broken open by the drunks who use this as a nocturnal meeting place and toilet. The eleventh century **Fadloune Mosque**, 1km further on the south side of the road, appears anonymously on numerous postcards of the island. A classic Jerban Ibadite mosque, it has buttressed walls and lantern-style minaret. It's no longer used for prayers, so non-Muslims can go in and look around (but beware of local layabouts claiming to be "the mosque guide", following you around and then demanding money for the privilege). Also in the compound is an underground cistern and an old flour mill. Another couple of distinctive Jerban **mosques** appear to the north of the road after another 8km or so: the **Ben Yakhlef** with its stumpy minaret is just by the road, with the **Mouzline**, like a sleeker version of the Fadloune, a little way beyond.

A kilometre west of the Fadloune Mosque, a turning southward, signposted "Jema'a el Gueïd" (the sign is only readable if approaching from the west), leads after 1km to yet another mosque, not especially outstanding. However, turn left in front of the grocery store opposite the mosque, follow the tarmac to a school, and continue around the school on the unsurfaced track: straight ahead of you at the next junction is **Qasr Hamida Ben Ayed**, a largely ruined eighteenth-century Ottoman palatial mansion built for the local governor. Seven hundred metres to your left is another ruined mansion called Dar Mustapha. The mansions can also be found by taking the Sedghiane turn-off from the Midoun–Houmt Souk road, continuing through **Sedghiane** till the tarmac ends (3km from the main road), and heading off down the track to the left; Qasr Hamida Ben Ahmed is on your right after 1km, and the track to your left leads back to the main road. A bike ride here makes a very pleasant excursion into the heart of the Jerban countryside.

A more picturesque route from Midoun to Houmt Souk is by way of Mahboubine and El May, through the vineyards and fruit and olive groves. **MAHBOUBINE**, a couple of kilometres northwest of Midoun, is itself little more than a central square, a couple of cafés and the nineteenth-century **El Kaateb Mosque**, inspired by the Blue Mosque in Istanbul. All along the winding road, behind the high banks (or *tabia*), are traditional Jerban houses (*houch*), each commanding the *menzel*, or estate, of a different family. The sand tracks to the north of the road here lead past one *menzel* after another, through a district best explored by bicycle.

△ Crocodiles at Djerba Explore, Ras Taguermes

El May and the Jewish villages

Right in the centre of Jerba, 8km west of Mahboubine and 9km south of Houmt Souk, **EL MAY** is most notable for its fifteenth-century fortified Kharijite **Mosque of Umm et Turkia**. As with the Zaouia of Sidi Brahim in Houmt Souk, the mosque's low walls are supported by thick buttresses, and are themselves a metre and a half thick, while the minaret is a squat, rounded stump. The windows however are less typical of classic Jerban mosques. A Saturday **market** takes place around the walls; other signs of business include two **banks** and a **post office** (country hours). **Buses** pass through here regularly between Houmt Souk and Midoun or Sedouikech.

Hara Sghira (Er Riadh)

Two kilometres from El May, towards Houmt Souk, the road turns off left for Guellala (see p.431). On the way is a Jewish settlement called **HARA SGHIRA** (Small Ghetto), now officially **Er Riadh**. Buses between Houmt Souk and Guellala pass through several times a day.

Hara Sghira's **synagogue of El Ghriba** ("The Miracle"; Mon–Thurs & Sun 7.30am–5pm, Fri until 2pm) is 1500m out of the village down a well-signposted road. The original synagogue was apparently constructed at the place where a holy stone fell from heaven; an unknown woman arrived, miraculously, at the same time, to direct operations. It is said that the synagogue's silver key will be thrown back to heaven if the Jews ever leave Jerba. The present building, dating only from 1920, is covered inside with rather garish tiles. An inner sanctuary contains several manuscripts, including one of the oldest Torahs in the world. One plaque on the wall offers a benediction for the Supreme Combatant, Bourguiba, and another asks for donations (not optional – less than half a dinar and you will promptly be shown the door).

The synagogue is a place of pilgrimage for Jews from all over North Africa on **Lag beOmer**, usually in May, the thirty-third day after the beginning of Passover, and a large new hostel for pilgrims reflects the importance of the site. Since the 2002 bomb attack (see box, p.440), security has been very tight, with airport-style metal detectors and baggage X-ray machines – you'll need to have your passport with you to visit.

It is possible to **stay** in Hara Sghira, at the small, smart new hotel called the *Dar Dhiafa* (℡75 671 166/7, ℻75 670 793, ⓦhoteldardhiafa.com; ❽), a tasteful conversion of four houses in the village, with traditional decor and all the modern conveniences of a tourist hotel, including two small swimming pools.

Hara Kebira (Es Souani)

The other Jewish village, **HARA KEBIRA** (now officially **Es Souani**), is near Houmt Souk and an easy walk from town (follow avenue Bourguiba south past the hospital and, at the next junction, take the road at eleven o'clock, between the Midoun and Kantara turn-offs). Rather more workaday than Hara Sghira, it boasts several synagogues, none as interesting as el Ghriba. The streets here are named after fruit and nuts rather than the usual array of politicians, dates and martyrs. The village also has a small *gargote*, the only kosher restaurant in the country, at 17 rue des Amandes (daily 8–11am & 5–8pm, closed Fri pm), off the main square.

One thing to look out for as you wander around the village are the symbols painted in blue on house doorways to ward off the evil eye. As well as the usual fish and hands, these include a five-armed version of the normally seven- or nine-armed *menorah* (Jewish candelabra).

The Jews of Jerba

Opinion about when **Jews** first came to Jerba is divided: some believe it was in 566 BC, following the fall of Jerusalem to Nebuchadnezzar; others say 71 AD, when the city was taken by Titus. The community today numbers about 1500, some of whom have returned here after emigrating to Israel.

Historically, Jewish **artisans** worked here as jewellers, playing a considerable part in developing the island's commercial reputation. Jerban Jewish colonies sprang up over much of the south of mainland Tunisia, often made up of shopkeepers or itinerant blacksmiths. But while they established small communities in remote villages, they kept their bonds with Jerba, returning to the island during the summer and for important religious festivals.

To begin with Jews were tolerated, but only while they kept to their own community and traditional occupations. Under the French their position improved, but they remained second-class citizens relative to the Europeans and European Jews. Their own attitude helped maintain this position, for while other communities took advantage of the educational and financial resources of world Jewish organizations, the Jews of Jerba rejected aid, preferring to keep their strict and distinctive form of Judaism untainted. Consequently they won a reputation as intransigent **traditionalists**, gained far less from the Protectorate than other communities, and became the target of French and Arab anti-Semitism.

The establishment of the state of Israel offered an opportunity to make a new life in the Promised Land, and by the early 1950s many Jews were leaving. After Tunisian independence the trickle of emigrants became a flood and the community shrank, only to revive slightly with the return of some Jews from Israel. Perhaps as a result of Bourguiba's attempts to encourage integration, overt anti-Semitism is rare, and Jerban Jews generally have good relations with their Muslim neighbours. However, anti-Zionism ("We have nothing against Tunisian Jews, it is only the State of Israel we object to") still forms a pretext for occasional outbursts of hatred. In 1985, a police officer, apparently incited by radio broadcasts from Libya, burst into the Ghriba in Hara Sghira and killed three worshippers before he could be restrained, but the worst attack by far came in April 2002 when a drifter and one-time smuggler from Ben Gardane blew up a tanker full of propane gas outside the synagogue in support of Islamic fundamentalism. As well as killing himself, the bomber murdered twenty people in the vicinity. The target was obviously chosen for its Jewish nature, but none of the victims were in fact Jewish – eighteen were tourists from Germany and France, and the other two were Tunisian Muslims. Although the bomber was Tunisian, this was no home-grown attack: the perpetrator had been to Pakistan and probably Afghanistan, where he was given $20,000 to fund it by members of al Qaida. Responsibility for the attack, giving details that only associates of the bomber could know, was claimed in a fax to a Pakistani newspaper by a group calling itself "the Islamic Army for the Liberation of the Holy Sites", a guise also used by al Qaida when it murdered 224 people in attacks on US embassies in Kenya and Tanzania in 1998.

The southeast coast

On the mainland southwest of Jerba are the small towns of **Jorf** and **Bou Grara** while, on the country's remote southeast coast, you'll find the nascent resort of **Zarzis** and the route into Libya via **Ben Gardane**. With most people heading for Jerba's lotus-eating shores, this corner of Tunisia is still rarely visited, though it could increasingly become the subject of tourist development over the next few years, if tourism in Libya continues to develop.

Jorf and Gightis

JORF is not the most inspiring town in Tunisia. If you're headed to Jerba, the frequent ferry services from here to Ajim ensure that you won't be stranded for long (see p.448). There are louages from Jorf to Medenine, but not to Gabès (either change at Medenine, or walk up to the turn-off and hitch). The only town between Jorf and Gabès is Mareth (see p.410), from where adventurous travellers can strike off to Toujane. En route to Medenine you could stop off to visit the Roman port of **Gightis** – though, as passing louages tend to be full, it can prove difficult to continue on afterwards.

Gightis

Established by the Phoenicians, **GIGHTIS** became a trading post under the Carthaginians. A large fleet could shelter here in what is now the Gulf of Bou Grara and, recognizing the site's strategic importance, the Romans attacked the city during the first two Punic wars. After the campaign of Julius Caesar from 46 to 40 BC, the Romans assumed control and for the next two hundred years Gightis flourished as a major port of Africa Proconsularis and Byzacenia. The Roman trade route went from Carthage via Hammamet, El Jem and Gabès to Gightis and then on to Oea, Leptis Magna and Ghadames in Tripolitania (modern Libya). The city was later sacked by the Vandals, but the Byzantines thought it worthy of restoration. With the Arab invasion of the seventh century, however, the port was destroyed and the site of Gightis covered over until excavations in 1906.

The **site** lies next to the main road (daily except Fri: April to mid-Sept 8am–noon & 3–7pm; mid-Sept to March 8.30am–5.30pm; 1.1TD), 1km south of the village of Bou Grara. It is not fenced off and you can go in at any time, although the *gardien* may come and ask you to pay the entrance fee. The large central square, the **Forum**, dates from the reign of Emperor Hadrian (117–138 AD) and is overlooked by a **temple** dedicated to Serapis and Isis. A long flight of steps leads up to the top of the red sandstone podium, but little remains of the columns or interior walls. The stone-flagged road down to the port begins by the arch at the other end of the forum and passes, on the left, the **Temple of Bacchus**. Behind the portico, where only the fragments of columns remain, is an underground passage and several small rooms, their purpose unknown. The **port** has long since silted up, but a partly submerged row of stones marks the site of a **jetty**, once 140m long. Stone foundations by the road also give an idea of the town's extent, stretching to the Capitol Temple, at the top of a slight hill and towering above the shops and houses. On the right-hand side of the forum as you face the sea are the **baths** and several scraps of mosaic. If you walk through the baths, away from the square, the **market** will be ahead of you and just to the right; built in the third century, it consists of a central courtyard surrounded by a walkway, fitted out with shops. Nearby are the remains of villas and a temple of Mercury.

Bou Grara and the Institut des Regions Arides

The new village of **BOU GRARA** stands just north of the ruins. From the rock, on the right of the site, there's a sweeping view of the inland sea, mud flats and the older fishing port down below. Although French naval architects believed they could build a second Bizerte in this natural harbour, the modern port never quite lived up to the promise of its ancient predecessor: the water was far too shallow to accommodate heavy military vessels and the plans were scrapped.

Six kilometres from Bou Ghrara towards Medenine, on the west side of the road, the **Institut des Regions Arides** (☎75 633 005) was set up to study the ecology and anthropology of desert regions, particularly those of Tunisia. This would be of little interest to tourists but for the fact that the Institute's most recent projects include a detailed study of the south's *ksour* (see p.453), and what looks set to be a very interesting **museum** of life in the desert region. Once open, the museum will contain archeological finds and antiques including agricultural equipment, plus a reconstructed working oil press, all well laid-out with explanations in French and Arabic.

Jerba to Zarzis and the Libyan frontier

Across the causeway from its namesake in Jerba, **El Kantara Continent** has nothing special to commend it except an old **Turkish fort** gazing languidly at Borj Kastil across the water. From here, there are two roads to Zarzis: a coastal road via **Hassi Jerbi**, passing the tourist hotels and beach zone, and a less scenic but more direct route via **Sidi Chammakh**. Until recently, few travellers ever bothered to go further east, but now that Libya has tentatively (though sporadically) started allowing entry to tourists, **Ben Gardane** and **Ras Ajdir** are slightly more on the beaten track.

Sangho

Some 12km down the coastal road, 9km north of Zarzis at **SANGHO**, you'll find a handful of hotels and "hotel clubs" by the beach but otherwise it's in the middle of nowhere. You can rent bicycles from both the *Oamarit* and the *Sangho*, and both have **car rental** desks – or you can rent a car from a couple of agencies outside, including Boulaaba by the *Hôtel Zyen* (☎75 705 097). Sports such as water-skiing, jet skiing and windsurfing are available on the beach, and horse-riding is also possible (there's a ranch opposite the entrance to the *Oamarit*).

Hotels

Hôtel Club Oamarit On its own turn-off from the Hassi Jerbi–Zarzis coast road ☎75 705 770, ℱ75 705 685, ℮oamarit@gnet.tn. Boasts indoor and outdoor swimming pools, and facilities for sports from mini-golf to archery. It also has several bars and restaurants, including a pizzeria, and a nightclub, plus appealing rooms separate from the main block. Full board only. ❽

Hôtel Giktis Next to the *Oamarit* ☎75 705 800, ℱ75 705 002. Quite well appointed for a three-star hotel, with two swimming pools and reasonably spacious rooms. ❼

Odysée Resort Just south of the *Sangho Club* ☎75 705 705, ℱ705 190. A modern adaptation of traditional Berber architecture, with forms reminiscent of Jerban mosques and the southern *ksour*. Berber carpets and motifs are used throughout – even the elevators are made of palm wood and lined with Berber rugs. The rooms are large and have balconies overlooking a pool terrace. ❾

Sangho Club Just off the coast road south of the *Oamarit* turn-off ☎75 705 124, ℱ75 705 715, ℮sangho.zarzis@planet.tn. More Club Med in style, with a variety of sports facilities. ❾

Sultana Residence Less than 1km south along the coast from the *Odysée Resort* ☎75 705 115, ℱ75 705 167, ℮www.residence-sultana.com. A tranquil, relaxing little place, it's like a classier version of a *pension de famille*, with a pool and a Jacuzzi, nine rooms, each one different, and a pier for sea swimming. Another little luxury they provide – the only place in Tunisia to do so – is mosquito nets.

Hôtel Zyen Just opposite the entrance to the *Sangho Club* ☎75 706 630, ℱ75 706 629. Comfortable and spotlessly clean, with its own bit of beach, a/c rooms with a large balcony, and a small pool. There's an upmarket restaurant (daily noon–3pm & 7–11pm), where you can get an ordinary menu for 9TD, with more expensive seafood menus also available ❻

Zarzis

Ten kilometres southeast of Sangho, **ZARZIS** has a good, long beach with new hotels, though it pales in comparison with Houmt Souk and much of Jerba. Even so, French officers considered it the cushiest posting in the south, a paradise compared with the parched heat of the interior. It was also the only place south of Gabès that suffered settlement by French colonists. Unfortunately, they didn't get on too well with the military, who feared that if too many colonists arrived they would lose their holiday resort to the civil administration, and did everything they could to make their lives difficult. The colonists, in turn, sent frequent complaints to the government, claiming that the army ruled with "the sword and the bull whip rather than any legal code". In the end, independence arrived before the military could be persuaded to abandon the town.

The main highlight in town is a small **museum** of locally discovered Roman artefacts (Tues–Sun: mid-April to mid-Sept 8am–noon & 3–7pm; mid-Sept to mid-April 9.30am–4.30pm; 2.1TD, cameras 1TD), in an old church on avenue Habib Thameur. There isn't much to see around Zarzis. Like Sfax, the town is surrounded by olive plantations, most of which were planted in the twentieth century. The **beach** at Zarzis's *zone touristique*, 3km north of town, near the village of **Souihel**, has the best swimming in the area, and the *Zarzis* and *Zita* hotels have decent swimming pools. Barriers at the hotels' entrances prohibit roaming Tunisians, but tourists should be able to get in.

Market days in the souk are Monday and Friday (Saturday in Souihel). An annual **sponge festival** is held in Zarzis in the last week of July, which is really just a series of concerts and other organized events aimed mainly at package tourists, and has little to do with sponges, though you might find some on sale.

Practicalities

If you're arriving from Jerba along **avenue Mohamed V**, then the third exit beyond **place de la Jeunesse**, the town's central roundabout, is rue Hedi Chaker, which leads to **place 7 Novembre**. From there, avenue Habib Thameur heads off towards the **port** and avenue Bourguiba towards Ben Gardane. The coastal road up to the *zone touristique*, 3km north of town along the coast, leads through a large military camp, so it's probably not the best place for an evening stroll.

Zarzis's **bus station** (℡75 684 372 for SRT services, ℡75 681 643 for SNTRI services) is down towards the port. As well as buses to Jerba, Medenine and other local destinations, there are services to Tunis, and a late-night departure to connect at Gabès with the early-morning train to Tunis. The *zone touristique* and Sangho can be reached by local bus #1 (10 daily). **Louages** leave just outside.

Place de la Jeunesse has a few **banks** (the Banque du Sud on av Mohamed V has an ATM), as does place 7 November; the **post office** (country hours) is just off the square. There are two **Internet offices**: Espace d'Internet on avenue Farhat Hached, about 200m west of place de la Jeunesse (daily 9am–10pm; 2TD/hr), and Publinet (daily 10.30am–10pm; 2TD/hr), just off avenue Farhat Hached, a block west of the *Hôtel Medina*. There's a Magasin Général **supermarket** at the junction of avenue 20 Mars and avenue Bourguiba. The **hospital** is on avenue 20 Mars (℡75 694 302), with an *infirmerie* opposite at no. 43, and a **night pharmacy** at the junction of 20 Mars and avenue Farhat Hached. The **police** station is also on avenue Farhat Hached (℡75 694 745). Avis have a **car rental** office (℡75 694 706) on the main road outside the hotels in the *zone touristique*, with smaller firms nearby.

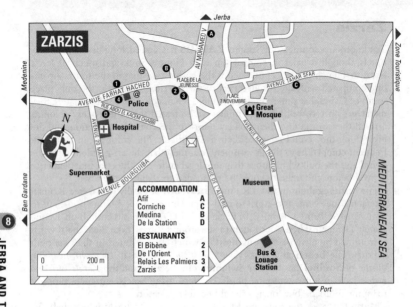

Accommodation

The *zone touristique* was originally home to three package **hotels** known as "*les trois zeds*": the *Zarzis* towards the northern end of the beach, the *Zita* just to its north (closed for renovation at last check), and to its south, the *Zephir*, now an all-inclusive club that can only be booked as part of a package tour. All cater for a mainly German clientele. In recent years, a few smaller hotels have opened up here, plus a number of restaurants. Zarzis itself has a number of budget hotels, most of them not too great and many often closed for no apparent reason.

Hotels

In town

Afif av Mohamed V ☎75 684 639. Bright and clean, slightly nicer than the *Corniche*. Bathrooms are shared. ❷

Corniche av Tahar Sfar, off pl 7 Novembre ☎ & ☎75 692 822. The best-value cheapie in Zarzis has very decent rooms, some en suite and some with a/c. ❶

Hôtel Medina (aka *Hôtel de Ville*) Off av Farhat Hached, near pl de la Jeunesse ☎75 691 901. The best hotel in town. The cool, clean rooms have private bathrooms, and there's a bar and restaurant. Rate includes breakfast. ❷

Hôtel de la Station av Farhat Hached ☎75 684 661. Simple, small, decent rooms, many with bathrooms. ❶

The zone touristique

Errachid On the main road about 100m south of the *Hôtel Zarzis* ☎75 706 762. A small, friendly,

good-value cheapie, clean and comfortable, with a sun terrace and kitchen on the roof. ❶

Nozha Halfway between the town and the *zone touristique* ☎75 694 593, ☎75 683 335. Quite cosy, with its own bit of rather exposed rocky beach. It is mainly known for its bar, where Libyan clients come to pick up prostitutes, but the rooms are fine (large and en-suite) and the trade is kept reasonably discreet. ❹

L'Oasis On the main road, across the street and a little to the south of the *Errachid* ☎75 706 483. A friendly, quiet little hotel, with self-catering apartments for 2–6 people, each with its own bathroom and kitchenette. ❸

Zarzis Northern end of the beach ☎75 684 160, ☎75 694 292, ☎zarzis.hotel@planet.tn. Reasonably classy as three-star package hotels go, with a clientele made up mainly of German sun-seekers. Wheelchair accessible. ❻

Ziha 100m off the beach just south of the *L'Oasis* ☎75 684 304, ☎75 694 680. A newer, fourth "zed"; the rooms are smaller than in the two sur-

8

viving original "zeds", and the pool (summer only) is more like a large bathtub, but the big downside is the rowdy bar full of drunken Libyans – definitely not female-friendly. **❹**

Eating

The best place to **eat** in town is the moderately priced *Relais les Palmiers* behind the filling station on place de la Jeunesse (daily noon–3pm & 7–10pm), with various sorts of couscous (including a vegetarian version), spaghetti and grills. Similarly priced, though with small portions, the *Restaurant el Bibène* very nearby on avenue Farhat Hached (daily 10am–9pm) serves decent food, notably prawns sautéed in garlic or in Provençal sauce. Cheaper eats (chicken, couscous, lamb chops and grills) can be had further west along avenue Farhat Hached at the *Restaurant Zarzis* (daily noon–2.30pm & 6–9pm), opposite at *Restaurant de l'Orient* (daily noon–11pm), and at *Restaurant de la Station* (daily noon–8.30pm) by the hotel of the same name on rue Abou el Kacem Chabbi.

More upmarket eating can be found in the *zone touristique*. *Le Pirate* (daily noon–midnight; ☏75 684 497) is the most prominent restaurant here (about 100m south of the *Hôtel Errachid*), with a popular open-air terrace, where you can eat dishes such as grilled bream for around 15–20TD. Slightly pricier, classier alternatives include *Le Château* just to the south (daily noon–midnight), where dishes include prawn kebabs and octopus provençale, and *La Pacha*, a little way north towards the *Hôtel Zarzis* (daily noon–midnight), with menus at 10TD and 15TD, and live music nightly from 8pm. There's a cheap rotisserie across the road from *La Pacha* and 50m south.

Southeast of Zarzis

The road south towards **Ben Gardane**, plied by buses and regular louages, skirts the **Sebkhet el Mellah**, a large salt flat that was the site of a mustard gas factory during World War I and today contains a massive salt mine. Seventeen kilometres south of Zarzis, a road leads to the village of **Biban**, at the end of a long spit. Beyond it (and not open to the public), an old Turkish fort, **Borj el Biban**, sits on a little island of its own. There are a few sandy beaches, mainly on the southern side of the spit, not up to Jerba's standards, but totally deserted. From the east, another spit stretches out towards Borj el Biban, the channel between them once marking the border with Libya.

The lagoon enclosed by the two spits, **Bahiret el Biban**, is full of fish and rich in bird life, notably flamingos, spoonbills and other waders. Easily accessible sites for spotting them can be found back on the main road, a few kilometres south of the Biban turn-off, where it crosses the western corner of the lagoon.

Ben Gardane

Off the beaten track for many years, **BEN GARDANE** is the last main town before the Libyan frontier, and a staging post on the route to Libya. The town is host to no fewer than three markets. The weekly Saturday **souk**, in the centre of town just south of avenue Habib Thameur, is very lively and far more agricultural than others in the south. There is also a **Libyan market**, similar to the one in Houmt Souk but bigger and less tourist-conscious, in a walled enclosure about a kilometre up the Zarzis road. This operates every day, but especially on Sundays when all the stalls are open. Finally, on the road to Mouamarat, 3km south of town (take the road south of the hospital, bear right at the fork after 500m and continue for a couple of kilometres), there is a Thursday-morning **livestock market**.

The road from Zarzis meets the road to Medenine at a roundabout where you will be dropped if **arriving** by SRT bus. Louages and SNTRI buses will leave you 50m from here up the Zarzis road (avenue 7 Novembre). Also off the roundabout is avenue Habib Thameur, which becomes the road to Ras Ajdir (turn right at the end and then bear left at the next roundabout). At the beginning of avenue Habib Thameur, there are shared yellow taxis (four places) to Ras Ajdir for the same price per place as a louage. The SRTGM **bus station** (☎75 710 026) is on the roundabout where the roads to Zarzis and Ras Ajdir meet. There are services to Gabès, Houmt Souk, Medenine, Ras Ajdir and Zarzis, though buses tend to peter out around midday. From the SNTRI office (☎75 711 400), there are departures to Tunis (via Sfax and Sousse, or by night via Kairouan), all passing through Medenine and Gabès; you'll find **louages** just opposite, and SRT buses (to Jerba, Zarzis and Ras Ajdir) by the main roundabout. Note that for Tripoli, you'll have to change at Ras Ajdir.

Ben Gardane has the usual **banks**, as well as moneychangers on avenue Habib Thameur, who buy or sell Libyan dinars and sell Tunisian dinars for hard currency. There's also a **post office** (country hours) at the eastern end of avenue Habib Thameur, and a Grand Magasin **supermarket**, about 50m towards Ras Ajdir from the post office.

There are around a dozen **hotels** in Ben Gardane. The biggest and poshest (which isn't saying much) is the *Pavilion Vert* on the Ras Ajdir road (☎75 710 103; ❷), with green-painted en-suite rooms and a reasonable restaurant. Friendlier and better value is the *Résidence Tines*, just next to the SNTRI office at 50 avenue 7 Novembre (☎ & ℉77 712 658; ❷ including breakfast), with spotless rooms, some en suite, plus its own parking lot, and a garden out back for coffee or pizzas. Cheaper options include the *El Ouns* (☎75 710920, ℉75 710 258; ❶), a dusty city hotel 100m down the Medenine road from its junction with the Zarzis road, also with en-suite rooms, but no hot water. For **food**, there are a number of cheap *gargotes* on the main road through town. If you prefer something a little more refined, try the moderately-priced restaurant at the *Pavilion Vert* (daily 10am–midnight), with grills, *kamounia* or couscous among the standard Tunisian options, or the *Restaurant Les Pyramides*, 200m down avenue Farhat Hached from the central roundabout (daily 10am–midnight), where you'll get grilled fish or brochettes at moderate prices.

On to Libya

The Tunisian frontier post for Libya is at **RAS AJDIR**, 33km east of Ben Gardane, and there are several police checks on the way. Although there is a Libyan embassy in Tunis (see p.118) and a consulate in Sfax (see p.277), it may be easier to arrange a visa from home. At Ras Ajdir, the prevailing atmosphere is one of complete chaos as you get out of your vehicle to go through the various **formalities**, which include filling out a departure card and getting your passport stamped.

There are 24-hour **exchange facilities**, but you should avoid using them if possible (apart from the queues, the rates are poor and they may decide on a whim not to change traveller's cheques). In any case, buying Libyan dinars is quite easy on the road to the frontier: moneychangers line the road all the way from Medenine, waving their wads of bills at passing cars. Ascertain the going rate before you start haggling (it's usually about three times the official rate). If you are coming from Libya, the same moneychangers will sell Tunisian currency for dollars, euros, sterling or Libyan dinars. Note that it is officially illegal to import or export Tunisian currency in or out of Tunisia, or to take Libyan currency into Libya.

There are always plenty of vehicles at the border, and you should have no difficulty finding **transport** to Tripoli, 196km away (4hr). Note that louages in Libya are called *taxi binasser*. Once over the border, the first thing you notice will probably be the superior state of the roads. **Arriving from Libya** at Ras Ajdir, you will find buses and plenty of louages to Ben Gardane, as well as buses to Gabès and Tunis, and occasional louages to Gabès.

Arabic place names	
Aghir	أغير
Ajim	أجيم
Ben Gardane	بنقردان
Bou Grara	بو غرارة
El Kantara	القنطارة
El May	الماي
Gightis	جيغتيس
Guellala	قلالة
Hara Kebira (Es Souani)	الحارة الكبرى (الصواني)
Hara Sghira (Er Riadh)	الحارة الصغرى (الرياض)
Houmt Souk	حومة السوق
Jerba	جربة
Jorf	جرف
La Seguia	السقية
Mahboubine	محبوبين
Mellita	مليتة
Midoun	ميدون
Ras Ajdir	رأس أجدير
Ras Taguermes	رأس تقرماس
Sangho	صنغو
Sedouikech	صدويكش
Sidi Mahares	سيدي محرس
Zarzis	جرجيس

Travel details

Buses

Ben Gardane to: Gabès (6 daily; 2hr 15min); Jerba (Houmt Souk; 3 daily; 2hr); Kairouan (1 daily; 6hr 30min); Medenine (6 daily; 1hr 20min); Ras Ajdir (5 daily; 40min); Sfax (2 daily; 4hr 30min); Sousse (2 daily; 7hr); Tunis (3 daily; 9hr); Zarzis (5 daily; 1hr).
Jerba (Houmt Souk) to: Ben Gardane (3 daily; 2hr); Bizerte (2 daily; 10hr); Gabès (11 daily; 2hr 30min); Kairouan (4 daily; 7hr); Medenine (5 daily; 2hr); Sousse (2 daily; 6hr 45min); Sfax (4 daily; 4hr 30min); Tataouine (2 daily; 3hr); Tunis (5 daily; 8hr

30min); Zarzis (8 daily; 1hr).
Ras Ajdir to: Ben Gardane (5 daily; 40min); Gabès (4 daily; 3hr); Kairouan (1 daily; 7hr); Medenine (2 daily 2hr); Tripoli (Libya; several daily; 4hr); Tunis (1 daily; 9hr 30min).
Zarzis to: Ben Gardane (5 daily; 1hr); Bizerte (1 daily; 10hr 30min); Gabès (7 daily; 2hr 30min); Jerba (Houmt Souk; 8 daily; 1hr); Jerba (Midoun; 2 daily; 1hr); Kairouan (2 daily; 7hr 30min); Medenine (9 daily; 1hr); Sfax (1 daily; 4hr); Sousse (1 daily; 6hr 30min); Tataouine (1 daily; 2hr); Tunis (2 daily; 9hr).

Louages

Ben Gardane to: Gabès (2hr 30min); Jerba (Houmt Souk; 1hr 45min); Medenine (1hr); Ras Ajdir (30min); Tataouine (1hr 20min); Tunis (9hr); Zarzis (45min).

Jerba (Houmt Souk) to: Ajim (20min); Ben Gardane (1hr 45min); Gabès (2hr); Medenine (1hr 20min); Sfax (4hr); Tataouine (2hr); Tunis (8hr 30min); Zarzis (1hr).

Ras Ajdir to: Ben Gardane (30min); Gabès (3hr); Tripoli (3hr 30min).

Zarzis to: Ben Gardane (45min), Gabès (2hr 30min), Jerba (Houmt Souk; 1hr), Medenine (1hr), Tataouine (1hr 45min); Tunis (9hr).

Ferries

Jorf to: Ajim (every 30min–2hr; 15min).

Domestic flights

Jerba to: Tunis (4–5 daily; 1hr–1hr 15min).

9

The Ksour

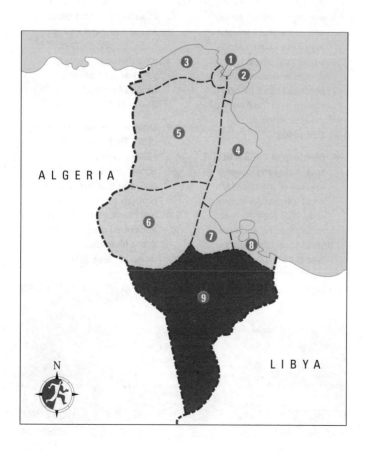

CHAPTER 9

Highlights

✳ **Metameur** A lovely old fortified granary (*ksar*; plural *ksour*) just outside Medenine, beautiful in the moonlight.
See p.457

✳ **Ksar Mourabtine** Abandoned, unrestored but still largely intact, this is one of the most rewarding of the ksour, standing among troglodyte homes and disused oil presses atop a hillside strewn with the fossils of Jurassic shellfish.
See p.462

✳ **Memory of the Earth tour** A day-trip covering one of the country's most interesting museums, plus hard-to-reach *ksour*, fossils, and prehistoric cave paintings.
See p.467

✳ **The Maztouria loop** A 48-kilometre circuit taking in some of the oldest, most interesting and best preserved of all the *ksour*, worth spending a couple of days exploring.
See p.469

✳ **Chenini** The most picturesque and most visited of the troglodyte Berber mountain villages, with its white mosque and rugged fortress.
See p.472

✳ **Douiret** The only one of the Berber mountain villages with tourist accommodation, and the only one that has been properly restored, with a subterranean mosque, ancient oil presses, and in the near future, a museum. See p.474

△ Chenini

9

The Ksour

Of all Tunisia, the **south**, the region that dips down towards the border with Libya and Algeria, is the most exciting and remote, and has long been this way. In the Middle Ages, Arab travellers avoided the area because the tribes were notorious for their lawlessness and banditry. It was a reputation that passed onto later generations: during the eighteenth and nineteenth centuries few European travellers entered the region, and only three are known to have visited **Medenine**, still the largest and most important town in the area. Even the intrepid James Bruce, who went on to discover the source of the Nile, preferred to take the boat from Gabès rather than risk his neck with these tribes. When the French invaded in 1881, they too gave the region a wide berth. It was many years before it was fully integrated, and remained under military administration until 1956.

With their steep escarpments, the south's arid mountains are impressive in themselves, but even more striking are the treasures hidden among them: the **ksour** (*ksar* in the singular), which are fortified communal granaries for the region's nomadic tribes, and the ancient Berber villages of **Douiret**, **Chenini** and **Guermessa**, as well as the much larger settlement of **Ghoumrassen**, all of which contain homes based around the cave dwellings (*ghar*) that were once typical of the region. Strange and extraordinary as monuments, they are even more remarkable as living settlements in so barren a land, though the culture that produced them is now under threat (see box, p.472).

The people themselves are another reason to visit: there's little of the hassle that you come to expect in the north, and people here are cool and reserved – in part, perhaps, due to the comparative absence of tourists. There are few hotels and facilities to attract visitors, and those who do come tend to be on whistlestop Land Rover tours. If you want to explore in more depth, you'll have to put up with "roughing it in a very moderate way", as the British explorer and colonialist Sir Harry Johnston put it in 1892.

Transport is the greatest problem you'll face in travelling independently. The road network is sparse, and joins modern French towns like **Zarzis** (see p.445), **Medenine** and **Tataouine**, rather than the more interesting villages. With

Market days

Monday Tataouine
Thursday Beni Kheddache, Tataouine
Friday Ghoumrassen, Ksar Jedid
Sunday Medenine, Remada

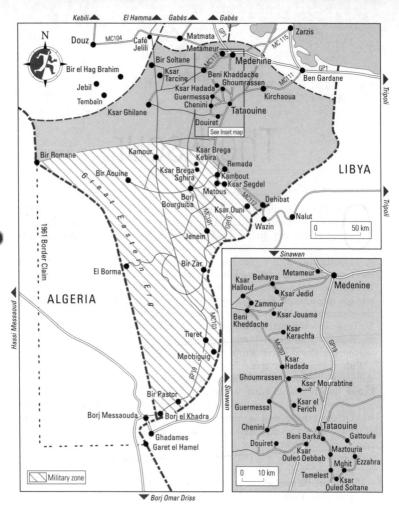

Tunisia's southernmost hotels and banks, Tataouine is a better base for exploration than Medenine. Buses are few and the louage service is less dependable than in the north, so you may have to hire a taxi, arrange a lift or hitch. Transport is always more frequent in the morning and often dries up completely by the afternoon, so the earlier you set out the better. But there's invariably some way of getting where you want, and the effort is generously rewarded. Having your own vehicle massively increases the accessibility of the more obscure sights, but if you intend going very far off the beaten track, especially in the far south, note the advice on desert driving on p.32.

Medenine and Metameur

Before the French occupation, **Medenine** was the focus of everything that mattered in the south, with a huge weekly market attracting merchants from as far afield as Tunis, Tripoli, Tebessa in Algeria, and even Bornu in present-day northern Nigeria. It was also the central granary of the **Touazine** and **Khezour**, tribes belonging to the powerful **Ouerghamma confederation**

Ghorfas, kala'a and ksour

Throughout the south, nomadic Berbers stored their grain in **ghorfas**, small stone cells (the Arabic word means "room") a couple of metres high and five to ten metres long. The cells were generally constructed on top of one another and side by side, at times reaching eight storeys. Individual units were always built in the same way, with grain sacks full of earth placed between the two side walls to act as a support during the construction of the roof. A layer of matting was placed over the top of these sacks, in the form of an arch, and then covered with clay, mortar and gypsum. When it had dried, the clay was chipped away, the sacks and matting removed to leave a gypsum-plaster ceiling, and a palm-wood door was fitted at the front. The rough inner walls were covered with gypsum plaster, usually with stucco figures such as hands or fish to ward off the evil eye, sometimes with inscriptions or geometric patterns, or spots on the ceiling representing rain.

In the tenth century, the Arab tribes of the **Banu Hilal** moved west into Tunisia from Egypt at the invitation of the Fatimids and with the promise of rich booty. In the first years of the Arab invasion, the Berbers retreated inland to the high mountaintops, building **forts** (*kala'a*) near their cave dwellings. Once the Arabs had occupied the fertile land the Berbers were forced into peace treaties and the *kala'a* were replaced by **ksour** (*ksar* in the singular, more correctly *gsour/gsar* in the local dialect), fortified granaries belonging to each tribe, where they could store and if need be defend their grain. *Ksour* were usually built in easily defensible positions, such as at the top of a rocky crag, and consisted of *ghorfas* built one next to the other in several storeys facing into a courtyard. The outer defensive wall of the *ksar* consisted of the back of these *ghorfas*, presenting a blank facade to the would-be assailant. The shape of the perimeter was dictated by the site, whether along a hilltop, as at Ksar Jouama, on a hillside, as at Ksar Ouled Soltane, or down in the more spacious river valley, like Medenine, where the less defensive position of the *ksar* is a mark of its builders' confidence in their military superiority.

But the *ksar* was not just a place to store grain. Often a mosque would be built just outside it. On Fridays the nomadic farmers would gather here to pray communally, and after prayer, they would spend some time together in the courtyard of the *ksar* drinking tea and exchanging news. Thus the *ksar* became the centre of the community as well as a place to store their food supply and if necessary defend it. The *ksour* and the *ghorfas* were not residential, but these days it is possible to **stay** in a *ghorfa* at Ksar Metameur (see p.457) and Ksar Hallouf (p.459), neither deluxe, but both very atmospheric.

In this chapter we cover the most accessible of the *ksour*, but if you want more comprehensive coverage, the Institut des Regions Arides (see p.442) has just completed a very detailed survey which they are due to publish in the form of a CD. It will be available in English, with a run-down of all the known facts about more than eighty *ksour*, plus numerous photos of each, and a map with zoom-ins to show you their exact location. Even for the non-specialist, it will make an excellent souvenir of the region, and will cover villages such as Chenini, Douiret and Guermessa, and Roman sites. The CD will be available from the Institut via their website, which was not yet on line when we went to press, but should be easy enough to find with a search engine.

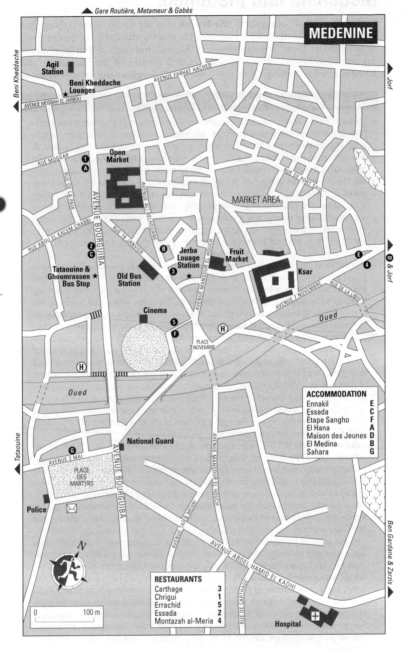

MEDENINE

Gare Routière, Metameur & Gabès

Beni Kheddache

Jorf

Agil Station

Beni Kheddache Louages

AVENUE FARHAT HACHED

AVENUE MOSBAH EL JARBOU

RUE MOGGAR

Open Market

RUE DE PORT SAID

RUE DE LA PAIX

AVENUE ALI BELHOUANE

MARKET AREA

AVENUE BOURGUIBA

RUE ABOU EL KACEM CHABBI

RUE 1ER JANVIER

Tataouine & Ghoumrassen Bus Stop

Old Bus Station

Jerba Louage Station

Fruit Market

Ksar

AVENUE MANSOUR EL HOUCH

AVENUE 7 NOVEMBRE

RUE DE LA LIBY

Oued

Cinema

PLACE 7 NOVEMBRE

Oued

ACCOMMODATION
Ennakil   E
Essada   C
Étape Sangho   F
El Hana   A
Maison des Jeunes D
El Medina   B
Sahara   G

Tataouine

National Guard

AVENUE 2 MAI

AVENUE BOURGUIBA

PLACE DES MARTYRS

AVENUE MANSOUR EL HOUCH

Police

Ben Gardane & Zarzis

AVENUE HAFER MERRI

AVENUE ABDEL HAMID EL KADHI

N

RUE DE CARTHAGE

0   100 m

RESTAURANTS
Carthage   3
Chrigui   1
Errachid   5
Essada   2
Montazah al-Meria 4

Hospital

of Berber-speaking tribes (see box, p.460), who had moved from Ghoumrassen on the advice of their marabout, Sidi el Assaibi. As a base for the confederation, Medenine grew rapidly from about 1800, and, at its height, the town's *ksar* had some eight thousand *ghorfas*. The French established their southern headquarters here and the town's jerry-built appearance hasn't improved much since. Nevertheless Medenine is the regional centre, and you'll have to pass through it at some point, probably even stay the night.

On the whole, Medenine's *ksar* is a disappointment, but it forms an introduction to those to the west and further south, which, although originally far smaller, are much better preserved. One of these is the *ksar* at **Metameur**, just a short bus ride from town.

Medenine

Sadly, the **ksar** at **MEDENINE** has gradually been demolished since the early twentieth century, when the tribes began to store their grain in silos near the fields rather than carry it all the way into town. One large *ksar* courtyard remains right in town on avenue 7 Novembre, its **ghorfas** converted into curio shops. Busloads of holidaymakers are driven in to look at it, and nearby cafés double their prices for anyone looking remotely like a tourist. There are some more *ghorfas* behind it, mainly abandoned, but up to three storeys high and giving a much better idea of the original construction.

The main **market** area is just to the north of the *ksar*. There are stalls out every day, but more so on market day, Sunday, when they take up a large part of the *oued* just south of boulevard 7 Novembre as well.

Practicalities

The town centre is concentrated down by the Oued Medenine el Gueblaoui at **place des Martyrs**, where you'll find the **post office** (city hours). Here **avenue Bourguiba**, the main road in from Gabès, meets the roads to Tataouine (av 2 Mai), Jorf (av 7 Novembre) and Ben Gardane (av Abdel Hamid el Kadhi). The main roundabout, **place 7 Novembre**, with a very gaudy tiled sculpture, is 100m up towards Jorf.

Moving on from Medenine

For a list of destinations and journey times, see Travel details on p.481.
Most buses and louages leave from the *gare routière*. There are ten daily **buses** to Tunis, five overnight, with three day and two night services going via Sfax and Sousse, the rest via Kairouan, including one that continues to Bizerte.

Eight daily buses (six SRT, two SNTRI) serve Tataouine, five continuing to Ghoumrassen, which also has three direct services. SRT services for Tataouine and Ghoumrassen stop in the town centre, so it isn't necessary to go up to the *gare routière* to catch them, but the bus may well fill up at these stops, leaving standing room only. The stops on avenue Bourguiba south of *Hôtel Essada*, and avenue 2 Mai west of place des Martyrs. Some services to Jorf and Jerba stop at the old bus station, so it's worth checking whether your bus calls there as it could save you a haul up to the *gare routière*.

Louages for Gabès, Ghoumrassen, Sfax, Tataouine and Tunis all leave from the *gare routière*, but those for Zarzis, Jerba and Ben Gardane usually leave from the old louage stand off rue 18 Janvier near the old bus station. Louages for Beni Kheddache leave from the rue Mosbah el Jarbou, just off av Bourguiba, as do *camionnettes* for Ksar Hallouf. Buses to Beni Kheddache also stop there.

Arriving from most places by bus or louage, you'll probably be dropped at the **gare routière**, 2km out of town on the Gabès road. Here taxis wait to ferry new arrivals into town for about 1.2TD. Only if you're coming from Jerba, Zarzis or Ben Gardane will louages drop you off in the town centre, as will some buses from Jerba and Jorf, before proceeding to the **old bus station** on rue 18 Janvier. Buses from Tataouine also stop in the centre of Medenine before continuing up to the *gare routière*.

Banks are mostly by place 7 Novembre, or on avenue Bourguiba up above its junction with rue 18 Janvier. A couple have ATMs, as does the post office. A rota system ensures that one bank is always open on Saturday and Sunday mornings. There's a **cinema** at the top of a pedestrianized area between avenue Bourguiba and place 7 Novembre, and a **hammam** the other side of avenue Bourguiba just by the *oued* (daily except Wednesday: men 5am–noon & 6pm–midnight; women 1–6pm), with another at 24 avenue 7 Novembre (similar hours). For essential supplies, there's a Grand Magasin **supermarket** at 18 avenue Bourguiba. Better than the state **hospital** on the Ben Gardane road (☏75 640 830) is the **Polyclinique Ibn Arfa** on rue de la République, just off the Tataouine road about 500m west of place 7 Novembre (☏75 640 157). There's a night pharmacy at 46 avenue Bourguiba.

Accommodation

Medenine's **hotels** have improved somewhat in recent years and, though there aren't many of them, they offer decent cheap and mid-range options. In addition to the hotels in town, there is accommodation at the nearby *ksar* of Metameur (see opposite). Clean four-bed dorms are available at the *Maison des Jeunes* on rue des Palmiers (☏75 640 338; dorm beds 5TD), unsignposted in a group of white buildings about 500m past the *ksar*, on the left as you head out of town. It operates a 10pm curfew.

Hotels

Ennakil av 7 Novembre ☏75 640 592. Could do for a night if the other budget hotels are full: beds are variable, some are very soft, none have sheets, and the shared toilets and showers could be better, but it's friendly, and the rooms are clean if bare. ❶

Essada 87 av Bourguiba ☏75 640 300. Simple, clean rooms, with windows opening onto a central terrace. Some rooms have a shower. ❶

Hôtel Étape Sangho pl 7 Novembre ☏75 643 546 ☏75 640 550. The best hotel in town, and not a bad place, with comfortable rooms and a bar, though rather impersonal. Off-season, they may offer you a rate no higher than the best rooms at the *Sahara*. ❺

El Hana av Bourguiba ☏75 640 690. A simple, respectable hotel, with its own parking space out back, and private shower in some rooms. ❶

El Medina av Ali Belhouane ☏75 630 200. A new place boasting cosy rooms with ceiling fans and nice firm beds, but the showers and toilets, all shared, are not kept clean. ❶

Sahara av 2 Mai ☏75 640 007. Offers reasonable comfort in en-suite rooms. Those on the top floor are the cheapest, those on the lower floors (with a/c & TV) cost more. There's also a restaurant. Rate includes breakfast. ❸

Eating and drinking

Medenine is not a place for gourmets. The best of the cheap **eating** is the *Restaurant Errachid* off rue 18 Janvier (daily 5am–10pm), by the side of the *Hôtel Étape Sangho*, with great barbecued meat and fish, though it's worth asking them to leave out the greasy cold chips that usually accompany it. Alternatives in the same price range include the *Restaurant Chrigui* on avenue Bourguiba (daily noon–4pm & 6–9pm) by the *Hôtel el Hana*, the *Restaurant Essada* at 91 avenue Bourguiba (daily 7am–midnight) by the hotel of the same name, and the *Restaurant Carthage* (daily 6am–11pm), a *gargote* at rue 18 Janvier special-izing in stews. For more refined meals, the *Restaurant Café Patisserie Montazah* *al-Meria* at 89–93 avenue 7 Novembre (daily 10am–9pm) serves pizzas and grills indoors or in a pleasant back garden overlooking the *oued*, and is also a good place to stop for a coffee and a pastry. For a **beer**, your best bet is the bar of the *Hôtel Sahara*.

Metameur

The 600-year-old *ksar* of **METAMEUR** has a dramatic silhouette, standing isolated in the plain. Though quite small, with three courtyards and *ghorfas* that reach only three storeys, it's remarkably well preserved and hasn't been converted wholesale to tourist use. It's a six-kilometre bus ride from Mede-nine along the Gabès road, or an easy enough hitch from the top of avenue Bourguiba in Medenine to the turn-off, from where it's a one-kilometre walk to the village.

The village was founded around the thirteenth century by a local marabout, Sidi Ahmed Ben Adjel, who set up shop in a cave, and the local nomads who followed him. Today the village is still occupied by Sidi Ahmed's descendants, the **Temara**, and the descendants of his followers, the **Harraza**. At one time each Berber Harraza family would pay its Arab Temara masters in wheat, barley, oil and the much-prized local wood. In autumn and winter the *ksar* is barely used by the Temara and Harraza tribespeople, as they're out in the plains with their herds; it is at its busiest in summer. On Fridays the **Mosque of Sidi Ahmed Ben Adjel**, housing the saint's tomb, draws a congregation mainly comprising nomads from the surrounding pastures.

The best preserved of the *ksar's* courtyards has been adapted to make a **hotel**, called *Hôtel les Ghorfas* (☏97 560 533, ℱ75 656 458; ❸), with accommodation in some of the *ghorfas* including supper and breakfast, or you can camp or park a camper van for the same price. The enthusiastic proprietor is on hand to tell you about the region, and usually has some kind of artistic exhibition on. It's certainly a lovely place to spend the night, though the accommodation is rather rustic (there are hot showers, but they're a bit temperamental). By the entrance, the *Café Ghorfa* is open until midnight and serves snacks such as *briks*, as well as tea, coffee and *chicha* pipes.

The road from Metameur west to Toujane and Matmata is now surfaced all the way to Douz.

Over the Jebel Haouaia

Although there's a main road south from Medenine straight to Tataouine (the GP19), with a branch off to Ghoumrassen (see p.460), it goes through the plain, a route that's uniformly dull. A spectacular alternative is to make a detour to the west via **Ksar Jouama**, **Beni Kheddache** and **Ksar Hadada**, straight through the rugged mountains of **Jebel Haouaia**, where some of the most impressive *ksour* sit perched on mountain spurs.

If you plan on doing this, take note that it's not easy. Sparse **public transport** runs southwest from Medenine as far as Beni Kheddache, and north from Tataouine to Ghoumrassen, and thence to Ksar Hadada; but making the connection without your own car involves hitching the 22km between Beni Kheddache and Ksar Hadada. If you decide to hitch, start early as the road is very quiet.

Medenine to Beni Kheddache

Six daily buses, plus regular louages, run west along the road from Medenine to Ksar Jouama and Beni Kheddache. All of them leave from the beginning of avenue Mosbah Jarbou (left off avenue Bourguiba, at the top of the hill by the Agil station). Failing that, you could try hitching from further along the same road.

The bus from Medenine stops briefly after 20km at **KSAR JEDID** (New Ksar); from Medenine, louages and *camionettes* from the Beni Kheddache stop also head to Ksar Jedid, as well as with Ksar Hallouf. Only one storey high, Ksar Jedid was built in 1916 when the security imposed by the French army allowed the mountain tribes to store their grain safely in the plains. This was the first stage in the process of abandonment: within twenty years, the tribes had stopped using *ksour* altogether, keeping their grain in unprotected silos near the fields.

From Ksar Jedid the road climbs the escarpment for 8km – where the view from the top is amazing – to **KSAR JOUAMA** and the modern village of the same name. The *ksar*, dramatically perched on the scarp, with sheer drops on three sides, is just visible to the south of the road on the crest of a steep hill. A path from the road, a little walk back from the bus stop and village shop, leads past a deserted mosque to the bottleneck of the *ksar* and its entrance gate. An inscription gives the date 1177 AH (1763–4 AD), though it may well have been constructed earlier. The Jouama tribe, who founded it, apparently on the ruins of a much older fortified Berber village, were part of the Brega, who moved up here after abandoning their base south of Remada at the end of seventeenth century (see p.479). Decades of disuse have taken their toll – the outer wall is now crumbling and some of the **ghorfas** have collapsed – but it still makes a strong impression. If you've taken an early bus, it's possible to stop off at Ksar Jouama and continue on the next one – if you can attract the driver's attention. Otherwise try hitching, as it's a busy road.

BENI KHEDDACHE is 8km further on, a large village that used to be another mountain *ksar*. British traveller Reginald Rankin (see p.561), who came here in the 1890s, described it as "a sort of Saharan Windsor", with walls 20m high and 90m long and a courtyard covering eighteen thousand square metres. Unfortunately it was demolished by the French just before World War II to make way for a market. However, a few **ghorfas** survive behind the **mosque**, whilst the *ksar* has become a settlement – a village and market centre for the surrounding tribes. Souk day is Thursday.

There are no hotels in Beni Kheddache; the nearest place to sleep is 2km away at Zammour (see below). A kilometre up the Zammour road, and right at the top of a hill, the moderately priced *Restaurant Le Bedouin* has terrace eating and great views (daily 9am–9pm, though best to check in advance; ☎75 637 258). The last bus back to Medenine goes at about 6pm, and there are louages and pick-ups to Medenine and Ksar Hallouf. The piste heading west to Ksar Ghilane (see p.475) is pretty well impassable without 4WD.

Zammour and Ksar Hallouf

Just 2km north of Beni Kheddache (driving west, bear right where the road forks) is **ZAMMOUR**, where a track leads up to a **ksar**. Small and largely ruined, it compensates with great views. Louages and a couple of daily buses connect Zammour with Medenine. There is a "**station touristique**" in Zammour (☎ & ⓕ75 637 196; ❷ including breakfast) where you can sleep in a former cave dwelling, which is cosier than it sounds, with hot showers and hot meals available.

Beyond Zammour, 8km of tarmac and 4km of piste bring you to **KSAR HALLOUF**, a small thirteenth-century *ksar* overlooking a fertile valley. It's worth climbing up for the views of the plain, with Jerba visible in the hazy distance. In the *ksar*, as well as a traditional camel-worked olive press, there's a **hotel**, *Relai Ksar Hallouf* (☎75 637 148, ℗75 637 320; half board ❹), where you can spend the night in a *ghorfa*, equipped with toilets and cold showers. It's a bit rustic, but it's in a beautiful spot and even if you don't want to stay, you could just stop off for a reasonably priced couscous dinner. Overlooking the *ksar* is a strange curiosity: a circular wall, less than a metre high with a gap facing the rising sun. Opposite the gap is a small altar, where candles are burnt and coins left as offerings. Supposedly this is a marabout, but it's actually pagan in origin (cf the shrine of Lalla Mna in Le Kef, p.313). Dust from the altar is used as "medicine" against illness, and the shrine is in regular use, though there's a mosque below it, disused and in ruins.

Camionettes run a shuttle service to Beni Kheddache and Medenine. The partly unsurfaced road from Zammour to Hallouf is passable in a regular car, as is the road to Behayra and Ksar Jedid, of which the first 4km is also unsurfaced.

Beni Kheddache to Ksar Hadada

The road south over the plateau from just outside Beni Kheddache heads towards Tataouine via Ksar Hadada and Ghoumrassen, winding across the hillocky **plateau** of the Jebel Haouaia, through dense plantations of olive and figs that use the same *jessour* technology as in the Matmata (see p.406). General Jamais, commanding a punitive expedition into the region in 1883, called it "a true paradise in the desolation of the south", and the contrast with the desert plains is, indeed, staggering.

The plateau is the home of the **Haouaia** (also spelt Khawaya), intractable enemies of the French. Part of the Ouerghamma confederation (see box, p.460), they are one of the few communities who still practise transhumance, the seasonal movement from pastures in the desert to the coastal plain. In the winter months they camp in the plain or in the **Dahar** – the arid plateau to the west of the mountains – returning to their fields in summer for the fig and olive harvests. Since the early twentieth century, however, the Haouaia have abandoned their *ksour* and now live in scattered houses and cave dwellings among their fields.

One of the most impressive of the old *ksour*, **KERACHFA**, dating from the fifteenth or sixteenth century, can be reached along a turning (surfaced) to the east 10km down the road from Beni Kheddache. The **ksar** is a ruin of startlingly Gothic appearance on a spur overlooking the plain. Most of the *ghorfas* have collapsed, but outside the main gate is a fitfully used **underground mosque**. Follow a path around the spur and you come to two abandoned **oil presses**, still in good repair.

Eleven kilometres south of the turn-off to Ksar Kerachfa, and just south of a pillar marking the boundary between the administrative regions of Medenine and Tataouine, life-size mother and baby **iguanadon dinosaurs** by sculptor Abdelaziz Krid overlook the road from an outcrop of rock dating back to the Cretaceous period (144–68 million years ago). There is a parking place below the dinosaur sculptures where you can stop, and a path up to get a closer look. Iguanadon was one of the most successful dinosaur species, and also one of the first to be discovered, back in 1825. A herbivore that probably lived in herds, it was around 9m from head to tail, and usually moved on all fours, though it could rear up to reach food or defend against predators. Iguanadon remains were discovered a few kilometres north of here, near Beni Kheddache, by French palaeontologist Albert de Lapparent in 1951.

Continuing south on the main road, you pass over the plateau and eventually sight the white minaret and silver dome belonging to the mosque of **KSAR HADADA** (sometimes called Ghoumrassen Hadada). The *ksar* here is no longer used for grain storage; half of it was used for a time as a hotel, and then as the set for the Mos Espa slave quarters in the *Star Wars* prequel, *The Phantom Menace*. Restoration is in train, but it isn't being done very well, and in the part that was tarted up to be a hotel, the cement used for the refacing is already falling away. None of the *Star Wars* film set remains.

The only **public transport** from here is by bus or louage to Ghoumrassen, from where there are buses to Tataouine and Medenine.

Ghoumrassen and south to Tataouine

Squeezed into a sharp-sided valley, **GHOUMRASSEN**, 5km south of Ksar Hadada, is an ancient settlement built around a craggy mountain. French officers found traces of a Roman fort nearby, with inscriptions now lost in a museum somewhere. In the fourteenth century the historian El Tijani, accompanying the Hafsid ruler of Tunis on the hajj, stopped at Ghoumrassen for three months. He encountered a community at war with its Arab neighbours, living in caverns within the rock in the shelter of a fortress, the **Kala'a Hamdoun**.

The *kala'a* has now gone, its site marked only by a few pieces of wall at the top of the spur overlooking the main part of the town, next to the white **tomb** of the marabout Sidi Moussa Ben Abdallah (the near-legendary figure who united the Ouerghamma; see box below), the texture of its walls reminiscent of

The Ouerghamma confederation

The Hilalian invasion by Arab tribes from Egypt in the mid-eleventh century displaced the Berber nomads who had occupied the fertile Jefara plain south of Gabès until that time. Driven westwards into the hills, they had to be content with mounting raids on their former territory. In the sixteenth century, a marabout by the name of **Sidi Moussa Ben Abdallah** established a *zaouia* at Ghoumrassen, and managed to unite the local feuding tribes, both Arab and Berber, into a confederation called the **Ouerghamma**, which became a formidable military force, controlling both the mountains and the plain. The security created by the confederation enabled the Ouerghamma, a century later, and on the advice of another marabout, **Sidi el Assaibi**, to build a new capital in the middle of the plain at Medenine.

Of all the Ouerghamma tribes, the most feared were the **Ouderna**, based in the Jebel Abiadh south of Tataouine. A 1916 report by British military intelligence claimed that the bey's army "dreaded" the Ouderna, and indeed as late as 1875, the Ouderna defeated a beylical army and seized two cannons from it. By 1883, however, along with most of the Ouerghamma, they had submitted to **French rule**. Nonetheless, a number of rebels from the Khezzour and Touazin tribes fled to Libya, from where they launched raids for some time before the French were able to secure the border.

During World War I, when both France and Italy were ranged against the Ottoman empire, the Ouderna again attempted an uprising against French rule, hoping to join with Berber rebels who had all but ousted the Italians from northwestern Libya, and to return both Libya and Tunisia to Ottoman rule. The Allied victory and the destruction of the Ottoman empire put paid to those plans for good.

melted candle-wax. A path cut into the mountain leads up to them. The craggy ridge running eastward from the marabout is marked by natural rock bridges.

Below, the **cave dwellings**, or *ghar*, remain, cut into the softer strata at the base of the spur. Most consist of a single room, a cooking area near the front and a raised living quarter behind, but some of the larger *ghar* have several rooms separated by massive pillars of stone. A walled courtyard called a *houch* at the front provides a private living area; the outer wall is usually a raised *ghorfa* used for storage. Few families now live in the *ghar*, as they are considered dangerous due to frequent rock falls from the cliff onto courtyards below. As you wander round you can see the devastation these have caused, so do take care.

Each of the five spurs on the northern side of the mountain shelters a separate part of the community, with another group living at Ksar Hadada. These have long been at odds and, during the French occupation, when they were brought under the command of a single sheikh, there was frequent fighting. With the construction of the new town in the valley in the 1890s, however, the community was linked together and peace finally achieved.

A one-storey *ksar*, **Ksar Rosfa**, dating to the early part of the last century, is marked by a huge telecommunications aerial on the hill south of town. It can be reached from the main Tataouine road by the "Ghoumrassen 4km/Tataouine 21km" marker, or from the town centre by taking the street between nos. 277 and 279, and then the fourth right after the *oued*. The main reason for making the fifteen-minute climb is not the *ksar* itself, but the great view it gives over the whole of Ghoumrassen. Immediately below it, houses built against the mountainside are in fact extensions of original cave dwellings which now make up the back room, opening onto the patio of the house.

Ghoumrassen is also the site of the northernmost prehistoric **cave paintings** in Africa, which are 5000–10,000 years old. Unfortunately, most are well worn by weather and vandalism, and hard to find, or even to make out when you do. One site is just at the western end of town, where the road to Ksar Ferech and Tataouine meets the road to Ksar Hadada and Beni Kheddache; the cave paintings are on the south side of the road, just east of the junction, behind a green metal barrier, in reddish-brown paint on the white rock, and very faded. There are some others better preserved, but you would really need a guide to find them – if you are interested, inquire at the Memory of the Earth Museum in Tataouine (see p.466), or at the Association des Amis de la Memoire de la Terre (T75 860 540), as the cave paintings feature in their Memory of the Earth tour.

A track leading north from the eastern end of town, motorable with care, leads after a kilometre or so to **KSAR BENI GHEDIR**, a one-storey plains *ksar* like Ksar Rosfa and Ksar Jedid. Restored in 2000, this ksar features a traditional oil press, complete with decorations in the plasterwork on the inside of the arches, featuring a Koranic inscription, spots representing rain, and symbols against the evil eye such as pentagram stars, hands, and fish. The ksar features on the tour run by the Association des Amis de la Memoire de la Terre, who plan an agricultural implements museum here.

Practicalities

If you don't reach Ghoumrassen via the Jebel Haouaia (see p.457), you can take the direct bus via the GP19 from Medenine, or get a bus or louage from Tataouine. A market town, Ghoumrassen is very lively during the Friday **souk**, which attracts tribespeople from Nefzaoua seeking the region's esteemed olive oil. Most of the town's shops are on the long main street. There are lots of **cafés** and **patisseries** selling the Ghoumrassen speciality, *ftair* (doughnuts), but

Moving on from Ghoumrassen

For a list of destinations and journey times, see Travel details on p.481.
The most direct route to Medenine and Tataouine commences at the eastern end of the main street. Roads to Guermessa, Tataouine via Ksar el Ferech, and Beni Kheddache via Ksar Hadada branch off at the other end of town. The **bus station** (☎75 869 031), a block south of the main street between nos. 41 and 43, has services to Ksar Hadada, Medenine and Tataouine. On schooldays, there are 6am, 5pm and 6pm buses to Guermessa and Ksar Mourabtine. **Louages** leave from the main street near the bus station (between nos. 45 and 119). **Hitching** to Guermessa shouldn't be too much of a problem: the tarmac road there branches off the main Tataouine road just out of town.

no hotels. If you need a **bank**, however, you'll find two, plus a Grand Magasin **supermarket**, and a **post office** (country hours).

Ghoumrassen to Tataouine

The more direct route of the two routes to Tataouine from Ghoumrassen heads east out of town. A turn-off after 8km leads to **Ksar Mourabtine**, 4km off the main road and accessible by bus (2 daily; school days only). The small *ksar* here, built in 1800 and abandoned in 1973, is largely intact, with up to four storeys of *ghorfas* standing on a crag overlooking the village. Outside the entrance is the mosque, with a number of abandoned oil presses round to its left. The path up to the *ksar* climbs through the village burial ground and past a number of abandoned *ghar* in the crag, and many of the stones here include fossils of sea animals from the Jurassic period, when this area was underwater. From the top, you can see as far as Guermessa and Chenini to the southwest. Though well off the beaten track, this *ksar* is definitely worth a visit if you have the means to get here, and also features on the Memory of the Earth tour (see p.467).

Via Ksar el Ferich

At the western end of Ghoumrassen is the junction where the Ksar Hadada and Guermessa roads meet, and the start of more scenic route to Tataouine. This heads southward, passing after 8km the large but unimpressive **KSAR EL FERECH**, built in 1911, whose two storeys of *ghorfas* lie flat on the plain. Like Ksar Jedid (see p.458), it's another example of the post-colonial *ksour*, and far less imposing than the mountain-top *ksour* of yore. There's a pretty marabout and oil press just outside the entrance, and inside the *ksar*, a café and moderately priced restaurant (advance orders only; ☎98 212 627), where you can stop for a break, and even take a ride around the *ksar* on a camel. It is possible to camp here and even stay in a *ghorfa* – contact the café for details. The *ksar* lies 1500m north of the modern village of Ferech.

Half a kilometre south of the "Ghoumrassen 10km/Tataouine 15km" marker, the unexcavated remains of **Dakyanus**, a Roman fort, lie 200m east of the road, but all that can be seen are few blocks of stone, and a mound showing the fort's outline. Holes in the ground here are the burrows of jerboas, hunted by the jackals and foxes which, like their prey, tend to come out only at night. A little way south, and a couple of kilometres before the Chenini turn-off, the *Hôtel Dakyanus* (☎75 832 199, ☞75 832 198, ☒www.dakyanushotel.com; 6x), with cool rooms and a 25-metre pool (summer only), offers a cheaper but less stylish alternative to the *Sangho*, 7km further down the road (see p.466).

Overlooking the road at the Chenini turn-off are two **bunkers** in the hillside, dating from the 1930s and built at the same time as the Mareth Line (see p.411) to defend the route north against a possible Italian invasion. The road to Tataouine continues past the Memory of the Earth Museum (see p.466) to meet the Remada road at place de la Memoire de la Terre, 2km south of town.

Guermessa

The traditional Berber village of **GUERMESSA**, 8km southwest of Ghoum-rassen, sees far fewer tourists than its sister villages of Chenini and Douiret to the south, with which it has much in common (see p.472), perhaps because it was rather difficult to reach until recently. Even now, despite surfaced roads from Tataouine and Ghoumrassen, and the three daily school **buses** to Ghou-mrassen, it's not exactly well connected and has few facilities.

According to legend, Guermessa was founded following the arrival in the region of two holy men, Sidi Ibrahim, son of a marabout from Kairouan, and Sidi Bando, his slave. When they asked for water to wash before praying, the local residents shame-facedly had to admit that they didn't have enough, whereupon the heavens opened up and a downpour ensued, a sign that led Ibrahim and Bando to remain here preaching the Koran. Sidi Ibrahim's *zaouia* (tomb) stands below the original village, long abandoned and now just a ruin. The village that superseded it grew up around the *zaouia* of Ibrahim's son, Sidi Hamza, built around a spur with a ruined **kala'a** on its peak. A distinctive paved **pathway** leads up to it from the valley below, no mean engineering achieve-ment considering the size of the slabs. Although the village is still inhabited, the construction of a new village in the plains is gradually drawing families away, and within a decade or so it too will most likely face abandonment.

The flat-topped hill above the village, **Ras el Metmana**, is the scene of a unique ritual in the wedding celebrations of Guermessi men. Before the wed-ding itself, the groom comes up here with his friends to stamp his footprint into the ground as a mark of farewell to bachelorhood.

Tataouine (Foum Tataouine)

FOUM TATAOUINE – meaning "the mouth of the springs" – evokes an image of the desert outpost, a palm oasis surrounded by drifting sand. *Star Wars* fans on the other hand may remember it as the name of Luke Skywalker's home planet, the film having been largely shot in the south of Tunisia (see box, p.364). Either way, the reality is rather different, for the town is new, busy and drab, built by the French administrators on a site some 50km south of Mede-nine that had previously been just a caravan halt with a spring. The French decided it was a good site for a military base, administrative centre and souk, and moved their government offices here from Douiret in 1890, that same year beginning construction of the marketplace, which opened for business in 1892. Within a few years, market traders were building homes here, and the town's first mosque (on the Medenine road, next to the *Hôtel Jawhara*) was opened to meet their spiritual needs in 1898. At the beginning of the twentieth century, the French had great expectations of the market as a focus of Saharan trade. It was not to be, as trade had already dwindled and what was left passed through Tripoli, where ivory and gold could be sold openly.

Tataouine has a certain inexplicable charm – don't be surprised if you find yourself making excuses to delay leaving. Though the town has little of historic interest in itself, some of the most impressive sites in Tunisia lie within a radius of 25km. To the north and west, you could fill a week or more seeing places such as Ghoumrassen, Guermessa, Ksar Hadada, Chenini and Douiret, while to the south are the well-preserved *ksour* of the Jebel Abiadh, which can be explored as a loop starting and finishing at Tataouine. Public transport to these places is sparse, but scooters and bicycles can now be rented in town.

Arrival and information

Tataouine's main street, **avenue Bourguiba**, is a continuation of the main road from Medenine. **Avenue Ahmed Tlili** splits off from it near the centre of town and heads out toward Remada and most of the *ksour*. Avenue Bourguiba continues through the town centre to meet **avenue Hedi Chaker**, which is the road out to Ezzahra. About halfway between these two junctions stood a statue of Habib Bourguiba, now replaced by a fountain and tableau marking the centre of town. SRT buses arrive at a bus station just 100m up the road from here, at the junction of rue 1 Juin and avenue Ahmed Tlili. SNTRI services from the north, and the bus that meets the overnight train from Tunis to Gabès, will drop you at the new **gare routière**, a kilometre from town on avenue Bourguiba, and about 1TD from the centre by taxi. Most **louages** will bring you to a yard round the corner off rue 2 Mars, unless you're arriving from Ben Gardane, in which case you'll be dropped on rue 18 Janvier by *Hôtel de la Station*, or from Remada, in which case you will end up on rue 1 Juin by the tableau.

Tataouine has two **tourist offices**: the ONTT, on avenue Bourguiba just east of the tableau (July & Aug daily 7.30am–1.30pm & 5–7pm; Sept–June Mon–Thurs 8.30am–1.30pm & 3–5.45pm, Fri & Sat 8.30am–1pm; ☎75 850 686),

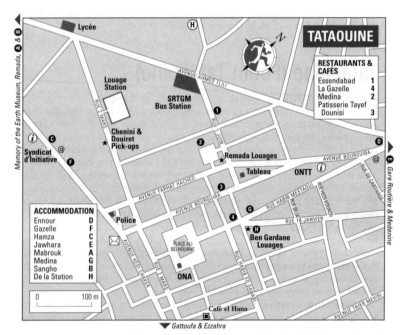

For a list of destinations and journey times, see Travel details on p.481.

SNTRI departures leave from the *gare routière* (☎75 862 138). There are three daily **buses** for Tunis – a morning and an evening service via Sfax and Sousse, and an evening service via Kairouan, plus a bus to Gabès that connects with the overnight train to Tunis. Buses operated by SRTG Medenine run from the bus station at avenue Ahmed Tlili (☎75 860 031). **Local buses** from here to Chenini, Ezzahra, Ksar Ouled Debbab and Ksar Ouled Soltane are not frequent.

Most **louages** operate out of the yard on rue 2 Mars (☎75 862 874), except for those to Ben Gardane, which leave from just by the *Hôtel de la Station*, and those for Remada, which leave from rue 1 Juin by the tableau.

Functioning like louages, **camionettes** and Peugeots head out to villages around the region, taking eight passengers instead of five, for around 1TD a place. They are most plentiful before midday, so set out early. For Chenini, Douiret, Maztouria and Ksar Ouled Soltane, they leave from rue 2 Mars, just north of avenue Farhat Hached. For Gattoufa and Ezzahra, they leave from in front of the *Café el Hana*, three blocks south of place Ali Belhouane.

A group of up to four people may be able to negotiate a deal with a **taxi** to one or more of the local *ksour* and Berber villages, so long as the driver is licensed to operate in the area you want to visit, or is otherwise prepared to risk problems with the police for taking you there. Taxis can usually be found in place 18 Janvier (where rue 18 Janvier meets rue Habib Mestaoui) or on rue 1 Juin. Expect to pay around 6–8TD each way to places such as Chenini, Douiret and Guermessa (plus around 5TD/hr for the driver to wait while you look around).

9

and the much more informative Syndicat d'Initiative on avenue Hedi Chaker (Mon–Thurs 8.30am–1pm & 3–5.45pm, Fri & Sat 8.30am–1pm; Ramadan Mon–Thurs 8am–2pm, Fri & Sat 8.30am–1pm; ☎75 850 850), a couple of hundred metres west of its junction with avenue Bourguiba.

Accommodation

There isn't a huge choice of **accommodation** in Tataouine. The cheap hotels are in town and not all that great. A couple of kilometres south of town however, there is an excellent three-star hotel, the *Sangho*, and the *Mabrouk* next door allows you to pitch a tent or park a camper. You can also camp at the very pleasant *El Borj*, 3km south of town in Rogba, off the Remada road (☎75 851 539; 10TD per car or campervan, 5TD per tent). There's a restaurant and pizzeria on site, plus clean toilets and hot showers.

Hotels

Ennour 107 av Bourguiba ☎75 860 131. A little rudimentary, with basic rooms, but adequate for the price, with two nice terraces, shared showers and toilets, and a café downstairs; ask for a room with an exterior window. ❶

Gazelle av Hedi Chaker ☎75 860 009, ®75 862 860. The top address in the town itself, rather drab but with decent en-suite, a/c rooms. It's best to phone ahead or arrive early, as it's often fully occupied by tour groups. ❹

Hamza av Hedi Chaker ☎75 863 506. The rooms are bright, with clean, shared bathrooms and a/c available for a supplement, but the prices are

steeper than other places in this bracket. The staff's attitude also leaves much to be desired. Rate includes breakfast. ❷

Jawhara 82 av Bourguiba ☎75 860 621. A good-value, friendly cheapie on the Medenine road with large, clean rooms, some en suite (the communal toilets aren't great) and all with ceiling fans. Ask for a second sheet if your bed only has one. Breakfast is available in the café downstairs for very little extra. ❶

Mabrouk rte de Chenini, 2km south of town, just up the Chenini/Ghoumrassen turn-off ☎75 862 805, ®75 850 100. Opposite the Memory of the Earth Museum, this is a lower-priced alternative to the *Sangho*, with smallish a/c rooms. Staff are surly though, and it's not especially recommended for lone female travellers. Camping is possible on the bare plot opposite, and campers can use the hotel's facilities. **❺**

Medina rue Habib Mestaoui ☎75 860 999. Rather run down, though still not bad for the price, with communal bathroom facilities (hot water mornings only) and a great view from the roof terrace. **❶**

Sangho rte de Chenini ☎75 860 102, ℗75 862 177, ℮sangho.tatouine@planet.tn. Just up the Chenini/Ghoumrassen turn-off, 2km south of town.

A cut above the usual three-star traps – very classy, with tasteful bungalow rooms and full facilities including a pool. Public areas have interesting displays of historic photographs, World War II artillery cases, Roman columns and fossils, and there's even a herb garden. **❻**

Hôtel de la Station rue 18 Janvier ☎75 860 104. A ramshackle but longstanding backpacker's favourite, where friendly staff make up for the slightly rudimentary rooms (some of which have their own shower) and sporadic hot water. **❶**

The Town

Tataouine was built as the far south's administrative centre and **garrison town** and the military presence is still strong today – be careful not to incur the wrath of army personnel by climbing the rocks behind the military camps along the Remada road for the view. As late as 1950 the soldiers outnumbered the civilians by three to one. Most of them were members of a penal battalion of the French army and French Foreign Legion, and many were German. Indeed, in the 1930s, German was the town's third language.

Tatouine's modern **marketplace**, off avenue Bourguiba in place Ali Belhouane, is very lively, and it's worth trying to coincide with the souk held on Mondays and Thursdays. The square fills with merchants from all over the south buying sheep in the early summer, olives in the autumn and locally made blankets year-round. Other merchants, mainly from Jerba, sell groceries and plastic knick-knacks. It's always very colourful, with tribespeople coming in from distant villages and nomadic encampments, and pedlars stocking up with the goods they subsequently sell from their camels' backs to people in the remotest communities.

In March the **Festival of the Ksour** enlivens the town in pale imitation of Douz's Saharan Festival, with mock traditional marriages and a rather tame pop concert. Further information can be obtained from the festival committee (☎75 851 833).

The Memory of the Earth Museum

Tatouine's main place of interest is the **Museum of the Memory of the Earth** (daily 9am–7pm; 1.5TD), 2km south of town on the Chenini/Ghoumrassen turn-off. The junction for the turn-off has been rechristened place de la Memoire de la Terre, and is graced with a large sculpture of the globe. Petrified tree trunks stand in among the date palms at the junction's northwest corner, and 200m down the turn-off, a life-size model of a **spinosaurus dinosaur** by sculptor Abdelaziz Krid looms ferociously on the hillside overlooking the road. Spinosaurus was a carnivore of the Cretaceous period whose remains have been discovered in the region.

The museum itself, a silver-roofed building, has displays of fossils, half-size sculptures of an iguanadon and a pterodactyl. There are also explanations of local fossil beds: Tatouine is on an outcrop of rock from the Jurassic period (144–208 million years ago), when it was submerged, and so fossils from that period are of sea animals; the Dahar mountain range to the west however, is made of rock dating from the Cretaceous period (68–144 million years ago), when it was above water, and thus the fossils from here are of land animals such as dinosaurs.

Desert flora and fauna

Predictably, the **stony desert** or *hamada* that covers much of the southeast of Tunisia has a sparse wildlife population, but the sand desert in the southwest has even less. Neither habitat owes very much to Mediterranean influence, with the huge Sahara to the south dominating the ecosystem. **Plants** are thin on the ground, but the wonder is that they can survive at all. They do this by special adaptation, their leaves often reduced to thin strips to reduce water loss to a minimum. Another strategy evolved by some plants is to have swollen leaves which can store water; cacti are best known for this, but many other plants do it too.

The small **desert mammals** are almost entirely nocturnal, feeding on plants and seeds in the cool of the night. The big ears of the **jerboas** are not just for acute hearing – they may also serve a temperature control function in the same way as an elephant's ears do. On the other hand, **lizards** are mostly active by day – though they're hard to see since they have a surprising turn of speed.

Birds fall into two groups – those that concentrate around the oases, and the true desert dwellers that live out in the inhospitable wastes. In the oases themselves **palm doves** have their "home" habitat, and they've spread to the rest of Tunisia's towns in much the same way as the collared dove has done in northern Europe. If you're truly devoted, rubbish tips are worth exploring for scavenging ravens. Out in the desert and away from the villages and oases, you'll come across many of the steppe birds – larks, wheatears, cream-coloured coursers, shrikes and so on. Lurk around any area of oasis water in the early morning and the reward may be a flock of fast-flying **sandgrouse** coming in to drink.

Tataouine is a good base for seeing desert wildlife, with the full range of species. The Tataouine region was the last part of the country where ostriches were found in the wild, though any sighting today of a large long-legged bird with a black and white neck is likely to be the **Houbara bustard** – a rare and endangered species, endangered all the more in Tunisia by visiting parties of Saudi princes whose sole aim is to hunt the bird. Traditionally this is done with falcons, but the Saudis are not above using guns if that proves easier. The meat of the Houbara bustard is supposedly an aphrodisiac, which makes it much prized in certain quarters, and it is the traditional prey of Saudi falconry. Saudis come to Tunisia and other North African countries to hunt the Houbara bustard because they have driven it to near extinction on the Arabian peninsula.

The museum is run by a local association called L'Association des Amis de la Memoire de la Terre, who offer a **Memory of the Earth tour** of the area, visiting Ksar Mourabtine (see p.462), Ksar Beni Ghedir (see p.461), Ghoumrassen's prehistoric cave paintings (see p.461), Guermessa (see p.463) and two fossil sites. The tour costs 20TD per person not including transport – if you don't have your own, the museum can arrange it for you. For further details or to arrange a tour, ask at the museum, call ☎75 850 244 or e-mail Ⓔmemoireterre@yahoo.fr.

Nearby ksour

Within walking distance just to the south of town are some interesting *ksour*. **Ksar Megabla** is the easiest to reach from Tataouine: just head down the Remada road for about 1km, then turn right (alongside a little park), cross the *oued* and continue along the surfaced road towards the mosque straight ahead. The *ksar*, originally put up in 1408 or 1409, is well preserved, with three-storey *ghorfas* and the remains of storage racks and broken pottery, but children here may harass visiting tourists with demands for money or pens, and have been known to turn nasty if refused. There's another *ksar* on a hill to the left of the Remada road, opposite the turn-off – one of a number called **Ksar**

Deghaghora – but it overlooks a military camp and you're not welcome up there, especially with a camera. A third *ksar* within walking distance of town is **Ksar Gurga** (see opposite).

Eating and drinking

When it comes to **food** in Tataouine, you're not exactly spoilt for choice. The best cheap place in town is the *Restaurant Essendabad*, just across rue 1 Juin from the bus station (Mon–Sat noon–3pm & 5.30–8.30pm), with passable fish soup and lamb chops, though the chicken and chips is liable to arrive luke-warm. Another cheap place, serving similar staples, though not as good, is the *Restaurant Medina* (Mon–Thurs & Sun 8am–8pm), in a little square off avenue Farhat Hached and rue 1 Juin, where you can eat outside. The *Hôtel Gazelle's* moderately priced restaurant (daily noon–3pm & 5.30–8.30pm) is slightly more upmarket and serves treats like chicken chasseur and chocolate mousse, as well as being the only place where in town you can get a **beer**. For anything posher, you'll have to trek down to the *Sangho* hotel where you have the choice of à la carte restaurant or a rather pricier buffet, with more moderately priced wood oven pizzas in summer.

The café at the *Hôtel de la Station* serves freshly squeezed orange and carrot juice. A Tataouine speciality, now common all over the country, is the **kab el ghezal**, or *corne de gazelle*, a sweet pastry horn filled with honey and nuts. *Cornes de gazelle* are available at any patisserie in town, but were in fact invented by Tayef Dounisi, whose patisserie is at 62 avenue Bourguiba, although better ones can be had at *La Gazelle* opposite the *Hôtel de la Station*.

Listings

Banks There are several banks in town, mostly on av Farhat Hached and av Bourguiba. ATMs can be found at the Banque du Sud at the western end of av Bourguiba, and Banque de l'Habitat on the same street opposite the end of rue Habib ed Dababi.

Hammam The most convenient hammam is down a side street by the Mobil garage, opposite the bus station – bear left after 20m and it's at the end of the street (daily: men 4am–8pm men, women 6am–5pm women).

Hospitals and clinics The hospital is 9km north of town, at the Ghoumrassen turn-off from the Medenine road (☏75 870 114). There's a nighttime emergency medical service (☏75 862 004) behind the Garde Nationale office, opposite the *Hôtel Gazelle*, and in the same location you'll find the surgery of local GP Dr Lassoued (☏75 860 638). Dr Dr Habib Belhedi in rue Habib Ghandour is the local dentist (☏75 860 540).

Internet access The best office is Kssournette on av Bourguiba (daily 8am–midnight; 1.8TD/hr),

nearly opposite *Hôtel Ennour*. Cheaper but not well run is LM Net Service, between the hotels *Gazelle* and *Hamza* on av Hedi Chaker (daily 8am–midnight).

ONA crafts shop In the southwest corner of pl Ali Belhouane.

Pharmacy There's a night pharmacy on the corner of rue Habib Mestaoui and rue de Carthage.

Police The main station is at pl des Martyrs (☏75 860 814).

Post office On avenue Hedi Chaker opposite the western end of av Bourguiba (city hours), but closed for renovation at the time of writing, with a temporary post office on av Bourguiba 500m east of the junction with av Ahmed Tlili.

Supermarket El Fawz, by the market in pl Ali Belhouane.

Swimming pool The well-run municipal pool is some way from the centre, 500m up the Ben Gardane road on the northeastern edge of town (daily except Mon 10am–noon & 1–6pm).

The Maztouria loop

To the east and south of Tataouine stretches the mountain range of **Jebel Abiadh** ("White Mountains"), home of the **Ouderna** tribe – the most powerful in the south and part of the Ouerghamma confederation (see p.460) – and of several smaller Berber communities. Though *ksour* and villages litter the mountains, the sites aren't as dramatic as Douiret and Chenini, to the west of Tataouine (see pp.474 and 473); even so, they're still pretty impressive, and have the great advantage of being free of tourist parties.

The Berbers living in these mountains lacked the independence enjoyed by the larger communities at Douiret, Chenini and Guermessa, and most shared their village with semi-nomadic groups who claimed Arab origins, or else the village was closely linked to a neighbouring nomadic tribe's *ksar*. Some French anthropologists – ever eager to find and stir up differences between Arab and Berber – maintained that the Ouderna, the dominant tribe, had Berber serfs who paid them olives, figs and wool in return for "protection". It was, they claimed, "a veritable slavery such that the Ouderna can spill the blood of his Berber client without fear of the law". In reality there were bonds between the supposedly Arab nomads and the sedentary Berber villagers, but these represented an exchange of services: in return for agricultural produce the nomads guarded the herds of their sedentary neighbours, who thus gained access to widely dispersed pastures without the trouble of a lifestyle on the move.

Tarmac reaches all the way round from Tataouine through the villages of **Maztouria**, **Tamelest**, **Gattoufa** and back, and the *ksour* here can be visited in a 48-kilometre loop from Tataouine. It's too far to cycle in a day, with a lot of climbing in the hot sun, but certainly possible by car, visiting – if you've a mind to – every single *ksar* en route. You could also negotiate a deal with a taxi, especially if there's a group of you. Though *camionettes* and even buses get as far as Ksar Ouled Soltane in one direction (3 buses daily), and Ezzahra in the other (2 daily), they don't as yet link, with 10km in between that you would have to hitch or walk; there is little to see on this stretch in any case. The Maztouria loop is described here from Tataouine to Ksar Ouled Soltane, then to Ezzahra and back to Tataouine, but you may of course wish to do all or part of it the other way round.

Beni Barka

A kilometre south of Tataouine, where the *oued* crosses the Remada road just south of Ksar Deghaghora (see opposite), a paved road to the east signposted "Beni Barka" takes you up into the Jebel Abiadh proper. This road passes a large number of *ksour* in varying states of repair, though you'd need to be a serious enthusiast to want to visit all of them. The first is the deserted **Ksar Gurga**, on your right after 1km and still within walking distance of Tataouine.

After another 4km, you'll see the village of **BENI BARKA** on your right, pitched atop the escarpment as you approach along the valley floor. Alight here to walk up the steep track to the top. Beni Barka was formerly an important market, the centre of a thriving Berber community linked to the Arabs of Ksar Ouled Debbab, but most of it is now in ruins. Even so, the **entrance gate**, dating from the fourteenth century or earlier, is spectacular, standing on the edge of the cliff and offering good views across the plain. The village has been deserted in favour of the many new cave dwellings in the surrounding slopes, some of them excavated 8m into the rock. As you walk up to the old village, look out for ripple marks in the rocks and fossils of ammonites and other sea molluscs, proof that this area has not always been desert.

Maztouria and Tamelest

South of Beni Barka, the road passes a number of desolate *ksour*. **Ksar Zoltane** is up on the west side of the road, about 1km south of Beni Barka. A couple of kilometres further south, a road branching off eastward brings you after 5km to the small, circular **Ksar Tounket**. Meanwhile, 7km south of Beni Barka is the new village of **MAZTOURIA**, around 20km southeast of Tataouine, where many of the surrounding people have settled near a spring.

As you enter Maztouria, you pass more abandoned *ksour* up to the west of the road – a rough but passable track leads up to them from just south of the Ksar Tounket turn-off. The first, round and compact, is **Ksar Ouled Aoun**. It is followed by three rectangular *ksour*, starting with **Ksar Aouadid**, now largely restored, whose massive stone walls are highly impressive, giving it the look of a fortress. Large iron-clad doors guard the entrance, whose archway still bears part of its original eleventh-century inscription. Next is **Ksar Kedim** (or Ksar Zenetes), also on the right overlooking Maztouria, which has been very carefully restored. According to the inscription inside the arch of its huge gateway, it was built in 1072 AD, shortly after the Hilalian invasion. Built as a place of residence rather than a grain store, it predates all the other *ksour* by some six centuries, hence its name – *kedim* meaning "old". It is usually ascribed to the Zenetes, the ancestors of the region's Berber tribes. Inside, part of the decoration is intact on some of the *ghorfas*' doorways and there is an underground **well** reached by a tunnel. The next *ksar* is **Ksar Dahar** (also known as Ksar Deghaghora), entered through a strange tunnel-like gateway, and accessible via a track leading up from the main road in the middle of the village.

Six kilometres south of Maztouria is the village of **TAMELEST**, also built to settle the region's nomads. Overlooking the village is the *ksar* of the same name, the thirteenth-century granary of the **Ouled Chehida**, the Ouderna's most powerful group. In 1915 their sheikh led the only full-scale tribal revolt against the French. Although the Ouderna managed to overwhelm the telegraph stations in the south, the French garrisons held out, and within a month the tribespeople were defeated by a column from the north and forced into Libya as refugees. Much of the damage done to this *ksar*, and others in the Jebel Abiadh, dates from this period.

Ksar Ouled Soltane

The road splits 2km beyond Tamelest. **Ksar Sedra**, with a number of cave dwellings in the rock beneath it, overlooks the right fork; the left leads to **KSAR OULED SOLTANE**, 3km away and (along with Ezzahra) one of the best-preserved *ksour* in the south, its *ghorfas* now refaced to their original state, though with cement rather than the original materials. Ksar Ouled Soltane was built by the Ouled Chehida (of whom the Ouled Soltane are descendants) on low land where it can be seen for miles around, a tribute to their confidence in troubled times. To get to the entrance, walk around the top of the hill, past the mosque and next to the shops and **café**. The two courtyards inside date from the fifteenth and the nineteenth centuries respectively and are connected by a passage made from palm wood. *Ghorfas* rise four storeys high and are still used to store grain and olives. On Friday afternoons the courtyards function as meeting places for the community, the majority of whom spend most of the year in the pastures with their herds of sheep, goats and camels. Thus, not only is the *ksar* intact but so is the way of life that goes with it. The explanation for this, unique in the south, lies in the Ouled Chehida's reluctance to migrate to the cities, along with the *ksar's* continued isolation from tourism. It's a community with a strong identity and a traditional lifestyle, one of the few left in Tunisia.

Two and a half kilometres beyond Ouled Soltane, at **Mghit**, the road forks: bear right for Ezzahra. Three kilometres further, or 5km from Ezzahra, a track branches off southward to **Ksar Grimissa**.

Ezzahra

The *ksar* at **EZZAHRA**, 21km south of Tataouine via Gattoufa, is almost a twin to Ksar Ouled Soltane. Like Ouled Soltane, it consists of two courtyards, both very well preserved, and it is still a meeting place where the community come on Fridays to pray. Thus Friday afternoons here, as at Ouled Soltane, have the feel of a sabbath (though the Muslim Friday is not really a sabbath in the Christian sense). The first and more recent of the *ksar's* two courtyards is the one used as a meeting place, and one of the *ghorfas* functions as a grocery store, but the second courtyard is much more impressive, with up to four storeys of *ghorfas*. Ezzahra can be reached by *camionette* from *Café el Hana* in Tataouine, and twice daily from Tataouine by bus.

Four kilometres north of Ezzahra, a track to the east of the road leads 3km (the last part very rocky, but motorable with care) to **Ksar Beni Yakzer**. Tall, imposing and built partly into the side of a rocky crag next to two small marabouts, Beni Yazker looks like the setting for a ghost story, and is actually a lot more impressive from the outside than within, being largely ruined. Beneath it, more *ghorfas* are built into the rock.

Gattoufa and Beni Blel

The villages of Gattoufa and Beni Blel stand next to each other, 10km south of Tataouine and 11km north of Ezzahra. Between them, a road branches off to **Beni Mhira**, 23km distant and host to an annual festival of traditional games in early March (it is Beni Mhira rather than Gattoufa or Ezzahra that is signed from Tataouine in this direction). The *ksar* at **Beni Blel**, adjoining the village mosque, is not in a marvellous state of repair, though it does reach up to four storeys high, but **GATTOUFA**, less than 1km north, has two rather more interesting *ksour*. The smaller and more recent of the two, **Ksar Gattoufa**, stands at the southern end of the village and, though only two storeys high, is in a good state and still partly in use, with a water cistern in the centre. The other, **Ksar Jellidet**, at the northern end of the village by the post office and the mosque, is derelict but not too ruined, with *ghorfas* up to three storeys high. *Camionettes* stop in front of Ksar Gattoufa, and there is a café opposite. Gattoufa is linked to Tataouine by a road that twists and writhes, with lovely scenery all the way.

Chenini and Douiret

The region's most famous attractions, the troglodyte Berber villages of **Chenini**, **Douiret** and **Guermessa** (the last of these is covered on p.463) are all startlingly alike, each with its *kala'a* and ruined village atop a craggy hill, counterbalanced by a white mosque, with a new village beneath. Where they differ chiefly is in their accessibility, and the number of visitors they receive, but they do also have slightly different sights to offer. Chenini is the village that receives the most visitors (eager would-be guides wait to greet you), while Douiret is much less visited – in particular by tourist buses – and is consequently much more laid-back, Guermessa even more so. Douiret is also the only one of the three with accommodation, and will undoubtedly be the most rewarding to visit when its museum opens.

Life in the Berber villages of Ghoumrassen, Guermessa, Chenini and Douiret has traditionally revolved around **agriculture**. Considerable effort was put into the construction of *jessour* (agricultural terraces; see p.406) and cisterns so that trees can be planted in the arid landscape. Although sheep and goats were once raised here, too, they were a small part of the economy and the villagers never participated in the transhumance of their nomad neighbours.

One solution to the poverty of the region was **emigration**. Young men would go to work in the city for a few years and then return to their village, spending the money they had saved on a bride price or a new *jessour*. Emigrants from each village had a specialist profession: the Douiri and Guermessi worked as vegetable market porters, the Ghoumrassini sold doughnuts, and the Chenini newspapers. Today, however, the young men go further afield, often to France and Libya, stay away longer and marry outside the community. Many do not return. As you look round the villages, you'll notice that women vastly outnumber men, most of whom are old – evidence that emigration is killing the community. This is doubly sad, since these villages represent the last of the region's Berber culture.

Berber was the predominant **language** in Tunisia under the Romans, but after the Arab conquest it was quickly overtaken by Arabic – the language of the new religion, of law and government. Berber only survived in the communities of the south, and here too it was in gradual decline. By the end of the nineteenth century Berber was only spoken as a first language in Douiret, Chenini and Guermessa and, with the French occupation, the extension of government to the south and the imposition of Islamic law, Arabic finally made inroads here, too. However, migration and the consequent dispersal of the Berber population was the death-blow. Now, only older people in Chenini and Douiret speak the language. Young people can understand it, but their children probably won't. In Guermessa, nobody now speaks Berber. This continuing decline of the Berber language in Tunisia contrasts sharply with the revival of Berber languages in Morocco (where Berber is now taught in schools, and Berber-language programmes shown on television), and with the militancy of Berbers in Algeria to defend their culture against this sort of erosion.

This process of Arabization continued during the **colonial period** despite the efforts of the French to separate the Berbers from their Arab neighbours. French anthropologists claimed that they were in fact Europeans who had migrated to North Africa at an early date. While the Arabs were caricatured as lazy, sly and tyrannical, the Berbers were supposedly industrious, honest and democratic (all considered evidence of their purported European origins), and for these reasons worthy of a privileged place in Tunisian society. In reality of course, the French were attempting to divide and rule, and the Berbers, on the whole, refused to play the game. While accepting many of the privileges offered by the government, including an independent administration and large tracts of Arab land, they remained just as hostile to the French as their Arab neighbours.

Chenini

Most people approach the ruggedly scenic **CHENINI** along the paved road directly from Tataouine, 20km away. You can squeeze into a *camionette* from rue 2 Mars in Tataouine, take a taxi (around 20TD return including waiting time, but you may have to haggle) or hitch, which is easiest on market days (Mon & Thurs) when trucks return to Chenini at noon.

Intensely dramatic in its size and desolation, Chenini is best seen from a distance, each row of dwellings clinging to the steep mountainside and fronted by *ghorfas*. Reginald Rankin, travelling in the 1890s, was mightily impressed:

473

△ Ksar Ouled Soltane

"I have seen nearly all the so-called wonders of the world and unhesitatingly say that the cave dwellings of the Saharan troglodytes seem to me the most wonderful thing of all." An inscription in one of the *ghorfas* gives the date 590 AH (1194–5 AD), but the village is certainly older than that.

As at Ghoumrassen, the **ghar** are mostly inhabited and are dug into soft strata on the slopes below the fortress. Several levels of cave dwellings form bands around the spur that are joined by steep walkways. You can visit a working camel-drawn **oil press**, an underground communal bakery, and even enter some of the houses, but you'll usually be charged, so fix a price before you enter. This is increasingly a problem, as Chenini has suffered from overexposure to parties of tourists, most of whom arrive in the morning. If you want the place more to yourself, go later in the day.

While Chenini itself is something special, the views from here are also quite outstanding. For a leisurely **walk** with brilliant vistas, follow the path up from the mosque in the village, along the hillside above the underground mosque (see below), down to a spring where the villagers collect water.

Even older than the village around the *kala'a* is an abandoned village a kilometre along the escarpment. Here only the **Jemaa Kedima**, an underground mosque, survives. Below the leaning minaret are two interconnected rooms, one housing the **tomb** of a marabout, the other those of the **Seven Sleepers**. According to folk legend – quite a common one in the region – seven Christians were imprisoned in this underground hiding place during the Roman occupation. Four centuries later, when their cell was opened, they awoke as if they had been asleep. All that time, however, their bodies had continued to grow, so that they were now just under 4m tall. Only when they had been converted to Islam did they die, their bodies buried here in these long tombs.

Chenini has a **post office** and a **restaurant** run by Tataouine's *Hôtel Mabrouk* (daily 7am–3pm), serving couscous, *gargoulette* and *mechoui*, mainly to tour groups. The very rough back route to Guermessa leaves the Tataouine road 6km back from Chenini, and is just about passable in a car if you go slowly, though a 4WD vehicle is preferable. The road to Douiret is surfaced, but for the intrepid, there's an eight-kilometre footpath over the mountain, although it's not easy to follow – enlisting the help of a guide might be a wise idea.

Douiret

The turning for Douiret is off the Remada road, 8km south of Tataouine at **Ksar Ouled Debbab**. Now abandoned, though used for a time as a hotel, Ouled Debbab is the largest *ksar* of the tribe of the same name. Although some members of the tribe claim an exotic Arab Hilalian line of descent, they probably share the indigenous origins of **DOUIRET**, 20km down the road, utterly Berber and immediately impressive, though unlike at Chenini, the **ghar** here, inhabited by 3500 people in 1850, are now mostly unoccupied. A new village was built on the plain in the 1960s, offering modern conveniences like electricity and running water. Most villagers have set up home there, or moved further afield to Tunis or even France; fewer than twenty residents now remain in the old village.

The village and the surrounding *jessour* (see p.406) have seen a large amount of **restoration** by the Association pour la Sauvegarde de la Nature et la Protection de l'Environnement de Douiret (ASNAPED). Their main project in the village is the construction of a **museum of traditional life** in what used to be a troglodyte family home. It is now being restored to show how people lived here, illustrated with the items they used in their everyday home life. Next door, the association are setting up a **study centre** in a small building that was briefly an office of administration in the late nineteenth century before the French base moved to Tataouine.

Perched on the mountain above is the white **Nakhla Mosque**, setting off the soft colour of the mountainside. The mosque has been restored, and will shortly be open to visitors. The façade is modern, but the inner prayer hall at the back, built into the rock, is at least as old as the village itself, dating back to the thirteenth century; it may be even older, as Donatist Christians in the region under the Romans and Byzantines used to gather in underground churches to pray, and this chamber could have been one of them. Indeed, Roman coins have been found in the ruined **kala'a** perched on a peak at the very top of the village, some 700m high. If you climb up onto the precarious rubble of the *kala'a*, the panoramic views over the surrounding desert are stunning.

Wandering around Douiret, you can find **oil presses** (three of them in use), **bakeries** and **inscriptions** in remarkably good condition. On the plain below is an old **graveyard** with the whitewashed tombs of revered marabouts, and there is another ancient subterranean mosque, the **Kerma Mosque**, by an ancient fig tree to the west of the village.

Practicalities

Like Chenini, Douiret can be reached by **camionette** from rue 2 Mars in Tatouine, or you could negotiate a deal with a taxi driver to bring you up here. Camionettes back to Tataouine are most easily located in the new village. Other vehicles will usually give people lifts, too.

Above the museum and study centre, ASNAPED have opened a small *auberge* where you can **stay**, called *Résidence de Douiret*. In a carefully restored troglodyte home, it has clean showers and toilets and hot and cold running water (℡75 878 066, ℻75 860 540; ❷ including breakfast). It's best to book ahead if you plan to stay here. There's a **restaurant** (℡97 497 242) up above it where you can get meals, but again you should give them notice.

Ksar Ghilane

An oasis situated where the *hamada* (stony desert) meets the *erg* (sand desert), **KSAR GHILANE**, 75km west of Tataouine, used to be a frighteningly desolate place. Such was its importance that the Romans built a **fort** to defend it, one of a chain, the *limes* (pronounced "lee-mess"), that extended the full length of the colonial frontier. Ksar Ghilane is linked traditionally with the **Nefzaoua** area south of the Chott el Jerid (see p.374), and in particular with Douz, since it is part of the area used traditionally by that town's Mrazig people to pasture their flocks.

With a 4WD, you could **drive** to Ksar Ghilane: there are routes off the Chenini–Douiret road, from Beni Kheddache, and off the Douz–Matmata road. If you are going to Ksar Ghilane under your own steam, it is wise to bring supplies, as there are no grocery stores in Ksar Ghilane, and everything costs that little bit more here. Without a 4WD, the only way to get here (short of paying to ride in a supply truck from Douz) is with a **tour** from Douz, Zaafrane or Tozeur, or from places further afield such as Jerba or Gabès; see the accounts of these towns – in particular p.380 – for details.

The safest and easiest route is the **pipeline road** which branches off the Douz–Matmata road at the *Café Jelili*, 32km west of Matmata, 68km east of Douz. The piste is well maintained and can even be traversed in a normal car, although it's a juddery 84km and you are very likely to get stuck in sand drifts, so 4WD is preferable. Thirty-seven kilometres south of the *Café Jelili*, there's another pitstop at **Bir Soltane**, a well whose sweet water is renowned throughout the region, and often taken by the tankerful to places like Douz, where it is much preferred to the rather brackish tapwater. The *Café les Deux Frères* here serves beverages to thirsty travellers. A detour from here, for those with 4WD and an insatiable appetite for ruins, follows a piste to the east, just 300m south of Bir Soltane, turning south after 8km towards **Ksar Tarcine**, the remains of what was originally the Roman *limes* fort of Tibubuci. After another 11km, you'll see it on top of a hillock lying 4km to the west of the piste. Back on the pipeline road, there's a surfaced turning leading west for the final 17km to Ksar Ghilane.

Entering Ksar Ghilane, the first thing you come across is the village, built to house people working in the oasis to the north and servicing the growing tourist industry. The **spring**, a tepid 25°C, is in the oasis just past the campsites, and emerges in a pool that you can bathe in. The only other sight as such is the **Roman fort**, 3km northwest in the desert. Since motor vehicles are prohibited from driving over the dunes to it, the only way to reach it is by foot (take water and sun protection) or camel. Just south of the village is a **monument** to the column of African and French troops under General Leclerc, who passed through here in 1943 on their way from Lake Chad – over 2000km across the desert on foot – to take the Fezzan (southwest Libya) on behalf of the Allies and link up with Montgomery's Commonwealth forces in Tripoli prior to their assault on the Mareth Line (see p.504).

Accommodation and eating

There are three **campsites** in Ksar Ghilane, plus one to the south, all of which provide bedouin-style tents to sleep in, plus a four-star hotel where the rooms are deluxe tents. The first site you come to is *Campement le Paradis* (☎75 470 255, ℻75 470 515), run by Douz-based tour firm Mrazig Voyages, which offers the choice of a traditional Bedouin tent (per person, 15TD for bed and breakfast, 30TD full board) or a deluxe tent that sleeps eight, though a smaller group or even a couple may be lucky and get one to themselves off-season. You can also pitch your own tent, though few people do. Bathroom facilities are nice and clean, and the tents are situated away from the generator. The *Campement Ghislane*, right next to the spring (☎75 460 100, ℻75 460 110), has full-board accommodation in Bedouin tents (30TD per person) and decent bathroom facilities. A little further afield is *Campement el Bibène*, between the oasis and the military barracks (☎75 470 178, ℻75 470 135; 23TD per person including breakfast). All the campsites have restaurants and bars, and serve moderately priced meals in principle at any time of the day or night. It is also possible to camp *sauvage* in the dunes, and there is a fourth campsite, *Campement Aïn Essbat* out in the desert 17km south (☎ & ℻75 471 599; 20TD per person b&b, 33TD full-board). For those who want to experience with the wilderness without roughing it, the *Relais Pansea* (☎75 900 506, ℻75 621 872; ❼) – essentially a four-star **hotel** – has a pool, an observation tower to survey the oasis and watch the sunset, and deluxe en-suite tents.

Remada and the extreme south

REMADA, 70km south of Tataouine, is yet another garrison town imposed on the south by the French and has nothing of great interest. When the French arrived, there was a small oasis and the remains of a **Roman fort** nearby, part of the *limes* (see p.475), now incorporated into the army base. In the 1970s and 1980s, when relations with Libya were tense, this area was considered a first line in the defence of Tunisia against possible Libyan incursions, especially after seven "terrorists" were caught crossing the border in 1986, with the 1980 Gafsa incident (see p.341) still fresh in people's minds. Since then, relations between the two countries have improved, and it is the border with Algeria, and the threat of incursion by that country's fundamentalist rebels, that now preoccupies the Tunisian authorities.

There's nowhere to stay in Remada, and unless you're heading further south, your best bet is to return to Tataouine by bus or louage before they dry up around 3pm. If you get stuck, you'll just have to throw yourself on the mercy of the local police, who may have a spare cell for the night. The only **restaurant** in town is very basic, and you're just as well off buying food from one of the shops. Bring enough dinars with you as there's no bank either. **Market day** is Sunday.

Dehibat and around

There are two buses a day from Remada to **DEHIBAT**, and it's also a fairly regular run by louage. The village has been taken over by the army but the old **ksar**, now a barracks, is still there. There's nowhere to stay in Dehibat, though you're only likely to be here if you're self-sufficient and equipped for desert travel.

From the 1880s until 1911, sovereignty over this tiny village was disputed between the French and the Turkish administration of Libya. The local Berber tribe, the Dehibi, had deserted the village to live in Matmata and Douiret a century earlier, but the French paid them to return and substantiate their claim. Eventually, when the Italians invaded Libya, the French persuaded them to concede the village and its lands, but when Italy entered World War I on the side of the Allies in 1915, Libyan rebels in Tripolitania (northwestern Libya) saw a golden opportunity to return Islamic rule with Turkish and German backing. Having driven the Italians from most of northwestern Libya, they crossed the border and laid siege to Dehibat, hoping that a military victory here would provoke a rebellion against the French in Tunisia. They gained the support of several southern Tunisian tribes, and the Ouderna in particular rose up in rebellion, but the French sent in 30,000 troops to relieve Dehibat, and the rebels failed to make much headway in Tunisia. In Libya however they continued to hold out until the Allied victory in Europe cut off their support. Today's military presence here indicates Tunisia's continued insecurity over the district, although smuggling is another possible reason for it.

Dehibat used to be a point of entry into Libya, but the border crossing here was closed at last check (by Libya). Until it re-opens, the only authorized crossing is at Ras Ajdir on the coast (see p.446). Even when the border at Dehibat was open, passport and customs checks were much more stringent down here, and took somewhat longer than at Ras Ajdir. From Wazin, on the Libyan side, there is transport to Nalut, 47km away, where there are connections to Ghadames, Tripoli and the rest of Libya.

West of Dehibat are the ruins of **Ksar Ouni**, which was at one time an important regional centre, and the first Berber village built in the area. It's reached via a piste that turns off the Remada road about 10km northwest of Dehibat, passing the modern village of **Ouni Jedid**. Ksar Ouni contains a number of troglodyte dwellings, a handful of oil presses, and a mosque with an inscription dating it to 549 AH (1154–5 AD), but its most intriguing feature is the remains of a lookout tower, unique in the region, which has led to the suggestion that this was originally a *ribat*.

The far south

There aren't many sights as such in the remote areas of the far south. What most people come for is the scenery, especially the massive sand dunes of the **Great Eastern Erg**, along with the remoteness few tourists get to see, plus the chance to spot wildlife such as the elusive gazelle (for more on desert wildlife, see box p.467).

Travelling south from Remada and Dehibat, or beyond **Kamour** on the pipeline road south of Ksar Ghilane, requires a **permit** from the Gouvernorat in Tataouine. At one time, these were very difficult to obtain, but nowadays are issued routinely so long as you have transport; a guide is also strongly advisable. Apart from the road to Dehibat, none of the roads south of Remada are surfaced, and there is no public transport, so if you don't have a 4WD, you'll have to go on an organized tour. Either way, the people to contact are in Tatouine: either Ali Béchir at the Syndicat d'Initiative (BP 108, 3200 Tataouine; ☎75 850 850, 🅕75 850 999), or Dr Habib Belhedi of the Association des Amis de la Memoire de la Terre (☎75 860 540, 🅔memoireterre@yahoo.fr), either of whom can arrange permit, guide and transport. It is best to apply for the permit in advance in writing or by email, stating the names, birth dates and passport numbers of all the people in your party, plus the number of vehicles you are taking, a rough itinerary (include all the places you might visit), and the dates when you're arriving in and departing the area. You can apply in person at the Syndicat d'Initiative, where the permit can usually be issued on the same working day if you arrive early enough.

As well as working at the Syndicat, Mr Béchir runs a firm called Sahara Atlas, which organizes 4WD **tours** in the far south (around 100TD per person per day, for a group of four or more). Besides the vehicle and a guide, he can organize tents, sleeping bags and food.

West of Remada

The Demmer mountains to the south and west of Remada contain a number of **abandoned villages**, whose collapsed ruins, plus the eroded landscape of their *jessour*, are all that remains of a once-flourishing economy. Between the sixteenth and eighteenth centuries, the tribes abandoned a total of 25 villages between Douiret and Dehibat. Why they left remains a mystery: the French colonialists blamed the expansion of the Ouderna into the region, though climate change and plague epidemics may also have played a part. More recently, it has been suggested that the Berbers supported the expansion of Ottoman power into this region in the early seventeenth century, an expansion opposed by local nomadic Arab tribes such as the **Traïfa**. When the Traïfa rebelled against Turkish rule in the 1670s, Ottoman troops stationed in the region called on the Berber villagers for support. This marked the end of the villagers' relationship with the Traïfa, who had allowed them to pasture animals in their lands and offered military protection against brigands in return for annual tribute. The Traïfa may even have responded by expelling the Berbers from their villages. Although the Traïfa rebellion was quashed by the Ottomans in 1696, the Berbers' precarious position in this remote area was largely dependent on a relationship with the nomads, and it was probably the ending of this link which forced the Berbers to leave.

Ksar Brega Kebira and Ksar Brega Sghira

The scenario above may well be reflected in the legend of **Ksar Brega Kebira** and **Ksar Brega Sghira**, two abandoned villages situated some 15km north-west of Remada. They're accessible from the piste to Borj Bourguiba that leaves the Tataouine–Remada road around 29km north of Remada, 42km south of Tataouine. Brega Kebira, the larger of the two villages (*kebira* meaning large, *sghira* small) is also the more spectacular, especially at sunset.

The story goes that every year the Brega paid annual tribute to the Traïfa for pasturage and protection, but the demands became more onerous until one year a woollen shawl was required from every Brega family in addition. Reluctantly, the Brega came up with the goods, but the Traïfa claimed there was a deficit, which they made up by seizing the shawl from the daughter of the Brega's sheikh (holy man). In the face of this humiliation, the sheikh left the village that night and took the road north. In the morning, his neighbours found two pigeons under an upturned wooden bowl outside his house. One, in full plumage, flew away when the bowl was lifted. The other, completely plucked, was unable to fly, but had this message in verse attached to its leg: "The one that takes off will regain a land of security and comfort; the one that remains will be left without shirt or plumage." Seeing this, the remaining villagers set off after him, burning their homes behind them. When the Traïfa chief heard of this, he realized he had gone too far, and sent messengers asking the Brega to return, but their chief responded with a curse: "May your men be consigned to flames. May the women of your tribe be taken by your Black slaves. May your soldiers be turned into dead meat." The curse did not take long to be realized: when the Turks put down the Traïfa rebellion, it was with great brutality. The men were massacred, and the women taken as camp concubines by the Ottoman troops, many of whom had the status of slaves.

Apart from its legend, Ksar Brega Kebira has a **subterranean mosque**, similar to those at Douiret (see p.474). It is said to have been founded by Oqba Ibn Nafi on his way north to bring Islam to Tunisia, and inscriptions found here have been attributed to a companion of the Prophet Mohammed, although the use of Maghrebi as opposed to Middle Eastern script makes this unlikely. Like the mosques at Douiret however, this one may originally have been a clandestine Donatist church in the period before Islam.

Ksar Segdel

Another possible trip from Remada is to the villages in the **Jebel Segdel** mountain range to the south and southwest. It's possible to reach the village of **Ksar Segdel** on foot, an eight-hour hike southward over a flat plain – you may be able to find a guide at the Maison du Peuple (a sort of cultural centre), beyond the marketplace on the Borj Bourguiba road. Otherwise you will need a 4WD and to follow a less direct route. Heading west out of Remada towards Borj Bourguiba, you pass a checkpoint some 9km from Remada at **Kambout**, after which you take a turn-off to the left towards the abandoned village of **Matous**. Beyond Matous, the road turns eastward to reach Ksar Segdel, perched high on an escarpment above a canyon with great views, but it's a tough climb. The village, topped by a *kala'a*, consists of three levels of troglodyte dwellings driven horizontally into the rock. Some are more sophisticated than others, fronted with walls that are faced and decorated, one with pictures of boats. This may have been the residence of a Traïfa chief, since the Segdel, who lived here, were big allies of the Traïfa, and allowed them to move into the village and set up a command centre for their war against the Turks. The biggest battle took place in the *oued* below the escarpment, and resulted in a victory for the Traïfa, which gave them control of the region. The victory proved short-lived however, and Segdel was abandoned when the Ottomans finally crushed the Traïfa revolt. Today the only residents of the village are said to be jackals.

Borj Bourguiba to Borj el Khadra

Southwest of Kambout, the main piste continues to **Borj Bourguiba**, 37km southwest of Remada. This military prison and settlement takes its name from the ex-president, who was interned here under the Protectorate (when it was called Borj le Boeuf). Ironically enough, the prison held many of Bourguiba's own political enemies in the 1970s and 1980s.

South of Borj Bourguiba, there is little in the way of settlements, ancient or modern, bar a handful of military posts and oil terminals, yet the main piste south (the MC101) was once a major trading route, plied for centuries by caravans travelling between Ghadames and the coast. South of Tataouine, the only sources of water were wells, and the caravan route followed a trail between them. Borj Bourguiba was originally just a well in the desert – called Bir Kecira – as was **Jenein**, 57km to its south, which isn't much more today. As a source of water however, it was an important stop on the road, and the French set up a military base here in 1898 to maintain control over it. The next well was 33km further south at **Bir Zar**.

To the west of the caravan trail lies the Great Eastern Erg, a vast sand desert of massive dunes, which stretches all the way down the west side of the southernmost tip of Tunisia. About halfway between Borj Bourguiba and Jenein and Bir Zar, a piste leads southwest to meet the pipeline road from Ksar Ghilane, off which, 18km further south, a piste leads west into the erg, finally reaching the oil terminal at **EL BORMA**. Here you will probably have to show your travel permit several times. Although it is an oil terminal, you can't just pull into the petrol station and buy fuel; first you have to go to the administration building of the oil company SITEP, who will issue you with a coupon that you exchange for fuel, and which will cost about a third more than usual. SITEP also have **accommodation** here (T75 642 880; half board ❺), mainly for the benefit of their workers, though you should be able to take a room if there's one free.

The area south of El Borma is dominated by huge dunes, and El Borma is a possible base for exploring them via a difficult piste that leads southeast from El Borma deep into the erg. This is **gazelle** country, so keep your eyes peeled – you are only likely to see them at a distance. MC101 continues south to meet the pipeline road, along which, after a further 26km, you reach **TIARET**, another well on the caravan trail, 56km south of Bir Zar. Tiaret is also an oil terminal, and there was a direct piste linking it with El Borma that was once much used by oil tankers, but it is now so well sanded up that it is pretty much impassable. The oil company TRAPSA have a **guesthouse** at Tiaret (T75 853 619; ❺), mainly for their workers.

Seventeen kilometres southeast of Tiaret is another ancient well at **Mechiguig**. A monument here commemorates the death in 1896 of the nutty rightwing French aristocrat, the Marquis de Morès, who advocated a French–Islamic front against what he believed was a conspiracy of Jews and Anglo-Saxons to rule the world at the expense of France and the Latin race. While on an ill-conceived expedition to give support, and possibly arms, to the Mahdists holding out against British rule in Sudan, Morès was killed by his Chaamba camel drivers and Tuareg supply brokers, following a row over payment. When his camel refused to turn and flee, Morès rather foolishly shot the beast, which keeled over on top of his rifle, sealing his fate. To ensure the inclusion of Mechiguig in their territory, the French stationed a garrison here and christened it Fort Pervinquière. In 1915, when the tribes of western Libya rebelled against colonial rule (see p.477), the Italian garrison at Sinawan were forced to flee across the border here to ask the French for protection.

Ninety-four kilometres south of Tiaret, **Bir Pistor** was one of five new wells sunk along the old caravan route by the French. The main point of interest here is an area 6km to the southeast which is known for its profusion of **desert roses**.

Borj el Khadra

Beyond Bir Pistor, the piste continues for 19km to **BORJ EL KHADRA** (also called Borj el Hattaba, formerly Fort Saint), at the southernmost tip of Tunisia, where the borders of Libya and Algeria meet. The fort was built by the French in the 1920s to mark the extent of Tunisian territory. During World War II it was taken by two hundred Italian troops, despite a brave attempt to hold out by its twelve French and Tunisian defenders, but was retaken for Free France four months later by General Leclerc's column of mainly West African troops in an action to protect Montgomery's flank in the run-up to the Battle of Mareth (see p.410). Nor was this the fort's last taste of action. During the Bizerte crisis of 1961 (see p.172), when France still controlled Algeria, Tunisian troops based here laid siege to two French forts across the border in pursuit of a territorial claim. Before independence, the Tunisia–Algeria border south of Bir Romane had been considered "provisional", and a 1910 treaty mentioned Garet el Hamel, 30km south of Borj el Khadra, as the southernmost point on Tunisia's border with Libya. As a result, Tunisian president Habib Bourguiba now claimed a border that ran due south from Bir Romane and due west from Garet el Hamel. The French sent in their air force to relieve the siege, attacking Borj el Khadra, and a cemetery near the fort here is the last resting place of more than two hundred Tunisian soldiers who were killed. A ceasefire came into effect at the same time here as in Bizerte, and the two issues were settled together.

Today, you cannot legally cross the **border** at Borj el Khadra, and even if you could, there's nothing very exciting on the Algerian side (the nearest important town being the oil terminal at Hassi Messaoud, 500km northwest), though there is a route south to Borj Omar Driss, over pistes to Tamanrasset and into West Africa. On the Libyan side, the ancient and fascinating former caravan terminus of Ghadames beckons – indeed, you can see it – but the only way to reach it at present is to go all the way up to Ras Ajdir on the coast and come back down on the other side of the frontier.

Travel details

Buses

Ghoumrassen to: Gabès (3 daily; 2hr 15min); Guermessa (3 daily; schooldays only; 20min); Ksar Hadada (7 daily; 10min); Ksar Mourabtine (3 daily schooldays only; 20min); Medenine (8 daily; 1hr); Tataouine (7 daily; 45min); Tunis (2 daily; 9hr).

Medenine to: Ben Gardane (6 daily; 1hr 20min);

Beni Kheddache (6 daily; 45min); Bizerte (1 daily; 9hr); Gabès (16 daily; 1hr); Ghoumrassen (8 daily; 1hr 30min); Jerba (Houmt Souk; 5 daily; 2hr); Kairouan (5 daily; 5hr); Ras Ajdir (2 daily; 2hr 15min); Sfax (6 daily; 3hr); Sousse (6 daily; 5hr 30min); Tataouine (6 daily; 1hr); Tunis (11 daily; 8hr); Zammour (2 daily; 1hr); Zarzis (9 daily; 1hr).

Tataouine to: Chenini (2 daily; 40min); Ezzahra (2 daily; 40min); Gabès (6 daily; 2hr 15min); Ghoumrassen (7 daily; 45min); Jerba (Houmt Souk; 2 daily; 3hr); Kairouan (1 daily; 5hr 30min); Ksar Ouled Debbab (2 daily; 30min); Ksar Ouled Soltane (1 daily; 40min); Maztouria (1 daily; 20min); Medenine (6 daily; 1hr); Remada (1 daily; 2hr); Sfax (2 daily; 4hr); Sousse (1 daily; 6hr 30min); Tunis (3 daily; 8–9hr); Zarzis (1 daily; 2hr).

Arabic place names

Beni Barka	بني بركة
Beni Kheddache	بني خدّاش
Bir Zar	بئر زار
Borj Bourguiba	برج بورقيبة
Borj el Khadra	برج الخضراء
Chenini	شنّي
Dehibat	ذهيبة
Douiret	دويرات
El Borma	البرمة
Ezzahra	الزهراء
Gattoufa	قطّوفة
Ghoumrassen	غمراسن
Guermessa	قرماسة
Jenein	الجناين
Ksar Ghilane	قسر غيلان
Ksar Hadada	قسر حدادة
Ksar Hallouf	قسر الحلوف
Ksar Jedid	قسر الجديد
Ksar Jouama	قسر جمعة
Ksar Kerachfa	قسر كراشفة
Ksar Nrega Sghira	قسر المرابطين
Ksar Ouled Soltane	قسر أولاد سلتان
Ksar Segdel	قسر سقدل
Maztouria	المزطورية
Mechiguig	المشاقيق
Medenine	مدنين
Metameur	ام التمر
Remada	رمادة
Tamelest	التمليست
Tataouine	تطاوين
Tiaret	تيارت
Zammour	زمّور

Louages and camionettes

* indicates a route served by camionette.

Ghoumrassen to: Ksar Hadada (15min); Medenine (1hr); Tunis (8hr 30min).

Medenine to: Ben Gardane (1hr); Beni Kheddache (30min); Gabès (1hr); Ghoumrassen (1hr); Jerba (Houmt Souk; 1hr 20min); Ksar Hallouf* (1hr); Sfax (3hr); Tataouine (45min); Tunis (7hr 30min); Zammour (40min); Zarzis (1hr).

Tataouine to: Ben Gardane (1hr 20min); Chenini* (40min); Douiret* (40min); Ezzahra* (40min); Gabès (1hr 45min); Gattoufa* (20min); Jerba (Houmt Souk; 2hr); Ksar Ouled Soltane* (40min); Maztouria* (15min); Medenine (40min); Remada (1hr 20min); Tunis (8hr); Zarzis (1hr 45min).

Contexts

Contexts

The historical framework

Tunisia has a long, dense and complicated history. The region was host to some of the earliest tool-making human cultures and centre of the still dimly understood Carthaginian Empire. The Romans left a clear mark and Islam arrived early in the faith's history at the end of the seventh century. Modern Tunisia is a comparatively recent creation, but the roots of the country in its present shape go back to the eighth century.

Prehistory

Around a million years ago, **early hominids** were living in North Africa's tropical climate, hunting with the primitive tools known as "pebble culture". These gradually gave way to heavy hand-axes, until, about 50,000 years ago, the discovery of fire encouraged what was by now almost *Homo sapiens* to live in fixed settlements. A culture known as **Aterian** began to make smaller, more specialized tools, and the next step forward was the arrival about 10,000 years ago of Caucasoid Proto-Hamites from western Asia. These people were probably fair-skinned, buried some of their dead, spoke a language related to ancient Egyptian, and made the most sophisticated tools yet: barbed arrows and long, thin blades, which have been found near Gafsa and have given their name to the influential culture (Capsian Man) found as far away as Kenya.

The blades found at Gafsa have been dated to around 6000 BC, and for the next 4000 years **Capsian people**, perhaps with some infiltration from further east, continued to live in caves and survive by hunting and gathering. About 2000 BC the introduction of metals from Sicily brought Tunisia into the Bronze Age, but it was still a relatively small-scale society of nomadic hunters that the Phoenicians encountered when they arrived at the beginning of the first millennium BC. Contemporary Greek accounts consistently distinguish "Libyans" from "Ethiopians" in North Africa, and the Libyans were descended from the Proto-Hamites, fair-skinned in contrast to the "Ethiopians" (Black Africans), and still speaking their remote Libyc language. The Greeks called them *barbaroi*, a name originally attached to any people who did not speak Greek and which gave rise to the term "Berber". Today's pure Berbers, of whom there are very few in Tunisia (most live in Algeria and Morocco), are the descendants of these Proto-Hamites.

The Carthaginian Empire 814–146 BC

The **Phoenicians** were a maritime trading nation, originally drawn to North Africa from their home in what is now Lebanon because they needed staging posts for the long haul across the Mediterranean. Traders supreme of the ancient world, they were already heavily involved in exploiting the resources of Spain and beyond (principally metals), and the colonies they founded on Tunisia's coast, such as Sousse, Utica and Bizerte, were important transit points.

Carthaginian civilization

Unfortunately, so little has survived of Carthaginian civilization that we are forced to rely almost entirely on Greek and Roman accounts, which deserve the same caution as modern Western descriptions of, say, Iran. By the seventh century BC Homer was describing a typical Phoenician as "grasping and well versed in deceit". "Phoenician faith" was a proverbial Roman term for dishonesty, and Roman mothers used to tell their children "Hannibal's coming" to make them quiet.

The Carthaginians seem to have succeeded in antagonizing many of the people they came across. Hannibal crucially failed to secure any local support during his long stay in Italy, and the Romans later claimed to have had little difficulty in persuading North Africa's Berbers to transfer their allegiance. A simplistic explanation for this might be found in the Carthaginian **commercial vocation**. Their exploits in pursuit of profit were legendary. Two of these – fifth-century BC voyages west round the coast of Africa and north as far as Brittany – may be apocryphal, but at the very least they reflect Carthaginian interest in distant markets.

The competitiveness which made them such successful traders left them ill-equipped to get on with others, or even among themselves. The **Truceless War** (241–237 BC) is a graphic example. Carthage had always relied on its naval strength, recruiting mercenaries whenever a land army became necessary. When peace was made at the end of the First Punic War, there were no funds to pay the mercenaries. The authorities tried to solve the problem by sending the mercenaries off to Sicca (Le Kef), but with the support of the oppressed Berbers they turned on their erstwhile masters and a four-year struggle of unrelieved brutality ensued. After hiring yet more mercenaries, the Carthaginians finally won – but the episode indicates a reliance on wealth rather than loyalty, manifestly an unsuitable policy for a country aspiring to Great Power status.

From what can be gathered of **Carthaginian society**, it was oligarchical and conservative and permanently divided into jealous factions, which prevented any unified policy from being carried out. Power was concentrated in the hands of the ruling aristocratic families (or whichever one had the support of the army) and, although many of the native Berbers were technically free, in practice the tribute demanded made them resentful of their effective subjection.

Characteristically for such a society, **religion** and art remained essentially anti-humanistic. The most important gods were **Baal** and his consort **Tanit**, and their worship included child-sacrifice – a practice which, somewhat hypocritically, made the Romans throw up their hands in horror. But details of the less lurid aspects of their religion are barely known. At first the gods were worshipped at *tophets* (holy places), just a sacred area with perhaps a small shrine to hold a divine effigy, but gradually, under Greek influence, these became more substantial, with a monumental porch and a courtyard attached. By the fourth century BC some Greek cults were even introduced, though in modified form. **Carthaginian art** was almost all derived from foreign sources – Egyptian, then Greek – and much of what little there is consists of uneasy attempts to reproduce what had been seen elsewhere. There are few original characteristics, and the most distinctive Carthaginian image – the symbol of the goddess Tanit, a bare circle balanced on a triangle – only proves the anti-humanist trend.

It is difficult to imagine what Carthaginian **towns** looked like; only domestic housing has so far been uncovered, at Kerkouane and Carthage, with none of the great public buildings which characterized Greco-Roman civilization. Under Greek influence, though, more regular civic planning may have come in. Outside their cities the Carthaginians eventually adapted very successfully after early disinterest. Their expansion into the Sahel and the Medjerda Valley after the fifth century BC was successful enough to be mentioned by Agathocles's expedition of 310 BC, and a Carthaginian scholar, Mago, produced a treatise on farming that was so highly regarded that the Roman Senate ordered its translation in 146 BC.

Traditionally, the earliest of these ports was founded around 1100 BC, **Carthage** itself in 814 BC. Part of this ancient tradition was the myth of the foundation of Carthage (Qart Hadasht – New City) by Queen Dido (or Elissa) and a band of exiled nobles from the Phoenician homeland. The myth may reflect a genuine influx of the Phoenician ruling class, caused by Assyrian pressure at home in the ninth century BC; but it may just be a later rationalization of Carthage's supremacy among the cities in North Africa. There is little archeological evidence to support the gap between the foundations, and ninth-century BC dates all round may be more accurate.

At first, the Phoenician trading posts were more or less isolated enclaves on the coast. Links with the homeland were strong, and there was no reason to use the hinterland for more than immediate needs. Towards the end of the seventh century BC, however, a rival for Punic (Phoenician) trade domination appeared as **Greeks**, based in southern Italy and Sicily, began to extend their reach through southern France and eastern Spain. Conflict was inevitable, and the Phoenician cities amalgamated for security under Carthage – though the relationship was never to be easy. Fighting through the sixth century went Carthage's way, but in 480 BC the Battle of Himera in Sicily resulted in a decisive Greek victory. Forced from now on to fight its own battle for survival in the western Mediterranean, Carthage became increasingly independent of the homeland and simultaneously extended its control over the Tunisian hinterland: the Carthaginian Empire was born. The year 396 BC saw another bad defeat in Sicily followed by domestic upheavals; then in 310 BC the Greek king of Syracuse, Agathocles, having boldly eluded a Carthaginian army which had landed in Sicily, was able to descend on Cap Bon and devastate North Africa for three years.

This episode was the last to involve Greeks against Carthage. **Rome** had been gradually superseding the Greeks in Italy and Sicily, and henceforth Carthage's struggle for domination of the Mediterranean basin and Europe was with this formidable opponent. The first of three famous **Punic Wars** (263–241 BC) consisted mainly of naval skirmishes around Sicily, but also included one episode of war on land which became enshrined in Roman national legend. The Roman general **Regulus** landed with an army in Africa and had some success before being defeated and captured along with his force. He was allowed to return on parole to Rome to plead before the Senate for acceptance of Carthaginian terms, but when this was refused he kept his word as a man of honour and returned to certain death and a place in the pantheon of Roman national heroes. Roman versions of the story dwell with loving detail on the grief of his family and the brutality of his death at Carthaginian hands.

Carthage finally lost the war and had to accept Roman terms, surrendering its fleet and agreeing on spheres of influence in Spain. It was to Spain, however, that the Carthaginians soon turned their attention. After preliminary manoeuvring by both sides, the Carthaginian general **Hannibal** deliberately moved over the agreed border in 218 BC and proceeded to make his legendary march (with elephants) through France and over the Alps. Although he won initial victories at Trasimene and Cannae, he remained isolated in Italy for several years with no support, either locally or from home, which would enable him to take Rome. This was in part because the Roman Scipio had been tying down Carthaginian forces at home, and in 202 Hannibal was finally compelled to return. Scipio defeated him at the **Battle of Zama** in central Tunisia, winning the official title "Africanus". Hannibal fled to Asia Minor (modern Turkey) – and to his own place in Roman legend as a dreaded but respected opponent.

Carthage had to surrender its fleet again, and to refrain from training elephants. Although Carthaginian power had now been effectively nullified, for many Romans a threat remained as long as the city physically existed. The arch-conservative Cato used to end every speech in the Senate, whatever the subject, with the phrase "Carthage must be destroyed." A story goes that one day he came into the Senate and deliberately spilt some ripe figs onto the floor. Questioned, he replied that these were Carthaginian figs – the implication being that a Carthage this healthy was one Carthage too many.

The hawks won the day, and in 150 BC a third war was provoked, culminating in the final, apocalyptic **sack of Carthage** in 146 BC. Descriptions of this are predictably lurid, and the ruins were ploughed over with the proverbial salt to ensure that they remained barren. The Carthaginian Empire was well and truly obliterated, and the Romans set up the province of Africa in northern Tunisia.

Roman Africa 112 BC–439 AD

The immediate attitude of the **Romans** to their acquisition in Africa was less than positive. The destruction of Carthage had been a preventive measure designed to protect the Straits of Sicily and ensure the safety of Italy: there were no plans for colonization, and the province of Africa consisted of no more than the Carthaginians had controlled, roughly everything east of a line from Thabraca (Tabarka) to Thaenae (Sfax).

Even so, Romans seem to have moved to Africa on their own initiative. In 112 BC, it was the native king **Jugurtha**'s misguided slaughter of Romans living at Cirta (Constantine in Algeria) which forced the Senate to intervene in Africa against his rampaging; presumably these were traders who had moved in to exploit the new territory. Jugurtha was king of Numidia, the native kingdom that stretched west from the Roman border through Algeria. He was the grandson of Massinissa, a Numidian king who had provided invaluable support for the Romans against Carthage in the second century BC; now that the Carthaginian threat had gone, however, there was no more incentive to support the Romans than there had been to support Carthage previously. The Romans had created a power vacuum in their province which they were eventually going to have to fill.

Jugurtha was finally defeated in 105 BC, and a few veterans were settled in the north of the province. It was only in 46 BC, however, when Julius Caesar finally won the Roman Civil War against Pompeii at the Battle of Thapsus (near Mahdia), that **colonization** really took off. The existing province was extended to the west by a line running south from Hippo Regius (Annaba in Algeria), and to the east by the addition of Tripolitania (western Libya), and renamed **Africa Proconsularis**. As a symbol of the Roman presence, **Carthage** was refounded in 44 BC.

Under the Roman Empire (from 30 BC), growth in Africa was phenomenal, made possible by a combination of political and economic factors. Politically, Africa was for two centuries one of the most stable provinces of the empire. Where a small part of France required four Roman legions (of 6000 men each) to maintain its defences, the whole of Roman Africa needed only one. Its base moved steadily further west during the first century AD, from Haïdra on the Tunisian border to Tebessa in Algeria, and Lambaesis near Batna, also in

Life in Africa Romana

There were two levels of **society** in the Roman province of Africa: a wealthy, urban, Romanized people, and a poorer, rural native population. A good deal is known about the rich, because they left behind material remains that can be seen everywhere in Tunisia today, but the life of the rural Berber population remains obscure. Although limited opportunities for social advancement did exist, the essential gap between the two groups was never eradicated, and the alienation of less privileged Berbers was an important factor in the eventual disintegration of imperial culture. To be fair to the Romans, most of those better off were of local origin: when one speaks of "Romans", this is usually a reference to Romanized Africans. There was opportunity for imperial citizens to make good – as never under Carthage – and many made the most of it, as the number of African senators and emperors shows.

The most striking fact about the **towns** is that there were so many: literally hundreds. These smallish settlements of 5000–15,000 inhabitants provided homes for farming landlords, markets for their produce – and a perfect environment for one-upmanship. In the absence of any external pressures, wealth was diverted into civic and private rivalry: local plutocrats put money into buildings and facilities on which their names would be prominently displayed. The ensuing prestige translated without too much difficulty into political office.

The basic aim was **Romanization**, and this meant building institutions which fostered Roman values. The spiritual heart of any self-respecting town was the **Forum**, a regular paved space enclosed by colonnades and surrounded by administrative and religious buildings. The most important of the town's religious buildings, the **Capitol**, was almost always in the Forum: it was dedicated to the Capitoline trio of Jupiter, Juno and Minerva, patrons of the empire. Other temples and shrines served cults which were a curious mixture of Roman and local influences; the Carthaginian goddess Tanit, for instance, was given a Roman name, Caelestis (Heavenly One), and worshipped all over Africa Proconsularis. Priesthood was a temporal matter, open only to those of a certain social status and thus closely tied to political authority.

Baths may not seem like an obvious imperial building, but they became almost synonymous with Roman civilization. They were magnificent buildings, their soaring vaulted ceilings impressive products of Roman engineering, and the activity they housed made them central to imperial life. Surrounded by mosaics and statuary, citizens of all ranks could pay a small fee and spend hours there. Bathing was only a small part of the ritual, which also included exercising in gymnasia, reading in libraries or just sitting around. Other public facilities such as theatres and amphitheatres were usually set on the outskirts of town, not far from the vast cemeteries of ostentatious mausoleums which lined approach roads. By 250 AD, the countryside was crisscrossed by 20,000km of roads, aqueducts and bridges.

In material terms Roman Africa was a great success, though historians have tended to exaggerate Rome's achievement. Culturally Roman Africa, best known for its lawyers, was less spectacular. Nevertheless the **mosaics**, used to decorate private homes and public buildings, reached heights in Africa almost without equal – perhaps partly because there was so little other artistic activity. The greatest name in **literature** was Apuleius, author of The Golden Ass, who was born in modern Algeria; others were Tertullian and St Augustine, the Christian writers. But these Christian names are a reminder of how briefly the empire flourished. Once its citizens lost faith in the imperial dream, from the third century onwards, the physical fabric also began to crumble. No great Roman buildings were erected after 250 AD, and those already standing went unrepaired. The only new constructions were churches, often built in the ruins of older temples and baths, and the Vandals that came later inherited a way of life that was only a shadow of its former incarnation.

Algeria; and a line of frontier forts was established, running westwards from the Chott el Jerid and east from Ghadames at the southern tip of Tunisia. Within the province, the characteristic network of Roman roads grew, but they were designed to facilitate trade rather than defence.

The **agricultural trade** in question was the basis of Roman Africa's economy. In the first century AD, the province provided two-thirds of Rome's grain requirements, to Egypt's one-third. As Rome's population swelled, the supply of grain grew to supreme importance – this in the era Juvenal coined the phrase "bread and circuses". When bad weather one year kept grain ships from sailing, there was widespread panic in Rome. Accordingly, the Romans invested a great deal of time and expertise in developing the province's infrastructure, maximizing the potential which the Carthaginians had barely touched on – they only had themselves to feed, after all. In the second century AD, olive oil production began to be encouraged in the Sahel, and other prod-ucts included a gaudy yellow marble (from Chemtou); purple dye; wild animals for amphitheatre displays; coral; wood; and plain domestic pottery – which by the second century was being exported all over the Empire.

Throughout the first two centuries AD there was hardly an interruption in Roman Africa's steady increase in prosperity and importance. By about 200 AD as many as one-sixth of Roman senators were of African origin and, in the Severans from Tripolitania, North Africa provided a dynasty of emperors. In 180, however, there was a portent of things to come. The proconsul of Africa tried twelve Christians and executed them when they refused to recant their faith. The rise of **Christianity** in Roman Africa, signalled also by the polemical writings of Tertullian, was a symptom of the problems threatening the Empire throughout its unwieldy expanse.

In 238 Thysdrus (El Jem) was the scene of a revolt which spread over the Empire and ushered in half a century of great unrest. The golden age was over and, while commitment to the imperial way of life steadily dropped, Christi-anity became more widespread. In 312 Emperor Constantine was converted and the Empire became officially Christian. Constantine was trying in effect to restore the Empire to the hearts of its people, but in Africa he was foiled by the **Donatist** schism in the local Church. This was caused by Christians unwilling to accept priests who had renounced their faith in the face of persecution; to avoid being "tainted" by such priests, they formed their own communion. One famous supporter of the official Church, who spent his life trying to heal the rift, was St Augustine of Hippo.

Throughout the fourth and fifth centuries the Empire gradually crumbled in the face of internal tyranny and external aggression. One such tyranny in Africa, under Gildo (386–98), put Rome in a quandary: whether to put the upstart down, risking disruption of the all-important grain supply, or just to cut their losses. In the end, Gildo and his 70,000 men were suppressed. The external problem, raiding by local tribes, was equally serious. One theory holds that the tribes had a secret weapon which decisively increased their combat strength – the camel; more likely, internal dissension was too great for organ-ized resistance on any scale. Donatist supporters probably aided the **Vandals**, a Germanic tribe which invaded North Africa from Spain in the 420s. Their capture of Carthage in 439 put an end to the Roman era, and effectively cut the area off from western Europe. From now on, the region's loyalties would lie in a different direction.

The Vandals and the Byzantines (439–646)

One of the northern tribes which harassed the Roman Empire to its end, the **Vandals** were a Germanic tribe of Arian Christians who worked their way through Spain into Africa. If the Donatist Berbers hoped that they would be rewarded for their support against the Romans, they were sadly mistaken. Religious persecution continued – including destruction of religious and other images, the Vandals' most famous characteristic. If half the Roman statues in the Bardo Museum, for example, seem to have had their noses and penises knocked off, that is down to the Vandals.

Religion apart, the conquerors found what remained of Roman luxury fatally congenial – there are reports of a great pleasure palace south of Carthage. They never got any further than northern Tunisia and, after the death of **King Genseric** in 477, a succession of weak rulers tried unsuccessfully to levy extortionate taxes from the ever-rebellious Berbers.

After little more than a century, the Vandals offered a tempting target to the resurgent eastern half of the Roman Empire, now established in Byzantium (modern Istanbul). The great Emperor Justinian had grandiose plans for recovering the lost realms of the western empire, and to this end dispatched **Belisarius**, his general, in 533. Belisarius sailed with his army to Sicily, now held by the Ostrogoths, hoping to exploit their differences with the Vandals. In the event, the landing and conquest were so easy that this was unnecessary.

The same cannot be said for the next century of **Byzantine rule**. As virtual absentee landlords, hoping to exploit the territory, the Byzantines found themselves no more able than the Vandals to control the insurgent Berbers of the west and south. They made a more concerted effort, building massive fortresses whose ruins are almost the only reminder of their presence, but the Berbers were gradually proving that they could not be ruled by force alone, and Tunisia was too remote from Byzantium to be a prime concern. In 646 the Prefect Gregory declared the province independent of Byzantium, but his new state lasted only a year before falling to the **Arabs**.

The first Arab rulers 647–800

When the first wave of **Arab invaders** hit North Africa from the east and defeated and killed the Byzantine Prefect Gregory at Sbeïtla in 647, their new religion of Islam was less than 50 years old. After victory at Sbeïtla, the first invaders stayed long enough only to collect their share of the rich booty distributed. It was the third Islamic wave, led by **Oqba Ibn Nafi**, which finally put down roots, after advancing northward through the country from Ghadames in Libya to make Tunisia part of a vast Arab empire ruled by the **Umayyad Caliphs** from Damascus. Ibn Nafi founded Kairouan as regional capital in 670. The rest of the seventh century was taken up with quelling the last of the Berber resistance, led most famously by a legendary Jewish queen, Kahina; but in the eighth century it was with Berber converts in their army that the Arabs advanced to Spain (and ultimately as far as Poitiers in central France).

However, as with Donatism four hundred years earlier, the Berbers turned to heresy as a way of asserting their independence. It took the form of **Kharijism**, a movement hostile to central government, which denied any need for the caliph to be an Arab, advocating instead his election from among all true believers (see p.432). This idea became very popular among the Berbers, who rose in rebellion under its banner. First defeated outside Kairouan in 742, they went on to conquer the city in 757 but were driven out four years later and their movement pushed into the south of the country, which remained part of a Kharijite state until 909. The Ibadites of Jerba are all that remains of it today but, paradoxically, it was Kharijism which brought Islam to almost all Berbers, making Islamicization of North Africa far more lasting than Romanization had ever been. Disaffection continued, but the Berbers now broadly shared a faith with their rulers.

The Aghlabids 800–909

By the end of the eighth century, the **Abbasid caliphs** – who had usurped the Ummayads in 749 and moved their capital to Baghdad – were finding it ever harder to hold onto Spain and North Africa. When Ibrahim Ibn Aghlab put down a military rebellion and declared himself governor in 800, Tunisia became independent in all but name. The caliph who accepted this situation, incidentally, was Haroun al-Rashid of *Arabian Nights* fame. For a century, Ibn Aghlab's descendants, the **Aghlabids**, controlled the whole country bar the Kharijite south. Unpopular in religious circles because of their dissolute life-style, the Aghlabids tried to make up for it by constructing and embellishing religious buildings throughout their domain. They also built a series of walled cities and *ribats*, most importantly Sousse, from where, in 827, they launched a successful invasion of Sicily. The island remained in Islamic hands until the eleventh century, and in 846 an Arab raiding party even managed to attack Rome and sack St Peter's.

The Aghlabids' building programme, their conquest of Sicily and raids on Italy, and their concern for irrigation and agriculture, made their reign something of a **golden age** for Tunisia. Their effect on culture was also strong: by the time their emirate fell, more people in Tunisia spoke Arabic than Berber.

Fatimids and Zirids 909–1148

Meanwhile, yet another heresy was finding fertile ground in North Africa. The **Ismailis**, a Shi'ite faction, sent one **Abu Abdullah** to Algeria as a missionary for their cause. He soon converted a number of formerly Kharijite Berbers, who joined him to invade the Aghlabid state in 903. When they took Kairouan six years later, the Syrian Ismaili leader Obaidallah Said decided to come to Tunisia and take over, but was imprisoned en route by Kharijites in Sijilmasa, Morocco. Abu Abdullah struck west and attacked the Kharijites, destroying their state ruled by the **Rustamid** dynasty based at Tahirt in what is now Algeria, and which controlled Jerba and the south of Tunisia. On his liberation, Obaidallah declared himself Mahdi (see p.256) and took political power. Claiming descent from the Prophet's daughter Fatima, he began the

Fatimid dynasty and built a new capital at Mahdia. He showed his gratitude to Abu Abdullah by having him assassinated.

Obaidallah and his successors made themselves highly unpopular through their attacks on the orthodox Sunni faith of most of their subjects – they had a distinguished lawyer flogged in the Great Mosque at Kairouan and various prominent Sunni theologians assassinated – and the extortionate taxes they levied to finance overseas military exploits. It was the Kharijites, however, who rose up against them. Led by **Abu Yazid** from Tozeur, they besieged Mahdia in 944 and Kairouan the following year. The revolt was not crushed until 947.

In fact, the Fatimids were never primarily interested in Tunisia: they had their eyes on Egypt, and then the caliphate itself. Obaidallah launched an abortive **campaign against Egypt** in 914–15 but, driven out by an army from Baghdad, had to be content with consolidating his power base and establishing control of Morocco and Sicily. In 961, however, his great-grandson El Muizz seized an opportune moment and finally achieved the long-desired conquest of Egypt, founding the forerunner of modern Cairo. The Fatimids ruled Egypt until overthrown by Saladin in 1171. They left Tunisia in the charge of their nominees, the **Zirids**.

This arrangement lasted until 984, when the Zirids, under pressure from their subjects, withdrew allegiance to the heretical Fatimids, later transferring it to the Sunni caliphs in Baghdad. The Fatimids responded by unleashing against their former representatives the **Banu Hilal**, a restive nomadic tribe who had been causing them trouble in Egypt. The Fatimids persuaded the Hilalians and another tribe, the Banu Suleim, to migrate westward with the promise of free land and rich booty. The Banu Suleim stopped in Libya, but the Banu Hilal descended on Tunisia in an orgy of destruction – Ibn Khaldoun compared them to a swarm of locusts – which may in reality have been merely the culmination of an already advanced process of disintegration. At any rate, they were more than a match for the Zirids, who abandoned Kairouan (sacked by the Banu Hilal in 1057) and holed up in Mahdia, leaving cities such as Tunis, Sfax, Gabès and Gafsa virtually independent, and the countryside under the control of **nomads** who had little understanding of sedentary agriculture and little use for the infrastructure in place. This **infrastructure**, which had since Roman times helped to keep the region unified, fell into disuse. The country reverted to the fragmented condition of early Phoenician times – a few isolated coastal centres, and an unproductive stateless interior. This disarray was exploited by maritime Europeans: the **Normans** recaptured Sicily in 1072, then took Jerba and ports on the east coast, and finally Mahdia in 1148, thus ending the last remnants of the Zirid state.

Almohads and Almoravids 1159–1229

The Normans were evicted by the **Almohads**, a religious movement from Morocco which followed the teachings of a revolutionary preacher named Ibn Tumart, whom they had declared Mahdi. After driving the ruling **Almoravids** out of Morocco and Spain into final refuge on the Balearic Islands, the Almohads turned their attention eastwards to Tunisia. They took Tunis in 1159 and Mahdia the following year, and came to control an area stretching from Spain to Libya, uniting the Maghreb under a regime based in Marrakesh.

Although **Islam** reached virtually all the Berbers, largely through the medium of rural marabouts, society was little more homogeneous than under the Romans. The rulers – whether Aghlabid, Fatimid or Zirid – had little in common with most of their subjects. The resentment of the ever-oppressed Berbers was felt even in the most apparently stable periods – hence, for example, the secluded palaces built by the Aghlabids outside Kairouan. Occasionally this found focus in a leader such as Abu Yazid from Tozeur and the rulers were forced to defend themselves.

Urban society, however, flourished. Scholarship, law and education centred on mosques and the religious tradition (see p.523), and, in the first centuries Arab culture here (as elsewhere) was able to absorb and disperse the knowledge it acquired during its rapid expansion. A specific example in Tunisia was the introduction around Gabès of silk culture, which had first been encountered in China. **Ibn Khaldoun**, a truly original thinker, was born in Tunis in 1332 and lived through an eventful 74 years, which took in scholarship, exile and high political office. His best-known work, *Al Muqaddimah* (see p.563), set out historical principles way ahead of its time. He saw history as a cycle reflecting the relative power of desert tribes and an urban state. The tribes were strong because life in the desert was harsh, they were constantly at war with their neighbours, and shared *assabiya*, the solidarity that derived from common descent and interests. The cities (and the states they supported) were, by contrast, weak, because the luxury of urban life corrupted people's bodies and their society. Tribes that were greedy for the wealth that control of a city offered, could defeat and take over a state that was internally weak. But, as the new rulers settled into the same mould, they also succumbed ultimately to another tribe. And so history unfolded in a cycle of dynastic rise and fall, but not progress.

The physical breadth of Arab culture played a large part in spreading knowledge. The geographer **Ibn Battuta**, born in Tangier in 1304, is estimated to have travelled 120,000km in his life. Even in early centuries, before the advent of the Ottoman Turks, it was a surprisingly cosmopolitan society – much more so than the bloodthirsty and intolerant image fostered by its Christian opponents. The Fatimid general Jawhar (Pearl), who captured Egypt in 970, had been a Christian eunuch slave in Sicily, which was itself a remarkable example of its period: when the Normans recaptured Sicily for Christendom in the eleventh century, they found the Arab culture so congenial that they happily made the most of it while at the same time raiding the Tunisian coast. In 1270 Louis IX's expeditionary force at Carthage found itself fighting against the army of Frederick of Castile, who had been engaged by the sultan.

Islamic art, however, took a very different form from that of Europe. The ban on human and animal images removed the narrative core of representative art, leaving an emphasis on disembodied form that came to be seen in **architecture** as well as in the **decorative arts**. For all their surface brilliance, Islamic buildings are distinguished most by their manipulation of space, whether in a courtyard or a dome. In a Christian cathedral, large spaces are intended to be filled; but while spaces in mosques – whether courtyards or prayer halls – are also filled, it is when empty that they have most significance, symbolizing the all-embracing nature of Islam. Early architecture in Tunisia – the Great Mosques at Kairouan, Sousse, Tunis and Sfax – illustrates this aspect particularly well.

Later buildings from the Hafsid period onwards became locked into a more conservative and provincial style, with an emphasis on decoration rather than space. The classic elements of Tunisian architecture are the horseshoe arch (a more restrained version than elsewhere in the Maghreb) and internal stucco decoration, a skill first brought by Andalusian artisans. Along with other features – tiles, doorways, relief patterns on minarets – these make for a tradition that is at its best extremely elegant; at its worst, trivially pretty. Certainly the majesty of the early buildings was lost when the Fatimids took their skills to Cairo in the tenth century.

The Almohads' rule saw a massive growth in **Sufism** and an atmosphere of religious turmoil, but their biggest threat in Tunisia came in 1184 when they tried to subjugate the Balearic Islands. Pre-empting attack, the Almoravids under **Ibn Ghaniya** launched an invasion of Tunisia and set up a base in the Jerid. From there, they went on to conquer most of the country; but just as Tunis fell to them in 1203, an Almohad force captured their home base of Majorca and cut off their armies. With no naval support, Ibn Ghaniya was unable to defend Tunis, and over the next two years his forces were beaten back by the Almohads until they held only Mahdia, which fell in January 1206. Ibn Ghaniya, forced out into the Waddan region of what is now southern Algeria, returned to southern Tunisia in 1212, holding out until he was finally dispatched from the country fourteen years later.

The Hafsids 1207–1574

Having regained Tunisia, the Almohads left it in the hands of a governor whose family, the **Hafsids**, ruled it from then on, declaring independence in 1229 when the Marrakesh regime repudiated Ibn Tumart's teachings. Many saw the Hafsids as the Almohads' legitimate heirs.

The Hafsids made **Tunis** their capital and gave the country the new orientation it needed. Contact with Europe was re-established after a gap of several centuries, and the trading state created by the Hafsids is recognizably the direct ancestor of modern Tunisia.

Mediterranean relations were both friendly and hostile, mutually threatening and beneficial. The Hafsids sent ships to Valencia in 1238 to help the Muslim citizens defend themselves against the Christian kingdom of Aragon; but, with Valencia's fall, they opened trading relations with Aragon. These grew to such an extent that eventually a large number of Christians lived in Tunisia under Aragonese protection, and were even allowed to preach their religion.

This did not prevent a **crusade** (the eighth crusade) being led against Tunisia by Louis IX of France. Louis's expedition was prompted by a desire to convert the Hafsid Sultan el Mustansir and by debts owed to French traders in Tunis; but after taking Carthage, the French king died suddenly of plague (he was later canonized).

Trade was now booming in the Mediterranean, and Tunis was exploiting it more successfully than anyone. Complex agreements were signed with European states such as Venice, Pisa and Genoa. There was also trade across the desert with West Africa, and in 1262 an embassy even arrived from Norway.

Hand in hand with trade went piracy – the two were often indistinguishable – and the **corsairs of Barbary** (as North Africa was now known in Europe) became the legendary scourge of Christian merchants, plundering their goods on the high seas and selling their crews into slavery. Christian corsairs were just as efficient as their Muslim counterparts, and Genoa and Pisa had their own slave markets. Credit arrangements between Barbary and Europe included provisions for ransoming captured merchants and sailors.

With the proceeds of these activities, **El Mustansir** (1249–77) created a kingdom in Tunis that was recognized as the leading monarchy in the Islamic world. Cultural life flourished and building programmes established what became Tunisia's classic style of architecture, influenced by the Andalusian artisans who were encouraged to immigrate from Spain.

After El Mustansir's death, however, the Hafsid state was riven with internal strife and became so weak that Tunisia began to disintegrate into small **city-states** once again – Gabès, Gafsa and Tozeur being the main ones. Christians from Sicily occupied Jerba in 1284 and the Kerkennah Islands in 1286, and the region was twice split with rival sultans in Tunis and Bougie (Algeria). One result of this split was the arrival of the Arab tribe from which most of southern Tunisia's nomads claim descent, the **Banu Suleim**, who had settled in Libya after being invited to migrate westward with the Banu Hilal by Egypt's Fatimid rulers back in the tenth century (see p.494). In attempting to wrest control of Hafsid territory from his Bougie-based rival, Tunis's sultan **Abu Hafs** (1284–95) called on the Banu Suleim for support, promising them feudal overlordship in much of the countryside, the Banu Hilal having largely moved further west to pastures new in the meantime. As nomads, the Banu Suleim had no experience in managing agriculture, and their domination of the Sahel devastated the olive industry, but in the south their descendants eventually worked out a stable system in which the sedentary Berbers supplied them with a tribute of agricultural products in return for military protection and pasturage rights. The split in the Hafsid sultanate meanwhile was healed again in 1370, when the Bougie sultan, **Abul-Abbas**, captured Tunis, took control of all the city-states and islands, and reunited the country, beginning a Hafsid revival that lasted another century. In 1390, he even saw off a joint European expedition against Mahdia.

The Hafsids continued to rule until 1574 although their state was in decline, losing any real power after 1534. Even so, they had presided over a settled and prosperous era lasting more than three hundred years, one to which Tunisians still look back with some pride.

Spanish–Turkish rivalry 1534–74

The sixteenth century in the western Mediterranean was glamorous but violent. Moorish civilization in Spain was being toppled by the resurgent Christians and, encouraged by the capture of Granada in 1492, the Spanish launched naval raids on the ports of the Maghreb with some success. Opposition to these Christian corsairs came from the **Barbarossa** brothers, Aruj and Khair ed Din, who based themselves on Jerba and set about winning back the Maghreb for Islam. After Aruj died in 1518, Khair ed Din petitioned the **Ottoman Turks** for support: still exhilarated by their capture of Constantinople in 1453, they needed no second invitation to contest such a vital region with the infidels, and Tunisia became the front line of an east–west confrontation.

In 1529 Barbarossa took Algiers, then in 1534 he expelled the now abject Hafsids from Tunis, at the same time taking control of the east coast and Kairouan. This was too much for the Spanish, who sent a massive army in 1535 and restored the Hafsid **Moulay Hassan** as a puppet ruler. Events continued at this sort of pace for the next half-century, with Spain, France, Turkey, Naples and other powers all disputing the North African coast. In 1536 Francis I of France allied himself secretly with the Ottoman sultan against their common enemy, Charles V of Spain. Fully supporting the pope's denunciation of this unholy pact, Charles tried to make his own arrangement with the real regional power, Barbarossa, under which Barbarossa would become Spanish viceroy of the North African coast in return for helping to crush France and Turkey. This eventually fell through, however, and in 1544 Charles and Francis managed to resolve their differences in another treaty which nullified the previous two at a stroke.

Fighting in the field was fierce – the pyramid of skulls which stood on Jerba until 1849 was the result of one clash between Turks and Spanish – but the Turks gradually gained the upper hand. **Dragut**, a pirate who had been enslaved by the Spanish and ransomed by Barbarossa, had extended his control from Jerba as far as Kairouan by 1557, and a flurry of activity at Tunis brought the war to a close. Taken from the Spanish in 1569 by an Algerian Turk, it fell to Don John of Austria in 1573, and then for the last time in 1574 to the combined Ottoman forces of Algiers, Tripoli and Turkey itself.

Early Ottoman rule 1574–1704

Tunis (like Algiers) was made a **regency** of the Ottoman Empire, governed by a complex system which only helped to intensify internal strife. Power was divided between the **bey**, a civil administrator in charge of the taxes levied from every town; the **dey**, a military commander with access to the proceeds

Refugees

One by-product of the Muslim–Christian struggles of the sixteenth century had a lasting impact on all the countries of the central Maghreb: the immigration of **Spanish Muslims** following their expulsion by the triumphant Christians in 1609.

Relations between the Muslims of the Maghreb and Spain had always been close, especially after the fall of Seville in 1248 and ensuing Christian advances. The Hafsid rulers of Tunis, who had previously held high command in Spain, were particularly welcoming and perhaps 100,000 immigrants arrived during the three centuries of their rule. Beginning in 1609, though, pressure on Muslims and Jews to leave Spain unless they converted to Christianity became a formal expulsion: in the provinces of Valencia, Andalusia and Murcia in 1609, Aragon in 1610, and finally in Catalonia, Castile and Extremadura.

In 1609 alone, 80,000 refugees arrived in Tunisia at a time when the entire population of Tunis was probably around the same figure. The wealthy urban elite were encouraged to settle in prestigious streets set aside for them: Rue des Andalous in the southwest of the Tunis Medina is the most obvious example. Smaller-scale artisans went to existing smaller towns in the north such as Jedeida and Tebourba. And the majority, rural farmers, founded small communities in three main areas: the northeast corner of the country, between Tunis and Bizerte, the fertile base of Cap Bon, in towns like Soliman and Grombalia; and the Medjerda Valley, from Medjez el Bab westwards.

Religion apart, these immigrants were more Spanish than North African and spoke Spanish rather than Arabic. When their writers composed satires against the Spanish Inquisition, they wrote in Castilian verse. More than a hundred years after their arrival, in the early eighteenth century, the French traveller Peyssonel found the inhabitants of Soliman and Tebourba still speaking Spanish. Their food and clothing were different and, with their eyes always on their abandoned homeland, they were reluctant to dilute their culture by marrying outside their community.

Eventually they became assimilated, but the Andalusian immigrants have left a lasting imprint on Tunisian culture. The single most visible and concentrated remnant of Andalusian immigration is **Testour** (see pp.302–304), a small farming town in the Medjerda Valley with a recognizably Spanish flavour.

of foreign trade and piracy; and the **pasha**, the Ottoman sultan's representative. At first it was the deys who controlled the country: Othman Dey (1598–1610) and Youssef Dey (1610–37) were two commanders who left their mark on the architecture of Tunis, and by building up the fleet to renew its activities in the Mediterranean. In 1604 Jerba was brought back under Tunis's control. But while the deys were busy with foreign and military affairs, Murad Bey and his son Hammouda Pasha (who combined the offices of bey and pasha), were strengthening their grip on domestic power, starting the first line of hereditary beys, known as the **Muradids**. Firearms and the professional Turkish army allowed them to hold power far more effectively than any previous government and, unlike the Hafsids before them, they faced no threat of a tribal coup.

As the century wore on, European traders were allowed back into the country. The first permanent French consulate was built in the Tunis Medina in 1659, and an agreement was signed with Britain in 1662. Not that trade was any more tranquil than it had been before – in 1654 the British Admiral Blake bombarded and destroyed the pirate base of Porto Farina (Ghar el Melh). But contact with the outside world boosted the opportunities for trade and began a short period of relative prosperity.

The Husaynids 1704–1883

The Muradid line of beys came to an end at the beginning of the eighteenth century, when an Algerian invasion had to be repulsed. The successful commander was **Husayn Bin Ali**, a Turkish soldier of Greek origin based in Le Kef, who took control of the country on the basis of his success. Despite his Ottoman ties, he came to identify more and more with internal Tunisian interests, and from this time on the Ottoman connection, never very strong, was little more than nominal.

Such problems as Husayn had were closer to home. Having groomed a nephew, Ali Pacha, to succeed him, Husayn produced a son who naturally replaced Ali as heir. Ali responded by rebelling against his uncle, enlisting the support of the ever-hopeful Algerian Turks. Husayn was defeated once near the border at Le Kef in 1735, then killed at a battle near Kairouan in 1740. Now Husayn's sons in turn obtained Algerian support against the usurper: they too were defeated near Le Kef (1746), but ten years later succeeded in expelling Ali Pasha from Tunis. After seeing off (with some difficulty) their over-enthusiastic Algerian supporters, **Ali Bey** (1759–81) and **Hammouda Bey** (1781–1813) made Tunis once again a secure, prosperous and independent power in the Mediterranean.

But whatever their success in international politics, the beys failed to bring Tunisia fully under their control. Even at its apogee under Hammouda Bey, the Husaynid state only governed the cities, the Sahel and the Tell. In the steppes of central Tunisia and in the far south the **tribes** were virtually autonomous. They paid their taxes irregularly, when forced to by a *mahalla* (military expedition), and though they might admit the bey's sovereignty as commander of the faithful, they would not allow him to intervene in their affairs.

The early years of the nineteenth century were the turning point of modern Tunisia. Under Hammouda Bey the economy and the state had been strong, but in following years both collapsed under assault from Europe. Cooperation between European navies after the Treaty of Aix-la-Chapelle in 1816 effectively put an end to Mediterranean piracy, an important source of revenue for the beys. To make up the loss they increased taxes on trade and agriculture, which placed a heavy burden on the economy. At the same time industrialization gave European manufacturers a competitive edge that enabled them to subvert Tunisian products, first in the Mediterranean and then in the domestic market. By the 1840s Tunisia's balance of trade surplus had become a deficit.

Tunisia was also beleaguered politically. In 1830 France had seized the Beylik of Algiers on the feeblest of excuses, and in 1836 it signalled its interest in Tunisia by sending a fleet to discourage a Turkish invasion. To secure foreign protection without falling under the control of any one power, the beys had to offer trading concessions to each of the European governments in turn, thereby aggravating the country's economic decline.

Ahmed Bey (1837–55) attempted to strengthen the state through internal reform, extending his control of local government and founding a **European-style army**. But this failed. The government could not afford these expenses and had to increase taxes and borrow from abroad. Furthermore, by employing French military advisers and going on a state visit to France in 1846, Ahmed Bey brought Tunisia firmly into the French camp, and once they had a grip they would not let go. Ahmed's successors, Mohammed Bey (1855–59) and Mohammed es-Sadok Bey (1869–82), were less dedicated to government reform than to a life of luxury. Their reckless expenditure on palaces and neglect of the administration brought the country to the brink of collapse. Not only did they contract debts at disadvantageous rates but, in 1864, the doubling of the **poll tax** led to a widespread revolt. At one point the European consuls, fearing that the capital would be overrun, packed their bags and were ready to leave. In the end the revolt fizzled out when the government backed down and the tribes fell out with each other. But by then the government's weakness was clear to all inside and outside Tunisia.

The scramble for Tunisia

Unable to increase taxes, the Tunisian government was virtually bankrupt. Trying to keep itself afloat, the country borrowed at ever-increasing rates from European (mainly French) banks in a spiral encouraged by the European powers. By 1869 Tunisia's main creditors – France, Britain and Italy – feared the Tunisian government would be unable to service these debts and that this might serve as a pretext for one of the powers to invade. In a rare moment of international cooperation they set up an **International Financial Commission** that effectively supervised every act of the Tunisian administration. Behind the scenes, however, the powers were jockeying for position. They fought among themselves to secure the contracts awarded by the bey – the TGM railway in Tunis, for instance – and influence at court.

The only Tunisian who came close to arresting this decline was **Kherredin**. As a minister in Mustapha Khaznader's government (1857–64) he had masterminded a form of constitutional monarchy that guaranteed the **civil rights** of Tunisian and foreign citizens (the name of which, *destour*, meaning "constitution" in Arabic, eventually gave its name to the pro-independence Destour Party). But jealousy at court and his unpopular pro-Turkish policies had led to his dismissal in 1862. When he returned from retirement in 1869, to head first the International Financial Commission and then the Bey's government, he realized that Tunisia's only hope was to play one power against another while strengthening from within. He reformed the administration, local government and the legal system, and seemed set to restore government control over the tribes and their finances. A rapprochement with Turkey enabled him to set the British and Germans, who did not want the ailing Turkish Empire broken up, against the French and Italians, who did, and so postpone the threatened French invasion.

Kherredin's government was short-lived (1870–77). Despite his reforms, the economy was still weak, and when he tried to embroil Tunisia, as a loyal country of the Ottoman Empire, in Turkey's war with Russia, the French consul was able to galvanize opposition at court and have him overthrown. Without his directing hand the administration foundered. Worse still, the French were able to secure an agreement on the division of the Ottoman Empire with Britain and Germany at the Congress of Berlin in 1878. In return for Cyprus, Britain gave France a free hand in Tunisia. And so Tunisia's fate was sealed. France's only rival in Tunisia was now Italy – a new nation eager to join the colonial powers – and when the Italians appeared to be getting the upper hand at court the French decided to act.

In 1881 France announced that 9000 Khroumir tribesmen had raided Algeria, an action they had actually encouraged, and that it was compelled to defend its territory. A force of 30,000 men was sent across the border, occupying first Le Kef and then Tunis, where the bey signed the **Treaty of Ksar Said** in 1881, ceding to the French all control over foreign affairs.

The French protectorate 1881–1956

The bey had given in without a fight, ordering his garrisons to surrender; in the words of a Tunisian song, "he sold his people like vegetables". Even so, resistance continued piecemeal among the tribes, led by a former *caid* (provincial governor), **Ali ben Khalifa en-Naffati**. But when Sfax fell in July 1882, bombarded into submission by nine ironclads and four gunboats, and then Kairouan in October, many of the tribespeople submitted. The remainder (100,000 people, a tenth of the population) fled to Libya as dissident refugees. There, disappointed by the sultan's indifference and starving in squalid camps, they gradually gave in. By 1885 there were probably fewer than 1000 dissidents left.

Having defeated all opposition, the French secured their control of Tunisia. In 1883 the **Treaty of the Bardo** recognized the bey as the nominal ruler but forced him to comply with any "suggestions" made by the French Resident General. Thus, while Tunisian administrators retained executive powers, the French alone made policy, which was less aggressive in Tunisia than in Algeria. There the French exerted direct control, and evicted Algerians to make way for colonists after repeated rebellions; in Tunisia they were more clandestine, advancing similar policies through law reform, usually with spurious claims to Islamic legitimacy. But the results were very much the same.

Large colonial estates were established in the Tell and Sahel by dispossessing Tunisians who lacked titles to their land. Tens of thousands of independent farmers were reduced to landless day-labourers. Iron, lead and phosphate mining concessions were granted to French companies. Taxation increased markedly but government expenditure only met the needs of the colonists. A Tunisian-sponsored colonization fund was established in 1897 to encourage

French immigration. Roads, wells and dams were built to facilitate colonization, not local development. Railways and ports were provided for the export of Tunisian resources to the metropole. Markets and advantageous tariffs allowed French goods to flood Tunisia, swamping local industry and draining precious local capital. In short, colonization upturned the local economy.

Within less than twenty years European settlers made up almost five percent of the population: 25,000 were French, but they were outnumbered by some 70,000 Italians. Most of the French colonists were government officials. They monopolized the higher echelons of the administration; few Tunisians achieved higher rank than a clerk. The **Italians**, fleeing impoverishment in southern Italy, set up small farms and businesses. Competition between the two communities was rife, occasionally violent. Eventually the French, fearing that their colonists would be overwhelmed by the militant Italians, many of whom were fervent supporters of Mussolini, had to restrict their immigration to redress the imbalance.

During World War I, the Ouderna in southern Tunisia launched a revolt against French rule in support of the Ottoman Empire, which had lined up against France. But there was little Tunisian **resistance**, at first, because its urban elite, always cosmopolitan, was not over-resentful of the French presence. Life for them, particularly those around the bey, was still very comfortable, and the resentment of the poorer classes had no outlet beyond sporadic outbreaks of violence. Those who sought reform, moreover, were admirers of France's material and economic power. These **Young Tunisians** wanted co-operation with "mother France", not confrontation: they wanted to learn before seeking full independence.

Unfortunately, the French were by no means as conciliatory. Led by the newspaper publisher de Carnières, a strong colonial lobby opposed every reform. They saw **education** as a particular threat because it would make Tunisians unsuitable for the role they were born to fill, that of servant and labourer. Their efforts were rewarded by cuts in the education budget and restriction of primary education to fewer than ten percent of the population.

Elitist and intellectual, the Young Tunisian movement could not rally popular support. Nor, despite demands for a wide range of constitutional rights, could its successor, the **Destour Party**, formed in 1920. Dominated by members of Tunisia's small professional and entrepreneurial middle class, they too were out of touch with the grass roots of Tunisian society. Their nationalism came across in a blend of nostalgia and legal hair-splitting rather than an active and broad-based campaign for independence.

Throughout the 1920s, however, growing resentment was fuelled by the economic depression. Violent demonstrations against French containing measures gave it some expression, but there was little organization. Ever more reactionary, Destour had nothing to offer, and a new organ was needed to channel popular nationalism. It was to meet this need that a group of rebels formed the breakaway **Neo-Destour Party** in March 1934 in Ksar Essaf. Their secretary-general was **Habib Bourguiba**, whose background epitomized the ideals of the new party. Born in 1903 into a lower-middle-class Monastir family, Bourguiba grasped the few opportunities that were allowed to him. He won a scholarship to the Sadiki College in Tunis, then another to study in Paris, where he became a lawyer and married a French woman, returning to Tunis in 1927. His political activism did not actually begin until 1932, when he founded a newspaper, *L'Action Tunisienne*; two years later the new party was formed.

The French were quick to spot the threat posed by this new opponent. Six months after Neo-Destour's foundation, they declared the party illegal and, for the first of many times over the next two decades, arrested Bourguiba, who was able to identify and give voice to popular aspirations in a way that the old Destour Party never had. For the first time ordinary people acquired some (albeit outlawed) political muscle. Bourguiba was a formidable populist, and Neo-Destour immediately drew massive support for its aims of self-determination and a return to Islam. Ever the pragmatist, Bourguiba could be heard in these years advocating a return to the veil for women.

When Bourguiba was arrested after another violent demonstration in 1938 he was quietly interned in France to avoid any suggestion of weakness in Tunisia. But French insecurity, and popular unrest, continued through the 1930s, fuelled by the situation in Europe and the growing ambition of **Mussolini's** Fascist Italy. Having helped themselves to Libya in 1912, and Ethiopia in 1936 – to the horror of the ineffectual League of Nations – the Italians had rampant hopes of a new African empire, and they had always felt cheated of Tunisia.

Tunisia in World War II

Ironically, when France fell in **World War II**, the **Italians** took Bourguiba to Rome, hoping for his support in their claim. Since, however, he trusted Italy and Germany's puppet Vichy regime in France even less than the Free French, he consistently supported the Allies, even when the **Germans** landed in Tunisia in November 1942.

The Germans had invaded in response to a double Allied advance: British and Commonwealth forces across the desert from Egypt (after El Alamein), and the Americans from Algeria following the **Operation Torch** landings of November 1942. The Allies needed Tunisia as a base to invade Italy, "the soft underbelly of Europe"; the Nazis needed it to control the Sicilian Channel and thereby cut off Allied shipping from Egypt and India. By the end of the month the Allies had the west of the country, but as winter set in they found the going harder than anticipated and, in February, **Rommel's** retreating forces found a weak spot in the Americans' defences at **Kasserine** and inflicted a serious defeat. In spite of this setback, American forces held the line before the Algerian border as Commonwealth troops streamed into Tunisia from the east. By this time too, the Allies were able to decode Rommel's most secret messages, learn his plans in advance, and identify and sink German supply ships.

The Germans held the **Mareth Line**, built south of Gabès in 1936 by the French as an African Maginot Line. By stealth, however, and using routes thought impassable by the Germans, **Montgomery's** Eighth Army managed to get round the line, and control it by the end of March 1943, linking up with the Americans to the west. They were also joined by General Leclerc's column of mainly African Free French troops, who had marched across the desert from Chad to take southwest Libya. Over the next month, the Allies advanced through the country; their toughest battle was at **Takrouna**, which fell to New Zealand troops on April 19. On May 7, the Allies took Tunis and Bizerte, leaving the Germans only Cap Bon, for which a fierce battle was expected. In the event, however, German forces in Cap Bon surrendered only two days later.

The campaign fought in Tunisia is little known compared with the "glamour" of Tobruk and El Alamein, but the Allies alone suffered **15,000 dead**. Without Tunisia, moreover, the invasion of Italy would not have been possible.

The struggle for independence 1945–56

After the war, the French took up much where they had left off. To all appearances, Bourguiba's political support for the Allies, and the military support of many Tunisians who had fought for them, had very little effect on his relations with the colonialists – but French intransigence would almost certainly have been hardened still further had the Tunisians supported the Axis.

Bourguiba had moved from jail in France to Rome before returning to Tunisia in 1942, but he found himself as unwelcome as before by the authorities. On March 25, 1945, he made a dramatic escape by fishing boat from Kerkennah (see p.285) to avoid arrest. He went to Cairo, and spent the next few years travelling world capitals to drum up support for his country's cause, with considerable success. A born showman, he took to the stage of world politics with some panache.

Back at home, popular nationalism was growing steadily. The **UGTT**, a Tunisian-only trade union federation formed in 1946, became an important vehicle of resistance in Bourguiba's absence. A strike in Sfax in 1947 was put down violently. By 1950 the French were ready to talk, and even accepted Bourguiba as a negotiator. After he put forward proposals in Paris, which included safeguards to French interests in Tunisia, a government was installed in 1951, headed by **Mohammed Chenik**, who had led a nationalist administration against the Axis occupation. But, in a pattern that was repeated later in Algeria, the first signs of concession from the French home government produced a sudden hardening in the resistance of the Tunisian French. Under pressure from them, the French government reversed its policy. Bourguiba was exiled to Tabarka, then France, and **violence** escalated. In December 1952, **Farhat Hached**, secretary-general of the UGTT and a close friend and ally of Bourguiba, was gunned down in Tunis by the **Red Hand**, a group of French settler terrorists.

This only attracted international sympathy for the Tunisians: the Latin American countries had succeeded in getting their problems onto the UN agenda, and a resolution was passed calling for the resumption of **French–Tunisian talks**. There were those in France and Tunisia who thought the issue could be squashed, including a repressive French resident-general immortalized for stating: "there can be no question of putting Monsieur Bourguiba on trial. Tunisians, who are apt to forget easily, have already almost forgotten his name." But if there was no legal outlet for nationalism, the guerrilla gangs who began to appear in the hills showed that it could not be simply ignored. In 1954 France suddenly reversed its policy, worried by recent disasters in Indo-China and fearing that, if they did not come to an agreement with Bourguiba, more radical politicians might gain the upper hand. Pierre Mendès-France came to Tunis with plans for internal self-government. After many months of talks, agreement was reached in June 1955, and Bourguiba returned to Tunis to an ecstatic welcome.

The agreement, however, only gave Tunisia limited internal autonomy – foreign policy and some aspects of the economy were still to be controlled by France – and this gave Bourguiba's traditional opponents an angle of attack. They claimed that he had compromised and betrayed the Tunisian nation – this was the time in the 1950s when pan-Arabism, inspired by Nasser in Egypt, was running strong. Bourguiba's leading opponent, **Salah Ben Youssef**, defeated politically in December 1955, took to guerrilla warfare with Egyptian and Algerian support. By 1956, though, his revolt had been suppressed; Ben Youssef escaped to Cairo, and five years later was murdered in Frankfurt.

Bourguiba had always retained the support of the people, and he was well aware that full independence was within his grasp; on **March 20, 1956**, soon after Morocco, Tunisia became an independent state.

Tunisia under Bourguiba 1956–87

In the years following independence Bourguiba set up the political and legal framework for the kind of state he had envisaged. **Elections** for the national assembly resulted in a virtually clean sweep for Bourguiba's **Front National**. The 1959 constitution gave Bourguiba wide powers as president, including nomination of government and civil service personnel, and initiation of legislation. Since all members of the assembly were nominees of the party (restyled the Parti Socialiste Destourien or **PSD**), the government became Bourguiba's personal fiefdom. The small Communist Party was banned in 1963, leaving a one-party state. Bourguiba immediately set about bringing in the sweeping social reforms he had long sought. New marriage laws gave women a more powerful voice, and outlawed polygamy (though it was never very widespread). Women were given the franchise, equal pay was made statutory, family planning introduced on a wide scale, and education for women strongly encouraged (see p.534).

Another area of planned reform was **religion**. Bourguiba downgraded the great Zitouna University in Tunis to a theological faculty of the modern university, and even attempted to end the tradition of Ramadan (see p.524), obtaining support from the religious establishment with an ingenious argument: to be engaged in a jihad (holy war – the Islamic equivalent of a crusade) excuses you from observing Ramadan, so the Tunisian "*jihad*" against underdevelopment extends to all of its people. What is remarkable is not the ingeniousness of the argument nor that it ultimately failed, but Bourguiba's audacity in challenging such a basic thread of Tunisian life, and in getting official support from the mufti of Tunis. The main centre of resistance to change was the holy city of **Kairouan**, which had previously also opposed the enforcement of monogamy; the citizens pointedly observed Ramadan a day early, simultaneously with Cairo, in a gesture of Arab solidarity.

It took several years to hive off the last remnants of the **colonial presence,** occasionally at some cost. The first of the problems was the naval arsenal at Bizerte, where the French had stayed on after independence because of NATO's decision that it was a vital link. In 1958, at the beginning of the Algerian war of independence, French planes from Algeria bombed the border village of **Sakiet Sidi Youssef**. Tunisia responded by demanding that France evacuate its base in Bizerte. The French refused, and in the resulting **Bizerte crisis** of July 1961 the Tunisian army saw action for the first time when it attempted to evict the French by force. Some 1300 Tunisian lives were lost before the French agreed to leave in October 1964. Also in 1964, Bourguiba **nationalized** the land of remaining French settlers, though relations with France were soon back to normal, helped by Bourguiba's pro-Western **foreign policy**.

While Gamel Abdel Nasser's regime in Egypt was challenging British, French and American influence in the region and making war against Israel – increasingly an American protégé whose statehood no Arab country would recognize – Bourguiba voiced approval of US bombing in Vietnam and implied that the Palestinians should negotiate peace with Israel. In 1968, Tunisia even boycotted the Arab League because of what it felt were pro-Soviet tendencies.

At home Bourguiba had other problems, caused largely by the rise of **Ahmed Ben Salah**. Once a leader of the UGTT, Ben Salah had been forced out after daring to claim an equal role for the unions in government. However, in 1961 the president switched course, appointing Ben Salah as Minister of Planning, and began to direct the country along an increasingly leftist course. Collectivization was introduced, particularly in agriculture, with co-operatives being formed out of the old peasant smallholdings. Bourguiba went around the country on well-publicized outings where he was shown riding through prickly-pear fences, a traditional symbol of the smallholder's pride. But in 1969 Bourguiba decided that collectivization was a failure. Ben Salah and his policies were purged, and the country was given a violent twist to the right.

The Ben Salah affair was typical of Bourguiba's avowedly **autocratic style** of government, guided by the demands of the moment rather than by any longterm overriding principles. By appointing a **prime minister** to deal with executive matters – from 1969 – and so putting himself somewhere above everyday politics, he made himself a figure of almost royal detachment. When mistakes were made he could sacrifice a subordinate, such as Ben Salah, and enhance his own reputation by appearing to correct misjudgements that were ultimately his own responsibility. Ever a master of political infighting, as well as the wider stage, Bourguiba resisted an attempt at the beginning of the 1970s to reduce his influence within the party, and in 1974 he was elected president for life.

As the 1970s wore on, however, Tunisia's international reputation for political stability in the developing world was being threatened. Early in the decade the government began to legislate against strikes, and the country's **human rights** record brought it to the attention of Amnesty International. Deteriorating relations between the government and unions eventually came to a head when a strike in the mining industry was followed in January 1978 with the first **general strike** since independence, called by the UGTT. The strike was violently suppressed by government forces and arrests were made, and then in June the Socialist Democratic Movement was (illegally) formed. On the second anniversary of the general strike the mysterious **"Gafsa incident"** (see p.341), possibly a Libyan-backed coup attempt, was clearly an attempt at destabilization, however badly calculated.

By now, though, the government promised **political liberalization**. In 1981 other political parties were legalized – providing, that is, they were representative, constitutional, "preserved national gains", and rejected fanaticism, violence and foreign dependence. This, in effect, meant that the government could choose and manacle the opposition by rejecting the applications for legalization made by parties they considered too popular. As it was, the PSD/UGTT federation won all 136 seats in the 1981 **election**, the first free election since 1956, prompting complaints of electoral malpractice from the recently formed Socialist Democrats and Popular Unity Movement.

Even more serious was the question of **Islamic fundamentalism**. Like every moderate Arab state, Tunisia was worried by the prospect of the Iranian Revolution spreading to its own shores and, as early as 1979, the government had banned the fundamentalists. In 1981 two religious movements appeared, the Mouvement de la Tendence Islamique (**MTI**) and the Rassemblement

CONTEXTS | The historical framework

Nationale Arabe (**RNA**), only to be banned just before the elections. Soon after, over a hundred of their leaders were summarily arrested and sentenced to long prison terms – arrests that presaged a new era of repression.

But in the absence of a legal opposition, discontent with the regime found other channels, fuelled by high **unemployment**, **poverty**, and **repression** administered by the police and the Destour Party's unofficial militia. In January 1984, following an announcement that the government **bread subsidy** would be removed, **rioting** broke out in the south and west (the country's poorest regions), and quickly spread to Tunis. After street battles in which at least eighty people were killed, Bourguiba announced restoration of the subsidy, and the riots ended almost as suddenly as they had begun. The Interior minister was made the scapegoat and resigned, and the government raised the price of bread again after a couple of months, but everyone knew that the riots had shaken the leadership, a tacit understanding that hardened government attitudes towards the opposition – and encouraged the regime's opponents to redouble their efforts.

Bourguiba's decline

The UGTT under **Habib Achour**, a rival of Bourguiba's since the 1950s, dissociated itself from its electoral alliance with the PSD and began to campaign against the government's economic and human rights records, so in January 1986, Bourguiba had him arrested and imprisoned with twenty other union leaders on trumped-up charges. After continued student unrest and a series of bomb attacks on ministry buildings, **General Zine el Abidine Ben Ali**, the officer who commanded the riot troops in 1984, was appointed Minister of the Interior. Police appeared on the campuses, 1500 students were arrested, a publishing house with fundamentalist sympathies was closed down, and a purge of the civil service and armed forces began. Nor did it stop there.

Bourguiba now divorced and exiled his wife, Wassila, a formidable woman with her own political aspirations, and, under the guise of an anti-corruption campaign, arrested her relatives and minions. Then he dismissed Prime Minister Mohammed Mzali, whom he had only just publically named as his successor, and replaced him with economist **Rachid Sfar**. The November 1986 elections were a sham, boycotted by even the recognized opposition parties. As for the fundamentalists, Bourguiba privately described them as a menace to the secular state he had created, saying that their destruction would be the last great service he could render his country.

Early in 1987 the police began arresting suspects on the streets and soon more than 2000 people had been jailed, among them **Rachid Ghannuchi**, the new leader of the MTI. The Tunisian League of Human Rights complained about torture and detention without charge, only to find its offices closed and its leader under arrest. Men shaved off their beards to avoid suspicion. Rachid Ghannuchi and ninety other Islamists were charged with promoting terrorism and conspiring with Iran to overthrow the state. The campaign of repression sparked off a series of retaliatory **demonstrations and bombings**. In August the fundamentalists planted bombs at four hotels near Monastir injured twelve tourists and threatened Tunisia's vital tourist industry.

Fortunately, the government backed down from further confrontation. Amid rumours of Bourguiba's ill health, Rachid Sfar then resigned as prime minister, to be replaced by General Ben Ali. Within a week, in November 1987, Ben Ali had seized power in a **palace coup**. Bourguiba was diagnosed as senile and forced to retire, and Ben Ali's opponents and rivals were placed under house

Throughout Tunisia, you will come across street names commemorating key dates and personalities from the country's recent history. The following is a brief run-down.

Bechir Sfar (1856–1917) and **Ali Bach Hamba** (1876–1918) were two early nationalists who co-founded the Young Tunisians movement in 1907. A famous speech by Sfar in 1906 is considered one of the key events in the development of Tunisian nationalism, and he was known as the "second father of the reawakening", the first being the Turkish official **Kherredin** (see p.501). Next in the sequence of nationalist movements was the Destour Party, founded in 1920 by **Abdelaziz Thaalbi** (1874–1944), but soon to be overtaken by the Neo-Destour Party, founded on March 2, 1934, at the Congress of Ksar Hellal by the young French-educated lawyer **Habib Bourguiba** (1903–2000).

Among Bourguiba's colleagues in the movement were **Hedi Nouira**, **Habib Thameur** (1909–49) and **Ali Belhouane** (1909–58), a teacher at Sadiki College. On **April 9, 1938**, Belhouane led an anti-French demonstration in Tunis that ended in violence, with as many as a hundred people killed; the result of the demonstration was the banning by the French authorities of Neo-Destour and the arrest of Bourguiba and other leaders.

After Bourguiba's hurried departure from Tunisia in March 1945, a reconstituted Neo-Destour received valuable support from the UGTT national union movement (Union Générale Tunisienne de Travail), among whose leaders were **Habib Achour** and **Farhat Hached** (assassinated in 1952). Negotiations for independence proceeded with Bourguiba in exile on the island of La Galite off Tabarka (see p.192), but on **June 1, 1955** he made a triumphant return to Tunis to supervise the final stages, and on **March 20, 1956** the final protocol was signed in Paris. Following independence, Bourguiba served as president until **November 7, 1987**, when he was peacefully deposed by the current incumbent Ben Ali.

arrest while a new administration was formed. Bourguiba remained under house arrest in Monastir until his death in April 2000.

Tunisia under Ben Ali

Once in power, Ben Ali pursued a policy of **national reconciliation**, releasing 5000 political prisoners over the next six months, including Rachid Ghannuchi. He reduced government interference in the internal politics of the UGTT and began to introduce **political reforms**, banning imprisonment without trial, relaxing political censorship and putting the presidency up for election every five years. A number of opposition parties were recognized by the state and allowed to operate, so long as they were not anti-constitutional, religious, ethnic nor regional, and Ben Ali announced another name change for the ruling party, henceforth to be known as the Rassemblement Constitutionnel Démocratique (**RCD**).

At the RCD's first conference in 1988, Ben Ali promised free expression and free **elections**. The latter materialized the following year, and resulted in the RCD taking all the seats and, apparently, eighty percent of the vote. Their main challengers were Islamic fundamentalists who, banned from fighting the election as a party, fought as independents and obtained up to a quarter of the vote in some areas and some 14 percent overall. The MTI, now called Hizb en

Tunisia's foreign relations

Relations between Tunisia and its **neighbours**, especially Libya, have had their ups and downs. In the late 1970s Tunisia accused Libya of interfering in its internal affairs, and it was generally believed that Libya had backed the "Gafsa coup" in 1980. After Tunisia lost a border dispute settled at the International Court of Justice, tension increased. In 1985 the Libyan Voice of Vengeance radio station called on Tunisians to massacre their Jewish community and police shortly after arrested seven suspected "terrorists" crossing the border. Libya then expelled 31,000 Tunisian workers, most of them illegal immigrants. Libyan troops began to mobilize and Bourguiba prepared for war, and though arbitration by Kuwait prevented military conflict, relations between Tunisia and Libya remainded sour.

Since Ben Ali took power there has been a dramatic improvement. Libya compensated the workers expelled in 1985, opened its frontier with Tunisia and settled a dispute between the two countries over Mediterranean oil fields. The 1980s also saw the foundation of the **Arab Maghreb Union** (UMA), encompassing Algeria, Mauritania, Morocco, Libya and Tunisia, though it has not lived up to the dreams of Maghrebian unity that greeted its creation, and has since pretty much fizzled out.

Ben Ali has been successful in maintaining good **relations with the West**, in particular France and the USA. America was the first country to recognize Tunisia's independence and bonds between the two countries have since been solid. Tunisia has American **Peace Corps** workers and military advisers, and many Tunisians believe that Ben Ali, who was trained in the USA, came to power with America's tacit support if not positive blessing. Tunisia certainly is a valuable US ally, lying as it does between Algeria and Libya, and the naval base at Bizerte is among the most strategic in the Mediterranean.

Relations with the West came under most strain during the 1991 **Gulf War**, when Tunisian public opinion strongly supported Iraq's leader, Saddam Hussein, seen as a champion of the Arab nation against Western interests. The fundamentalist opposition, funded largely from Saudi Arabia, was unable to capitalize on this feeling and Ben Ali successfully outflanked them, opposing American intervention, but not strongly enough to alienate his Western friends. Since then, he has been eager to increase links with Europe, particularly France.

One undercurrent of tension between Tunisia and the EU lies in the number of Tunisian and other Maghrebian nationals eager to **migrate** to Europe in search of a better life. Tighter immigration controls in Europe have resulted in a huge increase in the number of Maghrebians attempting to evade border controls and enter the EU illegally. Most illegal Tunisian immigrants end up in France and Italy, where they play a vital role in the informal economy, but where they are also the victims of racism and exploitation, and where many drift into petty crime. Italy in particular has an alarming number of young Tunisians in its jails, and in 1998 signed a treaty with Tunisia to allow for the repatriation of illegal immigrants. Following another agreement between the two countries, signed in 2003, Tunisian forces have themselves begun to patrol offshore waters and arrest illegal migrants, who face prosecution in Tunisia if caught.

Another possible source of friction between Tunisia and the EU lies in the field of **human rights**. In 1995, the EU signed an Association Agreement with Tunisia, which binds the parties to respect human rights and democratic principles. Since then however, Tunisian government harassment of human rights organizations, arrests of activists, and attacks on press freedom have prompted European parliamentarians to pass a series of resolutions expressing concern at the situation. Meanwhile, and despite his 1997 declaration that there were no political prisoners in the country, Ben Ali released 500 in November 1999, and another batch in May 2001, but Amnesty estimate there are still hundreds more in Tunisian jails.

Nahdha ("Renewal Party"), but still illegal, dismissed the elections as fraudulent, and Rachid Ghannuchi moved to Paris where he felt freer to speak out.

Political **liberalization** continued, with more amnesties and talk of legalizing Hizb en Nahdha, but when this proved to be little more than talk Hizb en Nahdha began to step up its activities. In December 1989, a group of fundamentalist students began a hunger strike in protest at government attempts to close the faculty of theology at Zitouna University in Tunis. Allegations of government inaction following the **January 1990 floods**, which killed thirty people and left thousands homeless, added fuel to the movement, together with a strike by municipal workers, riots in Nefta and Sidi Bou Zid, and clashes in Sfax and Kairouan between police and students associated with Hizb en Nahdha. The alarm bells really started ringing when fundamentalists scored a massive victory in Algerian municipal elections in June 1990. Arrests began in September as repression set in. Twelve opposition publications were closed and Hizb en Nahdha's student organization banned. Meanwhile, moves were made to bring the legal opposition into the establishment fold. Small political parties posing as a parliamentary opposition were given free seats in 1991 by-elections, and guaranteed **handouts** from the pork barrel. The illegal opposition were portrayed as "terrorists", with allegations of bomb-making and coup attempts.

Tensions reached a climax in 1992. While the government in Algeria cancelled general elections that were about to be won by the FIS Islamist party, the Tunisian government held mass trials of the 300 principally **Islamist dissidents** who had been arrested a year earlier. Most were sentenced to lengthy terms in prison. Tried in absentia, Rachid Ghannuchi received a life sentence, although he was subsequently granted political asylum in Britain.

The trials attracted criticism in the West from human rights observers such as Amnesty International, which reported torture and harassment of Islamists and their women relatives. The government, supported by legal "opposition" parties, and by prominent Tunisian women activists, protested its innocence. Meanwhile, the regime continued to consolidate its position. In 1994, **Ben Ali** was re-elected president, officially winning 99.9 percent of the vote. The ruling RCD gained 97.7 percent, but four legal "opposition" parties were guaranteed a share of parliamentary seats somewhat larger than their tiny percentage of the poll would normally warrant.

In February 1995, Algerian-based fundamentalist guerrillas attacked a frontier post at Chebika, killing Tunisian Garde Nationale officers. This was interpreted by some as a warning from Algerian Islamists to the Tunisian government not to support the Algerian regime. In July 1995, meanwhile, the government attempted to clamp down on media freedom by imposing strict controls on the use of TV satellite dishes, and later that year banned broadcasts to Tunisia by Italian TV station RAI Uno. In October 1995, Mohammed Mouada, leader of one of the legal opposition parties, the MDS, was arrested on what were widely seen as trumped-up charges of working for Libya after he had publicly attacked the government for establishing a one-party state. He was sentenced to eleven years' imprisonment along with a party colleague, but later released conditionally, while the government extended representation of legal "opposition" parties at national and municipal levels. Nonetheless, criticism of human rights violations by Tunisia continues, with regular arrests of activists and allegations of a "widening circle of repression" by Amnesty. Despite this, Ben Ali declared on a visit to France that there were no political prisoners in Tunisia, and the official opposition were allowed to field token candidates at the 1999 presidential elections, which did not prevent Ben Ali from securing 99.45 percent of the declared vote.

The years 2000–2001 saw the government step up action against human rights groups, notably the officially recognized Ligue Tunisienne des Droits de l'Homme (LTDH) and the unrecognized (and therefore illegal) Conseil national pour les libertés en Tunisie (CNLT), but in the face of mounting criticism at home and abroad, Ben Ali promised in a press interview to introduce democratic reforms, and revisions to the press code relaxed political censorship slightly. In May 2002, a series of reforms were put to a referendum, their main aim being to allow Ben Ali to seek another term as president in 2004 elections. The proposals were approved, according to official figures, by 99.5 percent of voters. The referendum followed a government reshuffle in response to an attack by al-Qaida on the Ghriba synagogue in Jerba (see p.440), which killed twenty people, mostly tourists. In line with Western regimes, the government responded in December 2003 by introducing an anti-terrorist law with a new and much wider definition of what constitutes terrorism. Despite the presence of an increased number of opposition candidates, presidential elections in October 2004 were expected to return Ben Ali for a third term with, officially at least, an overwhelming majority.

Prospects

The **economy** remains shaky after the ravages of high inflation in the 1970s, but an IMF-imposed austerity programme has stemmed Tunisia's huge national debt and kept inflation at manageable levels – officially, at least, less than ten percent. Inevitably, this has involved unpopular measures such as an **earnings freeze** for public employees (the state is Tunisia's biggest employer), **devaluation of the dinar** and **abolition of food subsidies**.

As Bourguiba's heir, Ben Ali has in many ways had a hard act to follow. When future generations look back they will judge Bourguiba as the father of his country. Following independence, he provided Tunisia with the framework for a constitutional and secular democracy, even if the reality did not quite live up to the ideal. His self-identification with the country's destiny gave Tunisians a national cohesion lacking in many developing countries. Tunisia's standard of living is one of the highest in the developing world, with little of the extreme poverty experienced in Morocco and Egypt. All Tunisians have free access to education as far as university level and to free health services. Actual social progress may have lagged behind the radical legal framework introduced nearly forty years ago, but it is a mark of just how far Tunisia has come that it tends to be judged – not least by Tunisians themselves – by Western standards rather than those of Africa.

The tradition of secularism and development seems safe enough in Ben Ali's hands, but as his regime suppresses human rights groups and allows only tokenistic opposition, the question remains: how many of Bourguiba's vices has Ben Ali inherited along with his virtues?

Architecture

This brief account is an attempt to introduce and explain the design, development and function of Tunisian buildings. Besides religious architecture, Tunisia has a wealth of domestic architecture which, unadvertised and often hidden, can reveal just as much about Tunisia as any mosque or beylical palace. The best way to view domestic architecture is just to wander the medinas and the villages. Although you can walk into many of the semi-public outer courtyards, you should be sensitive – like most people, Tunisians get upset if strangers walk uninvited into their homes.

Tunisian buildings often bear a plaque stating the date of construction, or sometimes of restoration or additions to the building. Although the **calendar** and the old Arabic numerals are unfamiliar, if you treat this as a puzzle it's not difficult to solve. The Arabic numerals for 1 and 9 are easy enough and the others don't take long to become familiar with (see below). As for the years, the Islamic calendar began with the Hegira, Mohammed's flight to Medina in 622 AD (which was thus 1 AH). Moreover, the Muslim year is a little shorter than the Western. To convert AH to AD, you add 622, then subtract the original AH year multiplied by 3/100, ignore anything after the decimal point and you have the AD year in which that AH year began. Thus, for example, 1421 AH = 1421 + 622 − (3/100 x 1421), and therefore began in 2000 AD.

١	٢	٣	٤	٥	٦	٧	٨	٩	.
1	2	3	4	5	6	7	8	9	0

Mosques

Mosques usually follow the same basic plan, whatever their size, style and age, the most important model in Tunisia being the Great Mosque of Kairouan. All mosques face **Mecca**, the birthplace of Islam, the site of the Ka'aba (see p.524), the place of pilgrimage, and, most important of all, the direction of prayer. In the mosque this direction is shown by the **mihrab**, a shallow alcove in the *qibla* (literally, "the facing") wall. This is not an altar; the direction, not the niche, is sacred and representations of the Ka'aba are often placed there to emphasize this point. The mosque is built around the axis passing through the mihrab and at right angles to the qibla wall, so that the whole building faces Mecca. (Incidentally, toilets and beds are usually aligned at right angles to the axis so as not to profane.)

The mosque is a place of worship and a sanctuary, its separation from the world outside guaranteed by high, often windowless walls and strong gates. Inside, large mosques usually have a courtyard like houses do. The parallel is important, for Islam considers its adherents a family. At the *qibla* end of this courtyard, nearest Mecca, is the **prayer hall** – broad rather than long because the front row of worshippers receives greater *baraka* (blessing) from Allah than those behind. What restricts their breadth is the ability of worshippers at either end to hear the calls to prayer and so act in unison with the rest of the congregation.

The prayer hall has to be ritually pure, so it is usually separated from the rest of the mosque by a step or balustrade – before entering, worshippers must take off their shoes so that no dirt is carried in. The worshipper must also wash before prayer – either partially or totally depending on their state of ritual impurity – and a **washing fountain**, a well leading to the cistern below, is often provided in the centre of the courtyard (as at Kairouan's Great Mosque) or in a washing room to the side (as at the Zitouna Mosque in Tunis).

There are few interior features inside the prayer hall. The **imam** leads the prayer and preaches from a **minbar** – a pulpit, usually just a flight of steps in ornately carved wood, occasionally a permanent structure in stone. The imam sits on the second step from the top, the highest step being reserved for the Prophet. In the days before loudspeakers the imam's voice was repeated more loudly by the **muezzin** sitting on a raised wooden platform, or **dikka**, and then relayed through the congregation by strategically placed respondents, the *muballighun*. Today the only other piece of furniture is the **kursi es-sura**, the wooden lectern, usually placed next to the minbar. This is important because recitation (*tawliq*), considered a great art in Islamic society, is the basis of the service. Otherwise the prayer hall is bare. There are no pews (the congregation sit on a floor covered with carpets in richer establishments and halfa-grass matting in poorer), no elaborate screens, and no paintings, though mosques are usually decorated with geometric designs and calligraphic quotes from the Koran.

Other rooms or buildings may be added to this basic design according to the size and function of the mosque. There is usually a **minaret**, the most distinctive feature of the mosque on the skyline, from where the muezzin calls the faithful to prayer. In Tunisia, most minarets are square, a mark of mosques that follow the Malekite school of Islamic legal interpretation (see p.528). In Ottoman times, the Hanefite school of jurisprudence, strong in Turkey, gained influence here, and mosques following the Hanefite rite were built with octagonal minarets. Some mosques have **tombs**, often crowded against the qibla wall, sometimes the centrepiece and raison d'être of the building. Others have **dormitories** for pilgrims or students, or a school room and library. But all these are appendices to the basic plan, for, in essence, the mosque is simply the *mihrab* and the prayer hall. Most of the **masjid** – mosques used for daily prayer – are just that. It is only the larger congregational mosques used for Friday prayer, the **jema'a**, that have all these features.

Stylistically, a gradual move can be traced towards lighter construction and more ornate decoration over time. The first mosques, those of the Aghlabids, used heavy columns, frequently of Roman origin, massive construction, and little or no decoration. The prayer halls were, consequently, dark, and much more impressive in their sheer size than in their architecture. Later the Zirids introduced the first domes which gave prayer halls extra light and a sense of space. With brighter interiors artists were able to develop finer and more sophisticated decoration. Under the **Hafsids** these trends continued, with domes becoming larger and covering more and more of the prayer hall, and decoration becoming more detailed and sumptuous. Then, during the **seventeenth century**, Turkish architects revolutionized styles. The dome was extended to cover the whole prayer hall, the superstructure was reduced to a minimum, allowing for more windows, and Ottoman and Italian decorative features – the keel arch, painted tiles and stucco plasterwork – were adopted. Prohibitive construction costs prevented the architects of smaller-scale mosques from adopting the massive domes seen at the Mosque of Sidi Mehrez in Tunis, but more modest Ottoman ornamental features spread throughout the country. Since then, styles of construction have changed little, except that modern mosques are built in reinforced concrete and their tiles and arches are more likely to be mass-produced than handcrafted.

Other religious buildings

In addition to simple mosques, two other types of religious building are common in Tunisia. The **medersa** (often pronounced, and sometimes spelt, "madrassa") is a religious school where theology is taught, and often by extension, Islamic law and science. Traditionally, students generally would lodge as well as study here, so there are boarding rooms, usually small, as well as classrooms. Nonetheless, the medersa is centred on a mosque, so it will have a courtyard beyond the main entrance, typically with a fountain, and a prayer hall beyond that. Classrooms are also situated off the main courtyard, usually to the sides, while students' sleeping quarters are normally arranged around the upper floor. Medersas are generally to be found in the medina areas of large towns and cities – Tunis in particular has a large number.

More common in the countryside are **zaouias**, also called **marabouts**, though strictly speaking the marabout is the holy man – usually a Sufi hermit – buried inside. If renowned, he will attract pilgrims, especially on a specific day of the year known as a *moussem*, when a local festival is celebrated. A *zaouia* is typically a small whitewashed building with a small dome or **koubba**, often found among the ordinary tombs in a graveyard. A larger *zaouia* may have a prayer hall attached, and function like a mosque. It will certainly have a *mihrab*, though not usually a minaret. The holiness of the building is such that it is believed to bestow *baraka* on those who come to pray. Since one of the best ways to attract *baraka* is by giving alms, *zaouias* often function as centres for distribution of funds to the needy.

Walled cities and fortifications

As in Europe and the Middle East, cities in Tunisia were traditionally surrounded by a **wall**, and many of these walls, including those at Sousse, Sfax, Kairouan and Le Kef, are still largely intact. The purpose of the wall was defensive: at many times in Tunisia's history, cities were left to fend for themselves with central government unable to provide an army to fend off Christian invaders, rebel forces or marauding nomadic tribes.

The top of the wall was always accessible from the inside, with a protected **rampart** from which defenders could aim missiles at an attacking force. The wall would have **gates** (*bab*), usually two, to allow access, and these might be staggered so that an invader would have to turn two corners when passing through them, thus slowing down an invading force. Alternatively, as at Mahdia, the gate might be a *skifa*, a passageway, which defenders could close off with iron grilles or into which they could pour hot oil on those below. As times became more settled, new gates would be opened in the wall to allow freer access, and these would open directly into the city.

A walled city would have a **kasbah** or citadel, usually at the highest point, as a fortress to defend the entire city, and a last fallback should the walls be penetrated. The main **mosque** on the other hand would usually be right at the heart of the city, surrounded by market areas, with the cleanest trades nearest the mosque and the dirtier ones further away from it. Near the gates, there would be **fondouks** – merchants' "hotels", known in the Middle East as caravanserais – where visiting traders could stable their animals downstairs and themselves board upstairs. A fondouk therefore consists of two floors of rooms surrounding a large central courtyard; one of the best places to see this kind of building is Houmt Souk in Jerba, where several have been converted into tourist hotels. The other vital public building is of course the public bath, or hammam (see p.57). This follows a design that has barely changed since Roman times, with a changing room, then a succession of bathing rooms from a cool to a hot room, heated by a wood oven fed from outside. The hot room is usually surmounted by a dome with small glass windows in it, allowing light to enter, but preventing the heat from escaping.

Aside from walled cities, rulers have sometimes felt it necessary to construct fortifications in the countryside, or along the coast. In particular the Aghlabids felt it necessary in the ninth century to construct **ribats** along the coast to protect the country from Christian invaders, and these can still be seen today at Sousse and Monastir. Because the purpose of the *ribat* was to defend the faithful against the infidel, military service was seen as a religious activity and those who served there were seen as holy warriors. The *ribat* would be their home, and would therefore have sleeping quarters for those serving in its defence. Square and surrounded by thick walls, it also has a lookout tower on each corner. The Byzantines, and later the Ottomans, used a more European style of fort, usually called a **borj** or sometimes **ksar**, to defend or control strategic points in the country.

In the far south, from the tenth century, the Berbers were forced to build fortified villages to defend themselves against the invading Banu Hilal. These were topped with a fort called a **kala'a**. Nomadic tribes in the same region built fortified granaries called **ksour** (the plural of *ksar*) to defend their food supplies against their enemies. For more on these, see p.453.

Domestic architecture

For Tunisians, the **home** should be genuinely private. Walking around the medina in any city you are immediately struck by the lack of windows looking out onto the narrow streets. Those that exist have heavy bars or ironwork grilles, and doors leading into the houses are made of thick wood reinforced with iron studs. Tunisian houses look in towards the family, not out towards the wider world.

The traditional Tunisian home, as elsewhere in North Africa and the Middle East, is centred around a **courtyard** or **patio**, *wust al-dar* in Arabic. This is usually open to the sky, though it may be partially covered, and rooms are arranged around it. The courtyard provides fresh air and light, while its walls prevent the sun from shining directly into it, thus keeping it cool. Traditionally, the courtyard had a well or fountain, in the centre or in the wall to one side. Otherwise, it might have a a cistern, or *madjus*, under the floor, to collect and contain the rainwater that fell on the marble floors and the roofs of storage cellars. In courtyards where the fountain was not in the centre of the courtyard, its place there might be taken by a tree, typically an orange tree. In large mansions, the patio might even contain a whole garden.

The entrance from the street does not lead directly into the courtyard, but into a vestibule called a **skifa**. In a larger home, and especially in the medinas of northern cities such as Tunis, Bizerte, Sousse and Kairouan, this would be a **hall**, with benches built against the wall, where the man of the house could receive guests without taking them into the family quarters. The reason for doing this was so that within the home, the women could go about unveiled, protected from the sight of strangers. Even smaller houses without a *skifa*, typically in the old quarters of the Jerid towns such as Tozeur and Nefta, have a chicane-like passage that protects the courtyard from street view. A very large house might have been built with an outer courtyard, the *wust el-dwiriya*, where the men of the family could entertain visitors while the women were safe in the privacy of the inner patio. There might even be further courtyards so that a single building could accommodate numerous related families.

The living quarters, including bedrooms and kitchen, are arranged around the courtyard. Often, a gallery surrounds the courtyard on the upper floor, with bedrooms and living quarters off that. Rather than have separate bedrooms and living rooms, a traditional Tunisian home has rooms for the family to relax during the day, and where close friends are admitted, which then double as sleeping quarters at night. The lower floors, readily accessible through the courtyard, are often used for storage space.

In contrast to the plain and anonymous outside walls of Tunisian houses, the courtyards and the living rooms behind them displayed extravagant **decoration**. Since the Middle Ages floors have been made of tessellated slabs termed *keddal*, with designs of black and white marble (from the Jebel Ichkeul) in the wealthiest houses. In the seventeenth century hand-painted **tiles** from Tunis and Nabeul became popular (to be replaced by cheap Italian factory-made copies in the nineteenth century), and most houses have tiles up to shoulder-height on the walls. A fashion for ornate geometric **stuccowork** also developed in the seventeenth century, and in the houses of wealthier Tunisians this delicate tracery begins above the tiles and continues over the vaults. During the nineteenth century, **paintwork**, abandoned in the fifteenth century, regained favour, particularly on the wooden ceilings and rafters of upper floors. Consequently the houses of wealthy families were full of colour and ornamentation.

Architectural features changed with fashion. During the seventeenth century, when North Africa was opened up to Mediterranean (particularly Italian) influences, a **loggia** was often added to the courtyard, usually three "Moorish" arches on classical columns. More substantial houses had peristyle courtyards, surrounded by a balcony supported on vaults with ornate wooden balustrades. Twin windows were yet another Italian import.

Urban houses were crammed into the limited space inside the city walls, making housing densities very high. For this reason the city streets were narrow, convoluted and seemingly chaotic. Yet chaotic they certainly were not. Within the city each ethnic group occupied its own **fariq**, or quarter. In Tunis, for instance, the Jews were segregated in the Hafsia and surrounded by a wall, the Europeans down near the Bab el Bahr. Early on in the indigenous quarters there was no segregation by class or wealth; instead, the households were clustered in loose ethnic or family groups. Many of the streets were impasses, sometimes called **darb**, hidden from major thoroughfares by sharp bends. Family groups lived around these *darb*, which still bear their names. The street provided a sort of outer courtyard used by the wider family group.

This urban structure and building style began to change when the **French** arrived. The new grid cities they built – the **Villes Nouvelles** – became the favoured quarters of wealthy Tunisians, who gradually abandoned the medinas. Their new houses or, more often, apartments, reflected their aspirations to French culture and the assimilation of a new individualism. Boulevards and segregation by wealth replaced the equality of the medina's narrow streets; isolated houses replaced the intimacy of the *darb*; and the smaller house of the nuclear family replaced the huge segmented house of the extended family.

Independence accelerated rather than reversed the process of Westernization. The new Tunisian middle class soon assimilated the social values and tastes of their European predecessors and, with them, their architecture. Expensive **suburbs**, much like those around any southern European city, gradually surrounded the larger towns. Today some of the architects are returning to the details of traditional housing, using arches, painted (though factory-produced) tiles, and even stucco plaster, but the inspiration and the design remain fundamentally European.

The departure of the wealthy inhabitants has inevitably led to the **decline of the medinas**. Houses have been divided up into one-room apartments, *oukala*, where families live in appallingly overcrowded conditions. Without an influential political lobby, some of the medinas' residents go without electricity, water or mains drainage. The fabric of the buildings has also suffered from lack of repair, unsympathetic modifications and dangerous extensions on roofs and walls. Faced with deteriorating conditions and soaring rents, many of the original residents preferred to move out, if only to a dilapidated suburb on the outskirts of the city, leaving the medina to recent immigrants.

Rural domestic architecture has undergone the same transformation as urban architecture in the last century. Houses, usually of reinforced concrete, that follow the same pseudo-European design, are squeezing out traditional styles. Tunisia's architectural diversity is being replaced by a rather tacky and depressing homogeneity, though in recent years there have been moves against this. The Jerid for example has seen a revival of traditional brick-making (see p.358), and also making a comeback are domed and rounded roofs, which cool the interior of a room due to the convection currents they create.

A chronology: Tunisian events and monuments

10,000–6000 BC	Capsian Man appears throughout North Africa
2000 BC	Introduction of metals from Sicily begins Bronze Age
1100 BC	Earliest Phoenician settlements
c. 800 BC	Carthage and other major Phoenician ports founded
600–300 BC	Increasing conflict in western Mediterranean between Carthaginians and Greeks
310 BC	Expedition of Agathocles from Syracuse into Carthaginian territory
263–241 BC	First Punic War between Carthage and Rome, including Regulus expedition
218–202 BC	Second Punic War; Hannibal crosses Alps from Spain with elephants
150–146 BC	Third Punic War; Carthage sacked in 146. Very few Punic constructions remain after this time (scant remains at Carthage, houses at Kerkouane, funerary monuments at Maktar and Dougga)
112–105 BC	Jugurthine War in province of Africa
46 BC	Caesar defeats Pompeii at Battle of Thapsus: Roman Civil War; Carthage refounded
1–200 AD	Almost uninterrupted growth in prosperity of Africa as rich province of Roman Empire; control gradually extended west to Morocco, south to Chott. Roman town plans and buildings imposed throughout province: theatres, baths, temples, forums, amphitheatres, bridges, aqueducts; Romans build Dougga, Maktar, Sbeïtla, Thuburbo Majus
193	Severan dynasty begins with accession of Libyan emperor Septimus Severus, who puts up the triumphal arches at Haïdra and Dougga
235	End of Severan dynasty and of the Roman empire's golden era; El Jem amphitheatre possibly built in this period, but there are fewer and fewer Roman monuments from this time, with churches built in the ruins of older Roman buildings
312	Empire becomes officially Christian, but Donatist schism in Africa is vehicle for disaffection with imperial rule
429	Carthage falls to Vandal invaders from Germany

535	Byzantine invasion, inspired by Justinian and led by Belisarius, drives out Vandals. Many fortresses (Ksar Lemsa, Biar el Aouani, Borj Younga) indicate fragility of Byzantine control
647	Arab invaders defeat Byzantine Prefect Gregory at Sbeïtla
670	Third wave of invasion under Oqba Iba Nafi settles and founds Kairouan as capital
800–900	Prosperous Aghlabid dynasty rules Tunisia from Kairouan, capturing Sicily in 835, building Great Mosques at Kairouan, Tunis, Sousse and Sfax, *ribats* along the coast, notably at Sousse, Monastir and Houmt Souk, Jerba
909–970	Heretical Fatimids rule from Mahdia, building Great Mosque there and making additions to the Great Mosque at Sfax; they resist Kharijite revolt led by Abu Yazid (940), then move to Egypt from where, having lost control of Tunisia, they unleash the destructive Banu Hilal invasion
1059–1159	Khourassanid dynasty rules principality of Tunis during Hilalian invasions, building Great Mosque; Normans and other Christians raid east coast
1236–1534	Hafsid dynasty establishes Tunis as capital; there is a century of great prosperity and prestige, followed by gradual decline. The Tunis Kasbah and medersas are built; an influx of Andalusian artisans brings Moorish techniques such as stuccowork; first great souks in Tunis
1270	Abortive invasion (Crusade) by Louis IX (St Louis) of France
1300–1400	Mediterranean trade and Christian attacks; domestic insecurity
1534–81	Hispano-Turkish struggles for control of Tunisia and North African coast: Tunis taken by Turks (1534), Spanish (1535), Algerian Turks (1569), Don John of Austria (1573), combined Ottoman forces (1574); many Spanish and Turkish forts built along the coast (La Goulette, Bizerte, Kélibia)
1580–1705	Regency of Tunis part of Ottoman Empire, ruled by deys and beys; Othman Dey (1598–1610) and Murad Bey (1610–37) secure power; many Hanefite mosques with octagonal minarets put up, including Youssef Dey and Hammouda Pasha in Tunis, both with Italian influence, as well as Sidi Mehrez, whose style is more purely Turkish

1600–1700	Trade and piracy at their height; French consulate established in Tunis 1659, agreement with Britain on relations and trade 1662; Porto Farina (Ghar el Melh) bombarded by British Admiral Blake (1654)
1705	Husaynid dynasty established; Turkish connection increasingly nominal; security and prosperity bring lavish building programmes, including Tunis's Mosque of the Dyers, Mosque of Sahib et Tabaa, Dar Ben Abdallah, Dar Husayn and *medersas* throughout Tunis Medina
1700–1800	Tunisia's last great era before independence, under Ali Bey (1759–81) and Hammouda Bey (1781–1813)
1741	Expeditions against coral establishments at Tabarka and Cap Negre
1784	French and Venetian fleets bombard Tunisian ports
1830	French takeover in Algeria; slave trade ends, leaving Tunisia in increasing economic straits; Britain, France and Italy all manoeuvring for position; last luxurious buildings help bankrupt the country (palaces at Bardo, Mohammedia, arsenal at Ghar el Melh)
1860–64	Kherredin's constitutional reform; Sadiki College built in Tunis
1869	International Financial Commission takes over bankrupt Tunisia's finances; cathedrals built in Tunis and Carthage
1869–77	Kherredin prime minister; administrative and judicial reform, diplomatic measures to prevent colonization
1881	French invasion – on spurious excuse of Khroumirie raids – and colonization; French quarters founded outside medinas; Art Nouveau, neo-Moorish and, later, Art Deco colonial buildings go up in Tunis, Sfax and Sousse
1920	Nationalist Destour Party founded
1930	Catholic Congress at Carthage helps inspire Bourguiba's nationalism
1934	Neo-Destour Party founded and soon banned by French
1942–43	Tunisian Campaign, World War II
1952	Farhat Hached murdered by Red Hand terrorists; Tunisia problem discussed at UN
1955	Bourguiba returns to Tunis with internal autonomy
1956	Independence, March 20
1957	Declaration of Republic
1963	Bourguiba has mausoleum built at Monastir

1976	The first major strike, and demonstrations
1978	The first general strike since independence sparks a wave of government repression
1980	Gafsa "coup" attempt
1981	First free elections; accusations of vote-rigging
1984	Bread riots start in the south and spread to Tunis
1985	Conflict with Libya comes to the brink of war
1987	Bourguiba overthrown by Prime Minister Zine el Abidine Ben Ali
2002	Referendum gives Ben Ali right to seek third term in office

Islam

slam is Arabic for "submission", meaning submission to God, and a Muslim is one who submits to God and His laws. The founder of Islam was the **Prophet Mohammed** (sometimes spelt Muhammad), an Arab from the rich trading city of **Mecca**, in what is now Saudi Arabia, which was also a centre for poetry, an important art form in Arab culture. In about 610 AD Mohammed received the first revelation of the Koran, the word of God, dictated in verse via the archangel Gabriel (the first verse he received was almost certainly 96:1: "Recite in the name of your Lord who creates: creates man from a clot of blood"). Although God had sent messages for humanity to other prophets – the Torah to Moses, the Psalms to David and the Gospel to Jesus, who is recognized in Islam as a prophet but not as divine – these messages had, according to Islam, become corrupted. The Koran, written in verse, was unchangeable, and Mohammed was therefore the final prophet, the "seal of the prophets", after whom no further revelations were needed.

When Mohammed first preached his new creed in Mecca however, it did not gain immediate acceptance, especially as it threatened powerful interest groups. Mohammed and his followers were persecuted and eventually in 622 they fled to **Medina**, the city whose name has come to stand for all walled cities in the Arab world. This flight, called the **Hegira** (or Hijra), marks the beginning of a new era, symbolized by the adoption of a new calendar starting in 622 AD. The year 2000 saw the start of the year 1421 in the Islamic calendar, 1421 AH (see p.513 for more on Islamic dates).

The five pillars of Islam

The main characteristic of the new religion Mohammed founded was its directness, a reaction to the increasing complexity of the established faiths, and its essential tenet was simply: "there is no God but God, and Mohammed is His Prophet." There is no intermediary between people and God in the form of an institutionalized priesthood or complicated liturgy, and worship in the form of prayer is a direct and personal communication with God. As well as this central article of faith, the four other basic requirements in Islam are five-times-daily prayers, the pilgrimage (hajj) to Mecca, the Ramadan fast and the giving of alms: together these form the **five pillars** of Islam.

The five times for **prayer** (bearing in mind that the Islamic day begins at sunset) are sunset, after dark, dawn, noon and afternoon. Prayer can be performed pretty much anywhere, but preferably in a mosque. In the past and even today in some places, a **muezzin** would climb his minaret each time and call the faithful. Nowadays the call to prayer is likely to be prerecorded; even so, this most distinctive of Islamic sounds has a beauty all its own, especially when neighbouring muezzins are audible simultaneously. The message itself is equally moving: "God is most great. I testify that there is no god but Allah. I testify that Mohammed is His Prophet. Come to prayer, come to security. God is most great." In the morning another phrase is added: "prayer is better than sleep." The most easily recognizable phrase is "Allah-o-Akbar" (God is most great).

Prayer is preceded by **ritual washing** and is performed with the feet bare. Facing towards Mecca (the direction indicated in a mosque by the mihrab

– though prayer can be uttered anywhere), the worshipper recites the Fatiha, the first chapter of the Koran: "Praise be to God, Lord of the Worlds, the Compassionate, the Merciful, King of the Day of Judgment. We worship You and seek Your aid. Guide us on the straight path, the path of those on whom You have bestowed Your grace, not the path of those who incur Your anger nor of those who go astray." The same words are then repeated twice in the prostrate position, with some interjections of "Allah Akbar". It is a highly ritualized procedure, with the prostrate position symbolic of the worshipper's role as servant, and the sight of thousands of people going through the same motions simultaneously in a mosque (in a jema'a, rather than a masjid, or "local mosque") is a powerful one. Here the whole community comes together for prayer, led by an **imam**, who may also deliver the *khutba*, or sermon.

The **pilgrimage**, or hajj, to Mecca is an annual event, when millions come from all over the world to Mohammed's birthplace. Here they go through several days of rituals, the central one a sevenfold circumambulation of the **Ka'aba** (Arabia's most important shrine from ancient times, rededicated to Allah by Mohammed in 630), before kissing a black stone set in its wall. Islam requires that Muslims should go on the hajj as often as is practically possible, although for the poor it may well be a once-in-a-lifetime occasion. In Tunisia, from the earliest times to the French occupation, pilgrims assembled at towns along a well-established route, passing through Kairouan and Gabès, to join the *rakeb*, a caravan numbering thousands of people. They would then make the journey to Mecca by foot or camel. The French made it a lot easier. They didn't want just anyone going on the hajj, where they might pick up bad political habits like nationalism, so they restricted pilgrims to several hundred a year and laid on transport in the form of a special pilgrim boat. Now the government still helps many of the poor to make their hajj by air, and the month when all the pilgrims leave for Mecca is still a great time of celebration in Tunisia. The apocryphal story that seven visits to Kairouan equal one hajj to Mecca expresses the unusual reverence in which the city is held.

Ramadan is the ninth month in the Islamic calendar, the month in which the Koran was revealed to Mohammed. The custom of **fasting** is modelled directly on Jewish and Christian practice, and for the whole of the month believers must forgo all forms of consumption – food, drink, cigarettes, sex – between dawn and sunset. A few categories of people are exempted: travellers, children, pregnant women and warriors engaged in a jihad, or holy war. Given the climates in which most Muslims live, the fast is a formidable undertaking, but in practice it becomes a time of some intense celebration, as the abstinence of the day is more than compensated for by huge consumption during the night.

The Koran and the Hadith

The tenets of the Muslim faith are based solidly on the text of the **Koran** (more correctly spelt "Qur'an"). More than just a holy book, the Koran is the literal word of God: Mohammed wrote it down, but it was God who dictated it. What the Koran says therefore cannot be challenged, and one who submits to God's will must accept it, lock, stock and barrel, and obedience to the laws of the Koran lies at the heart of Islam. The Koran could be learnt even by those who did not read, and shortly after Mohammed's death it was codified and its 114 *suras* (chapters) put in order – not the order in which Mohammed had received them, but (apart from the first) starting with the longest and finishing with the shortest. Less authoritative than the Koran are the **Hadith**, or sayings of the Prophet. Because there is less certainty about which were genuine – a "safe" Hadith comes complete with an account of who exactly heard Mohammed say it – and because they emanated from Mohammed rather than God, the Hadith do not carry the same authority as the Koran, although they are used as a guide to the faithful.

Based on the five "pillars of faith" and firmly underwritten by the Koran and to a lesser extent the Hadith, Islam was an inspirational faith for the Arab people, but it was far from being exclusively Arab. All who convert to Islam are accepted as members of the community, regardless of their ethnic origin, a principle that gained the new religion wide acceptance in the course of the Arab advance, among Turks, Iranians and, in North Africa, the Berbers.

The old beliefs

Whatever success Islam had during its early period of rapid expansion, it did not entirely eradicate **pre-existing religion**. Animistic beliefs in the powers of stones and trees (as at Fernana) and rites of ancestor worship were incorporated into the new faith, as was a belief in *baraka*, the power given by God to some men to work miracles. These "saints", or **marabouts**, formed a pantheon of intermediaries between the people and God. Some had particular powers, to cure disease or generate rain, and prayers and sacrifices were made to them at their tombs for these services. Others acquired reverence as founder-guardians of a tribe.

Baraka was not only embodied in tombs, it was also transmitted through blood, and the descendants of these holy men enjoyed a particular respect – the sharifs, descendants of the Prophet, more than any other. Some of them could even perform miracles. Ascetics and preachers might also acquire the status of a marabout, at least during their lifetime. In the fifteenth and sixteenth centuries, Tunisia was flooded with these holy men, most of them coming from

The evil eye

The superstition that envious looks bring **bad luck**, though disapproved of by strict Muslims, is ingrained in Arab culture. Even when admiring something belonging to a friend, formulas are uttered to ward off this **"evil eye"**. More unlucky than the remarks of friends, however, are the jealous glances of strangers.

For this reason, various charms are used against the evil eye. One of the most common is the so-called **"Hand of Fatima"**. The Fatima referred to is the Prophet's daughter, although what connection there is between her and the symbol of the hand remains obscure. It may be that the five fingers of the hand, like the five points of the pentagram star, represent the five daily prayers or the five pillars of Islam. Certainly, the symbol is often combined with a Koranic quotation, or with the names of Allah and Mohammed written in Arabic script. Then again, the pentagram and the significance of the number five predate Islam and are often associated with Jewish mysticism. It is interesting to note that Jerban Jews share this belief in the evil eye, and use similar symbols to ward it off, even more than do their Muslim neighbours.

Another charm against the evil eye is the **fish**. Again, its origins are obscure, though it's believed that it was originally a phallic fertility symbol. Whatever the truth, you'll see charms against the evil eye all over the place, in the form of car stickers, hands and fish painted on houses, and cards pinned up on the walls of shops.

Morocco. During a later time of crisis, in the nineteenth century, another wave arose, warning of the approaching Armageddon.

The dualism of the older faith was also retained as a belief in **bori**, or evil spirits, and the evil eye. These led to rituals of exorcism, many of which were performed by Black Africans who were believed to be particularly powerful against the *bori*. You still see little bags of herbs around the necks of children to protect them against any harm, and the "hand of Fatima" (see box, p.525) is a widespread symbol, but today these beliefs are on the way out. They persist in remote rural areas where religious life still focuses on the marabout's tomb rather than the mosque.

Islam's development

By **800 AD**, the new religion was dominant over an area stretching from Afghanistan in the east to Spain in the west. Given the rapidity of this expansion, it was inevitable that Islam would acquire some of the trappings of the older religions to which it had been a reaction, in the form of hierarchical and doctrinal disputes.

Like most religions, Islam soon developed its own institutions and, with them, particular interest groups. In the early years there was an understanding that consensus legitimized authority, the law and religion. By the ninth century, however, the **ulema** (the learned ones) – that is, the imam and the sheikhs of the religious colleges – had come to monopolize the interpretation of the Koran and the Prophet's sayings. They became a religious establishment, wielding considerable power and controlling great wealth. Under their control the religion itself became increasingly intellectual and dogmatic. And so the scene was set for the division of the faithful.

The **first dispute** arose soon after the death of Mohammed, and has remained the biggest single split in the faith – equivalent to the Catholic–Protestant schism in Christianity. When the Prophet died, the spiritual leadership of the faith was the object of fierce contention among several Caliphs (rulers). A substantial minority felt that the new Caliph should be in direct descent from the Prophet, and their candidate was Ali, a cousin of the Prophet married to his daughter, Fatima. Eventually, Ali's supporters broke away from the **Sunni** mainstream to form the **Shi'a** branch of Islam.

Although the two groups agreed broadly in their respect for the Koran and its tradition (the Hadith), the Shi'ites were forced into a more allegorical interpretation of the Koran in order to support their claims for a divinely inspired leader. Even the orthodox Sunnis found themselves increasingly unable to agree on points of legal detail (all law was taken from the Koran), and by the twelfth century, four **madhabs**, or schools of legal thought, had been established within the Sunni community: Hanefite, Shafite, Malekite and Hanbalite. Together with two Shi'a madhabs, these still account for the great majority of Muslims.

But there were also smaller and more radical sects. The Kharijites, or "Secessionists", were one of the earliest (see p.440). Puritanical in the extreme, they held that anyone guilty of serious sin deserved death. The rigour of this sect appealed particularly to subject peoples such as the Berbers in North Africa, alienated by the excesses of their new rulers, the more so because the Kharijites denied any necessity for Arab leadership – the caliph, they said, should be elected for his piety from among all true believers.

Sufism, which remains a force in southern Tunisia, is not so much a breakaway sect as the name for a different emphasis within Islam, focusing on the ecstatic and the mystical rather than the intellectual niceties of Koranic interpretation. It is a blanket term for the many different brotherhoods, spread widely over the Islamic world, who evolved various practices in the attempt to attain some sort of mystic communion with God. The name Sufi derives from the word for "wool", after the simple woollen clothes worn by early ascetics. During the eighteenth and nineteenth centuries, many of these Sufi brotherhoods spread throughout the Islamic world, with lodges as far apart as Yemen and Morocco linked by allegiance to their founder's teachings and, in some cases, a well-structured administrative hierarchy. They became institutions – and, in the case of the Senoussi of Cyrenaica (in what is now Libya), a government with a state.

The secret of the Sufi groups' success lay in their ability to meet the religious needs of the community ignored by orthodox Islam. Some, such as the intellectual Rahamania, placed great emphasis on learning, whereas others adopted more colourful practices in order to reach a state of **religious ecstasy**. The Aissouia, better known as the "whirling dervishes", used self-flagellation and music to induce a trance. Many of these brotherhoods are still active in Tunisia, though their secrecy, unorthodox practices, wealth and ability to mobilize a large part of the population arouse great suspicion among the religious establishment and in the government.

With these basic institutions, Islam came to exert a profound influence over every aspect of life in one of the great civilizations of the world. Unlike Christianity – at least Protestant Christianity – which has to some extent accepted the separation of church and state, Islam sees no such distinction. The **sharia**, or religious law, is also civil law, and in a process of gradual accretion numerous layers have been added to the original code, the Sunna established by Mohammed's practices and examples. Many controversial practices, such as purdah (the seclusion of women), polygamy and slavery, have been declared not to be part of the original code – but remain very much a question of interpretation.

Perhaps Islam's most fundamental role was in **education**, which was based almost entirely on the Koran. Young children (mainly boys) whose parents could afford it were sent to the **kouttab**, or primary school, where they learned to read and write by learning the Koran (often all 6200 verses) by heart. If they continued their studies, it would still be under religious auspices because the great universities, such as al-Azhar in Cairo (founded by Fatimids from Tunisia in the tenth century) and the Zitouna in Tunis, were attached to mosques. Students might live and do some of their study in **medersas**, or residential colleges, but teaching was based at the mosque, and the syllabus remained religious. Law, grammar, science, logic – all were subsidiary to the Koranic tradition as handed down from generation to generation. For several centuries Arab philosophers and scientists produced work that built on the Greco-Roman achievements they inherited, which was hundreds of years ahead of contemporary Europe – their role in transmitting this culture to the European Renaissance has gone generally unappreciated.

Decline and crisis

Despite its vigour, there was also a very static element in Islam and, as it developed, Arab culture became oppressed by the weight of a **religious tradition** increasingly hostile to free enquiry. Anything that threatened the authority of the religious establishment was gradually suppressed, and the dynamism which had taken the Arabs so far in so short a time was replaced by a society unable to make the innovations that would keep them ahead of the fast-rising Europeans. The Arabs learned how to make paper from the Chinese when they captured Samarkand in 704, but refused for centuries to manufacture books mechanically because it was an invention unsanctioned by God and tradition.

At first this stagnation was relatively unimportant because the Arab world was so far ahead of Europe in every field. But as the pendulum began to swing in the other direction there was no facility for adapting to match the Europeans. Napoleon's expedition to Egypt in 1798 was the beginning of a century in which almost every Islamic country came under the control of one or other of the European powers. Under **colonial rule**, Islam became the focus of opposition. In Algeria and Libya, Sufi brotherhoods led the resistance movement, drawing the support of the masses with a call to the jihad, a war to protect their faith as much as their country. But by the time it came to fight the battles, the wars had already been lost to the factories of Manchester and Lille.

In the nineteenth and twentieth centuries, colonization inevitably led to something of a crisis in religious confidence. Islam had once been the basis of a great civilization and was now dominated by infidel foreigners. There were two alternatives: either Islam could try to adapt itself in some way to the essentially secular ways which had brought prosperity to the West, or it could reject Western influence entirely; by purifying itself, it might rediscover its former strength. In practical terms, few Islamic countries under Western control were in a position at first to adopt either alternative – but these were the poles between which Islamic thought was operating.

Following World War II, the **decolonization** process, accelerated in many countries by the contribution of Islamic consciousness to the nationalist movements, brought political autonomy. More importantly, oil brought economic self-sufficiency and the possibility of true independence from the West. The result was that many Islamic countries could now afford to reject Western values. Some countries, notoriously to Western perceptions, have chosen to return to or maintain a more or less traditional form of fundamentalist Islam. To see this course, as many do in the West, as a deliberate return to barbarism is a failure to understand the context. A return to the totality of Islam is to choose one consistent spiritual identity, one that is deeply embedded in the consciousness of a culture unusually aware of tradition.

Conflict with the West is another aspect of the return to Islam. Adoption of Islamic values signals a rejection of Western society's values – which are perceived as being based on greed and exploitation. The most extreme Islamic fundamentalists are not passive reactionaries thinking of the past, but young radicals, often students, keen to assert new-found independence. Islam has in a sense become the anti-imperialist religion and there is frequent confusion and even conflict between secular, left-wing ideals and more purely religious ones.

But the rejection of Western values does involve missing out on liberal trends from the West, notably sexual equality – trends which many people, not least in Tunisia, see as both desirable and also reconcilable with Islam (see "Women in Tunisia", p.534). The hope is that the supremacy of Islam, a vital part of national identities, can be maintained while shedding what are seen as its less desirable elements.

Islam in modern Tunisia

For a country now so advanced in its secularization, **Tunisia** has always had a strong religious **tradition**. After Mecca, Medina and Jerusalem, Kairouan is the most holy city for Muslims, still visited at the Mouled every year by visitors from all over the Islamic world. The university at Tunis's Great Mosque was long respected, and Tunisia's Malekite teachers still enjoy a high reputation. Yet at the same time there is a greatly revered Jewish shrine, the Ghriba, on Jerba, and although the Jewish population has diminished over the last thirty years tolerance is still unusually high.

The majority of Tunisians have always belonged to the **Malekite** school of the Sunni orthodoxy (their mosques easily recognizable by square minarets). The Turks brought with them the teaching of the **Hanefite** school (these mosques have octagonal minarets), which still survives among Turkish-descended families; but there is little (if any) conflict between the schools, and since both are Sunni the two groups can use each others' mosques. Between them, these groups account for the vast majority of Muslims in Tunisia; for the **Kharijites** of Jerba, and the **Sufis** of Nefta, see p.440 and p.369 respectively.

Despite these long traditions, though, Tunisia – or at least Tunis itself – has always had a **cosmopolitan** element and therefore remained more open to innovation. Kherredin's attempt to introduce constitutional government in 1860 was a failure, but it was a move that several Islamic states have still to make. After independence, Bourguiba, broadly speaking, tried to **secularize** the country – as far as possible with the religious establishment's support – and with some success. During the 1950s and 1960s, religious observance dropped steadily, particularly in Tunis and among the younger generation. At the end of the twentieth century the trend reversed. Local and foreign funding boosted the number of mosques more than three-fold. What is more, the mosques are now full, with predominantly youthful congregations.

Today Islam gives the young a sense of identity and solidarity in a world they see as hostile. It has also given them hope. The imams' calls for a **return to Islamic values** are interpreted by many as an indirect criticism of a government that has done so much to Westernize Tunisia, and of the middle classes who live affluently amid poverty. Political fundamentalists, such as those in the illegal opposition party, Hizb en Nahdha, have gone further, demanding that Islamic values and principles be applied in law and that government create an Islamic Republic along Iranian lines.

It is difficult to tell how many Tunisians would support such a radical constitutional change. Most have some sympathy with the fundamentalists' point of view but cling to their Westernized and materialist lifestyle. With evidence of willingness to adopt Western values, vital Western aid and co-operation have always been abundant. At the same time the Islamic tradition has to be respected enough for the country to remain in favour with wealthier Arab countries, for both political and economic reasons. Fundamentalism's most fervent supporters are among the **very poor** or the frustrated **lower middle class**. But to what extent their fundamentalism is a reaction to and expression of poverty and oppression or a genuine ideological commitment is unclear.

The governments of Bourguiba and, subsequently, Ben Ali have tried to deflect criticism and return moderate fundamentalists to the fold of legitimate politics. The authorities have proclaimed their Islamic credentials, stressing the pre-eminence of Islam as the official religion rather than the secular nature of the state. Ministers now make great show of their religious observance. Affronts to Islam, such as the sale of alcohol on Fridays, have been stopped, and the outward trappings of **Islamicization** have been adopted, with TV stations broadcasting the call to prayer and readings from the Koran.

These gestures may have appeased the moderates, but the **radicals** remained unmoved. As their opposition became more vocal, Bourguiba, who feared fundamentalism as a threat to both the Destour Party and the secular nature of the state he had created, grew determined to root out what he saw as a danger. Confrontation escalated into violence from 1985 to 1987, and Tunisia seemed set to fall into a downward spiral of repression, dissidence and terrorism. Repression of fundamentalism under Ben Ali indicates his similar determination to keep state and religion apart.

Traditional society

I n traditional Tunisian society (which today means in rural areas and the poorer parts of the cities), the **extended family** was the fundamental social group. Tunisians spent much of their social life with close relatives and also tended to marry within the family network (for a man, marriage to his father's brother's daughter was the ideal), and mutual obligations meant that families were tied economically. Land in rural areas, for instance, was usually co-owned with brothers or cousins. If a man wanted to build a house or clear some land he would call on his relatives to help, on the understanding that he would reciprocate later. In the same way, if he had financial difficulties, or needed money to celebrate his daughter's wedding in proper style, he could rely on support from his close relatives.

Wider social groups were defined in the same family terms by means of descent from a common ancestor. In this way traditional Tunisian society was composed of a series of ever larger families: the nuclear family, the extended family, a lineage, a village or tribe. The frequency and intensity of social interaction declined as the size of the social group increased but, even at the scale of village or tribe, there were still communal rights and reciprocal obligations that unified the group.

Individuals were identified by their **genealogy**: Ahmed Ben (son of) Mohammed Ben Ahmed Ben Slim, along a chain of names. A distant ancestor usually identified the individual's lineage inside his community, but if he travelled to another village he would adopt the village name; and if he went to a city, his tribe's name. There were no surnames that transcended social context; people were always a member of such and such a family.

The family also created **honour** in that reputation and good name derived from the achievements of ancestors and the length of an identifiable genealogy. People whose ancestors were sheikhs, marabouts, or even hajjis (those who have made the pilgrimage to Mecca) are always identified as such. The more esteemed the ancestor, the more detailed the genealogy. A *sharif*, for instance, will trace his ancestry right back to the Prophet Mohammed.

Because honour was derived from descent and was shared by an extended group, attacks on individuals could escalate into a **vendetta**. A family shamed had to take appropriate revenge (an eye for an eye, a tooth for a tooth) if honour was to be saved, and reciprocal attacks could build up into long-lasting feuds. Most of these vendettas began with verbal or sexual attacks on women, for in this patriarchal society it was here that honour was most sensitive. Murder might be resolved by the payment of *dia*, blood money, but an attack on a woman could never be paid off.

Breakdown of traditional values

Now that Tunisians are moving to the **cities**, traditional society is breaking down. Migrants leaving rural areas try to find accommodation near relatives or members of the same village community. The poorer suburbs of Tunis and Sousse, and the *ukalas* in the Tunis Medina are full of these transplanted rural communities. Many of the migrants return to their home for the summer marriage season, the highlight of communal life, when social bonds are reaffirmed by complex webs of visiting and hospitality. But they're no longer temporary residents in the city, returning to their village when they have earned enough to get married and set up their own farm; they are now committed to an urban lifestyle and look at the village as their origin – not their goal.

After a couple of years in the city the migrant's visits home become, typically, less frequent, and social life begins to cross communal barriers, with **marriages** often taking place outside the community. Most important of all, income differentials among urban workers discourage the mutual aid that formerly united members of the same family. Gradually the **individual**, with personal identity and interests, emerges, and distant family and community fade into the background.

Among these dislocated urban dwellers new allegiances and identities develop – those of **income and class**. A new ethos of personal advancement takes the place of the redundant ideals of the community and mutual aid and, with this, new conflicts emerge between rich and poor. It is this struggle, expressed in the battle between the governing party and the secular middle class on the one side, and the aspiring poor, newly educated and fundamentalist on the other, that characterizes Tunisian politics today.

Customs and celebrations

As traditional society has been subverted by new social structures, so **customs** have been replaced by more "refined" mores. Tunisians still love celebrations, marriages in particular, but in the cities they have lost much of their social significance and zest. If you want to see Tunisian customs at their liveliest, you have to go to the small towns and villages.

Every stage of the **life cycle** is associated with its own celebration and customs: birth, circumcision (in the far south, this includes some girls), marriage and death. It is only at **marriage**, however, that strangers are welcome. Paradoxically enough in this patrilineal society, marriage – the social relationship that crosses patrilineages – is the most public of all social events. It is a matter of honour that the celebration is as splendid and well attended as possible. Most of the village turns out, and unexpected guests, even foreigners, are always welcomed.

Marriage ceremonies differ from region to region, but they are always lengthy affairs taking several days, usually in the summer when migrants return home. The first days are spent in preparation. The bride has henna applied to her feet and hands and has all her body hair removed, before being taken to the groom's house where separate receptions are held, accompanied by much music, usually performed by hired singers, drummers and pipe-players, and ritual praise-singing. The ceremony and the communal celebration follow, usually a massive feast with more music and dancing. The consummation of the marriage is, however, the climax, and in rural areas sometimes a semi-public event, with the groom's mother present to confirm her daughter-in-law's virginity. More often the bloodstained bedsheet is produced as evidence and, at this news, guns go off and the music starts all over again.

The other major celebration in village and tribal life is the **ziara** or **moussem**, a communal pilgrimage to the tomb of a marabout, usually the community's "patron saint" or eponymous ancestor, again a summer event. In the past everybody participated, even in nomadic communities, where it was the only occasion in the year when everyone would camp together. As a communal – as much as a religious – activity it was important in re-affirming the bonds between members of the community. With everyone gathered around the tomb, visiting would take place, deals would be clinched and marriages arranged.

Pilgrims walked barefoot to the tomb, usually accompanied by music and singing, waving flags bearing religious slogans. There they made a communal prayer and then sacrificed an animal, sometimes a sheep but more often a bull. The **meat** was scrupulously divided into equal portions (symbolic equality being important in tribal life) and distributed to each of the families. The real celebration came afterwards, with feasting and dancing.

Today, sadly, these festivals are becoming less and less common. The disintegration of village and tribal life is partly to blame, but the real cause is the expansion of **religious orthodoxy**. Tunisia's imams have no place for the marabouts next to God and lambast the old faith. As new mosques have penetrated the remotest villages, the marabouts' hegemony has been broken and their legitimacy undermined by the attacks of the educated religious establishment. The government encourages the trend. It doesn't want the people's religious allegiance scattered among a series of local saints, but wants it centralized instead, where it is easier to control and manipulate. Consequently, schools throughout the country promote orthodox Islam and dismiss its local forms. As attendance at the mosques and schools increases, that at the *ziara* declines.

Women in Tunisia

When still a young child, I told myself that if one day I had the power to do so, I would make haste to redress the wrong done to women.

Habib Bourguiba

Before independence, Tunisian women shared the oppression experienced in most Arab countries. That their position has changed as much as it has is due largely to Habib Bourguiba's personal vision and his ability to institute far-reaching reforms. Almost the first thing he did after independence was to introduce the Personal Status Code, an attempt to improve the social position and treatment of women. Hitherto such issues had been controlled by the *sharia*, the Holy Law based on the Koran and the Hadith.

This discussion of the position of Tunisian women is followed by personal accounts of women travellers in the country.

Women's traditional status

In the eighth century the **Islamic code** had in fact improved women's status: the dowry (*mahr*) was paid to the bride instead of to her guardian; rights of inheritance and control of income were given to women, albeit in a very limited sense. Divorce, though solely a man's right, was to be effective only after a three-month waiting period, the *'idda*, and the husband was supposed to maintain his wife (though the responsibility fell mainly on her brothers) and offer some explanation for his conduct. These limited reforms were, however, later ignored.

Women were henceforth **veiled and segregated** to protect their virginity and reputation; **polygamy** remained common, **marriages** were contracted when the girl was young, and **divorce** proceedings became quite arbitrary. A man could repudiate his wife simply by pronouncing the *talaq* three times in three months – but the three were often all pronounced at once, with no recourse for the woman and no *'idda*. Although it was possible to guard against polygamy by inserting a prohibition in the marriage contract, and to receive a portion of the *mahr* on divorce, such measures were seldom taken. A married woman lived in a patriarchal family and was expected to produce sons at regular intervals. Likewise the institution of **habous**, a legal entail excluding women, meant that they rarely received property through inheritance as was their right; and in the courts, a woman's word was worth less than that of a man.

Women, on the whole, enjoyed greater freedom in **rural areas** than in the cities. They were able to walk about within the village without the veil, and enjoyed considerable influence over their husbands, and power over their dependants, within the home. Most women drew an independent income from the sale of artefacts or animal produce. Divorce was rare, partly because parents consulted their children over the choice of spouse, and partly because of the social stigma attached. Moreover, the proximity of their own family afforded wives a certain protection and shelter. Nevertheless, their status did not reflect the originally progressive reforms introduced by Islam.

Reform

It is against this background that the radicalism of Tunisia's **1956 Code** must be measured. In Turkey another great reformer, Mustafa Kemal (Ataturk), had simply abolished the *sharia* and introduced the Swiss Civil Code. Bourguiba, influenced by early twentieth-century women's rights campaigner **Tahar Haddad** (see p.387), and helped in certain areas by the more egalitarian personal laws of Tunisia's Malekite school of Islamic law, justified his own reforms from within the original Koranic texts and thus secured the support of Tunisia's spiritual head, the sheikh of Zitouna University. The marriage age was raised – to 19 for women, 20 for men – and informed consent made necessary. Polygamy was outlawed completely: Mohammed had stipulated that each wife should be treated equally and this was held to be impossible. *Sharia* and civil courts were merged together, divorce became a civil matter, and the formulaic *talaq* was abolished. The Koran itself states that arbitration is needed when there is marital discord: **divorce**, reasonably enough, is felt to be evidence of this. But although a woman can now sue for divorce on grounds of "mental incompatibility", alimony is not always granted. Bourguiba also encouraged people to think of the *mahr* as purely symbolic and gave his second wife a token one dinar. Custody of children has been restored to the woman at divorce, though only until the boy is 7 or the girl is 9. **Abortion** rights were introduced over the next fifteen years, along with an extensive and effective family-planning campaign. Legislation was passed on equal pay and, as the French left, opportunities for work were created. Women obtained **the vote** in two stages during 1956 and 1957.

Actual **social change** has been slow to follow these comparatively radical laws. A telling indication of the staying power of traditional attitudes is the assertion, frequently heard among young and otherwise liberal men, that women now have "too much power". Despite the efforts of the Union Nationale des Femmes Tunisiennes (UNFT), formed in 1956 to introduce the reforms to the country, female **illiteracy** is higher than male, far fewer women than men have attended secondary school and university, and many of the rural poor, especially the Berbers, are unaware of their legal rights. Opinion polls among the lower classes in the ever-expanding cities, heavily affected by unemployment, show a decline in support for a woman's **right to work**. Much of the independence that a job might otherwise bring can be frustrated by the difficulty of finding somewhere to live: it can be regarded as immoral for women to live alone, though it is becoming more acceptable, a change largely due to the need for unmarried students to rent when attending university away from home. Furthermore, it has been argued that male authority inside the family may actually have increased as a result of women entering the labour market, because money earned is often paid directly to a husband or male relative, or used for the dowry – the goods which the bride herself brings to a marriage.

The economic recession, combined with the upsurge of fundamentalism, may lie behind this reaction. Following the 1979 Iranian revolution, a number of women, particularly in the cities, took to wearing the Iranian-style headscarf, instead of the traditional Tunisian *sifsari* – the white veil-cum-cloak often gripped between the teeth to hide the face. Many have stopped wearing it since such a badge of support for Islamic fundamentalism invites unwelcome attention from the authorities. If support for fundamentalism grows however, Tunisian women may find themselves caught between the break-up of the extended family on the one hand – already causing problems of isolation in the cities – and new reactionary pressures on the other.

Women visitors to Tunisia

As outlined on p.57, a woman traveller in Tunisia (either alone or with a female or male companion) faces certain difficulties. With the right approach, skill and luck, some of these can be overcome, but, as the following personal and very different accounts show, the problems are enduring ones. Further feedback and comments from women travellers – and from Tunisian women and men – is always very welcome.

A surface liberalism

Linda Cooley taught in Tunisia for six years.

Tunisian women enjoy a measure of freedom and equality under the law unknown in many other Arab countries. Polygamy was abolished in the mid-1950s when Tunisia became independent. Divorce laws have been altered in women's favour. Most girls attend school. A reasonably large percentage of women are in higher education. Many women work outside the home. There are women in the professions and two women ministers in the government, and an established feminist group exists, which holds regular meetings in the Club Culturel Tahar Haddad on rue du Tribunal (☎71 564 695), in the capital's Medina.

But the presence of so many women in public can be misleading. It may lull you into a false sense of security when you first arrive and lead to false expectations of what you can and cannot do. If you walk around the capital (and remember that Tunis, Sousse and Sfax are very different from small-town and rural Tunisia), you will see women in jeans and the latest fashions, sometimes sitting in cafés, even girls walking along holding hands with their boyfriends. But what you cannot see and should know is that these same fashionably dressed girls have fathers who expect them to be home early, who expect them to be virgins at their wedding, and who may even expect them to marry a relative chosen by their parents. The clothes may have changed in recent years, the number of women at work may have changed, but, especially outside the big cities and tourist resorts, **social attitudes** remain unaltered. The Tunisian women you see in the streets are most often going to work or going home. The idea of a woman travelling abroad on her own, in this traditional Arab society, is understandably considered strange.

It is important to realize this before setting off on solo (or even two-women) travels. And to realize, too, how superficial are many of the Europeanized images – even in Tunis. **Bars** are not like those in France, but exclusively male domains, and if you wander in for a rest and a beer you will be stared at. Similarly, you can't expect to be able to chat to the man at the next table in the café about the best place to have lunch or the best time to visit the mosque, without your conversation being taken as an invitation to get more closely acquainted. **Western movies** have done an excellent job of persuading Tunisian men that all Western women spend their lives jumping in and out of bed with any willing male.

All this may sound somewhat offputting. Yet in six years living in Tunis, I often travelled alone, I travelled with my son and I travelled with another woman. Perhaps I was lucky, but apart from the unwanted attentions of a few men nothing happened to me. There is no part of the country that it is unsafe to visit – you can see everything.

But **travelling alone**, it is incredibly hard to get to know the people, and it is hard to relax, never being sure about how your behaviour will be interpreted if you do. I learnt to cope by avoiding direct eye contact with men, and above all never smiling at strangers. I once found myself being followed home because I inadvertently smiled at a man as we reached for the same tin of tomato sauce in the supermarket. It may irk you to keep your silence; not to answer like with like; not to show occasional disdain; but in the long run it will make your life more pleasant. After a while, the ignoring game becomes a reality; you really don't notice that anyone has spoken to you! If you cannot learn to ignore the hassle from men you will probably find yourself impatient to leave Tunisia after a very short time – it is an easy country for a woman on her own to dislike.

Travelling with a man makes it all much simpler. The stereotyped images on both sides (yours of pushy Arab men; theirs of loose foreign women) can be dispensed with and everyone can act naturally. Men will talk to you both as you're sitting in a café or waiting for a bus – and generally just for the pleasure of talking with someone different, nothing more. You may well get invited home to meet their families, where you'll be able to talk to the women in the home too, as, unlike in many other Arab countries, Tunisian women and men eat together.

You can also go to the **hammam** with the women of the house. This is very worthwhile, as it is the one place where women can meet traditionally as a group, away from all the pressures of a male-dominated society. Unless you speak Arabic, it is difficult to talk to the older women there, who rarely speak French, but they are more than willing to show you how to remove the hairs from your body, to henna your hair, to use tfal (a kind of shampoo made from mud) and to give you a thorough scrub with a sort of loofah mitten. You could, of course, go on your own to the hammam, but it's much better to go with a Tunisian woman, and introductions are almost exclusively made through men.

Another possibility is that, if you express curiosity, you may well find yourself invited to a **wedding** (you don't have to know the bride or groom – hundreds of people attend Arab weddings who hardly know the couple), or some other traditional event. Total strangers can be very hospitable when it comes to sharing their customs and food with you. I once had the most beautiful couscous brought out to the field where I was eating my picnic of cheese sandwiches; but then, I was with my son and a male companion.

Alone or with another woman it is all possible. But you do miss a great deal of what is, essentially, Tunisian life. Hopefully through more contact between foreign women and Tunisians a greater understanding will ensue on both sides, and the lone woman traveller will become more easily accepted. Meanwhile, ideas are changing – but very slowly.

From both sides of the fence

Dee Eltaïef is an English woman married to a Tunisian man and lives in Sousse.

Tunisia is one of the most **progressive** Muslim countries in the world as regards its treatment of women, who have equal opportunities in education and work, are allowed to drive, to travel abroad, to have private bank accounts, wear European clothes and watch European television, go to the cinema, choose their own husband and inherit according to the law. All of this may sound very mundane to a Westerner, but by comparison to other Arab or Muslim countries it is very enlightened.

But, despite these progressive laws which protect women's rights, **tradition** also plays an important role in their lives. Especially in villages and rural areas, though less so nowadays in cities and large towns, girls are brought up to be homemakers and mothers, and are schooled from an early age for their wedding day (considered to be the highlight of their life), the gathering of a trousseau and the very real possibility that their marriage will be arranged by their family. To be unmarried by the late 20s is definitely considered to be "on the shelf", regardless of a career. So by being a wife and then a mother, a girl's status in society is assured and recognized.

Traditional roles originate from economic practicalities as much as anything else. The man provides for his wife and children, and a woman's day-to-day duties involve a lot of **domestic work**, with stone floors that need daily washing, and extensive food preparation (cleaning fish, plucking chickens, shelling peas, grinding spices, as well as annual tasks like preparing couscous and sun-drying tomatoes). There are no frozen foods here and only limited tinned goods, and because many families do not have a refrigerator, food has to be bought and prepared on a daily basis. Few people have vacuum cleaners or washing machines, and rugs must be beaten and clothes washed by hand. If the house has no running water, this has to be collected from the well or pump. Bearing the chores in mind, it is understandable that women's work in the home can be considered full-time, especially if you add several children as well. There are few New Age Tunisian men so the bulk of these jobs are left to the women, although men still often do the shopping. Following this scenario, the children will be trained to help and invariably follow the parental roles, with girls bearing the brunt of domestic jobs, and boys encouraged in the education stakes in order to get a good job so they can support their future wives and children, as well as their parents in old age. The girls of the family are often married, do not have an income, and therefore cannot help out financially. So from an early age the roles are set.

There is tremendous **social pressure** for marriage. Even if a girl goes on to further education, this is still often seen as a secondary status to that of a married woman, and having a job and income does not give her the same level of independence as in Europe. Until she is married she lives in the family home, helps with domestic duties and pools any income for the benefit of the whole family. But there is always a background encouragement for her to find a husband and clean her own floors instead of her parents'. **Virginity** is still a desirable commodity, even in so-called sophisticated circles, and single parents and unmarried mothers are a rarity, there being considerable social stigma attached to pregnancy outside marriage. Tunisian society is interdependent on a vast network of family members and friends, meaning that there are very few places that a single woman could go to seek privacy. Even cities operate as large villages and there are few secrets in a country with only eight million inhabitants. The arranging of marriages still goes on today, although it tends to be more of a tacit approval of the couple's intentions rather than the go-between couplings of strangers.

From the **male point of view**, a husband wants his home well looked after; if his new wife is pretty, as well as a good homemaker, he considers it a bonus. The average Tunisian man will continue to socialize with his male friends after marriage, and is therefore not necessarily looking for intellectual compatibility in his wife; in fact, many believe that wives should be "moulded" by their husbands and a brilliant intellect in a woman is not a desirable characteristic. A man wants a wife to be the mother of his children and provide regular sex; he would expect to marry a virgin, probably several years his junior. Her parents will vet the prospective husband to make sure he is able to support a wife and children, and has a firm financial basis in order to buy the basic essentials for a home. He would also be expected to buy gifts for his prospective bride, usually in the form of expensive gold jewellery. This can be a costly investment from a man's point of view, so he's looking for value for money apart from anything else. He does not necessarily expect to be "in love", and if they are compatible in other areas it is assumed love will follow. The groom is not expected to be a virgin; in fact, he is expected to have sown his wild oats and be ready to settle down. As all married Tunisian girls are supposed to be virgins, and all prospective husbands expected to be men of the world, one can only presume that a certain amount of convenient temporary homosexuality can serve a purpose, as can the local prostitutes, the discreet wife of someone else or the nubile tourists who come on holiday.

With such a complex background, the stage is set for **tourists** to provide a very attractive alternative, which leads to many misunderstandings. Firstly, many female European tourists are not inhibited in consummating a relationship with an attractive Tunisian male. The Tunisian is happy to oblige, thus being provided with sex and a certain kudos among his friends in having "pulled" a European; if he plays his cards right he might get invited to Europe, be given gifts and have his beers paid for locally. It also does not spoil his chances of a good marriage later to a Tunisian girl when he's ready to settle down.

As Tunisian girls are simply not available for this type of relationship, one can perhaps understand the gravitation of Tunisian males to European tourists. The sexual licence shown in current films also creates an image of freedom and willingness. Many female tourists encourage the myth by not considering they have had a good holiday unless they have had several boyfriends. If the liaison gets as far as a mixed marriage, there may still be ulterior motives involved. As many of the boys who chase after tourists are not in a financial position to provide the gold dowry for a Tunisian bride, it is one way round a celibate life. Also many may use the marriage as an entrée into a European country, for which they would have no hope of getting a visa without the foreign wife.

Many Tunisian males with little personal experience of European cultures may be more influenced by what they see on television or what their own fertile imaginations can provide, so it's largely a question of clearly giving out the right signals. If you bathe topless, don't expect a lot of respect from any man who has seen your breasts. Conversely, if you behave circumspectly and immediately reprove any advances, double meanings or hint of familiarity, you will earn the respect of both Tunisian men and women as you travel through their country. You will also be setting a standard which other female travellers will be happy to follow, and, just as all Tunisians cannot be grouped in the same category, so they will understand that not all female tourists can be the same either. The best way to ward off unwanted attention is to completely ignore the whistles, questions or comments. Replying only fuels men's interest – they see it as "the green light," and move in for more serious chatting up. In Tunisia it is not considered rude to ignore a "hello" or equivalent in the street, however strange it may feel to you, and it is the only way to get the message across that you are not interested.

Changing attitudes

In **recent years**, attitudes have changed a lot, especially in larger towns like the capital, which tend to be more cosmopolitan, and in those with a heavy tourist influence like Sousse. One contributory factor is the continuation of mixed-sex education. Friendships are formed between boys and girls which don't necessarily end at the school gate. Another factor is the emergence of suitable venues where friends can meet casually, often places designed for tourists. In Sousse, for example, the tourist ghetto of Port el Kantaoui has always served this purpose, joined now by shopping malls, tourist cafés and an ice-cream parlour, to say nothing of discotheques. Tunisian couples are now actually walking and holding hands in public. Even ten years ago, this would have been considered very forward, except for newly married couples, identifiable by the bride's newly hennaed feet. Couples can also be seen on the beach together and in mixed groups during the summer season, with bikinis and swimming costumes on show.

Women's domestic role is also changing, convenience foods and domestic appliances making arduous household tasks easier to complete, while two other innovations have opened up the gate to more freedom and a changing climate among the young. The first of these is the increased numbers of young girls with a driving licence and access to a family car, and the second is easy access to mobile phones, which allows discreet phone calls between the opposite sex, as well as allowing parents to stay in contact with their daughters if they do go out, giving the modern Tunisian woman much more independence and mobility.

Survival skills

Dr Carol Higham travelled around northern Africa and lived in Tunis for eight months.

As a fair-skinned Caucasian, I turn pink when exposed to the sun, and during my travels it was obvious everywhere I went that I was not Tunisian. Repeated advances from men taught me some basic urban survival skills.

1. Dress modestly. You will see Tunisian women in miniskirts and tank tops, but you must remember that most of them, too, are harassed on a daily basis, and also that they have connections with Tunisia. When they are in their own neighbourhood, everyone knows their family, which gives them some degree of protection, an advantage that foreign women do not have. Dressing in a long skirt and modest blouse or T-shirt will give a certain amount of immunity, although you should still expect occasional unwanted advances. My neighbours and several women I knew taught me defence skills because they felt I dressed in a way that was respectful towards their society.

2. Wear sunglasses. I found this cut down on unwanted eye contact as well as allowing me to watch out for potential trouble on public transport.

3. Make contact with Tunisian women and older men. I found that Tunisians are very observant people. The men on the front desk of the hotel we booked into became protective of me within a week, and I found I could sit in the lobby without being hassled. In our second week, I had a bad allergy reaction to some food and remained in our room for several days. The maid, Hedia, took it upon herself to check on me, and in faltering French we talked. She was very helpful and just as curious about me as I was about her. In the market, I always bought from the older men as they tended to be polite and very helpful. One day, a young man walked up and kissed me; the stall owner went after him with a broom and apologized to me about his behaviour. From that time on, he called me *binte*, or "daughter", as did some of the other men – older Tunisian men do not approve of most of this licence and, if they consider you a friend or valued customer, they will use their influence to stave off young men.

Because I lived in a neighbourhood for eight months, I met and befriended several Tunisian women. I also found that being friendly to Tunisian women in shops sometimes led to friendships. Women who work outside the home are not only sympathetic to your problems but they also have solutions – they know where the largely hidden restaurants are that are patronized by women.

On the street, it is best to act like you're in a large, anonymous city, but, when dealing with people in shops and souks, behave as if it is a small town, always asking how people and their families are and what they recommend you buy. They will initially be suspicious but will soon become equally friendly. Remember, Tunisia is still a very family-oriented society: family connections are important, and the more connections you make, the more included you feel.

4. Be open to questions and curiosity. Often when I became friendly with women, they would ask me embarrassing questions. One woman wanted to know why I did not shave the hair on my arms and offered to remove it with hot sugar water. Several times on the TGM, older women would look through my shopping basket and ask me what a non-Tunisian was going to do with various products, then give me some good cooking tips. I always figured that if they were interested enough to ask the question and felt comfortable doing it, it was up to me to answer it.

5. Establish a pattern. I tried to patronize the same stores again and again and played on my one advantage: I was distinctive. Within a month or so of arriving, I felt perfectly comfortable exploring the souks by myself even though I spoke no Arabic, as the hawkers had come to recognize me and ignored me unless I entered their store. Then I found they were happy to answer questions and very helpful. The same was true of people in the corner stores and restaurants. We often ate at a little *gargote* on rue Ibn Khaldoun that served wonderful *kefteji*. One day I asked the cook what was in it. From that point on, I got special service and she would always give me *kefteji* no matter what I ordered. She would also send her son to clear a spot and wipe down the table for me. My husband found this both funny and irritating because he ended up eating standing up most of the time.

6. Overtip waiters. When I did not want to wait in the hotel lobby, I some-times went to the café in the *Hotel Africa* in Tunis. Here, I applied big-city techniques, spreading the newspaper all over my table and avoiding eye con-tact. I also overtipped the waiters, and by the second week a newspaper was unnecessary. I could read a book, while the waiters intercepted men headed for my table. I had another advantage in my own neighbourhood: as my hus-band not only spoke some Tunisian Arabic but also looked somewhat Tunisian, I became an accepted member of my neighbourhood community, and was able to go into local cafés alone, with the waiters always asking about him and staving off unwanted advances.

7. Don't be afraid to confront. Early in our stay, two young men began to follow me and call out comments. I initially ignored them, but when one of them grabbed my skirt I turned around and hit him with my market basket. They instantly scattered. It was then that I became aware of the café across the street, where the men were clapping at the show I had put on.

Later, I related this story to a Tunisian friend of ours who has a daughter. He felt that once young men cross the line of touching, they deserve what they get, and had taught his daughter where to kick and how to punch. I can count on one hand the times I had to get physical or even threaten to get physical with men. I found simply turning on someone who follows you and heading towards them screaming "Izzy" does wonders. If you feel threatened, create a scene. The aggressor will usually back off, or other people will intervene.

Tunisia is like anywhere else in the world, in that strangers are more open to problems. When I saw tourists wearing halter tops and tight shorts in the souks, yelling because someone had touched them, I used to wonder what would happen if they dressed like that and walked around at a street fair in New York or Chicago. As I look back on my nine months there, I realize that I spent most of the time alone, exploring the souks, markets and museums, and I really had very few problems. Once you establish relationships with people in Tunisia, you will see a whole other part of the country that is wonderful and delightful.

Wildlife

For a country a mere 800km long by 250km wide, Tunisia packs in an amazing variety of **habitats**. Although northern Tunisia will be familiar to anyone who knows the Mediterranean – a combination of limestone and sandstone hills, pine and cork oak forest, and agricultural land – as soon as you get south of the great Dorsale ridge of mountains that splits the country, you're into something totally different: steppe deserts north of the Chott el Jerid, and true rolling sand dunes to the south, with fertile oases punctuating both.

Any visitor from wetter climes has to keep the **lack of water** firmly in mind – it's the dominant factor. Although Tunisia includes the wettest place in North Africa (the cork oak forests around Aïn Draham), large areas of the south have an annual average rainfall of less than 50mm. And average rainfall totals are highly misleading: what actually happens is that there is no rain at all for years, and then a sudden deluge. This patchiness is common in the north as well, and is confusing for the average naturalist. It means that animals and plants have adapted to become highly flexible and unpredictable in their appearances. While in Britain you can go to a wood and see the same orchids flowering year after year, you can't always do that in Tunisia. After a very wet year, parts of the desert will bloom in a blaze of colour, the *sebkhas* will flood and suddenly support huge populations of wintering birds. After a very dry winter, annual plants may simply not germinate, some perennials will retreat into their bulbs or roots and not even flower, and the desert will remain devoid of vegetation.

Along with climate, **agriculture** is the other hugely important factor. The fertile north of the country has been used as an intensive agricultural belt from the first century BC right through to the French occupation, and agricultural pressures are no less intense now, with Tunisia's population growing at 2.5 percent annually. This has meant that the original forests have long since been cleared, and many of the scrubby Mediterranean hillside regions have been converted to arable land or greatly modified by the pressure of grazing. **Grazing** accounts for changes to the desert, too, with the familiar pattern of desertification being caused by a combination of overgrazing and climatic change. Many people who live in the south depend on wood for their cooking and heating; combine this with over seven million grazing animals and you can see why forests have degraded to scrubland and desert.

Seeing flora and fauna

Despite the loss of habitats, Tunisia still has abundant plant and animal life, and much of it can easily be seen. One problem is the lack of relevant **books**. Birds are fine – many of the standard field guides include North Africa – but **plants** are a problem since the only comprehensive guides to flora in Tunisia are highly technical, out of print, unillustrated, and in French. The following accounts therefore concentrate on species that can also be found in the northern Mediterranean, or which are covered in Oleg Polunin and Anthony Huxley's standard field guide, *Flowers of the Mediterranean* (Chatto, 1990).

It takes some practice to identify promising wildlife sites. Look for sites with a variety of different habitats, such as a hillside with woodland, scrub and rocky gorges. **Fresh water** is invariably a magnet and always worth checking out. **Deciduous woodland** is terrific, but give the monotonous olive groves a miss. For flowers, look for **colour**, which often indicates richness, especially on hillsides. A site with a **wide variety of plants** will tend to be richer in insects, and hence small birds and reptiles, too.

Spring is a good time to visit. Not only are the hillsides in full flower, but April and May are the best times for migrating birds passing through Tunisia on their way to breeding grounds further north. By **high summer** much of the country is burnt out, though good flowers are still to be found in the mountains and on the coast, and breeding is in full swing for summer migrant birds from further south. **Autumn** sees the return migration of European breeding birds, as well as a late flowering of many species of bulbs. **Winter** is the best time to visit the deserts of the south, with many of the desert plants choosing this time to flower (water permitting), and the winter season also sees the build-up of birds from Europe and Russia with huge concentrations of wildfowl and waders.

The **time of day** is important, too. While flowers, insects and reptiles can be watched right through the day and are best when it's hot, birds are most active at dawn and dusk. A walk through the woods within the first two hours of daylight can yield ten times as many birds as the same walk at midday.

Birds

Tunisia's **bird** population varies widely depending on the time of the year – it's more obviously affected by migration than in countries further north. During spring migration, the country can seem like the avian equivalent of Piccadilly Circus or Times Square in the rush hour, when summer visitors like **bee-eaters** arrive to breed from their winter quarters south of the Sahara; winter visitors, mostly **waders and wildfowl**, leave to migrate the thousands of kilometres to their breeding grounds in northern Europe; spring migrants such as **honey buzzards** pass through, sometimes in huge numbers; and the resident birds just stay where they are. In autumn, the same happens but in reverse. The best book on Tunisian bird-spotting, if you can get hold of it, is the Danish-published *The Birds of Tunisia* by Peter Thomsen and Peder Jacobsen (Jelling Bey Frykheri).

Farmland

Farmland can be rewarding, especially where the fields are small and broken up by trees or patches of scrub. **Finches** are much in evidence here – familiar **goldfinches**, **linnets** and **chaffinches** are joined by the yellow **serin**, a distant relative of the canary. **Nightingales** are a common summer visitor and the colourful and exotic **hoopoe** can be found wherever there are suitable old trees for nesting. Another abundant farmland species is the resident **corn bunting**, a heavy, brown bird with a monotonous song usually described as like the jangling of a bunch of keys. The song of the small resident **fan-tailed warbler** is no less monotonous, a repetitive "tsip" delivered in its undulating flight. Farmland attracts migrating **quails** and is often hunted over by **black kites** – long-tailed, with level wings – and marsh harriers, with equally long tails but wings tilted upwards. Black and white **great grey shrikes** are also found here, often perching on telegraph wires; they're joined in summer by their smaller, red-headed relative, the **woodchat shrike**.

Woodland and mountains

Deciduous **woodlands** are really only found in the Khroumirie region in the northwest of the country, and are home to many birds which, though common in Europe, are rare in Africa. Look for **woodpeckers, jays, wrens** and **tits** all year round, with **warblers, nightingales** and **wrynecks** in summer. Coniferous woodlands are less exciting, although **finches**, tits and some warblers are common.

The scrubby hillsides of the north are rewarding for small species. **Sardinian warblers**, with their glossy black caps, red eyes and scratchy song, are abundant. One species found only in North Africa is **Moussier's redstart**, an extremely beautiful small bird, with a striking plumage of orange, black and white. **Stonechats** are resident in this type of habitat, and the same zones are widely used as feeding stations by migrating **wheatears, warblers** and **wagtails. Barbary partridges**, another North African species, breed on these hillsides too.

Mountains, whether the forested hills around Aïn Draham, the limestone ridge of the Dorsale, or the barren massifs of the south, are the best place to see resident birds of prey. **Buzzards, eagles, vultures, kites** and **falcons** all use the rocks as breeding sites, gliding out over the surrounding plains in search of food. **Blue rock** thrushes, very like blackbirds but a superb powder-blue colour, are also found in mountains, as are **black wheatears** and **rock buntings**.

The coast

Tunisia's coastline varies from the rocky shore of the north, around Bizerte, to mud flats in the southeast. Predictably, this is the place for sea birds: a wide variety of gulls and terns spend the winter here, including the **slender-billed gull** and the **Caspian tern**. The latter is the largest of the terns of the region, almost gull-sized and with a very stout red bill. The islands off the north coast have colonies of two species of **shearwater**. But it's the tidal mud flats of the Gulf of Gabès that hold the most exciting birds, with huge wintering populations of waders (primarily **dunlin, sandpipers, stints** and **redshank**), along with large numbers of more exotic species such as **flamingos**, spoonbills and avocets.

Desert birds

Finally, the hills, *oueds* (dry stream beds) and oases of the deserts hold their own specialities. There is a truly bewildering variety of **larks** and **wheatears** around here, enough to tax the keenest ornithologist. One especially strange lark is the **hoopoe lark**, so called because of its long, decurved bill and black and white wings. Its song starts on the ground with a series of repeated notes, slowly ascending in pitch until the bird culminates with a final flurry of notes as it takes off vertically and then spirals down to start all over again. Another desert bird with an extraordinary call is the **trumpeter finch**, locally quite common.

Mammals

Although the top-of-the-food-chain predators such as lion and leopard were finally shot out early last century, there are still exciting species such as **jackal, wild boar, porcupine, mongoose** and **genet**, a beautiful tree-climbing carnivore with a spotted coat and a long ringed tail. The cats are still represented by wild cats and (it is said) lynx. Ignore anyone who says it's easy to see mammals: they're shy and often nocturnal, with good reason considering the long history of hunting. But the wooded mountains of the Khroumerie hold a good range of species, as do some of the limestone mountains like Jebel Ichkeul.

Further south, small desert rodents are of interest. **Desert rats**, **gerbils** and **jerboas** lope around the desert at night, and a species of **suslik**, *Psamnomys* (a sort of short-tailed ground squirrel with a characteristic upright "begging" posture), is common on the salt marshes and *sebkhas* of the south. Most of the larger desert antelopes have been reduced to the point of extinction by disturbance and hunting, but a programme to reintroduce **gazelle**, **oryx** and **addax** (as well as ostrich, only exterminated south of Medenine in the last century) is in progress at the national park of Bou Hedma. Fennec foxes (a beautiful desert fox with huge ears) certainly used to occur on Chott el Jerid but may have disappeared by now.

One final mammal that may still exist on the shores of Tunisia is the Mediterranean monk seal, which is down to its last few hundred, mostly in Greece and Turkey. Perhaps a few still hang on around some of the islands off the north coast.

Reptiles and amphibians

Throughout the country, reptiles and amphibians are much in evidence. **Lizards** and **skinks** are everywhere on the dry hillsides, small **geckos** come out in the evenings to pursue their useful insect-eating lifestyle on the walls and ceilings of older buildings, and **frogs** and **toads** croak a deafening spring chorus wherever there is fresh water. The handsome **painted frog** is widespread, blotched in brown and green. In the desert, you sometimes see **desert lizards** running like the wind on their hind legs from bush to bush. **Tortoises** and **pond terrapins** are both (locally) quite abundant. A dozen species of **snakes** also occur; although only some are poisonous, they do include several species of **viper**, and you should be cautious when out walking on rocky hillsides – shorts and sandals are perhaps not a good idea.

Insects and arachnids

Butterflies are the most obvious insects. In spring, huge numbers of the migrant **painted lady** cross Tunisia from further south, bound for Europe. It's a pretty extraordinary phenomenon, for although they breed in northern Europe, the population has to be renewed by migration every year, as the creatures only very rarely survive the northern winters in hibernation. **Clouded yellows**, a deep yellow with black wing-edges, undertake a similar migration but in smaller numbers. A small yellow butterfly with orange wingtips is likely to be the **Moroccan orangetip**, very common in early spring. Three striking species are the Cleopatra (*Gonepteryx*), like a huge brimstone but with orange patches on its yellow wings, and two species of **swallowtail**. Early summer is probably the time when butterflies on the wing are at their peak. Other striking animals of the lower orders include **praying mantises** and, of course,

scorpions (see box, p.24), which you are most unlikely to come across unless you go looking under rocks or bark.

Marine life

Finally, the **marine life** of the rocky northern coast is well worth mentioning. Some of the best snorkelling and diving in the Mediterranean is here around the **coral reefs** off Tabarka, Cap Serrat and especially off the marine national park of the Zembra isles. The coral holds extensive seaweed beds and numerous fish; sadly, spearfishing is much promoted as a tourist activity.

On the other hand, the Tunisian **fishing** industry is one of the best regulated in the Mediterranean, with the National Fisheries Board doing a superb job in ensuring that offshore fishing remains at a sustainable level. Apparently the weight of fish per area in Tunisian waters is some twenty times the weight in areas around Sicily, where trawling is notoriously exploitative. A trip round any fish market, and especially the big one in rue d'Allemagne in Tunis, gives some idea of the range and quality of what can be caught.

Flora

The flora of Tunisia stands at the crossroads between the Mediterranean flora of the north and the desert plants of the south. The forests of the Khroumirie have an almost northern European feel, with cork oak, flowering ash and even hawthorn growing above bracken, while only a few finely tuned species survive in the waterless desert conditions.

Farmland

Farmland hosts a colourful mass of plants in spring and early summer, especially around the field margins. Characteristic plants include **scarlet pimpernel** (confusingly, bright blue in much of the Mediterranean region), **poppies**, **marigolds**, **daisies** and **campions**. The borage family is well represented; most plants of this family have hairy stems and leaves, and five-petalled flowers which are often pink in bud but blue in bloom. The **common borage** has nodding star-shaped bright blue flowers (which you can eat in salads, incidentally), the **forget-me-nots** are in the same family and so are the **buglosses**. There are a number of different bugloss species (*Echium*) in Tunisia, but they all have blue or purple trumpet-shaped flowers with protruding pink stamens. One common species in this family that breaks the blue-flowered rule is **honeywort** (*Cerinthe major*), which has unusual chocolate-tipped yellow flowers hanging in a fused tube. Various **convolvulus** species are common: there are pink varieties in early summer and, in spring, a colourful species is the aptly named *Convolvulus tricolor* – blue around the edge, yellow in the middle, and white in between.

Although the uncultivated field margins have most of the farmland species, an occasional field will have escaped the attentions of the herbicide spray, and here you can see a blaze of colour from miles off, including the bright yellow of *Chrysanthemum coronanum*, the scarlet of poppies, and sometimes the nodding pink of **wild gladioli**. A plant to watch out for on grazed agricultural land is the **asphodel** (*Asphodelus microcarpus*). It grows up to 1m in height, with flowering spikes flung up from a narrow-leaved basal bulb; the flowers are pink with darker veins. It's the classic indicator species of **overgrazed land**, since livestock won't touch it, and it slowly takes over as other, more nutritious species are eaten away. In some parts of Tunisia the asphodel forms a virtual monoculture over large stretches of impoverished land.

One final group consists of introduced species. **Mimosa** or wattle is widespread, with long pendant strings of yellow flowers in spring. It's an Australian species, and well adapted to a hot dry climate. So are the **eucalyptus** (gum) trees, which have been widely planted both in forests and for roadside shade; it's hot enough for them to flower here, often very strikingly in a mass of yellow or red blossom.

On farms and around villages you're bound to see the **prickly pear**, a large cactus introduced to this side of the Atlantic, it is said, by Christopher Columbus. The **century plant** (*Agave americana*) is another American species, brought over from Mexico in the eighteenth century; it produces a huge flowering spike up to 10m high when it's ten to twenty years old, and then dies, although suckers around its edge may live on. Much smaller, but equally noticeable, is the **Bermuda buttercup**. A very common wayside plant, it flowers in spring in a sheet of absolutely brilliant yellow among bright-green, trefoliate leaves. Despite its name, it was introduced from South Africa, as was the **Hottentot fig** (*Carpobrotus*). This last species now dominates sandy cliffs and banks by the sea, with its mat of fleshy leaves and psychedelic pink or yellow flowers.

The coast

The **coastal areas** also hold many of these farmland plants, and were in fact their original habitat in many cases. Field margins are continually being disturbed, and the plough creates an ecological niche similar to the effect of the sea and shifting sand. Three common plants around the Tunisian coast are all familiar to British gardeners: **white alyssum** (*Lobularia manbma*), beloved as an edging plant by bedding-plant enthusiasts, grows sprawlingly with clusters of white flowers; **Virginia stock** (*Malcolmia mantima*) has tiny pink, red or purple four-petalled flowers; and the everlasting **sea lavender** (still known as *Statice*, although botanists have renamed it *Limonium*) has papery blue and white flowers.

Salt marshes are a common feature of the east coast, and inland there are vast dry salt lakes (*sebkhas*). These are often dominated by plants of the **glasswort** family – low shrubs with fleshy cylindrical stems and minute flowers. Only real plant freaks will want to sort them out down to species level, as they're a very difficult group.

Hillsides and mountains

The scrub-covered **hillsides** of the north, and the slopes of the wetter limestone mountains of the centre, form perhaps the classic Mediterranean botanical habitat, equivalent to the garigue of France or the matorral of the Iberian peninsula. Here you can find the aromatic shrubs of **rosemary**, **sage** and **thyme**, together with the **rockroses** (*Cistus*), with their profusion of flat white or pink flowers. Limestone hills tend to have a wider variety of ground flowers than the sandstone ones; peer under the bushes for many orchid species, as well as **irises**, including the delightful, tiny *Iris sisyrinchium*, which only flowers in the afternoon after the heat of the sun has warmed it. A notice-able spring species here, also common on farmland, is a small **valerian**, *Fedia cornucopiae* – low-growing with clusters of pink tubed flowers. It seems to be unpalatable to goats: you see it flowering profusely where everything else has been grazed out. One plant which is heavily grazed is the **dwarf fan palm** (*Chaemerops humilis*), a low-growing relation of the ubiquitous date palm; on ungrazed hillsides (if you can find any) it can sometimes be dominant.

Desert species

The **sand and stone deserts** south of the Dorsale mountains have a quite different flora. Plants are sparse, except in the oases, where many of the farm-land and hillside species mentioned above can be found, and they are high-ly adapted to the dry conditions. They survive in two ways. Sunlight is so abundant that they don't need big leaves to gather energy, so their leaves are reduced to **narrow stems** in order to reduce water loss by transpiration. The other technique is to try to store water, and some desert plants have fleshy, swollen leaves for this purpose. Many desert plants and shrubs have ferocious **spines**, too, as protection against grazing animals, although there's not much that can protect against the camel, which will even feed on prickly pear.

Peter Raine

Legendary Tunisia

ong before acquiring its present name, when it still belonged primarily to early Mediterranean civilization, the land of Tunisia featured in two of the greatest poems of European literature: Homer's *Odyssey* and Virgil's *Aeneid*. More than two thousand years later, this remote past drew many travellers to what was now a French colony, among them the writer Gustave Flaubert, whose novel *Salammbô* revisited one spectacular episode of the Carthaginian era.

In **Homer**'s epic of wandering and survival, the hero Odysseus, on his way home from Troy with a group of faithful but often foolish companions, must overcome a series of tests set by hostile gods and goddesses before finally being allowed to return to the island of Ithaca. Many of the episodes, such as the encounter with the one-eyed Cyclops, are part of European mythology, and the **Land of the Lotus-Eaters** (see passage on p.416) is among them.

There is an obvious and enduring fascination in the idea of a lifestyle emptied of cares by a mysterious substance, and it is not surprising that different places claim identity with Homer's idyllic land. Jerba's claim, however, is supported by ancient tradition. Describing the peoples of North Africa, the fifth-century BC historian Herodotus says of the Gindanes: "Within their territory, a headland runs out into the sea, and it is here that the Lotus-Eaters dwell, a tribe which lives exclusively on the fruit of the lotus. It is about the size of a mastic-berry, and as sweet as a date. The Lotus-Eaters also make wine from it." The geographical similarity with Jerba is unmistakable, though the lotus (a type of water lily depicted on ancient Egyptian tomb paintings) is apparently now extinct in Tunisia.

Virgil: the Aeneid

Like Odysseus, Virgil's hero Aeneas has difficulty escaping the seductive charms of this part of Africa, but the episode is much more emotionally and politically involved. Aeneas and Dido represent Rome and Carthage respectively, but Aeneas' choice between his love for Dido and his commitment to found a new Troy – that is, Rome – also represents the conflict between personal desires and public duty. Dido has given everything for Aeneas, alienating both the neighbouring Numidians, by rejecting marriage with one of their kings, and her own people, through her infidelity to her dead husband. Aeneas knows therefore that to abandon Dido will be to destroy her. At first he plans to leave secretly, but Dido realizes his intentions and, here, confronts him. Dido's eventual suicide on a funeral pyre symbolizes the inevitable destruction of Carthage by Imperial Rome.

The end of the affair

At last Dido accosted Aeneas, speaking first, and denounced him:

"Traitor, did you actually believe that you could disguise so wicked a deed and leave my country without a word? And can nothing hold you, not our love, nor our once plighted hands, nor even the cruel death that must await your Dido? Are you so unfeeling that you labour at your fleet under a wintry sky, in haste to traverse the high seas in the teeth of the northerly gales? Why, had you not now been searching for a home which you have never seen in some alien land, and had ancient Troy itself been still standing, would you have been planning to sail even there over such tempestuous seas? Is it from me that you are trying to escape? Oh, by the tears which I shed, by your own plighted hand, for I have left myself, poor fool, no other appeal, and by our union, by the true marriage which it was to be, oh, if I was ever kind to you, or if anything about me made you happy, please, please, if it is not too late to beg you, have pity for the ruin of a home, and change your mind. It was because of you that I earned the hate of Africa's tribes and the lords of the Numidians, and the hostility of my Tyrians also; and it was because of you that I let my honour die, the fair fame which used to be mine and my only hope of immortality. In whose hands are you leaving me to face my death, my Guest? I used to call you Husband, but the word has shrunk to Guest. What does the future hold for me now? My brother Pygmalion coming to demolish my walls, or this Gaetulian Iarbas, marrying me by capture? At least, if I had a son of yours conceived before you left, some tiny Aeneas to play about my hall and bring you back to me if only in his likeness, I might not then have felt so utterly entrapped and forsaken."

She finished. He, remembering Jupiter's warning, held his eyes steady and strained to master the agony within him. At last he spoke shortly:

"Your Majesty, I shall never deny that I am in your debt for all those many acts of kindness which you may well recount to me. And for long as I have consciousness and breath of life controls my movement, I shall never tire, Elissa, of your memory. Now I shall speak briefly of the facts. I had no thought of hiding my present departure under any deceit. Do not imagine that. Nor have I ever made any marriage-rite my pretext, for I never had such a compact with you. If my destiny had allowed me to guide my life as I myself would have chosen, and solve my problems according to my own preference, I should have made the city of Troy, with its loved remembrances of my own folk, my first care; and, with Priam's tall citadel still standing, I should have refounded Troy's fortress to be strong once more after her defeat. But in fact Apollo at Grynium, where he gives his divination in Lycia by the lots, has insistently commanded me to make my way to Italy's noble land. Italy must be my love and my homeland now. If you, a Phoenician, are faithful to your Carthaginian fortress here, content to look on no other city but this city in far-away Africa, what is the objection if Trojans settle in Italy? It is no sin, if we, like you, look for a kingdom in a foreign country. Each time the night shrouds the earth in its moist shadows, each time the fiery stars arise, the anxious wraith of my father Anchises warns me in sleep, and I am afraid. My son Ascanius also serves as a warning to me; I think of his dear self, and of the wrong which I do him in defrauding him of his Italian kingdom, where Fate has given him his lands. And now Jove himself has sent the Spokesman of the Gods – this I swear to you by my son's life and by my father – who flew swiftly through the air, and delivered the command to me. With my own eyes I saw the divine messenger in clearest light entering the city gate, and heard his voice with my own ears. Cease, therefore, to upset yourself, and me also, with these protests. It is not by my own choice that I voyage onward to Italy."

Throughout this declaration Dido had remained standing, turned away from Aeneas but glaring at him over her shoulder with eyes which roved about his whole figure in a voiceless stare. Then her fury broke:

"Traitor, no goddess was ever your mother nor was it Dardanus who founded your line. No, your parent was Mount Caucasus, rugged, rocky, and hard, and tigers of Hyrcania nursed you ... For what need have I of concealment now? Why hold myself in check any longer as if there could be anything worse to come? ... Has he spared a sigh or a look in response to my weeping, or has he once softened, or shed a tear of pity for one who loved him? Depth beyond depth of iniquity! Neither Supreme Juno, nor the Father who is Saturn's son, can possibly look with the impartial eyes of justice on what is happening now. No faith is left sure in the wide world. I welcomed him, a shipwrecked beggar, and like a fool I allowed him to share my royal place. I saved his comrades from death and gave him back his lost fleet … The Furies have me now, they burn, they drive …! So, now, it seems, he has his orders from Apollo's own Lycian oracle, and next even the Spokesman of the Gods is sent by Jove himself to deliver through the air to him the same ghastly command! So I am to believe that the High Powers exercise their minds about such a matter and let concern for it disturb their calm! Oh, I am not holding you. I do not dispute your words. Go, quest for Italy before the winds; sail over the waves in search of your kingdom. But I still believe that, if there is any power for righteousness in Heaven, you will drink to the dregs the cup of punishment amid sea-rocks, and as you suffer cry 'Dido' again and again. Though far, yet I shall be near, haunting you with flames of blackest pitch. And when death's chill has parted my body from its breath, wherever you go my spectre will be there. You will have your punishment, you villain. And I shall hear; the news will reach me deep in the world of death."

She did not finish, but at these words broke off sharply. She hurried in her misery away and hid from sight, leaving Aeneas anxious and hesitant, and longing to say much more to her. Dido fainted, and fell; and her maids took her up, carried her to her marble bedroom and laid her on her bed.

Taken from Book IV of the Penguin Classics edition, translated by W. F. Jackson Knight

Gustave Flaubert: Salammbô

In the nineteenth century, Carthage's abrupt and tragic end captured the imaginations of many Europeans, among them Gustave Flaubert. His impulse to write about ancient Carthage owed as much to the present as the past; on his first trip to the East in 1851, Flaubert had become obsessed with "the Orient", that mythical land created by feverish post-Romantic sensibilities. The plot of Salammbô, such as it is, follows the War of the Mercenaries (241–237 BC) – though with significant additions from the author, including the character of Salammbô, sex symbol supreme. For the bulk of the novel, Flaubert attempts to recreate the atmosphere of Carthage as an ancient Orient, something of a cross between a Cecil B. De Mille epic and a video nasty. It is also, however, highly imaginative, not to say fantastic, and a whole generation saw the Orient in terms quite as excessive as Flaubert's.

In this extract, Hanno, one of the Carthaginian generals, is in Utica snatching in typical style a brief respite from the rigours of campaigning against the Mercenaries, or Barbarians.

Hanno takes a bath

Three hours later he was still plunged in the cinnamon oil with which the bath had been filled; and as he bathed, he ate on a stretched out ox hide, flamingo tongues with poppy seed seasoned with honey. Beside him, his doctor, standing motionless in a long yellow robe, had the bath heated up from time to time and two boys leaning on the steps of the pool rubbed his legs. But the care of his body did not interrupt his concern for the welfare of the state, and he was dictating a letter to the Grand Council and, as some prisoners had just been taken, wondering what terrible punishment to invent.

"Stop!" he said to a slave who stood writing in the hollow of his hand. "Have them brought in! I want to see them."

And from the back of the room filled with white steam where torches cast spots of red three Barbarians were pushed in: a Samnite, a Spartan, and a Cappadocian.

"Continue!" said Hanno.

"Rejoice light of the Baals! Your Suffete has exterminated the greedy dogs! Blessings on the Republic! Order prayers to be offered!" He noticed the captives, and then roaring with laughter: "Ha ha! My brave men from Sicca! You are not shouting so loudly today! Here I am! Do you recognize me? Where are your swords then? What terrible men, really!" And he pretended to try and hide, as if he were afraid. "You demanded horses, women, land, judicial office, no doubt, and priesthood! Why not? All right, I will give you land, and land you will never leave! You will be married to brand new gallows! Your pay? It will be melted in your mouths in the form of lead ingots! And I will set you in good positions, very high, among the clouds, so that you can be near the eagles!"

The three Barbarians, hairy and covered in rags, looked at him without understanding what he was saying. Wounded in the knees, they had been seized and bound with ropes, and the ends of the heavy chains on their hands dragged along the floor. Hanno was angry at their impassivity.

"On your knees! On your knees! Jackals! Dirt! Vermin! Excrement! So they do not answer! Enough! Silence! Have them flayed alive! No! In a moment!"

He was puffing like a hippopotamus, rolling his eyes. The scented oil ran out beneath the bulk of his body, and sticking to his scaly skin made it look pink in the torchlight.

He went on:

"For four days we have greatly suffered from the sun. Crossing the Macar some mules were lost. Despite their position, the extraordinary courage ... Ah! Demonades how I am suffering! Heat up the bricks and make them red hot!"

There was a clattering of rakes and furnaces. The incense smoked more fiercely in its large burners, and the naked masseurs, sweating like sponges, squeezed over his joints a paste composed of corn, sulphur, black wine, bitches' milk, myrrh, galbanum, and styrax. He was tormented by constant thirst: the man in yellow did not give in to this craving and, holding out a golden cup in which steamed a viper's brew:

"Drink!" he said, "so that the strength of the serpents, children of the sun, may penetrate the marrow of your bones, and take courage, reflection of the Gods! Besides, you know that a priest of Eschmoûn is watching the cruel stars around the Dog from which your illness derives. They are growing paler, like the spots on your skin, and you are not to die of it."

"Oh, yes, that is right," repeated the Suffete, "I am not to die of it!" And from his purplish lips escaped a breath more noisome than the stench of a corpse. Two coals seemed to burn in place of his eyes which had no eyebrows left; a mass of wrinkled skin hung down over his forehead; his two ears, standing out from his head, were beginning to swell, and the deep creases which made semicircles around his nostrils gave him a strange and frightening look, like that of a wild beast. His distorted voice sounded like a roar; he said:

"Perhaps you are right, Demonades? In fact a lot of the ulcers have closed up.

I feel quite robust. Just look how I eat!"

Then less out of greed than for show, and to prove to himself that he was well, he attacked cheese and tarragon stuffing, filleted fish, pumpkins, oysters, with eggs, horseradish, truffles and kebabs of little birds. As he looked at the prisoners he revelled in imagining their punishment. However he remembered Sicca, and fury at all his pains burst out in insults at these three men.

"Ah! Traitors! Wretches! Infamous cursed creatures! And you exposed me to your outrages, me! Me! The Suffete! Their services, the price of their blood, as they call it! Oh yes! Their blood! Their blood!" Then talking to himself: "They will all perish! Not one will be sold! It would be better to take them to Carthage! I should be seen . . . but I have probably not brought enough chains? Write: send me . . . How many of them are there? Go and ask Muthumbal! Go! No mercy! Cut off all their hands, and bring them to me in baskets!"

But strange cries, at once hoarse and shrill, could be heard in the room, above Hanno's voice and the clattering of the dishes being set round him. The noise increased, and suddenly the furious trumpeting of the elephants broke out as if battle was starting again. A great tumult surrounded the town.

The Carthaginians had not tried to pursue the Barbarians. They had settled at the foot of the walls, with their baggage, their servants, their whole satrap retinue and they were making merry in their handsome pearl-edged tents, while all that remained of the Mercenary camp was a heap of ruins on the plain. Spendius had recovered his courage. He sent out Zarxas to Mâtho, went through the woods, rallied his men (losses had not been heavy) – and furious at having been beaten in battle, they reformed their lines, when someone discovered a vat of paraffin, no doubt abandoned by the Carthaginians. Then Spendius had pigs collected from the farms, smeared them with pitch, set light to it and drove them towards Utica.

The elephants, frightened by these flames, took flight. The ground sloped upwards, they were assailed by javelins, and turned back – and with mighty blows of their tusks and hooves they ripped, smothered, flattened the Carthaginians. Behind them, the Barbarians were coming down the hill; the Punic camp, with no defences, was sacked at the first charge, and the Carthaginians were crushed against the gates, for no one would open them for fear of the Mercenaries.

Dawn was breaking; from the west appeared Mâtho's infantrymen. At the same time horsemen came in sight; it was Narr'Havas with his Numidians. Jumping over the ravines and bushes, they drove the fugitives like hounds hunting hares. This reversal of fortune interrupted the Suffete. He cried out to be helped out of the bath. The three captives were still before him. Then a Negro (the same one who carried his parasol in battle) leaned over to his ear.

"Well now . . . ?" the Suffete slowly replied. "Oh! kill them!" he added brusquely.

The Ethiopian drew a long dagger from his belt and the three heads fell. One of them, bouncing amid the debris of the feast, jumped into the pool, and floated there for a while, with open mouth and staring eyes. The morning light was filtering in through cracks in the wall; the three bodies, lying on their chests, were streaming blood like three fountains, and a sheet of blood covered the mosaics, which had been sprinkled with blue powder. The Suffete soaked his hand in this still warm slime, and rubbed his knees with it: it had remedial powers.

Taken from the Penguin Classics edition, translated by A. J. Krailsheimer

Tunisian literature

Modern literature right across the Maghreb is tied up with questions of national and linguistic identity. Traditional local Arabic forms and language have wrestled with the language of their colonizers, and the best-known works internationally have mostly been written in French. Tunisia has yet to produce a writer as widely known as Morocco's Tahar Ben Jelloun or Algeria's Rachid Mimouni, nor does it have a resident foreign sage and interpreter to play the role that Paul Bowles did in Morocco. In the first half of the twentieth century, though, two extraordinary writers – both fated to die young – emerged from colonial Tunisia.

Abou el Kacem Chabbi

Abou el Kacem Chabbi (1909–34), a native of Tozeur, was the son of a judge who sent him at the age of 12 to study at the Zitouna mosque in Tunis. He subsequently studied law, but was more interested in poetry, which he read widely. Goethe, Lamartine and the Syrian-American Gibran Kahlil Gibran were particular influences.

By the age of 18 his own poetry was being published and in 1929 he delivered a famous and influential lecture in Tunis on "The Poetic Imagination of the Arabs". Rejecting the stifling weight of the past as represented by classical Arabic poetry, he made a plea for the poet's "freedom to imagine". His own work, while retaining the essentials of classical form and language, expresses a distinctly Romantic sensibility. The poems are full of solitary individuals yearning for self-expression, frequently in settings of mountains covered with rushing streams and leafy forests. Neither Tunis nor Tozeur has many of these, but Chabbi spent his summers in Aïn Draham and would have drawn inspiration from the scenery there. He died of a cardiac problem at 25, but not before achieving an extraordinary reputation. His poem The Will of Life *has been taught to schoolchildren across the Arab world. Like several of his poems, it hints at the frustrations of the colonized state in which Chabbi found himself and his country.*

The Will of Life

If one day the people should choose life
Fate is certain to respond.
The night will surely retreat,
and fetters be broken!
He who is not embraced by the longing for life
will evaporate in vacancy and be forgotten –
Grief to anyone not aroused by the breathing desire for life!
Let him beware the slap of oblivion!
This is what life said to me,
this is how its spirit spoke.

The wind muttered between the ravines;
"When I aspire to a goal,
I ride my wishes, forgetting caution,
face the wilderness, the rugged trails
and flaming days –

He who does not like scaling mountains
will live eternally in potholes."

So the sap of youth churned in my heart
as other winds raged within my breast.
I bent my head, listening to
the clap of thunder,
the chime of the draft,
the cadence of the rain.

When I asked the earth,
"Mother, do you hate mankind?"
She replied, "I bless those with ambition,
those who brave danger –
I curse the ones not keeping step with time,
who are content to live a fossil life.
The vibrating universe loves what moves
and despises the dead, forgetting their
greatness.
The horizon hugs no stiffened bird,
nor does the bee kiss a withered flower.
Not even graves would hold the dead,
save for the tenderness in my motherly heart!
Woe to one not longing for life!
Let him beware the curse of extinction!"

On an autumn night laden with boredom,
I was so drunk on starlight my sadness drank too.
I asked the dark
"Does life return the spring of youth
once it is withered?"
The lips of darkness did not move,
nor did the virginal dawn.
Then the forest gently spoke
like the quiver of a chord:
"Winter comes, winter of mist,
winter of snow, winter of rain,
and magic dissolves.
What budded and ripened,
the gleaming angles of fields
and quiet magic of the sky –
gone like branches
that fall with their leaves.
Now the wind tosses dead petals,
the flood buries them haphazardly.
All perish like a lovely dream
which shimmered in some heart then
disappeared.
Only the seeds remain, kernels of memory,
still embracing, even under the fog, the
snows,
the heaps of earth –
the shadow of life that never palls,

C

the green germ of spring
dreaming of birdcall,
the musk of flowers, the tang of fruit."

✧✧✧

The diaphanous night revealed a Beauty
that kindled the mind.
A strange magic was flung across the skies
as a giant wizard lit the glittering stars.
Incense drifted from flowers on the moon's quiet wings ...
a holy hymn ringing out in a temple!
Across the universe it was proclaimed:
Endeavour is the flame of life,
the heart of victory.
If the spirit chooses life,
Fate is certain to respond!

From Songs of Life, *translated by Lena Jayyusi and Naomi Shihab Nye*
(Beit al-Hikma, Carthage, 1987)

Ali Du'aji

*Another member of the same Tunis literary circle, Ali Du'aji (1909–49) wrote plays,
stories and songs, and edited literary journals. Like el Kacem Chabbi, he wrote in
Arabic but read much foreign literature: Chekhov, Flaubert, Jack London and Mark
Twain. Twain's influence in particular is detectable in the ironic modern tone of Du'aji's
observations of contemporary urban life. One of his most striking works,* Bar-Hopping
Along the Mediterranean, *a series of sketches describing a Mediterranean cruise in
1933, offers a rare glimpse of the dominant European culture through Tunisian eyes.*

*"At the Beach at Hammam-Lif", the short sketch reprinted here, is typical of Du'aji's
portraits of everyday Tunisian life. Deceptively casual, it carries more weight than might
at first appear. Its narrator, rootless and anonymous in the crowd, shares the dreamy
alienation of Albert Camus' Outsider, while the switches in cultural reference – from
Romeo and Juliet to the palace of the Alhambra in Granada – betray a Western and
Arab duality. In just a few elegant paragraphs, Du'aji conveys the complex texture of
Tunis's new urban culture: simultaneously old and new, Arab and Western.*

At the beach at Hammam-Lif

The car on the train was packed with a very heavy woman, and heavy she
was! Added to her weight, she wore a red cape, the same colour as her lips and
fingernails. Just as she filled the car with her flesh, she filled it with her movements, and with her son too. Wouldn't you know, her son had a big fat head
and he too was wearing red. I imagined that wearing red and being fat ran in
the family. The kid was screaming like he was crying, but he wasn't crying at
all. Everyone in the car was bothered by the screaming. They just wanted to
keep him happy by giving him what he wanted. The questions kept coming.
One person asked him what he wanted; another bounced him on his knee;
a third patted him on the nose. But the kid got angrier and screamed all the
more, as though he were screaming just for the sake of screaming. He didn't

want a sandwich, he didn't want a toy horn. To tell the truth, twenty minutes was all I could take of this little brat, and I decided to move to another car.

I didn't see anyone at first, and I went in thinking the coast was clear. That is, until I walked past the second compartment where I found a young couple whom we would classically refer to as "Romeo and Juliet". Romeo was over six feet tall, gaunt and very pale, with a long nose. He looked like a poet. Juliet was Sicilian, medium height, and wearing bright yellow, the way a king would wear an ermine robe. They were speaking in whispers and moving their hands a lot to overcome the loud noise around them. Romeo would put up his hands, then pull his left hand forward as though he were saying: "I love you and I'll kill your father with a dagger if ..." Juliet was rolling her fingers around as though she were answering: "I'll embroider you a scarf that you'll be proud to wear in front of the vice-consul."

It was unbearable, sitting next to a pair of lovers, seeing and hearing only gestures ... And for this I took the train? Yes, I took it to go to Hammam-Lif. What was important was that I get there. So I decided to leave all the cars altogether, sit out the journey on one of the car steps watching the telegraph poles and counting them where I could.

From the station to the beach, I walked quickly so I could get to see the bathers. What's nice is that it's not just the "nose" beach, but every-other-part-of-the-body beach as well, the thigh beach and the breast beach and ... and ... and ...

The beach was full of peanut and lemonade vendors, and of bathers too, and wonderful white sheets.

The peanut and lemonade vendors are notorious for their filthiness and arrogance. As for the bathers, men and women alike, stripped of their clothes and their modesty, they feel the heat at times and throw themselves into the water. When they get cold in the water, they stretch out exposing their bodies, catching the rays of the sun. And there they were, all day long, between hot and cold.

Tradition has it that a person who bathes all day long is considered one of the "in-crowd", while the person who gives up and gets dressed after half an hour is considered an outsider.

The white sheets are something else. Those wrapped up in them are creatures who follow the tradition of their grandmothers, covering their soft bodies. Keeping up with the times, they come out to the beach mocking this one's hair-do and that one's wrinkled trousers. There's one who forgets that she's veiled and shows you her pretty face. Then she remembers and disappears under her veil after electrically charging up four young men on the beach who had been watching her all the while.

Walking along that road I was imagining all those bodies dressed in Andalusian clothes with wide pantaloons, belly dancing in a courtyard at al-Hambra. Then, all of a sudden, a bird drilling in air manoeuvres dropped a bomb on my fez that I didn't notice. If it weren't for the passers-by laughing and pointing at my venerable head, I wouldn't have realized that there was something there that was arousing the curiosity of all these distinguished people. I took off the fez and found it decorated from that damned bird's bomb. Who was it who described the bird as an angel? If I found him, I'd show him a devil.

It was better that I not stay at Hammam-Lif nor at "the pool" after it got out that I was wearing the target for bird manoeuvres on my head. So I headed back. By the grace of God I found the train empty except for an old man who knew every single villa along the tracks that ran from Hammam-Lif to Tunis.

From Sleepless Nights, *translated by William Granara (Beit al-Hikma, Carthage, 1991)*

Mustapha Tlili

Educated in Paris and the US and a resident of New York, Mustapha Tlili (born 1937) writes – unlike el Kacem Chabbi and Du'aji – in French. Lion Mountain, first published in 1988, was his fourth novel. Set in an anonymous village, it is a stark exploration of national identity in post-colonial North Africa. The villagers, represented by the narrator's mother Horia and her Nubian steward Saad, who lost a leg at the Battle of Monte Cassino in World War II, share a strong sense of local identity and history. Though barely affected by the French, their community is threatened after independence by the new state's demand for central control, and the story's violent ending has a sense of tragic inevitability. In the extract that follows, the village receives its first representative of the new government.

Lion Mountain

The delegate, the new authorities' very first representative in Lion Mountain, wanted to enrol all adult males in the Party. The portrait Saad draws of him is hardly flattering. A short, slightly built young man, it seems. His forehead is low and narrow. He has a thin moustache. Like one of those circumflex accents Little Brother used to pen so neatly but with too much ink when he was still at school, the moustache sits upon a dry and bony face deeply pitted by smallpox. Petty malevolence made flesh and blood.

And the man appears to be very full of himself. Always sprucely turned out, with a perpetually dashing air. He invariably wears a three-piece suit of shiny black material. It seems that from the first day, nobody was left in any doubt at all about the man's colossal self-importance, arrogance and conceit, which he shows off at the wheel of a luxurious black Citroën, driving with ostentation and contempt through the narrow, stony streets of our poor little village at breakneck speed, making an incredible racket and leaving behind great clouds of dust.

As soon as he took charge of the Delegation, which had remained unoccupied for more than a year, our little village tyrant, who thirsted for influence and authority, selected – out of all the possible candidates to fill the office of public crier – Horia's retarded farmhand. Who would ever have imagined it?

And so from dawn to dusk for three days running, the Simpleton shouted his lungs out in every corner of Lion Mountain: in the Spring, our former French quarter; in the old village, from house to house and in front of every street stall; even at the doors of the mosque, as well as for the benefit of the ruminating camels in the livestock market, the exhausted mules and donkeys brutalized by the heat and human stupidity, assorted skeletal stray dogs, and the cackling chickens roaming freely over Highway 15 as it lay dreaming in the spring sunshine.

And what tidings did this inspired messenger bring? That the Party was the Motherland. That everyone should prove his great worth by acquiring a Party card – upon payment of a certain sum, of course. And no holdouts, or else! Recalcitrants risked losing their share of irrigation water. Close scrutiny would unmask the guilty ones.

Since what was at stake was the life or death of their crops and tiny plots of land, the source of all wellbeing for them and theirs, all male adults had felt they had no other choice but to accept their fate and trudge off, one by one, heads bowed in resignation, to the former police station now serving as head-quarters for the new authorities.

Horia's property was upstream, however, and too close to the spring to risk being deprived of its fair share of water. Following the example of the other villagers, and just to be on the safe side, Saad had nevertheless thought it wise to ask Imam Sadek for his advice. The latter, after careful consideration, had confirmed the Nubian's original opinion. No, Horia and Saad weren't at risk, that was quite true. Still, it was better to be practical, after all, and cooperate with the authorities. In a word, to avoid unnecessary complications, the imam had advised against causing any trouble, because he, too, was beginning to be apprehensive about the future.

As always, however, Saad will end up doing exactly as he pleases. As always, he'll insist on seeing things only in their simplest, most essential light. And to get to the heart of a problem, he had decided there was only one way to go.

His reasoning was crystal clear. The house isn't on fire, he told himself. The village is in no danger, right? Now, he, Saad, learned all he needs to know about danger at Monte Cassino. No one, and certainly not that scarecrow of a petty tyrant at the Delegation, has to cry danger while waving a Party card under his nose. If Horia, if Imam Sadek, or the Ouled El-Gharib clan were threatened, then, yes, it would be understandable. In which case, plenty of people can vouch for the Corporal's courage. Everyone knows what he can do. Even though he has only one leg left, through the fault of the Infidels, nobody doubts that if he had to, he would not hesitate to take up a weapon. Even . . . to take the machine gun from its hiding place under the ancient mulberry tree, the same gun the Simpleton discovered one day while chasing around after partridges, and which has been kept in perfect shape, unbeknownst to anyone, not even Horia, thanks to his secret but constant attention. No, really, decided the Nubian, the house is not on fire. Thank the Party anyway for having thought of him. And thanks also to Monsieur the Delegate and Madame the Motherland. It's very nice, all that, but really, no thanks.

From Lion Mountain, *translated by Linda Coverdale (Little Brown, 1990)*

Books

T unisian **literature** in English is rare, but if you read French, look out for the publications of Éditions Sindbad and Éditions Salammbô in Tunisia. They publish contemporary writers in their original language and in French translation.

In the reviews below, books that are especially recommended are denoted ⬧ . Books designated "o/p" below are out of print at the time of writing, but are still worth tracking down secondhand or in libraries, and some may be reprinted or published in a new edition. We've given the name of the publisher if they are based in Tunisia.

One firm specializing in reprinting original editions of early travellers' books on North Africa is Darf (227 West End Lane, London NW6 1QS; ☎020/7431 7009, ✪www.darfpublishers.co.uk). The Maghreb Bookshop (45 Burton St, London WC1H 9AL, ☎020/7388 1840, ✪www.maghrebreview.com), the English-speaking world's main specialist on the Maghreb, has a wide range of titles, including many out of print, and also publishes the *Maghreb Review*, the most important journal on the Maghrebian countries in English.

Travel writing

Early travellers

James Bruce *Travels to Discover the Source of the Nile in the Years 1768–73* (o/p). Deleted after the first edition, the Tunisia section is but a small part of this six-volume account of Bruce's journey from Algiers to Ethiopia. His fascination with people's behaviour, brilliantly conveyed in blunt and lively style, makes this some of the most entertaining travel writing ever published.

Norman Douglas *Fountains in the Sand* (o/p). A bigot, who saw the Chott, like just about everything else in Tunisia, as a symbol for the "sterility of the Arab soul," Douglas nonetheless writes in a compelling style about his travels around the Jerid.

Leo Africanus *History and Description of Africa* (translated by J. Pory, 1896;

o/p). The author, a Spanish Moor who converted to Christianity after being captured at sea by Christian corsairs, got his nickname from the pope, who encouraged him to write about the Arabs of Barbary. Not surprisingly, there's more than a whiff of propaganda in some of the accounts.

Reginald Rankin *Tunisia* (o/p). Wholly eccentric and spiced with prejudice, arrogance and sheer stupidity, but still a good read in spite, or because of, all that.

Sir Grenville Temple *Excursions in the Mediterranean* (1835, o/p). An early imperialist view of Tunisia. The author, something of a Romantic artist, produced some unlikely versions of the monuments and scenery he encountered.

Other travel writers

D. Bruun *Cave-Dwellers of Southern Tunisia*. Bruun was one of the first Europeans to live with the people of Matmata and Haddej, and his sympathetic 1898 account retains its interest.

Alexandre Dumas *Tangier to Tunis* (o/p). Dumas is not at his best here, and the editing has shortened the chapters on Tunisia, but there are some amusing vignettes in this rare translation of one of the many French travellers – Dumas visited in 1846.

Katy Hounsell-Robert *Katy in Tunisia* (Nigel Day). A chatty and readable modern account of an Englishwoman's jolly jaunts in Tunisia. At times not very well informed, but easy to identify with when travelling in the country.

Aldous Huxley "In a Tunisia Oasis" (in *The Olive Tree: The Collected Works of Aldous Huxley*). By far the best of a largely barren English tradition of travel writing on Tunisia, despite the snide and rather racist tone. The oasis in question is Nefta.

★ **Dahris Martin** *Among the Faithful*. In this charmingly written and well-observed account Martin, a young American woman who spent two years in Tunisia during the late 1920s, tells of events that befell her and the group of Tunisian friends she got to know.

Ancient history and literature

Saint Augustine *Confessions* and Peter Brown *Augustine of Hippo: A Biography*. The former is the saint's most accessible work, a spiritual autobiography, while Brown's classic biography contains much interesting background material on the Africa of Augustine's time.

Serge Lancel *Carthage*. An authoritative history of Carthage, translated from the French.

Livy *The War with Hannibal*. One of Flaubert's sources for *Salammbô*, this is the classic Roman account of the Carthaginian general whose attempt to take Rome was foiled by the inability of his elephants to negotiate the Alps.

Susan Raven *Rome in Africa*. A well-illustrated survey of Roman (and Carthaginian) North Africa.

Sallust *The Jugurthine War*. Concise but entertaining and at times rather melodramatic account by a Roman historian of the war between the Numidian king Jugurtha and the Roman Army under Marius.

★ **David Soren** *et al. Carthage* (o/p). Written by Carthage archeologists to accompany a museum exhibition that toured North America, this is a very readable introduction to the Carthaginian and Roman cultures of ancient Tunisia.

Virgil *The Aeneid*. Books I and IV of the great Roman epic poem tell the tragic love story of Queen Dido (founder of Carthage) and Aeneas (founder of Rome), an inspiration to artists of every age since.

Tunisian and Arab history

★ **Jamil M. Abun-Nasr** *A History of the Maghreb in the Islamic Period.* An authoritative history of the region by a distinguished Lebanese historian, but not exactly light reading.

Lisa Anderson *The State and Social Transformation in Tunisia and Libya, 1830–1980* (o/p). Don't be put off by the academic title, as this is a good review of Tunisian and Libyan political and social history.

Ernle Bradford *The Sultan's Admiral* (o/p). A very readable biography of Khair ed Din Barbarossa, giving an excellent taste of the corsair rivalries of the sixteenth century.

Leon Carl Brown *The Tunisia of Ahmed Bey, 1837–1856* (o/p). A fascinating insight into nineteenth-century Tunisia and the problems faced by an Arab government struggling to keep itself out of European clutches.

Julia A. Clancy-Smith *Rebel and Saint.* Subtitled "Muslim Notables, Popular Protest, Colonial Encounters (Algeria and Tunisia 1900–4)", this book looks at local community leaders and their reaction to colonial rule at the beginning of the twentieth century.

Albert Hourani *A History of the Arab Peoples.* If you have the time to read it, this expansive and panoramic view of Arab history is the best available.

★ **Charles-André Julien** *History of North Africa from the Arab Conquest to 1830* (o/p). An easier read than Abun-Nasr, which it compliments well, although the last English version was in 1970 (updated editions are available in French).

Ibn Khaldoun *The Muqaddimah.* A translation of the masterpiece by Tunisia's great fourteenth-century historian, whose fascinating mix of sociology, history and anthropology was centuries ahead of its time.

Charles Messenger *The Tunisian Campaign* (o/p). A pictorial history of World War II in Tunisia.

Kenneth J. Perkins *Historical Dictionary of Tunisia.* A concise but comprehensive reference book on the history of Tunisia, mainly since the Arab invasion, but also covering earlier periods.

W. Perkins *Tunisia: Crossroads of the Islamic and European Worlds.* The best pocket history of Tunisia available. Authoritative and a good read.

Barnaby Rogerson *A Traveller's History of North Africa: Morocco, Tunisia, Libya, Algeria.* A welcoming key to unlock the complexities of this area's culture and way of life.

Modern literature

Abou el Kacem Chabbi *Songs of Life* (Beit Al-Hikma, Carthage). Poetry doesn't translate any better from Arabic than from other languages, but this does at least provide a sense of the Romantic sensibility of Tunisia's national poet (see p.555).

Hedi Bouraoui *Return to Thyna.* Bouraoui, who writes in French, is one of Tunisia's most well-known novelists, but this is his only work that has been published in English.

Ali Du'aji *Sleepless Nights* (Beit Al-Hikma, Carthage). Short sketches translated into English (see p.557).

 Gustave Flaubert *Salammbô*. Sex, violence and more violence in Flaubert's "historical" account of Carthage's brutal civil war with its Mercenaries (241–237 BC), which really owes less to history than to its author's obsession with the fabulous Orient. An extraordinarily bad novel, but a very enjoyable read – see p.552 for an excerpt.

André Gide *Amyntas* (o/p). An early work by the French writer whose experiences in the North African colonies (including meeting Oscar Wilde) were a lasting influence.

Gisèle Halimi *Milk for the Orange Tree*. Halimi is a Jewish civil rights lawyer in France, part of whose autobiographical account paints a picture of her childhood in Tunisia.

 Monia Hejaiej *Behind Closed Doors*. A compilation by a Tunisian-American researcher of traditional women's oral literature in the form of tales by three expert storytellers from Tunis, reflecting their very different attitudes to life, love, sex and social norms.

 Patricia Highsmith *The Tremor of Forgery*. Set in 1960s Hammamet, this is a characteristically creepy piece of work by the author of the Ripley books. Although described by Graham Greene as her finest novel, it is only intermittently available.

Sabiha Khemir *Waiting in the Future for the Past to Come*. A novel written – unusually – in English by a Tunisian author, consisting of a series of interconnected stories about an imaginary coastal town called Korba during the decades following independence.

Amin Maalouf *Leo the African*. An interesting attempt by a Lebanese writer at the fictional autobiography of Leo Africanus, the Christian convert whose career mirrors the to-and-fro of the sixteenth-century Mediterranean (see p.561).

Albert Memmi *Colonizer and the Colonized*; *The Pillar of Salt*. Tunisia's most distinguished novelist, whose main theme is the problem of identity for North African Jews such as himself. Other books of his available in English include *The Scorpion* and *Jews and Arabs*.

 Mustapha Tlili *Lion Mountain*. Excellent characterization in this short novel about the tragic effects of progress, tourism and dictatorship on a remote Tell village (see p.559).

Islam and society

The Koran The word of God as handed down to the Prophet Mohammed is the basis of all Islam, and notoriously untranslatable. The OUP translation is better than N. J. Dawood's stultifyingly prosaic Penguin version. Other popular translations are by Marmaduke Pickthal and by Abdallah Yusuf Ali.

Nadia Abu Zahra *Sidi Ameur: a Tunisian Village*. Account by an Egyptian anthropologist of a village near Monastir in 1965–8, examining social change and village traditions. Especially good on the lifestyle of local women.

François Burgat *The Islamists in North Africa*. Slightly dated but still highly relevant examination of Islamic fundamentalism as a political movement in the region.

Jean Duvignaud *Change at Shebika* (o/p). An account by one of a group of French and Tunisian sociologists who spent a year in Chebika in the 1960s when it was an isolated village, describing the position of women, families, religion and work, but most of all the impact of social change on local tradition.

Jacques Jomier *How to Understand Islam*. A comprehensive, readable introduction to Islam.

N. Minai *Women in Islam* (o/p). A historical survey and an analysis of contemporary Arab society, looking at the changing status of women from the time of Mohammed, plus the customs and traditions at each stage of a woman's life, in different Muslim countries.

Lucette Valensi and Abraham Udovitch *The Last Arab Jews*. The definitive study of the Jerban community, its history, sociology and prospects. Good illustrations too.

★ **Justin Wintle** *The Rough Guide History of Islam*. A pocket-sized mine of information about the Islamic world from the time of the Mohammed through to the modern day.

Art and architecture

Georges Fradier and André Martin *Mosaiques Romaines de Tunisie* (Cérès editions, Tunisia). A coffee-table book of all those wonderful mosaics, and a great souvenir. The text is in French, but it's the pictures you really want.

Derek Hill and Lucien Golvin *Islamic Architecture of North Africa* (o/p). It's a sad comment that this is the best available introduction to Tunisian architecture. Intended originally as an artists' guide to Islamic patterns, the pictures are numerous but of variable quality; the fuller histori-cal introduction and notes on individual buildings are useful.

★ **Richard Pean** *Islamic Tunisia, Tunisia under the Beys, Saharan Tunisia, Tunisia's Berber Heritage, Roman and Punic Tunisia, Ancient Tunisia, Tunis Medina* (Regie 3). Published in English and other languages by Tunisia's National Heritage Agency, this is a series of seven highly informative souvenir booklets for tourists, illustrating the country's rich architectural and cultural heritage from different periods in its history, with colour plates throughout.

Language

Language

Language

rabic is a notoriously difficult language for Westerners to learn, and further complicated by its variation from country to country within the Arab world, not only in pronunciation but in vocabulary. Fortunately, however, Tunisia is virtually bilingual, and even in the remotest of places you will find someone who can also speak French. With even basic school French you'll find you can get in quite well. Included here are some very basic words and phrases, which you can supplement by bringing a comprehensive phrasebook, such as *French: A Rough Guide Dictionary Phrasebook*.

For all this, though, French was the language of colonialism and any attempt at Arabic – even the most stumbling – will be well received. If you want to learn the language seriously, the Bourguiba School in Tunis (see p.63) is highly recommended and exceptional value.

It's also useful to get to know some local **sign language**, as Tunisians are great gesticulators. The classic motion involves joining thumb and fingertips and holding the hand upwards; thoroughly infectious, this sign can mean almost anything, depending on the circumstances. Waved fiercely it conveys impatience; held quietly it means wait, patience; and shaken deliberately in conversation it claims ultimate authority for what's being said. As elsewhere in the Middle East, and round much of the Mediterranean, the word "no" is accompanied by a click of the tongue and toss of the head – flourishes which can at first seem contemptuously dismissive, but aren't intended that way. Also apt to be confusing is "come this way": with the beckoning hand pointing downward, it often looks as though you're being told to go away. Sex in general is indicated by cutting one hand against the other.

Tunisian Arabic essentials

The **transliteration** below is highly approximate, and intended to function phonetically. "Kh" represents a sound like the "ch" in loch, while "gh" represents a sort of gargling sound like a French "r"; "q" represents a sound like "k" but at the back of the mouth.

In theory, there are two singular forms of "you": *inti* when addressing a woman and *inta* when addressing a man. In most of Tunisia, however, *inti* is used for everyone (to the shocked surprise of non-Tunisian Arab men). A lot of words referring to "you" end in -*ik*; strictly speaking, when addressing a man this should be -*ak*. We've put an asterisk next to vocabulary where the words vary according to the sex of the person being spoken to.

Basics

Yes	Ayi, Aiwa	Excuse me	Samahanee
No	La	OK, agreed	Dacordu
Please	Minfadlik*	I	Ana
Thank you	Bark Allahufik*	You	Inti/Inta*
	/Shukran	She	Hiya

He	Huwa	Not good	Mish behi/Khayeb
We	Ihna	A lot	Barsha/Yasser
You (plural)	Intoo	A little	Shwaya
They	Hoom	Big	Kebeer
There is/are (or is/ are there?)	Famma (?)	Small	Sgheer
		New	Jedeed
There isn't/aren't	Famma aysh	Old	Kedeem
Good	Behi	Money	Floos

Greetings and farewells

Hello	Assalama	Good night	Tisbah ala khir
Good morning	Sabah el khir	Goodbye	Bisalama, Filaman
response:	Sabah en nour	My name's . . .	Ismi . . .
Good evening	Missa el khir	What's your name?	Sismik?*
response:	Missa en nour	Where are you from?	Mineen inti?/inta?*
How are you?	Ashnooa ahwalik*	I'm from . . .	Ana min . . .
Fine, thanks	Labes elhamdulillah	Bon voyage	Treq salama
And you?	Winti?, Winta?*	See you later	N'shoofik* minbad

Other common or useful expressions

Slowly	Shwaya shwaya		the future, repeated in response)
Go away	Imshi/Barra		
Later	Minbad	In the name of God	Bismillah (used when starting a meal or journey)
Never mind	Maalesh		
The same, same difference	Kif kif		
		Let's go!	Yalla, Nimshi!
Praise be to God	El Hamdulillah (used when mentioning any kind of good fortune, repeated in response)	Chill out	Wasa balek (lit: "lengthen your mind")
		Shame on you!	Shooma!
		I don't know	Maarfsh/Mish arif
God willing	Insh'Allah (used in any reference to hopes or	I don't understand	Mefehemsh/Mishfehem

Directions and travelling

Is there a . . . near here?	Fee . . . qareb min hina?	Left	Lisaar
Where is the . . . ?	Fayn el . . . ?	Right	Limin
Hotel	Nezel	Near	Qareeb
Restaurant	Mataam	Far	Bayeed
Bank	Bunk	Here	Hina
Train (station)	(Mahatat el) tran	There	Radi/Hinik*
Bus (station)	(Mahatat el) car	When?	Waqtesh?
Museum	Met-haf	Could you write it please?	Yoomkintnajim tek tabah minfadlik?*
Ruin	Athar	First	El uwel
Toilet	Mirhad	Next	El jai
Straight on	Ala tul	Last	El akher

Shopping and accommodation

Have you got . . . ?	Andik*. . . ?	That	Hadik
a room	Beet, Ghorfa	(Too) expensive	Ghalee (barsha)
a shower	Doosh	Still expensive	Mazal ghalee
Key	Miftah	Have you got	'Andik* haja. . . ?
Hot water	Ma skhoon	anything . . . ?	
Cold	Biird	. . . better	. . . khir
Can I have a . . . ?	Yoomkin aateeni	. . . cheaper	. . . arkhas
	wahad . . . ?	. . . bigger	. . . akbar
Can I buy . . . ?	Yoomkin ashtiri . . . ?	. . . smaller	. . . asghar
Can I see . . . ?	Yoomkin ashoofa . . . ?	I haven't got any	Ma'andish
How much is . . . ?	Kaddesh . . . ?	Open	Mahloul
This	Hada	Closed	Msakker

Times and days

What time is it?	Kaddesh loweqet?	Now	El an
One o'clock	El wahad	Later	Minbad
Five past one	El wahad wa draj	Today	El yoom
Ten past one	El wahad wa darjeen	Tomorrow	Ghudwa
Quarter past one	El wahad warbo'o	Yesterday	El barah
Twenty past one	El wahad warba'a	Sunday	El had
Twenty-five past one	El wahad wa khamsa	Monday	El tneen
Half-past one	El wahad wa nuss	Tuesday	El tlata
Twenty-five to two	El wahad wa sabaa	Wednesday	El arba
Twenty to two	El etneen ghir arba'a	Thursday	El khemis
Quarter to two	El etneen ghir arbo'o	Friday	Ej jemaa
Ten to two	El etneen ghir darjeen	Saturday	Es sebt
Five to two	El etneen ghir draj		

Numbers

1	Wahad	13	Talatashar	60	Sitteen
2	Zous/etneen	14	Arbatashar	70	Sabaeen
3	Tlaata	15	Khamstashar	80	Temaaneen
4	Arbaa	16	Sittashar	90	Tissaeen
5	Khamsa	17	Sabatashar	100	Mia
6	Sitta	18	Tamantashar	200	Miateen
7	Sabaa	19	Tisatashar	300	Tlaata mia
8	Tmaania	20	Ashreen	400	Arba mia
9	Tissa	21	Wahad wa ashreen	1000	Alf
10	Ashara	30	Talaateen	2000	Alfayn
11	Hadashar	40	Arbaeen	5000	Khams alef
12	Etnashar	50	Khamseen		

French essentials

Basics and greetings

Yes	Oui	Open	Ouvert
No	Non	Closed	Fermé
Good morning	Bonjour	Big	Grand
Good evening	Bonsoir	Small	Petit
Good night	Bonne nuit	Old	Ancien
Sorry/Excuse me	Pardon	New	Nouveau
How are you?	Ça va?	Hot	Chaud
Goodbye	Au revoir	Cold	Froid
Please	S'il vous plaît	Money	Argent
Thank you	Merci	Go away!	Va t'en!
Could you?	Pourriez-vous?	Stop messing me	Arrête de
Why?	Pourquoi?	about!	m'emmerder!
What?	Quoi?		

Directions and travelling

Where is the road pour . . . ?	Quelle est la route for . . . ?	Right	À droite
Where is . . . ?	Où est . . . ?	Straight on	Tout droit
Bus	Car, Autobus	Near	Proche/Près
Bus station	Gare routière	Far	Loin
Railway	Chemin de fer	When?	Quand?
Airport	Aéroport	At what time?	À quelle heure?
Train station	Gare	Write it down, please	Écrivez-le, s'il vous plaît
Ferry	Bac	Passport	Passeport
Lorry	Camion	Currency exchange	Change
Bank	Banque	Post office	Poste/PTT
Hammam	Bain maure	Stamps	Timbres-postes
Here	Ici	Left luggage	Consigne d'equipage
There	Là	Ticket (return)	Billet (de retour)
Left	À gauche	Visa	Visa

Shopping and accommodation

Do you have . . . ?	Avez vous . . . ?	(Too) expensive	(Trop) cher
. . . a room?	. . . une chambre?	Cheap	Bon marché
Shower	Douche	More (expensive)	Plus (cher)
Key	Clé	More (coffee)	Encore (du café)
Roof	Terrasse d'équipage	Less	Moins
How much/many?	Combien?	Enough	Assez
How much does that cost?	Combien ça coute?	Like this/that	Comme ceci/cela
		What is it?	Qu'est-ce que c'est?

Numbers

1	Un/Une	19	Dix-neuf
2	Deux	20	Vingt
3	Trois	21	Vingt-et-un
4	Quatre	22	Vingt-deux
5	Cinq	30	Trente
6	Six	40	Quarante
7	Sept	50	Cinqante
8	Huit	60	Soixante
9	Neuf	70	Soixante-dix
10	Dix	71	Soixante-et-onze
11	Onze	72	Soixante-douze
12	Douze	80	Quatre-vingts
13	Treize	81	Quatre-vingt-un
14	Quatorze	90	Quatre-vingt-dix
15	Quinze	100	Cent
16	Seize	200	Deux cents
17	Dix-sept	1000	Mille
18	Dix-huit	2000	Deux mille

Times and days

Now	Maintenant	Tuesday	Mardi
Later	Plus tard	Wednesday	Mercredi
Never	Jamais	Thursday	Jeudi
Today	Aujourd'hui	Friday	Vendredi
Tomorrow	Demain	Saturday	Samedi
Yesterday	Hier	Sunday	Dimanche
Monday	Lundi		

A glossary of Tunisian food and drink

Basics

French	Arabic	English
L'addition	El fatura/el hisaab	Bill, check
Beurre	Zibda	Butter
Bouteille	Darbooza	Bottle
Cassecroûte	Cassecroûte	Sandwich
Couteau	Sekina	Knife
Cuillère	Mirafa	Spoon
Fourchette	Farchita	Fork
Huile	Zit	Oil (invariably olive)

Oeufs	Adhma	Eggs
Olives	Zitoun	Olives
Pain	Khobs	Bread
Poivre	Filfel	Pepper
Salade	Salata	Salad
Sel	Melha	Salt
Sucre	Sukar	Sugar
Table	Taula	Table
Verre	Keson	Glass

Meat and poultry (viande/lahma)

Biftec	Habra	Steak
Boeuf	Bakri	Beef
Foie	Kibda	Liver
Mouton/agneau	Houli	Mutton/lamb
Poulet	Djaj	Chicken

Fish (poisson/samak)

In general, the French terms are used, even when speaking Arabic.

Calmar	Subia	Squid
Clovisses	Babush	Clams
Crevettes	Qambri	Prawns
Dorade	Jerrafe	Bream
Langouste	Fakrun b'har	Crawfish (rock lobster)
Loup de mer	Karus	Sea bass
Merou	Manani	Grouper
Mulet	Bowri	Grey mullet
Poulpe	Qarnit	Octopus
Rouget	Trilya	Red mullet
Roussette	Kalb el-bahr	Dogfish (rock salmon)
Sépia	M'dass	Cuttlefish
Sole	Sabidaj	Sole
Thon	Ton	Tuna

Vegetables (légumes/khadrawat)

Haricots	Loobia	Beans
Oignons	B'sal	Onions
Pois chiche	Houmous	Chick peas (garbanzo beans)
Pommes frites	Batata	Chips (French fries)
Pommes de terre	Batata	Potatoes

Fruit and nuts (fruits/fawakia)

Abricots	Mishmash	Apricots
Amandes	Louze	Almonds
Cacahuètes	Kakwiya	Peanuts

Cerises	Hbmluk	Cherries
Citron	Limon	Lemon/lime
Dattes	Tamar	Dates
Figues	Kermus	Figs
Figues de Barbarie	Hendi	Prickly pears (Barbary figs)
Fraises	Fraulu	Strawberries
Grenade	Rouman	Pomegranate
Melon	Battikh	Melon
Noix	Zouze	Walnuts
Orange	Burtuqal	Orange
Pomme	Tufah	Apple
Pêche	Khoukh	Peach
Pistaches	Fozdok	Pistachios
Raisins	Ainab	Grapes

Tunisian dishes

Brochette	Small kebab, usually of lamb (sometimes the Arabic term safud is used).
Brik à l'oeuf	One of Tunisia's great culinary curiosities – an egg fried inside a pastry envelope, the eating of which demands considerable ingenuity to avoid getting egg on your face. Sometimes made with tuna or vegetables, briks vary in quality, and are best when freshly cooked and piping hot.
Chakchouka	Vegetable stew based on onions, peppers and chick peas, usually topped with a fried egg.
Chorba	Soup; there are many varieties, most of which are spicy and delicious.
Couscous	The classic North African dish – steamed semolina grains, served with meat or fish, and vegetables.
Deglet Fatima	Fingers of filo pastry with egg or other filling.
Gargoulette	A special earthenware pot, and the lamb casserole that is cooked in it.
Harissa	Red chilli and garlic sauce added liberally to almost every thing.
Kamounia	Meat (lamb, beef and/or liver) stewed in a thick cumin sauce.
Kefteji	A vegetable stew like a spicy ratatouille, often served with meatballs.
Koucha	Lamb and potatoes in tomato sauce.
Lablabi	Bread soaked in chick-pea broth, usually with a raw egg scrambled into it to cook, and spices added on top, some times with tuna. Very cheap – the worker's staple – and made in front of you so you can ask them to hold back on this or that.
Mechoui	Grilled meat.
Merguez	Spicy sausage – eat it well cooked.
Mermez	Mutton stew.

Mloukhia	Jew's mallow, a leaf vegetable cooked with meat to make a green stew with a distinctive slimy texture that some people love and some hate.
Ojja	Similar to a chakchouka, but with egg scrambled into it rather than topped with a fried egg.
Riz Djerbien	Jerba rice, steamed like couscous with meat (usually lamb) and vegetables.
Salade mechouia	Not a salad in the usual sense, but a mashed, spicy mix of roasted vegetables served cold.
Shawarma	Marinaded lamb kebab on a vertical spit. Looks like a doner kebab but is insulted by the comparison.
Tajine	A kind of baked omelette, no relation to its Moroccan name sake.

Sweets (patisseries/halawiyet)

Baklava	Honey-soaked flaky pastry with a syrup-soaked nut filling – hazelnut is best.
Draw (sahlab)	Milk thickened with orchid root, sometimes topped with halva or cake. Increasingly rare, but sometimes served by cafés, especially in winter.
Ftair	Deep-fried batter pancake, somewhere between a doughnut and a fritter, usually available in the morning; a Ghoum rassen speciality.
Halva	Sesame-based sweet common throughout the Middle East.
Kab el ghazal (corne de gazelle)	Pastry horn stuffed with chopped almonds and syrup; a Tataouine speciality.
Loukoum	Turkish delight.
Mesfuf	Sweet couscous.
Millefeuille	French cream pastry.
Makroudh	Syrup-soaked semolina cake with a date centre; a Kairouan speciality.
Youyou	Ring doughnut.

Drinks (boissons/mashrubaat)

Bière	Birra	Beer
Café	Qahwa	Coffee
Citronade	Asir limon	Real lemonade
Eau	Ma	Water
Jus	'Asir	Juice
Lait	Halib	Milk
Lait de poule	Halib djaj	Milkshake with egg white
Lait fermenté	Rayeb (leben)	Soured milk
Thé	Té or shai	Tea
Vin	Sharab	Wine
Vin de palme	Laghmi	Palm wine

Glossary

Abbasids Dynasty of Caliphs who ruled the Arab Empire from Baghdad, 749–1258.

Aghlabids Arab dynasty, ruled northern and central Tunisia from Kairouan, 800–909.

AH Anno Hegirae (after the Hegira); Islamic date, the equivalent of AD, dated from Mohammed's flight to Medina (see p.523).

Aïn Spring.

Almohads Religious movement from Morocco, which came to control the whole Maghreb, from Marrakesh to Tunisia, in the twelfth century.

Almoravids Dynasty which ruled Morocco in the eleventh century and invaded Tunisia in the twelfth.

Arianism Christian heresy followed by the Vandals, based on an attempt to reconcile Christianity with Germanic pagan religions.

ASM Association de Sauvegarde de la Medina, an organization dedicated to preserving the architectural heritage of old Arab towns.

Autogare Bus and louage station.

Bab Door or gate.

Baksheesh Alms or tips.

Barbary European term for North Africa in the sixteenth to nineteenth centuries.

Basilica Roman building type with aisles, later used for churches.

Berbers The non-Arab native inhabitants of North Africa since about 4000 BC. Very few pure Berbers survive in Tunisia, though they form the majority in Morocco and Algeria.

Bey Ottoman official; in practice the ruler of Tunisia in the eighteenth and nineteenth centuries (the adjective is "beylical").

Bir Well (hole in the ground).

Borj Fort.

Burnoose Long woollen or camel-hair men's outer garment, often with hood.

Byzantine The continuation of the Roman Empire in the East, ruled from Byzantium (now Istanbul), which controlled Tunisia from 533 to 646 AD.

Camionette Pick-up truck, often used as a form of transport in remote rural areas.

Caldarium Hot room in a Roman bath.

Calèche Horse-drawn tourist carriage.

Capital Stone "Cushion" at the top of a column or pillar.

Capitol Central temple of a Roman town, equivalent to a cathedral.

Carthage Phoenician colony founded around the ninth century BC, which became capital of the Carthaginian Empire finally defeated by Rome and destroyed in 146 BC, but later refounded as a Roman city.

Cella Inner sanctuary of a temple.

Chéchia Red felt hat, like a soft fez.

Chicha (or sheesha) Café water pipe.

Chott Seasonal salt lake, which will be a flat, dry area for most of the year; the term also occasionally refers to a beach.

CNLT (Conseil National pour les Libertés en Tunisie). Civil liberties organization, not officially recognized, so not legally allowed to operate.

Corsairs Muslim and Christian pirates who operated in the Mediterranean from the thirteenth to the nineteenth centuries.

CPR (Congrès Pour la République) Illegal Social-democratic political party.

Croisement Road junction, turn-off.

Dar House or palace.

Dey Ottoman military officer of junior rank. Their control of troops meant they effectively ruled Tunisia in the early seventeenth century.

Donatism Fourth- or fifth-century dissident Christian church set up to avoid "contamination" by insincere Catholic priests.

Driba Entrance hall.

El Quds (El Qods, El Kuds) Jerusalem, the third holy city of Islam.

Erg Sand desert.

En nahdha See Hizb en Nahdha.

Ettajdid (Parti du Renouvellement) A faction of the former Communist Party, now a legal opposition party with seats in parliament.

Fatimids Dynasty of Ismaili Shi'ite Muslims who ruled Tunisia from Mahdia (909–984) and Egypt (961–1171).

FDTL (Forum pour la Démocratie et le Travail et les Libertés) Illegal left-wing political party.

Forum Enclosed open space at the centre of a Roman town.

Fondouk Inn, storehouse and sometimes trading base, also known as a caravanserai in the Middle East.

Gare routière Bus and sometimes louage station.

Frigidarium Cold room in Roman bath.

Gargote Cheap restaurant or café.

Ghar Cave.

Ghorfa Room – refers in particular to the cells used to store grain inside a ksar.

Ghriba Ancient Jewish synagogue.

Hadith Statements of the Prophet Mohammed as reported by his Companions.

Hafsids Dynasty that ruled Tunisia from Tunis, 1207–1574. Originally governors for the Almohads, they declared independence in 1236 when the Almohad regime in Marrakesh ditched Ibn Tumart's teachings, and were widely seen as the Almohads' true heirs.

Haj (or hadj) Pilgrimage to Mecca, or someone who has made this journey (older people are politely assumed to have done it, and so are addressed as hajj).

Hamada Stony desert.

Hammam (Turkish) bath.

Hanefite One of the four schools of orthodox Sunni Islam, founded in the eighth century. Widespread in Anatolia and brought by the Turks to North Africa, the school's mosques are distinguished by octagonal minarets. The school is less austere than the native Malekite school, laying some stress on commercial success.

Hilalians (Banu Hilal) Nomadic Arabs who invaded Tunisia in the eleventh century, were outside the control of its Zirid rulers, and severely disrupted its infrastructure.

Hizb en Nahdha (Renewal Party) Illegal fundamentalist political party, formerly the MTI.

Houch Jerban house, which looks like a small fortress (see p.419).

Husaynids Dynasty of beys who ruled Tunisia from 1705 until (nominally) 1956.

Hypostyle Hall supported by pillars, as in many prayer halls of mosques.

Ibadite Member of the main branch of Kharijism.

Imam Roughly the Islamic equivalent of a Protestant pastor; leads the congregation of a mosque in prayer.

Impasse Blind alley.

Infirmerie Clinic staffed by nurses for dealing with general medical complaints.

Ismaili Shi'a splinter formed on the death of the sixth Shi'ite imam (equivalent to the Sunni caliph), which claimed that only descendants of his son Ismail could be given the title of imam.

Jebel (or djebel) Mountain.

Jedid/Jedida (also djedid/djedida) New.

Jema'a (or djema'a) Great Mosque, or Friday Mosque (Grande Mosquée), the central place of worship in any town. During the week citizens may worship at the masjid, a smaller local mosque, but on Fridays they worship together at the jemaa, to hear the imam's homily.

Kala'a Stone hill fort.

Kasbah Citadel of a walled city.

Kebir/Kebira Large, big.

Kedim/Kedima Old.

Kef Rock.

Kharijites The "Secessionists", an early heretical sect, still surviving in Jerba, which found eager adherents among the Berbers in the first years of the Arab conquest (see p.432).

Khourassanids Dynasty of princes who ruled the Tunis region during the eleventh century.

Koubba Dome, and by extension a small domed building, especially the tomb of a marabout.

Kouttab Koranic primary school.

Ksar (plural ksour). Communal fortified granary built mainly in the south.

Lalla Female saint.

Limes (pronounced "lee-mess") Chain of forts built along the frontier of the Roman Empire.

Louage Shared taxi (see p.28).

LTDH Ligue Tunisienne des Droits de l'Homme, a Tunisian human rights group, barely tolerated by the government.

Maghreb "West" in Arabic, used of the countries of the Maghrebian confederation (Morocco, Algeria, Tunisia, Libya and Mauritania), especially the first three.

Mahdi The "divinely guided one", whose impending arrival is Islam's equivalent of the Second Coming (see p.256). Of the various people who have claimed to be the Mahdi, three are referred to in this book: Obaidallah, founder of Mahdia and the Fatimid dynasty; Ibn Tumart, founder of the Almohads; and Mohammed Ahmed, who liberated Sudan from the British in 1886.

Malekite School of orthodox Sunni Islam, founded at Medina in Arabia in the eighth century and dominant in North Africa for many centuries, with mosques distinguished by square minarets. More rigorous than the Hanefite, it is considered the purest school by many.

Malouf (or maalouf) Andalusian-based traditional folk music.

Mamelukes Caste of soldiers, originally slaves, who ruled Egypt for 250 years and retained high office in the Ottoman empire.

Marabout Holy man, and by extension his place of burial. These tombs, dotted all over the North African countryside, are often centres of cult worship. Marabouts played a vital role in spreading Islam among the Berbers.

Masjid Small local mosque, for everyday (rather than Friday) prayer.

MDS (Mouvement des Démocrates Socialistes) Legal "opposition" political party, with an illegal dissident wing.

Medersa (also medressa, madrassa) Residential college of Islamic education, usually in the form of a courtyard surrounded by students' cells. These colleges spread throughout the Islamic world from the thirteenth century onwards, generally as state foundations teaching the local orthodoxy.

Menzel Dwelling place – in Jerba refers to the family houch and the enclosure around it.

Midha Ritual washing and latrine facility attached to mosque.

Mihrab Niche indicating the direction of Mecca (and of prayer).

Minaret Tower attached to a mosque from which the muezzin gives the call to prayer.

Minbar Pulpit from which the imam delivers his sermon at Friday prayers in a jemaa.

Moussem Annual local celebration held in honour of a marabout.

MTI (Mouvement de la Tendance Islamique) Illegal fundamentalist political party, renamed Hizb en Nahdha in 1989.

Muezzin Mosque official who gives the call to prayer.

Muradids The first hereditary line of beys who ruled during the seventeenth century, nominally under the Ottoman sultan.

Nador Watchtower.

ONA (also ONAT) Organisation Nationale de l'Artisanat (Tunisien). The national crafts organization: their shops are expensive but useful for indications of prices to bargain for elsewhere.

ONTT Office Nationale de Tourisme et Thermalisme (National Office of Tourism and Spas).

Ottoman Empire based in Constantinople (Istanbul) from the fifteenth century to World War I, to which Tunisia belonged as a regency.

Oued A wadi; a creek or seasonal river which may only carry water for a few days a year.

Ouerghamma Tribal confederation, based at Ghoumrassen and later Medenine, which dominated the far south of Tunisia from the sixteenth to the nineteenth century (see p.460).

Palaestra Roman gymnasium.

PCOT Parti Communiste des Ouvriers Tunisiens; Illegal Tunisian Communist party.

PDP Parti Démocratique Progressiste; illegal left-wing political party.

Peristyle Court enclosed by columns.

Phoenicians First great trading nation of Mediterranean history. Originally from what is now Lebanon, they founded trading posts (some of which became the Carthaginian Empire) along the southern Mediterranean coast from around the eleventh century BC.

Pressing Dry cleaner.

Protectorate The period of French control (1881–1956). The beys stayed, and French rule was largely indirect and less repressive than in neighbouring Algeria.

PSD Parti Socialiste Destourien, the title of the ruling political party from 1964 (before that it was called the Neo-Destour Party) until 1988, when it was renamed the RCD.

PSL (Parti Social Libéral) Legal "opposition" political party.

PTT Postes, Télécommunications et Télédiffusion: post office.

Publinet Public Internet office.

PUBLITEL Public telephone office.

Punic Of Carthaginians and their culture.

PUP Parti de l'Unité Populaire; legal "opposition" political party.

Qibla Direction of prayer, physically indicated by the mihrab.

Ras Headland or cape (literally: "head").

RCD Rassemblement Constitutionnel Démocratique; ruling political party, formerly the PSD.

Ribat Monastic fortress, a building type which sprang up on the North African coast in the ninth century. Marabout originally meant "an inhabitant of a ribat".

Rustamids Kharijite dynasty who ruled the south of Tunisia from Tahirt, modern Tagdemt in Algeria (761–909; see p.244).

Sabat Room built in vault over narrow street.

Sahel Coast (see p.215).

Schola Institutional Roman building.

Sebkha Salt-encrusted mud flat or salt lake.

SGHIR/SGHIRA Small.

Shi'a Branch of Islam whose split from the Sunni majority in the seventh century remains the biggest schism in the faith. Shi'ites emphasized the spiritual side of Islam in reaction to the power of the Umayyad caliphs (see p.526). Almost no Tunisians today are Shi'ite.

Sidi Lord, saint – title of holy men.

Sifsari A light women's outer garment wrapped around the body, which can also be used as a veil if held between the teeth. Tunisia's answer to the sari.

Skifa Narrow passage, entrance, vestibule.

SRT Societé Régionale des Transports (Regional bus company).

SOCOPA (Societé de Commercialisation des Produits de l'Artisant) Marketing organization for ONA.

Souk Originally a covered urban market, now used of any kind of market, but especially a weekly one.

Stela (plural stelae) Tombstone.

Sufi Unorthodox sects in Islam which take their teachings, often with mystical associations, from one originating teacher. Some cults spread throughout the Islamic world, transmitted by zaouias.

Sunni Islamic orthodoxy; the vast majority of Muslims are Sunni, though they belong to a particular school, such as the Malekite or Hanefite.

Tambour Wooden drum.

Taxiphone Public telephone for national and international calls.

Tophet Phoenician burial place.

Tourbet Islamic mausoleum.

Triclinium Roman dining room.

Tuaregs Nomadic Saharan Berbers.

UDU (Union Démocratique Unioniste) Legal "opposition" political party.

Ukala Large old building subdivided into residential or business premises.

UMA (Union du Maghreb Arabe) Union of Maghrebian countries, whose members are Tunisia, Algeria, Libya, Mauretania and Morocco.

Umayyads Dynasty of Caliphs who ruled the Arab Empire from Damascus, 661–749. The same family ruled Spain from 756 until 1031.

Vandals Germanic tribe who sacked Carthage in 439 AD and ruled in Tunisia until 535 (see p.493).

White fathers Order of monks cloaked in white burnoose-style habits; founded in 1870 and based originally in Carthage, later in Thibar.

Zaouia A sanctuary around a marabout's tomb, a seminary-type base for his followers, and by extension his followers as a group or cult.

Ziara Annual local celebration held in honour of a marabout.

Zirids Dynasty that ruled Tunisia in the eleventh century. Originally governors for the Fatimids, they declared independence in 984, but by 1057 ruled not much more than Mahdia.

Zitouna Olive tree.

Rough
Guides
advertiser

Rough Guides travel...

UK & Ireland
Britain
Devon & Cornwall
Dublin
Edinburgh
England
Ireland
Lake District
London
London DIRECTIONS
London Mini Guide
Scotland
Scottish Highlands & Islands
Wales

Europe
Algarve
Amsterdam
Amsterdam DIRECTIONS
Andalucía
Athens DIRECTIONS
Austria
Baltic States
Barcelona
Belgium & Luxembourg
Berlin
Brittany & Normandy
Bruges & Ghent
Brussels
Budapest
Bulgaria
Copenhagen
Corfu
Corsica
Costa Brava
Crete
Croatia
Cyprus
Czech & Slovak Republics
Dodecanese & East Aegean
Dordogne & The Lot
Europe
Florence
France

Germany
Greece
Greek Islands
Hungary
Ibiza & Formentera
Iceland
Ionian Islands
Italy
Languedoc & Roussillon
Lisbon
Lisbon DIRECTIONS
The Loire
Madeira
Madrid
Mallorca
Malta & Gozo
Menorca
Moscow
Netherlands
Norway
Paris
Paris DIRECTIONS
Paris Mini Guide
Poland
Portugal
Prague
Provence & the Côte d'Azur
Pyrenees
Romania
Rome
Sardinia
Scandinavia
Sicily
Slovenia
Spain
St Petersburg
Sweden
Switzerland
Tenerife & La Gomera
Tenerife DIRECTIONS
Turkey
Tuscany & Umbria
Venice & The Veneto
Venice DIRECTIONS
Vienna

Asia
Bali & Lombok
Bangkok
Beijing
Cambodia
China
Goa
Hong Kong & Macau
India
Indonesia
Japan
Laos
Malaysia, Singapore & Brunei
Nepal
Philippines
Singapore
South India
Southeast Asia
Sri Lanka
Thailand
Thailand's Beaches & Islands
Tokyo
Vietnam

Australasia
Australia
Melbourne
New Zealand
Sydney

North America
Alaska
Big Island of Hawaii
Boston
California
Canada
Chicago
Florida
Grand Canyon
Hawaii
Honolulu
Las Vegas
Los Angeles
Maui
Miami & the Florida

Keys
Montréal
New England
New Orleans
New York City
New York City DIRECTIONS
New York City Mini Guide
Pacific Northwest
Rocky Mountains
San Francisco
San Francisco DIRECTIONS
Seattle
Southwest USA
Toronto
USA
Vancouver
Washington DC
Yosemite

Caribbean & Latin America
Antigua & Barbuda
Antigua DIRECTIONS
Argentina
Bahamas
Barbados
Barbados DIRECTIONS
Belize
Bolivia
Brazil
Caribbean
Central America
Chile
Costa Rica
Cuba
Dominican Republic
Ecuador
Guatemala
Jamaica
Maya World
Mexico
Peru
St Lucia
South America

ROUGH GUIDES ADVERTISER

Rough Guides are available from good bookstores worldwide. New titles are published every month. Check www.roughguides.com for the latest news.

...music & reference

Trinidad & Tobago

Africa & Middle East
Cape Town
Egypt
The Gambia
Jordan
Kenya
Marrakesh
  DIRECTIONS
Morocco
South Africa, Lesotho
  & Swaziland
Syria
Tanzania
Tunisia
West Africa
Zanzibar
Zimbabwe

Travel Theme guides
First-Time Around the
  World
First-Time Asia
First-Time Europe
First-Time Latin
  America
Skiing & Snowboarding
  in North America
Travel Online
Travel Health
Walks in London & SE
  England
Women Travel

Restaurant guides
French Hotels &
  Restaurants
London
New York
San Francisco

Maps
Algarve
Amsterdam
Andalucia & Costa del Sol
Argentina

Athens
Australia
Baja California
Barcelona
Berlin
Boston
Brittany
Brussels
Chicago
Crete
Croatia
Cuba
Cyprus
Czech Republic
Dominican Republic
Dubai & UAE
Dublin
Egypt
Florence & Siena
Frankfurt
Greece
Guatemala & Belize
Iceland
Ireland
Kenya
Lisbon
London
Los Angeles
Madrid
Mexico
Miami & Key West
Morocco
New York City
New Zealand
Northern Spain
Paris
Peru
Portugal
Prague
Rome
San Francisco
Sicily
South Africa
South India
Sri Lanka
Tenerife
Thailand

Toronto
Trinidad & Tobago
Tuscany
Venice
Washington DC
Yucatán Peninsula

**Dictionary
Phrasebooks**
Czech
Dutch
Egyptian Arabic
EuropeanLanguages
  (Czech, French, German,
  Greek, Italian,
  Portuguese, Spanish)
French
German
Greek
Hindi & Urdu
Hungarian
Indonesian
Italian
Japanese
Mandarin Chinese
Mexican Spanish
Polish
Portuguese
Russian
Spanish
Swahili
Thai
Turkish
Vietnamese

Music Guides
The Beatles
Bob Dylan
Cult Pop
Classical Music
Country Music
Elvis
Hip Hop
House
Irish Music
Jazz
Music USA

Opera
Reggae
Rock
Techno
World Music (2 vols)

History Guides
China
Egypt
England
France
India
Islam
Italy
Spain
USA

Reference Guides
Books for Teenagers
Children's Books, 0–5
Children's Books, 5–11
Cult Fiction
Cult Football
Cult Movies
Cult TV
Ethical Shopping
Formula 1
The iPod, iTunes &
  Music Online
The Internet
Internet Radio
James Bond
Kids' Movies
Lord of the Rings
Muhammed Ali
Man Utd
Personal Computers
Pregnancy & Birth
Shakespeare
Superheroes
Unexplained
  Phenomena
The Universe
Videogaming
Weather
Website Directory

ROUGH GUIDES ADVERTISER

Also! More than 120 Rough Guide music CDs are available from all good book
and record stores. Listen in at www.worldmusic.net

Rough Guide Maps, printed on waterproof and rip-proof Polyart™ paper, offer an unbeatable combination of practicality, clarity of design and amazing value.

ROUGH GUIDES ADVERTISER

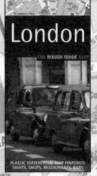

CITY MAPS
Amsterdam · Athens · Barcelona · Berlin · Boston · Brussels · Chicago · Dublin · Florence & Siena · Frankfurt · Hong Kong · Lisbon · London · Los Angeles Madrid · Marrakesh · Miami · New York · Paris · Prague · Rome · San Francisco Toronto · Venice · Washington DC and more...

US$8.99   Can$13.99   £4.99

COUNTRY & REGIONAL MAPS
Algarve · Andalucía · Argentina · Australia · Baja California · Brittany · Crete Croatia · Cuba · Cyprus · Czech Republic · Dominican Republic · Dubai · Egypt · Greece · Guatemala & Belize · Iceland · Ireland · Kenya · Mexico · Morocco · New Zealand · Northern Spain · Peru · Portugal · Sicily · South Africa · South India · Sri Lanka · Tenerife · Thailand · Trinidad & Tobago · Tuscany · Yucatán Peninsula · and more...

US$9.99   Can$13.99   £5.99

Athens

1843533146

Lisbon

1843533154

London

1843533162

Paris

1843533170

San Francisco

1843533189

Venice

1843533537

PUBLISHED AUGUST 2004

Amsterdam

1843533065

Antigua & Barbuda

1843533197

Barbados

1843533200

Marrakesh

1843533219

New York City

1843533227

Tenerife & La Gomera

1843533225

US$10.99 · Can$15.99 · £6.99

DIRECTIONS

Visit us online
roughguides.com

Information on over 25,000 destinations around the world

ROUGH GUIDES ADVERTISER

- **Read** Rough Guides' trusted travel info
- **Share** journals, photos and travel advice with other readers
- Get exclusive Rough Guide **discounts** and travel **deals**
- Earn membership points every time you contribute to the
  Rough Guide **community** and get **free** books, flights and trips
- Browse thousands of CD reviews and artists in our **music** area

stay in touch

ROUGH GUIDES ADVERTISER

roughnews

**Rough Guides' FREE
full-colour newsletter**

News, travel issues, music reviews,
readers' letters and the latest
dispatches from authors on the road

**If you would like to receive
roughnews, please send us your
name and address:**

Rough Guides, 80 Strand
London, WC2R 0RL, UK

Rough Guides, 4th Floor, 345 Hudson St,
New York NY10014, USA

newslettersubs@roughguides.co.uk

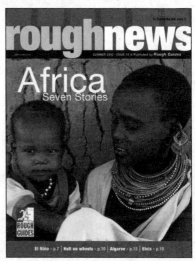

Don't bury your head in the sand!

Take cover!

with Rough Guide Travel Insurance

Worldwide cover, for Rough Guide readers worldwide

UK Freefone **0800 015 09 06**
Worldwide **(+44) 1392 314 665**
Check the web at
www.roughguides.com/insurance

Insurance organized by Torribles Insurance Brokers Ltd, 21 Prince Street, Bristol, BS1 4PH, England

NOTES

small print and
Index

A Rough Guide to Rough Guides

SMALL PRINT

In the summer of 1981, Mark Ellingham, a recent graduate from Bristol University, was travelling round Greece and couldn't find a guidebook that really met his needs. On the one hand there were the student guides, insistent on saving every last cent, and on the other the heavyweight cultural tomes whose authors seemed to have spent more time in a research library than lounging away the afternoon at a taverna or on the beach.

In a bid to avoid getting a job, Mark and a small group of writers set about creating their own guidebook. It was a guide to Greece that aimed to combine a journalistic approach to description with a thoroughly practical approach to travellers' needs —a guide that would incorporate culture, history and contemporary insights with a critical edge, together with up-to-date, value-for-money listings. Back in London, Mark and the team finished their Rough Guide, as they called it, and talked Routledge into publishing the book.

That first *Rough Guide to Greece*, published in 1982, was a student scheme that became a publishing phenomenon. The immediate success of the book – with numerous reprints and a Thomas Cook prize shortlisting – spawned a series that rapidly covered dozens of destinations. Rough Guides had a ready market among low-budget backpackers, but soon also acquired a much broader and older readership that relished Rough Guides' wit and inquisitiveness as much as their enthusiastic, critical approach. Everyone wants value for money, but not at any price.

Rough Guides soon began supplementing the "rougher" information about hostels and low-budget listings with the kind of detail on restaurants and quality hotels that independent-minded visitors on any budget might expect, whether on business in New York or trekking in Thailand.

These days the guides – distributed worldwide by the Penguin group – offer recommendations from shoestring to luxury and cover more than 200 destinations around the globe, including almost every country in the Americas and Europe, more than half of Africa and most of Asia and Australasia. Our ever-growing team of authors and photographers is spread all over the world, particularly in Europe, the USA and Australia.

In 1994, we published the *Rough Guide to World Music* and *Rough Guide to Classical Music*; and a year later the *Rough Guide to the Internet*. All three books have become benchmark titles in their fields – which encouraged us to expand into other areas of publishing, mainly around popular culture. Rough Guides now publish:

- Travel guides to more than 200 worldwide destinations
- Dictionary phrasebooks to 22 major languages
- History guides ranging from Ireland to Islam
- Maps printed on rip-proof and waterproof Polyart™ paper
- Music guides running the gamut from Opera to Elvis
- Restaurant guides to London, New York and San Francisco
- Reference books on topics as diverse as the Weather and Shakespeare
- Sports guides from Formula 1 to Man Utd
- Pop culture books from *Lord of the Rings* to Cult TV
- World Music CDs in association with World Music Network

Visit **www.roughguides.com** to see our latest publications.

Rough Guide credits

Text editor: Richard Lim
Layout: Andy Hilliard
Cartography: Karobi Gogoi
Picture research: Mark Thomas
Proofreader: Tamara Collof-Bennett

....

Editorial: London Martin Dunford, Kate Berens, Helena Smith, Claire Saunders, Geoff Howard, Ruth Blackmore, Gavin Thomas, Polly Thomas, Richard Lim, Lucy Ratcliffe, Clifton Wilkinson, Alison Murchie, Fran Sandham, Sally Schafer, Alexander Mark Rogers, Karoline Densley, Andy Turner, Ella O'Donnell, Keith Drew, Andrew Lockett, Joe Staines, Duncan Clark, Peter Buckley, Matthew Milton; **New York** Andrew Rosenberg, Richard Koss, Yuki Takagaki, Hunter Slaton, Chris Barsanti, Steven Horak
Design & Pictures: London Simon Bracken, Dan May, Diana Jarvis, Mark Thomas, Jj Luck, Harriet Mills; **Delhi** Madhulita Mohapatra, Umesh Aggarwal, Ajay Verma, Jessica Subramanian

Production: Julia Bovis, John McKay, Sophie Hewat
Cartography: London Maxine Repath, Ed Wright, Katie Lloyd-Jones, Miles Irving; **Delhi** Manish Chandra, Rajesh Chhibber, Jai Prakesh Mishra, Ashutosh Bharti, Rajesh Mishra, Animesh Pathak, Jasbir Sandhu, Karobi Gogoi
Cover art direction: Louise Boulton
Online: New York Jennifer Gold, Cree Lawson, Suzanne Welles, Benjamin Ross; **Delhi** Manik Chauhan, Narender Kumar, Shekhar Jha, Rakesh Kumar
Marketing & Publicity: London Richard Trillo, Niki Smith, David Wearn, Chloë Roberts, Demelza Dallow, Kristina Pentland; **New York** Geoff Colquitt, Megan Kennedy
Finance: Gary Singh
Manager India: Punita Singh
Series editor: Mark Ellingham
PA to Managing Director: Julie Sanderson
Managing Director: Kevin Fitzgerald

SMALL PRINT

Publishing information

This seventh edition published February 2005 by **Rough Guides Ltd,**
80 Strand, London WC2R 0RL.
345 Hudson St, 4th Floor,
New York, NY 10014, USA.
Distributed by the Penguin Group
Penguin Books Ltd,
80 Strand, London WC2R 0RL
Penguin Putnam, Inc.
375 Hudson Street, NY 10014, USA
Penguin Group (Australia)
250 Camberwell Road, Camberwell
Victoria 3124, Australia
Penguin Books Canada Ltd,
10 Alcorn Avenue, Toronto, Ontario,
Canada M4V 1E4
Penguin Group (New Zealand)
Cnr Rosedale and Airborne Roads
Albany, Auckland, New Zealand
Typeset in Bembo and Helvetica to an original design by Henry Iles.

Printed in China

© Daniel Jacobs and Peter Morris

No part of this book may be reproduced in any form without permission from the publisher except for the quotation of brief passages in reviews.

608pp includes index
A catalogue record for this book is available from the British Library

ISBN 1-84353-396-0

The publishers and authors have done their best to ensure the accuracy and currency of all the information in **The Rough Guide to Tunisia**, however, they can accept no responsibility for any loss, injury, or inconvenience sustained by any traveller as a result of information or advice contained in the guide.

1   3   5   7   9   8   6   4   2

Help us update

We've gone to a lot of effort to ensure that the seventh edition of **The Rough Guide to Tunisia** is accurate and up-to-date. However, things change – places get "discovered", opening hours are notoriously fickle, restaurants and rooms raise prices or lower standards. If you feel we've got it wrong or left something out, we'd like to know, and if you can remember the address, the price, the time, the phone number, so much the better.

We'll credit all contributions, and send a copy of the next edition (or any other Rough Guide if you prefer) for the best letters. Everyone who writes to us and isn't already a subscriber will receive a copy of our full-colour thrice-yearly newsletter. Please mark letters: "**Rough Guide Tunisia Update**" and send to: Rough Guides, 80 Strand, London WC2R 0RL, or Rough Guides, 4th Floor, 345 Hudson St, New York, NY 10014. Or send an email to **mail@roughguides.com**

Have your questions answered and tell others about your trip at
www.roughguides.atinfopop.com

Acknowledgements

Thanks from **Daniel** to: Habib Aljan, Abdoul Azaiz (*Restaurant Ouled Azaiz*, Matmata), Ahmed Barka, Dr Habib Belhedi (Association des Amis la Memoire de la Terre), Mohammed Ben Madani (Maghreb Bookshop, London), Abderrazak Cheraït, Dee Eltaïef, Kamel Laroussi and Dr Mohamed Neffati (Institut des Régions Arides), Arafat Sghaier (*Amis du Camping*, Kebili), Matthew Teller, Melita Tilley, *Résidence Karim* in Tozeur and *Hôtel 20 Mars* in Douz. Thanks also to the ONTT in London, Bizerte, Douz and Gafsa; to the Syndicat d'Initiative in Tamerza; to David Buckton and Elena Angelidis of the British Museum's Byzantine Antiquities Department; and, for their contributions to the text during the preparation of previous editions, Charles Farr, Adrian Fozzard, Jens Finke and Simon Foster.

From **Sam**, thanks to: Kais Mohdi at the *Belle Vue* in Hammamet, Mme Ben Yaala Nejia at ONTT Nabeul, M. Mabrouk at Sidi Daoud, Dee Eltaïef, the ONTT in Skanès and Kairouan, ASM in Le Kef, Saadi Adel at Haïdra, Daniel Jacobs, and Katy Tuthill.

Readers' letters

Thanks to all the readers who have taken the time to write in with comments and suggestions (and apologies if we've inadvertently omitted or misspelt anyone's name):

Anita Athi, Lucy Bale, Kat Birch, Donna Bystrican, Deborah Dalton, Allan Davis-Johnston, Eric and Margaret Dunkerley, John Easton, Gerald Fimberger, Nick Fisher, Michael Frost, Clare Fuller, Janice Fullman, James Grigg, Michael Hanna, Mary Hayes, Charles Hinton, Bernadette Horton, Mrs J.E. Hughes, David C. King, Martin Kraus, David Lumb, Jon Maclachlan, Paul and Jackie McPate, Jane Oliver, David Page, Janette Paterson, Oliver Pearce, Megan Remmer, Anthony Rowland, Sarah A. Smith, Frank and Monique van Beuningen-van Otterloo, and Chris Van Court.

Photo credits

Cover credits
Main picture: Sidi Bou Saïd
Back top picture: Sbeïtla © Powerstock
Back lower picture: Sahara Desert, Douz
  © Jon Arnold
small front top picture: Fadloune
  © Jon Arnold
small front lower picture: Camel
  © Robert Harding

Introduction
Monastir Beach © Les Polders/Alamy
Women collecting water at desert oasis
  © Hans George Roth/Corbis
Detail of door © Sam Thorne
Tozeur © Catherine Desjeux, Bernard
  Desjeux/Corbis
Tiled Archway and Minaret of the Great
  Mosque, Tunis © Royalty-free/Corbis
Jebel Zaghouan © Sam Thorne
Mosaic depicting the triumph of Neptune,
  Bardo Museum © Hans Georg Roth/Corbis
Tunis Medina © Sam Thorne
Chéchia maker © Steve Outram/Alamy
Star Wars © Lucasfilm
Tunisian tile depicting man smoking a *chicha*
  © Dave Bartuff/Corbis
Fruit vendor, Sfax © Ric Ergenbright/Corbis
Charms against the "Evil Eye" © Daniel
  Jacobs

Things not to miss
The Bardo © Dennis Marsico/Corbis
Ksour © Daniel Jacobs
Couscous © Photolibrary.com
Bathing in a hammam © Kurt-Michael
  Westermann/Corbis
Amphitheatre, El Jem © Chris Homes/Wild
  Place Photography/Alamy
Sidi Bou Saïd © Sam Thorne
Carthage © Sam Thorne
Camel © Ksar Ghilane/Corbis
Mahdia walls © Ray Roberts/Alamy
Festival of the Sahara © Hans Georg Roth/
  Corbis
Matmata © Chris Howes/Wild Places
  Photography/Alamy

Dougga © Sam Thorne
Cork oaks © Natalie Pecht/Alamy
The Great Mosque, Kairouan © Christine
  Osborne/Corbis
Hammamet beach © Nik Wheeler/Corbis
Jerba mosque © Daniel Jacobs
Kerkouane © Sandro Vannini/Corbis
Brik à l'oeuf © Daniel Jacobs
Troglodyte Berber village © Daniel Jacobs
Bizerte © Alamy
Sfax Medina © Wilmar Photography/Alamy
Kerkennah fishing boat © Michele Molinari/
  Alamy
Desert dunes © Robert Van der Hilst/Corbis
Nefta © Ruggerd Vannin/Corbis
Star Wars set © Daniel Jacobs
Tabarka © Hans Georg Roth/Corbis
Chott el Jerid © Daniel Jacobs
Sbeïtla © C. Bowman

Black and whites
The cathedral, Tunis © Jose Fuste Raga/
  Corbis
Rue Jemaa Zitouna, Tunis © Sam Thorne
Hammamet © Celestial Panoramas Ltd/
  Alamy
Hot springs, Korbous © Chris Howes/Wild
  Places Photography/Alamy
Sidi Mechrig © Sam Thorne
Mosaic in the Amphitrite House, Bulla Regia
  © Vanni Archive/Corbis
Sfax city walls © Daniel Jacobs
Monastir's ribat © Sam Thorne
Jugurtha's Table © Hans Georg Roth/Corbis
View from Thuburbo Majus © Sam Thorne
Triumphal arch, Maktar © Sam Thorne
The mausoleums at Sidi Aïch © Daniel
  Jacobs
The Lézard Rouge © Paul Gapper/Alamy
Matmata © Hans Georg Roth/Corbis
Toujane © Daniel Jacobs
Qasr Hamida Ben Ayed © Daniel Jacobs
Crocodiles at Djerba Explore © Daniel
  Jacobs
Chenini © Daniel Jacobs
Ksar Ouled Soltane © Ray Roberts/Alamy

SMALL PRINT

Index

In this index, place names which usually begin with the definite article – in French or Arabic – are indexed as though the article is an integral part of the name. Thus "Le Kef" appears under L while "El Jem" appears under E. As there is no standard way of transliterating Arabic, you may need to try various spellings to find a place in this index, bearing in mind that Tunisian transliteration tends towards French spellings. Thus a place whose name starts with a *j* sound will often be spelt Dj . . ., while a place whose name starts with a *sh* sound will usually be spelt Ch . . . .

Map entries are in colour.

E

F

G

INDEX

I

INDEX

Map symbols

maps are listed in the full index using coloured text

▬▬▬▪	International boundary	@	Internet
▬ ▬ ▬	Chapter division boundary	ⓘ	Tourist office
▬▬▬	Motorway	ⓒ	Phone office
═══	Major road	◉	Accommodation
══	Minor road	▣	Restaurant
───	Unpaved road	★	Bus stop
▥▥▥	Steps	🅟	Fuel station
▬▬▬	Pedestrianized street	‿	Bridge
= = =	Track	⊠	Post office
⟩⋯⋯⟨	Underpass	✈	Airport
─ ─ ─	Tunnel	⊞	Hospital
─ ─ ─	Railway line	⚊	Campsite
▥▥▥	Funicular railway	Ⓗ	Hammam
--Ⓜ--	Metro line and station	◔	Swimming pool
-----	Path	∿	Spring/spa
─ ─	Ferry route	⚑	Golf course
───	River	⊼	Lighthouse
▬▬▬	Wall	♦	Mosque
ᴪᴪᴪ	Rocks	✡	Synagogue
/|\\	Hill shading	⚖	Market
⚞	Mountain range	⊞	Church
▲	Peak	▬	Building
⌂	Cave	⬭	Stadium
⁋⁋	Oasis	⁺⁺⁺	Christian cemetery
◠	Dune	▭	Jewish cemetery
⬭	Saltpan	▽	Muslim cemetery
⧫	Place of interest	▦	Park
∴	Ruin	▦	Beach
⚒	Quarry	▭	Swamp